October 8–11, 2013
St. Andrews, UK

Association for
Computing Machinery

Advancing Computing as a Science & Profession

UIST'13

Proceedings of the 26th Annual ACM Symposium on User Interface Software and Technology

Sponsored by:

ACM SIGCHI and ACM SIGGRAPH

Supported by:

Autodesk, Disney Research, Microsoft, Synaptics, Visit Scotland™, Google, SICSA*, SMART™, WACOM, FX Pal, IBM Research, Nokia, Samsung, Tactual Labs and Technicolor

Association for
Computing Machinery

Advancing Computing as a Science & Profession

The Association for Computing Machinery
2 Penn Plaza, Suite 701
New York, New York 10121-0701

Notice to Past Authors of ACM-Published Articles
ACM intends to create a complete electronic archive of all articles and/or other material previously published by ACM. If you have written a work that has been previously published by ACM in any journal or conference proceedings prior to 1978, or any SIG Newsletter at any time, and you do NOT want this work to appear in the ACM Digital Library, please inform permissions@acm.org, stating the title of the work, the author(s), and where and when published.

ISBN: 978-1-4503-2268-3 (Digital)

ISBN: 978-1-4503-2674-2 (Print)

Additional copies may be ordered prepaid from:

ACM Order Department
PO Box 30777
New York, NY 10087-0777, USA

Phone: 1-800-342-6626 (USA and Canada)
+1-212-626-0500 (Global)
Fax: +1-212-944-1318
E-mail: acmhelp@acm.org
Hours of Operation: 8:30 am – 4:30 pm ET

Printed in the USA

Foreword

It is our pleasure to welcome you to the 26th Annual ACM Symposium on User Interface Software and Technology (UIST) 2013, held from October 8-11th, in the historic town and University of St Andrews, Scotland, United Kingdom.

UIST is the premier forum for the presentation of research innovations in the software and technology of human-computer interfaces. Sponsored by ACM's special interest groups on computer-human interaction (SIGCHI) and computer graphics (SIGGRAPH), UIST brings together researchers and practitioners from many areas, including web and graphical interfaces, new input and output devices, information visualization, sensing technologies, interactive displays, tabletop and tangible computing, interaction techniques, augmented and virtual reality, ubiquitous computing, and computer supported cooperative work. The single-track program and intimate size, makes UIST 2013 an ideal place to exchange results at the cutting edge of user interfaces research, to meet friends and colleagues, and to forge future collaborations.

We received a record 317 paper submissions from more than 30 countries. After a thorough review process, the program committee accepted 62 papers (19.5%). Each anonymous submission was first reviewed by three external reviewers, and meta-reviews were provided by two program committee members. If any of the five reviewers deemed a submission to pass a rejection threshold we asked the authors to submit a short rebuttal addressing the reviewers' concerns. The program committee met in person in Pittsburgh, PA, on May 30-31, 2013, to select the papers for the conference. Submissions were finally accepted only after the authors provided a final revision addressing the committee's comments.

In addition to the presentations of accepted papers, this year's program includes a keynote by Raffaello D'Andrea (ETH Zurich) on feedback control systems for autonomous machines. A great line up of posters, demos, (the ninth) annual Doctoral Symposium, and (the fifth) annual Student Innovation Contest (this year focusing on programmable water pumps called Pumpspark) complete the program. We hope you enjoy all aspects of the UIST 2013 program, and that you get to enjoy our wonderful venues and that your discussions and interactions prove fruitful.

General Chairs

Shahram Izadi
Microsoft Research, UK

Aaron Quigley
University of St Andrews, UK

Program Chairs

Ivan Poupyrev
Disney Research, USA

Takeo Igarashi
The University of Tokyo

Table of Contents

Session 7: Vision

Session Chair: Tom Yeh *(University of Colorado at Boulder)*

Session 8: GUI

Session Chair: Wilmot Li *(Adobe Research)*

Session 9: Applications and Games

Session Chair: Xiaojun Bi *(Google)*

Session 12: Haptics

Session Chair: Sriram Subramanian *(University of Bristol)*

UIST 2013 Symposium Organisation

General Chairs: Shahram Izadi *(Microsoft Research, UK)*
Aaron Quigley *(University of St Andrews, UK)*

Program Chairs: Ivan Poupyrev *(Disney Research, USA)*
Takeo Igarashi *(The University of Tokyo, Japan)*

Doctoral Symposium: Patrick Baudisch *(Hass Plattner Institut, Germany)*
Steven K. Feiner *(Columbia University, USA)*
Sriram Subramanian *(University of Bristol, UK)*
Celine Latulipe *(University of North Carolina at Charlotte)*

Poster Chairs: Mira Contcheva *(Adobe Systems, USA)*
Daniel Avrahami *(Intel)*

Proceedings Chairs: Julie R. Williamson *(University of Glasgow, Scotland)*
Pedro Lopes *(Hasso Plattner Institut, Germany)*

Student Innovation Contest Chairs: David Kim *(Newcastle University, UK)*
Nikolai Marquardt *(University of Calgary, Canada)*
Gabriel Reyes *(Georgia Tech, USA)*

Social Media Chair: Aaron Genest *(University of Saskatchewan, Canada)*

Demo Chairs: T. Scott Saponas *(Microsoft Research, USA)*
Per Ola Kristensson *(University of St Andrews, UK)*

Local Organizing Chair: Miguel Nacenta *(University of St Andrews, UK)*

Sponsorship Chair: Daniel Wigdor *(University of Toronto, Canada)*

Registration Chairs: Merve Keles *(New York University, USA)*
Jakub Dostal *(University of St Andrews, UK)*

Student Volunteer Chairs: Eve Hoggan *(HIIT / University of Helsinki, Finland)*
Uta Hinrichs *(University of St Andrews, UK)*

Web Chair: Jim Young *(University of Manitoba, Canada)*

Mobile Chairs: Eiji Hayashi *(Carnegie Mellon, USA)*
Stephen Oney *(Carnegie Mellon, USA)*
Jason Wiese *(Carnegie Mellon, USA)*

Publicity Chairs: Paul André *(Carnegie Mellon, USA)*
Jun Kato *(The University of Tokyo, Japan)*

PC Meeting Coordination: Chris Harrison *(Carnegie Mellon, USA)*

Keynote Chair: Otmar Hilliges *(Microsoft Research, UK)*

Program Committee: Caroline Appert *(Université Paris-Sud)*
Olivier Bau *(Disney Research Pittsburgh)*
Patrick Baudisch *(Hasso Plattner Institute)*
Xiaojun Bi *(Google Research)*
Jan Borcher *(RWTH Aachen University)*
Fanny Chevalier *(University of Toronto)*
Gabe Cohn *(University of Washington)*
Allen Cypher *(IBM Research Almaden)*
Paul Dietz *(Microsoft Research)*
Steven Drucker *(Microsoft Research)*
George Fitzmaurice *(AutoDesk Research)*
David Forsyth *(University of Illinois at Urbana-Champaign)*
Krzysztof Gajos *(Harvard University)*
Hans Gellersen *(Lancaster University)*
Chris Harrison *(Carnegie Mellon University)*
Björn Hartmann *(UC Berkeley)*
Scott Hudson *(Carnegie Mellon University)*
Pourang Irani *(University of Manitoba)*
Johan Kildal *(Nokia Research Center)*
Per Ola Kristensson *(University of St Andrews)*
James Landay *(University of Washington)*
Wilmot Li *(Adobe)*
Kent Lyons *(Nokia Research Center)*
Nicolai Marquardt *(University of Calgary)*
Rob Miller *(MIT)*
Mark Newman *(University of Michigan)*
Alex Olwal *(MIT Media Lab)*
Ken Perlin *(New York University)*
Jun Rekimoto *(The University of Tokyo)*
Wolfgang Stürzlinger *(York University)*
Sriram Subramanian *(University of Bristol)*
Anna Vallgårda *(IT University of Copenhagen)*
Koji Yatani *(Microsoft Research Asia)*
Tom Yeh *(University of Colorado at Boulder)*

UIST 2013 Sponsors & Supporters

Sponsors: SIGCHI · ACM SIGGRAPH

Supporters

Platinum: Autodesk

Gold: Disney Research · Microsoft · Synaptics · Visit Scotland

Silver: Google · sicsa* The Scottish Informatics & Computer Science Alliance · SMART · wacom

Bronze: FX PAL · IBM Research · NOKIA Connecting People · SAMSUNG · Tactual Labs · technicolor

Keynote Talk

Humans and the Coming Machine Revolution

Raffaello D'Andrea
Swiss Federal Institute of Technology (ETH)
Zurich

ABSTRACT
The key components of feedback control systems — sensors, actuators, computation, power, and communication — are continually becoming smaller, lighter, more robust, higher performance, and less expensive. By using appropriate algorithms and system architectures, it is thus becoming possible to "close the loop" on almost any machine, and to create new capabilities that fully exploit their dynamic potential. In this talk I will discuss various projects — involving mobile robots, flying machines, an autonomous table, and actuated wingsuits — where these new machine competencies are interfaced with the ultimate dynamic entities: human beings.

Author Keywords
Robotics; feedback loop; flying machines; mobile.

ACM Classification Keywords
H.5.m. Information interfaces and presentation (e.g., HCI): Miscellaneous.

BIO

Spanning academics, business and the arts, Raffaello D'Andrea's career is built on his ability to bridge theory and practice: He is Professor of Dynamic Systems and Control at the Swiss Federal Institute of Technology (ETH) in Zurich, where his research redefines what autonomous systems are capable of. He is also co-founder of Kiva Systems (recently acquired by Amazon), a robotics and logistics company that develops and deploys intelligent automated warehouse systems.

Photo credit: James Duncan Davidson

He was also the faculty advisor and system architect of the Cornell Robot Soccer Team, four time world champions at the international RoboCup competition. In addition, he is an internationally exhibited new media artist, best known for the Robotic Chair (Ars Electronica, ARCO, London Art Fair, National Gallery of Canada) and Flight Assembled Architecture (FRAC Centre, France). Other creations and projects include the Flying Machine Arena, the Distributed Flight Array, the Blind Juggler, the Balancing Cube, and RoboEarth.

UIST'13, October 8–11, 2013, St. Andrews, United Kingdom.
ACM 978-1-4503-2268-3/13/10.
http://dx.doi.org/10.1145/2501988.2508466

Lumitrack: Low Cost, High Precision, High Speed Tracking with Projected *m*-Sequences

Robert Xiao[1] **Chris Harrison**[1] **Karl D.D. Willis**[2] **Ivan Poupyrev**[2] **Scott E. Hudson**[1]

Human-Computer Interaction Institute[1]
Carnegie Mellon University
5000 Forbes Avenue, Pittsburgh PA 15213
{brx, chris.harrison, scott.hudson}@cs.cmu.edu

Disney Research Pittsburgh[2]
4720 Forbes Avenue
Pittsburgh, PA 15213
{karl, ivan.poupyrev}@disneyresearch.com

ABSTRACT

We present *Lumitrack*, a novel motion tracking technology that uses projected structured patterns and linear optical sensors. Each sensor unit is capable of recovering 2D location within the projection area, while multiple sensors can be combined for up to six degree of freedom (DOF) tracking. Our structured light approach is based on special patterns, called *m*-sequences, in which any consecutive sub-sequence of *m* bits is unique. Lumitrack can utilize both digital and static projectors, as well as scalable embedded sensing configurations. The resulting system enables high-speed, high precision, and low-cost motion tracking for a wide range of interactive applications. We detail the hardware, operation, and performance characteristics of our approach, as well as a series of example applications that highlight its immediate feasibility and utility.

ACM Classification: H.5.2 [Information interfaces and presentation]: User Interfaces - Input devices and strategies.

General terms: Design, Human Factors

Keywords: Input devices, optical tracking, structured light.

INTRODUCTION

Movement is one of the fundamental ways we interact with the world around us. We can configure our limbs and bodies into innumerable poses, locomote around the environment, and manipulate objects within it. Unsurprisingly, motion tracking is a fundamental input channel for almost all forms of computing. In response, literally hundreds of approaches have been proposed to capture motion, from accelerometers to Z+RGB depth cameras. The rapidly growing area of embodied and gestural interaction [10] underlines the continuing importance of accurate, fast, and affordable motion tracking technology.

In this paper, we present Lumitrack, a novel sensing technique with several unique qualities. Foremost, our approach is *extremely precise*: results demonstrate sub-millimeter and sub-degree translational and rotational accuracy respectively. It also offers extremely *high frame rate* with *low latency*: peak speeds over 1000 tracking frames per second (FPS) delivered ~2.5ms behind real time. Moreover, the components of our system are relatively *small* and *low powered* (<1 watt), enabling integration into mobile devices. Finally, the necessary components could be very *inexpensive*: under $10 parts cost in volume. These qualities make Lumitrack a powerful and intriguing addition to the toolbox of sensors used by HCI researchers and practitioners. The sensing approach can be configured and scaled for use with a range of interactive systems including tangible games, drawing applications, and augmented reality.

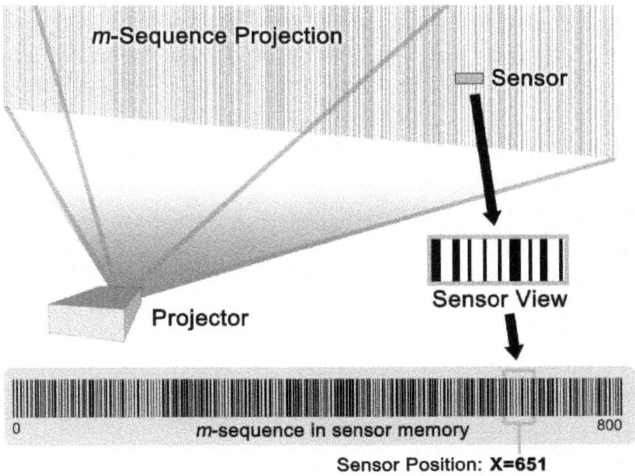

Figure 1. Lumitrack enables high speed, high precision, low-cost tracking by projecting a static binary pattern directly onto a linear optical sensor. A small section of this unique 'm-sequence' pattern falls onto the sensor, enabling 1D position to be recovered.

Lumitrack has two key components: projectors and sensors (see Figures 1 and 2). Our projectors emit a pattern of static structured light called a binary *m*-sequence [20]. These sequences have a special property: every consecutive subsequence of *m* bits within an *m*-sequence is unique. For example, in the following 7-sequence, the subsequence 1010001 appears exactly once:

000010001101110110000101101101010011110101100111 00
101011110011000111010001010000110010010111000100 11

UIST '13, October 8–11, 2013, St. Andrews, United Kingdom.

ACM 978-1-4503-2268-3/13/10...$15.00.
http://dx.doi.org/10.1145/2501988.2502022

In fact, any consecutive seven digits are guaranteed to only appear once. Our projectors use a 25-sequence where 1's are emitted lines of light and 0's are dark lines (no light).

The second component of our system is a small optical sensor. This must lie within the projection area to function. Because the projected area is big in relation to the sensor, only a small part of the *m*-sequence falls onto its surface (Figures 1 and 2). If at least 25 bits of the pattern can be seen (i.e., if the projector is sufficiently close), the sensor can determine where it lies within the projected field by looking up the subsequence's position within the full *m*-sequence (a pattern known to both the sensor and projector). This setup allows for 1D position to be resolved.

As we describe in depth later, Lumitrack uses two orthogonal 1D patterns, which allow the sensors to calculate X and Y position. Using more than one sensor, it is possible to resolve X, Y and Z positions, and even roll/pitch/yaw rotation – i.e., full six degree-of-freedom (6 DOF) tracking.

RELATED WORK

Motion tracking is a fundamental component of almost all interactive systems. Numerous approaches have been developed to sense and track motion using mechanical, inertial, acoustic, magnetic, and radio-based sensing techniques [35]. Most relevant to Lumitrack are optical sensing systems employing natural features, fixed markers, projected markers, structured light, or projections onto sensors.

Natural Feature Tracking

Natural features in a scene can be tracked using standard cameras to recover 3D information from a series of 2D images, i.e. using Structure from Motion (SfM) [13,27,34]. When combined with Simultaneous Localization and Mapping (SLAM) [9,36], camera pose can be estimated within a dynamically constructed map of the environment. Although powerful, natural feature tracking techniques are computationally expensive and challenging to implement in embedded systems and mobile devices.

Marker-based Tracking

Marker-based motion tracking systems instrument objects and the environment with physical markers to simplify the tracking process. A camera is used to detect the markers in the scene and estimate the location and, in some systems, the orientation of the marker. Marker-based systems can utilize printed 2D barcodes [7,15], retro-reflective or light-emitting points [5,40], hidden patterns [31,39] or printed patterns [2]. The Bokode system [22] images sections of illuminated lenslet-equipped barcodes using an out-of-focus camera. Finally, low latency, high precision commercial marker-based systems are available, but typically cost thousands of dollars.

Projected Marker Tracking

Marker patterns can also be dynamically projected onto surfaces in the environment for use with handheld devices [37,38], interactive tabletops [8], and augmented displays [11]. Projected markers can be identified and tracked using standard marker-based tracking techniques. These systems typically hide the obtrusive appearance of the projected markers using near-infrared projection [19] or temporal multiplexing [11].

Figure 2. A one-dimensional *m*-sequence projected in white onto a Lumitrack sensor. This is analogous to the setup illustrated in Figure 1.

Structured Light Tracking

Projecting geometric patterns on the environment, i.e. *structured light*, allows a camera to infer information about the structure and properties of the environment. A number of structured light schemes have been developed for 3D object digitization and recognition including M-arrays [24], de Bruijn sequences [26], bilinear de Bruijn sequences [16], time-multiplexed grey codes [3], and others [32]. Structured light has been used for interaction to simultaneously capture and display on objects and people [30], to localize mobile devices [17], and in a range of interaction scenarios using structured light depth cameras [12,23]. As structured light systems typically use a camera-projector pair, latency is a common and non-trivial issue [25].

Projector-Sensor Tracking

Projecting light directly onto an optical sensor enables spatial information to be directly communicated between projector and sensor. The dominant approach has been time-multiplexed projection. For example, in [14], spatial information is temporally communicated to photodiodes embedded in objects using LED clusters. [19] uses a specially-modified projector to project temporal grey code pattern within a monochrome display using an imperceptible change in modulation; sensors within the projection field then read the grey code patterns. PICOntrol [33] modulates the visible output of a projector to transmit time-multiplexed codes onto sensors within the projection field, which activate interactive functions upon detection of an appropriate code.

RFIG Lamps [28] projects time-multiplexed grey codes onto a collection of photodiode sensors. Each sensor computes its position within the projected image using the grey code. A similar approach is taken by Prakash [29], which further extends the sensors to include luminance and orientation sensors. Both systems bear similarities to Lumitrack, but the underlying principles are quite different. Prakash and RFIG Lamps are inherently time-multiplexed, whereas Lumitrack can project unchanging patterns. This opens the

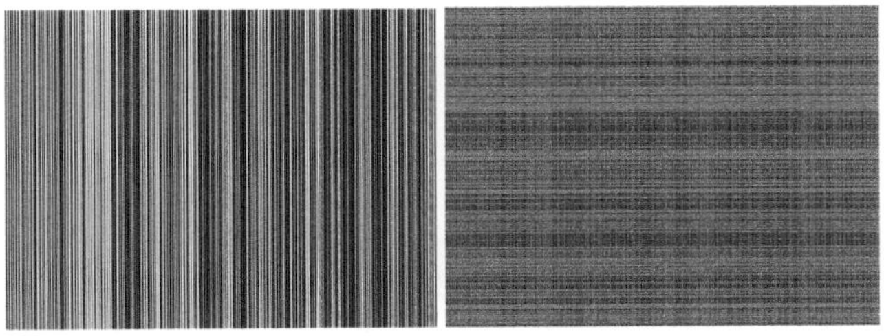

Figure 3. Left: 1D 25-sequence in black and white. Right: Two orthogonal 25-sequences, one rendered in blue and the other in red. Both images have a resolution of 800x600.

possibility of making Lumitrack's projector configuration much smaller and simpler – Lumitrack requires only a single projector, whereas Prakash requires one projector per bit of spatial resolution.

Although some time-multiplexed systems (e.g., [29]) can perform at comparable speeds to Lumitrack, using a single projected image vastly simplifies projector design. SpeckleSense [41], like Lumitrack, uses static projection for low latency tracking, but is limited to relative translation and distance approximation (whereas Lumitrack offers high frame rate *absolute* tracking). Finally, Bokode [22] can provide absolute tracking by imaging sections of a larger barcode using a lensed camera. In contrast, Lumitrack uses simple, lens-less optical sensors and operates at a significantly higher frame rate.

PROJECTOR IMPLEMENTATION

The *m*-sequence pattern can be projected using a static projector with a fixed pattern or a dynamic digital projector.

Static Projectors

Static projectors use a light source, focusing optics, and image source to emit a fixed pattern. Due to their simple design, static projectors can be compact, inexpensive, and lightweight. Our prototype static projectors are constructed using LED light sources, off-the-shelf focusing optics, and high-resolution films as image sources. We render our *m*-sequences onto black and white film at 8000dpi and insert the film into an off-the-shelf car door "gobo" projector measuring 4.6cm long by 2.2cm in diameter (Figure 4A, 4B). A visible light or invisible infrared LED can be used to power the projection. When projecting in infrared, special consideration needs to be given to the film's infrared transmission properties. Because many films are designed

Figure 5. The AAXA Technologies L1 projector emits a focus-free image using an LCOS panel and laser light.

to be transmissive to infrared, we use short wavelength 730nm infrared LEDs (Figure 4D) and continue to experiment with different films to maximize image contrast.

For prototyping purposes, we built a visible light, 2D *m*-sequence projector using a pair of static projectors (Figure 4C). Although our current prototypes use LED light sources, laser based projectors would have the advantage of focus-free operation provided a suitable *m*-sequence diffraction grating or image source could be designed and manufactured.

Dynamic Projectors

Focus-free dynamic digital projectors are readily available in compact 'pico-projector' form factors. Pico-projectors are currently being embedded in devices, such as mobile phones and digital cameras, and offer a unique opportunity for structured light tracking. Coherent laser light, producing crisp images at varying distances, is well suited for human interaction. With laser LCOS projection, a full, single-color image is projected at any instant in time. In contrast, scanning laser projectors rely on the human eye to integrate a single moving point into an image over time. The 'full-frame' property of laser LCOS projection allows us to rapidly track the projected *m*-sequence.

We use the L1 LCOS laser projector produced by AAXA Technologies [1], which projects time-multiplexed RGBG images at 800x600 resolution. This projection artifact is used to our advantage by displaying the X-axis *m*-sequence in the red and blue channels, and the Y-axis *m*-sequence in the green channel (Figure 5). By temporally multiplexing orthogonal *m*-sequences, we eliminate cross-talk between the projected axes. Using a digital projector allows us to not only track projector motion, but to also render interactive graphics onto the environment around the sensor (Figure

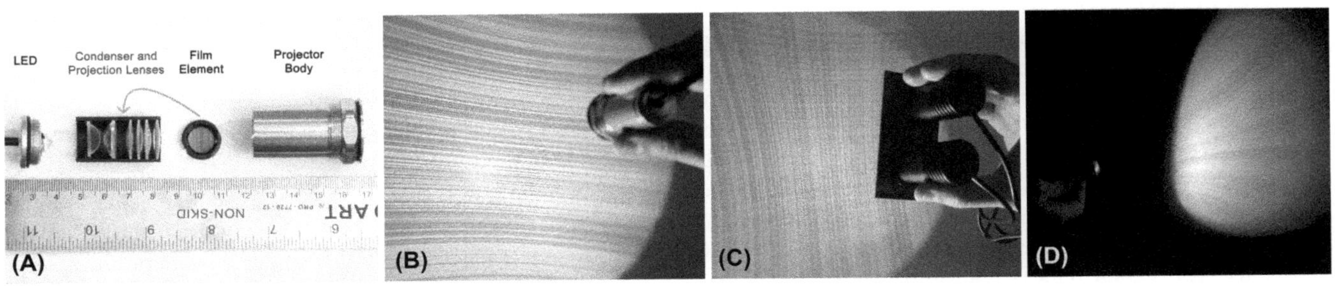

Figure 4. (A): An exploded view of a 1D static projector. (B): Projecting the 1D *m*-sequence onto a wall. (C): A two-axis static projector that emits orthogonal *m*-sequences, one in red and another in blue. (D): Projecting the 1D *m*-sequence in IR.

15). Although we primarily use visible light for prototyping purposes, we ultimately envision the use of two or more frequencies of IR light to hide the tracking patterns.

Generating *m*-Sequences

The projected *m*-sequences consist of a binary pattern in which every *m*-bit subsequence (window) is unique. For tracking robustness, we further constrain our *m*-sequences in several ways. We limit the maximum number of consecutive identical bits (a *run* of bits) to three and require that every window contain at least one run of length exactly one. These requirements assist with accurate recovery of the spatial frequency of the pattern received on the linear sensors. Finally, we require that the bit-patterns of different windows differ in at least two places, to ensure that single bit-flips caused by noise could not result in an incorrect identification. To create *m*-sequences that fulfill these constraints, we use a sequential generate-and-test approach with backtracking. We use a window size of m=25 for an 800-bit sequence suitable for an 800x600 projection resolution. We used the same approach to find two separate 800-bit sequences with no windows in common, opening the possibility of sequence switching as an additional information channel.

SENSOR IMPLEMENTATION

The Lumitrack sensor unit consists of a custom printed circuit board connected to a microcontroller. The microcontroller processes sensor data into X/Y positions, which are sent to a computer over USB for interactive applications.

Sensor Hardware

The sensor unit consists of a pair of TSL202R 128x1 linear optical sensors manufactured by AMS. The two linear optical sensors are mounted perpendicular to each other (Figure 2). This configuration of two 1D sensors has the distinct advantage of enabling 2D sensing, with a quadratic reduction in total pixels relative to a 2D camera sensor (e.g., 128x128 pixels vs. 2x128 pixels). With fewer pixels to read, we can achieve high frame rates. The optical sensors are highly responsive to a broad spectrum of light, including infrared. An ARM Cortex M3-based 72Mhz Maple Mini board is used to run our custom C software [18].

Sensor Sampling

The sensor sampling process is initiated by a timer interrupt, which interrupts the main pattern matching process. It uses both of the Maple Mini's analog to digital converters (ADCs) to sample the linear sensors, one ADC per sensor. By initiating both ADCs simultaneously and waiting for them to both return, the system can sample at a very high rate. We further utilize the high-speed sampling options of the Maple's ADCs to sample at a rate in excess of 1 million samples per second. This reduces the CPU time spent in the sampling process and allows for more time to perform signal processing. By using DMA, the speed could be further improved to a theoretical maximum of 5 million samples per second. Reading both sensors completely takes a total of 101 μs. The sensor data is read into two arrays of integers; because this process may interrupt the pattern matching process, double-buffering is used to ensure data integrity. The raw data collected from one linear sensor is shown in Figure 6A.

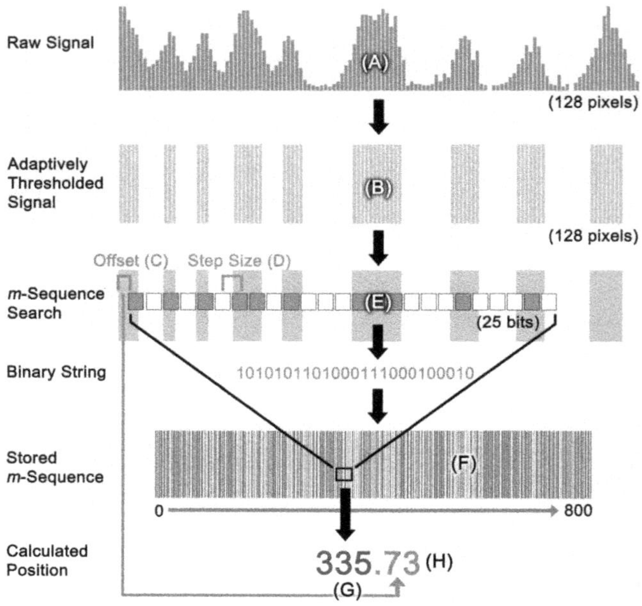

Figure 6. First, our embedded software reads the illumination values from a linear optical sensor (A). This signal is then adaptively thresholded (B). Next, the software exhaustively tests different offsets (C) and step sizes (D), testing to see if the pattern (E) exists in a stored *m*-sequence (F). If a sub-sequence match is found, a gross position estimate is yielded (G). The offset (C) provides fractional position accuracy within the m-sequence (H).

Between each sampling burst, the linear optical sensors accumulate the electrical charges from their photodiode array. This time period, called the *integration time*, is controlled by the timer period. Adjusting the integration time is a key parameter in optimizing the system performance. At close range, the integration time should be short to avoid saturating the sensors, while at long range, the integration time should be longer to improve sensitivity.

Adaptive Thresholding and Quick Rejection

For each linear optical sensor, the variance of the analog values is computed. If this value falls below a certain threshold, the system infers that a pattern is not present, and skips the computation. This happens roughly 50% of the time when using our L1 projector due to the projector's color time multiplexing: the pattern aligned with the sensor's orientation is only active half of the time. The quick rejection mechanism allows for more computation time for the other sensor, allowing for a higher overall frame rate.

The sampled analog values (Figure 6A) are adaptively thresholded with a specific window size to produce a binary pixel array (Figure 6B). The thresholding algorithm produces a 1 if the analog value under consideration is larger than the mean across a window centered on that value, and otherwise outputs a 0. The window size is adjustable, and constitutes another key parameter for performance optimization purposes. At short range, the window size should be small to accommodate a denser arrangement of bits, while at long range, the window size should be large because fewer bits will fall on the sensor.

m-Sequence Searching

The pattern falling on the linear sensor consists of a subsequence of the *m*-sequence. Each bit (projected line) of the sequence covers multiple pixels of the sensor and the step size (number of pixels from one bit to the next) varies based on the distance from the projector to the sensor. For example, in Figure 6, a single unit line falls onto approximately 4 sensor pixels. Furthermore, the offset from the edge of the linear sensor to the start of the first complete bit also varies with the precise position of the projector.

Thus, there are two unknown parameters: the *offset* and the *step size* (Figure 6C and 6D). To determine these two parameters, we run an exhaustive search algorithm over possible step size and offset parameters. We use 16.16 fixed-point arithmetic to enable fine-grained search parameters without the overhead of floating-point computations on the embedded ARM chip. We test step sizes from 2 to 5 pixels in increments of 1/7 of a pixel, and offsets from zero up to the step size in increments of a whole pixel. This results in a total of 63 parameter combinations. For each of these combinations, we sample the thresholded pixel array to obtain an *m*-bit integer, which is looked up in a fixed (precompiled) hashtable that maps subsequences to their index in the *m*-sequence. If the parameter combination is correct, the lookup should succeed (assuming no sensor or sampling errors occur). Note that this lookup is performed for every parameter combination. With our standard 800-bit 25-sequence, there are 2^{25} possible 25-bit sequences and less than 2^{10} valid sequences, so the chances of a false-positive lookup are less than one in 2^{15}. If a lookup succeeds, the Maple Mini sends the looked-up index (i.e., the linear position) and the step size and offset parameters over the USB serial port.

Sub-unit *m*-Sequence Tracking Precision

The offset from the sensor's edge to the start of the first complete bit (Figure 6C) offers a way to compute the projector's position with sub-unit accuracy. If the pattern moves by a single pixel on the sensor, the offset will change by one pixel even if the looked-up *m*-sequence index remains the same. By dividing the offset by the step size, we obtain a fraction of a position unit, which can be added to the position to obtain a higher-precision position estimate.

Computer Software

The computer-side software is written in C++ and runs on a Macbook Pro. It communicates via USB with the Maple's emulated serial port at 115200 baud. Because of the serial port's limited bandwidth, a hard limit of 2300 five-byte updates can be received per second; our system very nearly approaches this maximum. The serial port is continually polled by a background thread that pushes received updates into a queue. With multiple connected sensors, each sensor gets a background thread; the threads are synchronized to ensure that the data is up-to-date. Interactive applications query the queues every frame to retrieve the most recent data points. In the case of multiple sensors, our code library provides methods for estimating and filtering the 2 DOF, 4 DOF and 6 DOF positions.

2 DOF Tracking

With a single sensor, we can resolve an X/Y projected position. These two degrees of freedom can be used in two ways. First, if the projector is held still and not translated, the X/Y positions landing on the sensor can be interpreted as two rotational degrees (pitch and yaw), as seen in the sword demo described later (Figure 13). Alternatively, by translating the device without changing the orientation of the projector or distance to the sensor plane, the X/Y positions are interpreted as translations within the projector's plane and can be translated to X/Y screen-space coordinates, as is done in the spray painting demo described later.

4 DOF Tracking

With two sensors, it is possible to track four degrees of freedom: the X/Y center of the tracked points, the angle of the line joining the points relative to the horizontal, and the distance between the points. The inverse of the distance between the points can be used to calculate the approximate distance from the projector to the sensors.

6 DOF Tracking

The "holy grail" of tracking is to track all six degrees of freedom – three spatial dimensions and three rotational dimensions. At a bare minimum, three sensors (six linear sensors) are required, but for robustness we chose to use four sensors to provide an over-determined system. Solving for the six degrees of freedom amounts to solving for a 3D (4x4) projection matrix which projects the 3D positions of the four sensors onto the sensed 2D positions within the projector's projected image. This treatment ignores camera distortion parameters (intrinsic parameters), which we found to be minimal with the L1 projector.

To reduce the number of independent variables in the projection matrix, we calibrated and fixed as many variables as possible. The four sensors are arranged in a custom-built, planar mount with tight tolerances (<1mm). This arrangement is suitable for e.g. affixing sensors to the corners of a computer display (Figure 18, right). We calibrated the projector's vertical and horizontal throw precisely to fix the projection matrix's scaling parameters. The projection matrix then becomes $P = STR$, where S is the calibrated standard projection matrix (derived from the projector's throw and aspect ratio), T is a translation matrix, and R is a 3D rotation matrix. Because the linear sensors on our custom PCB are slightly offset, we end up with a set of four pairs of equations, one per sensor: $(Pp_x)_x = q_x$, $(Pp_y)_y = q_y$ where p_x and p_y are the 3D positions of the starting end of the x and y linear sensors, (q_x, q_y) is the 2D tracked position reported by the sensor, and $(P)_x$, $(P)_y$ denote the x/y coordinates of P.

With these eight equations and tracked positions, we perform Gauss-Newton iteration to find a solution which min-

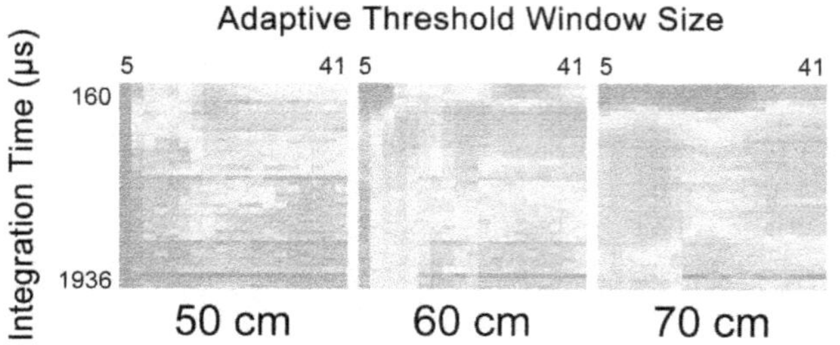

Figure 7. Results from our parameter optimization tests. A red to green scale is used, which indicates low and high tracking rates respectively. Note that as the distance increases, a longer integration time is needed to maintain optimal performance.

imizes the total squared error $\sum \| (Pp_x)_x - q_x \|^2 + \| (Pp_y)_y - q_y \|^2$, also known as the total squared reprojection error. This yields estimates for the six degrees of freedom. Finally, these estimates are smoothed with a 1€ filter [6] to reduce jitter in the estimates during rapid movement.

Parameter Optimization

We performed an experiment to determine the optimal values for integration time and adaptive threshold window size. We wrote a simple Maple mini program to step through the possible combinations of parameters. For each combination, the program performed pattern detection for 500ms and reported the number of successful X data points captured within that time. We ran the program at three distances to the sensor, 50cm, 60cm, and 70cm. The results are summarized in Figure 7. At longer distances, higher integration times are generally more advantageous. Using the data collected by this approach, future implementations could automatically select appropriate sensing parameters to achieve optimal performance over a wider range of distances and lighting conditions. For fixed window sizes, we found that a window size of 23 works well across distances.

SYSTEM PERFORMANCE AND EVALUATION

To quantify and convey the strengths of our system, we conducted a series of experiments that sought to evaluate key aspects of our system, including tracking precision, frame rate, latency, and power consumption.

Tracking Accuracy

To evaluate the spatial accuracy of Lumitrack, we attached our sensor onto a commercial grade, two-axis CNC platform, having a step size of 1 mil (0.0254mm). We mounted

Figure 8. Points recorded by sensors during raster pattern scan.

the L1 projector 65cm above the sensor plane and configured it to emit our standard *m*-sequence pattern.

We created a custom control program to repeatedly move the platform to a random location within the projected field. The program recorded values streaming from the sensor for one second, which were saved for later analysis. We ran this test for 14 hours, collecting data for 8400 random locations (trials). In total, we collected more than 5.6 million tracking frames. We discarded 221 trials that had no tracking frames for one or both axes, and 139 trials that had a measurement error greater than 25mm (errors of this magnitude were most likely caused by error frames).

Across the remaining 8040 trials, the average Euclidean distance error was 0.532mm (SD = 0.616mm). Except for 14 outliers, the maximum error was 1.297mm. At the testing distance of 65cm, the average error translates into a rotational accuracy of 0.0469°. For comparison, [29] achieved a mean error of 5.8mm (at 300cm) at ~500 FPS.

We also instructed the CNC platform to trace a 1.5cm raster pattern, also at a distance of 65cm. This took 136.0 seconds, during which time our sensor continuously collected 109,363 position values (an average of 804 tracking FPS). The raw data is plotted in Figure 8.

Effects of Distance on Tracking Frame Rate

To evaluate the tracking frame rate performance of Lumitrack at various projector-sensor distances, we used the CNC platform to move the projector away from the sensor by increments of 1.0cm. At each stop, the control program recorded the values streaming from the sensor for one se-

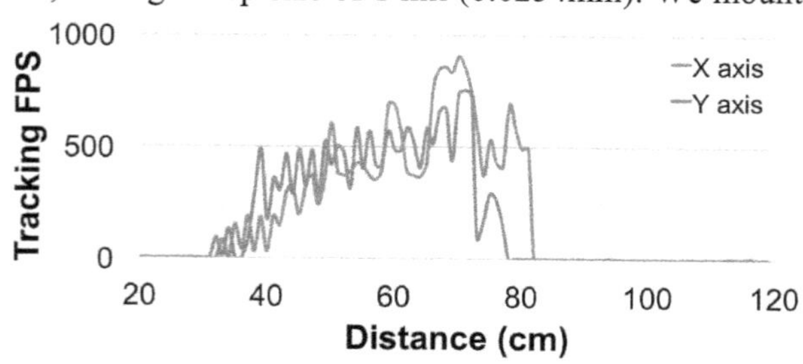

Figure 9. System tracking response for each axis at varying distances between sensor and projector.

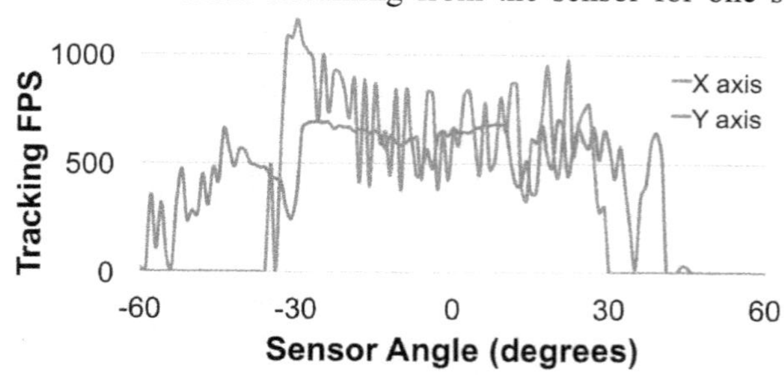

Figure 10. System tracking response for each axis at varying angles between sensor and projector.

cond. Figure 9 shows the number of X-axis (blue) and Y-axis (red) tracking frames obtained in one second as a function of distance. Note that the frame rates in Figures 9 and 10 are ½ maximum due to temporal multiplexing of the projector.

Note that the sensor parameters used in this experiment were set to the optimal parameters for a distance of 70cm; nevertheless, Lumitrack was capable of tracking at over 500 total tracking frames per second at distances of 40 to 75cm. Adaptive integration time and windowing will help to increase this range further in future work.

Effects of Rotation on Tracking Frame Rate

We also evaluated the tracking frame rate of Lumitrack under three rotational conditions: sensor rotation, projector pitch, and projector yaw. In each condition, we affixed the rotating component to a rotary table with a step of 1/80°.

In the first condition, the sensor was rotated on the platform while the projector remained fixed. The sensor was oriented so that the Y-axis linear sensor was perpendicular to the table, and the X-axis linear sensor was parallel to the rotating surface. The results, summarized in Figure 10, show that the perpendicular Y-axis sensor picked up frames over a wide range of angles (from -60° to 40°), whereas the X-axis sensor's range was slightly more limited (-35° to 30°).

In the second and third conditions, we mounted the projector to the rotary table and kept the sensor fixed. We observed that the sensor picked up tracking frames at near maximum speed as soon as the edge of the projection covered the sensor, and so we conclude that the field of view in this case is constrained only by the projector.

Latency

The total system performance is affected by latency at multiple levels. With the time-multiplexed image from the AAXA projector, only one coordinate (X or Y) is tracked at any given instant of time. Thus, the average latency to obtain sensor reads on both coordinates is equal to half the time spent displaying a single color frame, or around 2 ms (0.5/240 s) for the AAXA projector.

The tracker's sensor latency due to the integration time is around 440μs on average. Processing the sample takes an average of 1250μs on the Maple, so the average processing latency is 1900μs (half of the time to process the previous sample, plus the time to process the current sample). Finally, the data are sent over a serial connection running at 115200 baud. Since this connection can receive at most 2000 positions per second, it contributes up to 500μs of latency, or an average of 250μs. Thus, the input latency immediately due to our system is around 2600μs (2.6ms), which is more than enough to provide a fluid interaction

# Sensors (DOF)	**User w/ Sensor**	**User w/ Projector**
One (2D position)	*Spray painting* (Figure 11)	*Draw App* (Fig. 12) *Sword* (Figure 13)
Two (3D pos. + Z rotation)	*Airplane Yoke* (Fig. 14) *AR Spaceship* (Fig. 15)	*Highway escape* (Figure 16)
Four (3D Pos. + X/Y/Z rot.)	*Avatar head* (Figure 17)	*Helicopter* (Figure 18)

Table 1. Categorization of example applications based on sensor-projector configuration and number of sensors.

The latency of the sensor configuration is negligible compared to the latency of the operating system and application, and is likely to be imperceptible to an end user [25]. By comparison, other sensing technologies such as the Microsoft Kinect [21] operate at much lower frame rates (e.g., 30 FPS), resulting in noticeable input delays.

Error Frames

During the tracking accuracy analysis, around 7500 tracking frames belonging to the high-error trials were discarded. Not all frames in these trials were erroneous frames, but we can infer from this that the error rate is at most 1 in 750 frames. During the raster pattern test, 50 erroneous positions were identified by a post-hoc analysis of the data. This is an error rate of 1 in 2000 frames. Thus, the true error rate lies between 0.05% and 0.13% of all frames.

Power Consumption

The power consumption of the sensor, including microprocessor, is about 55mA at 5V, or around 275mW. The microprocessor's power consumption is about 35mA alone, and no special effort has been made to decrease this. We believe that this could be substantially improved with microprocessor power optimizations and low-power sensor components. The dual static projector configuration shown in Figure 4C consumes about 600 mW. In order to function with high ambient brightness or at a larger distance, more power would be required. The AAXA L1 projector we used consumes 7.5W.

EXAMPLE APPLICATIONS

To showcase our system's capability and utility, we developed a series of example applications. We categorize the application space based on two criteria: *Projector/sensor configuration* and *number of sensors*. Projector/sensor configuration denotes whether the sensor is held/worn by the user and the projector is mounted in the environment or vice versa [41]. As both the sensors and projector can be made lightweight and portable, either approach is viable for real-time tracking. The number of sensors used determines the degrees of freedom possible for tracking. Table 1 provides a taxonomic overview of our demo applications. Please also see the Video Figure for demonstrations.

One Sensor (2 DOF)

User with Sensor

We modified an off-the-shelf spray paint can, replacing the paint nozzle with a Lumitrack sensor (Figure 11). A button was provided to spray digital paint onto a computer monitor by toggling the transmission of tracking frames. The projector was mounted to the top of the monitor, providing a 2D tracking volume in front of the display.

User with Projector

In the first example application, the user manipulated the projector much like a laser pointer, controlling a cursor on the laptop screen (Figure 12) by translating or rotating. But-

Figure 11. Digital spray-painting example application.

tons on the projector allowed the user to toggle between three different m-sequence patterns which had no m-bit subsequences in common. The sensor was aware of all three patterns, so in addition to being able to compute its X/Y position within the projected pattern, it was also able to know what m-sequence was active. We bound these three patterns to a pen, eraser and cursor tool, enabling a basic, free-space painting application.

Figure 12. Example painting application. Users can translate and rotate the projector to draw and erase; modes are switched using buttons on the projector.

We used a sword prop for our second example application, which was augmented with a projector (Figure 13, left). On-screen, a virtual sword tracked with the user's rotational movements (Figure 13, Right). One could imagine using this in a sword dueling game requiring high precision and fast reaction times.

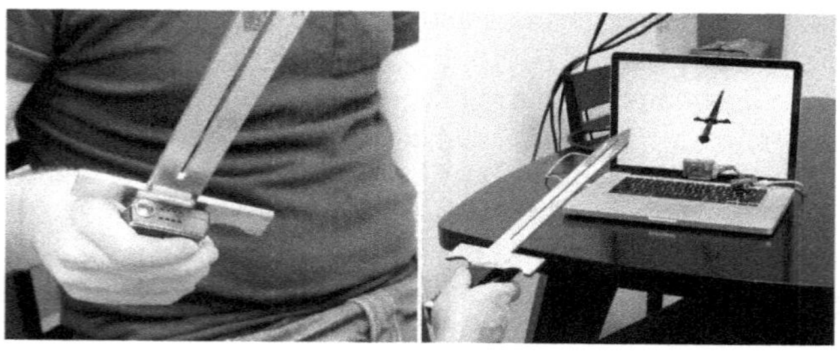

Figure 13. Tracking a projector-augmented sword.

Two Sensors (4 DOF)

User with Sensor

We fabricated an airplane yoke with sensors embedded in the upper grips (Figure 14). Like its real-world counterparts, this yoke could control the pitch (nose up/down via pull/push inputs) and roll (left/right bank via left/right turn inputs) of a virtual plane.

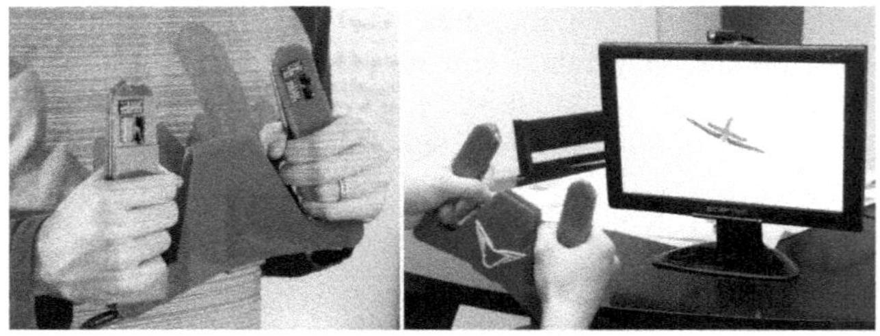

Figure 14. Lumitrack-instrumented airplane yoke used to control a virtual plane.

We also created a projected augmented reality application. A small spaceship model with fitted with two sensors (Figure 15). We affixed our L1 projector above a play space, facing downwards, blanketing an area with the two orthogonal m-sequences needed for tracking (Figure 15, right). Additionally, we took advantage of its dynamic projection capabilities to superimpose afterburner graphics and plasma weapon fire. The user can also steer the ship; a star field with parallax is rendered in the background to provide the illusion of directional travel.

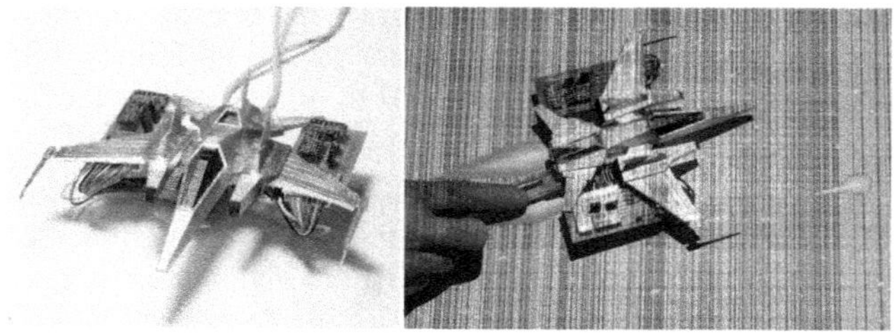

Figure 15. An example augmented-reality application. In addition to projecting m-sequences, the spaceship model (left) is augmented with afterburner and weapon graphics (right).

User with Projector

We 3D printed a small car model to sit top of our L1 projector. This car could be translated on a table's surface in front of an augmented laptop running a simple racing game (Figure 16). The player's onscreen car mirrored the user's real-world movements. To capture this movement, two sensors were placed on the front bezel of the laptop.

Four Sensors (6 DOF)

User with Sensor

We created a four-sensor rig that could be worn on the users head. This provided the 3D position and pose of the face. As a proof of concept, we created an avatar head (Fig-

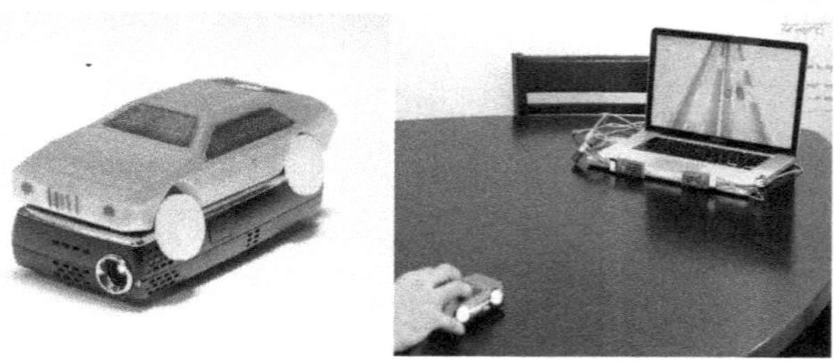

Figure 16. We created a highway racing game where users can translate a car prop on the tabletop to control their in-game car.

ure 17) that followed the user's position by rotating and translating. The avatar also mirrored the Z-rotation of the user's head (i.e., side-to-side tilting of the head).

Figure 17. Using 6 DOF tracking of the user's head, we created an avatar head that always faces the user.

User with Projector

As a final demo, we affixed a projector to the sleds of a 3D printed helicopter. This model could be moved and rotated in three dimensions, which was reflected by an onscreen virtual helicopter. In a flight simulator experience, this could be used control a virtual helicopter (e.g., tilting forward for forward movement).

Figure 18. A projector-augmented helicopter model, which could be used to control an on-screen helicopter with six-degrees of freedom.

LIMITATIONS AND DRAWBACKS

Ambient Light. As with all optical systems, Lumitrack is sensitive to changes in ambient light in the environment. Performance degrades sharply when a significant amount of ambient light is present. We envision increases in projector brightness and optical sensor response will improve the robustness of our system in varying lighting conditions.

Working Volume. The working volume in which interaction can take place is limited by a number of factors including the projector brightness, throw ratio, projection angle, and pattern density. Increasing the tracking distance requires a combination of brighter projection, larger sensors, and higher projection resolution, while reducing the minimum tracking distance requires higher sensor resolution. Our evaluation results demonstrate Lumitrack can be used for motion tracking within the spatial range of many typical applications.

False Positives. The use of parameter search to locate the m-subsequence renders the system prone to false positives – resulting in unwanted skips and jumps in the tracked position. These are made relatively rare by selecting a large m value (window size), but can still occur. Denser patterns with correspondingly higher m values, combined with more intelligent m-sequence search approaches, can help mitigate this problem.

Multi-User Scenarios. In our current approach, the sensor unit is unable to sense position if multiple projectors overlap, restricting use to single-user applications. Time-multiplexing, based on sensed proximity or other means, could resolve this issue and is the focus of future work.

Laser Safety. Depending on the sensing configuration, laser light can potentially be exposed to the user's eyes. LCOS-based laser projectors, however, are significantly safer than their scanning laser counterparts [4]. The use of IR laser light may require modifications to increase the projector throw ratio and minimize light exposure.

CONCLUSIONS AND FUTURE WORK

We introduced Lumitrack, a novel technology for high speed, high precision, low-cost tracking. In future work we envision extending the Lumitrack system in several ways. Firstly, developing color + infrared projectors will enhance the user experience and enable greater interaction with projected content. Secondly, optimizing our m-sequences to consider higher density encoding schemes (e.g., transition based schemes) and multi-resolution arrays that could enable increased range. Additionally, higher resolution pico-projectors are slated for release (e.g., HD resolution), which will offer improved tracking. Simultaneously, higher resolution linear optical sensors are already on the market (e.g., the TSL1402R is 400 PPI). Finally, we aim to reduce the size of our sensor unit by half to enable integration into a wider range of devices and objects.

ACKNOWLEDGMENTS

Funding for this work was provided in part by a Google Ph.D. fellowship, a Qualcomm Innovation Fellowship, NSERC, and NSF grant IIS-1217929.

REFERENCES

1. AAXA Technologies. http://www.aaxatech.com/
2. Anoto Digital Pen. http://www.anoto.com/
3. Bergmann, D. New approach for automatic surface reconstruction with coded light. In *Proc. Remote Sensing and Reconstruction for Three-Dimensional Objects and Scenes*. Vol. 2572, SPIE, 1995, 2-9.
4. Buckley, E. Eye-safety analysis of current laser-based LCOS projection systems. *J. Soc. Information Display.* 18(12), 2010, 1051-1057.
5. Cao, X., Forlines, C. and Balakrishnan, R. Multi-user Interaction Using Handheld Projectors. In *Proc. UIST '07*, 43-52.
6. Casiez, G., Roussel, N., Vogel, D. 1€ Filter: A Simple Speed-based Low-pass Filter for Noisy Input in Interactive Systems. In *Proc. CHI '12*, 2527-2530.
7. Celozzi, C., Paravati, G., Sanna, A. and Lamberti, F. A 6-DOF ARTag-based tracking system. *IEEE Trans. Consumer Electronics*, 56(1), February 2010, 203-210.
8. Chan, L.-W., Wu, H.-T., Kao, H.-S., Ko, J.-C., Lin, H.-R., Chen, M.Y., Hsu, J. and Hung, Y.-P., Enabling Beyond surface Interactions for Interactive Surface with an Invisible Projection. In *Proc. UIST '10*, 263-272.

9. Davison, A., Reid, I., Molton, N. and Stasse, O. MonoSLAM: Real-time single camera SLAM. *IEEE Trans. Pattern Analysis and Machine Intelligence.* 29(6), 2007, 1052-1067.

10. Dourish, P. Where the Action is: The Foundations of Embodied Interaction. MIT Press, Cambridge, Mass., 2001.

11. Grundhöfer, A., Seeger, M., Hantsch, F. and Bimber, O. Dynamic Adaptation of Projected Imperceptible Codes. In *Proc. ISMAR '07*, 1-10.

12. Harrison, C., Benko, H. and Wilson, A. D. OmniTouch: Wearable Multitouch Interaction Everywhere. In *Proc. UIST '11*, 441-450.

13. Hartley, R. I. and Zisserman, A. Multiple View Geometry in Computer Vision. Cambridge University Press. 2004.

14. Heo, S., Han, J., Choi, S., Lee, S., Lee, G., Lee, H., Kim, S., Bang, W., Kim, D. and Kim, C. IrCube tracker: an optical 6-DOF tracker based on LED directivity. In *Proc. UIST '11*, 577-586.

15. Kato, H. and Billinghurst, M. Marker tracking and HMD calibration for a video-based augmented reality conferencing system. In *Proc. IWAR '99*, 85-94.

16. Kawasaki H., Furukawa R., Sagawa R. and Yagi Y. Dynamic scene shape reconstruction using a single structured light pattern. In *Proc. CVPR '08*, 1-8.

17. Köhler, M., Patel, S.N., Summet, J.W., Stuntebeck, E.P. and Abowd, G.D. TrackSense: infrastructure free precise indoor positioning using projected patterns. In *Proc. Pervasive '07*, 334-350.

18. Leaf Labs. http://leaflabs.com

19. Lee, J., Hudson, S. and Dietz, P., Hybrid Infrared and Visible Light Projection for Location Tracking. In *Proc. UIST '07*, 57-60.

20. MacWilliams, F. J. and Sloane, N. J. A. Pseudorandom sequences and arrays. *Proceedings of the IEEE.* 64(12), 1976, 1715-1729.

21. Microsoft Kinect. http://www.xbox.com/kinect

22. Mohan, A., Woo, G., Hiura, S., Smithwick, Q., and Raskar, R. Bokode: imperceptible visual tags for camera based interaction from a distance. In *Proc. SIGGRAPH '09*, Article 98, 8 pages.

23. Molyneaux, D., Izadi, S., Kim, D., Hilliges, O., Hodges, S., Cao, X., Butler, A. and Gellersen, H. Interactive Environment-Aware Handheld Projectors for Pervasive Computing Spaces. In *Proc. Pervasive Computing '12*, 197-215.

24. Morita, H., Yajima, K. and Sakata, S. Reconstruction of Surfaces of 3-D Objects by M-array Pattern Projection Method. In *Proc. ICCV '88*, 468-473.

25. Ng, A., Lepinski, J., Wigdor, D., Sanders, S. and Dietz, P. Designing for low-latency direct-touch input. In *Proc. UIST '12*, 453-464.

26. Pagès, J., Salvi, J. and Forest J. A new optimised De Bruijn coding strategy for structured light patterns. In *Proc. CVPR '04*, 284-287.

27. Pollefeys, M., Gool, L. V., Vergauwen, M., Verbiest, F., Cornelis, K., Tops, J. and Koch, R. Visual modeling with a hand-held camera. *International Journal of Computer Vision.* 59(3), 2004, 207-232.

28. Raskar, R., Beardsley, P., van Baar, J., Wang, Y., Dietz, P., Lee, J., Leigh, D. and Willwacher, T. RFIG lamps: interacting with a self-describing world via photosensing wireless tags and projectors. In *Proc. SIGGRAPH '04*, 406-415.

29. Raskar, R., Nii, H., de Decker, B., Hashimoto, Y., Summet, J., Moore, D., Zhao, Y., Westhues, J., Dietz, P., Inami, M., Nayar, S., Barnwell, J., Noland, M., Bekaert, P., Branzoi, V. and Bruns, E. Prakash: lighting aware motion capture using photo-sensing markers and multiplexed illuminators. In *Proc. SIGGRAPH '07*, Article 36, 11 pages.

30. Raskar, R., Welch, G., Cutts, M., Lake, A., Stesin, L. and Fuchs, H. The office of the future: a unified approach to image-based modeling and spatially immersive displays. In *Proc. SIGGRAPH '98*, 179-188.

31. Saito, S., Hiyama, A., Tanikawa, T. and Hirose, M. Indoor Marker-based Localization Using Coded Seamless Pattern for Interior Decoration. In *Proc. VR '07*, 67-74.

32. Salvi, J., Fernandez, S., Pribanic, T. and Llado, X. A state of the art in structured light patterns for surface profilometry. *Pattern Recognition,* vol. 43, 2010, 2666-2680.

33. Schmidt, D., Molyneaux, D. and Cao, X. PICOntrol: using a handheld projector for direct control of physical devices through visible light. In *Proc. UIST '12,* 379-388.

34. Shiratori, T., Park, H., Sigal, L., Sheikh, Y. and Hodgins, J. Motion capture from body-mounted cameras. In *Proc. SIGGRAPH '11*, Article 31, 10 pages.

35. Welch, G. and Foxlin, E. Motion Tracking: No Silver Bullet, but a Respectable Arsenal. *IEEE Comput. Graph. Appl.* 22(6), November 2002, 24-38.

36. Welch, G., Bishop, G., Vicci, L., Brumback, S., Keller, K. and Colucci, D. The HiBall tracker: High performance wide-area tracking for virtual and augmented environments. In *Proc. VRST '99,* 1-10.

37. Wienss, C., Nikitin, I., Goebbels, G., Troche, K., Göbel, M., Nikitina, L. and Müller, S. Sceptre: an infrared laser tracking system for virtual environments. In *Proc. VRST '06*, 45-50.

38. Willis, K.D.D., Poupyrev, I., Hudson, S. E. and Mahler, M. SideBySide: Ad-hoc Multi-user Interaction with Handheld Projectors. In *Proc. UIST '11*, 431-440.

39. Willis, K.D.D., Shiratori, T. and Mahler, M. HideOut: Mobile Projector Interaction with Tangible Objects and Surfaces. In *TEI '13.*

40. Woltring, H. New possibilities for human motion studies by real-time light spot position measurement. *Biotelemetry,* 1(3), 1974, 132-146.

41. Zizka, J., Olwal, A. and Raskar, R. SpeckleSense: fast, precise, low-cost and compact motion sensing using laser speckle. In *Proc. UIST '11*, 489-498.

PneUI: Pneumatically Actuated Soft Composite Materials for Shape Changing Interfaces

Lining Yao[1], Ryuma Niiyama[1], Jifei Ou[1], Sean Follmer[1], Clark Della Silva[2], Hiroshi Ishii[1]

[1]MIT Media Lab
Cambridge, MA 02139 USA
{lining, ryuma, jifei, sean, ishii}@ media.mit.edu

[2]MIT EECS
Cambridge, MA 02139 USA
clarkds@ mit.edu

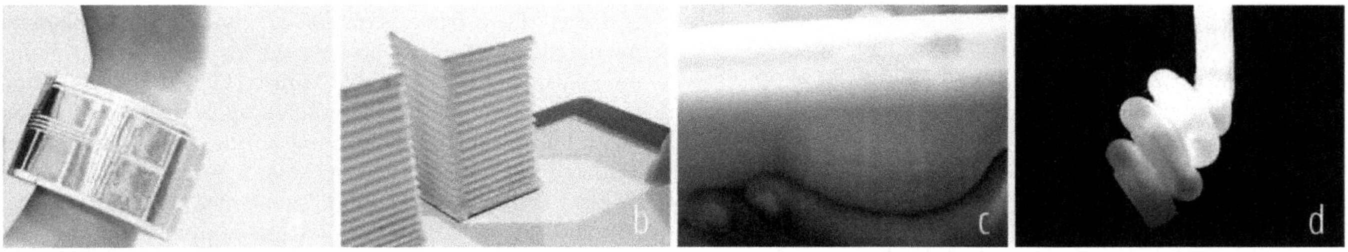

Figure 1: Application demonstrations. (a) A shape changing mobile. (b) Height changing tangible phicons. (c) A transformable tablet case. (d) A shape-shifting lamp.

ABSTRACT
This paper presents PneUI, an enabling technology to build shape-changing interfaces through pneumatically-actuated soft composite materials. The composite materials integrate the capabilities of both input sensing and active shape output. This is enabled by the composites' multi-layer structures with different mechanical or electrical properties. The shape changing states are computationally controllable through pneumatics and pre-defined structure. We explore the design space of PneUI through four applications: height changing tangible phicons, a shape changing mobile, a transformable tablet case and a shape shifting lamp.

Author Keywords
Soft Composite Material; Pneumatic System; Soft Actuator; Soft Robotics; Human-Material Interaction; Shape Changing Interface; Radical Atoms; Organic User Interface

ACM Classification Keywords
H.5.2. User Interfaces: Haptic I/O; Prototype

INTRODUCTION
Hard bodies with construction of rigid structural and electronic elements have limited the form, function and interaction of shape changing interfaces in HCI [37]. Thus a range of technologies in HCI have been developed to enable soft and organic interfaces, including flexible sensing techniques [28], dynamic stiffness [3], texture and buttons on malleable surfaces [6, 7], soft deformable surface output [1, 13], and 2.5D shape display with elastic covers [18]. In contrast, inspired by marine organisms that sense and accomplish drastic body deformation and locomotion by soft actuators [28], we take a holistic view of the material itself and envision a composite material that integrates input sensing and active shape output. Materials with different mechanical properties can be combined to form separate structural layers for the soft composites, which can be utilized to create shape changing interfaces without rigid mechanical elements. This research is driven by the vision of Radical Atoms [11], which proposes a group of physical materials as a dynamic manifestation of digital information.

While the study of soft motion and mechanisms is a growing topic in robotics, approaches and techniques in soft robotics have not been fully explored in HCI. In this paper, we presented PneUI, pneumatically actuated soft composite materials, that follow three principles: 1) the shape output is computationally controllable through pneumatics and pre-defined structure; 2) the material should enable either isotropic (uniform in all orientations) or anisotropic (directionally dependent) deformation determined by the intrinsic properties of the composite; 3) the material should integrate both input sensing and active shape output. Examples of utilizing shape changing primitives for HCI applications are illustrated in Figure 1.

In this paper, we first describe the design considerations of applying our soft composite materials for HCI. We then talk about the layered structures of soft composite materials and explain the composites' active shape output and input

UIST'13, October 08 – 11, 2013, St. Andrews, United Kingdom.
Copyright © 2013 ACM 978-1-4503-2268-3/13/10...$15.00.
http://dx.doi.org/10.1145/2501988.2502037

sensing capabilities in separate chapters. Finally, we describe pneumatic control systems and applications.

We present the following main contributions:

- Creation of pneumatically actuated soft composite materials, which integrates both input sensing and active shape output.
- Development of a framework for creation and testing of selected materials, structures, soft fabrication processes, and pneumatic control systems to construct soft composite materials.
- Primitives of soft shape changing at both macro and micro scales, including curvature change of surfaces, unidirectional volume change of solid geometries, and dynamic texture change.
- Development of two techniques that embed sensing into composite material and interfaces: 1) conductive pads composited on structural layers for sensing shape output and gestural input using capacitive and electric field sensing; 2) liquid metal embedded in elastomeric air channels for sensing deformation of soft surfaces.

RELATED WORK

Soft Robotics

Soft robotics is an emerging domain that is dedicated to robots comprised of soft components including soft actuators, flexible sensor/circuits, and soft bodies [10]. In contrast to other techniques for shape change, such as spatial arrangement of actuated modules [20], self-foldable chains [9], self-foldable surfaces [8, 15], soft robotics often focuses on pneumatic actuation of elastomeric channels and bladders. Pneumatic actuation is chosen because air is a lightweight, compressible and environmentally benign energy source [32].

While a primary focus of soft robotics is the improvement of the robot's performance and the exploration of the bio-inspired mechanism itself, there is a large space to introduce soft robotic technology in constructing shape changing interfaces. One design space is to explore not only isotropic, but also anisotropic deformation with soft composite materials: an elastomer by itself deforms uniformly under stress; however, by compositing different structural layers with various mechanical properties, the orientation of deformation can be pre-defined [19]. We build on this work by exploring other topologies, integrating sensing, and applying these concepts to HCI.

Shape Changing User Interfaces

The exploration of Shape Changing User Interfaces in HCI is still in its infancy, as techniques for shape change, flexible sensing and interaction techniques are being developed [2, 37]. Shape-Changing Mobiles [9] are actuated by RC servo motors to provide tapering of the back of the mobile phone. Densely arranged linear actuator arrays have demonstrated successful results in presenting complex 2.5D relief forms [18]. Those rigid mechanisms can achieve controllable transformations, yet not compliant, making it hard for these systems to conform to intricate shapes and limiting the amount of possible shape change states. Shape memory alloy (SMA) based actuators have been used to bend surfaces [1]. It has been integrated into mobile devices [27, 5] allowing for edges to be bent. SMA is lightweight and strong for its weight, but often slow.

In the field of HCI, pneumatic inflation has also been explored as an approach for shape change. Volflex [12] is a volumetric display consisting of independently controlled balloons. Deformable convex or concave hemispherical membranes with rims can be used for an inflatable multi-touch display [35]. Inflatable Mouse [13] is a shape-shifting mouse that can change the volume by using an air balloon and a built-in pump. Closely related to our work, Harrison explored dynamically changeable physical buttons on a display, with a variety of different materials for creating soft and ridged buttons, and integrated multi-touch sensing on the surface through diffuse illumination, pressure sensing for input [7]. Granular jamming [3], which can also be controlled pneumatically, can provide malleable surface with adjustable stiffness, and allows for passive shape change. In contrast to jamming, this work focuses on pneumatic actuation – allowing for active shape change.

The types of shape change in HCI have been categorized as: orientation, form, volume, texture, viscosity, spatiality, adding/subtracting and permeability [26]. We chose to focus on curvature, volume and texture as shape change primitives because we believe those encompass a large space of shape change in mobile and tangible applications, as demonstrated by past work [9, 6, 27].

Flexible Sensing Techniques

A range of sensing techniques on soft surfaces has been explored in HCI, optical sensing [3] and flexible capacitive sensing [3, 31] are among common approaches. "Sensing through structure" has been introduced to sense the deformation of flexible surfaces and structures [33, 8].

In Soft Robotics, sensing through the deformation of the surface itself is a unique approach afforded by the elastic nature of soft materials. A range of stretchy sensors, bend sensors and pressure sensors have been built [1, 22,16, 17].

Soft Fabrication

We choose fabrication processes that are feasible in common fabrication laboratories. One notable case is Soft Lithography [25], which is used to generate 3D structures within elastic polymers. Soft roboticists adapted the process for fabricating elastomer, especially silicon rubber, with integrated air bladders and channels. This process requires high precision equipment and fabrication processes, such as high resolution molds, spin coaters, and precise deposition process.

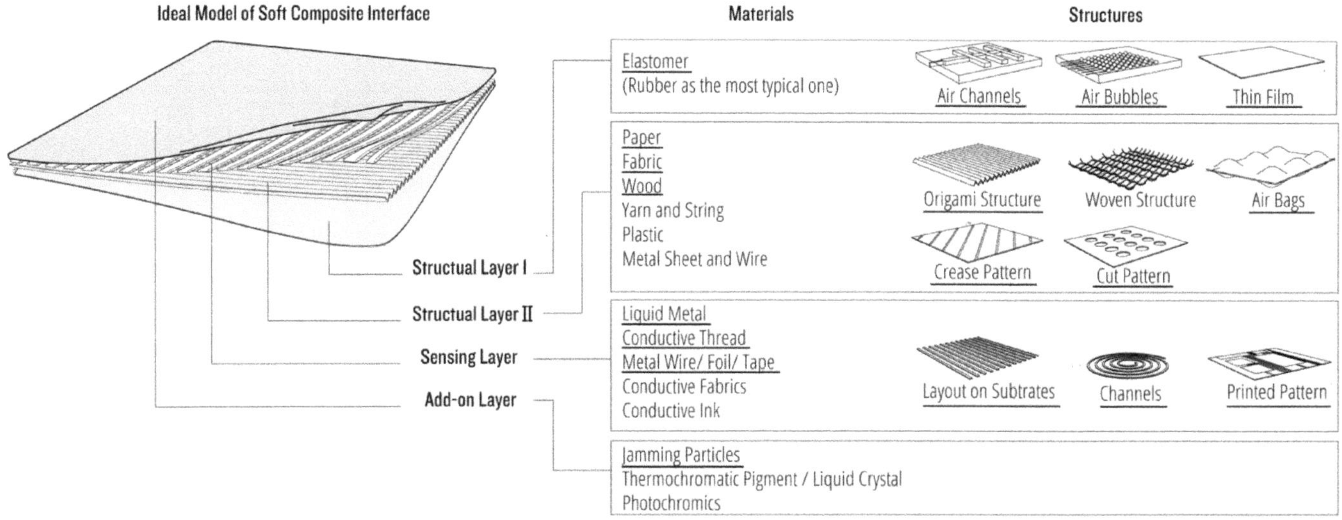

Figure 2: Diagram of composite structure. Structure Layer I responds isotropically to stress; Structure Layer II enables anisotropic deformation in response to air pressure; Sensing Layer enables the sensing of both hand input and shape output; Add-on Layer manipulates other material properties rather than the shape change, either haptically or visually. The underlined materials and structures are the ones that have been tested out.

SOFT COMPOSITE INTERFACE FOR HCI

Pneumatic soft composites provide many opportunities for designing significant and novel applications for HCI, primarily as an enabling technology for shape changing user interfaces. Shape change can be used to convey information to the user about computational state and provide dynamic affordances. By combining a sensing layer in the soft composite interface, PneUI interface can sense a range of inputs and outputs.

Information Representation

Shape change, both at the macro and micro level, can be used to convey computational states to users as a type of display. For example, smaller scale shape change, which we call texture change, has previously been shown to enable a separate haptic channel for representing or communicating information [6]. Pneumatic soft composites provide dynamically controllable texture patterns that can vary density, frequency and sequence. A shape changing iPad case is introduced in the paper as an example of dynamic textures.

Dynamic Affordances and Ergonomics

Shape change can also provide new ways for users to interact with devices on demand. In addition to dynamic physical affordances, adaptable shapes can increase economic performance for specific tasks. We develop a prototype of mobile phone that can change shape and motion for different use cases.

Sensing Modalities

We categorize the achievable sensing modalities into: 1) sensing gestures on the surface, 2) gestures hovering over the surface, 3) gestures that deform the surface, and 4) air deforming the surface. The first three are input modalities, and the last one is shape output. Further, the innate characteristics of soft interface could afford a wider variety of manipulations to deform the surface, such as pushing, stretching, bending, embracing, stroking and squeezing. A system of shape changing tangible phicons is developed to demonstrate different gesture sensing modalities.

STRUCTURE OF THE SOFT COMPOSITE MATERIAL

Layered Structure

Our pneumatically-actuated soft composite material is designed to enable both isotropic and anisotropic deformation in response to air pressure. The composite material is fabricated with three main layers, including two structural layers and one sensing layer (Figure 2). One structural layer utilizes an elastomeric polymer (or elastomer) as the main material to enable isotropic shape deformation. To go beyond isotropic deformation, an additional structural layer includes a range of materials with different elasticity to create constrained anisotropic deformation in response to air pressure. Moreover, conductive materials, either solid or liquid, such as conductive thread and liquid metal, are composited as the sensing layer to sense both input and output. Finally an add-on layer can be composited to control other material properties other than active shape output. For example, Jamming particles can control surface stiffness to give haptic affordances or lock shapes in a certain state [3]; and thermochromic liquid crystals can be injected into air channels of elastomer to change the color of surfaces.

Materials Choices

Each layer of the composite includes one or more materials with extrinsically designed structures. These structures can enhance or modify the deformations caused by pneumatic inflation. For example, copy paper itself has relatively low elasticity, however, origami structure enables increased flexibility in a specific directions. Further, composited conductive layers can form a sensing network. For example, placing electrodes onto 3D substrates enables sensing the 3D shape output through changes in capacitance.

Selecting different materials from Figure 2, and layering them in different orders allow the construction of multiple soft composite materials. The choice of materials is driven both by the type of shape change we want to achieve and also materials that we think other researchers would have ready access to, so as to make our work more accessible. The underlined materials from Figure 2 are the ones that have been verified during our exploratory experiments. We constructed the table assuming that air is the main actuation method. By introducing a greater variety of energy sources, we could composite additional ranges of active materials, such as heat-driven shape memory alloys and thermoplastics.

SHAPE CHANGING PRIMITIVES

We choose curvature, volume and texture to explore how soft pneumatic composite materials provide a range of deformation behaviors and thus enable or enhance shape changing interfaces on both the macro and micro level (Figure 3).

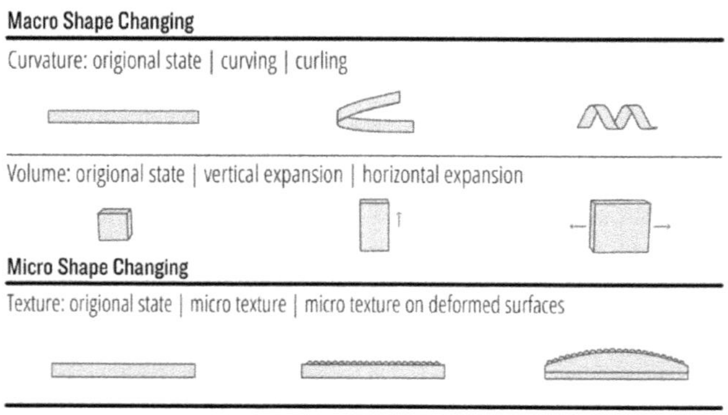

Figure 3: Shape changing primitives: curvature, volume and texture.

Curvature Change on Surfaces - Bending and Curling

The soft mechanical alphabet [2] describes the combination of compression and elongation to generate curvatures at given points of a surface. This is the basis to create physical forms under the constraints of preserved topological equivalents. We introduce two types of composite materials to generate such surface curvatures, utilizing compression and elongation behaviors with inflatable airbags (Figure 4). For both cases, crease patterns on the paper layer or the location of airbags define the position of the deformation. Air pressure determines the degree of curvature.

Elongation with Elastic Airbags for Bending and Curling

This composite material includes three layers, a silicon layer with embedded airbags connected with air channels, a paper layer with crease patterns, and a thin silicon layer at the bottom to bond and protect the paper layer (Figure 5).

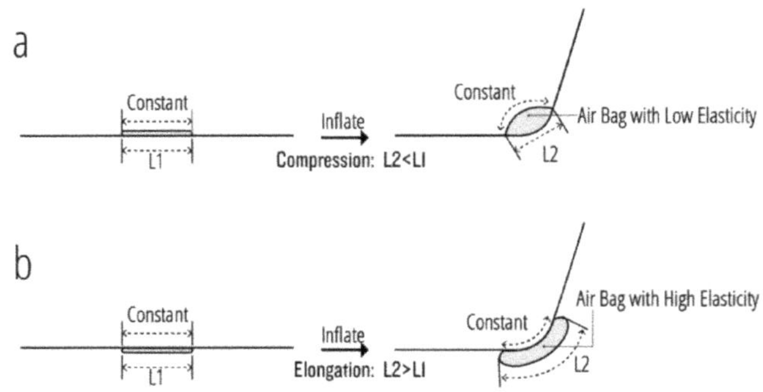

Figure 4. Surface curvature can be determined by the compression of airbags with low elasticity (a), or the elongation of airbags with high elasticity (b).

While soft actuators have been introduced before [19], our work focuses on introducing paper composite with various crease patterns to control the bending behavior. When inflated, the inner airbags function as actuators to generate elongation and force the surface to bend towards the opposite direction.

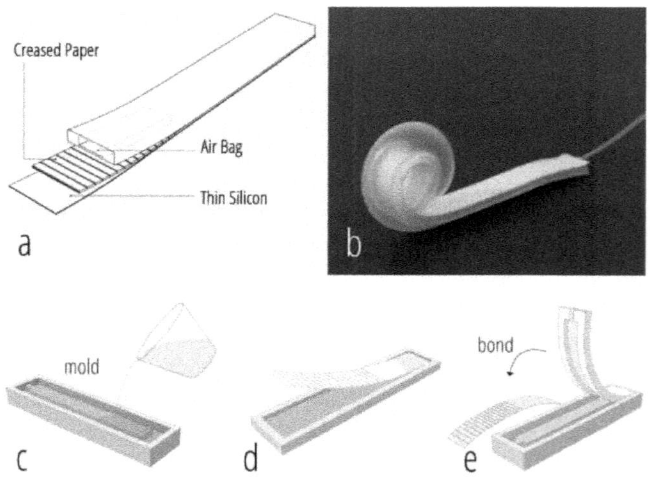

Figure 5: (a, b) Structure of the composite. (c, d, e) Fabrication process. (c) Pre-mixture of silicon (EcoFlex 00-30, Smooth-on, Inc) is poured into a 3D printed mold designed to form a shape with air channels. (d) Creased paper is soaked into the same silicon mixture. (e) Silicon and paper layer are peeled off molds separately once thermally cured. Two layers are then bonded with uncured silicon.

In this case, dynamic control of the curvature is determined by two factors: air pressure and crease pattern. First, air pressure can control the degree of curvature. Our experiments show how pumping additional air will make a single bending (Figure 6d) turn into a curling with continuous bending (Figure 6e). Secondly, the design of paper crease patterns will affect the deformation. We vary three factors of crease patterns in our experiments: density, location and angle. Figure 6a and 6b indicate how density affects the sharpness of bending. Low density creases enable sharper bends and by varying the location of crease, we can control the bending location on the surface (Figure 6c and 6d). Laying out the crease lines diagonally (Figure

6f) generates helical shapes instead of curling on a single plane (Figure 6e). Finally, through Figure 6g and 6h we demonstrate a variation of on-surface pattern cuts on thin pieces of wood instead of paper. It shows similar bending and curling behaviors.

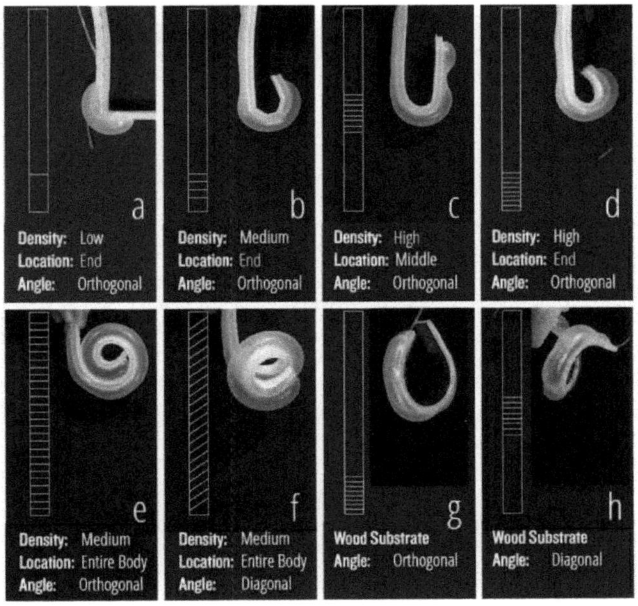

Figure 6: (a, b) Crease patterns with varied density; (b, c) Crease patterns at varied location; (d, e) (e, f) Crease patterns with varied angles; (g, h) Crease patterns on thin wood.

To apply the aforementioned approaches of dynamic control of shape changing states, we test how specifically designed crease patterns and respective control of airbags can make a flat circular shape morph into different spatial structures with three stands (Figure 7a). We also show a progressive transformation from a line to a square (Figure 7b).

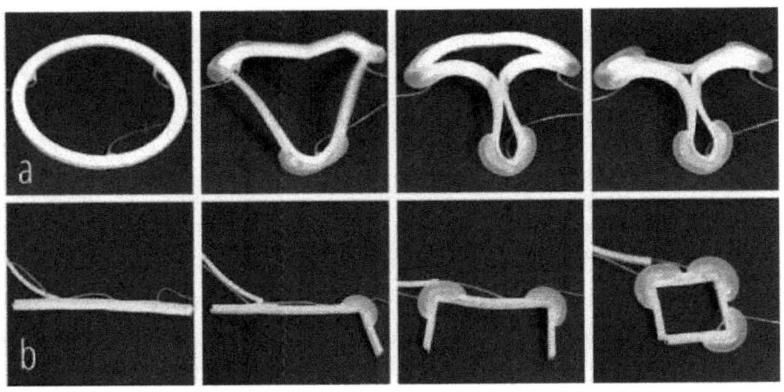

Figure 7: Specifically designed crease patterns and respective control of airbags enabling dynamic transformation of shapes.

Compression with Nonelastic Airbags

This composite material includes two layers: a plain paper layer and plastic airbags with low elasticity (Figure 8a). Airbags are fabricated using plastic welding and glued with the paper layer. While inflated, the airbags behave like the biceps (the muscle to pull the arm up), and compresses itself to cause the surface to bend. The inflation of nonelastic airbags happens on the same side as the surface bends towards (Figure 8). Experiments indicate that muscle like nonelastic airbags have stronger bending force than aforementioned elastic airbags, and can bend thicker paper or surfaces made from thin wood or plastic.

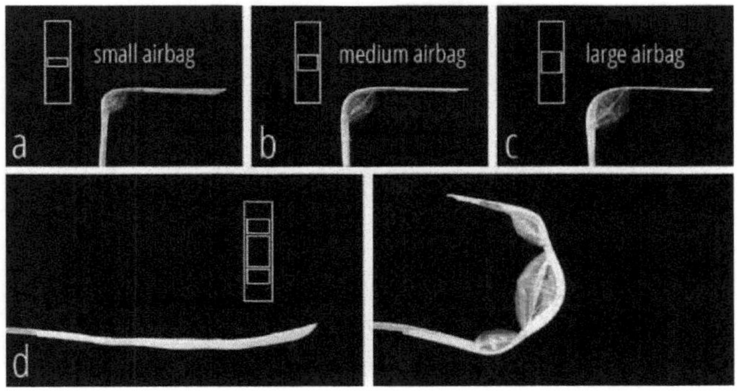

Figure 8: (a, b, c) Curvature control by size of the airbag. (d) Combination of the two different airbag sizes.

Unidirectional Volume Change of Solid Geometries

Origami is adapted through engineering methods to create 3D structures out of paper folds [36]. Inspired by the work in soft robotics that combines origami with elastomers to build soft actuators [19], we explore the orientational volume changing behaviors. We do this through compositing a range of origami structures with elastomers. The origami structures are spin coated and sealed with silicon (EcoFlex 00-30, Smooth-on, Inc), allowing the volume change to be actuated with air transported into the hollow space (Figure 9). Direct manipulation can also deform the shape.

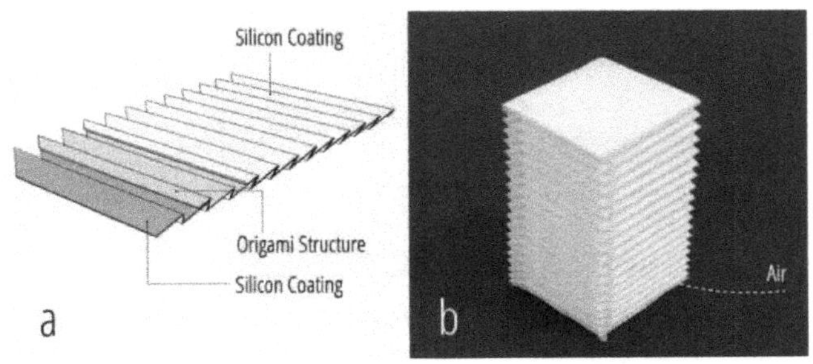

Figure 9: (a) Structure of the composite surface that forming the volume. (b) Air is pumped into the hollow space for actuation.

Three orientational volume changing behaviors are explored: 1) linear elongation, 2) angular expansion and 3) rotatory elongation. Accordion structure folded from V-pleats [24] enables linear elongation (Figure 10a). Utilizing the same pleating pattern and bonding one side of the folds with silicon, we are able to achieve angular expansion (Figure 10b). Lastly, rotatory elongation can be achieved with cylindrical structures folded with triangular pleats (Figure 10c) [29]. In this case silicon serves three functions: sealing the origami structure for air actuation, coating the paper surface for enhancing material durability, and constraining elasticity of origami structure within a specific range.

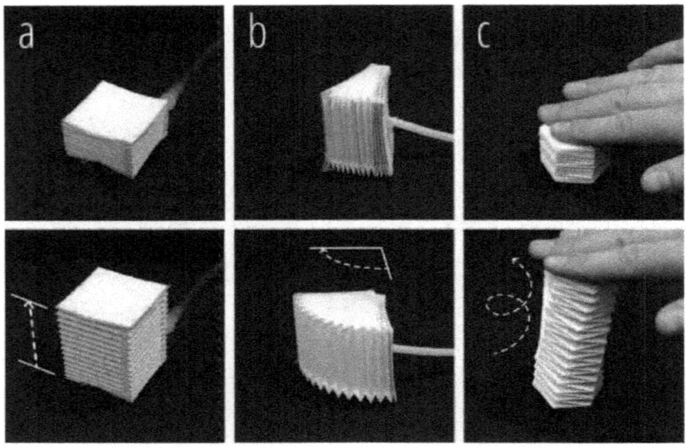

Figure 10: (a) Linear elongation. (b) Angular elongation. (c) Rotatory elongation.

Dynamic Texture Change

We perceive the change of texture as a local and micro level shape changing behavior occurring on the surface. Two approaches are examined to generate textures on soft surfaces: fabricating air bubbles inside elastomer and compositing fabric with cut patterns. Conductive threads, such as plated silver type threads, can be embedded in the composite material for human touch and gesture sensing.

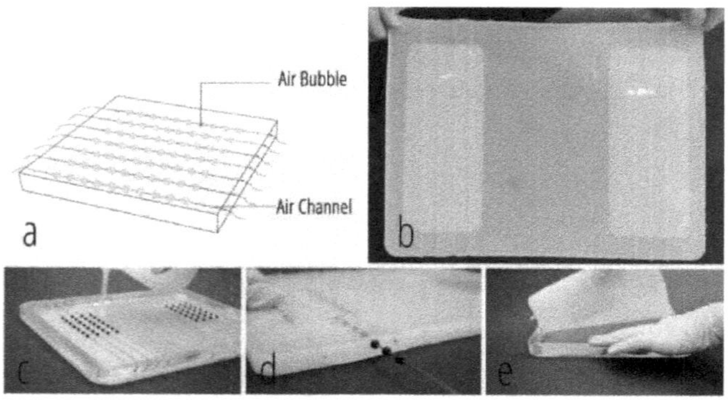

Figure 11: (a, b) Structure of the composite material. (c, d, e) Fabrication process. (c) Pouring pre-mixture of silicon into a mold with threads of beads suspended in the mid-air. (d) Thermally curing the silicon and peeling it off the mold. (e) Pulling the beads out of the silicon for the final sample.

Fabricating Air Bubbles inside Elastomer

In the sample from Figure 11, each column of air bubbles can be inflated separately. We can vary the density, frequency and sequence of texture by pumping and vacuuming air in separate columns at different times. The combination of the three factors is capable of communicating different types of information, such as directional signals and speed. Also, by compositing a second silicon layer with bigger airbags, we can combine deformation on both macro and micro level, to create texture patterns on a deformable, 3D surface.

Compositing Fabric with Cut Patterns

Another approach to generate texture on soft surfaces is to composite flexible material with cut patterns (Figure 12). Elastic fabric (Spandex) was chosen due to its compliance under stress when composited with silicon.

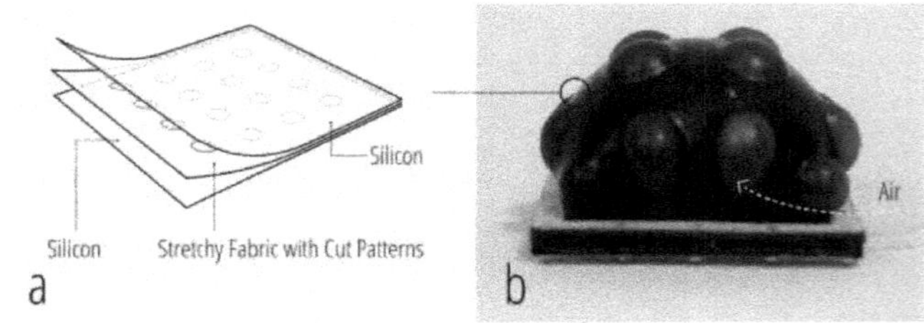

Figure 12: (a) Structure of composite material. (b) Fabric constraints of deformation in local areas of surface.

The difference in the elastic modulus of fabric compared with silicon creates multi-state deformation. We demonstrate that the same surface will deform from macro to micro level as air pressure is increased (Figure 13).

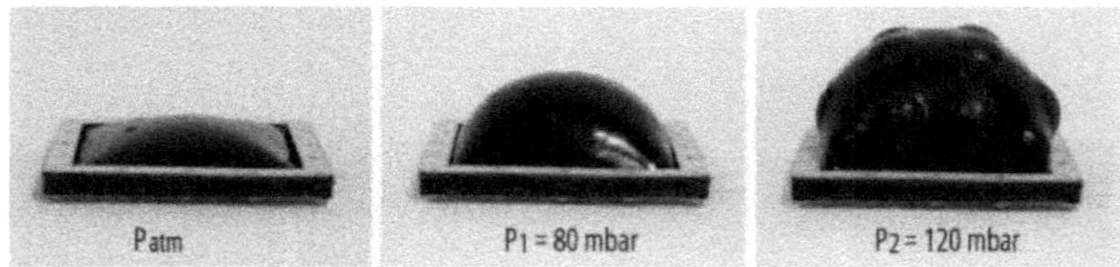

Figure 13: As the increase of air pressure, the surface deform from global to local region.

One advantage of a fabric-elastomer composite is the ease of designing and fabricating different patterns. Rather than making customized molds for textures, patterns can be quickly designed and cut with digital fabrication methods, such as laser cutting. Figure 14 shows a variety of texture patterns we have explored.

Figure 14: Different textures are generated due to different cut patterns on the fabric composite layer.

COMPOSITE SENSING LAYER

To sense input and output, we have explored different sensing techniques, including compositing electrodes to sense global structural change, and embedding fluid conductors to sense local surface deformation with high sensitivities. The cause of shape deformation can be air or human gestures.

Composite Thin and Flexible Circuitry

Flexible circuitry, which is cut out of copper tape or printed by an inkjet printer with conductive ink, can be composited as a sensing layer in the soft composite material. We designed customizable electrode patterns to sense direct touch and near range proximity by measuring the capacitance between human fingers and the electrode network. A coating of silicon layer on top of the sensing pads enables insulation. Multilayer circuitry can be composited with silicon layers in between. Further, through the application of shape shifting lamp, we have also demonstrated the possibility of compositing rigid electrical components, such as surface mounted LEDs, within soft bodies.

Composite Sensors on Folding Structures

In the case of using origami as a supporting and constraining structure, electrodes made from copper tape can be composited with paper folds to sense structural deformations. These deformations can be caused by either pneumatic actuation or direct manipulation. The separation distance between folds correlates to the capacitance between the electrodes as shown in Figure 15. For a linear accordion, four electrode pairs on both sides of the structure were sufficient to measure the height of each side. Other electrode placements can be extended to sense additional geometrical folding structures.

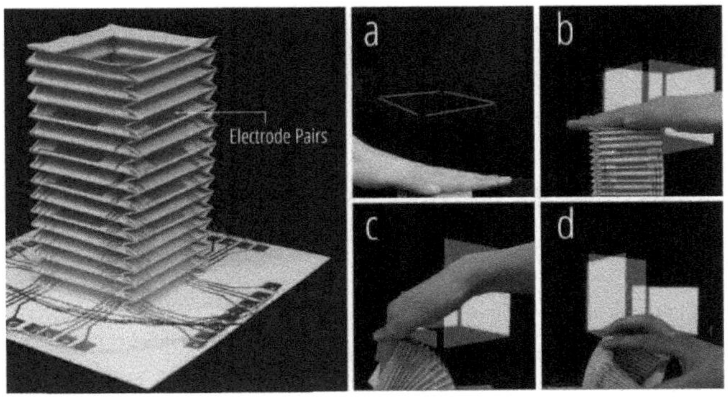

Figure 15: Four pairs of electrodes on adjacent faces of the folds are used to sense geometrical deformation. (a, b) Sensing the height. (c) Sensing side bending. (d) Sensing diagonal bending.

Measurements are taken by stimulating one electrode with a square wave and then reading the induced voltage on the adjacent electrodes. Readings are taken at time T after the rising and falling edges of the square wave, and the difference between these measurements is averaged for 23 cycles (Figure 16). Because the time constant of an RC circuit is dependent on C, as C changes, the voltage at time T changes, allowing for relative changes in capacitance to be measured. Sensor data for each side is averaged and then passed through a windowed time average in order to eliminate noise. The value for each side is then unity-normalized to determine the relative height of each side.

Composite Liquid Metal in Elastomeric Channels

Soft robotic engineers have shown how to construct elastic sensing surfaces by injecting conductive liquid metal (eGaIn) into inner channels of elastomer [1]. The resistance of liquid metal changes in response to the deformation of the channels.

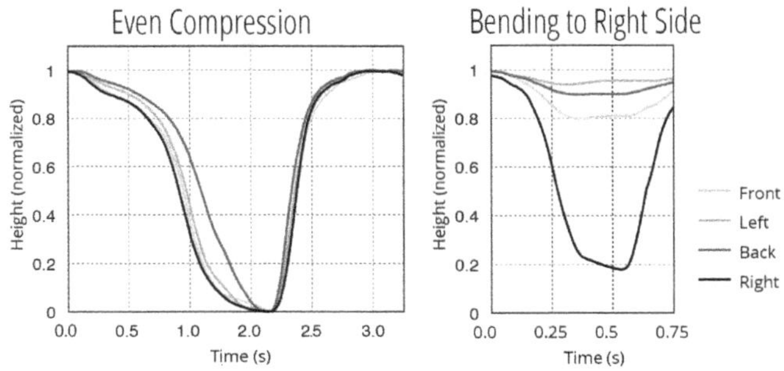

Figure 16: Relative side heights for various deformations of a linear accordion

We adapt this sensing technique to fabricate the top layer of the composite material. It can sense surface deformation through both direct manipulation and air actuation (Figure 17). These conductive channels can also be used for capacitive sensing.

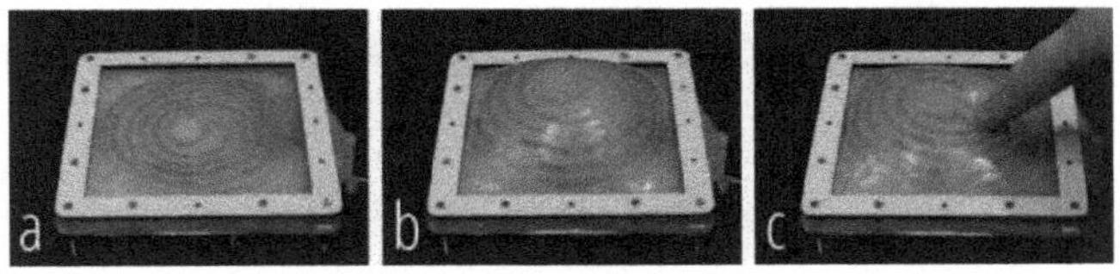

Figure 17: The resistance of liquid metal sensor changes in response to the deformation of the elastomeric channels through either air actuation (b) or direct manipulation (c).

PNEUMATIC CONTROL SYSTEMS

The pneumatic control system energizes the soft composite material. Air can be either injected into air channels inside elastomer, or introduced into the space wrapped around by the composite material.

There are three modes to control the airflow in and out of the soft composite material: supply, exhaust, and close. The supply/exhaust is the mode to inflate/deflate an air bag. The close mode stops the airflow to air inside the composite. Figure 18 shows a pneumatic control circuit consisting of two 3-port solenoid valves, an air compressor, and a vacuum pump for a single air bag.

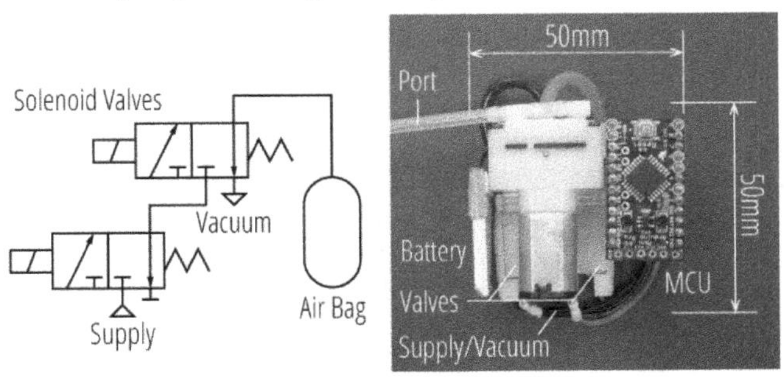

Figure 18: (Left) Basic pneumatic circuit for single air bag; (Right) self-contained pneumatic system

We use a large-sized stationary air compressor (Silent Aire Tech., Super Silent compressor 50) and a vacuum pump (Rocker Scientific, Oil-Free Pump 300) for experiments. However, typical tethered pneumatic systems with a stationary air compressor limits use in portable applications. Therefore, we developed a miniature pneumatic control system with small solenoid valves (SMC, Series S070), a pump used as both supply and vacuum (Koge Electronics, Series KPV), and lithium polymer battery (3.7V, 110mAh). The system indicates feasibility of a further mobile application. The noise levels of the systems are 40dB and 72dB for the stationary air compressor and the miniature pump used in the portable system, respectively (catalog value).

APPLICATIONS

We build four prototypes to explore the potential of shape changing interfaces enabled by the soft composite material. Different soft fabrication processes that combine structural layers with sensing layers are described in brief.

Shape Changing Mobile: Fabricating Multi-state Bending Surfaces

The shape changing mobile is a flexible body that enables multiple bending states, to give users dynamic affordances for various use cases. The surface will animate between flat and bending state when a call comes in. It can morph from a bar shape to a curved phone shape if a user answers the phone call; when placed over the user's arm, it turns into a wearable wristband (Figure 19).

The fabrication of the shape changing mobile is based on one type of the aforementioned primitives: curvature change on surfaces. Touch sensing pads are composited on both upper and bottom side to detect direct touch.

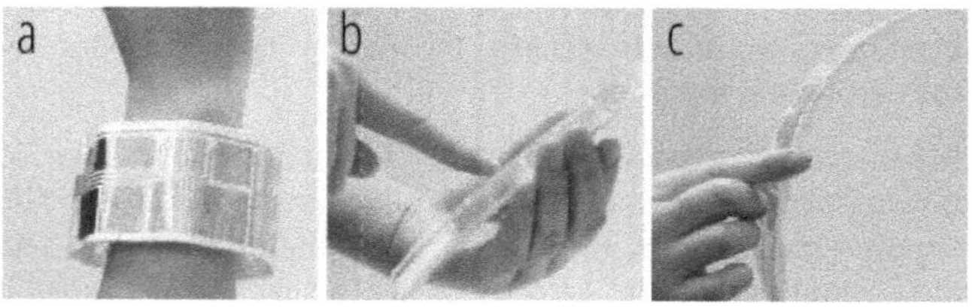

Figure 19: (a) Wrist band mode (b) Bar mode (c) Phone mode

Height Changing Tangible Phicons: Origami Composite with Sensing

This application demonstrates the controllability and connectivity of multiple height-changing objects mediated by graphics (Figure 20). The system casts computationally generated digital shadows on a graphic touch screen corresponding to the height of the box and imaginary time. Users can change the height of the box by push/pull and release the top. In addition, a user can change the height of the box by editing the digital shadow with drag gesture. This application is intended for computer-aided urban planning in which total capacity of the buildings is one of the conditions. By making bridge between boxes, users can also examine the height of the boxes without changing total volume of the multiple boxes.

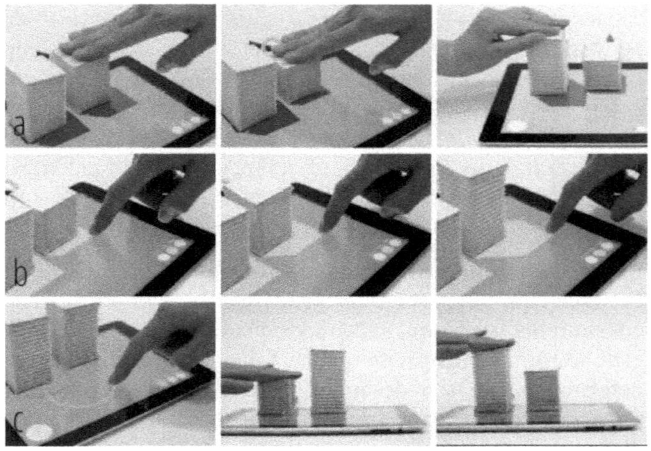

Figure 20: (a) Direct push/pull height-changing of the box with shadow simulation (b) Height-changing by editing digital shadow (c) Connecting two boxes with bridge and setting total volume constraint

The construction is based on linear elongation of shape changing primitives. The composite sensing techniques of the folding structure is adapted to sense the height change of the buildings. The main fabrication process includes pasting electrodes on paper, folding origami structures, dip coating and spin coating with silicon.

Transformable Tablet Cases: Fabricating Multilayer Airbags

For this prototype, while bigger airbags are inflated as grippers for a car racing game controller, columns of smaller air bubbles on top can be inflated sequentially to directions through haptics (Figure 21).

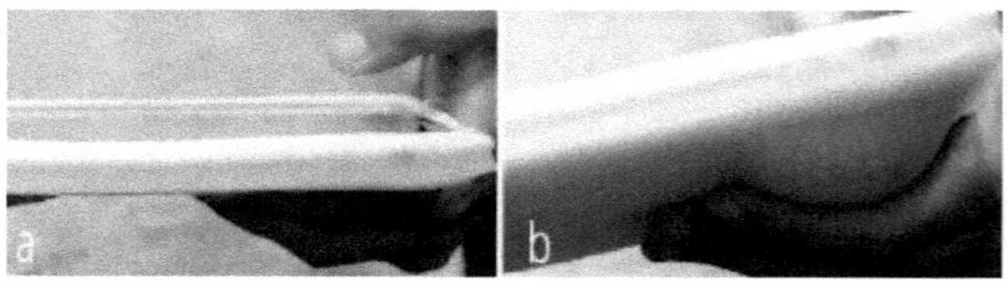

Figure 21: (a) Flat tablet cover in initial state. (b) Macro volume change for forming grips and micro volume change for haptic sensation.

This prototype demonstrates the hybrid of macro and micro level shape change, based on the isotropic deformation behavior exhibited by homogeneous elastomer. Flexible texture layer is molded on top of the bigger airbags. The fabrication involves multi-stage molding and casting. To keep the prototype thin and light, we embed two flat Mylar pieces during the casting process, to create two flat yet inflatable airbags below finer texture bubbles.

Shape-shifting Lamp: Soft Lithography with Embedded Sensing and Light

This lamp supports large deformation from a straight strip shape to a rounded bulb shape. Users can pull the strip like pulling the chain of a conventional lamp. The strip is the illuminating light itself and it starts to curl and light up.

This demonstrates Shape-changing combined with optical properties (Figure 22).

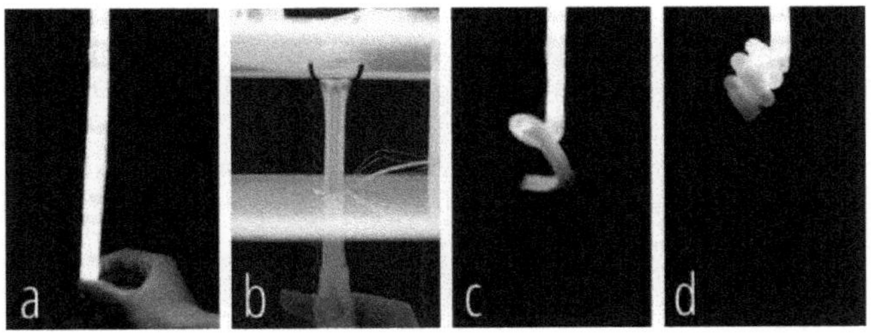

Figure 22: (a, b) Lamp in straight state capable of user input by pulling the entire body. (b) Silicon with embedded liquid metal as pulling sensor. (c, d) Lamp in bulb state by curling

The construction of the lamp is inspired by one type of shape changing primitives: the curling behavior under curvature change on surfaces. Silicon with embedded liquid metal is fabricated as pulling sensor, which is attached to the top of the lamp stip. Soft lithography is adapted for fabricating the shape-shifting lamp. Before the casting process, surface mounted LEDs are soldered on top of flexible copper strips. We then bond the copper strips with a paper substrate with angular cut patterns. The two layers, paper layer and air channel layer, are bonded together with half cured silicon.

LIMITATION AND FUTURE WORK

While the current soft composite materials have unique limitations in both design and fabrication processes, it opens up exciting directions to explore in the future.

Compositing Active Material

The current fabrication process allows the interfaces to morph between two shapes, by designing certain structure layers that composite with airbags. It is still desired that the interface can have multiple shape-changing states that can be dynamically controlled in real-time. This could be achieved by introducing other active stimulus and compositing a wider range of active materials. For example, by embedding memory alloy or heat reactive polymers, and combining two actuation sources (air and heat respectively), we might be able to achieve more flexible control of shape changing states. This is a step closer towards programmable, dynamically controllable, shape changing interfaces.

Variations of Source for Actuation

Current stationary system has limited mobility. We have shown an untethered mobile pneumatic system in the previous section. However the pumping and vacuuming speed drops significantly in the mobile system. Another issue of the pneumatic system is the continuous noise of the pump. The noise can be reduced with an insulation enclosure.

Future work is required to explore new approaches to enable smaller, faster and more integrated pneumatic control systems. Exploring other types of fluid rather than air to actuate and deform the soft composites is also an exciting direction, and it may enable new interaction behaviors. For example, Helium, or hot air can let inflated surfaces float in air or water. Using chemical reactions to generate gas sources may help eliminate hard pneumatic control systems.

Extension of Shape Changing Behaviors

Other types of shape changing behaviors are yet to be explored systematically. A broader and systematic exploration of shape changing primitives could increase use cases in the design of shape changing interfaces. For example, topological change, including creating holes on surfaces, can give interesting affordances for interaction. Locomotion as a bio-inspired mechanism can be achieved with programmable constraints in the material structure [32]. Shape locking is currently implemented with solenoid switches. However, stiffness changing materials, such as Jamming particles, can be adapted to lock shapes or introduce dynamic constraints.

3D Printing as a Promising Fabrication Approach

Soft fabrication requires handwork and time-consuming cast molding processes. This issue could be improved by using enhanced 3D printing technology. While current commercially available 3D printers are not able to print material with high elasticity, we envision printing elastic polymer will be feasible in the near future. It is helpful for constructing complex air channels, combining soft and hard materials, and additional automatic fabrication process.

CONCLUSION

We have presented various types of shape-changing interface enabled by pneumatic soft composite materials. By introducing constraints through materials with pre-programmed structures, we can design and control the direction, location and angle of deformation. We demonstrated shape-changing primitives, and present a framework and test results of the selection of materials, structures, soft fabrication processes, and pneumatic control systems to construct soft composite materials. The soft composite material is a fusion of sensing and actuation on the single-piece of malleable material. This approach creates new opportunities to employ shape-changing interfaces by using responsive materials.

CONCLUSION

We thank Chengyuan Wei, Daniel Leithinger, Ken Perlin, Sheng Kai Tang, Jie Qi and David Mellis for their willingness to brainstorm ideas, Hiroshi Chigira for sharing his network platform, James Weaver and Mike Tolley for their suggestion on 3D printed molds, and Nan-Wei Gong for her support on the inject printed conductive pads.

REFERENCES

1. Coelho, M., Ishii, H., and Maes, P. Surflex: a programmable surface for the design of tangible interfaces. *In CHI EA '08*, ACM (2008), 3429-3434.
2. Coelho, M. and Zigelbaum, J. Shape-changing interfaces. *Personal and Ubiquitous Computing 15*, 2 (2010), 161–173.

3. Follmer, S., Leithinger, D., Olwal, A., Cheng, N., and Ishii, H. Jamming user interfaces: programmable particle stiffness and sensing for malleable and shape-changing devices. *In UIST '12,* ACM (2012), *519-528.*
4. Frey, M. CabBoots: Shoes with integrated Guidance System. *In TEI '07*, ACM(2007), 245–246.
5. Gomes, A., Nesbitt, A., and Vertegaal, R. MorePhone : A Study of Actuated Shape Deformations for Flexible Thin-Film Smartphone Notifications. *In CHI* '13, ACM (2013), 583–592.
6. Harrison, C. and Hudson, S. Texture displays: a passive approach to tactile presentation. *In CHI* '09, ACM (2009), 2261–2264.
7. Harrison, C. and Hudson, S.E. Providing dynamically changeable physical buttons on a visual display. *In CHI '09*, ACM (2009), 299–308.
8. Hawkes, E., An, B., Benbernou, N.M., Tanaka, H., Kim, S., Demaine, E. D., Rus, D., and Wood. R. J. Programmable matter by folding. *PNAS 107*, 28 (2010), 12441–12445.
9. Hemmert, F., Hamann, S., Löwe, M., Zeipelt, J., and Joost, G. Shape-changing mobiles: tapering in two-dimensional deformational displays in mobile phones. *In CHI EA '10*, ACM (2010), 3075–3079.
10. Ilievski, F., Mazzeo, A.D., Shepherd, R.F., Chen, X., and Whitesides, G.M. Soft robotics for chemists. Angew. Chem.Int. Ed., *50*, 8 (2011), 1890–1895.
11. Ishii, H., Lakatos, D., Bonanni, L., and Labrune J.B. Radical Atoms : Beyond Tangible Bits , Toward Transformable Materials. *Interactions* 19, 1 (2012), 38–51.
12. Iwata, H., Yano, H., and Ono, N. Volflex. *In SIGGRAPH '05*, ACM (2005).
13. Kim, S., Kim, H., Lee, B., Nam, T.-J., and Lee, W. Inflatable mouse: volume-adjustable mouse with air-pressure-sensitive input and haptic feedback. *In CHI '08*, ACM (2008), 211-214.
14. Knaian, A.N., Cheung, K.C., Lobovsky, M.B., Oines, A.J., Schmidt-Neilsen, P., and Gershenfeld, N.A. The Milli-Motein: A self-folding chain of programmable matter with a one centimeter module pitch. In *IROS '02*, 1447–1453.
15. Koizumi, N., Yasu, K., Liu, A., Sugimoto, M., and Inami, M. Animated Paper: A Toolkit for Building Moving Toys. *Computers in Entertainment 8*, 2 (2010).
16. Kramer, R.K., Majidi, C., Sahai, R., and Wood, R.J. Soft curvature sensors for joint angle proprioception. In *IROS '11, IEEE/RSJ* (2011), 1919–1926.
17. Kramer, R.K., Majidi, C., and Wood, R.J. Wearable tactile keypad with stretchable artificial skin. In *IROS '11, IEEE/RSJ* (2011), 1103–1107.
18. Leithinger, D., Lakatos, D., DeVincenzi, A., Blackshaw, M., and Ishii, H. Direct and gestural interaction with relief: a 2.5D shape display. *In TEI '10*, ACM Press (2010), 221–222.
19. Martinez, R. V., Fish, C.R., Chen, X., and Whitesides, G.M. Elastomeric Origami: Programmable Paper-Elastomer Composites as Pneumatic Actuators. *Advanced Functional Materials 22*, 7 (2012), 1376–1384.
20. Murata, S., Yoshida, E., Tomita, K., Kurokawa, H., Kamimura, A., and Kokaji, S. Hardware design of modular robotic system. In *IROS '10, IEEE/RSJ* (2010), 2210–2217.
21. Park, Y., Chen, B., and Wood, R. Soft artificial skin with multimodal sensing capability using embedded liquid conductors. IEEE Sensors, 12, 8 (2012), 2711-2718.
22. Park, Y., Chen, B., and Wood, R. Design and Fabrication of Soft Artificial Skin Using Embedded Microchannels and Liquid Conductors. *Sensors Journal, IEEE 12*, 8 (2012), 2711–2718.
23. Park, Y.-L., Majidi, C., Kramer, R., Bérard, P., and Wood, R.J. Hyperelastic pressure sensing with a liquid-embedded elastomer. *Journal of Micromechanics and Microengineering 20*, 12 (2010), 125029.
24. Paul Jackson. Folding techniques for designers. Laurence King Publishers, 2011.
25. Qin, D., Xia, Y., and Whitesides, G.M. Soft lithography for micro- and nanoscale patterning. *Nature protocols 5*, 3 (2010), 491–502.
26. Rasmussen, M., Pedersen, E., Petersen, M., and Hornbæk, K. Shape-changing interfaces: a review of the design space and open research questions. *In CHI* '12, ACM (2012), 735–744.
27. Roudaut, A., Karnik, A., Löchtefeld, M., and Subramanian, S. Morphees : Toward High " Shape Resolution " in Self-Actuated Flexible Mobile Devices. *In CHI* '13, ACM (2013), 593–602.
28. Rekimoto, J. SmartSkin: an infrastructure for freehand manipulation on interactive surfaces. *In CHI '02*, ACM (2002), 113–120.
29. S.D. Guest, S. Pellegrino. The Folding of Triangulated Cylinders, Part 1: Geometric consideration. *J. Appl. Mech*. 1994. 61(4): 773-777.
30. S. Vogel, Life in Moving Fluids: The Physical Biology of Flow. Grant, 1981.
31. Sergio, M., Manaresi, N., and Tartagni, M. A Textile Based Capacitive Pressure Sensor. Sensors, 2002.1625–1630.
32. Shepherd, R.F., Ilievski, F., Choi, W., et al. Multigait soft robot. *In PNAS '11. 108*, 51 (2011), 20400–3.
33. Slyper, R., Poupyrev, I., and Hodgins, J. Sensing through structure: designing soft silicone sensors. *In TEI '11*, ACM (2011), 213 - 220.
34. Steltz, E., Mozeika, A., Rembisz, J., Corson, N., and Jaeger, H.M. Jamming as an enabling technology for soft robotics. In *SPIE Smart* '10.
35. Stevenson, A., Perez, C., and Vertegaal, R. An inflatable hemispherical multi-touch display. *In TEI '11*, ACM (2011), 289–292.
36. Thomus Hull. Project Origami: Activities for Exploring Mathematics. A K Peters/CRC Press, 2006.
37. Vertegaal, R., and Poupyrev, I. Organic User Interfaces. Communications of the ACM. 51, 6 (2008), 26–30.

Paper Generators: Harvesting Energy from Touching, Rubbing and Sliding

Mustafa Emre Karagozler[1], Ivan Poupyrev[1], Gary K. Fedder[2], Yuri Suzuki[1]

[1] Disney Research Pittsburgh,
4720 Forbes Avenue,
Pittsburgh, PA 15213 USA
{emre.karagozler, ivan.poupyrev}
@disneyresearch.com

[2] Department of Electrical and Computer Engineering
and The Robotics Institute
Carnegie Mellon University,
5000 Forbes Avenue,
Pittsburgh, PA 15213 USA

ABSTRACT

We present a new energy harvesting technology that generates electrical energy from a user's interactions with paper-like materials. The energy harvesters are flexible, light, and inexpensive, and they utilize a user's gestures such as tapping, touching, rubbing and sliding to generate electrical energy. The harvested energy is then used to actuate LEDs, e-paper displays and various other devices to create novel interactive applications, such as enhancing books and other printed media with interactivity.

Author Keywords: Energy harvesting, touch, gestures, tangible computing, paper electronics, interactive books.

ACM Classification Keywords

H.5.m. Information interfaces and presentation: User Interfaces-Graphical user interfaces; Input devices & strategies.

INTRODUCTION

This paper presents the design and exploration of a new energy generation technology that harvests electrical energy from touching, tapping and rubbing gestures applied by users to thin, flexible, paper-like structures. These gestures actuate LEDs, e-paper displays, buzzers and IR transmitters. The energy harvesting structures are assembled from inexpensive everyday materials such as common paper and Teflon® sheets; they are flexible, light and durable. Our energy harvesting technology can be easily embedded into everyday objects, such as printed books, postcards and board games, enhancing them with rich interactivity without requiring batteries or external power sources (Figure 1).

The Paper Generators presented in this paper are based on *electrets* that have been exploited for decades in designing sensors and MEMS-based energy harvesting devices [17]. We demonstrate that electret-based energy harvesting can be effective at the macro scale when human gestures are carefully matched to the design of structures producing electrical power. Developing, exploring and evaluating interactive power generators based on electrets are some of the major contributions of this paper.

Figure 1. Paper Generator harvests energy from rubbing and activates the e-paper display, revealing the word "hello".

It is important to highlight the differences between our approach and power harvesting/scavenging technologies popular today. Traditional power harvesting techniques often focus on *incidental* collection of "wasted" energy, such as the electromagnetic radiation around cell towers, ambient vibrations, or even the motion of a beating human heart [13, 20]. In this work, we explore *explicit* power generation where users actively generate power to achieve desired results [14]. In this respect our work follows the tradition of hand-wound radios and human-powered interaction devices such as Peppermill [18] and InGen [4] among others.

There are multiple applications of our power generating devices. In this paper we explore applications in designing interactive self-powered printed books where the reading experience is enhanced with simple interactivity that is either happening *locally* on the book itself or *remotely*, by triggering external computing devices. Augmenting paper books, notebooks and other paper products with computer-driven interactivity has been a burgeoning area of research and development [8, 3, 15]. In particular, we were inspired by such work as Electronic Popables [15] where traditional pop-up books were instrumented with a range of sensors, light sources and actuators to enhance reader experience.

ACM 978-1-4503-2268-3/13/10<$15.00.
http://dx.doi.org/10.1145/2501988.2502054

Although exciting and enjoyable, the need for electrical power limits the feasibility of interactive books by increasing their cost, weight, and size, and by decreasing their shelf life. Developing a basic set of interactive elements that allow for the design and development of self-powered interactive books is another contribution of this paper.

In the rest of the paper we present the principles, design, implementation, application and evaluation of our technology. The main contributions of this work are as follows:

1. We propose a novel energy harvesting technology based on electrets that allows harvesting energy from a variety of human gestures such as touching, tapping and rubbing. The energy harvesting structures are made from thin, flexible commonly available paper-like materials.

2. We design a set of energy harvesting structures and matching gestures that can effectively generate electrical power. We call them Paper Generators, and they form the building blocks that allow for the design of self-powered interactive devices, such as paper books, posters and cards.

3. We implement a number of interactive self-powered scenarios in printed form that demonstrate the use of Paper Generators for actuating interactive devices, such as LEDs, e-paper displays, IR transmitters and rotating needles.

RELATED WORK

Generating power from human motion requires designing devices that convert the motion of the human body into other forms of energy. Some of the earliest convertors were designed, perhaps, during the early Stone Age when humans learned to produce fire by rubbing two pieces of wood together. Modern convertors or *power generators* focus on the generation of electrical power from a wide range of human activities, such as walking, running, riding a bicycle, or moving various mechanical devices [13, 9].

Often there is a distinction made between passive and active energy generation [14]. In the case of passive harvesting, the energy is collected in the background, then blended into everyday human activities, such as walking or breathing [16]. These devices are often designed to be undetectable to the user wearing them; they do not require conscious attention or learning how to use them.

In the case of active energy harvesting, the human has to consciously perform actions leading to the creation of electrical power that can either be stored or used immediately [4, 18]. One of the earliest known devices designed to produce electrical power from human motion was the survival radio developed during WW2 [10]. Today, there is a wide variety of hand-cranked electrical devices such as flashlights and radios. Furthermore, a number of research projects have explored the use of the human power generation in various interaction devices, such as remote controls [4, 18]. In this paper we are following the same direction by focusing on active harvesting of electrical power from human activities.

The central element in any energy generation device is the *generator*, a device that converts one form of energy into another. Numerous generators for human power generation have been explored, such as piezo-based devices that produce power from pressure and vibration, electrostatic vibration generators, thermal convertors, magnetic induction-based generators and RF-based electrical generators [7, 9, 11, 13, 20]. The underlying principle of electrical power generation defines the efficiency of generation and the type of required human actions, e.g., piezo generators might have to be shaken, while a magnetic induction-based generator might require the user to turn a crank. Designing power harvesting and generation devices, therefore, has to be considered from the user interaction perspective because different interaction activities require quite different power generators. In this sense, we can consider human power generation a user interface design problem.

In this paper we propose a novel method of human-based electrical power generation by moving two electrodes with induced charge relative to each other. The physical principles behind electret design have been known for a long time and used in developing sensors, such as microphones, as well as MEMS-based harvesters that convert ambient vibration into electrical power [17]. Recently the electret principle was utilized to convert human finger tapping into power to actuate an array of flashing LEDs [19], an important first step in exploring this power harvesting approach at the macro scale. The reported devices, however, required complex and expensive microfabricated structures, i.e., silver coated nanowires deposited on a plastic substrate. The energy harvester presented in this current paper differs from [19] in structure and function and uses common materials that do not require microfabrication. While only a single mode of operation was investigated in [19], we demonstrate a variety of structures that allow for the use of different gestures and interactions in a broad variety of applications.

PRINCIPLE OF OPERATION

Energy harvesting devices typically employ a magnetic or electric field source, such as a small battery, a permanent magnet, or a permanent electret [12]. In our application, the field source is the semi-permanent charge on the surface of a thin and flexible sheet of PTFE (polytetrafluoroethylene), commonly known by its brand name – Teflon. When the sheet is rubbed with ordinary newspaper, opposite-polarity charges σ_P and σ_T accumulate on the surfaces of the paper and PTFE due to the triboelectric effect (Figure 2a). Because PTFE has a lower electron affinity than paper, charge σ_T is negative [2]. This charge on the PTFE sheet can then act as an electric field source.

When the PTFE sheet is brought near conductive objects, e.g., sheets of aluminum (Figure 2b), the charge on the PTFE attracts free charges of opposite polarity σ_1 and σ_2 that are available in the conductors. These charges accumulate on the surface of the conductors, as shown in Figure 2b.

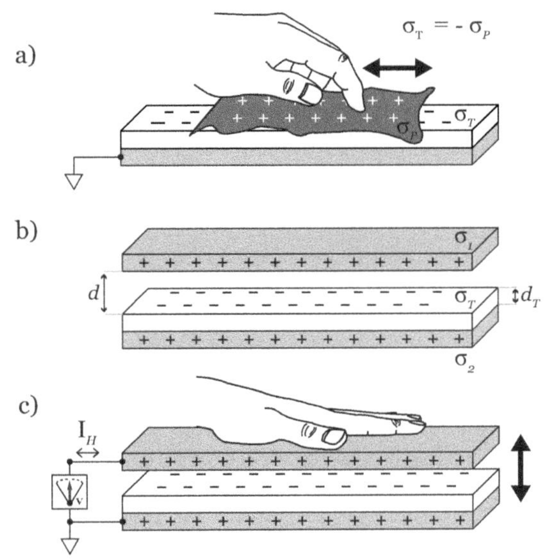

Figure 2. Principle of operation: a) The PTFE sheet is charged by rubbing it with newspaper; b) opposite polarity free charge is induced on the surface of electrodes; c) when the electrodes move relative to each other, a potential difference is created.

The operation of the Paper Generators relies on the *movement* of the two conductive sheets relative to each other and the electric field source, i.e., PTFE. As the relative positions of the sheets change, the distribution of the induced charges, the electric field, and the total capacitance between the sheets change, resulting in an electric potential difference between the conductors (Figure 2c). Hence, the mechanical movements of the sheets and the field source are converted into electrical potential energy that can do work.

It is important to emphasize that although the fundamental principles of operation are relatively simple, a broad variety of movements and gestures can be used to generate power by designing structures that are highly optimized for specific gestures. Different materials for electrodes and electret can also be used. In the next section we analyze the most basic structure shown on Figure 2.

Paper Generator Model

The structure of the Paper Generator that we used for analysis is as follows: a 50 μm, 14-by-8 cm PTFE sheet is stacked on top of a 127 μm thick sheet of silver-coated polyester (henceforth "electrode") with its silver-coated side facing the PTFE. A second electrode is placed above, with its silver-coated side facing the PTFE. The top electrode is supported by a 5 mm thick piece of flexible foam rubber on the sides, which separates it from the bottom PTFE-electrode stack by a gap of approximately 5 mm and allows for the deformation of the top electrode in the center. The top surface of the electrode is covered with common paper, providing stiffness to the top electrode. The whole structure is then attached to a large sheet of paper. All sheets are attached to each other and to the page using common adhesive tape. Wires are attached to the electrodes using silver-filled conductive epoxy (MG Chemicals 8331) to provide electrical connection. Figure 3a shows the energy harvester, with the top electrode opened, revealing the construction. Figure 3b shows the generated signal on the oscilloscope screen as the user brings the electrodes into contact with each other by pressing on the top electrode.

Analysis

We analyze the operation of the energy harvester in two modes by investigating both *short circuit current* and *open circuit voltage*. These give us upper bounds for the current and voltage that can be supplied by the Paper Generators as a power source. For simplicity, we assume that initially both electrodes are connected to a common ground (Figure 2c). Therefore, any excess negative charge is discharged to the ground, leaving a net positive charge on the electrodes to counter the electric field created by the charged PTFE.

Short Circuit Current

When the two electrodes are connected to each other through a small resistance, they are at the same potential at the steady state (Figure 2b). Because the electric field inside the conductors is zero at the steady state, the charge density in equilibrium on the bottom sheet, σ_1, the top sheet, σ_2 and the PTFE, σ_T, are related to each other as:

$$\sigma_1 + \sigma_T + \sigma_2 = 0, \qquad (1)$$

indicating that the total charge on the electrodes is equal but opposite in polarity of the total charge σ_T. In (1), the bound charges due to polarization of the dielectric (PTFE) are omitted, as their net effect is null. The potential difference, V, between the electrodes can be found by the line integration of the electric field between them [18]. It will be zero because the electrodes are shorted:

$$V = \int_0^{d_T+d} \vec{E}\cdot \mathrm{d}l = \frac{\sigma_1}{2\varepsilon_0}\left(\frac{d_T}{\varepsilon_T}+d\right) - \frac{\sigma_2}{2\varepsilon_0}\left(\frac{d_T}{\varepsilon_T}+d\right) + \frac{\sigma_T}{2\varepsilon_0}\left(-\frac{d_T}{\varepsilon_T}+d\right) = 0, \qquad (2)$$

where ε_T is the relative dielectric permittivity of PTFE (≈2, [7]), d_T is the thickness of the PTFE sheet, d is the distance between the PTFE and the top electrode, and ε_0 is the dielectric permittivity of free space (Figure 2b). Defining the electrical thickness of PTFE as $d_{TE} = d_T / \varepsilon_T$ and combining (1) and (2) we get:

$$\sigma_1 = -\sigma_T \frac{1}{1 + d_{TE}/d}, \text{ and } \sigma_2 = -\sigma_T \frac{1}{1 + d/d_{TE}}. \qquad (3)$$

Therefore, the charge on the top and bottom electrodes is dictated by the distance, d; and by changing it mechanically, induced charges can be moved between the sheets (Fig-

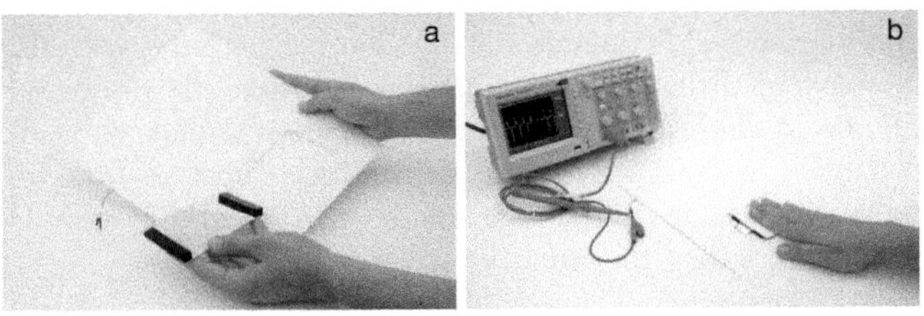

Figure 3. a) The Paper Generator. b) A signal is generated when the electrodes come into contact with each other.

ure 2c). If an electrical load, such as a resistor or an LED, is connected between the two electrodes, the current flowing through the load *will do electrical work*.

Let's assume that the initial and final distances between the electrodes are d_i and d_f, their surface areas are A, and they move for Δt seconds. The average harvested current, I_H, flowing from the top electrode to the bottom electrode can be calculated as:

$$I_H = \frac{\Delta Q}{\Delta t} = \frac{A(\sigma_1^f - \sigma_1^i)}{\Delta t} = \frac{A\sigma_T}{\Delta t}\left(\frac{d_i}{d_i + d_{TE}} - \frac{d_f}{d_f + d_{TE}}\right). \quad (4)$$

Equations (3) and (4) suggest that when the top electrode is brought closer to the PTFE, ($d_f < d_i$), the current is negative; flowing from the bottom electrode to the top. When the top electrode is moved further away, ($d_f > d_i$), the current is positive and flows in the opposite direction. When the top electrode is brought into contact with PTFE, ($d_f = 0$), the total charge flowing out of the top electrode increases with the PTFE surface charge density, the electrode surface area, and the initial distance. The average current also depends on the speed of the electrode movement, i.e., the faster the electrode movement and the smaller the Δt, the larger the current spike.

Open Circuit Voltage

When the electrodes are not connected to a load, their potential difference is free to change with distance d. Assuming that the initial and final distances between the sheets are d_i and d_f respectively, and the initial potential difference is zero, the potential difference at the final state is:

$$V_f = \int_0^{d_T + d_f} \vec{E} \cdot \mathrm{d}l = \frac{\sigma_2 - \sigma_1}{2\varepsilon_0}(d_{TE} + d_f) - \frac{\sigma_T}{2\varepsilon_0}(d_{TE} - d_f). \quad (5)$$

Combining (5) and (3) we get:

$$V_f = \frac{\sigma_T}{\varepsilon_0} \cdot \frac{d_{TE}(d_i - d_f)}{d_i + d_{TE}}. \quad (6)$$

Therefore, for the case where $d_f = 0$, i.e., when the top plate moves down to make contact with the PTFE, the voltage between the plates reaches:

$$V_f = \frac{\sigma_T}{\varepsilon_0} \cdot \frac{d_{TE} d_i}{(d_i + d_{TE})}. \quad (7)$$

Because σ_T is negative, the contact voltage is also negative. According to (6), the voltage approaches infinity as the top sheet is moved farther away ($d_f \to \infty$), which is impracticable. This is because the analysis presented is based on a parallel plate capacitor model, which assumes that there are no fringing fields outside the capacitor. In reality, with the increase of distance, d, the parallel electrode plates behave like point charges, and the electric fields dissipate with the distance. Therefore, the analysis presented here is valid for separation distances that are smaller than or comparable to the side length of the electrodes.

Measurements

We measured the *short circuit current* by connecting a small resistor between the two electrodes, and the voltage drop across the resistor was measured using a Tektronix P2220 voltage probe (10 MΩ, 16 pF). Because the short circuit current is on the order of hundreds of microamperes, a 1 kΩ load provided enough voltage drop to be separated from noise while still being approximated as zero volts.

Figure 4a demonstrates the current spikes measured from three separate "taps" using the test energy harvesting apparatus described above. Each tap consists of a large negative current spike reaching up to −500 μA lasting 1-4 ms. When the user's hand is lifted approximately 100 ms after initial contact, a positive current flows, restoring the original charge distribution as the plates return to their initial position. The speed of recoil depends on the spring constant and elasticity of the foam rubber and the top sheet. The typical recoil current peak is a lot smaller (≈ 30 μA) lasting up to 50 ms, allowing for a total charge of ≈ 400 nC to flow back.

The *open circuit voltage* of the energy harvester was measured using a Tektronix P5122 high voltage probe (100 MΩ, 4 pF). The voltage between the two electrodes was measured relative to the bottom sheet while the user taps the top sheet, bringing the two into contact. It results in a sharp negative voltage drop followed by a positive spike during recoil as seen on Figure 4b. The negative drop dissipates because once the contact between top and bottom sheets is established, the voltage diminishes due to the finite input resistance of the probe. This allows for a new charge distribution to be established. Similarly, a positive voltage spike occurs as the top sheet recoils. The negative voltage spikes routinely reach −600 V, and recoil voltage spikes can go up to 1200 V, especially when a new charge distribution is achieved with a long pause between contact and recoil.

We measured the power output of the Paper Generators under varying resistive loads, from 1 KΩ to 10 MΩ. Load resistances were connected at the output of the paper gener-

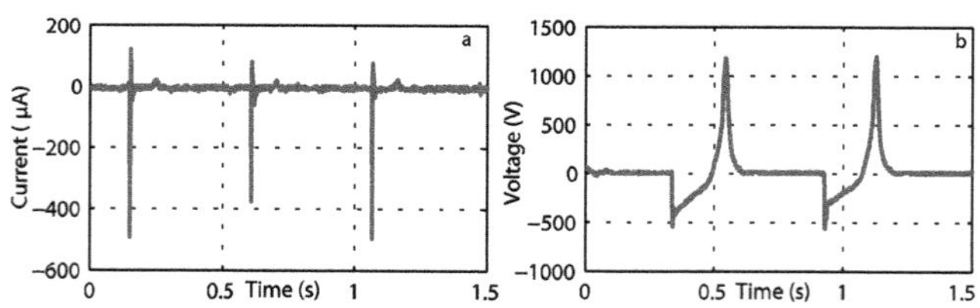

Figure 4. a) The short circuit current of three taps; b) The open circuit voltage during two taps.

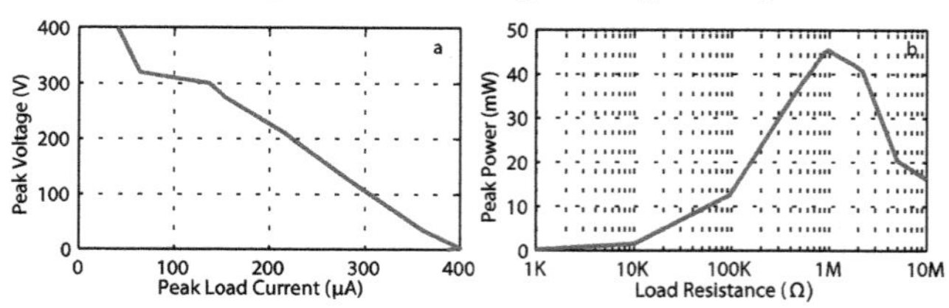

Figure 5. a) VI load line of the Paper Generator; b) Peak delivered power versus load resistance.

Peak short circuit current	−500 MΩ
Peak open circuit voltage	−600 V
Output resistance R_{out}	1.08 MΩ
Peak voltage at R_{load} =1 MΩ	−210 V
Peak current at R_{load} = 1 MΩ	−210 μA
Total charge moved (short circuit), C	400 nC
Electrical work per tap, R_{load} =1 MΩ, E_c	60 μJ
Average peak power, R_{load} = 1 MΩ	44 mW

Table 1. Summary of measurements

ators and the voltages spikes across them at contact were measured. The values were corrected for oscilloscope probe loading. To minimize the effects of variability between taps, peak values of multiple taps were measured and averaged. Figure 5a plots the peak (negative) voltage of varying load resistors versus peak currents calculated using Ohm's law. The output resistance can be calculated by fitting a line to the curve on Figure 5a which gives us R_{out} = 1.08 MΩ. This is not strictly a Thévenin equivalent resistance, because the voltage and current characteristics of the generator are dynamic and depend on multiple parameters, including tapping speed and contact area. Nevertheless, it can be considered an output resistance for design purposes.

Figure 5b plots the peak power delivered versus load resistances, including probe loading. The maximum peak power is delivered at ≈ 1 MΩ, consistent with the observation from the load line characteristics. Because the peak and average delivered power depend on the square of the current, the total electrical work done per tap, which includes contact and recoil, depends on the speed of the tap. Although the total charge that moves from one electrode to the other at each tap is constant, a faster tap creates higher currents, producing more electrical work even though the current has a shorter duration. Table 1 summarizes the electrical properties of the paper generator that we measured in this section. In addition to peak voltage, current and power, the total electrical work per tap was measured. At tens of microjoules, the electrical work per tap is up to one hundred million times smaller than the energy content of a AA battery. The measurement results presented in Table 1 are taken from a particular user's gestures and vary with speed and contact force. While the application of these gestures is not precise, these measurements establish the output characteristics of paper generators within an order of magnitude.

PAPER GENERATORS

In the previous section, we described a novel energy harvesting technology based on the electret principle; in this section, we demonstrate how this technology can be effectively used to design human-powered, interactive systems.

The principles of power generation that we discussed are simple, and yet they allow for the design of a surprisingly large variety of energy generating structures that permit the use of many different human gestures. A comprehensive investigation of all possible structures is beyond the scope of this paper. Here we discuss some of the most basic designs and illustrate how they can be used to produce more complex power generating structures (Figure 6).

An interactive system based on our energy harvesting technology includes the following three components: 1) *Paper Generators*, energy generating structures made of paper and producing electrical energy from human gestures, 2) *Harvesting Circuits*, electrical circuits that regulate energy produced by Paper Generators, and 3) *Application Components* that use electrical energy produced by Paper Generators.

Materials

Materials that can be used to build Paper Generators are common and inexpensive. A *substrate* is used as a foundation of the design and can be any electrically-proper material, such as paper, PET films, fabric, plastic or wooden sheets, among others. The *electrical conductors* are overlaid on substrates in various patterns that are printed using conductive inks, e.g., silver inks, silkscreen printed with conductive paints (e.g., nickel-based paint), or made with conductive films (e.g., silver or aluminum-coated polyester films) commonly used in gift wrapping and known under the Mylar® brand name. The *charge-storage* materials are used to store electrical charge, the most commonly used is PTFE–also known under the Teflon® brand name. Finally, *conductive bonding* materials are used for connecting electrical components to Paper Generators or for connecting parts of the Paper Generators. These may be silver-based conductive epoxies or copper tapes with conductive adhesive on both sides. The possibility of using a variety of common materials is an important advantage of our technology, allowing for numerous potential applications.

Designing Paper Generators

Figure 6 demonstrates Paper Generators that we designed. We started with the most basic structures and then designed progressively more complex generators adapting from the pop-up book design mechanics. The designs below were produced using photo paper, and the conductive patterns were printed using a customized Epson WorkForce 30 inkjet printer and Novacentrix® silver-based inks. PTFE films were attached using 3M™ spray adhesive. Conductive silver-based epoxy and conductive copper adhesive tape were used for connecting parts of the Paper Generators and interfacing to the electrical components. Below we present the generator design.

The Tapping Generator converts tapping or pressing on the paper flap into electrical power (Figure 6-1). Tapping or pressing are simple, intuitive gestures that everyone is familiar with through everyday experiences and have numerous uses in interactive applications. The generator utilizes the layered structure described previously: PTFE film overlays a printed electrode on the bottom and a second printed electrode on top, forming a bridge. The electrode on the top is connected to the bottom sheet using conductive tape.

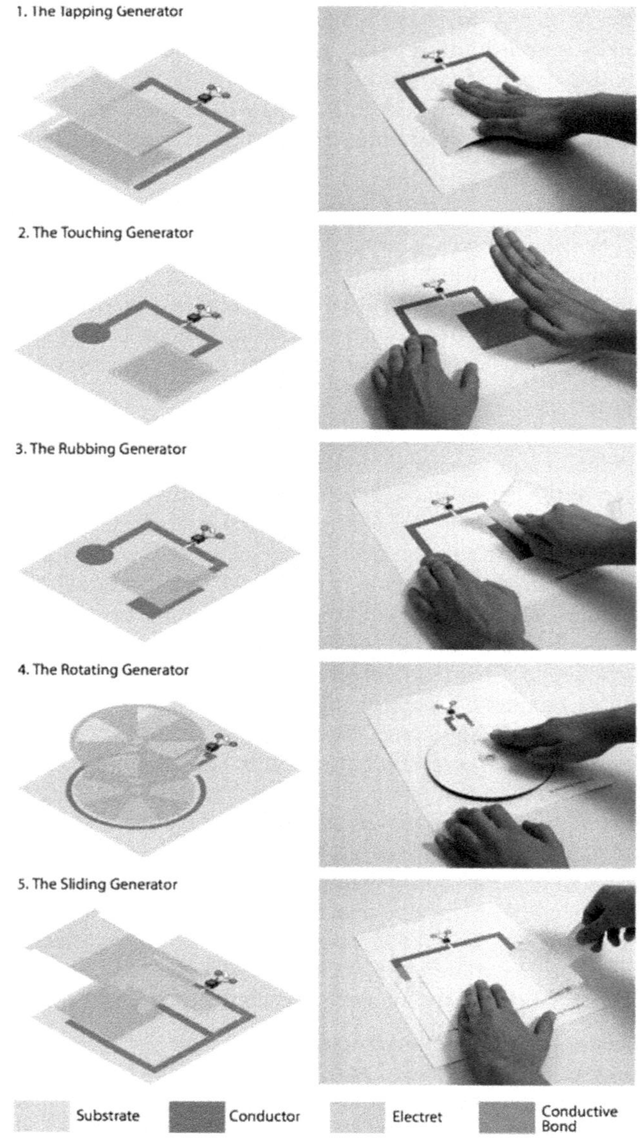

Figure 6. Paper Generators.

When tapped, the top sheet bends and makes contact with the stack, creating a voltage spike. The electrode recoils into its original position when the user's hand is retracted.

The Touching Generator is a variation of the Tapping Generator in which a user taps the bottom PTFE-electrode stack with his or her bare hand, replacing the top electrode (Figure 6-2). The advantage of this design is that it has no moving parts; the circuit is completed through the body by touching the second electrode with the other hand. The human body has enough conductivity to pass high voltages and, because the currents are minuscule, the temporary charges that accumulate in the body are not perceivable.

The Rubbing Generator utilizes a rubbing gesture where the user simultaneously touches one of the electrodes with one hand and rubs the second electrode with a sheet of PTFE (Figure 6-3). The PTFE sheet moves repeatedly on and off the surface of the electrode, creating a change in the induced charge. The principles of its operation are the same as in tapping, except the human hand forms a moving electrode and motion is horizontal rather them vertical. Rubbing generators produce the most power because a rubbing gesture can be performed rapidly with increased pressure, maximizing contact with the electrodes. In fact, because PTFE provides very low friction, users can apply high amounts of pressure effortlessly.

The Rotating Generator is a more complex implementation of rubbing generator. The segmented electrodes are printed on a disk, sliding on and off the bottom electrodes by means of rotation with PTFE film sandwiched in between (Figure 6-4). Unlike with rubbing generator the user does not have to touch a second electrode. To connect electrodes on the top rotating disk to the energy harvesting circuit on the bottom, overlapping circular rails are printed both on the rotating top disk and the bottom sheet (Figure 6-4).

The Sliding Generator is based on the same principle as the rotating generator except it allows power generation by sliding a sheet with a printed electrode on and off the electrode on the bottom sheet (Figure 6-5). Similar to the rotating generator, linear rails are used to connect the top sliding electrode to the harvesting circuit mounted on the bottom.

The designs above demonstrate how basic power generation principles can be used to create new energy generating structures uniquely adapted to specific applications.

Harvesting Circuits

The energy created by the Paper Generator is regulated using circuitry connected between the electrodes. There are two basic strategies to utilize the harvested energy: *immediate* and *charge and release.*

In the *immediate use* strategy, energy produced by Paper Generators is regulated and then immediately applied to an interaction device, such as LEDs or e-paper displays as we discuss later. For regulation, a high-voltage bridge rectifier chip (Vishay Semiconductor, DF10S) is used to convert the AC voltage spikes to a DC signal (see Figure 7a). This DC signal is then connected to an appropriate electrical load. A double-pole, double-throw slider switch is used to reverse the polarity of the output if needed. While the circuit design for this strategy is trivial, because the amount of electrical power generated is very low, its applications are limited.

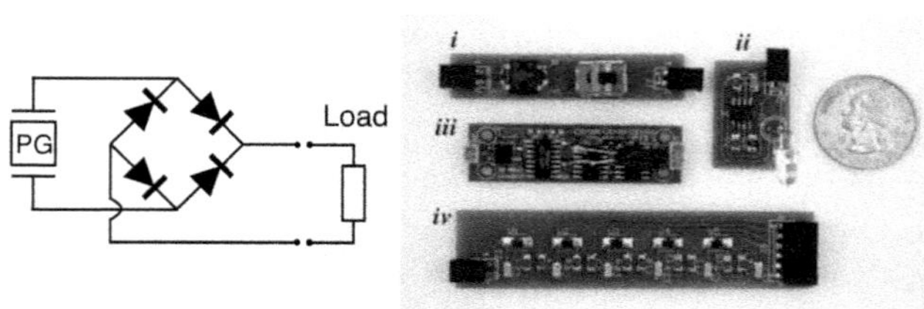

Figure 7. Left: Paper Generator connection to bridge rectifier. Right: the printed circuit boards for (i) rectifier and switch, (ii) IR transmitter (iii) EH301 (iv) zener diode-capacitor array.

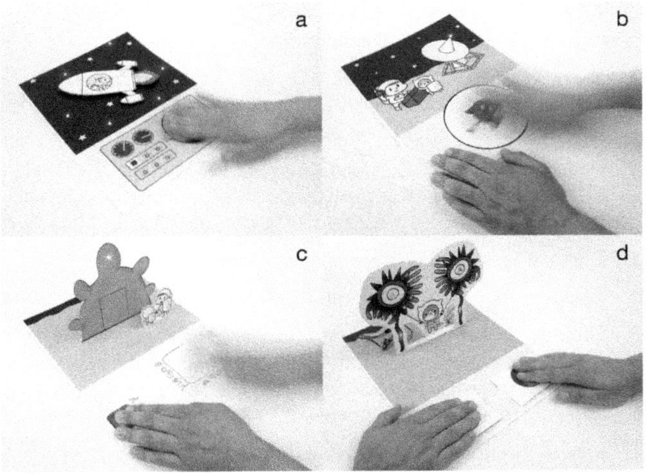

Figure 8. Driving LEDs with Paper Generators

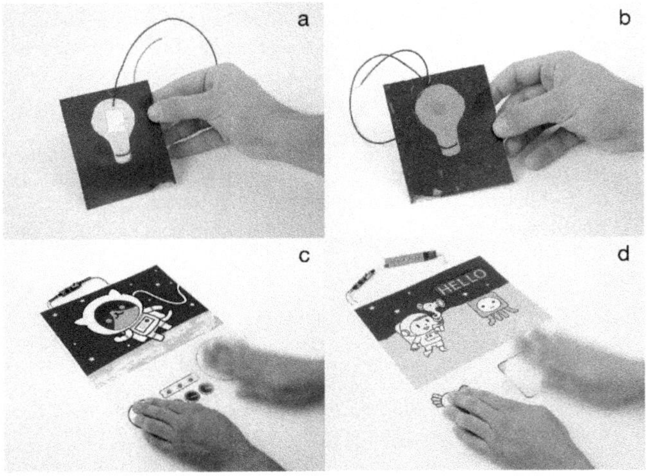

Figure 9. Driving e-paper with Paper Generators

In *store-and-release* harvesting, the electrical energy is used to charge a capacitor and only released to the load when a certain amount of energy is reached. This results in significantly increased power delivery and can be used in applications where a large amount of energy is required, such as a buzzer, or IR communications. To implement this circuit, we incorporate the EH300/EH301 energy store-and-release device from Advanced Linear Devices [1].

APPLICATIONS

We investigated applications of Paper Generators by implementing several interaction scenarios that enhance traditional printed books' storytelling with various output devices, such as LEDs, e-paper displays, sound buzzers, and wireless IR communication, among others. All of the applications that we present can be used with any of the Paper Generators, however, some devices are better suited for some of the applications than others.

LEDs and LED arrays can be very effectively driven by Paper Generators to provide a visual feedback to the user during interaction with the book. In *immediate use* configuration, multiple LEDs are connected in series at the output of the energy harvesting circuit. Because the voltage spikes created by the Paper Generator can reach up to hundreds of volts, it is possible to connect many LEDs in series and have enough voltage drops across each LED to produce bright lights. For example, in Figure 8a the stars and engine of the paper rocket light up each time the user taps on the "power" paper button: the faster and stronger the taps are, the more visible the lights are and, therefore, the "faster" the rocket flies. In Figure 8b, a light on the transmission antenna blinks repeatedly when the user rotates the disk on Rotating Generator, the blinking frequency would depend on the speed of rotation.

In the *store-and-release* configuration the user has to repeatedly rub or tap the generator to accumulate enough energy to flash an LED. It can communicate level achievement and suggest the story progress. For example, in Figure 8c the light on top of the alien house flashes after the user rubs it for a certain amount of time. In another example (Figure 8d), two Paper Generators are combined and readers have to tap on their respective Paper Generators until both alien flowers flash, indicating that the cat is released.

In designing LED-based applications we observed that phosphor-based LEDs, which are generally blue and white, are most suitable as the phosphor allows for prolonged light emission, making it more visible.

Electronic paper (e-paper) displays, such as E Ink's ePaper displays [5], are an especially suitable application for the Paper Generators as they require high voltages but very low switching current and no static power to keep the images on. To create a static image on the e-paper, we apply a layer of conductive epoxy to the back of the e-paper film (Figure 9a). When voltage from the Paper Generators is applied to the hardened epoxy, the image on the front appears (Figure 9b). Very little current is needed to toggle the e-paper display; in the case of rubbing generators a single rub is often sufficient. In Figure 9c, the face of the cat becomes visible when the user rubs the electrode of a Paper Generator.

We can also create simple animations by segmenting the image and connecting the individual segments to Power Generators through a passive capacitor-zener diode array (Figure 7-iv), which allows sequential voltage buildup at different nodes. With this circuit, the letters in a word, e.g., "hello", in Figure 9d, can be made to appear sequentially as more energy is harvested. By switching the polarity of supplied voltage, the letters can be made to disappear.

E-paper displays are some of the most expressive and impressive applications of Paper Generators. Only the bridge rectifier circuitry is sufficient to implement e-paper displays. Building conductive patterns on the back of the e-paper requires careful attention. Indeed, the back of the e-paper film is fragile and damaged easily if conductive patterns are not carefully applied. Furthermore, the film is sensitive to solvents. Many solvent-based conductive materials, such as silver-based tracing pens, cannot be used.

IR communication can be implemented using Power Generators to trigger an external computing device allowing for enhanced paper books with dynamic electronic media. For example, an animation on a screen can be triggered by interacting with a paper book. Store-and-release harvesting configuration is used to power a classic 555 IC oscillator, which then modulates an infrared LED that transmits data to an IR decoder connected to a remote computing device. By varying the frequency of oscillation, we can create unique frequency signatures for different Paper Generators, allowing us to build complex paper-based interactive controllers. In such a scenario any classic paper book can be used to control interactive storytelling on various devices, such as laptops, TVs and tablets.

Sound and mechanical motion can be also created using Paper Generators. For example, we have incorporated a single frequency audio buzzer (Mallory Sonalert, MSR516NR) with the store and release circuitry that creates a buzz, providing the user with an audible response.

In addition, we have incorporated analog voltmeter needles that create mechanical motion. The energy released from the store-and-release circuitry activates the needle. The spring-loaded needles then move back to original position.

DISCUSSION AND CONCLUSIONS

We have presented Paper Generators: a new energy harvesting technology that generates electrical energy from a user's interactions with paper-like materials. The generators can be assembled from off-the-shelf materials, such as PTFE sheets and Mylar, and they can be flexible, light and inexpensive. This paper presented analysis that predicts the current-voltage characteristics of the energy harvester and characterized it through measurements.

We have also defined the basic user gestures and physical structures that allow us to create effective Paper Generators. We evaluated the technology to enhance paper books with simple interactivity. The design is, of course, not limited to books. We envision added interactivity for any printed matter, including books, postcards, posters, board games and many others.

The technology does have certain limitations. The need to implant the initial charge into PTFE is one of the issues that potentially limit the interactive application of Paper Generators. It can be solved by permanently implanting charges into a PTFE sheet using such techniques as corona discharge. We will continue investigating and improving the Paper Generator technology in our future work.

ACKNOWLEDGEMENTS

The authors would like to thank Keiko Nakao, Joanna Dauner, Kaitlyn Schwalje, Spencer Diaz and Lanny Smoot for their help and E Ink for supplying the e-paper displays.

REFERENCES

1. Advanced Linear Devices. EH300/301, Epad Energy Harvesting Modules, http://www.aldinc.com/pdf/EH300.pdf .
2. Alphalab Inc., B. Lee, PhD. http://www.trifield.com/content/tribo-electric-series/.
3. Back, M., Cohen, J., Gold, R., Harrison, S., and Minneman, S. Listen reader: an electronically augmented paper-based book. In Proc. CHI 2001, ACM Press, (2001), pp. 23–29.
4. Badshah, A., Gupta, S., Cohn, G., Villar, N., Hodges, S., Patel, S. Interactive generator: a self-powered haptic feedback device. In Proc. of CHI 2011, ACM, (2011), pp. 2051–2054.
5. E Ink, ePaper display. http://www.eink.com/.
6. EnOcean. http://www.enocean.com/.
7. Ghodgaonkar, D., Varadan, V., Varadan, V. Free-space measurement of complex permittivity and complex permeability of magnetic materials at microwave frequencies. *IEEE Trans Instrumentation and Measurement* (39) 2, (1990), pp. 387–394.
8. Liao, C., Guimbretiere, F., Hinckley, K., and Hollan, J. Papiercraft: A gesture-based command system for interactive paper. ACM TOCHI, (14), 4, 2008, 18.
9. Mateu, L., Moll, F., et al. Review of energy harvesting techniques and applications for microelectronics. In Proceedings of SPIE, vol. 5837 (2005), pp. 359–373.
10. Meulstee, L., and Rudolf F. Wireless for the warrior. Volume 4, Clandestine Radio, (2004).
11. Mitcheson, P. D., Green, T. C., Yeatman, E. M., and Holmes, A. S. Architectures for vibration-driven micropower generators. *Microelectromechanical Systems, Journal of,* 13 (3), (2004), pp. 429–440.
12. Mitcheson, P. D., Yeatman, E. M., Rao, G. K., Holmes, A. S., and Green, T. C. Energy harvesting from human and machine motion for wireless electronic devices. Proceedings of the IEEE (96) 9, (2008), pp. 1457–1486.
13. Paradiso, J. A., and Starner, T. Energy scavenging for mobile and wireless electronics. *Pervasive Computing*, IEEE (4) 1, (2005), pp. 18–27.
14. Pierce, J., and Paulos, E. Designing everyday technologies with human-power and interactive microgeneration. In Proceedings of the DIS 2012, ACM, (2012), pp. 602–611.
15. Qi, J., and Buechley, L. Electronic popables: exploring paper-based computing through an interactive pop-up book. In Proceedings of TEI 2010, ACM, (2010), pp. 121–128.
16. Shenck, N. S., Paradiso, J. A. Energy scavenging with shoe-mounted piezoelectrics. *Micro, IEEE 21*, 3 (2001), 30–42.
17. Sterken, T., Fiorini, P., Baert, K., Puers, R., and Borghs, G. An electret-based electrostatic μ-generator. In 12th International Conference on Transducers, Solid-State Sensors, Actuators and Microsystems, IEEE, vol. 2, 2003, pp. 1291–1294.
18. Villar, N., and Hodges, S. The peppermill: a human-powered user interface device. In Proceedings of TEI 2010, ACM, (2010), pp. 29–32.
19. Zhong, J., Zhong, Q., Fan, F., Zhang, Y., Wang, S., Hu, B., Lin Wang, Z., and Zhou, J. Finger typing driven triboelectric nanogenerator and its use for instantaneously lighting up leds. Nano Energy (2012).
20. Zurbuchen, A., Pfenniger, A., Stahel, A., Stoeck, C., Vandenberghe, S., Koch, V., and Vogel, R. Energy harvesting from the beating heart by a mass imbalance oscillation generator. *Annals of biomedical engineering 41*, 1 (2013), pp. 131–141.

Touch & Activate: Adding Interactivity to Existing Objects using Active Acoustic Sensing

Makoto Ono, Buntarou Shizuki, and Jiro Tanaka
University of Tsukuba, Japan
Tennoudai 1-1-1, Tsukuba, Ibaraki, Japan 305-8571
{ono,shizuki,jiro}@iplab.cs.tsukuba.ac.jp

ABSTRACT

In this paper, we present a novel acoustic touch sensing technique called *Touch & Activate*. It recognizes a rich context of touches including grasp on existing objects by attaching only a vibration speaker and a piezo-electric microphone paired as a sensor. It provides easy hardware configuration for prototyping interactive objects that have touch input capability. We conducted a controlled experiment to measure the accuracy and trade-off between the accuracy and number of training rounds for our technique. From its results, per-user recognition accuracies with five touch gestures for a plastic toy as a simple example and six hand postures for the posture recognition as a complex example were 99.6% and 86.3%, respectively. Walk up user recognition accuracies for the two applications were 97.8% and 71.2%, respectively. Since the results of our experiment showed a promising accuracy for the recognition of touch gestures and hand postures, Touch & Activate should be feasible for prototyping interactive objects that have touch input capability.

Author Keywords

Touch; grasp; gestures; sensors; acoustic classification; tangibles; machine learning; prototyping; support vector machine; piezo-electric sensor.

ACM Classification Keywords

H.5.2 [Information interfaces and presentation]: User Interfaces - Graphical user interfaces; Input devices & strategies.

General Terms

Human Factors.

INTRODUCTION

Interactive objects that have touch input capability are still challenging to prototype, even while touch input is increasingly used in many consumer products such as mobile devices or tablets. Even engineers spend much time on circuit design and hardware configuration. This is because prototyping usually requires the developers to redesign the objects many times, which involves replacing sensors frequently especially in the early stage of prototyping.

UIST'13, October 8–11, 2013, St. Andrews, United Kingdom.

http://dx.doi.org/10.1145/2501988.2501989

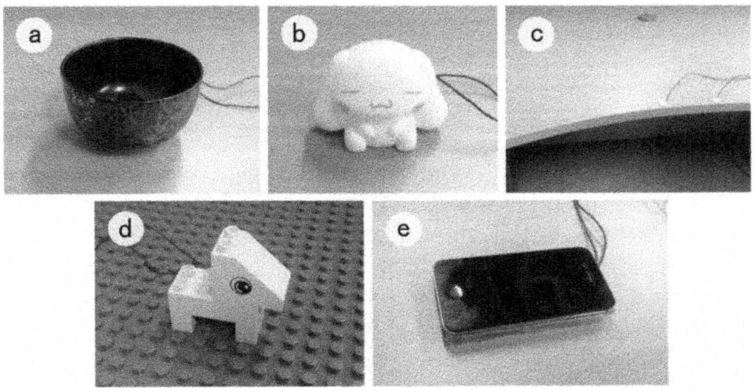

Figure 1. Examples of applicable objects: a) ceramic bowl, b) plastic toy, c) wood desk, d) Duplo block, e) mobile device (hard case).

Moreover, grasps, a kind of touch with rich context, have been explored intensively in recent years, and many grasp sensitive objects have been elaborated. For example, Kim et al. recognized hand grip patterns on mobile devices by embedding 64 capacitive sensors into mobile devices [32]. FlyEye [51] spread optical fibers across a surface, with their other ends attached to a camera, to prototype grasp sensitive surfaces. Taylor et al. developed objects with 23-72 capacitive sensors on their surfaces to explore how the way users hold and manipulate physical objects can be used as inputs [47]. HandSense [53] detected how a mobile device is held using four capacitive sensors, each of which has an antenna made of a tin sheet and is actively shielded by guard electrodes wrapping the antenna on three sides to improve sensitivity. MTPen [44] is a stylus, whose body's surface has multi-touch sensing capability using conductive ink, which detects how the user grips the stylus. FlexAura [33] detects how the user grips an object by using a flexible range finder, which is an 16×24 array of infrared LEDs and phototransistors. Note that these works all use many sensors, specialized hardware, or complicated hardware configuration; thus grasp sensitive objects are also challenging to prototype.

In this paper, we describe Touch & Activate, a novel acoustic touch sensing technique that enables prototyping interactive objects that have touch input capability rapidly and easily. It recognizes a rich context of touches, including grasps on existing objects, such as those shown in Figure 1, by attaching only a vibration speaker and a piezo-electric microphone paired as a sensor. As a result, developers can concentrate on the design of touch input rather than be overly concerned with circuit design or hardware configuration.

Our sensing technique is based on the resonant property of solid objects, which is highly sensitive to the way objects are touched. This leads to the following additional advantages: since most solid objects have this property, our approach is applicable to existing solid objects and does not require conductivity or magnetism on them and is thus safe; our sensing technique can estimate rough positions of touch and different postures of touch (e.g., pinch or press) on a single position; due to the sensitivity, developers can assign a position and/or posture of touch to an action quickly by training the system using machine learning. These advantages provide developers with possibilities to flexibly design various styles of interaction with the object.

RELATED WORK

Prototyping Physical Objects

Many tools have been developed to lower the barrier to physical prototyping. Phidgets [14] are packaged devices consisting of sensors and actuators that can be programmed with a well-defined software API. Arduino [1] and mbed [2] are electronics prototyping platforms that can be programmed via offline or online IDE. d.tools [25] is a prototyping environment that integrates prototype designing, testing, and analyzing into the visual programming interface. .Net Gadgeteer [48] provides a similar packaged module that can be programmed by using .Net Micro Framework. Prototyping with these abovementioned tools usually involves the use of off-the-shelf sensors. This means that while the prototype, once made, can work stably, the forms (i.e., shape and size) of sensors used are restricted to the ones commercially available. Therefore, developers may need to search for other forms of sensors when they want to examine prototypes of various shapes and sizes. Since this scenario occurs frequently in the early stage of prototyping, a more flexible approach is required.

Prototyping tools targeting touch sensitive prototypes have also been proposed. BOXES [28] is a tool with which developers can construct touch sensitive prototype from existing objects by attaching thumbtacks and foil to the objects. Tactile Tape [27] is a one-dimensional touch sensor that can be used to add touch sensitive areas on existing objects. Wimmer et al. explored how to extend time domain reflectometry in order to make thin, modular, and deformable surfaces and devices touch sensitive [52]. Midas [42] helps developers create their custom sensor layouts by the GUI editor. These previous works construct touch sensitive prototypes from everyday objects by attaching conductive elements to each position that will be touched. Meanwhile, our approach does not require these elements except for a pair of a speaker and a microphone. This does not only make the hardware configuration easier, but also makes the instrumentation used for sensing less obtrusive than the above approaches.

Physical prototyping tools using machine learning and pattern recognition techniques have also been proposed. Exemplar [24] is a design tool with which developers can prototype sensor based applications by demonstration for sensor-based interaction. PICL [12] is a portable in-circuit learner with which dvelopers can also prototype sensor-based applications with standalone machine learning hardware. Our approach employs machine learning to label acoustic response (i.e., frequency response in our study) as touch gestures.

Touch Sensing Technologies

Recent innovative touch sensing technologies have lowered the barrier to incorporating touch sensing into prototyping and broadened sensing capabilities. FTIR [17] enabled multi-touch surface to be made for low-cost using frustrated total internal reflection. OmniTouch [18] is a wearable depth-sensing and projection system that realizes interactive multi-touch applications on everyday surfaces. KinectFusion [30] can be used to realize multi-touch interactions on any physical surfaces, including complex ones, by using a Kinect camera. Although these vision based touch sensing technologies detect touched positions in high resolution, they require large footprints or high performance hardware for image processing. Touché [41] and Capacitive Fingerprinting [20], the works that mainly inspired us, found that the Swept Frequency Capacitive Sensing technique can detect a touch event and recognize complex configurations of human hands and body. However, Touché requires conductivity of objects. This means that, when developers apply it to non-conductive objects, they have to coat the objects with conductive ink or tape.

Acoustic Sensing

Researchers have explored many acoustic-based input techniques. These techniques are classified into passive and active approaches.

Passive approaches detect a user's input by capturing and analyzing sounds generated by the user's actions. The Sound of One Hand [3] recognizes fingertip gestures such as tapping, rubbing, and flicking by analyzing bone-conducted sound generated by the actions. Stane [36] classified sounds generated by actions such as scratching or rubbing its textured surface. Scratch Input [19] explored an acoustic based input technique using the unique sounds generated by scratching a surface of a textured material. Acoustic Barcodes [23] are tactile barcodes that, when an object like a fingernail or phone runs across the notches, identify a binary ID from the produced sound. Paradiso et al. employed multiple microphones to estimate tapped positions on a large sheet of glass based on time difference of arrival [37]. Pham et al. also employed a single microphone to localize tapped positions in non-planner objects based on time reversal [39]. Skinput [22] used bio-acoustic sensors to estimate the tapped position on the skin. TapSense [21] and Pedro et al. [34] identified the type of objects, or the part of the finger, being used for tapping from sounds generated by tapping the surface. MicPen [29] is a pressure sensitive stylus that estimates the amount of pressure applied to the stylus' tip from the scratch noise generated by dragging surfaces with its tip.

Active approaches transmit sounds using speakers, and capture and analyze the response to the sounds. Active Sonar [45] mounted on submarines and fishing boats is its typical example. It detects surrounding objects and measures distances to them by transmitting pulses of sounds and timing the response to the sound. Surface Acoustic Wave (SAW) touch screens [5] is another representative active approach. It consists of one glass sheet with a transmitter, a receiver, and reflectors. The transmitter emits SAW, which is an acoustic wave traveling on the surface of a material exhibiting elasticity, and they are reflected by reflectors that are lined up along the edges of the panel. When a finger touches the screen, the wave is absorbed. The absorption is observed by the receiver to localize the touch.

Other active approaches have also been explored in recent years. SoundWave [16] senses in-air gestures by measuring Doppler shifts. Takemura et al. proposed a wearable sensor system that estimates the angle of an elbow using a speaker and two microphones that capture bone-conducted sound in the elbow [46]. Collins estimated positions of a touch on flat surfaces by analyzing the frequency response of the surface using a single transmitter and one or two receivers [9]. It is similar to SAW touch screens in localizing touch from acoustic waves, but different in that it dose so by analyzing the frequency response with a simple instrumentation.

The advantage of active approaches for touch detection, such as those of Brenner and Fitzgibbon [5] and Collins [9], is that the system generates its own sounds and detects the changes in the sounds caused by the user's actions. This enables even the detection of gentle touches or varying pressures of touch, where almost no sound is produced. Although our approach is similar to that of Collins [9] in analyzing the frequency response of the acoustic wave, we extend it to classify grasp or farther context of touch on everyday objects and demonstrate a rapid prototyping method for interactive objects that have touch input capability with machine learning.

SENSING PRINCIPLE

All objects have their own resonant property represented by the resonant modes, natural frequency, and modal damping. The property depends on its own shape, material, and boundary condition. At present, this property has been applied to durability evaluation and vibration suppression of structures in the field of structural mechanics [11, 43].

Our study focuses on the boundary conditions among them. When an object is touched, the boundary condition changes. As a result, its resonant property also changes. The changes in the resonant property are observed as different resonant spectra. Figure 2 shows an example where a ceramic bowl touchable in different ways (Figure 2a-d) shows unique resonant spectra accordingly (Figure 2A-D). Therefore, if the object's shape and material are static, the change in the boundary condition caused by touching, grasping, and others can be observed as the change in the resonant property.

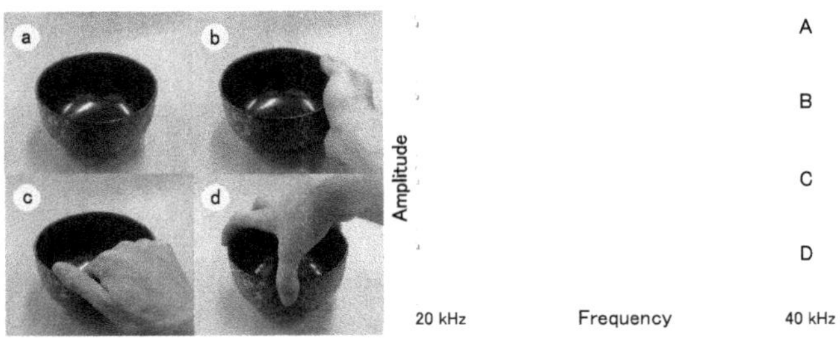

Figure 2. Resonant spectra of a ceramic bowl with different ways to touch. When the bowl is touched as shown in a-d, the resonant spectra of A-D are observed, respectively.

Our approach uses this phenomenon to estimate how an object is touched by analyzing resonant property. We use experimental frequency response testing to analyze resonant property. In general, this method involves vibrating the object at a wide frequency range using an actuator, such as an impact hammer, electrodynamic shaker, or vibration speaker, and capturing the frequency response by using a sensor, such as an accelerometer or piezo-electric microphone. In the field of structural mechanics, a theoretical modal analysis such as Finite Element Method (FEM) is then employed to calculate the details of the boundary condition. However, this requires detailed information about the shape and material of structures, and its calculation costs are high. On the other hand, we employ machine learning with frequency response labeled as touch gestures. This enables the estimation of touch gestures on an object whose structure information is unknown with lower calculation costs.

TEST SYSTEM OF TOUCH & ACTIVATE

We implemented a test system on the basis of the above sensing principle. Figure 3 shows the overview of our test system.

Hardware

Our test system consists of a vibration speaker, a piezo-electric microphone, and a computer running software for signal processing and machine learning.

We use a bimorph piezo-electric vibration speaker (Figure 4 left; Thrive OMR20F10-BP-310, 0.3 mm thick, 21 mm in diameter) to vibrate the object. The vibration speaker can transmit sounds by vibrating the object directly. We also use a unimorph piezo-electric microphone (Figure 4 right; Murata 7BB-20-6L0, 0.2 mm thick, 20 mm in diameter) to capture the vibration response. To vibrate an object with sufficient power, piezo elements with a bimorph structure are preferred to unimorph ones. Thus, we used a bimorph piezo element as an actuator and selected a smaller, thinner one that can be easily attached to any surface. In contrast, we used a unimorph piezo element as a microphone because the power is unnecessary for capturing the vibration response and it is less expensive than a bimorph one.

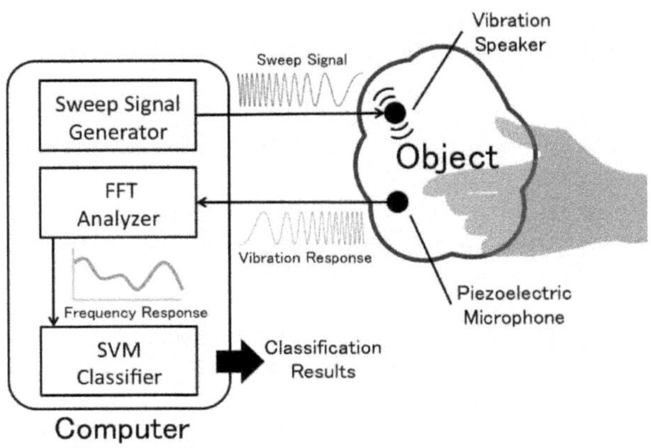

Figure 3. Overview of our test system.

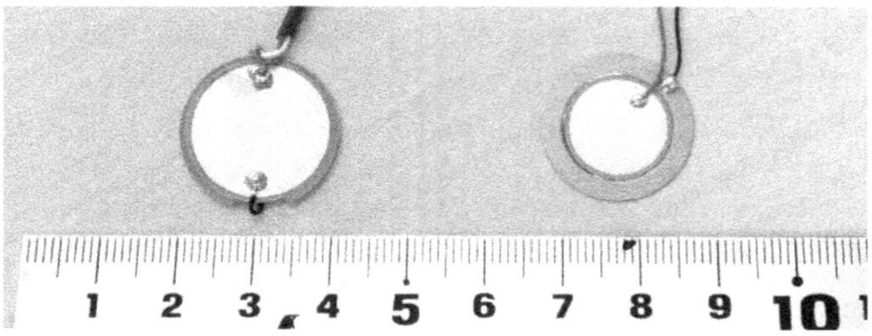

Figure 4. Vibration speaker and piezo-electric microphone.

These piezo elements are attached to various objects with double-sided tapes. Double-sided tapes are suitable as a mounting method in the early stage of prototyping using existing objects because this allows developers to remove the instrumentation from the objects easily. Instead, glues are appropriate for the final stage of prototyping because glues will provide lower mechanical impedance, making the actuation power necessary for the sensing lower. Moreover, glues connect piezo elements and objects tightly while eliminating ease to remove the instrumentation.

The signals current to/from the piezo elements are amplified and connected to a computer (Apple MacBook Air, CPU: Intel Core 2 Duo 1.4GHz, RAM: 2GB) via an USB audio interface (Native Instruments Audio Komplete 6) and processed by the software mentioned below.

Software

The software consists of three modules: Sweep Signal Generator, FFT Analyzer, and SVM Classifier. We used the BASS library[1] for audio I/O.

The Sweep Signal Generator we programmed generates sinusoid sweep signals from 20kHz to 40kHz, whose frequency increases linearly in 20 ms, at a 96kHz sampling rate. The module plays the signals repeatedly via the USB audio interface through the vibration speaker. The module also fades in/out both end of each period of the signals so as to suppress the impulse noise caused by the frequency gap. When the object is vibrated by the speaker, some sounds are emitted from the object to the air. We use 20k-40kHz sound since it is inaudible to humans [8] and robust to the contact noise produced by touching the object.

The FFT analyzer converts the vibration response captured from a piezo-electric microphone into the resonant frequency response. The module samples audio at 96kHz, which is the same rate generated by the Sweep Signal Generator, to obtain the high-frequency signal that ranges in 20k-40kHz, and uses the FFT with 8192-point hamming window vectors (85 ms long and overlapped with 20 ms) to compute the signal's 4096-point frequency vectors from 0 to 48kHz. This sampling does not need to be synchronized with the Sweep Signal Generator because the window vector of 8192 samples include at least four cycles of the sweep signal. This ensures that the frequency response we want is included in all window vectors at any moment during sampling while there are subtle differences depending on the phase of each sampling section. We then extract 400-point features representing from 20kHz to 40kHz with down-sampling. The purpose of down-sampling is to speed up recognition. To do this, we first determined the valid 400 frequency points that we use as features when the software is started. This is because there are many invalid frequency points (showing almost 0 value) within a raw frequency spectra, as the frequency resolution of the FFT is higher than that due to the sweep signal. Thus, we determined the valid 400 frequency points by applying peak detection algorithm to the raw frequency spectra.

The SVM Classifier classifies the touch gestures in real-time using a Support Vector Machine (SVM) implemented in LIBSVM [6] . We used the RBF kernel with default parameters as a kernel function for SVM. The parameters of the kernel can be tuned through a grid search to improve the accuracy. The 400-point features extracted by the FFT Analyzer are passed to the classifier every 20 ms (i.e., all data extracted by the FFT Analyzer are passed). Before the classification, the classifier must be trained for each gesture. For the informal training in the very early stage of prototyping, the module provides developers with a simple training mode where developers can train it by pressing any key (except the space bar) while performing a gesture. While a key is pressed, all features are passed to the classifier as training data labeled as its key code. After the training for all gestures is finished, the classification is started by hitting the space bar. For the formal training such as used in an evaluation and exhibition of the prototype, developers can use an auto-controlled training mode, where the training session for each gesture transits automatically at regular time intervals and the classifier can be trained by equal number of training data in each gesture.

APPLICATIONS

In this section, we demonstrate applications to show the broad range of sensing capabilities of Touch & Activate. We set up the applications using three types of objects: everyday objects, Duplo blocks, and a mobile device.

Everyday Objects

Our approach can make everyday objects touch or grasp sensitive. To show this, we applied Touch & Activate to three objects that have different shapes or material properties.

Ceramic Bowl

First, we made an interactive media art by applying Touch & Activate to a ceramic bowl (8 cm height, 14 cm in diameter). A bowl has several ways to be held depending on the user's manner and context (e.g., if its content is very hot, we may grasp the bowl as shown in Figure 2d). Such manner and context are often utilized in interactive media arts. Touch & Activate allows artists to create an interactive media art using real-world objects rapidly and easily. We trained the system to recognize four touch gestures as shown in Figure 2a-d and associated them with corresponding sounds.

Plastic Toy

Toys are an indispensable part of children's daily life. Interactive toys that can speak or move in response to children's actions are increasingly common. However, they are generally still more expensive than static toys. By using Touch & Activate, users can add interactivity to the existing static toys

[1] http://www.un4seen.com/

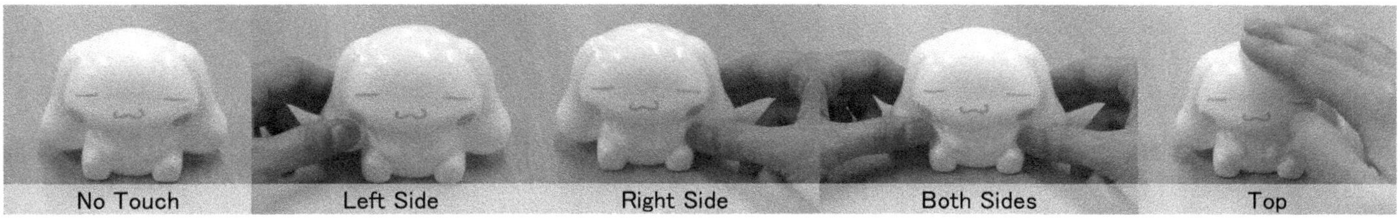

Figure 5. Five touch gestures applied to the plastic toy.

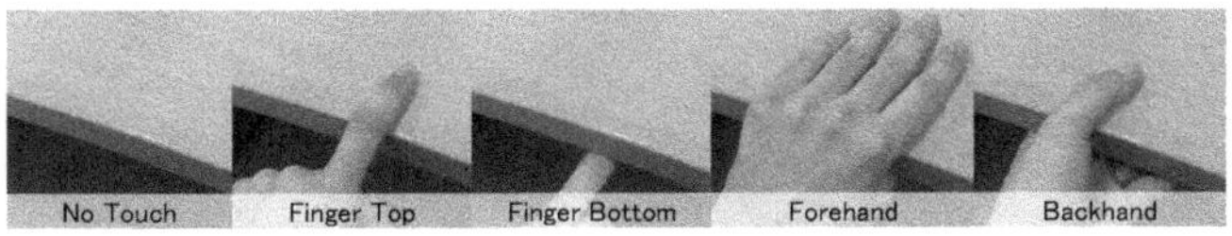

Figure 6. Five touch gestures that are applied to the laboratory desk.

that children have and love. As such an example, we applied Touch & Activate to a cheap plastic toy that is normally used as a money box. We trained the system to recognize five touch gestures on the toy and associated corresponding sounds to the positions, giving a new lease of life to an otherwise static object (Figure 5).

Wood Desk

When a large object such as a desk is used, its sensitive area is limited to the small space between the speaker and microphone. This is because the vibration traveling on the object is dampened when the distance is long. We attached the piezo-electric elements to the edge of a laboratory desk (1.5 cm thick, 120 cm wide, 75 cm deep) made of wood at intervals of 15 cm and trained the system to recognize five touch gestures on the desk (Figure 6) and confirmed the gestures can be recognized locally.

Duplo Blocks

Lego or Duplo blocks can be easily assembled to create a variety of models and are often used for rapid prototyping [10]. In our study, we attached two piezo-electric elements to the inner sides of a single piece of Duplo block (2×4, arch shaped) as shown in Figure 7a. We then made four different prototypes using the same piece of Duplo block as a base to add interactivity to the prototypes.

Music Player

First, we prototyped a simple music player that utilizes six studs on the block as discrete buttons representing play, stop, previous, next, volume up, and volume down (Figure 7b). The system recognizes the touch events on the respective buttons and sends corresponding commands to the iTunes music player via Apple Script. The system supports repeat actions in the event of continuous touch.

Interactive Animal Body

DuploTrack [15] infers the assembly arrangement of the Duplo blocks and tracks the assembly process. Our approach, albeit limited, can also estimate the assembly arrangement such as position and direction, as well as the shape of the added block. This is because the added block, depending on its arrangement and shape, produces a change in the boundary condition, hence the resonant property of the object will also

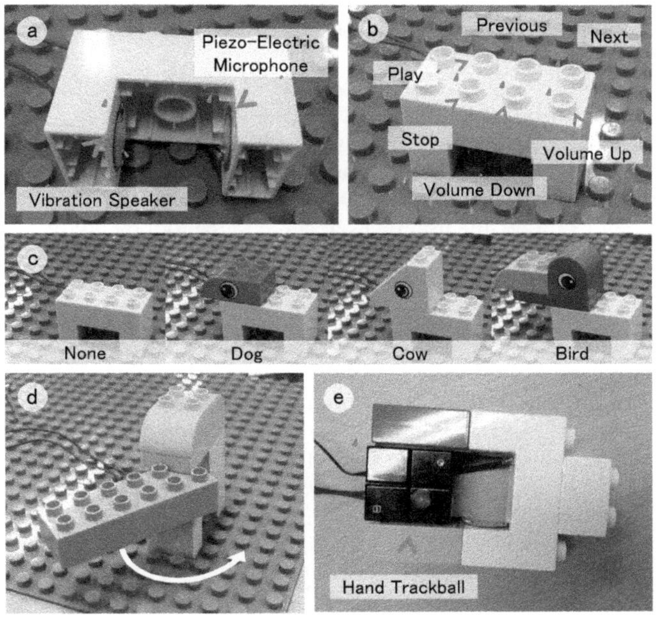

Figure 7. Examples of applications using Duplo blocks: a) a base block attached piezo-electric elements, b) music player, c) interactive animal body, d) six stage lever, and e) multi-functional input device.

change accordingly. We made a prototype of this called interactive animal body (Figure 7c) consisting of one body part, which is the base block, and three other blocks representing three animals' heads (dog, cow, bird). The system was then trained to play a corresponding sound when one of the three heads is added to the body.

Six Stage Lever

As another example of recognition of change in boundary condition without touch or grasp, we made a prototype called six stage lever (Figure 7d). In this prototype, a block which serves as a lever, is attached to the base block. By moving the lever, we can change the base block's boundary condition, thereby changing the resonant property. As the lever can be moved in a continuous manner, the resonant property can also be changed continuously. We trained the system to recognize six distinct angle of the lever with six different labels. This lever can be applied to the previous music player to control the volume.

Multi-Functional Input Device

Other studies have proposed input devices with multi-functions that can be selected by changing the way the device is held [40, 49, 44]. We developed a similar multi-functional input device (Figure 7e) designed for a paint appli-

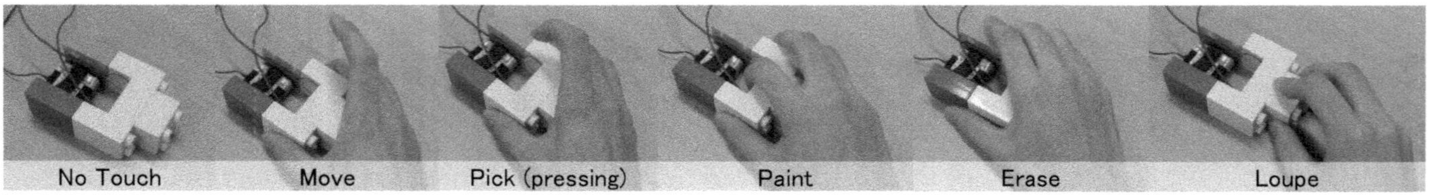

Figure 8. Tools of the multi-functional input device designed for a paint application and corresponding ways to grasp. No Touch) The device is not used. Move) This tool used to just move the mouse pointer is selected by holding out sides of the base block. Pick) By applying pressure to the base block in using move tool, pick mode is selected, with which users can create a selected area and then move the pictures in the area to another space by dragging. Paint) This tool used to paint the canvas is selected by hooking the finger in the base block. Erase) This tool is selected by holding the device deeply. Loupe) This tool can zoom into the canvas around the mouse pointer, which is selected by holding the yellow end of the device.

cation by embedding a super-mobile hand trackball (Sanwa Supply 400-MA018) upside down into the Duplo blocks. The mouse pointer movement is flipped horizontally using USB Overdrive[2]. The device has five input tools that can be selected by changing the way the device is grasped (Figure 8). For example, the user can select the loupe tool by holding the yellow end of the object.

Mobile Device

Many researchers have developed grasp sensitive mobile devices to explore how the user interface of mobile devices can be improved using postures and pressure when holding the device [13, 32, 7, 47, 53]. Most researches used multiple touch sensors to recognize hand postures and pressure. Although GripSense [13] can detect the posture and pressure on commodity mobile devices by using built-in sensors, it relys on the swipe or touch gesture on a touch screen to recognize the postures. Our approach is applicable for recognizing the hand posture and pressure on mobile devices. We made a grasp sensitive case by attaching two piezo-electric elements to the bottom of a transparent hard case for iPhone 4S (Figure 9). As the structure is wobbly when the device is mounted on the case due to the thickness of the two elements and cables, we glued six plastic beads (white ones in Figure 9; 5 mm thick, 5 mm in diameter) on the case to achieve the uniformity in thickness. Then, we tested the prototype to recognize hand posture and pressure.

Posture Recognition

Many applications on recent mobile devices are used with the user holding the device in a unique hand posture. For example, during a call, the user's thumb is on one side while the other four fingers are on the other side of the mobile phone. When using the camera function of the device, users usually hold the four corners of the device with both hands. Therefore, if the holding postures can be recognized, the device can be taught to launch the applications associated with these postures automatically [32, 47]. Additionally, the operational performance and usage of the device differ between different hand postures due to its touch behavior and possibility [4]. If the device can recognize the hand posture of the user, it can adjust the UI accordingly such that maximum ease of use can be achieved (e.g., optimizing keyboard layout and algorithm [4], hand posture based screen rotation [7]). Touch & Activate provides easy hardware configuration to researchers who want to implement these interactions. To test this, we trained the system to recognize six hand postures (Figure 10; determined by referring to [32]) that consists of feasible combinations of three applications (call, sms, camera) and three holding-hand conditions (left handed, right handed, two-handed).

Pressure Recognition

Although a mobile device that has a touch screen as its primary input device allows several multi-touch gestures, single-touch operations using the thumb are still often used because the vast majority of users prefer single-handed interaction with the mobile device [38, 31]. In single-touch operations, however, the interaction with the touch screen is limited because only the thumb can be used. On the other hand, if the grip pressure of the hand can be recognized as a form of control, single-handed interaction with the mobile device will improve (e.g., pressure based zoom-in/out [35, 13], menu selection [50], non-verbal communication during phone call [26]). Touch & Activate can also recognize the grip pressure on the mobile device because applying the pressure changes the boundary condition of the device, and it can be used to implement these interactions. To test this, we trained the system to recognize three levels of pressure (i.e., support, hold, and grasp as shown in Figure 11) and confirmed the levels can be recognized. This example application shows that our technique also can be used to test these pressure based interactions without additional pressure sensors.

[2]http://www.usboverdrive.com/USBOverdrive/Information.html

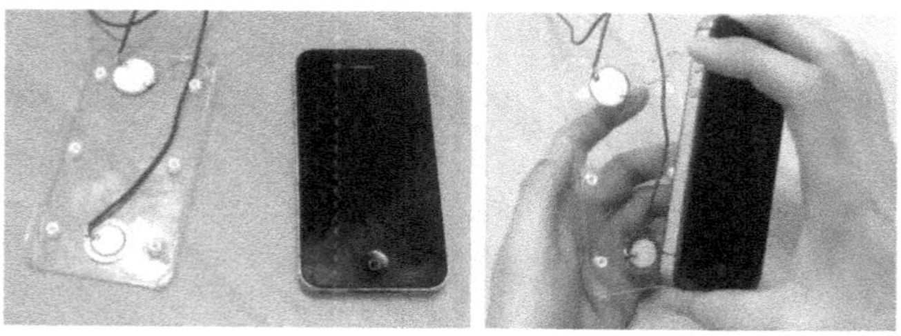

Figure 9. iPhone 4S and a grasp sensitive case with Touch & Activate.

Figure 11. Three hand postures for pressure recognition. The "grasp" posture is grasping the device applying pressure strongest.

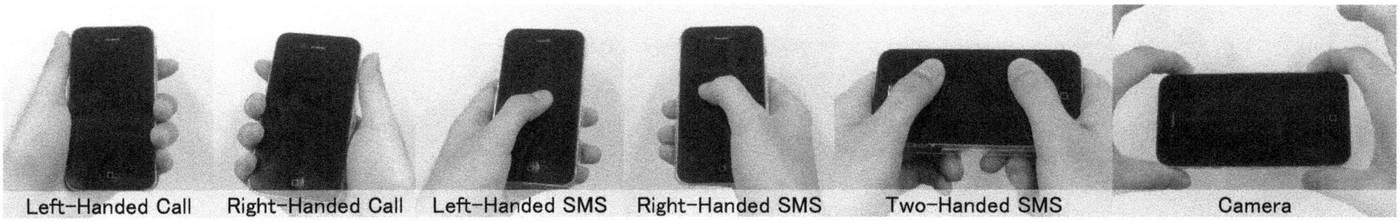

Figure 10. Six hand postures for posture recognition.

LIMITATIONS

Although Touch & Activate is applicable to various objects, our approach could not prototype fully touch-enabled objects due to the instrumentation. Moreover, it has limitations in material, size, and shape of objects; and noise will affect the recognition in some cases.

Materials

As Touch & Activate uses the vibration of objects for its sensing, the material of objects that are applied to need to conduct the vibration efficiently. In general, elastic modulus, a measure of the stiffness of materials, affects the conductivity of vibration of objects. If a material exhibits lower elastic modulus (such as gel, clay, and rubber), our approach is difficult to apply to it because this characteristic damps the vibration. In contrast, we confirmed that a material exhibiting high elastic modulus (such as wood, metal, plastic, and ceramic) generally works well.

Size

Even in the material that conducts the vibration efficiently, the vibration is dampened with the distance from the source. Thus, if the objects are large, the sensitive area is limited to a small area between the speaker and microphone as shown in the wood desk application. Extending the sensitive area requires extra sensors (i.e., speakers or microphones) or a more powerful amplifier. However, in our tests so far, most handheld-sized objects can be made touch and grasp sensitive by using a casual amplifier (e.g., consumer USB audio interfaces) and a single speaker and microphone pair.

On the other hand, if the objects are too small, there is little interaction space and developers might feel that the instrumentation is obtrusive in the prototyping. To remedy this issue, we recommend using smaller piezo elements as a sensor, because the surface area of the elements barely affects the sensitivity of the high frequency component. We confirmed even 15-mm-diameter piezo elements work well in our test.

Shape

The shape of objects also limits the sensing capability in some cases. For instance, a symmetrical object cannot recognize as many gestures as an asymmetrical object, where, due to its symmetry, the same resonant frequency is provided by the symmetric touch gestures. In such case, developers must displace the sensor from the axis of symmetry if they want to distinguish between the gestures. Moreover, if the objects that do not have clear touch points due to having too complex a shape (e.g., spiked surfaces), our approach is difficult to apply to them because our approach requires a clear change in the boundary condition.

Noises

In our technique, noise will affect the accuracy in some cases. When the speaker and microphone are placed close together, especially if they are on the same surface, the accuracy might be lowered because the reflected sounds with Doppler shifts are caused by moving hands or some objects passing above the sensors and affect the frequency response captured from the microphone. To avoid this, both piezo elements should be placed sufficiently apart, or the microphone should be covered with some material such as rubber to prevent it from capturing the noise caused by Doppler shifts.

Our current implementation of Touch & Activate cannot recognize touch gestures with certainty when a high impact is applied to the object. This is because a consumer audio hardware usually clips such sounds from the microphone and the high frequency in the signal, which is necessary to obtain the resonant property, is lost. In other words, if an audio hardware with a wide dynamic range is used, our approach can be used with a passive one (e.g., TapSense [21]) and further interactions combined with impacts, such as "tap and hold", can be detected, because our approach uses a very high frequency, which is not affected by tapping.

However, our approach is robust in noisy environments because little noise in air can be transformed as vibration of the object and the most of the noise is reflected. Due to this robustness, our system worked successfully when we demonstrated Touch & Activate in a noisy hall of an academic conference, where 65 demonstrations were presented simultaneously and over 400 people participated and had discussions.

EVALUATION

For our evaluation, we conducted a controlled experiment to measure the accuracy and trade-off between the accuracy and number of training rounds using the two applications: the plastic toy as a simple example and the posture recognition as a complex example.

Participants

Our experiment had 10 participants (seven males, three females) ranging in age from 22 to 32 years old. All participants were smartphone users and had used the device from between one week to three years.

Procedure

We collected the data for our evaluation by asking each participant to perform the following task for each application independently (i.e., we used the auto-controlled training mode described in the Software section).

Participants were shown a picture of one of the gestures selected from the gesture set (five touch gestures for the plastic

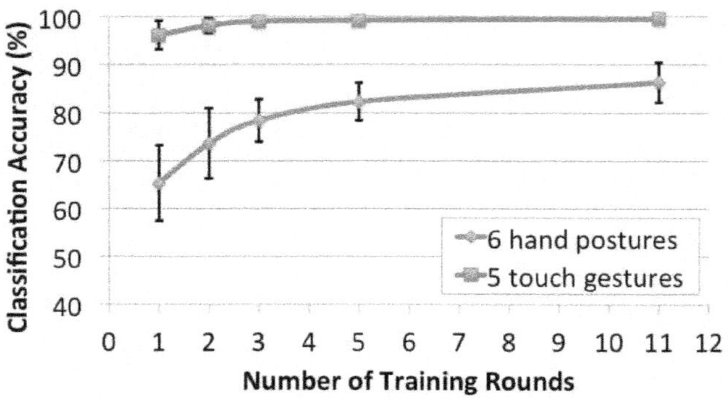

Figure 12. Accuracy using a per-user classifier.

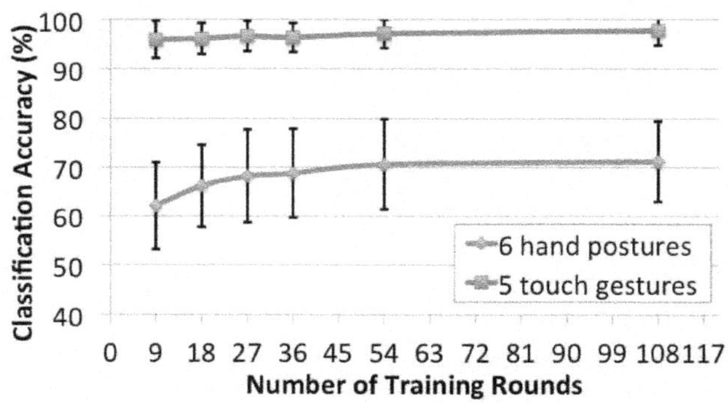

Figure 13. Accuracy using a general classifier.

toy shown in Figure 5 and six hand postures for the posture recognition shown in Figure 10) for seven seconds in a randomized order and asked to perform the gestures. While performing a gesture, the participants were also asked to continuously adjust the gesture's posture to make the system give the same label to slightly different postures of the gesture. This is necessary because our technique is so sensitive that it can detect even subtle differences in postures that the participants cannot. In the last second, because the participants were performing the gestures stably now, we collected the 40 pieces of frequency response data, which is representing the feature vectors in the last second. Seven seconds after seeing the previous picture, the participants were shown the next picture. This procedure was repeated until all gestures were performed (one round). Each participant performed 12 rounds, yielding 480 pieces of data per user per gesture.

In total, 24000 pieces of data (10 participants × 5 gestures × 12 rounds × 40 data) for the plastic toy and 28800 pieces of data (10 participants × 6 postures × 12 rounds × 40 data) for the posture recognition were collected, respectively. The entire experiment took approximately 25 minutes per participant (seven minutes for the plastic toy, nine minutes for the posture recognition, and nine minutes for the explanation and questionnaire) to complete.

RESULTS

By using the data, we evaluated two types of classifier for each application: per-user classifiers and general classifiers. We used a LIBSVM (RBF kernel, c=1.0, g=0.0025), which is the same SVM library used in our test system, in all training and classification processes.

Per-User Classifiers

To understand the feasibility of Touch & Activate for individual users, we assessed the accuracy of user-specific classifiers. We trained the classifier with 11 rounds of data collected from a single participant, and tested on the rest round data. All train/test combinations were tested and averaged per participant (i.e., 12-fold round-independent cross validation). This process was also tested for each participant's data and we averaged the accuracies. In the results, the plastic toy including five touch gestures achieved an accuracy of 99.6% (SD=0.36%). On the other hand, the posture recognition including six hand postures achieved an accuracy of 86.3% (SD=4.2%).

To understand the trade-off between the accuracy and number of training rounds for individual users, we also tested the accuracy when the system is trained with different amounts of data. To do this, we first divided the per-participant data into two, three, four, and six segments (e.g., we divided the per-participant data consisting of 12 rounds data into two segments: first-sixth rounds of data and seventh-twelfth rounds of data). Then, six-, four-, three-, and two-fold cross validations were performed on both segments. The results were averaged and are plotted in Figure 12. The plastic toy with only one round of data achieved an accuracy of 96.2% (SD=3.0%). The posture recognition with one round of data maintained an accuracy of 65.3% (SD=7.9%). By using five rounds of data, the accuracy jumped to 82.3% (SD=3.9%).

General Classifier

To understand the feasibility of Touch & Activate for "walk up" users, we assessed the accuracy of a general classifier. We trained the SVM with nine participants' data and tested on the other participant's data (all-combinations, i.e., 10-fold participant-independent cross validation). In the results, for the plastic toy achieved 97.8% accuracy (SD=2.9%) that is about 2% lower than per-user classifiers. On the other hand, the posture recognition maintained 71.2% accuracy (SD=8.2%).

We calculated the trade-off curves between the accuracy and number of training rounds (Figure 13). Note that 10-fold participant-independent cross validation was performed on all results with different numbers of rounds of data while six-, four-, three-, and two-fold round-independent cross validations were performed on per-user classifier's results. In the results, the plastic toy keeps a high accuracy of 96.0% (SD=3.8%) even with nine rounds of data (one round of data per participant). On the other hand, the posture recognition maintained 62.1% accuracy (SD=8.9%) with nine rounds of data and accuracy mostly stopped improving at around 54 rounds of data (five rounds of data per participant).

DISCUSSION & FUTURE WORK

As the results of our experiment showed a promising accuracy for the recognition of touch gestures and hand postures, Touch & Activate should be feasible for prototyping interactive objects that have touch input capability. Especially for a simple application such as the plastic toy, Touch & Activate provides a very rapid prototyping experience using existing objects. Note that, as Figure 12 shows, training with only one round of data resulted in 96.2% accuracy in the plastic toy, which is high enough for developers to test their ideas by themselves, and collecting one round of data requires only 35 seconds (7 seconds × 5 gestures). Even for a complex application such as the posture recognition, the touch or grasp input should be available with a promising accuracy of 86.3% after a few minutes of training; collecting 11 rounds of data takes 7.7 minutes (7 seconds × 6 postures × 11 rounds), which is much shorter than time spent designing circuits and configuring hardware using multiple sensors. Note that in our experiment, we presented a gesture for seven seconds to ensure that the participants could understand the gesture and perform it without fail. In practice, less time is necessary to train the system to recognize a gesture (it was approximately three seconds for each gesture in our development), supporting rapid prototyping.

Resonant property of solid objects, which is used for touch sensing in Touch & Activate, is highly sensitive to changes in the boundary condition. To stabilize the recognition, developers have to continuously adjust the touches while training the system to recognize the gestures. Moreover, when the system is trained once, the piezo elements positions must be fixed to recognize the gestures using those training data because the resonant property also differs even if the relative positions of sensors remain unchanged.

While we still cannot find any general rule for the sensor's placement with which Touch & Activate provides the best performance for the recognition, there are some rules to avoid limitations: 1) avoid the axis of symmetry in the symmetric objects, 2) place them sufficiently apart when Doppler shifts occur, and 3) place them in an area that do not needed to be touched. In future work, we plan to explore the general rules of placement.

Although our primary focus is on providing easy hardware configuration for adding touch input capability to existing objects, prototyping these objects still requires some programming for implementing actions, whose processes are difficult for non-engineers. In future work, we plan to remove this difficulty by adopting easy authoring methods proposed in other works (e.g., record-and-replay [24, 28, 42] and visual programming [25]) to help developers implement actions.

In our current implementation, the portability of the objects with Touch & Activate is restricted because of the wired connection to the computer. Since this might discourage developers from stretching their imagination in designing the interaction, we plan to implement the wireless sensor module of Touch & Activate. The module will be the one similar to the wireless Swept Frequency Capacitive Sensing module of Touché [41] with an additional amplifier to vibrate the objects; hence, its running time will be limited due to the power consumption of the amplifier. Therefore, we also plan to measure the trade-off between the degree of the amplification (i.e., power consumption) and the accuracy in sensing. However, we believe that power consumption would not impose any problem even in the wireless setup because our technique requires short time to train a gesture for rapid prototyping.

CONCLUSIONS

We presented a novel acoustic touch sensing technique called *Touch & Activate*. It can detect a rich context of touches including grasp and changes in other boundary conditions on existing objects, by attaching only a vibration speaker and a piezo-electric microphone paired as a sensor. This provides easy hardware configuration for prototyping interactive objects that have touch input capability. We demonstrated with a number of applications that our approach's broad range of sensing capability can be used in prototyping a variety of interactive objects. We conducted a controlled experiment to measure the accuracy and trade-off between the accuracy and number of training rounds of our technique. From its results, per-user recognition accuracies with five touch gestures for the plastic toy and six hand postures for the posture recognition were 99.6% and 86.3%, respectively. Walk up user recognition accuracies were 97.8% and 71.2%, respectively. This suggests Touch & Activate should be feasible and accessible for prototyping interactive objects using existing objects.

REFERENCES

1. Arduino - HomePage. http://www.arduino.cc/, Accessed: June 2013.
2. mbed - Rapid Prototyping for Microcontrollers. http://mbed.org/, Accessed: June 2013.
3. Amento, B., Hill, W., and Terveen, L. The sound of one hand: a wrist-mounted bio-acoustic fingertip gesture interface. In *CHI EA '02*, 724–725.
4. Azenkot, S., and Zhai, S. Touch behavior with different postures on soft smartphone keyboards. In *MobileHCI '12*, 251–260.
5. Brenner, M.C., and Fitzgibbon, J.J. Surface acoustic wave touch panel system, Feb.17 1987. US Patent 4,644,100.
6. Chang, C.-C., Lin, C.-J. LIBSVM: a library for support vector machines., http://www.csie.ntu.edu.tw/cjlin/livsvm
7. Cheng, L.-P., Hsiao, F.-I., Liu, Y.-T., and Chen, M.Y. iRotate grasp: automatic screen rotation based on grasp of mobile devices. In *UIST '12 Adjunct*, 15–16.
8. Christopher, D. Frequency Range of Human Hearing. In *The Physics Factbook*. 2003.
9. Collins, T. Active acoustic touch interface. *Electronics Letters 45*, 20 (24 2009), 1055 –1056.
10. Cralg, L. Right–rapid–rough. *Ask Magazine*, 13 (2003), 12–15.
11. Ewins, D.J. *Modal testing: theory, practice and application*, vol.2. Research studies press Baldock, 2000.
12. Fourney, A., and Terry, M. PICL: portable in-circuit learner. In *UIST '12*, 569–578.
13. Goel, M., Wobbrock, J., and Patel, S. GripSense: using built-in sensors to detect hand posture and pressure on commodity mobile phones. In *UIST '12*, 545–554.
14. Greenberg, S., and Fitchett, C. Phidgets: easy development of physical interfaces through physical widgets. In *UIST '01*, 209–218.
15. Gupta, A., Fox, D., Curless, B., and Cohen, M. DuploTrack: a real-time system for authoring and guiding duplo block assembly. In *UIST '12*, 389–402.
16. Gupta, S., Morris, D., Patel, S., and Tan, D. SoundWave: using the Doppler effect to sense gestures. In *CHI '12*, 1911–1914.

17. Han, J.Y. Low-cost multi-touch sensing through frustrated total internal reflection. In *UIST '05*, 115–118.
18. Harrison, C., Benko, H., and Wilson, A.D. OmniTouch: wearable multitouch interaction everywhere. In *UIST '11*, 441–450.
19. Harrison, C., and Hudson, S.E. Scratch input: creating large, inexpensive, unpowered and mobile finger input surfaces. In *UIST '08*, 205–208.
20. Harrison, C., Sato, M., and Poupyrev, I. Capacitive fingerprinting: exploring user differentiation by sensing electrical properties of the human body. In *UIST '12*, 537–544.
21. Harrison, C., Schwarz, J., and Hudson, S.E. TapSense: enhancing finger interaction on touch surfaces. In *UIST '11*, 627–636.
22. Harrison, C., Tan, D., and Morris, D. Skinput: appropriating the body as an input surface. In *CHI '10*, 453–462.
23. Harrison, C., Xiao, R., and Hudson, S. Acoustic barcodes: passive, durable and inexpensive notched identification tags. In *UIST '12*, 563–568.
24. Hartmann, B., Abdulla, L., Mittal, M., and Klemmer, S.R. Authoring sensor-based interactions by demonstration with direct manipulation and pattern recognition. In *CHI '07*, 145–154.
25. Hartmann, B., Klemmer, S.R., Bernstein, M., Abdulla, L., Burr, B., Robinson-Mosher, A., and Gee, J. Reflective physical prototyping through integrated design, test, and analysis. In *UIST '06*, 299–308.
26. Hoggan, E., Stewart, C., Haverinen, L., Jacucci, G., and Lantz, V. Pressages: augmenting phone calls with non-verbal messages. In *UIST '12*, 555–562.
27. Holman, D., and Vertegaal, R. TactileTape: low-cost touch sensing on curved surfaces. In *UIST '11 Adjunct*, 17–18.
28. Hudson, S.E., and Mankoff, J. Rapid construction of functioning physical interfaces from cardboard, thumbtacks, tin foil and masking tape. In *UIST '06*, 289–298.
29. Hwang, S., Bianchi, A., and Wohn, K. MicPen: pressure-sensitive pen interaction using microphone with standard touchscreen. In *CHI EA '12*, 1847–1852.
30. Izadi, S., Kim, D., Hilliges, O., Molyneaux, D., Newcombe, R., Kohli, P., Shotton, J., Hodges, S., Freeman, D., Davison, A., and Fitzgibbon, A. KinectFusion: real-time 3D reconstruction and interaction using a moving depth camera. In *UIST '11*, 559–568.
31. Karlson, A.K., and Bederson, B.B. Understanding single-handed mobile device interaction. Tech. rep., Dep. of Computer Science, Univ. of Maryland, 2006.
32. Kim, K.-E., Chang, W., Cho, S.-J., Shim, J., Lee, H., Park, J., Lee, Y., and Kim, S. Hand grip pattern recognition for mobile user interfaces. In *IAAI '06*, 1789–1794.
33. Liu, S., and Guimbretière, F. FlexAura: a flexible near-surface range sensor. In *UIST '12*, 327–330.
34. Lopes, P., Jota, R., and Jorge, J.A. Augmenting touch interaction through acoustic sensing. In *ITS '11*, 53–56.
35. Miyaki, T., and Rekimoto, J. Graspzoom: zooming and scrolling control model for single-handed mobile interaction. In *MobileHCI '09*, 11.
36. Murray-Smith, R., Williamson, J., Hughes, S., and Quaade, T. Stane: synthesized surfaces for tactile input. In *CHI '08*, 1299–1302.
37. Paradiso, J.A., Leo, C.K., Checka, N., and Hsiao, K. Passive acoustic knock tracking for interactive windows. In *CHI EA '02*, 732–733.
38. Parhi, P., Karlson, A.K., and Bederson, B.B. Target size study for one-handed thumb use on small touchscreen devices. In *MobileHCI '06*, 203–210.
39. Pham, D., Ji, Z., Yang, M., Wang, Z., and Al-Kutubi, M. A novel human-computer interface based on passive acoustic localisation. In *HCII '07*, 901–909.
40. Rekimoto, J., and Sciammarella, E. ToolStone: effective use of the physical manipulation vocabularies of input devices. In *UIST '00*, 109–117.
41. Sato, M., Poupyrev, I., and Harrison, C. Touché: enhancing touch interaction on humans, screens, liquids, and everyday objects. In *CHI '12*, 483–492.
42. Savage, V., Zhang, X., and Hartmann, B. Midas: fabricating custom capacitive touch sensors to prototype interactive objects. In *UIST '12*, 579–588.
43. Schwarz, B.J., and Richardson, M.H. Experimental modal analysis. *CSI Reliability week* (1999).
44. Song, H., Benko, H., Guimbretière, F., Izadi, S., Cao, X., and Hinckley, K. Grips and gestures on a multi-touch pen. In *CHI '11*, 1323–1332.
45. Stewart, J., and Westerfield, E. A theory of active sonar detection. *Proceedings of the IRE 47*, 5 (1959), 872–881.
46. Takemura, K., Ito, A., Takamatsu, J., and Ogasawara, T. Active bone-conducted sound sensing for wearable interfaces. In *UIST '11 Adjunct*, 53–54.
47. Taylor, B.T., and Bove, Jr., V.M. Graspables: grasp-recognition as a user interface. In *CHI '09*, 917–926.
48. Villar, N., Scott, J., Hodges, S., Hammil, K., and Miller, C. . NET Gadgeteer: a platform for custom devices. *Pervasive Computing* (2012), 216–233.
49. Vogel, D., and Casiez, G. Conté: multimodal input inspired by an artist's crayon. In *UIST '11*, 357–366.
50. Wilson, G., Stewart, C., and Brewster, S.A. Pressure-based menu selection for mobile devices. In *MobileHCI '10*, 181–190.
51. Wimmer, R. FlyEye: grasp-sensitive surfaces using optical fiber. In *TEI '10*, 245–248.
52. Wimmer, R., and Baudisch, P. Modular and deformable touch-sensitive surfaces based on time domain reflectometry. In *UIST '11*, 517–526.
53. Wimmer, R., and Boring, S. HandSense: discriminating different ways of grasping and holding a tangible user interface. In *TEI '09*, 359–362.

Fiberio: A Touchscreen that Senses Fingerprints

Christian Holz and Patrick Baudisch
Hasso Plattner Institute, Potsdam, Germany
{christian.holz, patrick.baudisch}@hpi.uni-potsdam.de

ABSTRACT

We present Fiberio, a rear-projected multitouch table that identifies users biometrically based on their fingerprints *during* each touch interaction. Fiberio accomplishes this using a new type of screen material: a large fiber optic plate. The plate *diffuses* light on transmission, thereby allowing it to act as projection surface. At the same time, the plate *reflects* light specularly, which produces the contrast required for fingerprint sensing. In addition to offering all the functionality known from traditional diffused illumination systems, Fiberio is the first interactive tabletop system that authenticates users during touch interaction—unobtrusively and securely using the biometric features of fingerprints, which eliminates the need for users to carry any identification tokens.

Author Keywords

Touchscreens; multitouch; user identification; fingerprints.

ACM Classification Keywords

H5.2 [Information interfaces and presentation]: User Interfaces. Input devices & strategies.

INTRODUCTION

Several researchers have proposed techniques that allow interactive tabletop systems to distinguish users during interaction. The ability to associate each touch with a particular user has allowed such systems to personalize interaction [21], log user activity [2], and ensure that only the authorized users can access private objects [31] or perform privileged activities [6].

A number of existing approaches address this challenge. Unfortunately, they either require users to carry identification tokens, such as RFID tags [28], rings [30], or marker gloves [21] or they can only distinguish among a small group of users, for example by recognizing their shoes [29], their hand contours [31], or the chairs they sit in [6].

Researchers have therefore pointed to fingerprint recognition as a possible solution to the problem. Fingerprint-based authentication is secure [20] and—in conjunction with touch interaction—would be unobtrusive for users. First steps in this direction include a separate fingerprint scanner placed *next* to the touchscreen [32] and an interactive fingerprint scanner without a screen (Ridgepad [15]). These prototypes point out the challenge in designing such a system, i.e., to sense fingerprints and display a computer-generated image *in the same space at the same time.*

UIST'13, October 8–11, 2013, St. Andrews, United Kingdom.
Copyright © 2013 ACM 978-1-4503-2268-3/13/10...$15.00
http://dx.doi.org/10.1145/2501988.2502021

Figure 1: *Fiberio* is a rear-projected tabletop system that identifies users based on their fingerprints *during each interaction*—unobtrusively and securely. The shown application uses this to verify that the respective user has the authority to perform the current activity, here approve invoices above a certain value. The key that allows Fiberio to display an image *and* sense fingerprints at the same time is its screen material: a fiber optic plate.

This challenge boils down to two contradicting requirements with respect to the screen material. On the one hand, the screen has to reveal fingerprints, i.e., produce contrast between the ridges and valleys of the fingerprint. Known solutions require a *specular* screen surface to accomplish optical fingerprint scanning. On the other hand, to be used as a display, the screen has to allow the rear-projection to produce a visible image, which requires the screen material to be *diffuse*. Unfortunately, specular and diffuse are contradictory requirements for such a surface.

These contradictory requirements eliminate a number of candidate technologies that appear suitable at first glance. Tabletops based on frustrated total internal reflection [13], for example, cannot generate the contrast between fingerprint valleys and ridges and thus do not afford scanning users' fingerprints with sufficient quality.

In this paper, we demonstrate how to resolve this contradiction. We present Fiberio, a multitouch table that recognizes fingerprints during touch interaction. As shown in Figure 1, Fiberio authenticates users while interacting with the table.

FIBERIO

Figure 2 shows Fiberio's hardware configuration, which is essentially a *diffused illumination* [22] setup: a 19″ screen ("diffuser"), a projector that rear-projects onto the screen, an infrared illuminant that illuminates the screen from behind, and cameras that observe touch input on the screen.

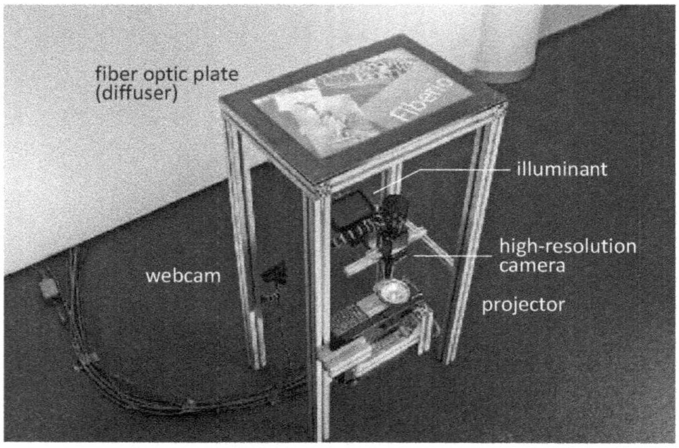

Figure 2: Our *Fiberio* prototype is a standard diffuse illumination setup, except that the diffuser is a fiber optic plate.

What distinguishes Fiberio from a regular diffused illumination setup is the nature of the diffuser: At first glance, Fiberio's diffuser appears like a sheet of frosted glass, but it is a 3mm thick, 4233dpi fiber optic plate. Its 40 million optical fibers run perpendicular to the surface and transmit light between the top and the bottom of the screen. Such plates, typically marketed for shielding CCD sensors from X-ray radiation in medical applications, are being produced in large numbers today and we repurpose them without modification in our prototype.

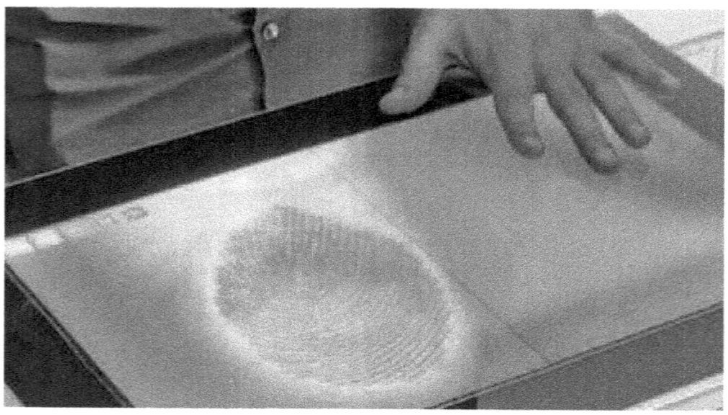

Figure 3: Fiberio displaying a region of its high-resolution raw input image, revealing the user's fingerprint.

In Fiberio, this fiber optic plate resolves the aforementioned contradiction. As we describe in detail in the section "working principle", the fiber optic plate (1) diffuses light on transmission. This causes the light coming from the projector located below the screen to scatter, allowing users to see the image on the surface from all locations around the table. (2) With the correct illumination setup, the fiber optic plate creates a specific type of specular reflection: *frustrated Fresnel reflection*, which is different from the type of reflection used in FTIR-based tabletop systems. This setup causes the infrared light that illuminates the plate from below to produce a visible contrast between fingerprint ridges and valleys, which allows the high-resolution infrared camera below the table to capture fingerprints (Figure 3). Because of the fiber optic plate, Fiberio is capable of *simultaneously* displaying images and capturing fingerprints.

Example Scenario: Collaborative Approval of Invoices

Since Fiberio identifies users during touch interaction, it supports a wide range of applications that require *secure* authentication. Figure 4 shows one of the examples we have implemented. A bank clerk and his manager approve invoices by pressing the 'pay' button on each invoice. When the invoice exceeds the clerk's approval limit as shown in Figure 4a, Fiberio refuses the transaction until (b) the clerk asks the manager to (c) approve the invoice. He does so by pushing the same button the clerk had pressed. This time, however, the transaction is performed under the manager's credentials, verified against his higher approval limit, and approved.

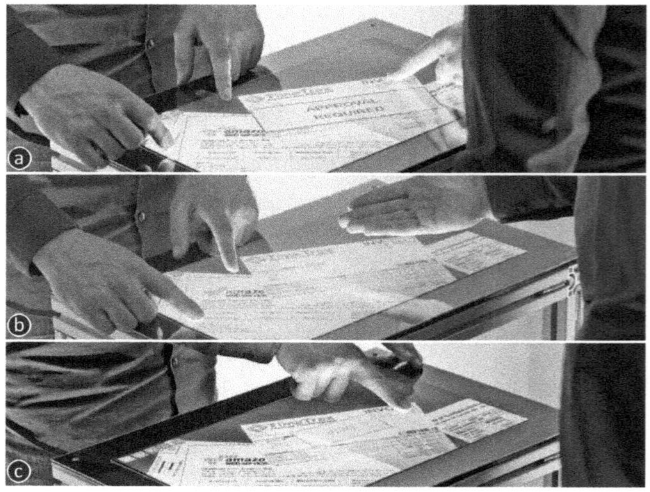

Figure 4: Example scenario. A bank manager (left) and clerk (right) approve invoices. (a) When the clerk encounters a bill above his approval limit, Fiberio refuses the payment. (c) The manager completes the transaction, pushing the same button.

Fiberio enables this scenario by authenticating users during each touch interaction and, in this scenario, by retrieving their approval limit from a database. Fiberio does so by authenticating users based on their fingerprints—integrated seamlessly into regular interaction. Fiberio thereby avoids the need for login procedures or identification tokens.

CONTRIBUTION

The main contribution of this paper is a prototype multi-touch table that identifies users biometrically on every touch interaction—securely and unobtrusively. We achieve this ability by capturing fingerprints *and* displaying a computer-generated image at the same time on the same surface, thereby implementing technology whose existence has been hypothesized since the late nineties [32]. Our solution is based on a new type of screen material, i.e., a fiber optic plate. We also demonstrate fingerprint processing at interactive rates (21ms processing time per frame) and a demo application in which Fiberio continuously authenticates users during interaction.

RELATED WORK

Fiberio is related to optical tabletop systems, applications of glass fibers, user identification, and fingerprint sensing.

Optical tabletop systems

Fiberio primarily inherits properties from diffused illumination systems, such as Holowall [22] and the Microsoft Surface table [25]. Such systems capture the light reflected by objects through their diffuser to detect touch or recognize fiducial markers. The diffuser such systems typically use, however, blurs all the details of the user's finger as well as those of objects above the surface [4].

Applications of glass-fiber bundles in HCI

A number of systems in HCI have exploited the capability of optical fibers to transmit light. For example, FiberBoard integrates optical sensing into a small form factor by folding the optical paths of its camera system [18]. Lumino channels light through tangibles, thereby allowing tabletop systems to sense stacked objects [4]. FuSA^2 projects color effects onto a large plastic fiber bundle and uses the same fibers to sense hovering hands [26].

User identification

To achieve reliable user authentication on tabletops, researchers have typically equipped users with identification tokens, such as rings that flash unique sequences of light (e.g., IR Ring [30]) or using fiducial markers to produce touch input (e.g., attached to a glove [21]).

Other approaches eliminate the need for such tokens, but in exchange are limited to identifying users only within a small group of users. Such approaches include identifying users based on the color of their shoes (Bootstrapper [29]) or the contours of their hands (HandsDown [31]). Capacitive touchscreens may identify two stationary users based on their electrical impedance after calibration [14].

Finally, a series of tabletop systems are able to *distinguish* users that simultaneously interact with the table. For example, DiamondTouch electrically connects users' chairs to the surface of the tabletop, closing a circuit when a user touches the table [6]. While this associates a user around the table with each touch contact and thus distinguishes users reliably, this approach is limited to a small number of stationary users. Other systems have associated touch events with users around the table by tracing their arm to the edge of the table using the reflections of the user's arm above the tabletop (e.g., [35]) or by instrumenting the table with sensors to capture users' arms and bodies around the table (e.g., Medusa [2]). Note that while these last systems reliably *distinguish* users, they do not *identify* them.

In contrast, Fiberio builds on fingerprint identification, which allows users to be authenticated unobtrusively and securely during each interaction.

Fingerprint recognition

Fingerprints are widely used for biometric identification feature, because they exhibit unique patterns of structural features that make such authentication reliable [3, 20].

Researchers have *simulated* interactive fingerprint-based devices, such as to invoke finger-specific functions [21,32]. Researchers have also directly used fingerprint scanners to control the mouse cursor (e.g., as relative [9] or absolute touchpad [1]) or for detecting gestures [12]. In our previous work, we used fingerprint recognition to improve touch accuracy (Ridgepad [15]).

To incorporate such high-resolution fingerprint sensing into touchscreens, in-cell technology has been hypothesized to one-day capture the diminutive structure of fingerprints. In-cell screens place photocells between screen pixels, allowing touchscreens to perceive the reflection from structure above the display. Sharp showed an image of a fingerprint captured on a small 2.6″ touchscreen using in-cell technology and VGA input resolution [5], but it is unclear if the quality and resolution sufficed for processing. Samsung ships a 40″ in-cell touchscreen (Microsoft PixelSense [25]), though with only ~27dpi input resolution, i.e., a factor of 20 too low for high-quality fingerprint scanning. Future in-cell systems may or may not offer the size and resolution required for reliable fingerprint scanning at 500dpi [20].

While in-cell screens afford scanning fingerprints, scanners achieve the highest contrast by optically sensing the specular reflections on polished waveguides.

BACKGROUND: OPTICAL FINGERPRINT SENSING

In order to record fingerprints, a camera needs to produce sufficient *contrast* between a fingerprint's ridges and valleys. Existing diffused illumination systems do not produce this contrast, because the skin of the user's finger diffusely reflects light and because the system's diffuser further blurs those reflections, thereby discarding all the structural details [22].

Prism-based fingerprint scanning yields excellent contrast

As shown in Figure 5a, prism-based fingerprint scanners achieve excellent contrast by shining light through a light diffuser and into a large solid glass prism [34]. (b) Since the light hits the top surface at an oblique angle, any blank part of the surface reflects the light directly into the camera, causing such areas to appear bright. (c) Whenever human skin touches the surface (i.e., the ridges of the fingerprint make contact), the light reflection is *frustrated*. That is, the light exits the prism and enters the finger, where the skin diffuses the light. Thus, little to no light reaches the camera, causing fingerprint ridges to appear dark in the image. The fact that valley locations *reflect* light whereas ridges *absorb* it produces a stark contrast, allowing such devices to capture fingerprints that are high in quality *and* contrast.

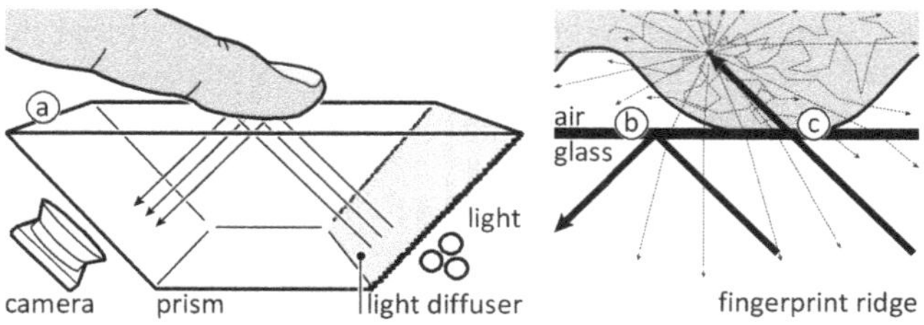

Figure 5: (a) Optical fingerprint scanners produce crisp contrast between fingerprint ridges and valleys using a prism. (b) Rays from the illuminant are totally reflected at the prism surface, causing such locations to appear *bright* as the camera sees directly into the light source. (c) Light escapes the prism (i.e., the reflection is frustrated) where fingerprint ridges touch the surface, causing ridges to appear *dark*.

Unfortunately, prism-based fingerprint scanning cannot be integrated into touch*screens*, because the prism construction does not allow these devices to produce visual output. The reason is that, as discussed above, the prism-based design requires a *specular* surface; projection, however, can only image on a *diffuse* surface.

Fingerprint scanners based on glass fibers

A number of input-only fingerprint scanners have been proposed that exploit *Fresnel reflection* inside glass fibers, a type of reflection that occurs whenever light travels from one medium to another [19], such as glass and air or glass and human skin. While the contrast between ridges and valleys is lower than in prism-based scanners [23, 20], such systems require no lens as glass fibers guide the light directly onto the sensor [23, 27].

Fingerprint scanners based on glass fibers have used slanted glass fibers and illuminate the fiber bundle from the side [10, 24] or from below [7] to produce reflections off the user's finger. Similar to prism-based scanning, light is reflected inside the fibers and guided back onto the sensor, but these reflections are frustrated once a finger touches the fibers. Other setups employ straight glass fibers, illuminate the finger through the space between the fibers, and capture the reflected light guided onto the sensor using the fibers [11]. Alternative setups use solid bundles and place them away from the camera (e.g., [17]). They illuminate the user's finger through the bundle while the camera captures all reflections. However, all such setups face the challenge of optimally illuminating the user's finger to produce light reflections that are high in contrast. While good illumination is easy to achieve for small surfaces, such as those that accommodate single fingers, their approach does not scale to larger surfaces.

While none of the previous fingerprint scanners produce *visual output* (they use glass-fiber bundles for scanning only), Fiberio offers an interactive touch*screen*.

Touchscreens based on FTIR cannot sense fingerprints

As mentioned in the introduction, touchscreens based on *frustrated total internal reflection* [13] cannot be enabled to capture fingerprints. The primary reason is that such systems employ compliant surfaces to act as diffusers and at the same time facilitate sensing touch input. Their structure is coarse, however, which dampens touch input to the extent that fingerprint ridges cannot leave distinct impressions on the waveguide. Such surfaces thus blur all the details required for fingerprint sensing.

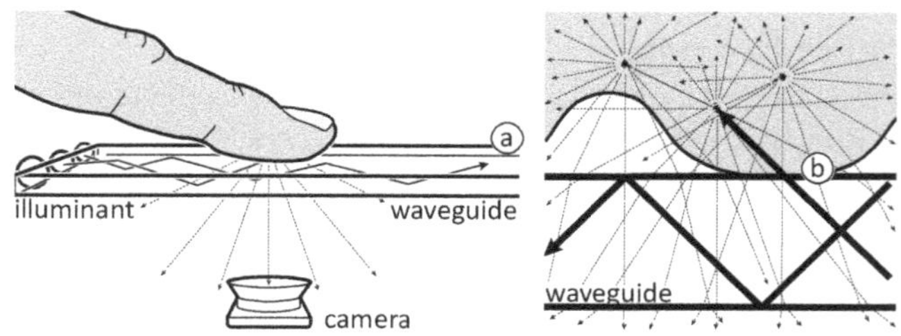

Figure 6: (a) Han's FTIR setup [13] does not afford high-contrast fingerprint scanning, even if we eliminate the compliant surface. (b) When a finger touches the surface (i.e., waveguide), fingerprint ridges frustrate the internal reflection, thus light escapes and enters the fingerprint ridges, which diffuse the light and consequently illuminate adjacent valleys. Therefore, FTIR setups illuminate the *entire* finger upon touch. Since the camera observes the entire finger and thus sees a finger that is illuminated as a whole, such system cannot resolve fingerprints with high contrast.

Even if we eliminate the light-diffusing property of the surface by removing the diffuser, the design of FTIR will still not produce the contrast required for fingerprint scanning. Figure 6 illustrates such a device without a compliant surface. When the finger touches the surface, the light escapes the waveguide and enters the ridges of the fingerprint. (b) The finger's skin, however, *diffuses the light* at a depth of 1mm, which causes the light to spill over into adjacent valleys [10, 33]. Unfortunately, the camera below the waveguide captures this diffused light for ridges and valleys alike. The finger thus appears illuminated as a whole with very little contrast between ridges and valleys.

FIBERIO'S WORKING PRINCIPLE AND OPTICAL PATH

As explained above, the key innovation behind Fiberio is that the fiber optic plate allows the screen to serve as a *diffuse* surface for projection and simultaneously act as a *reflective* surface for fingerprint scanning. We now describe the details of the optical path that enables this.

Diffuse transmission

The diffusion of projected images inside Fiberio's fiber optic plate is the result of two independent effects: (1) ring diffusion and (2) microstructural effects inside fibers.

Ring diffusion: As shown in Figure 7, light rays shone onto a fiber optic bundle with relatively large-diameter fibers (1mm) form a cone on exit. This cone manifests itself as a *ring* on a projection surface, here a table surface 5cm below the bottom surface of the fiber optic bundle.

Figure 8 explains this effect. (a) Looking into a glass fiber from one end, a light ray hits the surface of the fiber. (b) The ray enters the fiber and on its way down, the ray describes the shape of a star polygon. (c) We inject a

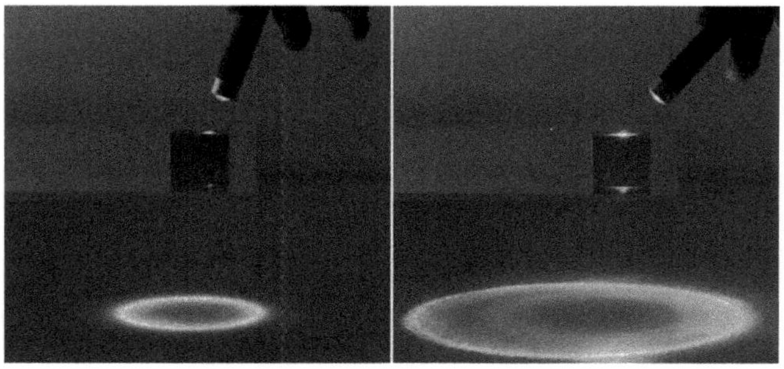

Figure 7: Pointing a laser at a fiber optic plate causes it to diffuse incident light into a ring. The angle of incident light thereby determines the radius of the ring, here small and large. The shown fiber optic bundle contains large-diameter fibers (1mm) and rests 5cm above a table surface.

second ray, parallel to the first, but at a small offset. We see how the slight offset causes the star polygon of the second ray to be made from more obtuse angles, allowing this ray to travel a greater angular distance and thus exiting in a different direction. (e) Looking at the fiber from the side, we see that the exit angle along this axis is always identical to the angle on entry. (d) With multiple rays varying by how much they "rotate" inside the fiber, but exiting at the same angle with respect to the fiber, rays form a ring.

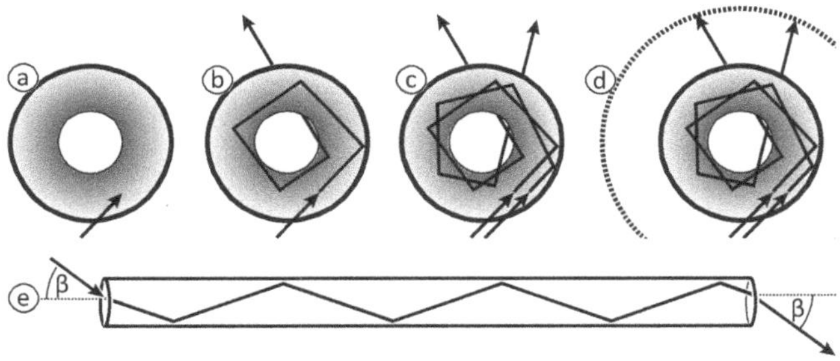

Figure 8: Each fiber diffuses parallel incident light into rings. (a) A fiber viewed top-down. (b) A ray enters the fiber and bounces down the fiber in a rotary pattern. (c) A parallel, but slightly offset ray exits into a different azimuth direction. (d) This variation in azimuth causes a ring, because (e) all rays have a constant exit angle with respect to the fiber.

Microstructural effects inside fibers: In contrast to the large-diameter fibers, a fiber optic plate made from very small-diameter fibers produces not only ring diffusion, but also much more diffuse light scattering as shown in Figure 9. This is essential for making Fiberio's projected image visible from all sides. At 6μm, each fiber in our fiber optic plate is only an order of magnitude larger than the wavelength of the light it transports, causing transmitted rays to scatter due to diffraction effects. In addition, the light reflected inside the fibers is subject to the microstructure of each fiber's core and cladding [19], which produces variations in reflection angles inside each fiber. Due to the thinness of such fibers, light is frequently reflected inside the fibers, which causes microstructural effects to manifest themselves in a stronger scattering of light upon exit.

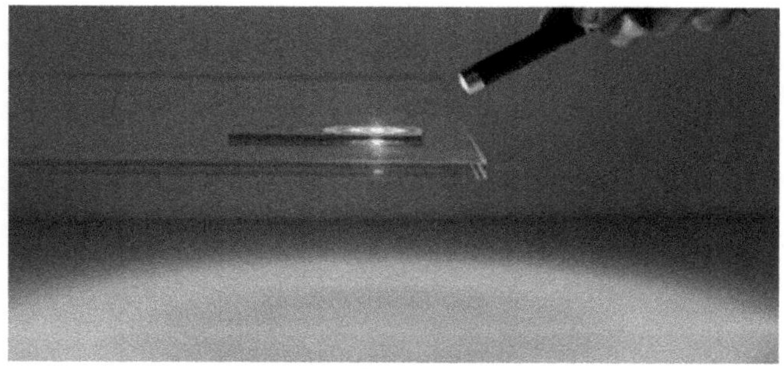

Figure 9: A fiber plate with a multitude of very small-diameter fibers (6μm) blurs ring diffusion, which scatters the incoming light into all directions. This is the basis for good light diffusion, which we need to produce an image on a touchscreen. The fiber plate rests 5cm above the table. The image on the plate is visible even from extreme angles.

As shown in Figure 9, the light diffusion produced by the fiber optic plate exhibits a mild hotspot around the ring. We account for this in Fiberio's setup by mounting the projector at an angle with respect to the fiber optic plate to further increase the amount of light diffusion.

In summary, the fiber optic plate diffuses light while *conducting it along* the fiber; this is different from the traditional way of diffusing light while passing through a diffuse *surface*. Diffusing light while conducting it allows Fiberio to maintain a specular surface, which is key to generating the contrast required for fingerprint capturing.

Sensing fingerprints using frustrated reflections

The specular reflection of light at the *top* surface of the fiber optic plate is what allows Fiberio to capture fingerprints. These reflections occur when the light *exits* fibers.

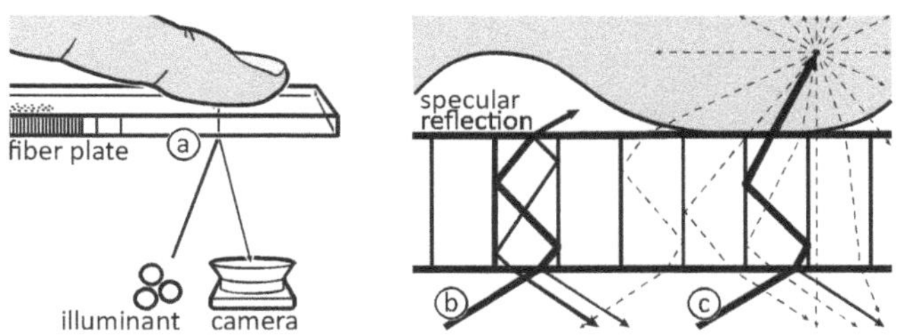

Figure 10: (a) The illuminant shines light onto the fiber optic plate. (b) A portion of the incoming light is reflected at the top of the fiber, traveling back down the fiber, where the camera observes it. (c) A fingerprint ridge touching the fiber, in contrast, frustrates the reflection at the top end of the fiber, so that only little light travels back down the fiber, causing this spot to appear dark to the camera.

As illustrated by Figure 10a, Fiberio shines infrared light onto the fiber optic plate from below. Some light is reflected at the bottom surface, but most light enters and travels up the fibers (Figure 10b). A large portion of the light exits the fibers, but the remaining portion is reflected at the top surface; the reflected light then travels back down inside the fibers and exits at the bottom, where Fiberio's camera observes it. Due to the reflection at the top surface of the plate, locations of fingerprint valleys and areas around the finger appear "brighter" in the resulting image.

If, however, a fingerprint ridge makes contact with the top end of the fiber (Figure 10c), the reflection at the top surface is frustrated and *almost all* light exits the glass fibers. Only a negligible fraction of light travels back down the fiber, so that this point appears "dark" to the camera.

The contrast between the light reflected at the top surface and the frustrated reflection allows Fiberio to sense fingerprints. Compared to prism-based scanning, this mechanism offers less contrast, because it returns only a small percentage of light. Since we use a camera with very low noise, however, we obtain a good signal-to-noise ratio. Fiberio thus extracts high-quality fingerprints from the captured images with fingerprint edges that appear very sharp.

In the optimal case, all light reflections are frustrated at the top surface when a fingerprint ridge is in contact. However, this requires that the skin of the finger be in direct contact with the fibers. In the case of a very dry finger (or dust on the skin), the frustrations may fail to occur at some locations, causing only a partial fingerprint to appear.

To address this, we created a thin compliant surface by pouring a layer of silicone onto the fiber plate. After having cured, the silicone increased the quality of the fingerprint. At the same time, it reduced the polished impression upon touch, which impeded dragging to a small extent.

In practice, we found no compliant layer to be necessary even for dry fingers, because over time the user's fingers leave small amounts of remnant grease on the surface. This facilitates the process of light coupling into dry skin without affecting the quality of projection or fingerprint sensing.

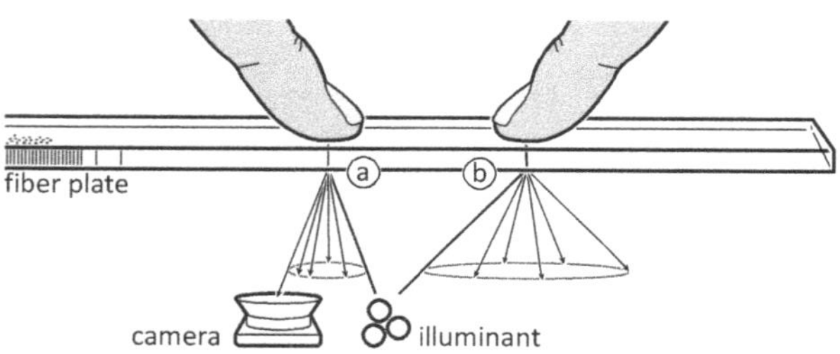

Figure 11: The light that comes back down the fiber is subject to same ring diffusion that we described earlier in terms of projection. While the camera will see reflections off the fiber plate's surface at location (a), reflections from location (b) will be invisible, because the camera does not sit on the same ring.

Placing the illuminant and camera for optimal contrast

We explained in the previous sections how the fiber optic plate enables scanning fingerprints at particular locations; to enable fingerprint scanning across the entire large surface of Fiberio, the location of camera and illuminant become important. The illuminant needs to shine light at the entire screen from below while the camera has to be placed so as to capture the reflected light coming back down the fibers. Figure 11 illustrates the challenge. The light that comes back down the fiber is subject to same ring diffusion that we described earlier in the context of projection. To enable the camera to capture reflections across the entire surface, we need to place the camera so that it is in the optical path of the returning light. We explored three solutions.

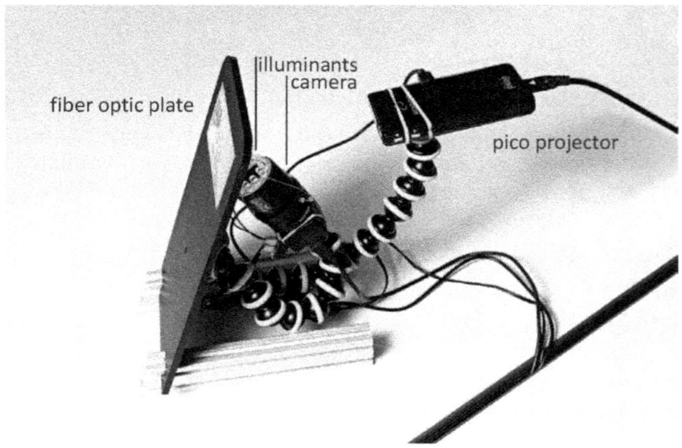

Figure 12: This earlier prototype placed the illuminant *around* the camera to approximate a shared location of camera and light source. Camera and illuminant were tilted with respect to the screen to prevent the camera from seeing the reflection of the illuminant in the fiber optic plate (hotspot).

Solution 1: Shared location for camera and small illuminant

Our first solution was to place the illuminant in the same location as the camera—or *around* the camera to approximate a shared location of camera and light source (Figure 12). This arrangement causes light to ring-diffuse back into the camera for *all* locations on the screen as shown in Figure 13. In the shown design, we offset both camera and illuminant from the screen and mounted them at an angle in order to prevent the camera from seeing the direct reflections of the illuminant (i.e., hotspots).

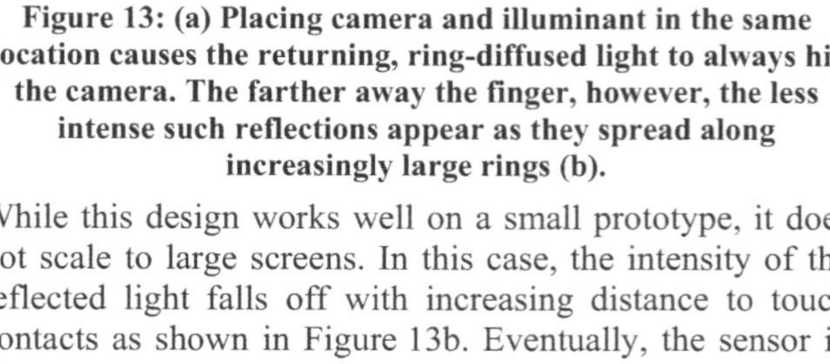

Figure 13: (a) Placing camera and illuminant in the same location causes the returning, ring-diffused light to always hit the camera. The farther away the finger, however, the less intense such reflections appear as they spread along increasingly large rings (b).

While this design works well on a small prototype, it does not scale to large screens. In this case, the intensity of the reflected light falls off with increasing distance to touch contacts as shown in Figure 13b. Eventually, the sensor in the camera will not be sensitive to resolve the contrast between fingerprint ridges and valleys for far-away touches, causing the resulting fingerprints to appear noisy. Since we scaled Fiberio to its current 19″ size, we switched to designs that illuminate the screen using a large homogenous illuminant.

Solution 2: Using a large homogenous illuminant

Our current Fiberio prototype uses evenly distributed illumination across the entire surface. The illuminant uniformly shoots light at the fiber optic plate from below, creating one evenly illuminated area. Since light intensities are roughly identical across the entire surface, no single hotspot occurs and thus no area of oversaturation or undersaturation in the camera image.

As shown in Figure 14, we prototyped two approaches to create a light source that evenly illuminates the fiber plate. In an earlier prototype, we placed a uniform area illuminant below the fiber optic plate (here Acrylight LED [8]) as shown in Figure 14a. The main limitation of this solution was that it produced low contrast, as the reflected light from the fingerprint not only competes with light reflected directly off the bottom of the fiber optic plate, but the illumination layer also shines light directly into the camera. We addressed this with yet another iteration on our design.

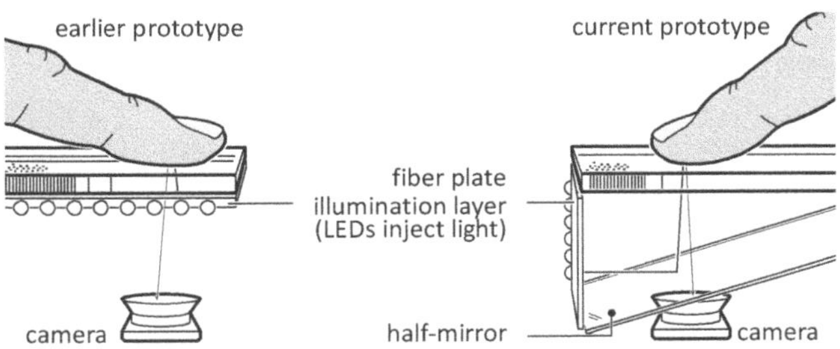

Figure 14: Fiberio evenly illuminates the entire surface, creating one even reflection to see fingerprints across the whole surface. (left) An earlier prototype used Acrylite LED below the fiber plate. (right) Our current prototype uses a half-mirror that reflects illuminations from the side.

Current solution: even illumination via a half-mirror

Figure 14b illustrates the conceptual setup that we use in our current prototype as shown in Figure 15. It continues to use Acrylite LED to illuminate a large area. However, we now place the sheet at the side of the table and use a half-silvered mirror to reflect illumination to the fiber optic plate. This prevents the camera from seeing the illuminant layer directly and thus avoids the loss of contrast that characterized our earlier design.

The resulting design works well and since this setup illuminates the screen using a large illuminant, the solution scales well to large screens, even beyond the 19″ of our current Fiberio prototype.

DETAILS ON HARDWARE SETUP

As shown in Figure 2, Fiberio offers a 40cm×25cm screen surface (16″×10″, 19″ diagonal). This surface we implement by tiling two 25cm×20cm fiber optic plates (Incom B7D59-6), which are polished and feel like a piece of glass.

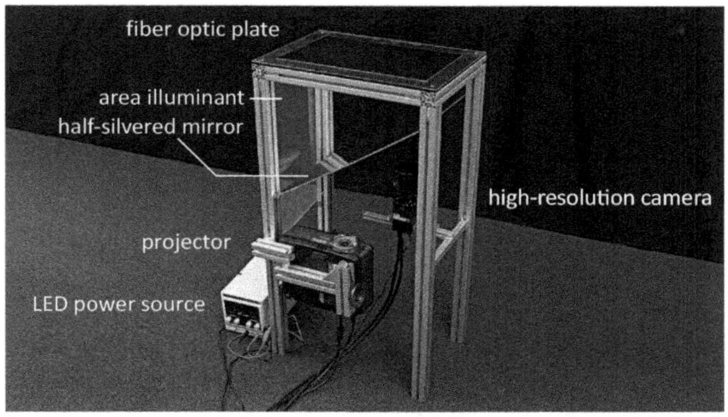

Figure 15: Our current prototype illuminates the fiber optic plate evenly, creating optimal reflections for the camera to resolve fingerprints at all locations on the touch surface. We use an area illuminant (Acrylite LED with light injected from the sides) mounted to the side of the table and a half-silvered mirror to reflect illuminations. All sides of the table are normally covered with black cloth to prevent reflections from the environment in the camera image (here we left out the covers to show the inner components of the system).

The BenQ short-throw projector pointed at the screen offers a resolution of 1024×768px. A hot mirror in front of the projector prevents interference with the cameras. Due to its high resolution, the fiber optic plate has no impact on the resolution of the projected image; each fiber measures 6 microns, whereas a projected pixel measures ~390 microns and thus covers a multitude of fibers. Projected images are visible even from extreme angles (Figure 9), because of the numerical aperture of the fibers we use (1.0). The refractive index of their core (1.8) and that of the cladding (1.49) allows for maximum acceptance and exit angles of 90°.

A frame made from a 40mm aluminum profile system holds Fiberio's components in place. Fiberio's height of 38″ is designed to minimize fatigue on the standing workstation.

To achieve fingerprint scanning across Fiberio's entire surface at a resolution needed for reliable scanning (500dpi [20]), our setup would require a camera resolution of 8000×5000 pixels. In our prototype, we used a high-resolution camera (Teledyne Dalsa Falcon2, 4000×3000px, 60fps, 6ms shutter speed), which observes only a sub region of Fiberio's surface (20cm×15cm). We supplemented this approach with a web camera to enable touch interaction across the entire surface (Sony PS3, 640×480px, 75fps), which we set up in a diffused illumination arrangement. Both cameras and the projector are calibrated to a shared world-coordinate system.

While our prototype setup using a half-mirror achieves the best illumination across Fiberio's whole surface, the switch to scanning prints on only a quarter of the surface allowed us to reduce the footprint of the table. We therefore substituted the half-mirror with one 4W infrared illuminant.

IMAGE PROCESSING

Currently, Fiberio locates and tracks all touches based on the low-resolution camera, implementing a typical diffused illumination processing pipeline [22]. When touches enter the region observed by the high-resolution camera, Fiberio locates fingerprints, extracts them along with their features, and matches features against the records stored in its fingerprint database.

Future versions of Fiberio will cover the entire screen either using a 2×2 array of high-resolution cameras or using a single camera and a high-speed pan and tilt mirror.

Fingerprint processing pipeline

To extract the locations and directions of fingerprint features, i.e., ridge endings and bifurcations (so-called *minutiae*), which allow identifying users, we implemented the algorithms commonly used to process fingerprints [20]. Figure 16 illustrates our pipeline.

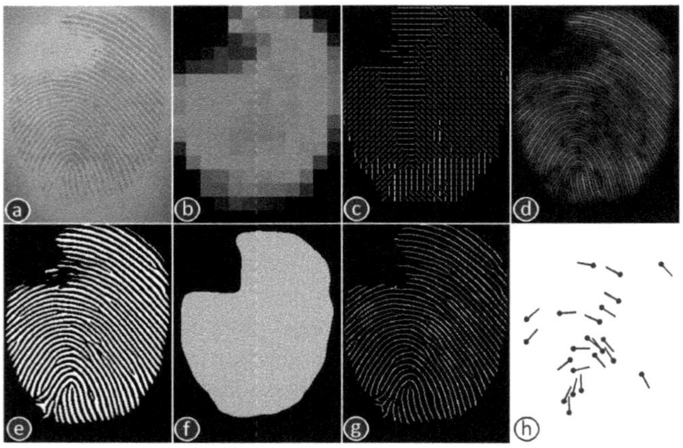

Figure 16: Fingerprint processing pipeline (images are cropped). (a) Raw image, (b) areas of high standard deviation, (c) flow field, (d) Gabor filter, (e) binarized fingerprint, (f) mask, (g) skeleton and (h) extracted locations and orientations of all fingerprint features.

The 768×768 pixel raw image shown in Figure 16a contains the reflections from the user's finger. Fingerprint ridges appear as dark lines inside a brighter area. Fiberio starts by removing possible luminance gradients by subtracting a low-pass copy from the image. (b) Fiberio locates fingerprints by calculating the standard deviation of brightness values for 16×16-pixel subregions in the image. High brightness deviation indicates the presence of adjacent ridges and valleys. Fiberio uses this to produce a mask—all further processing takes place inside this area.

To improve the contrast of the fingerprint, (c) Fiberio computes the direction of the main gradient across all 8×8-pixel subregions, resulting in the flow field of the fingerprint. We input the flow field into (d) a Gabor filter, which improves the edges in the fingerprint according to their orientation, thereby smoothing noisy and interrupted ridges. (e) Binarizing the result now brings out a sharp contrast between ridges and valleys in the fingerprint.

To extract the locations of all minutiae from the fingerprint, Fiberio obtains (f) a refined mask of the fingerprint and (g) derives the skeleton of the binarized fingerprint. The skeleton reveals the locations and orientations of minutiae; locations in the skeleton that have three neighboring pixels are bifurcations, whereas locations with only one neighbor are ridge endings as shown in Figure 16h.

To match two fingerprints based on their minutiae, Fiberio finds the best spatial alignment of both point sets using Bozorth matching [20]. It then computes a matching score based on the number of minutiae that match in terms of location and angle. When Fiberio compares an observed fingerprint to fingerprints in its database, it requires fingerprints to match in at least 10 minutiae locations.

GPU acceleration and resulting performance

Fiberio runs touch recognition, fingerprint extraction, matching, and graphics using parallel threads, allowing it to stays responsive to user input at all times. Since processing fingerprints is computationally expensive, we implemented our pipeline in CUDA 4.2 to run on the GPU (NVidia GTX 680), which allows our system to run at interactive rates.

Extracting all minutiae from the raw fingerprint image currently takes Fiberio 21ms per frame. We expect this to get even faster with newer graphics cards. The speed of matching fingerprints currently increases linearly with the number of records in the database (0.55ms per record).

EVALUATION

The purpose of our evaluation was to verify that Fiberio's sensor setup captures fingerprints with sufficient quality to allow it to recognize users reliably. To evaluate identification performance, we compared 30 fingers (three fingers per each of the 10 participants, ages 20–32, 2 female).

Apparatus: We conducted this evaluation using an earlier version of our prototype, which featured a lower-resolution camera (8.8MP Flea3). Considering that the image sensor of that camera was inferior to that of our current camera and we used our current algorithms for processing input, the results from this evaluation apply to our current prototype. The study apparatus was set up to capture fingerprint images at a resolution of 500dpi and 8ms shutter time. We performed all processing on a 2.2 GHz Intel Core2 Duo processor with 4 GB of RAM and an NVidia GTX 680 graphics card using the described algorithm. The projector was switched off.

Task and procedure: As shown in Figure 17, participants touched the screen region captured by the high-resolution camera during each trial, each time using one of their right hand's index, middle or ring finger. Participants thereby used their finger pad for touch input and repeated input five times, performing fifteen trials overall. Due to the limited frame rate of the camera we used during the evaluation, participants were required to hold a touch for around 400ms. This allowed the camera to capture frames reliably. This is no longer required for our current system due to the substantially larger frame rate of our current camera. For each trial in the evaluation, Fiberio processed only a single frame, namely the one in which the area of the touch

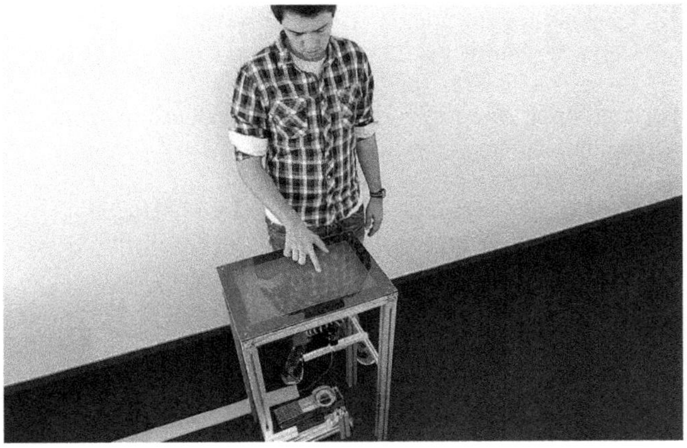

Figure 17: A study participant during the evaluation. The prototype was configured to provide no feedback.

contact was maximal across the entire event. Participants received no feedback during the evaluation.

Processing: The evaluation resulted in 150 captured fingerprints, from which we extracted the minutiae sets and created a database. We then performed minutiae-based matching on each of the captured prints against all 149 other records.

Results and Discussion: The cross-validated analysis resulted in 148 of 150 fingerprints being *correctly* matched, 0 *wrong* matches, and 2 *no matches* (i.e., samples that produced less than the minimum number of 10 minutiae needed for identification). The average processing time for matching a minutiae set against all others was 267ms.

These findings show that Fiberio identifies users reliably by their fingerprints and at interactive rates. Since the speed of user identification scales linearly with the number of samples in the database, this process runs asynchronously to still support responsive interaction.

Of course, participants used their finger pads when providing input, which allowed for optimal feature extraction. While flat fingers exhibit more than 100 minutiae, fingertips contain fewer features ($0.18/mm^2$ [34]). However, 12-15 visible features suffice to identify users when touching, which fingertips may provide depending on their tilt. Fiberio's height of 38″ facilitates touching with flat finger angles, which is optimal to extract a multitude of features. While users might be less careful during regular use, a live system could produce feedback on their touch events and ask for repeated input upon unsuccessful identification.

Note that a lack of visible features in a touch does not lead Fiberio to misidentify users. If a fingerprint exhibits too few features, Fiberio does not attempt to identify users.

CONCLUSIONS

In this paper, we presented Fiberio, a touchscreen that senses fingerprints. The key to making this possible is the fiber optic plate, which offers both specular reflection and diffuse transmission.

While our key contribution certainly is a touchscreen that performs user identification and secure authentication during interaction, Fiberio also implements a standard diffused illumination table. This results in additional desirable properties, such as the ability to recognize fiducial markers and detect objects that hover above the surface, such as the user's fingers and hands as shown in Figure 18. On the flip side, similar to other diffused illumination setups, Fiberio's rear projection requires space and it is susceptible to interference by strong infrared light sources in the environment.

A positive side effect of the fiber optic plate is that Fiberio is inherently free of parallax. Users see the projected output *on top* of Fiberio's screen; when users touch that output, Fiberio's cameras see this touch contacts exactly where it occurs, because touch contacts appear at the bottom surface of the fiber optic plate. Combined, this allows for particularly precise input.

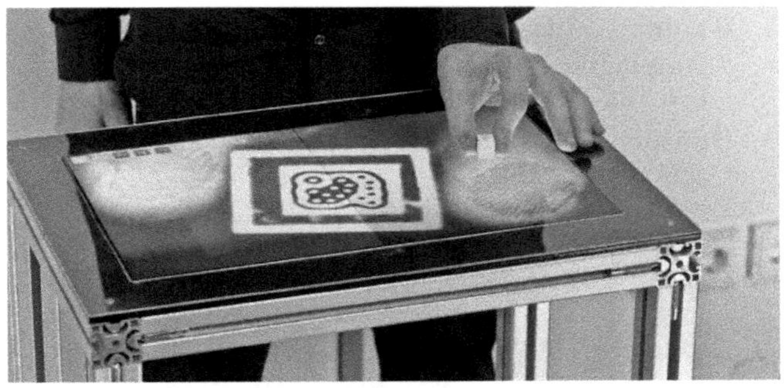

Figure 18: Fiberio recognizes touch, but also hovering objects (here fingers) as well as fiducial markers. The fiducial marker on this tangible object measures only 3mm×3mm.

Finally, Fiberio is subject to the same limitations as other biometric authentication mechanisms, such as the risk of spoofing using fake fingerprints [20], as well as concerns in terms of surveillance and respecting users' privacy. To evaluate Fiberio's capabilities in identifying users amongst a large population, a deeper evaluation of the system with a large number of participants of a large span of ages and a wider range of demographics.

In summary, Fiberio opens up a lot of new possibilities for interactive systems. For fifteen years, researchers have hypothesized the existence of a touchscreen with biometric authentication, be it for activity logging [6], high degree-of-freedom touch input [32], and high-precision touch input [15] by modeling touch as a 3D input operation [16]. These are all possible now based on the principles of Fiberio and our future work includes implementing such use-cases on our prototype. While Fiberio's current configuration does not translate to mobile devices, we plan on exploring flat form factors using in-cell technology [5] or integrating a wedge that folds the optical path as part of future work.

ACKNOWLEDGEMENTS

We sincerely thank Raimund Mückstein and Andreas Steinbacher for many insightful discussions about glass fibers as well as feedback on this paper. We thank Andy Wilson for discussions around fiber optics and the first version of our prototype. We thank David Benedict from Incom and Werner Sklarek from Schott for providing the fiber optic plate used in our prototypes. Thanks to Christoph Sterz for his help with the photos and the video.

REFERENCES

1. Akizuki, S. Touch Pad Having Fingerprint Detecting Function and Information Processing Apparatus Employing the Same. *US Patent 6,360,004*. 2002.
2. Annett, M., Grossman, T., Wigdor, D. and Fitzmaurice, G. Medusa: A Proximity-Aware Multi-touch Tabletop. *Proc. UIST '11*, 337–382.
3. Ashbaugh, D.R. Quantitative-Qualitative Friction Ridge Analysis: An Introduction to Basic and Advanced Ridgeology. *CRC Press*, 1999.
4. Baudisch, P., Becker, T. and Rudeck, F. Lumino: Tangible Blocks for Tabletop Computers Based on Glass Fiber Bundles. *Proc. CHI '10*, 1165–1174.
5. Brown, C.J., Kato, H., Maeda, K. and Hadwen, B. A Continuous-Grain Silicon-System LCD With Optical Input Function. *Solid-State Circuits*, 42(12), 2007, 2904–2912.
6. Dietz, P. and Leigh, D. DiamondTouch: a Multi-User Touch Technology. *Proc. UIST '01*, 219–226.
7. Dowling Jr., R.F. and Knowlton, K.L. Fingerprint Acquisition System with a Fiber Optic Block. *US Patent 4,785,171*. 1988.
8. Acrylite LED (EndLighten). http://goo.gl/6AdiH
9. Ferrari, A. and Tartagni, M. Touchpad Providing Screen Cursor Movement Control. *US Patent 6,392,636*. 2002.
10. Fujieda, I. and Haga, H. Fingerprint Input Based on Scattered-Light Detection. *Applied Optics*, 36(35), 1997, 9152–9156.
11. Fujieda, O. and Sugama, S. Fingerprint Image Input Device Having an Image Sensor with Openings. *US Patent 5,446,290*. 1995.
12. Gust, L.A. Compact Optical Pointing Apparatus and Method. *US Patent 7,102,617*. 2006.
13. Han, J.Y. Low-Cost Multi-Touch Sensing Through Frustrated Total Internal Reflection. *Proc. UIST '05*, 115–118.
14. Harrison, C., Sato, M. Poupyrev, I. Capacitive Fingerprinting: Exploring User Differentiation by Sensing Electrical Properties of the Human Body. *Proc. UIST '12*, 537–544.
15. Holz, C. and Baudisch, P. The Generalized Perceived Input Point Model and How to Double Touch Accuracy by Extracting Fingerprints. *Proc. CHI '10*, 581–590.
16. Holz, C. and Baudisch, P. Understanding Touch. *Proc. CHI '11*, 2501–2510.
17. Hossu, D. Device for Measuring Elevations and/or Depressions in a Surface. *US Patent 8,149,408*. 2012.
18. Jackson, D., Bartindale, T. and Olivier, P. FiberBoard: Compact Multi-touch Display Using Channeled Light. *Proc. ITS '09*, 25–28.
19. Kenyon, I. The Light Fantastic: A Modern Introduction to Classical and Quantum Optics. *Oxford University Press*, 2008.
20. Maltoni, D., Maio, D., Jain, A. and Prabhakar, S. Handbook of Fingerprint Recognition (2nd Edition). *Springer*, 2009.
21. Marquardt, N., Kiemer, J., and Greenberg, S. What Caused that Touch? Expressive Interaction with a Surface through Fiduciary-Tagged Gloves. *Proc. ITS '10*, 139–142.
22. Matsushita, N. and Rekimoto, J. HoloWall: Designing a Finger, Hand, Body, Object Sensitive Wall. *Proc. UIST '97*, 209–210.
23. Meghdadi, M. and Jalilzadeh, S. Validity and Acceptability of Results in Fingerprint Scanners. *Proc. MMACTE '05*, 259–266.
24. Memon, S., Sepasian, M. and Balachandran, W. Review of Fingerprint Sensing Technologies. *Proc. INMIC '08*, 226–231.
25. Microsoft Pixelsense (SUR40). http://goo.gl/Awpta
26. Nakajima, K., Itoh, Y., Yoshida, A., Takashima, K., Kitamura, Y. and Kishino, F. FuSA2 Touch Display. *SIGGRAPH '10 Emerging Technologies*, Article 11.
27. O'Gorman, L. An Overview of Fingerprinting Verification Technologies. *Elsevier Information Security Technical Report*, 3(1), 1998, 21-32.
28. Olwal, A. and Wilson, A.D. SurfaceFusion: Unobtrusive Tracking of Everyday Objects in Tangible User Interfaces. *Proc. GI '08*, 235–242.
29. Richter, S., Holz, C. and Baudisch, P. Bootstrapper: Recognizing Tabletop Users by their Shoes. *Proc. CHI '12*, 1249–1252.
30. Roth, V., Schmidt, P. and Güldenring, B. The IR Ring: Authenticating Users' Touches on a Multi-touch Display. *Proc. UIST '10*, 259–262.
31. Schmidt, D., Chong, M., and Gellersen, H. HandsDown: Hand-contour-based User Identification for Interactive Surfaces. *Proc. NordiCHI '10*, 432–441.
32. Sugiura, A. and Koseki, Y. A User Interface Using Fingerprint Recognition: Holding Commands and Data Objects on Fingers. *Proc. UIST '98*, 71–79.
33. Welch, A. The Thermal Response of Laser Irradiated Tissue. *Quantum Electronics*, 20(12), 1984, 1471–1481.
34. Xia, X. and O'Gorman, L. Innovations in Fingerprint Capture Devices. *Pattern Recognition*, 36(2), 2003, 361–369.
35. Zhang, H, Yang, X., Ens, B., Liang, H., Boulanger, P. and Irani, P. See Me, See You: A Lightweight Method for Discriminating User Touches on Tabletop Displays. *Proc. CHI '12*, 2327–2336.

Bayesian Touch – A Statistical Criterion of Target Selection with Finger Touch

Xiaojun Bi **Shumin Zhai**
Google, Inc.
Mountain View, CA, USA
xjunbi@gmail.com zhai@acm.org

ABSTRACT
To improve the accuracy of target selection for finger touch, we conceptualize finger touch input as an uncertain process, and derive a statistical target selection criterion, *Bayesian Touch Criterion*, by combining the basic Bayes' rule of probability with the generalized dual Gaussian distribution hypothesis of finger touch. The Bayesian Touch Criterion selects the intended target as the candidate with the shortest *Bayesian Touch Distance* to the touch point, which is computed from the touch point to the target center distance and the target size. We give the derivation of the Bayesian Touch Criterion and its empirical evaluation with two experiments. The results showed that for 2-dimensional circular target selection, the Bayesian Touch Criterion is significantly more accurate than the commonly used Visual Boundary Criterion (i.e., a target is selected if and only if the touch point falls within its boundary) and its two variants.

Categories and Subject Descriptors
H5.2 [Information interfaces and presentation]: User Interfaces. - Graphical user interfaces.

Keywords
Finger Touch; Target Selection; Bayes' Rule

INTRODUCTION
Finger touch has been widely adopted as a major input modality for various computing devices. It is direct, intuitive, always-available, and easily extensible to multi-touch. It has become the default interaction modality for Post-PC computing devices such as smartphones and tablets, and is even being integrated on regular PCs (e.g., touchscreen laptops).

Using finger touch to select a target among a set of candidates (target selection) is one of the most basic, important and frequently-performed finger touch tasks. However, it also suffers from the obvious "Fat Finger" problem. For smaller targets on the screen, it lacks the necessary precision to hit the intended one every time.

UIST'13, October 8–11, 2013, St. Andrews, United Kingdom.
ACM 978-1-4503-2268-3/13/10.
http://dx.doi.org/10.1145/2501988.2502058

Numerous methods have been proposed to improve the accuracy of target selection with a bare finger. Most of them attempted to map the input to the *intended touch point*. For example, Holz and Baudisch [10] proposed a method of estimating the intended touch point based on the 3D angle of the finger; Weir et al. [5] proposed mapping the raw sensor data or the touch location reported by the device to the intended touch point based on the historical touch behavior of a specific user. These techniques improve the touch accuracy by various degrees. However, employing them on current products would require either extra sensors [10] to measure finger postures, or knowing the specific user ID and her historical touch data [5].

Different from the previous research, we address the target selection problem with another approach. Instead of attempting to map finger touch to a single intended point, this approach conceptualizes finger touch input as an uncertain and ambiguous process. We keep the reported touch point unchanged, but devise statistical algorithms of deciding the intended target among distractors from the uncertain finger touch.

Current devices, by default, follow the *Visual Boundary (VB)* criterion to decide a target for a selection task: a target is selected if and only if the touch point falls within its boundary. Our experiment shows that this is a very erroneous criterion. Previous research [10] also reveals that to keep the error rate below 4%, the target size needs to be at least 4.3 mm wide if using this criterion.

The VB criterion matches the real word analogy of physical buttons with clear and deterministic edges. The underlying assumption is that the contact point is the point of interest and has to be within the visible boundary of the target However, this may not be the best analogy to finger touch on a purely visual target.

To reflect the inherent uncertainty of finger touch, we propose a statistical criterion of finger touch target selection — the *Bayesian Touch Criterion (BTC)*. We derive *BTC* by treating the touch event as a statistical signal of the user's intention and inferring the probability of the intention accordingly. Specifically this decomposes to two steps. One is applying the Bayes' rule to estimate the probability of each object being the intended target given a signal. The other is to use the dual Gaussian distribution principle recently discovered about finger touch (Bi, Li and Zhai [4]). By combining an absolute precision component and a relative (to target size) precision component we built a Gaussian distribution of a given target's touch point distribution. These two steps lead to *BTC*, which serves as a principled criterion for ranking target likelihood.

BTC computes the *Bayesian Touch Distance (BTD)* between candidate targets and the touch point, and selects the candidate with the shortest *BTD* as the most probable target. The *BTD* between the touch point s and the target candidate t is:

$$BTD(s,t) = \frac{(s-c)^2}{2(\alpha W^2 + \sigma_a^2)} + \frac{1}{2}\ln(\alpha W^2 + \sigma_a^2) \qquad \text{Eq. 1}$$

where s is the finger touch coordinates reported by the device, W is the width of t, c is the center of t, α and σ_a are constants which can be measured via a separate experiment.

We conducted two experiments to show that *BTC* significantly reduced the error rate of target selection by 70% over VB, and by 26% and 6% over its two other variants, respectively. The accuracy improvement was achieved only using the touch point reported by device, without any extra sensing information.

RELATED WORK

Understanding Finger Touch

As a key input modality for touch screens, touch input has been extensively studied by many researchers. Wang and Ren [13] studied the properties of five fingers for touch input. Their results showed that the touch points followed bivariate Gaussian distributions, with the standard deviation varying across fingers. The touch points tended to spread wider for thumb and little fingers than index, middle and ring fingers. Azenkot & Zhai [1] and Henze et al.[9] studied the patterns of a special class of target selection tasks: entering text on a touchscreen keyboard. Both studies showed that touch points followed bivariate Gaussian distributions over the intended target key, often with more than 10% of touch points falling off the target key on a phone-sized device. The means of the Gaussian distributions were close to the key centers, but often with a small bias in different directions depending on hand posture (index finger vs. thumb), and regions of the keyboard [1]. Bi, Li and Zhai [4] proposed the dual Gaussian distribution hypothesis to interpret the distribution of touch points for Fitts' tasks [6], a special type of target selection tasks. They further derived the Finger-Fitts law (FFitts law) based on that hypothesis. Their study results validated the hypothesis and showed that the FFitts model had stronger predictive power than the conventional form of Fitts' law [6], which only models one of the two distributions in the dual Gaussian hypothesis.

Building on the literature, we apply the dual Gaussian distribution principle [6] to model the distribution of touch points based on the size and location of the target candidate, and combine it with the Bayes' rule to improve touch selection accuracy.

Improving Touch Accuracy

As target selection plays a critical role for touchscreen interaction, a sizable amount of research has been conducted to improve its accuracy.

Holz and Baudisch's [10] research showed that the offsets of touch point locations from the intended point were affected by the angles between the finger and the touch surface (i.e., pitch, roll and yaw). Their research showed that the accuracy could be substantially improved if the offset was compensated according to the user and posture. Such information can be obtained by either 3D tracking or scanning the fingerprint. In the following studies [11], they discovered that users relied on the visual features of fingers such as finger outlines and nail outlines for placing the touch point. Their findings suggested that the pointing accuracy could be substantially improved by tracking fingers with cameras from above.

Weir et al. [5] proposed a machine learning approach for learning a function that mapped an input (the devices' reported touch location or the raw sensor value) to the intended touch location. The study results showed that using the intended touch location substantially improved the accuracy.

Henz et al. [8] used a game published at the Android Market to collect a large number of touch events (more than 120 million). Based on the collect data, they trained a function that shifted the touch events to reduce the error rates. Evaluated by an updated version of the game, the trained function can significantly reduce the error rates.

Most of the methods proposed in the literature required extra information in addition to the touch location reported by device (e.g., 3D posture of the input finger [10, 11], or a user's touch history [5]). Distinguished from the previous research, the Bayesian Touch Criterion improves the touch interaction accuracy with the reported touch location only, which could be easily implemented on current touch screens without adding extra sensors or obtaining any prior user data.

Handling Input with Uncertainty

Since modern input modalities (e.g., finger touch) are usually ambiguous, researchers have proposed handling these inputs as uncertain events. Williamson [14] proposed framing the input as a continuous control process. In his view, the system a user interacts with continuously infers a distribution over potential user goals, and provides continuous feedback about its beliefs as it does so. Schwarz et al. [12] proposed carrying the uncertainty of input forward all the way through in the interaction, and deciding the final action via a mediation process. Complementary to Williamson's [14] and Schwarz et al.'s [12] work in general frameworks for handling uncertain inputs, we focus on a specific input modality: finger touch. We treat the finger touch as an uncertain process, and apply probabilistic theory to improve input accuracy.

BAYESIAN TOUCH

A Bayesian View of Target Selection

Target selection problems can be formulated as follows:

Let $T = \{t_1, t_2, \ldots, t_n\}$ be the n target candidates on a touchscreen. Given a touch point s, the conditional probability that t ($t \in T$) is the intended target is $P(t|s)$. Determining the intended target is equivalent to finding t^* that maximizes $P(t|s)$:

$$t^* = \underset{t}{\operatorname{argmax}}\, P(t|s) \qquad \text{Eq. 2}$$

From Bayes' rule, $P(t|s)$ can be computed as:

$$P(t|s) = \frac{P(s|t)P(t)}{P(s)} \qquad \text{Eq. 3}$$

where $P(t)$ denotes the prior probability of selecting t without the observation of s, $P(s|t)$ is the likelihood function which expresses how probable the touch point s is if t is the intended target, and $P(s)$ is the normalization constant.

Since $P(s)$ is a constant, we have:

$$t^* = \underset{t}{\operatorname{argmax}}\, P(t|s) = \underset{t}{\operatorname{argmax}}[P(s|t)\,P(t)] \qquad \text{Eq.4}$$

Because the distribution of the touch point is Gaussian, the likelihood function can be written in the form (for 1-dimensional target):

$$P(s|t) = P(s|\mu,\sigma^2) = \frac{1}{(2\pi\sigma^2)^{1/2}}\exp\{-\frac{1}{2\sigma^2}(s-\mu)^2\} \quad \text{Eq. 5}$$

where s is the location of the touch point, μ and σ^2 are the mean and variance of the touch point distribution if t is the intended target.

As a common practice, maximizing the likelihood function is converted to minimizing the negative log likelihood function, which is in the form

$$-\ln P(s|t) = \frac{1}{2\sigma^2}(s-\mu)^2 + \ln\sigma + \frac{1}{2}\ln(2\pi) \qquad \text{Eq.6}$$

From Eqs. 4, 5 and 6, we have;

$$\begin{aligned} t^* &= \underset{t}{\operatorname{argmax}}[P(s|t)\,P(t)] \\ &= \underset{t}{\operatorname{argmin}}[-\ln P(s|t) - \ln P(t)] \\ &= \underset{t}{\operatorname{argmin}}\left[\frac{1}{2\sigma^2}(s-\mu)^2 + \ln\sigma + \frac{1}{2}\ln(2\pi) - \ln P(t)\right] \\ &= \underset{t}{\operatorname{argmin}}\left[\frac{1}{2\sigma^2}(s-\mu)^2 + \ln\sigma - \ln P(t)\right] \qquad \text{Eq. 7} \end{aligned}$$

$P(t)$ can be estimated from user history or design expectations (some targets are expected to be used more often than others). It is usually dependent on the application. In text input, for example, such information may come from language modeling or its simplest form, a lexicon [15]. Some letter keys are more likely than others given a context. In the most conservative and most unfavorable case of no prior knowledge about where the intended target is, we can assume that every candidate in T has an equal probability to be selected. Under this assumption, Eq 7 becomes:

$$t^* = \underset{t}{\operatorname{argmin}}(\frac{1}{2\sigma^2}(s-\mu)^2 + \ln\sigma) \qquad \text{Eq. 8}$$

We define the Bayesian Touch Distance (BTD) as:

$$BTD(s,t) = \frac{1}{2\sigma^2}(s-\mu)^2 + \ln\sigma \qquad \text{Eq. 9}$$

Eqs 8 and 9 show that finding the target t^* given a touch point s is equivalent to finding a value for t^* that minimizes the Bayesian Touch Distance. If candidates are not equally probable prior to s, $-\ln P(t)$ should be added to $BTD(s,t)$. Using $BTD(s,t)$ to decide the selected target is also referred as the *Bayesian Touch Criterion (BTC)* hereafter. In this paper we focus on the general target selection tasks in which we assume each candidate has an equal prior probability.

The Dual Gaussian Distribution Hypothesis

To compute $BTD(s,t)$, we need to know s, μ and σ. The touch point s is reported by the device. In this section, we propose an approach to estimate μ and σ from the size and location of target t. The method is derived from the dual Gaussian distribution hypothesis.

The dual Gaussian distributions hypothesis was initially introduced and verified by Bi, Li, and Zhai [4]. It considers the distribution of touch points (X) as a sum of two independent Gaussian distributions X_r, and X_a. Formally, this hypothesis can be expressed as:

$$X = X_r + X_a \sim N(\mu,\sigma^2) \qquad \text{Eq. 10}$$

μ and σ^2 are:

$$\mu = \mu_r + \mu_a \qquad \text{Eq. 11}$$

$$\sigma^2 = \sigma_r^2 + \sigma_a^2 \qquad \text{Eq. 12}$$

X_r is extrinsic to the user's motor control limit and relative to target properties (particularly size). The variance of X_r results from the speed-accuracy tradeoff of the user. It reflects to which degree the user has chosen to comply with the task precision. It is independent of the precision of the selection implement (e.g., pen or finger).

X_a is intrinsic to the motor control system, reflecting the absolute precision of a cursor, pen, or finger-based input method. It is independent of the user's desire to follow the specified task precision. X_a is negligible in a cursor-based input method, but significant in finger touch-based methods, particularly when the finger width is wider ("fatter") than the target width.

In the current work, we generalize the dual Gaussian distribution hypothesis from Fitts' tasks—which are special target selection tasks involving both amplitude (A) and target width (W)—to the more general target-selection tasks which are predominantly characterized by W alone. In tasks such as successive target selection with a single pointer, A is well-defined. In other tasks, such as alternating two thumb typing, or a single finger touch from a resting position off the screen, A is less well-defined.

Similar to the form in Fitts' tasks, we hypothesize that the touch point distribution X, if t is the intended target, is a sum of two independent Gaussian distributions: X_r and X_a.

Unlike Fitts' tasks in which the desired task precision is specified by A/W (A is the movement amplitude and W is the width of t), the precision is specified solely by W in target selection tasks.

In accordance with the underpinning of Fitts' law, at least in its original form, W affords the degree the touch points are expected to spread out. If the task precision is exactly complied with, no more, no less, we can expect $W \approx 4.133\sigma_r$, which means 96.4% touch points fall within the target. In practice a user might tend to over/under utilize W.

Note that it is σ_r instead of σ that is proportional to W. The reason is that X_a is irrelevant to the precision of the task, and should be removed when considering to what degree the user decides to comply with the task precision.

Assuming that σ_r is proportional to W, we have

$$\sigma_r^2 = \alpha W^2 \qquad \text{Eq. 13}$$

where α is a constant.

Replacing σ_r^2 in Eq. 12 with Eq. 13, σ^2 can be computed as

$$\sigma^2 = \sigma_r^2 + \sigma_a^2 = \alpha W^2 + \sigma_a^2 \qquad \text{Eq. 14}$$

Note that both α and σ_a^2 are constants and can be measured independently of the task. Eq. 14 shows that the variance (σ^2) is linearly correlated to the target size W^2, and the linear regression between σ^2 and W^2 has a non-zero intercept on σ^2-axis due to the low absolute precision of finger touch (σ_a^2).

Previous research [1, 8, 10] has shown that μ may have a small offset from the center of t (denoted by c). However, the magnitude and direction of the offset vary with individuals [10], finger vs. thumb [1], finger angle [10] and other factors. Across these factors, it is reasonable to expect the central tendency as

$$\mu \approx c. \qquad \text{Eq. 15}$$

Eqs 14 and 15 essentially predict μ and σ from the size and center of t. Replacing μ and σ in Eq. 9 with Eqs 14 and 15, we have

$$BTD(s,t) = \frac{1}{2\sigma^2}(s-\mu)^2 + \ln\sigma$$

$$= \frac{(s-c)^2}{2(\alpha W^2 + \sigma_a^2)} + \frac{1}{2}\ln(\alpha W^2 + \sigma_a^2), \qquad \text{Eq. 16}$$

where s is touch point location, W is width of t, c is the center of t, α and σ_a are constants.

Eq. 16 shows that $BTD(s,t)$ is computed based on the square distance of the touch point to the center of the target, the size of the target, and the finger absolute touch precision σ_a^2.

Two-Dimensional Circular Target Selections

With some simplifications, we generalize BTC to 2-dimensional circular targets. The derivation shows BTC for 2-dimensional circular target selection tasks is equivalent to finding the target that minimizes $BTD_2(s,t)$, the 2-dimensional Bayesian touch distance between the touch point s and the target candidate t.

Touch Points Distribution for 2-Dimenstional Circular Targets. Previous research shows that touch points approximately follow a bivariate Gaussian distribution for a 2-dimensional target selection [1, 8, 13].

$$X \sim N(\mu, \Sigma) \qquad \text{Eq. 17}$$

The correlation (ρ) between x and y coordinates of the touch points is small, but varies depending on the locations of the targets, and could be either negative or positive [1, 8]. Across various locations, it is reasonable to expect $\rho \approx 0$. μ and Σ of the distribution then become:

$$\mu = \begin{pmatrix}\mu_x \\ \mu_y\end{pmatrix} \qquad \text{Eq. 18}$$

$$\Sigma = \begin{pmatrix}\sigma_x^2 & 0 \\ 0 & \sigma_y^2\end{pmatrix} \qquad \text{Eq. 19}$$

where μ_x and μ_y are means, and σ_x and σ_y are standard deviations in x and y directions respectively.

According to the definition of bivariate Gaussian distribution, the negative log likelihood function becomes:

$$-\ln P(s|\mu,\Sigma) =$$

$$\frac{1}{2}\left[\frac{(s_x-\mu_x)^2}{\sigma_x^2} + \frac{(s_y-\mu_y)^2}{\sigma_y^2}\right] + \ln\sigma_x + \ln\sigma_y + \ln(2\pi), \qquad \text{Eq. 20}$$

where s_x, and s_y are coordinates of the touch point s.

$BTD_2(s,t)$, the generalization of $BTD(s,t)$ (Eq. 9) for 2-dimensional circular targets, becomes

$$BTD_2(s,t) = \frac{1}{2}\left[\frac{(s_x-\mu_x)^2}{\sigma_x^2} + \frac{(s_y-\mu_y)^2}{\sigma_y^2}\right] + \ln\sigma_x + \ln\sigma_y \qquad \text{Eq. 21}$$

2-Dimensional Dual Gaussian Distributions Hypothesis. To compute $BTD_2(s,t)$, we generalize the dual Gaussian distribution hypothesis to 2-dimensional circular targets.

Similar to the 1-dimensional targets, we hypothesize that the distribution of touch points for a 2-dimensional circular target is the sum of two independent Gaussians: X_r and X_a.

$$X_r \sim N\left(\begin{pmatrix}\mu_{rx}\\ \mu_{ry}\end{pmatrix}, \begin{pmatrix}\sigma_{r_x}^2 & 0\\ 0 & \sigma_{r_y}^2\end{pmatrix}\right) \quad \text{Eq. 22}$$

$$X_a \sim N\left(\begin{pmatrix}\mu_{ax}\\ \mu_{ay}\end{pmatrix}, \begin{pmatrix}\sigma_{a_x}^2 & 0\\ 0 & \sigma_{a_y}^2\end{pmatrix}\right) \quad \text{Eq. 23}$$

where μ_{r_x} and $\sigma_{r_x}^2$ are the mean and variance of X_r in the x direction, μ_{r_y} and $\sigma_{r_y}^2$ for X_r in the y direction, μ_{a_x} and $\sigma_{a_x}^2$ for X_a in the x direction, and μ_{a_y} and $\sigma_{a_y}^2$ for X_a in the y direction. Since we expect $\rho \approx 0$ for X, it is logical to expect $\rho_r \approx 0$ and $\rho_a \approx 0$ for X_r and X_a, respectively.

Similar to the 1-dimensional tasks, we assume both σ_{r_x} and σ_{r_y} are proportional to the size of t (the diameter d), and the μ is close to the center c (c_x , c_y) of t. The touch point distribution (X) of t can be expressed as:

$$X \sim N\left(\begin{pmatrix}u_x\\ u_y\end{pmatrix}, \begin{pmatrix}\sigma_x^2 & 0\\ 0 & \sigma_y^2\end{pmatrix}\right)$$

$$= N\left(\begin{pmatrix}c_x\\ c_y\end{pmatrix}, \begin{pmatrix}\sigma_{r_x}^2 + \sigma_{a_x}^2 & 0\\ 0 & \sigma_{r_y}^2 + \sigma_{a_y}^2\end{pmatrix}\right)$$

$$= N\left(\begin{pmatrix}c_x\\ c_y\end{pmatrix}, \begin{pmatrix}\alpha_x d^2 + \sigma_{a_x}^2 & 0\\ 0 & \alpha_y d^2 + \sigma_{a_y}^2\end{pmatrix}\right) \quad \text{Eq. 24}$$

Replacing μ_x, μ_y, σ_x and σ_y in Eq. 21 with the estimations in Eq 24, we have:

$$BTD_2(s,t) = \frac{1}{2}\left[\frac{(s_x-\mu_x)^2}{\sigma_x^2} + \frac{(s_y-\mu_y)^2}{\sigma_y^2}\right] + \ln\sigma_x + \ln\sigma_y$$

$$= \frac{1}{2}\left[\frac{(s_x-c_x)^2}{\alpha_x d^2+\sigma_{a_x}^2} + \frac{(s_y-c_y)^2}{\alpha_y d^2+\sigma_{a_y}^2}\right] + \frac{1}{2}\ln(\alpha_x d^2 + \sigma_{a_x}^2)$$

$$+\frac{1}{2}\ln(\alpha_y d^2 + \sigma_{a_y}^2) \quad \text{Eq.25}$$

Note that α_x, σ_{a_x}, α_y, and σ_{a_y} are constants and can be measured via a separated experiment.

After generalizing the dual Gaussian distribution hypothesis to the 2-dimensional circular targets, $BTD_2(s,t)$ can be computed based on touch point location s (s_x, s_y), center c (c_x, c_y) and diameter (d) of t.

EXPERIMENT 1. MODELING TOUCH INPUT

Theoretically, *BTC* builds on Bayes' theorem and the dual Gaussian distribution hypothesis. In many steps of derivation we made simplifications and assumptions. Fundamentally, we applied mathematical (quantitative) reasoning to human behavior. The reliability of such a process should not be taken for granted without empirical confirmation. In the rest of the paper we seek experimental verifications of *BTC*.

Though the original dual Gaussian distribution hypothesis has been verified by Bi, Li and Zhai [4] in tasks where participants selected a target with a certain size (W) over a distance (A), we first conducted an experiment (Expt. 1) to verify the generalized dual Gaussian distribution hypothesis for 2-dimensional circular target selection tasks where the task precision is solely specified by the target size W.

More specifically, Expt. 1 is to verify the prediction made by the generalized dual Gaussian distribution hypothesis (Eq. 24): variances (i.e., σ_x^2 and σ_y^2) are linearly correlated to the target size d^2, and have non-zero intercepts on the variance-axes due to the low absolute precision of finger touch (i.e., $\sigma_{a_x}^2$ and $\sigma_{a_y}^2$),

We also aimed to estimate α_x, σ_{a_x}, α_y, and σ_{a_y} via Expt. 1, which would be used to compute $BTD_2(s,t)$ for other target selection tasks.

Participants and Apparatus

We recruited 18 participants (3 females) between the ages of 26 and 49. Two of them were left-handed. All of them used touchscreen devices (e.g., smartphones) several times a day. The experiment was conducted on a Galaxy Nexus phone running Android OS 4.2. The capacitive touch screen was 11.94 cm in diagonal with an aspect ratio of 9:16 and a resolution of 720 × 1280 pixels. When a finger touched the screen, the approximate centroid of contact area between the finger and the screen was reported as the touch point.

Tasks

Each participant performed a set of typical target selection tasks. At the beginning of each trial, a green circle appeared on the screen and the participant was instructed to select it using the input finger as quickly and accurately as possible. The target turned yellow and the device played a successful beep sound if the target was successfully selected, otherwise an error sound. The next trial started as soon as the input finger was lifted off. The selection of the target was determined by whether the touch point fell within the target, which is a common criterion for selecting UI elements on current touchscreen devices.

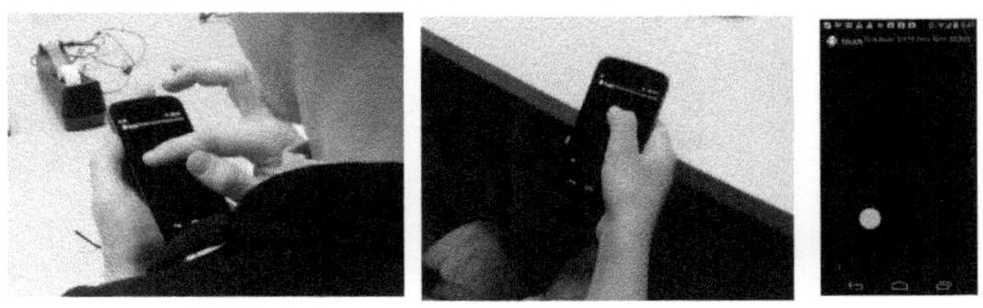

a b c

Figure 1. a: index finger posture. b: thumb posture. c: a target

Design

The study included 10 diameter (d) × input finger (f) conditions, with five levels of d (2, 4, 6, 8, 10 mm) combined with two levels of f (thumb and index finger). In the index finger condition, the participant acquired the target in a two-handed posture (Figure 1a), holding the device with one hand and acquiring the target with the index finger on the other. In the thumb condition (Figure 1b), the participant used a one-handed posture, holding it with one hand and using the thumb of the same hand to select it. Both postures are commonly used for interactions on touchscreen devices [1].

Each $d \times f$ combination included 80 trials. Trials with the same input finger (f) were grouped in a session. The order of trials in a session was randomized, as well as the location of the target in each trial. The order of sessions was counterbalanced across participants: half of the participant performed tasks with thumb first. A one-minute break was enforced before switching finger conditions.

In short, the study included:

18 (participants) × 2 (input finger) × 5 (target diameter) × 80 = 14400 trials.

Data Processing

We used the finger take-off position as the default location for a touch action. Trials with touch points 15 mm away from the target center were treated as outliers and discarded. The first 10 trials in each finger session of each user were treated as warm-up and were also excluded in the analysis. In total, 2% of trials were discarded and 14081 trials were analyzed.

Results

In agreement with previous research, the touch points followed bivariate Gaussian distributions for different target sizes. Shapiro-Wilk tests showed that touch points followed normal distributions for each user × target size ($p > 0.05$). Figure 4 shows three examples of touch point distributions.

To test the prediction from the dual Gaussian distribution hypothesis, we ran linear regressions for σ_x^2 vs. d^2, and σ_y^2 vs. d^2. Results are presented at Figure 2 & 3.

The regressions show strong linear relationships between the variance on each direction and d^2. The R^2 values are 0.93 for σ_x^2 vs. d^2 and 0.98 for σ_y^2 vs. d^2. Figure 2 & 3 also show non-zero intercepts on the y-axes.

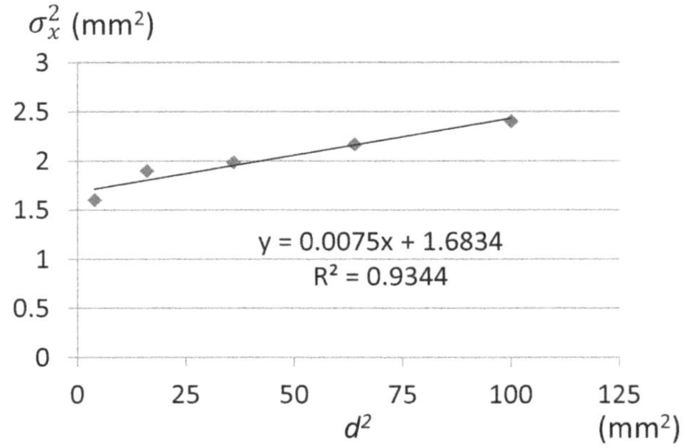

Figure 2. Regression between variance on *X* direction (σ_x^2) and target size (d^2).

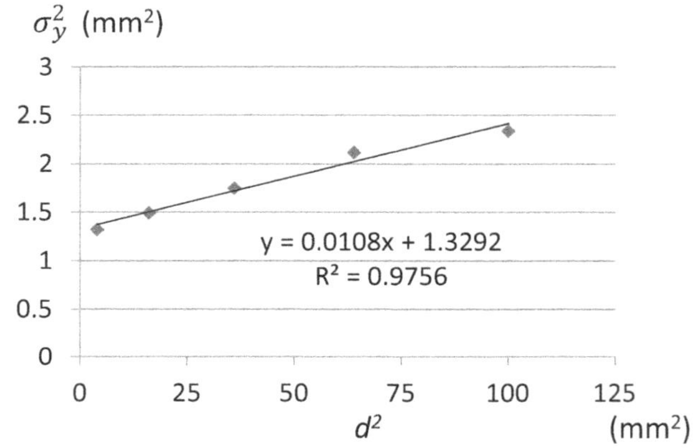

Figure 3. Regression between variance on *Y* direction (σ_y^2) and target size (d^2).

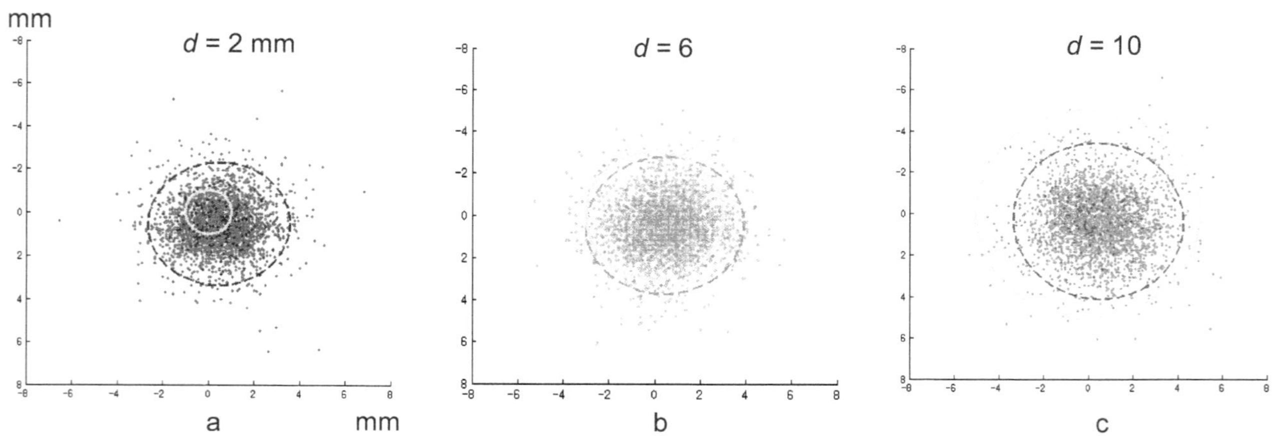

Figure 4. Distributions of touch points across all users for 3 target sizes. The yellow circles are the targets, and the dashed ellipses are 95% confidence ellipses. Touch point coordinates were calibrated with the origins at target centers.

The linear regressions provide the estimations of $\alpha_x, \sigma_{a_x}^2, \alpha_y,$ and $\sigma_{a_y}^2$, which are reported in Table 1.

α_x	σ_{ax}^2	α_y	σ_{ay}^2
0.0075	1.68	0.0108	1.33

Table 1. Constants $\alpha_x, \sigma_{a_x}^2, \alpha_y,$ and $\sigma_{a_y}^2$ computed from the linear regressions.

Replacing the constants in Eq.25 with the values in Table 1, $BTD_{2D}(s,\ t)$ can be computed as:

$$BTD_{2D}(s,t) = \frac{1}{2}\left[\frac{(s_x - c_x)^2}{\alpha_x d^2 + \sigma_{a_x}^2} + \frac{(s_y - c_y)^2}{\alpha_y d^2 + \sigma_{a_y}^2}\right] + \frac{1}{2}\ln(\alpha_x d^2 + \sigma_{a_x}^2) + \frac{1}{2}\ln(\alpha_y d^2 + \sigma_{a_y}^2)$$

$$= \frac{1}{2}\left[\frac{(s_x - c_x)^2}{0.0075d^2 + 1.68} + \frac{(s_y - c_y)^2}{0.0108d^2 + 1.33}\right] + \frac{1}{2}\ln(0.0075d^2 + 1.68) + \frac{1}{2}\ln(0.0108d^2 + 1.33) \quad \text{Eq. 26}$$

Thumb vs. Index Finger. Previous research [13] showed that the index finger and thumb have different precision, with the index finger slightly more precise than the thumb. The different properties of the index finger and thumb might lead to differences in $\alpha_x, \sigma_{a_x}, \alpha_y,$ or σ_{a_y} for different fingers.

To evaluate this, we ran regressions for data in thumb and index finger conditions respectively. Results are reported in Table 2.

	α_x	σ_{ax}	α_y	σ_{ay}
Thumb	0.0073	1.35	0.0113	1.18
Index	0.0075	1.24	0.0104	1.12

Table 2. $\alpha_x, \sigma_{a_x}, \alpha_y,$ and σ_{a_x} for thumb and index finger specifically.

Table 2 shows that the differences in $\alpha_x, \sigma_{a_x}, \alpha_y,$ or σ_{a_y} between the thumb and index finger are small. The biggest difference is for σ_{a_x}, with the index finger being 8% lower than the thumb condition. Both σ_{a_x} and σ_{a_y} are slightly greater for the thumb than for the index finger, indicating that the thumb has lower absolute precision.

Discussion

The study results strongly concur with the prediction made by the generalized dual Gaussian distribution hypothesis. The study results showed R^2 of linear regression was 0.93 between σ_x^2 and d^2, and 0.98 between σ_y^2 and d^2, indicating strong linear relationships between variances and target size d^2. Figure 2 and Figure 3 also show non-zero intercepts on the y-axis.

The study results also provide estimations of constants $\alpha_x, \sigma_{a_x}, \alpha_y,$ and σ_{a_y}. With these estimations, we can use Eq. 26 to compute $BTD_{2D}(s,t)$ for other 2-dimensional circular target selection tasks.

EXPERIMENT 2. EVALUATING BAYESIAN TOUCH CRITERION

The purpose of the study is to evaluate *BTC* by comparing it with other target-deciding criteria.

Participants and Apparatus

Eighteen participants (7 females) between the ages of 21 and 38 participated in the study. One of them was left-handed. All of them used touchscreen devices (e.g., smartphones) several times a day. Importantly, to ensure the external validity of the model parameters estimated from Experiment 1, none of them participated in the Experiment 1. The apparatus was the same as that in Experiment 1.

Task

Each participant performed a set of target selection tasks. Unlike the task in Experiment 1, in which each trial displayed only one green circle as the target, the tasks in Experiment 2 showed multiple grey circles as distractors in addition to the green circular target (Figure 5). The participant was instructed to select the target (i.e., green circle) as accurately and quickly as possible.

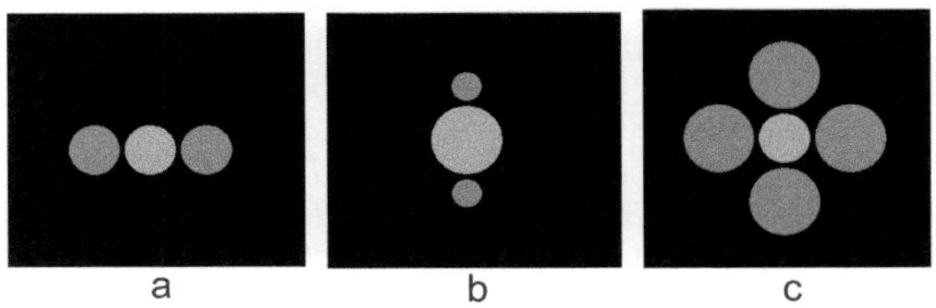

Figure 5. Three layouts of targets (green circles) and distractors (grey circles) used in the studies. The target and distractor sizes varied in the studies. The gap between the edge of the target and the edge of the distractor was 0.5 mm.

The task was designed to simulate the behaviors of UI elements on current touchscreen devices. If the touch point fell within a grey circle, the grey circle turned yellow and the device played an error sound, indicating a false selection. If the touch point did not fall within any circles, the device provided no feedback, indicating that nothing was selected. If the touch point fell within the green circle, the target turned green and the device played a successful sound. To encourage the participant to minimize errors, the participant needed to place the touch point within the boundary of the target (i.e., the *VB* rule) to continue to the next trial. Otherwise the trial repeated. The numbers of completed trials, remaining trials, and error rate were displayed at the right corner of the screen.

Design

The study included 54 target diameter (d_T) × distractor diameter (d_D) × distractor layout × input finger conditions.

Both d_T and d_D had 3 levels (3, 5, 7 mm), to represent small, medium, and large targets. Distractor layout also had 3 levels, which was illustrated in Figure 5. Input finger had 2 levels (thumb and index finger). Each condition had 20 repetitions with the location randomized each time. The process of the experiment was the same with that in Experiment 1.

In short, the experiment had:

$$3d_T \times 3d_D \times 3 \text{ distractor layout} \times 2 \text{ input finger}$$
$$\times\ 20 \text{ trials} \times 18 \text{ participants} = 19440 \text{ trials}.$$

Note that some trials might repeat multiple times until the targets were successfully selected.

Target Selection Criteria

We designed and evaluated four target selection criteria:

1) The *Bayesian Touch Criterion (BTC)*. We use α_x, σ_{ax}^2, α_y, and σ_{ay}^2 measured from Experiment 1 (Table 1) to compute *BTD*. The candidate with the shortest *BTD* is selected.
2) *Visual Boundary (VB)*. A circle is selected if and only if the touch point falls within it.
3) *Visual Boundary or Shortest Distance to Circle Boundary (VB/SDB)*. It applies the *VB* rule first. If the touch point does not fall within any circle, the selected target is the circle with shortest distance to the touch point from its boundary. This criterion is also equivalent to the bubble cursor [7] and many snap-to-target techniques.
4) *Visual Boundary or Short Distance to Circle Center (VB/SDC)*. It applies the *VB* rule first. If the touch point does not fall within any circle, the selected target is the circle with the shortest distance to the touch point from its center. This criterion is less common than *VB* and *VB/SDB* in practice.

Criterion 1 (*BTC*) is derived from statistical principles as shown earlier. Criteria 2 – 4 are common sense criteria of target selection to which we want to compare *BTC*. The metric of evaluation for all of these criteria is selection *Error Rate*, defined as

$$Error\ Rate = \frac{Number\ of\ Failed\ Selections}{Total\ Number\ of\ Selections}$$

Data Processing

We removed outliers and the trials in warm-up according to the same criteria as Experiment 1. In total, 3% of all trials were removed and 24214 trials were analyzed.

Results

Error Rate. Figure 6 shows the overall error rate for each selection criterion. As shown, *BTC* had the lowest error rate. The mean error rates were 5.9% for *BTC*, 19.6% for *VB*, 8.0% for *VB/SDB*, 6.3% for *VB/SDC*. ANOVA showed the target selection criterion had a significant effect on error rate ($F_{3,\ 51} = 152$, $p < 0.001$). Pairwise mean comparisons using the Bonferroni adjustment showed that *BTC* was significantly more accurate than all other criteria ($p < 0.001$).

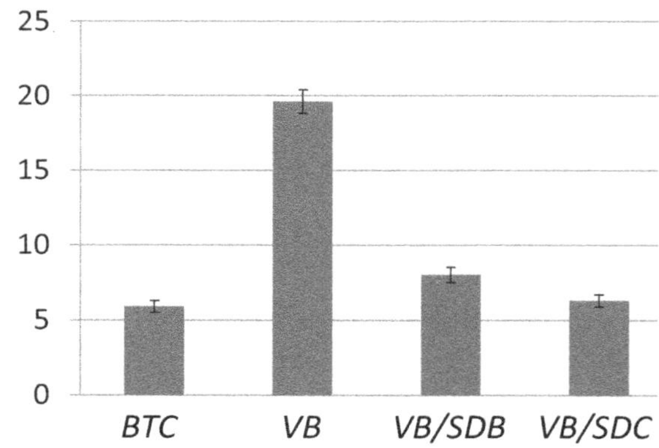

Figure 6. Mean and the standard error of mean (SEM) of Error Rate per target selection criterion.

Note that the *Visual Boundary (VB)* criterion resulted in the highest error rate, indicating that this commonly used criterion did not work well for finger touch under the experimental conditions tested.

ANOVA also showed that target diameter (d_T) ($F_{2,\ 34} = 110$, $p < 0.001$), distractor diameter (d_D) ($F_{2,\ 34} = 33$, $p < 0.001$), and distractor layout ($F_{2,\ 34} = 9.7$, $p < 0.001$) had significant main effects on error rate. Smaller targets or distractors led to higher error rates. The mean error rates for 3, 5 and 7 mm target diameter (d_T) were 20.5%, 6.0%, and 2.1% , and for 3, 5 and 7mm distractor diameter (d_D) were 11.8%, 8.7%, and 8.0%, respectively. The layout in Figure 5(c) resulted in the highest error rate, 10.9%. ANOVA did not show a significant main effect of input finger on error rate ($F_{1,\ 17} = 0.818$, $p = 0.378$).

ANOVA showed significant interaction effects for target diameter (d_T) × selection criteria ($F_{6,\ 102} = 314$, $p < 0.001$) and distractor diameter (d_D) × selection criteria ($F_{6,\ 102} = 41$, $p < 0.001$) on error rate. *BTC* outperformed other criteria with larger margins when targets were smaller or distractors were greater.

Touch Point Distributions. Since the participants in Experiment 2 were completely different from Experiment 1, it allowed us to evaluate the external validity of the dual Gaussian distribution hypothesis. We computed σ_x and σ_y from the recorded data (i.e., *observed*), and compare them with the values predicted from Eq. 26 (i.e., *predicted*). We define prediction error as:

$$Prediction\ Error = \frac{|Predicted - Observed|}{Observed} \times 100\%$$

As shown in Table 3, Eq. 26 is able to closely predict σ_x and σ_y. The prediction error was below 7.5% across all the conditions. In particular, the error was 0 for σ_y when $d = 5$ and 7 mm.

$d_T(mm)$		σ_x	σ_y
3.0	Observed	1.23	1.26
	Predicted	1.32	1.19
	Prediction Error	7.3%	5.6%
5.0	Observed	1.35	1.27
	Predicted	1.37	1.27
	Prediction Error	1.5%	0
7.0	Observed	1.37	1.36
	Predicted	1.43	1.36
	Prediction Error	5%	0

Table 3. Prediction Error by Target Diameter (d_T)

To evaluate whether *BTC* performs better with finger-specific tuning, we computed *BTC* with α_x, σ_{ax}^2,α_y, and σ_{ay}^2 in Table 2 for index finger or thumb input respectively. The mean (and SEM) of overall error rate across participants was still 5.9% (0.4%), almost the same as not using finger-specific parameters. t-test did not show a significant difference ($p \approx 1.0$) between using generic parameters (Table 1) and using finger-specific parameters (Table 2).

Discussion

BTC outperforms VB and its variants. The study results verified that *BTC* was the most accurate criterion in selecting a user-intended target, providing strong support to the theoretical analysis leading to *BTC*. In particular, the error rate of *BTC* was 70%, and 26% lower than *VB* and *VB/SDB*, respectively.

The study results also verified the external validity of the dual Gaussian distribution hypothesis and showed its strong predictive power: σ_x and σ_y predicted by Eq. 26 closely matched the empirical results observed from the data in Experiment 2 (Table 3).

BTC can be adopted regardless of input finger. The study results showed that using finger-specific *BTC* did not lead to substantial performance improvement. It is probably because parameters (i.e., $\alpha_x, \sigma_{a_x}, \alpha_y$, and σ_{a_y}) do not vary drastically across fingers. The results show *BTC* can be adopted regardless of the input finger type.

LIMITATIONS AND FUTURE WORK

The current work is meant to be an exploration of a new and principled approach to finger touch target selection. We studied the Bayesian Touch Criterion at a general and fundamental level. Applying the criterion to specific and practical UI designs will require further verification and modifications. For example, we assumed each touch point is always meant for one of the objects on the screen. There is no "dead space" between objects. This of course does not have to be true. While *BTC* can be used as the primary criterion in ranking target likelihood, additional criteria can still be combined in a specific UI design problem. For example, additional thresholds and filters can be applied to the final target selection.

To maintain a manageable scope of two experiments in a single paper, we limited the target and distractor sizes to a range commonly seen on smartphone-sized devices. We see the very strong predictive power of the Bayesian Touch Criterion within this range of sizes.

CONCLUSION

To improve the accuracy of touch input, we conceptualize finger touch input as an uncertain and ambiguous process, and devise a statistical *Bayesian Touch Criterion (BTC)* for deciding the intended target among distractors. In addition to the theoretical analysis, we conducted experiments to verify our theory, and empirically evaluate *BTC*.

Our investigations lead to the following conclusions:

1) The *Bayesian Touch Criterion (BTC)* is a principled criterion for deciding the target for finger touch. It selects the intended target as the candidate with the shortest *Bayesian Touch Distance* (*BTD*) to the touch point. *BTD* is a function of touch point s and the target candidate t. For 1-dimensional tasks, it is in the form:

$$BTD(s,t) = \frac{(s-c)^2}{2(\alpha W^2 + \sigma_a^2)} + \frac{1}{2}ln(\alpha W^2 + \sigma_a^2) \qquad \text{Eq.27}$$

where s is the location of touch point, W is the width of t, c is the center of t, α and σ_a are constants which can be measured via a separate experiment.

For 2-dimensional circular targets, we not only derived the equation for computing *BTD*, but also measured the parameters via an experiment. Our investigation shows the 2-dimensional Bayesian touch distance $BTD_2(s,t)$ is in the form:

$$BTD_2(s,t) = \frac{1}{2}\left[\frac{(s_x-c_x)^2}{0.0075d^2 + 1.68} + \frac{(s_y-c_y)^2}{0.0108d^2 + 1.33}\right]$$

$$+\frac{1}{2}\ln(0.0075d^2 + 1.68) + \frac{1}{2}\ln(0.0108d^2 + 1.33) \text{ Eq. 28}$$

where s_x, s_y are the coordinates of touch point s, c_x and c_y are the coordinates of the center of a target candidate t, and d is its diameter. The units of these variables are mm.

2) The empirical experiment for 2-dimensional circular target selection shows that *BTC* is significantly more

accurate than the typical target deciding method, *Visual Boundary (VB)*, and its two variants: *Visual Boundary/Shortest Distance to Circle Boundary (VB/SDB)* and *Visual Boundary/Shortest Distance to Circle Center (VB/SDC)*. *BTC* reduces the error rate by 70%, 26% and 6% over *VB*, *VB/SDB*, and *VB/SDC* respectively.

3) *BTC* is a basis for touch UI design. *BTC* has a foundational role in researching and designing future touch user interfaces. Actual and specific touch UI designs may combine it with many other concerns and criteria of target selection. We believe fruitful future work should be expected along the direction this work points to.

ACKNOWLEDGEMENTS

We thank participants in our studies, and the UIST paper reviewers for the insightful comments. We thank colleagues at Google, particularly Andrew Fowler.

REFERENCES

1. Azenkot, S. and Zhai, S. (2012). Touch Behavior with Different Postures on Soft Smart Phone Keyboards. *Proc. of MobileHCI'12*. 251 - 260.
2. Baudisch, P. and Chu, G. (2009) Back-of-device interaction allows creating very small touch devices. *ACM CHI*, 1923-1932.
3. Benko, H., Wilson, A. D., and Baudisch, P. (2006) Precise selection techniques for multi-touch screens. *ACM CHI*, 1263-1272.
4. Bi, X., Li, Y., and Zhai, S. (2013) FFitts law: modeling finger touch with Fitts' law. *ACM CHI*, 1363 – 1372.
5. Weir, D., Rogers, S., Murray-Smith, R., and Löchtefeld, M., (2012). A user-specific machine learning approach for improving touch accuracy on mobile devices. *ACM UIST* 465-476.
6. Fitts, P.M. (1954). The information capacity of the human motor system in controlling the amplitude of movement. *Journal of Experimental Psychology*, 47, 381-391.
7. Grossman, T., and Balakrishnan, R. (2005). The bubble cursor: enhancing target acquisition by dynamic resizing of the cursor's activation area. *ACM CHI*. 281-290.
8. Henze, N., Rukzio, E., and Boll, S. (2011). 100,000,000 taps: analysis and improvement of touch performance in the large. *Proc. MobileHCI* , 133-142
9. Henze, N., Rukzio, E., and Boll, S. (2012) Observational and experimental investigation of typing behaviour using virtual keyboards for mobile devices. *ACM CHI*. 2659-2668.
10. Holz, C. and Baudisch, P. (2010) The Generalized Perceived Input Point Model and How to Double Touch Accuracy by Extracting Fingerprints. *ACM CHI*, 581-590.
11. Holz, C. and Baudisch, P. (2011). Understanding Touch. *ACM CHI*, 2501-2510.
12. Schwarz, J., Hudson, S., Mankoff, J. and Wilson, A. (2010). A framework for robust and flexible handling of inputs with uncertainty. *ACM UIST*. 47-56.
13. Wang, F. and Ren, X. (2009) Empirical evaluation for finger input properties in multi-touch interaction. *ACM CHI*, 1063-1072.
14. Williamson J. (2006) Continuous Uncertain Interaction. *Ph.D. Thesis*. University of Glasgow.
15. Zhai, S. and Kristensson, P. O. (2013) The word-gesture keyboard: reimagining keyboard interaction. *Commun. ACM* 55, 9 (September 2012), 91-101.

Touch Scrolling Transfer Functions

Philip Quinn Sylvain Malacria Andy Cockburn

University of Canterbury
Christchurch, New Zealand
philip.quinn@canterbury.ac.nz,
sylvain@malacria.fr, andy@cosc.canterbury.ac.nz

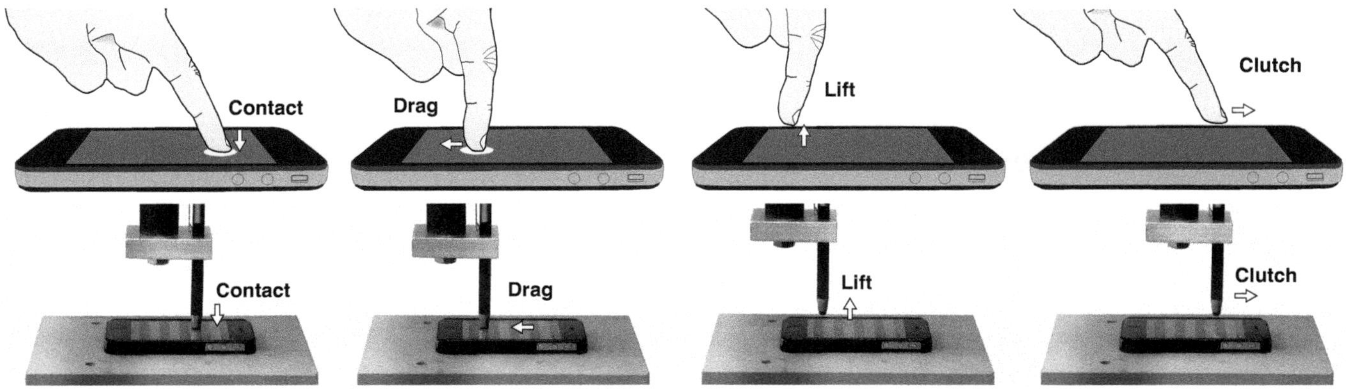

Figure 1. Transfer functions transform touch scrolling gestures (top) into scrolling output. These gestures can be simulated mechanically by SCARA robots (bottom) to reverse engineer the transfer functions.

ABSTRACT

Touch scrolling systems use a *transfer function* to transform gestures on a touch sensitive surface into scrolling output. The design of these transfer functions is complex as they must facilitate precise direct manipulation of the underlying content as well as rapid scrolling through large datasets. However, researchers' ability to refine them is impaired by: (1) limited understanding of how users express scrolling intentions through touch gestures; (2) lack of knowledge on proprietary transfer functions, causing researchers to evaluate techniques that may misrepresent the state of the art; and (3) a lack of tools for examining existing transfer functions. To address these limitations, we examine how users express scrolling intentions in a human factors experiment; we describe methods to reverse engineer existing 'black box' transfer functions, including use of an accurate robotic arm; and we use the methods to expose the functions of Apple iOS and Google Android, releasing data tables and software to assist replication. We discuss how this new understanding can improve experimental rigour and assist iterative improvement of touch scrolling.

ACM 978-1-4503-2268-3/13/10...$15.00.
http://dx.doi.org/10.1145/2501988.2501995

Author Keywords

Control-display gain; flick scrolling; scroll acceleration; touch interaction; transfer functions.

ACM Classification

H.5.2 [**Information interfaces and presentation**] User interfaces – *Interaction styles*.

INTRODUCTION

Gesture-based 'touch scrolling' allows users to scroll by simulating a direct physical interaction on the displayed content. Metaphors from the real world—such as the ability to *throw* the content with a velocity and *friction* that gradually slows it—assist with giving the user a scrolling mechanism that is perceived to be 'simple and natural'. Yet despite the perceived simplicity of gesture-based scrolling, sophisticated engineering underlies its behaviour. Close visual inspection of flick scrolling on an Apple iPhone, for example, will reveal that the scrolling velocity following a 'flick' gesture does not always follow simple physical laws, and that accelerated scroll speeds and rapid deceleration are sometimes applied.

The behaviour of touch scrolling techniques is determined by a *transfer function* [8, 17] that converts human input actions into a resultant scrolling output effect. These functions may attend to input parameters such as properties of individual gestures (such as their length, velocity, pressure, or direction), properties of a gesture sequence (such as the number of gestures issued in a rapid sequence or their period), properties of the document and viewport (such as the document's length or type of content), as well as attending to current system state and settings (such as scroll speed or friction setting). While any or all of these parameters *may* be used in any particular implementation, there is a lack of public information on which ones are actually used and on how they are used. Furthermore, there is a lack of fundamental human factors knowledge on how users choose to express their intentions for different scrolling velocities through gestures.

Given its role as a core component of touchscreen interaction, the transfer function that governs touch scrolling behaviour has received surprisingly little research attention (exceptions reviewed later). One reason for this is that the proprietary systems representing the state of the art are black-boxes that do not expose key aspects of their operation. Most platforms publicise and allow control over only a limited set of their built-in scrolling parameters. Another key reason is that there is a lack of methods that might allow inspection of the transfer functions. While recent work has disclosed techniques for inspecting transfer functions in mouse-pointing [4] and scroll-wheel operation [17], these methods rely on published USB standards for communication with external devices, and they therefore cannot be applied to touch scrolling.

The lack of information on touch scrolling transfer functions is a problem for researchers. It is a source of experimental imprecision because exact system settings can not be reported or replicated, and it impedes the iterative refinement of touch scrolling systems because key behaviours (both human and system) are unknown. For example, Aliakseyeu et al. [1], Lee et al. [13], and Tu et al. [19] all implement and evaluate touch scrolling transfer functions, where the baseline experimental control condition unintentionally differs from the behaviour of commercial devices.

We present four main contributions to resolve these problems. First, we present a human factors experiment to understand critical characteristics and limits of user actions when performing touch scrolling gestures. Second, we describe methods that facilitate reverse engineering the parameters used by touch scrolling transfer functions. These include controlled software simulation, and use of a high-quality Selective Compliant Articulated Robot Arm (SCARA) to precisely control input gestural actions. Third, we present results of using the methods to compare the transfer functions used by Apple iOS (iPhone and iPad) and Google Android. The results show some similarities, but also substantial differences in their transfer functions, suggesting that any experiment involving gestural scrolling is likely to be influenced by the platform on which it is conducted. Fourth, we release the source code for the tools used to extract, emulate, and test these transfer functions; to serve as documentation of the current state of the art and a foundation for iterative improvement.

BACKGROUND

The term 'scrolling' is often used informally in HCI to refer to any geometrical translation of the information displayed

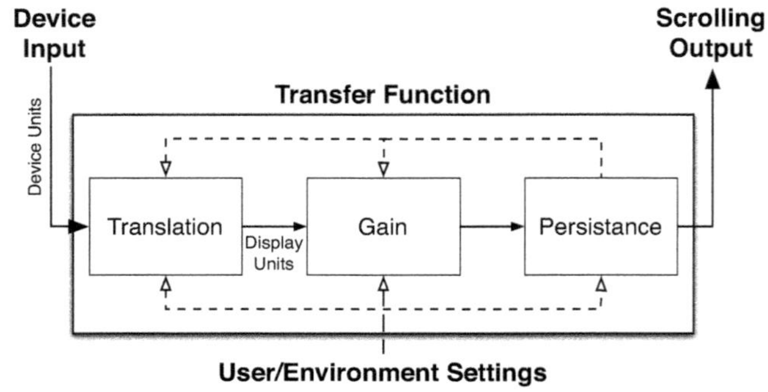

Figure 2. Conceptual low-level depiction of scrolling transfer functions (adapted from Quinn et al. [17]).

within a viewport, which permits diagonal or elliptical movement where the information is translated on two dimensions concurrently. However, this usage is inconsistent with the origin of the word 'scroll', which constrains movement to one dimension at a time. In this paper we use the word 'scroll' to refer to one-dimensional translation of the viewport. This section provides background on scrolling transfer functions and prior techniques.

Scrolling Transfer Functions

Transfer functions are responsible for converting human device manipulations into resultant output effects [8]. Several researchers have noted the important role that scrolling transfer functions have on user performance [e.g. 7, 20], but prior scrolling studies have been inexact on the transfer functions used due to a lack of methods for analysing, reporting, and controlling their settings.

Casiez and Roussel [4] recently made similar observations on the lack of tools for analysing and controlling mouse pointing transfer functions, causing in imprecise 'experimental bricolage'. Consequently, Casiez and Roussel [4] developed a USB mouse emulator (the *EchoMouse*) and software libraries to resolve these problems. Quinn et al. [17] adapted the EchoMouse to analyse scrolling transfer functions used with commercial scroll-wheel devices. Figure 2, adapted from Quinn et al. [17], shows three conceptual transformations that can occur in such a function: (1) *translation* converts device units into display units, such as millimetres of finger displacement into pixels of scroll translation; (2) *gain* amplifies or attenuates the input signals; and (3) *persistence* allows state memory to influence future behaviour, such as counting the number of repeated flick actions, or applying effects across time (such as momentum). The transfer function can also be influenced by user settings and by the environment (e.g. the length of the document or display pixel density).

Quinn et al. found substantial differences between the parameters used by different scroll-wheel driver vendors, and between the ways the parameters are used. For example, some apply different levels of gain across scroll direction and cumulatively apply gain across repeated scroll-wheel actions, others attend only to scroll-wheel velocity, and some attend to the duration of input. The diversity of approaches demonstrated that supporting scrolling through a wheel is surprisingly complex.

Touch Scrolling Techniques

With touch input, users can readily express several parameters in addition to those expressible via. scroll-wheels: many gestural forms are possible—linear [e.g. 1, 13], elliptical [e.g. 2, 18], or oscillatory motion [e.g. 14]; pressure can be varied [e.g. 9, 16]; as can the number of points of contact, and the type of limb contact [e.g. 6].

In this paper, we focus on linear (or near-linear) gestures. We use the term 'drag' to describe the action of moving the finger across the touch surface, independent of system feedback, and we use the term 'flick' to describe rapid finger movement at the point that it disengages from the touch sensitive surface. The basic elements of linear gestures are conceptually simple, as depicted in Figure 1: (1) users make *contact* with the surface; (2) they *drag* their finger(s) on the surface; (3) they *clutch* their finger or fingers (possibly initiating a *flick*), which involves lifting the contact(s) from the surface to regain a convenient space for subsequent contact to repeat the drag; and (4) they *disengage* from the surface when complete, and may (5) *grab* the surface by placing their finger back on the display and holding their position. Despite the apparent simplicity of these actions, they allow many parameters of expression that could be used by a transfer function to influence scrolling output.

Contact and Drag

During *contact* and *drag*, users can control parameters including gesture length, contact time, velocity, acceleration, contact area, orientation of contact area, limb use, pressure, and location. Multiple contacts (e.g., two finger scrolling) and bimanual contacts (e.g., two thumbs 'running' on the surface) could also be used. Example transfer functions using many of these parameters are available in commercial and research systems: for example, the perpendicular distance between the slider axis and finger location governs the control granularity of the playhead in Apple's iOS 'Music' application, and researchers have examined the use of pressure to control zoom [16] and inertial speed [3].

The user's perception of a transfer function's behaviour during *contact* and *drag/flick* is likely to be influenced by whether the interaction is *direct* or *indirect*. With direct interaction the touch surface is coincident with the output display, which affords a perception of physical direct manipulation. However, the expected effect of this manipulation has been debated—whether the user's movement should be interpreted as moving the viewport (moving the content in the opposite direction to the finger's movement), or whether the content moves with the finger [11, 12]—with contemporary implementations favouring the latter. This perception is enhanced through physically inspired behaviours, such as the ability to 'throw' the content with simulated momentum and friction. While these behaviours typically use a 1:1 mapping from contact movement on the surface to output effect, Kwon et al. [12] suggests that users are tolerant of mapping discontinuity, particularly when scrolling large distances.

Indirect interaction, such as trackpad scrolling, involves a separation between the input surface and the displayed content, which diminishes or eliminates the need for a 1:1 mapping. Indeed, multi-finger scrolling on trackpads has typically reversed the directional binding used on 'direct' manipulation devices, with downward dragging actions scrolling towards the end of the document rather than the beginning. The disconnect between input and content can be used to allow the user more precise control over their scrolling actions; for example, Hinckley et al. [9] describe several ways in which motion along a touch sensitive strip can be used to scroll, including automatic scrolling in response to pressure and accelerated scrolling in response to a finger's velocity across the strip.

Clutch and Repeat

Clutching and repetition are related as convenient repetition of linear gestures requires that a clutching action be performed. Clutching involves temporarily disengaging from the touch surface by lifting the finger, then repositioning it in the air to re-engage with the surface near the initial contact (however, certain styles of touch interaction negate the need for an explicit disengagement from the display [e.g. 2, 14, 18]).

Prior work with scroll wheels [10, 17] has used the count of successive clutching actions to increase scrolling gain to facilitate long distance scrolling. Equivalent methods could be used with touch scrolling by cumulatively applying gain across a sequence of repeated gestures. Furthermore, metaphors of inertia and friction can be used to support continued scrolling while the finger is out of contact [15, 21].

STUDY ONE: HUMAN SCROLLING MECHANICS

Designing a touch scrolling transfer function requires understanding the characteristics and limits of human input when gestures are expressed on devices. The lower-bounds of gestural scroll control are relatively clear—a user who slowly drags their finger across the touchscreen surface probably intends to scroll slowly, even if the rate is only a few millimeters per second. However, the mechanisms of rapid scrolling are unclear, with unknown factors including the following: what parameters do users choose to manipulate to signify an intention to scroll quickly; how fast do their fingers move; how long are the gestures; and how rapidly are gestures repeated?

The primary goal of this study is to gather data on the range and style of input that user's provide on touch devices to perform scrolling, answering questions such as those in the previous paragraph. In addition, the results are used to establish the range of values used to robotically probe devices in Study 2.

Prior experience with touch scrolling interfaces and scrolling feedback will influence users' expectations for scrolling behaviour. To reduce the impact of these factors the experiment

Figure 3. Devices and postures examined: held in one hand and operated with the other (iPhone: left, iPad: centre), and an iPhone held in one hand and operated with the thumb (right)

was conducted without any scrolling feedback. Instead, participants were asked to carry out whatever gestures seemed natural to achieve the requested scrolling velocities without any system response.

Method

We examined the participants' gestural actions when asked to imagine scrolling at three different speeds (browsing speed, comfortably fast, and maximally fast; detailed later) and in two directions (up and down). Three device and posture combinations were analysed: an Apple iPhone 4S held in one hand and operated with the index finger of the other hand; an Apple iPhone 4S operated with the thumb of the hand holding the device; and an Apple iPad 2 held in one hand and operated with the index finger of the other hand (Figure 3). These represent the most commonly observed operating postures of the devices. Devices were always held in a portrait orientation.

Subjects & Apparatus

Twelve volunteers (four female; mean age 26) participated in the experiment. All were right-handed post-graduate computer science students who owned and regularly used a touchscreen device (various vendors). Software logged all gesture events, and video captured the participants' postures and actions.

Quantization effects arising from the devices' digitisation of gestural movement will influence our results, particularly at high movement velocities and with short-duration gestures. To understand the magnitude of this issue we analysed the device event reports. The iPad and iPhone reported movement at 16 ms intervals. We tested the accuracy with which the coordinates of the edges of the display were reported by issuing very fast dragging gestures across the display edges, with results showing edges to be reported with ± 1 mm accuracy. However, the coordinates and time of the first event-report were variable when several seconds had passed since the previous contact (we assume the polling interval of the sensor panel is increased to conserve battery power). Similarly, the final event report when breaking contact frequently showed much a lower velocity than prior reports, which could be explained by the event being buffered until the device can confirm that contact has been lost. Our results, therefore, describe the human-factors of gestures *as observed by contemporary devices* (at the application-level).

Procedure

Participants were instructed that the experiment concerned how users perform scrolling gestures at different speeds and directions on touchscreen devices. They were told that they would not see the effect of their scrolling actions, but that they should issue gestures to control three speeds:

- *Browsing Speed:* "Imagine that you are scrolling through a list of songs, looking for something good to play."
- *Comfortably Fast:* "Imagine that you want to quickly scroll to the bottom of a long webpage or list."
- *Maximum Speed:* "Scroll as fast as you can."

One consequence of not showing scrolling feedback is that scrolling direction is ambiguous (pilot studies showed a tendency for participants to move their fingers downwards when instructed to scroll down, which would cause a document to scroll upwards, towards its start). We therefore instructed participants to move their fingers downwards for 'Down' tasks, and on how to hold the device with each posture.

The experimental software showed a title bar with the target speed for the next gesture set, the direction, and a numerical timer on the touchscreen. The rest of the display was a solid yellow colour except for a 'Tap to Begin' button in the centre of the display. Tapping the button caused the display to turn green; the timer began counting down from 6 seconds upon the participant's first contact with the screen. On reaching zero, the display turned red for 1 second before returning to the yellow 'tap to begin' state. Two initial trials at 'Browsing speed' were included to familiarise participants with the procedure (data discarded).

Each participant completed 18 six-second trials with each of the three device/posture combinations. The trials consisted of three repetitions of each direction and speed; all were completed with one posture before moving on to the next (posture order counterbalanced across participants). Within each posture, all trials at one speed (both directions, alternated across trials) were completed before advancing to the next speed.

Design

To reiterate, the experimental objective is to characterise human gestural actions in touch scrolling, resulting in several dependent variables. The maximum velocity attainable is a key value for understanding the range of values that must be processed by touch scrolling transfer functions, but we are also interested in various human and device characteristics that may help devices discriminate between user intentions for different scrolling velocities, including clutch time (or gesture frequency) and gesture length. The study factors, all within-subjects are as follows:

Speed ∈ *{browsing, comfortably fast, maximally fast}*
Device/Posture ∈ *{iPhone-thumb, iPhone-finger, iPad}*
Direction ∈ *{up, down}*

Device and *speed* were counter-balanced across subjects using a Latin Square; *direction* order was alternated.

Results and Analysis

Figure 4 uses box-whisker plots to show the cross-participant range, interquartile range, median, and mean values for three measures: maximum registered finger velocity (top), clutch time (middle), and gesture length (bottom).

Analysis of variance (with Greenhouse-Geisser sphericity corrections) of velocity shows significant main effects for *speed* ($F_{1.76,19.34} = 35.5, p < .001, \eta_p^2 = .76$), with means of 178, 399 and 560 mm/s at *browsing*, *comfortably fast* and *maximally fast*, respectively. The maximum velocity from any participant was 1378 mm/s with an upward gesture on the iPad. The main effect of *device/posture* was also significant ($F_{1.22,13.36} = 42.1, p < .001, \eta_p^2 = .80$), with thumb gestures on the iPhone slowest (mean 186 mm/s), then index-finger iPhone (390 mm/s) and iPad (560 mm/s). A significant *Speed×Device/Posture* interaction ($F_{2.60,28.57} = 18.5, p < .001, \eta_p^2 = .63$) is best attributed to the comparatively small difference between iPhone-thumb velocities across target speeds, as shown in Figure 4 (top). This interaction suggests that velocity may be a poor metric for discriminating between scrolling intentions—while it is likely to succeed for index-finger gestures, it could fail for one-handed thumb gestures. There was no effect of *direction* ($p = .05$), nor any other interaction.

Analysis of clutch time (Figure 4, middle) suggests that it is a fairly robust discriminator of the users' intention for different scrolling speeds. There was a significant effect of *speed* ($F_{1.30,14.25} = 16.4, p = .001, \eta_p^2 = .60$), with means of 536ms when *browsing*, 322 ms at *comfortably fast*, and 160 ms at *maximally fast*. *Direction* also showed a significant effect ($F_{1,11} = 5.6, p = .037, \eta_p^2 = .34$), with clutching after downward drags (mean 320 ms) slightly faster than upward ones (339 ms). No other main effects or interactions were significant. The results for clutch time suggest that users choose to increase the frequency of their gestures (reducing clutch time) when intending to scroll quickly.

Finally, analysis of gesture length showed that the device form-factor has a significant impact on gestures, with the larger size of the iPad encouraging much longer gestures (mean 92 mm) than the index finger or thumb on the iPhone (46 and 31 mm respectively)—$F_{1.39,15.31} = 75.12, p < .001, \eta_p^2 = .87$. There was no significant effect of *Speed* ($p = .35$), suggesting that gesture length is a poor metric for determining user intentions for different scroll velocities. No other effects were significant.

Observations of Subject Behaviour

Thumb gestures on the iPhone were expressed similarly, regardless of intended velocity, with interphalangeal articulation through contractor (down) or extensor muscles (up); explaining the relatively low variance in gesture length and velocity.

When using the index finger with the iPhone, several participants varied finger posture across velocity and direction. Approximately half of the participants used contractor-based interphalangeal articulation with the finger co-linear with the device to express downward gestures at *browsing* speed. Other participants used small amounts of finger contraction coupled with forearm movement to browse downward (with the finger at ~330° to device), and some used wrist ulna deviation with the finger substantially oriented across the device (~280°).

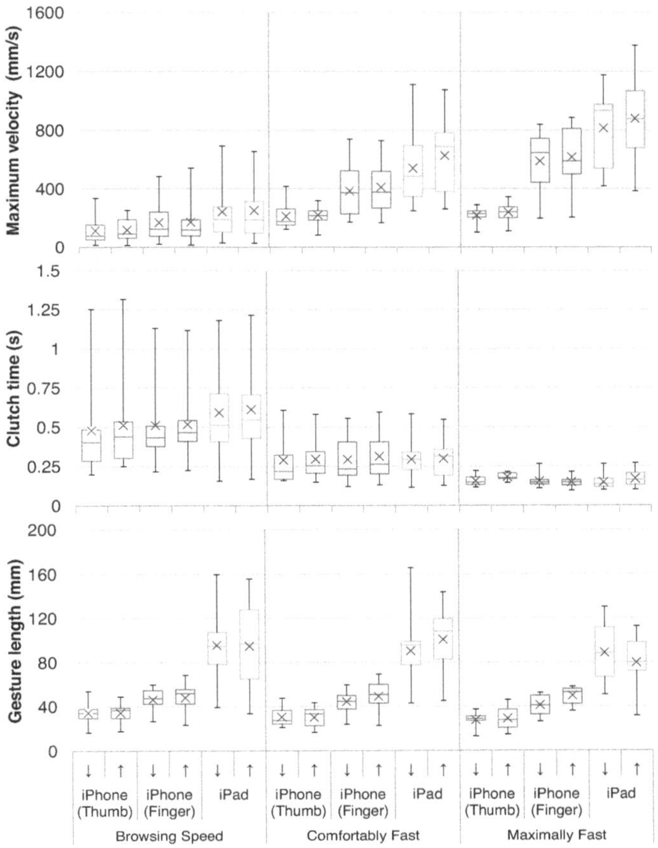

Figure 4. Box-whisker plots characterising the maximum velocity (top), clutch time (middle), and length (bottom) of gestures at three different target speeds with different device/posture combinations in up and down directions.

Upwards scrolling at browsing speed was less varied with most participants using radial deviation or lateral forearm movement with the finger oriented across the device. As the target speed increased to comfortably fast and maximally fast most participants switched to forearm-based movement with the finger pointing across the device. Broadly the same observations applied to the iPad, although few participants used interphalangeal articulation at browsing speed (using wrist or forearm movements throughout).

Discussion

These results provide insights into the parameters that people use to express their intentions for different scrolling velocities across different device form factors and postures. They also suggest the range of values that devices can expect users to express. We used the data from Study 1 to ensure that we probed a superset of human-expressible gestures in Study 2.

The primary finding is that clutch time is a reliable indicator of intended scrolling velocity, with users increasing gesture frequency to express a desire for faster scrolling. Gesture velocity also reliably differentiated between the intended scrolling velocities, but not when expressed with the thumb. Gesture length varied little between the intended velocities. One immediate implication of the clutch time finding is that transfer functions could allow accelerated scrolling by applying cumulative gain across repeated gestures.

For completeness we note some limitations in our method. First, as stated earlier, to focus on users' natural methods of gesture expression, we eliminated scrolling feedback. However, users will inevitably adapt their gestures to the output behaviour, and further work is needed to examine this relationship. Second, our method examined gesture data registered by the device, and quantization effects will introduce some error, particularly at high velocities. Regardless, transfer functions need to operate with registered data, so our results are indicative of what current devices can expect to receive. Third, physical properties of the device will influence gesture performance, including the surface material (e.g., glass vs. plastic), the existence of bezel edges or frames, and device size.

EXPOSING TOUCH SCROLLING TRANSFER FUNCTIONS

This section describes a variety of methods that can be used to examine touch-scrolling transfer functions, including the novel use of robotics to precisely emulate human movement.

Documentation and Source Code

Different vendors vary in their release of public information about scrolling. Google, for example, publishes the source code to their Android platform under an open source license, allowing open and complete inspection (however, device manufacturers can modify the open source code in a closed manner). Apple and Microsoft restrict public information to the API documentation about scrolling widgets (i.e., Apple's `UIScrollView` and Microsoft's `ScrollViewer` classes). This documentation describes properties that manipulate and can inspect limited aspects of the transfer function, but most details are absent.

Google Android

The following description highlights key elements of the transfer function in Android version 4.1 'Jelly Bean'.[1] Scrolling behaviour in widgets is built from several configurable components to perform input velocity tracking, gesture detection, and a deceleration function. To accommodate different device display densities, Android employs a measurement unit of 'density-independent pixels' (dp), where 1 dp is equivalent to one physical pixel on a 160 ppi (pixels per inch) screen. These values are scaled to the appropriate number of screen pixels for the display of a particular device.

The mechanics of these components is detailed in Study 2.

[1] `https://android.googlesource.com/platform/frameworks/base/+/jb-release/`

Simulators and Decompilation

When source code is unavailable, the vendor may provide device simulators or emulators that can be used to analyse behaviour. For example, Apple provides an iOS simulator that can be stimulated from other applications in the operating environment to simulate touch interaction. Furthermore, private APIs allow events recorded on the simulator to be replayed on an actual iOS device. Consequently, programmers can generate gestures on the simulator, edit the script describing the gestures (within certain constraints), and replay them on a device that is equipped to record the scrolling output resulting from the simulated gesture.

When a vendor does not provide tools supporting simulation or emulation, or if the reliability/fidelity of the tools is questionable, it is probable that the executable code can be disassembled and decompiled to reverse engineer a form of source code. For example, Microsoft ships the implementation of their scroll widgets in a virtual machine bytecode (CIL), which is amenable to disassembly.

Robotic Control

When simulators or emulators are unavailable, or if their fidelity is unknown, device behaviour is essentially a black-box, forcing analysts to guess how the device behaves based on unreliable observational methods. A major factor contributing to this problem is the lack of precision in human input control—the length, timing, speed, acceleration, direction, pressure, and other properties will vary substantially, regardless of attempts to control their consistency and accuracy.

To overcome this problem we used robotic control of touch contacts. SCARA robots (Figure 5) are particularly appropriate due to their high precision (±25 microns in three dimensions) and high maximum velocity (up to 11 m/s).

With programmable devices (such as phones and tablets) it is straightforward to write programs that log touch inputs and consequent scrolling output. However, when a device is non-programmable (e.g., an iPod Nano, which supports flick scrolling, but has no public methods for programming), it would be necessary to use high-speed video transcription to capture the scrolling output. It is important to log the contact data as well as the scrolling output in order to detect discrepancies between the intended robotic contact and that registered/processed by the device's touch sensor and firmware. For example, in this way we discovered discrepancies in the data describing a first contact after a pause of several seconds without contact (described earlier in Study 1).

STUDY 2: TRANSFER FUNCTION ANALYSIS AND RESULTS

We analysed the touch scrolling transfer functions supported by several contemporary devices using a variety of methods: Google Android functions using its source code (described earlier); Apple iPhone 4S and iPad 2 (both running iOS version 5.1.1) using the iOS Simulator on Mac OS X to emulate touch events that were subsequently recorded and replayed on actual

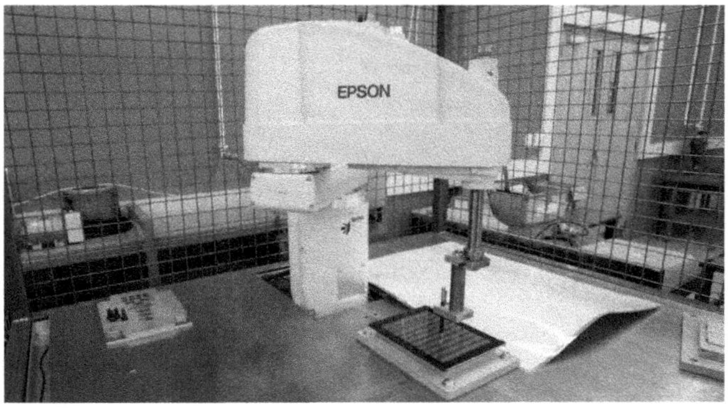

Figure 5. An an Epson G10-651S SCARA robot performing flicking gestures on an Apple iPad.

devices; and Apple iPhone 4S and iPad 2 using a SCARA robot. The iPhone and iPad were analysed using both robot and touch emulation methods to facilitate cross-validation of methods; any discrepancy in results would suggest errors or imprecision in either the robot method or in the touch emulation stemming from the iOS simulator.

Method

For robotic analysis we used an Epson G10-651S SCARA to manipulate a Wacom Bamboo Stylus (Figure 1). The Epson SCARA allows precise movements (±25 microns in three dimensions) at up to 8 m/s. Robot movement was programmatically controlled. Data describing contact information and resultant scrolling effect was logged on the device.

With robotic and emulated analysis (Apple devices), and with programmatic analysis (Android), we created a series of scripts to barrage the devices with batches of 16 repeated identical flick gestures. Each successive batch varied one input parameter at a time: *gesture length*, 10–160 mm; *gesture speed*, 5–200 cm/s; *clutch duration*, 100–1000 ms; and *direction*, up and down. We also examined other factors such as document length to rule out their influence. Multiple levels of each factor were initially investigated, and when the results indicated that threshold values were used to control transfer function behaviour, additional gesture-batch probes were created to successively hone in on the threshold values. After each gesture batch was complete, software logged any residual scrolling and then reset the scroll view for the next gesture batch.

Note that the set of parameters examined is not exhaustive, and other factors such as *acceleration*, *pressure*, and *contact area* may also influence behaviour. For expediency, we focused on the most likely parameters under default system settings.

Results

The Apple and Android behaviours maintain a 1:1 mapping between finger movement and output scrolling effect while the finger remains in contact with the display. Doing so is likely to maximise the user's perception of direct control of a physical surface while touching. Both systems also apply a 'slop' (Android) or 'hysteresis' (iOS) threshold that requires a minimum touch displacement before interpreting the input as a scrolling action (Android: 8 dp, iOS: 10 points[2]) to prevent accidental or noisy input channels. Once the finger leaves the surface, however, the transfer functions can substantially amplify the output scrolling effect (applying gain) to assist the user in traversing long distances. The conditions under which gain is applied, and the levels of gain, are described below.

Cross validation of the iOS transfer functions between the simulation and the robotic methods showed nearly identical results. The following subsections describe the primary parameters influencing the transfer functions (a complete set of data collected is also available[3]).

Flick Detection

Not every gesture is considered a 'flick' by the system; when the finger lifts from the screen, both systems examine recent touch information to classify the user's gesture as either a flick or a drag.

For Android, when the finger lifts off the display, up to the last 20 events over the last 100 ms are sampled and smoothed using the first order coefficient from a linear least squares solution to determine movement velocity. If this velocity exceeds a threshold of 50 dp, a 'fling' event is triggered. The velocity of the fling are used by a 'scroller' object to calculate the distance and duration (configurable with a coefficient of friction parameter).

On iOS, finger velocity is sampled between the movement events received. When the finger lifts from the touch surface, the velocity of two prior movement samples (v_t and v_{t-1}) are combined: $V_t = [(v_t + v_{t-1})/2] - [(v_t - v_{t-1})/4]$. If the resulting velocity is greater than 250 points per second, the gesture is classified as a 'flick'. A further transformation is then applied: $\frac{1}{4}V_t + \frac{3}{4}V_{t-1}$, which is used as the flick velocity for the gain and simulated friction calculations.

Cumulative Gain

Figure 6 shows the output scrolling velocity across time when a series of sixteen identical flick gestures (30 mm long at a velocity of 135 mm/s and with a clutching time of 500 ms) are issued on the touch surface—results are generated using iOS touch simulation (6a), iOS robotic control (6b), and Android simulation (6c). Thick lines in the figures show when contact is registered on the surface of the device. Note that the output velocity closely matches the velocity of the input control while surface contact is registered.

Both iOS and Android apply cumulative gain across gestures, but the manner in which they do so differs. With iOS, cumulative gain is applied as the finger lifts after the fourth repeated gesture, giving an instant acceleration to a higher velocity than that of the finger's movement. The scroll velocity is gradually

[2]The correspondence between points and physical pixels is determined by a device dependent 'scale factor' (either 1 or 2 on current non-'retina' and 'retina' devices, respectively).

[3]`http://cortex.p.gen.nz/reserach/scrolling`

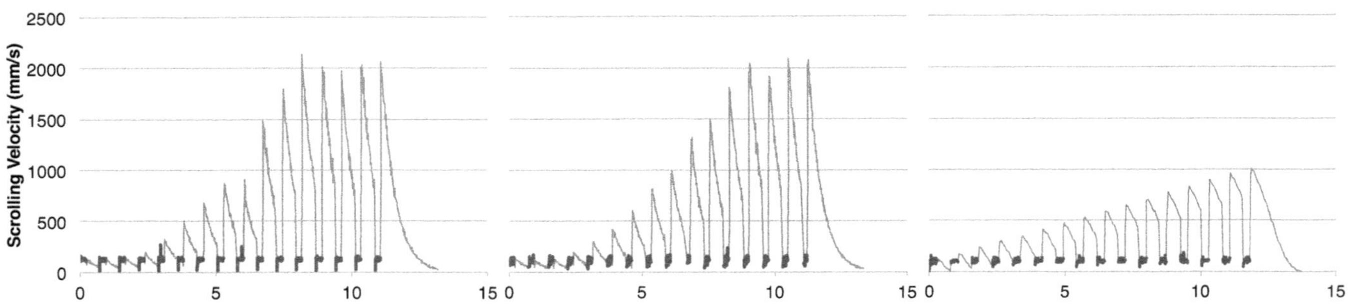

(a) iOS Simulator. (b) iOS Robot. (c) Android Simulator.

Figure 6. Scrolling velocity across time (seconds) recorded following repeated gestures of 30 mm length, 135 mm/s velocity, and 500 ms clutch time using: (a) the iOS simulator, (b) iOS via. SCARA, and (c) Android code execution. Thick lines indicate touch contact.

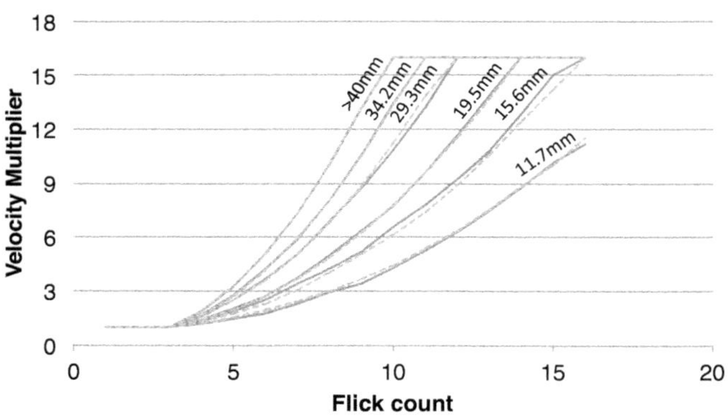

Figure 7. iOS (iPhone) velocity multiplier across successive flicks at different levels of gesture length and two levels of velocity (135 mm/s: dashed lines; and 300 mm/s: solid lines).

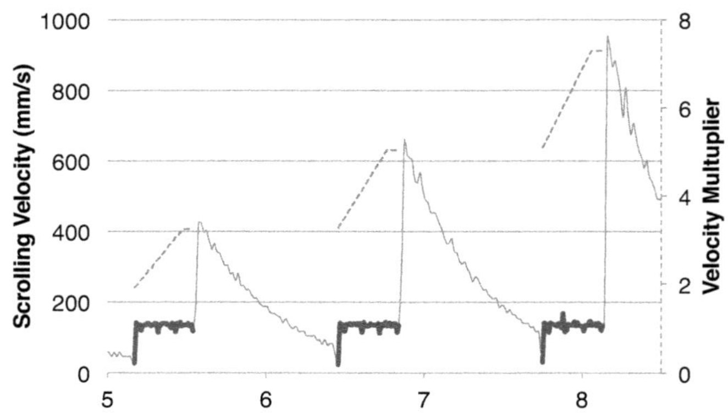

Figure 8. A detail of scrolling velocity from Figure 6a, shown with the value of the velocity multiplier (red, dashed line).

attenuated while contact is off the display, simulating friction. The iOS plots (Figures 6a and 6b) show that gain is capped; in this case after the 12th gesture.

When an Android Scroller's 'flywheel' function is enabled, any residual scroll velocity remaining during deceleration is added to the velocity of the next flick (Figure 6c). Unlike iOS, Android begins this amplification on the second flick and does not cap the maximum level of gain. Figure 6c shows scroll velocity gradually increases when receiving identical gestures to those used in Figures 6a and 6b. More precisely, Android approximates the actual residual scroll velocity based on the time spent since the previous flick gesture and the duration of contact for the current one, and adds it to the last flick velocity.

We found no evidence that the iOS transfer function attends directly to clutch duration, except for applying an $\sim$900 ms timeout between gestures to be considered part of a gesture series. Android incorporates clutch time as a component of the deceleration effect.

Gesture Length and Direction

The cumulative gain applied across flicks on iOS is controlled by a multiplier on the flick velocity. Figure 7 shows how the value of this multiplier increases across successive flicks as the length and velocity of each flick increases. Only gesture length was found to influence the rate at which the multiplier increases, with longer gesture lengths (up to a maximum of $\sim$40 mm) increasing the velocity the fastest. The multiplier was progressively raised until it reached a cap of 16×.

This behaviour can be seen in Figure 8, which shows detail of the scrolling velocity and the velocity multiplier across the fifth to seventh repeated gesture. Note that input and output velocity are identical while the finger is in contact, but the multiplier increases during this contact until release, when it is applied. More precisely, the value is incremented from the fourth contact onward by $\frac{1}{480}(k-1)$ for each point of finger movement (where k is the number flicks made in the series) until it reaches the cap. The cap is 1 before the fourth flick, 16 from the tenth onward, and $cap(k) = cap(k-1) + 0.45(k-1)$ for the intervening values.

Our analyses showed no difference in the application of gain across scroll direction, except that all methods reset cumulative gain across gestures when scroll direction changed.

Simulated Friction

Simulated friction effects slow the scroll velocity while the finger is out of contact with the surface. Figure 9 shows the

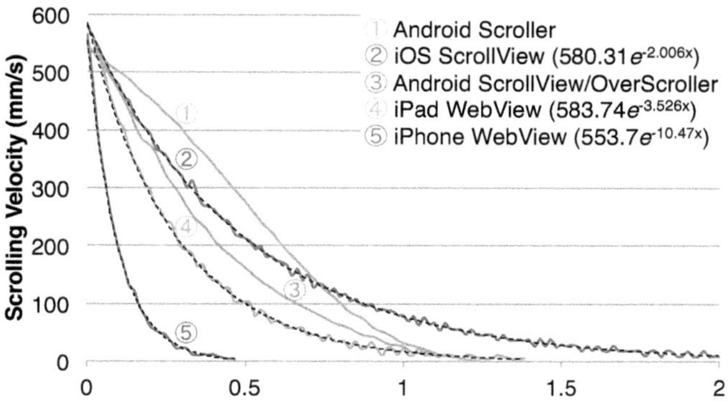

Figure 9. Friction/deceleration effects across time (seconds) following release on the iPad and iPhone with a `UIScrollView` (e.g., lists) and `UIWebView` (e.g., web browser), and the two scrollers provided on Android.

observed fall off curves with iOS, which vary with the type view displaying the content (`UIScrollView` for lists, and `UIWebView` for web content), and is configurable by developers (via. the `decelerationRate` property of `UIScrollView`). Exponential regression curves show accurate models of the observed behaviour, explaining more than 98% of the variance in all cases. `UIScrollView` effects are identical between the iPad and the iPhone; however, the `UIWebView` applies higher levels of friction on the iPhone.

Android's deceleration function depends on the 'scroller' used by the widget. Those that are provided by the system use either an `OverScroller` (scroll, list, and web view widgets) or a `Scroller` (gallery and text view widgets). Their behaviour can be customised, but the curves produced by their default parameters are shown in Figure 9. Regression curves did not produce accurate models of the observed behaviours; each class pre-computes a spline curve from piecewise functions.[4]

DISCUSSION

The results exposed the primary components of the iOS and Android touch scrolling transfer functions. We developed methods to analyse the transfer functions, conducted a human factors study to understand how users choose to control scroll velocity and to establish the range of values that should be used to probe the devices, and we deployed the methods to analyse the implementations of contemporary devices.

We revealed both substantial similarities and differences between iOS and Android. Similarities include: the maintenance of 1:1 correspondence between finger and scroll velocities while in contact; the application of cumulative gain across successive gestures; and progressive retardation of scroll velocity when the finger is out of contact. Differences include the iOS use of a capped scroll gain multiplier that is applied after the fourth successive flick gesture, while Android simply adds any residual scrolling velocity to the current gesture's velocity.

[4] `core/java/android/widget/OverScroller.java`, lines 606–637; `core/java/android/widget/Scroller.java`, lines 75–99.

Opportunities to Improve Scroll Transfer Functions

A primary reason for exposing these transfer functions is to facilitate their iterative refinement. Our results highlight three main opportunities for doing so, as follows.

In-Contact Gain. There are interesting opportunities in relaxing the 1:1 mapping of finger motion to scroll motion during contact. Figure 6 shows that the scroll velocity is continually slowed to that of the finger during contact. This is appropriate when scrolling slowly, because it helps maintain a sense of direct manipulation, but beyond some threshold it is unlikely that users will notice a breakdown of the mapping—allowing amplified scroll velocities throughout the drag and clutch operations. Implementing this relaxation would require careful design to ensure that a tap and hold gesture to stop scrolling was interpreted as such, at the user's expected scroll position.

Clutch-Time Dependent Gain. The human factors study suggested that users reduce clutch time (increasing gesture frequency) when they want to scroll faster, which could be explicitly incorporated as a parameter in gain functions.

Document-Length-Dependent Gain. Cockburn et al. [5] allows a 1:1 mapping at slow rates of input expression and a gain level that is determined by document length at high rates of input. This approach seems appealing for mobile devices that have small viewports and potentially very long views.

Facilitating Rigour in Touch Scrolling Studies

Another reason for exposing the transfer functions is to facilitate experimental rigour in touch scrolling studies. The methods described in this paper allow researchers to establish the functions used in any system used for baseline comparison. We recommend that future researchers examining touch scrolling systems report at least the following components of their experimental transfer functions: (1) the mapping used while the finger is contact with the display; (2) the function used to apply gain; (3) the deceleration function; and (4) the device resolution, and how physical touch movement is mapped to display pixels.

We are also releasing the data tables collected in our study, revealing the range of touch input we tested and the complete system response, and the source code to several tools used in gathering this data. These tools and data are available at: `http://cortex.p.gen.nz/reserach/scrolling`.

Limitations of Robotic Testing

SCARA robots provide a method of controlling and testing touch sensitive devices that do not allow direct programmatic control. While they allow extremely accurate control over the timing and location of discrete contacts, our experience suggests their velocity control is less stable. Our model allowed two modes of control, 'Continuous Path' (CP) and 'Point-to-Point' (PTP). In PTP mode the arm stops at each specified point in (x, y, z) space, while in CP it interpolates between points and attempts to maintain a constant velocity. Although it allows extremely rapid acceleration (up to 5 m/s^2, rocking its 2 tonne concrete mounting block), the resultant velocities logged on the device were not as constant as desired (see Figure 6b). Despite this limitation, robotic analysis revealed similar results to those generated with the simulator. It is worth noting that for closed devices, such as the Apple Magic Trackpad, robot control may be essential to analyse behaviour.

CONCLUSIONS

Touch scrolling is a fundamental component of mobile interaction, yet there has been little public research into how current methods achieve their behaviour. This is a problem for researchers, as they lack information on which to base iterative improvements, and experimental comparisons against contemporary systems may be confounded by failing to attend to a key parameter embedded in closed, proprietary systems. We have presented methods that can be used to reveal the parameters employed by touch scrolling transfer functions, and used the results of a human factors study to inform an examination of Apple iOS and Google Android touch scrolling transfer functions. We found interesting properties in both the human interaction features that change with a user's scrolling intentions, and the properties of touch input that are attended to by the system. These methods and results, together with the data tables and software accompanying the paper, provide a firmer foundation for research seeking to improve touch scrolling transfer functions and validate their effectiveness.

ACKNOWLEDGEMENTS

This work was supported by a Royal Society of New Zealand Marsden Grant 10-UOC-020.

REFERENCES

1. Aliakseyeu, D., Irani, P., Lucero, A., and Subramanian, S. Multi-flick: an evaluation of flick-based scrolling techniques for pen interfaces. In *Proc. CHI '08*, ACM (2008), 1689–1698.
2. Ausbeck, Jr., P. J., US. Patent No. 7446754. U.S. Patent and Trademark Office (Washington, DC, 2008).
3. Baglioni, M., Malacria, S., Lecolinet, E., and Guiard, Y. Flick-and-brake: finger control over inertial/sustained scroll motion. In *Proc. CHI EA '11*, ACM (2011), 2281–2286.
4. Casiez, G., and Roussel, N. No more bricolage! Methods and tools to characterize, replicate and compare pointing transfer functions. In *Proc. UIST '11*, ACM (2011), 603–614.
5. Cockburn, A., Quinn, P., Gutwin, C., and Fitchett, S. Improving scrolling devices with document length dependent gain. In *Proc. CHI '12*, ACM (2012), 267–276.
6. Harrison, C., Schwarz, J., and Hudson, S. E. Tapsense: enhancing finger interaction on touch surfaces. In *Proc. UIST '11*, ACM (2011), 627–636.
7. Hinckley, K., Cutrell, E., Bathiche, S., and Muss, T. Quantitative analysis of scrolling techniques. In *Proc. CHI '02*, ACM (2002), 65–72.
8. Hinckley, K., and Wigdor, D. Input technologies and techniques. In *The Human-Computer Interaction Handbook: Fundamentals, Evolving Technologies, and Emerging Applications*, J. A. Jacko, Ed., 3rd ed. CRC Press, 2012, ch. 9.
9. Hinckley, K. P., Bathiche, S. N., Cauthorn, J. H., and Sinclair, M. J., U.S. Patent No. 6690365. U.S. Patent and Trademark Office (Washington, DC, 2004).
10. Hinckley, K. P., and Cutrell, E. B., U.S. Patent No. 7173637. U.S. Patent and Trademark Office (Washington, DC, 2007).
11. Johnson, J. A. A comparison of user interfaces for panning on a touch-controlled display. In *Proc. CHI '95*, ACM Press/Addison-Wesley (1995), 218–225.
12. Kwon, S., Choi, E., and Chung, M. K. Effect of control-to-display gain and movement direction of information spaces on the usability of navigation on small touch-screen interfaces using tap-n-drag. *Int. J. Ind. Ergonomics 41*, 3 (May 2011), 322–330.
13. Lee, J., Lee, D., and Chung, M. K. Evaluation of mapping functions for one-handed flick operations on a mobile device. In *Proc. MobileHCI '11*, ACM (2011), 123–131.
14. Malacria, S., Lecolinet, E., and Guiard, Y. Clutch-free panning and integrated pan-zoom control on touch-sensitive surfaces: the cyclostar approach. In *Proc. CHI '10*, ACM (2010), 2615–2624.
15. Ording, B., Forstall, S., Christie, G., Lemay, S. O., and Chaudhri, I., U.S. Patent No. 7786975. U.S. Patent and Trademark Office (Washington, DC, 2010).
16. Quinn, P., and Cockburn, A. Zoofing! Faster list selections with pressure-zoom-flick-scrolling. In *Proc. OZCHI '09*, ACM (2009), 185–192.
17. Quinn, P., Cockburn, A., Casiez, G., Roussel, N., and Gutwin, C. Exposing and understanding scrolling transfer functions In *Proc. UIST '12*, ACM (2012), 341–350.
18. Smith, G. M., and schraefel, m. c. The radial scroll tool: scrolling support for stylus- or touch-based document navigation. In *Proc. UIST '04*, ACM (2004), 53–56.
19. Tu, H., Wang, F., Tian, F., and Ren, X. A comparison of flick and ring document scrolling in touch-based mobile phones. In *Proc. APCHI '12*, ACM (2012), 29–34.
20. Zhai, S., and Smith, B. A. Multistream input: an experimental study of document scrolling methods. *IBM Systems Journal 38*, 4 (1999), 642–651.
21. Zimmerman, J., and Martino, J. A., U.S. Patent No. 6690387. U.S. Patent and Trademark Office (Washington, DC, 2004).

Controlling Widgets with One Power-up Button

Daniel Spelmezan[1,2] **Caroline Appert**[2,1] **Olivier Chapuis**[2,1] **Emmanuel Pietriga**[1,3]

[1] INRIA
91405 Orsay, France

[2] Univ Paris-Sud & CNRS (LRI)
91405 Orsay, France

[3] INRIA Chile (CIRIC)
7561211 Santiago, Chile

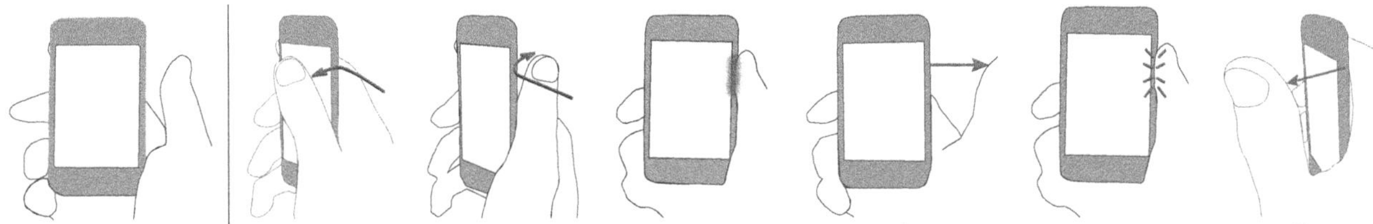

		(a)	(b)	(c)	(d)	(e)	(f)
EVENTS	*initial*	*discreteDown* (proximity)	*discreteUp* (proximity)	*continuousDown* (pressure)	*continuousUp* (proximity)	*click* (pressure)	*quickRelease* (proximity)

Figure 1. Gestures performed on and around the *Power-up Button*.

ABSTRACT
The Power-up Button is a physical button that combines pressure and proximity sensing to enable gestural interaction with one thumb. Combined with a gesture recognizer that takes the hand's anatomy into account, the Power-up Button can recognize six different mid-air gestures performed on the side of a mobile device. This gives it, for instance, enough expressive power to provide full one-handed control of interface widgets displayed on screen. This technology can complement touch input, and can be particularly useful when interacting eyes-free. It also opens up a larger design space for widget organization on screen: the button enables a more compact layout of interface components than what touch input alone would allow. This can be useful when, e.g., filling the numerous fields of a long Web form, or for very small devices.

Author Keywords
Mobile device; Proximity input; Pressure input

ACM Classification Keywords
H.5.2 [Information Interfaces and Presentation]: User Interfaces - Input devices and strategies (e.g., mouse, touchscreen)

INTRODUCTION
Touch input enables users to interact with display surfaces in a straightforward manner, by directly manipulating content and controlling widgets with their fingers. This simple interaction paradigm has favored the wide adoption of touch input on mobile devices. However, it has some limitations. First, accommodating control widgets reduces the area dedicated to the display of actual content, a resource that is already scarce on small devices. Second, users face occlusion and precision issues inherent to direct finger input [9]. This makes touch input inadequate in some contexts. For instance, users cannot operate their device eyes-free even for simple operations. Browsing songs in a music player, discarding an incoming phone call, or using the device as a remote controller to perform basic actions on a public display, requires taking the device out of one's pocket and looking at it.

A number of alternatives to touch input have been investigated, that expand interaction to the back of the device [1, 5, 9], to its sides [6, 10], and to the space above and around it [2, 4, 7, 8]. Many of these alternatives, however, are not very practical, no matter how interesting they might be. Instrumenting the finger with additional hardware [4] is inconvenient; around-the-device interaction [2, 7] does not allow users to both hold and operate the device with a single hand. Introducing physical buttons on the device's sides does not cause such issues, but their limited expressive power makes them better at complementing touch input rather than at providing full interface control [6]. One option would be to increase the number of such buttons, but this approach is impractical for small devices [5]. Another option is to extend the expressive power of those buttons.

Our *Power-up Button* enables users to perform numerous actions using a single controller located on the side of the device adjacent to the thumb. The controller does not occupy more space than a regular button would, yet provides a much higher level of expressive power compared to scroll wheels and joysticks that were used in some commercial devices. The *Power-up Button* consists of one proximity sensor superimposed on one continuous pressure sensor. Combined with the gesture recognizer we developed, it allows users to trigger a set of four discrete events and two continuous events using simple gestures performed on and around the button while operating the device with a single-hand (Figure 1). A single *Power-up Button* enables users to control, e.g., a music player eyes-free: pause and resume playback, adjust volume settings, and navigate both within and across songs.

UIST'13, October 6–9, 2013, St. Andrews, United Kingdom.

http://dx.doi.org/10.1145/2501988.2502025

We first give descriptions of our hardware prototype and event recognizer, that enables the *Power-up Button* to discriminate 2D gestures even though the underlying technology is based on one-dimensional sensing capabilities. We then explain how events were consistently mapped to actions that allow users to control all widgets of an application, providing an alternative to touch input when the latter is not practical; and conclude with directions for future work.

HARDWARE PROTOTYPE

Figure 2 shows the hardware prototype. The sensing hardware comprises four components: a force-sensitive resistor (Interlink Electronics FSR400 Short), an infrared proximity sensor (Vishay VCNL4000) that is mounted on a Sparkfun breakout board, an Arduino Pro Mini, and a custom-designed printed circuit board. Our sensor layering is similar to that of [3, 8], with one significant difference: our hardware detects continuous pressure input instead of switch-on/off events, and continuous proximity input instead of hovering.

The casing for the pressure sensor was produced by a 3D printer (Figure 2-a). This casing has a gap of 2 mm where the sensor and a thin piece of rubber are inserted. The rubber uniformly translates the applied pressure to the sensor's active area, which has a diameter of 5 mm.

The proximity sensor has an integrated ambient light sensor and signal processing circuit for suppressing ambient light by signal modulation. Its nominal sensing range is 200 mm. This sensor is placed inside a casing that was produced by a laser cutter. At the top of the casing is a small window (5×5 mm), which is centered above the proximity sensor at a distance of 2 mm (Figure 2-b). The window constrains the sensor's cone-shaped detection zone to an angle of $\sim \pm 20°$, and decreases the detection range to $\sim$50 mm for the user's thumb.

The printed circuit board (Figure 2-c) is powered by an iPod touch 4G (iOS 5.0). This board has an op-amp based circuit that linearizes the output of the pressure sensor. The Arduino samples sensor data at 25 Hz and sends the measurements to the iPod over the serial port. The iPod applies a low-pass filter and normalizes the output from both sensors.

The output of the proximity sensor depends on the properties of the sensed object, including reflectivity, size, material, color, and inclination inside the detection zone. To calibrate the sensor for our setup we measured the actual distance to one of the author's thumb at intervals of 5 mm, and linearly interpolated between the sensor readings.

The dimensions of the prototype button is $20 \times 16 \times 11$ mm ($L \times W \times H$), which matches the size of the large breakout board where the proximity sensor is mounted. It could actually be made much smaller in more advanced prototypes, as the sensing unit is tiny ($3.95 \times 3.95 \times 0.75$ mm).

GESTURES AND INTERACTION EVENTS

To demonstrate the potential of the *Power-up Button*, we designed a set of gestures that can be discriminated using the technology described above when the button is operated using the thumb of the hand that holds the device (Figure 2). We considered both motor and physiological aspects, ending up

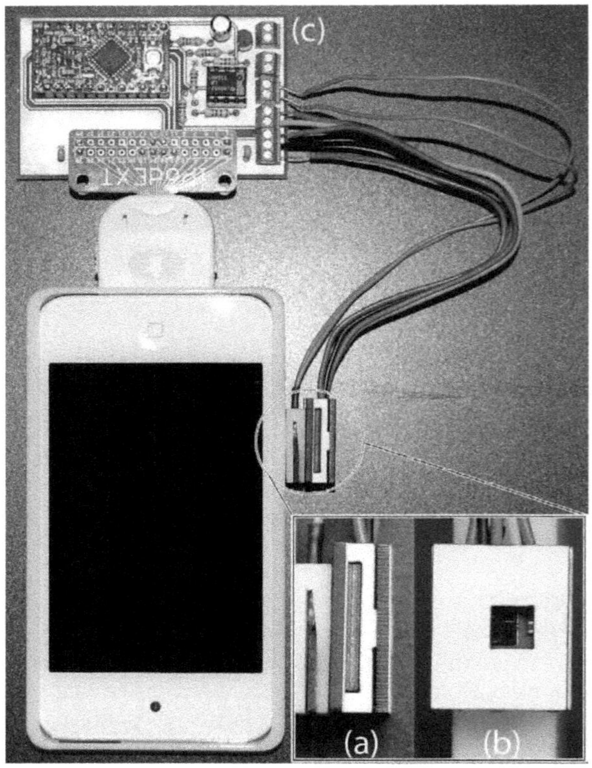

Figure 2. Our prototype, equipped with a button for sensing pressure and proximity. The sensors are placed inside custom-built plastic casings. (a) Side view of the pressure and proximity sensors. (b) Front view of the window above the proximity sensor. (c) Circuit board.

with a set of gestures that are easy to perform and that will not cause too much fatigue even when performed in sequence. To control the *Power-up Button*, users move their thumb within the device's plane towards or away from the button (Figure 1-(c,d,e)), and out of the device's plane towards either the front or the rear of the device (Figure 1-(a,b,f)). We implemented a recognizer to discriminate between these two-dimensional gestures with one-dimensional sensing capabilities only.

Gesture Recognizer

Our recognizer is implemented as a finite state machine in which final states are one of the following interaction events: *discreteDown*, *discreteUp*, *click*, *quickRelease*, *continuousDown* and *continuousUp*. Transitions are triggered by input variations on the pressure and proximity sensors. For the two continuous events, a first-order control is initiated as soon as the corresponding state is reached, letting users adjust the rate by varying the pressure intensity or the distance to the button.

Events and Pressure

To recognize *click* and *continuousDown* events, the *Power-up Button* analyzes the profile of the normalized pressure intensity that the thumb applies to the device. When the user starts pressing the force sensor, the state machine waits for a short amount of time (500 ms)[1] to decide if the pressure is released or sustained. Releasing the pressure before the timeout occurs triggers a *click* event if the initial force exceeded 1N. If

[1]This value minimizes accidental activation of rate-based control.

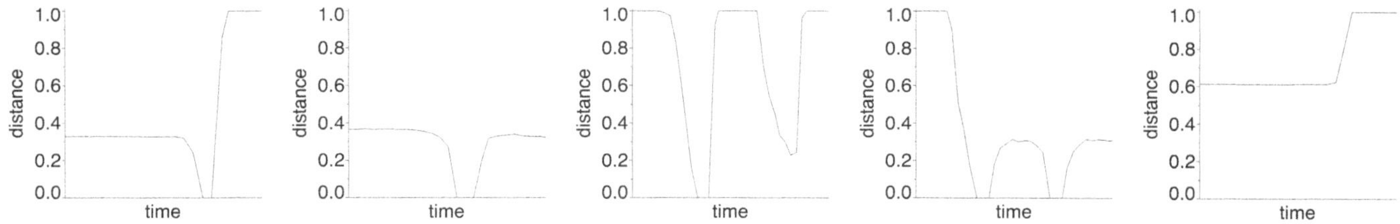

(a) *discreteDown* (b) *discreteUp* (c) *discreteDown*$^+$ (d) *discreteUp*$^+$ (e) *quickRelease*

Figure 3. Proximity profiles for discrete events (time scale = 1 sec). *discreteDown*$^+$ **and** *discreteUp*$^+$ **show two consecutive gestures (time scale = 1.5 sec).**

the pressure is sustained, the state machine triggers *continuousDown*, enabling pressure-dependent *continuous* control.

Events and Proximity

The *Power-up Button* analyzes the profile of the normalized distance between the device and the thumb. The distance is $d = 1$ if the thumb is too far away from the sensor's detection zone (`OutOfRange`), $d = 0$ if the sensor is occluded (`Touch`), and $d \in]0..1[$ if the thumb is close to the button (`Prox`). In addition, our algorithm examines how the distance changes over time ($\Delta d = d_t - d_{t-1}$, uniform sampling frequency) to detect changes in direction ($\Delta d > 0$ and $\Delta d < 0$) and gesture speed.

This low-level input allows our recognizer to identify the *discreteDown*, *discreteUp*, *quickRelease* and *continuousUp* gestures. The main challenge lies in discriminating orthogonal gestures *discreteDown* and *discreteUp*, as the proximity sensor only captures the orthogonal distance between the thumb and the edge of the device. We call these gestures orthogonal because the thumb is leaving the device's plane either towards the front of the device (*discreteDown*) or towards the rear of the device (*discreteUp*). Figure 3-(a,b) shows typical sensor readings for these gestures. Both gestures must begin in the proximity range (`Prox`), touch the button (`Touch`) and leave the device's plane in one direction or the other. This final part of the movement can be discriminated because of the anatomy of the hand, that makes moving the thumb away from the user (adduction) harder than moving it towards her (abduction). This results in sensing `OutOfRange` for *discreteDown* gestures and `Prox` for *discreteUp* gestures.

The recognizer for *discreteDown* and *discreteUp* accepts several profiles for a single gesture, making the repetition of such gestures in clockwise and counter-clockwise directions easier to perform. The initial position for both gestures becomes optional, allowing users to start their gesture either in proximity range `Prox` (Figure 3-(a,b)) or `OutOfRange` (Figure 3-(c,d). For *discreteDown*, users can either touch the button or pass close enough to it in mid-air (Figure 3-(c)). Below are typical sequences of low-level events that trigger discrete navigation events ($\nearrow$) in our state machine:

Two *discreteDown* performed in a row (Figure 3-(c)):

`OutOfRange` $\rightarrow$ `Touch` $\rightarrow$ `OutOfRange` $\nearrow$
$\rightarrow$ $\texttt{Prox}_{(\Delta d \neq 0)}$ $\rightarrow$ `OutOfRange` $\nearrow$

Two *discreteUp* performed in a row (Figure 3-(d)):

`OutOfRange` $\rightarrow$ `Touch` $\rightarrow$ $\texttt{Prox}_{(\Delta d > 0)}$ $\rightarrow$ $\texttt{Prox}_{(\Delta d \leq 0)}$ $\nearrow$
$\rightarrow$ `Touch` $\rightarrow$ $\texttt{Prox}_{(\Delta d > 0)}$ $\rightarrow$ $\texttt{Prox}_{(\Delta d \leq 0)}$ $\nearrow$

Figure 3-e shows that the *quickRelease* gesture is easily recognized based on a speed threshold at which the thumb must leave the $\texttt{Prox}_{(\Delta d = 0)}$ without touching the button ($\Delta d > s$ with $s = 0.5 \cdot (1 - d_{t_{initial}})$). Finally, the *continuousUp* gesture is recognized when the thumb remains in the detection zone for more than 500 ms.

Controlling Widgets

To evaluate the expressive power of our button, we demonstrate how the set of interaction events it generates can be used to control any widget of an existing graphical application. Table 1 lists the set of widgets commonly available on small devices[2] and how we can use *Power-up Button* events to fully control them. As we do not rely on touch input to detect which widget owns the focus, interaction events must also be dedicated to navigation in the widget hierarchy.

- *click* selects a widget. For a group of widgets, this event drills down to widgets that are located one level deeper in the widget hierarchy (navigation from parent to child).
- *discreteUp* and *discreteDown* increase and decrease the current value of a widget by one unit. For a group of widgets, these events move the input focus to the previous or next widget that are located at the same level in the widget hierarchy (navigation between siblings).
- *continuousUp* and *continuousDown* increase and decrease the current value of a widget using rate-based control.
- *quickRelease* moves up to widgets located one level up in the widget hierarchy (navigation from child to parent).

Figure 4 illustrates a scenario in which a user sets the value of a radio button that is not visible in the current viewport, which is scrollable. At the beginning, the viewport is outlined in blue to indicate that the input focus is set to the scrollbar. A *click* turns the outline of the viewport red (scrolling enabled) so that the user can bring the set of radio buttons in the viewport through the use of *continuousUp* and *continuousDown* events. She then *clicks* to move the input focus from the scrollbar to the first widget that is visible in the viewport (i.e., the group of radio buttons) and *clicks* again to access the level where she can control the set of individual buttons. She then navigates to the second radio button with a *discreteDown* event and *clicks* to select it. Finally, *quickRelease* commits the button selection and brings the input focus back to the group of radio buttons.

[2]Our implementation uses the iOS widget set. A *stepper* is an iOS widget that contains *plus* and *minus* buttons to set a discrete value.

EVENTS	BUTTON	STEPPER	CHECK BOXES AND RADIO BUTTONS	COMBO BOX	SLIDER	SCROLLBAR
click	invoke		select option	show list box	begin tracking	begin scrolling
quickRelease				dismiss list box	end tracking	end scrolling
discreteUp		increase value	highlight prev. option	highlight prev. list item		
discreteDown		decrease value	highlight next option	highlight next list item		
continuousUp					increase value*	scroll upward*
continuousDown					decrease value*	scroll downward*

* *(rate-based, speed depends on pressure level / proximity)*

Table 1. Interaction events and their mappings to navigation actions for widget control.

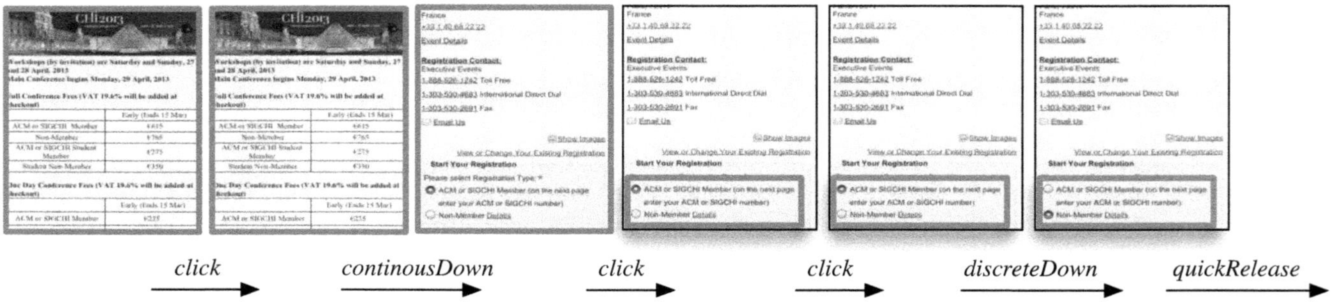

Figure 4. Selecting radio button Non-Member.

The exercise that consists of controlling all widgets is a demonstration of what the *Power-up Button* could do, pushed to the extreme. The more relevant use cases we envision involve a smaller set of controls like, e.g., discarding phone calls or controlling a music player. The latter basically consists of a slider for setting the volume, and a few buttons for navigating across and within songs. Considering only gestures relevant to the application or widget in focus can also help increase the recognizer's accuracy.

CONCLUSION AND FUTURE WORK

The *Power-up Button* is a physical button that combines pressure and proximity sensing to complement touch input on a mobile device for, e.g., controlling an application eyes-free. We present a set of simple gestures and a recognizer that let users manipulate an application on their mobile phone by moving the thumb of the hand that holds the device. We demonstrate that such a button alone can provide users with an expressive power high enough to control all usual widgets.

However, the *Power-up Button* has a few limitations. First, this technology captures mid-air gestures with one-dimensional sensing capabilities only. While it is an important advantage to be pluggable on any small device, it also means that the recognizer is potentially more permissive. Second, as with any gesture-based interaction, users must have clues to discover and learn possible gestures. This requires adding feedback to guide and assist novice users. However, informal testing with colleagues revealed that a short initial training period makes users both able to control the *Power-up Button* without triggering accidental events and to get a clear understanding about how to control a collection of widgets.

As future work, we plan to conduct controlled empirical studies to formally evaluate the two aspects mentioned above. We also plan to explore other gesture sets and other physical configurations for the button. For instance, the *Power-up Button* could be positioned on the back side of a mobile device to perform gestures with the index finger. It could also be placed on one of the sides of a mouse to enable users to operate it with the thumb while operating all over controls as usual.

REFERENCES

1. Baudisch, P., and Chu, G. Back-of-device interaction allows creating very small touch devices. In *Proc. CHI '09*, ACM (2009), 1923–1932.
2. Butler, A., Izadi, S., and Hodges, S. Sidesight: multi-"touch" interaction around small devices. In *Proc. UIST '08*, ACM (2008), 201–204.
3. Choi, S., Han, J., Lee, G., Lee, N., and Lee, W. Remotetouch: touch-screen-like interaction in the tv viewing environment. In *Proc. CHI '11*, ACM (2011), 393–402.
4. Harrison, C., and Hudson, S. E. Abracadabra: wireless, high-precision, and unpowered finger input for very small mobile devices. In *Proc. UIST '09*, ACM (2009), 121–124.
5. Harrison, C., and Hudson, S. E. Minput: enabling interaction on small mobile devices with high-precision, low-cost, multipoint optical tracking. In *Proc. CHI '10*, ACM (2010), 1661–1664.
6. Holman, D., Banerjee, A., Hollatz, A., and Vertegaal, R. Unifone: Designing for auxiliary finger input in one-handed mobile interactions. In *Proc. TEI '13*, ACM (2013).
7. Kim, J., He, J., Lyons, K., and Starner, T. The gesture watch: A wireless contact-free gesture based wrist interface. In *Proc. ISWC '07*, IEEE Computer Society (2007), 1–8.
8. Rekimoto, J., Ishizawa, T., Schwesig, C., and Oba, H. Presense: interaction techniques for finger sensing input devices. In *Proc. UIST '03*, ACM (2003), 203–212.
9. Wigdor, D., Forlines, C., Baudisch, P., Barnwell, J., and Shen, C. Lucid touch: a see-through mobile device. In *Proc. UIST '07*, ACM (2007), 269–278.
10. Wilson, G., Brewster, S. A., Halvey, M., Crossan, A., and Stewart, C. The effects of walking, feedback and control method on pressure-based interaction. In *Proc. MobileHCI '11*, ACM (2011), 147–156.

Improving Structured Data Entry on Mobile Devices

Kerry Shih-Ping Chang[1], Brad A. Myers[1], Gene M. Cahill[2], Soumya Simanta[2], Edwin Morris[2], Grace Lewis[2]
[1]Human-Computer Interaction Institute, [2]Software Engineering Institute
Carnegie Mellon University
{ kerrychang, bam }@cs.cmu.edu, { gmcahill, ssimanta, ejm, glewis }@sei.cmu.edu

ABSTRACT
Structure makes data more useful, but also makes data entry more cumbersome. Studies have found that this is especially true on mobile devices, as mobile users often reject structured personal information management tools because the structure is too restrictive and makes entering data slower. To overcome these problems, we introduce a new data entry technique that lets users create customized structured data in an unstructured manner. We use a novel notepad-like editing interface with built-in data detectors that allow users to specify structured data implicitly and reuse the structures when desired. To minimize the amount of typing, it provides intelligent, context-sensitive autocomplete suggestions using personal and public databases that contain candidate information to be entered. We implemented these mechanisms in an example application called Listpad. Our evaluation shows that people using Listpad create customized structured data 16% faster than using a conventional mobile database tool. The speed further increases to 42% when the fields can be autocompleted.

Author Keywords
Personal information management (PIM); data entry; structured data; mobile devices; autocomplete

ACM Classification Keywords
H.5.2 [Information interfaces and presentation]: User Interfaces – Input devices and strategies.

General Terms
Human Factors; Design.

INTRODUCTION
Various mobile personal information management (PIM) applications have been developed to support people's need to record and consume information while they are on the go. One of the key factors that affects whether users can and will use a PIM application is how easily, quickly and accurately they can *enter* data [4,6,10,11]. The most intuitive way, suggested by prior research, is simply entering data as an unstructured note [4,6,11]. Unstructured PIM applications (e.g., Memo, Notes) let people enter any text they want, and the simple "open and type" interaction is often preferred by mobile users who are in a hurry and can only devote limited attention to the devices [6,18].

UIST'13, October 8–11, 2013, St. Andrews, United Kingdom.
Copyright 2013 ACM 978-1-4503-2268-3/13/10 $15.00.
http://dx.doi.org/10.1145/2501988.2502043

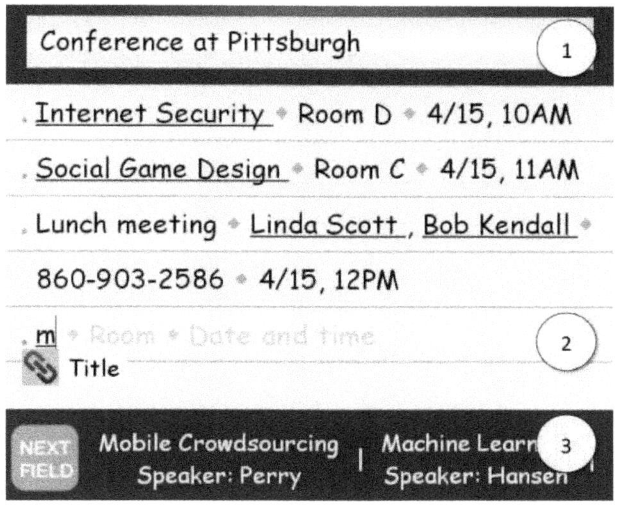

Figure 1. The Listpad Interface. The user is creating a list of to-dos for a conference, where (1) is the title box, (2) is the editing interface, with a label for the type and name of the field currently being edited, and a gray hint text suggesting a possible structure for the current item, and (3) Listpad's autocomplete suggestions are to the right of the "Next Field" button, showing possible values for the current field.

In contrast, structured PIM applications (e.g., Contacts, Calendar) provide a set of predefined fields for users to fill in when creating a new item. This structure increases the usefulness of the data and is highly utilized in these applications to support searches, visualization of the data in calendar and map views, and data sharing. However, entering structured data is much less flexible than entering an unstructured note. Structured applications force users to enter data in predefined formats. They also restrict the kinds of data that can go into the application by their predefined fields, while prior studies have found that a significant amount of what people want to store does not fit into these fields [4]. Most structured PIM tools have limited customizability, and even if customizable, require users to tediously go through multiple screens to select types and names for each field (e.g., see [9,14,20]). These downsides drive users back to entering unstructured data into the "notes" field in these applications or just into a separate plaintext note [6], but then the data loses all the advantages of structure. The ease and flexibility of unstructured text input motivates us to rethink the design of interfaces for creating structured data on mobile devices. We show that we can bring the benefits of unstructured input to make creating structures and entering structured data more fluid on mobile devices.

Another barrier to effective use of both structured and unstructured PIM applications on mobile devices is the difficulty of typing on today's touchscreen keyboards, which can be slow and error-prone due to the small key size and the lack of tactile feedback [18]. Minimizing the amount of typing can thus be beneficial to users in their interactions with mobile applications. Most smartphone input systems have a built-in dictionary that provides word suggestions for users as they type, or dictionary-based input techniques like ShapeWriter [21] and Swype [19]. This occasionally proves useful, but much of the data entered in PIM applications is likely to not be in the dictionary (e.g., proper names, addresses, etc.). Similarly, speech recognition systems do not work well for entering data into PIM applications because speaking this kind of data is often awkward and error-prone.

An insight that motivates our design is that when users are entering a value, they are often giving the system more information about the data than just the text. For example, the data typed in a "location" field in a Calendar is likely to be some place's name. The data a user types often already exists in some local or online database. For example, the entry in the "location" field is likely to be some place in the current city and could be looked up using a web service such as Google Places. Similarly, the data in a "person" field is likely to be found in that user's contact book or on Facebook or LinkedIn. Another insight is that data is often highly inter-dependent, so that after entering one value, the next value entered might also be about the same thing, such as the phone number of a location. Because entering structured data inevitably increases users' cognitive load compared with entering an unstructured note (even simply reading the structure requires more attention from the user), we hypothesized that we could compensate users by using these local and online public databases to provide *autocomplete suggestions* based on the structure to save users some of the effort in typing.

To demonstrate our approach to addressing these issues, we developed Listpad, a new PIM application for Android that allows users to create customized structured data in an unstructured, notepad-like interface, where users can add structure to the text as they are entering the data (see Fig. 1). By "structure," we refer to both the format of individual fields (like a time or place or plain-text), and also the specific sequence of fields in a record (such as that a record has a time, a name, then a location). Our goal is to design an interface that places minimum restrictions on how users can enter data, so that it is as quick to use as a note application, while still providing the ability to let users easily create and reuse customized structure for data. Furthermore, Listpad eases data entry by augmenting the built-in autocomplete mechanism with a rich collection of local and online data based on the type of the field and the user's context.

In summary, this paper makes the following contributions:

- A novel data entry technique that lets users create and reuse flexible customized structures and enter structured data in an unstructured, notepad-like interface.
- The novel use of public and personal databases as sources to provide autocomplete suggestions, which are then used to provide rich hyperlinking among data items and subsequent contextual autocompletes.
- An instantiation of these techniques in an Android application called Listpad, which was shown in a within-subjects evaluation to be faster compared to a mobile notepad application (AK Notepad [1]) and a conventional mobile database application (Memento [14]). People were 16% faster using Listpad to create customized structured data in the phone compared to using Memento. In addition, with the help of autocomplete, this difference increases to 42% faster, and Listpad was even able to outperform the notepad application by 18% when autocomplete can help with data entry.

SCENARIO

Here we describe a scenario where Jim, a graduate student, is attending a conference in Pittsburgh and uses Listpad to record a list of his activities. We use this scenario to give an overview of how someone could use Listpad. Later we will explain our system in detail.

A day before the conference, Jim wants to make a to-do list for the conference, such as interesting talks he wants to attend, on his phone. Jim notices that the conference provides a mobile app, but the app does not let him add any personal items like his lunch meeting or make any annotations. So he uses Listpad, which provides fully flexible data entry. Jim first downloads the conference programs in an Excel file and imports it to Listpad's database. Then he starts a new list in Listpad. Jim begins by entering some talks he wants to attend. Jim sets Listpad to use the conference program he just imported as the source of autocomplete suggestions. Now as he types, he sees that Listpad searches the programs and suggests talks that match what he has entered. Fig. 1 at 3 shows that just after typing a single letter, Jim finds the full name of the talk among the suggestions. Jim quickly autocompletes the field, and Listpad further suggests other information about the talk, such as the time, location and speaker. Again, Jim uses the suggestions and enters the talk's time and room. Jim enters a few more talks and his lunch meeting and saves the list. By default Listpad displays data in a list view (Fig. 5 at 1). Jim chooses to display his list in a day view (Fig. 5 at 4), where he can view the talks by their times of the day in a calendar. Later while listening to a talk, Jim thinks of a cool idea. He opens his list in Listpad, and quickly adds a new field to the talk and types in the idea.

During the conference, Jim talks to his friends and finds that several universities have parties at night. He wants to quickly write down the times and locations of the parties. Jim opens the same list in Listpad and starts adding the party information. When he is about to enter where the party is held, he links Listpad to Google Places, an online location database. Now as he types, Listpad uses Google Places as the source to provide autocomplete suggestions (Fig. 3 at left). The places returned are sorted by their distances from his current location. Again, just after a few taps Jim finds the place he wants among the suggestions, and using the autocomplete he quickly fills in the name, address and phone number of each place. Later in the day, Jim opens Listpad and views his list in a map view (Fig. 5 at 2), which plots the restaurants on a map using their locations.

RELATED WORK

The design of our data entry technique is inspired by prior studies on how people record information in real life. Research has found that a large amount of information that people record is in the format of a *list*, which consists of multiple items with similar structure. Examples are to-do lists, desired items, login/password information, etc. [2,4,13]. Therefore, Listpad particularly focuses on supporting mobile entry of lists of this kind of information. The need for structured data has been well addressed in [11], as the authors argue that structured data is the "*lingua franca*" of many daily applications from music players to productivity applications, all of which rely on specific data structures to provide their services. Most complaints about structured PIM tools are due to two reasons. First is that these tools are often too rigid and lack customizability as to the kinds of data that can be stored. Studies have found that much personal information is unable to fit into the existing structures provided by applications [4]. In order for the data to be storable, the user sometimes must pick an arbitrary field in which to put the data, even though the description of the field does not match the data [6]. As a result, a key feature we designed in our mechanism is to let users define customized structures to fit their needs. Also, studies reported that people naturally tend to record information tersely, often using abbreviations or partial sentences [2,13], whereas most structured tools require rigid and full entry of data or force users to enter data through standard GUI widgets.

Another problem identified in the literature is that entering structured data requires more cognitive load for the users because they have to read extra GUI elements [11] and enter the information into the rigid, structured format, which users may want to avoid if they need to enter data in a hurry [6]. Therefore, Listpad lets users type in data in their preferred formats and uses flexible data detectors [12,17] to extract the values. For example, Listpad recognizes date information in different formats, such as "Sept. 19" or "9/19", and does not force users to enter dates through date input widgets. Listpad also lets users link self-defined fields to local or online databases which are then used for autocomplete suggestions. Many mobile systems and computer text editors (such as Emacs) provide autocomplete using dictionary words or the users' typing history. Listpad's autocomplete is different in that its autocomplete suggestions come from data sources that are relevant to the user-defined structure, and can be from on-line web services. For example, the autocomplete suggestions for a "book" field could be book names from Google Books.

The idea of letting users enter structured data using unstructured text has been explored in several prior systems for desktop computers. Inky [15] is a command line tool for entering data quickly into well-known structured desktop PIM applications such as Email or Calendar. The interface provides graphical feedback to suggest what field the data will go into. Listpad focuses on a different problem, which is to facilitate creating *customized* structured data instead of entering data into existing structures in other applications. Jourknow [11] lets users enter plaintext notes and automatically adds context-related information to the note, such as when and where it is created. Similar to Inky, Jourknow can extract structure from plaintext and use it as input for well-known structured PIM tools based on predefined grammars, such as creating a calendar event by typing "Meet David at 3pm". Again, our work is different from Jorknow as we focus on the creation of customized structured data. Jourknow also allows users to create customized structured data using Notation3 syntax [3], which uses many extra punctuation characters. We feel that such syntax is not intuitive to learn and also is not suitable to use on mobile devices because it would require much extra typing and frequent switching between the letter and symbol keyboards.

Mobile database applications are designed for creating customized structured data on mobile devices. Examples are commercial tools such as Memento [14], Tap Forms [20] and HanDBase [9]. All of these use a traditional form-based interface and a similar procedure to set up the database as is used on desktop computers: they require the user to first specify the type and name of each field in the database, and then use entirely different screens to enter the data items. Users can add or delete a field after the database is created, but the changes will affect all the items in the database. In contrast, Listpad lets users do all these operations in the same editor and uses data detectors to help identify the type and name of a field, so that users do not necessarily have to specify everything explicitly. Listpad also allows users to flexibly add or delete any field in an individual item without affecting other items. Most of the mobile database applications allow users to build links to cross-reference to other entries in its database. Selecting a desired entry requires the user to go through multiple form interfaces. In Listpad, we make such linking more fluid and extend the idea to include connecting to online web services. To make the interface more integrated, we use these entries as autocomplete suggestions for the user while typing in the data.

Despite having many shortcomings, mobile database applications are apparently successful commercial products. For example, Memento, which we used for our user study, has between 100,000 to 500,000 installs on Google Play, showing that there is a demand for entering and viewing structured data on mobile devices.

LISTPAD

In Listpad, we define a *list* as a collection of *items*. Each item has one or more customizable *fields*. Whereas most lists have a fairly uniform structure, this is not a requirement – in fact every item could have a different structure. In the scenario, Jim's list has items of three different structures: one for presentations having the fields *time*, *talk*, and *room*, the lunch meeting with *event*, *people*, *phone number*, and *time*, and some items about parties with *time*, *place*, *address* and *phone*. All lists are created and edited in a notepad-like interface (Fig. 1 and Fig. 2). The title of the list can be added or modified through the textbox at the top. Below this textbox are all items in the list. Each item starts with an orange bullet, which is automatically displayed when the user enters a new line. Within an item, fields are separated by the blue diamond symbols, which are inserted using the blue "Next Field" button (Fig. 3 at 1).

Just as if it was a plaintext editor like Notepad, the user can edit the text freely, for example to delete a diamond symbol or a new line anywhere using the regular delete key, or moving the cursor and adding a diamond or new line anywhere. This would be useful to split a string into two fields, or delete a return to merge two items into one. We designed this feature to make creating structured data a very flexible process. The user can always type in unstructured data if in a hurry, or the user might copy and paste unstructured data from the web or elsewhere. Later, the user can add structure to the data by inserting the blue diamonds and then viewing and editing the list in the structured layout.

The decision to use a special character (the blue diamond) as the separator for fields was made to avoid the use of more common characters that often appear *in* data. For example, many data types use commas internally, such as names ("Olsen, Jr.") addresses ("3rd Street, Apt. 3"), and dates ("Oct. 7, 2012"). Rather than requiring users to disambiguate and correct possibly erroneous parsing or use unfamiliar special characters (as in [11]), we decided to add an easy-to-hit and unambiguous button to separate fields.

Listpad uses a label under the text that the cursor is at to show the type and name of the field (Fig. 2 at 1). The label icon represents the field type, and the label text is the field name. The default type and name are "text" and "Field *n*", where *n* is the number of the field in an item (Fig. 2 at 4). However Listpad will detect and change the type and name based on the value that the user types (see next section). Alternatively, the user can tap on the label to bring up a dialog box, where the field type can be changed through a dropdown list and the field name can be edited (Fig. 2 at 2).

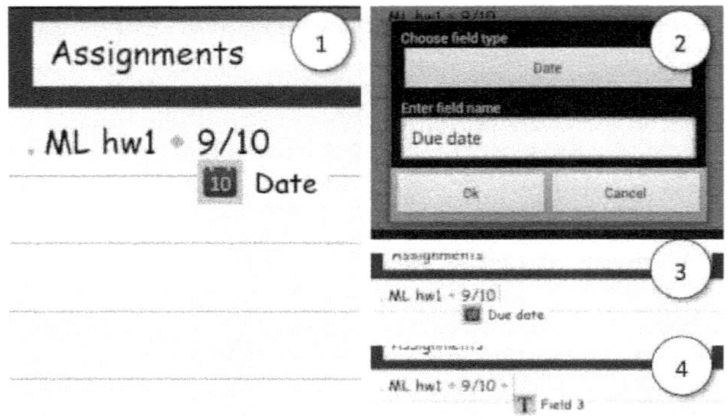

Figure 2. (1) The user is editing a list that has one item with two fields. The label shows the type (the calendar icon) and name (the label text) of the second field, both being "Date", because Listpad detects that the field value ("9/10") is in a date format. The user could tap on the label and bring up (2) the dialog box to change the field type and name manually. (3) The label updates after the user changes the field name to "Due date". (4) The user presses on the "Next Field" button to start a new field. The label moves to the new location and shows the default field type "Text" and name "Field 3".

When the user moves the cursor to another field by either tapping on it or inserting a diamond symbol to start a new field, the label moves to the new location and shows the new current field type and name (Fig. 2 at 3 and 4).

Data Detectors

Listpad currently supports 10 different data types: *text*, *number*, *phone*, *date*, *time*, *date and time*, *address*, *email*, *website*, and *link*. Except for "link" (see the next section) and text, for the rest of the eight data types Listpad provides corresponding data detectors to try to recognize the type of the current field value to see if it matches any of the predefined formats. When the system detects a type format other than a basic string, it updates the field type and name on the label in real time. Note that this use of data detectors is quite different from current smartphones or prior research [12,17], where the type is used to provide actions when tapping on the data in a plaintext note. In Listpad, the inferred types are persistent, and are used to define the structure for fields. (Tapping on the fields can also still invoke actions in Listpad, as discussed below.)

The default field name for a field is the name of the type (e.g., Fig. 2 at 1). Sometimes the default names are sufficient. For example, in our scenario when Jim enters the time of a talk, he just uses the default field name "date and time". If the user manually assigns a type to the field using the dialog box, the data detectors will no longer run. If the value that the user enters disagrees with the manually-specified type format, Listpad assumes that the user wants to consider the new value to be of the specified type, and simply allows it. For example, there might be a phone number format that Listpad currently does not recognize, such as an international number. This is an example of a design decision in the direction of flexibility and ease of entry. Of

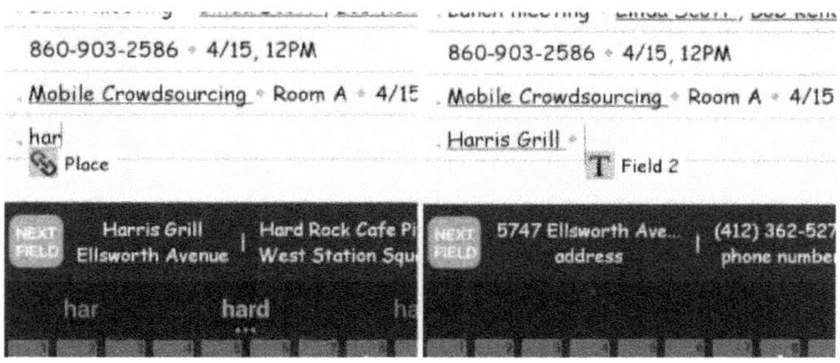

Figure 3. (Left) After the user sets the field to link to Google Places, the default field name becomes "Place", and search results from Google Places are shown as autocomplete suggestions. (Right) When the user starts a new field, Listpad shows options for the user to import more information about the selected place from the linked database.

course, *uses* of that item will be affected if Listpad does not understand the format. For example, unrecognized dates and times will not be shown in the calendar view. But some uses still work. For example, tapping on a phone number will always open the dialing application and attempt to dial that number, even if Listpad does not recognize the phone number format. In the future we plan to make the data detectors customizable by the users.

Autocomplete Suggestions

In addition to data detectors, another process that constantly runs in the background while the user types is the autocomplete engine that generates suggestions. Android has built-in autocomplete suggestions using a dictionary that comes with the default keyboard (Fig. 3 at left, the blue text). Listpad's autocomplete suggestions are placed right above Android's autocomplete suggestions and next to the "Next Field" button (Fig. 1 at 3 and Fig. 3), and can be scrolled horizontally left and right to see more suggestions. The user can choose from either list. Listpad's autocomplete suggestions come in the following categories.

Built-in Keywords

Listpad has a set of built-in keywords that are used by the data detector to recognize certain types, such as date keywords ("January" ~ "December", "Monday" ~ "Friday", "/"), time keywords ("AM", "PM", ":"), and address keywords ("Road", "Street", "Avenue"…). These are added to the autocomplete list to facilitate entering these types of data. For example, "AM" will be shown if the field value seems to be in a 12-hour clock format. Considering the fact that mobile information needs are highly contextual, we add three more "context keywords" in the autocomplete word list, which are "today", "current time" and "current location". These words, when in the suggestion bar, are shown in blue to signify that they are not the actual text that will be inserted into the field.

Values of Fields in the Same List

The same fields in items in the list may reuse values entered into that field in previous items. For example, when entering an assignment list, the value in the *course* field may be

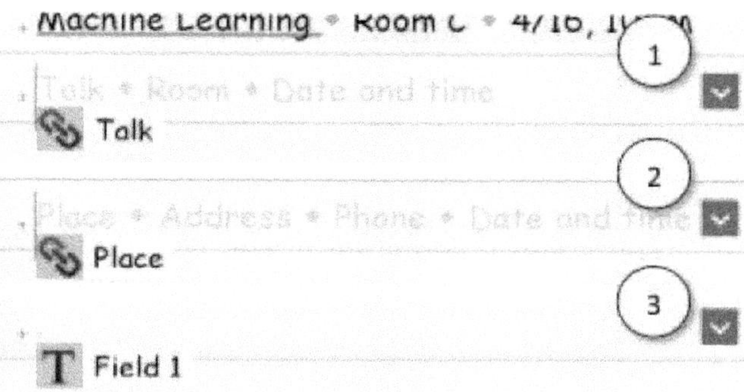

Figure 4. (1) When the user starts a new item, Listpad uses gray text to suggest a possible structure for it. (2) The user can tap on the brown button to switch to a different structure, or (3) choose a blank structure to start define a new item.

repeated in multiple items because a course can have multiple assignments. Listpad searches for fields in other items that have the same field type and name as the current field, and includes their values as autocomplete suggestions.

Local and Online Databases

As mentioned earlier, in Listpad we explore the possibility of using local personal and online databases based on our observation that data is often highly interdependent. The idea is that if the data is already somewhere in another database, then the user should be able to simply reference the value instead of retyping it. Unlike the other autocomplete engines already discussed that look for possible suggestions independent of the field types, the autocomplete engine for local and online databases is only activated when the user has set the field type to "link" to a particular data source. This design decision was made for two reasons: first, sending a request to the databases on every keystroke would use up system resources because it requires Internet access. Second, searching through multiple on-line databases using the incomplete string that the user enters might return many irrelevant results. Asking the user to pick from these results may cause more cognitive load than just typing in the value. Therefore, we thought it was an appropriate tradeoff to require the user to help Listpad narrow down the search space to a particular kind of data so that Listpad can present accurate suggestions.

To set up the link to a local or online database, the user first sets the field type to "link" using the dialog box shown in Fig. 2 at 2, and then selects the desired source name from a list of available sources in a popup menu. After the user picks a source, the default field name changes to match the source (e.g., Fig. 3 at left). Then when the user types in the field, the field value is sent as the query string to the connected data source every time that the user enters a character, and the returned search results are shown as autocomplete suggestions.

Listpad uses an extensible architecture that allows new data sources to be added, often without programming [5]. Some example sources we have used with Listpad include two local – Android's People (the contact app) and Listpad's

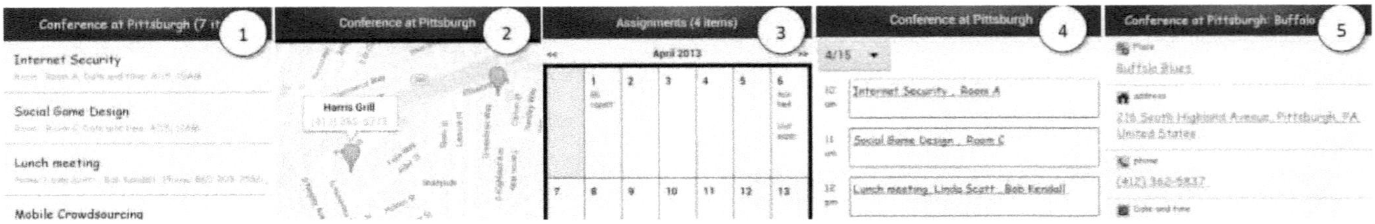

Figure 5. Listpad supports viewing a list in (1) a list view, (2) a map view, (3) a calendar month view, (4) a calendar day view, and a note view (not shown here, which displays a list as what it looks like in the editor). Clicking on an item entry in (1), (3), (4) or a marker in (2) opens (5) a detail view that shows all fields in the item, including the field types and names.

own databases - and five online databases – Google Places, Rotten Tomatoes (a movie database), Last.fm (a music database), Google Books, and Wine Searcher. The users can add new sources for autocomplete to Listpad in two ways. First, the user can import Excel files to Listpad's database, as Jim does in the scenario. Second, if the source is a remote online database, Listpad's architecture allows it to be added to the system as a plug-in. Furthermore, Listpad provides a web configuration tool, called Spinel, which allows end-users to create these plug-ins for Listpad without writing any code. The design of this architecture is explained in detail elsewhere [5]. Here, we will only briefly introduce it in the implementation section below.

After the user selects an autocomplete suggestion, Listpad not only inserts the full string for the user, but also provides autocomplete options for *other* fields of the selected item when the user moves to the next field (Figure 3 at right). If the user taps on a suggestion, not just the field value but also the field type and name will be autocompleted. Besides helping the user quickly enter other related information of an item, these autocompletes also serve another purpose: autocomplete has become a popular way for users to *explore* an information space and therefore serves as implicit queries [16]. For example, if a user has just entered "Bob" in the first field of an item, Listpad will then provide in its autocomplete menu the other information that it knows about Bob as possible values for other fields, which could help users understand what information is available and also helps them ensure that they have the right person without having to leave Listpad.

Entering a New Item and Reuse of Existing Formats

The user can press the "return" key to start entering a new item. Gray text appears on the new line to suggest a possible structure of this new item, based on the existing items in the same list (Fig. 4 at 1). The user can tap on the brown arrow button to cycle among the different structures that have been used for other items in this list (Fig. 4 at 2), and the last choice is a blank structure (Fig. 4 at 3) to start to define a new structure.

Viewing a List, Sorting and Searching

In addition to helping with the *entry* of the data through autocompletions, the structure of the data also enables Listpad to provide multiple views and sorting of the items, and actions when a user taps on items. Listpad provides:

1) A list view, where each item is displayed in a list layout showing its first field as the title and the rest of the fields in a line of small gray text under the title (Fig. 5 at 1). The user can sort the items in alphabetical order, number order (if the items have *number* fields), time order (if the items have *date* or *time* fields), and distances from the current location (if the items have *address* fields).

2) A note view, which shows the list just as in the editor. We provide this view in case the user only wants to enter unstructured notes. This makes Listpad fully capable of being used as simply a traditional notepad application.

3) A map view, where each item with an *address* field is plotted on a map showing its first and second non-address fields as a popup when the marker is tapped (Fig. 5 at 2).

4) A month view, where each item with a *date* or *date and time* field is displayed in a month calendar (Fig. 5 at 3), showing its first non-date field as the title.

5) A day view, which is similar to the month view, but for a single day. It displays items with a *time* or *date and time* field in a day calendar (Fig. 5 at 4).

In the list, map, month and day view, tapping on an item or a marker opens a detail view (Fig. 5 at 5) that shows all fields in the item, including the field types and names, in a list layout. In this view, Listpad provides actions on various types of data. For example, phone numbers are linked to the dialing application and addresses are linked to Maps. A link field is linked to its source item. For example, Place names from Google Places are linked to their Google Places webpage. Person names from the People contacts list are linked to their record in People.

Finally, Listpad currently supports free text search through all items. We are adding structured searching and filtering to the system, so that users will be able to search on individual fields or filter based on the structured value, such as only viewing places near me.

IMPLEMENTATION

Data structures

One of the challenges in implementing Listpad was to design an efficient database structure to store highly-dynamic, yet flexibly-structured data. We used db4o [7], an open source object-oriented database system, to host all of our data. In the database, each item in a list consists of a *value* object and a *format* object. The value object holds an ArrayList of the field values in an item. Each value object has an ID that links it to a format object that has an ArrayList of types and names that specify the types and names of the fields in the value object. Every time a new item is created, the system searches in the database to see if there is any existing format object that is the same as the newly created format object. If so, the system links the newly created value object to the existing format object, then stores only the value object. If not, then the system links the newly created value object to the newly created format object, and stores both of them in the database. Listpad uses Lucene [8] to do indexing and searching of text.

Adding new online data sources

Listpad accesses all online data sources through their official web APIs. Listpad uses two types of APIs for each source. One is a "search" API that searches the database by the query string. The other is a "detail" API that retrieves the full record of an item given its ID returned in the search result. To enable new data sources (new APIs) to be added dynamically without recompiling the system, each data source is stored as a separate JSON file that describes the usage of its APIs, including the authentication parameters, the request URLs, and the paths to the desired fields from the returned models. We called this JSON file a data source "plug-in". All plug-ins are put in a designated folder on the mobile device. When Listpad starts, it reads all plug-in files inside that folder to determine what sources are available. Installing a new data source requires simply putting a new plug-in file into that folder on the phone.

Currently, this plug-in architecture supports data sources that provide REST web APIs and return JSON data. Because the plug-in itself is just a JSON file, anyone who is familiar with how web APIs work can create a new plug-in using any text editor. We also provide a web-based configuration tool that lets people create a new plug-in using a web-based GUI without programming. Full details are described elsewhere [5].

USER STUDY

We evaluated the design of Listpad using a within-subject study. A key innovation in Listpad is allowing users to add structure to data on the fly while typing in a notepad-like interface. Therefore, we thought it would be interesting to compare Listpad with two different extremes – a conventional mobile database application that requires the structure to be defined beforehand and uses standard form interfaces for all editing, and a plain-text notepad application in which users only enter unstructured data. We hypothesized that Listpad would be slower than the notepad when structure was being created, but the time could be compensated for when Listpad could autocomplete the data by linking to a relevant source using the structure. We selected the Memento Database [14] for the mobile database application and AK Notepad [1] for the notepad application because of their high ratings on the Google Play marketplace. All participants used the experimenter's phone for the study, which is a Samsung Galaxy Nexus. Participants used Android's default keyboard, with its autocomplete using the built-in dictionary, to enter the data in all three applications.

Tasks

We designed five tasks to assess different aspects of our prototype system. All tasks relate to entering structured data into the phone. The data was presented to participants in a table on paper. For Listpad and Memento, participants had to enter an exact item as given, with the same field name, type and value for each field in the same order. If the field structure did not exist, participants had to create the structure themselves. For AK Notepad, however, because there was no notion of items and fields in the notes, we asked participants to ignore the field type and field name and simply enter the field values in order, to use commas to separate each field, and to press "return" to start a new item. From our observations, this is a common format when people create a list of things in their own notes.

The first task was to add two items to an existing "Account and Password" list. For both the first and second tasks, all needed structure was already set up in the existing list and therefore participants did not need to create or modify any of the structure. In the first task, participants typed the values into the correct fields. We used this task as a warm-up task and to ensure that participants understood Listpad's way of specifying structured data. The second task was to add two items to an existing "My CDs" list. This task was similar to the first one, but this time, Listpad linked the fields to Last.fm to provide autocomplete suggestions. We hypothesized that participants would enter data faster with Listpad, since this time the data could be autocompleted. The third task was to create a new list named "My shopping list" that has two items in it. This task required participants to create the structure in Listpad and Memento and manually enter the values. We hypothesized that with Listpad, participants would spend less time creating customized structured data than with Memento. The fourth task was to create a new list named "Restaurants" that has two items. This task was similar to the third one, but using Listpad participants only needed to set up the first field as a link field to Google Places, and the rest of the fields could be autocompleted. We hypothesized that Listpad would be much quicker than Memento with the help of autocomplete for creating the structure. The fifth task was to modify the "Restaurants" list by adding two new fields to it without the help of Listpad's autocomplete. We hypothesized that Listpad would help participants be quicker when modifying an existing structure compared to Memento. For each task, we designed three sets of data for the participants to enter using the three different tools. For tasks one to four, each data set had 82~87 characters. For task five, each data set had 27 characters. We randomly assigned datasets to tool to guard against any differences. We found no significant dif-

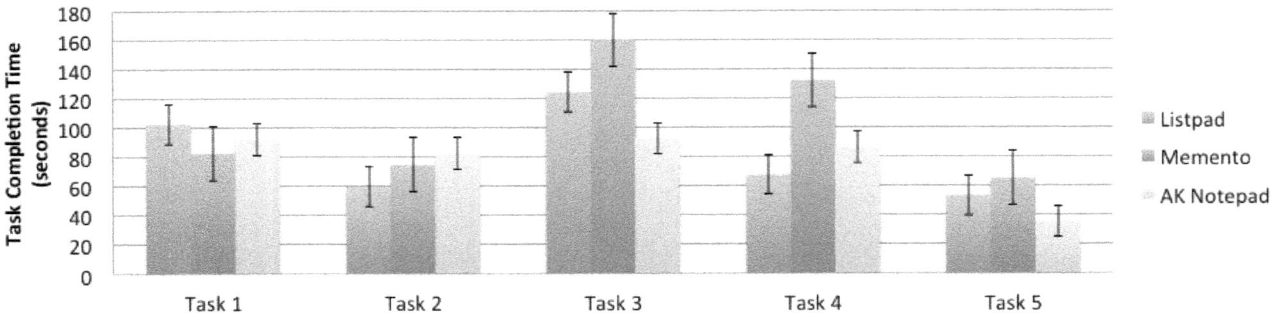

Figure 6. The average task completion time of Listpad, Memento and AK Notepad. Shorter bars are better.

ferences in the time that participants spent on each task entering different data sets, showing that we were successful at matching difficulty among the datasets.

Participants

Fifteen paid participants (ages 22-35) were recruited, all students or staff in our university. All participants used Android phones as their primary phones, so they were familiar with the Android UI in general. Participants rated their expertise with using computers and Android phones on a 7-point scale from "no experience" to "very experienced". The average rating for using computers for all participants was 6.67 and for Android was 5.6. None of the participants had used Memento or AK Notepad before. However, all participants had used other notepad applications, at least on regular computers, and they were all familiar with the form input interface because it is also used in other common Android applications such as People and Calendar.

Procedure

We randomized the order of the tools and the order of the data sets given to each participant. For each tool, the participants first received a short tutorial that covered how to create a list. We did not show participants the features in the tool that were irrelevant to the tasks, such as sorting and searching. The participants practiced with the tool as part of the tutorial. The data for the practice tasks was presented in the same table format as the real tasks, but the data structure was completely different. The whole tutorial took about 15 minutes for Listpad and Memento and 8 minutes for AK Notepad. After the tutorial, the participants began the first real task, as described above. The experimenter measured the time participants spent on each task. Participants were told to work quickly and carefully, and to enter the exact words that were on the sheets, except that they did not have to worry about upper and lower case. If the participants mistyped anything, they were asked to correct it. The correction time counted as part of the final task completion time. After finishing all five tasks, participants moved to the next tool, received the tutorial and did the tasks. After finishing all three tools, participants filled out a short survey to provide feedback. The study took between 60 and 75 minutes, depending on how fast the participant could type.

Results

Across all tasks, in addition to *performance* (time) we were evaluating the *usability* of the three tools by watching for any breakdowns and asking participants for their preferences. A paired-samples t-test was conducted to compare the time that participants spent on each task using different tools. The results are reported below and in Figure 6.

Task 1: Participants completed the task faster with Memento ($M=88.47s$, $SD=19.78$), than with AK Notepad ($M=93.74s$, $SD=17.7$) or Listpad ($M=101.47s$, $SD=21.75$). The difference between Memento and Listpad was significant ($t(14)=3.19$, $p<0.01$). We observed that some participants still appeared to be learning how to use Listpad during this first task. Because all participants were already familiar with entering data in a form interface, we suspect that the difference between Memento and Listpad on the first task was likely due to this learning effect. In all subsequent tasks, times in Listpad matched or beat Memento. The difference between Listpad and AK Notepad was not statistically significant.

Task 2: Participants spent significantly less time when using Listpad ($M=56.59s$, $SD=9.6$) than using Memento ($M=72.3s$, $SD=20.31$; $t(14)=5.55$, $p<0.01$) and AK Notepad ($M=76.52$, $SD=22.63$; $t(14)=5.31$, $p<0.01$). This result shows that participants understood how to use Listpad's autocomplete suggestions, and were able to use autocomplete to cut down their data entry time by an average of 24%. There was no significant difference between the Memento and AK Notepad times.

Task 3: Participants completed this task significantly faster using Listpad ($M=131.62s$, $SD=37.58$) than using Memento ($M=156.14$, $SD=29.89$; $t(14)=3.76$, $p<0.01$) by 16%. The result shows that the way Listpad lets people define structure while entering data could significantly shorten the time needed to create customized structured data. Both Listpad and Memento were slower than AK Notepad, where no structure is needed ($M=98.82s$, $SD=25.47$; $t(14)=4.89$, $p<0.01$; $t(14)=12.23$, $p<0.01$). The result confirms our hypothesis that specifying structure does require extra time.

Task 4: We found that Listpad's autocomplete significantly shortens the time participants needed to create and enter structured data. Participants were 42% faster using Listpad ($M=70.75s$, $SD=9.73$) than using Memento ($M=120.95s$, $SD=30.37$; $t(14)=9.01$, $p<0.01$) and 18% faster than using AK Notepad ($M=82.62$, $SD=20.04$; $t(14)=3.04$, $p<0.01$). The difference between Notepad and Memento was also significant ($t(14)=10.08$, $p<0.01$). The result shows that participants with the help of autocomplete could create structure and enter data even faster than creating an unstructured note that only contains the values of the fields. Although in order to get the autocomplete suggestions with Listpad, participants had to set up the structure for the first field, the time later saved by the autocomplete on subsequent fields was considerably more than the time spent defining the first structure.

Task 5: Participants completed this task significantly faster using Listpad ($M=55.32s$, $SD=11.81$) than using Memento ($M=65.27s$, $SD=13.3$; $t(14)=3.75$, $p<0.01$) by 15%. Participants spent less time using Notepad ($M=29.27$, $SD=10.9$) than both Listpad ($t(14)=8.78$, $p<0.01$) and Memento ($t(14)=13.32$, $p<0.01$). The result is consistent with the result in Task 3: Listpad helps people modify structure significantly faster than Memento, but it is still faster to have no structure at all.

Subjective Results

In the survey we asked participants to rate the three tools on a 7-point scale from "very hard" to "very easy" in various scales, including ease of *learning* and *entering and editing data*. Participants rated AK Notepad as the most easy-to-learn tool. It received higher rating ($M=6.13$, $SD=0.92$) than both Memento ($M=4.87$, $SD=1.3$; $t(14)=5.10$, $p<0.01$) and Listpad ($M=5.2$, $SD=1.42$; $t(14)=2.43$, $p=0.03$). For ease of entering and editing data, participants rated Memento as the hardest-to-use tool. It received lower rating ($M=4.73$, $SD=1.49$) than both Listpad ($M=5.93$, $SD=1.39$; $t(14)=2.55$, $p=0.02$) and AK Notepad ($M=5.47$, $SD=1.25$; $t(14)=2.13$, $p=0.05$). Listpad was rated highest, but the difference between Listpad and AK Notepad is not significant.

Finally, we asked participants to rate how they liked the tools on a 7-point scale from "don't like it at all" to "like it a lot". Participants rated Listpad ($M=6.21$, $SD=0.89$) higher than both Memento ($M=4.6$, $SD=1.18$; $t(14)=4.46$, $p<0.01$) and AK Notepad ($M=4.21$, $SD=1.37$; $t(14)=4.16$, $p<0.01$).

DISCUSSION

The study confirms several interesting possible use cases for Listpad in real life. All participants reported Listpad's autocomplete as the feature they liked the most among the three tools. They described the autocomplete to be "fast", "saved a lot of typing", and that it "makes finding and entering data a lot easier". On average, Listpad received the highest rating in "the ease of entering and editing data". Although we told participants not to worry about the upper and lower case of the data, many participants still tried to have the letters correctly capitalized. One person insisted on entering all the upper and lower case letters correctly. He later wrote in the survey that the *correctness* of the data was more important to him than the speed of entering data, so he really liked the autocomplete.

The main usability issue we found with Listpad was the delay caused by the network connection when showing the suggestions from online databases. The delay was not a problem for most participants, as their average speed of entering data was still faster using autocomplete even with the delay. We did find one participant who could type so fast that he had to pause for a noticeable amount of time to wait for the suggestions to show up. However, that participant still liked the autocomplete feature and said it was "fun to hit a button and have the whole address just pop up."

10 out of the 15 participants reported that they had notes or lists of items on their own phone. Participants' notes covered a wide range of topics. The most common ones were to-do and shopping lists, followed by lists of ideas, expenses, movies, books, songs/albums, food, contact details, reminders, login/password info, discount cards, favorite quotes and recipes. We were excited to see these examples because many of them include public information and could be easily entered and put into structures by using autocomplete from available web services. For example, information in a shopping list could be autocompleted using the data from Amazon or grocery store web data sources.

Participants liked that in Listpad they could create structure as they were entering the data, which they said was easier and more intuitive than Memento, where they had to use separate interfaces for entering data and creating the field structures. All participants successfully utilized the data detectors in Listpad to set up the structure, which saved time compared to Memento where they had to manually assign both a type and name for every field. Participants expressed interests in using Listpad in real life and suggested practical features they would like, such as connecting Listpad to Google Drive and grouping lists with folders.

Limitations

Our study has several limitations. First, the study was run in a quiet lab setting, which was different from real life where people are often distracted or interrupted by the environment. However, we suspect that this would affect all three tools and therefore would not change our main study findings. Second, in the study, we asked the participants to enter the exact same words as given. This requirement was necessary in order to compare data entry times, but it also violated the reality that people sometimes use abbreviations when entering data on mobile phone. For the tasks where Listpad did not provide autocomplete (tasks 1, 3, and 5), we believe this again would equally affect all three tools and should not change the comparative findings. For the tasks where Listpad did provide autocomplete (tasks 2 and 4), the time differences between Listpad and the other tools may decrease if abbreviations were allowed. However, it would not change our main findings about autocomplete, which is that it ensures that users can enter *correct* and *complete* data quickly. Finally, all our participants were fluent with typing on the touchscreen. For novice users who do not type on touchscreens well, using more GUI-like input widgets (such as a calendar widget) to enter some data may be faster and easier. We are considering adding a way to popup these kinds of widgets from Listpad's autocomplete bar.

CONCLUSIONS AND FUTURE WORK

We have presented a new data entry mechanism that facilitates creating customize structured data on mobile devices. It allows users to define structure while entering data using an unstructured, notepad-like interface, and uses data detectors to help determine the structure. The design was shown to be usable and more efficient than conventional mobile database applications and was preferred by experienced smartphone users. In addition, autocomplete using local and online data sources lets people create structured data even faster than entering unstructured notes in a note application.

Future work can be in many directions. First, we can extend the Listpad to allow storing multimedia data such as images and audio. Second, we can explore ways to automatically identify relevant local or online databases to use as autocomplete sources. One possibility is to use the list titles or tags. For example, lists having a "people" tag by default could link to Facebook's database. Third, we can allow syncing personal lists with their linked data sources after the lists are entered to keep them up to date. Using the conference scenario for example, if Listpad is linked to an online conference program database and one talk is moved to another room, the room information in user's personal list will automatically get updated. Finally, we can explore using Listpad-like data entry for conventional PIM applications like contacts. We feel that these interaction mechanisms are a starting point on the way to making many different kinds of data entry on mobile devices more efficient.

ACKNOWLEDGMENTS

We would like to thank Ruogu Kang for her help with the statistics for the paper. This material is based upon work funded and supported by the Department of Defense under Contract No. FA8721-05-C-0003 with Carnegie Mellon University for the operation of the Software Engineering Institute, a federally funded research and development center. This material has been approved for public release and unlimited distribution. DM-0000293

REFERENCES

1. AK Notepad on Android. https://aknotepad.com/
2. Bellotti, V., Dalal, B., Good, N., Flynn, P., Bobrow, D.G., and Ducheneaut, N. What a to-do: studies of task management towards the design of a personal task list manager. *Proc. CHI,* ACM (2004), pp. 735–742.
3. Berners-Lee, T. and Connolly, D. Notation3. http://www.w3.org/TeamSubmission/n3/
4. Bernstein, M., Van Kleek, M., Karger, D., and schraefel, m.c. Information scraps: How and why information eludes our personal information management tools. *ACM Trans. Inf. Syst. 26*, 4 (2008), 24:1–24:46.
5. Chang, K.S., Myers, B.A., Cahill, G.M., Simanta, S., Morris, E., and Lewis, G. A Plug-in Architecture for Connecting to New Data Sources on Mobile Devices. *Proc. VL/HCC,* IEEE (2013), to appear.
6. Dai, L., Lutters, W.G., and Bower, C. Why use memo for all?: restructuring mobile applications to support informal note taking. *CHI'05 extended abstracts* ACM (2005), pp. 1320–1323.
7. db4o. http://www.db4o.com/
8. Apache Lucene. http://lucene.apache.org/
9. HanDBase. http://www.ddhsoftware.com/handbase.html
10. Kalnikaité, V. and Whittaker, S. Software or wetware?: discovering when and why people use digital prosthetic memory. *Proc. CHI*, ACM (2007), pp. 71–80.
11. Van Kleek, M., Bernstein, M., Karger, D.R., and schraefel, mc. Gui --- phooey!: the case for text input. *Proc. UIST*, ACM (2007), pp. 193–202.
12. Lieberman, H., Nardi, B.A., and Wright, D. Grammex: defining grammars by example. *CHI'98 conference summary*, ACM (1998), pp. 11–12.
13. Lin, M., Lutters, W., and Kim, T. Understanding the micronote lifecycle: improving mobile support for informal note taking. *Proc. CHI*, ACM (2004), pp. 687–694.
14. Memento Database. http://mementodatabase.com/
15. Miller, R., Chou, V., and Bernstein, M. Inky: a sloppy command line for the web with rich visual feedback. *Proc. CHI*, ACM (2008), pp. 131-140.
16. Mooty, M., Faulring, A., Stylos, J., and Myers, B.A. Calcite: Completing Code Completion for Constructors Using Crowds. *Proc. VL/HCC*, IEEE (2010), pp. 15–22.
17. Nardi, B.A., Miller, J.R., and Wright, D.J. Collaborative, programmable intelligent agents. *Commun. ACM 41*, 3 (1998), pp. 96–104.
18. Oulasvirta, A., Tamminen, S., Roto, V., and Kuorelahti, J. Interaction in 4-second bursts: the fragmented nature of attentional resources in mobile HCI. *Proc. CHI*, ACM (2005), 919–928.
19. Swype. http://www.swype.com/
20. Tap Forms. http://www.tapforms.com/
21. Zhai, S. and Kristensson, P.O. The word-gesture keyboard: reimagining keyboard interaction. *Commun. ACM 55*, 9 (2012), 91–101.

DigiTaps: Eyes-Free Number Entry on Touchscreens with Minimal Audio Feedback

Shiri Azenkot, Cynthia L. Bennett, Richard E. Ladner
Computer Science & Engineering | DUB Group
University of Washington
Seattle, WA 98195 USA
{shiri, bennec3, ladner}@cs.washington.edu

ABSTRACT
Eyes-free input usually relies on audio feedback that can be difficult to hear in noisy environments. We present *DigiTaps*, an eyes-free number entry method for touchscreen devices that requires little auditory attention. To enter a digit, users tap or swipe anywhere on the screen with one, two, or three fingers. The 10 digits are encoded by combinations of these gestures that relate to the digits' semantics. For example, the digit 2 is input with a 2-finger tap. We conducted a longitudinal evaluation with 16 people and found that DigiTaps with no audio feedback was faster but less accurate than with audio feedback after every input. Throughout the study, participants entered numbers with no audio feedback at an average rate of 0.87 characters per second, with an uncorrected error rate of 5.63%.

Author Keywords
Eyes-free text entry, blind, touchscreen, mobile devices.

ACM Classification Keywords
H.5.2. Information interfaces and presentation: User interfaces — Input devices and strategies. K.4.2. Computers and society: Social issues – assistive technologies for persons with disabilities.

1. INTRODUCTION
Touchscreens are accessible to blind people with screen readers like Apple's VoiceOver [1], which provide continuous audio feedback to guide a user's interaction. To find a virtual button, for example, the user moves her finger across the screen as VoiceOver speaks descriptions of touched UI elements. Then, to press the button, the user performs a second gesture such as a double-tap. In addition to VoiceOver, researchers have proposed many other eyes-free interaction techniques [2,6,7,13,19,20], which also heavily rely on audio feedback.

UIST'13, October 8–11, 2013, St. Andrews, United Kingdom.

http://dx.doi.org/10.1145/2501988.2502056

Figure 1. A blind person enters numbers with DigiTaps. The white circles at the bottom of the screen mark her touch points.

Eyes-free methods that require the user's auditory attention can be difficult to use in noisy environments like a street corner, or quiet environments like a library where playing sounds is inappropriate. One can wear headphones to address these problems, but blind people often feel that headphones are clumsy and unsafe. Headphones can block sounds a blind person uses to perceive her environment, such as obstacles in one's path and traffic [3,25,27].

We introduce eyes-free interaction with *minimal audio feedback* that enables blind users to interact with a device with little to no auditory attention. In prior work, we developed minimal-audio methods for conveying directions for a wayfinding application that used only a touchscreen and vibration [2]. In the current paper, we explore eyes-free number input with minimal audio feedback. To our knowledge, we are the first to investigate eyes-free interaction with minimal audio feedback for blind people.

We present *DigiTaps*, an eyes-free number entry method with minimal audio feedback for touchscreen devices. DigiTaps can potentially be used in a variety of contexts: when making phone calls, interacting with automated voicemail systems, entering addresses in GPS-based applications, and entering personal identification numbers (PIN). To enter a number with DigiTaps, a user taps or swipes the screen with one or more fingers (e.g., a two-finger tap, a one-finger swipe), as shown in Figure 1. The DigiTaps gestures "feel" different, so people can discern whether they touched the screen with one finger or two. A user performs one to three gestures to enter a digit, according to a code that is derived from the semantics of the digits.

We evaluated DigiTaps as an eyes-free, minimal-audio input method in a longitudinal study with 16 people (six blind, ten sighted). Participants entered sets of digits with and without audio feedback. We found that removing audio feedback produced significantly higher entry rates, but also higher error rates. Participants entered digits at a mean rate of 0.87 characters per second (CPS) (SD = 0.32) with no audio feedback, and a mean uncorrected error rate of 5.6% (SD = 14.8). This seems much faster than VoiceOver, as we found in prior work that participants entered four-digit PINs in 7.5 seconds (about 0.53 CPS) [5].

In summary, our contributions include the design and evaluation of DigiTaps, a novel method for nonvisual number input with minimal audio feedback.

RELATED WORK

Eyes-free input has received much attention from the human-computer interaction community. Recent work has focused mostly on making touchscreens accessible to blind people, relying heavily on text-to-speech. By contrast, DigiTaps was designed and evaluated to support eyes-free entry with minimal audio feedback.

Tap2Count [11], a number input method by Hesselman et al., is a number entry method on large surfaces. Like DigiTaps, Tap2Count gestures relate to the digits semantics and seems appropriate for eyes-free entry with minimal audio feedback. To enter a digit with Tap2Count, a user touches the screen with the number of fingers of the input digit (two hands may be required). DigiTaps is better suited for a small screen than Tap2Count, where the user may be unable to touch the screen with more than 3 fingers.

The *de facto* standard eyes-free text entry method for smartphones is Apple's VoiceOver screen reader [1], which has interaction techniques that were first presented in Kane et al.'s Slide Rule [13]. Android devices have a similar screen reader called TalkBack [10]. There are no official estimates, but it is evident that VoiceOver has been broadly adopted by blind people. VoiceOver enables a user to explore the screen speaking the labels of UI elements that are being touched. To make a selection, a user performs a second gesture: a double-tap or split-tap (touching a second finger to the screen). One must listen carefully when searching for buttons on the screen, which can be especially difficult when selecting one of many small keys on the on-screen keyboard. In prior work, we found that blind people entered text with VoiceOver at a rate of just 4.5 words per minute [4]. Other work confirms that text entry is arduous and error-prone [4,6,21].

Several eyes-free systems have been proposed for blind people to address the difficulty of text entry with VoiceOver [2,5,6,7,19,20]. For example, Bonner et al [6] designed No-Look Notes, an eyes-free keyboard with larger targets, where two button presses are required to enter one character. They found that entry rates with No-Look Notes were still low, at 1.32 words per minute (WPM). Azenkot et al [2], Frey et al [7], and Oliveira [20,21], proposed eyes-free techniques for blind people based on Braille. Azenkot et al's Perkinput and Frey et al's BrailleTouch use multi-finger touches similar to those we use in DigiTaps. However, DigiTaps gestures can be performed anywhere on the screen with no need for calibration [2]. Also unlike DigiTaps, Braille-based approaches require knowledge of Braille dot patterns.

Researchers have also explored eyes-free input for sighted people [7,17,23]. Lyon et al. found that removing visual feedback did not adversely affect text entry with the chording Twiddler keyboard [15]. While the Twiddler has physical keys, the efficiency of chording input inspired the DigiTaps gestures. MacKenzie et al. [16] also developed and evaluated an eyes-free, base-4 text entry method using a joystick called H4-Writer. Like DigiTaps, H4 writer uses prefix-free codes to represent characters efficiently, but it is probably more difficult to learn than DigiTaps because its codes do not relate to the semantics of the inputs.

Graffiti and Unistroke [9] are gesture-based text entry methods that resemble printed characters and are potential eyes-free input methods with minimal audio feedback. While they are efficient for sighted people [28], they are not appropriate for blind people who may not know what printed letters look like [14]. DigiTaps gestures require no knowledge of printed characters.

THE DESIGN OF DIGITAPS

The discussion in the previous section leads us to four design goals for numeric entry. We strive to develop a method that is (1) eyes-free, (2) minimal-audio while being (3) efficient and (4) learnable. Efficiency and learnability are important for widespread adoption.

DigiTaps Gestures

To enter a digit with DigiTaps, a user performs one, two, or three gestures anywhere on the screen. The gestures used for digit entry are a one-finger swipe, a one-finger tap, a two-finger tap, and a three-finger tap. A BACKSPACE is entered with a 2-finger swipe. Swipes can be oriented in any direction.

During our formative studies, we considered using a four-finger tap. It was difficult for people to touch a surface with four fingers simultaneously, however, because the smallest finger, the "pinky," was typically much shorter than the other three fingers. Also, some people could not easily fit four fingers on a phone's screen, so we decided to use gestures that involved up to three fingers at a time.

DigiTaps Codes

After designing the DigiTaps gestures, our goal was to create a code that uses just four symbols to represent 10 digits. Usually, we use 10 symbols, the standard digits 0–9, to encode numbers using place values. One possible way to encode 10 digits with four gestures is to use base-4 notation. The 10 digits would be represented by 0, 1, 2, 3, 10, 11, 12, 13, 20, 21, respectively. This encoding could be difficult to learn, however. Can people quickly learn that the digit 5, for example, is represented by 11 in base-4? Furthermore, there is ambiguity in this encoding: if the digit 1 is represented by a one-finger tap, how would the system distinguish the entry of digit 5, input with two one-finger taps, from the entry of two 1's, which are also input with two one-finger taps. To resolve this ambiguity we could use a fixed-length, base-4 code to represent the 10 digits. This code would be 00, 01, 02, 03, 10, 11, 12, 13, 20, and 21 for digits 0 to 9, respectively. There is no ambiguity, but the code is less efficient and could still be difficult to learn.

To reduce the number of gestures per digit, we use prefix-free codes that allow for a varying number of symbols per digit with no ambiguity. The prefix-free property means that no symbol sequence for one digit is a prefix of another [12]. In the original base-4 code, 1 is a prefix of 11, which was ambiguous and led us to define the fixed-length base-4 code. In a prefix-free code, such ambiguity cannot happen and the number of symbols per digit is lower than in a fixed-length code. If all the digits are equally likely, the average number of symbols per digit is the sum of the lengths of the codes for all digits divided by 10.

As such, we developed a learnable, prefix-free code called DigiTaps$^{2.1}$ (first introduced in [22]). The digits can be derived by adding the symbols 0, 1, 2, and 3, entered by gestures, as shown in Table 1. For example, 0 is represented by a one-finger swipe, 1 by a one-finger tap, and 2 by a two-finger tap. The digit 3 is represented by a three-finger tap followed by a one-finger swipe, or 3 + 0. Similarly, 4 is represented by a three-finger tap followed by a one-finger tap (3 + 1). We represent 6 with two three-finger taps and a one-finger swipe (3 + 3 + 0). The digits 3 and 6 need a final one-finger swipe to ensure the code is prefix-free. The digit 9, however, is represented by three three-finger taps (3 + 3 + 3), since three three-finger taps are not a prefix to another input.

DigiTaps$^{2.1}$ uses 2.1 symbols on average per digit, which is close to the two symbols per digit of the fixed-length base-4 code, without the complexity of base-4 notation. An optimal prefix-free code, however, uses 1.8 symbols per digit. There are $6 \cdot 10!$ [1] $= 21{,}772{,}800$ distinct optimal codes, but are any as learnable as DigiTaps$^{2.1}$?

We developed a second code, DigiTaps$^{1.8}$, which has an optimal number of symbols per digit (see Table 1). In DigiTaps$^{1.8}$, the one-finger swipe represents either 0 or 10. It represents 10 when it is the first gesture in a two-gesture digit, and the digit is derived with subtraction. For example, the digit 7 is represented by a one-finger swipe followed by a three-finger tap (10 – 3). Similarly, the digits 8 and 9 are represented by a one-finger swipe followed by a two-finger tap (10 -2) and a one-finger tap (10 – 1), respectively. In all other cases, the one-finger swipe represents 0. The digit 3, for example, is represented by a three-finger tap and a swipe (3 + 0). DigiTaps$^{1.8}$ and DigiTaps$^{2.1}$ have the same codes for five of the 10 digits.

Table 1. DigiTaps Gestures.

Digit	DigiTaps$^{2.1}$	DigiTaps$^{1.8}$
0	1-finger swipe	1-finger swipe, 1-finger swipe
1	1-finger tap	1-finger tap
2	2-finger tap	2-finger tap
3	3-finger tap, 1-finger swipe	3-finger tap, 1-finger swipe
4	3-finger tap, 1-finger tap	3-finger tap, 1-finger tap
5	3-finger tap, 2-finger tap	3-finger tap, 2-finger tap
6	3-finger tap, 3-finger tap, 1-finger swipe	3-finger tap, 3-finger tap
7	3-finger tap, 3-finger tap, 1-finger tap	1-finger swipe, 3-finger tap
8	3-finger tap, 3-finger tap, 2-finger tap	1-finger swipe, 2-finger tap
9	3-finger tap, 3-finger tap, 3-finger tap	1-finger swipe, 1-finger tap

DigiTaps Feedback

DigiTaps provides haptic and optional audio feedback that "clicks" when a gesture is entered and speaks each digit. DigiTaps' haptic feedback enables users to determine whether the system detected their gesture correctly so they can correct errors inline. In formative studies, we found that (1) participants were sometimes unsure whether their touches were registered by the system, and (2) the system sometimes registered a swipe when a tap was entered and vice versa. Thus, DigiTaps gives two kinds of haptic feedback. When the user touches the screen, the device vibrates. If the touch produced a swipe, the system pulses an extra vibration. There is no extra pulse for a tap, so the user knows which gesture was registered.

EVALUATION

We evaluated DigiTaps to find out whether it was a viable method for use with minimal audio feedback. We compared DigiTaps entry (1) with and without audio feedback, and (2) with the DigiTaps$^{2.1}$ code and the DigiTaps$^{1.8}$ code.

Methods

Participants

We recruited 16 participants to complete the DigiTaps longitudinal study (six blind, 10 sighted). Blind participants had a mean age of 45 (range: 31-57), and sighted

[1] There are 6 ways to pick the two one-symbol codes from 4 symbols, and then there are 10! possible assignments of the 10 digits to the 10 resulting codes.

participants had a mean age of 28 (range: 22-34). All had experience using touchscreen devices. We recruited blind and sighted participants through mailing lists that were affiliated with blindness organizations and university communities, respectively.

Procedure
Blind and sighted participants completed the same study procedures with one exception: sighted participants held the phone under the table (as in Clawson et al.'s study [7]), while blind people held the phone in their preferred position. Participants completed six sessions that lasted about 35 minutes each. Sessions were at least two hours, but no more than four days, apart.

In each session, participants entered sets of random four-digit sequences under four conditions: with each DigiTaps code and each feedback method (haptic only or haptic with audio). In sessions 2 - 6, participants entered 15 sequences in each condition. In session 1, they only entered sequences with audio feedback for each code, since they were still learning the codes.

We counterbalanced the order of the DigiTaps codes but did not counterbalance the order of feedback methods. We were concerned that participants would confuse the two codes if they were alternating between them and no audio feedback was given.

Apparatus
We developed an instrumented prototype of DigiTaps that ran on two Galaxy Nexus phones. The phone screens were 4.65 inches long.

Design and Analysis
The experiment had three within-subject factors: *Code* ($DigiTaps^{2.1}$ and $DigiTaps^{1.8}$), *Session* (1-6), and *FeedbackMethod* (Audio or Haptic). We computed the characters per second (CPS) and uncorrected error rate to assess speed and accuracy, respectively, following the formulas and algorithms described by Wobbrock and Myers [29,30]. The uncorrected error rate measures the frequency of errors that were not corrected by the user and appear in the final transcribed strings. Another accuracy measure, the corrected error rate, measures the frequency of errors that the user corrected. It is subsumed by the CPS, however, so we exclude it from our report.

We assessed the normality of our data through graphical means (plotting histograms and boxplots). CPS was normally distributed so we modeled it with a linear, mixed-effects model using *Participant* as a random effect. The uncorrected error rate was not normally distributed, which is usually the case with error rates. We therefore compared sample means of uncorrected error rates with Wilcoxon Signed Rank tests. We use significance levels of $\alpha = 0.05$.

Results

Entry Rate
We found that DigiTaps entry with no audio feedback was faster than with audio feedback, and that the $DigiTaps^{1.8}$ code was faster than the $DigiTaps^{2.1}$ code. This resulted in a significant effect of *Code* ($F_{(1,15)} = 6.90$, $p = 0.02$) and *FeedbackMethod* ($F_{(1,154)} = 27.28$, $p < 0.01$) on CPS. Participants significantly improved their entry rate over time, yielding a significant effect of *Session* ($F_{(1,156)} = 27.28$, $p < 0.01$) on CPS. Their improvement was about the same with both codes and feedback methods, resulting in no significant interaction effects. Table 2 shows the mean entry rates for each condition and Figure 2 shows the entry rates over all sessions of the study.

Table 2. Mean CPS rates for each DigiTaps feedback method and code.

	$DigiTaps^{1.8}$	$DigiTaps^{2.1}$
Haptic feedback	0.89 (SD = 0.31)	0.85 (SD = 0.32)
Audio feedback	0.82 (SD = 0.36)	0.78 (SD = 0.34)

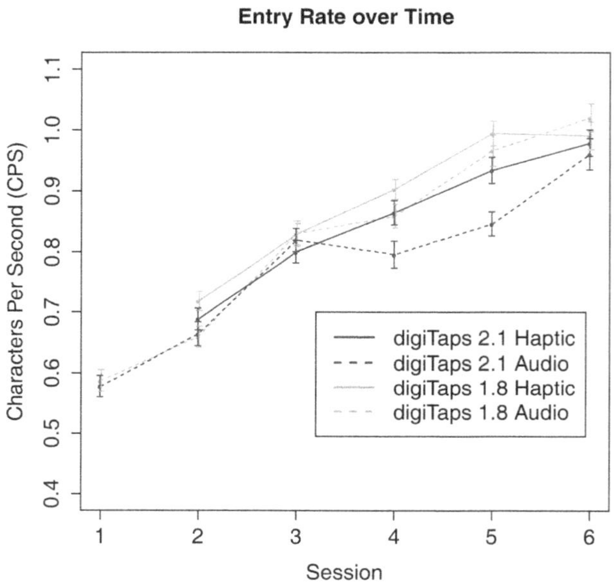

Figure 2. Entry rates for the six sessions of the study. The error bars show the standard error of the means. Higher numbers are better.

Accuracy
The uncorrected error rate was higher for haptic feedback than for audio feedback. This resulted in a significant effect of *FeedbackMethod* ($W = 5$, $p < 0.01$) on Uncorrected Error Rate. There was no significant difference between the uncorrected error rates for $DigiTaps^{2.1}$ and $DigiTaps^{1.8}$. Participants made fewer errors as the study progressed, and we found a significant effect of *Session* ($F_{(1,156)} = 15.69$, $p < 0.01$) on the uncorrected error rate. Table 3 shows the mean

entry rates for DigiTaps feedback methods and codes and Figure 3 shows how they changed over time.

Table 2. Mean uncorrected error rates for each DigiTaps feedback method and code.

	DigiTaps$^{1.8}$	DigiTaps$^{2.1}$
Haptic feedback	5.58% (*SD* = 14.6)	5.68% (*SD* = 15.0)
Audio feedback	2.17% (*SD* = 8.96)	2.22% (*SD* = 8.7)

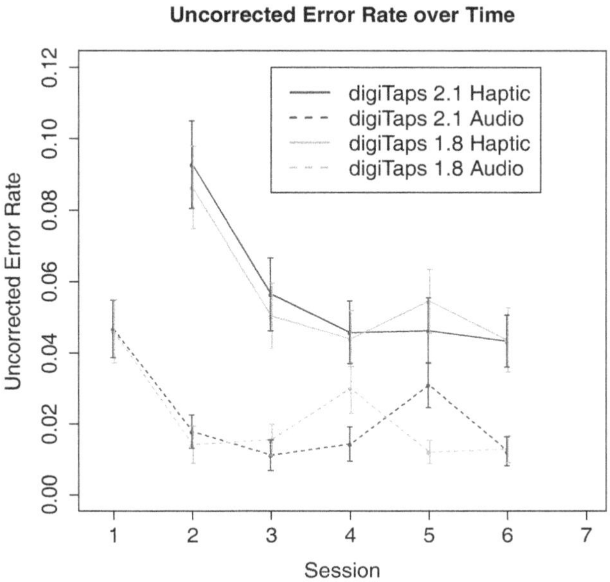

Figure 4. Uncorrected error rates for the six sessions of the study. The error bars show the standard error of the means. Lower numbers are better.

Subjective Preference

We asked participants which method they preferred at the end of the study. Twelve (71%) out of the 16 participants preferred DigiTaps$^{1.8}$, citing its speed and the lower number of taps per digit. A one-sample Pearson Chi-Square test of proportions showed that this preference was significantly different than chance, ($\chi^2_{(1,N=16)} = 4.00$, $p = 0.046$).

DISCUSSION

Overall, we believe the speed and accuracy results show DigiTaps is a promising eyes-free technique. Prior work [5] showed that blind iPhone users entered a familiar 4-digit PIN in 7.52 seconds on average with VoiceOver. With DigiTaps, blind and sighted people entered randomly generated four-digit sequences in 7.01 seconds after only the first study session. During the final session, they entered four-digit sequences in 4.1 seconds on average. Moreover, participants' rate of improvement (shown in Figure 2) suggests their entry speed will continue to increase with more practice.

Number entry with only haptic feedback was faster but also less accurate than entry with haptic and audio feedback. The former was faster probably because users did not pause after each entry to hear the spoken digit, and did not correct as many of their errors. We were pleased that by Session 6, the uncorrected error rate was still rather low, at only 4.6%. However, it is difficult to draw conclusions from the comparison of methods of feedback, because we did not counterbalance the order of the audio and haptic conditions in the study. There may have been carry-over fatigue or learning effects from the audio condition. Nonetheless, it seems likely that performance with only haptic feedback was not substantially *worse* than with audio feedback.

There was a small, albeit statistically significant, difference between entry rates between DigiTaps codes. DigiTaps$^{1.8}$ was faster than DigiTaps$^{2.1}$ with no speed-accuracy trade-off. Surprisingly, even though most participants felt DigiTaps$^{2.1}$ was easier to learn, performance with both codes was nearly equal in the first session. In later sessions, the difference in speeds between the codes was small, but most preferred DigiTaps$^{1.8}$.

We believe our results show that DigiTaps offers a new approach to eyes-free input that requires *minimal* audio feedback. Blind people would still need audio feedback to confirm the numbers they entered were correct; they would also need audio feedback for any other verbal output from their device. However, they wouldn't be as reliant on the audio feedback when entering numbers with DigiTaps. A blind person could sit in a loud café and comfortably enter a number without holding the device up to his or her ear. DigiTaps could be useful for sighted people as well. A sighted person could enter a street address while walking and glance down to ensure it was correct. Eyes-free minimal audio interaction would enable people to use their touchscreen devices more comfortably in a variety of situations.

CONCLUSION

We have presented DigiTaps, an eyes-free number entry method with minimal audio feedback. The design of DigiTaps was guided by learnability, efficiency, and complete eyes-free accessibility. We conducted a longitudinal study with 10 sighted and six blind participants, finding that entering numbers with DigiTaps was faster but less accurate when audio feedback was removed. We believe this trade-off shows that DigiTaps is a promising method for entering numbers in situations where it is difficult to hear a device's audio feedback. DigiTaps, along with other interaction techniques that require minimal audio feedback, will enable blind people to use mobile devices in a wider range of contexts.

ACKNOWLEDGEMENTS

The authors thank Jacob O. Wobbrock, and all study participants. This work was supported in part by AT&T Labs, the National Science Foundation under grant CNS 0905384, and grant IIS-0952786, the US Department of Education under grant H327A100014, and Google.

REFERENCES

1. Apple Inc., iPhone Accessibility. http://www.apple.com/accessibility/iphone/vision.html. Accessed June 19, 2013.
2. Azenkot, S., Ladner, R.E., and Wobbrock, J.O. Smartphone haptic feedback for nonvisual wayfinding. *Proc. ASSETS '11*, ACM Press (2011), 281.
3. Azenkot, S., Prasain, S., Borning, A., Fortuna, E., Ladner, R.E., and Wobbrock, J.O. Enhancing independence and safety for blind and deaf-blind public transit riders. *Proc. CHI '11*, ACM Press (2011), 3247-3256.
4. Azenkot, S., Wobbrock, J.O., Prasain, S., and Ladner, R.E. Input finger detection for nonvisual touch screen text entry in *Perkinput*. *Proc. GI '12*, Canadian Information Processing Society (2012), 121–129.
5. Azenkot, S., Rector, K., Ladner, R.E., and Wobbrock. J.O. PassChords: Secure Multi-Touch Authentication for Blind People. *Proc. ASSETS '12*. New York, NY: ACM (2012), 159-166.
6. Bonner, M., Brudvik, J., Abowd, G. Edwards, K. No-Look Notes: Accessible Eyes-Free Multi-Touch Text Entry. *IEEE Pervasive Computing '10*. Heidelberg: Springer (2010), 409--426.
7. Clawson, J., Lyons, K., Starner, T., and Clarkson, E. The Impacts of Limited Visual Feedback on Mobile Text Entry for the Twiddler and Mini-QWERTY Keyboards. *Proc. ISWC'05*, IEEE (2005), 170–177.
8. Frey, B., Southern, C., Romero, M. BrailleTouch: Mobile Texting for the Visually impaired. *Proc. UAHCII '11*. Heidelberg: Springer (2011), 19-25.
9. Goldberg, D. and Richardson, C. Touch-typing with a stylus. *Proc. CHI '93*, New York, NY: ACM (1993), 80–87.
10. Google, Android Accessibility. http://eyes-free.googlecode.com/svn/trunk/documentation/android_access/index.html. Accessed June 18, 2013.
11. Hesselmann, T., Heuten, W., and Boll, S. Tap2Count. *Proc. ITS '11*, New York, NY: ACM Press (2011), 256–257.
12. Huffman, D. A. A method for the construction of minimum-redundancy codes. *Proc. IRE* (1952). 40(9), 1098-1101.
13. Kane, S.K., Bigham, J.P. and Wobbrock, J.O. Slide Rule: Making mobile touch screens accessible to blind people using multi-touch interaction techniques. *Proc. ASSETS '08*. New York: ACM Press (2008), 73-80.
14. Kane, S. K., Wobbrock, J. O. and Ladner, R. E. Usable gestures for blind people: understanding preference and performance. *Proc. CHI '11*. New York: ACM Press (2011), 413-422.
15. Lyons, K., Plaisted, D., and Starner, T. Expert Chording Text Entry on the Twiddler One-Handed Keyboard. *Proc. ISWC* '04, 94–101.
16. MacKenzie, I.S., Soukoreff, R.W., and Helga, J. 1 thumb, 4 buttons, 20 words per minute: design and evaluation of H4-writer. *Proc. UIST'11*, New York, NY: ACM Press (2011), 471–480.
17. MacKenzie, S., and Castellucci, S. Reducing visual demand for gestural text input on touchscreen devices. *Proc. CHI EA'12*. New York: ACM Press (2012), 2585-2590.
18. MacKenzie, I. S., and Zhang, S. X. The design and evaluation of a high-performance soft keyboard. *Proc. CHI'99*. New York: ACM Press (1999), 25-31.
19. Mascetti, S., Bernareggi, C., and Belotti, M. (2011). TypeInBraille: a braille-based typing application for touchscreen devices. *Proc. ASSETS '11*. New York: ACM Press (2011), 295-296.
20. Oliveira, J., Guerreiro, T., Nicolau., H, Jorge, J., and Gonçalves, D. BrailleType: Unleashing Braille over touch screen mobile phones. *INTERACT* '11. Heidelberg: Springer (2011), 100-107.
21. Oliveira, J., Guerreiro, T., Nicolau, H., Jorge, J., and Gonçalves, D. Blind people and mobile touch-based text-entry: acknowledging the need for different flavors. *Proc. ASSETS '11*. New York: ACM Press (2011), 179-186.
22. Ruamviboonsuk, V., Azenkot, S., and Ladner, R. E. Tapulator: a non-visual calculator using natural prefix-free codes. *Proc. ASSETS '11*. New York: ACM Press (2011), 221-222.
23. Silfverberg, M. Using Mobile Keypads with Limited Visual Feedback: Implications to Handheld and Wearable Devices. (2003), 76–90.
24. Southern, C., Clawson, J., Frey, B., Abowd, G., and Romero, M. An evaluation of BrailleTouch: mobile touchscreen text entry for the visually impaired. *Proc. MobileHCI'12*. New York, NY: ACM Press (2012), 317-326.
25. Stein, D. Stop, Look, and Listen: Quiet Vehicles and Pedestrian Safety. The Braille Monitor. National Federation of the Blind (2005). https://nfb.org/images/nfb/publications/bm/bm05/bm0506/bm050605.htm. Accessed June 18, 2013.
26. Story, M. F. (1998). Maximizing usability: the principles of universal design. *Assistive technology*, *10*(1), 4-12.
27. Strothotte, T., Fritz, S., Michel, R., et al. Development of dialogue systems for a mobility aid for blind people. *Proc. ASSETS'96*, New York, NY: ACM Press (1996), 139–144.
28. Tinwala, H., and MacKenzie, I. S. Eyes-free text entry on a touchscreen phone. *TIC-STH '09 IEEE Toronto International Conference* (pp. 83-88).
29. Wobbrock, J.O. Measures of text entry performance. In *Text Entry Systems: Mobility, Accessibility, Universality*, I. S. MacKenzie and K. Tanaka-Ishii (eds.). San Francisco: Morgan Kaufmann (2007), 47-74.
30. Wobbrock, J.O. and Myers, B.A. (2006). Analyzing the input stream for character-level errors in unconstrained text entry evaluations. *TOCHI* 13 (4), 458-489.

Haptic Feedback Design for a Virtual Button Along Force-Displacement Curves

Sunjun Kim and Geehyuk Lee
Department of Computer Science, KAIST
Daejeon 305-701, Republic of Korea
{kuaa.net, geehyuk}@gmail.com

ABSTRACT
In this paper, we present a haptic feedback method for a virtual button based on the force-displacement curves of a physical button. The original feature of the proposed method is that it provides haptic feedback, not only for the "click" sensation but also for the moving sensation before and after transition points in a force-displacement curve. The haptic feedback is by vibrotactile stimulations only and does not require a force feedback mechanism. We conducted user experiments to show that the resultant haptic feedback is realistic and distinctive. Participants were able to distinguish among six different virtual buttons, with 94.1% accuracy even in a noisy environment. In addition, participants were able to associate four virtual buttons with their physical counterparts, with a correct answer rate of 79.2%.

Author Keywords
Haptic; tactile feedback; virtual button; force-displacement curve; rigid surface

ACM Classification Keyword
H.5.2. Information interfaces and presentation (e.g., HCI): User Interfaces - Haptic I/O

INTRODUCTION
A virtual button on a touchscreen lacks haptic feedback when compared with a physical button. A physical button provides both force and tactile feedback, which stimulate kinesthetic and cutaneous senses, respectively. Nevertheless, technology for the provision of force feedback on a touchscreen, has not yet matured, and this is especially so for mobile devices [8]. Studies on haptic feedback for a touchscreen have so far focused mainly on tactile feedback through tactile actuators [4, 8, 10, 13, 14]. Therefore, most haptic feedback designs for a virtual button ignore kinesthetic feedback and focus on modeling "click" vibrations that occur at the state-transition moments of a button [1, 4, 8, 10, 11, 12, 13].

UIST'13, October 8–11, 2013, St. Andrews, United Kingdom.

http://dx.doi.org/10.1145/2501988.2502041

A physical button provides haptic feedback throughout its full travel range – from the moment of touch, through the point of collapse, to the bottom of the button travel. On the other hand, most current haptic feedback designs for a virtual button provide haptic feedback only for the point of collapse, for the reason that we mentioned above. This is clearly an oversimplification of the haptic feedback of a real button, and we speculated that haptic feedback for a virtual button would be more realistic and distinctive if kinesthetic feedback before and after the point of collapse is also considered in a haptic-feedback design.

A physical button has its own force-feedback characteristics. These characteristics are represented by force-displacement curves that describe in a quantitative manner the kinetic characteristics. For this reason, most button manufactures provide force-displacement curves in their datasheets. As an example, Figure 1 shows the force-displacement curves of three different types of buttons manufactured by CHERRY Corp [2]. In the following, we will use the term "force graph" to refer to a pair of force-displacement curves for pressing and releasing strokes. As the force graphs show, a physical button provides diverse haptic feedback at different displacement points. The diverse haptic feedback makes users feel depth, repulsive force, and the rigidity of a button while they push or release a button.

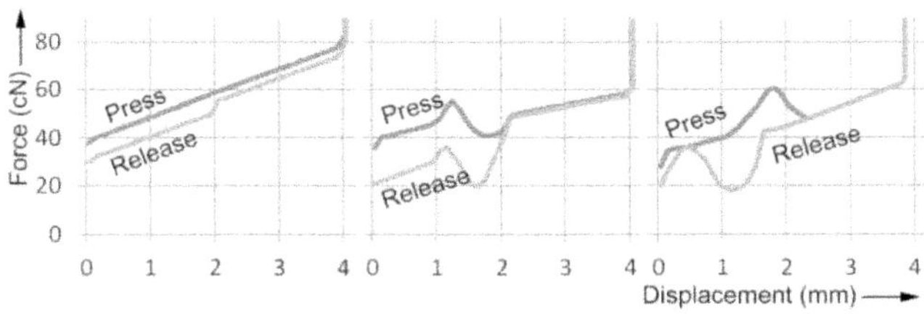

Figure 1. Force graph of variety of physical buttons (CHERRY MX keyswitches [2])

In this paper, we propose a haptic-feedback method for a virtual button, taking into account the entire length of a force-displacement curve, in order to provide haptic feedback throughout the full travel range of a button. We partition the force-displacement curves into a *slope* section, a *jump* section, and a *bottom-out* section, as illustrated in Figure 2, and then, considering the main characteristics for each section, we design the corresponding haptic feedback. For the *slope* region, we adopt the idea of haptic illusion introduced by Kildal [5, 6]. This technique makes possible the sensation of a kinetic movement on a rigid surface and uses only vibrotactile stimuli. For the *jump* section and the *bottom-out* section, we use a burst wave whose frequency, duration and envelope are determined on the basis of a force graph; this produces the sensation of a collapse and a collision. In this way, the proposed method provides haptic feedback along the entire length of a force-displacement curve.

We expected that haptic feedback generated by the proposed method would make a virtual button on a touchscreen feel more distinctive and realistic. In order to determine whether this was the case, we conducted two experiments: a pairwise discrimination test between six different types of the virtual buttons and a pairwise matching test between four types of the virtual buttons and their physical counterparts. The experimental results confirmed that the proposed method is effective for generating a variety of discriminable virtual buttons; also, the virtual buttons were realistic enough match physical buttons with a similar force graph.

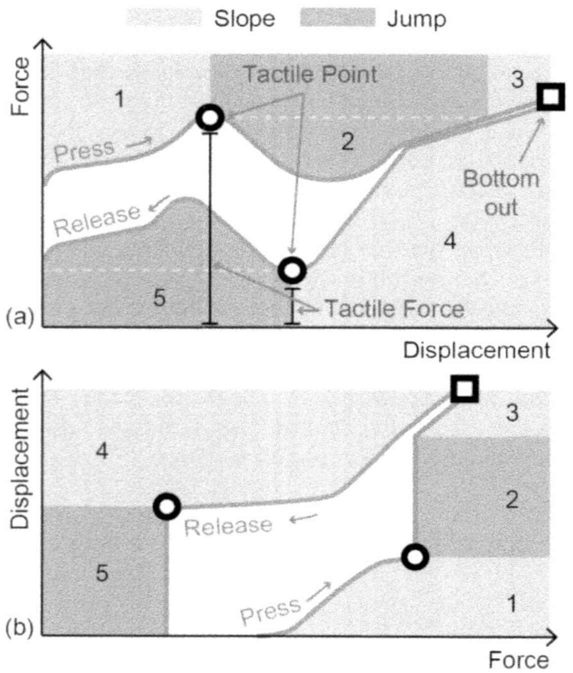

Figure 2. (a) Force-displacement graph of a tactile button (b) Displacement-force graph of the same button

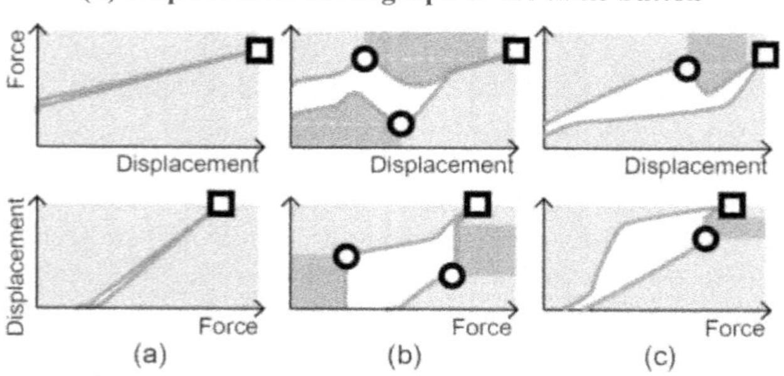

Figure 3. Force graphs of (a) a linear button, and (b, c) two different tactile buttons

RELATED WORK

Haptic feedback studies for a virtual button on mobile devices often rely only on tactile feedback [1, 4, 5, 7, 9, 10, 11, 13]. In these studies, various actuators have been tested to generate vibrotactile stimuli, such as eccentric vibration motors [9, 12, 10], electromechanical voice-coil actuators [4, 5, 12], and piezo actuators [1, 7, 9, 11, 13]. After Fukumoto and Sugimura [5] introduced the Active Click concept, a number of studies [1, 9, 11, 13, 12] designed and evaluated various vibrotactile stimuli for a virtual button. The latter mostly examined or compared static and predefined waveforms with various amplitudes, envelopes, frequencies, and durations. In contrast, [3, 10, 15, 16] propose haptic stimuli that are dynamically generated. Nashel and Rázzaque [10] designed a virtual button feedback that modulates the frequency of the vibration along with the finger pressure or lingering time. Weiss et al. [16] introduced buttons with adjustable resistances using electromagnet force. In their study, participants could distinguish different buttons with various spring resistances. Doerrer and Werthschuetzky [3] utilized force-displacement curve for a push button simulation; their experimental device can generate force feedback throughout the full range of travel. Similarly, Scilingo et al. [15] used a force-displacement curve to model a simulated softness. These haptic feedback methods [3, 15] are more systematic, in that they are based on force-displacement curves, but they are as yet not applicable to mobile devices because they require a bulky mechanism.

MODELING A BUTTON WITH A FORCE GRAPH

Before we introduce the main idea, we first define and clarify our terminology. Some terms are explained through the illustrations in Figure 2.

- **Press/release curve**: a force-displacement curve for the pressing/releasing stroke.
- ***Tactile point***: a local maximum point on a press curve, and a local minimum point on a release curve.
- ***Tactile force***: force at a *tactile point*.
- ***Jump***: A section of a curve where a sudden displacement occurs. Typically, this appears as a valley after a *tactile point* in force-displacement graph (Figure 2a), and as a vertical line in displacement-force graph (Figure 2b). This sudden displacement accompanies a burst of vibration and a clicking sound.
- ***Slope***: the rest section of a curve without *jump*. The curve in this section is monotonically increasing or decreasing. The displacement changes continuously as the force changes.
- ***Bottom-out***: a bottom-out occurs when the displacement reaches its maximum travel.

Figure 2 illustrates both the force-displacement graph (Figure 2a) and the corresponding displacement-force (reverse function) graph (Figure 2b) of an abstracted tactile button model. In this graph, a press curve starts with a *slope* until a *tactile point* (1), followed by a *jump* (2), and then followed by another *slope*, until a *bottom-out* point (3). A release curve starts with a *slope*, until a *tactile point* (4), followed by a *jump* all the way to a complete release (5).

Different physical buttons have different force graphs, as shown in Figure 1 and Figure 3. Their operational characteristics are described in force graphs, which indicate the number and the location of *tactile points* and *jumps*, the gradient of *slopes*, and the magnitude of *tactile force* at *tactile points*. By convention, a button with no *tactile point* is called linear button, and a button with one or more *tactile point* is called tactile button.

DESIGNING VIRTUAL BUTTON FEEDBACK FROM A FORCE GRAPH

In this section, we describe the design of virtual button feedback for each phase of a force graph: *slope*, *jumps* and *bottom-out*. Because of the limitations mentioned in the preceding sections, force feedback devices are not yet applicable to mobile devices. Therefore, we consider using only vibrotactile feedback.

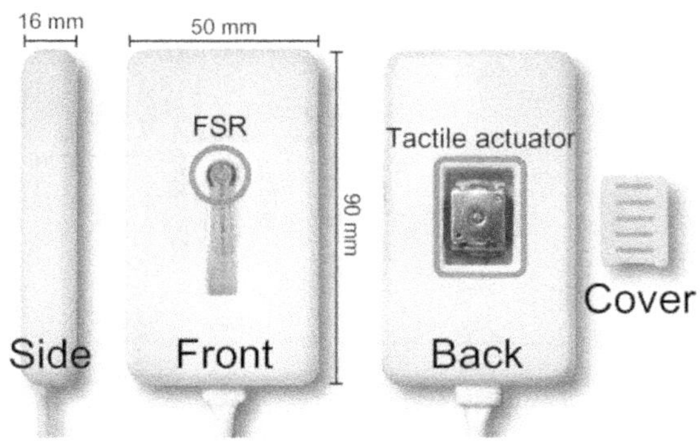

Figure 4. Virtual button feedback device

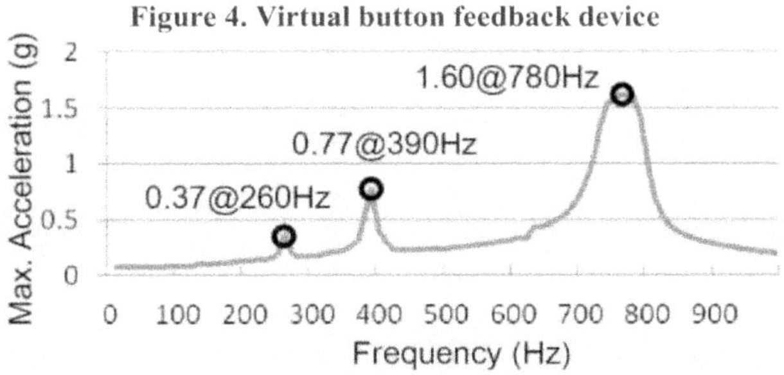

Figure 5. Frequency response of the mobile phone mockup

Apparatus

We implemented a mobile phone mockup that resembles the device in [6]; the implementation consists of a FSR400 force sensor from Interlink Electronics [1] and an electromechanical surface transducer from SparkFun Electronics[2] (Figure 4). The force sensor was calibrated to measure a normal force on the device, up to 12N. We used a MMA7260Q accelerometer to measure the frequency response of the actuator (Figure 5). The actuator played a $2V_{pp}$ sinusoidal waveform at frequencies ranging from 10Hz to 1000Hz. The device resonates at 260Hz, 390Hz, and 780Hz, and the corresponding audible noise, measured 30cm from the device, was 55dB, 60dB, and 95dB, respectively.

The output of the force sensor is transmitted to the PC through a USB 2.0 interface, at a refresh rate of 425Hz. An interface program, implemented in C#, processes sensor data and sends signal messages to a sound synthesizer by UDP packets. The sound synthesizer was implemented with Pure Data [3]; it dynamically generates a waveform in response to the signal messages. Overall, the mean latency from the force sensor to the vibration transducer was measured and was about 51.12ms (N = 50, SD = 1.65).

Slope Feedback Generation

In the *slope* region, a force change is directly translated to a displacement change. The main challenge here is the mapping between a displacement and a vibrotactile stimulus. Sensing a displacement change is done more by the kinesthetic channel of the body than by the tactile channel. To deal with this problem, Kildal [5, 6] proposed a haptic illusion concept. He implemented an illusory elastic material with a friction grain model. He found that a kinesthetic illusion of compliance can be rendered with a low-latency (~60ms) vibrotactile feedback device.

Following his studies, we implemented a similar friction grain model. As illustrated in Figure 6, when a displacement changes over a grain, it generates a brief burst of vibration – a "grain signal". A grain signal consists of a 150Hz sinusoidal wave with an inverted saw-tooth envelope. We distributed grain signals evenly along the displacement range (20 grains/mm), and, therefore, a movement along a gentle slope will generate more grain signals, whereas a movement along a stiff slope will generate fewer grain signals. If a new grain signal comes during playing the previous signal, the new one is played immediately. This may cause unwanted high-frequency harmonics; hence, we add a low-pass filter with cutoff frequency of 150Hz at the end of the signal processing steps.

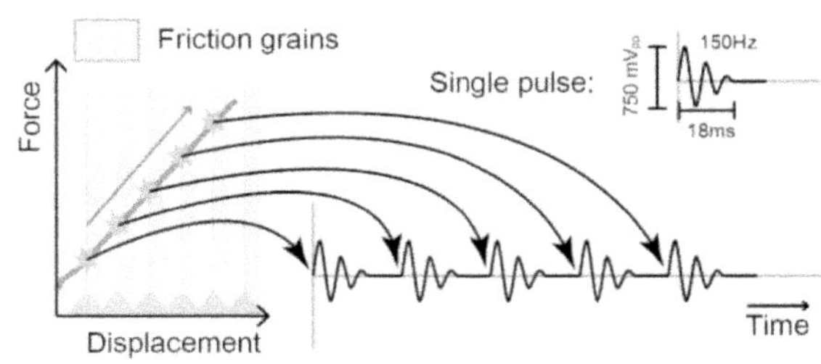

Figure 6. The friction grain model is applied to *slope* feedback generation. When a displacement changes over a grain, a brief burst of vibration is generated.

[1] http://www.interlinkelec.co.jp/
[2] https://www.sparkfun.com/products/10917
[3] http://puredata.info/

Jump Feedback Generation

We designed the haptic feedback for *jump* with a burst sinusoidal wave whose duration and amplitude are determined on the basis of a force graph. *Jump* in a physical button often generates a distinctive vibrotactile feedback. The vibrotactile stimulus for this region has been extensively investigated by previous works [1, 4, 9, 11, 13, 12]. Based on these previous studies, we concluded that a burst of a single signal is sufficient for *jump* feedback.

As illustrated in Figure 7, the duration of the signal is proportional to the change of displacement. This mapping is based on simple common sense: a longer distance takes more time to cross. Further, the amplitude of the signal is proportional to the area between the press or release curve and the horizontal line from the *tactile point*. A broader area means a more abrupt change in force. We reflect this to the intensity of the stimuli. Lastly, the frequency of the signal is predetermined from the resonant frequency of the device, which is 390Hz. This will generate clear amplitude differences from the *slope* signals. For the releasing *jump*, we chose a slightly higher frequency (410Hz), because releasing strokes are often faster than pressing strokes.

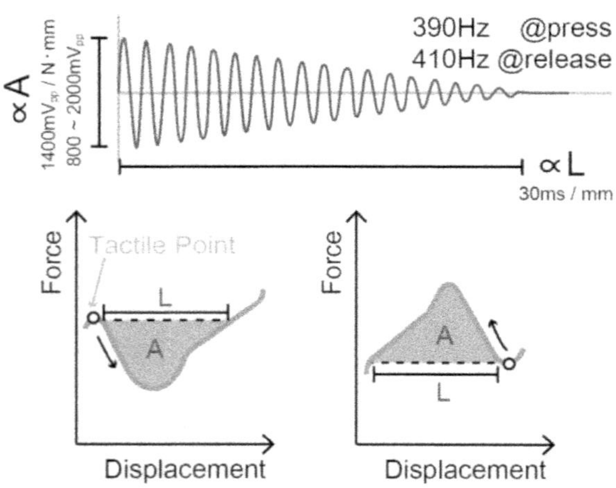

(a) Pressing jump (b) Releasing jump

Figure 7. Parameters of *jump* feedback generations

Bottom-out Feedback Generation

Bottom-out is the end point of a button press operation. We designed a *bottom-out* signal with a 200Hz sinusoidal burst with an increasing 30ms saw-tooth envelope (Figure 8). Compared with the *jump* feedback, the frequency here is slightly higher, and the amplitude is increasing instead of decreasing. We chose this vibrotactile feedback design in order to produce a "sudden stop" sensation. The resulting haptic feedback was effective but was not as effective as *slope* feedback or *jump* feedback. Nevertheless, we believe that this is a final touch to complete our haptic feedback design for a virtual button covering the entire length of force-displacement curves.

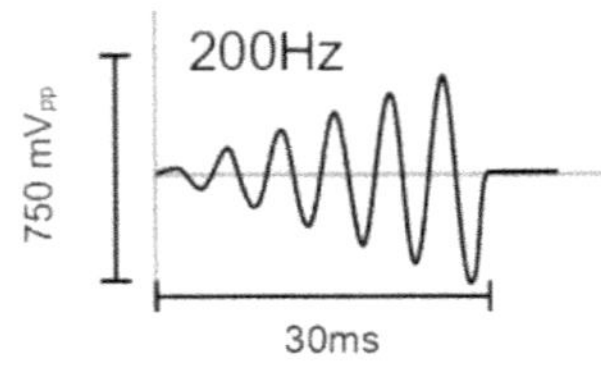

Figure 8. *Bottom-out* feedback

EVALUATION

In order to verify the effectiveness of the proposed haptic feedback design, we asked the two questions:

> "Will different force graphs actually generate different and discriminable virtual button sensations?"
>
> "Will people be able to match a virtual button and a physical button if the two have similar force graphs?"

To answer the first question, we designed six different types of virtual buttons and conducted a pairwise discrimination test. To answer the second question, we prepared four different physical buttons, and designed four virtual buttons based on the force graphs of the physical buttons. We then asked participants to find matching virtual and physical button pairs

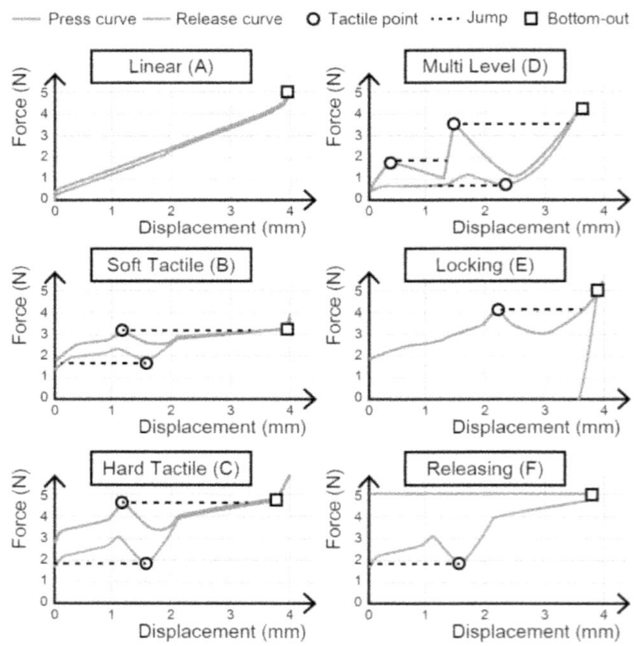

Figure 9. Force graphs of six virtual buttons.

Virtual Button Designs

We designed force graphs for three virtual buttons **A**~**C** on the basis of physical buttons from CHERRY Corp [2] and another three virtual buttons **D**~**F** on the basis of artificially designed force graphs. Figure 9 shows the force graphs of the six buttons. Button **A** is a linear switch. Buttons **B** and **C** are tactile switches with different *tactile forces*. Button **D** is a two-level button, such as a camera shutter. Buttons **E** and **F** are not actually a separate buttons but represent the unlocked state and the locked state of a self-locking button. Once a force graph is given, the software module of the previous section generates haptic feedback for a virtual button automatically.

Experiment 1: Discrimination between Virtual Buttons

An ABX test was employed to see how well each pair of different virtual buttons can be distinguished. In each trial, a participant compared three buttons: two different known buttons α and β[4] and one unknown button X that is randomly selected from α and β. We informed participants that α and β were different, but did not tell them what button (**A**~**F**) is assigned. Participants were asked whether α = X or β = X. We made a list of 15 pairs out of six buttons, multiplied that number by ten, and then shuffled the list of 150 pairs to generate a test set for a participant. As a result, each participant tested each pair ten times. In this test, a participant is considered to be able to discriminate between two buttons when there is at most one error in ten trials ($p<0.05$).

Measure \ Group	*Normal*	*Noisy*
Avg. time (SD)	20.9 min (6.2)	23.3 min (8.4)
Aggregated Errors / Trials	8 / 1350 (0.59%)	46 / 1350 (3.41%)
ABX test result # Fails / Total	1 / 135 (0.74%)	8 / 135 (5.93%)

Table 1. Summary of the test result (10 trials per one ABX test)

(a) *Normal* group

	A	B	C	D	E
B	0				
C	1	0			
D	0	0	2		
E	0	0	1	1	
F	1	2	0	0	0

(b) *Noisy* group

	A	B	C	D	E
B	3				
C	2	5			
D	1	3	10		
E	0	4	5	5	
F	1	4	1	0	2

Table 2. Total discrimination errors by all participants
White: no participant failed the ABX test
Light gray: one participant failed the ABX test
Dark gray: two participants failed the ABX test

Because the mockup device makes an audible sound, we divided participants into *Normal* and *Noisy* group. *Normal* group performed the tests in a quiet and calm environment. In contrast, *Noisy* group wore 3M earplugs and Bose QC15 noise-cancelling headphones playing an ambient raining sound[5] to block the sound generated by the mockup. We recruited nine participants (Ages from 20 to 27 (avg = 23.4), 7 Males and 2 Females) for *Normal* group, and another nine participants (Ages from 18 to 26 (avg = 22.7), 7 Male and 2 Females) for *Noisy* group. Participants were undergraduate or graduate students. All were right-handed they performed the tests with their right hands. Before the test, they tried every feedback freely, for about 3 minutes.

Table 1 and Table 2 show the results of the ABX test. The gray boxes in Table 2 indicate that at least one participant failed the ABX test with given pairs of virtual buttons. *Noisy* group clearly showed more errors, and the most confused pair was **C**-**D**. In this case, the first *jump* of button **D** tends to be masked by the more intensive second *jump*, and therefore button **C** and **D** generate similar feedback signals. Nevertheless, even in the worst case, seven out of nine participants could successfully discriminate between two different buttons.

Experiment 2: Matching Physical and Virtual Buttons

Buttons **A**, **B**, and **C** are generated on the basis of datasheets of real physical buttons. The self-locking button (**EF**) also resembles a real self-locking button, although we could not find a datasheet for it. For this button, we present **E** and **F** alternately. Thus, we had four virtual buttons with physical button counterparts. The mapping between the two sets is shown in Table 3.

A	CHERRY Corp. MX switch black (linear type, Figure 1-left)
B	CHERRY Corp. MX switch brown (tactile type, 55cN *tactile force*, Figure 1-middle)
C	CHERRY Corp. MX switch white (tactile type, 65cN *tactile force*)
EF	ALPS Electronics, self-locking switch (extracted from Apple Extended Keyboard II[6])

Table 3. Four virtual buttons and their physical button counterparts. EF means that the feedback is alternating between E and F at each button actuation.

Without giving them any additional information about the buttons, we asked the participants to find equivalent virtual and physical button pairs. Participants were allowed to freely try four virtual buttons and four physical buttons during the experiment. The 18 participants of Experiment 1 participated again in this experiment. The matching task took about 5 minutes for each participant.

Nine participants could make perfect matches between virtual and physical buttons. Of the other participants, three participants swapped **C** and **EF**, another three participants swapped **B** and **C**, one participant swapped **A** and **B**, and two participants were confused between three buttons. Overall, the participants correctly matched 79.2% (76 correct matches per 96 trials) of a given virtual button. In

[4] Conventionally, stimuli labels of ABX test is named A, B, and X. However, we use α, β, and X here to avoid confusion with virtual button labels from **A** to **F**.

[5] `http://www.rainymood.com`

[6] This keyboard was manufactured in early 1990s. ALPS Electronics no more produces keyboard switches now.

addition, after we gave the right answers, with short explanations, most participants agreed with the mappings between the virtual and physical buttons.

Post-Experiment Interview

After participants performed two experiments, we asked them to enunciate, in natural language, what they felt of the virtual buttons. Almost all reported a button-like sensation for buttons **B, C** and **D**, all of which have distinctive *tactile points* on both press and release curves. Fifteen participants reported a smooth feeling on button **A,** but three participants disliked its uncertain operational feel. Four participants reported unpleasant feelings on button **E,** because it does not provide any tactile feedback during a releasing stroke, and, for similar reason, nine participants considered button **F** is unpleasant. Some participants had a favorite button: three picked button **A**, two picked button **B**, five picked button **C**, and one picked button. In summary, participants could feel and report rich and diverse haptic sensations when playing with the virtual buttons in the experiments. Their preferences varied from person to person.

CONCLUSION AND FUTURE WORK

We proposed a haptic feedback method for a virtual button based on the force graph of a physical button. The distinguishing feature of the proposed method is that it provides haptic feedback not only for the *jump* section but also for the *slope* sections before the *jump* section in the force graph. We conducted two user experiments to show that the resultant haptic feedback is realistic and distinctive. In the first experiment, participants were able to distinguish six different virtual buttons quite successfully. The confusion rate was about 5.9% in a noisy environment and less than 1% in a quite environment. In the second experiment, participants were able to associate four virtual buttons with their physical counterparts at a correct answer rate of 79.2%.

The main contribution of the current study is that it was an original attempt to enhance the haptic feedback of a virtual button by providing vibrotactile feedback along the entire length of a force-displacement curve. Experimental results show that the proposed method is indeed effective.

Another contribution of the current study is that it provides a systematic design-method for virtual button haptic feedback on the basis of a force graph. In other words, the design of haptic feedback for a virtual button can be done almost mechanically given the force graph of a physical button counterpart. This design method will enable haptic feedback design for a virtual button to be based solidly on our existing knowledge of physical buttons.

A shortcoming of the current study is the lack of comparison with a base case, e.g., the case of click-only feedback. The current haptic feedback design is clearly richer than that of the base case, but we are yet to determine if it will be really more distinguishable and realistic. The first task in a future study is a more rigorous evaluation of the proposed haptic feedback method in comparison with other options.

ACKNOWLEDGEMENT

This work was supported by the IT R&D program of MKE/KEIT. [KI10041244, SmartTV 2.0 Software Platform]

REFERENCES

1. Chen, H.-Y., Park, J., Dai, S., and Tan, H. Design and evaluation of identifiable key-click signals for mobile devices. *Haptics, IEEE Transactions on 4*, 4 (2011), 229–241.
2. CHERRY Corperation. MX series keyswitches. http://www.cherrycorp.com/english/switches/key/mx.htm.
3. Doerrer, C., and Werthschuetzky, R. Simulating push-buttons using a haptic display: Requirements on force resolution and force-displacement curve. *EuroHaptics 2002*.
4. Fukumoto, M., and Sugimura, T. Active click: tactile feedback for touch panels. *CHI 2001 Extended Abstracts*.
5. Kildal, J. 3d-press: haptic illusion of compliance when pressing on a rigid surface. *ICMI-MLMI 2010*.
6. Kildal, J. Kooboh: Variable tangible properties in a handheld haptic-illusion box. *Haptics: Perception, Devices, Mobility, and Communication*, vol. 7283. Springer, 2012, 191–194.
7. Kim, J., Dai, X., Cao, X., Picciotto, C., Tan, D., and Tan, H. A masking study of key-click feedback signals on a virtual keyboard. *Haptics: Perception, Devices, Mobility, and Communication*, vol. 7282. Springer, 2012, 247–257.
8. Koskinen, E. *Optimizing tactile feedback for virtual buttons in mobile devices*. PhD thesis, Helsinki University of Technology, 2008.
9. Koskinen, E., Kaaresoja, T., and Laitinen, P. Feel-good touch: finding the most pleasant tactile feedback for a mobile touch screen button. *ICMI 2008*.
10. Nashel, A., and Razzaque, S. Tactile virtual buttons for mobile devices. *CHI 2003 Extended Abstracts*.
11. Pakkanen, T., Raisamo, R., Raisamo, J., Salminen, K., and Surakka, V. Comparison of three designs for haptic button edges on touchscreens. *Haptics Symposium*, IEEE (2010).
12. Park, G., Choi, S., Hwang, K., Kim, S., Sa, J., and Joung, M. Tactile effect design and evaluation for virtual buttons on a mobile device touchscreen. *MobileHCI 2011*.
13. Poupyrev, I., and Maruyama, S. Tactile interfaces for small touch screens. *UIST 2003*.
14. Poupyrev, I., Maruyama, S., and Rekimoto, J. Ambient touch: designing tactile interfaces for handheld devices. *UIST 2002*.
15. Scilingo, E., Bianchi, M., Grioli, G., and Bicchi, A. Rendering softness: Integration of kinesthetic and cutaneous information in a haptic device. *Haptics, IEEE Transactions on 3*, 2 (2010), 109–118.
16. Weiss, M., Remy, C., and Borchers, J. Rendering physical effects in tabletop controls. *CHI 2011*.

Transmogrification: Casual Manipulation of Visualizations

John Brosz[1], Miguel A. Nacenta[2], Richard Pusch[1], Sheelagh Carpendale[1] Christophe Hurter[3]

[1]University of Calgary, Canada
{jdlbrosz,sheelagh}@ucalgary.ca
rapusch@alumni.ucalgary.ca

[2]School of Computer Science
University of St Andrews, UK
mans@st-andrews.ac.uk

[3]University of Toulouse
ENAC, France
christophe.hurter@enac.fr

ABSTRACT

A transmogrifier is a novel interface that enables quick, on-the-fly graphic transformations. A region of a graphic can be specified by a shape and transformed into a destination shape with real-time, visual feedback. Both origin and destination shapes can be circles, quadrilaterals or arbitrary shapes defined through touch. Transmogrifiers are flexible, fast and simple to create and invite use in casual InfoVis scenarios, opening the door to alternative ways of exploring and displaying existing visualizations (e.g., rectifying routes or rivers in maps), and enabling free-form prototyping of new visualizations (e.g., lenses).

Author Keywords

Visualization; image deformation; multi-touch.

ACM Classification Keywords

H.5.2 Information interfaces and presentation: User Interfaces - Graphical user interfaces.

INTRODUCTION

We live in an information world and, thanks partly to the web, this information is increasingly visual. Visual representations of data appear often at work and in our social lives; for example, in newspapers and other websites we regularly encounter graphical evolutions of economic indicators for the last few years, or maps that display the most expensive neighborhoods in the city. These data visualizations are necessarily limited to specific representations, usually constrained by the format (e.g., paper, raster images on websites), and by the representation choices of the designer.

Naturally, no representation can be perfect for all purposes, for all people, or for all data. Tversky [53] has discussed how all maps (also a type of visual data representation) omit some information and may scale, simplify, reduce dimensionality, regularize, or even use inconsistent scale and perspective in order to better fulfill their purpose (which can be practical, aesthetic, or even political). Similar constraints apply to other types of static and dynamic visualizations. Even dynamic information visualizations cannot foresee all the needs and preferences of viewers [28]. Although InfoVis programming languages (e.g., [5]) and end-user software systems (e.g., Tableau[1]) are sufficiently expressive to create a great range of purpose-adapted representations, producing visualizations with these tools takes significant time and effort. Often this is not even an option since, despite the current push for open data, most often the data behind a representation is not directly available.

In this work we aim at allowing viewers to easily explore alternative representations. To do this we created the Transmogrification Canvas (TC), a tool that allows quick, real-time, flexible transformations of the representation of 2D visuals. Transmogrifiers—the core technique of the TC—are novel interface elements that adapt graphical deformation techniques to enable the transformation of an arbitrary original shape into another shape.

Using Transmogrifiers people can create custom transformations of existing graphics that are adapted to the person's specific visualization purpose, preference, and cognitive abilities. The specially crafted interface works in real-time on any existing visual material, and without the need for programming. The TC is designed to allow people to sketch, transform, and compare visualizations from one or multiple sources in a way that fits real-life situations, where people discussing a graph would like to make a point through a visual representation while still keeping pace with the conversation.

The contribution of this paper is three-fold:

- The concept of transmogrification: an application of graphical deformation to enable cartographic and visualization manipulations.
- A novel integrated set of interaction and animation techniques that enable quick and flexible transmogrification in real-time.
- A desktop multi-touch tool that integrates these techniques and animations into a coherent interface.

AN EXAMPLE SCENARIO

Maria likes to go on long bike rides. She carries equipment that measures her position and altitude through GPS, as well as her heart rate. After processing her data, her software creates the map and graphs in Fig. 1.A. To investigate the data further, Maria starts the Transmogrifier Canvas, which captures the map and graphs from the desktop. She creates a route trace on the map with her finger and then transforms it into a rectangle. This rectification represents her ride as

[1]http://www.tableausoftware.com/

UIST'13, October 8–11, 2013, St. Andrews, United Kingdom.

ACM 978-1-4503-2268-3/13/10...$15.00.
http://dx.doi.org/10.1145/2501988.2502046

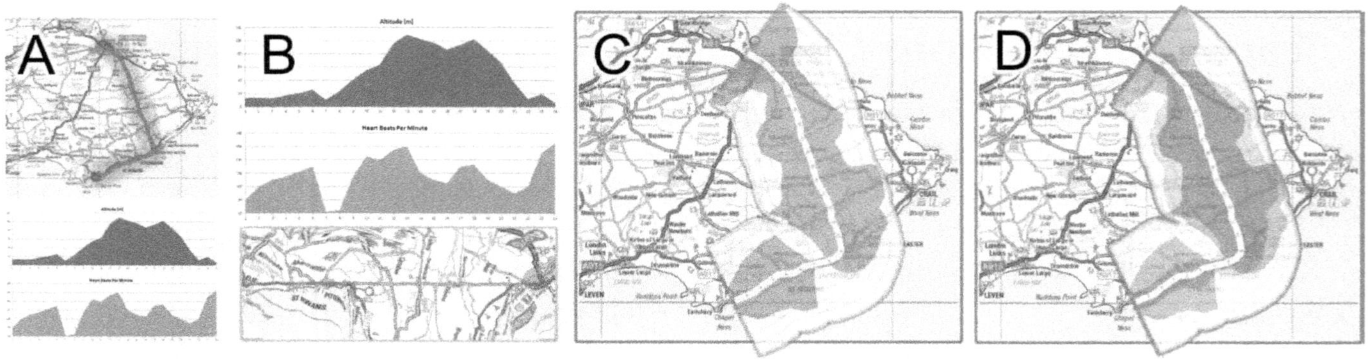

Figure 1. A) Cycling data: a map with a route and area graphs with average altitude (purple) and heart-rate (orange) at each kilometer. B) The rectified route map aligned under the linear graphs enables comparison of the measured variables to the map features. C) The heart-rate graph wrapped around the route in the map shows effort in spatial context. D) Same as C, but with multiple variables. Map used contains Ordnance Survey data © Crown copyright and database right 2013.

a straight path from start to finish and she then resizes and moves it to lie under the graphs of altitude and heart-rate (see Fig. 1.B). This shows her how the different towns and intersections correspond to the different stages of her ride. She can quickly identify the name of the town where she stopped for lunch by looking at the correspondence between the rectified map and the graphed area of low heart rate.

To get a further overview of where she put in the most effort, she applies a transformation to plot her heart rate upon the map itself. Figure 1.C represents the effort (heart rate) at each point in the route, encoded in the width and amount of orange beside the route. Now she can easily identify that she worked hardest along the inland road. Finally, she applies the same transformation of the altitude graph to the map and overlays this with the transmogrified heart rate to see how one influenced the other (Fig. 1.D).

RELATED WORK

While motivated by Casual Infovis [40], our interaction techniques can be applied to non-casual scenarios and audiences. In this section we review related work in four subsections: the closest related tools, visualization and cartographic techniques, graphical deformation algorithms, and animation.

Related Tools

Most closely related to our work is Savva et al.'s ReVision [44], which uses machine learning techniques to analyze images of charts, extract chart type and infer the data, and then create alternative chart designs and styles. This approach supports one of Transmogrifiers goals (re-representation of an existing visual), but it is not real-time, it still requires significant knowledge for re-representation, and does not allow arbitrary transformations of shape. Also, while ReVision is 96% accurate classifying the infographic type, it is much less accurate in extracting the data; for instance, it was only $\sim 64\%$ successful at extracting data from the charts. In exchange, if successful in extracting data, ReVision would usually be more accurate, and its results avoid some of the problems that we discuss in the Limitations section.

SketchVis [7] and NapkinVis [10] both create visualizations through sketches on interactive surfaces. These share with transmogrifiers the goal of quickly generating data visualizations without the need for programming. However, they are different in that they require access to the underlying data, do not operate on existing visualizations, and are focused on a few possible visualization types. Additionally, other tools exist that leverage multi-touch for drawing (e.g., [49]).

Related Visualization and Cartographic Techniques

The use of graphic deformation underlies many infovis techniques. A common type are local magnification techniques, which can be divided into two main categories (after Cockburn et al. [13]): overview+detail and focus+context. With overview+detail the magnified area is presented spatially separate from the context; focus+context techniques place the magnified region within the context by compressing some amount of the context area. Alternatives exist where transparency is used instead of compression [37], where context regions are hidden in folds [47], or where the lens automatically adapts its shape to match objects of interest [38].

Agrawala and Stolte [1] deform maps to reproduce characteristics of hand-drawn route maps, such as portraying the important turns and landmarks for a route without requiring an accurate representation of space. For this same goal of automatic creation of route maps Kopf et al. [27] make use of nonlinear optimization to non-uniformly adjust the position, scale, and orientation of an automatically determined subset of relevant roads. Bottger et al. [6] use image deformation to globally deform street-level map images to match the layout of an abstracted metro map/schematic.

Most of the techniques above can be simulated, reproduced, or approximated through the interactive use of transmogrifiers. Transmogrification provides a way of thinking about deformations as well a generalized interface to reproduce and prototype these deformations and many more.

Finally, there are related techniques based on spatial transformation and selection that are outside the scope of transmogrifiers. For example, magic lenses [4, 22] present information from a different or processed layer of spatial data in situ, within the spatial context, and Histomages [12] enable 2D selection operations in the transformed color histogram space.

Deformation Algorithms

Transmogrification is based on the ability to deform graphics. Computer graphics research has a long tradition of research in image deformation, which is often referred to as *tweening* (deformation has often been used to generate in-be*tween* frames for animations). Within tweening we review morphing and image deformation algorithms. Several of the following algorithms serve as base and are adapted to work with the constraints of transmogrifiers (see also *Implementation*).

Morphing. Morphing algorithms provide transitions where one object changes into another. Typically a set of correspondences are used to create a series of images that smoothly transition from an image to another. Although morphing was first achieved by simply cross-dissolving images [59], current approaches [48, 29] make use of image deformation style techniques, including one-to-one morphing. Reilly & Inkpen [42] and Haunert and Sering [19] provide examples of cartographic morphing—respectively deforming Cartesian maps into schematic maps and clarifying road knots.

Image Deformation. Image deformations encompass a variety of techniques designed to allow images to be manipulated as if they were flexible objects. These are applied to alter images, interpolate between keyframes, or even animate entire sequences. Usually deformations are enabled through placing and altering the positions of handles. There are many varieties of handles utilized for this task including points [24, 58, 25], lines [3], skeletons [8, 21], bones [46], lattices [60], sketches [15, 57], and cages [30, 56, 32]. Alternative interactions exist, for instance Schiwietz et al. [45] assign physical properties and create deformations by applying force vectors.

Many of these techniques, such as that of Igarashi et al. [24], break the image into small polygons and frame the problem as that of minimizing distortion. Other techniques, such as Lipman et al.'s [30], make use of different coordinate calculations with various shape preserving qualities to transform pixel coordinates. While minimization provides a physical basis for such manipulations, it also limits their scope. For transmogrification we can override these physically-plausible restrictions and instead seize the opportunity to alter imagery in a more abstract fashion.

Optimization-based deformation techniques work by moving pieces of the image to new locations and then attempting to make the rest of the image fit, providing a globally coherent reorganization of the image. These techniques are less useful for transmogrification, where the final shape is determined interactively rather than algorithmically.

In our exploration of algorithms we found that skeleton-type handles that allow for simple selection of visual elements are best suited for our purpose when combined with multi-touch interaction. Consequently transmogrifiers expand upon existing skeletal deformation techniques [8, 21], as discussed in the Implementation section below.

Animation

We provide animations to help viewers find correspondences between transformed and untransformed images. Tversky et al. [54] surveyed research in the cognitive value of animation and found that it can be beneficial if it helps to portray extra information. This is the case for transmogrifiers, where animation is used to depict correspondences between 2D spaces that are not explicit otherwise. Other researchers have found benefits in animation for different domains such as tree visualization [2], common statistical graphs [20], and hierarchies [43]. These and other uses and studies of animation in information visualization (e.g., [16, 14, 23, 22]) inspire and inform the animations available in our tool.

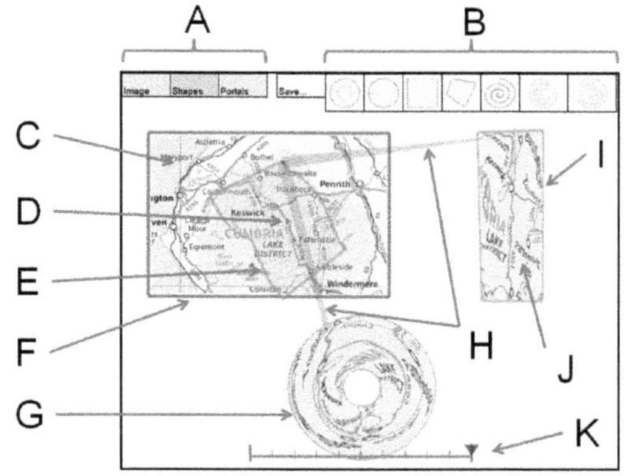

Figure 2. The basic interface of the Transmogrifier Canvas, containing two transmogrifiers. A) menu, B) shapes palette, C) imported image, D) control point, E) source shape (single-touch trace), F) imported image edge, G) destination shape (ring), H) transmogrifier lines, I) destination shape (rectangle), J) transmogrified image, K) animation control.

TRANSMOGRIFICATION

Transmogrification is a technique designed for casual information exploration that allows people to easily take a personally selected part of the visual data and transform its geometry interactively. Transmogrification is instantiated by transmogrifiers, which are interface elements that implement adaptations of existing skeleton-based image deformation algorithms [8, 21], can be animated in different ways, and are controlled with multi-touch interaction techniques.

Transmogrifiers operate on any chosen area of an image—that is, they can start from any arbitrarily shaped region—and transform its contents to fit a chosen resulting shape. These shapes can be regular geometrical shapes or free-form shapes created interactively to fit a particular feature of the original representation. For example, a square area can be transformed into a circular area, and a curved free-form area can be transformed into a rectangular area. We call the shape that determines the area to be transformed the *source*, and the intended shape of the transformation the *destination*. Fig. 2 shows two transmogrifiers sharing the same origin.

Interface

Interaction with transmogrifiers is designed to support two basic goals: enabling a flexible set of transformations that adapt to the underlying data, and allowing people to generate a large number of different explorations in a short time. To enable a large set of manipulations, source and destination can be chosen from a set of predefined shapes (rectangle, circle, quadrilateral, spiral, ring) available through a tool palette (see Fig. 2.B), created on the fly through single- and

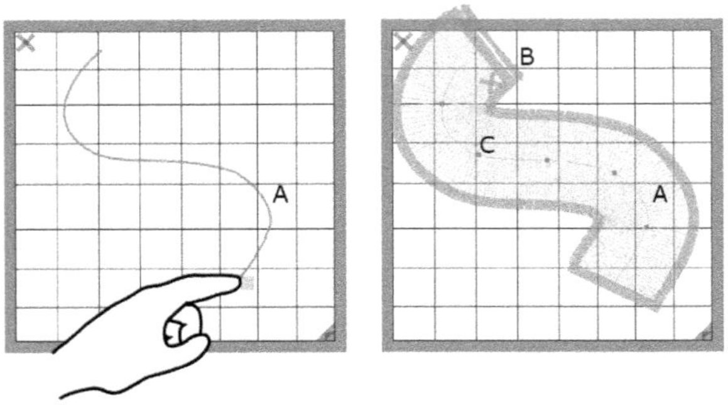

Figure 3. A single-point trace shape is created by dragging on free space. A) Spine, B) thickness control, C) sampling handles (red points).

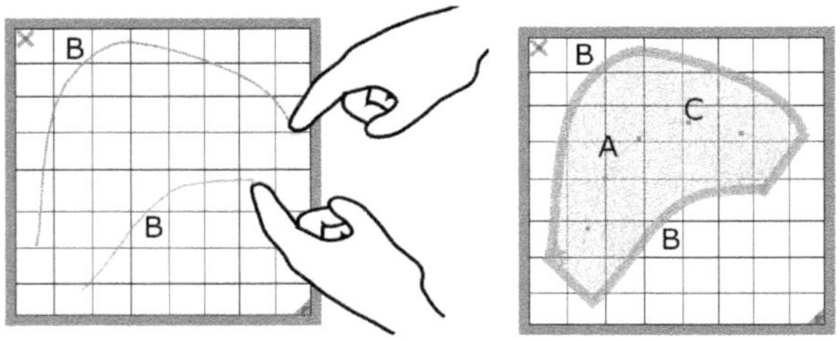

Figure 4. A double-point trace shape is created by dragging two fingers on free space. A) Spine, B) borders, C) sampling handles (red points).

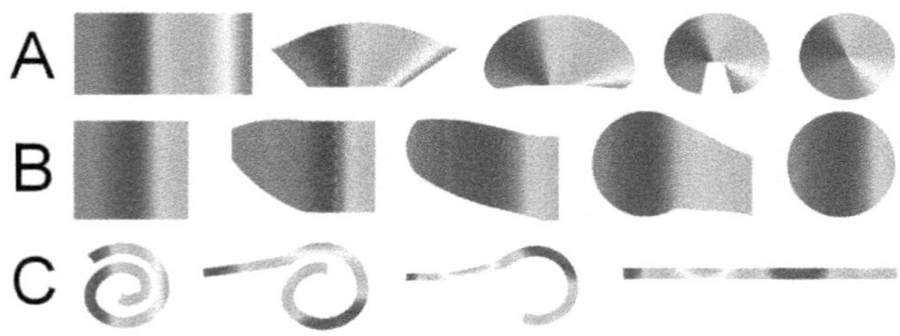

Figure 5. Implemented animations shown with coloured texture with the source shape (left), the destination (right), and tweened shapes (middle). A) Ring quadrature, B) path distance delay, and C) ribbon.

multi-point finger traces, or defined through bezier curves. The multiple combinations of source and destination shapes support different usages.

A transmogrifier is created by dragging a finger from an existing shape into another. The shape under the start of the drag gesture becomes the source and the shape under the finger at touch release becomes the destination. A red transparent tapered line starts thick on the source and narrows to the destination, indicating the presence of a transmogrifier (Fig. 2.H).

Shapes can be translated, scaled and rotated with multi-touch interaction techniques (e.g.,[35]). Most shapes have control points that enable further modifications, such as the quadrilateral, where corners can be adjusted, or the ring, where the size of the interior circumference can be enlarged.

One of the main features of transmogrifiers that enables data-centric flexible analysis are *trace-shapes*. A trace-shape is created by touch-tracing a line on any region of the image space. This allows generation of arbitrary source and destination shapes that can follow the shape of the original graphical data on the screen. For example, with this multi-touch technique it is easy to create a source shape that follows the contour of elements in the image such as coastlines in a map. There are two types of trace-shape: single- and double-point.

In single-point trace-shapes, the analyst generates a line around which a shape is grown with constant width (Fig. 3). We call this central line the *spine*, which is related to Hsu et al.'s reference backbone [21]. The width of the shape is constant, but it can be modified through a control that appears at the start side of the shape (Fig. 3.B). Trace-shapes also provide handles along the trace to modify the local sampling densities, which allow compression or expansion of parts of the image longitudinally along the spine.

The double-point trace-shape is more flexible than the single-point because it enables dynamic variation of thickness along the trace, which allows a larger range of possible shapes. In exchange, it is harder to control because the additional degrees of freedom may make difficult to attain accurate traces [35]. However, while tracing with double-points one's fingers do not occlude the middle content being traced (Fig. 4).

For traces that require more precision, we implemented a bezier curve drawing technique that works similarly to the single-point trace-shape. Bezier-generated shapes can also be translated, scaled or rotated with the usual gestures. Alternatively, the TC provides a "magnet" mode where traces are algorithmically aligned with nearby edges using our variant of Snakes [26], with the input points being aligned with the first-order gradient of a blurred internal image copy.

Animations

Transmogrifications are usually non-linear transformations which can be potentially hard to understand. To facilitate seeing the relationship between the original and transmogrified space we incorporate animation, which has previously been shown to be successful in supporting comprehension during transformation in infovis (e.g., [43, 14, 20, 2]).

When a transmogrifier is created, a default animated transformation from origin to destination is shown. The viewer can replay this animation at her desired speed by dragging a slider that appears at the bottom of the interface (Fig. 2.K).

A virtually infinite variety of combinations of origin and destination shapes implies that animations that are good for one transformation might not be good for another. To address this we implemented three different animation types, selectable through a menu in the TC interface. We chose these according to two criteria derived from previous work and our own experimentation: we try to maximize the number of pixels moving in the same direction (consistency), and we try to avoid twists and folds during the animation (clarity).

The animations are: *ring quadrature*, *path distance delay*, and *ribbon* (Fig. 5). Ring quadrature provides transitions from shapes in Cartesian coordinates to shapes in polar coordinates; path distance delay interpolates between shapes progressively from one end of the shape to the other; ribbon unwinds long, curving shapes. Future work should address the feasibility of automatic animation selection.

The Transmogrification Canvas

Transmogrifiers exist within the Transmogrification Canvas. Although the general interface is designed to take advantage of the multi-touch paradigm, during the design of the application we decided that—for some functions—menus, buttons, and sliders are preferable to invocation gestures that are sometimes difficult to discover and remember [36]. The following subsections describe the functionality of TC that goes beyond the individual transmogrifiers, and how it interacts with the wider computing context.

General Interface

TC has a basic menu/palette that appears on the top left corner of the window (2.A). Large elements enable touch interaction, although indirect input is also possible for systems with mouse input. The shapes sub-menu in TC offers the standard shapes; however it can also save custom-made transmogrifiers, which become part of the palette (Fig. 2.B). Transmogrifications can be turned into source raster images. The menu also contains options to select the animation type.

Multi-transmogrifier Functionality

Beyond pure transmogrification functionality, the TC provides a workspace to combine and compose different transmogrifiers for more power. For example, transmogrifiers can not only share the same canvas space, but TC allows transmogrifiers to share the same origin shape, which is useful to compare alternative transformations of the same data.

Because a transmogrifier can be turned into a source image with the press of a button, we can chain multiple transmogrification operations, creating a 'transmogrification pipeline' reminiscent of Lark [51]. This operation, combined with the

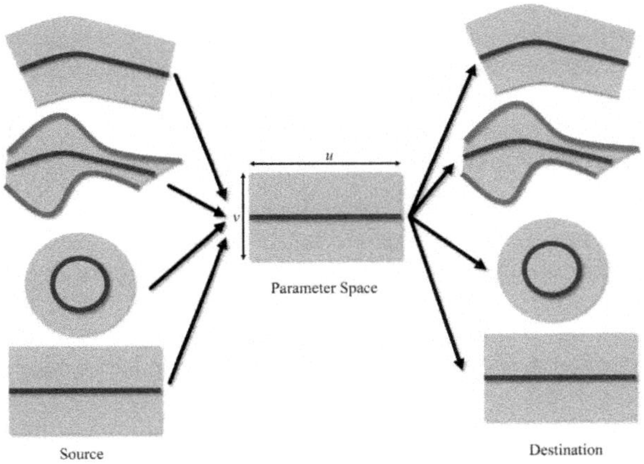

Figure 6. Transmogrification parameterizes a variety of source shapes (left) into parameter space (middle) and then re-maps it to any destination shape (right). Spine curves are shown as dark blue. From top to bottom the shapes are single-trace, double-trace, circle, and rectangle.

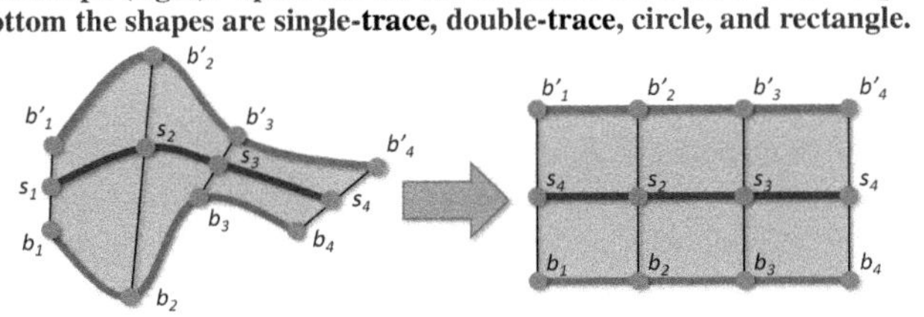

Figure 7. To render a transmogrifier, we calculate the image's texture coordinates along the source's spine, s, and boundary curves, b' & b (left). These coordinates are used to render the transmogrifier shape with texture coordinates placed along the equivalent destination curve.

ability of a transmogrifier to operate on adjacent images enables a powerful *image transformation algebra* that we will return to in the Examples and Discussion sections.

The TC and its Computing Context

TC is designed to integrate in people's workflow through multiple features. First, images to transmogrify can be imported into the canvas through a *load* option that accesses the user's operating system image files. Additionally, transmogrified images can be saved back to the hard-drive or copied into the system clipboard for use in other applications.

The TC can also be a sophisticated visualization and exploration tool when accessing web or other program's visualizations. By assigning a system-wide keystroke (e.g., Shift+PrtScr) TC can take a snapshopt of the current state of the desktop and import it into a screen-sized TC window.

Lastly, TC has a multi-display mode in which the canvas can operate, in real-time, on objects that are present in other screens. This is a powerful feature, since it enables real-time interaction with transmogrified visualizations or even videos, which are updated in real time. This is possible without the need for interfacing our software with each specific visualization. Additionally, this feature allows viewers to configure personalized transmogrified information dashboards of information from other screens, a powerful generalization of the WinCuts concept [50]. To better understand the real-time desktop features, please refer to the Video Figure.

IMPLEMENTATION

This section describes our implementation to enable other researchers to reproduce our work; additionally, we report on how we adapted existing techniques, highlighting our contributions and providing a rationale for our choices.

Spines and Parameterization

The key element of the implementation of transmogrifiers is the deformation algorithm that maps the source shape into the destination shape. For this we extend the skeleton-based approach of Hsu et al. [21]. Our algorithm requires that we define each shape through three curves: two boundary curves at the edges of the shape, and a spine somewhere between them (see Fig. 6). Based on those curves, the algorithm creates a parameterization of the source space that it uses to render it onto the destination. The destination space is a shape defined by a different set of spline and boundary lines (see Fig. 7).

With an equivalent parameterization in the source and the destination, we can then map the source area between the source's spine and boundaries to the shape defined by the destination's spine and boundaries. The parameterization of the shape's area is based on a linear interpolation between the spine, $f_s(u)$, and the boundary curves, $f_b(u)$ and $f_{b'}(u)$, where u is the parameter that expresses the distance of a point along the curves, and v the parameter that describes the relative position of a point between the curves:

$$f(u,v) = \begin{cases} (1-2v)f_b(u) + 2vf_s(u) & v \leq \frac{1}{2}; \\ (2-2v)f_s(u) + (2v-1)f_{b'}(u) & else \end{cases}$$

where $v \in [0,1]$.

Parameterization of standard shapes is easy to achieve (e.g., we parameterize the circle using polar coordinates); for trace-shapes we use piecewise linear parameterization of the touch traces. Once this is established, the rest of the process uses the texture coordinates to reshape the source area to fit the destination area. This is done by calculating the image's texture coordinates along the source's spine and boundary curves. These coordinates are used on the destination shape curves' positions, rendering textured quad strips between the spine and each boundary (Figure 7).

We adopted this algorithm for four reasons: a) it is sufficiently flexible to provide a wide variety of transformations; b) it preserves the continuity of the source and destination shapes; c) the visual presence of spines and borders facilitates the understanding of transformations (as opposed to, e.g., formulae); and d) it lends itself to trace-based interaction and, specifically, multitouch input (see next subsection).

Our implementation described thus far differs from Hsu et al.'s Skeletal Strokes [21] because the latter are constrained to rectangles as source shapes and only introduce arbitrary shapes as destination shape. We can use arbitrary shapes for both source and destination; in the following sections we show multiple examples that need this flexibility. Additionally, Hsu et al. do not offer an interface for the flexible manipulation of their parameters. In contrast, transmogrification is an interactive technique at heart. The following sections describe adaptations of our algorithm that derive directly from the interactive nature of transmogrifiers.

Defining the Spine and Boundary Curves

As seen above, the main input for the algorithm is the curves that define the source and destination shapes. These are defined in different ways depending on the type of shape. For example, in a quadrilateral we choose two opposite sides as boundaries, and the median line as spine; in a circle the boundary lines are the circumference and the circle's center, and the spine is a circle at half the radius. For trace-shapes the definition of the curves is built into the interaction and requires some extra considerations.

Single-point trace shapes. In these shapes the touch-trace generated by the analyst determines the spine, but the raw input has to be processed before it can be used due to the noisy touch input and irregular sampling provided by the input device. We interpolate the input linearly to subpixel resolution and then filter and decimate this signal [11]. The sampling of the spine curve is regularized according to arc-length along the spine. The viewer can alter the sampling by manipulating the handles described in the Interaction section.

To generate the shape, we expand from the spine outwards, perpendicular to the spine's tangent until boundary curves at the desired width are created. As noted by Hsu et al., this can result in wrinkling or folding on the inside of boundary curves (Figure 8). Figure 9 shows the solution proposed by Hsu et al. [21], which only works for small loops, and our solution, which avoids the area becoming unnaturally stretched by distributing points along the path to the loop's centroid (for larger loops). While this was not a concern in their scenario,

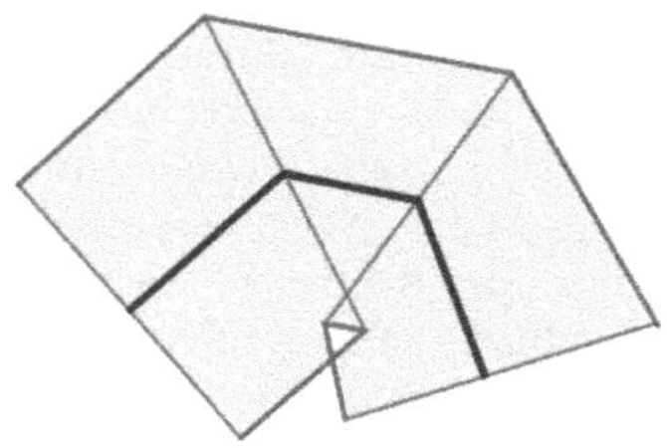

Figure 8. If only the tangent is used, growing the spine into the trace-shape produces overlaps (white triangle at bottom). Dark blue: trace (spine); red: path tangent; light blue: constructed bounding curves.

Figure 9. Repairing a self-intersection in a boundary curve (left). Center: moving sample points formerly within the loop onto the intersecting line segment. Right: To reduce stretching, we distribute loop points between the intersection and the loop's centroid instead.

we need to consider it because we use trace shapes as source shapes. For larger loops with more than three points in the loop we distribute points along a path to the loop's centroid.

Double-Point Trace. In a double-point trace-shape the touch-traces determine the boundary curves, and the spine is interpolated midway between them. Both boundaries are captured simultaneously, but care must be taken to match the sampling of both curves.

The piecewise curves resulting from each trace are linearly re-sampled based on input time so that each curve has the same number of points. Once both curves have an equal number of sample points the same interpolation and filtering process described for the single-point trace is applied. The parameterization for all three curves is based on the spine distance (as opposed to one of the boundaries).

Note that it is possible to use touch timestamps instead of distance to generate alternative sampling patterns. This opens a number of interesting possibilities that have not been considered in previous work. Moreover, our algorithmic modifications also support non one-to-one mappings, where source areas can appear more than once in the destination shape. In other words, transmogrifier shapes can fold upon or loop over themselves, making the same source pixels appear multiple times in the transmogrified image.

EXAMPLES

This section illustrates usage of transmogrification to achieve alternative visualizations in a range of scenarios.

Path Rectification and Deformation

Maps are typically represented as projections onto Cartesian planes. Distances and areas as measured in these representations usually revert to approximately Euclidean distances, which can be perceived reasonably accurately through direct sight. However, there are instances where we need to see distances beyond "straight line" distance. A straightforward example of this is J. H. Colton's visualization of river's length,

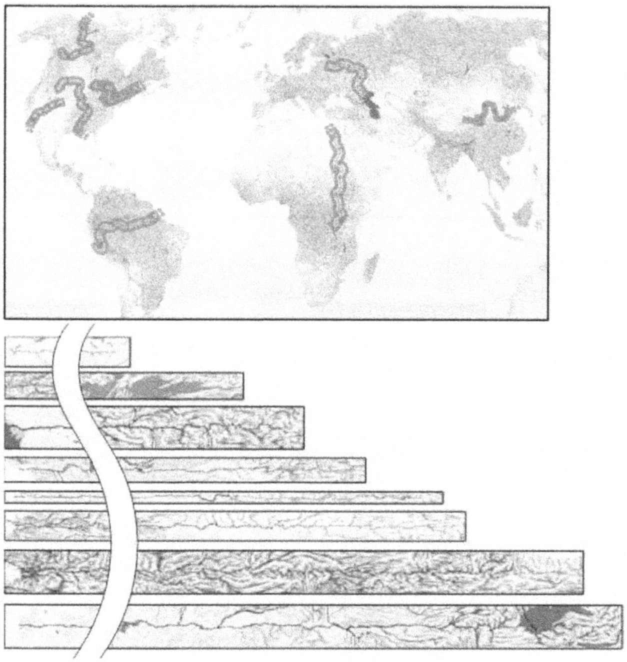

Figure 10. Straightening rivers. Top: rivers are traced on a map (in green), and transmogrified into a straight shape to present the river's length for visual comparison while retaining local context. River imagery is screen capture of National Geographic's World Rivers Water Map (http://bit.ly/bVOMkq). From top to bottom: the Colorado, St. Lawrence, Volga, MacKenzie, Yellow, Mississippi, Amazon and Nile. Mid section of the rivers omitted for space.

recently analyzed by Tufte [52], p. 77. Because it can be difficult to compare the lengths of rivers as displayed in their own locations, with different bends and orientations, Colton decided to "hang rivers to dry" in a visualization that, (a) is straightforward to understand, (b) provides a quick, visual answer to the question of distance, and (c) preserves local context and much of the graphical information of the rivers contained in their original graphical representation. What was a compelling but likely a painstakingly difficult visualization to produce for Colton is interactively trivial with a single-point trace transmogrifier (see Figure 10). All that is needed is to simply trace one's finger along the path of the river. This technique can enable quick visual calculations of distance to other elements such as roads, paths, and coastlines. Precision will depend on multiple factors such as the accuracy of the initial representation, whether the 'magnet' mode is on, the accuracy of the tracing, and the sampling algorithm.

When transmogrification is used to straighten roads, as in the opening scenario of the paper (Fig. 1.B), the resulting imagery is close in spirit to Matthew Paris's medieval pilgrimage maps [18]. Essentially, the resulting maps abstract away turns and provide a representation where the reader sees to the left or to the right what the travelers would see as their trip progresses.

The example in Fig. 11 uses spatial adjustments achieved through spine scaling for the route from Los Angeles to Las Vegas. The left part of the figure is an undistorted cutout of

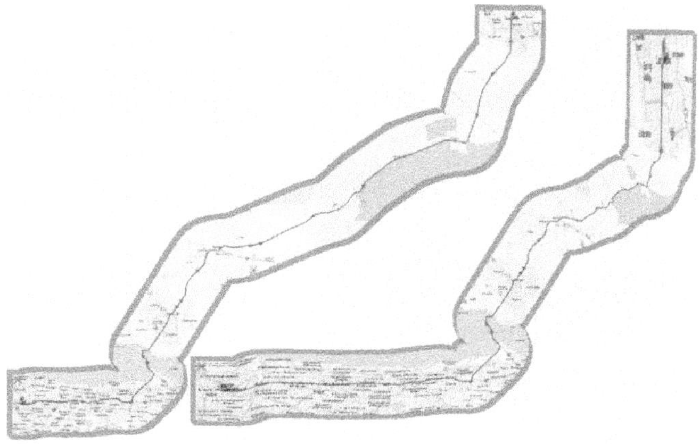

Figure 11. Compressing the highway between Las Vegas and Los Angeles. Left: original route cut from surroundings. Right: route transmogrified to show more details around cities and less across the desert.

the map; the right part shows a transmogrification of the route where sampling is intentionally varied. It has been manipulated to provide more detail in the areas that contain more important information (the details such as curves and turns within each city), and less detail in the long straight roads crossing the Mojave Desert. This manipulation is reminiscent of the route maps that people draw when sketching directions, and of those generated by Agrawala and Stolte [1] and Kopf et al. [27]. However, here we only adjust scale along the spine of the transmogrifier; adjusting scale in the dimension perpendicular to the spine can be achieved through a two-finger trace. Adding semantic zoom capabilities requires further work.

Straightening trajectories can offer additional benefits beyond the above length comparisons or traveler-centric maps. For example, transmogrifiers can help represent spatial data that encodes other visual variables. Fig. 12 (left) is an actual route visualization of aircraft taking off from Lyon airport; it shows how the aircraft take different routes that reach high altitudes (in red to blue) at different stages. Optimizing altitude profiles is important because it affects fuel consumption. However, the layout and the turns in the trajectories make color-coded altitude profiles difficult to compare. Fig. 12 (right) shows an alternative representation that rectifies the routes. We discussed this visualization with an air traffic controller, who was able to confirm insights from the graph that are otherwise difficult to perceive in the original layout (e.g., current routes going to the East have less steep profiles, despite heading towards the Alps).

Changing Visualization Layouts

There are multiple instances of visualizations that can benefit from dynamically adjusting their layout geometries; for example, circular or square layouts of trees might be preferable depending on whether the visualization is meant for a single person or a group of people on a tabletop [51]. Fig. 13 shows how an icicle plot is transmogrified into a sunburst tree, and the transmogrifier in Fig. 14 turns a circular chord visualization [33] into a rectangular layout.

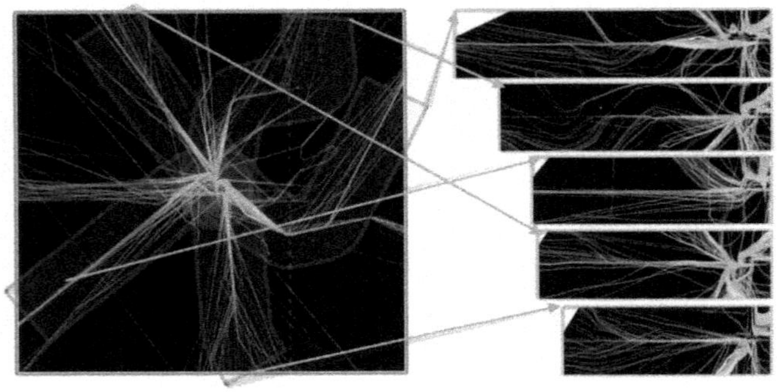

Figure 12. Left) One day of recorded aircraft positions taking off from Lyon airport. The color corresponds to the aircraft altitude (blue for low altitudes, red for high altitudes). Right) The rectified routes. Grey arrows added for clarity.

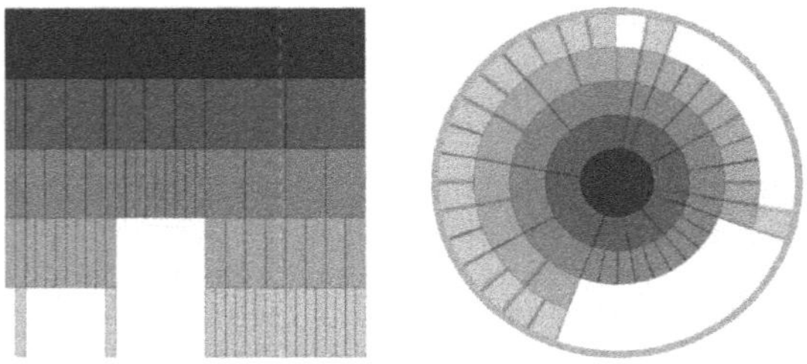

Figure 13. Transmogrification of an icicle plot to a sunburst tree.

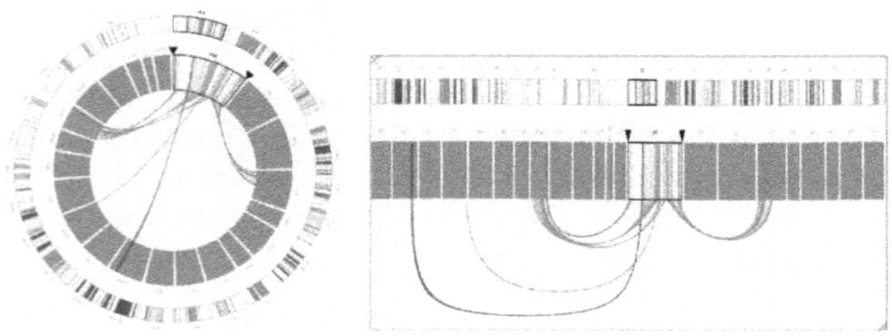

Figure 14. Transmogrification of a circular chord visualization (left) to a rectangular layout (right). Technique from [33].

A different example of visualization re-representation is the reverse of path rectification shown in the opening scenario (Fig. 1.C), where a variable is shown in its spatial context by warping to a path. More complicated geometry transformations can take advantage of the free-form shapes to, for example, adjust a stacked graph [55] by straightening the base line of a data region (Fig. 15).

The recursive features of the TC also enable composite manipulations, such as the elimination of part of the data in a circular graph by first transforming to a square geometry, clipping, and then transforming back to circular (Fig. 16). Note that similarly to removing data, we can add or merge data from multiple sources into a single graph.

DISCUSSION

Just as we often find solutions to problems by testing different alternatives in our minds, generating visual alternatives of visual data sets may be the key to new insights. Conversely, the ability to reverse distortions in representations should also facilitate analyzing data that would otherwise be partially obscured. Many existing techniques are currently being used by analysts and artists precisely for these purposes; for example,

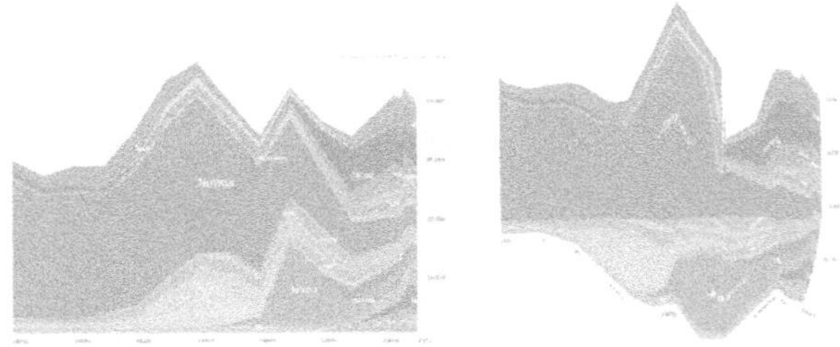

Figure 15. Transmogrification of a stackedbar graph can be used to straighten the base of one of the regions. Left: stacked graph; right: transmogrification. Technique from [55].

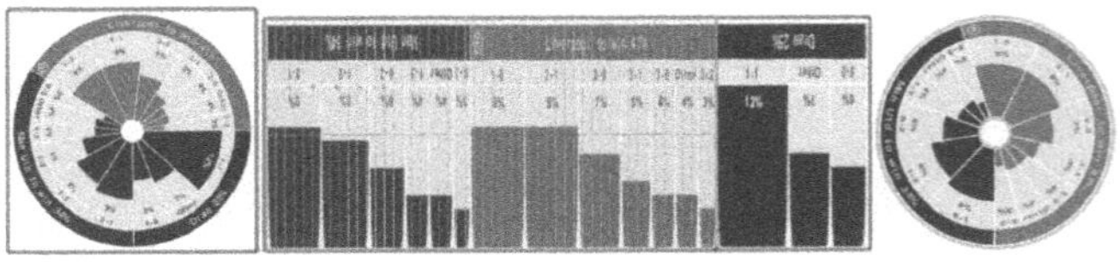

Figure 16. Transmogrification of a Nightingale chart into a bar chart, and then back to Nightingale with a subset of the data.

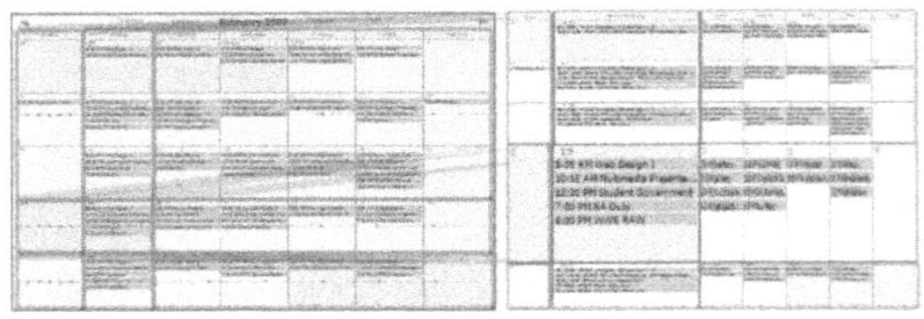

Figure 17. Use of several transmogrifiers to create a Table Lens [41].

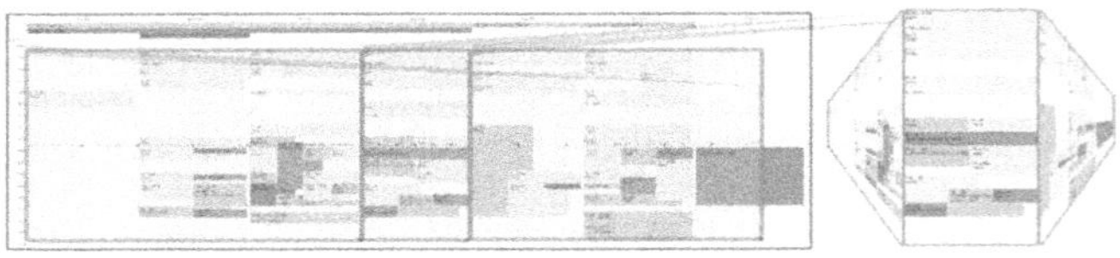

Figure 18. Use of three transmogrifiers to create a Perspective Wall [31].

collages and sketches (digital and paper) are often useful to reorganize data representations of images or data sets. However, it is difficult to find examples of techniques that allow us to quickly use non-linear and arbitrary transformations, especially in a casual setting.

With Transmogrification we extend existing knowledge and algorithms from computer graphics to serve the purpose of information assessment and exploration, particularly in initial stages where a quick look at an alternate view could confirm or refute an idea. We have found that multi-touch manipulation and tracing input lends itself particularly well to the control of graphical distortion techniques, where the large parametric space would be tedious and difficult to control through a single point (e.g., a mouse). Moreover, from our own experience with the system and during demonstrations, we speculate that the directness of touch interaction is particularly suited for deformation techniques because most of our experiences of deformation come from the physical world (e.g., stretching, folding of papers, cloth or other pliable or plastic materials [34]).

From the point of view of information visualization, we see transmogrification as the natural evolution of existing distortion-based techniques such as lenses [9], Melange [17], or Perspective Wall [31]. Recreations of a TableLens and a Perspective Wall with transmogrifiers are shown in

Figures 17 and 18. In fact, it is possible to think about transmogrifiers as a generalization of lenses and portal techniques. However, its flexibility and the possibility to transform visuals in arbitrary ways enables a qualitatively different way to use them; instead of applying a technique to an image, we create an ad-hoc interaction technique where visual results are based on direct interaction with the image. This information-centric perspective represents an inversion of most current techniques in visual data exploration.

We have found that transmogrifiers can be also useful to prototype and replicate many existing visualizations. In particular, the ability of the canvas to work as a transmogrification overlay on top of existing interactive visualizations makes it a powerful tool to explore questions about visualizations and about the data itself; for example, would a graph show the same effect if straightened out? How would this look on a perspective-wall? Is there a clear relationship between house prices and distance to the coast?

Although it is too early to say, we think that the composability and bidirectionality of transmogrifications will enable a large set of unexplored avenues. A common problem-solving strategy in physics, math, and engineering is to transform the data into another domain or geometry (e.g., the frequency domain, complex vector space), solve an easier problem in the transformed domain, and transform the solution back to the original domain. Transmogrification enables a similar process for spatial representations.

Finally, this paper is focused on the application of transmogrification to information visualization. During the development of transmogrifiers and the TC we have found many potential applications for collaborative environments (e.g., reproducing Cut-outs [39]), image editing (e.g., correcting perspective or drawing in perspective), and art and entertainment (e.g., creating caricatures and fabric patterns).

LIMITATIONS AND FUTURE WORK

Visualization tasks are sometimes focused on representation accuracy. The interactive nature of transmogrifiers and their reliance on touch traces might make it difficult to achieve shape-accuracy, even with the 'magnet' mode. For example, in the hanging rivers example above, the length of a river will be affected by the person's tracing accuracy which, in turn, is affected by the fat-finger problem. Although we see this more as a consequence of the sketch-like and approximate nature of transmogrification than as a problem, there are additional input techniques (e.g., input offset) that could enable better precision when needed.

Our implementation has been refined to avoid deformation artifacts when possible, but deformation of raster images always implies the risk of making text and other symbols less readable. We built a parallel version of transmogrifiers that addresses this problem through vector rendering. Given an initial point within the source shape we calculate its position in the destination shape. In this way, text or other primitives such as lines or glyphs can simply be drawn at their transformed position as shown in Figure 19. Future work is to automatically extract labels from source raster images (similarly to Savva et al. [44]) and alter transmogrifications to preserve text, or recognize and vectorize text and symbols to present in dual vector-raster transmogrifications.

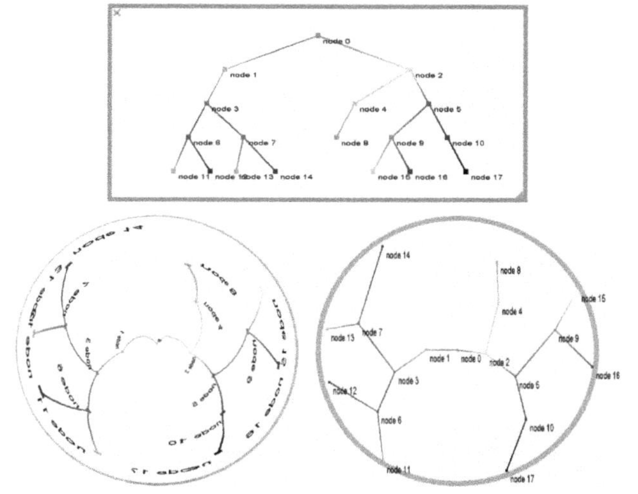

Figure 19. Transmogrification of a rectangular tree source (top) to circular destinations. Left: raster-based result. Right: vector-based result.

CONCLUSION

In this paper we have presented transmogrification, a visual exploration technique based on arbitrary transformations of 2D shapes. The technique is based on the transformation of arbitrarily-shaped source areas of the image into equally arbitrary destination regions. Through the adaptation of graphic transformations based on a spine, and using novel interaction techniques for the specification of shapes based on multi-touch traces, we enable people to design transformations based on the existing image and create real-time alternative visualizations quickly. We also presented examples that explore the application of transmogrifiers to visual map exploration, distortion compensation, and layout transformation.

ACKNOWLEDGEMENTS

We thank the reviewers and the InnoVis group. Research support was provided by the Natural Sciences and Engineering Research Council of Canada, SurfNet, GRAND NCE, AITF, Smart Technologies Inc., and the School of Computer Science at the University of St Andrews.

REFERENCES

1. Agrawala, M., and Stolte, C. Rendering effective route maps: improving usability through generalization. In *Proc. SIGGRAPH*, ACM (2001).
2. Bederson, B., and Boltman, A. Does animation help users build mental maps of spatial information? In *IEEE InfoVis* (1999).
3. Beier, T., and Neely, S. Feature-based image metamorphosis. In *Proc. SIGGRAPH*, vol. 26, ACM (1992).
4. Bier, E. A., Stone, M. C., Pier, K., Buxton, W., and DeRose, T. D. Toolglass and magic lenses: The see-through interface. In *Proc. SIGGRAPH*, ACM (1993).
5. Bostock, M., Ogievetsky, V., and Heer, J. D3: Data-driven documents. *IEEE TVCG 17*, 12 (2011).
6. Bottger, J., Brandes, U., Deussen, O., and Ziezold, H. Map warping for the annotation of metro maps. *IEEE CG&A 28*, 5 (2008).

7. Browne, J., Lee, B., Carpendale, S., Riche, N., and Sherwood, T. Data analysis on interactive whiteboards through sketch-based interaction. In *Proc. ITS*, ACM (2011).
8. Burtnyk, N., and Wein, M. Interactive skeleton techniques for enhancing motion dynamics in key frame animation. *Commun ACM 19*, 10 (1976).
9. Carpendale, S., and Montagnese, C. A framework for unifying presentation space. In *Proc. UIST*, ACM (2001).
10. Chao, W., Munzner, T., and van de Panne, M. Poster: Rapid pen-centric authoring of improvisational visualizations with napkinvis. In *Posters Compendium*, InfoVis (2010).
11. Cherlin, J. J., Samavati, F., Sousa, M. C., and Jorge, J. A. Sketch-based modeling with few strokes. In *Proc. SCCG*, ACM (2005).
12. Chevalier, F., Dragicevic, P., and Hurter, C. Histomages: fully synchronized views for image editing. In *Proc. UIST*, ACM (2012).
13. Cockburn, A., Karlson, A., and Bederson, B. B. A review of overview+detail, zooming, and focus+context interfaces. *ACM Comput. Surv. 41*, 1 (2009).
14. Dragicevic, P., Bezerianos, A., Javed, W., Elmqvist, N., and Fekete, J.-D. Temporal distortion for animated transitions. In *Proc. CHI*, ACM (2011).
15. Eitz, M., Sorkine, O., and Alexa, M. Sketch based image deformation. In *Proc. VMV* (2007).
16. Elmqvist, N., Dragicevic, P., and Fekete, J. Rolling the dice: Multidimensional visual exploration using scatterplot matrix navigation. *IEEE TVCG 14*, 6 (2008).
17. Elmqvist, N., Henry, N., Riche, Y., and Fekete, J.-D. Melange: space folding for multi-focus interaction. In *Proc. CHI*, ACM (2008).
18. Gaudio, M. Matthew paris and the cartography of the margins. *Gesta 39*, 1 (2000).
19. Haunert, J.-H., and Sering, L. Drawing road networks with focus regions. *IEEE TVCG 17*, 12 (2011).
20. Heer, J., and Robertson, G. Animated transitions in statistical data graphics. *IEEE TVCG 13*, 6 (2007).
21. Hsu, S. C., Lee, I. H. H., and Wiseman, N. E. Skeletal strokes. In *Proc. UIST*, ACM (1993).
22. Hurter, C., Telea, A., and Ersoy, O. Moleview: An attribute and structure-based semantic lens for large element-based plots. *IEEE TVCG 17*, 12 (2011).
23. Hurter, C., Tissoires, B., and Conversy, S. Fromdady: Spreading aircraft trajectories across views to support iterative queries. *IEEE TVCG 15*, 6 (2009).
24. Igarashi, T., Moscovich, T., and Hughes, J. F. As-rigid-as-possbile shape manipulation. *ACM Trans. Graph. 24*, 3 (July 2005).
25. Jacobson, A., Baran, I., Popović, J., and Sorkine, O. Bounded biharmonic weights for real-time deformation. *ACM Trans. Graph. 30*, 4 (2011).
26. Kass, M., Witkin, A., and Terzopoulos, D. Snakes: Active contour models. *IJCV 1*, 4 (1988).
27. Kopf, J., Agrawala, M., Bargeron, D., Salesin, D., and Cohen, M. Automatic generation of destination maps. *ACM Trans. Graph. 29*, 6 (2010).
28. Kostelnick, C. The visual rhetoric of data displays: The conundrum of clarity. *IEEE Trans. Prof. Commun. 50*, 4 (2007).
29. Lee, T.-Y., Lin, Y.-C., Sun, Y. N., and Lin, L. Fast feature-based metamorphosis and operator design. *Comp. Graph. Forum 17*, 3 (1998).
30. Lipman, Y., Levin, D., and Cohen-Or, D. Green coordinates. *ACM Trans. Graph. 27*, 3 (2008).
31. Mackinlay, J. D., Robertson, G. G., and Card, S. K. The perspective wall: Detail and context smoothly integrated. In *Proc. CHI* (1991).
32. Meng, W., Zhang, X., Dong, W., and Paul, J.-C. Multicage image deformation on gpu. In *Proc. VRCAI*, ACM (2011).
33. Meyer, M., Munzner, T., and Pfister, H. Mizbee: A multiscale synteny browser. *IEEE TVCG 15*, 6 (2009).
34. Mikulecky, K., Hancock, M., Brosz, J., and Carpendale, S. Exploring physical information cloth on a multitouch table. In *Proc. ITS*, ACM (2011).
35. Nacenta, M. A., Baudisch, P., Benko, H., and Wilson, A. Separability of spatial manipulations in multi-touch interfaces. In *Proc. GI*, Canadian Info. Proc. Society (2009).
36. Nacenta, M. A., Kamber, Y., Qiang, Y., and Kristensson, P. Memorability of pre-designed and user-defined gesture sets. In *Proc. CHI*, ACM (2013).
37. Pietriga, E., and Appert, C. Sigma lenses: focus-context transitions combining space, time and translucence. In *Proc. CHI*, ACM (2008).
38. Pindat, C., Pietriga, E., Chamuis, O., and Puech, C. Jellylens: Content-aware adaptive lenses. In *Proc. UIST*, ACM (2012).
39. Pinelle, D., Stach, T., Stuckel, D., Nacenta, M., Dyck, J., and Gutwin, C. Cutouts: A flexible interaction infrastructure for tabletop groupware. In *Ext. Abs. CSCW* (2006).
40. Pousman, Z., Stasko, J., and Mateas, M. Casual information visualization: Depictions of data in everyday life. *IEEE TVCG 13*, 6 (2007).
41. Rao, R., and Card, S. K. The table lens: merging graphical and symbolic representations in an interactive focus+context visualization for tabular information. In *Proc. CHI*, ACM (1994).
42. Reilly, D. F., and Inkpen, K. M. Map morphing: making sense of incongruent maps. In *Proc. GI*, Canadian Info. Proc. Society (2004).
43. Robertson, G., Cameron, K., Czerwinski, M., and Robbins, D. Animated visualization of multiple intersecting hierarchies. *Information Visualization 1*, 1 (Mar. 2002).
44. Savva, M., Kong, N., Chhajta, A., F.-F., L., Agrawala, M., and Heer, J. Revision: automated classification, analysis and redesign of chart images. In *Proc. UIST*, ACM (2011).
45. Schiwietz, T., Georgii, J., and Westermann, R. Freeform image. *IEEE CG&A* (2007).
46. Shen, Y., Ma, L., and Liu, H. An MLS-based cartoon deformation. *Visual Comput. 26* (2010).
47. Slack, J., and Munzner, T. Composite rectilinear deformation for stretch and squish navigation. *IEEE TVCG 12*, 5 (2006).
48. Smythe, D. B. A two-pass mesh warping algorithm for object transformation and image interpolation. Tech. Rep. 1030, ILM Comp. Graph. Dept., Lucasfilm, California, USA, 1990.
49. Sun, Q., Fu, C.-W., and He, Y. An interactive multi-touch sketching interface for diffusion curves. In *Proc. CHI*, ACM (2011).
50. Tan, D. S., Meyers, B., and Czerwinski, M. Wincuts: manipulating arbitrary window regions for more effective use of screen space. In *Ext. Abs. CHI*, ACM (2004).
51. Tobiasz, M., Isenberg, P., and Carpendale, S. Lark: Coordinating co-located collaboration with information visualization. *IEEE TVCG 15*, 6 (2009).
52. Tufte, E. R. *Envisioning Information*. Graphic Press, 1990.
53. Tversky, B. Some ways that maps and diagrams communicate. In *Spatial Cognition II*, vol. 1849 of *LNCS*. Springer, 2000.
54. Tversky, B., Bauer Morrison, J., and Betrancourt, M. Animation: can it facilitate? *Int. J. Hum-Comp Studies 57*, 4 (2002).
55. Wattenberg, M. Baby names, visualization, and social data analysis. In *IEEE InfoVis* (2005).
56. Weber, O., and Gotsman, C. Controllable conformal maps for shape deformation and interpolation. *ACM Trans. Graph. 29*, 4 (2010).
57. Weng, Y., Shi, X., Bao, H., and Zhang, J. Sketching MLS image deformations on the GPU. *Comp. Graph. Forum 27*, 7 (2008).
58. Weng, Y., Xu, W., Wu, Y., Zhou, K., and Guo, B. 2d shape deformation using nonlinear least squares optimization. *Visual Comput. 22* (2006).
59. Wolberg, G. Image morphing: a survey. *Visual Comput. 14* (1998).
60. Yang, W., and Feng, J. 2d shape manipulation via topology-aware rigid grid. *Computer Animation and Virtual Worlds 20*, 2-3 (2009).

TextTearing: Expanding Whitespace for Digital Ink Annotation

Dongwook Yoon
Cornell University
Information Science
Ithaca, NY 14850
dy252@cornell.edu

Nicholas Chen
Microsoft Research Cambridge
21 Station Road
Cambridge CB1 2FB, UK
nchen@microsoft.com

François Guimbretière
Cornell University
Information Science
Ithaca, NY 14850
francois@cs.cornell.edu

ABSTRACT
Having insufficient space for making annotations is a problem that afflicts both paper and digital documents. We introduce the TextTearing technique for *in situ* expansion of inter-line whitespace and pair it with a lightweight interaction for margin expansion as a way to address this problem. The full system leverages the dynamism of digital documents and employs a bimanual design that combines the precision of pen with the fluidity of touch. Our evaluation found that a simpler unimanual variant of TextTearing was preferred over direct annotation and margin-only expansion. Direct annotation in naturally occurring whitespace was least preferred.

ACM Classification Keywords: H5.2. Information interfaces and presentation (e.g., HCI): User Interfaces

Author Keywords: e-reading, documents, annotation, whitespaces, margins, bi-manual interaction, layout

INTRODUCTION
Written annotations are a crucial aspect of engaged reading activities. Among the many roles that annotations play include demarking important passages, tracking reading progress, and recording interpretations about the text [10]. Paper documents provide a number of affordances that cater to annotation activities [14]. For instance, blank spaces in the document—margins, within-text spaces, and blank pages—offer readily available regions where annotations can be created with minimal interruption to the reading process. Moreover, the spatial proximity of these regions to the text provides context [5] and implicitly connects annotations with the text to which they refer [11]. Paper materials are not perfect, however. Pages have a set amount of space for markup, which can be insufficient at times [12].

Support for annotation is less robust when it comes to digital documents. Although many software tools support free-form inking with touchscreens or pen digitizers,

UIST'13, October 8–11, 2013, St. Andrews, United Kingdom.
Copyright © 2013 ACM 978-1-4503-2268-3/13/10...$15.00.
http://dx.doi.org/10.1145/2501988.2502036

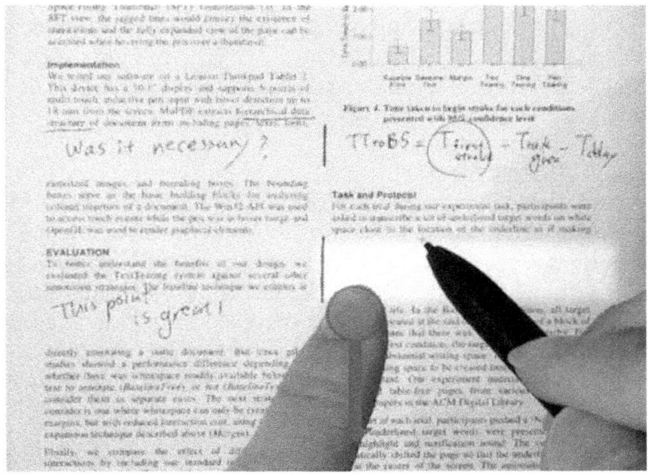

Figure 1. The TextTearing system allows additional writing space to be created between lines of text using a downward tearing gesture. The expanding region is highlighted. The red arrow indicates touch gesture opening a space. The blue shadow is a dynamic palm rejection region.

writing on electronic screens tends to place more demand on the available annotation space [1]. However, the dynamic nature of digital documents provides an avenue for workarounds. Existing strategies such as comment boxes, digital Post-it™ notes [13], and the ability to insert blank pages expand the space for annotations. Unfortunately, these come at the cost of fluidity and can disrupt the reading process [14]. Moreover, displaying these types of annotations (in overlaid windows alongside the text, for example) can result in the main text being obscured or unpredictable annotation layouts.

We introduce an interaction called TextTearing that addresses these problems. With this technique, users can tear open (i.e., expand) the whitespace between adjacent lines of text. This allows users to create blank space where it is needed, while maintaining the overall logical structure of the text and avoiding occlusions. We describe an initial design of our system, which includes our approach for rearranging document elements, a two handed tearing interaction based on Zeleznik et al.'s work [18], and a palm rejection system that makes it possible to implement this technique on commodity hardware. A complementary technique for expanding the page margins is also described.

Our evaluation of TextTearing compares it against a baseline where there is ample whitespace to directly write, a condition with expandable side margins, a two-handed version using an alternative tearing gesture, and a pen-only tearing technique based on pigtail gestures [7]. Our results showed that margin expansion was comparable to the baseline conditions, which were fastest because they required no interaction. However, the two highest ranked techniques in terms of user preferences employed tearing. In contrast, the baseline condition came in last, suggesting that the placement of the writing space makes a difference. Among the tearing techniques, the pen-only pigtail technique had a preference advantage over our initial design and could potentially be faster in practice.

RELATED WORK

Agrawala and Shilman [1] explained that differing physical characteristics between electronic displays and paper means that digital ink annotations are often larger and sloppier. As a result, what whitespace is available is more impacted. Their DIZI approach is to offer a zoomed-in writing pad to counteract the natural tendency to write larger, but because DIZI preserves document layout it provides no facilities for creating additional space.

Digital documents offer a unique capability to bypass the physical constraints of paper documents, however. Chang et al. introduced the notion of fluid documents, which dynamically adjust their layout in order to display secondary information [2]. We follow this strategy but apply it in the context of annotation creation.

Zeleznik et al. [18] created a bimanual gesture for inserting and removing whitespace within a digital canvas to solve similar problems of limited writing space encountered when working through math problems. In their system, this feature is activated when a touch following a pen stroke manipulates a feed forward widget. We used a simplified version of this approach in the initial design of our system. Our study provides performance data about different variations of this interaction technique.

LiquidText used various multi-touch gestures to collapse, rearrange, highlight and extract portions of a document [16] and GatherReader [8] explored how these tasks could be further enhanced using pen + touch interactions [9]. Although the interactions in these systems bear a resemblance to TextTearing, they serve fundamentally different purposes. In these other systems the interactions assist in juxtaposing or gathering different parts of a document whereas the interactions in TextTearing are designed to help the user make *in-situ* ink annotations.

TEXTTEARING

Spatial proximity between annotations and the primary text provides context [10], helps maintain continuity of attention, and serves as an implicit connection between the annotation and the text [11]. Thus, the central goal of our system is to give readers access to writing space anywhere beside printed text. To accomplish this, we let users create an expandable region of whitespace by adjusting the spacing between lines of text. As the region grows, the content below it is shifted lower in the page. In the following sections, we first describe the algorithms we use to make the system applicable to a wider variety documents; specifically, those with multiple columns. Then, we present the interaction for performing the space expansion.

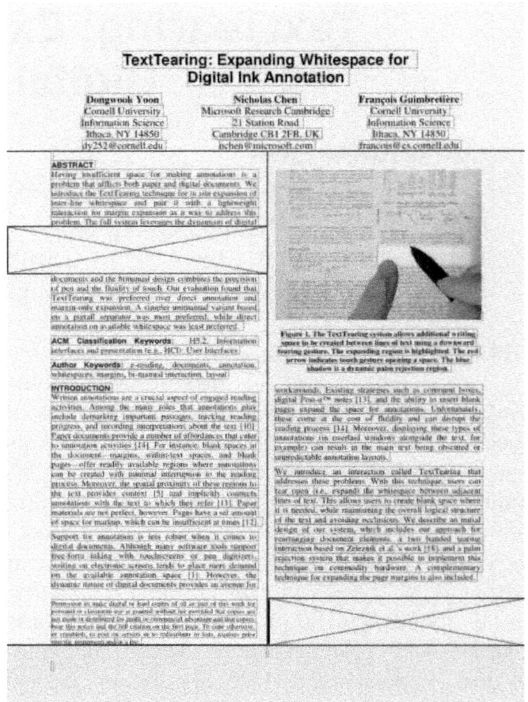

Figure 2. The dynamic document layout model. Boxes with an "X" are movable regions of the document. The area above and below the columns are each a single block. The left column has two text block and one region produced using TextTearing; the right, one text blocks and one tearing region.

Handling Multi-Column Layouts

To reduce undesirable effects of layout modification, such as introducing spurious spaces in adjacent columns, or collisions of shifted text into other elements, it is important for the system to understand the visual structure of the document and to enforce some modification constraints.

Our first task is to identify the position of text columns. Since our system targets PDF documents, we leverage layout information about the start and end points of the lines of text on a page. We first remove short lines of text from our analysis. Then, we use the midpoint between minimum and maximum horizontal line positions to identify the position of the alley between columns. Once that is done, we assign each line and figure into either of the left column, the right column, or leave it alone if it doesn't fall cleanly on either side. Once lines have been classified into the columns, the unclassified text is placed into either the header or footer depending on whether they are above or below the column bounding boxes. A typical structure our algorithm produces is shown in Figure 2. We currently only support two-column page layouts but this algorithm can be easily extended to handle layouts with more than two well-defined columns.

The extracted document structure dictates how the document expands. Tearing operations will always maintain the relative relationships between the header, columns, and footer. For instance, if space is created in one column, then the text below it will be pushed downward, which will in turn push the footer downward, creating whitespace at the bottom of the adjacent column if needed (Figure 2). Enforcing this high-level structure isolates expansion to a single column, which results in more predictable behavior and helps preserve spatial relationships in the document. In this first prototype we did not consider the case in which a tearing operation crosses over a long stroke such as the line in a callout, for example. This could be addressed by augmenting our system with the annotation reflow technique proposed by Golovchinsky and Denoue [4].

Annotations are anchored to neighboring pieces of text to accommodate subsequent movements of that text. This is done by first grouping strokes that are created in rapid succession (< 0.5s separation interval) together and then setting the stroke coordinates to be relative to the location of the closest piece of text so that when the text moves, so do the strokes.

Tearing Interaction

A guiding principle for the tearing interaction is that it should be precise (since lines could be closely spaced) and introduce minimal overhead compared to ordinary inking. Hinckley et al. showed that pen + touch input combines the lightweight nature of touch with the accuracy of pen input [8, 9]. For this reason, we adapt the pen + touch approach Zeleznik et al. employed to create blank space in Hands-on-Math [18]. In our system, users create additional space by hovering the pen tip over a target location and then use the finger on their other hand to "tear" the surrounding text apart. To avoid false positives that can occur when users are panning with the pen near the screen, we require that the initial finger touch must be within 16.5 mm of the line of text the pen is hovering over. Since we do not overload the hovering state, it is not necessary to have a feed forward widget like the one in Hands-on-Math.

Dynamic Palm Rejection

To provide pen + touch input along with a comfortable writing environment, we needed some way to reject touch events generated when the palm of the hand holding the pen inadvertently comes in contact with the screen. We noticed that Vogel et al.'s occlusion silhouettes model [17] provided a conservative estimate of the projection of the hand on the screen. Therefore, this model can be used to compute the area where the palm could possibly make contact with the screen. The palm rejection system can then reject any contact points in this area. Remaining touch points are passed to our application to be used for the tearing interaction as well as for panning and zooming when the pen is over the screen.

Margin Expansion

The tearing interaction described above could conceivably be used for expanding page margins as well. We discovered, however, that it was more straightforward to simply expand the margins when users pan past the current page extents. The expansion behavior does not interfere with page turning since our system uses a side tap to turn pages. Support for page turning with swipe gestures can be achieved using either a swipe starting on the bezel or a threshold mechanism to differentiate panning from swiping. Although we only enable this capability for the horizontal margins, this simplified interaction could be used for vertical margins as well.

Viewing the Original Document Layout

A three-finger touch gesture shows an alternative view of the document in which the dynamically generated whitespace regions are collapsed. This collapsed view of the document can be useful for checking the original document appearance or for ensuring that a full page can be displayed on the screen.

In the collapsed view, each collapsed area is represented by a jagged underline that reflects the projection of ink strokes onto the tear line. While maintaining this quasi-mode, hovering the pen over a jagged line overlays the associated annotation region over the page in a semi-transparent window. We also prototyped a "spring loaded" version of the software that collapses newly created regions by default. In this alternative design, keeping the pen tip in hover range keeps the newly expanded region open, and exiting the range restores the original document layout. Our experience with the technique suggested that a more effortless and stable way to maintain the quasi-mode is needed, however.

The collapsed view of the document may also be useful for maintaining a constant page aspect ratio for alternative visualizations such as Space-Filling Thumbnails (SFT) [3]. In the SFT view, the jagged lines would continue to convey the existence of annotations and the fully expanded view of the page can be accessed when hovering the pen over a thumbnail.

Implementation

We tested our software on a Lenovo Thinkpad Tablet 2. This device has a 10.1" display, multi-touch input supporting up to 5 simultaneous points of contact, and inductive pen input with hover detection up to 18 mm from the screen. We used the MuPDF library in conjunction with

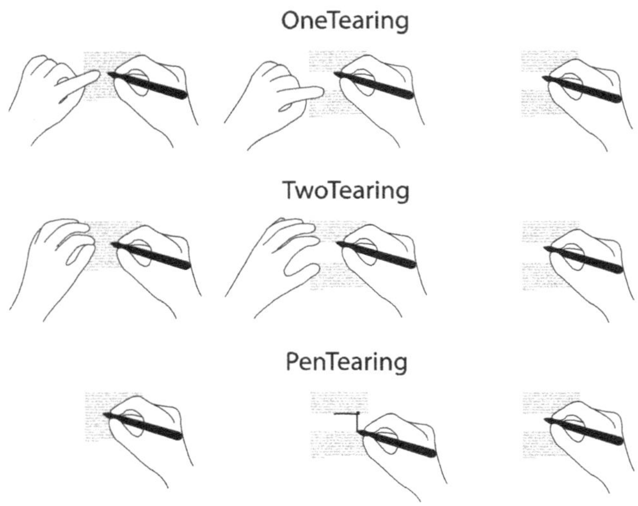

Figure 3. Tearing gestures considered in the experiment

OpenGL to render PDF documents onto the screen. MuPDF provided the hierarchical data structure of document items including page boundaries, text, raster images, and bounding boxes. The bounding boxes served as the basic building blocks for analyzing the column structure of a document. The palm rejection scheme currently used in Windows 8 does not support simultaneous bimanual interaction as it disables all touch input events when the pen is in hover range. We were able to work around this issue by using the RawInputDevice Win32 API to access touch events while the pen was in hover range.

EVALUATION

To better understand the benefits of our design, we evaluated the TextTearing system against several other annotation strategies. The baseline technique we employ is directly annotating a static document. But since pilot studies showed a performance difference depending on whether there was whitespace readily available below the text to annotate (*BaselineFree*), or not (*BaselineText*), we consider them as separate cases. The next strategy we consider is one where whitespace can only be created in the margins, but with reduced interaction cost, using the margin expansion technique described above (*Margin*).

Finally, we compare the effect of different tearing interactions by including our standard tearing technique presented above (*OneTearing*) along with two alternatives (Figure 3). The first alternative (*TwoTearing*), replaces the single finger non-dominant hand (NDH) interaction with a two finger NDH interaction resembling the gesture used for zooming on multi-touch devices. While hovering the pen, spreading one's fingers from a pinching position increases the size of the whitespace region. A possible benefit of this approach is that the positions of the NDH fingers map directly to the expansion region. The second alternative (*PenTearing*) uses a single handed pen interaction based on pigtail delimiters [7]. In this condition, a long horizontal line (> 12.0 mm) followed by a pigtail starts the tearing operation. The centroid of the stroke points preceding the crossing point indicates where the whitespace expansion should occur. The pen stroke is then extended downwards to specify the size of the expansion. The trigger is distinctive enough that it does not seem to interfere with writing activity. We considered but ruled out using the pen barrel button as a trigger since it can be error-prone [15].

Task and Protocol

For each trial during our experiment task, participants were asked to transcribe a set of underlined target words on white space close to the location of the underline as if making notes in real-life. In the BaselineFree condition, all target words were located at the end or the beginning of a block of text to guarantee that there was writing space nearby. For the BaselineText condition, the target was at least four lines away from substantial writing space. The tearing conditions required writing space to be created immediately below the underlined text. Our experiment materials consisted of picture and table-free pages from various two-column formatted papers in the ACM Digital Library.

At the start of each trial, participants pushed a 'Next' button and the underlined target words were presented with a visual highlight and notification sound. The system then automatically shifted the page so that the underlined words were at the center of the screen. The automatic centering removed page adjustment performance as a factor so that the measured time better reflects the amount of time it takes the participant to find or create writing space. Our implementation required a one-time iterative calibration procedure to manually tune the 5 parameters of the hand occlusion model (e.g., hand radius, forearm angle, etc.). This process could be made automatic, however [17].

Each technique was tested in one block. A block consisted of an introduction to the technique, a practice phase with 18 trials, and an experimental phase with 13 trials. The order of the techniques and materials was counterbalanced using a 6×6 Latin square. At the end of each block, participants were interviewed and completed a paper-based NASA Task Load Index survey (TLX). After all blocks were finished, the participant sorted 5 cards, representing the baseline and the four other techniques we tested, by preference. There were 12 participants in total (10 females, 2 males, average age 23.2 years old). Participants were paid $10 for the hour-long experiment.

RESULTS

Measurements of the elapsed time were computed starting from when the underlined target words are shown to the beginning of the first inking stroke. We accounted for the skewed distribution of human reaction time by taking the median value of a block's trials. We used Greenhouse-Geisser correction when we could not assume sphericity and the Bonferroni correction for pairwise comparisons.

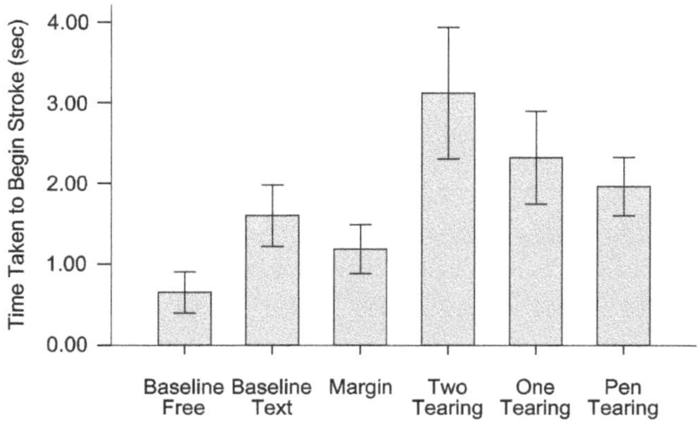

Figure 4. Time taken to begin stroke for each conditions presented with 95% confidence level

Errors
We counted an error whenever participants opened a space below a line other than the one that was underlined. A one-way repeated measure ANOVA on error rate showed a marginally significant effect of technique ($F(1.56, 17.17) = 3.73$, $p < .054$, partial $\eta^2 = .25$). TwoTearing (M = 13.69%, SD = .044) showed a significantly higher error rate than PenTearing (M = 2.78%, SD = .054, $p < .05$), due to small panning motions induced by the first finger prior to the second finger touching down. OneTearing fell in the middle (M = 7.63%, SD = .024) but the differences were not significant. We also measured the occurrence of false tearing activations for the pigtail gesture and found a single case across all trials (0.6%) that occurred when the participant was writing in cursive.

Total Space Opening Time
A one-way repeated measure ANOVA on the total space opening time showed a significant effect of technique ($F(2.47, 27.18) = 19.5$, $p < .001$, partial $\eta^2 = .64$). BaselineFree was the fastest condition (M = .65 sec, SD = .4, $p < .004$) followed by the Margin condition (M = 1.19 sec, SD = .48) that was marginally faster than BaselineText (M = 1.60 sec, SD = .60, $p < .067$) with both significantly faster than all tearing techniques ($p < .037$). It was somewhat surprising that the Margin technique performed in between the two baseline conditions that required no interaction at all. We believe that even though extra time was required to perform the margin expansion it is offset by the savings from not having to find a place to write.

For the tearing-enabled interactions, TwoTearing was the slowest (M = 3.12 sec, SD = .37) but the difference was only significant versus PenTearing (M = 1.96 sec, SD = .57, $p < .005$), but not OneTearing (M = 2.32 sec, SD = .91, $p < .098$). Given the large difference in means, we looked more carefully at our data and discovered that an overly cautious participant caused a large increase in the variance. Re-running the analysis without this participant resulted in TwoTearing being significantly slower than both of the other techniques ($p < .005$). The difference between PenTrearing and OneTearing was not significant ($p < .18$). To better characterize differences between OneTearing and PenTearing, we decomposed the total space opening time into 3 components: the time it took to begin tearing (T_{begin}), the time for the tearing action (T_{Tear}) and the time it took to start writing after the tearing action was completed ($T_{1^{st} stroke}$). We found that most of the difference between the two techniques were from T_{Tear}, with PenTearing being faster ($t(11) = 5.43$, $p < .0001$).

Subjective Preferences
We performed a Friedman test on the ranking data we gathered at the end of each session. We found a significant difference in ranking ($\chi^2 = 46.80$, $p < .001$), with PenTearing (1.25) coming first followed by OneTearing (2.25), Margin (3.17), and TwoTearing (3.75). The baseline technique was the last (4.58). The TLX showed that TwoTearing required the highest effort ($F(2.81, 30.87) = 5.78$, $p < .003$, partial $\eta^2 = .34$). No other significant differences were observed.

DISCUSSION
PenTearing was the most preferred, and rated higher than the Baseline techniques even though it was 3 times slower than direct annotations. We believe this effect illustrates that directly writing in naturally occurring space is not necessarily desirable even though it can be done quickly. This interpretation is in line with Agrawala and Shilman's observations about the difficulties of writing on electronic documents [1]. Additional studies are needed to determine how our expansion-based techniques compare to a zooming scheme like DIZI.

The fact that two of the tearing techniques were preferred over margin annotation reinforces the notion that the spatial positioning of the annotation is important. One participant noted that creating a space below the target text for writing resulted in less occlusion from the writing hand compared to annotating beside the target text (i.e. writing in the margin). We believe that reduced occlusion, along with ergonomic and semantic benefits from being able to position annotations flexibly, are advantages that TextTearing would bring to real-world annotation tasks.

Participants' preference for the one-handed, pen-only, tearing technique over the two-handed ones was surprising given the expected advantages of bimanual interaction [6]. Participants told us that PenTearing was a simpler one-step gesture. They also pointed out that without hover as a mode delimiter, PenTearing allowed the pen tip to remain on the screen, which resulted in more stable targeting. Finally, participants mentioned that performing the tearing interaction using a single hand produced less occlusion than using two hands and freed the ND hand for other, unrelated, tasks. From an implementation standpoint, the simpler input hardware required is an additional advantage of the one-handed technique. We believe, however, that additional investigations of bimanual versus unimanual modalities in the context of real-world activities are needed to definitively confirm these advantages.

Palm Rejection

Despite the fact that users were required to have the pen in the hover zone before resting their palm on the screen, no participant thought avoiding these false-positives was burdensome. One situation where the occlusion model failed was when users rotated the screen prior to writing, such as to squeeze text into a narrow space during a baseline interaction. This situation could potentially be remedied by using on-board motion sensors. It bears noting that the palm rejection functionality is still useful even with a technique like PenTearing because it enables other touch gestures, such as navigation, while the pen is in the hover volume.

CONCLUSION AND FUTURE WORK

In this paper, we presented TextTearing, an interaction technique for expanding the whitespace between text lines. We also described a palm rejection technique for enabling pen + touch input. We conducted an experiment comparing three variations on the TextTearing technique against each other as well as against margin expansion and a baseline system with no expansion capabilities. Participants rated TextTearing techniques highly, which suggests that TextTearing is a desirable method for supporting annotation. The pen-only and one-finger tearing variants were faster than the two-finger variant and the pen-only technique was the most preferred.

In future work, we hope to see TextTearing used as part of a deployable document viewer to observe its effectiveness for a full range of real-world practices against methods such as DIZI [1] or sticky notes. Furthermore, studying the impact of TextTearing on annotation consumption tasks such as reading, searching, maintaining, and sharing would complement the research presented in this paper.

ACKNOWLEDGEMENTS

Yoon gratefully acknowledges support from the Kwanjeong Educational Foundation. This work was made possible by a generous gift from FX-PAL. We would like to thank Ken Hinckley and Michel Pahud at Microsoft Research for their technical assistance in managing pen and touch events simultaneously.

REFERENCES

1. Agrawala, M. and Shilman, M. DIZI: a digital ink zooming interface for document annotation. Human-Computer Interaction-INTERACT 2005, (2005), 69-79.
2. Chang, B.-W., Mackinlay, J.D., Zellweger, P.T., and Igarashi, T. A negotiation architecture for fluid documents. In Proc. UIST 1998, ACM Press (1998) , 123–132.
3. Cockburn, A., Gutwin, C., and Alexander, J. Faster document navigation with space-filling thumbnails. In Proc. CHI 2006, ACM Press (2006), 1-10.
4. Golovchinsky, G. and Denoue, L. Moving markup: Repositioning Freeform Annotations. In Proc. UIST 2002, ACM Press (2002), 21-30.
5. Golovchinsky, G., Price, M.N., and Schilit, B.N. From reading to retrieval: freeform ink annotations as queries. In Proc. SIGIR 1999, ACM Press (1999), 19–25.
6. Guiard, Y. Asymmetric division of labor in human skilled bimanual action: the kinematic chain as a model. Journal of motor behavior 19, 4 (1987), 486–517.
7. Hinckley, K., Baudisch, P., Ramos, G., and Guimbretiere, F. Design and analysis of delimiters for selection-action pen gesture phrases in scriboli. In Proc. CHI 2005, ACM Press (2005), 451-460.
8. Hinckley, K., Bi, X., Pahud, M., and Buxton. B. Informal information gathering techniques for active reading. In Proc. CHI '12 (2012), 1893–1896.
9. Hinckley, K., Yatani, K., Pahud, M., et al. Pen + touch = new tools. In Proc. UIST 2010, ACM Press (2010), 27-36.
10. Marshall, C.C. Annotation: from paper books to the digital library. In Proc. DL 1997, ACM Press (1997), 131–140.
11. Marshall, C.C. Toward an ecology of hypertext annotation. In Proc. HYPERTEXT 1998, ACM Press (1998), 40–49.
12. Pearson, J., Buchanan, G., and Thimbleby, H. Improving annotations in digital documents. In Proc. ECDL 2009, Springer-Verlag (2009), 429-432.
13. Pearson, J., Buchanan, G., and Thimbleby, H. The reading desk: applying physical interactions to digital documents. In Proc CHI 2011, ACM Press (2011), 3199-3202.
14. Sellen, A. and Harper, R. The Myth of the Paperless Office. MIT Press (2003).
15. Song, H., Benko, H., Guimbretiere, F., Izadi, S., Cao, X., and Hinckley, K. Grips and gestures on a multi-touch pen. In Proc. CHI 2011, ACM Press (2011), 1323-1332.
16. Tashman, C.S. and Edwards, W.K. LiquidText: a flexible, multitouch environment to support active reading. In Proc. CHI 2011, ACM Press (2011), 3285-3294.
17. Vogel, D. and Balakrishnan, R. Occlusion-aware interfaces. In Proc. CHI 2010, ACM Press (2010), 263-272.
18. Zeleznik, R., Bragdon, A., Adeputra, F., and Ko, H.-S. Hands-on math: a page-based multi-touch and pen desktop for technical work and problem solving. In Proc. UIST 2010, ACM Press (2010), 17-26.

Content-Based Tools for Editing Audio Stories

Steve Rubin*, **Floraine Berthouzoz***, **Gautham J. Mysore**†, **Wilmot Li**†, **Maneesh Agrawala***

*University of California, Berkeley
{srubin,floraine,maneesh}@cs.berkeley.edu

†Adobe Research
{gmysore,wilmotli}@adobe.com

ABSTRACT
Audio stories are an engaging form of communication that combine speech and music into compelling narratives. Existing audio editing tools force story producers to manipulate speech and music tracks via tedious, low-level waveform editing. In contrast, we present a set of tools that analyze the audio content of the speech and music and thereby allow producers to work at much higher level. Our tools address several challenges in creating audio stories, including (1) navigating and editing speech, (2) selecting appropriate music for the score, and (3) editing the music to complement the speech. Key features include a transcript-based speech editing tool that automatically propagates edits in the transcript text to the corresponding speech track; a music browser that supports searching based on emotion, tempo, key, or timbral similarity to other songs; and music retargeting tools that make it easy to combine sections of music with the speech. We have used our tools to create audio stories from a variety of raw speech sources, including scripted narratives, interviews and political speeches. Informal feedback from first-time users suggests that our tools are easy to learn and greatly facilitate the process of editing raw footage into a final story.

Author Keywords
Audio editing, storytelling, transcript-based editing, music browsing, music retargeting

ACM Classification Keywords
H.5.2 Information Interfaces and Presentation (e.g. HCI): User Interfaces - Graphical user interfaces

INTRODUCTION
Audio stories are an engaging form of communication that are commonly heard in podcasts, radio programs and audiobooks. But, creating a compelling audio story requires careful editing and production. Starting from the raw recorded speech, experienced producers select and combine the most salient content and then refine individual sentences to improve the phrasing and rhythms of the speech. Many audio stories also include a musical score that plays under the speech. Producers choose music that enhances the emotion of the story and then adjust the length and volume of musical sections to both complement and emphasize key moments in the speech. In short, creating an effective audio story requires making a number of high-level editing and design decisions that together define the narrative arc and emotional tone of the story [7, 8, 20, 24, 33].

Most existing audio editing systems provide all of the functionality necessary to support such editing and production tasks. However, these systems force producers to manipulate the speech and music at the level of the audio waveform. As a result producers must map their high-level story editing and design goals onto a sequence of low-level editing operations — e.g. selecting, trimming, cutting and moving sections of a waveform. Manually applying each of these low-level edits is often tedious and usually very time-consuming.

In this paper we present a set of tools that analyze the audio content of raw speech and music tracks and thereby allow producers to work at a much higher level. Our tools address challenges that span the process of creating audio stories, from (1) navigating and editing speech, to (2) selecting appropriate music for the score, and (3) editing the music to complement the speech. Using these tools the producer can focus on developing the content and emotion of the story while our system automatically applies the appropriate low-level operations on the audio waveforms.

Our audio editing system includes the following key features:

Transcript-based speech editing. To help producers navigate and edit raw speech recordings, our interface includes a transcript view of each speech track. As in previous transcript-based speech editing systems [10, 14, 40], producers can directly modify the transcript text, and our system propagates the corresponding edits to the speech waveform. However, unlike previous systems, our transcript view groups similar sentences, so that the producer can quickly listen to different versions of a line and insert the best one into the story. The transcript view also marks pauses and breaths in the speech to help the producer refine phrasings while maintaining a natural sounding rhythm.

Multi-feature music browsing. To help producers find the appropriate music to score a story, our system includes a music browser that supports searching for songs based on several different features, including emotional characteristics, tempo, key, or a crowdsourced set of keywords associated with the music. In some cases, a producer may need several different songs that sound similar to form a coherent score that does not sound repetitive. For these situations, our browser provides a similarity search that takes a single song as input and finds other songs that are similar in timbre.

Structure-based music editing. To help producers integrate music into a story, our system includes two types of music

UIST '13, October 8–11, 2013, St. Andrews, United Kingdom.
ACM 978-1-4503-2268-3/13/10.
http://dx.doi.org/10.1145/2501988.2501993

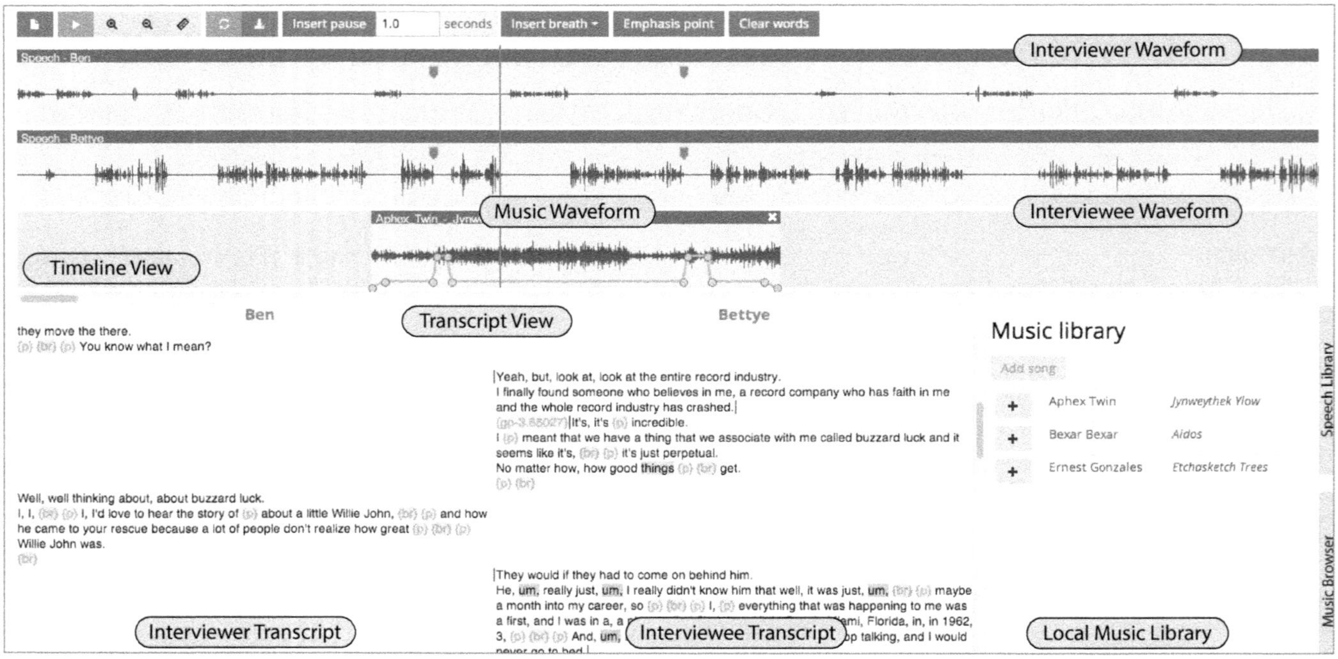

Figure 1. Our editing interface features two views of each speech track: a traditional waveform view, and a text-based transcript view.

editing tools that make it easy to retarget music to fit the speech. Our *simple music retargeting tool* allows the producer to interactively extend or shorten a section of music while maintaining a natural sounding result. Our *constrained retargeting tool* automatically restructures a song to match a desired length while also highlighting one or more emphasis points in the speech.

We have used our tools to create audio stories from a variety of speech sources, including scripted narratives, interviews, and presidential speeches. We also report on informal evaluation where we asked users to create audio stories from raw speech recordings using our system. The results demonstrate that our tools enable first-time users to produce high-quality stories that contain a variety of edits to raw speech and music. User feedback suggest that our tools are easy to learn and greatly facilitate the production of audio stories.

RELATED WORK

Traditional digital audio workstations (DAWs) like Adobe Audition [1] and Avid ProTools [2] allow producers to edit waveforms in a multi-track timeline interface. These systems provide a wide variety of low-level signal processing tools [11, 13, 28, 44] for manipulating audio waveforms, but their interfaces are very complex. Moreover, because they are designed to serve as general-purpose audio production systems, they include many features that are not directly relevant for creating audio stories.

Hindenburg Systems [5] develops tools that are designed specifically for producing audio stories, stripping away much of the complexity of full-fledged DAWs while simplifying common tasks in audio journalism like managing the relative volume levels of the speech and music tracks. Despite these usability improvements, Hindenburg still adheres to the standard waveform-based metaphor of audio editing and forces producers to directly edit the waveform.

Researchers have investigated several alternatives to direct waveform-based navigation and editing. Barthet et al. [9] segment podcasts into speech and music so that listeners can jump to the different sections. Fazekas et al. [17] split songs into verse and chorus to similarly enable quick navigation. In the context of video editing, researchers have developed tools that leverage higher-level structural annotations. Davis [15] proposes video editing tools that make extensive use of metadata (e.g. camera settings and semantic annotations) to describe the content of the raw footage. Users can then browse and rearrange the footage through an iconic representation of the metadata. Li et al. [25] enable faster browsing of video clips by automatically marking shot boundaries and enabling pitch-preserving rapid audio playback. Likewise, Girgensohn et al. [19] present a system that automatically filters out unsuitable video clips based on an analysis of the camera motion. Unlike these systems, our work focuses on using a transcript of the speech track to navigate and edit audio stories.

We build on several previous techniques for text-based navigation and editing. Whittaker and Amento [40] show that users strongly prefer editing voicemail through a transcript instead of a waveform, even when automatic speech recognition produces significant errors in the transcript. However, because they focus on voicemail recordings, their work did not investigate how to produce high-quality edited output. Casares et al. [14] and more recently, Berthouzoz et al. [10] present video editing systems that include speech-aligned transcript editors to enable more efficient navigation and editing of video. We extend this approach to the domain of audio editing and provide a number of additional transcript-based editing tools (e.g. grouping similar sentences and editing breaths).

Researchers have also developed tools for browsing large collections of music based on a variety of low-level features (i.e., tempo, timbre, volume, etc.) [26, 31, 30]. However, these tools are designed to serve as general-purpose music browsers for music discovery and designing playlists. None of them integrate into an audio editing system.

Example-based music synthesis and retargeting is an active area of research [22]. Lu et al. [29] describe a method for generating *audio textures* that takes an audio track as input and reshuffles its frames to generate a similar-sounding track. Zils and Pachet's [43] Musical Mosaicing system synthesizes a target waveform by sequencing snippets from a database of music. The EchoNest, a company that provides a robust API for music analysis, has demonstrated tools for extracting the structure of a song and then retargeting it to play indefinitely [23, 39]. In concurrent work, Wenner et al. [38] have developed a music retargeting algorithm that preserves user-specified constraints. Our music retargeting tools similarly consider the structure of a music track to extend or shorten it in a natural sounding manner. However, unlike previous techniques we also impose retargeting constraints based on combined features of the music and speech tracks.

AUDIO EDITING INTERFACE

We have developed a set of tools that are designed to help producers edit raw speech and music tracks into audio stories. We first describe the interface to these tools (Figure 1) and then present the content-based analysis algorithms that enable each tool in the ALGORITHMIC METHODS section.

Transcript-based speech editing

The producer starts by loading raw speech tracks into the editing interface. In Figure 1, the producer is editing the two tracks of an interview between Ben Manilla and recording artist Bettye Lavette. Our system displays two different views of each track: the timeline view shows the audio waveform, and the transcript view shows the corresponding text. Each speaker's transcript appears in a separate column of the transcript view and the text alternates between the columns as the speakers talk back and forth.

Each transcript is time-aligned with the corresponding waveform, so that selections and edits made to the text are reflected in the waveform and vice versa. All edit operations (i.e. cut, copy, paste, delete) in the transcript view occur at the word level (Figure 2). Our system snaps selections to the nearest word boundary to prevent the producer from breaking words into fragments. The transcript view helps the producer quickly navigate to specific parts of a speech track and edit the content of the story.

With interviews it is essential for the speech tracks to stay in sync with one another as the producer makes edits. Our system provides a linked editing mode that automatically maintains such synchronization. If the producer deletes part of a track for one speaker, our system deletes the corresponding

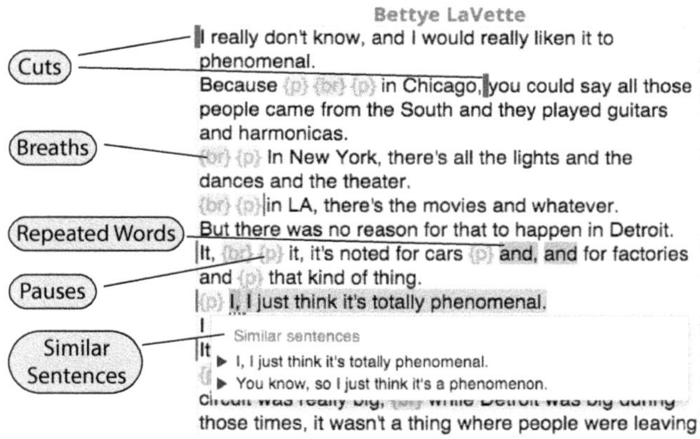

Figure 2. The transcript view allows producers to edit the story at the word level. This view marks cuts, breaths, pauses, repeated and unnecessary words, and similar sentences, all of which enable the producer to quickly edit the speech.

region from the waveform and transcript of all linked tracks. Similarly if the producer inserts text into the transcript of one speaker, our system inserts background *room tone* into the corresponding regions for the linked speakers. Producers usually capture room tone at the start of a recording session and our system automatically treats relatively silent segments from the beginning of the track as room tone.

Speakers often record multiple versions (or takes) of the same sentence to try variations in voicing or wording. Producers must then choose the most appropriate take for the story. Our system analyzes the transcript to identify retakes and underlines sentences in the transcript view for which similar alternatives are available. Clicking on the underline opens a drop-down showing the similar alternatives (Figure 2). The producer can listen to any of these takes and select her favorite without having to search for retakes through the entire raw recording.

After editing together a rough cut of the raw tracks, the producer next focuses on refining individual sentences to improve the flow of the speech. Our system identifies 'uhs', 'ums' and repeated words and highlights them in red so that the producer can easily delete them (Figure 2).

The transcript view also explicitly marks the breaths and pauses that occur in each speech track (Figure 2). These tokens help the producer maintain the natural patterns of speech as she edits the story. For example, speakers typically take a breath and pause for a moment before uttering each new sentence [7]. After rearranging sentences in the transcript view the producer can immediately check that the breath-pause combination occurs between sentences. The producer can also split a long sentence into two sentences by typing a ('.') in the transcript view, and our system automatically inserts the breath-pause combination before the next sentence. Finally, the producer can manually add or remove breaths and pauses as necessary. Pauses often serve to emphasize the preceding speech and give the listener time to reflect on what was said. Thus, the producer may choose to insert pauses at different points in the speech, to emphasize particular thoughts

Figure 3. The music browser allows producers to filter by emotion, find similar sounding songs, and sort by low-level feature.

that the speaker may have originally rushed through. The default pause length is 250 ms, and the producer can manually adjust its length as necessary. Our system fills the pause with background room tone.

Multi-feature music browsing

Producers often add a musical score to an audio story in order to emphasize specific moments or emotions [7, 8]. To help producers find the appropriate music, our system provides a music browser (Figure 3). By default, our browser includes a collection of 90 songs that are commonly used in radio stories, but the producer can add other songs to the browser as well. Each song listing includes a '▶' button, to play a snippet of the song. When the producer finds a song that she likes, she uses the '✚' button to add the song to the local music library, which appears to the right of the transcript view (Figure 1). If the producer has a specific song in mind, she simply searches for the song by name. Otherwise, the producer can search for music in several different ways.

Finding music that fits an emotion

Producers often use a musical score that matches the emotion of a particular moment in the speech. Our music browser allows the producer to quickly find emotionally appropriate music by coarsely filtering the songs based on a measure of their emotion. Specifically, we use Russell's circumplex model of 'valence' and 'arousal' to measure the emotion of the songs [36]. Valence ranges from "misery" to "pleasure," and arousal ranges from "sleepy" to "activated." With our browser, the producer can filter the music to only see songs that corresponds to one of the four quadrants of the valence/arousal plane (Figure 4). For example, to find happy and upbeat music, the producer can select the high valence, high arousal quadrant Q1.

Figure 4. Russell's circumplex model of emotion.

Finding similar-sounding music

In some cases, the producer may wish to find a few different songs that all sound similar in order to form a musical score that is coherent but does not repeat songs. Using our browser, the producer first finds one song that she likes and then clicks the '≈' button. The browser then sorts the library to show the songs that are closest in timbre to the selected song. Timbre reflects the instrumentation of a song and we have found it to be a good indicator sound similarity.

Searching by feature

Our browser also lets producers sort the music based on several low-level features that we compute from the music: *tempo*, *mode* (major or minor key), and *danceability* (a feature from The EchoNest [4]). For example, if the producer is looking for an up-tempo song for her story, she can sort in descending order based on tempo and listen to songs starting from the top of the list.

Searching by keyword

Producers can also search for music using descriptive keywords (e.g., find *chill* music). To support this type of search, our browser retrieves tags that have been assigned to songs by users of last.fm [6], a music-tracking social network with ~50 million registered users and information on ~45 million songs. Thus, the producer can simply type *chill* into a search box to find all the music that has been tagged with this keyword.

Structure-based music editing

Once the producer has added songs to the local music library, the next step is to combine the music with the speech track. We provide standard waveform-based editing tools that allow the producer to add a song to the timeline, trim and reposition it as necessary, and specify a spline to control the volume. However, we also provide a set of higher level tools that help the producer retarget music (i.e. extend or shorten it) to match the length of a corresponding speech segment.

Simple music retargeting

At times producers may find a segment of music that is appropriate for a particular section of the speech, but is the wrong length. If the music is too short, the producer first select the subsegment she would like to extend and then clicks the '↻' button that appears on the waveform. Our system automatically extends the music by adding a seamless loop to the selected subsegment. The producer can click this button as many times as necessary to bring the music to the desired length (Figure 5). In order to minimize repetition in the music, our system finds and adds the longest loop that occurs

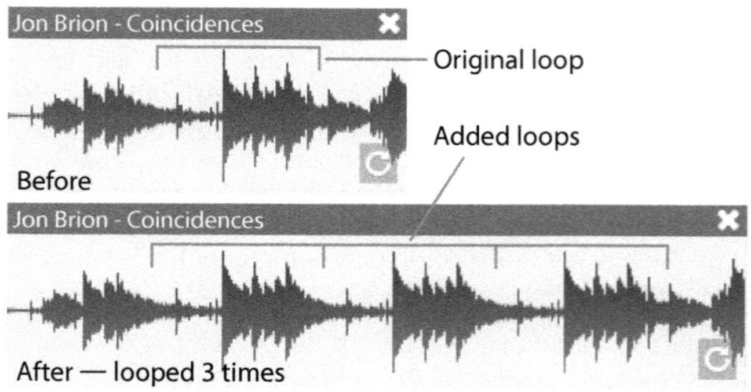

Figure 5. A musical segment before and after simple retargeting. Our tool finds a loop in the orginal segment (before) and in this case the producer repeats the loop three times in the final segment (after).

within the selected subsegment. Likewise, if the music is too long, the producer can click the '↻' button to remove audio from the selected subsegment.

Constrained music retargeting
Music usually contains a small set of *change points* that mark significant transitions in timbre, harmonic structure, or volume. Producers often emphasize a moment in the story by adding a *musical underlay* that aligns a music change point with an important point in the speech. Such underlays fade in the music before the emphasis point in the speech, then pauses the speech while the music solo plays at full volume, and finally fades out the music as the speech resumes. Rubin et al. [34] recently showed how to automatically detect change points in music and presented a semi-automated tool for creating a musical underlay that aligns one change point with one speech emphasis point. Our system includes this functionality – the producer marks an emphasis point in the speech, selects a song, and the system automatically produces the underlay.

In some cases, however, the producer may wish to use a single piece of music to continuously score a section of speech containing multiple speech emphasis points (Figure 6). In this situation the producer must align each emphasis point with a different music change point without stopping the music. Yet, the time between music change points rarely matches the time between speech emphasis points. Given multiple emphasis points and a song, our system automatically retargets the music by analyzing its structure and generating a new version that meets the alignment constraints.

ALGORITHMIC METHODS
Our audio editing tools all rely on algorithms that analyze the content of the raw speech and music tracks.

Obtaining the transcript
We obtain a transcript of the raw speech tracks using the crowdsourced transcription service, CastingWords.com [3]. It costs $1.00–$2.50 per minute of audio, depending on the desired turnaround time. By default the service produces *sanitized* transcripts that excludes words like 'uh', 'um', 'so' etc. However, our audio editor is designed to highlight such words in the transcript and let producers decide whether or not to remove them. Therefore we specify that the transcription service should produce *verbatim* transcripts. While automatic speech recognition software is continually improving, we have found that they cannot match the quality of crowdsourced transcription.

Aligning the transcript to the speech track
Once we have obtained the verbatim transcript of the speech track, we align it to the audio using the Penn Phonetics Lab Forced Aligner (P2FA) [42], which is built on the HTK (HMM toolkit) speech recognition software [41]. This aligner computes perceptual linear prediction (PLP) features to model each phoneme in the speech audio and applies a dictionary of word-to-phoneme translations on the text. It then uses the Viterbi algorithm for hidden Markov models to compute the maximum likelihood alignment between the speech and transcript. The aligner also inserts "pause" tokens into the transcript when there is a silent gap in the speech.

In practice we have found that transcripts frequently contain some words that are not in the P2FA word-to-phoneme dictionary (e.g. proper names, jargon, etc.). Therefore, we have extended the P2FA algorithm so that whenever it encounters such an unknown word, it uses the CMU Sphinx Knowledge Base Tool [35] to algorithmically determine the word's pronunciation. Although the resulting phonemes may be incorrect, we have found that the aligner is far more accurate when it has phonemes for every word in the transcript than when it is missing phonemes for some words.

Detecting breaths
Audible breaths are subtle but important elements in the natural rhythm of speech. The P2FA tool contains a model of breaths and can successfully align transcripts that contain explicit tokens indicating breaths. However, our crowdsourced transcripts do not indicate breaths because it is difficult for human transcribers to detect them reliably. Nevertheless we have developed an automated procedure that uses the initial transcript alignment and P2FA to detect breaths.

We assume that breaths can only occur in the segments already labeled as pauses in the initial alignment. Using P2FA we align each pause with a transcript containing a single breath token. The aligner returns a score indicating its confidence that the alignment is correct. If the score is greater than an empirically chosen threshold and the detected breath is longer than 100 ms then we accept the alignment and insert the breath token into the transcript.

If the producer manually adds a breath to the transcript we randomly select one of the detected breaths and insert the corresponding breath waveform into the timeline.

Detecting multiple takes of a sentence
Speakers sometimes record multiple takes of a sentence one after another. At other times they revisit lines later in a recording session. To identify such re-takes we cluster all of the sentences in the transcript so that each cluster contains all variations of a given sentence in the raw recording.

To build these clusters we first compute the similarity between each pair of sentences in the transcript using the Levenshtein string edit distance. If the edit distance is less than a threshold α we mark the pair as similar. Because the edit distance depends on the length of the strings, we have found that setting α to half the length of the longer sentence works well in practice. Intuitively, this threshold allows sentences marked as similar, to differ in about half of their characters. We then treat each sentence as a node in a graph and add an edge between each pair of similar sentences. Each connected component of this graph forms a cluster of similar sentences. When a producer clicks on an underlined sentence in the transcript view we show all of the sentences in the corresponding similarity cluster as the alternate takes.

Multi-feature music browsing
Our music browser contains a collection of songs and provides a set of tools designed to help producers quickly find

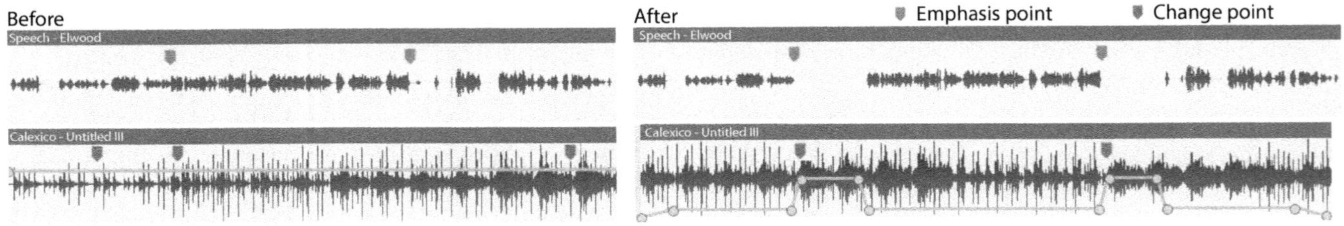

Figure 6. In constrained music retargeting, the producer selects multiple speech emphasis points (red markers) and a piece of music (before). Our system automatically identifies music change points (green markers) and aligns them with the emphasis points, by extending or shrinking the music as necessary, while preserving the local beat-level structure of the music (after).

appropriate music for scoring their audio stories. It relies on a set of five features (tempo, mode, danceability, timbre and valence/arousal) that characterize different aspects of each song in the collection.

We compute tempo and mode (major or minor key) using standard algorithms from music information retrieval and signal processing [16]. For the danceability feature we query the EchoNest [4] web service. They describe this feature as a combination of beat strength, tempo and tempo variability. We compute the timbre feature using mel-frequency cepstral coefficients (MFCCs) [27], which analyze the spectral characteristics of the song. For each song, we compute one 13-dimensional MFCC feature for a 15 second frame that begins 30 seconds into the song. Since MFCCs are a high dimensional feature we don't directly expose them to the producer. Instead when the producer searches for similar-sounding songs using the '≈' button we compute the nearest songs based on the Euclidean distance between their MFCCs. To support fast nearest-neighbor lookups, we store the MFCCs in a k-d tree.

The emotional controls in our browser filter songs based on the quadrants of the valence/arousal plane in Russell's circumplex model of affect [36] (Figure 4). Valence/arousal values are based on human perception, and can vary from person to person, so there is no direct way to compute them. Instead, following Schmidt et al. [37], we use a machine learning approach to estimate the valence/arousal for each song. The MoodSwings Turk dataset [37] contains a set of songs with corresponding valence/arousal values that were collected from workers on Amazon Mechanical Turk. We compute MFCCs for each of these songs and then perform multiple linear regression to build a mapping from the MFCCs to valence/arousal. Given a new song from our collection we first compute its MFCCs and then apply the regression model to predict valence/arousal values.

Structure-based music editing

Our interface allows the producer to extend or shorten a segment of music while preserving the local, beat-level structure of the song. To enable such music retargeting we first segment the song into beats using the approach of Ellis and Poliner [16]. We then consider how the beats are related to one another. A transition from beat m_i to beat m_{i+1} sounds natural because it respects the original progression of the music. To estimate whether a transition from beat m_i to beat m_j where $j \neq i+1$, would sound natural, we follow the approach of Jehan and Sundram [23] and compute a transition cost matrix T such that

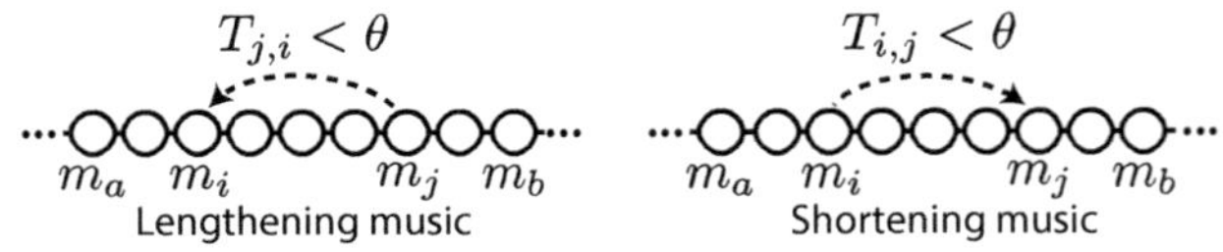

Figure 7. For simple music retargeting, we lengthen music by finding low cost transitions to earlier beats in the music. The producer can click a button to repeat such loops in the track. To shorten music, we find low cost transitions to later beats. The producer can than choose to delete the in-between beats.

$$T_{i,j} = \frac{D_h(m_{i+1}, m_j)}{\sigma_h} + \frac{D_t(m_{i+1}, m_j)}{\sigma_t}$$

where $D_h(m_i, m_j)$ is the Euclidean distance between the chroma features [16] (a measure of harmonics) for beats m_i and m_j and $D_t(m_i, m_j)$ is the distance between their MFCCs, while σ_h and σ_t are the standard deviations across all of the harmonic and timbre distances, respectively. Entries in this transition cost matrix are low for beats m_i and m_j if the timbre and harmonic features of beat m_j are close to the corresponding features of beat m_{i+1}. Thus, a low cost suggests a natural sounding transition.

We use this transition cost matrix T to enable simple and constrained music retargeting.

Simple music retargeting

In simple retargeting the producer can press a button to extend a segment of music by adding a loop to it. As shown in Figure 7, given a music segment from beat m_a to beat m_b we look for beats m_i and m_j such that $a \leq i < j \leq b$ and the transition cost from m_j to m_i is low (i.e. $T_{j,i} < \theta$). A low transition cost ensures that playing the music from beat m_i to beat m_j and then looping back to m_i sounds natural. In music, longer loops are often less noticeable and therefore we look for the m_i and m_j that maximize $j - i$ subject to the other constraints.

We tune the cost threshold θ to trade-off between finding more loops with higher average cost (high θ) or fewer loops with lower average cost (low θ). We have empirically found that setting θ with respect to the mean and standard deviations of the harmonic and timbre distances provides a good balance:

$$\theta = \frac{\mu_h - \sigma_h}{\sigma_h} + \frac{\mu_t - \sigma_t}{\sigma_t}.$$

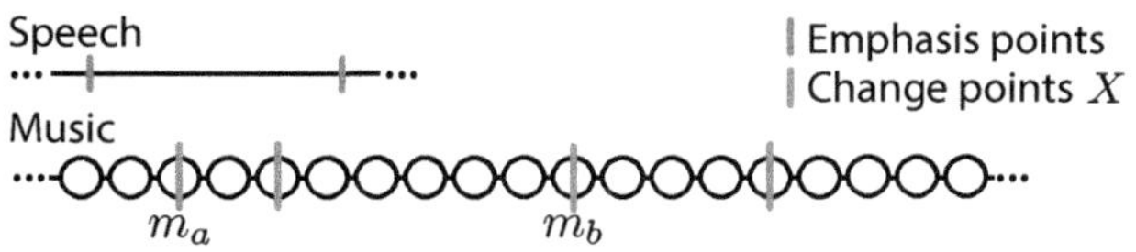

Figure 8. A constrained music retargeting problem in which producer has marked a pair of speech emphasis points (red markers) and selected song. Our system computes the music change points (green markers). We use a dynamic programming approach find a sequence of beats in the music that fit the length of the speech segment such that only the first and last beats change points.

Our interface also allows producers to shorten a segment of music. In this case we search for beats m_i and m_j where $a \leq i < j \leq b$ with $T_{i,j} < \theta$ and $j \neq i+1$. The low transition cost from m_i to m_j ensures that we can safely remove the audio between those beats (Figure 7).

Constrained retargeting

In constrained retargeting the producer wishes to add a continuous musical score to a section of speech containing multiple emphasis points. Moreover, she requires each speech emphasis point to match a change point in the music.

Consider the constrained retargeting problem in Figure 8. The producer has marked a pair of speech emphasis points and selected a piece of music for the score. We automatically find the set of change points X in the selected music using Foote's [18] method for analyzing the *novelty* of each beat based on several audio features including MFCCs, chroma and RMS energy (a measure of volume).

To retarget the music we first compute the number of beats n required to fill the length of time between the speech emphasis points. Note that because the average beat length can vary from song to song we compute n based on the average beat length for the selected song. Our goal is to find a natural sounding sequence of n beats in the music where only the first and last beats are change points. In other words no beat in the sequence other than the first and the last can be in X.

Our algorithm searches for the lowest cost sequence of beats that fits these constraints. We define the cost c of a sequence of n beats starting at beat m_a and ending at beat m_b as $c(m_a, m_b, n)$. To compute $c(m_a, m_b, n)$ we must find the beat $m_k \notin X$ that minimizes the cost of an $n-1$ beat sequence from m_a to m_k plus the cost of a 1 beat sequence from m_k to m_b. That is,

$$c(m_a, m_b, n) = \min\{c(m_a, m_k, n-1) + c(m_k, m_b, 1) \mid m_k \notin X\}$$

We set the cost of a 1 beat sequence (i.e. the base case) using the transition cost matrix $c(m_a, m_k, 1) = e^{T_{a,k}}$ so that we favor low-cost transitions. We use dynamic programming to efficiently find the optimal sequence of n beats subject to this recursive cost formulation.

In practice we search for the lowest cost sequence of n beats for each permutation (m_a, m_b) of change points in X. In some cases it is impossible to find a low-cost sequence with exactly n beats. Thus we give the algorithm additional flexibility by allowing the sequence length n to vary by a few beats. We make up for the difference in length by extending or shrinking the pauses that typically follow speech emphasis points in a musical underlay.

Rendering audio

When rendering speech that has been edited, we insert a short crossfade (5 ms long) at each cut to ensure that the cut remains inaudible. Without such crossfades it is sometimes possible to hear faint pops or clicks at a cut. To further improve audio quality we snap edits to zero-crossing points [21], which are the least likely points to cause a click in the generated audio. Our music retargeting algorithms generate a sequence of beats. We render these beats to an audio file by concatenating them in order and inserting a crossfade between any two successive beats m_i and m_j where $j \neq i + 1$. These crossfades again serve to hide pops and clicks at loop points in the final rendered audio.

RESULTS

We have used our tools to compose seven audio stories from a variety of raw speech sources including scripted narratives, interviews and political speeches. Table 1 describes the content of each story. All seven final results as well as the original raw recordings can be found on our supplemental website[1] for this paper.

We significantly edited each of the raw recordings to focus the final story on the most important content. The final edited length is usually much shorter than the raw recording length and the total number of cuts indicates the amount of editing we performed. It took us about a half hour to edit each story using our tools. We instrumented our speech and music editing tools to log their usage during each editing session as shown in the table.

As reflected in the usage numbers, we made extensive use of the transcript editor to clean-up and reorganize the speech. Although we used the text delete tool most often, we also used text copy/paste to move words, phrases and sentences. The raw speech recordings for scripted narratives (Elwood and Bullwinkle) often included a large number of re-takes, while interviews and political speeches contained fewer such alternates. When such alternates were available we usually previewed them and selected the best version for the final story. We occasionally had to insert breaths after such rearrangements to maintain the natural rhythm of the speakers.

We added a musical score to all of the stories except for Phone. We used the constrained music retargeting tool to emphasize key moments in the speech for the six other stories. In three of the stories (Photoshop, Obama, LaVette) we also extended some of the music segments by adding loops using our simple retargeting tool.

Limitations. In using our system we also identified two main limitations. First, we found that errors in transcription or in alignment sometimes generated audible artifacts (e.g. clicks, noise, etc.) in the edited speech. We leave it to future work

[1] http://vis.berkeley.edu/papers/audiostories

					Transcript editing usage				Music retargeting usage	
Name	Description	Raw length	Edited length	Total cuts	Text delete	Text copy/paste	View re-takes	Breath insertion	Simple loops	Constrained retargets
Elwood	Scripted blues show narration	17:11	1:51	14	43	20	5	6	0	1
Bullwinkle	Scripted story about TV show	8:24	1:24	29	29	9	17	6	0	1
Photoshop	Interview about imaging technology	12:22	3:17	64	195	24	2	9	8	3
Obama	Inaugural speech	18:22	2:42	21	61	1	2	0	7	7
Rickard	Interview with math professor	1:07	:54	19	28	1	0	1	0	3
LaVette	Interview with blues singer	8:47	1:45	30	60	18	0	7	19	1
Phone	Lower-quality clip from LaVette	:47	:19	11	41	4	0	7	0	0

Table 1. We constructed seven audio stories using our system and instrumented each of our tools to record usage statistics. Total cuts refers to the number of crossfades that were added by our system when rendering the final audio story. Text delete and text copy/paste refer to usage of basic transcript-based editing tools. View re-takes indicates how many times we previewed different takes of a sentence using similar sentence dropdowns. Breath insertion is the number of times we either added breaths directly or by typing a ('.'). Finally, we counted both the number of loops added to music, and the number of constrained music retargets we used in each editing session.

to provide an interface that allows users to correct inaccuracies in the transcript or in the alignment. Second, we found that in some cases our system was unable to segment a music track into beats (e.g., ambient music with an ambiguous tempo). Poor beat segmentation led to failures in constrained music retargeting. It may be possible to mitigate this problem by adding a music retargeting option that uses constant-sized windows instead of beat-sized windows.

INFORMAL USER EVALUATION

We conducted an informal user evaluation to gauge the utility of our editing interface. We recruited four participants with a range of experience using existing audio editing software: two experts, one casual user, and one novice. We started each session with a 10-minute demonstration of all our editing tools and then asked the participant to create a short audio story from a raw interview recording. At the end of the session, we solicited written qualitative feedback on the features of our interface. In total, each session lasted 50 minutes.

Overall, the results from the study were extremely encouraging. Each participant was able to successfully produce a high-quality audio story that contained significant edits to the speech and music. All of the participants also offered strong positive feedback about the content-based editing capabilities of our interface. One participant wrote, ""*This is what narration audio editing should be – it's hard to imagine why I'd want to do it any other way.*"

They were most enthusiastic about the transcript-based speech editing tools, which they felt would greatly facilitate the process of editing raw footage into a final story. In particular, they liked the two-column transcript view for linked interview tracks and the ability to quickly modify pauses, breaths, and unnecessary words. One participant said that he thought two-column interview editing was great because *"It made it very easy to see which person's audio I was working on. It's critical to be able to see which speaker is saying what, and I wouldn't get this from a waveform editor (without the tedium/time cost of re-listening to the audio)."*

Participants were also impressed with our music editing tools and felt that our simple and constrained retargeting features allow them to rapidly experiment with musical scoring ideas that would otherwise be prohibitively time-consuming to try out. One participant wrote that constrained music retargeting was *"such a great way to experiment with what might work. Great for trial and error creation."*

The feedback on the music browsing tools was also generally positive. Three of the four participants thought that emotion-based filtering and timbre-based similarity search would be useful. However, we observed that participants spent less time working with the music browser than with our other editing tools. It may be that participants were reluctant to spend too much time searching for music due to the time constraints of the study. Also, one participant noted that he was not as interested in the music browser for this task because he does not personally like audio stories with musical scores.

CONCLUSION AND FUTURE WORK

Audio can be an engaging medium for storytelling. We have presented a set of tools designed to help producers create high-quality audio stories. A key aspect of our tools is that they analyze the content of the raw speech and music tracks to provide higher-level editing capabilities than general-purpose audio editing systems. With our tools producers can focus on building the narrative arc and setting the emotional tone of the story while our system handles the low-level details of editing the audio waveforms.

We believe there are several fruitful directions for building more advanced content-based editing tools. For example it may be useful to apply natural language sentiment analysis [32] techniques to the transcript to identify the most positively or negatively charged sentences. Similarly it may be possible to apply prosody analysis methods [12] to determine which alternate take a sentence is the "angriest". Such analysis could aid a producer in identifying speech emphasis points and in scoring the story based on the emotion of the speech.

Audio stories are typically crafted to fit a certain amount of time. However, some listeners may want to listen to a longer version of the story with more detail, or a shorter, summarized version. Similarly, some listeners may prefer one kind of music in the score while another prefer a different type of music. Future work could investigate how to automatically generate stories of different lengths with personalized scores, from one *master* edit.

ACKNOWLEDGMENTS

We would like to thank Kurt Andersen, Ben Manila, and Julia Wetherell for providing the raw audio recordings we used in this work. We also thank the production staff at WNYC's Studio 360 including Leital Molad, David Krasnow, Michele Siegel, Jenny Lawton, John DeLore, Sean Rameswaram and Alana Harper for showing us how to create compelling audio stories.

REFERENCES

1. Adobe Audition. http://adobe.com/audition, Apr. 2013. Accessed: 2013-04-02.
2. Avid ProTools. http://avid.com/protools, Apr. 2013. Accessed: 2013-04-02.
3. CastingWords. http://castingwords.com/, Apr. 2013. Accessed: 2013-04-02.
4. The EchoNest API. http://developer.echonest.com/docs/v4, Apr. 2013. Accessed: 2013-04-02.
5. Hindenburg Journalist Pro. http://hindenburgsystems.com, Apr. 2013. Accessed: 2013-04-02.
6. Last.fm. http://last.fm/, Apr. 2013. Accessed: 2013-04-02.
7. Abel, J., and Glass, I. *Radio: An Illustrated Guide*. WBEZ Alliance Inc., 1999.
8. Abumrad, J. Music: A force for good (and sometimes evil). http://www.thirdcoastfestival.org/library/450-music-a-force-for-good-and-sometimes-evil, 2005. Accessed: 2013-04-02.
9. Barthet, M., Hargreaves, S., and Sandler, M. Speech/music discrimination in audio podcast using structural segmentation and timbre recognition. *Exploring Music Contents* (2011), 138–162.
10. Berthouzoz, F., Li, W., and Agrawala, M. Tools for placing cuts and transitions in interview video. *ACM Transactions on Graphics (SIGGRAPH Conference Proceedings) 31* (2012).
11. Blesser, B. Audio dynamic range compression for minimum perceived distortion. *IEEE Transactions on Audio and Electroacoustics 17*, 1 (1969), 22–32.
12. Boersma, P. Praat, A system for doing phonetics by computer. *Glot International 5*, 9/10 (2002), 341–345.
13. Boll, S. Suppression of acoustic noise in speech using spectral subtraction. *IEEE Transactions on Acoustics, Speech and Signal Processing (TASSP) 27*, 2 (1979), 113–120.
14. Casares, J., Long, A. C., Myers, B. A., Bhatnagar, R., Stevens, S. M., Dabbish, L., Yocum, D., and Corbett, A. Simplifying video editing using metadata. *Proceedings of the 4th conference on Designing interactive systems (DIS)* (2002), 157–166.
15. Davis, M. Editing out video editing. *IEEE MultiMedia 10*, 2 (2003), 54–64.
16. Ellis, D. P., and Poliner, G. E. Identifying cover songs with chroma features and dynamic programming beat tracking. *IEEE International Conference on Acoustics, Speech and Signal Processing (ICASSP) 4* (2007), 1429–1432.
17. Fazekas, G., and Sandler, M. Intelligent editing of studio recordings with the help of automatic music structure extraction. *Audio Engineering Society Convention* (2007).
18. Foote, J. Automatic audio segmentation using a measure of audio novelty. *IEEE International Conference on Multimedia and Expo (ICME) 1* (2000), 452–455.
19. Girgensohn, A., Boreczky, J., Chiu, P., Doherty, J., Foote, J., Golovchinsky, G., Uchihashi, S., and Wilcox, L. A semi-automatic approach to home video editing. *Proceedings of the 13th annual ACM symposium on User interface software and technology (UIST)* (2000), 81–89.
20. Glass, I. The transom review: Ira Glass. http://transom.org/?p=6978, June 2004. Accessed: 2013-04-02.
21. Golding, B. Digital editing basics. http://transom.org/?p=7540, Jan. 2001. Accessed: 2013-04-02.
22. Jehan, T. *Creating music by listening*. PhD thesis, Massachusetts Institute of Technology, 2005.
23. Jehan, T., and Sundram, J. The EchoNest remix earworm. https://github.com/echonest/remix/tree/master/examples/earworm, Apr. 2013. Accessed: 2013-04-02.
24. Kern, J. *Sound reporting: The NPR guide to audio journalism and production*. University of Chicago Press, 2008.
25. Li, F. C., Gupta, A., Sanocki, E., He, L.-w., and Rui, Y. Browsing digital video. *Proceedings of the SIGCHI conference on Human factors in computing systems (CHI) 1*, 6 (2000), 169–176.
26. Lillie, A. S. *MusicBox: Navigating the space of your music*. PhD thesis, Massachusetts Institute of Technology, 2008.
27. Logan, B. Mel frequency cepstral coefficients for music modeling. *International Symposium on Music Information Retrieval (ISMIR)* (2000).
28. Louizou, P. C. *Speech Enhancement: Theory and Practice*. CRC Press, 2007.
29. Lu, L., Wenyin, L., and Zhang, H.-J. Audio textures: Theory and applications. *IEEE Transactions on Speech and Audio Processing 12*, 2 (2004), 156–167.
30. Pachet, F., Aucouturier, J.-J., La Burthe, A., Zils, A., and Beurive, A. The cuidado music browser: an end-to-end electronic music distribution system. *Multimedia Tools and Applications 30*, 3 (2006), 331–349.

31. Pampalk, E., and Goto, M. Musicrainbow: A new user interface to discover artists using audio-based similarity and web-based labeling. *International Conference on Music Information Retrieval (ISMIR)* (2006).

32. Pang, B., and Lee, L. Opinion mining and sentiment analysis. *Foundations and trends in information retrieval 2*, 1-2 (2008), 1–135.

33. Purcell, J. *Dialogue editing for motion pictures: a guide to the invisible art*. Focal Press, 2007.

34. Rubin, S., Berthouzoz, F., Mysore, G. J., Li, W., and Agrawala, M. Underscore: Musical underlays for audio stories. *Proceedings of the 25th ACM Symposium on User Interface Software and Technology (UIST)* (2012), 359–366.

35. Rudnicky, A. Sphinx knowledge base tool. http://www.speech.cs.cmu.edu/tools/lmtool-new.html, Apr. 2013. Accessed: 2013-04-02.

36. Russell, J. A. A circumplex model of affect. *Journal of personality and social psychology 39*, 6 (1980), 1161–1178.

37. Schmidt, E. M., and Kim, Y. E. Modeling musical emotion dynamics with conditional random fields. *International Symposium on Music Information Retrieval (ISMIR)* (2011).

38. Wenner, S., Bazin, J.-C., Sorkine-Hornung, A., Kim, C., and Gross, M. Scalable music: Automatic music retargeting and synthesis. *Computer Graphics Forum (Eurographics conference Proceedings) 32*, 2 (2013), 345–354.

39. Whitman, B. Infinite Jukebox. http://labs.echonest.com/Uploader/index.html, Apr. 2013. Accessed: 2013-04-02.

40. Whittaker, S., and Amento, B. Semantic speech editing. *Proceedings of the SIGCHI conference on Human factors in computing systems 24*, 29 (2004), 527–534.

41. Young, S., Evermann, G., Kershaw, D., Moore, G., Odell, J., Ollason, D., Valtchev, V., and Woodland, P. The HTK book. *Cambridge University Engineering Department* (2002).

42. Yuan, J., and Liberman, M. Speaker identification on the SCOTUS corpus. *Journal of the Acoustical Society of America 123*, 5 (2008), 3878.

43. Zils, A., and Pachet, F. Musical mosaicing. *Digital Audio Effects (DAFx)* (2001).

44. Zolzer, U. *DAFX: Digital Audio Effects*. Wiley Publishing, 2011.

Panopticon: A Parallel Video Overview System

Dan Jackson, James Nicholson, Gerrit Stoeckigt, Rebecca Wrobel, Anja Thieme, Patrick Olivier
Culture Lab, Newcastle University
Newcastle upon Tyne, UK.
{dan.jackson, james.nicholson, g.stoeckigt, r.wrobel, anja.thieme, p.l.olivier}@newcastle.ac.uk

ABSTRACT
Panopticon is a video surrogate system that displays multiple sub-sequences in parallel to present a rapid overview of the entire sequence to the user. A novel, precisely animated arrangement slides thumbnails to provide a consistent spatiotemporal layout while allowing any sub-sequence of the original video to be watched without interruption. Furthermore, this output can be generated offline as a highly efficient repeated animation loop, making it suitable for resource-constrained environments, such as web-based interaction. Two versions of Panopticon were evaluated using three different types of video footage with the aim of determining the usability of the proposed system. Results demonstrated an advantage over another surrogate with surveillance footage in terms of search times and this advantage was further improved with Panopticon 2. Eye tracking data suggests that Panopticon's advantage stems from the animated timeline that users heavily rely on.

Author Keywords
Multimedia tools; video surrogates; video browsing; surveillance video.

ACM Classification Keywords
H.5.1 Multimedia Information Systems

INTRODUCTION
The volume of digital video data has grown dramatically in recent years. By the end of 2012 video accounted for half of consumer Internet traffic and, by 2016, 1.2 million minutes of video is forecast to transfer over the Internet every second [16]. Supporting applications such as video browsing, selection and editing within this information-dense resource requires interface technologies that provide efficient representations of video content. However, gaining a rapid visual overview of video data, and searching long videos for specific information, are both challenging and time consuming activities [2].

Video surrogates allow users to view a more efficient representation in lieu of the original video. Storyboard surrogates are the most popular form of video overview [1] and are typically presented in a grid layout with time increasing (not necessarily uniformly) left-to-right, top-to-bottom. This organization allows the user to see the representative frames simultaneously while maintaining their temporal relationship. The result is that storyboards are able to present users with an overview of the context, but at the expense of losing the motion information from the video.

The purpose of this paper is to describe a new video surrogate system, *Panopticon*, and compare it with other commonly implemented systems in terms of users' seeking experience and gist comprehension. Panopticon is distinctive in that it does not remove any of the frames and therefore does not compromise on context. This is achieved through the animation of the timeline which results in an overview of the video that displays all frames within an approximate 10 second time window. Based on this maximization of contextual information to aid visual search, we hypothesized that Panopticon would help users find information in videos faster than other surrogates. To test our assumptions we ran a series of evaluations in the form of two user studies to determine how users performed when asked to find information in previously unseen videos. The results from these studies show evidence that Panopticon's animated timeline is an improvement upon existing static systems for some categories of video – i.e. unedited and especially surveillance videos.

We first present relevant literature before introducing the two user studies, where Panopticon is compared to *VideoBoard* – a video surrogate system similar to those found in video editing applications – and a popular online video player, *YouTube*. The first study focused on highlighting the differences in search times between video types and participants' ability to understand the gist of the video. In the second study we evaluated an improved version of Panopticon based on feedback from participants. We conclude with a discussion on the differences between systems and videos and present the wider implications of this work.

BACKGROUND
The increased affordability of personal video recorders and smartphones have made the capture of personal video simple and convenient, resulting in rapidly expanding content libraries. With the rise of faster broadband internet connections to homes, YouTube has become one of the most popular internet video content libraries in the world

UIST'13, October 08 – 11, 2013, St Andrews, United Kingdom.
Copyright 2013 ACM 978-1-4503-2268-3/13/10…$15.00.
http://dx.doi.org/10.1145/2501988.2502038

[2]. The availability of large amounts of video has created a new problem for users [4] – the need to find specific scenes or information in videos, or the need to take in the information quickly from potentially long videos. To address such needs YouTube, for instance, introduced features that facilitate contextual information for users when seeking and searching through videos: by holding and moving the play-head at any point, the interface presents the user with time-dependent context (see Figure 1, approximately 30 seconds at any one time for a 30 minute video). However, the implementation not optimal for long videos [2].

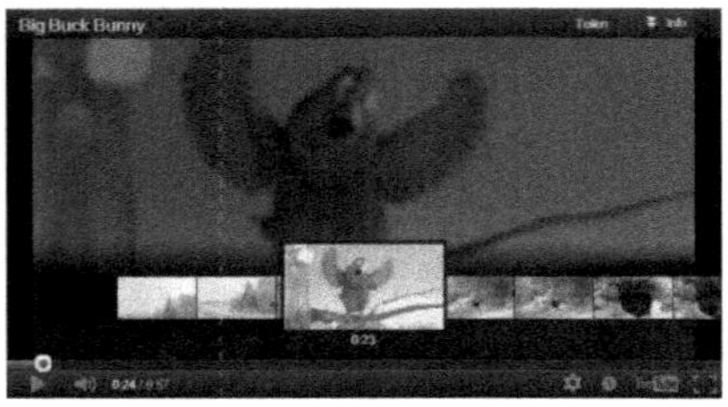

Figure 1. YouTube interface showing local context.

Video surrogates refer to an efficient representation of a video that can be used as a point of reference, for example, in the decision to view the full video or not. A variety of video surrogates are currently available – e.g. storyboards, slideshows and fast-forwards (for an overview see Shoeffmann et al. [11]). More recently, multimodal surrogates incorporating audio and visual features have been developed and evaluated (e.g. [8]). While results have been encouraging the use of audio is not always practical (e.g. in a loud office environment, or from the lack of necessary equipment). Gil et al. [5] proposed a novel text-based method for obtaining an overview of a video using tags with high participant satisfaction, but Wildemuth et al. [15] suggest using matching surrogates for media – for example text surrogates for text and video surrogates for video – in order to minimize complications in the decision-making process.

The video surrogate literature has focused on gist comprehension [3, 12] but little research has been done on the suitability of surrogates for searching and seeking information within videos. Tse et al. [13] investigated both gist comprehension and object recognition in surrogates in the context of playback speed and simultaneous displays and concluded that static simultaneous displays (such as 12 static frames representing points in the video) were better for identifying objects than a dynamic single display (such as a series of frames being played one after the other in a single position). More recently, Matejka et al. [9] proposed Swifter, an enhanced system for video scrubbing that presents scenes in a grid layout to facilitate scene identification. This technique was found to be an improvement over existing video scrubbing methods (e.g. utilized by YouTube, Netflix, etc.) and suggests that the storyboard grid layout could be beneficial for video search.

Popular video editing applications such as *iMovie* and *Final Cut Pro* utilize a 'timeline' feature where the entirety of the video is summarized in a storyboard-like approach. For the purposes of video seeking and searching, work in the area of visual search by Hollingworth [7] has shown that a preview of a scene – with either the target present or not present – improves the search times for that target over the no-preview condition. With this in mind, the use of a storyboard layout as a video surrogate is preferred, given the additional context presented by the illustration of the whole video. Work by Christel [1] confirms this preference for storyboards for video visualization.

An interesting area where surrogates may be of some use is video surveillance. In some systems, surveillance video search is done automatically, but user input on decisions is still necessary at times. For example, it is common for alerts to be automatically triggered when unusual events are spotted, but the resulting alert is received without the video footage in order to save bandwidth. It is possible to request the footage at the expense of the bandwidth but then the decision arises between downloading more than just the event for context or save resources and potentially miss important information [6]. The use of a suitable video surrogate in this situation would alleviate the bandwidth concerns while not compromising on context.

In general, existing video surrogates either present a static view of the context, losing valuable motion information, or a dynamic representation that is removed from the context of the video as a whole. In the following section, a new video surrogate system is described, Panopticon, which is designed to take advantage of context in visual search.

THE PANOPTICON SYSTEM

In the Panopticon system, a grid of thumbnails is displayed adjacent to a traditional video player (see Figure 2). The grid serves as a seek area and displays a 'timeline' where the whole video is presented in the form of thumbnails representing approximately every tenth second (depending on the video duration). Displaying frames from a video in parallel is a powerful method of providing the user with a rapid overview of the video, and by animating the thumbnails appropriately, the user can easily follow any part of the video without the need to seek.

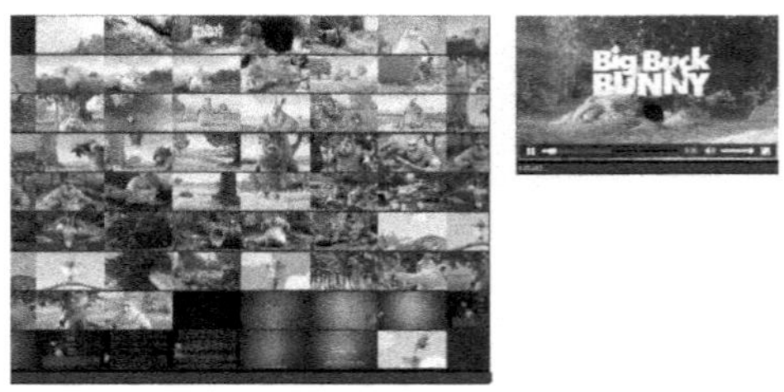

Figure 2. Panopticon interface. Left: dynamic timeline, right: video player.

Unlike other surrogates, Panopticon retains all of the frames from the original source – thereby preserving both the motion information and the overall context. Each of the thumbnails is animated in a loop by advancing the frame indices presented to the user over time. For example, the first thumbnail could play the first 10 seconds from the start of the video (0:00 until 0:10) and then restart. In parallel, the second thumbnail plays the next 10 seconds (time 0:10 to 0:20), and so on. This provides a consistent spatiotemporal layout – the opening scene of a video will always stay in the top left corner, and the end of a video will always be in the bottom right.

As each thumbnail reaches the time the next thumbnail started from (after 10 seconds) the thumbnail videos loop – for example, the first thumbnail ends at 0:10 and directly jumps back to 0:00 while the second thumbnail starts again at 0:10. To prevent this from causing a spatial discontinuity – so that a user does not have to adjust their gaze every 10 seconds when following the video – the grid is animated so that it slides smoothly to the right over time. By the time the first thumbnail has played its content, its position is where the second thumbnail originally started – when the loop occurs, the thumbnails reset to their original location, yet no visual jump is perceived. This makes it possible to smoothly follow the content at any point, without confusion.

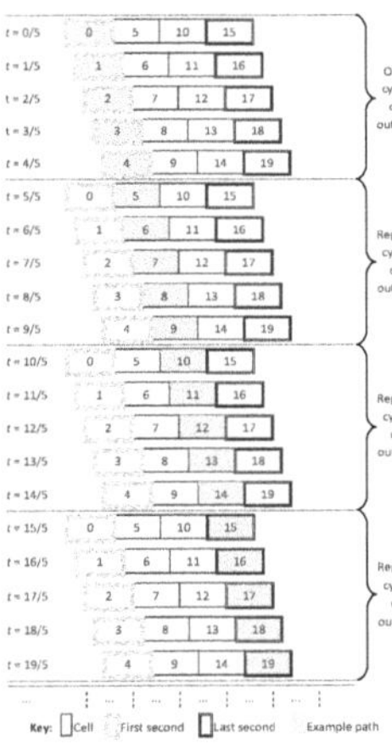

Figure 3. An example of a single-row Panopticon grid over time. Video frame indices shown at each time step, *t* (5 fps, 1 sec. cell interval, 4 sec. duration). One uninterrupted path through the video is highlighted.

Figure 3 shows an illustration of the Panopticon technique using a single-row grid for brevity. The start of the video remains on the left, the end remains on the right. An overview of all 20 frames has been given after just the first five steps, and yet any sub-sequence (even the whole video) can be followed without interruption. Moreover, it can be seen that the displayed sequence repeats in the same period as the interval between each grid cell (in this example, every five frames). These five frames, when repeatedly looped, represent exactly all that is required to be shown to the user. This fact enables the whole Panopticon overview to be computed once as a very short video loop and used in resource-constrained environments (such as web browsers). An interactive example of the Panopticon system is available online[1].

The discontinuity at the end of each line is minimized as the grid cells slowly fade out at the end of a line once they have faded in at the start of the next line, allowing the user time to adjust their gaze to the duplicate cell below.

In selecting the parameters of a Panopticon display, thumbnail sizes are maximized (while preserving aspect ratio) to produce a grid layout that provides a between-thumbnail time close to a chosen interval (e.g. 10 seconds). A minimum limit on thumbnail size (for legibility) means that, for longer videos, the interval must grow, to the detriment of easily identifying momentary actions.

VideoBoard comparison system

Based on previous work in the area of video surrogates, we predict that a static video surrogate system will facilitate information search within videos when compared with a video player such as YouTube. To this aim, we have created *VideoBoard,* a storyboard presentation with a video player (see Figure 4), which mimics commercial video editing software by providing fine-grained seek previewing of frames between thumbnail representations when moving the mouse pointer over the thumbnails.

Figure 4. VideoBoard interface. Left: static timeline, right: video player.

Based on the work by Hollingworth [7], we predict that Panopticon, a system that preserves all the context of the source, will facilitate information search when compared with VideoBoard.

STUDY 1

This initial study was designed with the aim of comparing user performance in searching previously unseen videos with Panopticon and two other systems – VideoBoard and YouTube – using three different video types. Participants were evaluated in both object recognition and gist comprehension.

Design

A 3×3 factorial mixed design was used to evaluate the time taken (seconds) for participants to find information with one of three video systems: Panopticon, VideoBoard, and

[1] http://di.ncl.ac.uk/panopticon

YouTube. Participants were required to find information in three separate videos: edited footage, unedited footage and surveillance footage.

Participants

A total of 36 participants (13 female, 23 male) aged 21 – 48 years (M = 27) were recruited from the university. They were randomly assigned to one of the three video conditions (Panopticon n=12, YouTube n=12, VideoBoard n=12). Participants were provided with refreshments, but were not financially compensated.

Materials

Three video systems were used for evaluation in this series of studies: Panopticon (Figure 2), VideoBoard (Figure 4), and YouTube (Figure 1). Panopticon is described in more detail in the previous section. VideoBoard was comprised of a static timeline on the left of a video player with each thumbnail representing every tenth second. The static thumbnails were animated on mouse-over events. This system was inspired by storyboard surrogates that are becoming increasingly popular [1] but added the feature of presenting all video frames on demand (i.e. mouse-over) similar to popular video editing programs like iMovie and Final Cut Pro. Finally, YouTube represents one of the most popular interfaces for video delivery [2] and has recently begun using preview thumbnails for context while seeking.

Three different videos (~30 min in length) were chosen to represent different application areas: an edited video, an unedited video, and a surveillance video. The edited footage – an extract from "Beverly Hills Ninja" – aimed to represent a standard film where users may want to find a specific scene (e.g. an action scene in a movie). The unedited footage – filmed sequences of a park, city center, and market area – aimed to represent personal videos and life-logging where users may want to find a specific event (e.g. when the family encountered a squirrel). Finally the surveillance footage – static camera footage of an office entrance during a normal working day – aimed to represent a pre-identified key time in a video where a user may want to find a specific person.

To assess gist comprehension, a forth video of the same duration was used – an extract from the movie "Soccer Mom". We chose the movies ("Beverly Hills Ninja" and "Soccer Mom") as they were freely available to download, had a chronological narrative, were in color, and were not known as bestselling titles.

Participants were asked four different questions for each video to assess how quickly specific occurrences could be found in the videos. The rationale behind the questions was the same for all videos: it was important that none of the occurrences were too close together, i.e., finding the answer to one question should not already give away the answer to the next one. Furthermore, it was important that participants understood the questions without knowing the videos. So questions never mentioned names or other things that would have been better understood if participants had seen the video before. Also, it was important that occurrences were distinct, e.g. there was only one tray being carried out of the room, and there was only one lorry turning in the road. We left out any technical terminology which may not have been understood by all participants.

Procedure

Once participants had been briefed, and informed consent collected, they were introduced to their randomly-selected system. Participants were given up to 10 minutes to explore and familiarize themselves with the different functionalities of their system, using both a practice video ("Big Buck Bunny") and practice questions.

Following the practice, participants were given the four questions (in counterbalanced order) corresponding to the first video, both on paper and read aloud by the researcher. We made sure that participants understood the questions before starting a stopwatch to record completion time, and participants were asked to answer the questions verbally. The accuracy of the measured performance time was ensured through a video recording of the screen and additional audio recording of the overall session.

Once participants had satisfactorily answered all four questions for a video, the same procedure was used for the following two videos. The order of the videos presented was also counter balanced. To assess how well participants would understand the narrative of a video, a fourth video was presented at the end and participants were given exactly five minutes to review the footage. Afterwards, participants had to write a short summary about everything they had understood from the video.

Study 1: Quantitative Results

Search Times

A two-way mixed ANOVA was carried out on the time data with System (Panopticon, VideoBoard, YouTube) and Video (edited, unedited, surveillance) as the independent and repeated factors respectively.

A main effect of System was found, $F(2,33)=20.567$, $p<.001$, where participants were significantly faster with Panopticon (288.50 sec.) than with YouTube (1252.83 sec., $p<.01$) and VideoBoard (321.06 sec., $p<.01$). A significant difference was also found in speed between VideoBoard and YouTube ($p<.05$).

A main effect of Video was also present, $F(2,32)=88.662$, $p<.001$, where significant differences in search times were observed between all three video types ($p<.001$) with the unedited footage being the fastest, and surveillance video the longest.

An interaction effect was found between System and Video, $F(4,66)=7.939$, $p<.001$ (see Table 1) with no differences between systems for the edited video. However, for the unedited video YouTube was significantly slower than both Panopticon (t(22)=3.305, p<.010) and VideoBoard (t(22)=2.325, p<.05). No difference was found between Panopticon and VideoBoard.

Video	Panopticon	VideoBoard	YouTube	*F(df)*	*p*
Narrative movie	288.50 (85.40)	308.17 (134.21)	325.33 (163.37)	0.24 (2,33)	.79
Unedited footage	109.58 (31.47)	131.25 (66.01)	215.00 (105.92)	6.74 (2,33)	< .01
Surveillance footage	235.50 (117.48)	523.75 (195.91)	712.50 (124.16)	30.73 (2,33)	< .01
Total time	626.08 (179.12)	963.17 (303.56)	1252.83 (193.99)	21.88 (2,33)	< .01

Table 1. Mean times in seconds (standard deviations in brackets) for the four questions of each video (left) in each condition (top).

For the surveillance video, significant differences in search times were found between Panopticon and VideoBoard (t(22)=4.371, p<.001), Panopticon and YouTube (t(22)=9.667, p<.001), and between VideoBoard and YouTube (t(22)=2.819, p=.010).

Gist Comprehension

A list of requirements was created to evaluate the summaries written by participants of their understanding of the last video. This list contained 25 entries of the most important parts of the storyline (e.g. "Family: 3 kids"). Two researchers independently classified the summaries. Final scores were matched and emerging disagreements discussed and resolved. One point was awarded for each correctly mentioned entry.

System	Panopticon	VideoBoard	YouTube	*F(df)*	*p*
Mean Score (SD)	9.25 (2.96)	5.58 (2.88)	5.33 (2.87)	6.85 (2,33)	<.01
Range	5-14	1-10	2-11		

Table 2. Participants' scores in the gist comprehension task. ANOVA reveals significant differences between the conditions.

Table 2 shows the final scores of participants in each video condition. A one-way ANOVA found that participants included a significantly higher number of important aspects in their summaries when using Panopticon in contrast to the other video systems. (Panopticon vs. YouTube, p<.01; Panopticon vs. VideoBoard, p=.01; YouTube vs. VideoBoard, p>.05)

Study 1: Qualitative Findings

Following the completion of Study 1, participants were asked to fill out an open-ended questionnaire asking them about their experience using one of the three systems. These responses were analyzed using Content Analysis by one researcher and verified by a second researcher.

Participants were in agreement that the grid-style timeline – present in both Panopticon and VideoBoard – was an important feature. More specifically, participants agreed that the timeline allowed them to see an overview of the video and use that to scan the most appropriate areas of the video first.

Finding specific information was generally perceived to be more appropriate in unedited or surveillance footage rather than edited footage where fast transitions made it difficult for the viewer to focus. However, not all participants were in agreement, suggesting that the ease of spotting information depended on various factors.

A major difference between the two surrogates that participants pointed out was the absence of all frames from the overview in VideoBoard. Participants noted that while it was not an ideal implementation to have large a number of frames hidden, the timeline still helped in finding information faster than with a regular video player. The fact that the system allowed the participants to preview the hidden frames on demand was an added bonus.

Despite a generally favorable perception of Panopticon, participants pointed out a number of problems with the system. The most common issues included thumbnails that were too small and at times made it difficult to identify objects. Participants also commented that the inability to pause the timeline for a quick search made them feel as if they were being overloaded with information.

PANOPTICON REDESIGN

Study 1 was replicated using a Tobii X60 eye tracker with the aim of understanding participants' behavior when searching for information in videos. The variable under investigation comprised of Mean Visit Duration – the average time (in seconds) participant spent looking at a feature (timeline or video player) per visit to the area.

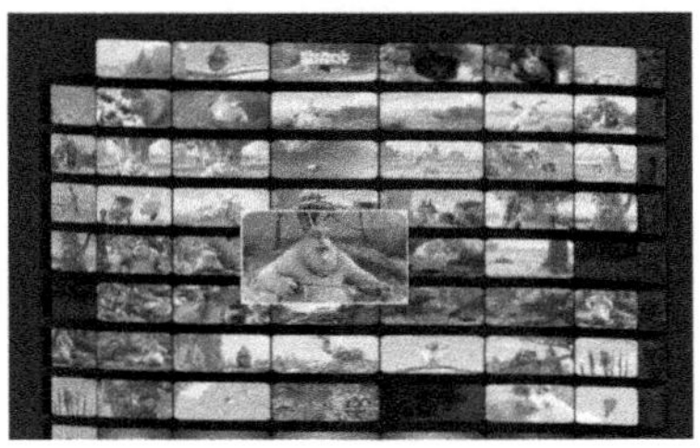

Figure 5. Panopticon 2 Interface, showing video playback within the overview.

It was observed that participants spent significantly longer on the timeline window than on the video window with Panopticon (p<.001) and VideoBoard (p=.001). These results support the qualitative findings indicating users' preference of using the timeline over the video window. It was also found that participants viewing the unedited (p<.010) and surveillance (p<.001) videos spent significantly longer on average on the timeline window than on the video window. Motivated by these findings, coupled with the qualitative feedback from Study 1, Panopticon was redesigned. This 'Panopticon 2' contained three core changes: the integration of the video player into the timeline, larger thumbnails, and a pause functionality.

Firstly, the video window was directly integrated into the timeline window (see Figure 5) in order to facilitate the search for information. In this configuration, the user may keep their focus on the timeline while spotting relevant events and objects in their peripheral vision [10]. Additionally, participants should not waste time switching between the timeline and video window – as indicated by the eye tracking gaze plots (see Figure 6 and Figure 7).

Secondly, the size of the thumbnails was increased as a result of participant feedback. For a given length of video, there is a trade-off between maximizing the thumbnail size (to retain resolution) and minimizing the interval between cells (so an overview is given in a short time). A practical compromise was reached by showing a windowed view over a range of the video, and the user may vertically scroll over the overview. This still maintains the coherency of the rendered output – exactly the same output appears at the same time in a loop, albeit at different vertical positions.

Finally, a key-press 'pause' functionality was implemented to satisfy participants who found the initial experience with the system overwhelming.

STUDY 2

A second study was carried out to evaluate Panopticon 2. Based on the changes made from participant feedback and the eye tracking results, it was expected that participants would be able to find information more quickly using this new system.

Method

A repeated measures design was used to evaluate the time taken (seconds) for participants to find information with Panopticon 2. Participants were required to find the information in the same videos: edited footage, unedited footage and surveillance footage. 13 new participants aged 18-24 (M=20.7 years old) took part in this study (8 female and 5 male). They were recruited from university and were compensated accordingly.

Participants were first taken through a demo with the new Panopticon version to familiarize themselves with it. They were then presented with the three videos and the related questions to each video. Videos and questions were both presented in a random order. Time was recorded for each question via stopwatch after the questions were read aloud.

Results

A two-way mixed ANOVA was carried out on the time data (seconds) of the three different videos and the video system (Panopticon, VideoBoard, YouTube, Panopticon 2) as between-subject factor. A main effect of video was found, $F(2,44)=93.02$, $p<.001$, with significant differences between all three videos ($p<.001$). A main effect of system was also present, $F(3,45)=123.79$, $p<.001$ showing significant differences between all systems ($p<.010$) with the exception of Panopticon and Panopticon 2.

An interaction was found between video and system, $F(6,88)=17.12$, $p<.001$, where participants searching within the surveillance video were significantly faster with Panopticon 2 (29 sec.) than with Panopticon (72.12 sec.), $t(23)=3.131$, $p<.010$. .No difference was found between systems for the edited video, but for the unedited video YouTube was significantly slower than both Panopticon ($p<.010$) and VideoBoard ($p<.05$). No Difference was found between Panopticon and VideoBoard.

DISCUSSION

The majority of past work on video surrogates has primarily focused on gist comprehension and largely ignored object recognition [3, 12]. In this paper, we have looked at object recognition as well as gist comprehension with Panopticon, a new video surrogate system. Results from two user studies demonstrated that participants using Panopticon were faster in recognizing objects than those using VideoBoard and YouTube with unedited footage (e.g. life-logging, personal video) and surveillance video. An improved version of the system, Panopticon 2, further enhanced the performance of users with surveillance footage, but not with the other two video types. Panopticon also proved to be significantly better than both VideoBoard and YouTube in gist comprehension.

Participants using the YouTube player were the slowest at finding information within videos and this could be attributed to the fact that they had to view more of the video due to less frames being available at once in the timeline. The eye tracking data found that participants using Panopticon and VideoBoard spent longer on average viewing the timeline, while no such difference was observed for participants using the YouTube player. In other words, participants using YouTube spent similar amounts of time viewing the timeline and watching the video. Given the differences in timeline design between the YouTube player and the other two systems, it is reasonable to suggest that YouTube's poorer results were due to the lack of a comprehensive overview.

Surveillance

Panopticon was clearly superior to the other two systems with the surveillance footage. This was the case across both studies and was further reinforced by participant feedback.

The heat maps from the eye tracking data (see Figure 6) clearly show how participants using Panopticon were able to identify the key areas within the timeline more easily than those using VideoBoard – given that very little time was spent looking away from the key areas. The fundamental difference in design between Panopticon and VideoBoard was the animation of the key-frames in the

Panopticon timeline. Since participants were significantly faster finding information in surveillance videos with Panopticon when compared with VideoBoard, it is possible to conclude that the animated key-frames were the main factor in the improvement of information search in surveillance. A look at the mouse clicks for the systems also shows that clicks were fairly equally distributed over the whole window for VideoBoard while they were concentrated in key areas for Panopticon. This observation is corroborated by feedback from participants who complained about the 'hidden frames' in the VideoBoard timeline, which resulted in them having to mouse over regions to find the required objects.

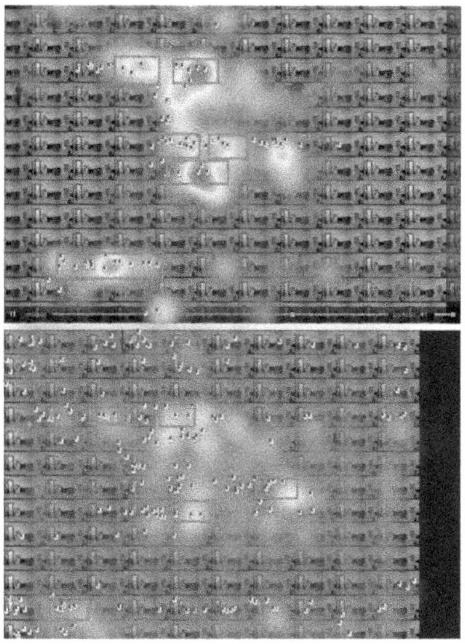

Figure 6. Panopticon (top) and VideoBoard (bottom) heat maps for surveillance video, with key areas (red boxes) and mouse clicks (red dots) shown.

Possible applications for Panopticon in the context of security could be twofold. In an implementation where an area is monitored automatically and alerts are triggered when unusual activity is detected, a generous amount of footage could be downloaded as a Panopticon movie in order to preserve all information from the footage while also saving browsing time and bandwidth. Instead of the offending event being presented to an expert in isolation, much richer contextual footage could be included. In an implementation where an area is monitored in real-time, Panopticon can be modified to work with a "live" view. For example, the lower-right corner showing "now", and "now-10" to the left of that, forming a grid of time. As the "now" view is constantly updated, the other thumbnails would not have to move in order to keep this relative, yet consistent, spatiotemporal layout. This view could serve as a fall back system where the user can quickly skim footage from the past few minutes for missed information. In both of the described scenarios Panopticon could add value to surveillance systems, and the usability of such a system amongst security professionals should be evaluated.

Edited Video

Interestingly, the YouTube player was comparable to VideoBoard and Panopticon for finding information in an edited video. A look at the heat maps for the edited video for Panopticon and VideoBoard (see Figure 7) shows little difference in spread of gaze time for both systems, suggesting that participants using Panopticon were not able to identify the key areas of the video as easily as with, for example, the surveillance video (Figure 6). As a result, participants had to employ a seeking approach similar to that used with VideoBoard. Participants viewing the edited video were required to view more of the video in the video player than participants viewing the other two videos – as demonstrated by the Feature and Video interaction – further supporting the notion that participants were unable to quickly spot important segments in the timeline.

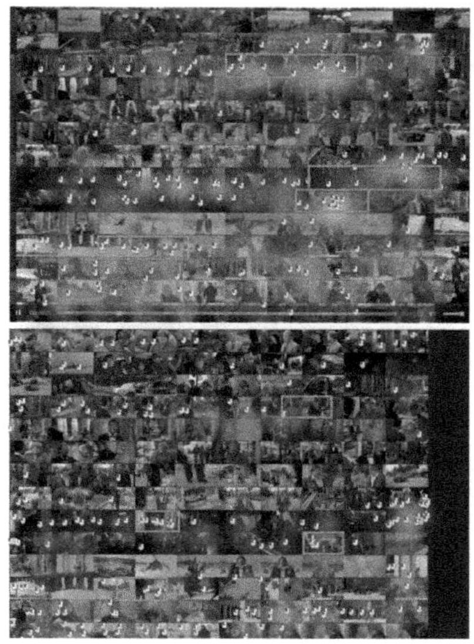

Figure 7. Panopticon (top) and VideoBoard (bottom) heat maps for edited video, with key areas (red boxes) and mouse clicks (red dots) shown.

A potential interpretation of this finding, supported by participant feedback, is that the storyboard timeline design does not lend itself for searching in edited, narrative-driven videos with fast transitions. Participants had to resort to watching more of the video which meant that they were using the surrogate system in a similar way to the video browsing system – and hence no significant differences in search times. Previous work seems to suggest that repetitive footage is not represented well with surrogates [14] but this notion was not supported by our findings.

Limitations

There are a number of limitations that have to be taken into consideration in this study. The questions used for the surveillance video were slightly different to those used for the other two videos. Two questions for the surveillance footage asked participants to count actions (e.g. the number of times a person passed through a door) which added another layer to solely searching. The different questions explain why the surveillance video took the longest to complete across all systems, but as the same four questions were used for all three systems the differences found should be viewed as legitimate. Another limitation was that only one video was used for each type. With this in mind, it is possible that the video that was chosen for the edited condition happened to not suit storyboard timelines due to its structure and fast action sequences. Finally, this study evaluated the performance of participants searching for information in previously unseen videos. However, a common use case is to search in videos users are already familiar with, and it would be interesting to look at this scenario. For example, video editing with footage a user has shot themselves, or a user finding a scene in a movie they just finished watching in order to clarify plot details.

CONCLUSION

This paper presents a new video surrogate system, Panopticon, which does not remove any frames and uses a novel animated arrangement to maximize context to improve gist comprehension, object and event recognition in videos. The overview can be generated as a highly efficient repeated animation loop for resource-constrained environments. As an example, a 30 minute video can be presented as a 10 second loop which allows any sub-sequence (even the full 30 minutes) to be seamlessly followed.

A series of user studies demonstrated the superiority of the system with both unedited footage and surveillance footage over a popular video browsing system – YouTube. In addition, Panopticon was shown to be superior to another video surrogate system with surveillance footage, suggesting a particular niche in that application area. The eye tracking studies suggest that the advantage is the result of the animated timeline.

Much work remains in fully exploring this new technique. These studies have only used a uniform grid layout, and more general transform function need exploring (e.g. larger, slower moving cells where they represent more salient scenes). Additionally, despite the multimodal nature of video, additional data such as speech, music, and subtitles are not yet represented within the Panopticon.

ACKNOWLEDGEMENTS

We would like to thank Dermot McNaney, Tom Bartindale and Robyn Taylor for work on the associated video. This work was partly funded by the SiDE project.

REFERENCES

1. Christel, M. (2008). Supporting video library exploratory search: when storyboards are not enough. *In Proc. CIVR 08* (pp. 447–456).
2. Cunningham, S., & Nichols, D. (2008). How people find videos. *In Proc. JCDL '08* (pp. 201–210).
3. Ding, W. and Marchionini, G. A Study on Video Browsing Strategies. Tech. Report CS-TR-3790, UMIACS-TR-97-40, CLIS-TR-97-06, University of Maryland. 1997.
4. Divakaran, A., & Otsuka, I. (2007). A video-browsing-enhanced personal video recorder. *In Proc. ICIAPW '07* (pp. 137–142).
5. Gil, N., Silva, N., Dias, E., & Martins, P. (2012). Going through the clouds: search overviews and browsing of movies. *In Proc. MindTrek 12* (pp. 158–165).
6. Haering, N., Venetianer, P. L., & Lipton, A. (2008). The evolution of video surveillance: an overview. *Machine Vision and Applications*, *19*(5-6), 279–290.
7. Hollingworth, A. (2009). Two forms of scene memory guide visual search: Memory for scene context and memory for the binding of target object to scene location. *Visual Cognition*, *17*(1-2), 37–41.
8. Marchionini, G., Song, Y., & Farrell, R. (2009). Multimedia surrogates for video gisting: Toward combining spoken words and imagery. *Information Processing & Management*, *45*(6), 615–630.
9. Matejka, J., Grossman, T., & Fitzmaurice, G. (2013). Swifter: Improved Online Video Scrubbing. *In Proc. CHI 2013*. pp. 1159-1168.
10. Palmer, S. M., & Rosa, M. G. P. (2006). A distinct anatomical network of cortical areas for analysis of motion in far peripheral vision. *The European Journal of Neuroscience*, *24*(8), 2389–405.
11. Schoeffmann, K., Hopfgartner, F., Marques, O., Boeszoermenyi, L., & Jose, J. M. (2010). Video browsing interfaces and applications: a review. *SPIE Reviews*, *1*.
12. Song, Y., & Marchionini, G. (2007). Effects of Audio and Visual Surrogates for Making Sense of Digital Video. *In Proc. CHI 2007* (pp. 867–876).
13. Tse, T., Marchionini, G., Ding, W., Slaughter, L., & Komlodi, A. (1998). Dynamic key frame presentation techniques for augmenting video browsing. *In Proc. AVI 98* (pp. 185–194).
14. Wildemuth, B., Marchionini, G., Wilkens, T., & Yang, M. (2002). Alternative surrogates for video objects in a digital library: users' perspectives on their relative usability. *LNCS*, *2458*, 493–507.
15. Wildemuth, B., Sun Oh, J., & Marchionini, G. (2010). Tactics used when searching for digital video. *In Proc. of IIiX '10* (pp. 255–264).
16. The Zettabyte Era. Cisco Visual Networking Index White Paper, 2012. http://cisco.com/en/US/solutions/collateral/ns341/ns525/ns537/ns705/ns827/VNI_Hyperconnectivity_WP.pdf

Video Collections in Panoramic Contexts

James Tompkin[1,5] Fabrizio Pece[2] Rajvi Shah[1,3] Shahram Izadi[2,4] Jan Kautz[2] Christian Theobalt[1]
MPI für Informatik[1] University College London[2] IIIT Hyderabad[3] Microsoft Research[4] Intel VCI[5]

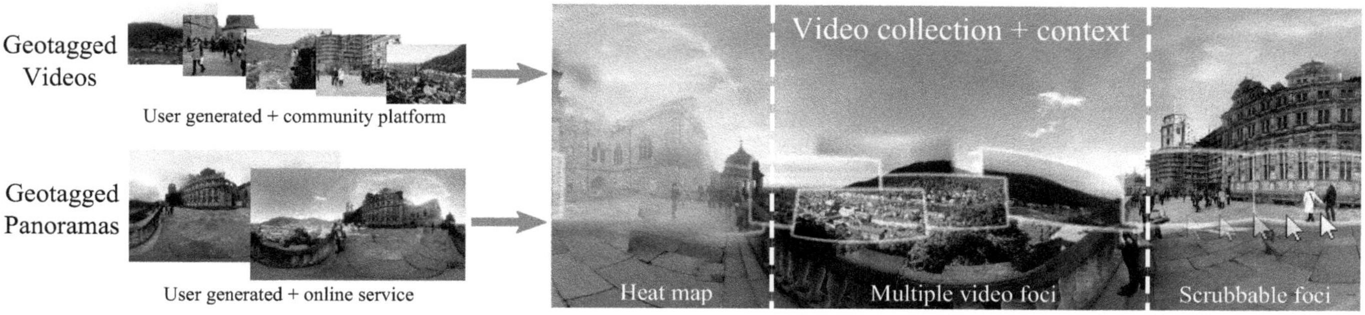

Figure 1: Panoramas are widely available online, and more and more video content of these places is shared online. With these data, our video-collection+context interface visualizes the dynamic changes within a collection. The right-hand side shows our spatio-temporal index as a heat map (*left*), inlayed video foci (*center*), and fast search with spatial mouse scrubbing (*right*).

ABSTRACT
Video collections of places show contrasts and changes in our world, but current interfaces to video collections make it hard for users to explore these changes. Recent state-of-the-art interfaces attempt to solve this problem for 'outside→in' collections, but cannot connect 'inside→out' collections of the same place which do not visually overlap. We extend the focus+context paradigm to create a video-collections+context interface by embedding videos into a panorama. We build a spatio-temporal index and tools for fast exploration of the space and time of the video collection. We demonstrate the flexibility of our representation with interfaces for desktop and mobile flat displays, and for a spherical display with joypad and tablet controllers. We study with users the effect of our video-collection+context system to spatio-temporal localization tasks, and find significant improvements to accuracy and completion time in visual search tasks compared to existing systems. We measure the usability of our interface with System Usability Scale (SUS) and task-specific questionnaires, and find our system scores higher.

Author Keywords
Video; video collections; panoramas; space-time exploration.

ACM Classification Keywords
H.5.2 User Interfaces: Evaluation/methodology, Interaction styles; H.5.1 Multimedia Information Systems: Artificial, augmented, and virtual realities, Evaluation/methodology.

http://dx.doi.org/10.1145/2501988.2502013

INTRODUCTION
The abundance of mobile devices with cameras has resulted in an ever increasing number of videos of places around the world. With geotagging, it is very easy to assemble a video collection containing many videos of the same location spanning a period of time. Such a collection can capture both the moment-to-moment dynamics of a location, the comings and goings, and its temporal evolution across days, months, seasons, or years. However, exploring these dynamic changes within places is difficult for users as existing interfaces do not explicitly connect the spatio-temporal content and display it within a unifying context. For example, a virtual tourist wishing to explore the dynamic events taking place over time in a famous square can only see videos in isolation, and has no easy tools to search within the space or time of the place.

Current mapping applications such as Google Maps link videos geographically and provide ways to find videos taken from the same place. However, they do not explicitly relate the changes over space and time into a single view for easy comparison, and users must watch videos in turn. State-of-the-art research systems for video collection browsing, such as Unstructured Video-based Rendering [2] and Videoscapes [31], try to find visual links within videos that all observe the same content either at the same time or across different times. However, often the contents of a geotagged video collection captured from the same place will not visually match because the videos all look out from approximately the same spot — we define these contents as 'inside→out'. For instance, two videos of a touristic vista might take in side-by-side views but never intersect. Further, for many interesting places, it is impossible to 'go around' and we can only 'look around', such as atop the Eiffel Tower. This forbids the application of existing vision-based matching systems which rely on cameras in different positions which converge to a common scene — we define these contents as 'outside→in' because the cameras surround the subject. As such, currently it is difficult to structure, relate, and explore 'inside→out' video collections.

To solve this problem, we introduce *Vidicontexts*, a system that embeds videos into the common context of a panoramic frame of reference. Vidicontexts extends the focus+context paradigm and enables the simultaneous visualization of individual videos as multiple foci, and through the context allows the exploration of how videos are spatially and temporally related even though there might be no direct visual match between them. This alleviates the difficulty of spatially and temporally exploring 'inside→out' video collections.

To this end, we align geotagged video from mobile devices to a panoramic context using orientation sensor data (if available) and time stamps. Omnidirectional panoramas exist for many places from online street mapping platforms, and recent work enables accurate pairing of geolocated images and panoramas [16]. Further, panorama stitching is a common easy-to-use application for mobile devices. These sources provide readily available contexts for our video collections.

We explore the application of our interface on different display/input devices: a flat desktop display with a mouse in both perspective and equirectangular projections, a tablet display with perspective projection driven by orientation sensors, and a spherical display with joypad or tablet controls. In a supplemental video, we demonstrate our system and the possible spatio-temporal interactions on various datasets and display types. We verify Vidicontexts utility with user studies that measure the accuracy and time taken of spatio-temporal video location tasks against existing systems. We also investigate the usability of Vidicontexts with two questionnaires, and find it compares favorably to two existing systems.

Our contributions are:

1. A system for exploring and manipulating video collections of places within panoramic contexts.
2. A demonstration of the flexibility of our representation with interfaces for different display devices.
3. A study that quantifies the performance benefit of our tools and assesses desirability and usability when compared to existing systems.

RELATED WORK

Panoramic Imaging

Panoramas make an attractive context as they provide wide or omni-directional views of an environment in a single image. There are many established methods to construct panoramas, including using special camera hardware or by stitching individual photographs [3, 5, 30] or videos [1]. Panoramas for hundreds of thousands of places are available through mapping portals such as Google Street View or photography platforms like Panoramio.

Omnidirectional panoramas can be rendered in a variety of ways. Recent work [20] has explored the influence of varying projections on how users are able to locate scene objects. Their work concludes that clear and understandable visualization of the panorama is more important than accurate spatial mapping to enable users to exploit the 360° content.

Spatio-temporal Media Exploration

Exploring large collections of unstructured images depicting the same location can be sometimes difficult or cumbersome. The research community has tried to solve this problem by developing spatio-temporal photo visualization applications. Photo Tourism [29, 28] is one example, as the program aims to arrange and display a set of images in a 3D space so that spatially-confined locations can be interactively navigated. Similarly, the PhotoScope work of Wu et al. [32] extends the standard photo browsing paradigm by visualizing spatial coverage of construction site photos on a 2D map, and by indexing them with a combination of spatial coverage, time, and content specifications.

RealityFlythrough [19] uses videos combined with GPS and orientation data as its input. Videos are situated in a 3D representation of the world, allowing the user to navigate freely while continually transitioning to the most appropriate video for the current view. The system provides the user with some sense of how the videos relate to one another spatially, but no further context is provided and only one video is ever played back at the same time.

Unstructured video-based rendering [2] combines contemporaneous video streams of the same scene or performance, and provides an intuitive 3D-aware interface to these videos. It requires an image-based 3D reconstruction of the scene from photographs beforehand. Tompkin et al. [31] introduce Videoscapes to explore sparse unstructured video collections. They build a graph of videos by visual similarity, exploiting this graph to generate 3D reconstructions at nodes, and then provide various different interfaces to explore this graph with seamless transitions. These works use 'outside→in' assumptions as mentioned earlier, and usually only show the spatio-temporal changes when transitioning between two videos at a time. Furthermore, they require substantial additional data, such as photos to reconstruct a geometric background model or a graph of hundreds of videos. In contrast to our 'inside→out' approach, without an enveloping context they would fail to show videos taken from the same place but with non-overlapping views of the scene.

Dale et al. [7] introduce a system for browsing multiple videos with a common theme, such as the result of a search query on a video sharing website or videos of an event covered by multiple cameras. This browsing companion enhances a primary video by showing thumbnails of other temporally synchronized video clips.

Spatially-enabled exploration of single videos in isolation has also been researched. Hermans et al. [12] visualize a single tripod video as a single augmented panoramic video. Dynamic foreground and background objects are segmented and decoupled to re-time motions in the original video footage. Pongnumkul et al. [26] introduce a map-based storyboard system that presents a single tour video with different coherent shots at different locations pinned to a map.

Focus+context and Video+context Applications.

Focus+context systems show a subset of information in full detail within a wider context of surrounding lower-density de-

Figure 2: The Vidicontexts interface. Different months of the fall season — rainy October, cloudy skies at twilight in November, snow in December — and dynamic objects are added to the summer scene context.

tail [6]. CamBlend by Norris et al. [23] extends focus+context interfaces to apply to panoramic video collaboration tools. A smaller focus window is moved around within a larger panoramic video to identify objects to viewers of the scene.

Neumann et al. [22] introduced 'live' augmented virtual environments, where video from static surveillance cameras is projected onto geometric models from LIDAR data of a city. Follow up work attempts live painting of the bare geometry environment with texture from video from a mobile observer [13]. de Haan et al. [8] overlay static security video feeds onto geometric models for virtual first-person viewing. Kim et al. [15] propose methods for augmenting aerial visualizations of Earth with dynamic video information. However, the natures of the data (aerial looking down vs. our many inside→out overlapping videos) dictate different and novel interaction tools. Moreover, the interactions in their work are speculative, while we demonstrate significant improvements in studies. These methods were extended to provide automatic camera control for tracking dynamic objects in virtual environments that have been augmented using multiple sparse static video feeds [27]. De Camp et al. [9] map an indoor environment spatially top down, where each room is covered by one omnidirectional camera feed.

Pece et al. [24] present a teleconferencing system with smartphone cameras to create a surround representation of meeting places. Live videos from smartphones is inserted into a static panorama using marker- and image-based tracking. However, this result is not used to develop a system for exploring the space and time of a video collection.

Similar to our work, Pirk et al. [25] enhance panoramas with embedded videos to create a new interactive medium. Videos are captured from tripods at the same time as the panorama is captured. Our paper creates and evaluates an interface for spatio-temporal visualization and interaction within video-collection+contexts, using heterogeneous hand-held videos captured at different times than the panorama, whereas their paper focuses on seamlessly blending videos into a panorama using hand-segmented dynamic objects.

VIDICONTEXTS SYSTEM

Vidicontexts[1] (Fig. 2) takes as input a panoramic image and a collection of videos with time stamps, GPS data, and orientation sensor data. We first track and align all videos within the panorama, which yields a sequence of homographies for each video. Next, we build a spatio-temporal video index for exploration. Finally, we provide an interface to explore the collection of videos within their panoramic context. In general, any task that requires spatial or temporal reasoning would benefit from our system. A user might browse a collection of videos to locate object in space/time, follow videos, infer temporal changes, highlight captured regions, filter and isolate video instances that belong to a particular time span or spatial bounds; broadly, relate videos within a collection. Sport, museum, cultural sites, social events, surveillance, and tourist videos could be browsed and analysed.

Capture and Context

Our panoramic contexts can come from online repositories such as Google Street View, panoramic cameras, and DSLR stitches, or from user-assisted tools included in many mobile devices. Although any suitable source could be used, to create the material for the demonstrations in this paper we use Microsoft Photosynth on smartphones and Microsoft Research's ICE for stitching photos from a DSLR. Next, we captured several example video collections ourselves from roughly the same location as the panoramas, returning to the same locations over time. We used Samsung Galaxy II and HTC OneX smartphones to capture both video, GPS location, and orientation data (from integrated accelerometer, gyroscope,

[1] http://gvv.mpi-inf.mpg.de/projects/Vidicontexts/

(a) Spherical projection (b) Localization with sensor data (c) Feature-based alignment (d) Panorama composition

Figure 3: (a) Videos a projected into a spherical coordinate system and (b) localized using orientation sensor data. Within this localization, SIFT features are extracted and robustly matched to estimate an alignment (c) for compositing (d).

and magnetometer sensors via the Android API). This camera orientation estimate provides an initial registration to the panoramic context. For online panoramas, pairing geotagged videos to geotagged panoramas can be difficult when GPS data is inaccurate. We assume existing work picks the closest geographical panorama from an online repository [16].

Video Alignment

Orientation data provides only approximate video alignment to the context. Accurate spatial localization is made difficult by *a*) hand-held video capture with jitter; *b*) time changes between context and videos, causing lighting changes, static and dynamic object changes, and broad scene appearance changes from seasonal variation; and *c*) the computational cost of alignment traded-off against the need to handle collections of videos. Despite variations in capture pose, we assume that the spherical panorama is a good proxy geometry for the scene, and we align the video frames to the spherical panorama using sensor- and feature-based image alignment (Fig. 3).

Spherical Projection:

We transform perspective videos into spherical projection with focal length metadata and pitch and roll orientation data from our smartphones [3]. If the focal length, pitch, and roll estimates are accurate, and if there is no parallax, then the spherically transformed video frames would be related to the equirectangular panorama by a translational model; however, due to errors in these estimates, we allow more freedom in the alignment transformation by using a homography model.

Feature Extraction:

We extract SIFT features [18] from the spherically-warped video frames and from the panorama. As feature extraction is a frame-independent task, we parallelize it.

Sensor-data based Localization:

We localize video frames approximately within the panorama using orientation data. Given this, we only match panorama features to video features within a bounding box 20% larger than the approximate localization. This reduces matching time and false matches significantly. For videos with no metadata or sensor readings, we perform an initial robust feature-based match between the panorama and the video to discover approximately the focal length, pitch, and roll angles.

Homography Estimation:

With 4 or more matches between frames and panorama, we can estimate a homography between each video frame and the panorama using the gold standard algorithm [11]. For further refinement, we use the estimated homography to find inliers from the initial set of matches and re-estimate the homography using inliers only [10]. This refinement step is repeated for three iterations in our experiments. As we have a strong expectation for a translation transformation, we perform conservative homography outlier rejection and remove homographies that are not projective or that have a large skew factor.

Estimation of Missing Homographies:

With outlier rejection, it is possible that no good homography is found for short sequences of frames. We approximate these missing homographies: with a neighboring valid homography as a starting point, we accumulate sensor orientation changes until we find a valid homography end point, and then integrate the resulting error over the length of the missing sequence.

Temporal Filtering:

Since frame homographies are estimated independently, some temporal jitter remains due to small but independent alignment errors. We bilaterally filter the frame corner positions over 30 frames in time to reduce temporal jitter. We modulate the contribution of each filter window position (temporal weight) by the image-space Euclidean distance from the center window position (range weight).

The solution we provide to the alignment problem in our system is not the final word as this is a hard problem in its own. Please see our supplemental material for implementation details of our alignment approach.

Spatio-temporal Index

With video alignment, we can construct a spatio-temporal index of where and when each video intersects the context. We iterate through each video and intersect its per-frame bounds against a grid of cells which cover the panorama. The choice of grid resolution depends on the size of the dataset and memory constraints. We set the cell resolution of this index to be $\sim 100 \times 50$ cells, which gives a moderate 40 pixel spatial precision across the panoramic context. Each grid cell stores the spans of frames per video which intersect it.

The spatio-temporal index can be visualized in many ways depending on the application. We choose to render the index with a gradient such as a heat map (Fig. 4). With this, users can see which regions of the context held the most 'attention' among the videos, and our spatio-temporal interaction tools then allow these videos to be found quickly. Selecting individual videos shows a per-video index which defines the spatial extent of the video. Heat maps for specific index

Figure 4: The spatio-temporal index displayed as a heat map to show attention over the context. This index allows quick spatio-temporal search and filtering of the video collection. This is computed globally (*top*) and per-video (*bottom*).

queries can be generated, e.g., video attention for a historic time span. Other visualizations would be possible, such as altering the saturation of the panoramic context locally for when it is important not to overlay further graphics onto the scene, or by displaying the path of the video by rendering a line joining the center-most grid cells along the path. Arrows on the line can show the progression of time, and color with a gradient can show where the video lingers.

Interface and Interaction

The Vidicontexts interface (Fig. 2) presents the context in either look-around perspective projection or as a full equirectangular map projection with an infinitely-rotating canvas. The user is free to pan, zoom, and smoothly switch between perspectives. Videos can be visually followed, or the context can be locked to follow individual videos. We also provide standard video playback controls. Our vidthieo-collection+context interface becomes more interesting as we provide tools for spatio-temporal interactions.

Temporally-driven Interactions

Each video has its own local timeline which appears when the video is selected. Unlike a normal video player, adjusting the timeline affects both the dynamic content within the video and the spatial position of the video in the context, and this provides a quick way to check the spatial extent of a video. This enables new applications: by adjusting the timelines of different videos and by setting A→B loop markers, the user can compose a novel arrangement of the videos within the context to highlight spatio-temporal changes.

As we have timestamps for each video, we also show a global timeline which displays the temporal extent of the video collection. Adjusting the ends of the timeline filters the video collection, for instance, to isolate videos from a particular day or month. The global timeline slider synchronously adjusts the playback of all videos in the collection, and allows the visualization of events which share the same time but otherwise have no visual overlap (Fig. 5). Such relations are difficult to explore when the videos are seen out of context. If multiple panoramas captured from the same position are available

Figure 5: The global timeline allows control over all videos at once and enforces temporal ordering. Here, two contemporaneously captured videos which never intersect are displayed synchronously and in context, allowing easy identification of the movements of a man (red).

and timestamped, then the global slider also switches between them. This shows temporal changes in the context: for instance, in the seasons or in the built environment.

Spatially-driven Interactions

Temporal scrubbing has a spatial equivalent: By dragging the mouse over the panoramic context, the user can spatially drag individual videos or all videos at once, providing a fast way to localize many videos at once. As videos aren't guaranteed to visit all locations in space, they scrub to their nearest position. The extents of each video individually and of all videos combined can be shown by visualizing the spatio-temporal index (Fig. 4), and this helps guide spatial exploration.

We also provide area-based spatio-temporal filtering (Fig. 6). By dragging a box over the context to describe a region of interest, the user queries the spatio-temporal index for sequences of frames which intersect the region. This is a very fast way to 'collage' an area of the context with video.

EVALUATION

As this paper describes a time-varying interactive system, we refer the reader to our supplemental video for our interface demonstration. Thus, this section describes performance and timings for the preprocessing and viewer, then describes our quantitative and qualitative interface evaluation to gauge both the improvement over existing interfaces for tasks and the desirability and usability of our interface. For all results shown in both the paper and the supplemental video, we captured our own datasets to jointly capture orientation data.

Performance timings

We process videos independently and, as feature extraction is frame independent, our technique is embarrassingly parallel. Video alignment was computed on an Intel Xeon 8 core 2.40GHz PC; see Table 1 for computation times. All panoramas are 4000×2000 pixels, and all video frames are

Figure 6: The spatio-temporal index makes searching simple. The user draws a bounding box over the region of interest, and our interface lays out all intersecting videos. The dynamic objects such as the red bus bring the scene to life.

Dataset	# Videos	# Frames	Alignment	Index
College grounds	15	30,426	6hr 10min	40sec
Castle vista	9	17,460	3hr 33min	25sec
New courtyard	11	21,518	4hr 26min	30sec
Neo-classical quad	20	26,635	6hr 16min	55sec
Indoor hallway	6	4,152	36min	16sec

Table 1: Computation times for alignment and spatio-temporal indexing (100×50 cells) for our datasets.

1920×1080 pixels. Our alignment code is written in MATLAB and C++, though GPU-accelerated matching algorithms may speed this up. The computation time for the spatio-temporal indices is also included in this table, and this performance scales linearly with the total number of cells.

The computational performance of our interface is defined by the number of videos visible. The rendering cost is minimal as we need only apply a homography to a pre-warped video and its feathered matte; however, the video decompression cost is large. Our implementation supports approximately 3 1080p HD videos at framerate at once. To cope with more videos, we store a reduced resolution version at a quarter scale, and only switch to full resolution if the user zooms in. While modern CPUs contain hardware to decompress 5+ videos at once, it is difficult to use this as our video format must support fast and exact seeking.

User Study

Design

Vidicontexts facilitates spatio-temporal exploration and comparison within video collections. While this is straightforward to understand and demonstrate, measuring whether our system provides significant benefits over existing video collection interfaces is non-trivial. Therefore, to evaluate Vidicontexts, we conduct a user study with two tasks that require participants to infer spatial and temporal information from a video collection. We compare Vidicontexts with *iMovie*, which offers a chronological browsing window and a resizeable timeline for fast preview, and against iMovie with the panoramic context image available for reference (*iMovie+pano* henceforth). Please see the supplemental document for further explanation of these two interfaces.

Tasks chosen to measure performance should represent general actions performed regularly by users. Common actions while exploring a place include looking for objects/actions in space and in time, following dynamic events within the place, and identifying when changes happen within specific times or areas of the place. As such, we select two tasks that involve counting and tracking events, in our case the comings and goings of people, within several videos. These tasks offer two reliable metrics which a) mimic common tasks performed when browsing a video collection, and b) can be extended to multiple system interfaces for comparison. In addition, we exclude possible tasks which would be trivial with one interface over another (e.g., in our interface, to find all videos which intersect part of the panorama). The resulting tasks are exemplars for real interactions which allow us to assess different systems and validate spatial and temporal understanding.

We wish to assess the accuracy with which participants can correctly obtain a spatial and temporal understanding of a collection of videos. Hence, in both tasks, we measured the completion time and accuracy expressed as errors in the people counts. Following the experiment, participants completed the standard System Usability Scale (SUS) questionnaire [4], which gathers subjective assessments of usability, as well as an additional questionnaire on the task experience (Tab. 3).

Tasks and Datasets

The *people counting* task requires participants to browse 20 videos from the *neo-classical quad* dataset (Fig. 4, 6) and identify the number of different people who sit on a set of benches. Videos differ in length and cover a large area of the environment. As different videos could depict the same person, or show a person sitting near the areas of interest, a participant could potentially make 20 erroneous counts. The maximum number of errors was manually counted.

The *people tracking* task asks participants to review 6 videos from the *new courtyard* dataset (Fig. 5) and track the number of different people who cross between two buildings. Here, the videos never fully track a person and do not overlap, so multiple synchronous videos must be analyzed to obtain the correct result. Videos differ in length, but they all cover a similar area of the environment. A participant could potentially make 12 erroneous counts (again manually counted).

Data Collection and Participants Selection

30 participants from the staff and student population at our university performed both tasks using one system each for a between-subjects design for the system independent condition, and a within-subjects design for the task. While we did not filter the study population for handedness and eyesight, we ensure gender balance was respected. Additionally, the participants were randomly assigned one of the three sys-

Condition	People Counting		People Tracking	
	Error	Time	Error	Time
iMovie vs. +pano	0.958	0.916	0.968	0.898
iMovie vs. Ours	0.040	0.017	0.049	0.014
+pano vs. Ours	0.107	0.023	0.012	0.005

Table 2: Significance (p-values) for each task and condition combination for both error and time to complete. Green values are statistically significant ($\alpha = 0.05$).

tems, within which the order of the two tasks was alternated to minimize the influence of learning effects. All subjects were introduced to their assigned system and to the tasks, and there was no mention of the overarching goal of the study. All participants were familiar with editing in general, and all received training with their system.

Procedure

Each participant performed two different tasks using the same system, with no time limit. Participants could use all features of each system, e.g., in iMovie and iMovie+pano, the built-in video scrubbing and thumbnail expansion. Each participant was given a detailed description of the system's interface and features, and as much time as they liked to familiarize before the task. Each task was conducted in series, with a briefing beforehand to explain the task. Following both tasks, the participant completed two questionnaires.

Hypotheses

We expect accuracy to vary with the sophistication of the spatio-temporal representation, and so we expect Vidicontexts to be more accurate. In turn, we expect iMovie+pano to be more accurate than iMovie alone. For completion time, we expect performance to vary according to the spatio-temporal controls available, and so we expect our system to require the least time. We expect all three conditions to score above average (75%) on the SUS. Finally, we expect Vidicontexts to obtain the highest score for the task-related questionnaire as we believe this is directly related to task performance.

Results

We provide a summary of our results here and in Figure 7, where box and whisker plots are reported for the completion time, the number of errors committed, and the significance for each task and condition combination; in the supplemental material we provide a full analysis description. We computed Analysis of Variance (ANOVA) using SPSS with the system used as the single factor and completion time/counting error as the dependent variable, with post-hoc Games-Howell tests for pairwise significance tests ($\alpha = 0.05$). Table 2 shows the significances of all compared systems. There was no significant difference between the iMovie and the iMovie+pano cases across all our experiments. When comparing iMovie against Vidicontexts, we see significant error reductions and significant time benefits for both counting and tracking tasks. One anomalous result is that our system is not significantly less eroneous than iMovie+pano in the counting case, though there are large differences between mean and std. dev. values.

Task-related question	iMovie	+pano	Ours
Easy to complete tasks	2.3	2.6	4
Understood video orientation in space	3.5	3.9	4.7
Understood relative video position	3	3.8	4.4
Understood space-time video overlap	2.8	3.8	4.3
Understood temporal order of videos	1.5	2.1	3.4
Environment representation confused	3.2	3.5	1.7
System has enough functions for tasks	3	2.5	4.4
#videos made remembering things hard	3.9	4.2	2.6
Overall mean	2.375	2.62	3.86

Table 3: System mean scores for the task-related questionnaire. The response scale varies between 1 and 5. The scale for negative questions was reversed for mean computation.

From the SUS questionnaire, only Vidicontexts scored above the average ($SUS = 77.5$), followed by the iMovie+pano ($SUS = 62.75$) and iMovie ($SUS = 59.5$) conditions. From this, our system can be classified as a Rank B system [17], whereas both iMovie and iMovie+panorama mode are Rank C systems. From the task-related questionnaire, Vidicontexts performed better than both iMovie and iMovie+pano conditions, scoring a significantly higher mean score of $M = 3.86$. Table 3 presents the mean score for each system and question.

DISCUSSION

User Study

For iMovie and iMovie+pano, user task strategy was to first expand the video thumbnails timeline to obtain an idea of where each video pointed, and then either to use the normal playback tools or to scrub through the videos as thumbnails. For the people tracking task, users played parts of the collection several times before answering. One user in both the iMovie and iMovie+pano conditions struggled to accomplish the task at all, and generally participants from these two conditions struggled more than participants from our condition. For Vidicontexts, most participants used the local video timelines to accelerate video localization in the panorama. The global timeline was frequently used by the participants in the tracking task, but rarely used for the counting task. No users struggled to complete the tasks with Vidicontexts.

In both tasks, Vidicontexts provided greater accuracy, and this agrees with our initial hypothesis. Our spatio-temporal representation combines necessary information to reduce task complexity over iMovie, and this is confirmed by significant error and time reductions. For instance, in the iMovie counting task, users need to spatially locate the video before counting people as only particular regions are of interest. In Vidicontexts, the user need only count people as the video is already spatially located. This reduction in complexity allows the user to perform only the task essential action.

Analysing the user task strategy confirms this explanation: In the counting task, for iMovie and iMovie+pano, users first expanded the video thumbnails timeline to spatially locate each video in turn, and then either used normal playback tools or scrubbed through the videos as thumbnails to count people.

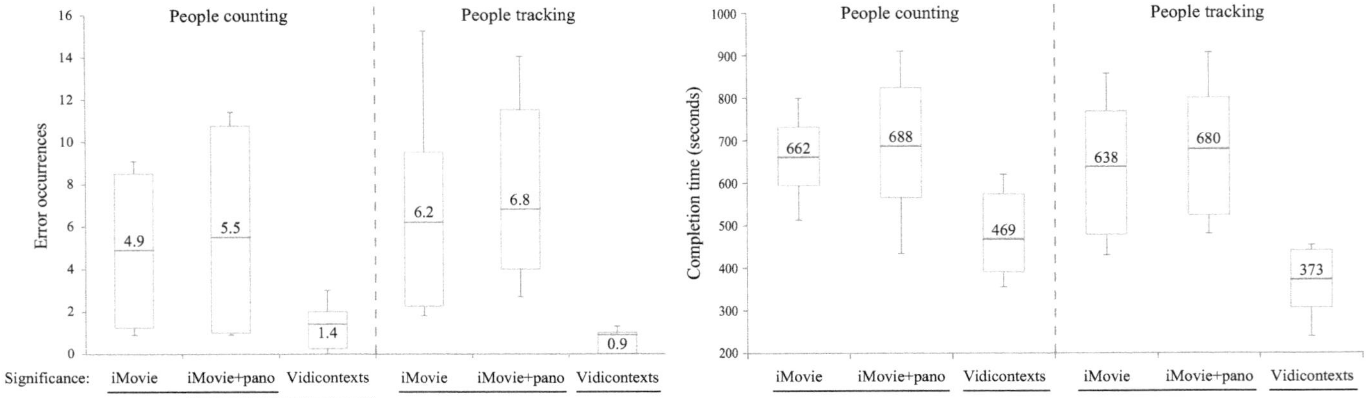

Figure 7: Box and whisker plots for each condition in both tasks. *Left:* Error occurrences. *Right:* Time to complete occurrences. First and third quartiles are reported in the upper and lower boxes, respectively. Any conditions whose name are underlined are considered statistically similar.

For Vidicontexts, participants could exploit the spatial alignment and only needed to search in time. Here, most used the local video timeline tool.

The people tracking task requires temporal and spatial alignment, and this increased cognitive load presented a challenge to users. In both iMovie conditions, users had to replay parts of the collection several times before answering. One user in both iMovie conditions struggled to accomplish the task at all, and generally participants from these two conditions struggled more than participants from our condition. For Vidicontexts, the global timeline maintains temporal alignment, and so this was frequently used by the participants in this task. No users struggled to complete the tasks with our system: the context representation combines necessary information and reduces task complexity.

Users were quick to familiarize with the new Vidicontexts system as video information is presented in a similar way to real life environments. This can help explain why users response to our system was also positive in terms of usability and desirability, as suggested by the much higher questionnaire scores for our interface than for the iMovie conditions. The individual questions reveal that participants considered our system the best tool to convey spatial and temporal information within the video collection, that they perceived our representation as less confusing, and that they thought our tools were more useful for exploration tasks. Additionally, participants agreed that, for tens of videos, our system improved recall; though we must not extrapolate this result to larger numbers of videos.

Finally, we observed a general trend in the preferred panorama projection. To complete the tasks, 80% of the population assigned to our system used equirectangular projection. This finding, in accordance with recent work by Mulloni et al. [20], shows that participants thought the 360°-at-once projection conferred more spatio-temporal information than the geometrically-correct perspective projection. We assume that users did not want to be constrained to a limited field-of-view for localization tasks.

Display applications

The video-collection+context representation fits display and interaction devices beyond desktop environments, such as tablets, spherical displays, and head-mounted displays such as Oculus Rift. These devices map the panorama to both virtual and real spatially-located spheres. Mobile devices naturally respect the geometry of 'inside→out' video collections, with a display that can respond to rotation and head movements (similar to [14]). With spherical displays, our context is displayed on a physical sphere in tandem with complementary joypad or tablet controller interfaces (Fig. 8, bottom row). Further, using contexts to join video collections has applications in augmented reality, especially when coupled with wearable computing devices such as Google Glass. Please see our supplemental material for detailed descriptions, and our supplemental video for demonstrations. Different displays provide different real and virtual geometries, and this might impact how users relate to and perform with the panoramic context. We leave this broad study for future work.

Use cases

Vidicontexts has many applications, including virtual tourism, surveillance, and shared browsing of an event. For example, sifting through footage and looking at patterns of behaviors over time within a place for a surveillance review; or, comparing and contrasting past events in a square, such as protesters contrasted against performers and musicians.

One particularly interesting example builds upon Naimark's Time Binoculars idea [21]: similar to the coin-operated binoculars common at vistas, a viewfinder allows users to "look around an actual site and see aligned augmentations of what they see, such as different times of day or different seasons, or historical views, or full-out Hollywood-style reenactments". Vidicontexts removes the need for fixed apparatus for these examples, and instead we imagine a smartphone or tablet app which guides users to spatial hotspots via GPS, from which they can use their mobile device as a viewfinder to explore the 'augmentations', or record new footage to add to the collection. For instance, a heritage site could create content especially for these experiences, such as re-enacted

Figure 8: Additional displays and interactions. *Left:* Spherical display with a joypad controlling a cursor. *Center:* A tablet acting as a proxy controller, where the spherical display mirrors the context of the tablet. *Right:* Tablet display in situ, showing a protest that no longer exist in the real environment.

druidic rituals at Stonehenge; or a city could collate videos into a walking tour, say, London in 2012, re-viewing royal wedding, diamond jubilee, and Olympic events.

Limitations

While panoramas are available for many locations in the world, and simple tools on smartphones make panorama capture easy, Vidicontexts still requires a panorama as we register each video individually to the panorama. With only sensor orientation data, videos could still be coarsely aligned within an empty context, though existing videos rarely have embedded orientation data. Future work could explore stitching videos to each other to build a context. Further, even with a panorama, Vidicontexts will fail if large changes have occurred in the environment between the panorama and videos. For instance, many historical videos may only partially match the environment as building development is likely to have occurred. Here, we would have to rely on inter-video homography estimation for times in the video which do not match the panorama, anchored between times which do match. With no visual similarity at all, again we could only rely on captured orientation data.

In this work, we show panoramic contexts and, with in-situ browsing, we show real world contexts; however, other potential contexts exist. One alternative is 3D geometry from laser scans, but these are not readily available. Another alternative is 3D geometry reconstructed from images online. However, often these techniques are brittle with small baselines and are generally less applicable. In contrast, panoramas are widely available and easy to capture, and so our panoramic approach is applicable to more varied places.

Many errors can affect the quality of video alignment to the context, including failures and artifacts in panorama stitching, incorrect or badly synchronized sensor data and camera metadata, large deviations from the proxy geometry assumption, large dynamic objects, and large static changes. The problem of temporally consistent video alignment is difficult even for state-of-the-art vision systems, and improving this is important future work. However, we posit that this improvement would cause a relatively small functional improvement in our interface, and instead we try to show that a useful and wanted system is still possible under these conditions. Further, while orientation sensor data can be bad, it does provide a fallback for cases where visual alignment will have difficulty, and modern smartphones produce fittings from sensor data that are acceptable for many video-collection+context applications (we show one such case in our supplemental video).

With dynamic object segmentation masks, we could build a second spatio-temporal index for manipulating dynamic content directly in a similar way – scrubbing, filtering, and searching – and this would increase the functionality of our interface. Dynamic objects from different videos could be composited into the same context, and index look-ups would create synopses where space-time is compressed to be only those instances and positions where dynamics occur. As segmentation is a hard vision problem, existing work performs this manually for small numbers of short videos [25], but this approach is infeasible for video collections.

Providing context with panoramas is a special case of the larger problem of aligning videos to a 3D virtual world. As such, we impose strict limitations on the source data and so bypass many problems that come with more difficult data. Our examples and experiment do not use real data from community video websites, and many challenges remain to provide context for these varied collections. Our work demonstrates the promise of video-collection+context techniques in general, and produces a system with immediate benefits over existing video collection exploration software for limited subsets of videos. Overall, we feel that our approach is sufficiently practical for the described use cases in online mapping and tourism to be applicable immediately.

CONCLUSION

Vidicontexts is a system for interacting with an 'inside→out' video collection within a panoramic context. We capture panoramas and videos with handheld smartphones, and visually embed the videos into the panorama. With a spatio-temporal index of the scene, we create novel interface tools to quickly search and filter the video collection. We extend our system for tablet devices with physical rotation and zoom, in situ with real world contexts, and to spherical displays. We conduct a task-based study to compare with existing systems: we find that Vidicontexts provides significant benefits to accuracy and time taken in localization tasks, that it is preferred both by SUS and for our tasks, and that it would be used frequently and recommended to friends/colleagues if deployed.

Acknowledgements

Anthony Steed, Mike Terry, Pan Ye, Antti Oulasvirta, Kwang In Kim, Will Steptoe, Peter Grindrod, and all our participants.

REFERENCES

1. Agarwala, A., Zheng, K., Pal, C., Agrawala, M., Cohen, M., Curless, B., Salesin, D., and Szeliski, R. Panoramic Video Textures. *ACM Trans. Graph. (TOG) 24*, 3 (2005), 821–827.
2. Ballan, L., Brostow, G. J., Puwein, J., and Pollefeys, M. Unstructured Video-based Rendering: Interactive Exploration of Casually Captured Videos. *ACM Trans. Graph. 29*, 4 (2010).
3. Benosman, R., and Kang, S. B. *Panoramic Vision: Sensors, Theory, and Applications*. Springer, 2001.
4. Brooke, J. SUS: A Quick and Dirty Usability Scale. In *Usability Evaluation in Industry*. Taylor & Francis, 1996.
5. Brown, M., and Lowe, D. G. Automatic Panoramic Image Stitching using Invariant Features. *International Journal of Computer Vision 74*, 1 (2006).
6. Cockburn, A., Karlson, A., and Bederson, B. B. A Review of Overview+detail, Zooming, and Focus+context Interfaces. *ACM Comput. Surv. 41*, 1 (2009), 2:1–2:31.
7. Dale, K., Shechtman, E., Avidan, S., and Pfister, H. Multi-video browsing and summarization. In *CVPR Workshops* (2012).
8. de Haan, G., Scheuer, J., de Vries, R., and Post, F. H. Egocentric Navigation for Video Surveillance in 3D Virtual Environments. *2009 IEEE Symposium on 3D User Interfaces* (2009).
9. DeCamp, P., Shaw, G., Kubat, R., and Roy, D. An Immersive System for Browsing and Visualizing Surveillance Video. *Proc. MM '10* (2010).
10. Farin, D. S. *Automatic Video Segmentation employing Object/Camera Modeling Techniques*. PhD thesis, Technische Universiteit Eindhoven, 2005.
11. Hartley, R., and Zisserman, A. *Multiple View Geometry in Computer Vision*, 2 ed. Cambridge University Press, New York, NY, USA, 2003.
12. Hermans, C., Vanaken, C., Mertens, T., Van Reeth, F., and Bekaert, P. Augmented Panoramic Video. *Computer Graphics Forum 27*, 2 (2008).
13. Hu, J., You, S., and Neumann, U. Texture Painting from Video. *Journal of WSCG* (2005).
14. Joshi, N., Kar, A., and Cohen, M. Looking at You: Fused Gyro and Face Tracking for Viewing Large Imagery on Mobile Devices. In *Proc. SIGCHI '12*, ACM (New York, NY, USA, 2012), 2211–2220.
15. Kim, K., Oh, S., Lee, J., and Essa, I. Augmenting Aerial Earth Maps with Dynamic Information from Videos. *Virtual Reality* (2011), 1–16.
16. Kroepfl, M., Wexler, Y., and Ofek, E. Efficiently Locating Photographs in Many Panoramas. In *Proc. SIGSPATIAL '10*, ACM (New York, NY, USA, 2010).
17. Lewis, J., and Sauro, J. The Factor Structure of the System Usability Scale. In *Proc. Human Centered Design*, Springer (2009), 94–103.
18. Lowe, D. G. Distinctive Image Features from Scale-Invariant Keypoints. *International Journal of Computer Vision 60*, 2 (2004).
19. McCurdy, N. *RealityFlythrough: A System for Ubiquitous Video*. Ph.d., University of California, San Diego, 2007.
20. Mulloni, A., Seichter, H., Dünser, A., Baudisch, P., and Schmalstieg, D. 360 degrees: Panoramic Overviews for Location-Based Services. *Proc. SIGCHI '12*.
21. Naimark, M. Time Binoculars. `http://www.naimark.net/projects/pending/timebinoculars.htm`, 2010.
22. Neumann, U., You, S., and Hu, J. Augmented Virtual Environments (AVE): Dynamic Fusion of Imagery and 3D Models. *IEEE Virtual Reality '03* (2003), 3–9.
23. Norris, J., Schnädelbach, H., and Qiu, G. CamBlend: An Object Focused Collaboration Tool. In *Proc. SIGCHI '12*, ACM (New York, NY, USA, 2012).
24. Pece, F., Steptoe, W., Wanner, F., Julier, S., Weyrich, T., Kautz, J., and Steed, A. Panoinserts: Practical spatial teleconferencing. In *Proc. SIGCHI '13*, ACM (New York, NY, USA, 2013).
25. Pirk, S., Cohen, M. F., Deussen, O., Uyttendaele, M., and Kopf, J. Video Enhanced Gigapixel Panoramas. *SIGGRAPH Asia 2012 Technical Briefs* (2012).
26. Pongnumkul, S., Wang, J., and Cohen, M. Creating Map-based Storyboards for Browsing Tour Videos. *Proc. UIST '08* (2008).
27. Silva, J. R., Santos, T. T., and Morimoto, C. H. Automatic Camera Control in Virtual Environments augmented using Multiple Sparse Videos. *Computers & Graphics 35*, 2 (2011).
28. Snavely, N., Garg, R., Seitz, S. M., and Szeliski, R. Finding Paths Through the World's Photos. *ACM Trans. Graph. 27*, 3 (2008).
29. Snavely, N., Seitz, S., and Szeliski, R. Photo Tourism: Exploring Photo Collections in 3D. *ACM Trans. Graph. 25*, 3 (2006).
30. Szeliski, R. *Computer Vision: Algorithms and Applications*, 1st ed. Springer-Verlag, 2010.
31. Tompkin, J., Kim, K. I., Kautz, J., and Theobalt, C. Videoscapes: Exploring Sparse, Unstructured Video Collections. *ACM Trans. Graph. 31*, 4 (2012).
32. Wu, F., and Tory, M. PhotoScope: Visualizing Spatiotemporal Coverage of Photos for Construction Management. *Proc. SIGCHI '09*.

DemoCut: Generating Concise Instructional Videos for Physical Demonstrations

Pei-Yu (Peggy) Chi[†‡], Joyce Liu[†], Jason Linder[‡], Mira Dontcheva[‡], Wilmot Li[‡], Björn Hartmann[†]
†: Computer Science Division, UC Berkeley and ‡: Adobe Research
peggychi@cs.berkeley.edu, joyce.liu@berkeley.edu, linder@adobe.com
mirad@adobe.com, wilmotli@adobe.com, bjoern@cs.berkeley.edu

ABSTRACT
Amateur instructional videos often show a single uninterrupted take of a recorded demonstration without any edits. While easy to produce, such videos are often too long as they include unnecessary or repetitive actions as well as mistakes. We introduce DemoCut, a semi-automatic video editing system that improves the quality of amateur instructional videos for physical tasks. DemoCut asks users to mark key moments in a recorded demonstration using a set of marker types derived from our formative study. Based on these markers, the system uses audio and video analysis to automatically organize the video into meaningful segments and apply appropriate video editing effects. To understand the effectiveness of DemoCut, we report a technical evaluation of seven video tutorials created with DemoCut. In a separate user evaluation, all eight participants successfully created a complete tutorial with a variety of video editing effects using our system.

Author Keywords
video; instructions; tutorials; demonstrations; how-to

ACM Classification Keywords
H.5.m. Information Interfaces and Presentation (e.g. HCI): Miscellaneous

INTRODUCTION
Do it yourself (DIY) instructional videos show viewers how to carry out physical tasks, such as craft projects, home improvement, repair, or cooking [30]. The availability of free video-sharing sites like YouTube and Vimeo has led to an explosion in user-generated video tutorials online [21]. Effective instructional videos use a range of video editing techniques, including subtitles, annotations, and temporal speed up effects, to concisely communicate physical procedures. However, producing high-quality videos requires significant time investment and expertise. In addition to recording possibly many takes, authors must review and cut the footage and then apply the appropriate editing effects [24]. Instead of investing this effort, many amateurs instead create videos that simply show a long uninterrupted recording of a demonstration. While such videos are easy to produce, they often include a lot of unnecessary footage (e.g., pauses, mistakes, long repetitive actions) that makes it difficult for viewers to focus on the most important steps and actions.

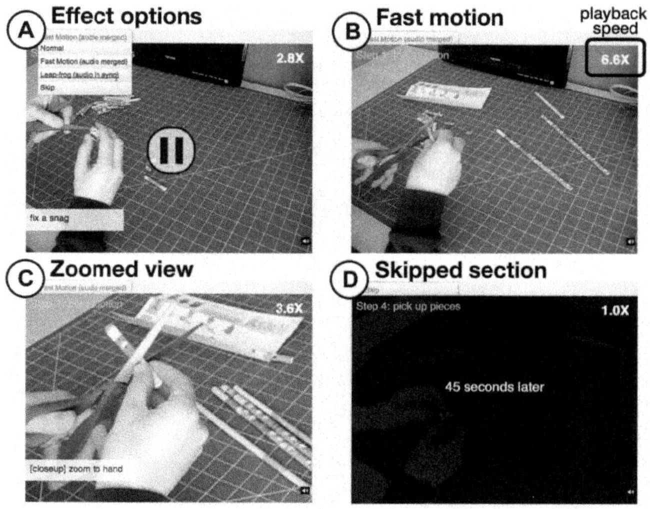

Figure 1. DemoCut automatically segments a single-shot demonstration recording and applies video editing effects based on user markers (A), including subtitles, fast motion (B), leap frog, zoom (C), and skip (D).

The goal of our work is to help amateur users produce effective instructional videos. We analyzed existing DIY videos and interviewed video authors to uncover key challenges in creating high-quality video tutorials: organizing long, single take recordings into meaningful steps; removing/condensing unnecessary or repetitive actions; and adding effects that emphasize important details in the demonstration. To address these challenges, we introduce DemoCut, a semi-automatic video editing system that generates concise instructional videos from recorded demonstrations (Figure 1).

With DemoCut, users record a single take of a narrated physical task demonstration and then roughly annotate the recording with markers that indicate high-level steps, important actions, supplies and mistakes. Based on these annotations, the system uses a combination of video and audio analysis to automatically organize the recording into meaningful segments and apply editing effects that make the tutorial more clear and concise. DemoCut supports both temporal effects that increase playback speed or skip segments, as well as visual effects, such as zooming, subtitles, and visual highlights. De-

UIST'13, Oct 08-11 2013, St Andrews, United Kingdom
ACM 978-1-4503-2268-3/13/10.
http://dx.doi.org/10.1145/2501988.2502052

moCut also provides an interface that allows users to quickly review and edit the automatically generated effects.

We used DemoCut to create seven video tutorials in five different DIY domains: electronics, crafts, art, repair and food. The generated videos were concise in terms of video length and descriptive instructions with low effect error rates. We also conducted a small user study where participants used our system to record and edit their own video tutorials. All participants successfully created a complete tutorial that included a variety of video editing effects, and the qualitative feedback on DemoCut was very positive. The participants felt that DemoCut enables a convenient workflow for creating concise video tutorials and that the automatic editing effects are particularly useful for speeding up repetitive actions.

In summary, the main contributions of this paper include:

- A light-weight annotation-based interface for editing instructional videos.
- A set of marker types for annotation derived from our formative work. Markers represent different types of moments that lead to different editing effects.
- A semi-automatic approach for editing DIY video that combines user annotation with audio and video analysis.
- A working implementation of this approach and a preliminary evaluation with both novice and expert video editors.

RELATED WORK

Current Practices around How-To Videos

The research community has been investigating the motivations of both authors and viewers of how-to videos and written tutorials. While one primary motivation is to share expertise, published videos also serve as a way to broadcast skill and as an online portfolio [30]. Authors may derive revenue through advertising or referrals [21]. Viewers, on the other hand, typically seek technical explanations, but are also searching for inspiration [29] and looking for validation of existing skills [21]. In aggregate, these studies suggest that how-to videos have a larger variety of purposes and uses than merely communicating technical content. In our work we strive to make authoring of how-to videos more accessible to amateurs while maintaining opportunities for adding individual style through control over editing effects.

Video Capture, Annotation and Editing

Capture. Several research and commercial systems guide users at capture time to yield higher-quality videos. Such systems often employ templates to help users capture sequences of distinct shots (e.g., Snapguide[1]) or suggest framing of the subject or camera view as in NudgeCam [7]. Computer vision algorithms, like face tracking, can be used to offer real-time feedback during such directed actions [10, 18, 7]. Instead of relying on templates, shot suggestions can also be bootstrapped through user dialogs [1]. In contrast to these systems, we work with a single long video take and do not require the author to manipulate the camera during capture. Many leisure activities, such as home repair or cooking, require use of both hands or involve getting one's hands dirty, so camera manipulation is not possible.

[1] http://snapguide.com/

Annotation. Researchers have investigated how to provide interactions that enable efficient, fluid annotation of video data, from the early EVA system [23] to more recent interfaces like VideoTater that leverage pen input [11]. We do not claim a contribution in the interaction techniques of our annotation interface and take inspiration from such prior work.

Editing. Frame-based editing of video is very time-intensive, as it forces users to operate at a very low level of detail. Editors can leverage metadata, such as transcripts [6] and shot boundaries [8], to give users higher-level editing operations at the shot level rather than the frame level. Computer vision techniques can automate certain effects, such as creating cinemagraphs [2, 20], automatically-edited lecture videos [17], zoomable tapestries [3] and synopses [27], or stabilizing shaky amateur videos [22]. When analyzing video is a matter of subjective taste, identifying salient frames can also be outsourced to crowd workers [5]. DemoCut also uses vision techniques for automatic editing. It differs from previous approaches in its focus on a particular application domain – physical demonstration videos. By focusing on a specific domain, DemoCut can make assumptions about the structure of the input and output video, such as the fact that there is a linear set of steps, and offer an interface and algorithms that make it easier to create high quality how-to videos.

Creating Effective Tutorials

There are many ways to produce effective tutorials. One approach is to track user behavior to automate tutorial authoring [13, 14, 9]. This method also opens the door to interactive tutorials that can respond to user progress [4, 26]. However, tracking user behavior in the physical world, rather than in software, remains a challenge. DuploTrack uses a depth camera to track progress and provide guidance for block assembly tasks [15]. Augmented reality applications overlay real-time information on top of the work area, usually through a head-mounted display. Such systems can provide visual highlights (such as arrows, text, closeup views, and 3D models) for machine maintenance [19], or interactive remote tutoring for repair tasks [16].

In this work we seek to support a wide variety of how-to tasks from craft to home repair and cooking where automatically tracking user activities is not yet possible. To support these tasks we propose a semi-automatic approach where the user marks important moments and the system automatically edits the video based on the user markers. Here we focus on the authoring of how-to videos, and we leave interactive tutorials for physical tasks to future work.

UNDERSTANDING CURRENT PRACTICE

To gain insight into the editing decisions that go into effective demonstration videos, we analyzed a set of 20 highly-rated videos on YouTube and interviewed six of the authors of these videos about their recording and editing processes.

Figure 2. We analyzed 20 DIY instructional videos. Examples included (clockwise from top left): Microcontroller circuit design, tablet screen replacement, custom shoe painting, and creating latte art.

Video Analysis

To cover a range of topics, we chose five different DIY domains (electronics/science, craft, home/repair, art, and food) from a popular DIY website[2]. We selected the first four videos on YouTube for each domain that satisfied a set of criteria chosen to ensure they were effective, including:

- Produced video: evidence of editing through cuts
- Camera angle: 1-2 static camera viewpoints
- Content: 1-2 instructors with audio narration
- Popularity: a minimum of 1000 views, with less than 10% dislikes from the total like-or-dislike ratings.
- Experience: authors with >5 published how-to videos.

20 videos from 20 distinct authors were coded in a week (Figure 2). The average length of these videos is 5 minutes and 5 seconds (*max*=9'08", *min*=1'54"), and the average view count is 269,426 (*max*=4,004,613, *min*=1,156). Although these tutorials cover various topics and tasks, we observed several common characteristics of the videos:

- **Narration.** All of the videos include narration that explains what is happening in the tutorial. Most authors seem to narrate during the demonstration (70%), while fewer authors record a separate voice-over track.
- **Speed-up effects.** Most videos (60%) include editing effects that speed up repetitive actions, such as screwing in fasteners or chopping vegetables. In many cases, authors break the sync between the audio and video tracks in these sped-up sections so that the narration plays continuously at normal speed with no long silences while the video plays at a faster speed.
- **Annotations.** Many videos (65%) include titles that add relevant information about the task, including descriptions of depicted objects or actions, measurements, elapsed time, and details that are not shown in the demonstration. Some videos also include other annotations (e.g., arrows, rectangular highlights) that emphasize important details.

This analysis suggests that authors apply a common set of editing techniques. Since the final videos convey limited information about the recording and editing processes, we interviewed several authors of the selected videos. We hope to learn what kind of footage they omitted and how much time they spent on editing. We also wanted to understand the rationale behind the edits.

[2]http://makezine.com/

ID	Category	Experience	Videos	Sample Project
P1	electronics	professional	48*	Body-mounted camera
P2	home/repair	amateur	162	Powder coating aluminum
P3	science	professional	45*	Develop caffenol film
P4	home/repair	amateur	717	Snowblower repair
P5	home/repair	amateur	33	Paintcan setup
P6	electronics	amateur	5	On-beat disco light

Table 1. Background information about interview participants. **** Numbers of videos published on personal YouTube channels, excluding those on the professional channels.***

Interviews with Tutorial Authors

We contacted the 20 YouTube account holders of the analyzed videos, and interviewed the first six who responded (all males, ages 17 to 48). One of the YouTube user accounts corresponded to a 3-person team, which we counted as a single participant (P6). Among the participants, two were professional tutorial makers, while the rest were amateurs. For editing, three used Apple Final Cut Pro, two Corel VideoStudio, and one Adobe Premiere. Table 1 summarizes other information about the experience of the authors.

Capture. Except for the team (P6), all of the participants record demonstrations individually without any assistants. P2–P6 use a single video camera, while P1 uses an extra camera to capture closeup shots. To keep the recording process simple, the amateur authors tend to capture demonstrations in one uninterrupted take, narrating the action as they go. Naturally, such recordings often include mistakes (e.g., walking out of frame to retrieve a forgotten tool) and long, repetitive actions. In contrast, the professional authors create a script beforehand and record the narration separately.

Editing. All of the participants mentioned the importance of editing the final video tutorial down to a reasonable length (5–10 minutes). The goal is to provide enough information to understand the demonstration, but at the same time keep the video lively and interesting. P2 described his strategy as follows: *"If you can get rid of it and the video content still gets through, get rid of it"*; *"The way to make your video sizzle is to have good cuts, good points."* As a result, authors spend much of their editing time deciding on cuts, segmenting the video, removing and merging shots, and adding visual effects to speed up repetitive actions. They also take time to add subtitles and annotations. As P4 explained, *"the filming is the easiest part; it is the editing that's the challenge."* Overall, participants reported that filming time takes from one hour up to one day, and editing time typically takes 6–12 hours, depending on the the complexity of the project.

DESIGN IMPLICATIONS

Based on our analysis of existing video tutorials and interviews with tutorial authors, we identified a few key aspects of the tutorial creation process that have important design implications for DIY video editing systems.

Working with single take, single camera footage. Most amateur authors record demonstrations in a single take with a a single camera. As a result, the captured footage often includes mistakes and long, repetitive actions.

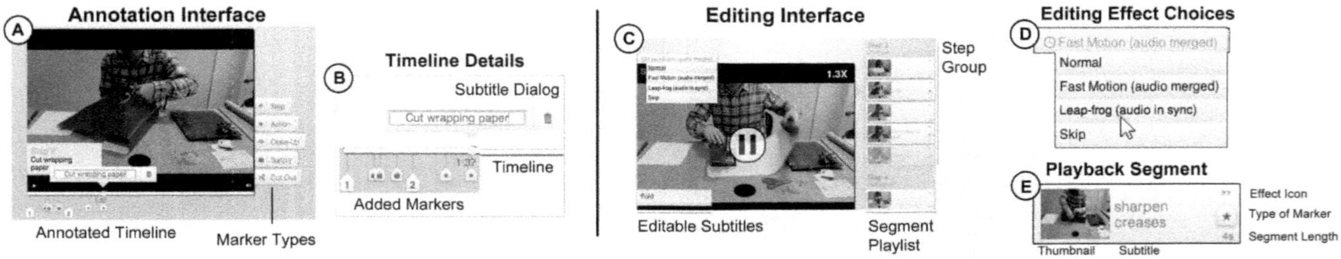

Figure 3. Users first add markers to their recorded video in the Annotation Interface (A). Each marker can be labeled with a descriptive string (B). The Editing Interface shows automatically generated segments with effect suggestions (C). Users can change the effect (D) applied to each segment (E).

Making concise videos. The most important design principle for creating effective DIY videos is to make them concise without sacrificing clarity. To this end, authors remove/condense unnecessary or repetitive actions so that the resulting video only contains salient footage.

Retiming audio and video tracks separately. One common technique for speeding up a video involves breaking the synchronization between the audio and video tracks so that they can be retimed separately. In cases where the narration refers to specific visual events, the tracks should remain aligned.

Emphasizing important information. Most effective DIY videos include titles, annotations and/or closeup views to emphasize relevant information and highlight key details.

Focusing on high-level editing decisions. Amateur users often struggle with low-level manipulation of cut points and timing in general-purpose video editors: A system should reduce the editing efforts and enable authors to focus on making simple choices for the final production.

We next describe how these considerations informed the design of DemoCut.

AUTHORING VIDEOS WITH DEMOCUT

To enable amateur users to produce effective video tutorials, the DemoCut video authoring system semi-automatically edits a long, single take recording into meaningful steps. Early testing revealed that users find it easier to locate specific *moments* in the video than to mark or edit *segments*. Therefore, our Annotation Interface asks users to mark important moments. DemoCut combines the user annotations with audio and video analysis to automatically generate a segmented video with editing suggestions: It removes or condenses unnecessary/repetitive actions and enables flexible synchronization between audio and video tracks. Titles, visual annotations and closeup views are applied to enhance the content. Users can review and revise these decisions in the DemoCut Editing Interface. This section reviews DemoCut from the user's perspective (Figure 4). The following section will describe our video analysis pipeline.

Annotating the Video

The purpose of the DemoCut Annotation UI is to collect high-level information that is difficult to extract automatically but useful in determining how to edit the video. We rely on users to distinguish important from unimportant actions and successful steps from mistakes. The user scrubs through the captured footage and adds markers for distinct moments, such as the instant when he cuts a sheet of paper (Figure 3A). DemoCut offers five types of markers for annotating a video:

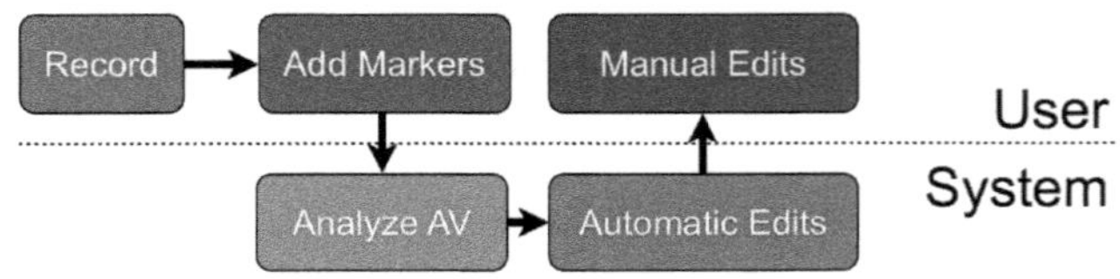

Figure 4. DemoCut users first mark their recorded video in the Annotation Interface. DemoCut then segments their recording and suggests video edits, which users can change in the Editing Interface.

- *Step*: indicates the start of a major part of the task
- *Action*: marks important moments
- *Closeup*: indicates moments where the action is happening in a small region of the video frame, e.g., for a detailed action such as fastening a small screw.
- *Supply*: indicates a tool or material used in the task
- *Cut-out*: indicates moments of the video that should be removed due to occlusion or a mistake in the performance.

This set of markers was derived from our observations of the structure of effective tutorial videos: actions are treated separately from supplies; zooming can direct the viewer's attention to a small area of the frame; and step divisions are used to divide actions into meaningful groups. Rather than specify start and end frames, users can place a marker on any frame of an important moment.

Users can add descriptions to markers (Figure 3B). These descriptions serve a dual purpose: they are used to generate automatic subtitles, and they are also shown as segment names in the Editing Interface to facilitate navigation. Users can also add visual highlights such as boxes and arrows to any marker.

Automatic Video Editing

Based on the user's markers, DemoCut automatically segments the raw footage and applies editing effects.

Temporal Effects

We designed four temporal effects to shorten a video. In addition to skipping a segment or leaving it unchanged, we consider the synchronization between the audio and video tracks: People are sensitive to changes in speech playback speed, but video can often be accelerated without loss of clarity. Therefore, our temporal effects accelerate or contract video but keep audio at normal speed.

Fast motion (with merged audio): When a segment includes several sections of narration with intermediate pauses, Demo-

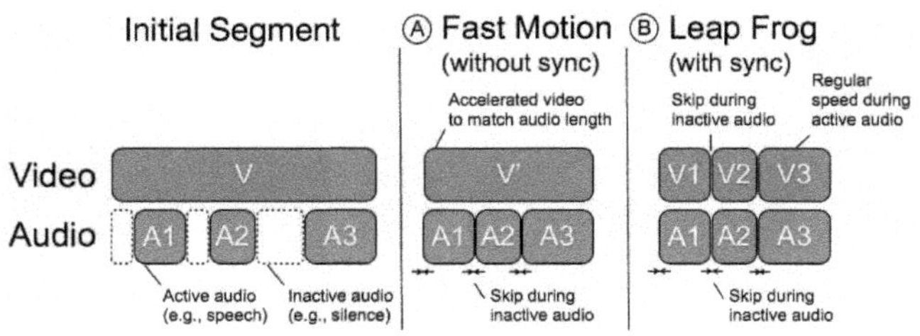

Figure 5. DemoCut accelerates playback of video with intermittent audio narration through Fast Motion (A) and Leap Frogging (B).

Cut removes the pauses and concatenates the audio segments. Then it speeds up the video so the total video length corresponds to the length of the concatenated audio (Figure 5A). This effect is appropriate if tight synchronization between audio and video is not required. For example, an author may describe general strategies for choosing supplies while measuring paper – here audio and video are independent of each other. In this case, DemoCut will accelerate the video to fit the length of the author's remarks.

Leap frog (with synchronized audio): If synchronization between audio and video is necessary, this effect plays video and audio at normal speed during active audio segments, and skips video in the interstitial segments (Figure 5B). Synchronization is important if the author's face is in the shot (so lip movement and audio match), if actions produce distinct sounds (like cutting paper), or if the narration refers specifically to actions, e.g., when pointing at an object and describing its properties. Since DemoCut cannot automatically decide whether synchronization is necessary, it applies the Fast Motion effect by default but offers users control to change that effect.

Skip: Depending on the length of the removed segment, DemoCut either applies a fade through black (for segments up to 15 seconds); or a fade to a title that indicates how much time has passed (e.g., "2 minutes later").

If these temporal effects are not appropriate, DemoCut plays the audio and video at the captured rate. We call this the *Normal* effect.

Visual Effects

In addition to manipulating time, DemoCut offers three visual effects to structure the video and to provide emphasis. These visuals appear for the duration of the segment DemoCut derived from the user's marker:

Subtitles: Text entered by the user in the marking phase is converted into automatic subtitles with two levels – a step heading that remains on screen for all segments within a step (e.g., "Wrapping the present"); and a subheading from individual event markers (e.g., "Sharpen creases").

Automatic zoom: When users create closeup markers, they also specify a rectangular region of interest. DemoCut automatically crops and enlarges this region of the segment.

Visual annotation: DemoCut overlays visual box or arrow annotation specified by the user in the marking stage.

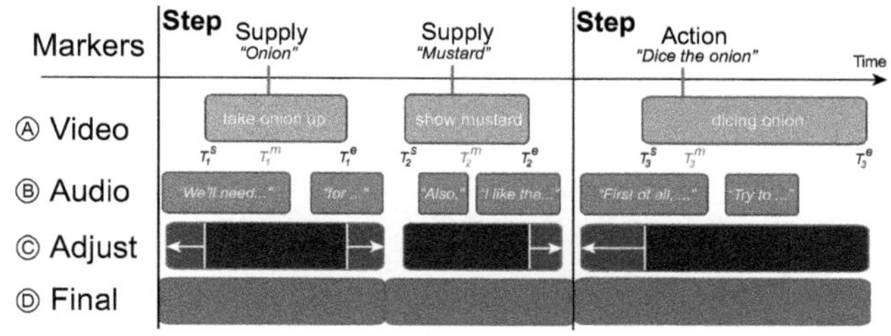

Figure 6. Given user markers, DemoCut analyzes both video and audio to segment the demonstration video and apply editing effects.

Reviewing and Editing

Since our automatic video and audio segmentation has a limited understanding of the video, it is likely that some editing decisions will be incorrect. For example, DemoCut's algorithms have no way of inferring whether audio-video synchronization will or will not be required in a given segment. In addition, automatic analysis may also lead to errors: if the narration is not correctly segmented, speech can be cut off mid-sentence. DemoCut's editor gives authors the opportunity to review and revise all editing decisions.

In the Editing Interface, the video is visualized as a set of segments (Figure 3E) flowing from top to bottom on the right side of the main video view (Figure 3C). There is no traditional timeline for two reasons: first, editing operations only apply to detected segments (we consciously prevent users from applying frame-level edits to keep with the goal of a semantic editor); second, because segments may come with labels entered by the user, a vertical layout makes it easier to read labels. Users can navigate to any segment by clicking on its thumbnail. Once selected, they can change which effect should be applied to a given segment (Figure 3D). Users can also modify any visual effects, to edit subtitles, resize the cropped region, or add/delete highlights. When satisfied with their choices, users can export a continuous video suitable for online video sharing platforms.

AUTOMATIC EFFECT DECISION PIPELINE

DemoCut performs several automated steps to convert the user-annotated input recording into an edited video tutorial. First, the system segments the recording into regions around user-specified markers. This segmentation considers both the similarity of video frames around each marker and the presence of narration in the audio track in order to determine the appropriate segment boundaries (Figure 6). DemoCut then automatically applies an temporal and a visual effect to each segment based on the type of the corresponding user marker and the properties of the audio/video content in the segment. The rest of this section describes these steps in detail.

Video Segmentation

Except for the step marker, all of the user-specified markers indicate important moments in the demonstration that correspond to some segment of the recording. In many cases, we can infer the duration of these segments by searching for video frames that look similar to the marked frame. For example, in Figure 7A, the similar frames before and after a supply marker show the author holding up a bottle of vinegar, and in Figure 7B, the similar frames around an action marker show the author grating cheese. For every marked frame T^m, DemoCut uses the following method to compute candidate start and end frames T^s and T^e for the corresponding segment. For the i-th marked frame T_i^m, our algorithm finds T_i^s by comparing T_i^m to earlier frames in the video until it reaches a previous marker at T_{i-1}^m, or until 5% of pixels (in grayscale) have changed by 20%. Similarly, the system finds T_i^e by comparing T_i^m to subsequent frames in the video. To optimize performance, DemoCut compares to frames sampled at 0.5 seconds and ignores overlaps between segments. Segment overlaps are resolved during boundary adjustment after incorporating the audio analysis.

Adjusting Segments with Audio Analysis

Adjacent segments can have different effects that change how video and audio are processed. To prevent such changes from interfering with a video's narration, DemoCut adjusts segment boundaries to align with audio activity boundaries.

Detecting non-silent sections

Since many DIY videos include prominent non-speech sounds such as chopping noises, power tools, etc., detecting speech automatically is a challenging task. We found that even state-of-the-art speech detection algorithms produce poor results in many cases. As a result, we take a more conservative approach; DemoCut automatically detects non-silent sections in the recorded audio and treats the background sound as part of the narration.

At a high level, our algorithm for detecting non-silent sections works as follows. We compute the "loudness" of each audio window, organize the windows into a histogram based on loudness, and then analyze the histogram to determine a minimum loudness threshold for non-silent windows. We then apply this threshold to categorize all audio windows as silent or non-silent. Finally, we filter this categorization to eliminate very short sequences of silent or non-silent samples. Here, we describe these steps in more detail:

Computing loudness. Given an input audio waveform sampled at 44.1 kHz (Figure 8A), we estimate loudness by computing the root mean square (RMS) energy [25] across the entire waveform. The RMS energy for a window of size n is $\sqrt{(\sum_n x_i^2)/n}$ where x_i is the value of the ith audio sample in the window. We set window sizes as 0.1 second with $n = 4410$. Prior to computing RMS energy, the audio is normalized and noise-reduced with Adobe Audition.

Computing loudness threshold. After analyzing the RMS energy profiles of several different types of DIY videos, we found that the vast majority of recorded audio represents background sound, which tends to have similar and fairly low RMS energy values. In contrast, user narration varies from medium to high RMS values based on the speaker's distance to the microphone and the sensitivity of the recording device. Based on this observation, we first compute a histogram of RMS energy for all windows in the audio track; the windows that correspond to background sound form a large mass at the low-RMS end of the histogram (Figure 8B). To distinguish these "silent" parts of the recording from the narration, we

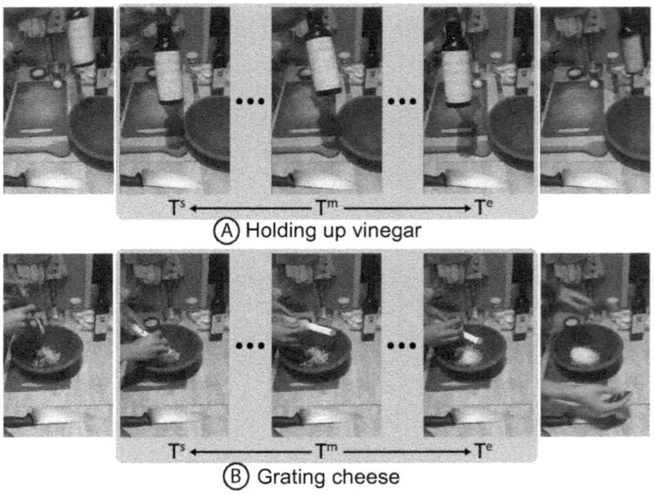

Figure 7. DemoCut looks for similar video frames before and after a marked frame T^m to find candidate start (T^s) and end (T^e) frames for the corresponding segment.

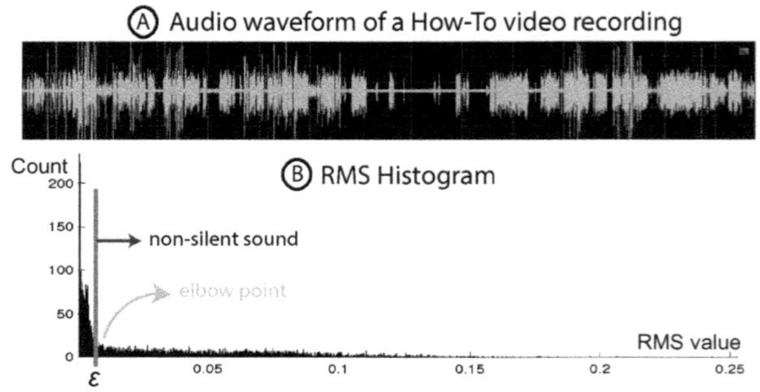

Figure 8. We use RMS energy of the audio to find silent and non-silent regions. We determine the threshold for silence by analyzing the histogram of the RMS energy.

smooth the histogram with a Gaussian kernel, find the minimum derivative point in the smoothed histogram, and set the loudness threshold ε to be the RMS energy value at this elbow point. Figure 8B shows the RMS histogram and loudness threshold for one of our example videos, "How to make salad dressing."

Categorizing silent/non-silent sections. To partition the audio track into silent and non-silent sections, we first label each window as silent or non-silent based on ε. This initial labeling often includes some very short silent and non-silent sections. Since many short silent sections correspond to short pauses between spoken words, we turn any silent sections that are shorter than 0.4 seconds into non-silent sections. Then, we discard any non-silent sections that are shorter than 0.8 seconds to account for any clicks and pops in the recorded audio. The 0.4 and 0.8 second thresholds for silent and non-silent sections were tuned experimentally, and we used these parameter values for all of our results.

Adjusting segment boundaries

In order to avoid cutting off an author's narration, DemoCut adjusts the video segment boundaries using the non-silent sections of the audio track (Figure 6). First, for any segment we find all of the overlapping non-silent audio sections and

Task	Category	Raw footage length	DemoCut video length	# of markers	# of segments	Incorrect Effects	# of non-silent sections	Audio misses	Audio cut-off	Audio false-positives
A: Xbee tutorial	electronics	7'01"	3'27"	16	30	0%	79	5%	0%	0%
B: Paper pipe robot	craft	10'55"	4'40"	18	30	20%	77	21%	12%	0%
C: Ribbons for straps	craft	10'03"	4'23"	39	46	7%	72	15%	7%	0%
D: Fixing front light	repair	6'32"	2'12"	21	33	9%	40	10%	3%	0%
E: How to make grassy head	art	9'28"	5'29"	29	44	5%	86	8%	2%	0%
F: How to make potato stamps	art	16'38"	4'05	30	45	7%	119	7%	3%	0%
G: How to make salad dressing	food	14'46"	5'38"	33	39	13%	121	6%	2%	0%
AVERAGE	-	10'46"	4'10"	26.4	38.1	9%	83.5	10.3%	4.1%	0%

Table 2. A list of how-to videos we recorded to assess the robustness of the DemoCut system.

then grow the segment so that it completely contains all of these non-silent sections. Next, DemoCut resolves overlapping segments: If any two segments overlap, the boundaries must be readjusted. If the overlap region is silent, the region is split into two equal parts and each is assigned to the corresponding segment. If the overlap region includes a non-silent audio section, DemoCut assigns this non-silent section to the segment that has more overlap with the section. If the overlap for both video segments is the same, DemoCut assigns the section to the smaller video segment. Finally, DemoCut addresses any gaps between segments. If a gap is less than 2 seconds, it is merged to the shorter adjacent segment. Otherwise, DemoCut creates a new segment for the gap. Note that such *unmarked segments* do not have a corresponding marker, but they may still show useful details of the demonstration.

Applying Effects

To automatically apply an effect to each computed segment, DemoCut first detects whether there is motion in the video. A segment is considered to be *static* (i.e., no motion) if less than 1% of pixels in the grayscale versions of consecutive frames have changed by more than 20%. To optimize for performance, the segment is sampled at 0.5 seconds for this comparison. DemoCut chooses effects as follows:

1. If the segment includes a *cutout* marker, apply *"Skip"*.
2. If the segment includes a *closeup* marker, apply *"Zoom"* to the entire segment.
3. If the segment includes any non-silent audio sections, apply *"Fast Motion"*.
4. If the segment is silent, static, and unmarked, apply *"Skip"*.
5. If the segment is silent but not static (either marked or unmarked), apply *"Normal"*.
6. For any marker with a text annotation, apply *"Subtitles"*.

IMPLEMENTATION

The video and audio analysis is implemented in Matlab. The Annotation and Editing Interfaces are implemented with standard Web technologies (HTML5, CSS3, and JavaScript). An Apache web server hosts these web pages and sends the user annotations to the back-end Matlab system.

EVALUATING AUTOMATIC EFFECT DECISION

To evaluate DemoCut's analysis engine, we recorded seven how-to tasks from the five categories we selected in the formative user study (Table 2). The tasks were recorded by 4 people (all authors of this paper) in 7 locations using a Sony camcorder or an iPad with a video resolution of at least 640x480 pixels. We used DemoCut to annotate the recordings and then examined the automatically generated tutorials.

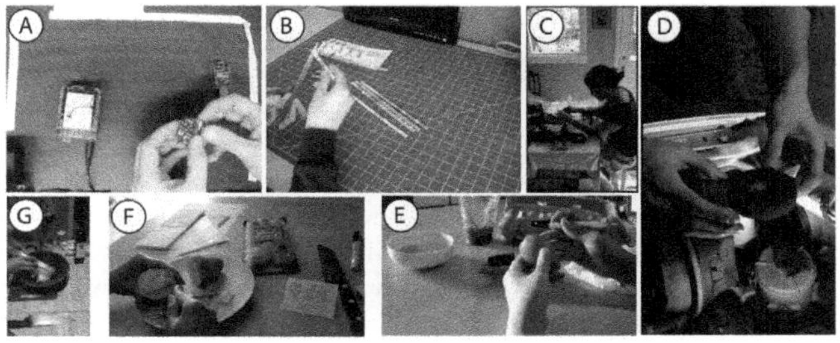

Figure 9. Illustrative frames from the seven videos used to assess DemoCut. Labels correspond to task labels in Table 2.

Overall, the resulting tutorials exhibit many of the desired characteristics outlined earlier in the paper. The automatically edited videos are concise: 2-5 minutes long and 2.5 times shorter than the original footage. In most cases, DemoCut successfully identified segments where the "Fast Motion" or "Skip" effects could be applied to condense the tutorial. For example, the edited salad dressing video uses "Fast Motion" to speed up repetitive actions like chopping an onion and grating cheese, and then skips the segment where the author leaves the frame to toast pine nuts. In addition, the automatically generated titles improve the clarity of the tutorials by adding valuable descriptions of steps, actions, supplies and indicating the elapsed time for skipped segments. In an electronics tutorial, titles like "sending data toggles LED" add important details that are not visible in the video.

There were some situations where the effects were not as successful. To get a more quantitative measure of DemoCut's performance, we counted several types of errors in the automatically generated videos:

Incorrect editing effects. In a few cases, the "Fast Motion" effect is applied to segments where the audio track should actually be in sync with the visuals. Also, when markers are very close to one another in time, DemoCut sometimes generates very short segments where the editing effects are hard to see. We identify these cases as incorrect editing effects.

Audio miss. We refer to any piece of narration that is not detected as a non-silent section as a miss.

Audio cut-off. We refer to any detected non-silent section that cuts off narration by ending too early or starting too late as a cut-off error.

Audio false-positive. We refer to any non-silent section that is neither narration nor significant activity or background sound as a false-positive.

Figure 10. Our user study setup

We report the incorrect edits as a percentage of the total number of segments and the three audio errors as a percentage of the total number of ground-truth narration sections. Table 2 shows all of the results from our analysis. Overall, we found low average error rates (less than 11%) for all of these problems. Also, note that most of these errors can be fixed by changing the automatically applied editing effects in DemoCut's reviewing and editing interface.

USER EVALUATION

To evaluate the usability and utility of DemoCut, we recruited 8 participants (4 males, ages 20-41) to create how-to video tutorials. We were especially interested in two questions: First, how much *effort* would participants have to invest to mark and edit their own tutorial videos with DemoCut? And second, what are the *qualities of the resulting videos* – both in terms of strengths and shortcomings?

Task and Materials

The participants were asked to create a tutorial for wrapping and decorating a present. We chose this task because it is relatively simple but still involves multiple distinct activities and steps that can be accomplished in 5-15 minutes. Possible steps include: measuring the gift size, cutting paper and ribbons, folding and wrapping, and decorating the present with ornaments. We offered the following supplies:

- *Present*: a rectangular gift box of size $9 \times 2 \times 4.5$ inches.
- *Tools*: scissors, utility knife, ruler, pencil, double-sided tape, transparent tape, and glue.
- *Wrapping paper*: a variety of wrapping paper rolls including plain, patterned, and textured.
- *Decorations*: ribbons (curling and fabric) in multiple colors, gift bows, stickers, and message cards.

To help them understand the context of the study, the participants were asked to watch three videos before visiting our lab. The videos were selected from the formative user study.

Procedure and Environment

The study was conducted in a quiet lab environment with static lighting. We used a tripod-mounted Sony camcorder to record the gift wrapping task (Figure 10), and a Macbook Pro running OS X and Google Chrome for DemoCut. The laptop was connected to a 30-inch monitor and external mouse and keyboard. Each study session lasted 60-90 minutes.

Introduction (15 minutes). The participants viewed a web-based tutorial that introduced the goal and procedure of the study. In the tutorial, the participants practiced annotating a one-minute demo video with five types of markers, reviewed a system-generated result, and modified video effects in the DemoCut Editing interface.

Filming setup and practice (5 minutes). The participants were asked to plan their gift-wrapping demonstration with any of the provided supplies. The camcorder was positioned either opposite the participants or behind them on the right and was angled down to capture their workspace on a conference table. The participants reviewed the camera's point of view and were told that any activities outside of the delineated workspace would not be captured. The participants were free to plan their task on paper or conduct a practice run.

Filming demonstration (10-20 minutes). The participants filmed their gift wrapping demonstration in a single take. The study moderator initiated and terminated the recording, but did not provide additional assistance.

Annotating and editing (30-45 minutes). The participants annotated their video with the DemoCut Annotation Interface and modified the generated video tutorial using the DemoCut Editing Interface.

Review of the final video and discussion (10 minutes). Finally, participants reviewed the final video, completed a questionnaire, and discussed the process with experimenters.

FINDINGS AND DISCUSSION

All of the participants successfully created a complete video tutorial of their gift wrapping technique using DemoCut during the study session. The average length of the recorded demonstrations was 8 minutes, and the final generated videos were just over 5 minutes long (45% shorter than the raw footage). On average, participants spent 15 minutes annotating the recordings and added 33 markers. Table 3 summarizes several other quantitative results from the study.

Here, we summarize a few key points from the responses to the questionnaire and the end-of-study discussions:

DemoCut interface and workflow. We received strong positive feedback about the DemoCut interface as a whole and the editing workflow that it enables. All participants agreed or strongly agreed that it was easy to annotate a recording using the Annotation Interface, and seven of them found it easy to use the reviewing and Editing Interface. P1 explained, *"This is very simple for beginning users and takes out some of the guess work around learning how to use different layers, speed effects, etc."*, and P2 described the workflow as, *"super easy and SUPER FAST!"* P6 also appreciated the simplicity of the interface: *"I like this a lot because there aren't thousands of different buttons to work with."* In addition, several participants noted how the automated components of the system reduced the amount of effort required to create an edited video: *"I could be lazier and still have a great video cause it did everything for me"* (P8), and *"Pre-segmentation (when it worked well) made it easy to zero in on the portion I wanted to modify"* (P4).

ID	Editing expertise (years)	Footage length	DemoCut video length	Final video length	Annotation time (mins)	# and types of markers used for annotation						Ave text length (words)	# of segments	Review & edit time (mins)	# of effects changed
						Total	Step	Action	Supply	Closeup	Cutout				
P1	5	3'51"	2'14"	2'14"	10	20	3	10	5	1	1	3.2	28	8	1
P2	3	7'16"	4'09"	4'14"	16	29	4	16	4	5	0	4	49	11	4
P3	10	10'57"	6'45"	6'45"	18	36	10	18	4	0	4	2.2	57	10	3
P4	2	9'16"	5'12"	5'38"	25	35	6	20	3	4	2	3.3	56	13	6
P5	0	7'17"	4'13"	4'07"	17	38	5	18	7	6	2	3	56	12	5
P6	0	6'28"	3'20"	2'48"	8	24	3	13	6	0	2	3.5	40	9	9
P7	0	10'08"	6'18"	6'02"	21	66	7	35	12	8	4	3.9	92	14	20
P8	0	8'58"	3'05"	3'03"	8	13	4	6	1	0	2	3.6	21	10	2
AVE	2.5	8'01"	4'24"	4'21"	15	33	5	17	5	3	2	3.3	50	11	6

Table 3. Quantitative analysis of the user evaluation.

Automatic editing effects. In general, the participants liked how DemoCut automatically removed or condensed parts of their recordings. Their feedback suggests that the automatically generated effects were particularly useful for speeding up repetitive actions like cutting and folding and skipping extraneous actions, such as removing the adhesive sticker from a bow. As P3 noted, these effects were generally successful because DemoCut *"correctly understood parts with no speech but long actions."* Another participant commented specifically on the fast motion with merged audio effect, and said *"(I) appreciate the automatic speeding up/slowing down of video to match speech."*

Reviewing and editing. As expected, there were some cases where participants decided to modify the automatic effects. Errors in the audio analysis can cause the narration within a segment to get cut off when fast motion effects are applied. To eliminate these audio artifacts, participants changed the segment effect from fast motion to normal mode. In cases where the narration referred to specific visual events, participants switched from the default fast motion with merged audio effect to leap frog with synchronized audio. Finally, in a few situations, participants decided to skip an annotated segment that they deemed unnecessary or unclear after reviewing the rest of the tutorial.

Quality of generated tutorials. Five of the eight participants said they were satisfied or very satisfied with the video tutorials that they created with DemoCut during the study. The remaining three participants had significantly more video editing experience, and they wanted to further refine their tutorials by adjusting some of the timing and cut points using more traditional low-level editing tools. However, even these participants agreed that DemoCut was *"good for a first pass of editing"* and provided *"helpful "smart" suggestions"* even though the system is *"limited in manual control."*

Default speed-up effects. The participants noted some limitations with the default editing effects. P5 explained that *"having the speed up of video be the default speed creates a stressful tutorial."* Some participants pointed out that there are some obvious cases where fast motion with merged audio should not be applied; for example, the effect *"does not work well if the person's face is showing (the speech and mouth movements would not match up)."* We agree with these comments and plan to use face detection and add an adaptive learner to improve the system.

Annotation guidelines. One observation from the study is that adding too many markers during the annotation phase can hurt the quality of the generated tutorial. Adding markers temporally close together leads to many short segments, and since DemoCut applies a video edit effect to each segment individually, the resulting tutorial may end up transitioning rapidly through several inconsistent effects (e.g., fast motion effects with various playback speeds). One way to address this problem is to make automatic editing decisions that span several consecutive segments. The participants offered a few other suggestions: P4 wonders *"if there are simple tips you could give to the user while recording that would make them more successful,"* and P8 suggested that seeing real-time effects while adding markers might help him understand how best to annotate the recording.

LIMITATIONS AND FUTURE WORK

Our implementation is based on several simplifying assumptions that limit generality. We assume a single, static camera position that shows all relevant actions and a quiet indoor environment with constant lighting and little background noise. In order to detect static shots that should be skipped, our video analysis assumes a static background. Our audio analysis assumes that all non-silent sections of audio are narration, but this may not always be the case. Loud non-speech sounds, such as chopping or the sound of a sewing machine, can lead to errors in our editing effect decisions.

As was pointed out by several of our study participants, making effect decisions individually for each segment can lead to inconsistencies in playback speed as the video transitions from segment to segment. A more global approach that looks at all video effects together and enforces smooth transitions between adjacent segments would help address some of these artifacts. In addition to addressing these limitations, we see several promising directions for future work.

Multiple camera footage. We designed DemoCut to work with footage from a single, static camera. One interesting avenue for future work is to consider footage from multiple cameras. Prior work has compared different camera views capturing physical tasks for remote collaboration [12, 28]. Similarly, DemoCut could try to automatically select the best view for each segment based on user annotations as well as the video content (e.g., choosing a zoomed view for closeups, switching to a different view when there are occlusions).

Support viewer's learning. In this work, we focus on producing well-edited video tutorials. However, we could also imagine generating different output formats, including indexed videos, step-by-step instructions, or mixed media tutorials, similar to those presented by Chi et al. [9]. Another natural extension would be to develop interactive components that monitor user actions and provide realtime guidance and feedback for general DIY tasks. Follow-up studies to understand viewer's learning experience would be useful for refining the automatic editing effects and interactive design.

Generalize to other instructional video domains. One exciting direction is to explore other areas where our techniques could be applied, such as software learning, music instruction, and video lectures. Each domain may require slightly different analysis and segmentation rules. For example, the system could use a log of executed operations to adjust segment boundaries for software tutorials, or incorporate pitch detection when analyzing music instruction.

CONCLUSION

In this paper, we presented DemoCut, a semi-automatic video editing system that helps users create clear and concise video tutorials of DIY tasks. The key idea behind our approach is to combine rough user annotations with simple video and audio analysis techniques in order to segment the input recording and apply appropriate editing effects. Our small user evaluation suggests that video authors are able to create effective video tutorials using DemoCut, and the qualitative feedback includes encouraging positive reactions to the annotation and editing workflow, as well as the automatic editing effects.

ACKNOWLEDGMENTS

Work at Berkeley was supported by Adobe and a Berkeley Fellowship for Graduate Studies. We thank the YouTube users (in alphabetical order) *donyboy73, Griffin Hammond on Indy Mogul, John NYCCNC, Matt Richardson on MAKE, mjfpieters, and TheMuskokaPainter* for sharing their insights on DIY tutorials in our interviews.

REFERENCES

1. Adams, B., and Venkatesh, S. Situated event bootstrapping and capture guidance for automated home movie authoring. In *Proceedings of MULTIMEDIA*, ACM Press (2005), 754–763.
2. Bai, J., Agarwala, A., Agrawala, M., and Ramamoorthi, R. Selectively de-animating video. *ACM Trans. Graph. 31*, 4 (2012), 66:1–66:10.
3. Barnes, C., Goldman, D. B., Shechtman, E., and Finkelstein, A. Video tapestries with continuous temporal zoom. *ACM Trans. Graph. 29* (2010), 89:1–89:9.
4. Bergman, L., Castelli, V., Lau, T., and Oblinger, D. Docwizards: a system for authoring follow-me documentation wizards. In *Proceedings of UIST*, ACM Press (2005), 191–200.
5. Bernstein, M. S., Brandt, J., and Miller, R. C. Crowds in two seconds. *Proceedings of UIST* (2011).
6. Berthouzoz, F., Li, W., and Agrawala, M. Tools for placing cuts and transitions in interview video. *ACM Trans. Graph. 31*, 4 (2012), 67:1–67:8.
7. Carter, S., Adcock, J., Doherty, J., and Branham, S. Nudgecam: toward targeted, higher quality media capture. In *Proceedings of MULTIMEDIA*, ACM Press (2010), 615–618.
8. Casares, J., Long, A. C., Myers, B. A., Bhatnagar, R., Stevens, S. M., Dabbish, L., Yocum, D., and Corbett, A. Simplifying video editing using metadata. In *Proceedings of DIS*, ACM Press (2002), 157.
9. Chi, P.-y., Ahn, S., Ren, A., Dontcheva, M., Li, W., and Hartmann, B. MixT: automatic generation of step-by-step mixed media tutorials. In *Proceedings of UIST*, ACM Press (2012), 93.
10. Davis, M., Heer, J., and Ramirez, A. Active capture: automatic direction for automatic movies. In *Proceedings of MULTIMEDIA*, ACM Press (2003), 88.
11. Diakopoulos, N., and Essa, I. Videotater: an approach for pen-based digital video segmentation and tagging. In *Proceedings of UIST*, ACM Press (2006), 221–224.
12. Fussell, S. R., Setlock, L. D., and Kraut, R. E. Effects of head-mounted and scene-oriented video systems on remote collaboration on physical tasks. In *Proceedings of CHI*, ACM Press (2003).
13. Grabler, F., Agrawala, M., Li, W., Dontcheva, M., and Igarashi, T. Generating photo manipulation tutorials by demonstration. *SIGGRAPH* (2009).
14. Grossman, T., Matejka, J., and Fitzmaurice, G. Chronicle: capture, exploration, and playback of document workflow histories. In *Proceedings of UIST*, ACM Press (2010).
15. Gupta, A., Fox, D., Curless, B., and Cohen, M. DuploTrack: a real-time system for authoring and guiding duplo block assembly. In *Proceedings of UIST*, ACM Press (2012), 389–402.
16. Gurevich, P., Lanir, J., Cohen, B., and Stone, R. TeleAdvisor: a versatile augmented reality tool for remote assistance. In *Proceedings of CHI*, ACM Press (2012).
17. Heck, R., Wallick, M., and Gleicher, M. Virtual videography. *ACM Trans. Multimedia Comput. Commun. Appl. 3*, 1 (2007).
18. Heer, J., Good, N. S., Ramirez, A., Davis, M., and Mankoff, J. Presiding over accidents: system direction of human action. In *Proceedings of CHI*, ACM Press (2004), 463–470.
19. Henderson, S., and Feiner, S. Exploring the benefits of augmented reality documentation for maintenance and repair. *IEEE Trans on Visualization and Computer Graphics 17*, 10 (2011), 1355–1368.
20. Joshi, N., Mehta, S., Drucker, S., Stollnitz, E., Hoppe, H., Uyttendaele, M., and Cohen, M. Cliplets: juxtaposing still and dynamic imagery. In *Proceedings of UIST*, ACM Press (2012), 251–260.
21. Lafreniere, B., Bunt, A., Lount, M., Terry, M., and Cowan, D. Looks cool, I'll try this later!": Understanding the faces and uses of online tutorials. *University of Waterloo Tech Report* (2012).
22. Liu, F., Gleicher, M., Wang, J., Jin, H., and Agarwala, A. Subspace video stabilization. *ACM Trans. Graph. 30*, 1 (2011), 4:1–4:10.
23. Mackay, W. E. Eva: an experimental video annotator for symbolic analysis of video data. *SIGCHI Bull. 21*, 2 (1989), 68–71.
24. Müller, E. Where quality matters: discourses on the art of making a YouTube video. In *The YouTube Reader*, Stockholm: National Library of Sweden (2009).
25. Panagiotakis, C., and Tziritas, G. G. A speech/music discriminator based on RMS and zero-crossings. *IEEE Transactions on Multimedia 7*, 1 (2005), 155–166.
26. Pongnumkul, S., Dontcheva, M., Li, W., Wang, J., Bourdev, L., Avidan, S., and Cohen, M. F. Pause-and-play: automatically linking screencast video tutorials with applications. In *Proceedings of UIST*, ACM Press (2011), 135–144.
27. Pritch, Y., Ratovitch, S., and Hendel, A. Clustered synopsis of surveillance video. In *Proceedings of AVSS*, IEEE Computer Society (2009).
28. Ranjan, A., Birnholtz, J. P., and Balakrishnan, R. Dynamic shared visual spaces: experimenting with automatic camera control in a remote repair task. In *Proceedings of CHI*, ACM Press (2007), 1177–1186.
29. Torrey, C., Churchill, E. F., and McDonald, D. W. Learning how: The search for craft knowledge on the Internet. In *Proceedings of CHI*, ACM Press (2009), 1371–1380.
30. Torrey, C., McDonald, D. W., Schilit, B. N., and Bly, S. How-To pages: Informal systems of expertise sharing. In *Proceedings of ECSCW*, Springer London (2007), 391–410.

Chorus: A Crowd-Powered Conversational Assistant

Walter S. Lasecki[1], Rachel Wesley[1], Jeffrey Nichols[2], Anand Kulkarni[3], James F. Allen[1], and Jeffrey P. Bigham[1,4]

Computer Science, ROC HCI[1]
University of Rochester
{wlasecki,james}@cs.rochester.edu
{rwesley2}@u.rochester.edu

MobileWorks, Inc.[3]
anand@mobileworks.com

USER Group[2]
IBM Research - Almaden
jwnichols@us.ibm.com

Human-Computer Interaction Institute[4]
Carnegie Mellon University
jbigham@cmu.edu

ABSTRACT

Despite decades of research attempting to establish conversational interaction between humans and computers, the capabilities of automated conversational systems are still limited. In this paper, we introduce Chorus, a crowd-powered conversational assistant. When using Chorus, end users converse continuously with what appears to be a single conversational partner. Behind the scenes, Chorus leverages multiple crowd workers to propose and vote on responses. A shared memory space helps the dynamic crowd workforce maintain consistency, and a game-theoretic incentive mechanism helps to balance their efforts between proposing and voting. Studies with 12 end users and 100 crowd workers demonstrate that Chorus can provide accurate, topical responses, answering nearly 93% of user queries appropriately, and staying on-topic in over 95% of responses. We also observed that Chorus has advantages over pairing an end user with a single crowd worker and end users completing their own tasks in terms of speed, quality, and breadth of assistance. Chorus demonstrates a new future in which conversational assistants are made usable in the real world by combining human and machine intelligence, and may enable a useful new way of interacting with the crowds powering other systems.

Author Keywords

crowdsourcing; conversational assistants; dialog systems; human computation; crowd-powered systems

ACM Classification Keywords

H.4.2 Information Interfaces & Presentation: User Interfaces

INTRODUCTION

Using natural language dialogue to interact with automated software has been a goal of both artificial intelligence and human-computer interaction since the early days of computing. However, the complexity of human language has made robust two-way conversation with software agents a consistent challenge [1]. Existing dialogue-based software systems generally rely on a fixed input vocabulary or restricted phrasings, have a limited memory of past interactions, and use a fixed output vocabulary. In contrast, real-world conversations between human partners can contain context-dependent terms or phrasing, require memory stretching back over the conversation and past history of interactions and shared experiences, require common sense knowledge about the world or events, or facts, and contain meaningful incomplete and partial statements. Conversational assistants like Siri were greeted with great excitement when first released, but still possess limited capabilities beyond a finite set of pre-defined set of tasks because they cannot truly *understand* the user [8, 9].

While individual humans have no difficulty in maintaining natural-language conversation, it is often infeasible, unscalable, or expensive to hire a human to act as a conversational partner for long periods of time or to support large numbers of conversational partners. In recent years, *crowd computing* has become a popular method to scalably solve problems that are beyond the capabilities of autonomous software by subcontracting the difficult aspects that only humans can solve to groups of paid humans over the web. In this model, *the crowd* refers to a transient pool of online, semi-anonymous workers recruited for short periods of time from online microtask marketplaces such as Amazon's Mechanical Turk[1] or MobileWorks[2]. Crowd computing can provide software with human intelligence often while maintaining the scalability of autonomous software, but presents new challenges in reliability, incentivization, and accuracy [14].

In this paper we present Chorus, a crowd-powered conversational assistant that allows a user to receive assistance on any online task through a two-way natural language conversation. Chorus is capable of performing any task that may be accomplished over the web using information that the user is comfortable sharing. Although it appears to the user that the assistant is a single individual, the actions and responses of

UIST'13, October 8–11, 2013, St. Andrews, United Kingdom.

ACM 978-1-4503-2268-3/13/10...$15.00.
http://dx.doi.org/10.1145/2501988.2502057

[1] www.mturk.com
[2] www.mobileworks.com

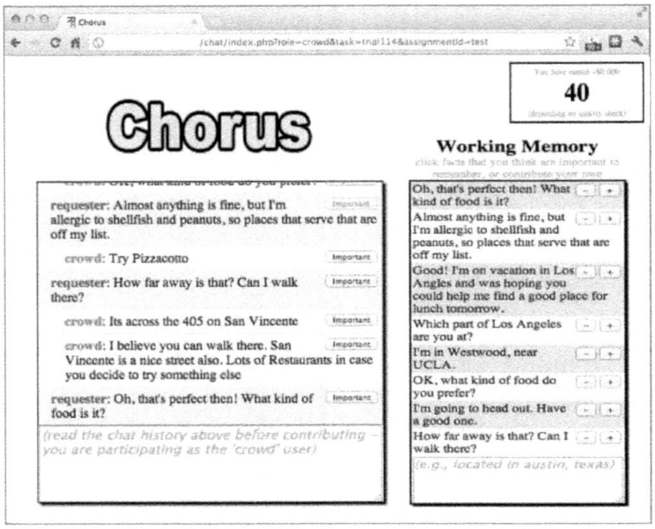

Figure 1. The Chorus interface for crowd workers encourages each worker to both propose responses and vote on the responses of others. Crowd workers can also make use of a collective shared chat history (working memory) that allows them to maintain continuity throughout the conversation, even as some leave and new workers join. The memory view is curated by a separate set of crowd workers. The "user" view is similar but removes the "Working Memory" section and only displays proposed messages once they have sufficient votes.

the assistant are actually the combined effort of a number of crowd workers that may come and go over the course of a single conversation. This approach enables real-time interaction, personalized answers, and takes the first steps towards robust conversational interaction for control over other systems, in addition to question answering.

As part of the crowd worker interface to Chorus, crowd workers generate, agree upon, and submit responses to end users (Figure 1). Key to Chorus are three components that support realistic conversations from multiple crowd workers. First, a *collaborative reasoning* system lets workers select reasonable responses from a number of crowd-produced suggestions, which allows the best responses to be forwarded on to the end user and removing potential responses that do not fit the flow of the conversation. It also allows the crowd to decide when a response is "good enough" and not to wait for another potentially better response. Second, a *dynamic scoring system* rewards workers for interactions that support the goal of consistent conversation, such as making useful statements or highlighting facts that are used later. Finally, a *curated memory system* lets workers promote salient portions of a conversation to a shared memory space, which provides a rapidly-accessible list of facts and statements that are sorted by importance (again judged by the crowd) that ensures new crowd workers are up-to-date with details of current or past conversations that may be relevant for providing future responses. These features enable the crowd to learn and remember information collectively, and allows crowd workers to be rewarded for their performance.

Our experiments with 12 users and 100 crowd workers demonstrate that Chorus can provide highly accurate and on-topic responses, answering over 92.85% of queries appropriately, and staying on-topic in nearly 96% of accepted responses, significantly better than unfiltered crowd responses. Using multiple workers also allows the average task time to fall from 103.4 seconds with just a single worker to 44.6 seconds because multiple workers have a better chance of finding the correct solution more quickly because they are able to search in parallel. Beyond user performance, we gain insight into user's usage and preferences regarding real-time personal assistants. More generally, Chorus demonstrates how crowd-powered communication may serve as a robust alternative for interacting with software systems.

The primary contributions of this paper are:

- Chorus, a crowd-powered conversational assistant able to assist end users consistently with general knowledge tasks;
- A game theoretic incentivization mechanism that encourages crowd workers to participate as part of a consistent conversational assistant;
- An evaluation with 12 end users and 100 crowd workers that both shows the advantage of our approach and offers several interesting qualitative observations about how crowd members work together to answer questions; and
- The description of a path forward from crowd-powered conversational assistants that will gradually introduce more machine intelligence into the process in order to lower costs and improve scalability.

RELATED WORK

Chorus builds on prior work in both real-time and offline human computation. Human computation [25] has been shown to be useful in many areas, including writing and editing [5], image description and interpretation [7, 26], and protein folding [11]. Chorus aims to enable a conversation with a crowd of workers in order to leverage human computation in a variety of new ways. Existing abstractions obtain quality work by introducing redundancy and layering into tasks so that multiple workers contribute and verify results at each stage [22, 13]. For instance, the ESP Game uses answer agreement [26] and Soylent uses the multiple-step find-fix-verify pattern [5]. Since these approaches take time, they are not always suitable for interactive real-time applications.

Many crowd computing applications have used the crowd to interpret natural language instructions provided by the user in applications such as image description [7], speech recognition [16], activity recognition [18], interface control [17], document editing [5], and even vacation planning [29, 15]. However, such systems require only a single round of communication, from the requester to the worker and back. The reason for this is that maintaining consistent communication with the crowd is inherently difficult because the pool of online agents is always changing and no individual worker can be relied upon to be available at a given time to respond to a query or to continue a dialogue for more than a few moments. Individual workers may fail to respond to queries quickly or intelligibly for various reasons including misunderstanding of task directives, laziness, distractions, or outright maliciousness. Furthermore, individual workers may experience delays that are beyond their control, such as network bandwidth variability, that make conversation inefficient. As a result, the crowd has historically been used only as a tool to interpret human instructions, rather than the foundation of a dialogue-based system itself.

Crowdsourcing Web Search and Question Answering

Prior work has looked at providing specific answers to a wide range of uncommon questions searched for on the web by having workers extract answers from automatically generated candidate webpages [6]. CrowdSearcher [2] introduced a model in which social search was combined with automated search by way of a structured query model.

Most Internet forums rely on groups of workers to answer queries. Contributors are expected to read through the thread history and gain context before submitting responses. Those submitting the original question can also respond to the answers provided, and give feedback concerning issues that the group has with the query. This is similar to what Chorus aims to elicit from web workers. The difference is that forums and similar systems typically generate answers offline, often taking hours or even days to arrive at a final answer. In order for Chorus to enable conversational interfaces, it needs to be able to provide real-time interactive responses. Other systems such as ChaCha[3] try to get answers back to users in nearly-realtime, but provide answers from individual workers without considering the history of the user. Another difference from typical forums is that participants in Chorus collectively participate in dialogue as though they were a single individual, instead of responding independently.

Real-Time Human Computation

Researchers have only recently begun to investigate real-time human computation. VizWiz [7] was one of the first systems to elicit nearly-realtime response from the crowd. It introduced a queuing model to help ensure that workers were available both quickly and on-demand. For Chorus to be available on-demand requires multiple users to be available at the same time in order to collectively contribute. Prior systems have shown that multiple workers can be recruited for collaboration by having workers wait until a sufficient number of workers have arrived [26, 10]. Adrenaline combines the concepts of queuing and waiting to recruit crowds (groups) in less than 2 seconds from existing sources of crowd workers [3]. Further work has used queuing theory to show that this latency can be reduced to under a second and has also established reliability bounds on using the crowd in this manner [4]. Work on real-time captioning by non-experts[16] uses the input of multiple workers, but differs because it engages workers for longer continuous tasks. These systems introduce a variety of methods for rapidly recruiting crowds for a task that we use in Chorus, but focus only on one-way interaction with the crowd rather than extended engagement.

Legion enables real-time control of existing user interfaces by allowing the crowd to collectively act as a single operator [17]. Each crowd worker submits input independently of other workers, then the system uses an *input mediator* to combine the input into a single control stream. Our work allows systems such as Legion to be more easily and naturally controlled by users by adding a conversational layer on top. Importantly, Chorus does not need to change the underlying system itself, making development of crowd systems with natural language interfaces more modular.

Organizational Learning

The idea of crowd memory and learning in continuous real-time and collective answer tasks is related to the organizational learning theory (summarized in [21]). Organizational learning has previously been demonstrated in continuous real-time crowdsourcing using Legion [20]. There learning was shown in implicit cases where new workers learned from experienced workers by observing the collective actions of the group. This means that activities in which information is ideally only provided once, such as conversation, cannot be accounted for using their model. Here, we instead aim to make the crowd's memory more explicit by having workers curate a knowledge base to be used by future workers in much the same way historians do on a societal scale by aggregating documents and other accounts of past events.

Measuring Human-Crowd Conversation

Several approaches have been proposed for measuring the effectiveness of conversational agents. One approach is to use reference answers, then compare agent-provided responses to these [12]. This approach falls short when rating dialogues that may not follow the fixed expected path, even when the response itself is valid. PARADISE [27] attempts to create a structured framework for evaluating spoken dialogue that is separate of the specific task being performed. However, because PARADISE tries to minimize completion time, it is generally biased in favor of shorter conversations, not just ones that accomplish a task more effectively. Another approach is to elicit subjective feedback from users of the system itself to get a more comprehensive notion of whether or not the system is helpful. Webb et al [28] explore measuring conversations for appropriateness, rather than via a fixed 'performance' metric.

In this paper, we evaluate the crowd's ability to hold a conversation using a combination of measuring appropriateness and obtaining user evaluations of the interaction. Since our metric must account for variations in Chorus that are not seen in automated systems, such as varying time to find the same answers, this gives us a more complete metric of the conversation without being biased towards speed alone. It also allows conversations to take one of many appropriate paths, which is important given the multitude of workers and opinions that Chorus will incorporate.

CHORUS

This section presents the Chorus system, first at a high-level through a scenario, and then through a discussion of the key challenges that Chorus faces and how they were addressed to create a functional system. A diagram of the Chorus system can be seen in Figure 2.

[3]www.chacha.com/

Scenario

To demonstrate the utility of crowd-powered conversational interfaces, we consider the following scenario. Susan is a mother of 3 who uses Chorus as an autonomous personal assistant while driving from work and picking up her daughter. When Susan is driving, she is situationally disabled [23], as she is unable to use her hands or divert her focus from the road. We will see how Chorus can listen to Susan's requests and interact with an interface on her behalf, much like a personal assistant.

When Susan first opens Chorus at the start of a drive, the system begins recruiting crowd workers from the web. Within a few seconds, the system is ready to begin responding. Since Susan is driving, she opts to use the voice input mode. She is on her way from a meeting to a store in downtown Chicago, IL to purchase a present for a birthday party, then needs to quickly head over to pick up her daughter and take her there. Since Susan does not know what kind of present is appropriate and is in a hurry, she asks Chorus to recommend a present for a 5-year-old boy that she can buy on the way home.

Individual workers in the crowd can listen to Susan's request, interpret the instruction and then develop their own response. These responses must then be merged into getting a single, unified response, which is a key challenge for Chorus that we call *achieving agreement*. Our method for achieving agreement involves a combination of crowd voting and similarity matching between existing answers, which we will discuss later. When a proposed response has sufficient agreement it is "locked in," presenting it to the user (Susan) via speech or text. Using workers for both response generation and selection has several advantages. First, involving multiple workers leads to an appropriate response more quickly and with more options explored than a single worker could do alone because each worker works in parallel with the others and typically on a different path because of the intrinsic differences between workers. Second, using workers to help achieve agreement improves accuracy since people are generally able to identify correct answers better than they can generate them [24].

Once Susan has asked for suggestions, one worker quickly returns "a Furby," but others have looked up Amazon reviews online and know that this product is not recommended for 5-year-olds. Workers propose a variety of alternatives at first, including some that cost over fifty dollars. The responses with high-priced items do not receive as many votes however, because most workers have noticed that in a previous conversation Susan had said she typically spends around twenty dollars on a gift. This is revealed in the "Working Memory" section of the crowd workers' interface. Ensuring that memory of previous interactions is integrated into crowd workers' decisions is another key challenge addressed by Chorus.

Some workers propose purchasing a specific action figure for twenty dollars, and find a nearby toy store that lists it in stock via its website. Finally, while verifying the route to the toy store, one worker sees a traffic report saying there is a major accident on Archer St that will not be cleared for at least an hour, so they propose an alternative store close to Susan's work: "take I-90 to the toy store on 444 W. Chicago Ave to avoid traffic on I-55 and an accident on Archer St You can buy an action figure there for twenty dollars." Other workers quickly check this option and see it is the best one. Within moments they switch their vote, and the action figure option is forwarded to Susan and spoken out loud by the application. The agreement and memory features of Chorus have ensured that crowd workers were able to generate a high quality response while taking into account information available to them from current and past conversations.

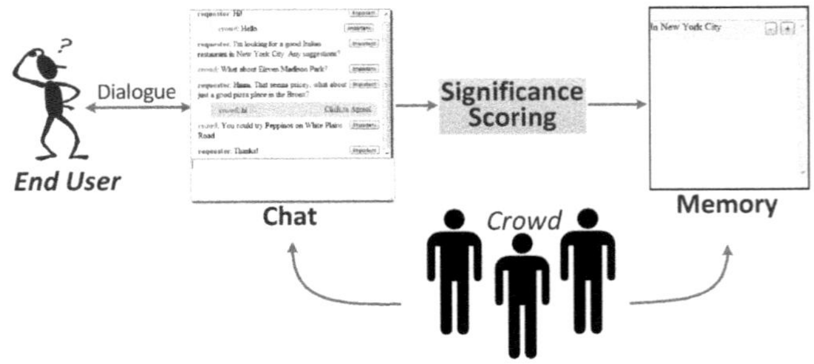

Figure 2. The Chorus system. Users first make a request, which is forwarded to the crowd. Workers can both submit responses and vote for those proposed by others. Responses are hidden from users until sufficient agreement between workers is achieved. Workers can also add information to the crowd's working memory by either voting on existing lines from the conversation, or adding summaries of key facts.

Challenge: Recruiting and Training Workers

To recruit workers in near real-time, we use a retainer pool [3] and a thresholding mechanism to ensure that a certain number of workers arrive to each conversation task simultaneously and when needed, similar to the method used in legion [17]. The number of workers required is configurable, and we explore this in our studies, described later.

To ensure that the workers were educated in the use of the interface and to test their competence for the task, we showed workers a 30 second video describing how to use the interface the first time they joined a task. After showing the video, we then sent workers through two guided tutorials before they could participate in the main task. The first tutorial required workers to correctly propose a response given a message and the second required the user to vote on a set of potential responses given a message. Both of these tutorials provided guidance on how to use the interface, and the correct answer for each tutorial task was extremely simple to deduce. Feedback was provided for incorrect answers and workers had as many opportunities as they wanted to try again if they failed. While these tutorial tasks were *very* simple, they had the effect of filtering out many lazy, idle, malicious, and confused workers, as well as any bots. Filtering the idle workers was particularly important, because in early trials many workers would join the retainer queue but then become idle while waiting for the task to begin.

Informally, we found that those that passed these tutorials were generally more engaged in the task and less likely to become idle. We also found that a majority of the workers who visited the tutorial pages did successfully enter the task.

Challenge: Achieving Agreement

There are at least two possible methods that Chorus could use to identify when agreement has been achieved among the crowd workers: an explicit voting method where crowd workers vote on others' responses, or an automatic method that attempts to identify agreement automatically by comparing the similarity of multiple suggested responses. In the current version of Chorus, we focus on only the explicit voting method.

The crowd worker interface for Chorus (Figure 1) shows all of the suggested responses and allows workers to vote on those responses. Workers may change their votes at any time, including retracting their votes. Chorus requires a majority of workers to agree on a response in order to lock it in, and the majority is calculated based only on the currently connected workers and their votes. If a worker disconnects from the system then their votes are removed, which prevents workers from trying to game the system by voting for a lower quality post and then disconnecting to lower the number of votes required to achieve a majority.

While the use of a voting method seems straight-forward, it is important to design a reward scheme that motivates workers to think carefully about their responses and their votes. A naive award scheme might reward workers for each response and vote that they put into the system, but this approach will simply yield a large number of low quality responses instead the higher quality responses that we wish to encourage.

To encourage workers to submit only accurate responses, Chorus uses a multi-tiered reward scheme that pays workers a small amount for each interaction with the interface, a medium reward for agreeing with an answer that subsequently gets enough votes from others to forward to the user, and a large reward for proposing an answer that the crowd eventually chooses. The difference between these reward values for each of these cases can be used to adjust workers' willingness to select one option over another. Our experiments used 20, 1000, and 3000 points for each value respectively, where 1000 points correlates to 1 cent. At this rate, workers can reasonably earn above the U.S. minimum wage for responding to questions and performing simple search queries, while still providing a reasonably priced service to the user. Furthermore, these numbers can be tuned by developers to best suit their application.

To prevent these rewards from being abused by workers, we also adjust the points over sequential inputs sent without any user feedback by reducing the value of each subsequent contribution. Reward values are reset with each user input. This means that the points given to workers for each contribution to the same response decreases, removing some of the incentive for workers to provide excess input. Since Chorus's goal is a consistent dialogue, reducing the number of responses a worker can submit without some kind of user input does not limit the system's functionality, so absolute limits can also be enforced if desired (we limited workers to 3 contributions per user message).

Challenge: Conversational Memory

Memory is an important aspect to any conversation because it allows participants to have a shared context, and history of events and topics covered. This reduces the total amount of information that must be conveyed by largely eliminating the need for information to be repeated, and allows more information to be transferred with each utterance as the conversation progresses.

Context is typically gained over the course of one or more conversations. However, since the crowd is dynamic, we must account for workers who join conversations that are already in-progress and may not have been around for previous conversations. The chat history logs contain this contextual information, but having each worker read through the entire conversational history with a particular user eventually becomes prohibitively time consuming and difficult. Instead, we need a means of directing users to the most important aspects of a conversation without making them parse extensive logs.

To support memory, we add the "Working Memory" section to the crowd workers' user interface. This area shows lines from previous conversations and summarized facts that may be useful when formulating responses.

In the initial version of the system, crowd workers were allowed to curate the memory while also producing and voting on potential responses. In this version, workers could move lines of dialog from the chat window into the working memory area if they believed that it would be useful later, or contribute summarized facts by entering them into the text field at the bottom of the section. Workers could also increase or decrease the importance of each line in the crowd's memory by voting, and the lines were sorted in descending order.

In our studies of the initial prototype, described later, we found that the overhead of asking users to perform both the "chat" task and this "memory curation" task was too much. For this reason, in the current version of the system we split these two tasks to different sets of crowd workers. Workers in the chat task are no longer able to add items to the working memory or change their order in the list. A second set of workers is then recruited for the memory task. They see a new interface that allows them to browse the conversation history, add items to the memory by selecting lines of dialog or typing in their own summaries of facts, and vote for facts they think are important, but cannot participate in the chat.

The chat task and memory task can proceed simultaneously, but work on the memory task does not have the same real-time requirements of the chat task. In fact, workers on the memory task can only be productive if there is a sufficient amount of new conversation content to process. Thus, workers for this task can be recruited only occasionally during a conversation depending on its speed and length, or after the end of a conversation.

Contributions to the collective memory are rewarded using the same multi-tiered point system described above for the chat task, although this may not be ideal given that this task is somewhat different. Further investigating the best reward scheme for the memory task is left for future work.

Challenge: Keeping Workers Engaged

In order to pay workers who may remain active in the task for different lengths of time fairly, we base payments on the number and accuracy of their contributions. This means that workers are paid based on their contributions to the conversation over any span of time, preventing them from being encouraged to leave sooner by paying a fixed amount. Furthermore, we expect workers will be encouraged to remain connected longer than they otherwise would because of the promise of continued pay and because they are compensated for their increased knowledge of the task as it continues, which makes it easier for them to respond quickly and accurately.

During our example, Susan only paid a small amount for workers to complete her task because workers were paid based on their useful input, and she was able to pay the crowd only for a small unit of time (a few minutes). This is considerably cheaper than hiring an individual, dedicated employee to serve as Susan's assistant when she may need it. It also provides quicker response time in many cases because workers are able to search for answers on many fronts at once.

Interface Design

To this point, we have focused on a particular interface design that forwards only the single agreed upon response to the user. This masks the fact that multiple crowd workers are actually providing responses in the back-end and creates the impression of talking to a single individual. We call this the Filter version of the interface.

We have also experimented with an alternate interface called Suggest, which allows the user to see multiple responses generated by the crowd as they are working. Some filtering is still performed on the responses, but at a reduced level compared to the Filter interface. This interface allows the user to provide feedback on the responses as they are being generated, which may help guide the crowd to provide a better answer even sooner.

In both interfaces, we also present the users and workers with a "typing" status indicator that tells the other party that a response is being composed, similar to the feature found in many instant messaging clients. To determine when the crowd response is being composed, Chorus checks if there were currently any active proposals that have not yet been forwarded to the user.

FORMATIVE STUDY

To begin exploring how to use the crowd as a conversational partner, we conducted a formative study with an early version of Chorus. This version used a simple voting mechanism that did not remove votes for users that disconnected before the required agreement threshold was reached, allowed crowd workers to curate the collective memory directly, and did not reduce reward values for actions leading to a single response. In addition, workers were not shown a tutorial before they began the task.

We recruited a 23-year-old user who had no prior experience with Chorus to have a series of conversations with it. This user carried out conversations starting with one of two questions: (i) Will dog breed `X` be good for my apartment? and (ii) what is the best place to eat near `Y`? The dog type and city in these questions were altered each iteration just in case any of the workers overlapped from a previous trial.

	Total Lines	Accurate Responses	Errors Made	Clarifications Asked	Questions Asked	Answers Provided
Consistency #1	24	9	0	0	4	4
Consistency #2	55	50	1	0	7	6
Consistency #3	33	11	0	0	2	2

Figure 3. Results for the conversations with Chorus..

In our analyses, we reviewed several hundred lines of conversation and interaction with Chorus, focusing on overall performance and conversational consistency. Over the course of the study, Chorus recruited a total of 33 unique workers, with an average of 6.7 workers contributing to each trial. Overall, Chorus filtered out 37.5% crowd responses and answered 84.62% of inquiries correctly (with useful information).

To investigate conversational consistency, we ran three experiments. In each, we used 3 conversations spanning a total of 112 lines suggested by the crowd. Each of these lines was hand-coded by two researchers as "on topic" or "off topic." This was filtered down to 70 lines by the curation system, and among these only a single off-topic line was spoken across all three conversations. A set of 13 questions were asked with 12 answered successfully by the crowd during the conversations. These results are summarized in Figure 3.

Throughout these experiments, we observed the crowd providing serendipity unavailable in traditional automated search, with workers suggesting outcomes not considered by the original participant and building on one another's responses. For instance, in a typical example, the requester provided Chorus with the query, "I am looking for a place to eat dinner." Chorus responded with "There is Asian Fusion joint on 3rd and Molly Ave. It serves amazing cuisine." Following a brief interlude, the crowd provided the additional, unsolicited suggestion, "I also saw a Groupon for 1/2 off!" This was a relatively frequent occurrence: in 26 accepted lines of discussion, workers prompted requesters with additional information concerning aspects not initially suggested as part of the starting query. These results (an effect of the information foraging behavior of groups) are deeper than those that would be obtained through search on a site such as Yelp, and suggests that there is additional utility in using conversations with humans as an intermediary when interacting with software. In particular, a crowd-based dialogue partner can significantly augment and improve the utility of software interfaces by providing parallelized search and the ability to recognize and provide relevant facts based on their personal knowledge.

EXPERIMENTS

To test the feasibility of using the crowd as a conversational partner, we performed experiments focusing on two different aspects: *(i)* conversational consistency (measured in terms of topic maintenance and coherent answers), and *(ii)* memory of past events (measured in terms of factual recall).

Conditions

Based on our formative study, we designed 3 variants of Chorus that we used in the study. We also included a control condition in which users simply searched the web for their own answers. The conditions were as follows (Figure 4):

- **Filtered:** This is the complete version of Chorus, which asks a group of workers to collectively propose answers to user's questions, and vote on one another's responses to find the best ones. This approach benefits from finding the best answers from a range of people, each with different sets of prior knowledge and approaches to search. However, requiring an explicit voting step prevents answers from being forwarded as quickly as possible.
- **Solo:** In this condition, Chorus is powered by a single worker. This means that there is no underlying collaborative search, or wide variety of prior knowledge. However, it also means that the system does not have to wait for workers to agree with one another, potentially reducing the response time.
- **Unfiltered:** In this condition, Chorus uses a crowd to generate responses, but does not require any agreement to forward them to the end user. This means users can benefit from the diversity of the crowd, while not reducing the speed at which individual answers are provided. However, because responses are not filtered, unhelpful or redundant responses might be included. Thus, this might not be as helpful to users who are occupied with other tasks during their search (e.g. driving or holding another conversation).
- **Google:** The fourth condition asked users to find information themselves using Google. This acted as a baseline for their feedback on the system.

Since chatting via an instant messenger is often not done as a stand-alone task, we allow users to use the web on a different task during our tasks, returning when they received a new message from the system.

In our experiments, the crowd was recruited from a combination of Amazon Mechanical Turk (90% approval rating or higher, composing 77% of our workers) and MobileWorks (no restrictions, composing 23% of workers). These workers were paid 25 cents to complete the interface training, plus an additional three cents for each contributed message accepted by Chorus, and one cent for each vote towards an accepted message contributed by another worker. Our tests used a total of 100 unique workers with at least 4-5 workers beginning each Filter and Unfiltered session (as well as workers coming and going throughout), and exactly 1 worker at any given time during single-worker sessions (described below).

Conversational Consistency and Dialogue

In our experiments we focused on the crowd's ability to generate reasonable responses to user questions. To help control for the potential complexity user questions and ensure results were not skewed by the varying types of participants' impromptu questions, underspecified task descriptions, or particular communication styles, we generated a script for each of our four tasks and asked our participants to follow the

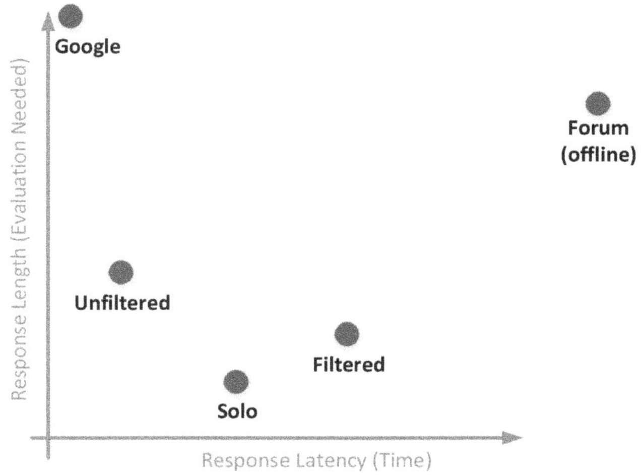

Figure 4. Tradeoff between speed and ease of parsing results. While Solo results in a small set of responses and reasonable response time, the answers also lack variation. Both Filtered and Unfiltered approaches give more broad answers interactively, but Unfiltered returns a result quicker. Older, offline methods, such as Forums, can return varied answers but don't return answers in real-time.

script as closely as they could, while still allowing the conversation to flow naturally as if would if they were talking to another person (all while following the persona laid out in the script). We used the following task goals to generate scripts:

- **(i)** Find information about things to do when traveling to Houston, TX that are not "too touristy".
- **(ii)** Discuss the options available for getting a dog, given the constraints of a small apartment near a park in Washington, D.C.
- **(ii)** Find an interesting dinner date idea that is more unique than just dinner and a movie.
- **(iv)** Get step by step directions about how to make lasagna. Users remember only after an initial response that they failed to mention the dish they want to prepare must be meat and gluten free.

Specifics of the tasks, such as location or dog size, was varied between trials in order to prevent workers from being able to just repeat responses from previous trials. Each participant was asked to complete all four scripts using three different versions of Chorus as well as Google to get a baseline for finding a solution to one of the scripted problems using a conventional search engine. Conversations were allowed to be free-form as long as the topic was addressed. For these tests, workers were not provided any chat history on which to base their answers, meaning that each test was treated as the crowd's first contact with a given user, and in fact the user had a different identity they played for each question asked. To prevent workers who may have previously completed a session from having an unfair advantage, we altered task details such as user city or preferences. As a baseline, we also compared users' performance on a conventional keyword search engine to find information. While we expect keyword search to be much quicker, because the user must define their own

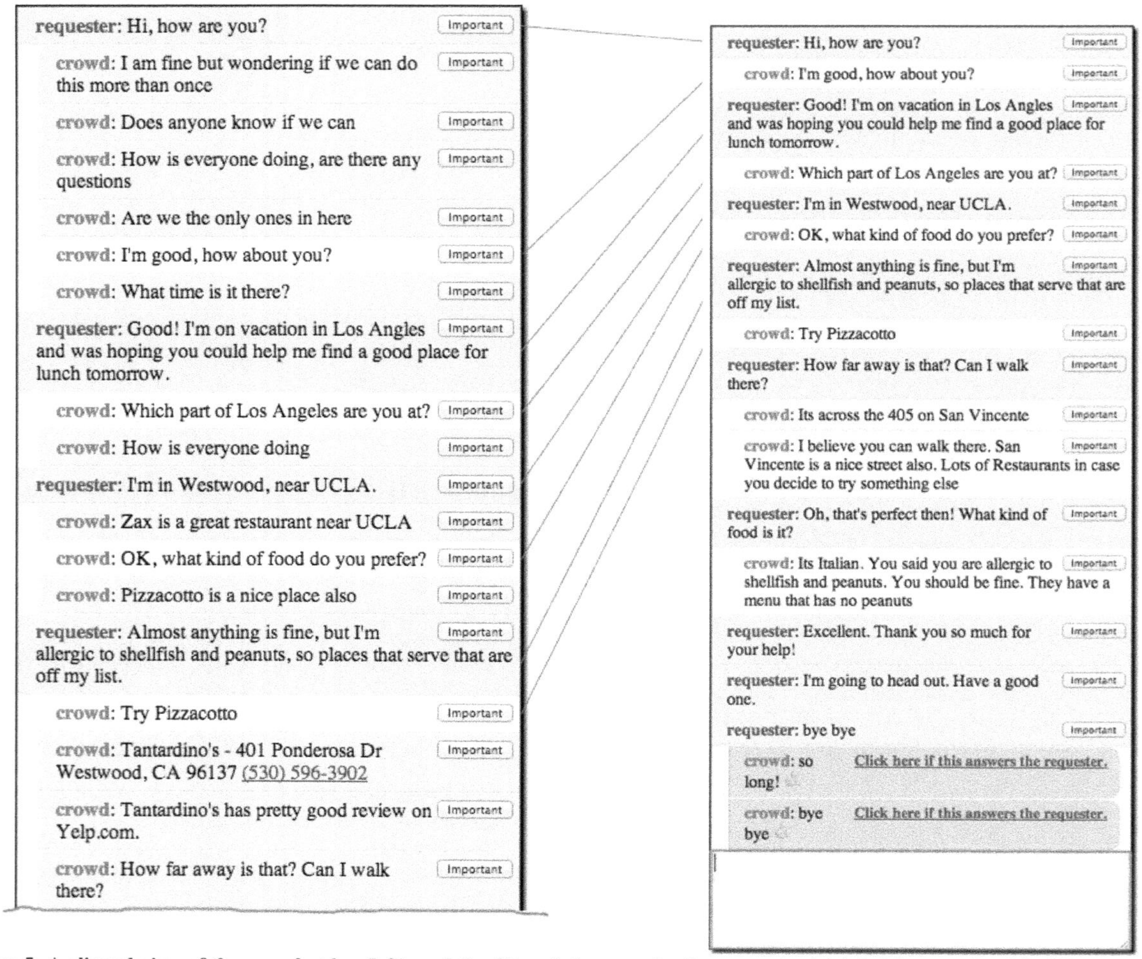

Figure 5. A clipped view of the raw chat log (left), and the filtered view seen by the requester (right). Messages in pink did not receive sufficient votes from the crowd to make it into the requester view. Some of these messages did not contribute to the conversation (e.g. new workers asking questions about the task in the beginning), while others were simply not chosen.

terms even when unfamiliar with a space, there is less potential for finding a useful answer that may not be closely related to the initial search terms.

Trials were spaced out over a period of four days and the order of the conditions randomized. We recruited 12 participants to act as users and hold conversations based on our scripts. They were asked to hold a conversation until Chorus provided an answer to their question (including followups), 15 minutes passed without a single response from the crowd, or 30 minutes total passed without a correct answer being given. Once done, four of the authors coded the responses according to the following scheme:

- **On-Topic:** The response furthers the topic of conversation that the user proposed by providing an answer or opinion related to the question that the user asked. If the relevance of a response is unclear, the user's response (correction or affirmation) is used to determine its status.
- **Off-Topic:** The response is either not clearly related to the user's current topic (including unsolicited information about the worker them self) or provides an instantly identifiable incorrect answer to the user's question (for example, Q:"What is the capitol of Texas?" A:"Outer space.")
- **Side Chatter:** Conversations between workers either about the task itself, or general conversations and queries.
- **No Code:** The response is blank, a correction or typo, or otherwise unintentionally not interpretable. This does NOT cover messages which are explicitly spam, which are classified as off-topic.

Each of the 960 messages in our dataset was coded by these four researchers, resulting in a Fleiss' Kappa score of 0.67 (strong agreement). Their ratings were then combined with even weight to score the success of the system. We found that 88.3 % of messages were classified as On-Topic, 9.3% of messages were Off-Topic, and 1.7% consisted of Side Chatter between workers. Out of all messages, just 68.6% were accepted, with a final accuracy visible to the user of 95.60%. This relative improvement of 8.3% was significant ($p < 0.05$).

We also tracked the number of user-generated queries and clarification details that were addressed completely in answers, partially addressed, or not addressed at all by the crowd. This gives us a measure of how well the crowd listened to the user (as opposed to just spouting off answers without correct details). We considered an information-containing message as addressed when the response did not violate any of the facts in the message, partially addressed if it violated some but not all, and not addressed if the response did not take the information in the message into account at all. We used the same rating scale for questions, but required that workers provided an *actionable* solution to the users. 92.85% of questions asked by users were addressed completely, another 3.38% were addressed partially, and only 3.77% were not addressed. In addition, many of those questions and facts that the crowd failed to answer or use were less important tidbits and followup questions similar to those that often go unseen the first time in any conversation or instant messenger. These results demonstrate that the crowd is very attentive to the information that users provide.

Individual Workers and Crowd Assistants
Across 24 tests involving the crowd-powered version of Chorus, 12 with filtering and 12 without, users' information goals were met 100% of the time. In contrast, when a single crowd worker was recruited to answer questions, the system was unresponsive in 2 tests, and failed to finish within the 30 minute bound in 2 more. This means that in a third of all uses, the single-worker version of the system could not complete the task requested. Workers might have been unresponsive because workers did not fully understand the task, queued multiple tasks (contrary to the task instructions) and were planning to get to ours later, lost connection, or some other unknown cause. Workers not responding in a reasonable amount of time may have likewise been for a variety of reasons such as a poor connection, long search times for a single piece of information (which took longer than 15 minutes to complete), or in a few cases, workers leaving as soon as they did the minimum amount of work possible. The reliability of the crowd over single workers recruited from these platforms is one of the primary benefits to using a group in user interaction domains, alongside improved response speed and increased opportunities for creative and novel answers.

Response Speed
To answer a question, workers either need to have prior knowledge of the answer, or find an answer via a web search. On average, individuals have less prior knowledge than a group does collectively, and so we expect individuals to need to search more often. Workers generally disengage from the dialogue to perform a search. Chorus is designed to leverage the prior knowledge of the group. When using Chorus, some workers can continue to engage in conversation with users to help find more helpful points, while others who believe they can find the answer go to search for specific information. Because the collective prior knowledge is larger, many questions may be answered without the need to search at all.

These factors combined result in a significant reduction in the average time until the user gets a first response from the crowd for a given question. Using a single worker, the average response time between a question and a response was 103.4 seconds, likely due to workers already being engaged in a search, or doing other tasks between responses. In the Suggest condition, there was a significant reduction of 56.9% ($p < 0.01$) in this delay, resulting in only a 44.6 second average response delay. The Filter condition also had a significant decrease of 51.5% ($p < 0.05$) over the single-worker case, with an average latency of 50.13 seconds.

	Total Lines	Accurate Responses	Errors Made	Clarifications Asked	Questions Asked	Answers Provided	Memory Successes	Memory Failures
Memory #1	138	53	30	3	5	3	4	2
Memory #2	63	15	1	1	4	2	1	0
Memory #3	30	29	1	1	3	3	1	0
Memory #4	28	7	0	2	3	2	2	0

Figure 6. Results for the conversations with Chorus including memory.

Individual conversations with Chorus averaged 11:21 minutes (median 10:51). While no user took more than 5 minutes on Google, a majority of people independently commented that they preferred Chorus due to the answers they received being easier to scan through and containing suggestions that would not have come up had they simply used a keyword search. In many cases this involved the crowd clarifying a question or suggesting a different search parameter (i.e. type of food in a given city specializes in), which would not have been done by a search engine. As a result, overall search time is can be a deceptive measure, since longer interactions frequently lead to much higher satisfaction with the final result.

Answer Diversity
Online searches for information can be limited by a user's preconceived notions of how to describe the information that is sought. The crowd permits access to a wider range of experience, prior knowledge, search methods, and creativity than any single individual. We observed that the crowd was able to come up with both diverse sets of answers, as well as diverse sets of variations on a given topic. For instance, when asked to provide a set of recommendations for restaurants in the Los Angeles area, crowd members suggested both commonplace suggestions as well as highly unusual ones. This can lead to more effective information provided to end users.

Memory
To test the system's ability to remember information over time, we ran an experiment that simulates new members of the crowd arriving to Chorus to find pre-populated short-and long-term memory logs. We wanted to find whether the crowd would be willing and able to use the highlighted history logs to bring themselves up to speed on the current conversation. We generated an artificial chat history and presented new workers with information pre-highlighted by the authors in the memory window. This simulates a prior chat interaction carried out by past participants in Chorus. In our test, the artificial chat history simulates a conversation between a user and Chorus concerning a trip the user is taking, and contains information about the user's dietary restrictions and the city they are visiting. We asked the crowd to 'continue' the conversation with a new live user, and asked them questions that assume background available from the memory, including suggestions for new restaurants in the area. The user's script assumed that the crowd had full knowledge of prior

requester: "Hi"
crowd: "hello"
Requester: "Do you know of 2 or 3 fun things that I can do in Houston that aren't too touristy?"
crowd: "A good place to eat in Boston is Neptune Oyster"
crowd: "Are you on a budget?"
requester: "Yeah I would rather they aren't too expensive."
crowd: "you always need to look at how expensive they are"
crowd: "this places can be very expensive"
crowd: "something good that i can request is for you to use google map"
crowd: "what kind of things are you looking to do? concerts, sports, etc?"
crowd: "Try googling eating on a budget in Boston."
requester: "Anything that's fun but not too touristy."
crowd: "and look for the areas you want to visit and check out the nearby restaurants"
crowd: "Do you enjoy outdoor activities?"
requester: "Yes."
crowd: "well if you go to Boston they have so many free"

Figure 7. In this conversation, the user is asking about Houston, but one of the crowd workers is confused and suggests facts about Boston. These proposals (in red) are not selected to be forwarded on to the user.

interactions, and did not contain reminders about facts previously mentioned. The user was free to specify these facts only if explicitly prompted by the crowd.

Between-Task Consistency

We ran four memory experiments. In each, we held 3 conversations spanning a total of 259 lines suggested by the crowd. This was filtered down to 104 lines by the curation system. The crowd was frequently successful in recalling facts using working memory. We separately recorded both successful use of the working memory to recall facts and failure to do so (Figure 6). In 8 of 10 conversations, the crowd was able to recall facts stored in the working memory from prior sessions, but in the remaining 2 scenarios required prompting. We found that prompted crowds displayed a cascade effect, where workers were rapidly able to identify forgotten facts when prompted and mark them as salient. This is likely because a user implying that the crowd should already know a fact makes the workers seek the information within the interface, helping them to notice previously missed information, then recover information that they initially bypassed.

DISCUSSION

The ability to hold consistent, in-depth, conversations with the crowd opens up a range of interaction possibilities. Our tests showed that the crowd was able to generate consistent and helpful responses to users with high reliability. We are currently working on deploying this system in a variety of situations, including more complex software such as restaurant reservation and flight booking applications. We are also investigating the idea of 'embodied crowds' via a mobile crowd-powered information kiosk that can answer general questions using Chorus to present users with a conversational interface.

Quality and Reliability

For many applications, we are interested in whether or not the crowd can respond with high quality feedback compared

requester: "thanks! how much does the space center visit cost?"
crowd: "GENERAL ADMISSION AT THE GATE ONLINE DISCOUNT Adults: $22.95 $11.45 Children (Age 4-11): $18.95 $9.45 Seniors: $21.95 $10.95"
requester: "great, and how much would it cost to do the houston zoo, the miller outdoor theatre,the space center, bowling all together?"
crowd: "How many adults and kids would be going?"
requester: "just a single adult"
crowd: "How long will you be staying in Houston?"
crowd: "It will about 150"
requester: "two days (full days)"
crowd: "It will cost around $150"
crowd: "I will be less if you buy tickets online!"
requester: "ok thanks for your help"
crowd: "You Welcome.Have a good day"
crowd: "There might be a city pass available from the local tourist office."
requester: "what does the city pass allow me to do?"
crowd: "CityPass attractions include: Space Center Houston (NASA) Downtown Aquarium Houston Museum of Natural Science Option ticket: Choose to visit either Houston Zoo or Kemah Boardwalk Option ticket: Choose to visit either Museum of Fine Arts, Houston or The Children's Museum of Houston "
requester: "perfect, i will do that. bye!"

Figure 8. In this conversation, the user was concerned with price. Not only does the crowd provide the information the user requested, but it also finds a "City Pass" – a less expensive way to do the activities that the end user wants to do that he didn't know about.

to what an expert individual might present. For example, in the restaurant finding task, proposing McDonalds as a solution might be valid answer, but not one that is always very helpful to the user. Qualitatively, in both the experiments we present in this paper and in continued testing, the crowd has consistently made very useful suggestions that went well beyond the minimum effort. This behavior is supported by the two-role (proposers and voters) system that requires only a small subset of the workers to seek out high-quality information, whereas the rest need only to identify the relative utility of an answer and agree with the best one by voting.

The possibility of using Chorus in real-world settings also means that important situations will arise in which an answer from the crowd must be trusted and thus needs to be as reliable as possible. A particular challenge is encouraging users to dig deeply into possible solutions. For example, a worker might propose an inappropriate restaurant to a user with a particular allergy, perhaps because the food served at the restaurant was not obvious from the name (e.g. "John's Grill" serving seafood). It is possible the other crowd workers will agree with the option without doing further (unrewarded) research.

In future work, our goal is to find ways to encourage workers to do these type of deep knowledge searches, then use redundant results of deep searches performed by different workers to increase the reliability of the system on critical tasks where the additional cost is warranted.

Difficulties

While our results showed very high rates of correct responses and low rates of unhelpful responses, there are still areas of difficulty. For instance, using the current method for curating crowd memory, only a limited number of facts can be remembered at once without requiring workers to complete a search task within the recorded memories themselves. Thus, over a

requester: "Hi, I want to know how to make lasagna?"
crowd: "Vegetarian or with meat?"
requester: "With meat, but I don't eat red meat."
crowd: "You can find a recipe for a lean lasagna made with turkey meat here: http://www.epicurious.com/recipes/food/views/Lean-Lasagna-230145"
crowd: "It makes 8 servings and takes 1 hour."
crowd: "Would you like another recipe?"
crowd: "Does that use any mushrooms?"
crowd: "It uses 1/2 cup chopped mushrooms. Would you prefer one without mushrooms?"
requester: "Yes, how about a recipe without mushrooms."
crowd: "Here is one made with Italian Turkey sasuage, no mushrooms: http://www.chow.com/recipes/30279-turkey-sausage-lasagna"
crowd: "Would you prefer a different recipe? Or does this work for you?"

Figure 9. In this conversation, the crowd helps the user search for a recipe appropriate for him to make lasagna. Not only does the crowd find relevant web pages and refine their search based on user feedback, but they also ask relevant questions about dimensions the user did not think to specify upfront (such as if the recipe should be vegetarian).

longer span of interactions, most facts would not be remembered by the assistant. in the future, our goal is to create a hybrid approach that learns from the importance of certain facts based on the topic of conversation, then is able to retrieve older pieces of information and display it to workers.

Payments
Another significant challenge in crowdsourcing systems that ask workers for variable input faces is adequately rewarding workers for their contribution. This is especially true of Chorus, where workers might spend anywhere from a few seconds to several minutes finding a response, but are only rewarded based on the number of answers accepted by other workers. While our incentive mechanism makes spending more time result in a better response will increase the likelihood that other workers find it important, there is still no way to determine exactly how valuable the response is.

One way to help solve this problem might be to vary the payment to workers based on the magnitude of the crowd's agreement with their response, since we observed that almost unanimous agreement (among active workers) on answers that were clearly useful or especially helpful. Another approach might be to let the user rate the helpfulness of each answer, which might also prove helpful to give workers ongoing feedback, or train automated conversational assistants.

From reviewing the results for our tasks though, we feel that workers were adequately compensated in the end. In fact, many even emailed us to say they would like to take more of these tasks if possible. This indicates both fair pay, and that workers like the conversational task.

FUTURE WORK
Chorus presents a wide range of potential future directions of work involving systems that have previously been limited by the robustness of automated conversational interaction systems, as well as providing a model for future crowdsourcing workflows. In this section, we discuss some of the potential issues that might arise for such applications.

Privacy
Crowds that are capable of learning about users over time introduce privacy concerns. As with many communication technologies, users must be mindful of the fact that others can view the information they provide to the system and adjust their behaviors and use of the system accordingly. To support this, developers must take care to make users aware of the fact that people, not just software, are used to support their system in order to facilitate these behavioral choices.

There are also a variety of tasks that Chorus could perform for users if not for issues of privacy. For example, if a user was comfortable giving the crowd their online banking login information, it would be possible for the crowd to pay bills and carry out other sensitive tasks. Such tasks might become more palatable if techniques could be developed to hide such sensitive information from the crowd workers while allowing them to perform the task. For example, workers might perform web-based tasks through a proxy that automatically hides sensitive information and restricts them from performing known malicious operations.

Merging the Crowd with Machines
The current version of Chorus relies heavily on human involvement in all areas of the interaction, but there is likely room for the strategic addition of machine learning algorithms throughout the process. For example, an automated dialog system could be employed to answer simple requests or an automated system might act as one of crowd workers alongside the other workers in suggesting or voting on responses. The advantage of this approach is that fewer crowd workers might be needed per conversation, or possibly not needed at all in the case of certain conversations, especially for those topics that have come up repeatedly in the past.

Playing a Role
In the current version of Chorus, the virtual agent does not have a pre-defined personality or play the role of a character, but these might be potentially advantageous features for the agent. For example, an agent acting as a customer support representative for a company might be given an agreeable and open personality. In another case, an agent might act as a character in a video game. In this case, the crowd must act consistently with beliefs that might not be held by any constituent member, and prevent biases and contradictory opinions from coming through in the response. One way this might be implemented is through integration with machine algorithms, as suggested above. For example, an algorithm might down vote some responses that it identifies as contradictory or manipulate the text of a "locked in" response to be more in line with the pre-defined personality of the agent.

Voice-Enabling Existing Interfaces
One of the most impactful uses of Chorus may be to enable semi-autonomous natural language interfaces for existing systems via both text and voice. In this work, we focus on tasks that the workers can individually perform then return with the results, such as a web search task or general question

answering. However, to allow users to control specific systems that they might not otherwise have direct access to, we need workers to be able to collectively control the current interface based on the knowledge of the situation and intention, and provide feedback that takes into account the current task and system state. A particularly advantageous use of Chorus might be for disabled users, such as blind [19] or motor impaired users, or ordinary users who are *situationally disabled* [23]. In such a use case, the crowd workers in the chat condition could be given direct access to an existing interface through a crowd control system, such as Legion [17].

CONCLUSION

We have presented Chorus, a crowd-powered conversational assistant that features natural two-way dialogue between the user and the assistant. While the assistant appears to be a single individual, it is actually driven by a dynamic crowd of multiple workers using a specially designed interface. We have demonstrated that Chorus can assist with a variety of tasks across domains, maintain consistency over the course of multiple interactions, and provide a new framework for cooperation among crowd workers. Chorus sets the stage for a rich new area of research in crowd-powered conversational assistants. Such assistants will be able to learn about the user's preferences over time, making them capable of improving the quality of interaction with the user as they gain experience. In this way, Chorus also acts to add a notion of agency to existing software, allowing them to complete tasks without the user's explicit guidance at every step. We believe Chorus represents not only an interesting system for assistance by the crowd, but potentially a more natural way to interact with current and future crowd-powered systems.

ACKNOWLEDGMENTS

This work is supported by National Science Foundation awards #IIS-1149709 and #IIS-1218209, and a Microsoft Research Ph.D. Fellowship.

REFERENCES

1. Allen, J. F., Schubert, L. K., Ferguson, G., Heeman, P., Hwang, C. H., Kato, T., Light, M., Martin, N. G., Miller, B. W., Poesio, M., and Traum, D. R. Enriching speech recognition with automatic detection of sentence boundaries and disfluencies. In *Journal of Experimental and Theoretical AI (JETAI) 7* (1995), 7–48.
2. Bozzon, A., Brambilla, M., and Ceri, S Answering search queries with CrowdSearcher. In *WWW 2012*, 33–42.
3. Bernstein, M. S., Brandt, J. R., Miller, R. C., and Karger, D. R. Crowds in two seconds: Enabling realtime crowd-powered interfaces. In *UIST 2011*, 33–42.
4. Bernstein, M. S., Karger, D. R., Miller, R. C., and Brandt, J. R. Analytic methods for optimizing realtime crowdsourcing. In *Collective Intelligence 2012*.
5. Bernstein, M. S., Little, G., Miller, R. C., Hartmann, B., Ackerman, M. S., Karger, D. R., Crowell, D., and Panovich, K. Soylent: a word processor with a crowd inside. In *UIST 2010*, 313–322.
6. Bernstein, M. S., Teevan, J., Dumais, S., Liebling, D., and Horvitz, E. Direct answers for search queries in the long tail. In *CHI 2012*, 237–246.
7. Bigham, J. P., Jayant, C., Ji, H., Little, G., Miller, A., Miller, R. C., Miller, R., Tatarowicz, A., White, B., White, S., and Yeh, T. Vizwiz: nearly real-time answers to visual questions. In *UIST 2010*, 333–342.
8. Bilton, N. With apple's siri, a romance gone sour. http://bits.blogs.nytimes.com/2012/07/15/with-apple's-siri-a-romance-gone-sour/.
9. Bonnington, C. Steve jobs would have 'lost his mind' over Siri, former employee says. www.wired.com/gadgetlab/2012/05/apple-siri-disappointment/.
10. Chilton, L. Seaweed: A web application for designing economic games. Master's thesis, MIT, 2009.
11. Cooper, S., Khatib, F., Treuille, A., Barbero, J., Lee, J., Beenen, M., Leaver-Fay, A., Baker, D., Popovic, Z., and Players, F. Predicting protein structures with a multiplayer online game. In *Nature 466*, 7307 (2010), 756–760.
12. Hirschman, L., Dahl, D. A., McKay, D. P., Norton, L. M., and Linebarger, M. C. Beyond class a: a proposal for automatic evaluation of discourse. In *Workshop on Speech and Natural Language*, HLT '90, ACL, 1990, 109–113.
13. Kittur, A., Smus, B., and Kraut, R. Crowdforge: Crowdsourcing complex work. In *UIST 2011*, 43–52.
14. Kittur, A., Nickerson, J. V., Bernstein, M., Gerber, E., Shaw, A., Zimmerman, J., Lease, M. and Horton, J. The future of crowd work. In *CSCW 2013*, 1301–1318.
15. Kulkarni, A. P., Can, M., and Hartmann, B. Turkomatic: automatic recursive task and workflow design for mechanical turk. In *CHI 2011*, 2053–2058.
16. Lasecki, W. S., Miller, C. D., Sadilek, A., AbuMoussa, A., R. Kushalnagar, and Bigham, J. Real-time captioning by groups of non-experts. In *UIST 2012*, 23–34.
17. Lasecki, W. S., Murray, K., White, S., Miller, R. C., and Bigham, J. P. Real-time crowd control of existing interfaces. In *UIST 2011*, 23–32.
18. Lasecki, W. S., Song, Y. C., Kautz, H., and Bigham, J. P. Real-time crowd labeling for deployable activity recognition. In *CSCW 2013*, 1203-1212.
19. Lasecki, W. S., Thiha, P., Zhong, Y., Brady, E. and Bigham, J. P. Answering Visual Questions with Conversational Crowd Assistants. In *ASSETS 2013*.
20. Lasecki, W. S., White, S., Murray, K. I., and Bigham, J. P. Crowd memory: Learning in the collective. In *Collective Intelligence 2012*.
21. Levitt, B., and March, J. G. Organizational learning. In *Annual Review of Sociology 14* (1988), 319–340.
22. Little, G., Chilton, L. B., Goldman, M., and Miller, R. C. Turkit: human computation algorithms on Mechanical Turk. In *UIST 2010*, 57–66.
23. Sears, A., Lin, M., Jacko, J., Xiao, Y. When computers fade: Pervasive computing and situationally induced impairments and disabilities. In *HCI International '03*, 1298-1302.
24. Sun, Y.-A., Dance, C. R., Roy, S., and Little, G. How to assure the quality of human computation tasks when majority voting fails? In *Workshop on Computational Social Science and the Wisdom of Crowds*, NIPS 2011.
25. von Ahn, L. Human computation. In *Ph.D. Thesis* (2005).
26. von Ahn, L., and Dabbish, L. Labeling images with a computer game. In *CHI 2004*, 319–326.
27. Walker, M. A., Litman, D. J., Kamm, C. A., and Abella, A. Paradise: a framework for evaluating spoken dialogue agents. In *Proceedings of the Association for Computational Linguistics*, ACL '98, Association for Computational Linguistics (1997), 271–280.
28. Webb, N., Benyon, D., Hansen, P., and Mival, O. Evaluating human-machine conversation for appropriateness. In *Proceedings of the Conference on Language Resources and Evaluation*, N. Calzolari, K. Choukri, B. Maegaard, J. Mariani, J. Odijk, S. Piperidis, M. Rosner, and D. Tapias, Eds., LREC'10, European Language Resources Association (ELRA) (May 2010).
29. Zhang, H., Law, E., Miller, R. C., Gajos, K. Z., Parkes, D. C., and Horvitz, E. Human computation tasks with global constraints. In *CHI 2012*, 217–226.

CrowdLearner: Rapidly Creating Mobile Recognizers Using Crowdsourcing

Shahriyar Amini*
Carnegie Mellon University
Pittsburgh, PA
shahriyar@cmu.edu

Yang Li
Google Research
Mountain View, CA
yangli@acm.org

ABSTRACT
Mobile applications can offer improved user experience through the use of novel modalities and user context. However, these new input dimensions often require recognition-based techniques, with which mobile app developers or designers may not be familiar. Furthermore, the recruiting, data collection and labeling, necessary for using these techniques, are usually time-consuming and expensive. We present CrowdLearner, a framework based on crowdsourcing to automatically generate recognizers using mobile sensor input such as accelerometer or touchscreen readings. CrowdLearner allows a developer to easily create a recognition task, distribute it to the crowd, and monitor its progress as more data becomes available. We deployed CrowdLearner to a crowd of 72 mobile users over a period of 2.5 weeks. We evaluated the system by experimenting with 6 recognition tasks concerning motion gestures, touchscreen gestures, and activity recognition. The experimental results indicated that CrowdLearner enables a developer to quickly acquire a usable recognizer for their specific application by spending a moderate amount of money, often less than $10, in a short period of time, often in the order of 2 hours. Our exploration also revealed challenges and provided insights into the design of future crowdsourcing systems for machine learning tasks.

Author Keywords
Crowdsourcing; crowdsensing; mobile interaction; gesture recognition; activity recognition; machine learning.

ACM Classification Keywords
D.2.2 **[Software Engineering]:** Design Tools and Techniques; H.5.2 **[Information Interfaces And Presentation]:** User Interfaces; I.5.2 **[Pattern Recognition]:** Design Methodology.

INTRODUCTION
Mobile users experience diverse interaction scenarios throughout everyday activities. These diverse scenarios call for novel input modalities and the use of context to provide users with intuitive and fast access to their mobile resources. Such interaction techniques often involve recognizing user context and intentions from mobile sensory input, such as accelerometer readings. However, creating recognizers is a time-consuming and expensive feat, often requiring expert knowledge in machine learning. This is beyond the reach of many developers. Thus, it is important to investigate how to empower developers to rapidly create recognizers for improving mobile user experience.

UIST'13, October 8–11, 2013, St. Andrews, United Kingdom.
ACM 978-1-4503-2268-3/13/10.
http://dx.doi.org/10.1145/2501988.2502029

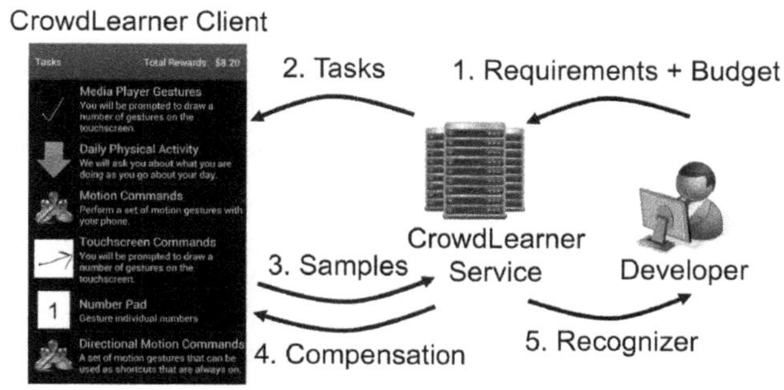

Figure 1. A developer submits a task and provides funds to run it on CrowdLearner. CrowdLearner publishes the task and compensates mobile workers who answer questions and label samples. CrowdLearner continuously builds and updates a recognizer and presents its performance to the developer.

Several off-the-shelf machine learning tools such as Weka [28] and GART [27], and lightweight recognition algorithms such as the $1 recognizer [29] have gained traction with developers and researchers. However, these tools often act more as libraries or even source code that do not encapsulate the complexity of creating recognizers from developers. High-level tools, such as Gestalt by Patel *et al.*, have been developed for using and understanding machine learning techniques [20]. Though promising, prior work has often left out data collection, a critical but time-consuming and labor-intensive step for producing efficient recognizers.

In this paper, we present CrowdLearner, a framework that employs crowdsourcing to enable an end-to-end solution for generating recognizers for mobile interaction. These recognizers, referred to as *mobile recognizers*, take in built-in mobile sensor input such as touchscreen events or accelerometer readings and infer target user actions, such as gestures or physical activities. CrowdLearner allows non-expert users (such as mobile app developers, researchers, and interaction designers), referred to here as *developers*, to easily create mobile recognizers by creating a recognition

* This work was done while the author was an intern at Google Research.

task and publishing it to mobile users, referred to here as *workers* (see Figure 1). Through CrowdLearner's web interface, a developer can create a recognition task by specifying a set of targets for recognition (i.e., classes in machine learning), the sensor inputs to use, data collection strategies and the amount of funds allocated for the task. With a high-level task description, CrowdLearner automatically determines the technical details for constructing the recognizer and scheduling data collection. CrowdLearner then collects and labels samples by relying on the wisdom and scale of the crowd, generates a recognizer, evaluates it, and presents its accuracy to the developer as the recognizer evolves with additional data collection. Once satisfied, the developer can export the recognizer for use in the intended application.

Our focus in this paper is to design and experiment with new frameworks and methods for creating mobile recognizers using crowdsourcing, instead of focusing on specific details such as featurization and classification techniques. This paper makes the following contributions:

First, we present an end-to-end framework for developers to rapidly create mobile recognizers that are specific to their tasks by ordering them. In doing so, we eliminate the overhead of recruiting and data collection, and reduce the need for expert knowledge of machine learning.

Second, we demonstrate two strategies as well as the supporting UI for collecting training data in the wild: *participatory* and *opportunistic* sampling, which complement traditional, laboratory-based data collection by allowing a more diverse and realistic set of observations. We also provide a *collaborative temporal* sampling model to further improve opportunistic sampling.

Finally, through deploying and experimenting with CrowdLearner, we reveal how developers and crowd workers reacted to this kind of system, and provide insights into designing such systems in the future.

RELATED WORK

Crowdsourcing has been used in the past to accomplish complex tasks by reducing them to smaller ones and validating the results from the crowd. Bernstein *et al.* use a Find-Fix-Verify approach to bring the wisdom of crowds to word processing [2]. Kittur and Kraut explore crowdsourcing with respect to creation of Wikipedia articles [15]. Heer and Bostock use crowdsourcing to assess visualization design [12]. Song *et al.* use real-time crowdsourcing to label unrecognized activities in activity recognition systems [25]. JANA is a commercial mobile crowdsourcing platform that rewards workers with airtime for performing tasks such as consumer research and product promotion. CrowdLearner uses crowdsourcing in a new light by automatically creating mobile recognizers for non-experts.

Prior work has explored how participants game crowdsourcing platforms and how to mitigate this problem [8, 14]. CrowdLearner workers perform simple tasks such as drawing a stroke gesture or labeling data samples (similar to Captchas [26]) to receive monetary compensation. Although we touch on mechanisms for validating sensor data, it is not our focus. As the first step to addressing the issue, we concentrate on enabling the end-to-end workflow for non-experts to create mobile recognizers using a crowdsourcing approach. However, the body of prior art focusing on validating crowd input would also prove useful in the case of CrowdLearner.

CrowdLearner is also closely related to crowdsensing [5, 7, 24] and *in situ* experience sampling [9, 10]. CrowdLearner shares the goal of previous work for collecting samples in users' natural environments. However, CrowdLearner goes beyond prior work by making sense of collected mobile sensor data and user labeling, and employing machine learning techniques to automatically generate recognizers for high-level events and user actions. In particular, CrowdLearner's data collection mechanisms and interfaces were designed for capturing mobile on-device sensor data and facilitating mobile user labeling, which are not designed for general mobile data collection purposes. As such, the outcome of CrowdLearner can be directly incorporated into developers' applications. Existing mobile crowdsensing platforms (e.g., CrowdLab [6], PRISM [7] and Medusa [21]) enable researchers and developers to run custom experiments on crowd devices. However, the level of knowledge required to setup and use these platforms place them beyond the reach of non-experts. CrowdLearner obviates the need for developers to have expert knowledge of sensing, data analysis, feature extraction, and classification.

Past work has looked at high-level tools for producing classifiers while reducing the need for expert knowledge of machine learning, e.g., MAGIC [1] and Exemplar [11]. CrowdLearner expands prior work by taking the event generation and data collection to mobile users' natural environments. It minimizes the burden on developers by eliminating recruiting and data collection. Furthermore, it creates recognizers for diverse devices that might be in use in the wild, rather than only a limited set of devices and sensors that are accessible to the developer.

INTERACTING WITH CROWDLEARNER

In this section, we discuss how a developer can create a recognition task and monitor its progress in CrowdLearner and how a mobile crowd worker interacts with the system to contribute labeled training data.

Developers: Creating a Recognition Task

To create a recognition task, a developer uses a web interface that streamlines task creation with a wizard. The wizard only requests a small amount of information, such as the targets to be recognized, sensors to use on a mobile device, data collection strategies and the amount of funds that the developer is willing to allocate for the task.

Adding a Task Description

The wizard includes four tabs for task *Description*, *Sensors*, *Targets*, and *Strategy*. On the Description tab, the developer provides basic information about a task, such as the task title, a short summary about the task, and a set of instructions for crowd workers to perform the task. Once the task is published, all this information is displayed on a worker's mobile device. For example, for the Motion Commands Task, the basic task information is as follows:

Title: Motion Commands; Summary: Perform a set of motion gestures with your phone; Instructions: Imagine you can operate your phone by moving it in certain ways, e.g., shaking the phone to ignore a phone call. We will ask you to perform a set of motions with your phone. Please hold your phone in one hand and make sure that your phone's screen is facing you when conducting these gestures. The top of your device should point away from you.

Selecting Mobile Sensors

On the Sensors tab (Figure 2), the developer selects sensor input for the recognizer to use. The developer can directly pick specific sensors from the list, such as Accelerometer, Microphone or Touchscreen. Based on the selected sensors, CrowdLearner automatically generates an appropriate feature vector for recognition (classification).

Alternatively, the developer can select a group of necessary sensors for recognizing high-level event types, such as Motion, Audio or Touch. These high-level event types are useful for developers who are less familiar with built-in sensors on mobile devices. For example, when a developer selects Motion, both Accelerometer and Gyroscope are selected, as they are typical sensors for inferring motion. Another advantage of this feature is that a developer can also explore how a sensor is typically used. When a sensor is selected, the corresponding high-level event type will be selected as well. For instance, selecting Microphone will also select the high-level event type, Audio.

Composing Recognition Targets

After choosing the sensors, the developer specifies the targets for the recognizer in the Targets tab (see Figure 3). The developer can give each target a name and describe it further by uploading an image or a video clip. Targets are presented to workers to perform actions or answer questions as instructed by the task. With images and video, developers can explain target actions that would otherwise be difficult to describe in text. For example, when instructing a worker

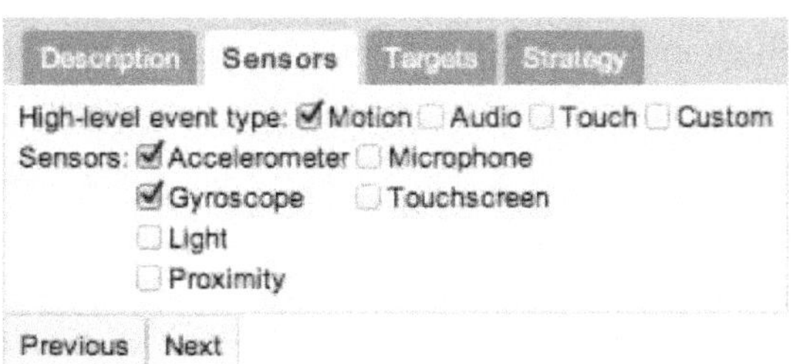

Figure 2. The developer selects which sensors CrowdLearner should sample. CrowdLearner decides on the set of features for training a recognizer based on the sensors.

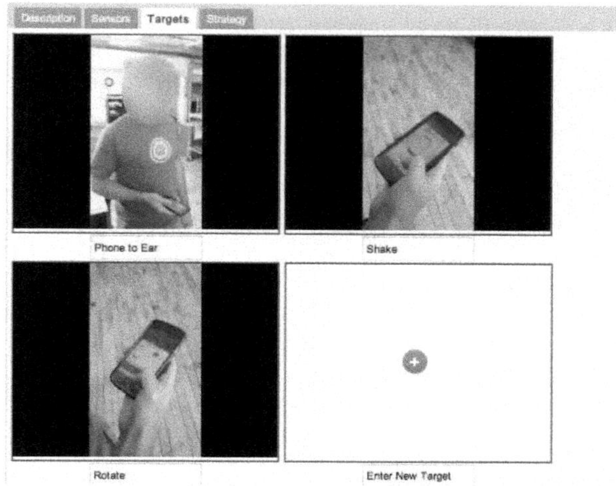

Figure 3. The developer specifies a set of targets along with images or videos for the task. The developer can add or edit targets in the wizard and view/play the media.

to perform a *Rotate* action in the Motion Commands task, the accompanying video for *Rotate* can easily explain how the worker should move his phone to perform the action.

Specifying Task Strategies

On the Strategy tab, developers provide the learning strategy and monetary constraints for performing the task. CrowdLearner supports two learning strategies: participatory and opportunistic sampling. The developer chooses between "*learn when I ask the user to do something*"—in a participatory fashion—or "*learn when something interesting happens*"—an opportunistic fashion. The developer decides on how she wants to collect data. For instance, for a task concerning touchscreen handwritten symbols, she would choose participatory sampling because this kind of behavior—writing specific symbols on the touchscreen—only happens when the worker is asked to do so. However, for a task concerning daily physical activity, she would use opportunistic sampling, as events can occur even when the phone is not in active use. The developer also selects the maximum number of questions a worker could answer, the compensation per question, and the total funds allocated for the task. These constraints ensure that the generated recognizer does not rely on samples from only a small group of workers, and that CrowdLearner does not go beyond the developer's budget. Once the developer is satisfied with the task, she can publish it to CrowdLearner, which automatically distributes the task to the workers.

Crowd Workers: Performing a CrowdLearner Task

CrowdLearner distributes a task to a worker's mobile device if the sensors required by the task are available on the device. On the mobile client's main screen, workers can see all available tasks and also check the rewards accumulated so far (Figure 1). After selecting a task, the worker will be greeted with the task instructions. On the next screen, he will see the amount of compensation received for each question answered (i.e., each sample contributed). If motivated, he can proceed to participate in the task. Depending on the type of task chosen, participatory or opportunistic, the worker performs the task through a different procedure.

Participatory Tasks

During a participatory task, CrowdLearner prompts the worker to perform a particular action (considered a question in CrowdLearner) at a time. The task repeats a Question and Answer pattern. On the Question screen (Figure 4), CrowdLearner instructs the worker the action to perform by showing the action name along with a pictorial or video description. On the following Answer screen (Figure 4), the worker has the opportunity to perform the action, redo it if needed, or skip it. The order of questions is randomized.

Once the worker understands the target action, he can go to next screen. Depending on the type of sensors that the task involves, CrowdLearner presents different screens to the worker. For a touchscreen gesture task, because a worker is expected to interact on the touchscreen, such as drawing a gesture symbol, CrowdLearner leaves the screen blank with only the name of the symbol and its associated media displayed at the right corner. The worker needs to recall the target gesture and draw it on the screen. Once finished, the worker can click on a button to go to the next question.

Unlike a touchscreen that stops sensing when a worker lifts his finger from the screen, sensors such as accelerometers continuously sense. As a result, we need a mechanism for the system and the worker to agree on the beginning and the end of sensing. For example, if a worker has to click a button to signal the system to stop sensing, the motion for stopping the sensing will be captured as part of the target action. In addition, the action that a worker is to perform puts the phone in a state where he cannot interact with the display. For instance, for the "Put the phone to ear" action in the Motion Commands task, we do not want workers to place the phone to their ear and then bring it down to confirm the answer. To address this issue, CrowdLearner employs a count down timer. Once a worker moves to the Answer Question screen, a timer starts and the worker is to perform the action before the timer ends (see Figure 4). The worker is instructed to not move the phone or perform any other actions until the timer runs out and he hears an audio notification. We currently use 3 seconds for the timer, which we empirically found is an upper bound for the execution time for many motion-related actions.

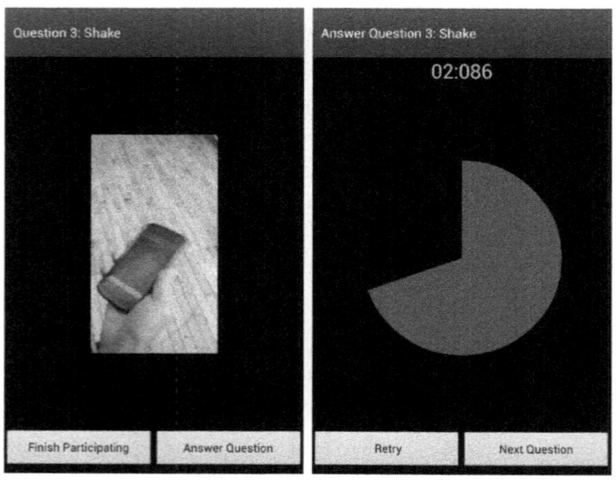

Figure 4. On the Question screen, workers are prompted to perform an action through a target and a pictorial or video description. On the Answer screen, workers perform the action instructed on the previous Question screen. A count down timer informs when to perform the action.

Opportunistic Tasks

An opportunistic task is designed to capture events (training samples) that do not occur at a predefined time, such as walking or biking. These events are difficult to capture using a participatory approach in which a worker is asked to perform a target action. When a worker signs up for an opportunistic task, such as one collecting daily physical activity samples, the worker does not need to perform any action at the signup. Instead, CrowdLearner will notify the worker to answer a question regarding an observed event. The answer to this question effectively labels a collected sample.

However, there is a dilemma in executing opportunistic tasks. When the system observes an event of interest during the day, asking a question about the event may disturb the worker's ongoing activity, e.g., the worker might be biking and having difficulty to take out the phone and answer a question. Therefore, it is impractical to ask a worker to answer the question immediately when an event occurs. To address this problem, we employ a notification and expiration mechanism. When an event of interest occurs, the system sends the worker's phone a notification along with a distinct vibration pattern. The worker does not have to answer the notification immediately.

When a worker joins an opportunistic task, the system plays a sample of the vibration pattern and instructs what the vibration means: "*CrowdLearner will send you a notification question along this vibration pattern whenever it observes something relevant to the task. You don't have to respond to the question right away, but remember your state at the time of vibration for answering the question later.*" We designed the vibration pattern to be similar to SOS in Morse code, which is distinctive from many vibration patterns used by other applications. However, a worker may not be able to answer the question for a while, which may lead to him forgetting the event. Therefore, CrowdLearner keeps the notification question available for a limited amount of time only. We chose 30 minutes to ensure that the workers are able to recall their state at the time of the vibration.

When selecting their state at the time of the event, workers have other choices available in addition to the targets specified by the developer. These choices consist of, "*Didn't have the phone on me*", "*Don't remember*" and "*None of the above*". Based on the answer selected by the worker, the event is used as a positive sample, a negative sample, or ignored. Positive samples confirm a certain type of event; whereas negative samples are discounted for a particular event. In an actual deployment, the system could avoid workers who provide too many negative samples to prevent workers from gaming the system.

Developers: Monitoring the Progress via a Dashboard

The developer can monitor the progress of the task through a web-based dashboard. The dashboard shows a list of all the tasks created by the developer. By selecting a task, the developer can view the accuracy of the recognizer and its progression through a chart. A table presents the accuracy and number of samples for each target. The developer can also view the total amount of funds allocated and remaining, the number of participating workers and sample, and the average number of samples per worker. The dashboard also allows the developer to allocate more funds to the task.

IMPLEMENTATION

In this section, we describe the technical details of our current implementation. These specific technical aspects are not our focus, but are essential for creating a fully-functional system that can be deployed in the wild to examine the workflow of CrowdLearner. We built CrowdLearner as a cloud service. It uses Google App Engine (GAE) to serve tasks and store training data, recognizers, and performance measures. We used Google Web Toolkit (GWT) for implementing the web-based task creation wizard and presenting recognizer evaluation. The CrowedLearner client, used by workers to perform tasks, is implemented based on the Android platform.

Sampling

CrowdLearner aims to abstract away sampling and data collection. Currently, it allows a task to leverage several popular mobile sensors as shown in Figure 2. CrowdLearner collects the profile for each type of device presented in the workers' pool of devices. These device profiles enable CrowdLearner to account for variations in device sensors and packaging by producing a recognizer for each type of device. A default sampling rate is set for each type of sensor at which samples from all devices are resampled, e.g., 40Hz for accelerometers.

Sampling Conditions for Opportunistic Tasks

For opportunistic tasks, we have a set of requirements before any data collection takes place to improve user experience and also to respect workers' computational resources. Opportunistic sampling takes place at random intervals throughout the day. In our current implementation, data collections are set to occur 30 to 90 minutes apart, which enable CrowdLearner to work around workers' daily routines. The sampling duration is set to be 30 seconds. Nevertheless, the sampling interval and duration should be developer-configurable in actual deployments.

Opportunistic sampling is activated upon satisfying several requirements. The mobile client checks local time to ensure that data collection takes place between 9am and 8pm. We made a usability trade-off here, in that we do not want to disturb workers at night. However, this prevents capturing events such as eating breakfast or brushing in the morning. We also require the worker's device to have at least 25% of its battery capacity charged, to prevent CrowdLearner from depleting the device's battery power.

Validating Samples

Prior work in crowdsourcing has used verification questions and obtaining multiple samples in order to validate samples [14]. CrowdLearner requests multiple samples from workers for each of the targets. Since CrowdLearner focuses on building recognizers, it can use classifiers that are resistant to outliers such as SVM as is the case with our current prototype. Alternatively, we can train a k-nearest neighbor classifier in parallel to detect and discard outliers, although false detection may skew sample distributions.

Feature Extraction

Feature extraction is dependent on the types of sensors selected. In CrowdLearner, each sensor employs a different process to generate features, e.g., a featurization for touchscreen traces might not be appropriate for accelerometer readings. When multiple sensors are selected for a task, CrowdLearner combines the feature vector of all sensors to form a single vector. This modular design allows us to easily incorporate new sensors when they become available. For accelerometer or gyroscope readings, we currently use common features such as means, standard deviations, FFT coefficients, cepstral coefficients, spectral entropy, correlations, and integrations [17]. For the touchscreen, we use features similar to prior work for gesture and handwriting recognition [19]. When combining the features from different sensors, we always concatenate them in the same order.

Generating a Recognizer through Continuous Learning

CrowdLearner continuously updates the recognizer as workers provide more samples and allows the developer to monitor the progress of the task and acquire the latest recognizer or one generated in the past at any time. We first seed our learning process with a *null* recognizer, which simply returns a null target for any sample received. We keep a counter for the number of errors that the recognizer has made for predicting each newly observed sample. Once the error count reaches a threshold—20 in our case, we generate a new recognizer with the data that has been collected, and reset the error counter and repeat the process.

In the beginning of the process, as more samples come in, the classifier is likely to make more errors and rebuilds (retrains) more frequently. With this *valved continuous learning* process, CrowdLearner continuously learns from the samples that it receives, but also does not spend too many cycles retraining a recognizer when it would only provide marginal benefit. As a proof of concept, we use an implementation of Linear SVM, which performs reasonably well and quickly for many classification purposes [3].

To present the learning progress to the developer, CrowdLearner visualizes the performance of a generated recognizer based on 10-fold cross validation that splits the collected samples based on workers.

EVALUATION

We deployed CrowdLearner internally in a large IT company to 72 participants (M=51, F=21) for a period of 2.5 weeks. We recruited workers by emailing company-wide lists, and sent the mobile client via email. We never met or had any direct contact with the workers. Our workers were between 18 and 55 years old, with approximately 75% of ages falling uniformly between 18 and 35. Workers had a variety of occupations including Administrative, Legal, HR and engineering. We evaluated CrowdLeaner through 6 recognition tasks. At the end of our study, we awarded workers monetary compensation for the credits earned by emailing gift certificates. Workers were paid $0.10 for each question they answered, and up to $10 per task. This remote hands-off deployment is a good approximation for a realistic crowdsourcing platform.

Experimental Tasks

We created 4 of the recognition tasks ourselves. The Media Player Gestures task was used to generate a recognizer for 10 stroke gestures for controlling a media player application: Play, Pause, Stop, Rewind, Fast Forward, Previous, Next, Accept, Reject, and Help. The $1 Recognizer Gestures task concerned 16 stroke gestures as defined by Wobbrock *et al.* [29]. The Phone Call Motion task involved 3 motion gestures for receiving phone calls: Shake, Rotate, and Place Phone To Ear. The Daily Physical Activities task was to detect four user activities: Still (sitting or standing), Walking, Biking, and Riding in a car or on a bus. The Daily Physical Activities task employed opportunistic sampling.

To understand how developers would react to CrowdLearner, we invited two developers, who were not involved with our project, to use CrowdLearner to create mobile recognizers that can be useful to their projects. One developer wanted to recognize handwritten digits 0 through 9 for a Number Pad application. The other developer created the Directional Motion task for recognizing 5 motion gestures: Left, Right, Up, Down, and Double Flip [22]. The directional commands are flicks toward the designated direction and back to the initial position similar to those defined in [18].

Experimental Results

To deal with device variation, CrowdLearner builds a recognizer for each type of device available in the worker pool. Table 1 shows the recognition performances for Galaxy Nexus devices, which were most common in our pool of devices. In general, the tasks involving touchscreen stroke gestures performed well and it took less than 2 hours and $10 for their recognizers to reach 80% of the final accuracy. With respect to motion gesture recognition, recognizers reached 80% of the final accuracy within 3 hours.

The Phone Call Motion task performed reasonably with 77% final accuracy. However, the Directional Motion task performed poorly with final accuracy of 42%. Upon our examination of the results, we noticed that the recognizer performed well with respect to detecting Double Flip and separating vertical and horizontal flicks. However, it failed to discern different directions within vertical or horizontal movements—it could not separate Up from Down or Left from Right. By carefully examining the collected data, we found although our current featurization mechanism for accelerometer and gyro readings is able to capture the overall movement profile of the phone, e.g., rotating versus shifting, it is ineffective to capture detailed sequence variation in motions such as these quick directional flicks. We can address this issue by introducing features that can better capture the temporal characteristics of motion or employing more advanced featurization techniques (e.g., [17]).

Opportunistic Learning

While the Daily Physical Activities task achieved 78% accuracy, it was most effective at recognizing sitting or standing events. Specifically, the produced recognizer detected over 99% of sitting events. However, it only recognized 2.5% of walking and 2.5% of riding in a car or bus activities and did not recognize any of the biking activities (3 total). We attribute this performance to the scarcity of non-stationary activities during data collection. Moreover, physical activity recognition using a single sensor pack with a non-static location on the body is challenging [17]. Nevertheless, we still observed some interesting trends when examining the data for the Daily Physical Activities task.

Based on our logs, the workers answered only 25% of all CrowdLearner opportunistic notifications. We observed that motion activities were generally sparse. In one week of data collection (including the weekend), we collected 285 samples for Still (sitting or standing), 40 for Walking, 3 for Biking, and 44 for Riding on a bus or in a car.

There are several ways to address the scarcity of sampled target events. One approach is to employ a base event detector that decides if an event of interest is likely happening so as to help CrowdLearner determine when to perform opportunistic sampling. However, developing an effective

Task (Number of Targets)	Workers	Samples	Time to 80% A*	Funds to 80% A*	Final Accuracy (A)
Media Player Gestures (10)	52	2119	1 hr	$5	99.2%
$1 Recognizer Gestures (16)	48	2200	1.5 hrs	$5	98.4%
Number Pad Gestures (10)	47	2473	1 hr	$10	95.2%
Phone Call Motion (3)	45	1487	3 hrs	$12	77.4%
Directional Motion (5)	34	1227	3 hrs	$5	42.2%
Daily Physical Activities (4)	30	368	2 hr	$3	78.1%

Table 1: Participation and Accuracy for CrowdLearner tasks (*80% of Final Accuracy).

base event detector itself might be challenging. A developer can create the detector in the laboratory or also in CrowdLearner.

By examining the occurrence of these activities (see Figure 5), we found the workers were most likely to be on the move during the evening, and often moved around noon-time. We conjecture that these events correspond to heading home from work and going for lunch, respectively. Considering the emerging trends, we devised a model for sampling events based on their occurrence, which we will discuss in detail in the Collaborative Temporal Sampling section.

Sampling in the Wild

To understand how CrowdLearner data, which is collected in the wild, is different from data collected in laboratories, we compared the dataset of CrowdLearner's $1 Recognizer Gestures task to the original $1 Recognizer dataset. The original dataset was collected in the laboratory from ten individuals and is published on the web [29]. CrowdLearner aims to collect and train on data generated in users' natural environments. To test out the theory that CrowdLearner data collection exhibits more variation than that conducted in a laboratory environment, we ran the $1 Recognizer algorithm—based on template matching (or the Nearest Neighbor)—on both datasets. To be comparable with the original $1 dataset, we limited our dataset to samples collected from 10 individuals only, and manually checked them for mislabeled data. When manually (visually) examining our entire dataset of 2200 samples, we found 19 outliers. 12 of these outliers were gestures for another label and 7 were not distinguishable to be any of the targets. Since each gesture might have an unequal number of samples in the CrowdLearner dataset due to the uncontrolled collection process, we sampled the original $1 dataset to have the same distribution as our dataset across the three gesture speeds present in the original $1 dataset. We then trained and tested the $1 Recognizer on all possible training and testing pairs across the two datasets. In all tests, we trained on half the data and tested on the remaining half.

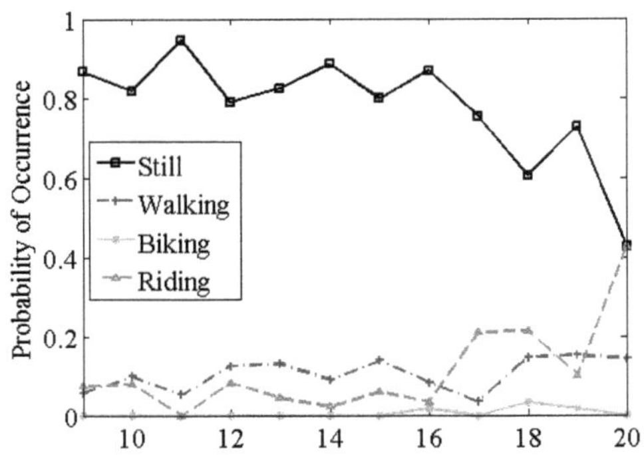

Figure 5. Probability of observing activities aggregated across users. Our workers were more likely to be on the move at noon and during the evening.

Training and testing on the $1 dataset produced an accuracy of 99.2%. This was not surprising as it is in line with the published performance of the $1 Recognizer. Training and testing on the CrowdLearner's $1 dataset produced 81.2% accuracy. However, the most interesting results were obtained when we trained on CrowdLearner's $1 dataset and tested on the original $1 dataset (87.9% accuracy) versus training on the original $1 dataset and testing on CrowdLearner's $1 dataset (77.7% accuracy). As $1 Recognizer is a template matching gesture recognition algorithm, these results indicated that gestures collected in the wild (via CrowdLearner) exhibit more variation. Specifically data produced by the crowd is more representative as it can describe data present in the $1 dataset, however, is not as describable using the $1 dataset templates.

Feedback from the Workers

At the end of our study, we asked our worker participants to provide feedback through a web-based survey. We asked workers general questions regarding CrowdLearner and also specific questions regarding each of the tasks. Participating workers rated ease of use, usability of the user interface, awareness of availability of tasks, adequacy of compensation per question, awareness of total rewards, and the possibility that they would perform tasks using the CrowdLearner app in the future on a 5-point Likert scale. More than 75% of the workers responded positively to each of the aforementioned attributes of the system (Agree or Strongly Agree).

Two worker participants commented that the instructions for motion-related tasks (target and associated video) were given too often and requested to be able to skip them faster. One worker mentioned that because of the audio notification for the count down timer, he was not able to perform the Phone Call Motion and Directional Motion tasks quietly during down times (e.g., on his subway commute) without disturbing others in his vicinity. This would suggest providing an option of audio or vibration notifications at the end of the count down timer. He preferred more silent tasks during these periods (e.g., Media Player Gestures).

With respect to the Daily Physical Activities task, most workers found the vibration helpful in remembering their state (85% Agree or Strongly Agree). Similarly, they found that knowing the time that the activity occurred was helpful (over 85% Agree or Strongly Agree). However, workers were divided with respect to usually not having their phone on them when the phone vibrated (median=Neutral) or not being able remember the event (median=Disagree). This confirmed our log-based finding that workers answered 25% of the opportunistic notifications. One worker did not find the vibration notifications useful as she used a pouch to hold her phone. Another worker suggested giving workers the ability to inform CrowdLearner about their activities beforehand: "allow the user to say 'I'm about to go Biking'" to enable sampling of non-stationary activities.

Feedback from the Developers

Both developers found CrowdLearner easy to use with respect to creating tasks and targets, associating media with targets, and monitoring the performance of the recognizers, responding positively with Agree and Strongly Agree on a 5-point Likert scale.

The creator of the Directional Motion task (referred to as C1 hereafter) commented that it would be useful to allow workers to try out a task without affecting the results for the recognizer, specifically for when they are unsure as to how to perform a certain gesture. This would be a valuable improvement as some worker participants also mentioned that they were not sure what to do when first starting a task. C1 felt that the produced recognizer was muddled by too many poor initial samples. He also felt that it would be useful to allow the developer to select a particular set of samples to train the final recognizer. The creator of the Number Pad Gestures task (C2) also suggested being able to select a specific set of samples for training and being able to look at and validate the samples provided by workers. C2 recommended adding information about whether the recognizer was able to classify the samples successfully, and presenting the developer with visualizations for clusters of samples to support inference of general types and trends.

COLLABORATIVE TEMPORAL SAMPLING

One important lesson that we learned from the experiment is that it is challenging to determine when to perform opportunistic sampling. Sampling uniformly in time can be inefficient, especially when some of the target events occur less frequently, such as biking or driving. By examining the dataset of the Daily Physical Activities task, we discovered that the occurrence of target events follows temporal trends. As a result, we devised a model to discover these trends in order to enable more intelligent sampling.

With this model, CrowdLearner can sample conditionally based on when an event of interest is likely to occur. More specifically, when a worker's device wakes up, it first checks with the CrowdLearner service to determine if the wake up time is associated with a period of uninteresting samples, e.g., when workers would be most likely sitting. If this is the case, CrowdLearner would inform the device not to sample. We present here the result of an offline analysis of the Daily Physical Activities task to evaluate our conditional sampling model.

The conditional sampling model consists of two components. One component captures general trends for the entire worker population, while the other captures trends for a specific worker. These two components perform in an online fashion in that they are trained based on prior days of data and then combined to decide whether to sample. When an opportunistic task first starts, any time of the day is a "good" time for sampling—a uniform distribution. However, each day, the model is updated to learn from prior days' samples. Both the individual and population components are trained in the same fashion. For the individual component, only a single worker's data is used for training, whereas for the global component, data from the entire population is used.

We train each component using a system of linear equations for each target, and add extra constraints to smooth the data. Specifically, we divide days to N timeslots, where N is dependent on the sampling interval. For our case, since we sample approximately once an hour, N is 168. Timeslots are indexed in day-major order with the first timeslot starting at 00:00 on Sunday. We add an equation to the system for each timeslot for a particular label, where the probability of occurrence of event x in that timeslot is defined as:

$$p_i = n_x / n_{total}$$

We also add constraints to smooth the probabilities:

$$(\lambda/2)p_{i-1} + (1-\lambda)p_i + (\lambda/2)p_{i+1} = p_i$$

λ is between 0 and 0.5 and controls the smoothing of each p_i. Additional constrains may be added to control variations in weekdays or weekends. Using this system of equations and a least squares solver, the probabilities of occurrence for each target can be computed to create a sampling model. Figure 6 presents the model for riding in a vehicle.

Once probabilities are generated for each target, sampling can be done to either obtain a more diversified set of samples, or a different criterion based on targets deemed interesting. We combine the individual and global models linearly:

$$p_i = (1-\alpha)p_i^{global} + \alpha p_i^{individual}$$

where α is between 0 and 1. α is learnt based on correct predictions using the individual component, in the following fashion:

$$\alpha(t+1) = \alpha(t) + \gamma\left(F\left(p_{i,t}^{individual}\right)\right)$$

where γ controls how quickly α updates, and F outputs 1 for correct predictions and -1 for incorrect ones. For our evaluation, we set alpha to be a constant of 0.5.

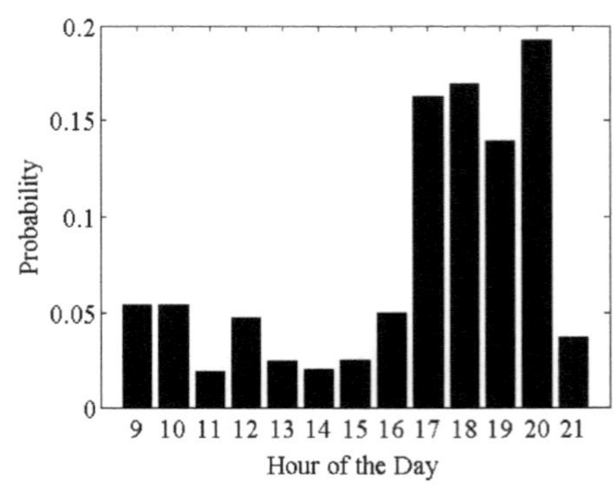

Figure 6. Global sampling model trained for riding in a vehicle based on data collected for the Daily Physical Activity Task. Workers are more likely to ride in a vehicle early in the morning and in the evening hours.

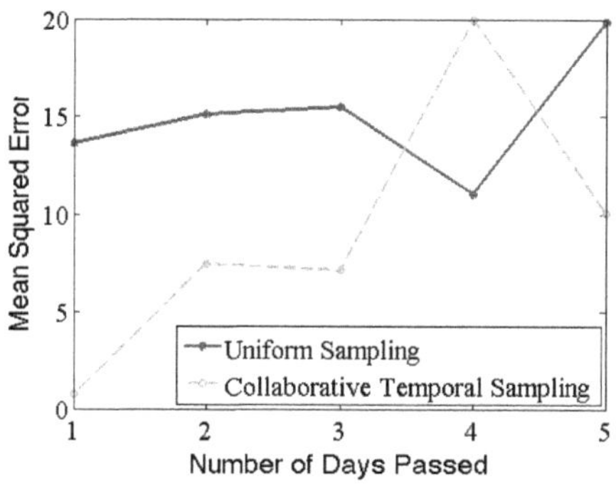

Figure 7. Collaborative temporal sampling performance compared to uniform sampling for the Riding in a Car or on a Bus target. The Collaborative Temporal Sampling model has a jump after the 4th day as the worker shifts to also drive in the morning.

Using the aforementioned approach, we created a sampling model for the Daily Physical Activity task and verified our results by training on prior days of data, and testing on current day's events. Specifically, we tested the model against a uniform sampling approach for the riding in a car or on a bus target. The results are based on data from the global model and one worker's individual model. Figure 7 shows the mean squared error (MSE) for the conditional sampling model and the baseline approach using uniform sampling. The error is computed as the temporal distance (as the number of hours) between when the model predicts an event would occur and when the event actually occurred. In Figure 7, we see a jump in MSE for our model after day 4. This corresponds to a shift from the worker's habits to also drive in the morning. We see great potential in using collaborative temporal sampling models to learn about people's activities in an opportunistic fashion. The model helps improve the answering rate for opportunistic sampling and optimizes the power and computation consumption on the worker's device to obtain useful samples.

CRITICAL REFLECTION

CrowdLearner is the first general end-to-end framework for non-machine learning experts to quickly create recognizers with ecologically valid data. It eliminates the effort for data collection and the technical barrier for training and testing recognizers. However, its machine learning component currently offers a single classification model and a limited set of features, which are insufficient for all kinds of recognition tasks. As our experiments indicated, CrowdLearner performed well for stroke gestures but less than ideal for motion-based recognition. We can address this issue by offering a suite of machine learning techniques and featurization mechanisms and enabling CrowdLearner to evaluate these alternatives in parallel—automatically selecting an optimal one for a specific task.

It is also possible to expose more learning parameters to the developer for finely tuning a recognizer. For example, popular ML toolkits such as Weka allow developers to adjust various ML parameters specific to a model. However, adjusting these parameters often requires the developer to have a deeper understanding about the machine learning techniques, which deviates from our motivation to support developers who have no ML expertise. We can potentially benefit from extensive work in interactive ML (e.g., [20]) that attempts to make it easy for average developers to adjust and iterate on ML techniques.

The performance of CrowdLearner is also impacted by sensors that are available on a target mobile device and the type of recognition task that the developer orders. Given the sensors on a mobile device, the targets in a task might be fundamentally ambiguous (e.g., sitting or standing still) or too fine-grained to be captured (e.g., minor gradual movements of the device). As such, it is crucial to communicate with developers about what CrowdLearner is capable of recognizing and explain reasons for poorly performed tasks.

Similar to much design-oriented work, iteration is essential. More relevantly, Patel *et al.* reveal the critical role that iteration plays in designing a machine learning method [20]. Currently, CrowdLearner supports in-flight changes such as adding more funds to a task, editing the task's name and instructions, adding or removing targets, and changing the targets' associated media. It would be valuable to explore a more systematic support for iteration in CrowdLearner. We can potentially add advanced iteration support that are conceptually akin to Version Control System mechanisms, e.g., versioning, merging and branching [23], for better managing changes and supporting collaboration in CrowdLearner.

CrowdLearner adopts a continuous learning concept by rebuilding and improving recognizers as more workers are added and more samples are collected. This process can be furthered by also automatically synchronizing the performance of the CrowdLearner recognizers that are active in the field. Specifically, these recognizers could send their incorrectly recognized observations to the CrowdLearner service for further improvement of recognition. CrowdLearner could also adopt active-learning concepts to achieve greater accuracy with fewer samples by requesting workers to perform specific gestures or actions [4], e.g., gestures that are often misclassified.

CrowdLearner mitigates the problem of variability in devices by maintaining profiles of workers' devices and building a recognizer for each type of device present. As an artifact of this approach, popular devices will have more training data and potentially more accurate recognizers. However, there still exists variability in samples with respect to workers. A problem that is inherent to the use of crowd workers is that characteristics such as age, gender, and physical attributes can affect the samples provided. We do not explore this problem ourselves, however, prior work by Lane *et al.* has presented promising results in using Social Networks to identify people with similar characteristics to build recognizers that are tailored towards individuals and more specific user types [16]. Similar approaches may be used in CrowdLearner to improve recognizer performance. Another solution would be to obtain demographic information from workers and perform intelligent crowd sampling based on demographics and trends, similar to how we use activity trends for the temporal conditional sampling.

CrowdLearner currently enables a "free market" in which developers determine the allocations of funds for tasks and workers freely opt in or out. However, it is valuable to offer additional support for fund allocation, such as suggesting how much a sample or interaction is worth. It is also worth investigating how to incentivize workers for specific targets, e.g., by increasing compensation for targets with fewer samples. In addition to using monetary compensation as a general incentive, we can potentially leverage game-based schemes (e.g., [13]) for certain tasks such that workers can motivate each other to contribute more quality data.

CONCLUSION

We presented CrowdLearner, a crowdsourcing platform that automatically creates recognizers for non-machine learning experts for mobile applications. CrowdLearner reduces the barriers presented by recruiting participants, data collection and labeling, and the technical knowledge required to train recognizers. We discussed our design and implementation of CrowdLearner as a cloud service and presented the findings of our evaluation through experimenting with 6 recognition tasks with 72 workers and 2 developers. Our results provide insight into designing future crowdsourcing systems for machine learning tasks.

REFERENCES

1. Ashbrook, D. and Starner, T. MAGIC: a motion gesture design tool. In *Proc. CHI 2010*, ACM Press (2010).
2. Bernstein, M.S., Little, G., Miller, R.C., Hartmann, B., Ackerman, M. S., Karger, D.R., Crowell, D. and Panovich, K. Soylent: a word processor with a crowd inside. In *Proc. UIST 2010*, ACM Press (2010).
3. Boser, B., Guyon, I.M. and Vapnik, V.N. A training algorithm for optimal margin classifiers. In *Proc. COLT 1992*, ACM Press (1992).
4. Burr, S. Active Learning Literature Survey. Comp. Sciences Tech. Report 1648, University of Wisconsin-Madison, 2009.
5. Campbell, A.T., Eisenman, S.B., Lane, N.D., Miluzzo, E. and Peterson, R.A. People-centric urban sensing. In *Proc. WICON 2006*, ACM Press (2006).
6. Cuervo, E., Gilbert, P., Wu, B. and Cox, L.P. CrowdLab: An Architecture for Volunteer Mobile Testbeds. In *Proc. COMSNETS 2011*, IEEE (2011).
7. Das, T., Mohan, P., Padmanabhan, V.N., Ramjee, R. and Sharma, A. PRISM: platform for remote sensing using smartphones. In *Proc. MobiSys 2010*, ACM Press (2010).
8. Downs, J.S., Holbrook, M.B., Sheng, S., and Cranor, L.F. Are your participants gaming the system? screening mechanical turk workers. In *Proc. CHI 2010*, ACM Press (2010).
9. Froehlich, J., Chen, M.Y., Consolvo, S., Harrison, B. and Landay, J.A. MyExperience: a system for in situ tracing and capturing of user feedback on mobile phones. In *Proc. MobiSys 2007*, ACM Press (2007).
10. Gajos, K.Z., Reinecke, K. and Herrmann, C. Accurate Measurements of Pointing Performance from In Situ Observations. In *Proc. CHI 2012*, ACM Press (2012).
11. Hartmann, B., Abdulla, L., Mittal, M. and Klemmer, S.R. Authoring sensor-based interactions by demonstration with direct manipulation and pattern recognition. In *Proc. CHI 2007*, ACM Press (2007).
12. Heer, J. and Bostock, M. Crowdsourcing graphical perception: using mechanical turk to assess visualization design. In *Proc. CHI 2010*, ACM Press (2010).
13. Henze, N., Pielot, M., Poppinga, B., Schinke, T. and Boll, S. My App is an Experiment: Experience from User Studies in Mobile App Stores. *International Journal of Mobile Human Computer Interaction* 3, 4 (2011), 71-91.
14. Kittur, A., Chi, E.H. and Suh, B. Crowdsourcing user studies with Mechanical Turk. In *Proc. CHI 2008*, ACM Press (2008).
15. Kittur, A. and Kraut, R.E. Harnessing the wisdom of crowds in wikipedia: quality through coordination. In *Proc. CSCW 2008*, ACM Press (2008).
16. Lane, N.D., Xu, Y., Lu, H., Campbell, A.T., Choudhury, T., and Eisenman, S.B. Cooperative Communities (CoCo): Exploiting Social Networks for Large-scale Modeling of Human Behavior. *Pervasive Computing*, IEEE (2011).
17. Lester, J., Choudhury, T. and Borriello, G. A practical approach to recognizing physical activities. In *Proc. PERVASIVE 2006*, Springer (2006).
18. Negulescu, M., Ruiz, J., Li, Y. and Lank, E. Tap, Swipe, or Move: Attentional Demands for Distracted Smartphone Input. In *Proc. AVI 2012*, ACM Press (2012).
19. Ouyang T. and Li, Y. Bootstrapping personal gesture shortcuts with the wisdom of the crowd and handwriting recognition. In *Proc. CHI 2012*, ACM Press (2012).
20. Patel, K., Bancroft, N., Drucker, S.M., Fogarty, J., Ko, A., and Landay, J.A. Gestalt: Integrated Support for Implementation and Analysis in Machine Learning Processes. In *Proc. UIST 2010*, ACM Press (2010).
21. Ra, M., Liu, B., La Porta, T.F. and Govindan, R. Medusa: a programming framework for crowd-sensing applications. In *Proc. MobiSys 2012*, ACM Press (2012).
22. Ruiz, J., and Li, Y. DoubleFlip: A Motion Gesture Delimiter for Mobile Interaction. In *Proc. CHI 2011*, ACM Press (2011).
23. Ruparelia, N. B. The History of Version Control. SIGSOFT Softw. Eng. Notes, 35, 1 (2010), 5-9.
24. Shepard, C., Rahmati, A., Tossell, C., Zhong, L. and Kortum, P. LiveLab: measuring wireless networks and smartphone users in the field. SIGMETRICS Perform. Eval. Rev. 38, 3 (2011), 15-20.
25. Song, Y., Lasecki, W., Bigham, J., and Kautz, H. Training Activity Recogntion Systems Online Using Real-Time CrowdSourcing. In *Proc. UBICOMP 2012*, ACM Press.
26. Von Ahn, L., Blum, M. and Langford, J. Telling humans and computers apart automatically. *Commun. ACM 47, 2* (2004), 56-60.
27. Westeyn, T., Brashear, H., Atrash, A. and Starner, T. Georgia tech gesture toolkit: supporting experiments in gesture recognition. In *Proc. ICMI 2003*, ACM Press (2003).
28. Witten, I. H. and Frank, E. *Data Mining: Practical Machine Learning Tools and Techniques*. Morgan Kaufmann, San Francisco, 2 (2005).
29. Wobbrock, J.O., Wilson, A.D. and Li, Y. Gestures without libraries, toolkits or training: a $1 recognizer for user interface prototypes. In *Proc. UIST 2007*, ACM Press (2007).

Cobi: A Community-Informed Conference Scheduling Tool

Juho Kim[1] Haoqi Zhang[1,2] Paul André[3] Lydia B. Chilton[4] Wendy Mackay[5]
Michel Beaudouin-Lafon[6] Robert C. Miller[1] Steven P. Dow[3]

[1]MIT CSAIL
Cambridge, MA, USA
{juhokim, rcm}@mit.edu

[2]Northwestern University
Evanston, IL, USA
hq@eecs.northwestern.edu

[3]HCI Institute, CMU
Pittsburgh, PA, USA
{pandre, spdow}@cs.cmu.edu

[4]University of Washington
Seattle, WA, USA
hmslydia@cs.uw.edu

[5]INRIA
Orsay, France
mackay@lri.fr

[6]Université de Paris-Sud
Orsay, France
mbl@lri.fr

ABSTRACT
Effectively planning a large multi-track conference requires an understanding of the preferences and constraints of organizers, authors, and attendees. Traditionally, the onus of scheduling the program falls on a few dedicated organizers. Resolving conflicts becomes difficult due to the size and complexity of the schedule and the lack of insight into community members' needs and desires. *Cobi* presents an alternative approach to conference scheduling that engages the entire community in the planning process. Cobi comprises (a) communitysourcing applications that collect preferences, constraints, and affinity data from community members, and (b) a visual scheduling interface that combines communitysourced data and constraint-solving to enable organizers to make informed improvements to the schedule. This paper describes Cobi's scheduling tool and reports on a live deployment for planning CHI 2013, where organizers considered input from 645 authors and resolved 168 scheduling conflicts. Results show the value of integrating community input with an intelligent user interface to solve complex planning tasks.

Author Keywords
Cobi; conference scheduling; mixed-initiative; constraint solving; crowdsourcing; community; communitysourcing

ACM Classification Keywords
H5.2 Information Interfaces and Presentation (e.g., HCI): User Interfaces - Graphical user interfaces

INTRODUCTION
Creating a compelling schedule for a large conference is a difficult task. Hundreds of accepted submissions must be scheduled into sessions across multiple days and rooms, while accounting for the multi-faceted preferences and constraints of organizers, authors, and attendees. Organizers aim to create thematic sessions, avoid scheduling related papers or the same presenters in opposing sessions, and generally make the program interesting for attendees with different interests.

Figure 1. A small group of organizers and associate chairs create a preliminary CHI program on paper.

To better understand this challenge, we observed the schedule creation process for CHI, the largest human-computer interaction conference: CHI 2013 received over 2260 submissions and accepted more than 500 to be scheduled in 16 simultaneous sessions spanning four days. Scheduling CHI involves two stages. Once papers are accepted, a small group of associate chairs help the conference organizers to roughly create categories and suggest sessions. Over the next two days, the organizers and a few assistants build a rough preliminary schedule (see Figure 1). The process is paper-based, collaborative, and time-consuming; its output is highly dependent upon the specific knowledge of the individuals in the room. In stage two, organizers refine the rough schedule to create the final program. They attempt to resolve conflicts, handle stray papers, respond to last minute changes, and generally look for ways to improve the program. The organizers use a script to check that no presenter is scheduled to be in two places at once, but otherwise, all changes are made manually. Interviews with past organizers revealed that the process was extremely time-consuming, and that resolving conflicts was "painstaking" due to schedule complexity and the lack of feedback on whether changes resolved existing conflicts or created new ones.

Despite organizers' best intentions and efforts, previous CHI programs often contained incoherent sessions, similarly-

UIST'13, October 8–11, 2013, St. Andrews, United Kingdom.

ACM 978-1-4503-2268-3/13/10...$15.00.
http://dx.doi.org/10.1145/2501988.2502034

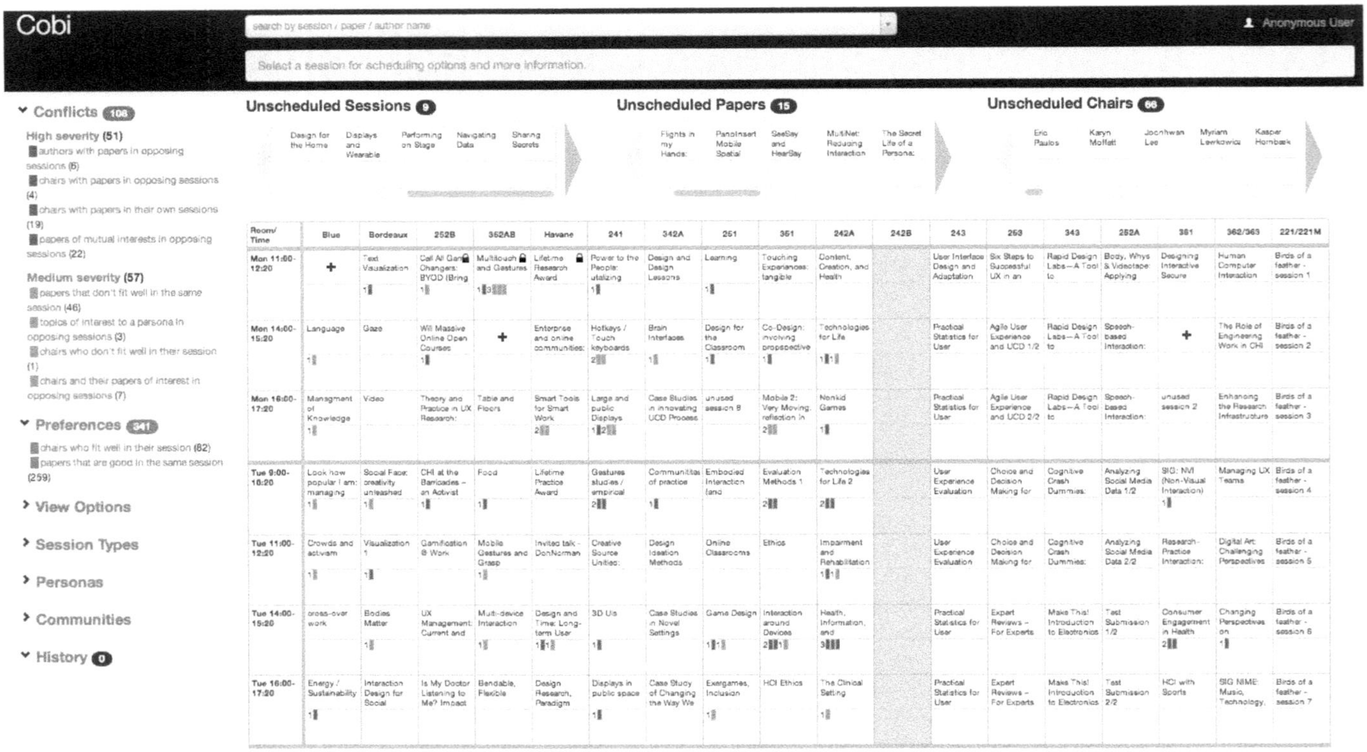

Figure 2. Cobi's scheduling tool consists of the top panel (top), the sidebar (left), and the unscheduled panel and main schedule table (right).

themed sessions that run in parallel, and author-specific conflicts. Several aspects of the process contribute to these problems. First, due to the organic nature of how organizers make connections between papers in stage one, many sessions have odd papers mixed in. Second, because the process does not capture affinities between papers in different sessions, it is difficult for organizers to make scheduling changes that lead to more cohesive sessions. Third, organizers are often unaware of the preferences of authors and attendees. This can lead to sessions of interest being scheduled at the same time. Finally, the lack of tools for managing constraints and the sheer size of the schedule make it difficult for organizers to make informed decisions when finalizing the schedule.

Cobi addresses these challenges by drawing on the people and expertise within the community, and embedding intelligence for resolving conflicts into a scheduling interface. The Cobi system consists of a collection of communitysourcing applications that elicit preferences, constraints, and affinity data from program committee members and authors, and an intelligent scheduling tool that provides organizers with helpful context and suggestions for improving the schedule. By engaging the community in the planning process, Cobi exposes the preferences and constraints of its members to the organizers and makes the planning process more transparent.

Cobi's scheduling tool (Figure 2) integrates community preferences and constraints with constraint-solving intelligence into a new kind of *community-informed mixed-initiative system*. The interface helps organizers visually spot problems and resolve them in the schedule. It highlights general, high-level conflicts such as scheduling a presenter in two opposing sessions. It also exposes more detailed, communitysourced preferences such as scheduling together papers that authors feel fit well in a session with their paper. When manipulating the schedule (e.g., assigning, moving, and swapping sessions, papers, and session chairs), the interface uses a constraint solver to help organizers make informed decisions by recommending edits that best improve the schedule and visualizing the consequences of potential edits. Organizers drive the system by applying their personal knowledge, choosing which problems to focus on, and making final decisions.

We deployed the Cobi system for planning CHI 2013. We recruited associate chairs to group sets of related papers, and authors to identify papers of interest and those that fit well in a session with their own paper. The process collected 1722 paper affinities from 64 associate chairs and 8651 preferences and constraints from 645 authors (covering 87% of accepted submissions). In addition, we asked candidate session chairs to submit their representative papers to determine their fit with sessions. The organizers used Cobi's scheduling tool to improve the preliminary schedule and assign session chairs. The tool helped the organizers resolve 168 conflicts as they created the final schedule. They found that the scheduling tool greatly simplified conflict resolution, while allowing them to combine their own knowledge with the machine intelligence and the community's input.

The paper proceeds as follows. We first discuss related work in communitysourcing and conference scheduling. We then share findings from a preliminary study and identify key design goals. We present Cobi's scheduling tool, focusing on the integration of community data, machine intelligence, and end-user interface. We report on our deployment at CHI 2013 and discuss the key lessons learned. The paper concludes with notes on future research directions.

RELATED WORK

Our work seeks to tailor tasks to the inherent incentives, interests, and expertise of diverse groups within a community. We draw from the broad literature on encouraging community contributions, both in online [10] and physical spaces [5], and on tasks ranging from collecting scientific data [4] to co-designing public transportation services [16]. In our work, community members contribute to solving a specific problem whose solution affects themselves and the community at large. With Cobi, we are exploring incentives, methods, and interfaces for collecting and incorporating multidimensional preferences and constraints from large numbers of individuals within a community into a single, cohesive outcome.

Previous research introduced mixed-initiative solutions to complex tasks such as aircraft scheduling [3] and manufacturing task scheduling [7] by modeling expert knowledge. To this line of research, Cobi contributes a community-driven approach, which raises the unique design challenges of incentivizing community members to express preferences, and mediating, encoding, visualizing, and acting on noisy and diverse community input. Interactive machine learning (IML) approaches such as CueT [1] and E-mazing [15] use a combination of human labor and machine learning. However, they take opposite approaches to the problem. IML supervises an algorithm with human input, while Cobi helps conference organizers make informed decisions with computations shown as visual feedback.

Automated scheduling is a well-studied problem in both computer science and operations research. Specific to conference scheduling, Sampson et al. [13] introduced formulations for maximizing the number of talks of interest attendees can attend. For the related problem of course scheduling, Murray et al. [11] introduced formulations for minimizing student and instructor conflicts subject to scheduling constraints. While automated scheduling is appropriate when the parameters and constraints of the optimization problem are well-specified, our interviews with past CHI organizers show that they attempt to tackle soft constraints and other tacit considerations. With Cobi's mixed-initiative, interactive optimization [6, 14], the machine plays a supporting role, providing intelligence and feedback for detecting problems and resolving conflicts. Organizers can thus better interpret and act on the community's input, which can be overwhelmingly rich, subjective, and incomplete at the same time.

Jacob et al. [8] developed a tangible interface for manipulating a conference schedule and checking constraints on a physical grid layout. Cobi extends this approach by accounting for input from the larger conference community.

There are several commercial systems for conference and course scheduling. One example is Confex's scheduling tool (`confex.com`), which detects and highlights hard conflicts in the schedule (e.g., scheduling a presenter in simultaneous sessions) but makes no suggestions about how to resolve them. Another example is UniTime (`unitime.org`), which first computes an optimal course schedule to minimize conflicts and then allows a user to make fine-grained adjustments while seeing the effect on conflicts. Our work presents an alternative approach in which the user is in control at all times while the system detects conflicts and provides suggestions for resolving them.

PRELIMINARY STUDY AND DESIGN GOALS

Our research team conducted hour-long semi-structured interviews and exchanged emails with five past and current CHI organizers, two of whom are co-authors on this paper. Discussions centered around the planning process at CHI and focused in particular on existing challenges and potential solutions. Conversations revealed three high-level goals that drove the design of the Cobi system and its scheduling tool:

Understanding paper affinities. Organizers stressed that "papers fit into sessions in complex ways" and that "getting a session together that makes sense is hard." While the in-person meeting created sessions that are mostly cohesive, organizers still needed to break open some sessions. Organizers noted that this is a "major pain point" and that it is "very hairy to break up a session" because swapping a paper with another paper requires each paper to fit well in the other's session. In order to capture paper affinities across sessions, organizers noted that you would need contributors "knowledgeable enough in the field to know that papers should or shouldn't be in the same session." Cobi draws on input from paper authors, who we hypothesize would know what other papers fit well in a session with their own.

Detecting conflicts automatically and providing feedback for resolving them. Organizers found it particularly difficult to know the consequences of moving a paper or session in the schedule, which requires reasoning about the conflicts that would be created in addition to those that would be resolved. One organizer noted that she "would (painstakingly) solve those [conflicts and] re-run [a constraint-checking script], usually showing that the problems I had solved had generated other author conflicts." In order to avoid thrashing and frustration, Cobi recommends moves and swaps that resolve the most conflicts and allows organizers to preview the effect of possible edits on conflicts.

Keeping the human in control. While an automated constraint solver can be used to resolve known conflicts, previous organizers felt that taking a purely automated approach would be impractical and would fail to capture the "many semantic constraints that are hard to express using machine understandable ways." The organizers also stressed the importance of being able to make sense of the schedule so that they can apply their knowledge and weigh the various demands of the community while scheduling.

COBI'S SCHEDULING TOOL

Once the program committee determines the accepted papers, Cobi's communitysourcing applications collect preferences, constraints, and affinity data from community members. This

Example Constraints & Preferences	*Possible Source*	*Rationale*
Papers that don't fit well together shouldn't be in the same session	Authors	Authors know what papers are related to theirs and care about which end up in a session with their own.
Papers of mutual interest shouldn't be in opposing sessions	Attendees	Knowing what attendees want to see can avoid scheduling talks of interest at the same time.
Chairs' area of research should match the topic of their session	Chairs' papers	We can collect papers from potential session chairs and check if they are related to the papers in a session.

Table 1. Examples of preferences and constraints encoded in Cobi that can be collected from community members.

input is then encoded and presented in Cobi's scheduling tool to help users (conference organizers) resolve conflicts and improve the schedule.

Encoding Preferences and Constraints

Cobi supports preferences and constraints over attributes at three entity levels: sessions, papers, and chairs. For example, a constraint may specify sessions that should not be concurrent (e.g., "sessions of interest to the ICT4D community should not oppose one another"), and a preference may state that a chair is a good fit for a session (e.g., "James Sysmaster is a good fit for the systems session"). At a high level, the goal is to create a schedule that violates few constraints and meets many preferences.

In early prototype testing, we found that most constraints and preferences of interest can be stated as conditions on a single entity or a pair of entities (e.g., "George Latewaker prefers to chair sessions in the afternoon" or "sessions on crowdsourcing and social computing should not oppose one another"). Further simplifying matters, paired-entity constraints of interest tend to describe relations over entities when they are in the same time or room, suggesting that we need only check conflicts between entities in such cases. Currently Cobi supports encoding paired entity constraints of the form "x and y should [not] be in the same session" and "w and z should [not] oppose one another," where x and y can be papers and chairs and w and z can be sessions, papers, and chairs.

Some constraints (and likewise preferences) may be *system-defined*, which refers to high-level, overarching constraints that can be stated using data from a submission management system (e.g., "a presenter should not be scheduled in opposing sessions"). Other constraints may be *community-defined*, which refers to more specific and perhaps more subjective wishes stated by community members (e.g., "Sessions A and B should be scheduled apart because Mary Liker is interested in papers in both sessions"). Table 1 provides examples of community constraints and preferences encoded in the current Cobi prototype and potential sources of community input that can be used to instantiate them.

While encoding system-defined constraints is straightforward, encoding community-provided constraints requires taking into account the potential sparsity, diversity, and subjectivity of the collected data. We may collect thousands of preferences and constraints, some of which are in direct conflict with others (e.g., an author may feel that his paper fits well in a session with another paper whose author disagrees). To account for such issues, an *input-mediation layer* aggregates responses before adding a constraint or preference in Cobi. For instance, we add a preference for two papers to be in the same session, only if the majority of people providing data about both papers agreed that they are related. We restrict two papers from being in opposing sessions only when many people express interest in seeing both papers.

In addition to managing the complexity of subjective data, the input-mediation layer can help focus the user's attention on salient constraints that matter to many community members. It can also be used to capture variance in the data and note an absence of data, so that the user can know when not to rely excessively on community input. The goal is to capture the community input at a level where the user can best act upon it: too little mediation makes it difficult to understand the community's wishes, and too much may end up hiding some of the useful information contained in the data.

Scheduling Interface

Cobi's scheduling tool (Figure 2) enables manipulating, scanning, and reviewing the schedule with support for conflict resolution and multi-faceted views. The interface keeps the user in control and provides advice on entity moves and swaps. It consists of three components: the top panel, the sidebar, and the unscheduled panel and main schedule table.

The top panel (Figure 2, top) allows the user to search for entities and displays information about the current operation. The sidebar (Figure 2, left) contains view modes and faceted browsing options to help the user analyze the current schedule. *Conflicts* and *Preferences* display conflicts and satisfied preferences in the current schedule and their counts. They are separated by type and grouped based on their severity. Counts update immediately following any change to the schedule, and provide immediate feedback on the effects of the user's actions on conflicts.

View options display different aspects of the schedule and help the user spot issues requiring attention. For example, the default *Conflict* view shows icons for conflicts that involve entities within a session. (Figure 2, right). Clicking on the *Duration* view option displays the length of each session, and allows the user to quickly identify ones with too many or too few papers. *Personas* and *Communities* allow the user to skim the schedule for various interest-based subgroups and check if the schedule is well-distributed across subgroups. The *History* option keeps track of all the scheduling operations and who performed them.

The unscheduled panel displays unscheduled sessions, papers, and session chairs. In addition to holding the entities to be scheduled, in initial testing we found that users needed

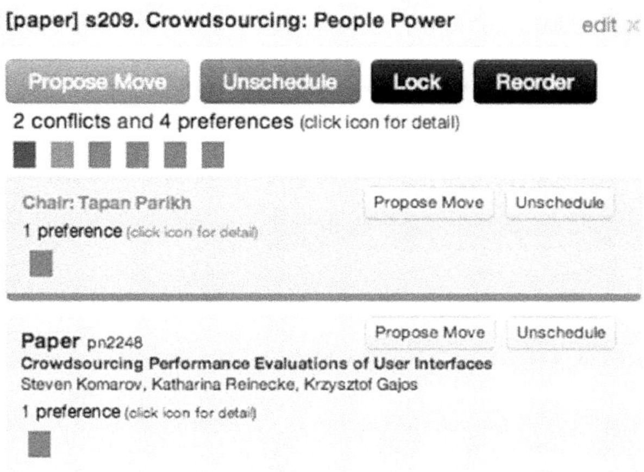

(a) View Mode

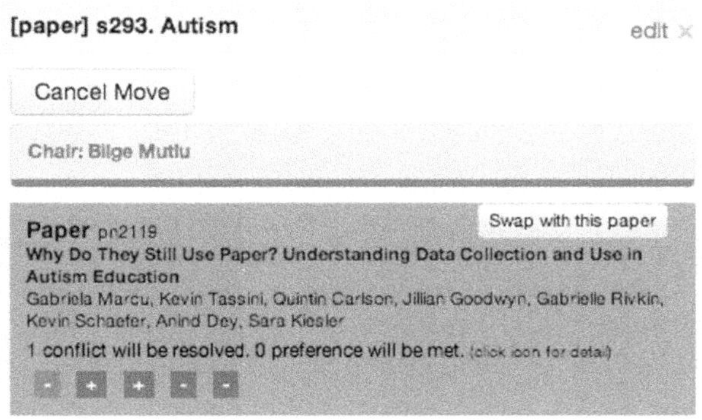

(b) Move Mode

Figure 3. Inner-session view in view mode and move mode. A recommended paper move is highlighted in green.

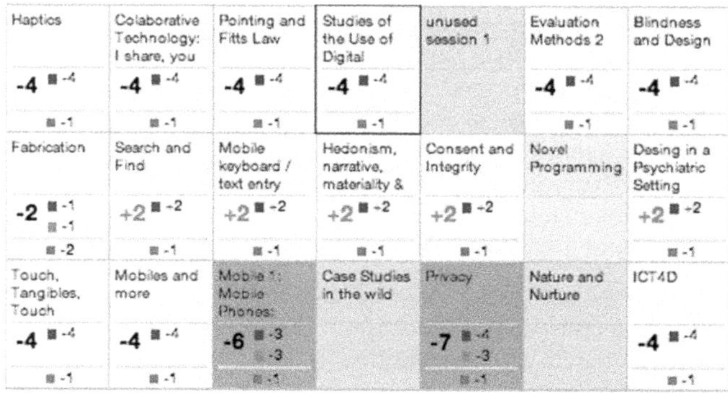

Figure 4. Move preview displays the change in the number of conflicts and preferences should the user swap the source session (shown in yellow) with each of the candidate target sessions. The system recommends sessions that minimize conflicts by highlighting them in green.

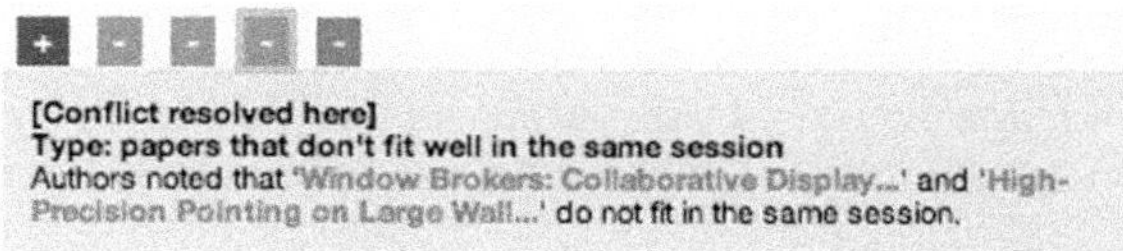

Figure 5. In move mode, conflict details preview the consequence of making a swap. By clicking on individual icons and following navigation links, the user can understand the specific conflicts and preferences that would be added or removed by making this swap.

a scratch space to construct a session without having to worry about where it is placed in the schedule. The unscheduled panel serves as this scratch space.

The main schedule table displays the entire schedule in a time table (Figure 2, right). Each cell displays a session name and additional information based on the view option (e.g., *Conflicts*). Clicking on a session displays details of the session (Figure 3(a)), which includes conflict information and details on its papers and chair. Here the user is provided with options for scheduling entities, unscheduling entities, swapping entities, reordering papers, editing titles, and locking sessions.

When working to resolve conflicts related to an entity, the user can click *Propose Move* on a session, paper, or session chair and enter *move mode*, which displays previews of the consequences of moving to an empty slot or swapping with a candidate entity (Figure 4). Each target cell displays the net change in the number of conflicts for swapping with entities in the cell, and cells highlighted in green represent recommended moves that would lead to the largest reduction in the number of conflicts. The user can scan different options, and click on cells to examine in detail the consequences of potential moves (Figure 3(b)).

For each empty target or target entity, Cobi displays an icon for each conflict that would be added or removed at the source and target by making the move. Clicking on the icon shows detailed information about the selected conflict or preference (Figure 5). Cobi adds links to all entities involved in the conflict or preference, so that clicking on the link highlights the selected entity. Since conflicts created or removed may also involve entities other than those being moved (e.g., a conflicting paper in an opposing session), this helps the user carefully understand which conflicts and preferences will be violated or met for which entities. Upon making a decision, the system displays the change briefly to allow the user to make sense of their decision, and returns to the view mode with updated conflict counts in the sidebar.

By using a combination of overview and detailed views, Cobi's scheduling tool aims to support quick scans as well as detailed investigations. It leaves the user in control of selecting which entities to work on and in what order, while making potential problems in the schedule evident via the conflict view and other view options. When making schedule changes, the system helps the user narrow down the set of candidates to consider, and understand visually the consequences of all possible moves on conflicts in the schedule. Since communitysourced data may be noisy or incomplete and the user may weigh various factors beyond the encoded preferences and constraints, Cobi leaves it to the user to make final scheduling decisions by applying their knowledge and making sense of recommendations from the tool.

Implementation

Cobi associates with each type of preference or constraint a lookup table containing pairs of entities that would be in conflict if particular conditions are met. Since Cobi only encodes constraints within a timeslot, conflict checking and resolution can be performed by simply taking pairs of entities in the same timeslot in the schedule and using the lookup tables to determine if they are in conflict. When computing the consequences of moves and swaps, the system uses the same lookup tables to determine which conflicts involving the source and target entities would be added or removed.

To help the user make sense of potential conflicts in the schedule, each constraint is associated with a *template message* that is instantiated with the entities in conflict when a conflict is detected. For example, a template message may state that "authors noted that x and y do not fit in the same session" and be instantiated with papers x and y that are in the same session and in the corresponding lookup table.

The scheduling tool allows multiple users to collaborate synchronously or asynchronously. The system keeps consistent transaction records on the database and pushes changes to users as they interact with the system. In cases of simultaneous, conflicting edits, the interface displays a message to the user with the failed operation, performs a local rollback, and updates with changes other users have made. Cobi also provides a polling API for other systems or interfaces to access its schedule state, which is useful when alternative visualizations or output devices are available (as in our deployment). The frontend web interface is built with HTML5, CSS3, and Javascript using the jQuery and Bootstrap toolkits.

DEPLOYMENT AND EVALUATION

We deployed the Cobi system for scheduling CHI 2013. Prior to deployment, a small group of organizers and associate chairs met in early December to produce a preliminary schedule by clustering accepted papers and making initial sessions. We deployed Cobi's communitysourcing applications between January 6 and February 12, 2013 to collect preferences, constraints, and affinity data from associate chairs, authors, and session chairs. This data was then encoded into Cobi's scheduling interface. Organizers used Cobi over a period of 42 days from February 10 to March 23, 2013. They took into account the community input, resolved session, paper, and session chair conflicts, and generally worked to improve the initial schedule.

To better understand the scheduling experience with Cobi, we collected quantitative and qualitative data from the organizers. We logged all operations the organizers executed using Cobi. A log entry includes the user responsible for the action, the action type, affected sessions or papers, and a snapshot of conflict counts as a result of the action. At the end of the deployment, we reflected on the process with each of the three CHI 2013 organizers individually (two are co-authors of this paper). Each session lasted 60-120 minutes, and was audio-recorded for later analysis. The organizers talked about high-level goals in scheduling, walked through the scheduling process, and described specific subtasks they were involved in. During the discussion they also tested the latest version of the Cobi scheduling tool that encoded the authorsourcing data, and provided feedback on the experience and usability.

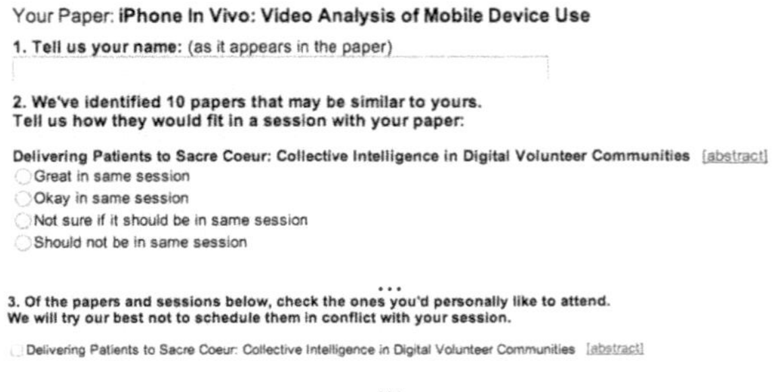

Figure 6. Authors were presented with a custom list of 20 papers and asked to judge which are related to their paper or of interest to them.

System-defined Preferences and Constraints

For sessions and papers, we used data from the submission management system to encode two constraints that sought to avoid scheduling paper authors in opposing sessions and sessions of interest to a persona in opposing sessions. The former constraint seeks to ensure that no presenter has to be in two places at once and that all authors can see their papers presented. The latter constraint seeks to keep sessions on a particular area of interest apart in the schedule.

For session chairs, we used data from the submission management system to encode constraints stating that chairs should not have papers in opposing sessions (for the same reason as authors), and that they should not chair sessions in which they have a paper (to avoid perceived conflict of interest).

Collecting and Encoding Community Input

We deployed three communitysourced initiatives that collected input from associate chairs, authors, and session chairs. To better understand paper affinities, we first recruited associate chairs to cluster papers in their area of expertise. The process collected 1722 paper affinities from 64 associate chairs (ACs). We then invited authors of accepted papers to identify papers that would fit well in a session with their own and that they are interested in seeing at CHI (Figure 6). To produce a small list of papers for authors to judge, we seeded suggestions based on affinities identified by ACs and by running TF-IDF (Term Frequency - Inverse Document Frequency) [9] comparisons on paper titles and abstracts. The process collected 8651 preferences and constraints from 645 authors, which covered 87% of accepted submissions. The high response rate suggests that authors were inherently interested in seeing their paper in a session with related papers and thus willing to contribute. For more information on the committee and authorsourcing stages, as well as empirical comparison of affinity creation methods, see André et al. [2].

Taking the collected authorsourcing data, Cobi's input mediation layer filtered and aggregated preferences and conflicts so that only those submitted by multiple authors were encoded. For papers, this led to encoding 923 constraints of the form "papers x and y are of mutual interests and shouldn't be scheduled in opposing sessions," 651 constraints of the form "papers x and y do not fit well in the same session," and 805 preferences of the form "papers x and y are good in the same session." For authors who also served as session chairs, we

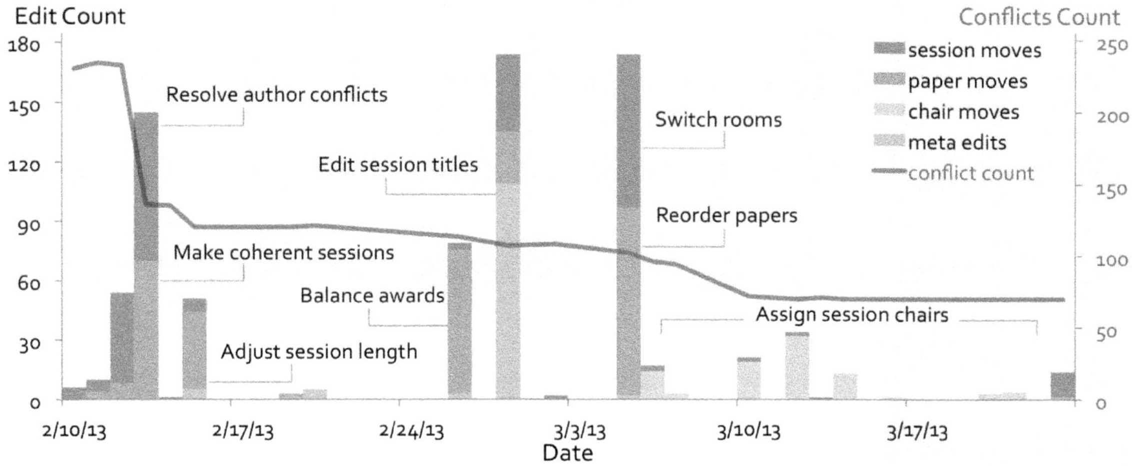

Figure 7. Representative subtasks during the CHI 2013 scheduling process are shown with associated operation types from the interface log. For example, the "Resolve author conflicts" subtask is associated with a cluster of session swap operations. Session, paper, and chair edits indicate scheduling operations involving those entities. Meta edits indicate non-scheduling operations, such as editing session titles and locking or unlocking sessions.

also added 243 constraints of the form "chair x is interested in a paper y in an opposing session." Due to time constraints in the deployment schedule, only the chair-related constraints were visible to organizers in the version of Cobi's scheduling tool they were using. For resolving other community-defined author conflicts, the organizers relied on visualizing the authorsourced data externally without the preview and recommendation support from Cobi.

In addition to the authorsourcing data, we collected representative paper samples from 165 potential session chairs, which we used to compute affinity measures on how well they may fit as chairs for a session. Using TF-IDF similarity between each session chair's papers and each session's papers, we produced affinity scores between chairs and sessions. Cobi encoded the affinity information as a preference for assigning a chair to a session when they are among the top 5 by affinity score, and a constraint when they are out of the top 25. To compute an initial assignment, we solved a linear optimization program to compute an assignment of session chairs that maximizes the sum of affinity scores.

Scheduling Process

Cobi was used in a number of scheduling meetings that involved the organizers and other collaborators. The version of Cobi that organizers used supported all session, paper, and session chair-related scheduling operations. It provided previews and recommendations for system-defined constraints, but as mentioned before, did not incorporate the authorsourcing data. For some of the meetings, Cobi was used in conjunction with a large wall display that visualized community data along with detailed session information and supported multiple users simultaneously exploring the schedule. The wall display did not include intelligence for resolving conflicts; the organizers relied on Cobi for conflict resolution and making actual changes to the schedule.

During the 42-day deployment, the three CHI 2013 organizers made 815 scheduling operations using Cobi's scheduling interface. We reconstructed the scheduling process by connecting organizers' description of the process with the interface usage log. Figure 7 shows the variety of subtasks that organizers faced during the scheduling process. By decomposing the scheduling problem into subtasks, organizers could focus on a particular aspect of the schedule at a given time.

The scheduling process proceeded in three high-level phases. In phase one (February 10 to February 17), organizers took the preliminary schedule from the technical program meeting and worked to resolve conflicts from violated system- and community-defined constraints. Organizers first moved papers so as to construct more coherent sessions based on the collected feedback from authors on which papers fit well in a session with theirs. Organizers then resolved all author conflicts by swapping sessions. While this eliminated nearly all of the existing system-defined conflicts, many sessions contained too few or too many papers. Organizers then moved papers to ensure that all sessions were at or under 80 minutes.

At the end of phase one, organizers had a mostly complete program. In phase two (February 17 to February 28), they worked to enhance themes and fine-tune the schedule to address special requirements. On the room level, they placed related sessions in the same or nearby rooms and sessions with awards in larger rooms. On the paper and session level, they distributed awards across sessions and reordered papers within a session so that they are presented in a logical progression. These subtasks generally did not involve conflict resolution, but the organizers used Cobi's conflict preview to ensure that changes would not introduce new conflicts. The organizers also made 122 session title edits to better capture and promote sessions and the papers within.

Once the organizers finalized the program, they worked in the final phase (March 1 to March 23) on assigning session chairs. Organizers first moved chairs out of sessions in which they had papers and corrected assignments where the chair was a poor fit. They then announced the initial assignments

Constraint Type	Related Entity	Data Source	Severity	Encoded	Initial	Final	Change
author with papers in opposing sessions	session (Figure 8)	system-generated	high	-	31	0	-31
topics of interest to a persona in opposing sessions	session (Figure 8)	system-generated	medium	-	6	4	-2
papers of mutual interests in opposing sessions	paper (Figure 9)	authorsourcing	high	923	40	19	-21
papers that do not fit well in the same session	paper (Figure 9)	authorsourcing	medium	651	129	42	-87
chair's paper in own session	chair (Figure 10)	system-generated	high	-	21	0	-21
chair's paper in opposing sessions	chair (Figure 10)	system-generated	high	-	6	0	-6
chair interested in opposing sessions	chair (Figure 10)	authorsourcing	medium	243	5	4	-1
chair in a session with a bad fit	chair (Figure 10)	chairs	medium	-	0	1	1
Total violated					238	70	-168
Preference Type		**Data Source**	**Severity**	**Encoded**	**Initial**	**Final**	**Change**
papers good in the same session	paper	authorsourcing	N/A	805	268	272	4
chair fits well in the session	chair	chairs	N/A	-	90	78	-12
Total satisfied					358	350	-8

Table 2. For all constraint or preference types in our deployment, the table shows the related entity, the data source for encoding, the severity level displayed in the tool, the total number of encoded items if authorsourced, the violation or satisfaction count from the preliminary schedule, the count in the finalized schedule, and the change in the count (highlighted if improved). There remains no conflicts for 3 of the 4 high severity types (highlighted). Soft constraints (medium severity) have more violations, which shows that scheduling involves multiple factors in addition to conflict resolution.

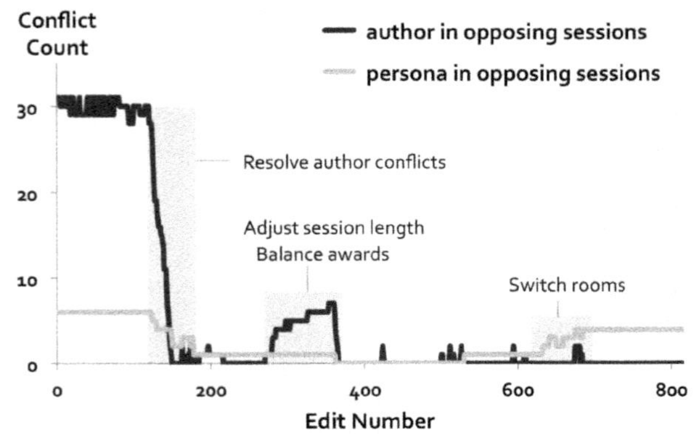

Figure 8. Change in system-defined conflicts over time. The organizers resolved 30 author conflicts during initial session making. When they were adjusting session lengths and balancing awards, the conflict count temporarily increased, but they resolved all of them shortly after. The organizers introduced three persona conflicts while they were switching rooms, but they chose not to resolve these conflicts due to other factors.

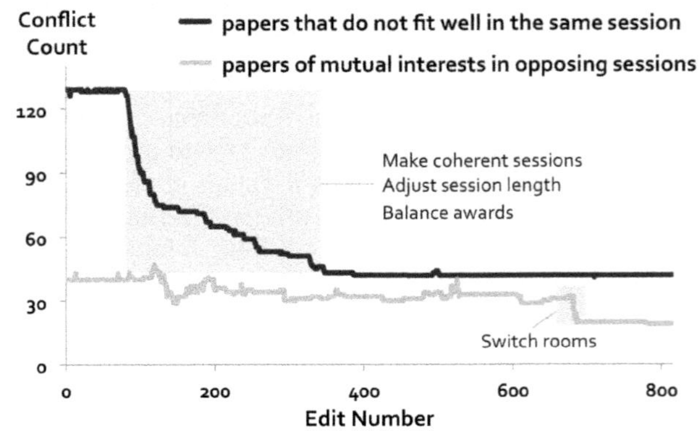

Figure 9. Change in community-defined conflicts over time. Organizers first attempted to make more coherent sessions with papers that did not fit well in the same session. After switching rooms, they resolved 11 conflicts to avoid having simultaneous sessions with similar topics.

to the session chairs, who provided additional feedback on fit and conflicts that the chairs resolved subsequently.

Conflict Resolution

The preliminary schedule from the technical program meeting included 238 conflicts. Organizers resolved 168 of them during the scheduling process. Table 2 summarizes changes in conflict counts for each constraint and preference type.

Schedule creation (phase one and two)

Organizers resolved all but four conflicts from system-defined constraints (Figure 8). Shortly after making more cohesive sessions (but in the same meeting), the organizers eliminated all 30 author conflicts in 29 minutes. This ensures that no presenter has papers in parallel sessions and that co-authors can attend all sessions that contain their papers. Persona conflicts were mostly absent because the in-person meeting to generate the initial schedule already took personas into account by scheduling sessions of interest to the same persona apart.

Organizers also resolved many of the community-defined conflicts (Figure 9). 21 of the 40 "papers of mutual interest in opposing sessions" conflicts in the initial schedule were resolved (53%), and 87 of the 129 "papers that do not fit well in the same session" conflicts were resolved (67%). Note that organizers made these changes using community-provided data and Cobi's paper-level operations, but without the previews and recommendations.

Session chair assignment (phase three)

During phase three (Figure 10), organizers resolved all 27 conflicts based on system-defined chair constraints. 6 conflicts involved chairs with papers in opposing sessions and 21 conflicts involved chairs with papers in their own session.

Reflection

Discussions with organizers revealed a number of key points on how Cobi supports the conference scheduling process and helps to resolve conflicts:

Simplifying conflict resolution with preview and feedback

The organizers commented that Cobi "trivialized conflict resolution" and was "a major stress reducer." Organizers noted

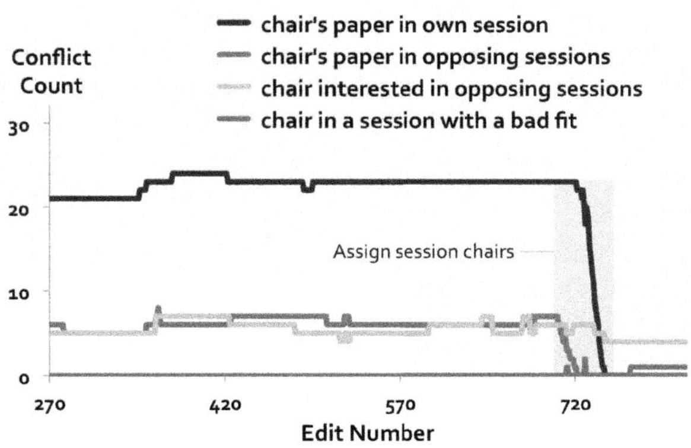

Figure 10. Change in session chair-related conflicts over time. Session chair assignment took place near the end of the scheduling process. The organizers resolved a majority of conflicts from the initial assignment by considering the individual constraints they collected from chairs.

that Cobi's visual previews aided in understanding the consequence of making a move, and immediate feedback accelerated conflict resolution. One organizer described the experience of resolving system-defined conflicts as follows: "It went really really fast, because we see a session that has conflicts, and the suggestions Cobi was giving were really good, and then we swapped things. It was almost a no brainer."

Enabling mixed-initiative problem solving

Cobi allowed organizers to use constraint-solving intelligence alongside their own knowledge of the schedule and of tacit constraints to improve the program. One organizer commented that "I was by and large driven by what Cobi was suggesting. As you make progress you can then progressively integrate other criteria that are not explicit in the system." In swapping sessions to resolve author conflicts, another organizer noted that he used Cobi's conflict previews to find good sessions to swap with that were in the same room, so as to resolve conflicts while maintaining the themes that were loosely assigned to rooms during the in-person meeting. Cobi also allowed organizers to be aware of causing potential conflicts even when they weren't working to resolve them. "We had Cobi up all the time to make sure that when we had a solution that we thought worked from the affinity point of view, that it didn't introduce new conflicts."

An important aspect of any mixed-initiative system is the user's trust in system recommendations. Organizers noted that their trust in Cobi grew over time. "For those of us who returned to the problem on multiple occasions, with a diverse set of short-term colleagues with varying expertise who came in to help, I think our appreciation of Cobi actually grew. We were looking at C&B [contribution & benefit] statements, as well as abstracts, and double-checking with our visitors, and Cobi kept coming up with great suggestions. So it stopped being based on following Cobi because it dealt with the areas that we knew, and became more fundamental, because it held up under scrutiny from a variety of visitors and when we delved into the details of various papers."

Intelligence powered by community input

Organizers commented on the value of having authorsourcing data during the scheduling process. In previous years, "authors saw their paper move from a slot they liked to a time they didn't and talked to the TP chairs." But this year, "we had virtually none of this. Authors were asked for input, most gave it, we tried hard to accommodate them, and almost nobody complained."

Organizers noted that authorsourcing data was particularly useful for understanding the affinity among papers beyond the initial sessions created at the TP meeting. "It helped with the more subtle issue of what happens when a paper moves out of a 'happy session'. Pairs of papers with a strong affinity are not in conflict if in the same session, and become conflicted if they move out of that session, but stay in the same time slot. This got lost over and over again in previous years and is the big win this year."

The organizers used a wall display to visualize authorsourcing data. Since the version of Cobi that organizers used at the time did not incorporate this data, organizers had to manually identify paper swaps that lead to more cohesive sessions. Later, when asked to test a version of Cobi's scheduling tool that encoded authorsourced preferences and constraints, organizers noted that having Cobi able to propose and resolve community-defined conflicts would have been valuable: "That is precisely what I was doing by hand with the authorsourcing data. And [the blue icon showing community preference] is absolutely useful." "I think if we had this earlier when we were doing the first round of improving the sessions, we would certainly have used it."

Weighing priorities and deliberately leaving conflicts

If Cobi makes it easy to resolve conflicts, why does the final schedule still include 70 conflicts? When asked this question, an organizer replied that for many of the remaining conflicts "we felt that they were minor or we decided that they weren't really conflicts." Since there are multiple factors that affect scheduling decisions, satisfying all constraints is sometimes not possible. An organizer commented that "it's also a question of opinion in some cases." In these cases the organizers made the final decision, which corresponds to Cobi's design goal to support decision-making while keeping the user in control at all times.

Mediating and visualizing community input

While the authorsourcing data provided a rich perspective on the community's preferences and constraints, the data was also sparse and noisy. In resolving authorsourced conflicts, organizers strived to understand the complexity of community input. Organizers used their wall display to visualize the raw community data, and attempted to account for the variance, quality, and weight of the data when making decisions. While organizers appreciated Cobi's aggregating authorsourcing data to remove noise and highlight salient conflicts, they also noted that visualizing the raw data was helpful and gave them more flexibility in using community input. Based on this feedback, we plan to develop other methods for mediating and visualizing community input, that can reflect its variance and quality while also maintaining simplicity.

Visualization improvements

Organizers noted a few areas for potential improvement in Cobi's visualization. A major issue raised was that Cobi can only display the details of one session at a time. While scheduling, organizers found that they often wanted to compare multiple entities. One organizer noted that "having to sequentially navigate multiple items worsens the experience a bit." To address these comments, we are currently exploring alternative visualizations for displaying detailed information for multiple sessions and are considering applying focus plus context techniques such as those found in TableLens [12]. The challenge is in providing additional context without distorting the schedule table in ways that hinder sensemaking.

Another solution to the visualization challenge is to leverage more space when available. For example, the wall display the organizers used for planning CHI 2013 was large enough to visualize detailed submission information in the global view. It allowed a group of people to collaborate on scheduling subtasks, although it lacked conflict resolution capability. A possible extension for Cobi is to directly connect to a large display so as to facilitate collaboration and enable the micro-outsourcing of scheduling tasks.

CONCLUSION AND FUTURE WORK

The Cobi system integrates community process, constraint-solving intelligence, and end-user interface to help organizers plan large conference schedules. Cobi's scheduling tool encodes community input as preferences and constraints, and helps organizers resolve conflicts by providing previews and recommendations when editing the schedule. A live deployment of Cobi for planning CHI 2013 demonstrated the effectiveness of collecting preferences and constraints from community members, and of the scheduling tool for simplifying conflict resolution and supporting informed decision-making.

The challenges of conference scheduling—understanding paper affinities, knowing what people want, and managing the solution complexity—are shared by conferences beyond CHI. We believe the approach presented in this paper generalizes to scheduling other academic conferences, and also to other events such as trade shows, film festivals, or university courses. More generally, the success of Cobi's deployment posits community-informed, mixed-initiative interaction as a novel approach for solving optimization problems, for which the goal is to collect important data from the community, use computation to guide the solution, and allow users to apply their tacit knowledge.

In future work, we plan to explore ways to further engage the community in the scheduling process. We wish to provide a generalized method for community members to express arbitrary constraints and preferences (e.g., travel plans and special considerations). We are currently working on an interactive interface that allows community members to specify a broader range of preferences and constraints. The collected input can then be encoded like other community-defined constraints, so that conflicts can be easily resolved using Cobi.

Another direction for future work is to extend the role of the community beyond providing data. Can hundreds of people collaboratively make sessions and resolve conflicts? We imagine that tools can support new ways of communicating, collaborating, and incorporating different opinions. Pursuing this research direction can lead to a new family of community-supported mixed-initiative systems that better mediates and visualizes diverse input from the community.

ACKNOWLEDGMENTS

We thank Patrick Baudisch, Kia Höök, Ed Chi, Pedro Lopes, Nirmal Patel, and members of the CHI community. This work is supported in part by Quanta Computer as part of the Qmulus project, by the Ford-MIT Alliance, and by NSF under awards SOCS-1111124 and SOCS-1208382. Juho Kim is partly supported by the Samsung Fellowship.

REFERENCES

1. Amershi, S., Lee, B., Kapoor, A., Mahajan, R., and Christian, B. Cuet: human-guided fast and accurate network alarm triage. In *Proc. CHI'11* (2011), 157–166.
2. André, P., Zhang, H., Kim, J., Chilton, L. B., Dow, S. P., and Miller, R. C. Community clustering: Leveraging an academic crowd to form coherent conference sessions. In *Proc. HCOMP 2013, in press* (2013).
3. Butler, K. A., Zhang, J., Esposito, C., Bahrami, A., Hebron, R., and Kieras, D. Work-centered design: a case study of a mixed-initiative scheduler. In *Proc. CHI'07* (2007), 747–756.
4. Evans, C., Abrams, E., Reitsma, R., Roux, K., Salmonsen, L., and Marra, P. P. The neighborhood nestwatch program: Participant outcomes of a citizen-science ecological research project. *Conservation Biology 19*, 3 (2005), 589–594.
5. Heimerl, K., Gawalt, B., Chen, K., Parikh, T., and Hartmann, B. Communitysourcing: engaging local crowds to perform expert work via physical kiosks. In *Proc. CHI'12* (2012), 1539–1548.
6. Horvitz, E. Principles of mixed-initiative user interfaces. In *Proc. CHI'99* (1999), 159–166.
7. Hsu, W.-L., Prietula, M. J., Thompson, G. L., and Ow, P. S. A mixed-initiative scheduling workbench: integrating ai, or and hci. *Decis. Support Syst. 9*, 3 (Apr. 1993), 245–257.
8. Jacob, R. J. K., Ishii, H., Pangaro, G., and Patten, J. A tangible interface for organizing information using a grid. In *Proc. CHI'02* (2002), 339–346.
9. Jones, K. S. A statistical interpretation of term specificity and its application in retrieval. *Journal of documentation 28*, 1 (1972), 11–21.
10. Kraut, R., and Resnick, P. *Building Successful Online Communities: Evidence-Based Social Design*. Mit Press, 2011.
11. Murray, K., Müller, T., and Rudová, H. Modeling and solution of a complex university course timetabling problem. In *Proceedings of the 6th international conference on Practice and theory of automated timetabling VI* (2007), 189–210.
12. Rao, R., and Card, S. K. The table lens: merging graphical and symbolic representations in an interactive focus + context visualization for tabular information. In *Proc. CHI'94* (1994), 318–322.
13. Sampson, S. E. Practical implications of preference-based conference scheduling. *Production and Operations Management 13*, 3 (2004), 205–215.
14. Scott, S. D., Lesh, N., and Klau, G. W. Investigating human-computer optimization. In *Proc. CHI'02* (2002), 155–162.
15. Stumpf, S., Sullivan, E., Fitzhenry, E., Oberst, I., Wong, W.-K., and Burnett, M. Integrating rich user feedback into intelligent user interfaces. In *Proc. IUI'08* (2008), 50–59.
16. Zimmerman, J., Tomasic, A., Garrod, C., Yoo, D., Hiruncharoenvate, C., Aziz, R., Thiruvengadam, N. R., Huang, Y., and Steinfeld, A. Field trial of tiramisu: crowd-sourcing bus arrival times to spur co-design. In *Proc. CHI'11* (2011), 1677–1686.

The Drawing Assistant: Automated Drawing Guidance and Feedback from Photographs

Emmanuel Iarussi
REVES / Inria Sophia Antipolis

Adrien Bousseau
REVES / Inria Sophia Antipolis

Theophanis Tsandilas
Inria - Univ Paris-Sud & CNRS (LRI)

(a) Interaction setup (b) Model and extracted guides (c) User construction lines and drawing

Figure 1. Our drawing assistant provides guidance and feedback over a model photograph that the user reproduces on a virtual canvas (a). We use computer vision algorithms to extract visual guides that enhance the geometric structures in the image (b). In this example, the user first sketched the block-in construction lines (c, blue) before drawing the regions and adding details. This guidance helps users produce more accurate drawings.

ABSTRACT
We present an interactive drawing tool that provides automated guidance over model photographs to help people practice traditional drawing-by-observation techniques. The drawing literature describes a number of techniques to help people gain consciousness of the shapes in a scene and their relationships. We compile these techniques and derive a set of construction lines that we automatically extract from a model photograph. We then display these lines over the model to guide its manual reproduction by the user on the drawing canvas. Finally, we use shape-matching to register the user's sketch with the model guides. We use this registration to provide corrective feedback to the user. Our user studies show that automatically extracted construction lines can help users draw more accurately. Furthermore, users report that guidance and corrective feedback help them better understand how to draw.

Author Keywords
Interactive drawing; pen-based interfaces; shape matching;

ACM Classification Keywords
H.5.2 [Information Interfaces and Presentation]: User Interfaces - Training, help, and documentation; I.3.4 [Computer Graphics]: Graphics Utilities - Paint systems

http://dx.doi.org/10.1145/2501988.2501997

INTRODUCTION
Drawing is the earliest form of visual depiction and continues to enjoy great popularity with paint systems like Adobe Photoshop, Autodesk SketchBook Pro and FiftyThree Paper which combine traditional pen-based interaction with the flexibility of digital media. However, drawing requires artistic skills that many people feel out of reach. Our goal in this work is to help users of digital drawing tools to improve their drawings by practicing long-standing traditional drawing-by-observation techniques.

A major challenge in drawing from observation is to trust what we *see* rather than what we *know* [24, 12, 10]. Our mental image of common objects is iconic and conflicts with the particular instance that we observe, resulting in distorted or simplistic drawings [13]. Drawing books and tutorials provide simple techniques to help learners gain consciousness of shapes that they observe and their relationships [12, 10, 18, 5, 17, 19]. Common techniques include drawing simple geometrical shapes – also known as *blocking in* – before drawing the subject of interest and checking for alignments and equal proportions. While very effective, these techniques are illustrated on few examples with static instructions and no corrective feedback. As it takes significant effort to generalize the techniques to arbitrary models, books and tutorials benefit only few dedicated learners.

Interactive technology and pen-based interfaces offer new possibilities for the dissemination of drawing techniques to a larger audience by providing assistance and encouraging practice. Recent work in this area includes the iCanDraw? system to draw faces [9] and ShadowDraw that suggests completion of the drawing as it is performed [21]. Following this line of work, we present an interactive drawing tool that assists users in the practice of long-standing drawing techniques advocated by expert teachers. Our *drawing assistant* helps users to practice these techniques from any model photograph and provides corrective feedback interactively. From a technical standpoint, we make two primary contributions:

Automatic visual guides to support drawing. Books and online tutorials on drawing abound with techniques that help people to observe shapes and draw them accurately. Many of these techniques share common principles implemented in different variations. We distill these principles and derive a set of visual guides, in the form of construction lines, that assist users in the process of drawing from a model. We extract visual guides automatically from photographs using simple computer vision algorithms.

Interactive drawing tool with corrective feedback. We integrate our visual guides into a drawing tool that displays guidance over a model photograph. Following recommendation from the drawing literature, we separate our interface into two display areas — model and canvas, as shown in Figure 1 — to encourage users to concentrate on the subject of the drawing rather than on the drawing itself. This interface design differs from existing methods that provide guidance directly on canvas. Our pen-based interface also allows users to navigate between the techniques they wish to practice and to draw construction lines in dedicated layers. We augment this interface with real-time registration between the drawing and the model to detect errors and distortions. We then provide corrective feedback by highlighting in the model alignments and equal proportions that are violated in the drawing.

We conducted two user studies to inform the design of our tool and evaluate our approach with a total of 20 users. Participants produced better drawings using the drawing assistant, with more accurate proportions and alignments. They also perceived that guidance and corrective feedback helped them better understand how to draw. Finally, some participants spontaneously applied the techniques when asked to draw without our tool after using it for about 30 minutes.

RELATED WORK

On-Canvas Guidance

Several systems assist the process of drawing by displaying guidance on the drawing surface. Projector-Guided Painting [15] decomposes a target painting into coarse-to-fine layers. Users paint over the projection of each layer, following guidance to orient individual brush strokes or to paint all the strokes of a given color. Similarly, PapARt [20] allows users to trace over a 3D scene projected on paper and Rivers et al. [25] extend this concept to project guidance for sculpture. ShadowDraw [21] provides guidance for freeform drawing by inferring potential models from the user sketch. At run time, the algorithm matches the drawing to a database of images and blends the best matches to form a *shadow* that suggests a completion of the sketch to users. Similarly, Limpaecher et al. [22] correct sketches traced over a picture by matching them against a database of drawings of the same picture.

All these methods are reminiscent of the traditional "paint-by-number" and "connect the dots" drawing books that guide people in placing individual strokes until completing complex artworks. While these approaches can give people confidence in their ability to draw, they do not help them observe and understand the underlying shapes, relationships and proportions of the drawn models.

Step-by-Step Instructions

A complex drawing can be easier to achieve if it is decomposed into a succession of simple steps. Several commercial applications propose step-by-step drawing tutorials, such as Nintendo Art Academy[1] and the "How to Draw" and "Learn to Draw" mobile applications. Unfortunately, these tools do not provide any corrective feedback to the inexperienced user. Sketch-Sketch Revolution [14] allows expert users of sketching software to generate tutorials for novice users. The system offers on-canvas guidance and feedback to replicate the expert strokes at each step of the tutorial. Finally, work in other domains has introduced systems that generate tutorials from demonstration for image editing [16, 6] and 3D modeling [8]. Such tutorials illustrate drawing techniques on pre-recorded examples rather than images of the user's choice.

Closer to our work are the iCanDraw? and EyeSeeYou systems [9, 7] that assist users in drawing faces and eyes respectively. These systems rely on face and sketch recognition algorithms to generate domain-specific instructions and textual or on-canvas feedback. We draw inspiration from these approaches, incorporating some of their design principles. However, our drawing assistant implements a different set of guides to draw arbitrary models . We also provide visual feedback that highlights alignments and proportions on the model photograph, helping people to see and correct the relationships between different parts of a shape. Our approach also draws inspiration from the system described by Soga et al. [29] which guides users to draw a still life scene using a data base of pre-recorded construction lines and advice.

3D Sketching

While our primary goal is to assist users in drawing from photographs, we believe that helping people to draw has the potential to benefit other applications that rely on sketches as input, such as sketch-based modeling. Several systems use construction lines [27] and sketching planes [2] to support 3D curve sketching. However, users of these systems create construction lines from imagination rather than from a model.

DESIGN GOALS

While most children enjoy drawing, many adults consider themselves incapable of drawing realistically and resort instead to iconic sketches of objects [13]. Edwards [12] suggests that people confront a frustrating *artistic crisis* around ten as their abstraction of the world — what they *know* — conflicts with their visual perception — what they *see*. For instance, children commonly draw cubes with squared faces and get disappointed by the result, as it bears unrealistic proportions and lacks perspective. To gain confidence and improve their drawing skills, people need to resolve this conflict and focus on the actual forms that they want to draw rather

[1] http://artacademy.nintendo.com/

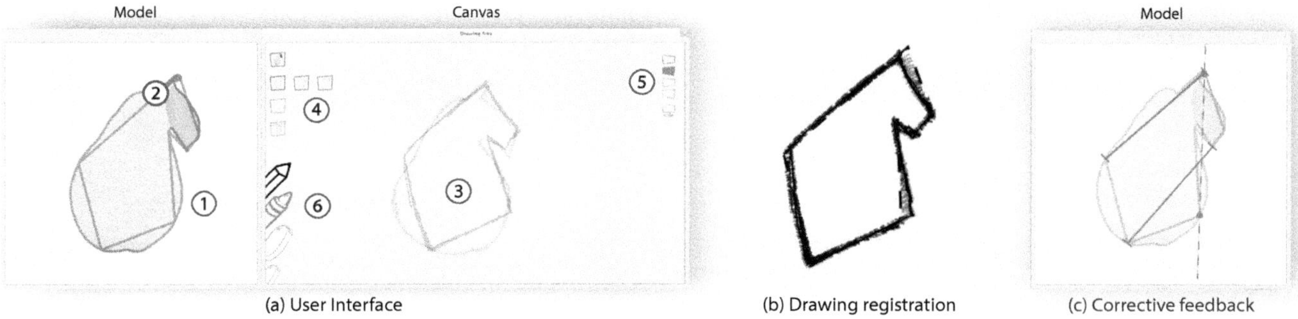

Figure 2. Our interface is composed of two display areas (a): the model area with the photograph and the visual guides, and the canvas area with the tools and the user's drawing. The user has used the drop-down list of tools (4) to activate a coarse block-in guide. The block-in guide is displayed over the model in blue (2). The user has reproduced the block-in guide over the canvas in the corresponding blue layer (5) and used these construction lines as a scaffold to reproduce a detailed contour (1,3). We offer simple drawing tools including a pencil, a pen and a small and big eraser (6). Our system registers the drawing in the active layer — block-in in this example — to estimate distortions (b) and shows on the model the erroneous alignments and proportions (c). In this example, the red dashed line shows a vertical alignment that has not been respected by the user and the dark blue segments show two distances that should be made equal.

than their symbolic representations: "You should set your symbol system aside and accurately draw what you see" [12]; "We should draw as if we know nothing, and were obedient only to what our eye tells us to draw" [10]. Dodson [10] also observes that "a common practice that weakens drawing effectiveness is concentrating too much on your paper and not enough on your subject". For this reason, art teachers advise students to "keep their eyes on the subject of the drawing most of the time, not on the drawing itself" [24, 12].

Inspired by these recommendations, we set the following design goals:

- Encourage users to focus their attention on the actual model rather than their drawing.
- Help users to practice *observation techniques* proposed by the drawing literature. These techniques should allow users to identify the shapes and their relationships on a model and to structure their drawings.
- Support corrective feedback to help users understand their errors and refine their drawings.

In addition to our three design goals, we also chose to focus on basic drawing techniques that apply to generic models, rather than domain-specific rules such as anatomy and perspective. This choice is motivated by the teaching approach of Dodson [10], who states that domain-specific principles "were developed to help us understand what we see, but they do not come first. Seeing comes first. When rules conflict with seeing, forget them and draw what you see."

SYSTEM OVERVIEW

Figure 2a illustrates the main interface of our interactive drawing assistant. It consists of two distinct areas that we display on two separate monitors. The *model* area shows the photograph, which acts as the model for the drawing task, while the *canvas* is the drawing area where the user interacts with the pen. We display the model on a vertical computer monitor and the canvas on a pen display, which mimics traditional drawing where the drawer alternates between observing the model and drawing on paper.

Given a model photograph that the user wishes to reproduce, we first run computer vision algorithms to extract visual guides that emphasize the shapes in the image. We derive these guides from traditional drawing techniques that we discuss in the following section. Our interface displays the detected guides over the model, and the user reproduces them on the canvas as construction lines that form a scaffold for more detailed contours.

Following our first and second design goals, we display visual guides in the model area to enforce users to observe the model before structuring their drawing by themselves. While this design requires extra effort from the user and can be less precise than on-canvas guidance, it is consistent with the teaching approach and recommendations of expert artists.

At run time, our system registers the construction lines drawn by the user with the corresponding visual guides (Figure 2b). We use this registration to estimate local distortions and to detect erroneous alignments and proportions in the drawing. The user can then ask for feedback based on this evaluation. The feedback highlights the parts that require extra attention over the model (Figure 2c) so that the user can understand what to observe to improve the drawing.

VISUAL GUIDES

Drawing books [12, 10, 5, 18] and online tutorials [17, 19] abound with recommendations to observe the shapes in a scene and identify their relationships. While most authors only present a subset of techniques and describe them in their own vocabulary and style, we distilled from these resources three main principles suitable for integration in a computer-assisted tool:

- Drawers should first lay down the main structure of the drawing with a coarse approximation of the shape.
- The coarse structure forms a scaffold to guide contour

drawing. Drawers should draw contours of large regions first and then details.

- Proportions and alignments should be verified to avoid distortions.

We refined these principles through informal user tests both on paper and the computer.

We articulate each principle around *visual guides* that help users construct their drawing. We then describe how to extract these visual guides from a photograph using existing computer vision algorithms. Our guides do not aim to match the style of a particular artist but rather to capture the common idea of drawing from coarse to fine. Art books also describe drawing as "a process which usually bypasses conscious thought and knowledge" [10] and we found simple vision algorithms, that are blind to the semantical content of the image, to be very effective to help the user "bypass" advanced cognitive processes[2]. To further simplify our analysis, we assume that users first separate the subject of the photograph from its background using an interactive foreground extraction tool like *GrabCut* [26].

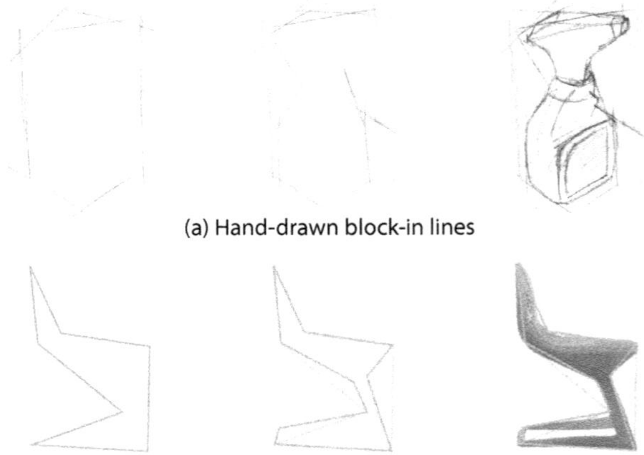

Figure 3. Blocking-in consists in first drawing a coarse approximation of the shape before adding details (after [19]).

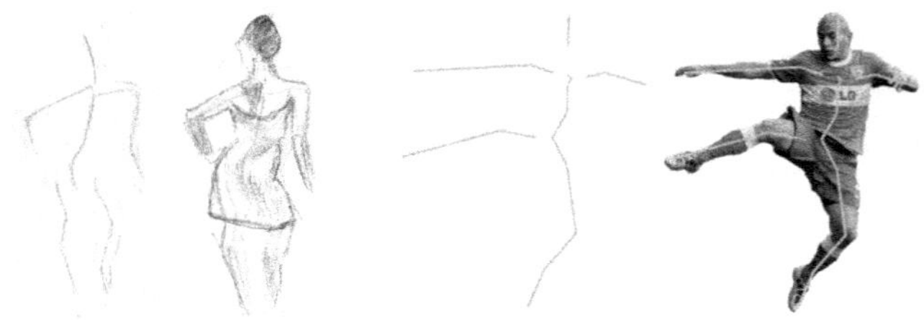

(a) Hand-drawn skeleton (b) Automatic extraction

Figure 4. In this example, skeleton lines enhance the main directions of the body parts. Note that the lines do not correspond to an accurate representation of an anatomical skeleton (after [5]).

Laying Down the Main Drawing Structure

Inexperienced drawers often strive to know how to start their drawing. A common recommendation is to first sketch the basic structure of the shape that will then serve as construction lines to support more complex details.

The *block-in* technique approximates the shape with a polygon [19] or with a collection of geometrical primitives like disks and rectangles [18]. We experienced with both approaches and our early tests with users revealed that using multiple disks and rectangles quickly produces cluttered visual guides that intersect inside the shape. We adopt instead the polygonal visual guide that artists often only apply on the main outline of an object to avoid clutter. This approach draws inspiration from sculptors who start with a block of wood or marble and remove matter from coarse to fine until they reach the final shape (Figure 3a).

Artists also use skeletons to enhance the structure of a shape [5]. While the block-in technique emphasizes the outer shell of man-made objects, skeleton lines depict the principal internal directions and are more suitable to elongated structures and characters, even though they do not necessarily correspond to an anatomical skeleton (Figure 4a).

Automatic extraction

Many algorithms could be used to generate a polygonal approximation of an object's outline. The only requirement is to preserve the overall shape in order to provide local guidance that prevents drifting away while drawing detailed contours. We use the *Douglas-Peucker* algorithm [11] which simplifies a shape by progressively removing vertices of its contour. We generate a coarse-to-fine approximation with two levels of detail containing seven and ten vertices (Figure 3b).

To extract the skeleton of an object, we use the medial axis algorithm [4] which generates the set of points having more than one closest point on the contour of a region. However, we found the medial axis of the main outline of an object to be too detailed. Instead, we first approximate the outline with the detailed polygon of the block-in guide and then compute its medial axis to obtain a skeleton composed of few line segments (Figure 4b).

Drawing Contours and Details

The block-in and skeleton guides form a coarse scaffold for drawing the detailed contours of color regions. Edwards [12] and Dodson [10] advise to consider these regions as abstract shapes that compose a "jigsaw puzzle". They recommend to draw the large regions first, then the smaller ones, merging adjacent regions that share similar tones (Figure 5a). Focusing on the abstract shapes of individual regions prevents us from thinking about the semantic of the object that the regions compose.

Automatic extraction

We guide users in identifying large and small regions by segmenting the image with the hierarchical algorithm of Arbelaez et al. [1] (Figure 5b). We chose this algorithm for its high score on the Berkeley Segmentation Dataset Benchmark [23] with respect to human ground-truth boundaries. We generate two levels of detail containing one and six regions.

[2] We provide the results of our visual guide extraction on 10 typical images as supplemental materials.

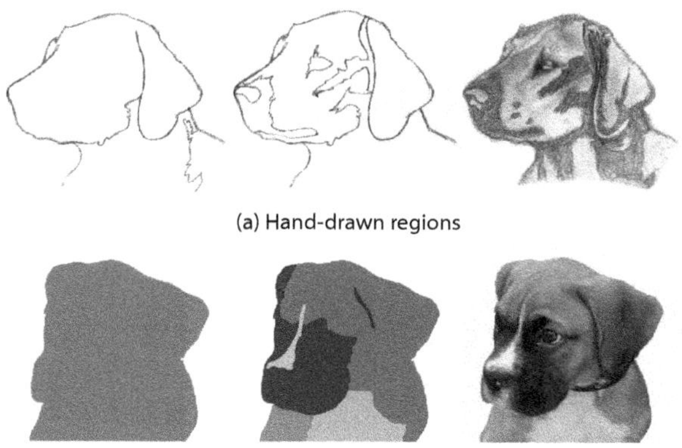

(a) Hand-drawn regions

(b) Automatic extraction

Figure 5. Considering a shape as a collection of regions helps to forget its iconic representation (after [10]).

(a) Sighting for alignments and proportions (b) Automatic extraction

Figure 6. Sighting facilitates the identification of alignments and proportions (after [10]).

Verifying Alignments and Proportions

It is often hard to judge and measure the distortions in a drawing with a naked eye. Artists make use of the "sight" (or "thumb-and-pencil") method to facilitate this task. They hold their pen or pencil at arms length between their eye and the object of interest and sight along it. Sighting helps them identify and estimate relative proportions and alignments [10] (Figure 6). While not explicitly stated in drawing books, we observed that artists only look for vertical and horizontal alignments, which are easier to reproduce. Sighting is especially useful when beginning a drawing to obtain well proportioned construction lines that then yield accurate contours.

Artists sometimes prepare their drawing by laying down a grid over the drawing surface [5, 18]. The grid serves multiple purposes, such as visualizing alignments and spacing and helping the artist focus on local areas in the drawing. The grid also serves as an alternative to block-in to capture the overall arrangement of shapes. Bradley [5] recommends to capture the most salient points of the subject with a non-uniform grid.

Automatic extraction

To emulate sighting, we first detect feature points that correspond to salient landmarks in the image. Many feature detectors could be used for this task and we found that the Shi-Tomasi corner detector [28] performs well for our purpose, both on photographs and line drawings. We then detect and sort pairs of aligned points. We favor pairs that form long lines close to vertical or horizontal because our first tests revealed that they were the most useful to prevent large distortions. For proportions, we detect points that form pairs of equal length. Following early comments from an expert user, we favor pairs that have a common point because users can more easily compare them using their pen as a compass. Finally, we build a non-uniform grid over the photograph by tracing vertical and horizontal lines through the n most salient corners ($n = 3$ in our implementation).

(a) Hand-drawn grid (b) Automatic extraction

Figure 7. A grid visualizes alignments and spacing and allows artists to focus on one cell at a time (after [5]).

REGISTERING VISUAL GUIDES AND USER INPUT

A key ingredient of our drawing assistant is the ability to evaluate error in the drawing with respect to the visual guidance. We perform this evaluation by registering each visual guide with its user-drawn counterpart in real time. We encourage users to draw different guides in different layers to facilitate registration, as we describe in the next section. Our registration builds both a dense correspondence between contours and a sparse correspondence between corners, which we use to provide different types of feedback.

Dense Correspondence between Contours

We first compute a dense correspondence between the guide and the user drawing to evaluate error along any portion of a contour. We base our registration on the *Shape Context* descriptor [3], which was designed for this purpose.

Shape Context represents a shape as a dense set of points where the descriptor of each point encodes the distribution of all other points relative to it. To register two shapes, the original algorithm first computes a one-to-one assignment between their respective point sets, and then estimates the transformation that best align the two shapes. Since the one-to-one assignment is a costly procedure, we adopt a faster approach and simply assign each point p of one shape to the most similar point q in the other shape. We use this assignment to estimate the affine transformation T_A between the two shapes:

$$\underset{T_A}{\operatorname{argmin}} \sum_p \|T_A(p) - q\|^2. \tag{1}$$

In practice, we always register the user drawing with respect to the guide so that each point in the drawing has a correspondence. Belongie et al. [3] suggest iterating the assignment and estimation steps to reject outliers from the initial assignment. We perform one such iteration, where we weight the matching costs $C(p, q)$ between a point and all other points by their residual after the initial transformation:

$$C'(p, q) = \|T_A(p) - q\| \; C(p, q). \tag{2}$$

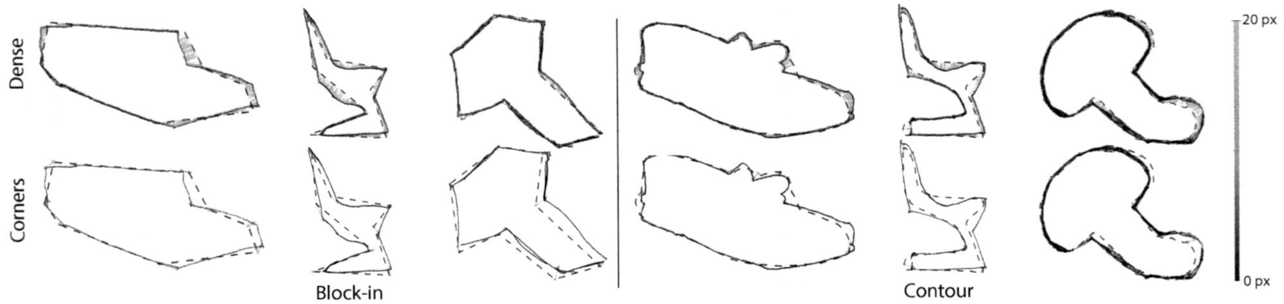

Figure 8. Results of our dense and sparse registration on drawings performed by three different users.

The affine transformation yields a registration robust to non-uniform scaling and shear. While this robustness is desirable for identifying accurate correspondences, we should account for the non-uniform distortions when evaluating the quality of the drawing. For this reason, we also estimate the *similarity* transformation T_S that best approximates the registration as a combination of rotation, translation and uniform scaling. We express the error ϵ for each point in the drawing as the distance between the transformed point and its correspondence:

$$\epsilon(p) = \|T_S(p) - q\|. \quad (3)$$

Sparse Correspondence between Corners

Our system relies on corner features to detect alignments and equal proportions. We register corners between the guidance and the drawing to verify that the user sketch satisfies the same alignments and proportions as the visual guide. We again use the Shape Context descriptor to perform this registration, using the affine transformation T_A computed from the dense correspondence to weight the matching cost of each pair of corners. In practice we use the inverse of this transformation since our goal is to find a correspondence between each corner of the guide and its most similar corner in the drawing. While we need to run the Shi-Tomasi detector [28] to extract corners from the user sketch and the region guide, we can directly use the vertices of the block-in and skeleton lines as robust corners for these guides.

We illustrate in Figure 8 our dense and sparse correspondence on block-in guides and contours drawn by three different users. We provide additional registration examples on other guides and images as supplemental materials.

USER INTERFACE DESIGN

Drawing books do not provide clear recommendations about which guides to use for a certain subject or how to combine different guides together. A guide can be more appropriate for a given subject depending on its form and complexity, while the experience and style of the user may also determine the use of a technique. Therefore, we offer users the freedom to experiment with different guides on the same model and decide by themselves which technique best suits their needs.

Visual Guides and Drawing Layers

The canvas area offers simple drawing tools — a pen to draw opaque strokes, a pencil to draw light strokes, a small and a big eraser. The left side of the canvas contains a menu to select and configure the techniques users wish to practice, which includes regions, block-in, skeleton and grid. Each technique is associated with a different color and each icon displays a miniature visualization of its effect on the model (Figure 2a(4)). A drop-down list gives access to levels of detail for the block-in tool (coarse and fine polygon) and the regions tool (coarse and fine regions, and original photograph). We make the block-in and skeleton techniques mutually exclusive because they have a similar goal and displaying them together produces clutter. In contrast, we always show the regions behind other guides as they form the basic elements of the final drawing. Finally, the grid is optional and can be combined with any other technique.

We enrich our drawing tool with a layering system that has two benefits. First, it helps users make the distinction between the guides that they sketch and the final drawing. Users can also hide the layers to visualize their drawing without construction lines. The second goal of the layering is to facilitate registration between the visual guides that we extract from the photograph and the guides drawn by the user. We assign one layer to each guide and compute a registration between each layer and the corresponding guide. We further help users to distinguish each layer by using different colors that correspond to the colors of the guides (Figure 2a(5)). When the user selects a guide, the system automatically activates the corresponding layer. The user can also select a layer and the system activates the corresponding guide. We then render the active layer and active guide on top of the other ones. Finally, we use semi-transparent strokes for the guidance layers to allow users see their drawing through the construction lines and subtle animated blending to communicate transitions between different guides.

Corrective Feedback

At any time, users can request feedback on their drawing by pressing a button on the pen tablet. We again follow our design goals and display feedback on the model to encourage users to observe it more carefully before applying corrections on canvas. We use the correspondence between the visual guides and the user drawing to generate two types of corrective feedback, as we illustrate in Figure 2c.

We first use our dense measure of error to highlight parts of the guides that are highly distorted. We use a color code that interpolates between the color of the guide (no error) and red (high error). We then use the registration between corners to display the alignments and relative proportions that the user drawing does not satisfy. This form of feedback mimics the traditional sighting technique. Dashed lines indicate alignments while pairs of colored lines indicate equal proportions. We adjust the opacity of these indications proportionally to the magnitude of the error, so that users can focus on the most erroneous parts and assess their progress as the indications become more transparent until disappearance.

We observed in a first version of our tool that the model can get highly cluttered in the presence of multiple indications of equal proportions. We avoid such clutter by first displaying the indications that share a common point, since those are easier to verify by the user. We also disable the proportion feedback when the region tool is active because the detailed contours yield too many candidate pairs of corners with equal length.

On-Canvas vs. On-Model Guidance

An important decision that we faced during the design process was whether to show guides not only over the model but also on the canvas. While we expected that on-canvas guidance would result in higher-quality drawings with less effort, we were afraid that it would distract users from observing the model, which would be contrary to our first design goal.

We conducted a pilot experiment to better understand the strengths and weaknesses of each design approach. Twelve participants (seven women and five men) tested three drawing interfaces that provided different levels of guidance: (I1) no guidance, (I2) guidance over the model, and (I3) guidance over the model and the canvas.

The use of corrective feedback was only applicable for I2. For each user interface, participants completed one practice task and two drawing tasks where they had to draw familiar objects from photographs. The order of presentation of the three interfaces was counterbalanced among participants. We kept the sessions short by focusing on the block-in technique and by limiting each drawing task to only 5 minutes, so that the entire study took around an hour to complete.

As we expected, I3 resulted in better drawings, reducing contour error by an average of 50% compared to the base user interface (I1). In contrast, I2 did not have any immediate benefits for such short drawing tasks. However, participants appreciated that I2 encouraged them to observe the model and replicate the visual guides on the canvas by themselves.

One commented that I2 *"is the most didactic solution for learning how to draw"*, while I3 *"is the most easy solution but people do not learn"*. A second participant agreed that *"to learn how to draw, I prefer the [I2] tool. It is convenient to have the corrections"* while another said *"I liked to do the block-in by myself with the [I1] tool"* but added that *"if I would have started by [I1], I would not have known how to draw the block-in guides"*. Participants also appreciated the use of corrective feedback: *"It is nice to have the feedback in [I2]. [I3] is good to draw fast."*

On the other hand, several participants liked the direct on-canvas guidance, and, as shown in Figure 9, they rated I3

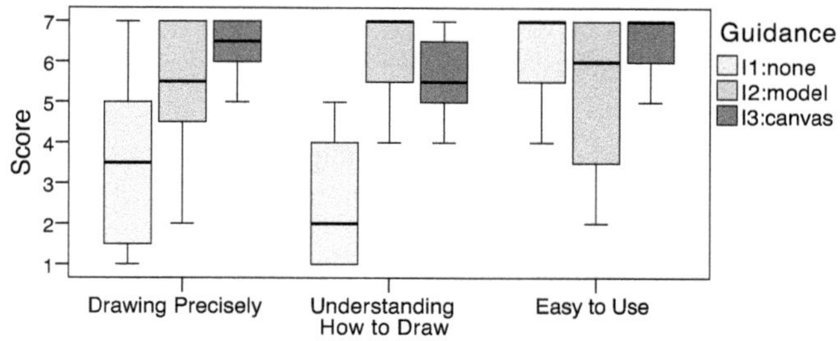

Figure 9. Pilot experiment: Boxplot summarizing the subjective user rankings (1 = not helpful, 7 = very helpful). The top and bottom of the box correspond to the first and third quartiles and the band inside corresponds to the median. The whiskers denote the score range.

relatively high. The tradeoffs among the three interfaces are perhaps best summarized by the following user comment:

"The three versions let me see the difference. It's the union of them that lets me understand the technique."

We decided to keep our tool simple and consistent with our initial goals by only showing guides over the model. However, we envision that future designs of the tool could accommodate all three levels of guidance within the same interface.

EVALUATION

We conducted a user study to evaluate the automatic guidance of our drawing assistant and get initial user feedback about its potential as a learning tool.

Method

Participants

Eight volunteers participated in the study — six women and two men, 23 to 43 years old. Their drawing experience ranged from 1 to 4 on a Likert scale from 1 (poor) to 5 (good), with a mean experience of 2.25 (below average). All the participants were right-handed.

Apparatus

Participants interacted with a Wacom Cintiq 12WX pen display. Model photographs were displayed on a 21" monitor.

Design and Procedure

Before each session, participants completed a brief questionnaire about their drawing experience. Each participant was then exposed to two versions of the drawing interface: our drawing assistant with on-model guidance and a base interface with no guidance. The order of their presentation was counterbalanced among participants, i.e., four participants started with the base interface, and four participants started with the guided one. The base user interface did not provide any mechanism for drawing on separate layers and we gave no instructions whether participants should make use of construction lines for this condition.

Participants were first given a short tutorial for each interface. Then, they completed a practice and a main drawing task that lasted 15 to 30 minutes. To observe the use of visual guides with different types of drawing subjects, we split participants into two groups (see Figure 12). The first group drew a roller skate and a trumpet and was advised to use the block-in guides. The second group drew two full-body characters and was advised to use the skeleton guides. We provide example sessions of each group in the accompanying video.

After the end of the session, participants completed a questionnaire to evaluate their experience with the tool. The whole procedure lasted 60 to 80 minutes.

Results

Figure 12 presents the drawings of each participant along with their mean contour error. This error is calculated by our similarity registration and provides an objective measure of the overall distortion of the drawing that we aim to correct for. Since some participants drew more detailed drawings than others, we performed a fair comparison by manually erasing any interior contours and measuring error on the main outline of the drawn subject only.

The average error was 24.6 pixels ($SD = 9.0$ pixels) for the base drawing interface and 13.2 pixels ($SD = 4.6$ pixels) for the guided one. Guidance resulted in error reduction ranging from 31% to 64% for all but Participant 5. This participant, who reported having previous training in drawing, explained:

"The [skeleton] guide is very clear and I understood quickly what I was supposed to do [but] following the guide was hard for me because I'm used to drawing in a different way. I think this is very useful for a beginner."

Our system was particularly effective for participants 1, 6 and 7 that had poor drawing experience. A close examination of their drawings without guidance reveals significant errors. For example, Participant 1 made the roller shoe too tall and the wheels too close apart and Participant 6 made the torso of the character too long, the right leg too short and the left leg too low. No such distortions appear in their guided drawing.

Figure 10 presents how participants evaluated the visual guides, the corrective feedback, and their overall experience of the tool's learning utility.

Guides: Overall, participants found the visual guides clear, helpful, and easy to use. Seven participants reported having made extensive use of the visual guides. Only Participant 5 reported that she made limited use.

Corrective feedback: While most participants appreciated the corrective feedback, their ratings varied from *Neutral* to *Good*. An analysis of the error evolution during the guided tasks reveals that by following the corrective feedback, Participants 1 to 7 managed to progressively reduce the error of their guides by an average of 34% ($SD = 9\%$). However, Participant 8 increased the error of the skeleton by 43% between his first and last request for feedback. The participant noted that *"trying to correct some specific parts sometimes makes other proportions wrong"*. We suspect that skeletons were harder to draw because they contained around 15 vertices forming disconnected segments, while the block-in guides form closed polygons of no more than 10 vertices.

Overall experience: All the participants, to a different extent each, agreed that the session helped them learn new things about how to draw: *"I discovered new concepts like regions and block-in. I learned a fairly easy technique to improve my drawings."* Similarly, they agreed that the interface can be useful for helping people learn how to draw.

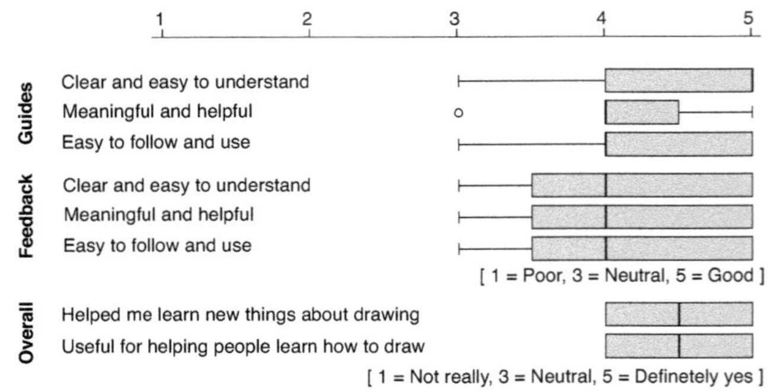

Figure 10. Subjective user evaluation of the drawing assistant. The dot represents an outlier.

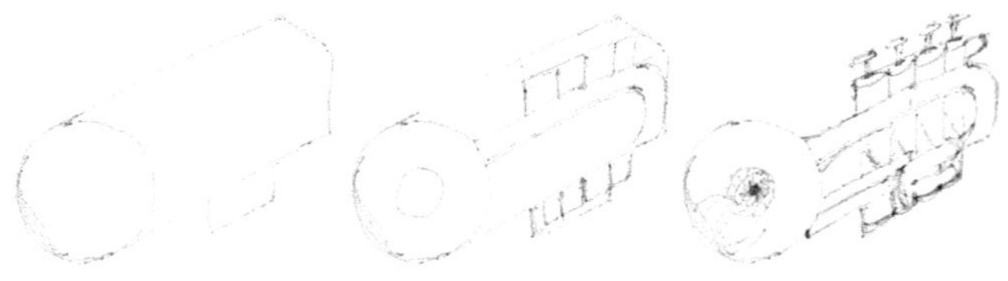

(a) User's block-in lines (b) Final drawing

Figure 11. Use of the block-in technique by Participant 4 for her second non-guided task.

Interestingly, participants who were first exposed to our drawing tool tried to apply the techniques practiced through the first task to the second non-guided task, despite the fact that the base interface did not encourage their use. Participant 6 drew a skeleton to structure her second drawing. Participant 8 used sighting to verify alignments and proportions. Participant 4 applied the sighting and block-in techniques (see Figure 11). According to this participant:

"I could apply the methods on my second drawing, and I think they were very useful to better reproduce the photo. I understood clearly the interest of the explained method."

This result is particularly encouraging as it shows that some users could quickly benefit from our tool.

Finally, some participants identified limitations and proposed areas for improvement. A participant observed that the *"first stages of the process provided a lot of help for learning to draw the volumes with right proportions"* but commented that she *"had some problems adding details"* as this stage of drawing was *"less assisted"*. Other participants pointed to the lack of support for different drawing habits, especially assistance adapted to more experienced drawers. Participants from an early informal study also suggested providing guidance not only for drawing shape but also for shading. Furthermore, some participants tended to mimic the clean style of our guides even though our registration is robust to more sketchy lines. They suggested that rendering guides in a sketchy style would have made them feel more relaxed.

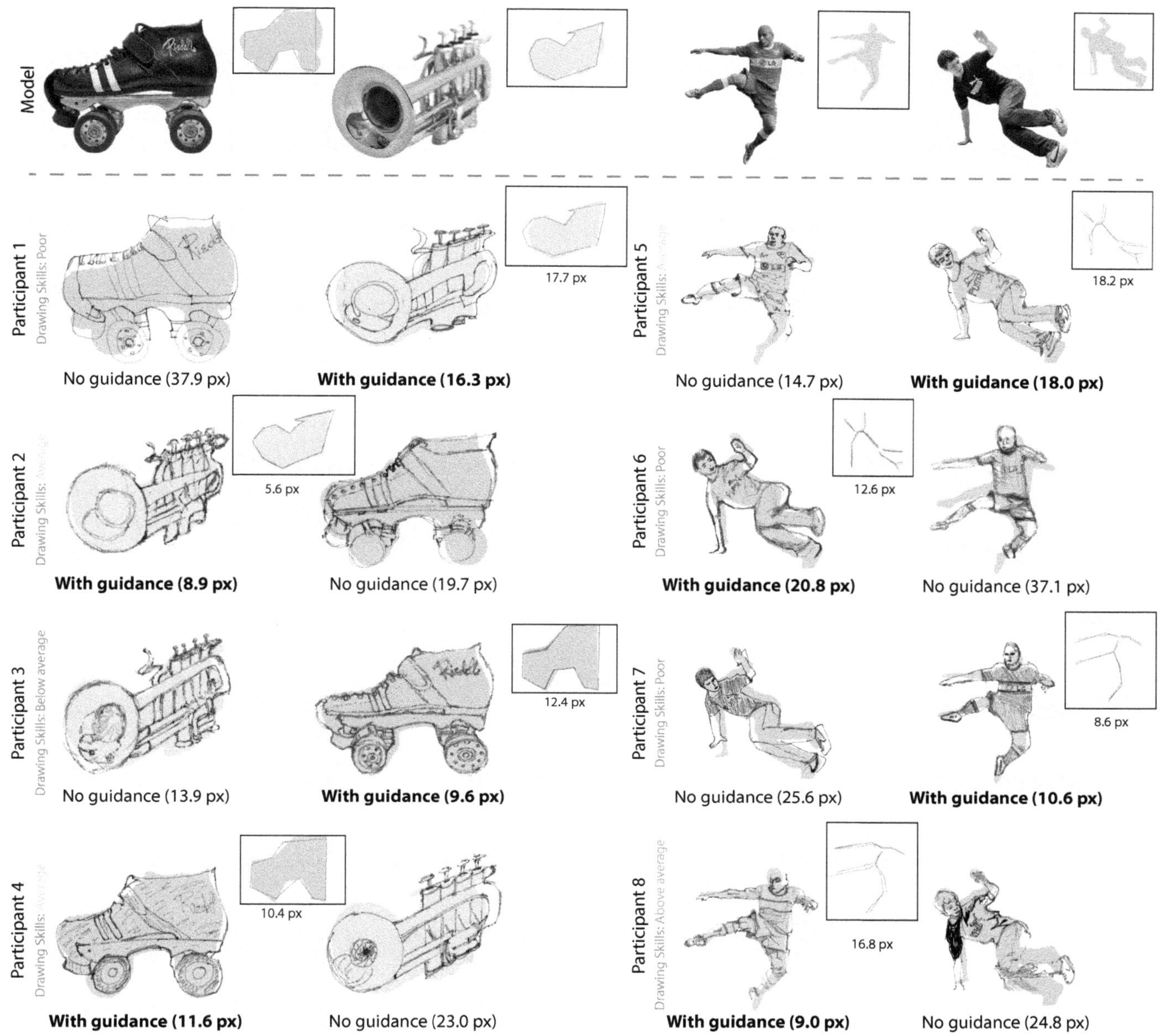

Figure 12. Drawings produced by the height participants, with and without our tool, in the order of completion. We provide as inset the drawn construction lines for the drawings performed with our tool. We display under each drawing the average error of the main contour, in pixels.

DISCUSSION

While we have selected simple and robust computer vision algorithms to extract our visual guides, they may fail to detect the desired features on some images. As a result, our system can sometimes miss alignments or proportions that could help users improve their drawing. Alignments and proportions alone are also sometimes not enough to show how to improve a drawing, as is the case in Figure 13 where our system did not identify any sighting guides to help the user move the legs apart. Traditional artists face the same limitations of sighting and resort to additional measurement techniques, which we could also integrate into our system. For example, some artists hold two pens as a compass to measure angles.

At several stages of the design process, we made the choice to avoid visual clutter by limiting the amount of guidance. For example, we chose to not show all the detected proportions at once and only use block-in on the main outline, not on the small internal regions. Despite these efforts, the feedback can be visually complex in the presence of many errors and we plan to explore alternative visualizations and interaction techniques to improve the balance between level of guidance and clarity. Nevertheless, participants judged our visualization clear and easy to understand overall and managed to apply the system's advice to correct their drawings.

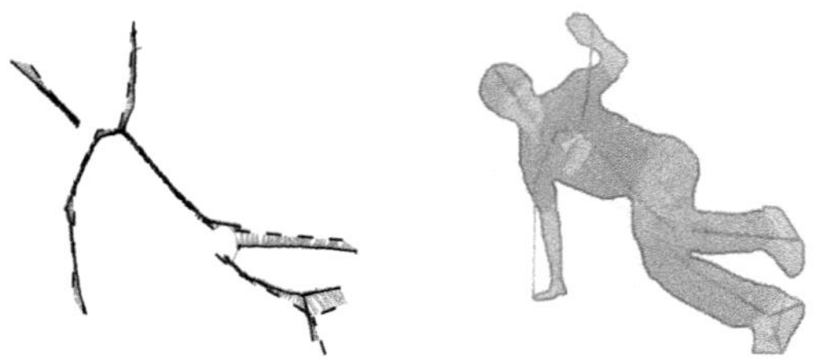

Figure 13. Limitation of our feedback. While the user drew most of the skeleton accurately, he did not manage to correct the legs that should be moved apart (a). Our feedback mechanism marked the distorted legs in red but did not suggest any relevant alignments and proportions (b).

Our system relies on well-known observational drawing techniques from the extensive drawing instruction literature. Assessing how people learn from these techniques represents an exciting but difficult research challenge. Such a study would have to observe users over a long period to measure significant learning behavior but also deal with unintended learning effects between conditions. Our study evaluates instead the quality of the produced drawings, which demonstrates that guidance and feedback have immediate benefits. Nevertheless, the users' subjective evaluation and the tendency to reproduce guides in the no guidance condition suggests that our system helps understanding how to draw.

CONCLUSION

We presented an interactive tool that assists users in drawing from photographs by providing guidance and corrective feedback inspired by traditional drawing techniques. Our system is based on automatically generated guidelines that apply to generic models. By combining pen-based interaction with a real-time registration algorithm, our tool encourages users to practice these techniques on model photographs of their choice. While we focused on generic techniques in this paper, domain-specific techniques could also be integrated into our system. We are especially interested in using computer vision algorithms to detect vanishing points that form the basis of perspective drawing. Finally, we plan to extend our approach with augmented reality technology, enabling users to practice drawing with real subjects.

Acknowledgments. We would like to thank all the volunteers who participated in our study. We also thank George Drettakis and Maneesh Agrawala for feedback and Lora Oehlberg for help with the video. Chair in Fig. 3 from ambientedirect.com, other pictures from Wikimedia Commons: dog in Fig. 1 by Emery Way, soccer player in Fig. 4 by Pallenestor, dog in Fig 5 by André Villeneuve, basketball player in Fig. 6 by Ildar Sagdejev, dancers in Fig. 7 and 12 by Alexander Zabara, trumpet in Fig. 12 by Guillaume Piolle, skate in Fig. 12 by ChrisEngelsma. This work was funded in part by Autodesk (research and software donations) and by ANR-12-JS02-003-01 DRAO.

REFERENCES

1. Arbelaez, P., Maire, M., Fowlkes, C., and Malik, J. Contour detection and hierarchical image segmentation. *IEEE Trans. on Pattern Analysis and Machine Intelligence*, 99 (2011), 1–1.
2. Bae, S.-H., Balakrishnan, R., and Singh, K. EverybodyLovesSketch: 3d sketching for a broader audience. In *ACM Symp. on User Interface Software and Technology (UIST)* (2009), 59–68.
3. Belongie, S., Malik, J., and Puzicha, J. Shape matching and object recognition using shape contexts. *IEEE Trans. Pattern Analysis and Machine Intelligence 24*, 4 (2002), 509–522.
4. Blum, H., et al. A transformation for extracting new descriptors of shape. *Models for the perception of speech and visual form 19*, 5 (1967), 362–380.
5. Bradley, B. *Drawing people: how to portray the clothed figure*. North Light Books, 2003.
6. Chi, P.-Y., Ahn, S., Ren, A., Dontcheva, M., Li, W., and Hartmann, B. Mixt: automatic generation of step-by-step mixed media tutorials. In *ACM Symp. on User Interface Software and Technology (UIST)* (2012).
7. Cummmings, D., Vides, F., and Hammond, T. I don't believe my eyes!: geometric sketch recognition for a computer art tutorial. In *Proc. International Symposium on Sketch-Based Interfaces and Modeling* (2012), 97–106.
8. Denning, J. D., Kerr, W. B., and Pellacini, F. Meshflow: interactive visualization of mesh construction sequences. *ACM Trans. on Graphics (Proc. SIGGRAPH) 30*, 4 (2011).
9. Dixon, D., Prasad, M., and Hammond, T. iCanDraw: Using sketch recognition and corrective feedback to assist a user in drawing human faces. In *Proc. of the International Conference on Human Factors in Computing Systems (CHI)*, ACM (2010).
10. Dodson, B. *Keys to drawing*. North Light Books, 1985.
11. Douglas, D. H., and Peucker, T. K. Algorithms for the reduction of the number of points required to represent a digitized line or its caricature. *Cartographica: The International Journal for Geographic Information and Geovisualization 10*, 2 (Oct. 1973), 112–122.
12. Edwards, B. *Drawing on the right side of the brain*. Tarcher, 1979.
13. Eitz, M., Hays, J., and Alexa, M. How do humans sketch objects? *ACM Trans. on Graphics (Proc. SIGGRAPH) 31*, 4 (2012), 44.
14. Fernquist, J., Grossman, T., and Fitzmaurice, G. Sketch-sketch revolution: an engaging tutorial system for guided sketching and application learning. In *ACM Symp. on User Interface Software and Technology (UIST)* (2011), 373–382.
15. Flagg, M., and Rehg, J. Projector-guided painting. In *ACM Symp. on User Interface Software and Technology (UIST)* (2006), 235–244.
16. Grabler, F., Agrawala, M., Li, W., Dontcheva, M., and Igarashi, T. Generating photo manipulation tutorials by demonstration. *ACM Trans. on Graphics (Proc. SIGGRAPH) 28*, 3 (2009), 66:1–66:9.
17. Hoddinott, B. Drawspace, http://www.drawspace.com/.
18. Hoddinott, B., and Combs, J. *Drawing for dummies*. 2011.
19. Kohr., M. Ctrl+paint, http://www.ctrlpaint.com/.
20. Laviole, J., and Hachet, M. Papart: interactive 3d graphics and multi-touch augmented paper for artistic creaton. In *3DUI - IEEE Virtual Reality Conference* (2012).
21. Lee, Y., Zitnick, C., and Cohen, M. Shadowdraw: real-time user guidance for freehand drawing. *ACM Trans. on Graphics (Proc. SIGGRAPH) 30*, 4 (2011), 27.
22. Limpaecher, A., Feltman, N., and Cohen, M. Real-time drawing assistance through crowdsourcing. *ACM Trans. on Graphics (Proc. SIGGRAPH)* (2013).
23. Martin, D., Fowlkes, C., Tal, D., and Malik, J. A database of human segmented natural images and its application to evaluating segmentation algorithms and measuring ecological statistics. In *IEEE International Conference on Computer Vision* (2001), 416–423.
24. Nicolaides, K. *The Natural Way to Draw: A Working Plan for Art Study*. Houghton Mifflin Co., 1969.
25. Rivers, A., Adams, A., and Durand, F. Sculpting by numbers. *ACM Trans. on Graphics (Proc. SIGGRAPH Asia) 31*, 6 (2012).
26. Rother, C., Kolmogorov, V., and Blake, A. "grabcut": interactive foreground extraction using iterated graph cuts. *ACM Trans. on Graphics (Proc. SIGGRAPH) 23*, 3 (2004).
27. Schmidt, R., Khan, A., Singh, K., and Kurtenbach, G. Analytic drawing of 3d scaffolds. *ACM Trans. on Graphics (Proc. SIGGRAPH Asia) 28*, 5 (2009).
28. Shi, J., and Tomasi, C. Good features to track. In *IEEE Conference on Computer Vision and Pattern Recognition* (1994).
29. Soga, M., Kuriyama, S., and Taki, H. Sketch learning environment with diagnosis and drawing guidance from rough form to detailed contour form. *T. Edutainment 3* (2009), 129–140.

AttribIt: Content Creation with Semantic Attributes

Siddhartha Chaudhuri *
Princeton University
sidch@cs.princeton.edu

Evangelos Kalogerakis *
U. Mass. Amherst
kalo@cs.umass.edu

Stephen Giguere
U. Mass. Amherst
sgiguere@cs.umass.edu

Thomas Funkhouser
Princeton University
funk@cs.princeton.edu

ABSTRACT
We present ATTRIBIT, an approach for people to create visual content using relative semantic attributes expressed in linguistic terms. During an off-line processing step, ATTRIBIT learns semantic attributes for design components that reflect the high-level intent people may have for creating content in a domain (e.g. adjectives such as "dangerous", "scary" or "strong") and ranks them according to the strength of each learned attribute. Then, during an interactive design session, a person can explore different combinations of visual components using commands based on relative attributes (e.g. "make this part more dangerous"). Novel designs are assembled in real-time as the strengths of selected attributes are varied, enabling rapid, in-situ exploration of candidate designs. We applied this approach to 3D modeling and web design. Experiments suggest this interface is an effective alternative for novices performing tasks with high-level design goals.

Author Keywords
content creation, exploratory interfaces, high-level attributes, relative attributes, semantic attributes, assembly-based modeling, interactive modeling

ACM Classification Keywords
H.5.2 Information Interfaces and Presentation (e.g., HCI): User Interfaces - Interaction styles; I.2.10 Artificial Intelligence: Vision and Scene Understanding - Shape

General Terms
Algorithms; Design; Human Factors.

INTRODUCTION
The ubiquity of visual media, and the growing interest in new applications such as collaborative virtual worlds and 3D printing, has led to a demand for interfaces suitable for novice users to engage in computer-aided visual design to produce their own content. This is especially true for three-dimensional content, which is notoriously difficult for novices to create [33]. A successful interface must make it as easy as possible for novice users to map a design goal to intuitive interactions so that they quickly reach the objective and feel confident that it has been achieved.

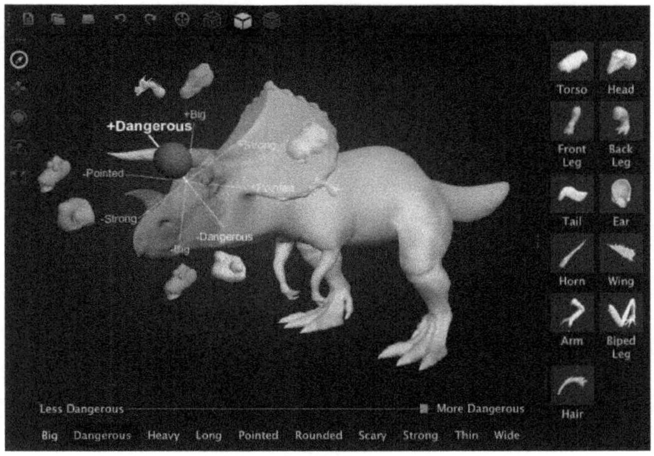

Figure 1: *A user explores novel virtual creatures by changing the strength of semantic attributes reflecting high-level design intent. The attributes, and their relative strengths for different parts, are learned from crowdsourced training data.*

Several types of state-of-the-art interfaces, such as drawing and sculpting tools [15,27], drag-and-drop component assembly [6,24] and design galleries [22,23,35] have been proposed to address this need. However, such interfaces have a common limitation: they do not provide a way to directly express a high-level design goal (e.g. "create a cute toy"). Instead, the goal must be reached by careful planning and execution of a series of low-level selection and editing commands — which requires previsualization, dexterity and time — or serendipitiously through largely unstructured exploration. The gap between how a person thinks about what she wants to create, and how she can interact with a computer to get there, is a barrier for the novice.

This paper introduces ATTRIBIT, an approach for quickly realizing high-level design goals by directly capturing design intent in *linguistic* terms. For example, the designer may want

*S. C. and E. K. contributed equally to this work.

UIST'13, October 8–11, 2013, St. Andrews, United Kingdom.

ACM 978-1-4503-2268-3/13/10...$15.00.
http://dx.doi.org/10.1145/2501988.2502008

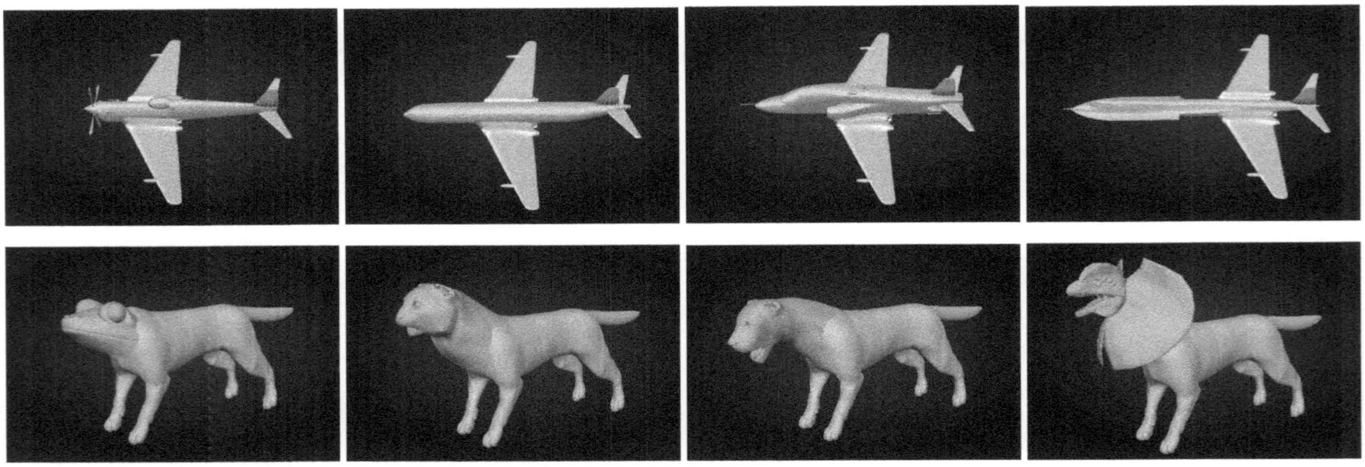

Figure 2: *Exploration with semantic attributes for 3D modeling. Top: Exploring less (left) to more (right) aerodynamic fuselages. Bottom: Exploring less (left) to more (right) scary heads. The adjectives "aerodynamic" and "scary," and the ranking of components under these attributes were learned from crowdsourced training data. The displayed components, left to right, have ~0%, 33%, 66% and 100% of the respective attribute strengths. All components are automatically positioned and glued.*

to make a virtual creature more "scary", or a web page more "artistic". Such requirements are natural for humans, yet cannot be directly expressed in current interfaces. Nor are they represented in the pioneering work of Coyne and Sproat [8] which focuses, by contrast, on configurational specifications ("the cat is facing the wall"). We seek a human-centric interface that lets us specify such objectives directly, without having to translate to computer-friendly abstractions.

ATTRIBIT is a data-driven interface for content creation that associates *relative semantic attributes* with design elements. A relative attribute [29] is one whose strength varies continuously (e.g. "strong"), as opposed to binary attributes, which are either present or absent (e.g. "quadruped"). ATTRIBIT directly supports actions such as "show me scarier heads" or "show me more artistic webpages". Of course, it is infeasible to capture all possible design objectives as individual attributes. However, complex concepts can usually be expressed in terms of simpler ones [25] (e.g. an airplane designed to win dogfights is typically "aerodynamic", "fast" and "military"). Hence, ATTRIBIT supports a wide range of design objectives beyond those corresponding to individual supported attributes.

Further, ATTRIBIT is an exploratory interface, supporting the notion of design as informed choice [3, 14]. It facilitates *targeted exploration* of the design space in terms of human-friendly, semantic axes of variation. ATTRIBIT uses domain knowledge learned from a database of exemplar designs to automatically assemble coherent designs from selected components. The designer can rapidly iterate over a large number of relevant candidate designs to find a suitable one, rather than spend time in painstaking geometric manipulation tasks to assemble each design. Instead of trying to visualize the result of assembling components, she can simply evaluate the finished design in-situ.

A key challenge in enabling this type of interaction is to develop automatic or semi-automatic techniques to infer high-level semantic attributes for design components. A second key challenge is to develop interfaces that allow targeted exploration of the design space based on these attributes.

To infer semantic attributes, we first crowdsource descriptive adjectives for design components from Amazon Mechanical Turk. Since real-world applications will have too many exemplar components for complete manual annotation, we leverage techniques from information retrieval, machine learning and computer vision to learn functions that map component appearance to attribute strengths, e.g. how scary an animal head is, or how artistic a web page title appears. The functions are learned from a training set of pairwise comparisons also gathered via Mechanical Turk. Finally, we introduce a statistical model for multiple components to be changed simultaneously and coherently as attribute strength is varied.

To enable exploration with high-level attributes, we introduce an interface that allows users to initialize a design with a coherent combination of components from a database, select a subset of these components, interactively increase or decrease the strength of an attribute using sliders, and observe changes to the whole design in real time as new database components corresponding to the updated attribute strengths are swapped in. The components are automatically assembled into a coherent design.

In this paper, we discuss ATTRIBIT chiefly in the context of modeling three-dimensional shapes: virtual creatures, aircraft and ships. To demonstrate that the method generalizes to other (non-3D) domains, we also describe an application to web page design. We present results of experiments with novice users, showing that the interface is easily mastered (in 10 minutes, by an 11-year-old) and can be used to rapidly construct compelling visual content. Finally, we discuss possible future applications of high-level attributes for design.

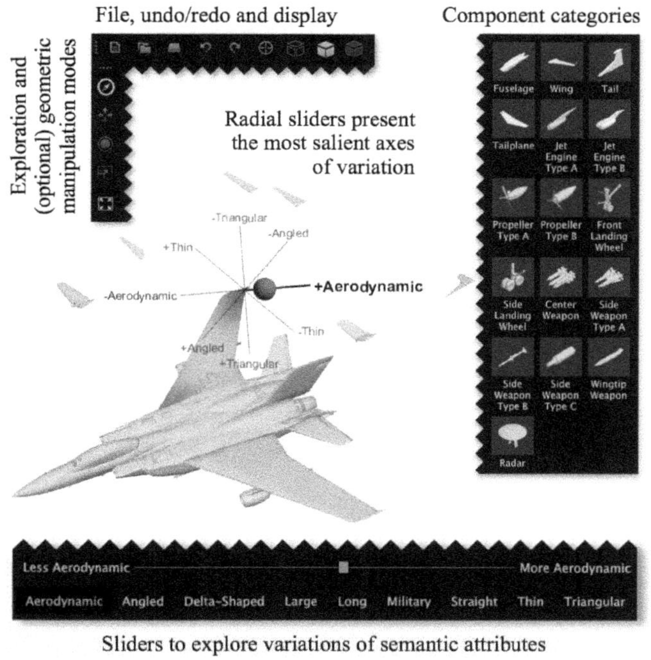

Figure 3: *Modeling interface. Sliders at the bottom and in a radial menu allow exploring novel designs by increasing (+) or decreasing (−) the strength of semantic attributes. Each radial axis approximates the direction of corresponding geometric variation: aerodynamic, angled and triangular wings are stubby and swept back, those with opposite properties are long and perpendicular to the fuselage. Here the user drags the violet handle towards "+Aerodynamic" to explore more aerodynamic wings. Red highlights indicate regions of high geometric variation under the current attribute — the tips are most salient because aerodynamic wings are swept back.*

INTERFACE

ATTRIBIT employs a database of exemplar designs, assumed to be compatibly segmented and labeled. E.g. creatures might be decomposed into head, tail, torso and legs, and airplanes into wings, fuselage, tailplane and engines. Novel designs are created by recombining components from different exemplars [6, 11, 17]. Repurposing successful elements from prior designs can be more efficient than reinventing them from scratch [13]. The space of possible designs is exponentially large: in comparison, the subset fulfilling a given design objective is infinitesimally small. The goal of ATTRIBIT is to facilitate access to this subset of suitable designs.

When the interface is first launched, the artist is presented with buttons on the right corresponding to categories of components from the domain (e.g., heads, torsos, legs, tails for animals; fuselages, wings, tails, engines for airplanes), and a modeling area in the center (Figures 1, 3). She can click buttons in any sequence to add initial components from the corresponding categories to the modeling area. Each initial component is chosen so that the assembled design is plausible, according to a statistical shape prior [17]. They are automatically positioned and stitched into a coherent, seamless design. Components are selected by clicking; selected components are removed with the Delete key. Components may be added and removed at any time, in any sequence. To allow fine adjustment in positioning if desired, our interface also provides translation, rotation and scaling controls.

Exploration Widgets

To explore semantic axes of variations, the user selects one or more components. Upon selection, exploration widgets appear on the screen. The first such widget is a tabbed panel of sliders at the bottom of the screen. Each tab is labeled with the name of an attribute that applies to at least one of the selected components (e.g. "Aerodynamic", "Dangerous", "Fast"). As the user drags a slider up (or down) the range, new components corresponding to higher (resp. lower) strengths of the attribute replace the current ones (Figure 2). Replacement, repositioning and re-stitching of assembled components happens automatically and in real time (Appendix).

The second widget is a set of sliders displayed as spokes of a wheel, positioned directly on the most recently selected component. The spokes have equal angular spacing (45°). Each pair of opposed spokes maps to increasing and decreasing directions of an attribute slider. For instance, the wheel might display "+Fast" and "−Fast" sliders along opposed spokes, corresponding to increasing or decreasing the strength of the "Fast" attribute respectively. One clicks and drags the central handle to explore replacements along any axis, or return to the center to pick a new one.

The wheel allows designers to efficiently evaluate the utility of different attributes with a single click (and subsequent dragging), instead of the click-heavy process of selecting and interacting with individual slider tabs. It displays the 4 attributes with largest geometric variation at the point c at the wheel center (the attribute of the current tab is always included for consistency). To estimate this variation for an attribute, we pre-align all parts in its ordered sequence to the current part using non-rigid ICP [1]. This lets us track c through the preceding and succeeding parts in the sequence of components ordered according to their attribute strength. The local geometric variation for the attribute is computed as the average displacement of the point through successive replacements, limited to K preceding and K succeeding parts in the sequence (we use $K = 3$). The length of this vector ("attribute saliency") determines inclusion in the wheel, and its screen-space direction determines the preferred orientation of the corresponding pair of opposed spokes (Figure 3).

The wheel can be repositioned by clicking at a different point on the selected part, whereupon the most salient attributes are recomputed at that point. We visualize regions of high geometric variation for the active attribute as a saliency map, highlighting more salient regions in red. This visualization provides information on how *semantic* variation manifests as *geometric* variation over a shape (Figures 1, 3). For instance, fast airplane wings have their tips swept back, so related attributes have high saliency at wingtips. The wheel is initially positioned at the most salient point.

The accompanying video shows several example interaction sessions with the ATTRIBIT interface.

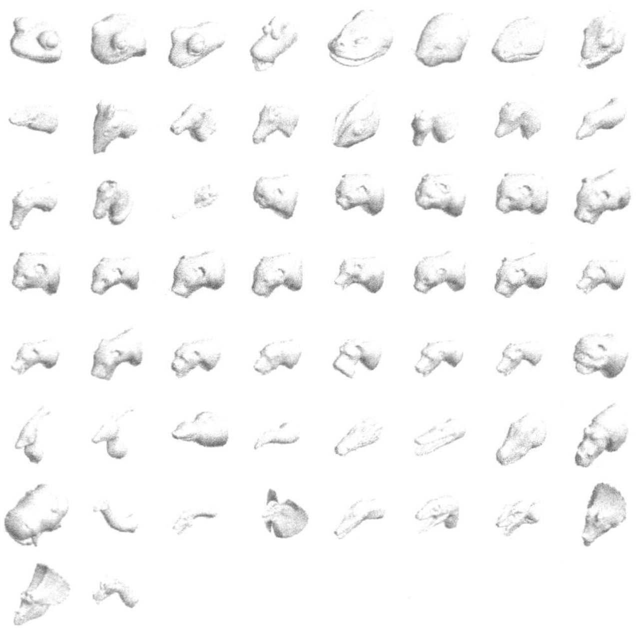

Figure 4: *Ordering of animal heads according to the "dangerous" attribute (top-left is the least dangerous head, sequence is in row-major order). The orderings are organized on sliders in the* ATTRIBIT *interface (Figure 1).*

LEARNING ATTRIBUTES

Recent computer vision research has shown that low-level image features can be mapped to "visual attributes" that correspond to properties observable in images and have human-designated names (e.g., smiling, natural, man-made) [2, 9, 10, 28, 31]. These visual attributes can serve as semantic cues in various image analysis problems. Our work is particularly inspired by the idea of "relative attributes" introduced by Parikh and Grauman [29].

ATTRIBIT uses relative semantic attributes to explore the design space. To achieve this, it learns mappings from features of design components to attribute strengths, based on crowd-sourced training data. For 3D shapes, the features include histograms of curvature and shape diameter, and view-based descriptors. We compute non-linear transformations of these descriptors as additional higher-level features. For details, please refer to the Appendix. By applying these learned mappings from features to attributes, ATTRIBIT automatically ranks components by attribute strength.

Attribute Selection

Our first task is to find adjectives describing attributes of each category of design component. Rather than picking attributes ourselves, we resorted to crowdsourcing to quickly find such adjectives. For each component category (e.g. "head", "fuselage"), we created web pages showing images of two randomly selected designs with highlighted components. For each such pair, we asked respondents in Amazon Mechanical Turk to complete one of the following statements with a suitable adjective (Type 1 questions):

- The left part is more ____ than the right part.
- The left part is ____ than the right part.
- The right part is more ____ than the left part.
- The right part is ____ than the left part.

We also asked about the role of the parts in influencing attributes of the whole design (Type 2 questions):

- The left part makes the shape look more ____ than the right part.
- The left part makes the shape look ____ than the right part.
- The right part makes the shape look more ____ than the left part.
- The right part makes the shape look ____ than the left part.

To obtain a consistent set of salient adjectives across a large sample of respondents, we followed Schelling [32]. Respondents were asked to suggest adjectives they thought *other* people would also select. In addition, to reduce spurious entries, we disallowed the adjectives "better", "worse", "brighter" and "darker." Our survey collected a total of 989 unique adjectives for 32 component categories. Then, we merged synonyms and corrected typos manually. For each component category, we selected the top 10 most common adjectives, omitting those selected < 5 times. For example, the top adjectives for torsos were: *large*, *long*, *thin*, *strong*, *rounded*, *heavy*, *dangerous*, *smooth*, *curved* and *muscular*.

Pairwise Comparison

After finding suitable attributes, we compute complete rankings of all components of each category for each attribute. Asking humans to manually rank thousands of components would be impractical. However, it is relatively easy for a person to compare two objects [29]. Hence, we collect a few pairwise comparisons as training data and automatically infer full rankings. We again created web pages showing pairs of designs with highlighted components. If an attribute was associated with Type 1 questions during attribute selection, we asked Mechanical Turk users to indicate which component in each pair has more of the attribute:

- The left part is more [adjective] than the right part.
- The left part is less [adjective] than the right part.
- The left part is as [adjective] as the right part.
- Neither part is [adjective].

If an attribute was associated with Type 2 questions, we asked which component contributes more to the global attribute:

- The left part makes the shape look more [adjective] than the right part.
- The left part makes the shape look less [adjective] than the right part.
- The left part makes the shape look as [adjective] as the right part.
- Neither part makes the shape look [adjective].

We posted at most 100 pairs for each category and for each adjective, for a total of 87650 comparisons. Each respondent compared 25 pairs and repeated the process for consistency. We rejected respondents whose answers for more than a third of the pairs differed across repetitions. Three different people evaluated each pair, yielding a per-pair confidence measure.

Learning to Rank Components

Given training pairs, we learn a ranking function that infers the strength of an attribute for each associated component. The function maps features of a component to its ranking "score", and thus generalizes to components not in the training comparisons.

For each component category and each associated adjective m, the input to the learning step is a set of training pairs $O_m = \{i, j\}$ in which component i has more of an attribute than j, and a set of training pairs $S_m = \{i, j\}$ in which components i and j have comparable attribute strengths. For each training pair and relative ordering thereof, we also have a confidence measure $c_{ij} \in [0, 1]$ defined as the fraction of respondents who agreed on this ordering. Each component i is represented in $\mathbb{R}^n$ by a feature vector $\mathbf{x}_i$ (for more details on the features used, please refer to the Appendix).

The ranking function r_m maps features to attribute strength:

$$r_m(\mathbf{x}) = \mathbf{w}_m \cdot \mathbf{x},$$

where $\mathbf{w}_m$ is a parameter vector, s.t. the maximum number of dissimilarity and similarity constraints is satisfied:

$$\forall (i,j) \in O_m : \ \mathbf{w}_m \cdot \mathbf{x}_i > \mathbf{w}_m \cdot \mathbf{x}_j$$
$$\forall (i,j) \in S_m : \ \mathbf{w}_m \cdot \mathbf{x}_i = \mathbf{w}_m \cdot \mathbf{x}_j$$

Learning the optimal ranking function is NP-hard [16]. However, we can introduce slack variables to relax the problem, as in Support Vector Machine (SVM) classification [29].

$$\begin{aligned} \text{minimize} \ & \frac{1}{2}\|\mathbf{w}_m\|_2^2 + \alpha \sum_{i,j} (\mathcal{L}(\xi_{ij}) + \mathcal{L}(\gamma_{ij})) \\ \text{s.t.} \ \ \mathbf{w}_m(\mathbf{x}_i - \mathbf{x}_j) \ & \geq \ 1 - \xi_{ij}, \quad \forall (i,j) \in O_m \\ |\mathbf{w}_m(\mathbf{x}_i - \mathbf{x}_j)| \ & \leq \ \gamma_{ij}, \qquad \forall (i,j) \in S_m \\ \xi_{ij} \geq 0 \ & \text{ and } \ \gamma_{ij} \geq 0 \end{aligned}$$

where ξ_{ij} , γ_{ij} are slack variables, $\mathcal{L}(\xi_{ij})$, $\mathcal{L}(\gamma_{ij})$ are loss functions to progressively penalize misranked training examples, and α weights the approximated error. Various loss functions can be employed — for example, in [29] quadratic loss functions $\mathcal{L}(\xi_{ij}) = \xi_{ij}^2$, $\mathcal{L}(\gamma_{ij}) = \gamma_{ij}^2$ were used. This problem is equivalent to solving the following unconstrained optimization problem [5]:

$$\begin{aligned} \text{minimize} \ \ \|\mathbf{w}_m\|_2^2 + \alpha & \sum_{i,j \in O_m} \ell(1 - \mathbf{w}_m(\mathbf{x}_i - \mathbf{x}_j)) \\ + \alpha & \sum_{i,j \in S_m} \ell(|\mathbf{w}_m(\mathbf{x}_i - \mathbf{x}_j)|) \end{aligned}$$

where the first term serves as a regularization term favoring sparse parameter vectors, and $\ell(\cdot)$ is the loss function penalizing misranked examples, e.g. quadratic loss: $\ell(t) = \max(0, t)^2$, or hinge loss: $\ell(t) = \max(0, t)$. In practice, we found the sigmoid loss function [4, 30] performed slightly better (see *Ranking Quality* section). We also consider the confidence c_{ij} for each pair, and weight the loss functions for similarity and dissimilarity constraints differently. Thus, the optimization problem we solve is the following:

$$\begin{aligned} \text{minimize} \ \ \|\mathbf{w}_m\|_2^2 + \mu & \sum_{i,j \in O_m} c_{ij}(1 - \sigma(\mathbf{w}_m(\mathbf{x}_i - \mathbf{x}_j))) \\ + \nu & \sum_{i,j \in S_m} c_{ij}\sigma(|\mathbf{w}_m(\mathbf{x}_i - \mathbf{x}_j)|) \end{aligned}$$

where μ, ν are weighting coefficients and $\sigma(t) = 1/(1 + \exp(-\lambda t))$ is the sigmoid function. The sigmoid loss function is not convex, so we start optimizing the parameters $\mathbf{w}_m$ with a quadratic loss function that is convex and can be minimized with Newton's method [5]. Then, we refine the parameters with a subgradient method for the objective function using the sigmoid loss, which practically converges as also shown in [12]. The weights λ, μ, ν are estimated using 5-fold cross-validation to minimize the number of wrong pairwise rankings in the validation sets.

Using Attributes as Additional Features for Learning

Some attributes, such as "strong", can depend on other simpler attributes, such as "large", "heavy", "thin" or other higher-level attributes, such as "dangerous". ATTRIBIT takes into account these inter-dependencies between attributes to learn them more effectively. Specifically, we first learn a model $r_m(\cdot)$ for each attribute using the base features. Then, we learn a new model $r'_m(\cdot)$ by enriching the feature vector with the scores of all other attributes inferred from the first trained models. We repeat the procedure to learn another model $r''_m(\cdot)$ using the attribute scores from the second trained models. This procedure further decreased test errors (see *Ranking Quality* section). Subsequent repetitions did not decrease errors significantly. Interestingly, many natural inter-dependencies of attributes are successfully captured in this way. E.g. the attribute scores for "strong" heads are strongly correlated with "larger", "heavier", more "dangerous" and less "thin" heads.

MULTIPLE COMPONENTS AND DESIGN PRIORS

ATTRIBIT also supports exploring variation in multiple components simultaneously. When more than one component is selected, some will possess the active high-level attribute and some will not. For example, the attribute "scary" exists for animal heads, but not for legs. We define a joint ranking score for multiple components that share the same active attribute, and infer plausible replacements for components that do not have the attribute.

Joint Ranking of Multiple Components

When multiple components $P = \{p_1, p_2, \ldots, p_n\}$, from categories $q_1, q_2, \ldots, q_n$ respectively, share a single high-level attribute m, we define a joint ranking score over them. First, the ranking scores r''^{q}_m for the components in each associated category q are normalized to $[0, 1]$. Let $R^{q_i}_m(p_i)$ the normalized scores for each component p_i in their associated category q_i. The combined score is defined as the sum

$R_m(P) = \sum_{i=1}^{n} R_m^{q_i}(p_i)$. Starting from the current configuration P, we greedily find the single component replacement that will improve the ranking score, defined above, by the smallest increment. We continue this process until no further replacements are possible — the resulting configuration has the maximum attribute strength under our definition. Similarly, we extend the ranking in the other direction, decreasing the score by minimal increments until we reach the lowest-strength configuration. The resulting ordering ranks configurations of n components under the attribute. We found this simple approach sufficient for our needs. More sophisticated techniques for combining attribute scores (e.g. with learned weights, or nonlinearly) may be considered in future work.

Inference

When a component does not share the active attribute, we perform inference to find a suitable replacement, given context from the rest of the design. This can be thought of as enforcing a design prior. For 3D shapes, we follow Kalogerakis et al. [17] to learn a probability distribution over the shape space that captures relationships between shape components. The distribution is defined over discrete and continuous properties, such as shape type, component styles, number and geometric features of components from each category.

Real-Time Inference

The 3D shape prior of Kalogerakis et al. [17] was designed for sampling novel shapes (not for inference). We developed a real-time inference technique for this model. Given a category q, the technique finds the component from q most compatible with the rest of the shape.

Inference is performed as follows. Let $\mathbf{X}_q$ be the model variables sufficient to identify the most probable component from category q, $\mathbf{X}_e$ be observed features of components from other categories existing in the shape, and $\mathbf{X}_u$ be unobserved shape variables. The unobserved variables include latent shape and component styles, and features from categories not observed in the current shape. The goal of inference is to compute the posterior

$$P(\mathbf{X}_q \mid \mathbf{X}_e = \mathbf{e}) = \frac{\int_{\mathbf{u}} P(\mathbf{X}_q, \mathbf{X}_e = \mathbf{e}, \mathbf{X}_u = \mathbf{u})}{\int_{\mathbf{u},\mathbf{q}} P(\mathbf{X}_q = \mathbf{q}, \mathbf{X}_e = \mathbf{e}, \mathbf{X}_u = \mathbf{u})},$$

where the integral is replaced by a sum for discrete variables. Since the denominator does not differentiate between different components (i.e. is a normalizing factor), we only need to compute the marginal distribution in the numerator. Computing the marginal distribution however requires summing over an exponential number of joint assignments to the variables $\mathbf{X}_u$, which makes its direct computation intractable. We resort to loopy belief propagation to approximate the marginal distribution [20]. Each factor in the model is mapped to a node in a "cluster graph". Belief propagation maintains a set of beliefs (marginals) over these nodes by passing messages along edges to exert the influence of one variable on another. If we mutually connect all nodes including a variable X, the messages would cycle endlessly, resulting in incorrect beliefs. Hence, we introduce auxiliary nodes involving individual variables that are connected to nodes containing the factors in which they appear. The resulting cluster graph has Bethe-style structure and guarantees there is only a single, non-cyclic path along which messages about a variable can flow. In each belief propagation iteration, messages are sent from all nodes to their neighbors synchronously. The beliefs typically converge after 5-10 iterations in under 50ms, allowing real-time approximation of the marginal distribution.

Organizing Components on Sliders

Components are placed on the slider for an associated attribute according to their attribute strength. To increase ease of use, the slider intervals are equally spaced (even if the ranking strengths are not). Second, to increase visual continuity and better organize components in the slider according to their types (so that, e.g., canine heads precede dinosaur heads for the "scary head" attribute, even if MTurk users judged some canine heads to be scarier than some dinosaur heads), the ordering is adjusted to group components by visual style, found by the design prior above. For this purpose, we define attribute strengths for each visual style as the average of the attribute strengths of components associated with this style. We place components on the slider based first on attribute strength of their style, then on their individual strength.

DATASETS

We implemented ATTRIBIT on three domains of 3D models: animals, airplanes and ships. The models were obtained from publicly available commercial libraries (Digimation, Dosch 3D). They were segmented and labeled semi-automatically [17]. Statistics for the datasets are shown in Table 1.

	Airplanes	Animals	Ships
# of source shapes	100	69	42
# of categories	7	11	14
# of components	881	593	639
# of attributes	59	81	21

Table 1: *Input datasets.*

COMPARING ATTRIBIT TO A CATALOG-DRIVEN INTERFACE

We ran an experiment to test the following hypothesis for 3D content creation: high-level attributes help accomplish certain types of content creation tasks more effectively than an alternative data-driven interface where components have to be located by searching catalogs. We chose this comparison for two reasons. The first reason is normalization: the two interfaces can operate on identical input databases, differing only in the semantic exploration aspects introduced in this paper. The second reason is that catalog-driven drag-and-drop interfaces have been shown to be highly accessible to first-time designers in both industrial [24] and academic [6] settings. We chose the state-of-the-art "Modeling by Assembly" (MBA) interface of Chaudhuri et al. [6], which leverages context-sensitive component suggestions. We restricted the experiment to novice users to discount the influence of prior experience with particular modeling interfaces, and because a goal of both ATTRIBIT and MBA is to be as accessible as possible to non-professionals.

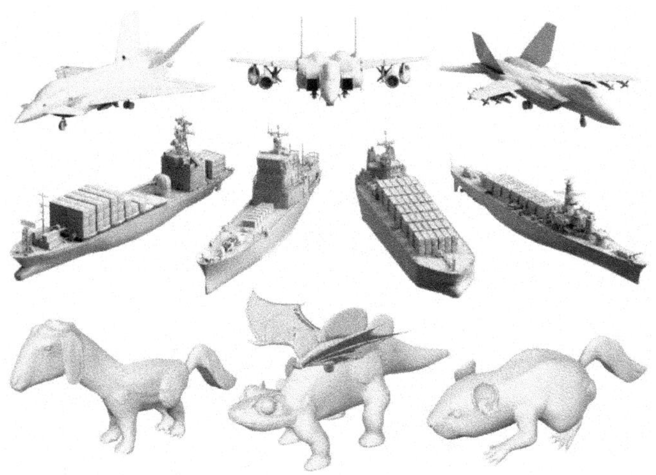

Figure 5: *Dogfight airplanes (top), high-security cargo ships (middle) and cute animals (bottom) created by novice modelers in 15 minutes with* ATTRIBIT. *Images of all 68 models created in the study are provided in supplementary material.*

Method

We recruited 37 persons ranging in age from 11 to 57 . Each reported zero prior 3D modeling experience. We asked them to perform the following content creation tasks:

Airplane. Create an airplane that is best suited to win a dogfight (one-on-one aerial combat) in a computer game.

Animal. Create the cutest possible toy for a small (~7-year old) child.

Ship. Create the best possible ship for carrying large amounts of valuable cargo across a sea infested by modern-day pirates.

The tasks were chosen to represent real-world open-ended design situations which did not directly correspond to maximizing any single attribute (e.g. no animal attribute was "cute" or any synonym thereof).

Each participant completed one task using MBA, and one using ATTRIBIT, with no indication of which interface was "test" and which was "control". We skinned the two interfaces identically and supplied them with identical segmented and labeled datasets. We also let MBA use the state-of-the-art probabilistic model of [17] (an improvement on [6]) and our real-time inference algorithm for component suggestions.

The choice and order of both tasks and interfaces were randomized. No participant was assigned the same task twice, to eliminate the influence of memory of available parts in designing new shapes. Each participant was given a 10 minute orientation with each interface and then allowed 15 minutes of unsupervised modeling time. In all, we collected 68 models: 13 airplanes, 13 animals and 8 ships with each interface (to balance the numbers, the last participant was assigned tasks and interfaces deterministically). A selection of the created models are shown in Figure 5. Images of all models are provided in the supplementary material.

Task	ATTRIBIT	MBA	Both good	Both bad
Airplane	**278**	142	163	19
Animal	**265**	196	53	102
Ship	**226**	166	150	96

(a) *Model better accomplishes goal of task.*

Task	ATTRIBIT	MBA	Both good	Both bad
Airplane	**199**	97	213	27
Animal	**192**	152	65	137
Ship	**183**	119	279	31

(b) *Model is more plausible.*

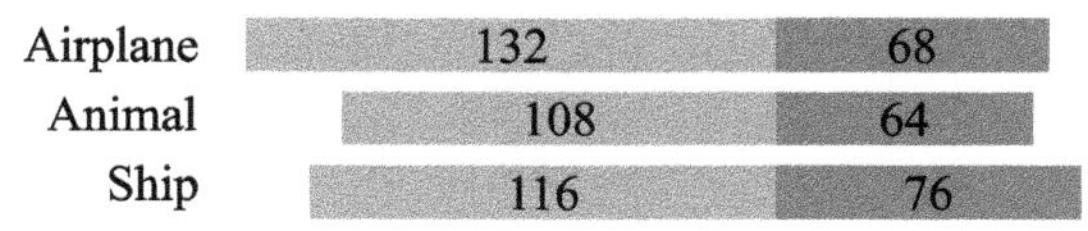

(c) *Model is better in both goal and plausibility. Green:* ATTRIBIT, *red:* MBA. *Statistics obtained from comparisons of the same pair of models under both questions.*

Table 2: *Distribution of votes cast in blind evaluations of user-created models by MTurk respondents. Overall, raters favoured* ATTRIBIT *models over those created with* MBA *[6].*

Evaluation

To evaluate how well the interfaces helped people accomplish tasks, we asked 71 Mechanical Turk respondents to do blind comparisons of the created models. Each respondent was asked 25 questions via a web survey. Each page of the survey showed renderings of two shapes. One shape was randomly selected from models created with ATTRIBIT, and the other from models for the same task created with MBA. The order was randomized. The respondent was asked to compare either how well the two models accomplished the task (better dogfighter, cuter toy, etc.), or how plausible they were. The rater could say one shape was better than the other, or both were equally good, or both were equally bad. After the rater had answered all 25 questions, (s)he was presented the same questions again in a different order, to check for consistency. Raters with ≥ 8 inconsistent responses were discarded.

The results are in Table 2. Shapes created with ATTRIBIT were preferred by proportions of 52.6% to 94.1% in terms of both goal achievement and plausibility (Table 2c). All preferences for ATTRIBIT in Table 2 are statistically significant according to a two-tailed Mann-Whitney U test with $p < 0.05$.

To see if participants actually found the semantic attributes useful for accomplishing tasks, we logged how often individual attributes were used for exploration. Table 3 shows the top attributes used to select the parts present in the final user models. The common attributes ("faster fuselages", "less scary heads", "more modern hulls") correspond to natural associations of adjectives with the tasks, which indicates that users benefited from semantic controls to achieve design goals.

We also observed that participants could more easily explore designs with ATTRIBIT, because parts do not need to be manually positioned. This is supported by statistics from program

Task	Part	Most Popular Attributes
Airplane	Fuselage	Fast, Military, Aerodynamic
	Wing	Delta-Shaped, Military, Aerodynamic
	Tail	Aerodynamic, Military, Less-Delta-Shaped
	Engine	Advanced, Fast, Strong
	Weapon	Dangerous, Less-Big, Pointed
Animal	Head	Less-Scary, Less-Big, Rounded
	Torso	Curved, Rounded, Large
	Leg	Less-Agile, Stubby, Long
	Tail	Curled, Less-Big, Bushy
	Ear	Curved, Long, Floppy
Ship	Hull	Fast, Less-Rounded, Modern
	Weapon	Large, Advanced
	Cabin	Modern
	Antenna	Military, Powerful, Tall
	Funnel	Less-Complex

Table 3: *Most popular attributes used to select final parts in user models. Part categories are ordered by decreasing frequency of replacements explored using their top attributes. Attributes for a part are ordered by decreasing frequency of replacements initiated using them. "Less-" indicates chosen parts came from the lower half of the ranking for the attribute (no prefix indicates parts were chosen from the upper half).*

logs: on average, participants saw 243.4 distinct designs with ATTRIBIT vs 24.6 designs with MBA, a 9.9x improvement.

Two participants told us that without ATTRIBIT, they would not have been able to fulfill the airplane and ship tasks as they lacked the necessary domain knowledge to assemble suitable models. Informal feedback from others also showed encouraging support for ATTRIBIT.

RANKING QUALITY AND COMPUTATIONAL COMPLEXITY

We evaluated our ranking method by test ranking error: the fraction of test pairs where the predicted relative ordering contradicts ground truth. We used leave-one-out mode, iteratively omitting one element from the training set and testing on all pairs containing that element. As a baseline, the human inconsistency (fraction of times a human ranking for a pair contradicted the majority vote) was 14.0%. The lowest average test ranking error (20.4%) was obtained with the sigmoid loss function and attribute strengths as additional features. Using only the sigmoid, hinge and quad loss functions, the average error was 20.9%, 21.1% and 21.1% respectively.

Training an attribute is $O(P \cdot D)$ where P is number of training pairs and D is feature vector size. Evaluating the ranking score per attribute is $O(N \cdot D)$, where N is component category size. Practically, training the model and ranking the parts for each attribute took ~10 minutes in Matlab on an i7.

APPLICATION TO WEB DESIGN

We believe high-level attributes constitute a viable design paradigm in many different visual (and possibly non-visual) domains. To demonstrate that our approach generalizes, we applied it to an important non-3D domain: web page design.

We collected 30 WordPress blog templates (`http://wordpress.com`), recreated by hand to have compatible DOM structure (background, body, sidebar, title font, header image). Since we focused on exploring attribute variations, we did not experiment with more sophisticated style transfer methods [21] to work with unmodified HTML sources: this forms an interesting avenue for future work.

Web page components were of two types: images and (styled) text. Their feature vectors comprised image and font descriptors respectively, as described in the Appendix. We set up Mechanical Turk surveys analogously to 3D shapes, replacing "shape" with "web page" in the survey text. The attributes learned for web page components were: *artistic, casual, cheerful, colorful, creative, cute, elegant, emphatic, modern, professional, romantic, simple* and *welcoming*.

At runtime, components were swapped into the current template by exchanging matched CSS/HTML blocks as attributes were varied with sliders. Joint ranking was performed on all components using a simple handwritten model that tries to maintain compatibility with dominant design elements (e.g. background) or between associated elements (e.g. title font and header image). The wheel widget was not relevant for this domain and was omitted. Two sequences of novel web designs created with ATTRIBIT are shown in Figure 6. The "casual" sequence progresses from bare, formal pages to bright, colorful pages, matching our intuition of "casual". A similarly meaningful progression holds for "artistic".

DISCUSSION

This paper introduces an approach for people to create visual content by exploring an assembly-based space of designs with commands based on linguistic terms. We also demonstrate a method to learn relative attributes for 3D shapes. During experiments, we find it is more effective for 3D modeling with high-level design goals compared to related prior work.

Although our initial results are encouraging, there are limitations of the current implementation and questions for future research. First, our interface based on sliders to control relative attributes is a first prototype. It will be interesting to explore other interactions for adjusting semantic attributes, e.g. using voice input and natural language processing.

Second, our current system only allows creation of new content by combining components of existing examples. It will be interesting to study how relative attributes can be mapped back to design parameters to synthesize completely novel designs, for example by incorporating attributes directly in probabilistic models of shapes and design patterns [17, 34].

Third, attributes that do not increase monotonically in the selected feature space cannot be learned effectively with the current method and would require a more complex approach.

Fourth, our assembly-based system leverages highly structured databases of examples containing consistent segmentations and alignments of components. While many data sets are available of this type, it would be nice to relax this constraint by inferring such structures automatically, for example using methods described in [18, 19, 21]).

(a) *Less (left) to more (right) "casual" novel web pages.*

(b) *Less (left) to more (right) "artistic" novel web pages.*

Figure 6: *Novel web page designs created with* ATTRIBIT *using components from 30 exemplars. Attributes learned for web pages were:* artistic, casual, cheerful, colorful, creative, cute, elegant, emphatic, modern, professional, romantic, simple, welcoming.

Finally, our study has considered design tasks only in the domains of 3D modeling and web page design. It will be interesting to investigate the range of application domains for which design with semantic attributes is possible.

ACKNOWLEDGMENTS

Discussions with Vladlen Koltun, Sergey Levine, Scott Klemmer, Jerry Talton and Karan Singh helped improve the paper. Mixamo Inc. provided the GUI artwork. David Mimno narrated the video. This research was supported by funding from Google, Adobe, Intel (ISTC-VC) and the National Science Foundation (CCF-0937139, CNS-0831374).

REFERENCES

1. Amberg, B. Optimal step nonrigid ICP algorithms for surface registration. In *CVPR* (2007).
2. Berg, T. L., Berg, A. C., and Shih, J. Automatic attribute discovery and characterization from noisy web data. In *ECCV* (2010).
3. Buxton, B. *Sketching User Experiences: Getting the Design Right and the Right Design*. Interactive Technologies. Morgan Kaufmann, 2010.
4. Carvalho, V. R., Elsas, J. L., Cohen, W. W., and Carbonell, J. G. A meta-learning approach for robust rank learning. In *SIGIR* (2008).
5. Chapelle, O. Training a support vector machine in the primal. *Neural Comput. 19*, 5 (2007).
6. Chaudhuri, S., Kalogerakis, E., Guibas, L., and Koltun, V. Probabilistic reasoning for assembly-based 3D modeling. In *SIGGRAPH* (2011).
7. Chen, D.-Y., Tian, X.-P., Shen, Y.-T., and Ouhyoung, M. On visual similarity based 3D model retrieval. *Computer Graphics Forum 22*, 3 (2003).
8. Coyne, B., and Sproat, R. WordsEye: an automatic text-to-scene conversion system. In *SIGGRAPH* (2001).
9. Farhadi, A., Endres, I., Hoiem, D., and Forsyth, D. Describing objects by their attributes. In *CVPR* (2009).
10. Ferrari, V., and Zisserman, A. Learning visual attributes. In *NIPS* (2007).
11. Funkhouser, T., Kazhdan, M., Shilane, P., Min, P., Kiefer, W., Tal, A., Rusinkiewicz, S., and Dobkin, D. Modeling by example. In *SIGGRAPH* (2004).
12. Guillory, A., Chastain, E., and Bilmes, J. Active learning as non-convex optimization. *J. Machine Learning Research 5* (2009).
13. Hartmann, B., Wu, L., Collins, K., and Klemmer, S. R. Programming by a sample: rapidly creating web applications with d.mix. In *UIST* (2007).
14. Hartmann, B., Yu, L., Allison, A., Yang, Y., and Klemmer, S. R. Design as exploration: creating interface alternatives through parallel authoring and runtime tuning. In *UIST* (2008).
15. Igarashi, T., Matsuoka, S., and Tanaka, H. Teddy: a sketching interface for 3D freeform design. In *SIGGRAPH* (1999).
16. Joachims, T. Optimizing search engines using clickthrough data. In *SIGKDD* (2002).
17. Kalogerakis, E., Chaudhuri, S., Koller, D., and Koltun, V. A probabilistic model for component-based shape synthesis. In *SIGGRAPH* (2012).
18. Kalogerakis, E., Hertzmann, A., and Singh, K. Learning 3D mesh segmentation and labeling. In *SIGGRAPH* (2010).
19. Kim, V., Li, W., Mitra, N., Chaudhuri, S., DiVerdi, S., and Funkhouser, T. Learning part-based templates from large collections of 3D shapes. In *SIGGRAPH* (2013).

20. Koller, D., and Friedman, N. *Probabilistic Graphical Models: Principles and Techniques*. MIT Press, 2009.

21. Kumar, R., Talton, J. O., Ahmad, S., and Klemmer, S. R. Bricolage: example-based retargeting for web design. In *CHI* (2011).

22. Lee, B., Srivastava, S., Kumar, R., Brafman, R., and Klemmer, S. R. Designing with interactive example galleries. In *CHI* (2010).

23. Marks, J., Andalman, B., Beardsley, P. A., Freeman, W., Gibson, S., Hodgins, J., Kang, T., Mirtich, B., Pfister, H., Ruml, W., Ryall, K., Seims, J., and Shieber, S. Design galleries: a general approach to setting parameters for computer graphics and animation. In *SIGGRAPH* (1997).

24. Maxis Software. *Spore*. 2008. `http://www.spore.com`.

25. Murphy, G. L. *The Big Book of Concepts*. Bradford Books, 2004.

26. Oliva, A., and Torralba, A. Modeling the shape of the scene: a holistic representation of the spatial envelope. *Int. J. Comput. Vision 42*, 3 (2001).

27. Olsen, L., Samavati, F., Sousa, M. C., and Jorge, J. Sketch-based modeling: a survey. *Computers & Graphics 33*, 1 (2009).

28. Parikh, D., and Grauman, K. Interactively building a discriminative vocabulary of nameable attributes. In *CVPR* (2011).

29. Parikh, D., and Grauman, K. Relative attributes. In *ICCV* (2011).

30. Perez-Cruz, F., Navia-Vazquez, A., Figueiras-Vidal, A. R., and Artes-Rodriguez, A. Empirical risk minimization for support vector classifiers. *Trans. Neur. Netw. 14*, 2 (2003).

31. Russakovsky, O., and Li, F.-F. Attribute learning in large-scale datasets. In *ECCV* (2010).

32. Schelling, T. C. *The Strategy of Conflict*. Harvard University Press, 1960.

33. Sproull, R. F. Parts of the frontier are hard to move. *Computer Graphics Forum 24*, 2 (1990), 9.

34. Talton, J., Yang, L., Kumar, R., Lim, M., Goodman, N. D., and Měch, R. Learning design patterns with Bayesian grammar induction. In *UIST* (2012).

35. Talton, J. O., Gibson, D., Yang, L., Hanrahan, P., and Koltun, V. Exploratory modeling with collaborative design spaces. In *SIGGRAPH Asia* (2009).

APPENDIX

Automatic Placement and Stitching

It can be tedious to assemble designs from components manually. For 3D shapes, we developed a placement algorithm to automatically readjust the assembly to accommodate newly added parts (re-scaled to have comparable relative scales [17]). A preprocessing step records "slots" for each part that connect it to others in its source shape. At runtime, we sort all parts in the assembly by decreasing average part scale of their categories, yielding a sequence $p_1, p_2, p_3, \ldots$. The first (canonically largest) part p_1 is held fixed. The second part p_2 is placed relative to it by identifying valid connection points between the two parts. If slots with matching labels (e.g. leg-torso) exist, they constitute these connection points. Else, we check if any part p_1' from the category of p_1 exists in the source mesh of p_2. If the check succeeds, we map the connection points between p_1' and p_2 to p_1 via non-rigid registration and use them to attach p_2 to p_1. If the check fails, we try with p_1 and p_2 exchanged. The process repeats with the next part in the sorted order. Parts are smoothly stitched together using the method described by Chaudhuri et al. [6].

Features for 3D Shape Components

The feature vector for a part comprises: i) low-level geometric features (same as [17]): part scales, histograms of curvature, shape diameter, and light-field descriptor values [7] — the dimensionality is reduced by PCA; ii) high-level features representing nonlinear transformations of the low-level features. Specifically, the high-level features are probabilities for the part to belong to each part and shape "style" estimated by a statistical model [17]. The probabilities characterize soft memberships of the part in these visual "styles", and also take into account the context of the parent shape of the part. This context provides additional useful information for the part (e.g. that it belonged to a dinosaur).

Features for Web Page Components

The feature vector for a web page component that is an image (background or header) includes: i) color histograms in CIE L*a*b space (4 bins per channel) and ii) the GIST descriptor [26] with a 4×4 spatial resolution, where each bin contains the corresponding image region's average response to steerable filters at 6 orientations and 4 scales.

The feature vector for a web page component containing text (sidebar/body/title) includes: i) histograms of curvature of character outlines (10 bins), ii) 32 Fourier coefficients of the signal representing the distance of the outlines to their centroids, iii) area coverage of characters w.r.t. their bounding rectangle, iv) aspect ratio of characters, and v) width of pairs of letters divided by their height. These features are measured for each character individually: we use the median values as final features. In addition, we include features from the CSS style: vi) a boolean indicating whether the font is italicized, vii) a boolean indicating whether the font is bold, and viii) the font size. Finally, each feature vector is augmented with non-linear transformations of the low-level features from a probabilistic model, analogously to 3D shape components.

dePENd: Augmented Sketching System Using Ferromagnetism of a Ballpoint Pen

Junichi Yamaoka
Keio University
5322, Endo, Fujisawa
yamajun@sfc.keio.ac.jp

Yasuaki Kakehi
Keio University
5322, Endo, Fujisawa
ykakehi@sfc.keio.ac.jp

ABSTRACT
This paper presents *dePENd*, a novel interactive system that assists in sketching using regular pens and paper. Our system utilizes the ferromagnetic feature of the metal tip of a regular ballpoint pen. The computer controlling the X and Y positions of the magnet under the surface of the table provides entirely new drawing experiences. By controlling the movements of a pen and presenting haptic guides, the system allows a user to easily draw diagrams and pictures consisting of lines and circles, which are difficult to create by free-hand drawing. Moreover, the system also allows users to freely edit and arrange prescribed pictures.

This is expected to reduce the resistance to drawing and promote users' creativity. In addition, we propose a communication tool using two *dePENd* systems that is expected to enhance the drawing skills of users. The functions of this system enable users to utilize interactive applications such as copying and redrawing drafted pictures or scaling the pictures using a digital pen.

Furthermore, we implement the system and evaluate its technical features. In this paper, we describe the details of the design and implementations of the device, along with applications, technical evaluations, and future prospects.

Author Keywords
Creativity Supporting Tools; Pen-based UIs; Sketching; Interactive Fabrication;

ACM Classification Keywords
H5.2 [Information Interfaces and Presentation]: User Interfaces.

General Terms
Design; Human Factors

INTRODUCTION
Until now, many researchers have attempted to expand the act of drawing by augmenting pens and paper by combining hand-drawn images and digital information. As a typical approach, pen-type input interfaces (e.g., pen tablets and digital pens) are often used. By using these devices, the system can capture hand-drawn information, process it, and show additional information. However, in these systems, the data outputs are limited to digital displays (monitors, projectors). In contrast, Willis et al. proposed "Interactive Fabrication [17]," a series of prototype systems that combine intuitive embodied interfaces and digital fabrication machines to empower a user's creativity via real-time interactions.

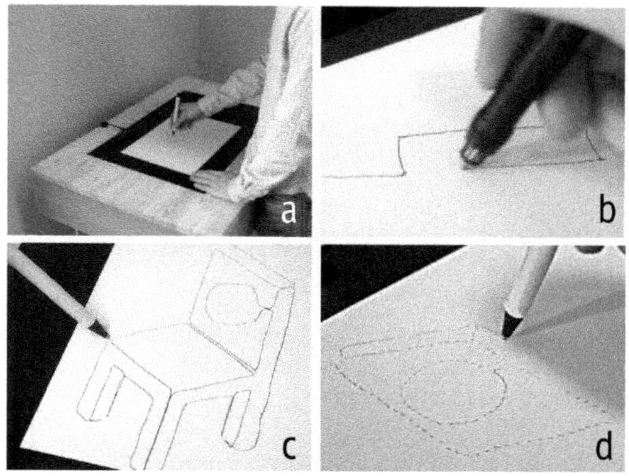

Figure 1. (a) Augmented sketching system *dePENd* that uses regular pens and paper and desk-shaped device. (b) The system enables users to draw exact shapes such as lines and (c) diagrams. (d) The system also allows users to edit and change pictures freely during the drawing process.

At this time, we incorporate such an interactive fabrication approach into the acts of drawing and writing with a pen. We propose a novel interface system called *dePENd* that augments the act of drawing using haptic guides. This system can control the motions of a pen directly, and assist and augment the act of drawing.

In our *dePENd* system (Figure 1), users place a piece of paper on a table and draw lines as usual without wearing any special equipment. They can use normal ballpoint pens with this interface. In fact, many tips of commercially available ballpoint pens can be attracted to magnets because they are made of a ferromagnetic material. We focused on this feature, and controlled the movement of the pen by moving the position of a magnet under the table. A significant feature of our system is its ability to influence the movements of pens to provide

http://dx.doi.org/10.1145/2501988.2502017

haptic guides. Because our system provides haptic guides for the fundamental movements of the user's pen, the user is able to draw diagrams and pictures consisting of lines and circles, which are difficult to draw by free-hand drawing. Therefore, it is expected that there will be less reluctance to drawing and a certain amount of influence on the users' creativity.

Moreover, users may be able to improve their skills by learning from the direct guidance of experienced artists. As another important feature of this system, owing to the use of magnetic ballpoint pens, the system also allows users to edit and arrange prescribed pictures freely during the drawing process aided by a computer.

In addition, digital pens can be used in this system to change actions interactively according to the user's movement. This enables users to adopt interactive applications such as copying and redrawing drafted pictures or scaling pictures.

In this paper, we present the details of *dePENd* and several applications of this system.

RELATED WORK

Prior to our research, a considerable number of studies were conducted on sketching, interactive fabrication, and interfaces using magnetic forces.

Support for Sketching via a Stylus Input

A considerable number of studies have focused on supporting users in sketching and improving their skills in digital environments. *SketchPad* [15], which is considered to be a pioneer of CAD software, alters traditional drafting by using a display and light pen. This system was implemented to change imprecise sketchy input into precise designs, and to duplicate drawings. *ScanScribe* [13] is a software tool that detects a group of drawn shapes, and allows users to move these freely. Unlike sketching with a pen and paper, digital functions such as copying, undo, scaling, and moving are more likely to let users experience the trial and error process and improve their overall design skills.

In addition, studies have been conducted not only on drawing using computers, but also on detecting drawn lines and shapes, and suggesting prospective shapes. *Pegasus* [5] is a software tool that automatically revises hand-drawn lines, while *ShadowDraw* [8] improves users' sketches. By predicting the pictures users want to draw and displaying these predictions as guides, this system allows users to draw the figures in an easier way.

These software systems support users with visual information via digital screens. In addition to providing visual aids, our system attempts to effect users' physical motions by manipulating the pen's movement during sketching.

Interactive Fabrication

Gershenfeld proposed personal fabrication [3], which was an effort to support rapid prototyping using automated machine tools such as 3D printers and laser cutters, which are connected to a computer network. Among these various machines, a plotter is a familiar tool for printing graphics.

As research that adopted an approach similar to our system, *the suspended pen on an XY plotter* [10] controls the position of a pen hung from a topside structure, while *the center pivot pen plotter* [2] draws and moves a pen in an arch. These are automatic drawing machines. However, these systems do not have functions for interaction during the drawing process.

Shaper [17], which is a steric modeling system that uses a computer-numeric controlled machine and transparent touchscreen, is a system developed in one of the studies on interactive fabrication that combines handcrafts and digital technologies. This system allows users to create steric sculptures intuitively by dispensing polyurethanes at the point where the touchscreen is touched. *Interactive Construction* [11] is a woodworking support system with a laser pointer and a laser cutter. As a user drafts a wooden board with a laser pointer, a computer transforms the hand-drawn lines into exact lines, and cuts these with a laser cutter. These studies allow users to design intuitively, unlike traditional designs using CAD systems. However, there is still room for improvement in terms of intuitive inputs, rather than actual modeling tasks.

As for a typical study on modeling support, *Haptic Intelligentsia* [7] is a handheld 3D printing machine that uses a haptic interface (*Phantom Omni* [14]) and a glue gun. As users dispense the glue under the guide of tactile feedback, the system creates input data for the sculptures. *Free D* [19] is a handheld digital milling machine consisting of a magnetic sensor, small milling machine, and computer. As users trace the wood, the tip of the milling machine slides along the outlines of the three-dimensional input data and creates the sculptures. These studies are similar to our research in terms of adding artifacts, arranging creations by hand, and modifying the way editing is done using the motion of machines as guides. In comparison with these studies, our research especially focuses on pen writing/drawing.

An example of a tool supporting sketching on paper in the same way as our study, which combines input and output, is *Digital Rubbing* [6]. This system allows users to copy graphics projected on a display using a pen device. As the tip of the pen device, which contains tablet sensors and solenoids, touches the graphics on the tablet display, the system extends the tip of the pen device, thereby drawing the same graphics on the paper by rubbing. A further example of a tool similar to our research is *Blind Self Portrait* [9], which is a system that allows users to draw their self-portraits automatically with their eyes closed. As a user places his/her pen on the table, the position of the table moves along the outline of a photograph that was taken beforehand, thereby allowing the user to draw his/her own face. *Self-Portrait Machine* [4] controls the pen's motions through a robotic arm attached to the user's hand.

In contrast to normal printers, these systems incorporate the merits of handcrafting in digital fabrications, because their artifacts can be changed by hand and a variety of user arrangements can be added. However, our research includes features that augment sketching and add interactive functions without having to wear or grab special devices.

Interfaces Using Magnetic Forces

In the research field of haptic displays and tangible interfaces, several systems have functions that involve moving physical objects or a user's fingers by using magnetic forces.

Actuated Workbench [12] and *Proactive Desk II* [18] are tabletop systems that can make physical objects placed on the table move using an array of electromagnets. These systems were designed to serve as intuitive interfaces with computers.

FingerFlux [16] also uses electromagnets under a projection screen. The aim of this research was to provide haptic feedback to users. By attaching a small magnet to a finger or a pen, the user experiences haptic force according to the position.

In comparison with these systems, our system aims to control the movement of a pen with a magnetic force and assist users with drawing.

BASIC DESIGN OF DEPEND SYSTEM

The augmented sketching system *dePENd* controls the motions of ballpoint pens by moving magnets. Users can draw shapes and pictures, which have been input into computers, using regular ballpoint pens. In other words, after spreading a piece of paper on a desk-shaped device and placing a regular ballpoint pen on the paper, a user can draw figures semi-automatically as the magnetic tip of the pen is controlled by a computer. Figure 2 shows an overview of the *dePENd* system.

For example, if users need to draw, they can handwrite diagrams such as circles and lines that exist on the computer. As an important feature of this system, because we use regular ballpoint pens, the system allows users to intervene and change the pictures freely during the machine-assisted drawing process.

As for the method of controlling the motion of the ballpoint pens, several approaches can be included. For example, *Phantom Omni* [14] uses arms with built-in actuators, while *SPIDAR* [1] uses motors and nylon strings. These methods are suitable for tactile presentation and controlling physical pens. However, we consider these interfaces to be unsuitable for daily use, because users must wear external devices on their hands to hold the pens. Thus, in our system, the ability to use regular ballpoint pens the metal tips of which are ferromagnetic allows users to make use of pens intuitively in daily life.

In addition, by using digital pens that have ferromagnetism similar to regular pens, the system can detect hand motions, which allows users to operate the system interactively. For example, the guides allow users to start drawing figures from any position, and can record and play back drawings/sketches of users with highly skilled drawing abilities. Moreover, digital pens enable functions such as copying and redrawing, which are difficult to achieve using ordinary sketching, and can be a novel method of sketching.

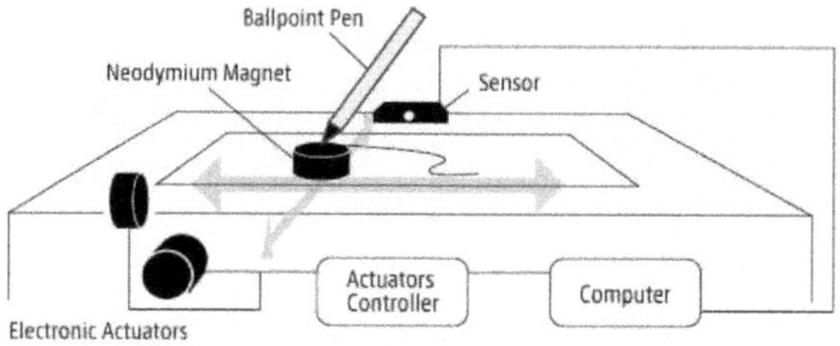

Figure 2. Overview of dePENd system.

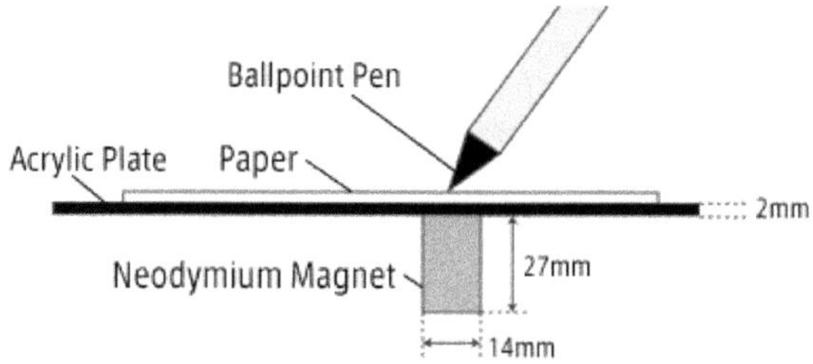

Figure 3. Size of magnets and acrylic boards.

Structure for Moving Pens

dePENd consists of a computer with input control programs and a desk-type device comprising a ballpoint pen, magnets, electric actuators, and controller. Because the electric actuators on the x and y axes control the positions of magnets, the system can change the positions of the absorbed tips of ballpoint pens.

In this research, ballpoint pens are used as the writing instruments. The material used for the tips of regular ballpoint pens is stainless steel with nickel, which is ferromagnetic. Therefore, the tips can be manipulated by the motion of the magnets. We used neodymium magnets; because the magnetic flux density of such magnets is high, they have strong magnetism. The neodymium magnets are round, with a 14-mm diameter and a height of 30 mm (Figure 3). The magnetic flux density is about 450 mT, and the adsorption power is about 12 kgf. Because the magnets are round in shape, the pen tips can move close to the center of the magnets. Moreover, the tips and magnets are physically close if there is paper or a board between them, because neodymium magnets are stronger than ferrite magnets. In addition, we use 1-mm-thick acrylic boards as the tops of the tables.

The two electric actuators on the x and y axes are electric sliders (Oriental Motor Co., Ltd., EZ limo EZSII), which are drives in ball screws. The movable ranges of these actuators are 500 mm on the x-axis and 300 mm on the y-axis, with a resolution of 0.01 mm and a maximum speed of 60 mm/s. The maximum thrust of an electric actuator is 43 N. In addition, photomicrosensors (Oriental Motor Co., Ltd., PAES-S) are placed at the origin of each coordinate axis. The system corrects errors by periodically moving the table position back to the origin.

A microcomputer (ATMEGA328P) is used to control the electric actuators. The system connects the microcomputer and controller using serial communication, and controls the actuators by sending the values of the motor's direction of rotation and speed from the controller to the microcomputer in real time. The transmitted values are the advanced data input or the input values from the digital pens. The current prototype includes both a controller and a microcomputer. However, in the future, the system will run with a controller only for moving the motors.

The values for controlling the motions of the ballpoint pen are calculated by the software on the controlling computer. Specifically, the software converts the data we want to draft into values for the motors' direction of rotation and speed. By sending the converted data to the controllers of the desk-type devices, the system can control the electric actuators and allow users to draw pictures.

System for Sensing Pens

Using a digital pen, which allows the coordinates of the tip of the pen to be acquired, instead of a regular ballpoint pen, is an attempt at allowing users to draw pictures at any position the pen is placed, along with interactive control such as duplicating the picture being drawn.

For the current system, we designed and developed the devices using digital pens (MVPen Technologies., Ltd., MVP-1), that is, versions with the ability to interact. Infrared and ultrasonic sensors (attached to the MVP-1) placed on the desk detect the position of the tip of the pen on the paper, as well as events that allow the tip to stay in touch with the paper (Figure 4).

The position of the pen is converted to coordinates for the controlling magnets, and the movement of the pen is linked to the movements of the magnets.

Specifically, the system is able to identify the position at which the user starts drawing, and record the shapes that are drawn, as described below.

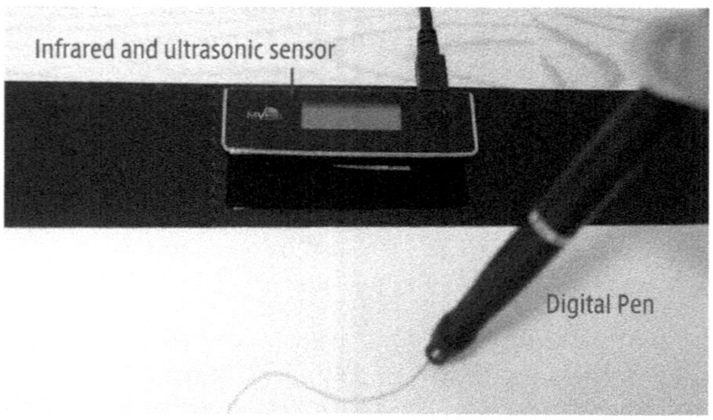

Figure 4. Infrared and ultrasonic sensors and Digital Pen.

BASIC FUNCTIONS OF DEPEND

By using this hardware, the system can guide the user's pen on the paper in various interactive ways. For interactive rapid prototyping, we developed the basic functions for drawing basic figures, drawing input pictures, and duplicating pictures that have been drawn. Each function is selected using key input. Here, we describe these basic functions.

Drawing Pre-set Data

The first function is drawing preset line pattern data. The data consist of a series of position information. When we use a regular ball point pen, we have to touch the pen on a certain point on the table to start drawing. In this case, there is a limitation in that the drawing pattern must be traversable. On the other hand, when we use a digital pen, we can point to the starting point of a drawing interactively. In the current implementation, we assigned the pattern data to several keys and change the drawing pattern using the keys.

Drawing shapes

In addition to preset data drawing, in this system, users can interactively determine what they want to draw in the drawing process. The second function is drawing basic shapes such as circles and lines. Usually, we use compasses and rulers to draw circles and lines. But our system allows users to draw various shapes using one device by moving magnets in constant directions and circles.

To draw shapes with various lengths and diameters and at different locations, the system uses digital pens. To draw a line, the user only needs to draw any two points on the paper. For example, after selecting the appropriate key for *the line drawing function*, the user draws a point at the location shown in point (a) in Figure 5 using a digital pen. Then, the user draws the next point (b), as shown in Figure 5, and the magnet moves to where the tip of the pen is positioned. The system then assists the user to draw the line by moving the tip of the pen toward the first drawn point. After moving the tip from point (b) to point (a) with the help of the magnets, the user can draw new lines by drawing a new point at any place and placing the tip of the pen at point (a) as the second point. By repeating this process, a user can draw various shapes such as triangles and squares. Changing the distance between the two points modifies the length.

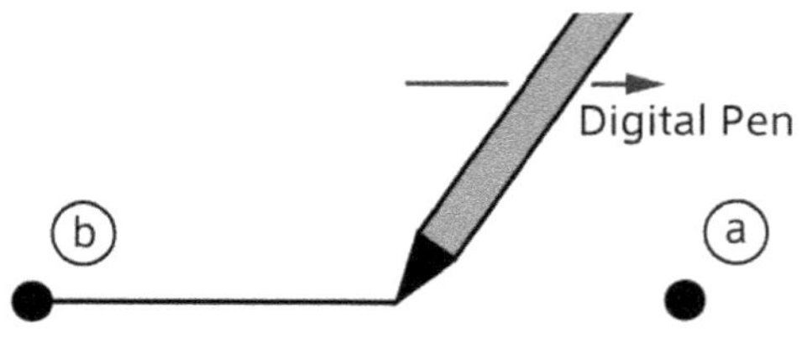

Figure 5. Line drawing function:To draw a line, the user only needs to draw any two points on the paper.

Similarly, to draw circles, *the circle drawing function* uses any two points. After selecting *the circle drawing function* via the appropriate key, the user draws the first point at the center of the circle using the digital pen (see point (a) in Figure 6), and the second point (b) shown in Figure 6, which sets the radius of the circle. After drawing the second point, the device draws a perfect circle automatically by moving the pen. The system allows the user to change the position of the circle by changing the position of point (a), and the size of the circle by changing the position of point (b).

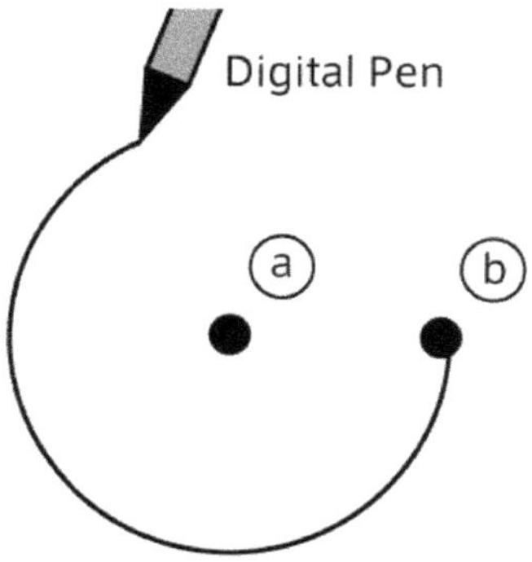

Figure 6. Circle drawing function.

The functions of drawing circles and lines can be combined. Figure 7 shows a picture of a chair drawn using *the line drawing function.*

Figure 7. Users can combine functions for drawing circles and lines.

Copy and Redraw Function

In addition to the functions for sketching precise lines and circles, we developed novel expressions by adding digital technology to sketching. For example, *the copy and redraw function* duplicates drawn pictures by using digital pens (Figure 8).

The computer records the distance from where the tip of the pen is released. Thus, when the user places the tip of the pen at any other point, the magnet automatically moves to the position of the tip, and the system allows the user to draw the recorded picture. Usually, it is difficult to exactly redraw the same picture when sketching. However, in our system, which can duplicate pictures exactly, users can draw crowds of characters and sketches through trial and error by changing the forms bit by bit.

Moreover, by recording the pen motions of experienced sketch artists, these motions can be used as guides and support to improve the drawing skill of inexperienced users.

Scaling

We also provided a scaling function to change the size of drawn pictures when copying them. First, the system records the drawing process using functions such as *the line and circle drawing functions* or freehand drawing using digital pens. After recording these processes and selecting *the scaling function*, users draw arrows to change the size of the picture(Figure 9). The computer calculates the coordinates according to the changed size. After changing the paper and using regular pens at the origin, the system allows the user to automatically draw the pictures according to the changes in size with a single stroke of the pen. The system changes the size of the picture according to the length of the arrows. Moreover, depending on the direction of the arrows, the change in size could be reversed.

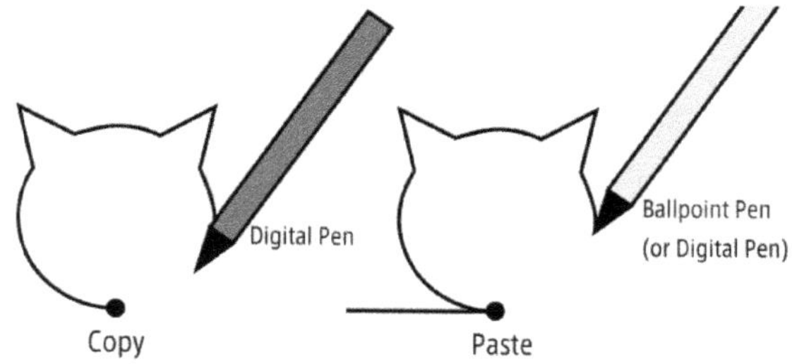

Figure 8. Copy-and-redraw function: users can duplicate drawn pictures.

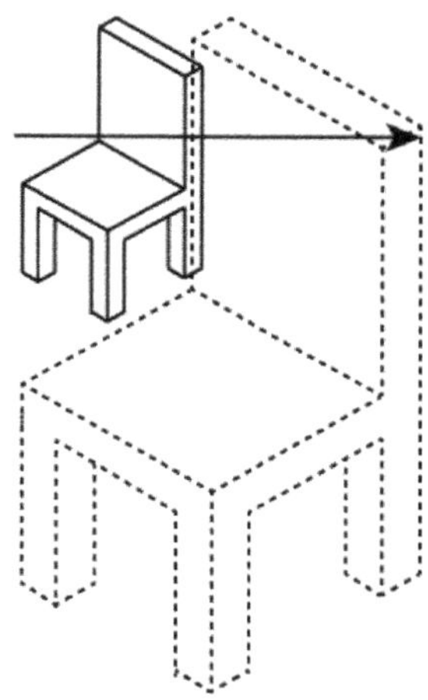

Figure 9. Scaling function. The system changes the size of the picture according to the arrows drawn by users.

ADVANCED USAGE EXAMPLES

Adding Additional Arrangements

A characteristic expression of our research is that users are allowed to add a hand-drawn arrangement to a drawing done by the computer. Specifically, the system uses the movement of a magnet as a guide for drawing. For example, when the system draws a circle using the movement of a magnet, the user can move the ballpoint pen slightly to add an arrangement manually.

For instance, users can modify any line to make it dotted or wavy (Figure 10). Likewise, users can change the colors in the drawing by using different colored ballpoint pens (Figure 11). While repeating the same pen motions, users can try various arrangements such as different forms and colors in their quest for new artistic expressions.

By using these techniques, this system supports the drawing of animations. Our system has the ability to draw the same picture repeatedly. Thus, while drawing a recorded picture, the user can add motions or change shapes partially by moving some of the shapes in the picture. Figure 12 illustrates how this can be done. This feature is expected to lead to the efficient creation of animations.

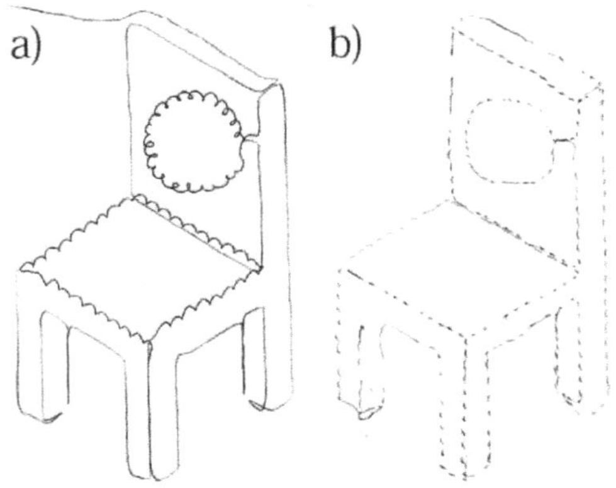

Figure 10. Adding an Arrangement: (a) wavy lines or (b) dotted lines.

Figure 11. users can change colors by using different-colored ballpoint pens.

Communication Function

Through communication between multiple devices, it is possible to create a drawing as a team. As the sender draws a picture on paper with a digital pen, the receiver moves his/her pen in the same motion in real time (Figure 13).

Furthermore, it is also possible to change the sender and receiver. Communication between desk devices uses the OpenSound Control protocol, with changes the sending or receiving taking place via switches. Although the input requires a digital pen to send data, the receiver can use a regular ballpoint pen. If the receiver draws with a regular pen, the pen must be placed at the origin at the start (Figure 14).

In this way, users can modify and draw pictures in collaboration with each other in real time. Moreover, because the motions of one person's pen can be sent to other people, users can share drawings with each other.

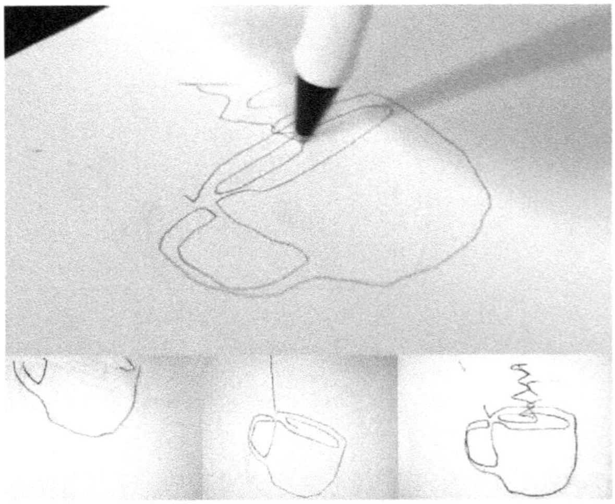

Figure 12. Users can add animation by moving some of the shapes in the picture.

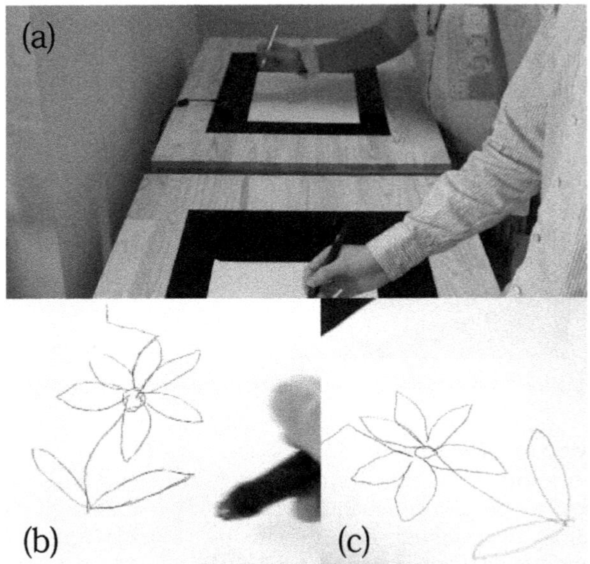

Figure 13. Communication function, (b) sender draws picture with digital pen, and (c) receiver moves his/her pen in same motion.

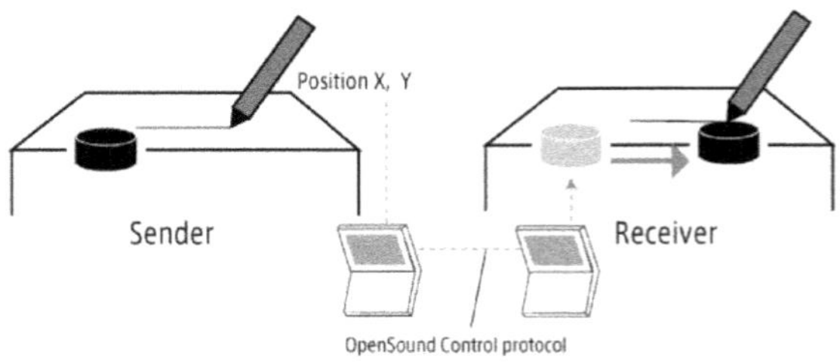

Figure 14. Communication function for system using OpenSound Control protocol.

This function is useful not only for drawing shapes, but also for education by allowing teachers to send examples of penmanship to their students.

TECHNICAL EVALUATION

We demonstrated this system at several events to obtain feedback from users (Figure 15). We next discuss several technical issues that we discovered through actions and experiences of these users.

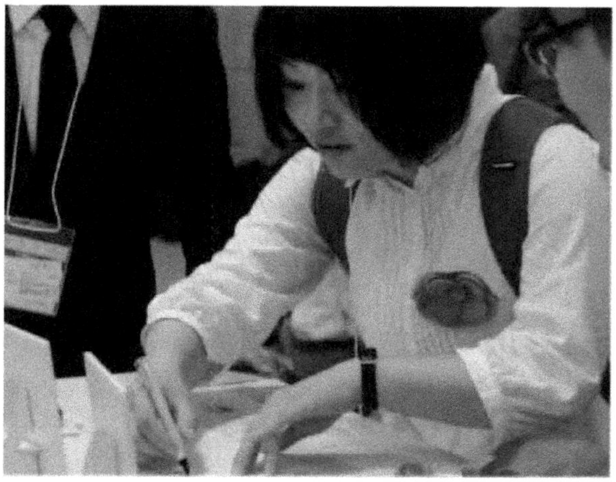

Figure 15. Demonstration at the event.

Attractive force of magnet

We measured the attractive forces by pulling spring balances attached to the ballpoint pen while changing the height of the neodymium magnet. The force ranged from 0.9 to 1.15 N according to the height of the magnet, which was 5 to 40 mm, as shown in Figure 16. This is the necessary force users need in order to separate the tip of a pen from the magnet. By using this force as a guide because it is necessary for the pen to adhere to the magnet we decided that the height of the magnet should be 30 mm.

However, because some users did not understand how to apply the pressure of the writing pen on the paper to achieve a magnetic force, they could not follow the motion of the magnets. In this case, by teaching them to grasp the pen lightly, they were able to determine the suitable pressure for writing.

Accuracy

We also examined the resolution of the pictures drawn using the devices. Because the magnets and pens are not completely fixed, the pens deviate from the center of the magnets. The tips of the pens can move from one edge of the diameter to the other.

In terms of precision, plotters, which can draw figures faithfully, are superior to our system. However, because users have room to move to a certain extent, increasing the diameter of the magnet would be effective for guiding and adding additions to the drawing/sketch. To differentiate our system from digital fabrication tools such as plotters, we considered increasing the diameter of the magnet.

Nevertheless, increasing the diameter of the magnet will decrease the accuracy of the drawn figures.

Speed of actuation

The maximum speed of the electric actuators used in this research was 60 mm/s. We investigated whether five subjects could draw circles with a diameter of 230 mm while the actuators moved at the maximum speed. We found that all the subjects were able to do this. Furthermore, we decided that the maximum speed for drawing using this device would be 60 mm/s.

Drawing patterns

This system allows users to draw with a single stroke. Users have to separate the pen from the magnet within the limit of the attractive force of the magnet. This is why we considered changing the line thickness by moving the devices along not only the x and y axes but also the z axis. In this way, users can feel a change in the attractive force of the pen and draw lines with various intensities.

Moreover, if we attach actuators such as solenoids to pens and adopt functions where the tip of a pen slides in and out such as with *Digital Rubbing* [6], the drawing will not be limited to a single consistent stroke. On the other hand, adding complex machinery for pens will create problems that make it hard to use.

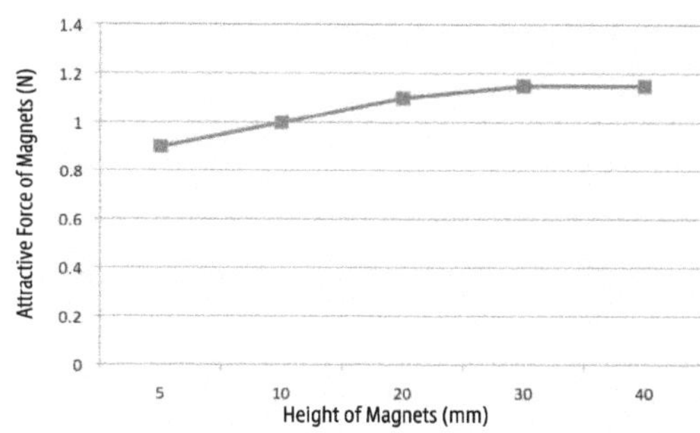

Figure 16. Relationship between the attractive force and the height of the neodymium magnets.

Size

The size of the device is relative to the size of the actuators. In this research, we developed two devices with different sizes: one with a length of 300 mm and width of 500 mm, and the other with a length of 150 mm and width of 150 mm. Users that tried this system mentioned that this device is more suitable for drawing long lines and large circles than drawing by hand, because it easily permits long strokes. However, to create miniature devices such as mobile devices, it would be advisable to use smaller actuators.

Sensing

In this research, digital pens with infrared and ultrasonic sensors were used for the stylus input. The detection range of the digital pens is a height of 210 mm and width of 297 mm. To increase this range, a possible improvement would be to attach a reflective material (3M, Scotchlite) to a regular pen and detect the position of the pen using infrared cameras.

CONCLUSION

In this paper, we proposed *dePENd* as an augmented handwriting system using the ferromagnetism of a ballpoint pen. By using electric actuators with a magnet, the system can control the pen's motion dynamically. Moreover, by using a digital pen as an input interface, various functions such as copying-and-redrawing and scaling can be realized.

As for the future work on this system, we plan to develop an intuitive interface for selecting functions during drawing. For example, by sensing the pressure exerted by the user on the pen, the device can assist when the pressure is weak and stop assisting when the pressure is strong.

Moreover, we intend to extend the system by detecting the writing motion and pressure of the user and create interactive motions of the pen, specifically, moving the magnet back to the position where the tip of the pen was disconnected, and allowing the system to draw the picture that the user intends to draw by predicting their motion.

In our research, we propose a method to support manual drawing by the computer. In the future, in order to create a new style of fabrication, we plan to develop various applications by using haptic guides not only for drawing but also for cutting or carving in other tools such as cutting machines.

ACKNOWLEDGMENTS

This research is supported by CREST, JST.

REFERENCES

1. Anusha Jayasiri, Katsuhiko Akahane, M. S. Haptic rnedering of dynamic image sequence using string based haptic device spidar. In *Proceedings of the 24th annual ACM symposium on User interface software and technology* (2012). Virtual Reality Conference of ICAT-EGVE-EuroVR (2012), DOI: 10.2312/EGVE/JVRC12/009-015,10.17-19.
2. Bynoe, D. Drawing Machine. http://dbynoe.blogspot.ca/2012/09/drawing-machine.html.
3. Gershenfeld, N. *Fab: The Coming Revolution on Your Desktop–from Personal Computers to Personal Fabrication.* Basic Books, Inc., New York, NY, USA, 2007.
4. hui Liao, J. Self-Portrait Machine. http://www.jenhui-liao.com/selfportraitmachine/.
5. Igarashi, T., Kawachiya, S., Tanaka, H., and Matsuoka, S. Pegasus: a drawing system for rapid geometric design. In *CHI 98 Cconference Summary on Human Factors in Computing Systems*, CHI '98, ACM (New York, NY, USA, 1998), 24–25.
6. Kim, H., Kim, S., Lee, B., Pak, J., Sohn, M., Lee, G., and Lee, W. Digital rubbing: playful and intuitive interaction technique for transferring a graphic image onto paper with pen-based computing. In *CHI '08 Extended Abstracts on Human Factors in Computing Systems*, CHI EA '08, ACM (New York, NY, USA, 2008), 2337–2342.
7. Lee, J. Haptic Intelligentsia. http://studiohomunculus.com/ portfolio/haptic-intelligentsia-humanprototyping-machine.
8. Lee, Y. J., Zitnick, C. L., and Cohen, M. F. Shadowdraw: real-time user guidance for freehand drawing. *ACM Trans. Graph. 30*, 4 (July 2011), 27:1–27:10.
9. McDonald, K. a. Blind Self Portrait. The 3rd Annual NYCR Interactive Show(2012).
10. Moon, H. Suspended Pen on an XY Plotter: The Drawing Machine. http://unanything.com/.
11. Mueller, S., Lopes, P., and Baudisch, P. Interactive construction: interactive fabrication of functional mechanical devices. In *Proceedings of the 25th annual ACM symposium on User interface software and technology*, UIST '12, ACM (New York, NY, USA, 2012), 599–606.
12. Pangaro, G., Maynes-Aminzade, D., and Ishii, H. The actuated workbench: computer-controlled actuation in tabletop tangible interfaces. In *Proceedings of the 15th annual ACM symposium on User interface software and technology*, UIST '02, ACM (New York, NY, USA, 2002), 181–190.
13. Saund, E., Fleet, D., Larner, D., and Mahoney, J. Perceptually-supported image editing of text and graphics. In *Proceedings of the 16th annual ACM symposium on User interface software and technology*, UIST '03, ACM (New York, NY, USA, 2003), 183–192.
14. Sensable. PHANTOM Omni. http://www.sensable.com/haptic-phantom-omni.htm.
15. Sutherland, I. E. Sketchpad: a man-machine graphical communication system. In *Proceedings of the May 21-23, 1963, spring joint computer conference*, AFIPS '63 (Spring), ACM (New York, NY, USA, 1963), 329–346.
16. Weiss, M., Wacharamanotham, C., Voelker, S., and Borchers, J. Fingerflux: near-surface haptic feedback on tabletops. In *Proceedings of the 24th annual ACM symposium on User interface software and technology*, UIST '11, ACM (New York, NY, USA, 2011), 615–620.
17. Willis, K. D., Xu, C., Wu, K.-J., Levin, G., and Gross, M. D. Interactive fabrication: new interfaces for digital fabrication. In *Proceedings of the fifth international conference on Tangible, embedded, and embodied interaction*, TEI '11, ACM (New York, NY, USA, 2011), 69–72.
18. YOSHIDA, S., NOMA, H., and HOSAKA, K. Proactive desk ii: Development of a new multi-object haptic display using a linear induction motor. *IEEE VR 2006* (2006).
19. Zoran, A., and Paradiso, J. A. Freed: a freehand digital sculpting tool. In *Proceedings of the SIGCHI Conference on Human Factors in Computing Systems*, CHI '13, ACM (New York, NY, USA, 2013), 2613–2616.

Mirage: Exploring Interaction Modalities Using Off-Body Static Electric Field Sensing

Adiyan Mujibiya
The University of Tokyo
7-3-1 Hongo, Bunkyo-ku, Tokyo 113-0033, Japan
adiyan@acm.org

Jun Rekimoto
The University of Tokyo
Sony Computer Science Laboratories, Inc.
rekimoto@acm.org

ABSTRACT
Mirage proposes an effective non body contact technique to infer the amount and type of body motion, gesture, and activity. This approach involves passive measurement of static electric field of the environment flowing through sense electrode. This sensing method leverages electric field distortion by the presence of an intruder (e.g. human body). *Mirage* sensor has simple analog circuitry and supports ultra-low power operation. It requires no instrumentation to the user, and can be configured as environmental, mobile, and peripheral-attached sensor. We report on a series of experiments with 10 participants showing robust activity and gesture recognition, as well as promising results for robust location classification and multiple user differentiation. To further illustrate the utility of our approach, we demonstrate real-time interactive applications including activity monitoring, and two games which allow the users to interact with a computer using body motion and gestures.

Author Keywords
Electric Field sensing; Off-body sensing; Motion detection; Activity recognition; Gesture recognition;

ACM Classification Keywords
H.5.2 [User Interfaces]: Input devices and strategies;

INTRODUCTION
Electronic devices with significant computational resources can now be carried mobile and becoming more ubiquitous. Such advancements lead to a growing research interest in new human-computer interfaces that go beyond the traditional paradigm of keyboard, mouse, and touch screen, including explorations on leveraging human body motion, gesture, and activity to support always-available computing, either with devices that people carry on their bodies, or using devices embedded in the environment.

UIST'13, October 8–11, 2013, St. Andrews, United Kingdom.
Copyright © 2013 ACM 978-1-4503-2268-3/13/10...$15.00.
http://dx.doi.org/10.1145/2501988.2502031

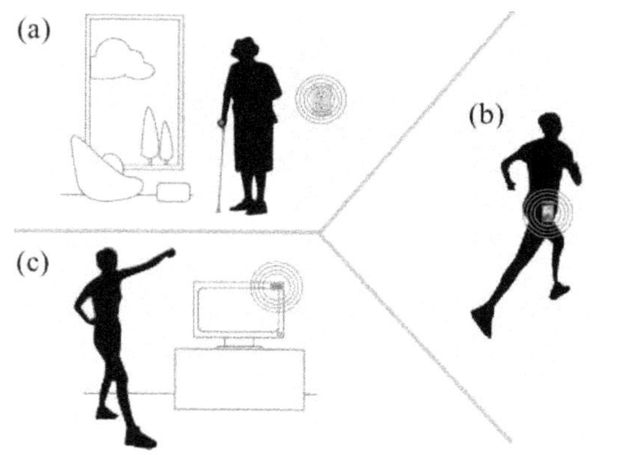

Figure 1. *Mirage* infers the type and amount of body motion, gesture, and activity by passively measuring ambient (off-body) static electric fields. Here we show three configurations representing supported application domains: (a) environmental sensor, (b) mobile sensor, and (c) peripheral-attached sensor.

Electric Field (EF) sensing offers strategic solution for these challenges, and recently has gain significant attention due to the availability of inexpensive electronic components to measure the relatively small signals. However, it is difficult to acquire stable and easily interpretable signal which is important to aggregate meaningful contextual information in a *passive* (for low-power and simple hardware implementation) and *non body contact* configuration (for broader support in interaction modalities). Our research addresses these issues to make EF sensing more accessible to interface designers.

We present *Mirage*, a novel sensing approach to infer the amount and type of body motion, gesture, and activity using non body contact technique leveraging human-generated body charge. *Mirage* utilizes passive (i.e., no additional signal transmission) static EF measurement through an electrode placed at a distance from the subject. Human body will induce EF distortions when performing motions. We leverage this phenomenon and show that human body motion and gesture produce significant signals at useful ranges. *Mirage* sensing principles robustly extract these signals by leveraging the design of sample-and-hold circuit in the Successive Approximation Register (SAR) Analog to Digital Converter (ADC), which is widely used in microcontrollers boards such as Arduino [4].

Mirage software system incorporates signal processing and analysis approaches to provide contextual information such as: 1) presence detection, 2) amount and type of body motion, whole-body gesture, and activity, 3) location classification, and 4) multiple user differentiation.

Mirage sensing approach requires no instrumentation to the user or electrical infrastructure. It can be configured as an environmental, mobile, or peripheral-attached sensor (Figure 1). Each setup represents different application domains with broad interaction modalities. The sensing hardware consumes as low as 1.8 μW, and only requires a single analog input of an off-the-shelf microcontroller. Moreover, the sensing unit met safety requirements, and inexpensive in both hardware and software.

The sensing technology proposed is *scalable,* e.g., motion and activity sensing is equally effective across user (no requirement for user dependent training) and across environment (across buildings and outdoor). The gesture recognition and location classification system requires minimal user dependent training and incorporates real-time segmentation and machine learning-based classification.

The specific contributions of this paper are:

1) Proposal and development of a novel non body contact passive static electric field sensing. This technique leverages the design of ADC in an off-the-shelf microcontrollers such as Arduino.
2) Description of the theory of operation and detailed implementation of the sensing system, including signal acquisition, signal processing, event detection, segmentation, feature extraction, and classification.
3) Presentation of results from a series of controlled experiments to demonstrate the usability of our technology including: a) activity recognition, b) whole-body gesture recognition, c) location classification, and d) multiple user differentiation. We also demonstrate *Mirage*'s usage in real-time interactive applications.

RELATED WORK

Motion sensing systems have been used in applications such as activity and gesture recognition, health and wellness monitoring, security and surveillance systems, and also elder care. Conventional methods have largely used infrared systems, computer vision techniques, or inertial sensors.

Infrared systems have been widely used for human motion sensing. However, these systems have limitations in high-rate of false detections and artifacts caused by the presence of illumination sources inside the surveillance area. Such systems often only detect the presence of a subject, and relatively difficult to infer activity or gesture. Also, these systems are impractical for deployment in large areas because they typically require significant power.

Alternatively, computer vision and depth sensing systems (e.g. Kinect [29] and Motion Capture system [26]) have been used for detecting body motion and gesture, mainly because they are gradually becoming inexpensive, and at the same time provide accurate measurement of three-dimensional sensing of body segments. The commercial success of these devices and the advancements of computer vision in general have stimulated the ideas of consumers and researchers alike, and have led to rapid growth in explorations (e.g. see [28]). Computer vision based approaches also provide measurement methods that do not require the user to wear any additional device, such as [16]. However, these approaches are limited in the potential scale of deployment due to their associated installation burden and cost. Also, these systems typically suffer from occlusion and require line-of-sight.

Body-mounted inertial sensors have been used extensively for the detection of human body motion and activity recognition [2,9,12,17,20]. These techniques often require users to place the sensors on the body, which can be cumbersome. Approaches for recognizing coarse subset of gestures using only a single device such as a mobile phone have also been proposed [1,22]. These approaches achieved impressive results with minimal instrumentation. Unfortunately, these approaches can only detect gestures involving body parts that are instrumented with sensors. Arguably, users prefer non body contact approach. In this work, we aim to perform unobtrusive off-body sensing that allows broader support on interaction design.

Other sensing methods such as microwaves-based approaches pose potential health and regulation problems. Simple pyroelectric systems have very slow response times (>100 milliseconds) and can only respond to changing signals. Methods involving lasers often require scanning which are line-of-sight and may cause eye damage.

Human motion detection systems that utilize quasi-electrostatic fields generated during walking have also been proposed [14,15]. However, the detection of the quasi-electrostatic fields is strongly affected by the electromagnetic fields generated by surrounding electrical equipment. Human body models describing the phenomenon of electrical charge during walking have also been proposed [3,25,27]. These models show that motion detection using passive static EF sensing is possible with complex analog circuitry and body instrumentation.

EF sensing has been used in HCI work for sensing gestures as means of user input [7,8,10,18,21,23,30,31]. These techniques use *active* approach, requiring time-varying signal transmitter and receiver that measure the signal at different location. Consequently, these solutions pose design complexity that can lead to additional power consumption. Pioneered by Rekimoto [19] and most recently Cohn et al. [6,7], human body motion detection using static EF sensing by *passively* measuring the voltage at a location on the user's body have been proposed. Such approaches enable low-power implementation. These techniques have been relied heavily on body-mounted sense electrode/s, which poses usability issues (e.g. rigidly fixing sense electrode/s to maintain direct contact with the skin at most of the time is difficult, and uncomfortable). Furthermore, it's technically challenging to differ the actual signal from the noise caused by sensor and skin displacement. Also, Cohn et al. in [6] proposed sensing of the voltage between the body and a small ground plane near the body, i.e. they did not have a ground reference; hence the signal was very weak such that they required heavy amplifications. Our method has a true ground reference so that the signals are much stronger. In broader interaction design point-of-view, decoupling the sense electrode from the user's body allows us to gain multitudes of interesting application domains we can explore.

We extend previous work by proposing sensing method that leverages much simpler hardware, while aggregating more stable and reliable signal. Furthermore, we also investigate multiple user differentiation and location classification using ambient EF fingerprints. We are not aware of previous work that has explicitly observed the usage of *passive (non-signal transmission)* sensing of *ambient (off-body)* static EF for HCI.

PASSIVE AMBIENT STATIC ELECTRIC FIELD SENSING

Off-Body Static EF Sensing Model

The human body is electrically charged during motion [3,24,26]. From Figure 2, the potential U_B of the human body when it is performing walking motion can be expressed as follows.

$$U_B = Q_B \frac{\varepsilon_a S + x C_B}{C_B \varepsilon_a S} \quad (1)$$

where C_B is a capacitance between the body and the environment, Q_B is the instantaneous charge of the human body during walking motion, ε_a is the permittivity of the air gap between the sole and the floor, and S is the effective sole area at a height x above the floor. The induced charge Q_e of the measurement electrode placed at a certain distance from the subject can be expressed as follows:

$$Q_e = C_d(U_B - V_e) \quad (2)$$

where C_d is the capacitance between the human body and measurement electrode, and V_e is the potential of the measurement electrode. From the Eq. (1) and (2), the induced current I_e flowing through the sensor electrode can be expressed as follows:

$$I_e = \frac{dQ_e}{dt} = C_d \frac{dU_B}{dt} = C_d Q_B \left(-\frac{x}{\varepsilon_a S^2} \frac{dS}{dt} + \frac{1}{\varepsilon_a S} \frac{dx}{dt} \right) \quad (3)$$

Assuming that the human body is a good conductor, the first term in Eq. (3) represents the current induced as the result of foot motion just before it is lifted off the floor. The second term represents the current induced as the result of foot and leg motion after the foot is lifted off the floor. Note that the second term is approximately proportional to the velocity of the foot. Therefore, in a scenario of body motion near the sensor electrode, it is possible to measure the current generated under perfect non body contact condition.

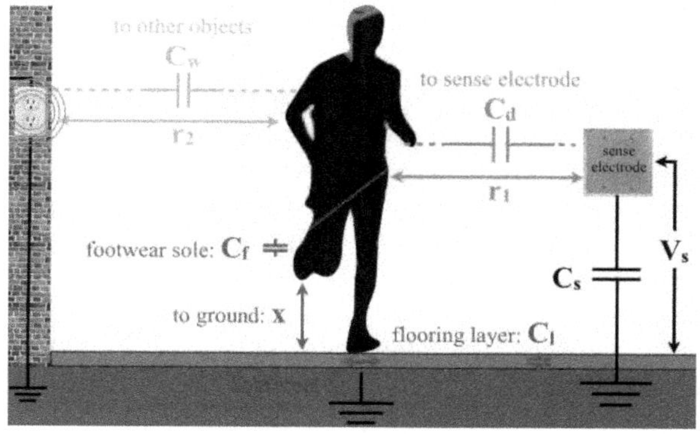

Figure 2. Circuit model of capacitive coupling between the user's body, the environment, and the sense electrode. The sensing voltage (V_s) is measured between the sense electrode and earth ground.

In practical conditions, a person walking or scuffing may develop potentials of over 1000 Volts depending on shoe sole thickness and resistance of the ground surface. Moreover, as s/he raises one foot his body capacitance to ground reaches a minimum and this in turn causes his potential to rise to a maximum. When both feet are momentarily making ground contact, the charge potential is lowest. These caused the characteristic of rise and fall in potential due to foot motion.

Sensing Parameters

A passive EF sensing is one in which the EF is generated external to the detector. If the sensor itself generates EF which is then perturbed by the object, the system is known as an active EF sensing. In this paper we deal with a passive detection system in which the ambient static EF is perturbed or distorted by the presence of an intruder (e.g. human body).

Previous work by Cohn et al. describes the theory of operation behind static electric field sensing when the device is placed on the body of the user being sensed [6]. In this previous work, a voltage is measured between the user's body and a small "local ground plane" that is located on the sensing device, but is electrical isolation from the body. In this work, the same static electric field phenomenon is leveraged, but the sensing device is not directly attached to the user's body, and therefore the important capacitances are changed as shown in Figure 2.

Firstly, we observe a capacitance C_B between the body and the environment. In Figure 2, this is separated into two capacitances: the coupling capacitance C_F between the user's feet relative to the ground, and the coupling capacitance C_w between the body and other objects in the environment, such as the walls. We assume that there are two highly resistive layers between the feet of the subject and the ground. One layer is the sole of the subject's footwear. The other is the surface of the floor. The capacitance C_F may be calculated as the sum of the capacitance C_f of the sole and the capacitance C_l of the surface of the floor. Therefore, C_B can be expressed as:

$$C_B = C_w + C_F = C_w + \frac{C_f C_l}{C_f + C_l} \quad (4)$$

Unlike the previous on-body sensing case, there is now a coupling capacitance between the body and the sense electrode (C_d), which is mostly a function of the proximity of the user to the sense electrode. The sensing unit is basically a sensor depicted as a probe or antenna of arbitrary shape connected to an ADC input of a microcontroller. It is assumed that probe's size and shape does not disturb the field being measured. Finally, the sensing voltage (V_s) is measured from the sense electrode to earth ground (i.e., across the sense capacitor C_s).

Since the sense capacitor (C_s) value is fixed, changes in any of the coupling capacitances result in an AC voltage change on the sensing voltage (V_s). For normal interactions, V_s is most affected by changes in (1) the distance between the user and the sense electrode–ΔC_d, (2) the user's contact area with the floor–ΔC_F (e.g., standing on one foot vs. two), and (3) the proximity of the user to other objects in the interaction space–ΔC_w.

IMPLEMENTATION

Hardware Approach

Previous work on sensing static electric fields required custom analog hardware to DC bias, amplify, and filter the signal before it could be sampled and used for motion classification [6,7,19]. In this work, we demonstrate the ability to sense static electric fields using simple and available commodity prototyping hardware. Our hardware implementation consisted of only an off-the-shelf microcontroller such as Arduino [4]. Arduino is a very popular embedded systems prototyping platform in the hobbyist, designer, and artist communities. Our implementation of the static electric field sensor requires no additional hardware besides an Arduino and a sense electrode, which can be made from foil.

Since we are interested in only an AC signal, we need to DC bias the signal in order to sample it using the single-ended analog-to-digital converter (ADC) on the microcontroller board. Traditionally, a DC level is established by adding a high impedance path to a reference voltage. Unfortunately, we would need an extremely large resistor value in order to avoid cutting off the 60 Hz signals we want to observe. In previous work, this was accomplished using custom hardware before the ADC.

In contrast to the previous approaches, we use a simple channel-switching method to DC bias the ADC signal (i.e. we implemented alternate-sampling of the internal voltage reference (VREF) and the analog input). In the case of Successive Approximation Register ADC, sampling the VREF will pre-charge the ADC input to a known level. This should establish a DC level when we switch back to sample the analog input (which shares that stored charge). Broad range of microcontroller boards such as Arduino incorporate Successive Approximation Register ADC in their design, due to low-cost and ease of interfacing.

Our hardware configuration requires no filtering before the ADC, because we do not utilize the raw EF samples as our main signal. Typically, when sampling low frequency EF, the extremely strong main noise (60 Hz) and it's harmonics will alias into the reading, which can cause the reading to clip as the AC amplitude becomes too high. Previous work such as [6] required hardware implementation of a low pass filter. Our approach can be implemented digitally in software, which supports easy deployment in already existing microcontroller boards.

Processing

Data acquisition

In our prototype, we used an off-the-shelf microcontroller (prototyped with ATmega 2560/328/168) and attached a sense electrode in one of its analog input. Each analog input available on the microcontroller potentially forms an EF sensor channel. Small electrode surface area may be sufficient if the sensing unit is placed near the human body, e.g. in-pocket sensing configuration. The microcontroller then stacked with lithium-ion battery pack for power, and a XBee for wireless communication to the signal processing PC. In scenarios that do not require wireless communication, the microcontroller was connected to a FTDI FT232RL USB to serial IC, thus further redirects all the communication with PC through a USB connection.

The data acquisition algorithm was implemented in AVR C firmware for the microcontroller. Each channel was sampled at 20 Hz, a sampling rate that would be considered too low for any significant noise other than EF disturbance that we are examining, but was able to represent the relevant spectrum for motion, gesture, and activity recognition. This reduced sample rate (and consequently low processing bandwidth) makes our technique readily portable to embedded processors with limited resources.

Real-time signal capture

Serial communication client written in Java was used for interfacing the sensing unit and PC. Furthermore, this program performed several other key functions. First, it provides live visualization of the data from our sensor/s, which is useful to identify distinctive features for analysis.

A single packet of our raw data stream consisted of a 10-bit sample of sense electrode reading (Figure 3, red line), and offset $\acute{o}$ (Figure 3, yellow line, multiplied by 100 for better visualization). We defined $\acute{o}$ as a ratio of ideal and actual VREF reading when measured against Vcc. It essentially shows very small fluctuations in Vcc. We accommodate these small fluctuations in our measurements to have more accurate ADC readings. In the case of ATmega 168/328, VREF is 1.1 V and Vcc is 5 V, hence:

$$\acute{o} = \frac{\frac{1.1}{5} \times 1023}{VREF\ reading} = \frac{225.06}{VREF\ reading} \quad (5)$$

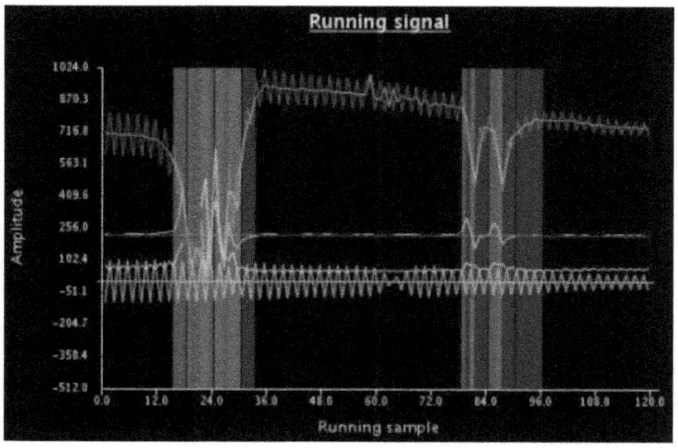

Figure 3. Signal acquisition in *Mirage*, showing raw sample (red line), DC component (green line), AC component (blue line), main signal (white line), event detection (green and yellow highlights) and gesture segmentation (grey highlights).

Our first treatment to the raw sense electrode reading was to apply a 3rd order Butterworth IIR low-pass filter with a 3 dB corner at 7 Hz. This filter reduces the high frequency component (higher than 7Hz) of sampled signal (Figure 3, green line). The DC waveform is then multiplied with ó. After multiplying the DC waveform with ó, we aggregate our signal that fluctuates relative to the magnitude of user's movements. This signal is plotted in Figure 3 (white line).

From the raw data stream (Figure 3, red line) we can also examine that the amplitude of the AC components also changes significantly during a gesture. This is mainly caused by changes of proximity between the body and electromagnetic sources in the environment (ΔC_w in Figure 2), in addition to changes in the frequency response. We extracted the AC components by applying a 3rd order Butterworth IIR high-pass filter with a 3 dB corner at 7 Hz to our raw data stream. The AC component of our signal is plotted in Figure 3 (blue line). To capture the AC amplitude in this signal, we compute the root-mean-square (RMS) over each window.

Analysis

To give a clear target on the signal features we need to explore, we focused our activity and gesture recognition study in the following domains:

1. Continuous activity recognition
   This domain focuses to recognize relatively long-duration activities. These problems generally have the property of using relatively long windows (since activities don't change rapidly) and not focusing on individual events. In this paper, we test our sensing approach to recognize when the user is standing still, walking, running, or doing jumping jacks.
2. Discrete activity recognition
   This domain focuses on repeated events, which have more tolerance to false negatives. In our study, we perform activity counting and activity density calculation (e.g. step per-second) from the aforementioned continuous activities (walking, running, and jumping jacks).
3. Gesture recognition
   This domain focuses on recognizing discrete command gestures, which generally have the properties of occurring slowly and infrequently, with high cost of false positives and false negatives. We investigate the feasibility of our system to detect, segment, and classify whole-body gestures.

Based on the aforementioned activity and gesture recognition targets, we implemented necessary signal analysis approaches such as event detection (including counting), gesture segmentation, feature extraction, and gesture classification.

Real-time event detection

In this stage, we aimed to detect real-time events of EF disturbances mainly caused by body movements to perform continuous and discrete activity recognition. Our system incorporates heuristic based adaptive threshold approach to detect these events. This simple approach is sufficient and effective for our signal mainly because the aggregated signal is clean, stable, and has predictable behavior. The signal rise and fall (as illustrated in Figure 3 by light green and light yellow highlights, also shown in Figure 7 and 8a) were direct effects of foot lift and foot land. Hence, continuous activities such as walking, running, jumping jacks, or standing still can be inferred simply by analyzing the signal amplitude and frequency. Our step-counting algorithm is based on threshold crossings, with rejection of crossings that are too close in time.

Real-time segmentation

Next, the program segmented inputs from the data stream into independent instances. Our system requires a real-time segmenter that automatically identifies gesture events from the live signal stream. We used similar adaptive thresholding method as the event detection described above, and then compute finite difference (i.e. sample-to-sample difference) of the signal in 1-second non-overlapping window. We set 1-second window because the designated gestures are unlikely to exceed 1-second period. By implementing this, the latency of our real-time segmentation algorithm is purely limited to sampling time (group delay of low pass filter). The mean value of the computed finite difference is then compared to a dynamic threshold aggregated from the adaptive algorithm similar to that implemented in our real-time event detection; if the absolute value of the mean is greater than the threshold, the system considers the current instance to be a gesture. The real-time segmentation results are illustrated in Figure 3 marked by light grey highlights.

Real-time feature extraction

In this stage, the program analyzed segmented signals and performs feature extractions. Below are the 77 features we exploited for our gesture classification:

- Signal waveform (20, Figure 3 – white line).
- DC & AC waveform (40, Figure 3 – green and blue line)
- Mean (1): average value of the signal over the window
- Median (1): the median signal value over the window
- Standard Deviation (1): the spreadness of the signal over the window
- Variance (1): the square of standard deviation
- Root Mean Square (1): The quadratic mean value of the signal over the window
- Zero Crossing Rate (1): The total number of times the signal changes from positive to negative or back or vice versa normalized by the window length
- Mean Crossing Rate (1): The total number of times the signal changes from below average to above average or vice versa normalized by the window length
- Signal spectrum (10): 20-points FFT of the signal.

Real-time classification

Our system classified these input instances into a set of gestures using Sequential Minimal Optimization (SMO) implementation of the Support Vector Machine (SVM) classifier found included in the WEKA [11]. Our system runs the new features against a previously trained model to produce gesture classification results.

Resolution and Signal-to-Noise Ratio

In the current configuration, our sensor has an update rate of 20 Hz. This is considered sufficient because we are dealing with body movements which are not likely to exceed 10 Hz. It is important to note that our system is capable of performing much higher refresh rate, but at the same time we also focused on reducing unnecessary data transfer to perform ultra-low power sensing.

Our sensing method passively measures noise in electric field due to body motion. To evaluate our signal, we choose the alternative Signal-to-Noise Ratio (SNR) definition, which is a reciprocal of the coefficient of variation of a set of samples taken over a period of time. We collected an hour-long sample of our signal and measured the mean and standard deviation. The mean was 224.65 (SD=2.59), hence the SNR is:

$$SNR = \frac{\mu}{\sigma} = \frac{224.65}{2.59} = 86.74 \qquad (6)$$

Note that our measurement includes variations from nearby electrical appliances, and also from the presence of experimenter who was standing still near the sense electrode during the data collection. This measurement scenario closely resembles actual usage scenario of *Mirage*.

EVALUATION

We designed and carried out a series of experiments to investigate the usability of our sensing approach, as well as to establish the baseline performance of the recognition engine. The experiment was conducted in 10 separate locations in 2 different office buildings. The office buildings had 4 and 3 floors with basements. We selected these locations to represent different flooring materials, building constructions, and surrounding electrical appliances, thus form a wide variety of ambient static EF. For a single location, experiments were conducted in a single visit.

Our participants were unique for every location, totaling in 10 participants (3 female), weighed between 47 and 84 kg (mean=65 kg), and height between 163 and 184 cm (mean=172 cm). Throughout our experiments, we did not require participants to use certain footwear. However, we did suggested participants to wear shoes, i.e. not barefooting. During our experiments, we avoid non-participants from entering the experiment space.

Activity Recognition

Setup

We developed a system that acquires signals produced by *Mirage* sensor, detects when a user is present, and recognize the amount and type of user's activity. To test the robustness of this system, we conducted evaluations where the participants in different locations performed the following activities: (1) participant not in the room, participant in the room and (2) standing still, (3) walking, (4) running, and (5) jumping.

To support these scenarios, we attached a 50 × 5 mm copper tape as our sense electrode on the notebook PC monitor frame and our microcontroller was connected to the notebook PC by USB cable (similar setup as Figure 4a, but attached on notebook PC monitor). The notebook PC was powered by internal li-ion battery.

Procedure

We instructed the participants to subsequently perform each of the designated activities for 10 seconds period at the

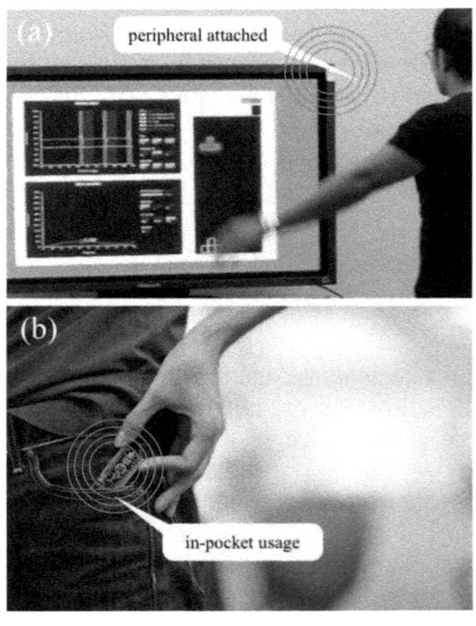

Figure 4. Setup used in our evaluation: (a) microcontroller with sense electrode attached to a monitor frame, and (b) microcontroller (with wireless connection) without additional sense electrode for in-pocket usage.

same location in the experimental space (i.e. without locomotion). In general, our signal exists regardless of locomotion. Participants performed activities within the sensible distance from the sensor (typically <2m). We also instructed the participants to count their steps during walking, running, and jumping activities. Participants then reported their counting results to the experimenter. We repeated this session 5 times for each of the participants. Overall, we obtained 250 samples.

The real-time event detection was done automatically during each session. Our system logs signal peaks and valleys together with their amplitudes, as well as signal frequencies obtained by spectral analysis (FFT). Combined, these data served as features for activity recognition. In this experiment, we set static thresholds for the aforementioned features to identify activities; therefore our activity recognition system does not require training.

Results

By comparing the aggregated activity recognition results with the ground truth data, we obtain 96.72% average accuracy (SD=5.35%) across 5 activities for 10 participants. Note that we used heuristic threshold to identify activities in a simple, low-power, and fast way (in contrast to machine learning based approaches), which can be extended to leverage more advanced recognition algorithm for supporting broader type of activities.

Furthermore, we compared the automated and self-reported step counting results; yielding an average of 8.41% error margin (SD=3.12%). Note that high-quality research grade pedometers available in the market have typical error margin of ±5% [5,22]. These results seem promising with plenty of headroom for fine-tuning.

Gesture Classification

Setup

To aggregate whole-body gestures, we extended our activity recognition system (which is basically a real-time event detection and heuristic threshold setting) with real-time segmentation, feature extraction, and SMO based classifier. We used the techniques described in the previous section. To evaluate this system, we recruited the same participants and adopted similar setup as our previous experiment. The designated gestures include: (1) left arm lift, (2) right arm lift, (3) left hand rotation, (4) right hand rotation, and (5) jump. We illustrate these gestures in Figure 5.

Figure 5. Stick figures describing the 5 gestures performed by participants in our gesture classification experiment.

Procedure

First, the participants were instructed to train themselves to perform the gestures. Soon after, the participants were instructed to subsequently perform each of the gesture for 5 times. To avoid over fitting, we treat the aforementioned session as one fold, and then we repeated the session for 5 times (5-fold). Overall, we aggregated 1250 samples of gestures. Our system performs segmentation and feature extraction automatically. It labeled and recorded each sample for our 5-fold cross-validation test. Prior to the test, we trained our SMO classifier in user dependent manner.

Results

The average accuracy across 10 participants and locations was 92.11% (SD=6.84%) when classifying between 5 gestures. These results are encouraging for explorations on inferring gestures from completely passive static EF sensing using no body contact approach. It also validate our assumption that *Mirage* would work equally well across a reasonably wide set of people and homes.

Location Classification

Setup

We conducted a study on location classification based on our hypothesis that different environments will give different fingerprints of ambient EF features. This is mainly caused by the variation of electrical appliances and electricity wiring that acts as electromagnetic sources. To be able to see wider range of the spectrum, we modified our sampling mechanism to sample only from the sense electrode. In this experiment, we sampled our ADC at 400 Hz, resulting in a spectrum width of 200 Hz, easily containing 60 Hz mains and its harmonics.

We measured EF fingerprint in 6 locations: (1) work desk, (2) meeting room, (3) kitchen, (4) hallways, (5) hardware lab, and (6) soccer field. The examples of the signals for each location are available in Figure 6. This ambient EF reading confirmed our hypothesis on the variability of EF fingerprints across different locations.

We recruited the same participants as previous experiments. The sensor was placed in the user's pocket, with no additional electrode attached to the analog input of the microcontroller (Figure 4b). This usage scenario works well to capture the EF fingerprint mainly because the human body acting as an antenna receives wide-range of frequency from the environment. Moreover, the analog input in close proximity to the body picks significantly stronger signal (ΔC_d in Figure 2).

Procedure

We instructed the participants to freely choose a spot at above locations, and remember it for the next round of data collection. Each location of every round naturally separated in time due to participants moving from one location to another. Hence the training and testing data were from the relatively same spot, but separated in time.

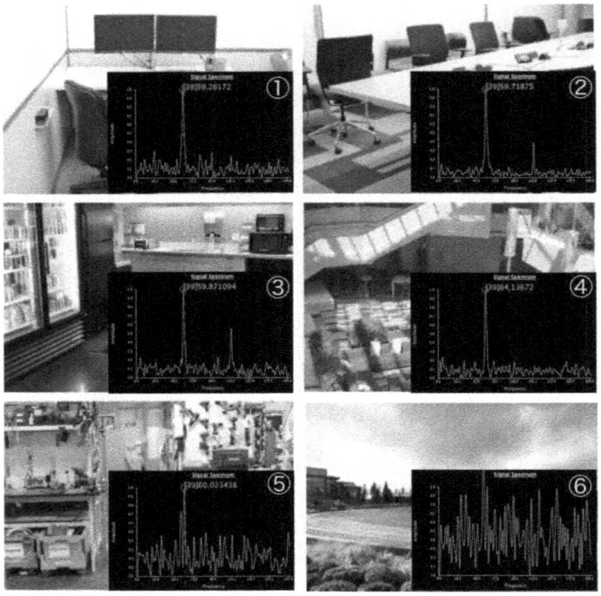

Figure 6. The ambient electric field fingerprints sampled from 6 different locations show distinctive features that we leveraged in our location classification.

At the measurement location, participants pressed a keyboard key to start collecting 100 samples of EF fingerprints (each consists of spectral features), which took approximately 100 seconds. We subsequently perform the data collection for all the locations and repeat it again for 5 rounds. Overall, we aggregated 30000 samples that were trained in user dependent manner.

Results

We performed 5-fold cross validation using our SMO classifier. The average accuracy was 98.12% (SD=4.47%) when classifying between 6 locations. This is impressive, given that the approach was simple, and there is still plenty of headroom to fine-tune the parameters.

Multiple User Differentiation

Setup

We conducted a study to leverage 2-channel *Mirage* sensor and Independent Component Analysis (ICA) algorithm to differentiate signal source coming from multiple user. In this experiment, we used the same implementation as our activity recognition, except that we had utilized two-channel *Mirage* sensor and applied ICA to the signals.

Procedure

We instructed 2 participants to perform foot motion (without locomotion) in a 2 × 2 m work desk cubicle. We also asked the participants to perform foot motion in different speeds relative to each other.

We applied our ICA based multiple user differentiation approach to the real-time signal. We observe the behavior of the signals and the aggregated independent components.

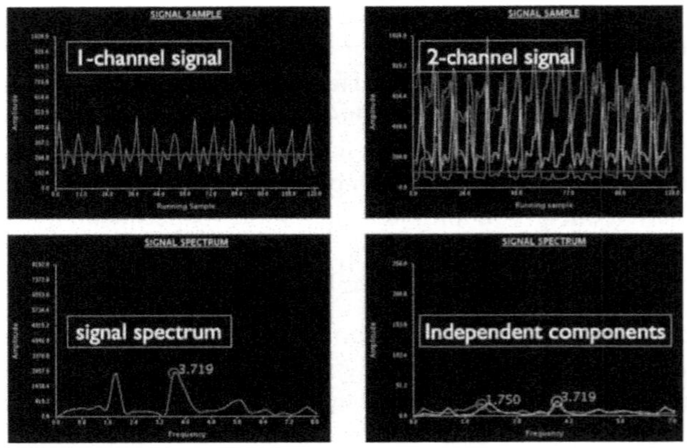

Figure 7. Multiple users differentiation using Independent Component Analysis (ICA). Upper left graph shows mixtures of signals captured by 1-channel sensor, and consequently mixed spectrum as shown in lower left graph. Using two-channel sensor and implementing ICA separates the independent components of the signal, revealing two signal sources as shown in lower right graph.

Results

Our system successfully aggregated independent components of the signals originated from 2 participants. We show an exemplary result in Figure 7, where a participant was walking and another participant was running.

Combining ICA with simple amplitude based proximity sensing has the potential to help multiple user tracking. ICA can also be used to filter out noise from the signal, especially in the crowded environment. Exploring user tracking and noise filtering using ICA remains future work.

Interactive Application

We developed three applications to demonstrate *Mirage* real-time interactive capabilities. The first application shows the capability of *Mirage* to perform activity monitoring. This application provides real-time visualization of the raw data stream, results of the signal processing (AC/DC components, signal, FFT of the signal) as well as context aggregation results such as standing still, walking, running, and jumping, with their respective speeds and step counts (Figure 8a).

The second application leverages activity detection to control the movement of a game character. Figure 8b shows a user playing the game where he tries to avoid obstacles by walking, running, and jumping.

The third application is a Tetris game, which the user controls were mapped to a player's whole-body gestures. Although a wide range of gestures can be trained, we leverage intuitive arm and foot motions such as: lifting left or right arm for left or right movement respectively, rotation gesture with one hand for Tetris block rotation, and jumping gesture to drop the block on the top of the stacks. In this application, we pre-trained the gesture classifier

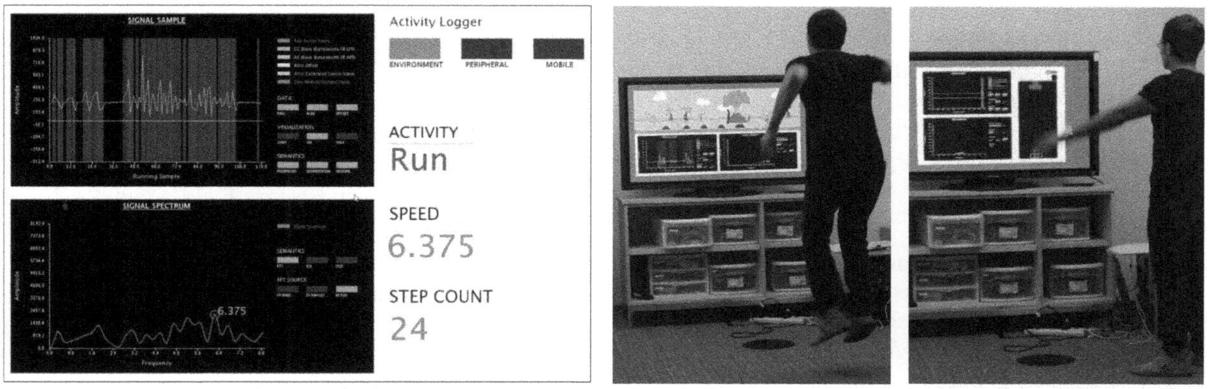

(a) Activity monitoring (b) Avatar-control game (c) Tetris game

Figure 8. Our interactive applications build on: (a) continuous and discrete activity recognition for activity monitoring, (b) discrete activity recognition embedded in an avatar-controlling game where a user has to physically walk, run, or jump to avoid obstacles, and (c) gesture recognition embedded in a Tetris game where user controls are mapped to whole-body gestures.

(SMO) using 10 examples of each gesture. Figure 8c shows the actual image of a user playing our Tetris game.

DISCUSSION

Through the experiments presented in this paper, we have shown that using the proposed off-body static electric field sensing, our system is able to perform activity recognition, gesture recognition, location classification, and multiple user differentiation in encouraging results. In addition, by developing three interactive applications we have demonstrated the ability to run our system in real-time. This section discusses the limitations of the current system, and future work to improve the system.

Limitations and Future Work

The EF strength E at a distance r away from a point charge Q is given by:

$$E = k\frac{Q}{r^2} \qquad (7)$$

where k is Coulomb's Law constant ($9.0\times10^9 N\,m^2/C^2$). Hence, the EF strength is inversely proportional to the square of the distance. Consistent with this, the sensitivity of our sensing approach is limited to a certain distance from the subject to sensor (ΔC_d in Figure 2). Fortunately, depending on the usage scenario this limitation can also be a *feature*. Limiting sensible space helps to avoid noisy signal, and useful to recognize events only from users who are nearby the sensors. This can also be a hint for proximity sensing. Also, by leveraging spatially distributed sensors we can upscale the usage to indoor location estimation.

Circuit model represented in Figure 2 and physics model represented in Eq. (1-4) note that the capacitance of the foot to the ground (C_F) and the body to nearby objects (C_w) influence the resulted sensing voltage (V_s). Hence, the resistance of user's footwear also highly influences the magnitude of our signal (i.e., the higher the resistance, the higher magnitude of the signal our system can capture). While we do not have exact solution for this particular limitation yet, our pilot experiments showed wide-range of footwear could produce detectable signal. Furthermore, our heuristic-base adaptive threshold approach also helps to detect marginal changes in the signal for further processing.

From the physics model represented in Eq. (2), capacitance between body and sense electrode (C_d) is directly proportional to the induced charge of the measurement electrode. Thus, the area size of the sense electrode also influences the magnitude of our signal (bigger electrode yields more sensitive system). Fortunately, using Mirage as a mobile sensor (e.g. in-pocket usage scenario) will mitigate this limitation; i.e., if the distance between the sensor and subject decrease, the signal magnitude will increase significantly. Using Mirage as peripheral attached sensor or environmental sensor also gives more headroom for attaching larger sense electrode.

For future iteration of this work, we plan to explore the interaction design space for *Mirage* in mobile devices, as well as exploring integration of *Mirage* in homes (interfacing with powerline). Also, we plan to further explore our multiple user differentiation to support multiple user tracking.

CONCLUSION

In this paper, we have presented a novel approach to infer the amount and type of motion, gesture, and activity, as well as location classification and multiple user differentiation using non body contact and passive static electric field sensing, namely *Mirage*. We have described the theory of operation and detailed implementation of the sensing system that leverages the design of ADC in off-the-shelf microcontrollers, which allows simple setup with no instrumentation on the user. *Mirage* systems can be extremely small, lightweight and low power. Since electric fields penetrate non-conductors, electrode sensors can be hidden, providing protection from weather and wear, while simultaneously adds the element of disappearing input interface. *Mirage* also works outdoor, enabling truly mobile solution. Results from our experiments have demonstrated that our system performs reasonably well for a series of activity and gestures. Additionally, we have presented results on location classification within a building and outdoor, as well as multiple user differentiation using ICA. We conclude with demonstration of an activity monitoring application, and two interactive applications showing immediate applicability and rich interaction design space enabled by *Mirage*.

ACKNOWLEDGEMENTS

We are thankful to Desney S. Tan, Shwetak N. Patel, and Gabe Cohn for their significant contribution in helping to understand passive electric field sensing and its principles of operation. We also thank anonymous reviewers for their thoughtful comments and subjects who participated in the experiments. This work is partially supported by Microsoft Research through Collaborative Research (CORE) Projects.

REFERENCES

1. Agrawal, S., Constandache, I., Gaonkar, S., Choudhury, R., Caves, K, DeRuyter, F. Using Mobile Phones to Write in Air. *Mobisys 2011,* 15–28.
2. A. Mansfield, and GM. Lyons. The Use of Accelerometry to Detect Heel Contact Events for Use as a Sensor in FES Assisted Walking. *Med. Eng. Phys.*, Vol. 25, pp. 879–885, 2003.
3. A. Ohsawa. Electrostatic Characterization of Antistatic Floors Using an Equivalent Circuit Model. *Journal of Electrostatics*, Vol. 51–52, pp. 625–631, 2001.
4. Arduino. http://arduino.cc/
5. C G Ryan, P M Grant, W W Tigbe, M H Granat (2006). The Validity and Reliability of a Novel Activity Monitor as a Measure of Walking. *British Journal of Sports Medicine*, 40 (40): 779–784.
6. Cohn, G., Gupta, S., Lee, T., Morris D., Smith J.R., Reynolds, M.S., Tan D.S., Patel S.N. An Ultra-Low-Power Human Body Motion Sensor Using Static Electric Field Sensing. *Ubicomp '12*, 99–102.
7. Cohn, G., Morris, D., Patel, S.N., Tan, D.S. Humantenna: Using the Body as an Antenna for Real-Time Whole-Body Interaction. *CHI '12,* 1901–1910.
8. Dietz, P. and Leigh, D. DiamondTouch: A Multi-User Touch Technology. *UIST '01*, 219–226.
9. FitBit. http://www.fitbit.com/
10. Fukumoto, M. and Tonomura, Y. Body coupled FingeRing. *CHI '97*, 147–154.
11. Hall, M., Frank, E., Holmes, G., Pfahringer, B., Reutemann, P., Witten, I.H. The WEKA Data Mining Software: An Update. *SIGKDD Explorations*, 11.1 (2009).
12. JRW. Morris. Accelerometry a Technique for the Measurement of Human Body Movements. *Journal of Biomechanics*, Vol. 6, pp. 729–739, 1973.
13. Junker, H., Lukowitz, P., Troester, G. Continuous Recognition of Arm Activities with Body-Worn Inertial Sensors. *ISWC '04,* 188–189.
14. K. Takiguchi, T. Wada, and S. Toyama. Human Body Detection that Uses Electric Field by Walking. *Journal of Advanced Mechanical Design, Systems, and Manufacturing*, Vol. 1, No. 3 pp. 294–305, 2007.
15. K. Takiguchi, and S. Toyama. Does a Dog Recognize his Master by an Electric Field? Generation and Transmission of an Electric Field Around a Walker. *Journal of International Society of Life Information Science*, Vol. 21, No. 2, pp. 428–433, 2003.
16. Michoud, B., Guillou, E., Bouakaz, S. Real-time and markerless 3D human motion capture using multiple views. *In Proc of Human Motion 2007*, 88–103.
17. Nike+. http://nikeplus.nike.com/plus/
18. Rekimoto, J. GestureWrist and GesturePad: Unobtrusive Wearable Interaction Devices. *ISWC '01*, 21–27.
19. Rekimoto, J. and Wang, H. Sensing GamePad: Electrostatic Potential Sensing for Enhancing Entertainment Oriented Interactions. *CHI EA '04*, 1457–1460.
20. R. Williamson, and BJ. Andrews. Detecting Absolute Human Knee Angle and Angular Velocity Using Accelerometers and Rate Gyroscopes. *Med. Biol. Eng. Comput.* Vol. 39, pp. 1–9, 2001.
21. Sato, M., Poupyrev, I., Harrison, C. Touché: Enhancing Touch Interaction on Humans, Screens, Liquids, and Everyday Objects. *CHI '12,* 483–492.
22. Scott, J., Dearman, D., Yatani, K., Truong,K.N. Sensing Foot Gestures from the Pocket. *UIST '10*, 199–208.
23. Smith, J.R. Field mice: Extracting hand geometry from electric field measurements. IBM Systems Journal, (35) 3.4, 1996, 587–608.
24. Susan D. Vincent, Cara L. Sidman. Determining Measurement Error in Digital Pedometers. *Measurement in Phys. Ed. and Exercise Science*, 7 (1): 19–24. 2003.
25. T. Ficker. Electrification of Human Body by Walking. *Journal of Electrostatics*, Vol. 64, pp. 10–16, 2006.
26. Vicon. http://www.vicon.com
27. V. Amoruso, M. Helali, and F. Lattarulo. An Improved Model of Man for ESD Application. *Journal of Electrostatics*, Vol. 49, pp. 225–244, 2000.
28. Wachs, J., Kölsch, M., Stern, H., Edan Y. Vision-based hand-gesture applications. *In Comm. ACM* 54.2, 60–71.
29. Xbox Kinect. http://www.xbox.com/en-US/kinect
30. Zimmerman, T.G. Personal Area Networks: Near-Field Intra-Body Communication. *IBM Systems Journal,* (35) 3.4, 1996, 609–617.
31. Zimmerman T.G., Smith J.R., Paradiso J.A., Allport D., Gershenfeld, N. Applying Electric Field Sensing to Human-Computer Interfaces. *CHI '95,* 280–287.

StickEar: Making Everyday Objects Respond to Sound

Kian Peen Yeo yeokianpeen@sutd.edu.sg
Suranga Nanayakkara suranga@sutd.edu.sg
Shanaka Ransiri shanaka@sutd.edu.sg
Augmented Senses Group, International Design Center, Singapore University of Technology and Design

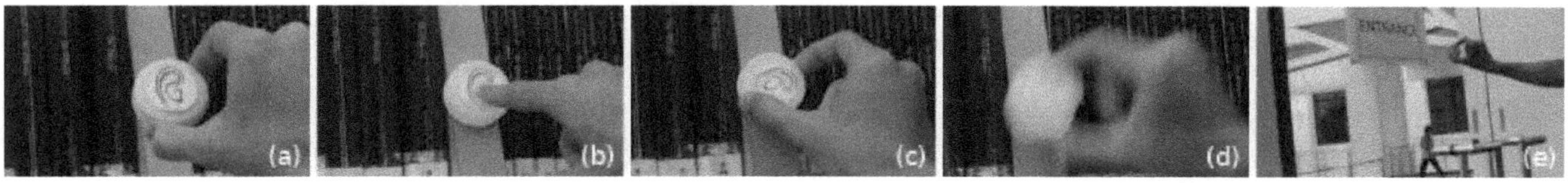

Figure 1. StickEar prototype: (a) Deploy on an object. (b) Press to activate. (c) Rotate to tune. (d) Shake to reset (e) Redeploy on another object.

ABSTRACT
This paper present StickEar, a system consisting of a network of distributed 'Sticker-like' sound-based sensor nodes to propose a means of enabling sound-based interactions on everyday objects. StickEar encapsulate wireless sensor network technology into a form factor that is intuitive to reuse and redeploy. Each StickEar sensor node consists of a miniature sized microphone and speaker to provide sound-based input/output capabilities. We provide a discussion of interaction design space and hardware design space of StickEar that cuts across domains such as remote sound monitoring, remote triggering of sound, autonomous response to sound events, and controlling of digital devices using sound. We implemented three applications to demonstrate the unique interaction capabilities of StickEar.

Author Keywords
Distributed tangible user interfaces (dTUI), wireless sensor networks, sound based interactions

ACM Classification Keywords
H.5.2. User Interfaces: Interaction styles; K.4.2. Social Issues: Assistive technologies for persons with disabilities

General Terms
Design

INTRODUCTION
Spatial anchoring of visual information on physical objects through the use of paperbound materials is a common method for leaving tangible bits of information to facilitate non-verbal communication. Tagging objects and places with visual information using product labels, price tags, and signboards etc., has become a part of our daily lives. Often these visual tags are static and always visible. Sticky notes are special purpose visual tags used for temporal anchoring of visual information, with the flexibility of being redeployed to another object and space [28]. With StickEar, we propose a method to empower people with the ability to deploy acoustic tags on any objects or space, and be well informed of acoustic cues that may be produced by an object or a location.

UIST'13, October 6–9, 2013, St. Andrews, United Kingdom.

http://dx.doi.org/10.1145/2501988.2502019

We live in a world surrounded by sensors. They can either be embedded in a device that we carry around, or be a permanent installation at a location [37]. While having a portable feature-packed device (such as a mobile phone) with multiple sensors embedded may seem to be an 'all-round' solution for many applications, it might not be a cost effective solution when having to deploy multiple devices at various locations. Hence, dedicated low cost sensor devices are often deployed in large sensor networks [4]. Distributed sensor networks pose a different problem, as they are often seen as an expert device that can be complicated to set up and deploy [25]. They are often semi-permanent installations that are not meant to be redeployed on a frequent basis. With StickEar [40], we want to bring together the advantages of portability, accessibility and re-configurability into a single system.

With StickEar, users can simply 'stick' a StickEar sensor node onto an object to enable sound based interaction. The tangible user interface of StickEar allows users to interact with the device by pressing, turning and shaking (Figure 1). Contributions of this work include a discussion of the interaction space of StickEar, exploration of associated hardware design space, development and evaluation of the prototype system, and demonstration of a few examples of StickEar enabled applications.

RELATED WORK

Sound based Interactions
Sounds generated by everyday objects (e.g. doorbell, microwave oven, etc.) and sound in spaces (conversation, thunder etc.) act as important awareness cues for us to understand the state of the world around us [18]. In addition, sound is perhaps the most natural 'active' form of two-way communication since human hear and produce sound naturally [10]. The use of sound as a output for tangible interactions has been explored in various research areas [17, 1]. Scratch Input [15] for example, transforms the unique sound produced when dragging a fingernail on a textured surface into various gesture inputs to the surface. PingPongPlus [21] is a novel interface for digitally augmented cooperative play. It uses the sound from a ball

hitting the table in a game of table tennis as an input to create a digital augmentation layer on the physical table. StickEar builds upon this concept of using sound as an input to transform objects into one that is interactive.

Tangible User Interfaces

Ishii and Ullmer proposed the concept of tangible bits as a means to bridge the gaps between the digital and physical world, as well as the foreground and background of human activities [20]. The use of dTUIs is demonstrated in Siftables, a research project which became a successful commercial product [27]. Siftables applies the technology and methodology from wireless sensor networks to a touch and gesture based TUI with graphical displays, allowing the physical interaction of digital information. In addition, Lucero et al. [24] implemented a network of mobile devices to demonstrate spacial and tangible interactions. In StickEar, we harness the idea of having wireless tangible bits but instead apply it on interactions with sound.

Connectivity

Interconnecting real-world objects in the digital domain provides an opportunity to perform collaborative and cooperative behaviours [12, 38]. Ninja Blocks [2] and Twine [3] are two commercial products that integrate wireless sensor monitoring into a cloud-based service over the Internet. They both feature an intuitive 'rule-based' configuration method to replace traditional programming for setting up the device. In addition, apart from the inbuilt sensors that come along with the device, they both allow external sensors to be connected through connectors. We recognize the potential of 'Internet of Things' [36], and the notion of these devices providing 'just in time information'. With StickEars, we want to provide users with the ability to stay connected and be aware of their surroundings, and at the same time, make the experience intuitive through an inbuilt TUI on the device.

Augmented Objects

Augmenting objects with digital capabilities is getting increasingly popular as computing power gets cheaper and smaller [22, 26, 5]. A framework for object augmentation was proposed by Guerrero et al. [11], and some researchers have focused on building generic and extensible infrastructure to make smart objects [32, 19, 35, 34]. Sensor network technology for object augmentation is challenging and interesting to the extent of overshadowing its applications [30, 33]. However, recently, Sato et al. [31] proposed a novel capacitive sensing technology, Touché, to enhance touch gestures on everyday objects and a rich set of potential application domains. StickEar follows a similar approach where we present a method to augment objects based on sound and present a compelling set of potential StickEar-enabled applications.

INTERACTION DESIGN SPACE

Through the design of a sound-based wireless TUI that is easy to deploy and configure, we seek to explore possible interaction techniques and gain insights on novel applications enabled by this device. The interaction space of StickEar is broad, covering both input and output domains. We identified four possible interactions that support the redeployability nature and collaborative structure of one or more StickEars: (a) Remote monitoring of sound events; (b) Remote triggering of sound output; Autonomous response to sound events; (d) Sound as a controller.

Remote monitoring of sound events (input)

A StickEar can be attached to an object or to a specific space to 'listen' for sound events. Attaching StickEar facing an object would capture sounds on and very close to the object whereas attaching StickEar facing outwards would capture sound events from a much wider space. A user could change the range of detection by adjusting the sensitivity of StickEar. StickEar as an input device opens up many application possibilities including security monitoring, ubiquitous data collection [23], activity monitoring [39] and as an assistive tool for the deaf [18]. In addition, as an input sound-monitoring device, we see a potential of deploying multiple StickEars for applications such as sound source localization [13].

Remote triggering of sound output (output)

Misplacing objects can be a frustrating experience, and one would often hope that the object could somehow respond to your calls and tell you where it is. StickEar as an output device could act as a 'voice' for inanimate objects. Finding appropriate sounds that add to the affordances of an object [6] would make this interaction more interesting. StickEar can even be used to transform everyday objects into sound sources [8] and multiple StickEars could potentially collaborate to provide a multichannel audio output.

Autonomous response to sound events (input/output)

In this interaction space, a StickEar is used as an input and output device at the same time. A sound input event triggers an immediate sound output on the same StickEar. This interaction can be explained with an example of using StickEar as a baby monitor. StickEar is placed near a baby's crib and configured to detect the sound of a crying baby. Upon detection, it responds immediately by playing a lullaby. This interaction could be based on the amplitude of the sound (exceeding a threshold) or, more interestingly, could be based on StickEar having the ability to perform classification of sound. Multiple StickEars in this interaction domain could be used to provide a better user experience for spaces such as museums and art exhibitions [16].

Sound as a controller (controller)

StickEar having the ability to perform classification of sound could function as a wireless controller using different sound inputs. For example, users could control personal digital devices or electrical appliances by snapping their fingers, tapping on StickEar or possibly 'talking' to it. Additionally, similar to PingPongPlus [21], a user would also be able to turn any surface into an interactive surface by attaching a single or multiple StickEars.

Apart from the above interactions, composite interactions between StickEars opens up new possibilities. One example scenario is where one StickEar is configured as an output device for locating objects, while another configured as an input device for sound event monitoring. A user triggers the alarm on one StickEars (configured as an output) but he/she is not in the range to hear the sound. However, another StickEar (configured as an input) within the vicinity can pick up this alarm sound and send a notification to the user informing him/her about the location of this sound event. This then allows a user to find an object from a remote location.

HARDWARE DESIGN SPACE

In the design of StickEar, our objective was to provide users with a device that enables sound based interactions with the environment. We want to emphasize on a wireless and portable device with a tangible user interface that is easy to deploy and configure. In this section, we will discuss the design space for possible hardware implementations that would support our proposed interactions.

Scope of recognition

We define two scopes of recognition: *level* and *class*. In its most basic configuration, the device is able to detect sound exceeding a user defined amplitude (*level*). This can be further sub-divided into two categories: localized detection of sound on or in close proximity to an object, or spatial detection of a particular space. Given the ability of the device to capture sound, it would be useful to be able to recognize a particular type of sound (e.g. clapping or knocking). As such, we define the second scope of recognition as the ability to recognize a certain type of sound (*class*).

Sound input measurement

We take into consideration two specific characteristics of sound (*amplitude* and *frequency*) for determining the required microphone hardware for sound measurement. The amplitude or loudness of sound is one factor that determines how far it can be heard from a distance. For example, softest sound a person can hear with normal hearing is 0 dB; normal conversation is about 60 dB; and baby screaming is about 110 dB. An amplifier circuit with tuneable gain settings gives users flexibility in detecting various sound *levels*. In terms of frequency, many common sounds at home fall in the range below $8kHz$ [10]. The sampling rate of the microphone signal should be at least $16kHz$ in order to capture these frequencies.

User input

A user physically interacts with the device to perform various tasks such as choosing between different modes of operation, tuning of sensitivity, executing or cancelling a selection and resetting. User inputs can be based on direct contact with the device such as pressing, turning, touching, shaking and bending. Indirect user inputs can be sound based, taking advantage of the microphone which is essential to the device. While a single capacitive touch screen would allow a user to perform these tasks through different touch gestures, it comes with high power consumption and large physical size. Use of traditional mechanical input devices such as push button switches and rotary encoders overcome some of these constraints. In addition, the affordances provided by these mechanical input devices and their corresponding functions are well established in many existing devices [9].

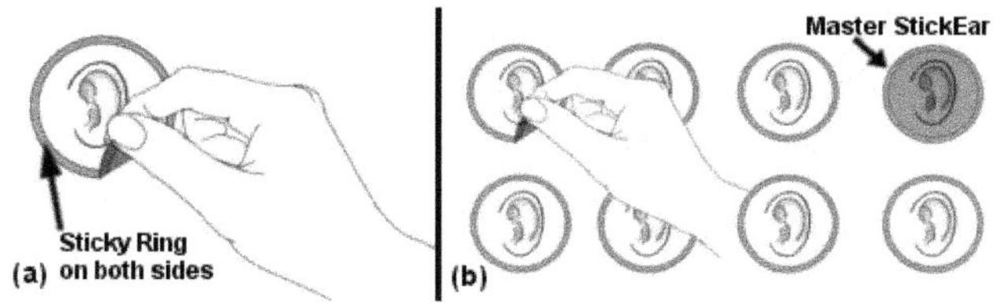

Figure 2. Envisioned form factor of futuristic StickEar

Output

Generally, feedback from StickEar to a user would be provided by using one or a combination of methods such as tactile, audio or visual. Audio and visual feedback in particular have an extended range while tactile feedback requires physical contact with the device itself. Audio feedback can be easily provided by a miniature speaker. Visual feedback in the form of display screens is popular because of the vast amount of information it can provide. However, the versatility of a single point light should not be underestimated. Harrison et al. [14] evaluated 24 different light behaviors from a single color light emitting diode (LED), of which eight were recommended for use in a mobile domain. With a tri-color LED, the amount of information that can be expressed can be multifold. For non-complex applications involving several different states, a single point light offers advantages in terms of power consumption and physical size.

Communication

Each StickEar could potentially have a direct internet access though a WIFI module built into it. Alternatively, connectivity could be achieved indirectly by establishing a local connection to a special StickEar that has an internet connection. Out of the numerous options for establishing wireless communication (bluetooth, WIFI, RF transceivers etc.), bluetooth and RF require low energy. However, an RF network with proprietary protocol might provide a computationally light weight and optimised solution in terms of power consumption and packet overhead.

Form factor

One of the motivations for StickEar came from the idea of sticky notes. Sticky notes come in a thin flexible paper material, with user inputs coming from an ink medium and providing an output that is visual based. Sticky notes unlike other writing mediums, offers a unique feature of being easily deployable through the use of a special non-permanent adhesive. The form factor of StickEar needs to be small, lightweight and possibly flexible too, so that it can be easily attached to flat or uneven surfaces using special reusable mounting tape or suction cup tape (Figure 2a). The electronics can be encapsulated in a waterproof flexible material that is acoustically transparent and users can interact with the device through touching, pressing and bending gestures. The device would be highly energy efficient and could harvest energy from its environment [29]. We envision

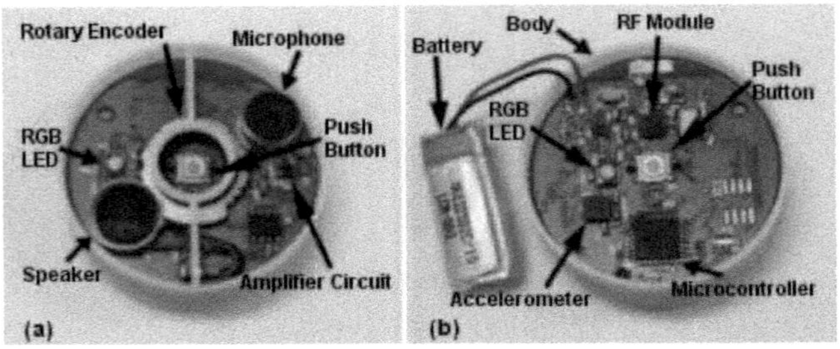

Figure 3. StickEar main board (a) front and (b) back.

that future StickEars will come as a sheet of stickers where users simply peel them off to attach to different objects (Figure 2b). It is important to design this thin form factor with a thickness that would not fundamentally change the user interactions.

STICKEAR

Based on the hardware design considerations in the previous section, we developed a proof-of-concept prototype of StickEar. The system consists of multiple StickEar sensor nodes that are wirelessly interconnected. In addition, a 'master StickEar' is used for relaying messages from sensor nodes to other external devices, if necessary.

Hardware Implementation

StickEar sensor node

At the heart of the StickEar sensor node is an ATMEGA328 8-bit microcontroller running at 8 MHz. A 3.3V lithium polymer battery provides power to the device. Inputs to the sensor node include a microphone, rotary encoder, push button switch and an accelerometer. A tri-color LED and speaker are used for visual and audio feedback respectively. Wireless connectivity between sensor nodes is provided by an nRF24L01 2.4 GHz radio transceiver. Hardware design of StickEar sensor node is shown in Figure 3.

Sound Acquisition: An omni-directional electret microphone with a sensitivity of -44 dB is used for capturing sound. An op-amp circuit configured as an inverting amplifier is used to amplify the signal from the microphone so as to maximize its dynamic range. In addition, the signal gain can be adjusted programmatically using a digital potentiometer. The amplified signal is then sampled at $20kHz$ by the microcontroller, allowing frequencies up to $10kHz$ to be measured accurately.

Input: In the current prototype, a user interacts with StickEar through three basic input gestures. By rotating a cylindrical ring sandwiched between the top and bottom faceplates (connected to a rotary encoder), a user can choose between different modes of operation as well as adjust the sensitivity. A push button switch located at the center of both the front and back of StickEar allows the detection of the pressing gesture. A 3-axis accelerometer (ADXL335) is used to detect a shaking gesture, which is associated with resetting the device to its main function selection menu.

Output: Two types of output feedback are available to the user. Visual output is provided by a tri-color LED located on both the front and back of the device. Different colors are used to represent a different mode of operation. Thus as a user cycles through the main mode selection menu, StickEar will light up with a corresponding color. A periodic blinking light sequence is used to indicate the occurrence of an event on the device. Also, a change in intensity of the light output provides an indication when adjusting the sensitivity. Audio output from a miniature speaker is used when StickEar functions as an output device to a remote sound triggering application.

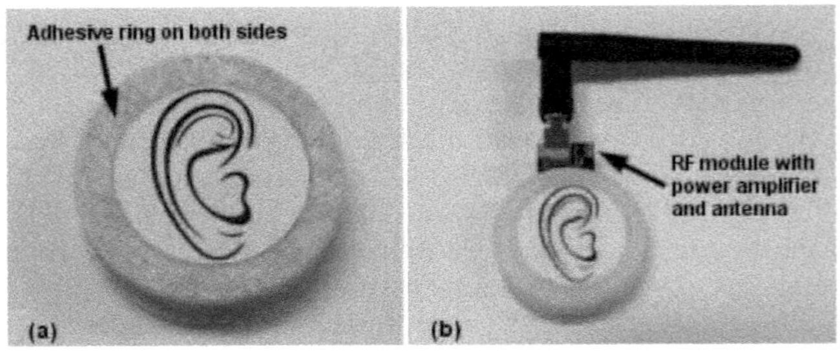

Figure 4. (a) StickEar sensor node. (b) Master StickEar

Form Factor: Current prototype version of the StickEar sensor node is a rounded shaped 3D printed plastic case (Figure 4a). The outer casing is designed such that it has a flat front and rear surface with reusable ring shaped adhesive along the perimeter of both sides. This allows the StickEar to be easily deployed and redeployed on different objects.To differentiate between localized and spatial hearing, an ear pictogram is printed on one side of the casing to indicate hearing directionality.

Master StickEar

The master StickEar uses an nRF24L01 transceiver with a power amplifier. It has a similar form factor to a StickEar sensor node except a more powerful RF antenna (Figure 4b) for an extended range of communication with other StickEar sensor nodes. A Bluetooth module in the master StickEar allows communication with a Bluetooth enabled computing device. We recognize the limitations with range in Bluetooth connectivity, but this current implementation is sufficient to demonstrate the interactions we are proposing. In the next design iteration, we would extend the connectivity of StickEars to be Internet enabled through a master StickEar that has an embedded WIFI module.

EXAMPLE STICKEAR APPLICATIONS

Based on the previous discussion on interaction design space, we developed three specific applications to demonstrate the capabilities enabled by the device. These applications allow StickEar to function as an input device, output device and/or a remote controller.

ObjectListener

In this particular application, StickEar operates as a remote input device, providing a notification to a user upon detecting a sound. An application on a Samsung Galaxy Nexus smartphone (service running in the background) was developed to establish pairing with the master StickEar for receiving notifications from sensor nodes. Setting up StickEar as an object listener is simple, as a user only needs to attach StickEar to the object (Figure 5a), initiate a one-time

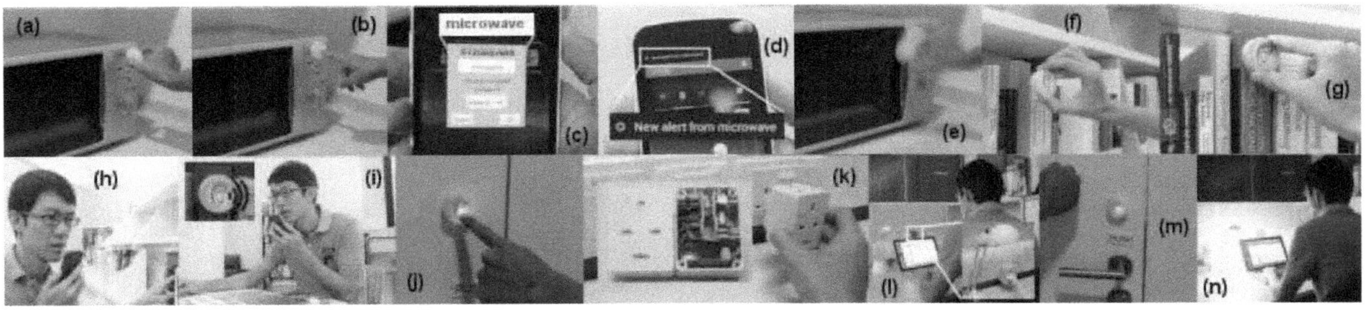

Figure 5. StickEar enabled interactions. (a) Deploying StickEar on a microwave; (b) Press to pair with the smartphone application; (c) Enter a text label and notification type; (d) Receiving an ambient alert form the microwave; (e) Unsticking and shaking to reset; (f) Redeploying on a bookshelf; (g) Rotating to select 'ObjectFinder' mode; (h) Assigning a voice tag; (i) Voice command to find an object (StickEar triggers an alarm); (j) Augmenting a door as a remote controller; (k) Augmented plug that receives notifications from 'master' StickEar; (l) Table lamp is connected to the Augmented plug; (m) Sound event on the door; (n) Table lamp lights up.

pairing request by manually triggering a sound event on the object for the first time (Figure 5b). This pairing request message is relayed to the smartphone application via the master StickEar. In response to the pairing request, a user provides a text entry (Figure 5c) to label the object which is then stored together with the wireless ID of the sensor node in the phone database. In addition, the user has the option to choose to receive either an alert (pop-up message on the screen) or ambient notification (task bar message) for subsequent sound events on that object (Figure 5d). To reuse and redeploy StickEar, a user simply detaches it from the object and gives it a shake to remove its association with the object (Figure 5e).

ObjectFinder

StickEar when used as an output device, can function as an object finder by producing a sound output that can be remotely triggered by a user. We developed another application on the same smartphone to enable StickEar as an object finder. An object can be tagged with a sound by attaching StickEar to the object (Figure 5f), selecting it to operate in output mode and initiate a pairing request to the mobile device by pressing on the exterior face plate of StickEar. Upon receiving the pairing request on the mobile application, the user can assign a voice tag to the object by speaking into the phone (Figure 5g), in which a speech to text service (Google Voice) will convert the voice tag into text, which is then stored in the application's database. To locate the object at a later time, the user can simply launch the application on his or her device and issue a voice command (Figure 5h). This then triggers an alarm sound output on the corresponding StickEar sensor node (Figure 5i).

LightController

In the last application example, we developed a sound awareness tool [18] for the deaf. We demonstrate this by modifying an electrical adaptor plug, adding the same RF module used in StickEar sensor nodes together with a microcontroller and a relay switch (Figure 5k). A deaf user connects the power supply of the device (in this case a table lamp – Figure 5*l*) into the modified plug and deploys a StickEar sensor node to an object or a location (Figure 5j). Whenever the sensor node detects a sound event (Figure 5m), it activates the relay on the plug turning the device on to inform the user (Figure 5n).

DISCUSSION AND CONCLUSION

In our preliminary experiments, we noticed that the external casing contributed to a drop in the sensitivity of sound reception of StickEar. Extending this range with a higher gain value on the amplifier would be challenging as it would also decrease the signal to noise ratio. It was difficult to implement advanced classification algorithms due to limited speed and memory of the microcontroller used. There was a need to balance between processing speed and power consumption, as a faster microcontroller would have high power requirements. However, initial experiments shows that, with limited speed and memory resources, StickEar can be trained to detect impulsive sounds.

In multi-user scenarios, to prevent data from being sent to a wrong master StickEar, a sensor node can be easily paired to the master by perhaps tapping both together to indicate their primary association. In terms of interactions, we plan to develop a comprehensive conceptual interaction model of the device. It is important to note that the social, economical and ethical effects of extensive integration of ubiquitous computing into our everyday life with devices like StickEar is yet to be determined [7]. We plan to conduct a user study to understand how users would react to some of the suggested applications, and possibly see if they would come up with any other novel interactions.

We would consider the possibility of a flexible multi-layered printed circuit board design to bring StickEar closer to a more sticker-like form factor. If an external casing is necessary to water-proof the electronic components, the casing can be printed on flexible material. It would be interesting to explore the acoustic properties of the casing material, having an acoustic transparent material on one side and an acoustic shielding material on the other. Alternatively, the use of directional microphones can be considered. Using a faster and more powerful microcontroller or digital signal processing chip would perhaps open up more possibilities given that it would be possible to have higher sampling rates and more complex algorithms for signal processing. To overcome the problem of power usage with a faster microcontroller, the firmware could be designed to be interrupt driven and set to low power mode during idle states. While the form factor of the current StickEar prototype is far from being a true thin sticker-like device as we envision for the future, the device was sufficient to provide us with capabilities to explore various possible sound based interactions.

In this paper, we presented StickEar as a tangible bit that can be redeployed and reused easily for sound-based interaction with everyday objects. Based on the explorations of the interaction and hardware design space, we implemented and evaluated a functional prototype of the StickEar system. StickEar enabled interactions were demonstrated by developing three specific example applications. We envision StickEar to be an empowering personal device that anyone would carry and use everyday to augment objects and spaces.

ACKNOWLEDGMENTS

This work was supported by the International Design Center of the Singapore University of Technology and Design.

REFERENCES

1. Jukebugs. **http://www.joriszaalberg.com**.
2. Ninja Blocks. **http://ninjablocks.com**.
3. Twine - Listen to your world, talk to the internet. **http://supermechanical.com**.
4. Akyildiz, I., Su, W., Sankarasubramaniam, Y., and Cayirci, E. A survey on sensor networks. *IEEE Communications Magazine 40*, 8 (2002), 102–114.
5. Beigl, M., Gellersen, H.-W., and Schmidt, A. Mediacups: experience with design and use of computer-augmented everyday artefacts. *Computer Networks 35*, 4 (2001), 401–409.
6. Blattner, M. M., Sumikawa, D. A., and Greenberg, R. M. Earcons and icons: their structure and common design principles. *Hum.-Comput. Interact. 4*, 1 (1989), 11–44.
7. Bohn, J., Coroama, V., Langheinrich, M., Mattern, F., and Rohs, M. Living in a world of smart everyday objects-social, economic, and ethical implications. *Human and Ecological Risk Assessment An International Journal 10*, 5 (2004), 763–785.
8. Delle Monache, S., Polotti, P., Papetti, S., and Rocchesso, D. Sonically augmented found objects. In *Proc. NIME 2008* (2008), 154–157.
9. Djajadiningrat, T., Wensveen, S., Frens, J., and Overbeeke, K. Tangible products: redressing the balance between appearance and action. *Personal Ubiquitous Comput. 8*, 5 (2004), 294–309.
10. Goldstein, E. B. *Sensation and Perception (7th Edition*. Wadsworth Publishing, 2006.
11. Guerrero, L. A., Horta, H., and Ochoa, S. F. Developing augmented objects: A process perspective. *Journal of Universal Computer Science 16*, 12 (2010), 1612–1632.
12. Guo, B., Zhang, D., and Wang, Z. Living with internet of things: The emergence of embedded intelligence. In *Proc. ITHINGSCPSCOM 2011*, IEEE Computer Society (2011), 297–304.
13. Guo, Y., and Hazas, M. Acoustic source localization of everyday sounds using wireless sensor networks. In *Proc. Ubicomp 2010*, ACM Press (2010), 411–412.
14. Harrison, C., Horstman, J., Hsieh, G., and Hudson, S. Unlocking the expressivity of point lights. In *Proc. CHI 2012*, ACM Press (2012), 1683–1692.
15. Harrison, C., and Hudson, S. E. Scratch input: creating large, inexpensive, unpowered and mobile finger input surfaces. In *Proc. UIST 2008*, ACM Press (2008), 205–208.
16. Hatala, M., Kalantari, L., Wakkary, R., and Newby, K. Ontology and rule based retrieval of sound objects in augmented audio reality system for museum visitors. In *Proc. SAC 2004*, ACM Press (2004), 1045–1050.
17. Helmes, J., Hummels, C., and Sellen, A. The other brother: re-experiencing spontaneous moments from domestic life. In *Proc. TEI'09*, ACM Press (2009), 233–240.
18. Ho-Ching, F. W.-l., Mankoff, J., and Landay, J. A. Can you see what i hear?: the design and evaluation of a peripheral sound display for the deaf. In *Proc. CHI 2003*, ACM Press (2003), 161–168.
19. Holmquist, L., Gellersen, H., Kortuem, G., Antifakos, S., Michahelles, F., Schiele, B., Beigl, M., and Maze, R. Building intelligent environments with smart-its. *Computer Graphics and Applications 24*, 1 (2004), 56–64.
20. Ishii, H., and Ullmer, B. Tangible bits: towards seamless interfaces between people, bits and atoms. In *Proc. CHI 1997*, ACM Press (1997), 234–241.
21. Ishii, H., Wisneski, C., Orbanes, J., Chun, B., and Paradiso, J. Pingpongplus: design of an athletic-tangible interface for computer-supported cooperative play. In *Proc. CHI 1999*, ACM Press (1999), 394–401.
22. Kawsar, F., Fujinami, K., and Nakajima, T. Augmenting everyday life with sentient artefacts. In *Proc. sOc-EUSAI 2005*, ACM Press (2005), 141–146.
23. Lifton, J., Feldmeier, M., Ono, Y., Lewis, C., and Paradiso, J. A. A platform for ubiquitous sensor deployment in occupational and domestic environments. In *Proc. ISPN 2007*, ACM Press (2007), 119–127.
24. Lucero, A., Keränen, J., and Jokela, T. Social and spatial interactions: shared co-located mobile phone use. In *Proc. CHI EA'10*, ACM Press (2010), 3223–3228.
25. Mainwaring, A., Culler, D., Polastre, J., Szewczyk, R., and Anderson, J. Wireless sensor networks for habitat monitoring. In *Proc. WSNA 2002*, ACM Press (2002), 88–97.
26. Matthews, T., Gellersen, H.-W., Van Laerhoven, K., and Dey, A. K. Augmenting collections of everyday objects: A case study of clothes hangers as an information display. In *Proc. PERVASIVE 2004*, Springer (2004), 340–344.
27. Merrill, D., Kalanithi, J., and Maes, P. Siftables: towards sensor network user interfaces. In *Proc. TEI 2007*, ACM Press (2007), 75–78.
28. Mistry, P., and Maes, P. Intelligent sticky notes that can be searched, located and can send reminders and messages. In *Proc. IUI 2008*, ACM Press (2008), 425–426.
29. Paradiso, J. A., and Starner, T. Energy scavenging for mobile and wireless electronics. *IEEE Pervasive Computing 4*, 1 (2005), 18–27.
30. Pauwels, E., Salah, A. A., and Tavenard, R. Sensor networks for ambient intelligence. In *Proc. MMSP 2007* (2007), 13–16.
31. Sato, M., Poupyrev, I., and Harrison, C. Touché: enhancing touch interaction on humans, screens, liquids, and everyday objects. In *Proc. CHI 2012*, ACM Press (2012), 483–492.
32. Siegemund, F., and Krauer, T. Integrating handhelds into environments of cooperating smart everyday objects. In *Proc. EUSAI 2004* (2004), 160–171.
33. Surie, D., Laguionie, O., and Pederson, T. In *Proc. ISSNIP 2008* (2008), 189–194.
34. Tapia, E. M., Marmasse, N., Intille, S. S., and Larson, K. Mites: Wireless portable sensors for studying behavior. In *Ubicomp EA'04* (2004).
35. Terada, T., Tsukamoto, M., Hayakawa, K., Kishino, Y., Kashitani, A., and Nishio, S. Ubiquitous chip: a rule-based i/o control device for ubiquitous computing. In *Proc. Pervasive 2004* (2004), 238–253.
36. Uckelmann, D., Harrison, M., and Michahelles, F. *Architecting the Internet of Things*, 1st ed. Springer, 2011.
37. Vetelino, J., and Reghu, A. *Introduction to Sensors*. CRC Press, 2010.
38. Weiser, M. The computer for the 21st century. *SIGMOBILE Mob. Comput. Commun. Rev. 3*, 3 (1999), 3–11.
39. Yatani, K., and Truong, K. N. Bodyscope: a wearable acoustic sensor for activity recognition. In *Proc. UbiComp 2012*, ACM Press (2012), 341–350.
40. Yeo, K. P., and Nanayakkara, S. Stickear: augmenting objects and places wherever whenever. In *Proc. CHI'13*, ACM Press (2013), 751–756.

Mime: Compact, Low-Power 3D Gesture Sensing for Interaction with Head-Mounted Displays

Andrea Colaço[1] Ahmed Kirmani[2,3] Hye Soo Yang[1] Nan-Wei Gong[1]
Chris Schmandt[1] Vivek K Goyal[2*]

[1]MIT Media Lab [2]Research Laboratory of Electronics [3]Department of Electrical Engineering
Massachusetts Institute of Technology

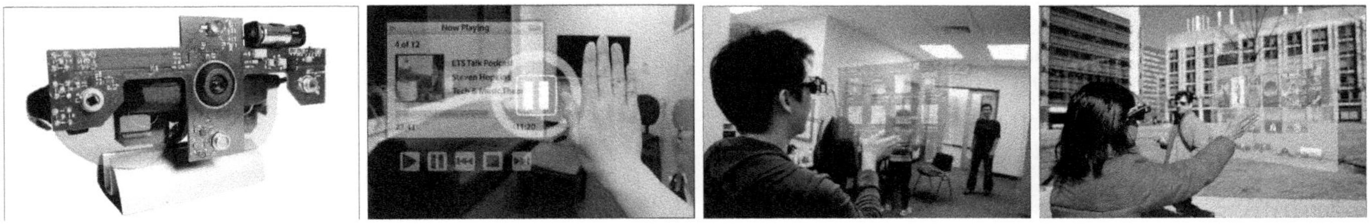

Figure 1: Mime is a compact, low power sensor for 3D gestural control of head mounted displays. It comprises a battery operated active illumination three-pixel time-of-flight (TOF) sensor, and a 2D RGB camera. Mime's real-time signal processing pipeline enables fast and precise 3D gestural control in cluttered environments, and in strong daylight and dynamic light conditions.

ABSTRACT

We present *Mime*, a compact, low-power 3D sensor for unencumbered free-form, single-handed gestural interaction with head-mounted displays (HMDs). Mime introduces a real-time signal processing framework that combines a novel three-pixel time-of-flight (TOF) module with a standard RGB camera. The TOF module achieves accurate 3D hand localization and tracking, and it thus enables motion-controlled gestures. The joint processing of 3D information with RGB image data enables finer, shape-based gestural interaction.

Our Mime hardware prototype achieves fast and precise 3D gestural control. Compared with state-of-the-art 3D sensors like TOF cameras, the Microsoft Kinect and the Leap Motion Controller, Mime offers several key advantages for mobile applications and HMD use cases: very small size, daylight insensitivity, and low power consumption. Mime is built using standard, low-cost optoelectronic components and promises to be an inexpensive technology that can either be a peripheral component or be embedded within the HMD unit. We demonstrate the utility of the Mime sensor for HMD interaction with a variety of application scenarios, including 3D spatial input using close-range gestures, gaming, on-the-move interaction, and operation in cluttered environments and in broad daylight conditions.

*Please address correspondence to {acolaco | akirmani | vgoyal } at mit.edu

UIST'13, October 8–11, 2013, St. Andrews, United Kingdom.

ACM 978-1-4503-2268-3/13/10...$15.00.
http://dx.doi.org/10.1145/2501988.2502042

Author Keywords

hand tracking, 3D sensing, gesture sensing, time-of-flight imaging, mobile, head mounted displays, glasses.

ACM Classification Keywords

H5.2 [Information interfaces and presentation]: User Interfaces. - Interaction Styles.

INTRODUCTION

Head mounted displays (HMDs) have gained widespread attention in anticipation of the launch of several consumer-priced units such as Google Glass[1] and Oculus Rift.[2] HMDs had already been successfully deployed in niche commercial applications such as flight navigation [15] and simulated training environments; with the promise of low-cost HMDs, users and developers alike are excited about the opportunities in applications and interface design.

Historically, hand-held point-and-click controllers [14], one-handed keyboards like the Twiddler [12], and voice commands have been the primary modes of interaction with HMDs. More recently, mobile devices like smart phones have been used as HMD controllers [7]. These conventional technologies have limitations: joysticks and keypad controllers as well as touch-based mobile devices are external to the HMD unit; these hand-held controllers are often inconvenient and undesirable in free-form interaction scenarios and mobile settings. Voice-activated control offers limited input functionality, it's accuracy greatly varies from user to user and depends on ambient noise levels. Voice input also raises user-privacy concerns when used in public spaces.

The limitations of conventional input technologies warrant development of new sensors for intuitive and effective free-form gestural input for HMDs. Even outside of the HMD use

[1]Project Glass. `www.google.com/glass`
[2]Oculus VR. `www.oculusvr.com`

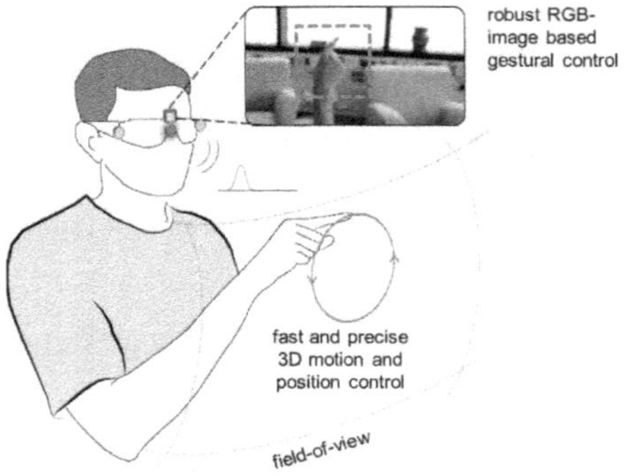

Figure 2: Mime combines a new TOF sensor for precise 3D tracking with RGB-image based gesture recognition.

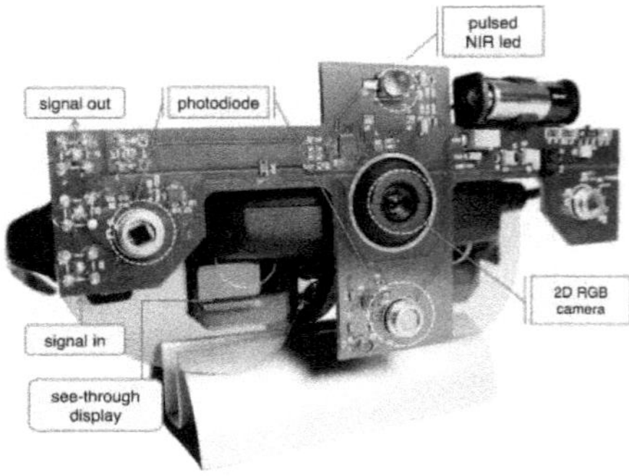

Figure 3: The battery powered Mime sensor prototype.

case, there has been great deal of recent research on close-to-body gesture sensing (see Related Work). A requirement for most of these interactions is a means of visually sensing the human hand in mobile, fast-changing and cluttered backgrounds. Short-range 3D gestural control meets several of the aforementioned performance metrics and design constraints. However, the use of depth sensors in mobile and wearable devices is currently prohibitive due to form factor and power considerations.

Design considerations: An input technology intended for HMD control and interaction should ideally possess the following characteristics:

- **Technical**: High accuracy, low power, low latency, small size, daylight insensitivity, and robust performance in cluttered, noisy and fast-changing environments.
- **User experience**: Interacting with the HMD should be intuitive and should not induce fatigue upon prolonged use. The input device must be able to support both motion- and position-controlled gestures in 2D and 3D.
- **User convenience**: The sensor should be embedded within the HMD to enable unencumbered user interaction. The user should not be required to wear markers [17] or external sensors [9, 20] or carry additional touch pads.

In this paper, to meet these needs, we introduce Mime—a compact, low-power 3D sensor for short-range and single-handed gestural control of HMDs. Mime provides fast and accurate 3D gesture sensing. The sensor's performance derives from a novel signal processing pipeline that combines low-power time-of-flight (TOF) sensing for 3D hand-motion tracking with RGB image-based computer vision algorithms for shape-based gestural control (see Figure 2).

The Mime sensor is built using off-the-shelf hardware and is easily reproducible. As shown in Figure 3, it comprises three unfocused, baseline-separated photodiodes; an omnidirectional, pulsed light-emitting diode (LED); and a standard RGB camera. Mime can be embedded in the HMD unit or attached as a peripheral, thereby eliminating the need for markers, hand-worn sensors, or mobile controllers.

Using the Mime hardware prototype along with Vuzix smart glasses,[3] we implemented a diverse range of gestures and applications that demonstrate the utility of our sensor, as well as the effectiveness of close-to-body 3D gestures as an input to HMDs. In our interactive scenarios, we use free-hand gestures for in-air 3D spatial input and interact with virtual displays while on the move, in cluttered environments and broad daylight conditions (see supplementary video and Applications section). Our paint-and-draw application and 3D game (Fruit Ninja) demonstrate the precise motion control and low latency of the Mime sensor.

Contributions

Our main contributions encapsulated in the development of the Mime sensor are summarized as follows:

1. A novel three-pixel TOF module for fast and accurate 3D localization and tracking of a single hand.
2. A signal processing framework based on parametric modeling of optical signals that allows accurate 3D hand localization despite a small baseline, low system bandwidth, and sub-Nyquist sampling of both space and time.
3. Fusion of 3D localization information provided by the TOF module with RGB image-based information to improve the accuracy and robustness of gestural recognition.
4. A compact, real-time hardware implementation of Mime built entirely using low-cost, off-the-shelf parts.
5. Integration of the Mime prototype with smart glasses to demonstrate interactive scenarios.

TECHNICAL OVERVIEW AND COMPARISON

In this section, we briefly overview Mime operation and highlight key technical distinctions from RGB cameras and depth sensors used in HMD input and control.

Operation and Assumptions

The Mime hardware comprises two modules:

1. A low-power time-of-flight triangulation module built using a pulsed LED and a linear array of three photodiodes.
2. A standard RGB camera module.

Mime operates by first using TOF triangulation for accurately localizing the 3D hand position in the sensor field-of-view (FOV) (see Figure 4(a)). This is based on assuming interaction with a single hand in the sensor FOV which produces a sharply-localized return time pulse. This is not unreasonable

[3]STAR 1200XL Augmented reality system. www.vuzix.com

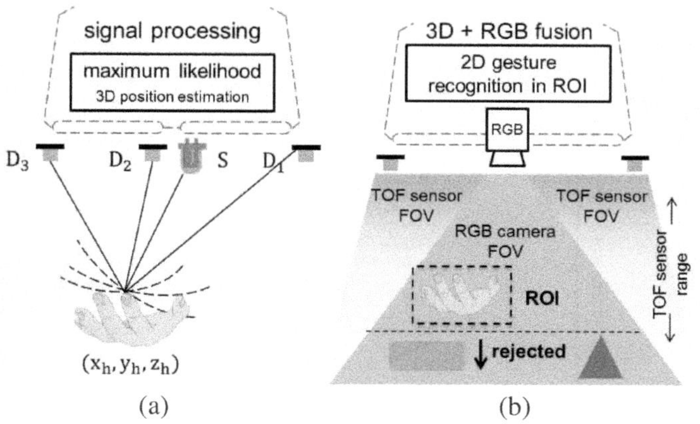

Figure 4: The signal processing pipeline for Mime. (a). The scene is illuminated using a pulsed LED and the backscattered light is time-sampled using 3 photodiodes. The time samples are processed using a maximum likelihood estimation framework to acquire 3D hand coordinates. (b) These coordinates are further used to identify a region-of-interest in the RGB image, and process it to recognize hand gestures.

since, in typical interaction scenarios, a user does not have objects in close proximity to his or her head—other than possibly a smooth surface like a wall, which results in a smooth temporal response and does not disrupt hand localization.

Once this region of interest (ROI) is identified, the corresponding RGB image patch is processed to obtain detailed hand gesture information using well-known computer vision techniques (see Figure 4(b)).

Mime is intended for short-range gesture sensing with a $0-4$ ft working range. This is adequate for close-to-body interaction, and essential for avoiding fatigue upon prolonged use.

Key Technical Distinctions

Hybrid RGB and TOF sensing: RGB image-based gesture input—including stereo methods—uses compact, low-power and ubiquitous 2D cameras; however, it is inaccurate, unreliable, and quickly fails in cluttered environments containing objects of different shape, color, and texture. In contrast, gesture recognition using depth cameras is robust and accurate even in complex scenes; however, 3D sensors that use active illumination are power intensive, sensitive to daylight, and require large heat sinks, and hence they currently are not used in mobile devices.

Mime is neither a general-purpose depth camera nor an RGB image-based computer vision system. It combines the advantages of RGB image-based techniques for gesture control and TOF-based 3D sensing while mitigating their respective disadvantages at the expense of generality.

Application-specific sensing: Mime is an application-specific sensor — it is only intended for single-handed gestural interaction. It sacrifices generality of use to simultaneously satisfy performance criteria (high precision and low latency) and technical constraints (low power and compact form factor). Thus, like the Leap Motion Controller and Digits [9], Mime is developed around the design philosophy of sacrificing generality for performance or power.

Disrupting the computer vision pipeline: The conventional vision pipeline involves capturing a full-resolution color image or depth map using a 2D sensor array, followed by processing it to identify and extract features of interest. Mime disrupts this standard processing pipeline for the specific problem of single-handed 3D gestural recognition. Mime directly senses the feature of interest, i.e., the 3D hand position, using a three-pixel TOF sensor. It further uses this 3D information to identify and process an ROI in the RGB image to extract finer features like orientations of fingers. In essence, Mime uses coarse 3D information to improve the accuracy and robustness of traditional RGB image-based gestural recognition by rejecting outliers and false positives.

Depth super-resolution: Mime's novel TOF signal processing framework achieves precise 3D localization and accurate range resolution relative to hardware specifications. The key step in this processing pipeline is 3D triangulation. To achieve fine range resolution relative to working range, conventional TOF-based triangulation systems require a combination of very short pulses, a large baseline, and an array with large number of detectors. Mime has a small baseline of $5-7$ cm compared with the working range of $0-1.2$ m; it also uses a broad light pulse and a matched photodetector with pulse width of 200 nanoseconds, and a sub-Nyquist sampling bandwidth of 5 MHz. Despite these low hardware specifications, Mime achieves centimeter-accurate 3D localization. This super-resolution is made possible through physically-accurate signal modeling and novel processing detailed later.

Daylight insensitivity: Like other mobile devices, smart wearables are intended to be used both indoors and outdoors. Strong ambient light (such as daylight) causes structured light sensors like Kinect or Leap Motion Controller to completely fail, and it significantly degrades the performance of TOF cameras even though they have background cancellation technology [11]. Moreover, HMD operation involves constantly-changing light conditions, to which the aforementioned devices are sensitive as well. Mime's signal processing only makes use of high-frequency information, enabling it to be robust to daylight and light fluctuations by rejecting low-frequency ambient light.

RELATED WORK

Emerging Gesture-Controlled Interfaces

The use of gestures for human-computer interaction is currently an active area. From a user-experience viewpoint, gestural control using 3D cameras has been demonstrated to be an intuitive, robust, and widely-popular input mechanism in gaming applications.[4] Several new technologies, such as the Leap Motion Controller[5] and compact TOF cameras,[6] are still being explored for gesture-controlled interfaces in the context

[4]Microsoft Kinect Sensor. `www.xbox.com/en-US/kinect`

[5]`www.leapmotion.com/product`

[6]PMD Camboard Nano. `www.pmdtec.com`

of personal computing spaces. While the effectiveness of gesture control for accomplishing daily computing tasks remains to be proven, researchers have recently demonstrated that 3D gesture input is at least as effective as touch input for mobile devices [8]. This finding raises interesting possibilities for smart wearables, like HMDs, which lack a dominant input interface like touch.

Close-to-body interactions: Several researchers have showcased the design of on-body and close-to-body gestural interfaces using a 3D camera mounted in different regions close to the user; OmniTouch [5] mounts the 3D camera on the shoulder of the user, and ShoeSense [1] mounts a 3D camera on a user's shoe facing up. Another class of examples uses motion capture systems such as the Vicon to create applications that track free-form hand movement, position, and orientation [2, 4]. The gesture pendant [18] is also an early example of gesture recognition in a wearable device. All the above examples clearly demonstrate the need for 3D gesture sensing in scenarios where the user is mobile, supporting our vision for building sensors that can eventually be embedded in mobile and wearable devices.

Gestural control with 2D cameras: Computer vision techniques allow the use of embedded 2D cameras to recognize hand gestures [13]. These gestures have been widely used for unencumbered line-of-sight interaction with mobile devices. Standard RGB image-based gesture recognition suffers from several technical problems: it has poor resolution and is not robust in cluttered environments, it is computationally complex for mobile processors, and it supports only a small dictionary of simple motion-cued gestures like waving. RGB image-based gesture recognition can be made more precise, robust and generic at the expense of using of additional elements like color markers or infrared trackers [18].

Gestural control with 3D cameras: Stereo cameras [19], TOF cameras [11], and structured light sensors such as from PrimeSense capture 3D scene structure in a depth map, which is then processed to identify gestures. 3D cameras retain all the advantages of standard 2D cameras but offer better performance and support complex gestures through acquiring position and motion cues in real time. The main limitations in using 3D sensors for mobile devices and smart wearables are high power requirements, bulky form factor, heat dissipation, and computational complexity.

In addition to the aforementioned gesture recognition systems, wearable sensors such as Digits [9] have also been proposed for precise full-hand tracking. Similar to hand-held controllers and voice input, wearable sensors allow non-line-of-sight user interaction.

Comparisons with Mime

Figure 5 shows the accuracy vs. power trade-offs comparing Mime with other real-time sensors useful for HMD interaction that are compact and enable unencumbered interaction. Compared with these other sensing modalities, Mime offers fast and precise 3D gesture sensing at low power.

As the fidelity and size of HMDs improve, we expect that unencumbered input will be an important user interface design

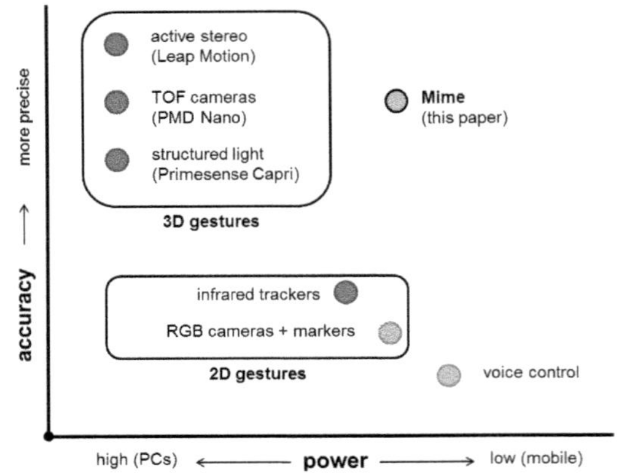

Figure 5: Accuracy vs. power comparison for compact, real-time HMD input technologies. The red dots denote devices with high daylight sensitivity, and green dots denote devices that operate under strong ambient light.

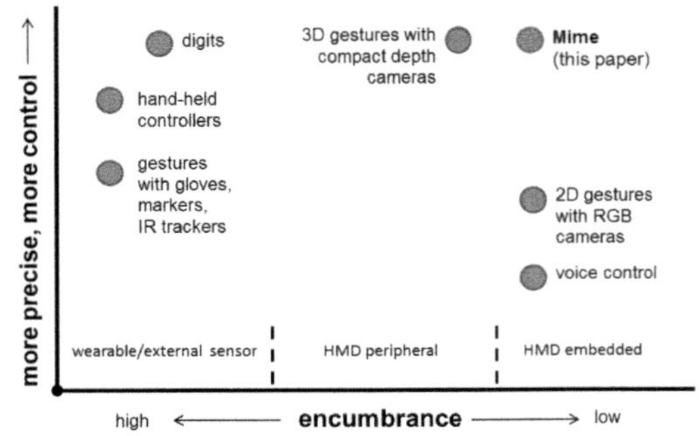

Figure 6: Performance vs. encumbrance comparison for HMD input technologies.

consideration for consumer applications and daily use cases. Figure 6 compares Mime with other input techniques on performance vs. encumbrance axes. Along with other 3D gestural control techniques, Mime offers high performance and unencumbered interaction, with the added advantage of being embedded in the bezel of the HMD unit.

MIME TOF MODULE: 3D HAND LOCALIZATION USING TIME-RESOLVED MEASUREMENTS

We now describe Mime's signal processing pipeline, which is based on parametric modeling of scene response [10]. The first step is the estimation of 3D hand position using time-resolved measurements.

Localization setup: As shown in Figure 7, there are three baseline-separated photodiodes, D_1, D_2 and D_3, with a total baseline length L. An incoherent, near infrared (NIR), pulsed light source, S, with repetition period T is co-located at the origin with D_2. The light source and photodiodes are omnidirectional and lack spatial resolution.

The user's hand, denoted by H, is considered to be a diffuse reflector with reflectivity ρ at unknown coordinates (x_h, y_h, z_h). For numerical reasons, we find it convenient to operate in spherical coordinates (R_h, θ_h, ϕ_h) rather than Cartesian coordinates. We denote the maximum range by R_{max}, so $0 \leq R_h \leq R_{max}$. Since Mime is a front-facing

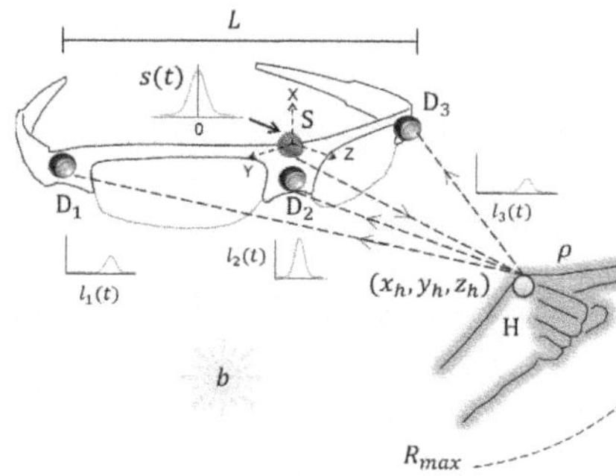

Figure 7: The Mime TOF sensing setup indicating the system variables and the geometric arrangements.

sensor, we also have $0 \leq \theta_h, \phi_h \leq \pi$. The placement of light source and sensors on a horizontal line creates two-fold vertical symmetry (i.e., even symmetry around $\phi = \pi/2$).

The hand is effectively modeled as a point source since temporal variations attributed to reflected light coming from different regions of H are at high frequencies relative to Mime's low system bandwidth and sub-Nyquist sampling rate.

The outputs of the photodiodes are digitized with a sampling period T_s. The analog-to-digital converters and LED pulsing are synchronized to measure absolute time delays.

Signal modeling: Denote the illumination pulse shape by $s(t)$. The light backscattered by the user's hand is incident at the photodiodes. Let $l_i(t)$ denote the scene impulse response from the source to photodiode i for $i = 1, 2, 3$. Using Lambert's law for diffuse reflectors we have

$$l_i(t) = \frac{\rho}{4\pi^2 \|HS\|^2 \|D_i H\|^2} \, s\left(t - \frac{\|HS\| + \|D_i H\|}{c}\right) + b,$$

where $\|\cdot\|$ denotes the Euclidean distance between two points in 3D space, c denotes the speed of light, and b is the contribution due to sunlight or other ambient light sources. Note that we have not included the effect of the cosine factor from Lambert's law because the change in perceived luminance is dominated by radial fall-off.

Sampling and background rejection: Let $h(t)$ denote the impulse response of the three identical photodiodes. We apply an analog notch filter with impulse response $f(t)$ at the output of the photodiode to filter out background signal at low frequencies (less than 100 Hz). The digital samples measured with sampling period T_s are

$$r_i[n] = \frac{\rho}{4\pi^2 \|HS\|^2 \|D_i H\|^2} \, g\left(nT_s - \frac{\|HS\| + \|D_i H\|}{c}\right),$$

$n = 1, \ldots, N = \lfloor T/T_s \rfloor$, where $g(t) = f(t) * h(t) * s(t)$.

Size, shape, orientation, and skin color of human hands: The reflectivity ρ includes the effects of both skin color and geometric parameters. Mime uses a fixed value of ρ obtained through calibration rather than an estimated value. The color factor is approximately constant because the illumination is at NIR wavelength [3]. The use of a single value of ρ despite variations in geometry is supported experimentally; radial falloff is the dominant cause of signal attenuation and a fixed value of ρ was sufficient to achieve desirable 3D localization performance irrespective of the variability in hand sizes and shape changes during gestural interaction. We also found that Mime's 3D localization accuracy decreases for small hands, simply because of decrease in signal-to-noise ratio (SNR).

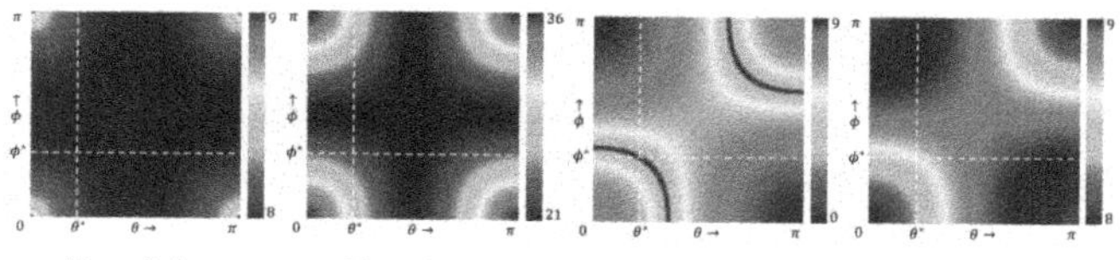

Figure 9: Slices of the 3D likelihood function for four values of radial distance R when the true value is $R^* = 0.46$ m. Parameters from the hardware prototype are used: illumination by a Gaussian pulse with duration 200 ns, baseline $2L = 10$ cm, $T_s = 30$ ns, $T = 100$ μs, and $SNR = 20$ dB.

Maximum likelihood (ML) hand localization: Given ρ, L, $s(t)$, T, T_s, and the $3N$ noisy data samples $\{r_i[n]\}_{n=1}^{N}$, $i = 1, 2, 3$, we would like to estimate the 3D hand position (R_h, θ_h, ϕ_h). We assume the noise is additive Gaussian, yielding a nonlinear least square estimation problem.

$$(\hat{R}_h, \hat{\theta}_h, \hat{\phi}_h) = \underset{P=(R,\theta,\phi)}{\arg\min} \sum_{i=1}^{3} \sum_{n=1}^{N} \left\{ r_i[n] - \frac{\rho \, g\left(nT_s - \frac{\|PS\| + \|D_i P\|}{c}\right)}{4\pi^2 \|PS\|^2 \|D_i P\|^2} \right\}^2$$

The hand position that minimizes the cost function is chosen as the estimate. This minimization is implemented using gradient descent in spherical coordinates that is initialized using a minimization on a coarse grid; we found the use of spherical coordinates to lead to a simpler cost function with fewer local minima. To further speed up computation, we keep track of previous estimates using a fast Kalman tracker; the estimates from the Kalman tracker are used to narrow the grid search.

Note here that even in the noiseless case, the problem is degenerate because of two-fold vertical symmetry. This appears as symmetry in constant-radius slices of the likelihood function, as shown in Figure 9. The degeneracy could be alleviated by adding a fourth photodiode at an off-axis location. Instead, we resolve this degeneracy by using the RGB camera to check for the presence of human hand in the ROI corresponding to the two degenerate solutions. Aside from the two-fold symmetry, fine vertical resolution is achievable even though the light source and sensors lie on a horizontal line.

The estimated 3D coordinate could lie anywhere on the hand surface, depending on the hand shape, position, and gesture. While this may seem a limitation, the position within the hand remains stable through hand motions, so the gesture identification and tracking performance is not affected.

Comparison with classical source localization: Conventional source localization based on TOF measurements using a detector array is solely based on time delay estimation; it does not incorporate any target reflectivity information. This is important because the target reflectivity is typically unknown, and inaccurate models or estimates for ρ introduce large errors in position estimation. First the samples $r_i[n]$ are used to estimate time delay or light path length,

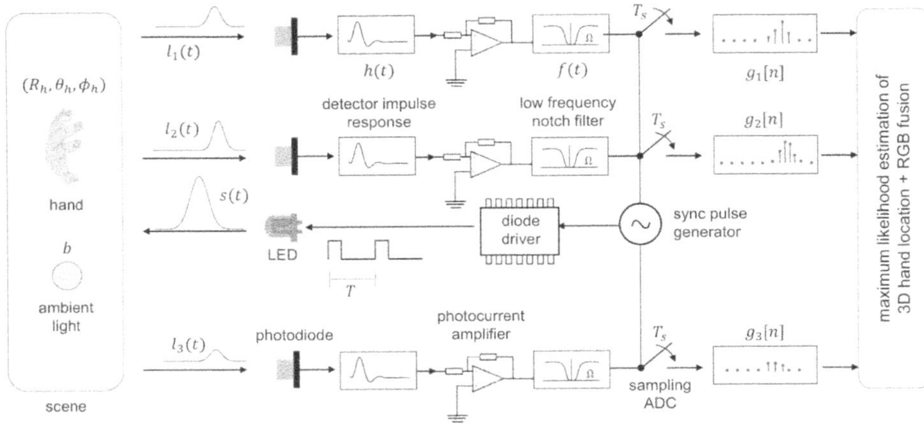

Figure 8: Mime data acquisition pipeline showing the system parameters and hardware components.

$\|PS\|+\|D_iP\|$, at each detector. Then, the individual delay estimates are used for 3D coordinate estimation using triangulation. It is well known that the estimation accuracy depends on system bandwidth, baseline, working range and SNR [6]. Mime's TOF processing pipeline achieves better localization accuracy by exploiting target reflectivity rather than discarding it. Incorporating a physically-accurate reflectivity model in the ML solution framework improves 3D position estimation accuracy.

Next, we discuss how the acquired 3D hand coordinates are used with RGB image-based gestural recognition.

REGION OF INTEREST RGB-IMAGE PROCESSING

The camera embedded in the HMD unit captures an RGB image of the scene in front of the user. This image alone may be used for hand gesture recognition using well-known computer vision techniques [19], but this approach has two problems: it does not possess range or depth information required for 3D gestures, and it has poor practical performance. Real-world scenes are complex and contain objects of various shapes, textures and colors which cause the conventional methods to fail.

Mime uses a RGB camera whose FOV is registered with the TOF sensor's FOV. Instead of processing the entire image to identify hand gestures, Mime uses the 3D hand coordinates to first select an ROI in the RGB image and then applies gesture recognition algorithms. Specifically, the ROI data is processed using skin color segmentation, followed by shape recognition, feature extraction, and gesture recognition using a trained SVM classifier [19].

Mime's approach of fusing the 3D information with RGB data via ROI identification is simple, yet powerful. It has two major advantages over traditional RGB gesture sensing: it significantly reduces false positives to drastically improve the robustness and accuracy of computer vision techniques, and computation overhead is reduced since only a small portion of the image needs to be processed to extract gestural information. In our prototype, the ROI window size is chosen based on the range value, R_h. Closer objects occupy larger pixel area in the 2D camera's FOV and therefore require a larger ROI window.

In the next few sections, we discuss the hardware implementation, calibration, gesture sensing and experiments to validate performance.

HARDWARE IMPLEMENTATION

The Mime sensor—shown schematically in Figure 8—is built using the following off-the-shelf optoelectronic components:

Light source: Our illumination source is a high-speed NIR (850 nm wavelength) LED with high peak power from OSRAM semiconductor (SFH 4236). The LED has half angle of 20° with diffusion of 90° over the range of interest and is eye safe. We pulse this LED using a laser diode driver from Maxim with high-peak current. High peak power leads to high SNR, and therefore we require less averaging via repeated pulsing. We use a low pulse repetition frequency of 10 KHz and a pulse width of 200 ns with a rise time of 70 ns (modulation bandwidth ≈ 5 MHz).

Photodiodes: We use fast PIN silicon photodiodes from Thorlabs (part no. FDS100) with a rise time of 50–70 ns (typical). The photodiode output is filtered using an analog notch filter to reject low frequency, followed by signal amplification using a Maxim low-noise amplifier (MAX 3806).

Sampling: We used a low-jitter 4-channel USB oscilloscope with a built-in function generator (PicoScope model 6404b) for sampling the amplified light signal and also to generate the sync signal to measure absolute time delays. We also use a scope bandwidth of 5 MHz (sub-Nyquist compared with pulse modulation) and a sampling period of $T_s = 30$ ns.

The Mime sensor was implemented in a compact form factor with careful circuit design. The sensor was mounted on a pair of Vuzix smart glasses that has a full-FOV see-through display for both eyes and a built-in RGB camera.

Calibration

FOV registration: We registered the FOVs of the RGB camera and the TOF sensor in the transverse or $x-y$ plane by

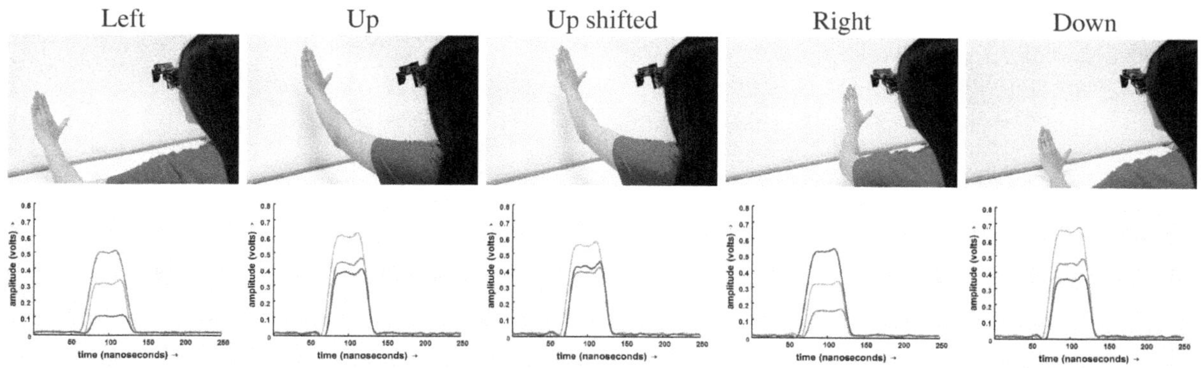

Figure 10: Sensor data visualization for varying hand positions. The red, green, and blue curves are the responses at the left, center, and right photodiode, respectively. Note that the sensor closest to the hand has the strongest response and least time shift. The Mime sensor has a vertical symmetry—the responses corresponding to *Up* and *Down* positions are very similar despite a large hand displacement. However, in the top and bottom vertical halves, Mime achieves perfect localization as demonstrated by significant changes in detected response as the hand moves from the *Up* to the *Up shifted* positions.

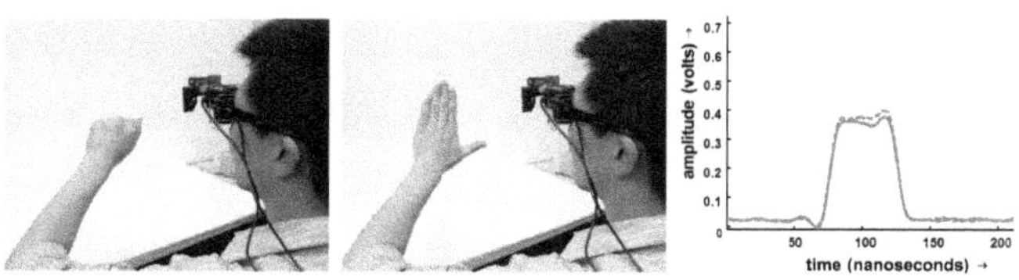

Figure 11: Radial fall-off dominates signal amplitude. The responses detected at a photodiode for a fixed hand position and varying hand gestures are very similar. This enables Mime to achieve robust 3D hand localization for different skin colors and gesture shapes.

tracking the user's finger in a clutter-free setup using both modalities. Using the $x-y$ coordinates generated by the RGB image-based and Mime's TOF sensor, we computed the rigid body transformation (rotation and translation) using point cloud registration algorithms [19].

System impulse response: The system impulse response $g(t)$ was measured by directly illuminating the photodiodes with the pulsed LED, sampling the output signal finely, and applying parametric curve fitting. We observed that our system response is approximated well by a Gaussian pulse shape.

Hand reflectivity: We estimated ρ empirically by measuring the photocurrent amplitude under strong diffuse NIR illumination to eliminate the effect of radial fall-off. To achieve this, we conducted this measurement in a dark room to eliminate background, and set the LED in a high-power continuous illumination mode. Also, as shown in Figure 11, the radial fall-off dominates the signal amplitude over the hand reflectivity and surface area.

PERFORMANCE EVALUATION

Localization accuracy and resolution: For gestural control applications, sensing changes in hand position is critical. We tested resolution, defined as the ability to detect small changes in hand position as it moves across the sensor FOV. Figure 10 shows plots of the data captured at two close hand positions. Although the variation in data is noticeable, it is still small. But using the ML estimation framework discussed earlier, Mime is able to successfully resolve this challenging resolution test case. Figure 10 also demonstrates the two-fold vertical symmetry in our system—the responses from the top and bottom halves are identical. The symmetry is resolved using the RGB camera. Adding a fourth, off-axis sensor would also allow us to resolve the ambiguity.

Figure 12: Mime operation in strong sunlight conditions.

Daylight insensitivity: In Figure 12, we show outdoor hand tracking in bright daylight. The depth is coded in the color and size of the tracked squares. Mime's accuracy and frame rates remain unaffected using our hardware-based low-frequency rejection. Notice the accurate performance despite the presence of pedestrians in the camera's FOV.

Power and working range: The bulk of the power in a system with active illumination is consumed by the light source. Mime's TOF illumination unit consumes 25 mW and the three amplified photodiodes require a total of 20 mW. Greater working ranges require stronger illumination and hence more device power. For the same working range of 4 ft, PMD's depth camera consumes 3.5 W, compared with the Mime TOF module's 45 mW total power budget. Such low powers make Mime an ideal candidate for mobile implementations. The mobile RGB camera consumes an additional 75 mW.

Latency: The Mime TOF system (data acquisition, transfer to memory, and computation) achieves a latency of $8-10$ ms, which translates to 3D localization at more than 100 frames per second (fps) (see supplementary video). When integrated with the RGB camera, the overall frame rate is limited by image capture operating at 30 fps.

Using the Mime sensor, we implemented a number of motion-activated and shape-based gestures.

GESTURE SENSING USING MIME

Gestures using 3D motion tracking: Mime's 3-pixel TOF sensor accurately captures 3D hand position at high frame rates. We track user's hand movement over time and implement several motion-controlled gestures using Mime's TOF module alone. These are swipe (left-to-right, up-to-down), point-and-click, zoom in and out using depth, circle and arc gestures (see Figures 13 and supplementary video). To verify repeatability we asked 3 users with different hand sizes to test each motion gesture implemented using our prototype. Mime achieved at least 95% detection accuracy and less than 3% false positive rates for all implemented motion gestures. Extensive user evaluation is a subject of future work.

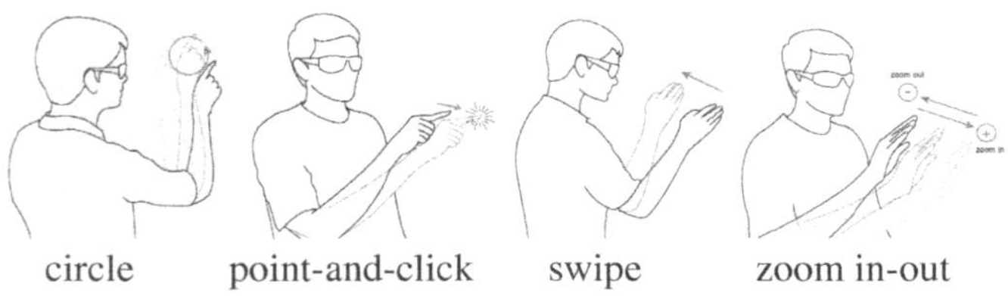

Figure 13: Motion-controlled gestures implemented using only the 3D coordinate data acquired by Mime's TOF sensor.

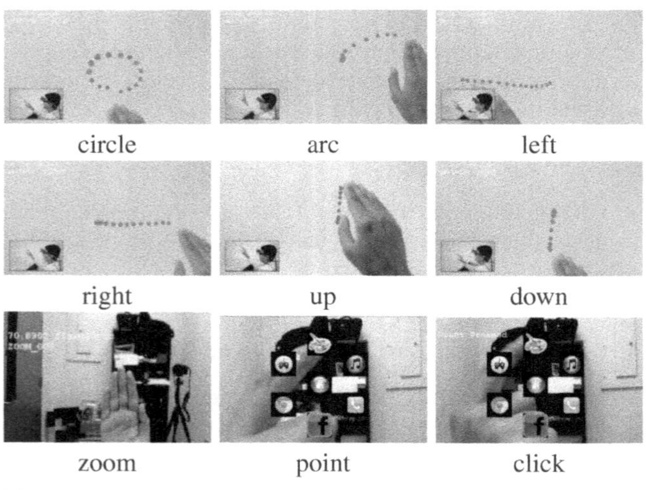

Figure 14: Implementation of 3D motion-activated gestures using only the 3D hand coordinates. Mime's motion tracking works accurately in cluttered environments.

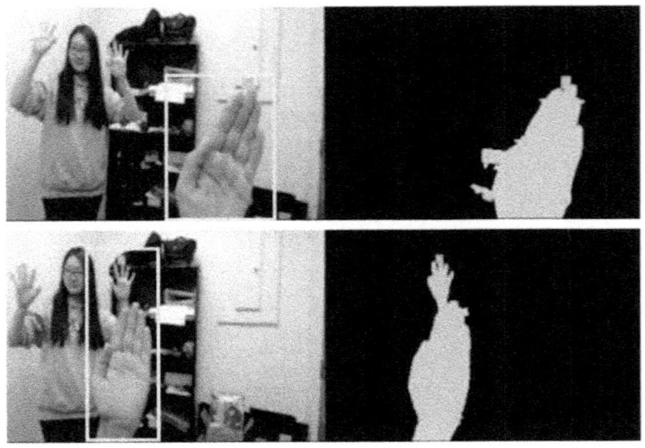

Figure 15: The Mime sensor's 3D localization data improves the robustness of RGB-image based gesture recognition. (Top) Notice that the skin colored targets (human hands) in the RGB camera's FOV are rejected because they do not fall inside the identified 2D ROI. (Bottom) Mime's algorithmic framework cannot be used to reject cases in which there are multiple skin-colored objects in the identified RGB ROI.

Shape-based gestures using RGB+3D data fusion: Using the RGB+3D fusion approach, Mime adds finer shape-based gestural control. By capturing finger arrangements, we implement gestures like holding fingers in an L-shape to take a picture, C-shape for crop, the OK gesture and thumbs-up (see Figure 18). We also note that Mime does not acquire a complete 3D hand model, as is captured by Leap Motion Controller or Digits [9]. Compared with these sensors, Mime supports fewer 3D gestures and has reduced accuracy; however, it also consumes less power and is not encumbering.

The performance of gesture recognition using 2D color images is well studied [13]. These methods work accurately in the absence of clutter, which causes outliers and false positives. In Mime's processing framework, such outliers are rejected using the 3D and 2D data fusion approach described earlier, thereby leading to an overall increase in system robustness and gesture recognition rates. To test how well Mime's clutter rejection works, we placed multiple user hands and faces in the Mime sensor's FOV. Only one of these hands was within the TOF sensor's range, and the goal was to identify the ROI containing this hand. As shown in supplementary video and Figure 15, Mime is able to successfully reject the outliers and increase detection accuracy.

INTERACTION TECHNIQUES AND HMD USE CASES

This section presents demonstrative styles of interaction utilizing the Mime sensor in various real-world HMD use cases. The Mime sensor was mounted on the Vuzix glasses; the application is seen through the display of the smart glasses. For each application, we highlight components of the Mime sensor that are utilized to make the interaction possible.

Augmented menu interaction: We demonstrate navigating an augmented interface through the glasses display (see Figure 16). The user navigates to any element by appropriately moving their hand to the target icon. Activating an application is achieved by controlling the z-dimension, that is, by

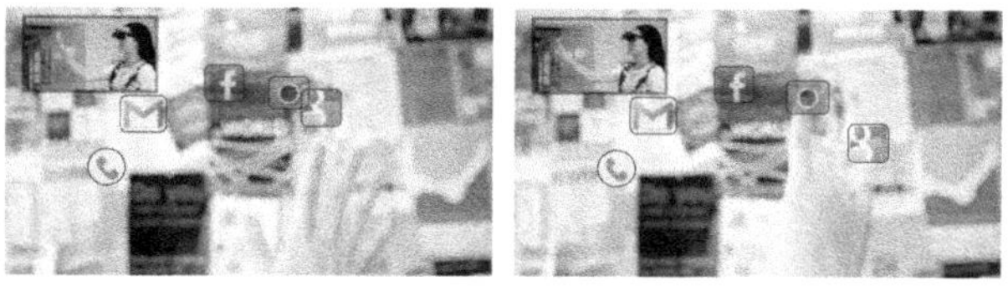

Figure 16: Augmented menu interaction using motion gestures: arc to activate menu, and point-and-click to select item.

an analog "push" gesture that is measured through relative z-motion over a highlighted icon. This example only requires the 3D TOF tracking without any RGB component. The resolution in all three dimensions is sufficiently accurate to achieve real-time, in-air menu navigation. Thus, this scenario is invariant to clutter in the environment, daylight presence, or poor lighting conditions. The in-air point and click requirements for such an on-the-go application are clearly achieved by the Mime sensor.

Using Mime's TOF module we also implemented swipe, zoom, arc and circles which are natural, intuitive gestures for navigating carousel-style interfaces.

In-air drawing and annotations: In the second use case we present an in-air drawing interface that tracks and visualizes a user's hand motion to create a paint trail (see Figure 17) as well as write and draw in air. We envision the applicability of this use case in generating quick annotations to documents on-the-go or simplifying search through drawing letters while skimming through a contact list for names that begin with a specific letter. Again, this set of applications only requires the 3D TOF tracking module and hence is invariant to the user's surroundings, making it ideal for quick input without the need for external keypads.

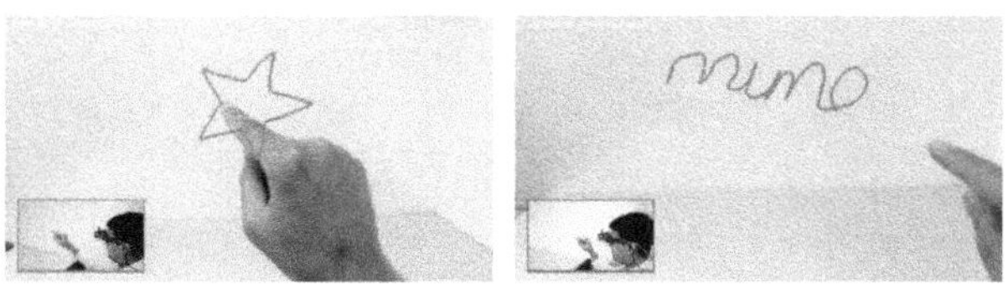

Figure 17: In-air writing and drawing implemented only using Mime's TOF sensor.

Interactive capture tools for photography: We now demonstrate how 3D tracking combined with ROI-based RGB processing provides fine gestural control. In this application we use the Mime sensor to allow manipulation of visual content as we capture it. While capturing pictures from a vantage point the user typically cannot manipulate it on the display screen itself because of the smaller degrees of freedom of control available and the inherently limited display size. Our application allows the user to manipulate visual content during the capture pipeline through gestures that map to the scene or region of interest being captured. The key concept is that the user is using gesture to interact with the image while the photo is being taken and the scene and desired view is fresh and alive.

As shown in Figure 18, the user makes an L-shaped gesture, which activates the camera and begins taking a picture. Depth based zoom allows the user to control focus. After gesturing

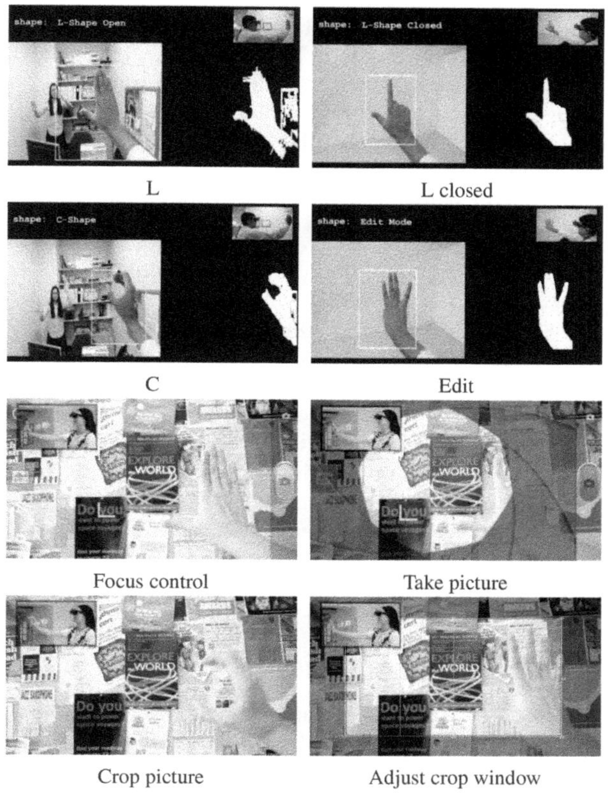

Figure 18: Interactive photography application with shape-based gestures implemented using Mime's 3D and RGB data fusion approach. All gestures work accurately even in cluttered environments with competing targets.

to the HMD to take the picture, the user crops the image and finalizes the selection using C-shape gestures. A key feature of smart glasses is the ability to capture visual information while we see it. Hence, input options that enable shortcuts to such applications will determine the utility of such features. In both these use cases first use 3D TOF information to localize the hand target and then use RGB processing to identify finer gestures in the ROI.

Immersive gaming: In addition to content consumption, portable devices are increasingly used for recreation. Bringing an immersive gaming experience closer to the user through HMDs has been explored in several contexts [16]. The Mime sensor provides gaming control without the need for additional controllers. We demonstrate fast and precise performance of the Mime sensor through a gaming application. Specifically, we use the Mime sensor to play the popular Fruit Ninja game (see supplementary video). The application requires short reaction times both by the user and the sensing system to effectively advance through the game.

LIMITATIONS

The sensor system introduced in this paper is designed to provide free-form input to always-on HMDs. The Mime sensor is optimized to capture interaction-specific input from the user—specifically, single-hand (and finger) tracking close to the HMD. This is an example of the increasing number of application-specific sensors that trade generality for performance in order to create a better experience for the user. However, a substantive understanding of the limitations of the sensor is necessary to evaluate the gamut of applications this input technique can support. Here, we will go over the limitations of the Mime sensor and optimal conditions of operation to provide the reader a holistic understanding of trade-offs.

1. **Single-handed operation.** The Mime sensor is designed for single-handed multiple-finger operation. This could prove to be a limitation for more complex gestural activity such as digital 3D sculpting.
2. **Multiple finger detection.** Since multiple finger detection relies on the RGB component of the Mime sensor, the performance of the detection algorithm will depend on the RGB sensor and its limitations.
3. **Region of interest definition.** The region of interest in the current Mime implementation is assigned as a function of distance measured under the assumption that closer objects occupy a larger FOV area. This can often lead to the presence of objects other than the hand in the ROI which will impact performance in the case of multi-finger detection.

OUTLOOK AND CONCLUSION

Here, we outline steps towards practical integration of the Mime sensor prototype with HMDs or other mobile devices.

1. For a standalone implementation of the sensor, sampling, analog-to-digital conversion and processing needs to be enabled on a micro-controller unit. Due to the sensor's low power requirements, battery operation is trivially extended.
2. Demonstrate multi-finger detection accuracy and tracking. This will require sophisticated computer vision processing within the ROI to mitigate the effect of extraneous objects that may lie within the ROI.
3. Introduce multiple-hand tracking and expand the set of gestures supported.

Placement of the Mime sensor on the HMD governs the set of supported gestures. The baseline requirement of the Mime sensor makes it ideal for placement along the HMD frame, facing the world. This configuration naturally elicits user interaction in front of their body, and may be useful in creating an immersive experience.

Close-to-body discreet interaction using subtle actions is highly desirable. This configuration is possible via a side-facing or downward-looking Mime sensor. Mime's highly precision tracking and localization makes it possible to accurately detect subtle gestural movements. Such Mime sensor configurations are subject of future consideration.

The use of computing systems is defined and limited by the set of input actions available to the user. Desktop systems limit the interaction space to the keyboard and mouse. The use of touch devices confines the user to the boundaries of the display itself. Emerging wearable displays like Google Glass attempt to dissolve the boundary between the display and the computing platform behind it, thereby making the user experience more mobile. While output to user is achieved through information overlaid on displays, designing responsive input to the system is essential for an effective on-the-go computing experience. The Mime sensor is one such effort to provide a compact, low-power 3D gesture sensor which is amenable to mobile size and power constraints.

Acknowledgements: This material is based upon work supported in part by the National Science Foundation under Grant No. 1161413 and a Qualcomm Innovation Fellowship. Special thanks to Dongeek Shin (MIT).

REFERENCES

1. Bailly, G., Müller, J., Rohs, M., Wigdor, D., and Kratz, S. ShoeSense: A new perspective on gestural interaction and wearable applications. In *Proc. ACM Ann. Conf. Human Factors in Comput. Syst.* (2012).
2. Chen, X. A., Marquardt, N., Tang, A., Boring, S., and Greenberg, S. Extending a mobile device's interaction space through body-centric interaction. In *Proc. 14th ACM Int. Conf. Human-Computer Interaction with Mobile Devices and Services* (2012).
3. Fredembach, C., Barbuscia, N., and Süsstrunk, S. Combining visible and near-infrared images for realistic skin smoothing. In *Proc. IS&T/SID 17th Color Imaging Conf.* (2009).
4. Gustafson, S., Bierwirth, D., and Baudisch, P. Imaginary interfaces: Spatial interaction with empty hands and without visual feedback. In *Proc. ACM Symp. User Interface Softw. Tech.* (2010).
5. Harrison, C., Benko, H., and Wilson, A. D. OmniTouch: Wearable multitouch interaction everywhere. In *Proc. 24th Ann. ACM Symp. User Interface Softw. Tech.* (2011).
6. Ho, K. C., Lu, X., and Kovavisaruch, L. Source localization using TDOA and FDOA measurements in the presence of receiver location errors: Analysis and solution. *IEEE Trans. Signal Process.* (2007).
7. Hong, Y., Lee, S., Lee, Y., and Kim, S. Mobile pointing and input system using active marker. In *Proc. IEEE/ACM Int. Symp. Mixed & Augmented Reality* (2006).
8. Jones, B., Sodhi, R., Forsyth, D., Bailey, B., and Maciocci, G. Around device interaction for multiscale navigation. In *Proc. Conf. HCI with Mobile Devices and Services* (2012).
9. Kim, D., Hilliges, O., Izadi, S., Butler, A., Chen, J., Oikonomidis, I., and Olivier, P. Digits: Freehand 3D interactions anywhere using a wrist-worn gloveless sensor. In *ACM UIST* (2012).
10. Kirmani, A., Colaço, A., Wong, F. N. C., and Goyal, V. K. Exploiting sparsity in time-of-flight range acquisition using a single time-resolved sensor. *Opt. Expr. 19*, 22 (Oct. 2011), 21485–21507.
11. Lange, R., and Seitz, P. Solid-state time-of-flight range camera. *IEEE J. Quant. Electron. 37*, 3 (2001), 390–397.
12. Lyons, K., Starner, T., Plaisted, D., Fusia, J., Lyons, A., Drew, A., and Looney, E. W. Twiddler typing: One-handed chording text entry for mobile phones. In *SIGCHI Human Factors in Comput. Syst.* (2004).
13. Mitra, S., and Acharya, T. Gesture recognition: A survey. *IEEE Trans. Syst., Man, Cybernetics, Part C: Appl. Rev. 37*, 3 (2007), 311–324.
14. Nelson, S. A., Lee, J. C., and Helgeson, M. A. Handheld computer apparatus. US Patent 6,911,969, 2005.
15. Newman, R. L., and Haworth, L. A. Flight displays II: Head-up and helmet-mounted displays. *Spatial Disorientation in Aviation* (2004).
16. Piekarski, W., and Thomas, B. ARQuake: The outdoor augmented reality gaming system. *Commun. ACM 45*, 1 (2002), 36–38.
17. Smith, R., Piekarski, W., and Wigley, G. Hand tracking for low powered mobile AR user interfaces. In *Proc. Sixth Australasian Conf. User Interface* (2005).
18. Starner, T., Auxier, J., Ashbrook, D., and Gandy, M. The gesture pendant: A self-illuminating, wearable, infrared computer vision system for home automation control and medical monitoring. In *IEEE Int. Symp. Wearable Comput.* (2000).
19. Szeliski, R. *Computer Vision: Algorithms and Applications.* 2010.
20. Thomas, B. H., and Piekarski, W. Glove based user interaction techniques for augmented reality in an outdoor environment. *Virtual Reality 6*, 3 (2002), 167–180.

uTrack: 3D Input Using Two Magnetic Sensors

Ke-Yu Chen[1], Kent Lyons[2], Sean White[2], Shwetak Patel[1]

University of Washington[1]
Seattle, WA (USA)
{kychen, shwetak}@uw.edu

Nokia[2]
Sunnyvale, CA (USA)
{kent.lyons, sean.white}@nokia.com

ABSTRACT

While much progress has been made in wearable computing in recent years, input techniques remain a key challenge. In this paper, we introduce *uTrack*, a technique to convert the thumb and fingers into a 3D input system using magnetic field (MF) sensing. A user wears a pair of magnetometers on the back of their fingers and a permanent magnet affixed to the back of the thumb. By moving the thumb across the fingers, we obtain a continuous input stream that can be used for 3D pointing. Specifically, our novel algorithm calculates the magnet's 3D position and tilt angle directly from the sensor readings. We evaluated uTrack as an input device, showing an average tracking accuracy of 4.84 mm in 3D space – sufficient for subtle interaction. We also demonstrate a real-time prototype and example applications allowing users to interact with the computer using 3D finger input.

ACM Classification: H.5.2 [Information interfaces and presentation]: User Interfaces. - Graphical user interfaces.

Keywords: Finger; interaction; magnetic-field; MF; sensing; 3D; pointing

INTRODUCTION

Wearable devices such as Google Glass[1] extend user experiences and increase interaction richness. While these types of devices offer a unique visual experience, input is a challenge. The user sees a virtual image in 3D space so there is nothing physical to touch or manipulate for input. Traditional input modalities are not appropriate in this case because they are mainly designed for 2D interactions[2,3]. Therefore, there is a strong need for a new, mobile, 3D input device. Such pointing devices need to be low-cost, low power, and easily accessible [3].

Commercial 3D pointing devices have been broadly used in recreational or medical systems[4,5]. However, these tools are designed for desktop computers and cannot be instrumented on the human body easily for wearable applications. To overcome this problem, researchers have leveraged acoustic characteristics to use human skin for mobile, always-existing input interfaces [5,9]. Unfortunately, these acoustic-based methods only detect discrete 2D fingertip events and may become brittle in noisy environments.

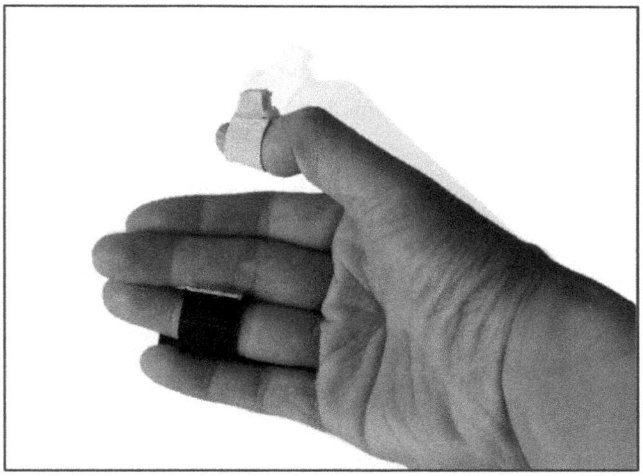

Figure 1. uTrack enables real-time 3D input from the thumb and fingers using one permanent magnet (thumb) and two magnetometers (ring finger).

In order to achieve truly 3D continuous cursor control, others explored computer vision techniques for finger-level gesture detection [10,11], including commercial products[6]. Vision-based techniques suffer from occlusion problems and are generally sensitive to lighting conditions, limiting their use in mobile contexts. To resolve these issues, some traditional approaches have used inertial sensors for cheap, occlusion-free arm gesture recognitions [14] or in-air writing [1]. While impressive, this previous work was either limited to 2D pointing or requires frequent recalibrations to resolve drifting errors.

To this end, we present *uTrack*, a pointing technique that enables 3D interactions for wearable devices. uTrack turns the user's thumb and finger into an input device using magnetic field (MF) sensing (see Figure 1). In particular, our algorithm calculates the magnet's x/y/z position plus an axis of orientation from the magnetic field vectors. Our system leaves the pads of the user's fingers free, and with only two

http://dx.doi.org/10.1145/2501988.2502035.

[1]Google Glass: http://www.google.com/glass
[2]HDE Finger Mouse: http://www.shophde.com
[3]Mycestro: http://www.inn-dev.com
[4]Novint: http://www.novint.com
[5]Phantom Omni: http://www.sensable.com
[6]Leap motion: https://www.leapmotion.com

attachment points needed on the back or sides of the fingers, there is flexibility in designing form factors based on this technology.

Specifically, the contributions of this paper are:

1. A novel, low-cost technique for turning the thumb into a 3D input device for wearable systems.
2. An algorithm that derives the magnet's 3D position and tilt angle from sensor readings with minimal instrumentation to the user.
3. An analysis demonstrating tracking accuracy across 3D space within a volume of 70 mm (W) x 30 mm (D) x 60 mm (H) and a study showing the use of a thumb for pointing with this technology.

RELATED WORK

There are various devices that can be used for pointing with wearable computers. Zucco et al.'s studies compare a variety of prop-based pointing techniques including a trackball, cursor key physical buttons, gyroscopic mouse, and touchpad [18]. These each require either two-handed use or a device held in the hand for operation. In contrast, uTrack instruments the hand and uses novel sensing to enable the interaction.

Next, there is a set of techniques that utilize on-body sensing to obtain input. Researchers have shown that the distinct sounds generated by the movements of the body can be used for gesture-based interactions [5]. Harrison et al. used skin as an input surface and identified the locations of finger taps by analyzing the bio-acoustic sounds propagating through the human body [9]. Other techniques have leveraged electromyography (EMG) for sensing hand movements [16]. A common issue with all of these techniques is that they rely upon machine learning techniques to recognize and classify the underlying data sensed from the user. As such they fundamentally offer discrete input, which is often mapped to symbolic actions as opposed to a continuous signal that can be used for direct manipulation.

Others have explored optical or computer vision techniques for hand input. For example, infrared (IR) proximity sensors have been used in various ways to obtain input [4]. An IR camera was mounted in a pendant form to image the hands with the Gesture Pendant [17]. Kim et al. put an IR camera on the wrist to see the hands [11] and Harrison et al. used a depth camera mounted on the shoulder [10]. While these methods enable accurate, continuous 2D or 3D positioning, they all require a line-of-sight view of the hands, which limits the applicability of these techniques. For instance, one could not use these techniques with a hand in a pocket.

Magnetic field (MF) sensing also has a long history in tracking human body dynamics and computer input. Polhemus uses MF sensing to track objects with 6 degrees of freedom (DOF) [15]. In this work, Raab et al. derived a series of transformations that convert the non-linear magnetic field equations into a set of linear equations that can be directly solved. However, this method requires *active* magnetic sources (*i.e.*, three powered, orthogonal electromagnetic fields). The need for active sources limits the mobility of this technology since users have to stay in the range of the signal sources, which are physically large to generate fields that can be sensed at a distance.

Some systems use arrays of magnetic elements to obtain the 2D or 3D position of a tracked magnet. For example, Wacom tablets use an array of coils under the surface and Liang et al. use an array of 192 Hall effect sensors [13]. Unfortunately, these techniques require a 2D sensor array with a size that corresponds to the sensed area and thus have limited applicability to wearable uses.

Some research has used permanent magnets worn on the body, creating a magnetic field that can be sensed for input. Abracadabra uses a magnet attached to a finger and tracks the radial position of the finger with respect to the watch face [8]. Nenya uses a magnetic ring and tracks rotation of the ring about the finger to obtain a 1D input to a watch [2].

In a sequence of work, Han et al. showed that it is possible to calculate a magnet's 2D position using a pair of magnetometers if one imposes some constraints on movement [6]. In particular, they decompose the sensed magnetic field into two different eigenspaces and derive a direct relationship between the sensed data and the magnet's x and y positions. A key limitation of this work is that the magnet and the sensors must remain axis aligned in order for the assumptions to hold [7].

uTrack is conceptually similar to Han et al.'s work [6, 7]; however, we derive a completely new algorithm to remove the fixed orientation limitation in [6] and extend the sensing capability. By using one permanent magnet and only 2 magnetometers, uTrack is able to track the magnet's x/y/z position plus an axis of rotation. We focus on the configuration shown in Figure 1 where the magnet is worn on the back of the thumb and the magnetometers are on the back of the ring finger; however, other geometries are also possible with this system.

MAGNETIC FIELDS AND SPACE TRANSFORMATION

In this section, we first introduce background knowledge on magnetic field sensing in 2D space and then detail how we convert our 3D sensor readings into this 2D domain.

We can completely describe the magnetic field emanating from a fixed magnet in 3D space using only 2 degrees of freedom. To do this, we define a plane called the *magnetic field space*, in which the sensor's center is at the origin, and its x-axis is oriented in the direction of the magnet's north pole. Any point in magnetic field space can be represented in (r, θ) polar form, where r is the distance between the magnet and the sensor, and θ is the angle between the sensor and the magnet's north pole. This is a two dimensional quantity as the magnetic field is symmetric about the magnetic pole. The magnetic field vector $\mathbf{H}$ can therefore be decomposed into its tangential and radial components, $\mathbf{H_r}$ and $\mathbf{H_\theta}$, as shown in Figure 2 and defined in below:

$$H_r = M \cos\theta / 2\pi r^3 \quad (1)$$

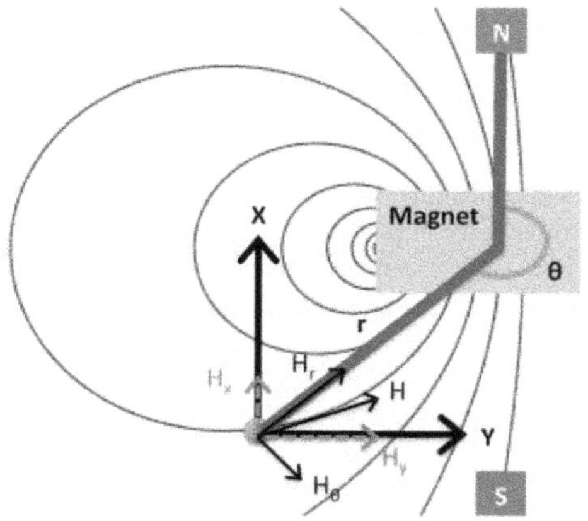

Figure 2. The magnetic field and the polar coordinate system. By decomposing the sensor vector **H** into two different eigenspaces, x and y positions of the magnet can be derived from H_x and H_y.

$$H_\theta = M\sin\theta / 4\pi r^3 \qquad (2)$$

where M denotes the magnetic moment [12]. These two equations describe the magnetic field anywhere on the plane defined by the magnetic field space.

The two orthogonal vectors $\mathbf{H_r}$ and $\mathbf{H_\theta}$ form the basis of this space. **H** can also be decomposed into another basis, $\mathbf{H_x}$ and $\mathbf{H_y}$ (Figure 2) which produces a Cartesian coordinate system with the sensor at the origin and the directions of $\mathbf{H_x}$ and $\mathbf{H_y}$ parallel to the x and y-axis of the sensor. By using similar approaches to [6], the sensor-magnet relationship can be derived as:

$$H_x = H_r\cos\theta - H_\theta\sin\theta = \frac{K[2(x_m)^2 - (y_m)^2]}{r^5} \qquad (3)$$

$$H_y = H_r\sin\theta + H_\theta\cos\theta = \frac{K(3x_m y_m)}{r^5} \qquad (4)$$

$$K = \frac{M}{4\pi},\ r = \sqrt{(x_m)^2 + (y_m)^2},\ \sin\theta = \frac{-y_m}{r},\ \cos\theta = \frac{-x_m}{r}$$

where x_m and y_m denote the magnet's Cartesian position in the magnetic field space. For a given vector pair $\mathbf{H_x}$ and $\mathbf{H_y}$, the magnet's positions x_m and y_m can be calculated from the nonlinear equations (3) and (4).

The relationship between the magnet and sensors can be derived through equations (1) to (4) *only if* the incident plane of magnetic field lines is known. The incident plane is the 2D space in which $\mathbf{H_r}$ and $\mathbf{H_\theta}$ are defined (*i.e.*, the magnetic field space). So if the magnet and sensor axes are aligned, a 3D magnetometer's sensor readings correspond directly to $[H_x, H_y, 0]^T$. This need for alignment is the fundamental constraint in Han's work, which requires the depth and orientation of magnet be held constant, and hence enables only 2D tracking [7].

Arbitrary Rotations

uTrack overcomes these limitations and allows the magnet to move and to rotate through any position in the 3D space. The key insight to make our system work is a space transformation between the 3D *sensor space* and the corresponding magnetic field space.

Figure 3 shows the incident plane and space transformation from the sensor space to magnetic field space. The transformation is achieved by the multiplication of sensor vector **H** with an unknown rotation matrix **T**. In 3D space, **T** can be defined with three Euler angles *R* (Roll), *P* (Pitch) and *Y* (Yaw), which are the rotation angles along sensor's x-, y- and z-axis respectively. Mathematically, this is denoted as below:

$$\begin{bmatrix} H_x \\ H_y \\ 0 \end{bmatrix} = TH = T_R T_P T_Y H \qquad (5)$$

Once H is converted to magnetic field space, the system can then solve x_m and y_m by applying H_x and H_y to equations (3) and (4). Finally, we need to reverse the transformation back to the original 3D sensor space:

$$\begin{bmatrix} x_s \\ y_s \\ z_s \end{bmatrix} = T^{-1}\begin{bmatrix} x_m \\ y_m \\ 0 \end{bmatrix} = T_Y^{-1}T_P^{-1}T_R^{-1}\begin{bmatrix} x_m \\ y_m \\ 0 \end{bmatrix} \qquad (6)$$

where x_s, y_s and z_s denote the magnet's x, y and z position in the sensor space. To find a solution, we must therefore find the unknown transformation matrix **T**. We will detail our searching algorithm in the next section.

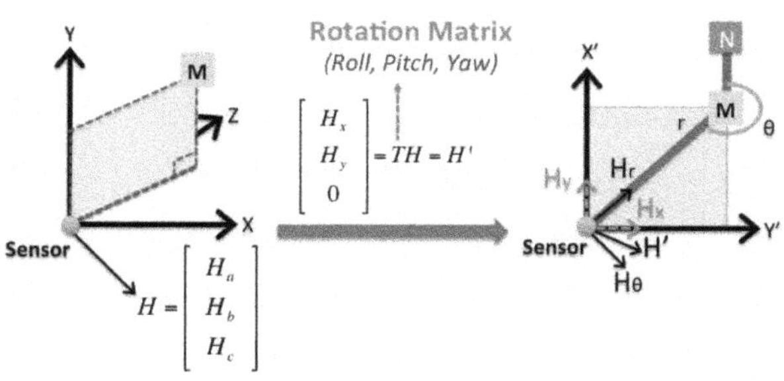

Figure 3. The incident plane of MF lines (blue rectangle) and space transformation. The rotation matrix **T** transforms the magnetic vector **H** from sensor space (left) into magnetic field space (right).

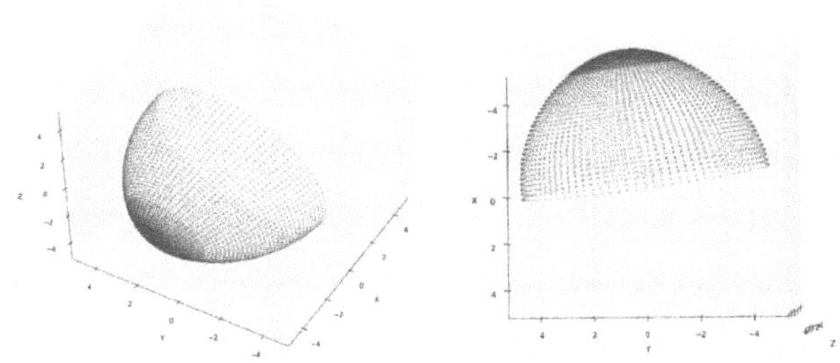

Figure 4. The search space for a given sensor vector **H** from the exhaustive search analysis. Each blue spot represents one combination of P, R and Y and its corresponding solution in the sensor space.

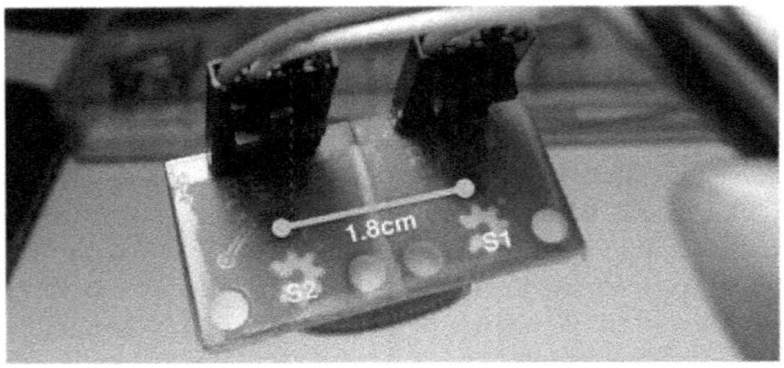

Figure 5. Using the second sensor. The aligned x axes of two sensors and the constant distance between them (1.8cm) are used in eliminating the ambiguity problem.

Understanding the Solution Space

To better understand the solution space, we performed an exhaustive search for a given sensor vector **H**. This analysis visits a subsampling of all possible combinations of R, P, and Y which satisfy the constraint of converting **H** to the vector $[H_x, H_y, 0]^T$.

Figure 4 shows the result of this exhaustive search for a single sensor reading. Each blue point represents a valid combination of R, P and Y and its corresponding solution in the sensor space. The banding is a result from our subsampling and the actual solution space would be a solid surface. This half-egg shape indicates the *ambiguity* in locating the magnet's 3D positions using only one sensor. For a given **H**, there are an infinite number of valid solutions to our equations. Thus, a single sensor is not sufficient to uniquely locate the magnet's 3D position.

Using a Second Sensor

The ambiguity can be resolved by adding a second sensor to the system with a known fixed position relative to the first sensor. In particular, we align both sensors, *S1* and *S2* so that their axes remain parallel, but there is an arbitrary shift along the x-axis of 1.8 cm (Figure 5). The axis alignment and constant distance between sensors is the key factor to resolve the ambiguity and locate the unique solution from two sensor readings.

Using this information, we are now looking for the set of rotation matrices that convert both sensor vectors to their correct magnetic field space. However, we note that the rotation matrixes, **T** and **T**', for S1 and S2 are different, but related. The offset along the x-axis means S2's incident plane needs to be rotated with one additional angle α about the S2's z-axis (Figure 6), that is, $\mathbf{T'} = \mathbf{T}\mathbf{T}_\alpha$.

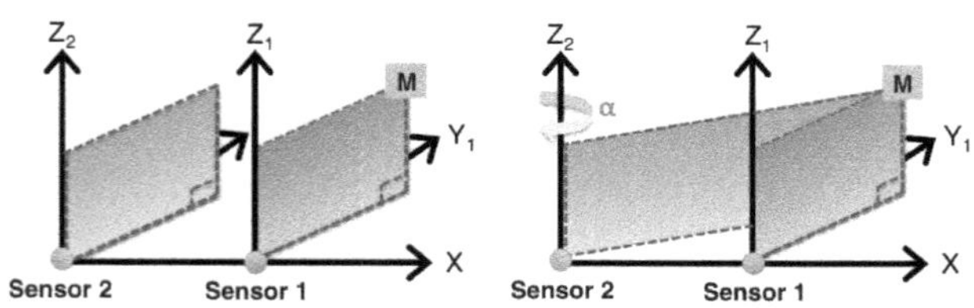

Figure 6. Magnetic field spaces for both sensors. If the same **T** is applied to both sensors, their spaces become two parallel planes, which is incorrect (left). Sensor 2 requires an additional rotation angle α to rotate it into the correct magnetic field space (right).

ALGORITHM

Figure 7 shows the system flow of uTrack. Given the non-linear nature of the system (*i.e.*, equation 3 and 4), we decided to use an exhaustive approach. The algorithm iteratively searches the three unknown angles R, P and Y for the rotation matrix **T** that eliminates the z component of S1 and converts **H** into the magnetic field space. Additionally, the angle α is used to rotate from the S1 magnetic field space to the corresponding field space of the second sensor, S2.

Now we label sensor readings from S1 and S2 as $\mathbf{H}_1$ and $\mathbf{H}_2$. The algorithm proceeds as below:

1. The system iteratively searches the three angles of **T** that converts $\mathbf{H}_1$ to a 2D vector $\mathbf{H}_{m1}$ (Eq. 5).
2. Once a candidate **T** is found, the system searches across α to find valid **T'** candidates which converts the S2 reading $\mathbf{H}_2$ into $\mathbf{H}_{m2}$.

   At this point, we have a set of rotations that satisfy our magnetic field readings. However, these candidates do not yet take into account the known physical displacement between the two sensors.
3. The two transformed magnetic field values ($\mathbf{H}_{m1}$ and $\mathbf{H}_{m2}$) are turned into spatial positions in the magnetic field space using a non-linear function solver (Eq. 3 and 4).
4. The solutions, $[x_{m1}, y_{m1}]^T$ and $[x_{m2}, y_{m2}]^T$, are then transformed back into the sensor space (Eq. 6). We denote these transformed solutions $\mathbf{V}_1$ and $\mathbf{V}_2$ as $[x_{s1}, y_{s1}, z_{s1}]^T$ and $[x_{s2}, y_{s2}, z_{s2}]^T$.
5. $\mathbf{V}_1$ and $\mathbf{V}_2$ represent the magnet's 3D position in their *respective* sensor spaces (see Figure 8, left). Since the sensors' axes are aligned and the distance between sensors is known (1.8cm), a valid solution pair $\mathbf{V}_1$ and $\mathbf{V}_2$ *must* satisfy,

$$V_2 - V_1 = \begin{bmatrix} x_{s2} - x_{s1} \\ y_{s2} - y_{s1} \\ z_{s2} - z_{s1} \end{bmatrix} = \begin{bmatrix} 1.8 \\ 0 \\ 0 \end{bmatrix} \quad (7)$$

   as shown in Figure 8 (right). This spatial constraint is the

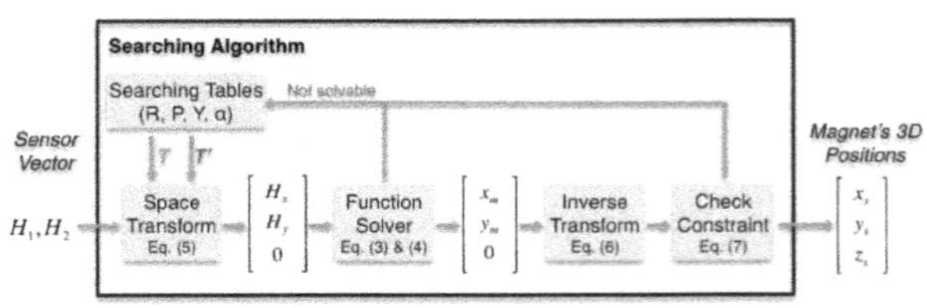

Figure 7. The searching algorithm finds three unknown angles R, P, Y and α, and converts **H** to the magnetic field space where the magnetics can apply. The magnet's 3D position is then calculated by the inverse transform.

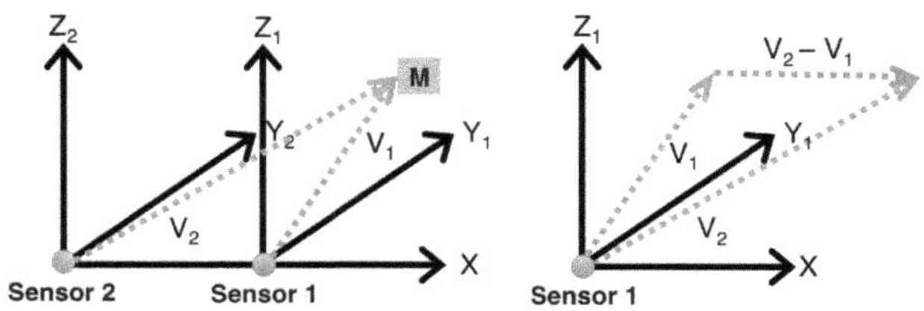

Figure 8. A valid solution pair (V_1, V_2) must satisfy the equation $V_2 - V_1 = [1.8, 0, 0]^T$. This key condition enables uTrack to identify a unique solution using only two sensor vectors.

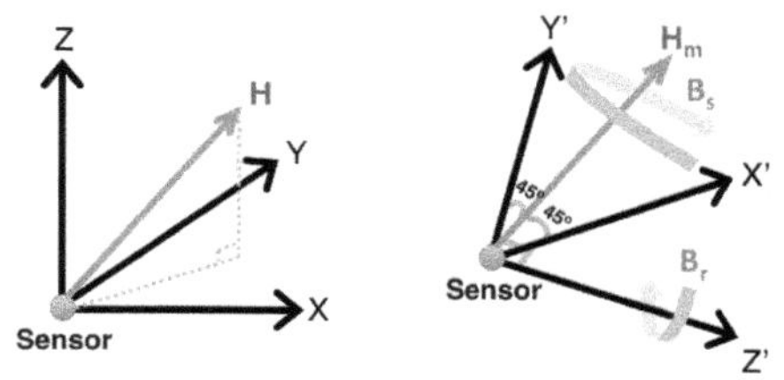

Figure 9. The orientation of a sensor before (left) and after (right) applying T_u to H. Our enhanced algorithm uses two angles B_s (spin) and B_r (rotate), which significantly reduces search complexity.

key element that enables uTrack to uniquely identify the magnet's 3D positions using *only* two sensors.

6. If at any point (1, 2, or 5) the system fails to pass the corresponding constraint, the system goes back to step 1 and continues until it finds a valid solution.

Optimization of the Searching Algorithm

In practice, the search through all angular permutations is not feasible, so we incorporated a small optimization based on the nature of the magnetic fields.

We first reduce the complexity of our algorithm by decreasing the number of angles to search for **T** from three to *two*. Intuitively, we apply a transformation to directly convert **H** to a 2D plane (i.e., making z component 0). At this point the system needs to search only two angles in this new 2D domain. To do this, we first convert **H** to its unit vector $\mathbf{H_u}$ and directly calculate the rotation matrix $\mathbf{T_u}$ that transforms $\mathbf{H_u}$ to a unit vector in the magnetic field space:

$$\begin{bmatrix} \frac{\sqrt{2}}{2} \\ \frac{\sqrt{2}}{2} \\ 0 \end{bmatrix} = T_u H_u \quad (8)$$

Next we multiply **H** by $\mathbf{T_u}$, which converts **H** to a 2D vector (called $\mathbf{H_m}$) with equal x and y values. It is noted that H_m is on the X'-Y' plane (*i.e.,* $\mathbf{H_m}$ is perpendicular to Z'-axis) and has no z component. We therefore can search only two angles B_s (spin) and B_r (rotate), which are the angles that rotate the sensors along $\mathbf{H_m}$ and Z'-axis (see Figure 9).

To further improve the efficiency, we track the delta movement instead of searching the whole space for each new sensor reading. That is, we keep B_s, B_r, and α from the previous solutions and use it as the starting search point for the current sensor reading. To this end, we divide the searching range of B_s, B_r and α (*i.e.*, -π to π) into 90 steps. Moving outwards from 0, we add the candidate delta rotation angle to the last B_s and B_r. This corresponds to the magnet's delta movement from the previous point. Once a valid combination from S1 is found (*i.e.*, satisfying Eq. 5), the system searches for a valid α using the same delta approach. The system stops searching when a valid answer pair ($\mathbf{V_1}$, $\mathbf{V_2}$) is found or exceeds an arbitrary searching upper bound (*i.e.*, ±8 degrees).

Figure 10. uTrack prototype (left) and the case with the two magnetometers (right). The data from two sensors are multiplexed and streams to Arduino.

EVALUATION OF TRACKING ACCURACY

Our first experiment is designed to understand the 3D pointing accuracy of the system with respect to ground truth. In the experiment, our uTrack prototype includes two 3-axis MEMs magnetometers (Honeywell's HMC5883), an I^2C multiplexer (NXP's PCA9527), and an Arduino Uno (Figure 10, left). The two magnetometers sample at 50Hz and are physically aligned along their x-axis as shown in Figure 5. Here we used a breakout module from Sparkfun for the magnetometers. A smaller custom board could be made to house both sensors. To ensure temporal consistency, the data from the two sensors is multiplexed through the I^2C mux and is streamed through the Arduino to the same computer. The magnetometers sit in a custom designed case to prevent unwanted movement or torqueing of the sensors (Figure 10, right). The computer for calculating the locations has a quad-core 2.8GHz CPU with 8GB of RAM running Mac OS X. The core algorithm was written in Python using the NumPy and SciPy libraries.

Experiment I: Pointing Accuracy

In the first experiment, we evaluate the accuracy of uTrack for obtaining the 3D position of the magnet. The ground truth for the magnet's 3D position was obtained using a PhaseSpace motion tracking system[7]. The PhaseSpace uses active LED markers to capture movements in real time and has 1 mm resolution. In this study, we utilized 6 cameras to capture movements of markers sampled at 480 Hz. The markers are attached on sensor 1 and the magnet.

In this experiment, the magnet was worn by the first author on the index finger; and, the sensors were affixed to the table. The researcher moved randomly in a 3D volume of ±80 mm (x-axis), ±60 mm (y-axis) and 0–80 mm (z-axis).

[7]PhaseSpace: http://www.phasespace.com

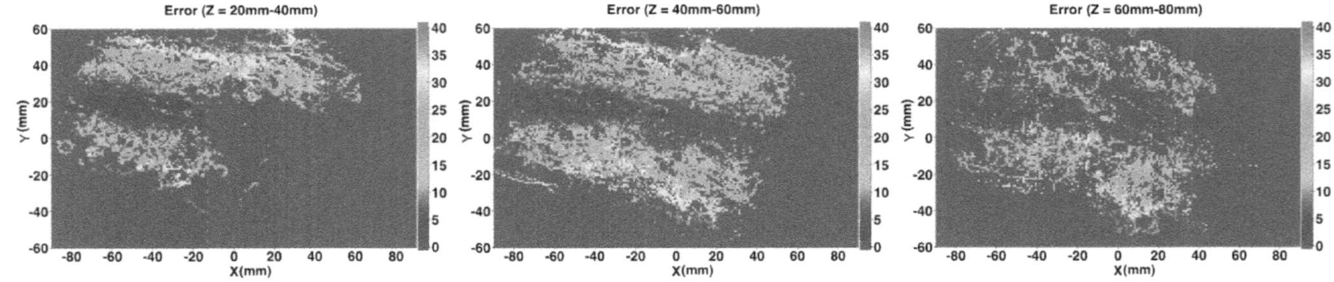

Figure 11. Tracking accuracy (unit: mm) of uTrack. The interactive space is divided into three 20 mm slices along the z-axis and shown in these three plots. The color indicates the amount of error in absolute position. The system is most accurate in the center of the volume, with a mean error of 4.82 mm.

This volume is much larger than what would be needed for our target mobile applications; however, we chose this relatively large volume to explore the limits of the system. The uTrack sensor data and 3D positions of the optical markers are saved on the same computer (*i.e.*, using the same clock and aligned in time) for off-line analysis. There were 39384 data points collected in total.

Results

Figure 11 shows Euclidean distance between the results of uTrack and the optical tracking results which we assume to be ground truth. The interaction space is divided into three 20 mm slices along z-axis to improve the visualization. In each slice, the mean of error for points with same x and y position is calculated.

For the entire volume of 38,400 mm^3, the mean Euclidean error is 24.54 mm (σ=9.17). This high overall error is caused by the environmental magnetic noise. In this study, we use a relatively strong magnet to overcome environmental interference such as the earth's magnetic field and surrounding electromagnetic fields. However, when the magnet moves away from the sensors, the data becomes noisier and therefore degrades the accuracy of the system. This can be seen in Figure 11 with increased error moving out from the center of the graphs. It is useful to note that the error in x-, y- and z-axis is 1.84 mm (σ=7.69), 2.72 mm (σ=5.51) and -13.80 mm (σ=19.04), respectively. This result indicates that the performance drop is mainly in the z-axis and the tracking on x-y plane remains quite accurate. Hence, despite the accuracy fluctuations in z-axis, uTrack is still capable of fine-grained controls on x-y plane and relatively coarse-grained controls on the z-axis.

We next explore the region where the points are within 10 mm of ground truth. In Figure 11, this region is depicted with the blue points and corresponds to a box of approximately 70 mm (W) x 30 mm (D) x 60 mm (H) (*i.e.*, the x-, y- and z-axes range from -70 mm to 0 mm, 5 mm to 35 mm and 20 mm to 80 mm, respectively). When we examine only this region, the error significantly reduces to a mean of 4.82 mm (σ=1.01). If the sensors are instrumented on the ring finger (Figure 12, left), this region approximately corresponds to the space that thumb can move around the fingers.

Besides the analysis of accuracy, we also evaluate the resolution of uTrack within the same volume of 10 mm accuracy. For this purpose, we calculate the Euclidean distance between two consecutive data points (*i.e.*, the relative movement) measured by the optical markers and the results of our system, and use their difference as the drifting error. The Euclidean mean error is 3.78 mm (σ=1.7), indicating $(25.4\ mm/3.78\ mm)^3 = 303$ dpci (dots per cube inch).

APPLICATION TASK EVALUATION

To further verify the feasibility of using uTrack in real applications, we conducted a second study. Here we had participants conduct three tasks.

Experiment II: User Evaluation

For the first task, we evaluated the performance of using our system for absolute cursor control on a monitor. Here, we had participants move the magnet in the x-y plane (i.e., parallel to the table), and in x-z plane (i.e., the vertical plane approximately aligned with the monitor). The participants are asked to move the cursor along a 120-pixel square on a 24-inch, 1920x1080 LCD monitor. This square corresponds to a 20 mm square of physical movement (*i.e.*, 1 mm magnet movement corresponds to 6 pixels on the display). When the participant moves the magnet in either of the two target dimensions, they can see the cursor moving on the screen and adjust their path in real time. Movement in the third dimension was allowed, but discarded and not represented onscreen with visual feedback.

Tasks 2 and 3 were more open ended. We explored the ability of uTrack for slow, fine-grained manipulation (task 2) and fast, coarse-grained (task 3) movements. For these tasks

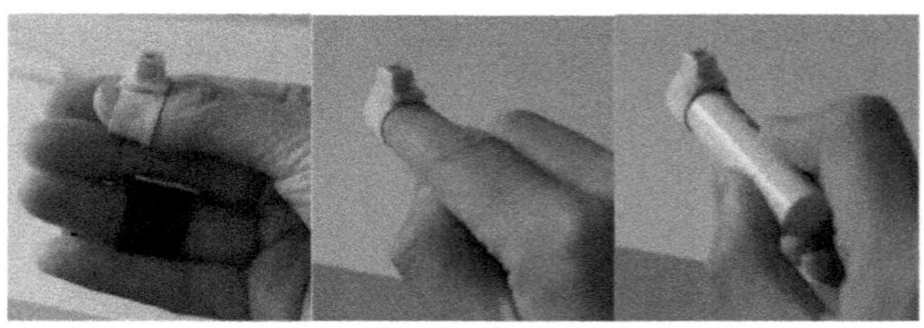

Figure 12. Three form factors using the thumb (left), the index finger (center), and a stylus (right) for 3D pointing.

	X-Y	X-Z	Avg.
Thumb	14.9	14.0	**14.5**
Finger	15.1	13.5	**14.3**
Stylus	14.6	14.2	**14.4**
Avg.	**14.9**	**13.9**	**14.4**

Table 1. Error in the cursor control task (in pixels).

participants manipulated a 3D model and played the Fruit Ninja game respectively. For these tasks, we only collected subjective feedback.

In experiment II, we explored three different physical configurations for uTrack (see Figure 12) in various scenarios. The first used the sensors on the ring finger and a magnet attached on the back of the *thumb* as the pointer. This is our original targeted one-handed pointing interaction. The second represents having two sensors in a device such as wristwatch and using the *index finger* of the opposite hand as a 3D pointer. Our third configuration would embed the two sensors in a mobile phone or tablet and use a *stylus* for 3D interactions. For scenarios two and three, instead of embedding the sensors into a device, we simulated the configuration by having participants use their non-pointing hand to hold the sensors in an appropriate configuration.

We recruited ten participants (6 males, 4 females) ranging in age from 22 to 33 years from a university. Eight participants have more than 10 years of experience with computers, while the other two participants reported having only an intermediate level of experiences with computers. Two participants were left-handed. One of the left-handed participants used their non-dominant hand for pointing and all other participants used their dominant hand. At the end of each session, the participants were asked to fill a questionnaire regarding their adaptation to these three input methods.

For all conditions, we smoothed the tracking path of the 3D points produced by our underlying algorithm by applying cosine interpolation and moving average (window size 10) on the tracking results.

Results

The results from the user evaluation for Task 1 are shown in Table 1. Because the system maps 6 pixels to 1 mm, the mean error of 14.4 pixels (σ=1.26) represents approximately 2.4 mm of movement error of the magnet (we excluded data from one participant as an outlier as the user had difficulty with the thumb condition). Since the participants move the finger or thumb in air without the benefit of a surface for support, this small error is likely due as much to the difficulty of the task as the underlying uTrack system. We also want to note that there was minimal training with this system and all participants started testing after only 30 to 60 seconds of practice.

All participants were able to successfully perform our other two open-ended tasks. We also asked participants for qualitative preferences for our different configurations. For Task 1, among three input methods, participants preferred the finger and stylus for cursor control. Participants indicated no preference between the three configurations for manipulating the 3D model and preferred the finger configuration for playing Fruit Ninja.

DISCUSSION AND FUTURE WORK

Our evaluation showed that uTrack enables 3D pointing with sufficient accuracy for real-time applications, and is perceived well by study participants. In this section, we discuss some opportunities for improving uTrack, the calculation of the magnet's tilt angle, and some future work.

There are several improvements we would like to explore with uTrack. First, our algorithm is relatively naïve in searching for the 4 unknown angles. For our prototype, this was sufficient to allow real-time performance using the computing power of a PC; however, a mobile solution would require a different implementation. It might be possible to derive some alternative linear formulations that allow for more efficient computation similar to [15].

Also, in order to reduce the search space, our current implementation utilizes deltas for tracking movements of the magnet. It requires a somewhat known starting point to seed the search. To resolve this, we constrain the magnet to stay in the first quadrant of the magnetic field space when the system is initially launched.

In addition to 3D positions, uTrack also tracks the tilt angle of magnet (4 degrees of freedom total). Here we define the tilt angle as the angle between the magnet's north pole and sensor's x-y plane. As described earlier, our algorithm searches for a rotation matrix **T** that converts **H** to the magnetic field space where x-axis is parallel to magnet's north pole. The direction vector of the magnet's north pole $\mathbf{V_N}$ can therefore be derived by:

$$V_N = T\begin{bmatrix}1\\0\\0\end{bmatrix} = \begin{bmatrix}V_x\\V_y\\V_z\end{bmatrix} \tag{9}$$

The tilt angle of magnet $\boldsymbol{\theta}_t$ can then be calculated by:

$$\theta_t = \arcsin\left(\frac{V_z}{\| V_N \|}\right) \tag{10}$$

Figure 13 illustrates some examples of angles that uTrack is able to detect. Evaluating and utilizing this additional degree of freedom would be an interesting area of future work. For

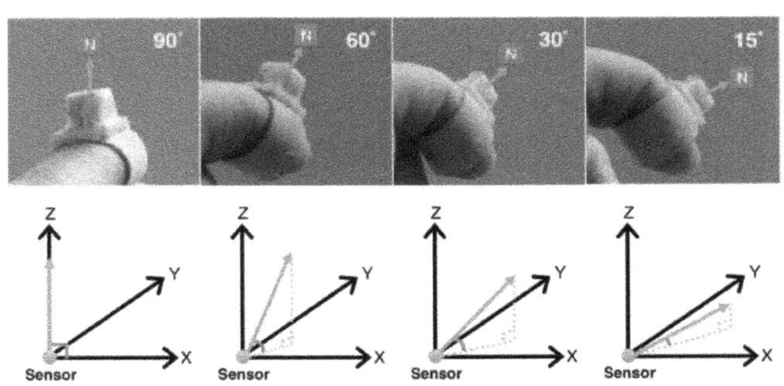

Figure 13. In addition to tracking 3D position, uTrack continuously tracks the direction of magnet's north pole to derive the magnet's tilt angle.

example, the tilt angle can possibly be used to enable "clicking", a proxy for pressure, or to switch the cursor from hover to click-and-drag mode.

Although the experiments in this paper were conducted while seated, we believe that uTrack will work equally well even when the user is in motion. To prove this, we informally conducted experiments in which a person utilized the system for 3D cursor control while walking around a building. Although the signal fluctuates more relative to the signal seen in a static location, the system appeared to be functional. We plan to further explore the ability to use uTrack in a noisy environment. An additional sensor may also be useful in these situations to help account for environmental magnetic field variations similar to Han et al. [6].

CONCLUSION

In this paper, we present a novel interaction technique using magnetic field sensing that turns the fingers and thumb into a 3D input device. Our evaluations show that for an active volume of 70 mm (W) x 30 mm (D) x 60 mm (H), we obtain an absolute positioning accuracy of 4.82 mm and 303 dpci. A user study showed participants were able to effectively use uTrack for several different pointing tasks.

This system requires only a single active module consisting of a *pair* of MEMs magnetometers that could be worn on a finger like a ring. We described how we derive the position of a permanent magnet attached to the back of the thumb. This configuration allows the user to move the thumb around fingers to provide a continuous, 3D input. As various forms of wearable computing become more commonplace, the need for a good mechanism for continuous pointing will become critical; uTrack provides such a solution.

ACKNOWLEDGEMENTS

We would like to thank Shigeyuki Seko for his help with our hardware and Daniel Ashbrook for his early feedback on magnetic field sensing. We would also acknowledge Vikash Kumar for assistance with the evaluation.

REFERENCES

1. C. Amma and T. Schultz. 2012. Airwriting: demonstrating mobile text input by 3D-space handwriting. In *Proc. of IUI* '12, pp.319-320.
2. D. Ashbrook, P. Baudisch, and S. White. 2011. Nenya: subtle and eyes-free mobile input with a magnetically-tracked finger ring. In *Proc. of CHI* '11, pp.2043-2046.
3. D. Ashbrook, J. Clawson, K. Lyons, N. Patel, and T. Starner. Quickdraw: The impact of mobility and on-body placement on device access time. In *Proc. of CHI*, 2008, pp.219-222.
4. A. Butler, S. Izadi, and S. Hodges. 2008. SideSight: multi-"touch" interaction around small devices. In *Proc. of UIST* '08, pp.201-204.
5. T. Deyle, S. Palinko, E.S. Poole and T. Starner, "Hambone: A Bio-Acoustic Gesture Interface," *Wearable Computers*, 2007, pp.3-10.
6. X. Han, H. Seki, Y. Kamiya, and M. Hikizu, Wearable handwriting input device using magnetic field. In *Proc. SICE'07*, pp.365-368.
7. X. Han, H. Seki, Y. Kamiya, and M. Hikizu, Wearable handwriting input device using magnetic field: 2nd report: Influence of misalignment of magnet and writing plane, Precision Engineering, July 2010, pp.37-43
8. C. Harrison and S. E. Hudson. 2009. Abracadabra: wireless, high-precision, and unpowered finger input for very small mobile devices. In *Proc. of UIST* '09, pp.121-124.
9. C. Harrison, and D.M. Tan, Skinput: Appropriating the Body as an Input Surface. In *Proc. of CHI* 2010, pp.453-462
10. C. Harrison, H. Benko, A.D. Wilson, OmniTouch: Wearable Multitouch Interaction Everywhere. In *Proc. of UIST* '11, pp.441-450
11. D. Kim, O. Hilliges, S. Izadi, A. D. Butler, J. Chen, I. Oikonomidis, and P. Olivier. 2012. Digits: freehand 3D interactions anywhere using a wrist-worn gloveless sensor. In *Proc. of UIST* '12, pp.167-176.
12. M.R. Kraichman, Handbook of Electromagnetic Propagation in Conducting Media, 2nd ed. Washington, D.C.; Head-quarters Naval Material Command, 1976.
13. R. Liang, K. Cheng, C. Su, C. Weng, B. Chen, and D. Yang, 2012. GaussSense: attachable stylus sensing using magnetic sensor grid, In *Proc. of UIST '12*, pp.319-326.
14. J Lementec and P. Bajcsy. Recognition of arm gestures using multiple orientation sensors: gesture classification. *Proceedings of the 7th International IEEE Conference on Intelligent Transportation Systems*, 2004, pp.965-970
15. F.H. Raab, E.B. Blood, T.O. Steiner, and H.R. Jones, Magnetic Position and Orientation Tracking System, Aerospace and Electronic Systems, IEEE Transactions on, Sept. 1979, pp.709-718.
16. T. S. Saponas, D. S. Tan, D. Morris, R. Balakrishnan, Jim Turner, and J. A. Landay. 2009. Enabling always-available input with muscle-computer interfaces. In *Proc. of UIST* '09. ACM, New York, USA, pp.167-176.
17. T. Starner, J. Auxier, D. Ashbrook and M. Gandy (2000), The Gesture Pendant: A Self-illuminating, Wearable, Infrared Computer Vision System for Home Automation Control and Medical Monitoring, In *Proc. of ISWC*'00, pp.87-94
18. J. E. Zucco, B. H. Thomas, K. Grimmer-Somers and A. Cockburn. 'A Comparison of Menu Configurations and Pointing Devices for use with Wearable Computers while Mobile and Stationary'. In Thirteenth International Symposium on Wearable Computers, Linz, Austria, September 2009. IEEE, pp.63-70

A Cuttable Multi-touch Sensor

Simon Olberding[1], Nan-Wei Gong[2], John Tiab[1], Joseph A. Paradiso[2], Jürgen Steimle[1]

[1]Max Planck Institute for Informatics
Campus E1 7, 66123 Saarbrücken, Germany
{solberdi, jtiab, jsteimle}@mpi-inf.mpg.de

[2]MIT Media Lab
75 Amherst Street, Cambridge MA 02142, USA
{nanwei, joep}@media.mit.edu

ABSTRACT
We propose cutting as a novel paradigm for ad-hoc customization of printed electronic components. As a first instantiation, we contribute a printed capacitive multi-touch sensor, which can be cut by the end-user to modify its size and shape. This very direct manipulation allows the end-user to easily make real-world objects and surfaces touch-interactive, to augment physical prototypes and to enhance paper craft. We contribute a set of technical principles for the design of printable circuitry that makes the sensor more robust against cuts, damages and removed areas. This includes novel physical topologies and printed forward error correction. A technical evaluation compares different topologies and shows that the sensor remains functional when cut to a different shape.

Author Keywords
Cuttable Electronics, Printed Electronics, Multi-touch Sensor, Capacitive Sensing, Ubiquitous Computing.

ACM Classification Keywords
H.5.2. Information interfaces and presentation (e.g., HCI):

General Terms
Human Factors; Design; Measurement.

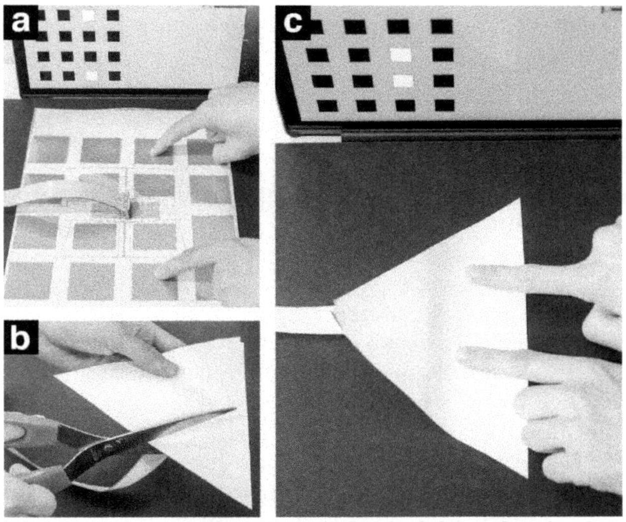

Figure 1: We contribute technical principles and an implementation of cut-robust printed multi-touch sensor sheets. a) The multi-touch sensor features a novel wiring scheme. b) This allows to sensor to be cut very much like a conventional material while (c) remaining touch-sensitive.

INTRODUCTION
Conventional electronic components and devices cannot be cut to customize their size and shape in an ad-hoc manner. Their rigid substrate is hard to cut, components are too expensive to be discarded and cutting irreversibly damages the electronic circuit. In contrast, people have always cut traditional materials for tailoring them to their specific needs. At home, people wrap packages with material, which is cut to shape; they cut protective films to cover books and devices of various sizes; and they create artistic shapes in paper craft. At the workplace, tailors cut textiles to fit the size of the customer, carpenters cut wood to build furniture, and designers or engineers cut cardboard and plywood to create physical prototypes.

This form of very direct manipulation enables people to quickly and easily create custom shapes and objects; in addition the direct manual interaction with the material encourages thinking by doing [7].

Printed electronics now enables for a novel paradigm, introduced in this paper: printed electronic components and devices can easily be tailored to a custom shape and size by ad-hoc cutting. This is possible because substrates are very thin and flexible, and printouts are cheap. However, current printed solutions take over the circuitry schemes from conventional electronics. Due to its internal layout, cutting parts off to adapt the shape will very likely break the electronics. Therefore we advocate that printed electronics requires novel electronic designs that can cope with its new material properties: designs that are robust against cuts and removed areas of the substrate.

As a first instantiation of this paradigm, we contribute a printed capacitive multi-touch sensor, which the user can tailor by cutting it to the desired size and shape (see Fig. 1). We present technical principles that make the circuit layout more robust against physical cuts and removed areas, taking inspiration from topology in biological systems and computer networks, as well as from coding theory. First, we contribute *novel topologies* for the circuit layout that are more robust against cuts. Second, we show how by *combining several topologies* in the same sensor sheet, a wider variety of cut-out shapes can be supported. Third, we contribute a principle for adding various *levels of redundancy* within each topology, proposing *printed forward error correction*.

We validate our technical contributions by a detailed *simulation*, an evaluation of the *electronic sensing properties*, and a *proof-of-concept implementation* of several letter-sized cuttable sensor sheets.

TOWARDS CUTTABLE MATERIALS WITH EMBEDDED MULTI-TOUCH SENSING

Our vision is that printed sensors will be so inexpensive that multi-touch sensing capability will become an inherent part of the material. For instance, manufacturers of protective foils will offer a product line that features multi-touch sensing. Paper manufacturers will offer paper, cardboard or adhesive labels, which have the printed multi-touch sensor embedded. Manufacturers of wooden boards will offer boards that feature the sensor. The user buys the material in one of several standard sizes and then cuts it to the desired size and shape, using tools such as scissors, razors, saws, or laser cutters. This very direct physical manipulation seamlessly integrates with existing practices for customization, prototyping and crafting. It stands in contrast with existing solutions, which either require the additional a step of designing the sensor at a computer [21] or by requiring an expert to design a customized sensing solution.

Cuttable multi-touch sensor foils, sheets and boards will be a ubiquitous resource, enabling a wide range of applications. For ubiquitous computing, people can easily add multi-touch input on pretty much any physical object or surface, by using an *adhesive multi-touch foil* that is cut to match the desired size and shape. As illustrated in Fig. 2 a-c, this enables people to easily touch-augment physical objects and devices. In prototyping and crafting, *touch-enabled paper, cardboard or plywood* empowers people to make models, prototypes and artwork interactive (Fig. 2d).

RELATED WORK

Shape-adaptable Multi-touch Sensors

The commonly used principle for the construction of a multi-touch sensor [17,22,28,20,11,4,18] is illustrated in Fig. 3. A set of electrodes is arranged on a regular two-dimensional grid. Each electrode senses one touch point. The electrodes are connected to a controller with a set of horizontal and parallel wires; each electrode is situated at the intersection of one horizontal and one parallel wire.

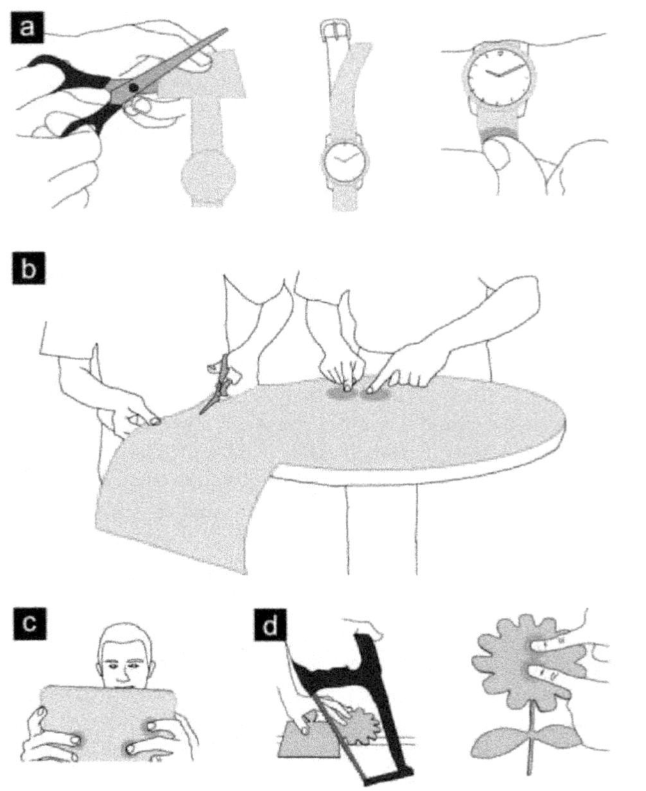

Figure 2: a-c) Easily touch-enable objects with a cuttable multi-touch foil. d) Build interactive objects, prototypes or paper craft out of raw materials with embedded sensing.

Therefore it can be uniquely addressed by the appropriate combination of two wires. The elegance of this approach is in requiring only a minimum number of wires. However, this grid topology is not designed for shape adaptation. It is not robust to cuts and removed parts. Since each wire addresses many electrodes, damage of a wire results in a burst effect: many electrodes become unusable and possibly large areas of the sensor stop working. Moreover, the controller connects to the sensor from its outer sides; in consequence these sides cannot be removed, preventing round shapes.

Some prior work has investigated means to realize shape-adaptable sensors. Additive approaches support shape customization by combining multiple interconnected active sensor tiles or nodes [4,12,14,15,19]. Subtractive approaches support customization by cutting. Our work draws inspiration from work by Wimmer et al. [31] and Holman et. al [8], who introduced cutting of a sensor strip for adapting its length. Wimmer et al.'s sensor is adapted in

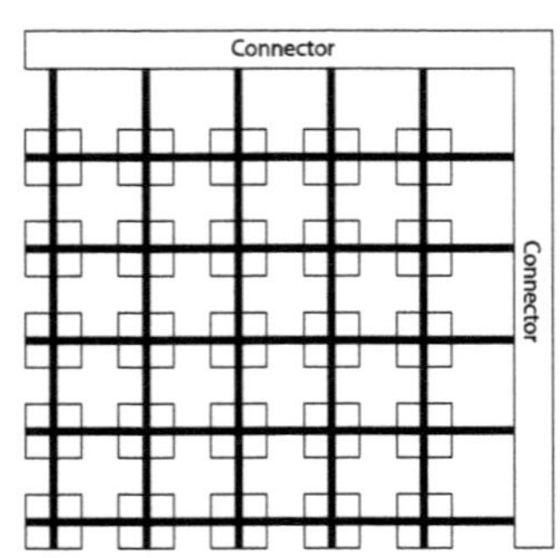

Figure 3: Concept of a traditional multi-touch pad.

shape by cutting a sensor wire to the desired length and laying it out using a space-filling curve. Alternatively, several prefabricated sensor tiles, each containing a wire, can be combined. While this elegant solution supports virtually any sensor shape, it is limited to single-touch input and requires a complicated sensing technology, Time Domain Reflectometry. Tekscan[24] developed a pressure sensitive shoe inlet that can be trimmed to fit different sizes. While the size can be varied, the shape itself is predefined due to the internal wiring. We extend upon prior work by contributing the first cuttable multi-touch sensor sheet.

Printed Electronics

Printed electronics is the key enabling technology for the approach presented in this paper, as this technology allows producing sensitive surfaces in large scale at very low cost and on a very thin substrate [25]. While inkjet printing of electronics [25] enables customized electronic circuits in small quantities, roll-to-roll printing [25] supports large sizes and high printing speeds. It is possible to print multi-layered electronic circuits and active electronic components, such as transistors, by combining conductive, semi-conductive and insulating inks on several layers [25]. While such active electronics are still on the level of basic research, printing of passive conductive circuits is already commercially offered [3]. To keep costs low and to enable a deployment in the near future, our solution only requires passive printed electronics.

Rapid Prototyping

Our work is also heavily inspired from prior research on rapid prototyping. A stream of previous work allows the user to make a physical prototype interactive. For instance, this is done by attaching electronic components on the prototype and connecting them by drawing conductive traces with a conductive pen [29], or by attaching thin lines of copper [16]. As an alternative to hand-drawn traces, VodooIO [27] introduced a specific foam substrate that wires electronic components that the user attaches on the material. This stream of work emphasizes on the importance of hand-crafting in rapid prototyping.

Another stream of research proposes digital fabrication [30,13] for creating interactive prototypes [9,21]. The Midas toolkit [21] enables the user to digitally design a custom touch sensor on a computer. The sensor then gets produced on a vinyl cutter and can be attached onto the object.

Our approach complements the above work in two ways. Using physical tools (such as scissors, knife or saw), the sensor can be iteratively customized in its shape before, during and after the crafting process. This contrasts with previous work [21] in which the sensor cannot be altered once it is designed and printed. But our approach also extends digital prototyping in the way that the user can plan digitally and then use a machine to cut the sensor sheet or sensor-enabled material into a desired shape.

REQUIREMENTS

Multi-touch sensors must fulfill a set of technical requirements, such as a specific spatial and temporal resolution, dynamic range and number of touch points. Shape-adaptable multi-touch sensors extend this set with several additional requirements that are specific to cutting. We identify four desirable properties, which a cuttable sensor sheet ideally should fulfill. Taken together, they define what is intuitively understood by "robustness" of the sensor to cutting.

Set of supported shapes: The sensor should support a large set of cut-out shapes, including convex and non-convex shapes. This means that all electrodes on the cut-out shape remain functioning.

Scale and aspect ratio invariance: The cut-out shape can be of any size and aspect ratio, as long as it fits on the sheet.

Besides these intrinsic properties of the shape, extrinsic characteristics are affected by where and how the shape is placed on the sensor sheet:

Rotation invariance: A specific shape should be supported no matter in which orientation it is placed on the sensor sheet.

Location invariance of the connector: The sensor sheet has a connector to tether it with the controller. It should be possible to locate this connector at several locations or even any location on the cut-out shape, to integrate well with the specific requirements of the application.

While a working solution does not have to support all of these requirements, supporting more of them increases its usability, as the user can cut a wider variety of shapes and place them more freely on the sensor sheet.

In the following sections, we contribute three principles to create more robust multi-touch sensors that better fulfill the above requirements.

TOPOLOGIES FOR CUTTABLE MULTI-TOUCH SENSORS

Multi-touch sensors are typically based on a matrix topology. As we have discussed in the related work section, this topology is not robust to cuts and removed areas and does not support a variety of cut-out shapes. In this section, we introduce novel basic wiring topologies for cuttable multi-touch sensors that are inspired by biological systems and computer networks. We show how they improve the robustness of the sensor against cuts and discuss which cut-out shapes they support.

Radial and tree structures are very common organization principles in biological systems, e.g. in blood and nerve systems, in the physical structure of plants and in fungal structures [6]. This ensures not only effective transmission, but also protects vitally important parts in an inner area of the system. Also in computer networks, star and tree structures are amongst the most central topologies [23]. Meshes are a further promising structure, often applied in computer networks, which however require active routing components.

In the following, we present star-based and tree-based topologies. Similarly to the conventional matrix topology, they lay out the electrodes on a regular grid. This ensures a consistent spatial resolution across all areas of the sensor. In contrast to the standard matrix topology, they use point-to-point connections between connector and electrodes to avoid burst effects, in which loss of a single wire would result in irreversibly damaging multiple electrodes.

Star Topology

The first layout follows the geometry of a star (Figure 4a). The connector, which is used to tether the sensor sheet with a controller, is placed in the center. Wires extend radially to the electrodes. This topology can be realized with two layers (wires are routed underneath the electrodes with proper shielding) or as a single layer (wires are routed around the electrodes).

The star topology has a number of desirable properties. Due to the circular scheme, all wires run towards the center of the sheet on the shortest path between the electrode and the connector. This reduces the likelihood of a wire getting cut while the corresponding electrode remains on the sensor. As outlined above, this is a problem of the classical matrix topology, in which an electrode can be affected by a cut at the very other end of the sensor. In the star topology, the electrode and its corresponding wire are always located within the same pie slice. Cuts in the remaining pie slices will never affect the electrode. Another benefit is that the topology is point symmetric. A shape is supported no matter how it is rotated around the controller.

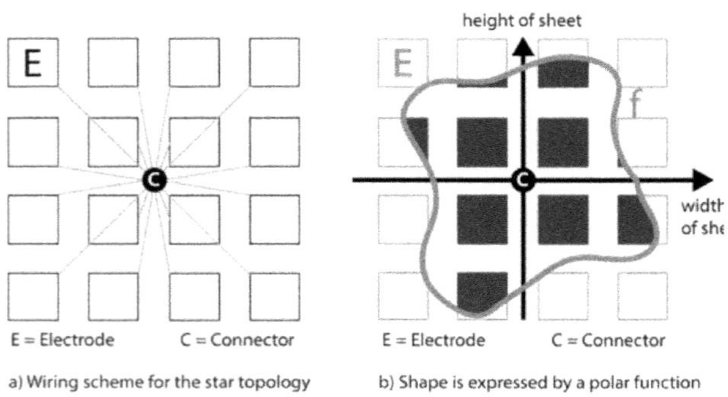

Figure 4: a) The star topology wires the connector radially with each electrode. b) The star supports shapes with outlines that can be defined by any positive polar function (green line). The blue filling indicates functional electrodes.

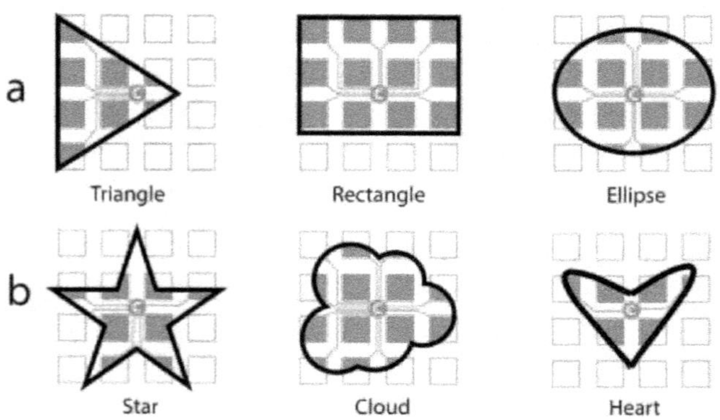

Figure 5: a) The star topology supports a large variety of convex shapes including triangles, rectangles and ellipses. b) It also supports shapes that introduce concavity, provided they are properly placed.

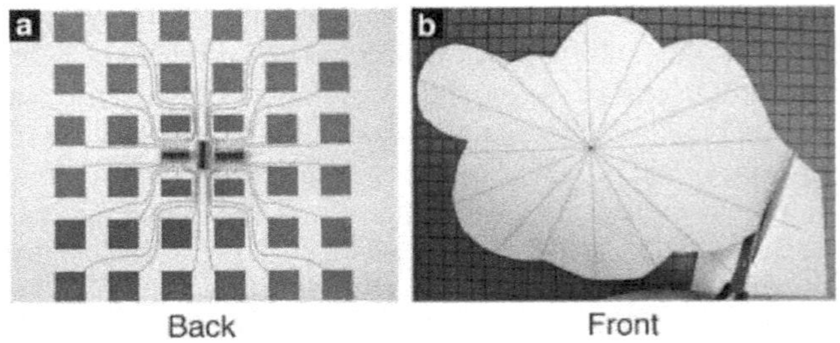

Figure 6: a) Backside of the fabricated multi-touch sensor featuring a grid of 6x6 electrodes. b) To guide the user, the front side features fine printed lines.

The full set of supported shapes can be mathematically modeled. The outline of the shape is defined by any polar function defining an outline that does not extend beyond the sheet (see Fig. 4b).

This topology supports a large variety of shapes, including triangles, convex rectangles and ellipses (see Fig. 5a). These shapes can be located anywhere on the sheet as long as the connector is inside the shape (realizing location invariance). Moreover, the shapes can have arbitrary scale and aspect ratio. The star topology also supports some non-convex shapes, such as "heart-like", "cloud-like" or "star-like" shapes, provided they are properly placed on the sheet (see Fig. 5b). However, it only partially supports more complex shapes, such as the ones depicted in Fig. 8.

We implemented a prototype sensor sheet in letter size, which is based on the star topology and has 36 electrodes (Fig. 6). We printed fine radial lines on the front side to communicate the wiring layout to the user. As a rule of thumb, the shape will be supported if each line is cut not more than once.

Tree topology

In the tree topology, all electrodes are orthogonally connected to one stream of wires, which is then connected to the controller (Fig. 6a). Through the indirection in how electrodes are wired with the connector, the tree topology supports shapes that are not supported by the star (and vice versa). This specifically includes shapes that introduce concavity, as depicted in Fig. 8a and b. Carve-outs are only partially supported (see Fig. 8c,d).

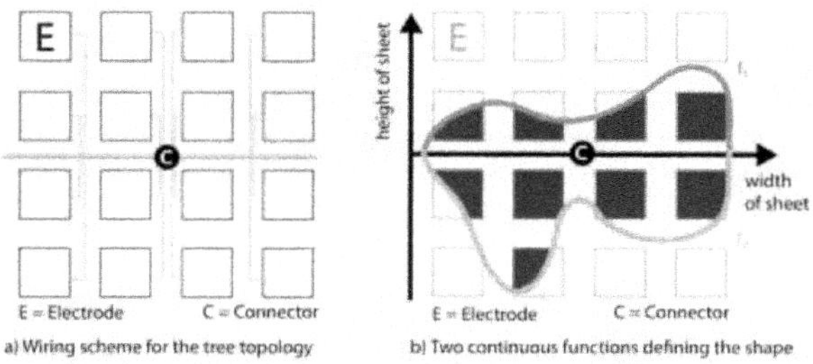

Figure 7: a) In the tree topology, all wires are routed to a central stem. b) The outline of the shape can be defined by two continuous functions. Functional electrodes are blue.

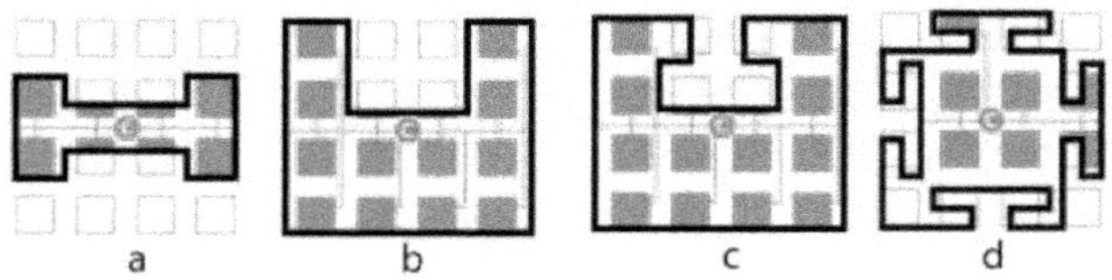

Figure 8: The tree supports carve-outs at the border of a shape (a,b). Puzzle-shaped connection pieces are partially supported (c,d).

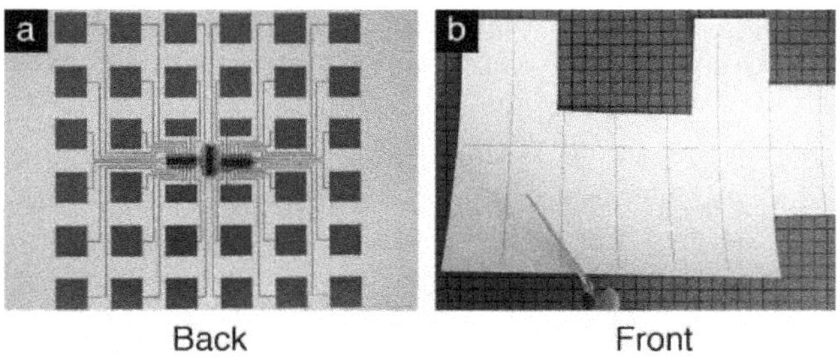

Figure 9: a) Prototype of a multi-touch sensor that implements the tree topology. b) As long as the user does not cut a line twice, the shape is supported.

The tree is not rotation invariant but supports different sizes and aspect ratios of the cut-out shape. The outline is defined by two continuous functions, whereby the stem of the tree is the x axis (see Fig. 7b).

We implemented a first instantiation of a letter-sized sensor sheet, depicted in Fig. 9. We printed fine lines on the paper to provide guidance about which cuts are supported.

ADDING REDUNDANCY BY COMBINING TOPOLOGIES

In this section we show how to further increase the robustness of the sensor and to support more shapes by combining two or more topologies in one sensor sheet. Since different topologies each have their unique strengths and drawbacks, combining them adds valuable redundancy and geometric robustness. Each electrode is connected to the connector via two or more potentially very different paths. Note that this does not increase the number of pins required at the hardware controller, since all wires from all layers that are connected to the same electrode are combined at the connector.

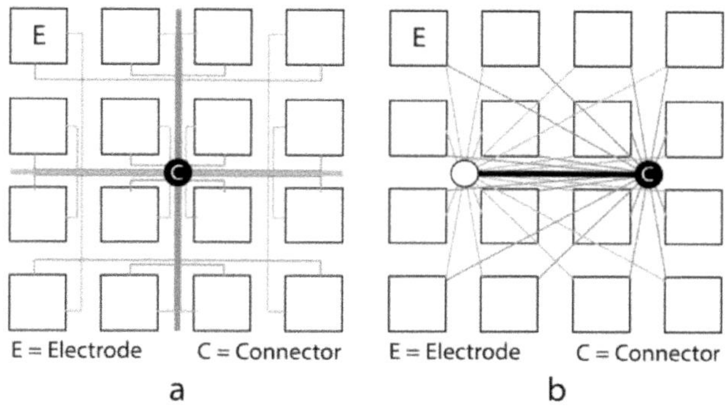

Figure 10: a) Overlaying two tree topologies improves rotation invariance. b) Overlaying two star topologies allows for wider range of supported shapes.

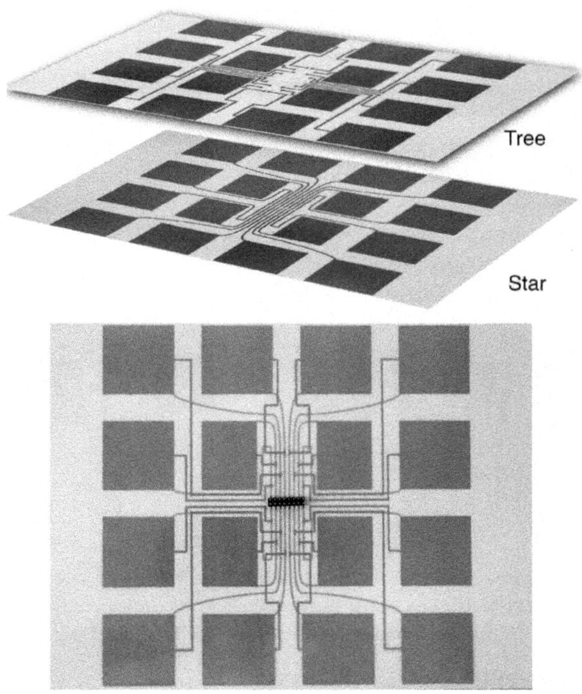

Figure 11: Prototype of a dual-layer sensor with overlaid tree and star topologies for a 4x4 sensor sheet. The tree topology is printed on a transparent PET film. Both layers are connected using 3M conductive z-Tape.

Conceptually, we distinguish between two cases: Overlaying (1) distinct topologies and/or (2) the same topology:

(1) combines the advantages of two distinct topologies. For instance, consider overlaying the star topology with a tree topology. This would support all shapes of Fig. 5 *and* Fig. 8a,b.

(2) can overcome some limitations, which are inherent to the specific topology, by repeating this topology in a rotated or displaced manner. For instance, consider overlaying two tree layouts rotated by 90 degrees around the center point (see Fig. 10a). This makes the layout invariant to 90 degree

rotations. Overlaying two star layouts in a displaced manner (see Fig. 11b) allows for supporting shapes with certain concave elements, which otherwise would be supported only by the tree (see Fig. 8a, b).

Mathematically, the outline of the shape can be divided in segments. As long as each segment can be represented by a valid function in at least one of the overlaid topologies, the shape is supported.

We implemented a first prototype of a sensor with two overlaid topologies, an overlay of a star and a tree. Figure 11a shows how tree and star are overlaid; Figure 11c shows the compound sensor.

INCREASING ROBUSTNESS WITHIN A TOPOLOGY

In this section, we contribute methods for encoding redundancy within a topology.

Basic Redundant Wiring

Figure 12 (a1) shows an example of an electrode that is cut in two pieces. While a considerable part of the electrode remains on the sensor sheet, it cannot be read, since the wire is cut off. Connecting each electrode with two redundant wires from its opposite sides makes the sensor robust to such situations (see Fig. 12 a2)). Moreover, this adds robustness to cases where one of the wires is damaged (see Fig. 12b). This rather simplistic form of redundancy requires the double amount of wires.

Figure 12: Basic form of redundant wiring: a cut on the electrode (a1) or a cut on the wire (b1) can be compensated for by adding a redundant wire (a2 and b2).

Printed Forward Error Correction

A more advanced solution adds redundancy with fewer wires. It is inspired from coding theory. Forward error correction (FEC) provides mechanisms to encode data in a redundant way to cope with errors in data transmitted via an unreliable channel [26]. Examples are the parity bit (error detecting) or the Hamming code (error correcting). The underlying idea is to calculate a redundant symbol as a function of several payload symbols.

Based on this principle, we contribute a solution to encode a FEC mechanism right on the printout; it involves a specific wiring scheme and a modified electrode design. Our approach is depicted in Fig. 13a. Both electrodes are read independently via direct wires a and b. In addition, a redundant wire c connects to both electrodes. In contrast to the above example of the parity bit, the sensor readings are not binary. Each electrode captures a dynamic range, so it gives

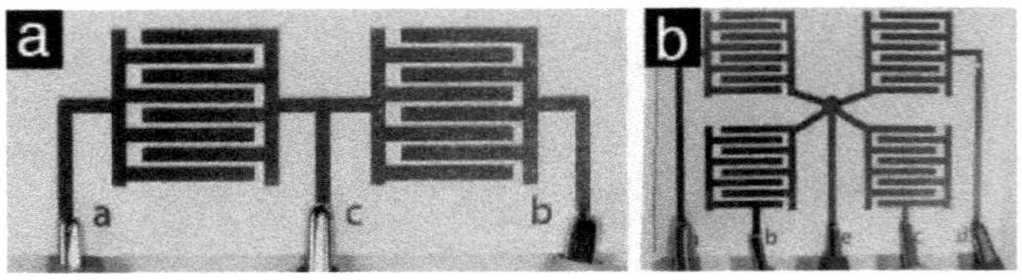

Figure 13: Printed forward error correction (FEC) for reconstructing sensor readings from a missing wire: a) 2+1 redundancy, b) 4+1 redundancy.

a continuous value. Nevertheless a combined reading of two or more electrodes can be designed, since the capacitance of two capacitors adds up if they are connected in a parallel circuit. Therefore, wire c connects to both electrodes in a parallel circuit; it adds up their respective capacitance. To prevent the wire c from generating a short-circuit between both electrodes, we split each electrode into two interdigitated parts which are mutually insulated. This ensures independent reading of a, b and c.

Redundancy: As long as any two wires of the block remain functional, the controller can reconstruct the value of the non-functional third wire, since $c = a + b$. If at any time the readings do not sum up (within a defined threshold) and one of the values is close to zero, it can be safely assumed this wire is not functional. Compared to the basic solution, this FEC approach reduces the number of redundant wires by 50%. However, only one of three wires can be removed instead of one of two wires.

The approach allows varying the proportion of redundancy in the encoding. Figure 13b shows how a block of 4 electrodes can be wired with one additional redundant wire. In this case, the number of wires added through redundancy is only 25% the number of payload wires. All electrode readings can be reconstructed as long as a maximum of one wire is broken, using the formula $e = a + b + c + d$. One sensor sheet may contain blocks of different redundancy levels; for instance outer areas, which are prone to cuts, could have more redundancy than inner areas. Theoretically, more electrodes can be connected with one redundant wire. In practice, the limit is defined by the sensing resolution of the controller. Beyond some point, imprecise readings, which add up, result in an imprecise reconstruction of a missing value.

Graceful degradation: The FEC encoding has one important beneficial side-effect. If two or more wires in a block are damaged, it is not possible to fully reconstruct the original sensor readings. However, due to the redundant wire, the sensing resolution gracefully degrades. If the redundant wire remains on the sensor sheet, it tells whether touch interaction is occurring somewhere in the block. Hence, the sensor is still providing data, yet with a reduced resolution in that area.

IMPLEMENTATION

We implemented our proof-of-concept prototypes with conductive inkjet printing. In contrast to larger-scale roll-to-roll processing, this allows us to easily experiment with different topologies and does not require a complex setup. The principles and technical solutions introduced in this paper transfer to other printing technologies that are capable of printing passive conductive traces. We are using silver ink to print conductive traces and electrodes on photo paper using an off-the-shelf inkjet printer [10]. The method requires no post-process sintering and is functional within minutes after printing. The sheet resistance is 0.21Ω/sq, with a thickness of 0.5 mm and a length of 50mm.

For the ease of implementation, we picked an electrode size of 20x20mm with an offset of 15mm. However, the approach supports smaller sizes; the maximum number of electrodes is defined by the microcontroller. Our wires have a minimum width of 0.5mm, which is defined by the printing process that we use. Industrial printing solutions allow for a much smaller width down to 40nm [5].

We realized the multi-layer sensor by printing each layer on a separate substrate and combining them with Z-Axis Electrically Conductive Tape from 3M [2]. This is an adhesive transfer tape with anisotropic electrical conductivity only on the z-axis, designed for interconnecting flexible circuits. The tape has the very important property that it can be easily cut. Our proof-of-concept implementation has two layers. We use scotch tape to insulate both layers from each other. In industrial-scale production, several conductive and insulating layers would be printed on top of each other, on the same substrate.

The implementation uses time-multiplexed loading mode capacitive sensing for detecting touch input. Processing of sensor readings is performed on an ATmega2560 microcontroller, which runs the Arduino CapSense Library [1] with a 10MΩ resistor per electrode. The controller features up to 48 input pins. To support a higher number of electrodes, multiple controllers can be connected. We picked a fairly large size for the ease of experimenting with different topologies. An industrial solution would support a much higher number of input pins per microcontroller. The connector is attached to the sensor sheet using 3M Z-Tape.

We normalize the raw data from partially cut electrodes. We used a simple calibration step. After cutting the sensor to a new shape, the user once moves her flat hand over the entire sensor, ensuring that the entire surface is covered. During this calibration step, the processor updates a calibration matrix, which holds one entry per electrode. Each entry stores the maximum capacitive value that is registered at this electrode during calibration. This maximum reading is proportional to the size of the remaining electrode.

EVALUATION

To validate the technical principles contributed in this paper, we performed two evaluations: (1) A mathematical simulation demonstrates that the proposed topologies support a variety of cut-out shapes. The results provide guidance in choosing a suitable topology. (2) A series of technical experiments demonstrate the technical feasibility of the principles.

Mathematical Simulation

Methodology

We implemented a simulation framework, which takes any sensor topology and any set of 2D shapes as input, modeled in SVG files. To account for the requirements listed above, the framework automatically scales, moves and rotates these shapes to simulate a large variety of cut-out shapes over the entire sensor sheet. As a performance index, it calculates the average proportion of the area on the cut-out that remains touch-interactive.

We simulate a *sensor sheet* with 266 x 266 mm, covered with a rectangular array of 26 x 26 electrodes, each sized 10 x 10 mm and spaced with 0.25 mm distance.

We simulate the following *topologies*: grid as the baseline (G), star (S), tree (T), overlaid star and tree (ST), overlaid tree and tree rotated by 90° around the center point (TT), as well as overlaid star, tree and rotated tree (STT).

In addition to the simulation of a multi-touch sheet that can be manufactured with industrial machinery, we also simulated the prototypes that we have built, using the dimensions and topologies introduced earlier in this paper.

We simulate the following *cut-out shapes*: triangle, rectangle, ellipse, star (Fig. 5), carve-out (Fig. 8b) and connector (Fig. 8d). Triangle, rectangle and ellipse are very basic shapes that are commonly used in a wide variety of tasks. Star, carve-out and connector are representing more complex shapes that are used in crafting and prototyping.

The minimum size of the shape has a bounding box of 150 x 150 mm, which is the width of an A5 sheet. A minimum of 16 non-uniform scales are randomly generated, with a maximum step size of 1.0. A minimum of 358 random locations are generated, with a maximum step size of 12.5 mm. A minimum of 8 random rotation angles are generated, with a maximum step size of 22.5 degrees.

The simulation algorithm calculates the performance index for each combination of $location_{(x,y)}$ * $scale_{(x,y)}$ * rotation of the shape as follows:

$$Sensing\_Coverage = \frac{A_{shape,el}}{A_{shape}} * \frac{A_{sheet}}{A_{sheet,el}}$$

with A_{shape} being the overall area of the cut-out shape, $A_{shape,el}$ being the area on the cut-out shape covered with sensor electrodes, A_{sheet} being the overall area of the entire sensor sheet, $A_{sheet,el}$ being the area on the entire sensor covered with sensor electrodes. The second fraction normalizes a more or less dense electrode arrangement on the sensor sheet. A partially cut electrode is considered functional if the remainder is still tethered to the connector and has at least 1/3 of the original electrode size. In this case, the readings are still clearly distinguishable from touching the wire. This is a conservative estimate.

The result is calculated as the average of the more than 30,000 simulated variations of each shape. Variations that do not entirely fit on the sensor sheet or do not contain the connector are not considered.

Results

As discussed above, the conventional grid topology, our baseline, supports only a few very specific shapes (most notably rectangles, and a few carefully selected polygons). In all cases, two sides of the shape must be straight lines that are laid out in a 90 degree angle. Moreover, these shapes have to be placed at one specific location on the sensor and must not be rotated.

Figure 14 shows the simulation results for the new topologies that considerably extend over the baseline. A large set of common shapes (triangles, rectangles, ellipses) can be placed at arbitrary locations and with any rotation on the sensor, yielding an average coverage of around 96%. The fabricated prototype has an average coverage of 86%. The tree topology performs less well, but still offers coverage above 83% (80% for the prototype).

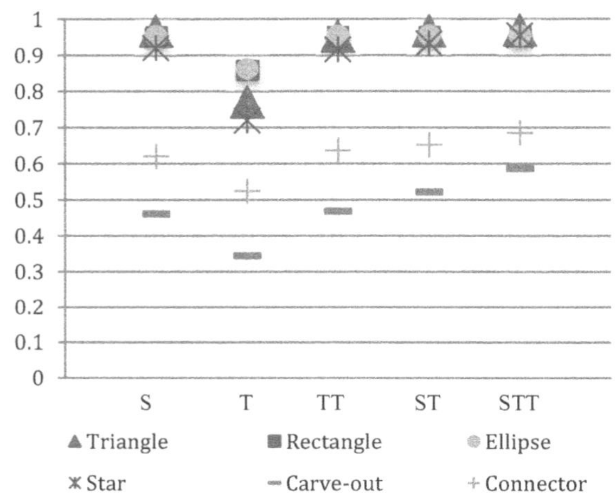

Figure 14: Sensing coverage of different shapes using various topologies. Shapes are freely rotated, translated and scaled on the sensor sheet.

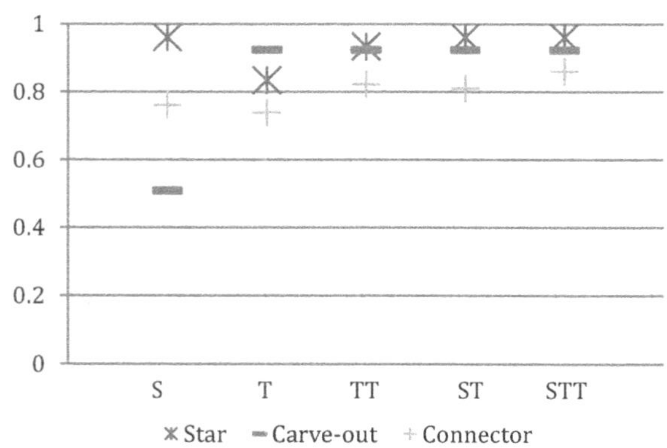

Figure 15: Sensing coverage of complex shapes when placed at one location without rotating, but with scaling.

Combinations of several topologies do not considerably increase the coverage for these simple shapes. In contrast, the coverage for complex shapes (star, carve-out, connector) is increased by using overlaid topologies. Particularly the combinations of star and tree improve the results. However, even with overlaid topologies, an average of roughly one third of the surface of the carve-out and connector shapes remain uncovered. This is because we simulate arbitrary placement and rotation on the sensor sheet.

For these complex shapes, we performed a second simulation in which we did not require location invariance and rotation invariance, but maintained scale invariance. From a practical perspective this means the user has to adjust the shape at a specific location and rotary angle. The results (Fig. 15) show that in this case even complex shapes are well supported. Even the most complex connector shape yields an average coverage of more than 85% (SD=1.6%).

Furthermore, we performed all simulations for topologies with redundant wiring added. This increased the results from 3% to 15%, with most improvement for the tree topology.

Technical Experiments

We conducted a series of technical experiments to demonstrate the technical feasibility of the principles. Since our implementation is based on a standard method for capacitive sensing, we did not evaluate basic touch sensing in detail, but rather focused on the critical technical aspects that are added by our contributions: we evaluated whether electrodes which fully or partially remain on the cut-out sensor are functional, whether dual-layer sensing is possible and whether the forward error correction can be realized.

Figure 16 shows a letter-sized sensor sheet that uses the star topology. It is cut into a user-defined shape (left part within the image). The sensor readings (right part) show that electrodes, which remain on the cut-out, are functional and capable of detecting touch input.

To evaluate the feasibility of cutting in more detail, we tested what is the minimum size of a partially cut electrode to

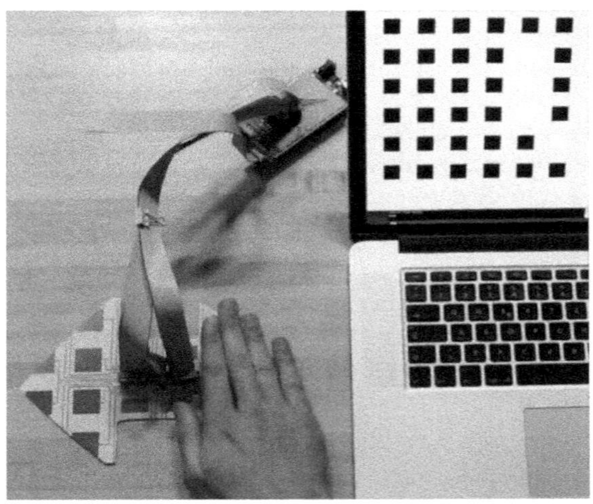

Figure 16: Normalized sensor readings of a partially cut sensor sheet.

Material/Electrode size	Wire	1/3	2/3	Full
Paper	0.34	1.90	5.30	8.12
Cardboard	0.06	0.13	0.26	0.34
Acryl	0.07	0.12	0.28	0.37
Plywood	0.06	0.10	0.22	0.32

Table 1: Capacitive sensor readings in pF of partially cut electrodes.

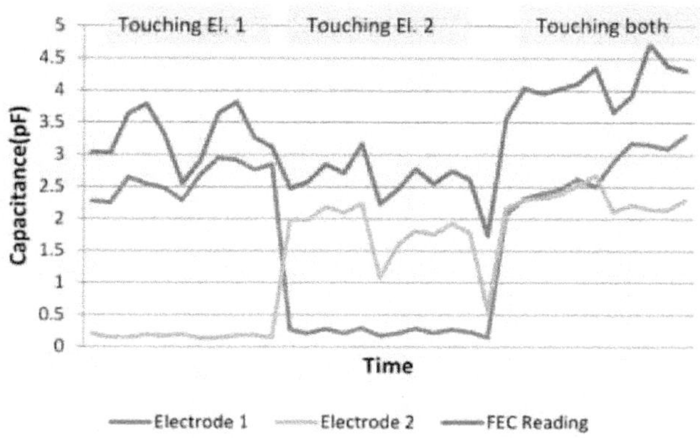

Figure 17: Capacitive sensor readings of a 2+1 redundant forward error correction block (depicted in Fig. 12a).

remain functional with a variety of materials the sensor is sandwiched into (paper, 3mm thick cardboard, 3mm acryl, 3mm plywood). If the electrode gets too small, it is not possible to reliably distinguish whether the user is touching the electrode or touching its wire. Table 1 shows data from electrodes of 2x2cm size, according to the dimensions used in the simulation. The data shows that if only 1/3 of the electrode remains, touch input can still be reliably analyzed.

In a third experiment, we studied whether a multi-layer sensor can be cut without creating a short circuit between the two layers. As expected, we were able to validate that the sensor remains functional and both layers independently connect the electrodes with the connector.

Last, we tested the forward error correction principle. Figure 17 shows the data plot for the setup illustrated in Fig. 13a. The data shows that the capacitive measurements of both electrodes roughly add up in the redundant FEC wire. The data demonstrates the feasibility of FEC, but shows that a proper selection of the threshold for sum detection is required, ideally set individually for each electrode. This could be done in the calibration step proposed above.

BENEFITS AND LIMITATIONS

Results from the evaluation show that the contributed sensor topologies support a variety of standard and more complex shapes. Those with a convex shape can be effectively supported by using just one layer with the star topology. They are rotation, location and scale invariant, providing a free-form cutting experience which comes close to cutting conventional, touch-insensitive materials. Overlaid topologies provide improved support for more complex shapes. Due to the infinite number of possible shapes, our validation can only provide some representative examples to shed light on the space of supported shapes.

We have not addressed how the sensor can cover three-dimensional shapes. This could be done by cutting a 2D shape and folding it to cover the 3D object, or by combining several distinct 2D shapes. We leave this for future work. While the substrate that is used in our prototypical setup is bendable, the printed traces are sensitive to strong bends (i.e. a notch). This can be overcome by using a print technology based on chemical deposition.

Our implementation of a cuttable Letter-sized sensor sheet has a lower number and density of electrodes than used in the simulation and is restricted to two layers. These restrictions are due to our prototypical manufacturing method. However, the dimensions were sufficient to test and validate the electronic properties of the sensor. The simulation results show what can be achieved with higher-density and multi-layer industrial fabrication.

The 1-pin-per electrode design requires more wires than the traditional grid, which raises questions of scalability. This is an inherent trade-off of the design space: either requiring fewer wires which comes at the cost of robustness, or making it robust to cuts using additional wires. In order to alleviate this issue we propose the following strategies: (1) While current print technologies can already realize wire widths of down to 40nm [6], which allows for a large number of wires on a single layer, wires can also be outsourced to one or more additional layers, using multi-layer printing. (2) Attaching multiplexers at the connector allows significantly reducing the number of input pins. (3) In a longer-term perspective, printing flexible multiplexers directly on the sensor sheet allows to bundle adjacent wires. Future work should also explore sensors with mixed topologies. These could comprise many smaller areas that are internally wired with the efficient grid design and connected with the controller using our more robust topologies.

Our implementation requires the connector to be located at one specific location on the sheet. Hence, only one shape can be cut out of a sheet. With larger sheets, this possibly wastes large portions of the material. Several spatially distributed access points on the same sheet could be realized by printing multiple layers with displaced topologies. This enables to cut several shapes out of one sheet.

The approach presented in this paper is compatible with a wide variety of non-conductive materials. As first examples, we discussed paper, cardboard, acryl and plywood. For use with transparent materials, the sensor grid could be made transparent using indium tin oxide (ITO).

CONCLUSIONS

In this paper, we contributed principles for a printed multi-touch sensor, which is robust against cuts and removed areas. The sensor can be embedded within conventional materials and touch-enable them, while maintaining the very direct customization possibilities of the material. The principles are inspired by topology and coding theory. We introduced novel topologies for the circuitry layout of multi-touch sensors that support a variety of cut-out shapes. Furthermore, we showed how to increase the set of supported shapes by combining several topologies and by printing a redundancy scheme that realizes a form of forward error correction. We evaluated strengths and limitations of the topologies in a mathematical simulation and presented a first proof-of-concept prototype to demonstrate the possibilities for crafting and prototyping.

We consider this first instantiation to be a point of departure for a novel interaction modality with printed electronics: physical cutting and shape adaptation. Future work should address other printed components and devices, including active ones, and show how these can be made robust for desired shape adaptations and against undesired damages.

ACKNOWLEDGMENTS

This work has partially been funded by the Cluster of Excellence Multimodal Computing and Interaction within the German Federal Excellence Initiative. We thank Pattie Maes for her valuable feedback and Yoshihiro Kawahara for technical advice.

REFERENCES

1. Arduino Capsense Library. http://playground.arduino.cc//Main/CapacitiveSensor?from=Main.CapSense. Accessed: April 2013.
2. Conductive Z Axis Tape. 3M. http://www.newark.com/3m/9703-25mm-x-33mtr/tape-conductive-z-axis-50micron/dp/95M4936?Ntt=3M+-+9703. Accessed: April 2013.
3. Conductive Inkjet Technology. http://www.conductiveinkjet.com. Accessed: April 2013.
4. Dietz, P. and Leigh, D. 2001. DiamondTouch: a multi-user touch technology. *Proc. UIST '01*, 219-226.
5. Feature size for printed electronics. http://www.semi.org/en/node/44156. Accessed: April 2013.
6. Fricker, M., Boddy, L. and Bebber, D. Network Organisation of Mycelial Fungi, 309-330, Springer Berlin Heidelberg. 2007.
7. Hartmann, B., Klemmer, S. R., Bernstein, M., Abdulla L., Burr, B., Robinson-Mosher, A., and Gee, J. Reflective physical prototyping through integrated design, test, and analysis. *Proc. UIST '06,* 299-308.
8. Holman, D. and Vertegaal, R. TactileTape: low-cost touch sensing on curved surfaces. *Proc. UIST '06*, 17-18.
9. Hudson, S. E. and Mankoff, J. Rapid construction of functioning physical interfaces from cardboard, thumbtacks, tin foil and masking tape. *Proc. UIST '06*, 289-298.
10. Kawahara, Y., Hodges S., Cook B., Zhang, C. Abowd G. Instant Inkjet Circuits: Lab-based Inkjet Printing to Support Rapid Prototyping of UbiComp Devices. *To appear in UbiComp'13*
11. Liu, S. and Guimbretière, F. FlexAura: a flexible near-surface range sensor. *Proc. UIST '12*, 327-330.
12. Mistree, B. F.T. and Paradiso, J. A. ChainMail: a configurable multimodal lining to enable sensate surfaces and interactive objects. *Proc. TEI '10,* 65-72.
13. Mueller, S., Lopes, P. and Baudisch, P. Interactive construction: interactive fabrication of functional mechanical devices. *Proc. UIST '12*, 599-606.
14. Paradiso, J.A., Lifton. J., and Broxton, M. Sensate Media - Multimodal Electronic Skins as Dense Sensor Networks. BT Technology Journal, Vol. 22, No. 4, pp. 32-44. 2004.
15. Pérez, G and Paradiso, J.A. B. S.N.A.K.E.: A Dynamically Reconfigurable Artificial Sensate Skin. B.Sc. Thesis. 2006
16. Qi, J and Buechley, L. Animating paper using shape memory alloys. *Proc. CHI '12*, 749-752.
17. Rekimoto, J. SmartSkin: an infrastructure for freehand manipulation on interactive surfaces. *Proc. CHI '02,* 113-120.
18. Rendl C., Greindl, P, Haller, M, Zirkl, M, Stadlober, B, and Hartmann. PyzoFlex: printed piezoelectric pressure sensing foil. *Proc. UIST '12*, 509-518.
19. Richardson, B., Leydon, K., Fernstrom, M., and Paradiso, J. A. 2004. Z-Tiles: building blocks for modular, pressure-sensing floorspaces. *Proc. CHI '02,* 1529-1532.
20. Rosenberg, I., Perlin, K., Hendee, C., Grau, A and Awad N. The UnMousePad: the future of touch sensing. *Proc. SIGGRAPH '09.*
21. Savage, V., Zhang, X., and Hartmann, B. 2012. Midas: fabricating custom capacitive touch sensors to prototype interactive objects. *Proc. UIST '12,* 579-588.
22. Song H., Benko, H., Guimbretiere, F., Izadi, S., Cao X., and Hinckley, K. Grips and gestures on a multi-touch pen. *Proc. CHI '11,* 1323-1332.
23. Tanenbaum, A. S., Wetherall, D. J. Computer Networks. Prentice Hall.
24. Tekscan. F-scan foot pressure mapping system. http://www.tekscan.com/3001E-pressure-sensor. Accessed: June 2013.
25. Tobjörk, D. and Österbacka, R. Paper Electronics. Adv. Mater. 23: 1935–1961. 2011
26. Todd K. Moon. Error Correction Coding: Mathematical Methods and Algorithms. John Wiley & Sons. 2005
27. Villar, N. and Gellersen, H. A malleable control structure for softwired user interfaces. *Proc. TEI '07*, 49-56.
28. Villar, N., Izadi, S., Rosenfeld, D., Benko, H., Helmes, J., Westhues, J., Hodges, S., Ofek, E., Butler, A., Cao, X., and Chen, B. Mouse 2.0: multi-touch meets the mouse. *Proc. UIST '09*, 33-42.
29. Wiethoff, A., Schneider, H., Rohs M., Butz, A. and Greenberg, S. Sketch-a-TUI: low cost prototyping of tangible interactions using cardboard and conductive ink. *Proc. TEI '12*, 309-312.
30. Willis K. D.D., Xu, C., Wu, K., Levin, G. and Gross M. D. Interactive fabrication: new interfaces for digital fabrication. *Proc. TEI '11*, 69-72.
31. Wimmer, R and Baudisch, P. Modular and deformable touch-sensitive surfaces based on time domain reflectometry. *Proc. UIST '11,* 517-526.

FingerPad: Private and Subtle Interaction Using Fingertips

Liwei Chan* Rong-Hao Liang*† Ming-Chang Tsai‡ Kai-Yin Cheng† Chao-Huai Su†
Mike Y. Chen‡ Wen-Huang Cheng* Bing-Yu Chen‡
*Academia Sinica †‡National Taiwan University
*{liwei,whcheng}@citi.sinica.edu.tw †{howieliang,keynes,domossu}@cmlab.csie.ntu.edu.tw
‡{r98944021,mikechen,robin}@ntu.edu.tw

ABSTRACT
We present FingerPad, a nail-mounted device that turns the tip of the index finger into a touchpad, allowing private and subtle interaction while on the move. FingerPad enables touch input using magnetic tracking, by adding a Hall sensor grid on the index fingernail, and a magnet on the thumbnail. Since it permits input through the pinch gesture, FingerPad is suitable for private use because the movements of the fingers in a pinch are subtle and are naturally hidden by the hand. Functionally, FingerPad resembles a touchpad, and also allows for eyes-free use. Additionally, since the necessary devices are attached to the nails, FingerPad preserves natural haptic feedback without affecting the native function of the fingertips. Through user study, we analyze the three design factors, namely posture, commitment method and target size, to assess the design of the FingerPad. Though the results show some trade-off among the factors, generally participants achieve 93% accuracy for very small targets (1.2mm-width) in the *seated condition*, and 92% accuracy for 2.5mm-width targets in the *walking condition*.

Author Keywords
Instant-available, private input, subtle interaction, eyes-free interaction, nail device, finger-mounted device.

ACM Classification Keywords
H.5.m. Information Interfaces and Presentation (e.g. HCI): Miscellaneous

General Terms
Design, Human Factors

INTRODUCTION
Recent developments have seen new proposals for glass-mounted displays for use in mobile computing. Though similar to head-mounted displays, glass-mounted displays (e.g., Google Glass) are specially designed to be lightweight, attachable, non-obstructive to natural vision, and with increased social acceptance.

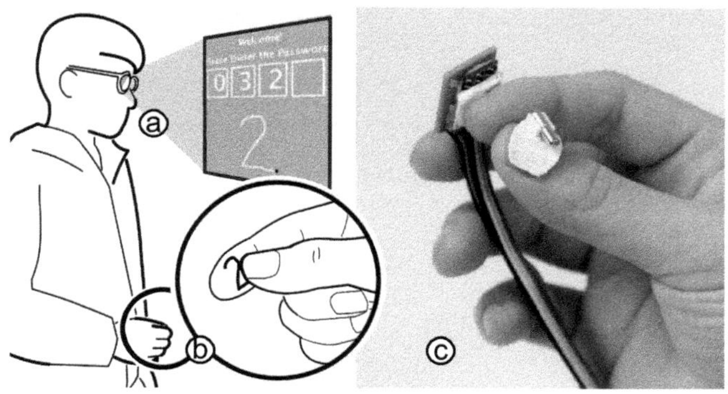

Figure 1. FingerPad enables touchpad function through pinch gesture. The user can (a) enter passwords to the private glass display (b) by drawing numbers with the thumb tip on the index fingertip. (c) The proposed technology is realized through magnetic tracking by adding a magnet and Hall sensor grid on the fingernails.

Although these types of displays permit personal and private visual outputs, their input methods may not offer the same privacy. For example, voice input is commonly used for glass-mounted displays because it is expressive and effective. However, voice input can be problematic in loud environments, and privacy issues arise with its use in public spaces (e.g., password input)[11]. Gesture input suffers from similar privacy concerns because input actions are easily observable.

To permit private input, recent research proposes subtle interactions [2, 10, 15], which are based on implicit movements and generally considered socially acceptable. For example, muscle interface [10] allows input through unobservable muscle movement. Foot gesture [12] detects subtle foot motions. Ring devices [1, 9] and fabrics [6] have been developed to support tap, spin, and slide inputs. Although these methods allow subtle inputs (and thus allow for privacy and social acceptability), they generally suffer from limited input space.

This paper presents FingerPad, a nail-mounted device that turns pinched fingertips into a touchpad, allowing private, and subtle interactions. As illustrated in Figure 1, the user treats the tip of their index finger as the touchpad, and their thumb as the touch stylus. FingerPad enables touchpad function using magnetic tracking, by adding a magnet and Hall sensors on the fingernails. Functionally, FingerPad resembles a touchpad that users can easily learn to use. Allowing for 2D touch input, FingerPad is suited for rich interactions, including pointing, menu selection, and stroke input.

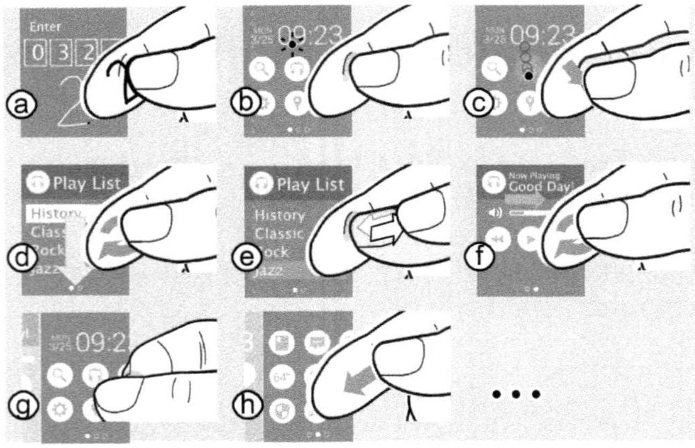

Figure 2. The walkthrough illustrates the use of FingerPad for glass displays. The graphics on the left of the subfigures are GUIs presented in the glass display view. Meanwhile, the graphics on the right of the subfigures are the suggested gestures that can be enabled using the proposed technique.

Benefits

Enabling touchpad functions through the pinch gesture suggests several benefits. (1) Private and socially acceptable: since the subtle movements between pinched fingers are naturally hidden by the operation hand, FingerPad is appropriate in contexts where privacy or social acceptance is a concern. (2) Highly mobile: owing to the dexterity and stability of the hands, FingerPad allows precise 2D input even while users are highly mobile, such as walking as tested in the study. (3) Natural haptic feedback: attachment of the device to the nails preserves natural haptic feedback from the fingertips, and dose not affect their native functions (e.g., griping small objects). (4) Instant availability: allowing for quick access (right under the fingertips), FingerPad can provide instant help between manual works (e.g., switching radio channels during hands on cooking). Additionally, by tracking through magnetism, FingerPad is occlusion-free (i.e., it can be used with the hands in the pocket).

SCENARIO

Figure 2 illustrates a scenario involving the application of FingerPad for private visual outputs, such as glass-mounted displays. Robin wears the glass display while on the train on his way to work. The glass display asks the subject, Robin, to provide an authentication password. Instead of using voice input, he chooses to use the FingerPad input owing to privacy concerns. (a) Robin individually writes four numbers on the tip of his index finger to unlock the glass application. (b) Robin presses on the tip of his index finger to enter the cursor mode, (c) then moves the cursor over the music app, and releases the pressure on his thumb to make a selection. (d) In the music list, he draws a circle on his fingertip to move to the Jazz category, and (e) clicks to enter the player page. (f) He then circles again to adjust the volume. (g) To jump to the home screen, he taps on the very tip of his index finger. Finally, (h) he swipes his thumb leftward, which takes him to the next app page, and plans to check the daily.

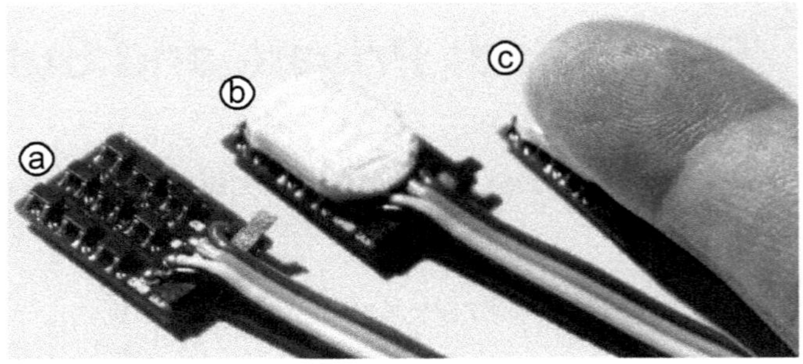

Figure 3. (a) The 3x3 sensor grid, and (b) a nail-shaped plate with a curved surface (c) suggesting fitness to the natural nail.

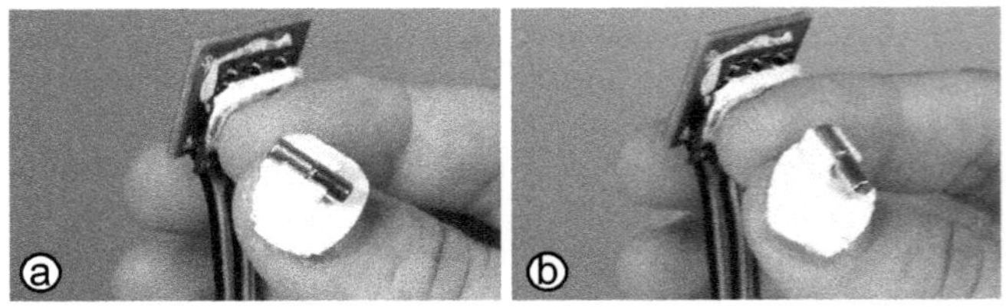

Figure 4. The magnet holder grips the magnet at a specific orientation. (a) The first design of the magnet holder. (b) The magnet orientation is pushed 30 degrees to the right to accommodate the bio-mechanism of the index and thumb fingers.

DESIGN CONSIDERATION

There are several possible methods to install 2D input capability on the fingertips, such as a fingerstall-like device with a touchpad added to the tip side, or a ring device [8] with a tiny optical mouse. Although fingerstalls and rings are reasonable forms, they can affect the native abilities of the fingertips. For example, fingerstalls influence the softness and friction of the fingertips, which are essential for gripping small objects. The ring mouse is a decent alternative, but constrains the finger. In comparison, FingerPad places no constraints on the fingertip, finger, and hand. To the knowledge of the authors, magnetic tracking is the only available solution that preserves the natural haptics of the fingers. However, the downside of magnetic tracking is that the device must be installed on two fingers.

PROTOTYPE

FingerPad is a pair of nail-mounted devices comprising a thin (2mm) magnetic sensing plate, and a plate of neodymium magnet. The sensing plate includes a 3x3 Winson WSH138 Hall sensor grid (Figure 3a), and each sensor is separated from the others by 2mm, which implies a total area of 12(W) x 12(H) mm^2. Each sensor element detects both N- and S-polar magnetic field intensities within the range 0 to 200 Gauss on a 512-point scale. An Arduino board with an ATmega32U4 microprocessor bridges the sensing plate and the computer. Based on the magnetic strength captured by the plate, FingerPad approximates the magnet position, transforms that position into finger-pad coordinates defined through user calibration (see the *Tracking* and *User calibration* sections), and sends these coordinates to the applications.

To attach the sensor plate firmly to the nail, we use a 3D printer to craft a nail piece that suggests the curved surface of a natural nail. As shown in Figure 3b, the sensor plate,

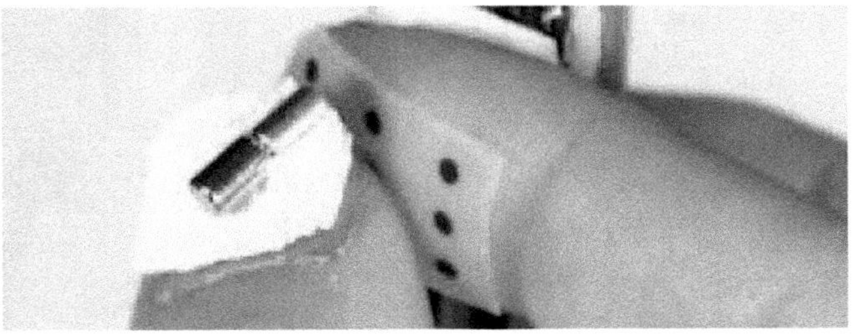

Figure 5. To guide the calibration, a translucent dot pattern is fixed to the index fingertip, thus helping to obtain good homographic transformations.

glued the nail piece, is further glued onto the nail of the user using twin adhesive tape. The use of glue helps users envision future nail devices that resemble artificial nails.

Another nail piece is created that holds the magnet and fixes its orientation. The magnet is placed such that the polar orientation of the magnet is parallel with the normal of the sensor grid when users place their thumb at the center of the tip of the index finger. Figure 4a shows the first design. To adapt the bio-mechanism of the thumb and index fingers, we improve the design by moving the magnet orientation 30 degrees to the right (Figure 4b). The magnet we used is a 3mm-diameter x 8mm-height cylindrical neodymium magnet, which allows effective sensing within 2.1cm using the sensor plate. Notably, this effective distance can be further extended with more sensitive magnetic field sensors, such as magnetometers [5].

Tracking

The finger-pad coordinate is presented as Cartesian coordinate. For the 3 x 3 sensor grid, the sensor at the lower left corner is set as the coordinate origin. The magnet position expressed in sensor-grid coordinates is approximated from bilinear weighting based on the magnetic strength read by each Hall sensor. Because the measured magnetic field strength is in fact a mix of quadratic and cubic attenuation, this approach merely approximates the magnet position. The *User calibration* section further regulates the positioning result.

Two strategies are applied to improve the positioning. First, the polarity of the magnet is positioned in parallel with the normal of the sensor grid, as shown in Figure 4b. Second, we exclude opposite polar values read by the sensors. When users tap on the edges of the index fingertip (e.g., the bottom area), the magnet orientation may deviate from the normal of the sensor grid, which leads some sensors to read opposite polar values.

User calibration

User calibration is performed to regulate the 2D positions calculated in the *Tracking* section, to the finger-pad coordinate in the index fingertip. To account for the non-linear mappings between the sensor-grid and the finger-pad coordinates, the finger-pad coordinate is divided into multiple sub-coordinates, and the nonlinearity is approximated by computing the homographic transformation between each sub-coordinate and the sensor-grid coordinate.

Typically, a homographic transformation can be determined by more than four pairwise correspondent points. To guide the calibration, a translucent dot pattern is fixed on the tip of the index finger. The dots are separated by 4mm in a Cartesian coordinate, and the 3 x 3 dot pattern suggests a normal fingertip size. We stick the pattern on the index fingertip area, as shown in Figure 5. The nine pairs of the correspondent points from the calibration process are then used to compute the homographic transformation for each of the four sub-coordinates. Provided the magnet orientation is correctly positioned, the calibration configuration can adapt well to fingers of different sizes and thickness.

Land-on detection

Although the Hall sensor plate can detect a hover state (e.g., when the thumb is near the index fingertip) based on the strength of the magnetic field, it is hard to determine when the thumb of the user contacts the index fingertip. To detect contact, an accelerometer is added to the Hall sensor plate to detect the impact associated with contact. Specifically, we calculate the derivative in the X-, Y-, and Z-axes, respectively, using a sliding window. Monitoring the values in the sliding window can identify a candidate for land-on when a positive derivative is followed by a negative one. Contact is only reported, when the thumb is simultaneously within the hover range. After contact, touch interactions by the user can be recognized until the thumb moves beyond the hover range.

Flick selection

While the upside of magnetic sensors is 2D tracking, whether users have released the pinch is tricky to determine from the observed magnetic strengths. We implemented take-off selection, which required the user to release the pinch sufficiently fast and far to produce a clear decrease in magnetic strengths. In the pilot, participants reported that fast take-off contradicted the sense of commitment. This problem was resolved by the second design, which used flick. In this design (1) users pushed to overcome the friction from the fingerprints, which better matched the sense of commitment. Additionally, (2) flick-up is more easily detectable because the magnetic-field intensity drops as a result of this motion in an inverse-cubic manner, compared to an inverse-square decrease in take-off selection.

We propose selection by flick, as illustrated in Figure 6. Moving the cursor over a target, the user makes a selection by flicking their thumb up. Upon exit from the hover state, we remove the cursor movement during the last 180 milliseconds (determined from a pilot testing) to eliminate unwanted cursor movement. The final cursor position determines the selection. The side effect of flick selection is that the user may experience unwanted cursor movement before the thumb exits the hover state.

APPLICATION

Based on the touchpad functions provided by the prototype, we implement the touch cursor, gesture input, and stroke input functions to demonstrate the capability of FingerPad. The implemented application is described in the Scenario section. The touch cursor function allows a user to use a long press

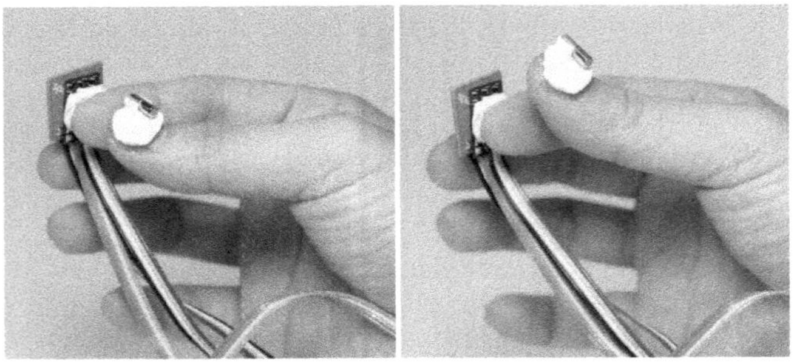

Figure 6. The user makes a selection by flicking the thumb up.

to enter the cursor mode, which reveals the cursor on the display (e.g., the glass interface). Movement of the thumb on the index fingertip allows the user to freely move the cursor. The flick selection then allows the user to make a menu selection. Swipe and circling gestures can be used in the gesture input. In a page view, the user can swipe left or right to view the subsequent or previous page. In a list view, the user can make a clockwise or counter-clockwise circling gesture to scroll down or up through the list. In terms of stroke input, the unistroke recognizer [14] is adapted for numeric input, which allows users to write the password or phone numbers.

USER STUDY

This study seeks to understand user performance in a mobile scenario that included seated and walking conditions. We proposed the flick method as a baseline method, and included the bimanual click method to reveal the upper-bound results. Finally, this study also seeks to determine how small a target users can select to learn the user limitations.

Task and Conditions

The participants are instructed to move the cursor over the target shown in the screen and make the selection using single-handed flick selection method or the bimanual clicker method with the non-pointing hand depending on the conditions. The target color changes when the cursor enters the target square. On successful selection, the target disappears and the next target appears on the screen. We measured task time and error rate for target side lengths of 10mm, 5mm, 2.5mm, 1.2mm and 0.6mm. The 0.6mm case is included to test user limitations. The experiment screen is a 13-inch macbook air. Only a sub-region (3-inch, 4:3) in the center of the screen is used. The cursor is absolute mapping.

In the *seated condition*, the participants sat on the chair in front of the table with the screen facing them. The participants , and were instructed to adjust the chair height such that they could rest their dominant hands on the table for support (Figure 7a). The participants ensured that they could see the smallest (0.6mm) target clearly. The screen was moved closer to the participants if necessary to achieve this. In the *walking condition*, subjects performed tasks on the treadmill. The screen was placed on top of the treadmill control platform, as shown in Figure 7b. In principle, the screen in both conditions was positioned at a normal reading distance (40cm). The treadmill was set to a normal walking speed (3.5 km/hour)

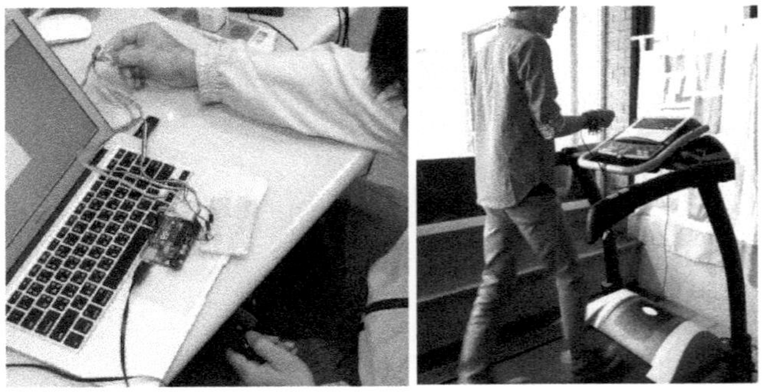

Figure 7. The study setup for the seated condition (left) and walking condition (right).

and participants adjusted this speed by up to 0.5km in either direction according to their preference.

Interface and apparatus

The participants wore the sensor part of the device on the index fingernail, and the magnet part on the thumbnail. Owing to differences in nail sizes and the way participants moved their thumbs on the index finger pads, participants were assisted in wearing the device, and adjusted the magnet holder orientation to accommodate interpersonal tapping habits. The pilot testing found that the thick fingers from some male participants could degrade the tracking performance using the original magnet setting. To avoid tracking errors, the magnet was replaced with a wider magnet (4mm-diameter x 8mm-height) that ensures the tracking performance.

Experimental design

The study design was 2 x 2 x 5 x 12 (Condition x Commitment method x Target Size x Target Position) with three repetitions for each cell. The Condition was the between-subject variable. The target sizes were 10mm, 5mm, 2.5mm, 1.2mm and 0.6mm, and the target positions were the 12 centroids of a regular 4 x 3 grid. For each trial, task completion time and errors were recorded. The different commitment methods were counterbalanced, and the target sizes and positions were randomized.

Participants

22 participants (10 female) with mean age 26.9 years old (*SD*: 3.9), ranging from 22 to 38 years olds, were recruited from the university. Each subject was rewarded by a small gift for their participation. The task took about 30 minutes. All participants were right-handed and had experience of using touch input devices.

Results and discussion

A multi-way ANOVA found there was a significant difference in completion time between different target sizes, and existed an interaction effect between the commitment method and the posture. While for the error rate, it found only [target size x posture] and [commitment method x posture] interactions. To further evaluate how these factors (i.e. the posture, the commitment method, and the target size) affected user performance, we did the following post-hoc tests.

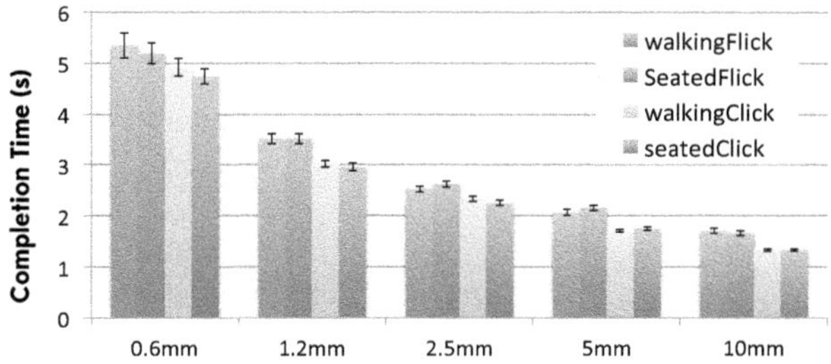

Figure 8. The study completion times, with 95% confidence intervals, of different target sizes in two commitment methods under the seated and walking conditions.

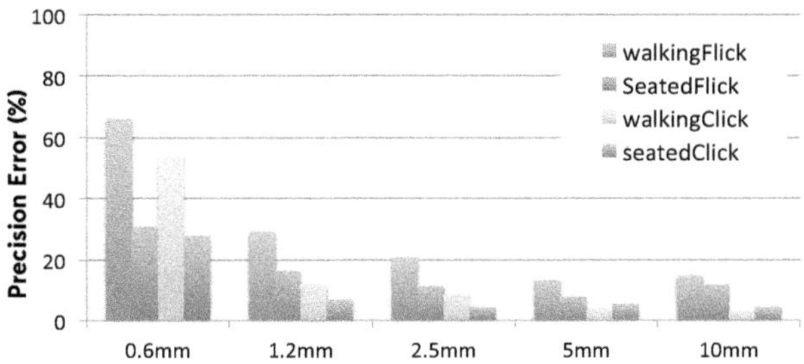

Figure 9. The study error rates of different target sizes for two commitment methods under the seated and walking conditions.

Posture

To analyze the data, we ran the pairwise *t*-test to determine whether posture affects user performance. Completion time did not differ significantly between the seated and walking conditions. However, error rate differed significantly between the two postures when the target size was below 2.5mm. In terms of design insights, if the system can detect user posture, it can adjust UI layout accordingly. For example, the system can provide seated users with a tight layout and compact information, and can provide walking users with a loose layout and abstract information. However, if users want a consistent user experience, the target size should be larger than 2.5 mm.

Commitment method

The pairwise *t*-test was run to determine whether different commitment methods for both postures affect user performance. The results showed that the clicker method was significantly faster than the flick method only for the walking posture. As for the error rate, while in the walking condition, the difference in error rate between the flick and clicker methods, were statistically significant. Regarding design insights, performance can be improved by choosing different commitment methods. However, there exists a trade-off between the two methods. Although the clicker method can perform better, it requires bimanual interaction. Compared to the clicker method, users can perform the task with only one hand, which frees the other hand.

Target size

The pairwise *t*-test was run to learn whether different target sizes affect user performance. For both completion time and error rate, the statistics show that 0.6mm differs significantly compared to all other target sizes for subjects adopting a walking or seated posture. Regarding completion time, 1.2mm differs significantly compared to 5mm and 10mm for subjects adopting a walking or seated posture. Hence, in terms of design, we suggest the control should exceed 1.2mm to maximize user experience.

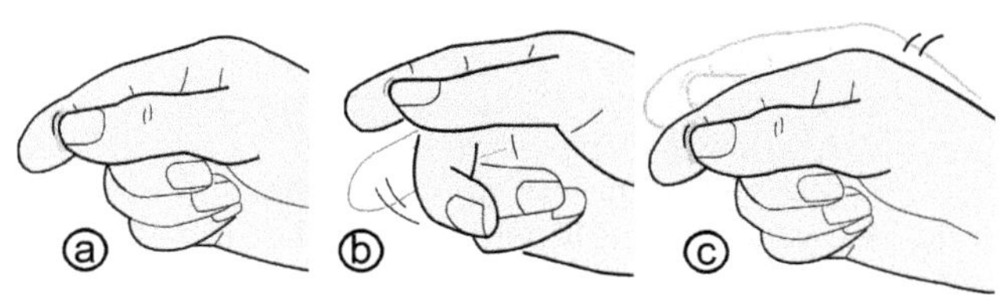

Figure 10. Other commitment methods described by the participants are as follows: (a) press, (b) move the middle finger, and (c) move the wrist.

Based on the results of the user study, we were also impressed by the ability of users in cursor control under the walking condition, even though cursor shaking was inevitable. When working on the smallest target, the participants reported that they reduced shaking by pressing hard during the pinch gesture. Specifically, they first moved the cursor to an area near the target, then squeezed the fingertips, and made minor adjustments to the cursor position to achieve fine control.

Summary

Generally, through the user studies, we can conclude three design insights. First, posture affects performance, but this influence is significantly decreased provided the target size is sufficiently large (e.g., larger than 2.5mm). Second, performance differs with commitment method. Based on considering comfort and convenience, alternative designs of the single-handed commitment methods can also be considered. For example, hard pressing (Figure 10a), moving the middle finger in the air (Figure 10b), or slightly twisting the wrist (Figure 10c) can be adopted. Third, the target size of the control buttons should not be too small, such as smaller than 0.6mm. Nevertheless, the system design should consider the trade-offs among the three factors.

RELATED WORK

This work is related to private and subtle interaction, and finger-worn devices, and magnetic tracking.

Private and subtle interaction

Several subtle interaction techniques have previously been proposed. Costanza et al. [2] used electromyography to sense subtle motionless gestures. Saponas et al. [10] used a similar technique to sense different finger gestures. Furthermore, Scott et al. [12] proposed using mobile devices located in the pocket of the user to sense foot gestures. Pinstripe [6] allows users to perform subtle interactions by pinching and rolling their clothes. Other works [1, 9] used rings as a subtle input device. Still, these techniques could only support limited gesture input. In contrast, FingerPad is functionally equivalent to a touchpad, which implies that it can provide more dimensions for the input space.

Finger-worn input devices

Several technologies have been proposed that use finger-worn devices to sense gestures. FingerRing [3] placed accelerometers on every finger to sense different chord gestures. UbiFinger [13] allowed control of house appliances through finger gestures by placing an IR transmitter and bending/touch sensors on the index finger together with an accelerometer on the wrist. Magic finger [16] extended the dimensions of touching gestures through a finger mounted camera. Since FingerPad uses pinched fingers as the input, it offers more privacy and subtlety than these works.

Magnetic tracking

Magnetic tracking has previously been used to sense gestures remotely. For instance, Han et al. [4] tracked a finger-mounted magnet for handwriting input. Similarly, Abracadabra [5] used a finger-mounted magnet to control a watch. Meanwhile, Nenya [1] used a magnet mounted in a finger ring for device control. Liang et al. [7] used a magnet mounted in a stylus and the Hall sensor array to enable input on arbitrary surfaces. Compared with these works, FingerPad provides more private and subtle input through pinched fingertips.

CONCLUSION

This paper presented FingerPad, a nail-mounted device that enables touchpad functions from users manipulating their index fingertips, allowing for private and subtle interaction on the move. The study shows good user ability to control a cursor using the pinch gesture with FingerPad. The statistics demonstrate that users can achieve 93% accuracy for very small targets (1.2mm-width) in the seated condition, and 92% accuracy for 2.5mm-width targets in the walking condition, which is sufficient for mobile usage. This study makes design insights based on exploration of three factors, namely posture, commitment method, and target size. Despite inevitable trade-offs among these factors, this study still demonstrates that the FingerPad can work well for subtle interactions.

In the future, although the FingerPad is intended for use with mobile glass displays, the technology could also be applied without visual support. Different commitment methods can be explored in the future to create different alternative gestures. Once devices designed for rich private output are invented, users will need to use them privately with a rich input device, and the input method should be sufficiently subtle to achieve social acceptability, as is achieved by the FingerPad.

ACKNOWLEDGMENTS

We gratefully acknowledge the helpful comments of the Associate Chairs and the anonymous reviewers. This paper was partially supported by National Science Council of Taiwan under NSC101-2219-E-002 -026, NSC101-2221-E-001-016, NSC102-2622-E-002-006-CC2, NSC101-2628-E-002-030-MY2, and the MediaTek Fellowship Award program.

REFERENCES

1. Ashbrook, D., Baudisch, P., and White, S. Nenya: subtle and eyes-free mobile input with a magnetically-tracked finger ring. In *Proc. ACM CHI '11* (2011), 2043–2046.
2. Costanza, E., Inverso, S. A., Allen, R., and Maes, P. Intimate interfaces in action: assessing the usability and subtlety of emg-based motionless gestures. In *Proc. ACM CHI '07* (2007), 819–828.
3. Fukumoto, M., and Suenaga, Y. FingerRing: a full-time wearable interface. In *Proc. ACM CHI '94* (1994), 81–82.
4. Han, X., Seki, H., and Hikizu, M. Wearable handwriting input device using magnetic field. In *Proc. IEEE SICE '07* (2007), 365–368.
5. Harrison, C., and Hudson, S. E. Abracadabra: wireless, high-precision, and unpowered finger input for very small mobile devices. In *Proc. ACM UIST '09* (2009), 121–124.
6. Karrer, T., Wittenhagen, M., Heller, F., and Borchers, J. Pinstripe: eyes-free continuous input anywhere on interactive clothing. In *Proc. ACM UIST '10* (2010), 429–430.
7. Liang, R.-H., Cheng, K.-Y., Su, C.-H., Weng, C.-T., Chen, B.-Y., and Yang, D.-N. GaussSense: attachable stylus sensing using magnetic sensor grid. In *Proc. ACM UIST '12* (2012), 319–326.
8. Ni, T., and Baudisch, P. Disappearing mobile devices. In *Proc. ACM UIST '09* (2009), 101–110.
9. Ogata, M., Sugiura, Y., Osawa, H., and Imai, M. iRing: intelligent ring using infrared reflection. In *Proc. ACM UIST '12* (2012), 131–136.
10. Saponas, T. S., Tan, D. S., Morris, D., Balakrishnan, R., Turner, J., and Landay, J. A. Enabling always-available input with muscle-computer interfaces. In *Proc. ACM UIST '09* (2009), 167–176.
11. Sawhney, N., and Schmandt, C. Nomadic radio: speech and audio interaction for contextual messaging in nomadic environments. *ACM Trans. Comput.-Hum. Interact. 7*, 3 (2000), 353–383.
12. Scott, J., Dearman, D., Yatani, K., and Truong, K. N. Sensing foot gestures from the pocket. In *Proc. ACM UIST '10* (2010), 199–208.
13. Tsukada, K., and Yasamura, M. Ubi-finger: Gesture input device for mobile use. In *Proc. APCHI '02* (2002), 388–400.
14. Wobbrock, J. O., Wilson, A. D., and Li, Y. Gestures without libraries, toolkits or training: a $1 recognizer for user interface prototypes. In *Proc. ACM UIST '07* (2007), 159–168.
15. Wolf, K., Naumann, A., Rohs, M., and Müller, J. Taxonomy of microinteractions: Defining microgestures based on ergonomic and scenario-dependent requirements. In *Proc. INTERACT '11* (2011), 559–575.
16. Yang, X.-D., Grossman, T., Wigdor, D., and Fitzmaurice, G. Magic finger: always-available input through finger instrumentation. In *Proc. ACM UIST '12* (2012), 147–156.

Pursuit Calibration: Making Gaze Calibration Less Tedious and More Flexible

Ken Pfeuffer
Lancaster University
Lancaster, United Kingdom
k.pfeuffer@lancaster.ac.uk

Mélodie Vidal
Lancaster University
Lancaster, United Kingdom
m.vidal@lancaster.ac.uk

Jayson Turner
Lancaster University
Lancaster, United Kingdom
j.turner@lancaster.ac.uk

Andreas Bulling
Max Planck Institute for Informatics
Saarbrücken, Germany
andreas.bulling@acm.org

Hans Gellersen
Lancaster University
Lancaster, United Kingdom
hwg@comp.lancs.ac.uk

ABSTRACT
Eye gaze is a compelling interaction modality but requires user calibration before interaction can commence. State of the art procedures require the user to fixate on a succession of calibration markers, a task that is often experienced as difficult and tedious. We present *pursuit calibration*, a novel approach that, unlike existing methods, is able to detect the user's attention to a calibration target. This is achieved by using moving targets, and correlation of eye movement and target trajectory, implicitly exploiting smooth pursuit eye movement. Data for calibration is then only sampled when the user is attending to the target. Because of its ability to detect user attention, pursuit calibration can be performed implicitly, which enables more flexible designs of the calibration task. We demonstrate this in application examples and user studies, and show that pursuit calibration is tolerant to interruption, can blend naturally with applications and is able to calibrate users without their awareness.

Author Keywords
Eye gaze calibration; Gaze interaction; Gaze interfaces; Eye tracking; Smooth pursuit eye movement.

ACM Classification Keywords
H.5.2. Information interfaces and presentation: User Interfaces

INTRODUCTION
Eye gaze is long established for human-computer interaction [29, 7, 8]. As input device, eye gaze has been shown to be fast and highly accurate while requiring no acquisition time [20]. Our eyes are always at the ready and naturally involved in attentive processes and selection of what we are interested in [24]. We can use our eyes to interact over a distance [23], and in combination with other modalities [22, 31]. However, although pervasive in usability labs, eye gaze is still rarely used in everyday interaction with computers. This is attributed to the calibration problem, as users are required to register the input space of their eye movement with the output space of a display before they can start to interact.

UIST'13, October 8–11, 2013, St. Andrews, United Kingdom.
Copyright © 2013 ACM 978-1-4503-2268-3/13/10...$15.00.
http://dx.doi.org/10.1145/2501988.2501998

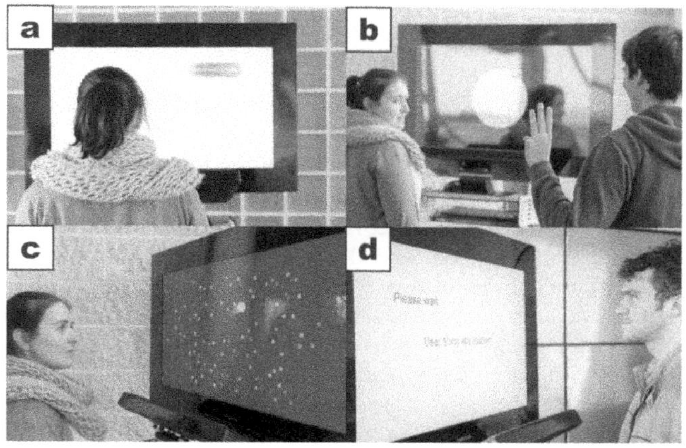

Figure 1: *Pursuit calibration* is based on moving targets (a), tolerates interruptions (b), can blend with application tasks (c) and calibrate users even when they are not aware (d).

State of the art eye tracking systems are based on remote gaze estimation using the pupil center and corneal reflections [5]. The movement of the pupil relative to reflections on the eye can be accurately tracked with a single camera, but a user calibration is necessary to register estimated gaze direction with the target interaction space. The registration requires sampling of eye gaze at known points, for which the state of the art procedure is to present the user with a succession of targets to fixate. Theoretically fewer points would suffice to establish the input-output mapping, but in practice five or more points are used, spread over the target space. Unfortunately, this is a process that presents users with a task that is of poor usability [14], often experienced as difficult [19], and frequently described as tedious [28, 16, 33].

We address the calibration problem by introducing *pursuit calibration* as a method that overcomes the rigidity of existing procedures. The method is based on the smooth pursuit eye movement that we naturally perform when we follow a moving object with our eyes [18]. Recent work demonstrated that smooth pursuits can be used to identify moving objects a user is looking at, by correlating the user's eye movement with the trajectory of the objects [26, 25]. We adapt this approach by basing calibration on presentation of a moving target to the user and continuous sampling of calibration points while the user follows the target. Because our method is based on correlation of eye and target movement, we can reliably determine when a user is attending to the target. Automatic detection of user attention to a known point is a fundamental advance over existing procedures, as it enables more flexible calibration task designs – there is no rigid start and end, calibration can stop and resume, and users need not be explicitly aware of the task.

Figure 1 illustrates pursuit calibration, and some of the advances the method provides over existing procedures. Instead of having to dwell on static points, users follow a moving calibration target (Figure 1a) during the whole procedure. The method is intelligent in collecting gaze data only when the user actually attends, and this can be done iteratively. If a user is interrupted during the calibration, they can simply resume and do not have to start all over again (Figure 1b). There is no need to make start or end of the calibration explicit, as calibration data can be automatically collected as soon as a user's attention is detected, and for as long as deemed necessary for a given application purpose. The calibration can thus be implicit, and blended into an application experience. Figure 1c illustrates the creative possibilities of leading from interaction with moving objects (here, shooting stars) smoothly to interaction with static content (star constellations). As calibration is implicit, it is not necessary that the user actively cooperates, and interfaces can be designed to calibrate users unawares. Figure 1d illustrates a waiting screen that provides an illusion of idle waiting while the system actually calibrates the user.

Our work makes four contributions. First, we introduce pursuit calibration and the concept of using correlation of eye and target movement for detecting user attention. Second, we provide a performance characterisation of the method against a baseline of state of the art static point calibration that shows that it is possible to achieve the same level of gaze estimation accuracy in potentially less time. Third, we demonstrate the method in three application examples that illustrate the flexibility gained for designing the calibration task. Fourth, we show that the pursuit calibration method is interruption-tolerant, and able to calibrate users without their awareness.

RELATED WORK

The requirement for user calibration is well recognised as a critical problem for wider adoption of eye gaze. Morimoto and Mimica, in their 2005 survey, concluded "although it has been thought for long that [eye gaze tracking devices] have the potential to become important computer input devices as well, the technology still lacks important usability requirements that hinders its applicability", pointing specifically at calibration as a task of poor usability [14]. It is not natural for users to dwell on static calibration markers, and the protocol of following through a succession of markers presented on the screen is dull and tiring for the eye. Schnipke and Todd's account of "trials and tribulations of using an eye-tracking system" [19] might be dismissed as dated but there is hardly any publication of eye-tracked user studies that does not report calibration problems. Villanueva et al., and others in eye tracking research, have described the calibration task as "most tedious" [28].

Consequently, calibration is a significant focus in eye tracking research. A common thrust is to develop advanced geometric models to reduce the number of calibration points that need to be sampled to achieve good accuracy (a generally agreed accuracy target is 1° of visual angle), for example to only two points [28, 16]. Commercial suppliers advertise "child-friendly versions" where only two points are used, and researchers have proposed single-point multi-glint calibration also with infants in mind [6]. However, although a single point with multiple reflections is theoretically sufficient, good accuracy generally requires additional points [27]. Pursuit calibration contrasts the quest for fewer calibration points, as it involves continuous collection of point samples while the user follows a moving target.

A range of work are aimed at using the eyes for interaction while avoiding calibration altogether. Eye gestures use relative eye movements to encode commands for computer input and thus do not require any registration with the output space [2]. Lightweight computer vision techniques have been used to detect attention to displays [21] and to classify whether users look straight at a display or to the left or right [32]. *Pursuits* correlate relative eye movements with the movement of objects on a display, and thus enable gaze selection of moving objects without estimating gaze direction [26, 25]. All these efforts have in common that they compromise expressiveness, whereas pursuit calibration is aimed at accurate registration of eye gaze with the output space. Other approaches aim to achieve good accuracy without calibration but rely on additional instrumentation [13], or longitudinal training for probabilistic gaze estimation [1]. Pursuit calibration, in contrast, does not avoid calibration but is aimed to make the process less tedious and more flexible.

Calibration Games [4] share our motivation to make calibration a more natural task. The system transforms the calibration into a game to make it more pleasant. Users perceived the calibration as more enjoyable while calibration data quality was not compromised by the game design. However they examine calibration in general while we focus on gaze calibration which they did not specifically address. Renner et al. [17] demonstrated playful integration of gaze calibration in a virtual reality environment. A dragonfly flew into the view of the user every time a calibration was required and directed the user from point to point. To ensure that the user

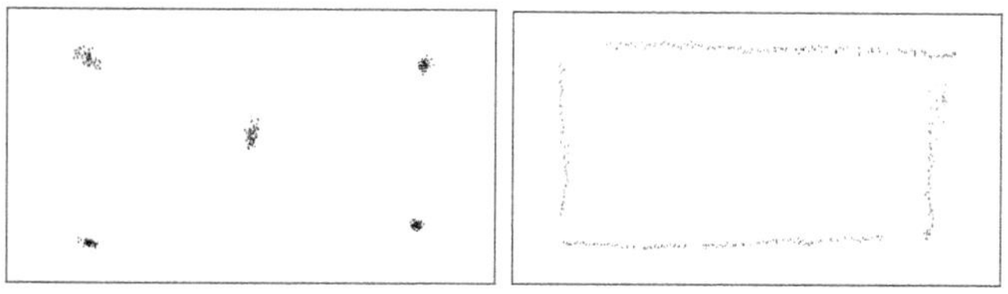

(a) Point clouds of a 5-point calibration. (b) Samples of a moving-target calibration.

Figure 2: Samples of a point-to-point and a moving-target calibration. Contrary to a point-to-point method, a moving-target calibration cannot average each point, however the samples are more equally distributed across the screen.

truly follows this target, the gaze estimation of the previous calibration was regarded. In a comparison to a standard point-to-point calibration, users found the guided approach more enjoyable.

A few papers present moving targets for calibration. Kang and Malpeli [9] calibrate their system to cats with moving targets, because fixations on stationary targets are often unreliable. Here, they use horizontally moving targets to calibrate the vertical eye position and vice versa. This resulted in an accurate calibration and emphasized the advantage of not relying on successful fixations. They also point out that this method is applicable to any species and any recording system. Kondou and Ebisawa [10] evaluated a gaze detection system with user head movements during calibration. Two point-to-point and one moving-target calibration methods were compared. The calibration with moving targets yielded the highest accuracy. These efforts show that calibration with moving targets is feasible and producing good results. However, our approach introduces automatic detection of user attention as an additional feature, achieved by correlation of eye and target movement.

PURSUIT CALIBRATION

The goal of a gaze calibration method is to collect samples of eye gaze at known points in the output space, in order to calculate an accurate gaze-to-display mapping. The pursuit calibration method approaches sampling in a novel way, by displaying a smoothly moving target to the user. The method automatically detects when the user is following the target with their gaze, by correlating the eye movement trajectory with the trajectory of the target. Only points on the display through which the target passes while the user is looking at it, are collected as samples for calibration.

Figure 2 illustrates how sampling of gaze points with pursuit calibration fundamentally differs from sampling with a conventional calibration procedure. A point-to-point calibration collects multiple gaze samples at each of a small number of points, typically at the corners and the centre of the display (Figure 2a). In contrast, pursuit calibration collects one sample for each display point at which the user followed the target. Since the target moves continuously, a larger number of display points can be sampled but each only once (see Figure 2b).

Method implementation

Pursuit calibration builds on recent work in which eye movement was correlated with the movement of screen objects, in order to determine which of a number of objects a user is looking at [25]. As in that work, our method takes uncalibrated gaze coordinates from the eye tracker as input, in the form of a synchronised time series. A moving window is used over which the gaze coordinates are compared with the coordinates of the moving target. The correlation is computed by using Pearson's product-moment correlation for the horizontal and the vertical gaze position. If the returned correlation coefficient lies above a defined threshold, the user must have followed the trajectory of the moving target with their eyes, and eye gaze is sampled at the current position of the target for later calibration. Both the size of the moving window and the threshold for correlation are controlled by the designer, and for this work have been based on Vidal *et al.*'s analysis of the Pursuits method [25].

Once sampling has been completed, the collected gaze points are fitted to a homography model, representing a perspective projection of gaze and screen plane. This is implemented with the homography computation of OpenCV, using RANSAC for outlier elimination with default parameter settings [3].

Design considerations

Attention detection. Automatic detection of user attention is the distinguishing feature of pursuit calibration. The design choices influencing attention detection are the length of time window and the threshold set for correlation of gaze and target movement. The confidence that a user is following a moving target increases with evidence over a longer time window, and with a higher threshold, but as a trade off will effect the sampling rate as more samples will fail the correlation test.

Path. A moving target for pursuit calibration can follow any path across the display. A main design consideration is to sample the target interaction space in a representative manner to obtain a well-balanced mapping. A pilot study in which we investigated the influence of the target's path indicated that the most accurate results are obtained when a path along the borders of the display is followed (see Figure 3). This is similar to a point-to-point calibration where the static points are often near the screen's edge.

Sample size. The more samples are collected, the more accurate the calibration will be, but also the more time consuming. The calibration task can be designed for calibration in a fixed amount of time, during which as many samples as possible are collected. Alternatively, target movement could continue until a desired number of samples have been collected.

Target velocity. Because the target is moving, its velocity is relevant as well. The velocity of a human smooth pursuit eye movements is limited to up to $30°/s$ [30], and greater speeds lead to catch-up eye movements. However, the detection rate for smooth pursuits also decreases when targets are too slow [26]. The speed of the target also affects the duration of the calibration: if the target moves slowly, it will take longer to sample the output space.

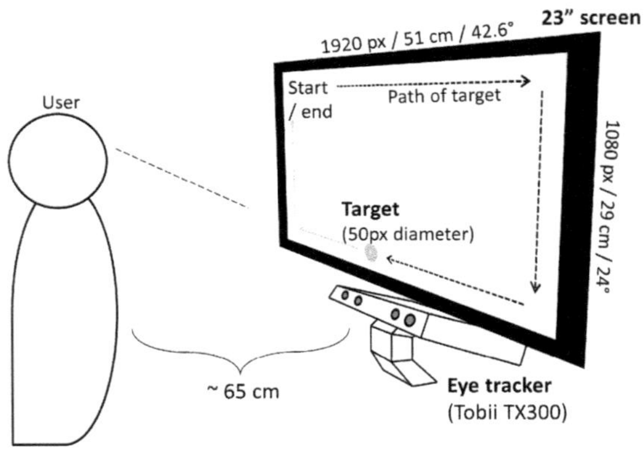

Figure 3: Moving target calibration setup during the accuracy evaluation.

ACCURACY EVALUATION

From a usability point of view, the most important factors for a successful calibration are its accuracy and how time-consuming it is. We therefore investigate the accuracy of pursuit calibration depending on its duration and target velocity. In order to make sense of the results, we compare it to a baseline point-to-point calibration procedure. We use the Tobii 5-points calibration to represent a standard of calibration for the eye-tracking industry. It takes 19 seconds overall, during which the user has to fixate on four points at screen corners and one at the center, and involves a moving target to guide the user from one point to another.

The calibration stimulus we evaluate is that of a target that moves along the borders of the screen in a rectangle (see Figure 3). We test two types of design: one where the speed of the moving target is constant, and one where it accelerates on straight lines and slows down when approaching a corner, for a smoother transition. The shorter the duration of the stimulus, the quicker the target travels. We conducted a pilot study to determine which range of speeds is feasible: four users performed each calibration, calibration duration was varied, speed varied with respect to duration and path of target remained rectangular. Data analysis resulted in the following ranges of durations/speeds for our study evaluation: for the constant speed case durations of $\{5, 10, 15, 20, 25, 30\}$ seconds, which in visual angles equates to a target speed of $\{23.3, 11.6, 7.6, 5.8, 4.7, 3.9\}°/s$, and for the accelerated speed durations of $\{5, 7.5, 10, 12.5, 15, 17.5\}$ seconds (target speed of $\{23.3, 15.5, 11.6, 9.3, 7.8, 6.6\}°/s$). Accelerated speed has lower durations because calibration was satisfying with shorter durations during the pilot study. The acceleration reached a peak speed of $35.77°/s$ and slowed down to $1.1°/s$ at the corners.

Participants performed 13 calibrations: first the Tobii baseline, then the twelve other in randomised order. In order to calculate the accuracy of each stimulus, after each calibration procedure we presented a test where participants had to fixate 16 equally distributed, static points appearing in random order, for two seconds each. Calibrated gaze data was collected for each of these points in order to calculate the accuracy by evaluating the difference between the mapped gaze and the real point position. During analysis, the first 0.8s and the last 0.2s were discarded as to compensate for the time participants' eyes need to travel to reach the target and for anticipation movements. After each task the user was instructed to a pause of at least 90 seconds to avoid eye fatigue effects. In total, the study lasted approximately 35 minutes.

15 paid participants between 21 and 32 years ($\mu = 25.6$, $\sigma = 3.97$, 4 female) took part in the study. Participants sat in front of a display coupled with a Tobii X300 remote eye tracker in a dimmed room (see Figure 3). Data was collected at 60Hz.

Results

Figure 4 shows the measured difference between the true position of points and the gaze collected, averaged over all 16 points. For the constant speed calibration (Figure 4a), all durations ≥ 10 seconds show marginal differences and achieved an accuracy under $1°$. The five second calibration procedure showed an accuracy 2.15 times higher than the one that lasted ten seconds, indicating that a target speed of $23.3°/s$ is less feasible when users calibrate with our rectangular path design.

Results for the accelerating target calibration (Figure 4b) confirm this observation, the five second procedure also being the worst with 9.96 times higher difference than the 7.5 seconds procedure. Here again, from duration $10s$ and above, tests show an accuracy of under $1°$. The baseline 5-points calibration resulted, as expected from the industry standard, also in less than a $1°$ error.

In order to evaluate how well the correlation method detected the participants' gaze, we plotted its detection rate in Figure 5. For both target movement types, more than half of the gaze data was detected by the correlation algorithm at ten seconds and above. The five seconds procedure yielded the lowest detection, which indicates that the target was moving too quickly to ensure robust detection. Undetected correlation is caused by too fast target movement, blinks of participants as well as sharp direction changes at the corners. At corners the user was often required to perform catch-up eye movements on the target, causing the eye and target correlation to be lost for a short time as shown in Figure 2b.

We also conducted a post-hoc analysis of how accuracy iteratively improves as the target travels across the screen. For the analysis we calculated the accuracy for each 100 ms, i.e. fitting all samples available so far into a mapping. Figure 6 represents this progressive accuracy for each constant speed procedure. It shows that the accuracy was not computable before at least 40% of its path was completed, which corresponds to the target being halfway between the top right and bottom right corner of the screen. This indicates the necessity to collect enough samples on both vertical and horizontal axis of the screen. This is rational, since samples on only one axis cannot produce an accurate mapping over two dimensions.

Shortly after the vertical axis samples are collected, accuracy drastically improves and stabilizes. The final accuracy is reached around 66% of its whole path, which corresponds to a location slightly after having moved over the bottom right

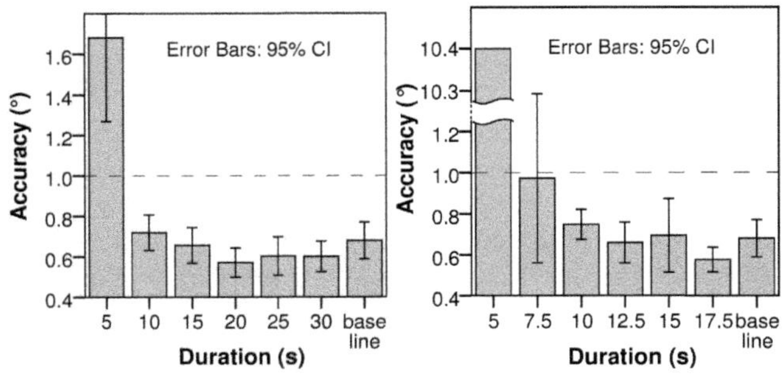

(a) Constant target calibration. (b) Accelerated target calibration.

Figure 4: Calibration accuracy results (in degree of visual angle) for each movement type and each duration.

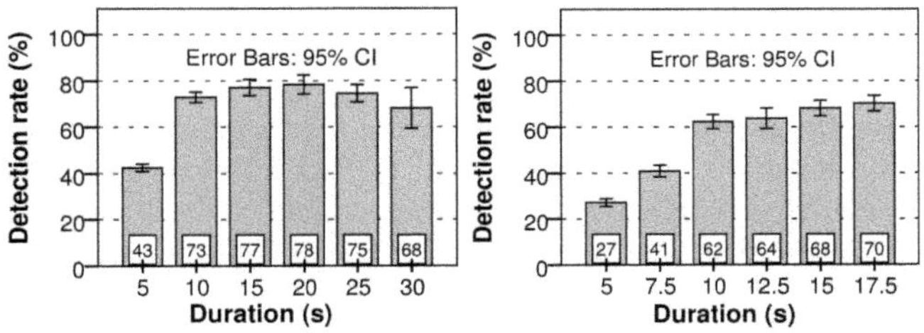

(a) Constant target calibration. (b) Accelerated target calibration.

Figure 5: Correlation detection rate: the ratio of detected gaze samples to overall possible samples in a calibration procedure.

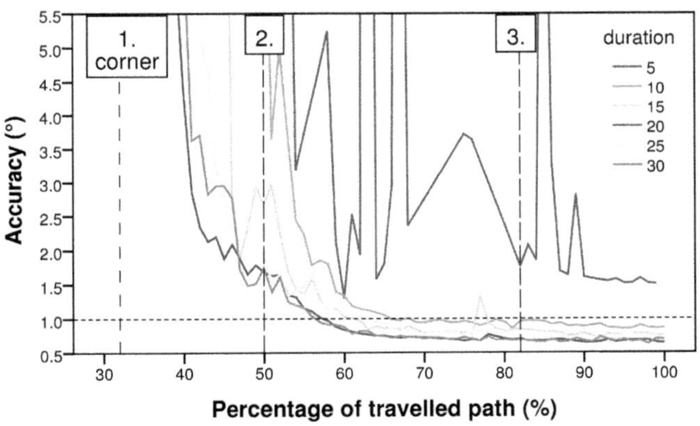

Figure 6: Analysis on how accuracy incrementally improves over time, for procedures with constant speed. Rectangles depict when the target encounters corners of the target path.

corner of the screen. This shows that the calibration procedure could have stopped at this point and thus significantly shortened the procedure duration, e.g. the ten second procedure could have already stopped at seven seconds.

These results show that a calibration with moving targets is a feasible alternative to a point-to-point calibration. Pursuit calibration yields an accuracy as high as the industrial baseline for the same time or even shorter durations, as short as seven seconds. Constant and accelerated target movement showed minor differences in accuracy. The study also showed that

	ATM	Stargazing	Waiting Screen
Settings			
Participants count (calibrated / all)	20/20 (12F)	30/37 (5F)	13/14 (5F)
Study duration (min)	5-8	3-5	3-5
Target speed (deg/s)	6.6	∼17.7	6.6
Target design	Simple circle	Shooting star	Text
Correlation threshold	0.3	0.7	0.3
Window size (ms)	160	80	80
Sample size threshold	200	100	200
Threshold per target	200 (1 target)	25 (4)	50 (4)
Results			
Calibration time(s)	7.8,12.4, 10.8	30.9(median)	13.6
Calibration time SD (s)	2.1, 3.8, 3.9	28	5.3

Table 1: Settings and results of the three application evaluations. For the ATM case, results indicate the calibration time for no interruption, on-screen interruption and off-screen interruption, consecutively. The calibration times presented for the on-screen and off-screen distractions exclude the time during which users were looking at the distractions.

the target does not need to travel across the entire screen, but rather needs to cover the full range of the two dimensions of the display.

APPLICATIONS

We designed three realistic applications that each emphasize different capabilities of pursuit calibration: the Automated Teller Machine (ATM) application demonstrates the interruption-proof capability of the method, the stargazing scenario shows the smooth blend between calibration and interaction, and in the waiting screen study users are calibrated without being conscious of it. All three applications also demonstrate how pursuit calibration does not require a clear start or end but adapts to the user. We implemented them to show the feasibility of the method and collect the time needed for users to calibrate on each system. For this purpose, we used a fixed number of samples as a calibration completion criteria, instead of a fixed duration as in the accuracy study. A summary of the settings and results of the three studies is shown in table 1.

ATM

Kumar et al. [11] suggested an eye-based ATM as it significantly increases security. This is based on accurate eye tracking to select the digits, enabled by a user calibration procedure. In real ATM situations users can get distracted, e.g. from passers-by, vehicles or barking dogs. During a normal calibration procedure, any eye movement to see outside the screen, caused by reflex, would void the calibration and lengthen the process. We evaluate the performance of pursuit calibration when these distractions occur (see Figure 7b).

We created an interface where an explicit calibration stimulus is shown: in realistic settings, users wanting to use an eye-based interface would be aware they have to undergo a calibration procedure. The moving target of the calibration follows a circular path within the interface (around the white circle at fig. 7a). Once calibrated a numeric keypad appears in the area where the calibration stimulus was located, allowing

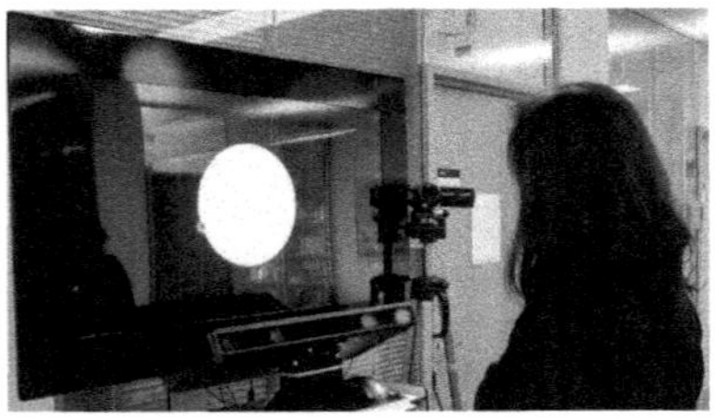

(a) A user calibrating to the ATM application by looking at the circular moving target.

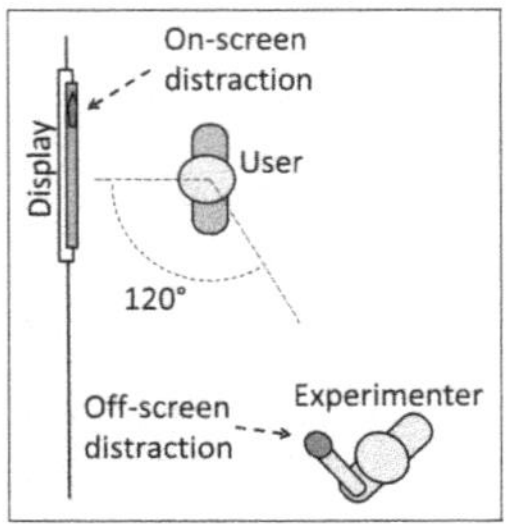

(b) Distraction positions when users interact with the interactive ATM application.

Figure 7: User study with the ATM application.

the user to enter a four-digits PIN by dwelling on the numbers for one second.

We evaluated the time needed to calibrate and complete the task for three cases: when no distraction interrupted the user, with an on-screen distraction and with an off-screen distraction. The on-screen distraction was a red circle shown for three seconds appearing when the calibration reached 100 valid samples, which was 50% of the total number of samples needed to complete the procedure. Users were instructed to voluntarily look at the target. The off-screen distraction was created by the experimenter, who gave an oral sign to the user to turn towards them and tell the number of fingers the experimenter was showing with their hand before returning to the calibration. This distraction created an interruption of 2.6 seconds (SD=1.5s) on average.

20 paid users aged between 19 to 31 years (mean=22.4, 12 female) took part in the user study. Participants stood in front of a 40" display with a Tobii X300 eye-tracker placed underneath (see Figure 7a). Data was collected at 60Hz. Each condition was repeated twice.

Results

The user study showed that all users calibrated without distraction in 7.8s, and needed an additional 4.6 seconds to complete the calibration in the case of an on-screen distraction, and 3 seconds for the off-screen case (see Table 1 for calibration times). These times correspond to the distraction durations and that users had to re-adjust to the calibration stimulus. The study showed that the method is robust against distractions during the calibration: users can look somewhere else for some time and resume calibration without having to start the procedure all over again.

Stargazing

Stagazing presents an interesting application, because it naturally includes static elements (stars) and moving elements (shooting stars). We use the shooting stars as the calibrating targets, while the stars are the objects users can interact with once calibrated. This is an example of how smoothly pursuit calibration can be integrated in an application, without separating it as a phase of its own.

We implemented an interface where a user can see stars glowing but cannot interact with them yet. Shooting stars appear randomly on four trajectories (see Figure 8b) and the user's eye is naturally attracted by them. The system detects when a user looks at a shooting star and collects samples for this area of the screen, while simultaneously notifying the user that something is happening by highlighting the shooting star in red. This means the calibration part was subtle but still noticeable. Once the calibration is complete, stars become gaze-aware and present additional information when looked at, such as their name and constellation lines (see Figure 8c).

The system was set up in a public area of the computer science department of a university (Figure 8a). It uses the same hardware and setup as the ATM study. Passers-by were encouraged to take part in the study by an experimenter that assisted them in placing themselves when needed.

Results

Based on application and video log we counted 247 passers-by of which 37 interacted with the system and 30 of them calibrated successfully (81%) in a median calibration time of 30.9 seconds (SD=28s, MIN=14.5s, MAX=120.8s). We report the median, as few users calibrated much longer because of poor eye detection caused by eye physiology [15], lots of head movements and interface design.

In general, users instantly understood that they could explore the stars and constellations by moving their eyes. Despite inexperience with eye-tracking, most users were able to calibrate with little assistance or instructions. This application demonstrates how calibration can be seamlessly integrated into an application without having a sharp transition or explaining to the user what their task is.

Waiting screen

This application investigates the feasibility of calibrating users when they are completely unaware that they are being calibrated. We aimed for the calibration to blend in the interface so that it is virtually invisible and the user does not have the impression that a task is required of them to enable the interaction. The methodology is based on Latane and Darley [12], in which users are in a waiting room waiting to be called for an arbitrary task while in reality the actual experiment investigates what happens during the waiting time.

In order to entice participants to use the system naïvely, we randomly invited passers-by in the university foyer of the management department. We described that users were to test an eye-based interface where they had to "click" on coloured circled by looking at them. They were told the goal of the experiment was to measure how fast people can select targets with their eyes and to perform as few head movement as possible therefore, but calibration was never mentioned in any way. They were shown a short example of the task so they could visualise it. After being placed in front of the system, a waiting screen appeared and the experimenter pretended to be "starting the system".

The waiting screen was designed to be the actual calibration procedure. It consisted of a study title and floating words enticing the user to wait (see figure 9). Words read "Please

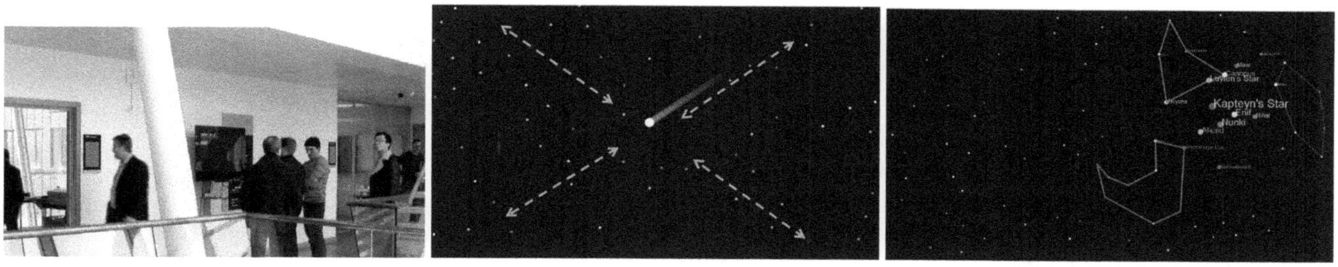

(a) Setup of the system and during the field study. The experimenter encouraged passers-by to participate and assisted in placing them when needed. (b) Calibration phase. The arrows show the trajectory of all possible shooting stars (arrows itself not part of the application). During runtime, one shooting star is shown at a time. (c) Interaction phase. Constellations and star names become visible when the user looks at them. The size of the visuals increased around the gaze direction of the user.

Figure 8: With the stargazing application, we design a seamless transition between calibration and interaction phase. Users first look at shooting stars and get calibrated. When the calibration finishes, the system switches to interaction mode. Users interact with a gaze aware interface that smoothly displays names and constellations wherever they look at.

wait" in five different languages, in order to distract the user enough during the waiting phase and subtely encourage them to keep reading. Our aim was to display a waiting screen that has movement in it for calibration, but is subtle enough so users do not get suspicious that it is part of the study. Words slowly faded in and out to enable a smooth experience. When 100 calibration points were collected, the task started automatically.

The setup was the same as the accuracy evaluation, where users were sitting in front of a display. We recruited 14 participants (5 female). The font size of the words was 30px, and the calibration point it was calibrating for was the exact centre of the word. As the user can gaze at any position within the word's bounding box, inaccuracy up to 30px in height and 30px×wordlength in width can occur. The task users performed after calibration is selecting 9 circular objects with a width of 250px.

Results

The last application showed that 13 of 14 users were calibrated in 13.6 seconds on average (SD=5.3s) and performed the circle task easily, without being aware of a calibration procedure. By using floating words, we were able to successfully

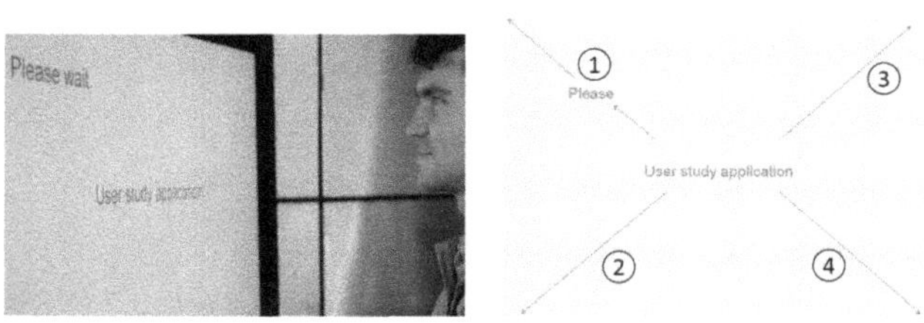

(a) (b)

Figure 9: A user calibrates by looking at a floating word (a). These words move through four trajectories (b). Arrows, circles and numbers are not part of the interface but illustrate path (arrows) and order of appearance (numbers) of attention attracting floating words. From 1 to 4, it consecutively shows 'Please', 'wait.', 'Bitte', 'warten.'.

catch the attention of the user to a moving target. However, as words are not exact points, the calibration accuracy decreased, which is why we used a coarse task after the calibration. This can be avoided by using different target design.

DISCUSSION

The detection of user attention in pursuit calibration presents a significant advance over previous methods, both in terms of calibration and usability. From a calibration point of view, a key advantage is that samples for calibration are only collected at points the user is known to have looked at. In conventional calibration, outliers can be filtered from a point cloud of samples at each display point, but the entire point cloud can be off target, resulting in a poor calibration.

The usability advantages lie primarily in the flexible calibration design enabled by our approach, where the user is not required to follow a rigid procedure. This renders eye based interfaces more realistic to use in everyday settings where distractions and interruptions are common. The method enables designers to introduce users to the application through calibration, rather than showing a separate necessary step to undergo before being able to interact. One can envision this kind of introduction with any kind of naturally moving objects: flying birds before discovering the highlights of a nature trail, racing cars followed by information on different car models, snowflakes falling and leading to the latest information on ski trails status, etc.

Pursuit calibration can be beneficial in application areas where users can not be assumed to cooperate actively toward calibration. An example may be infant eye-tracking studies: while it is hard to keep an infant's gaze focussed on one point, their attention can easily be caught by moving coloured objects. In eye-tracking studies, experimenters can more generally benefit from our method because it removes the need to manually check the accuracy of collected samples, which is now commonly required in the process. Our method can also calibrate users unawares which opens opportunities for casual interaction with public devices, as well as for studies in which it may be required that participants are not conscious of their eye movement being analysed.

Limitations

We used a high-range remote eye-tracker to evaluate the accuracy and usability of the method. However, pursuit calibration is not limited to such device and the method is generic. Because it is based on eye movement, it could work similarly with a mobile eye-tracker and off-the-shelf trackers. The requirement is that both eye data and screen coordinate system evolve in the same direction for the correlation to work.

In order for pursuit calibration to be integrated into applications, it requires careful interface design. The accuracy study showed that a target that is too quick is hard to follow for the eye, while one that is too slow avoids detection of correlation. In addition, the target's path needs to be equally distributed along the screen as well as cover both horizontal and vertical directions to attain high accuracy. This can be automated by using the iterative characteristic of pursuit calibration. Additionally, the calibration target should be as small as possible. Small targets offer an exact point the user can gaze at, while larger targets, such as words used in the waiting screen study, lead to more approximation and a less accurate calibration.

During the accuracy evaluation, we only tested a rectangle path along the borders of the screen. It would be interesting to conduct in-depth investigations of other paths, for example a circle path as used in the ATM application. Another interesting way to extend the accuracy evaluation would be to create a model of the accuracy obtained depending on the target path used. Such a model would allow the procedure to estimate when the desired accuracy has been reached, instead of calibrating until a certain number of samples are collected. This could further optimise the calibration target placement and shorten the calibration duration.

CONCLUSION

In this paper we introduced pursuit calibration as a novel method for gaze calibration. The method represents a radical departure from conventional approaches, as it calibrates eye gaze against a moving target, exploiting smooth pursuit eye movement to determine when the user is following the target. This leads to novel strategies for more intelligent sampling of calibration points, as well as usability advantages in tolerating user distraction and facilitating casual calibration. Pursuit calibration is simple in its core design but lends itself to implement gaze calibration in creative and innovative ways.

REFERENCES

1. Chen, J., and Ji, Q. Probabilistic gaze estimation without active personal calibration. In *Proc. of CVPR '11* (2011), 609–616.
2. Drewes, H., and Schmidt, A. Interacting with the computer using gaze gestures. In *Proc. of INTERACT '07*, Springer (2007), 475–488.
3. Fischler, M. A., and Bolles, R. C. Random sample consensus: a paradigm for model fitting with applications to image analysis and automated cartography. *Commun. ACM 24*, 6 (1981), 381–395.
4. Flatla, D., Gutwin, C., Nacke, L., Bateman, S., and Mandryk, R. Calibration games: Making calibration tasks enjoyable by adding motivating game elements. In *UIST '11* (2011), 403–412.
5. Guestrin, E., and Einzenmann, M. General theory of remote gaze estimation using the pupil center and corneal reflections. In *IEEE Trans. on Biomedical Engineering*, vol. 53 (2006), 1124–1133.
6. Guestrin, E. D., and Eizenman, M. Remote point-of-gaze estimation requiring a single-point calibration for applications with infants. In *Proc. of ETRA '08*, ACM (2008), 267–274.
7. Hutchinson, T., White, K.P., J., Martin, W., Reichert, K., and Frey, L. Human-computer interaction using eye-gaze input. *IEEE Trans. on Systems, Man, and Cybernetics, Part C 19*, 6 (1989), 1527 –1534.
8. Jacob, R. J. K. What you look at is what you get: eye movement-based interaction techniques. In *Proc. of CHI '90*, ACM (1990), 11–18.
9. Kang, I., and Malpeli, J. G. *Behavioral calibration of eye movement recording systems using moving targets*, vol. 124. Journal of Neuroscience Methods, 2003.
10. Kondou, Y., and Ebisawa, Y. Easy eye-gaze calibration using a moving visual target in the head-free remote eye-gaze detection system. In *Proc. of VECIMS '08* (2008), 145 –150.
11. Kumar, M., Garfinkel, T., Boneh, D., and Winograd, T. Reducing shoulder-surfing by using gaze-based password entry. In *Proc. of SOUPS '07*, ACM (2007), 13–19.
12. Latane, B., and Darley, J. M. Bystander "apathy". *American Scientist 57* (1969).
13. Model, D., and Eizenman, M. User-calibration-free remote eye-gaze tracking system with extended tracking range. In *Proc. of CCECE '2011* (2011), 1268–1271.
14. Morimoto, C. H., and Mimica, M. R. M. Eye gaze tracking techniques for interactive applications. *Computer Vision and Image Understanding 98*, 1 (2005), 4–24.
15. Nyström, M., Andersson, R., Holmqvist, K., and van de Weijer, J. The influence of calibration method and eye physiology on eyetracking data quality. *Behaviour Research Methods* (2012).
16. Ohno, T., and Mukawa, N. A free-head, simple calibration, gaze tracking system that enables gaze-based interaction. In *Proc. of ETRA '04*, ACM (2004), 115–122.
17. Renner, P., Lüdike, N., Wittrowski, J., and Pfeiffer, T. Towards continuous gaze-based interaction in 3d environments - unobtrusive calibration and accuracy monitoring. In *GI VR/AR workshop*, Shaker Verlag (2011), 13–24.

18. Robinson, D. The mechanics of human smooth pursuit eye movement. *The Journal of Physiology 180*, 3 (Oct. 1965), 569–591.

19. Schnipke, S. K., and Todd, M. W. Trials and tribulations of using an eye-tracking system. In *Proc. of CHI EA '00*, ACM (2000), 273–274.

20. Sibert, L. E., and Jacob, R. J. K. Evaluation of eye gaze interaction. In *Proc. of CHI '00*, ACM (2000), 281–288.

21. Smith, J. D., Vertegaal, R., and Sohn, C. Viewpointer: lightweight calibration-free eye tracking for ubiquitous handsfree deixis. In *Proc. of UIST '05*, ACM (2005), 53–61.

22. Stellmach, S., and Dachselt, R. Look & touch: gaze-supported target acquisition. In *Proc. of CHI '12*, ACM (2012), 2981–2990.

23. Turner, J., Alexander, J., Bulling, A., Schmidt, D., and Gellersen, H. Eye pull, eye push: Moving objects between large screens and personal devices with gaze & touch. In *Proc. of INTERACT '13* (2013).

24. Vertegaal, R. Attentive user interfaces. *Commun. ACM 46*, 3 (2003), 30–33.

25. Vidal, M., Bulling, A., and Gellersen, H. Pursuits: Spontaneous interaction with displays based on smooth pursuit eye movement and moving targets. In *Proc. of UbiComp '13*, ACM (2013).

26. Vidal, M., Pfeuffer, K., Bulling, A., and Gellersen, H. Pursuits: Eye-based interaction with moving targets. In *Proc. of CHI EA '13*, ACM (2013).

27. Villanueva, A., and Cabeza, R. A novel gaze estimation system with one calibration point. *IEEE Trans. on Systems, Man, and Cybernetics, Part B 38*, 4 (2008), 1123–1138.

28. Villanueva, A., Cabeza, R., and Porta, S. Eye tracking system model with easy calibration. In *Proc. of ETRA '04*, ACM (2004), 55–55.

29. Ware, C., and Mikaelian, H. H. An evaluation of an eye tracker as a device for computer input. *SIGCHI Bull. 17*, SI (1986), 183–188.

30. Young, L., and Sheena, D. Survey of eye movement recording methods. *Behavior Research Methods & Instrumentation 7* (1975), 397–429.

31. Zhai, S., Morimoto, C., and Ihde, S. Manual and gaze input cascaded (magic) pointing. In *Proc. of CHI '99*, CHI '99, ACM (1999), 246–253.

32. Zhang, Y., Bulling, A., and Gellersen, H. Sideways: A gaze interface for spontaneous interaction with public displays. In *Proc. of CHI '13*, ACM (2013).

33. Zhu, Z., and Ji, Q. Eye gaze tracking under natural head movements. In *Proc. of CVPR '05*, IEEE Computer Society (2005), 918–923.

Gaze Locking: Passive Eye Contact Detection for Human–Object Interaction

Brian A. Smith **Qi Yin** **Steven K. Feiner** **Shree K. Nayar**
Department of Computer Science, Columbia University
450 Comp. Sci. Bldg., 1214 Amsterdam Ave., New York, NY 10027 USA
{brian, qiyin, feiner, nayar}@cs.columbia.edu

ABSTRACT
Eye contact plays a crucial role in our everyday social interactions. The ability of a device to reliably detect when a person is looking at it can lead to powerful human–object interfaces. Today, most gaze-based interactive systems rely on gaze tracking technology. Unfortunately, current gaze tracking techniques require active infrared illumination, calibration, or are sensitive to distance and pose. In this work, we propose a different solution—a passive, appearance-based approach for sensing eye contact in an image. By focusing on gaze *locking* rather than gaze tracking, we exploit the special appearance of direct eye gaze, achieving a Matthews correlation coefficient (MCC) of over 0.83 at long distances (up to 18 m) and large pose variations (up to $\pm 30°$ of head yaw rotation) using a very basic classifier and without calibration. To train our detector, we also created a large publicly available gaze data set: 5,880 images of 56 people over varying gaze directions and head poses. We demonstrate how our method facilitates human–object interaction, user analytics, image filtering, and gaze-triggered photography.

Author Keywords
Gaze-based interaction; passive eye contact detection; human–object interaction; user analytics; image filtering; gaze-triggered photography; human vision.

ACM Classification Keywords
H.5.2 [Information Interfaces and Presentation]: User Interfaces—Input devices and strategies; I.4.8 [Image Processing and Computer Vision]: Scene Analysis

INTRODUCTION
Eye contact is a major form of nonverbal communication and plays a crucial role in our everyday social encounters. We use it to seek information (e.g., to see how something we say is received) and regulate interaction (e.g., by signaling when it is someone else's turn to speak), among other uses [1, 19, 40]. Interestingly, while we have a hard time determining the exact angle at which someone else is looking, we seem to be very good at determining when someone else is looking *at us* (i.e., at or very near our eyes), and are acutely aware of it [15].

UIST'13, October 8–11, 2013, St. Andrews, United Kingdom.

http://dx.doi.org/10.1145/2501988.2501994

Figure 1. Gaze locking. We propose the idea of sensing eye contact directly from an image in a passive, appearance-based manner. The main idea is to focus on gaze *locking* (a binary problem) rather than gaze tracking (a continuous problem) and exploit the special appearance of direct eye gaze. Our approach can be used to facilitate a wide range of applications.

Most gaze-based interactive systems today rely on gaze tracking. They find the exact angle users are looking at instead of sensing eye contact directly. Although gaze tracking has been extensively studied and current methods [2, 3, 18, 24, 36] are highly accurate, they suffer from several limitations that restrict their practical use. They generally work only over short distances (often 80 cm or less) [2, 3, 18, 24, 36] or with direct head poses [2, 18, 36], or require active infrared illumination [2, 3, 24, 36], intrusive equipment (such as head-mounted cameras), or extensive calibration [3, 24]. One exception is Shell et al.'s system [31], which does in fact sense eye contact directly, but also requires active illumination. To address these limitations, we make the following contributions.

Gaze Locking
We propose the idea of sensing eye contact directly from an image in a passive, appearance-based manner (Figure 1). The main idea is to focus on gaze *locking* (a binary problem) rather than gaze tracking (a continuous problem) and exploit the special appearance of direct eye gaze. In addition to being passive (no special illumination or hardware required), our approach is non-intrusive, calibration-free, and robust to distance and head pose. Like Shell et al.'s active method [31], it can be used to allow humans to interact with computers, devices, and other objects just by looking at them.

Sample Detector
As a proof of concept, we demonstrate that even a simple and lightweight gaze locking system can yield accurate and robust results. Our sample detector uses very basic features—the eye area's pixel intensities—yet achieves a Matthews correlation coefficient (a measure of accuracy for binary classifiers) of over 0.83 at long distances (up to 18 m) and large pose variations (up to $\pm 30°$ of head yaw rotation) without requiring calibration. This equates to a 92% accuracy on our training data set. It runs at over 20 FPS on a computer with an Intel Core i5-3470 processor, 8 GB of RAM, and an NVIDIA GeForce GTX 660M graphics card. A more advanced classifier could be used to improve accuracy even further.

Human Performance Evaluation
We performed a study to see how accurate people are at sensing eye contact and found several interesting results. For example, we found that people achieve MCCs of over 0.2 at distances of 18 m, and that their accuracy decreases roughly linearly over distance regardless of others' (horizontal) head orientations. We also found that people are often more accurate when they can only see one of the other person's eyes.

Gaze Data Set
To facilitate our human study and provide training data for our sample detector, we created a gaze data set of 56 people and 5,880 images, available at `http://www.cs.columbia.edu/CAVE/databases/columbia_gaze/`. It has more images and fixed gaze targets than any other publicly available gaze data set. To ensure robustness, our data set spans a variety of parameters: 5 head poses and 21 gaze directions per head pose. Our subjects were ethnically diverse and 21 of them wore glasses. We use our data set for gaze locking purposes, but it can serve as a very large resource for gaze tracking purposes as well.

Demonstration of Applications
Lastly, we show a few applications that gaze locking facilitates. First, since camera modules are becoming increasingly small and inexpensive to produce, we can allow any device to respond to eye contact by embedding a camera that serves as an eye contact sensor inside it. Our technique can thus serve as a backbone for allowing humans to interact with computers, devices, and other objects simply by looking at them. In addition, our method is passive and hence can be applied to any existing image. Therefore, it can be used to sort images on the web and on personal computers by their degree of eye contact, improving image search. Finally, we can incorporate a gaze trigger in cameras to capture group photos exactly when everyone in the group is looking straight back.

RELATED WORK

Gaze Estimation and Tracking
Not surprisingly, both gaze estimation and gaze tracking (gaze estimation at video rate) have been studied extensively in the past few decades. Hansen and Ji [17] and Morimoto and Mimica [26] provide excellent surveys of earlier work. Ideally, a gaze tracking system should be accurate, passive, non-intrusive, calibration-free, and robust to distance and head pose [26]. Unfortunately, current systems maintain accuracy at the expense of other qualities—they are predominantly active systems that work only at close range (80 cm or less).

For example, Morimoto et al.'s [24] and Beymer and Flickner's [3] feature-based techniques are accurate and robust to head pose, but are active, require calibration, and work only at close range. Baluja and Pomerleau's [2] and Tan et al.'s [36] appearance-based techniques are accurate and calibration-free, but are active, sensitive to head pose, and work only at close range. Hansen and Pece's [18] commercial off-the-shelf (COTS) system is passive and easy to calibrate, but is sensitive to head pose and again works only at close range. Nishino and Nayar's method [27] is passive and produces an image of what a person is looking at, but requires a high resolution image of the eye to provide useful results. Stiefelhagen et al.'s eye tracker [34] is passive and boasts an accuracy of up to 1.3°, but requires a fixed head pose and was only tested on four users at close range. They also developed an earlier gaze tracking system [33] that tracks only head pose and not eye gaze direction. Our gaze locking approach can be applied to any image (including those from COTS products or even from the Web) and is accurate, passive, non-intrusive, calibration-free, and robust to distance and head pose.

Lastly, Cadavid et al. [6] use spectral regression to passively detect whether an infant is looking at his or her parent's face, but their work differs from our gaze locking approach in three important respects. First, their system does not perform gaze locking since the camera is not worn by (and co-located with) the parent, but rather shows a third-party view. Second, neither the precision nor accuracy of their approach was directly tested. The parent's face subtends a large solid angle with respect to the infant (resulting in a large "sweet spot" for detection), and the system's underlying positive and negative samples were manually labeled by human coders viewing a simultaneous video recording showing both the infant's and parent's faces. We prove that our sample detector has a precision of 5°, allowing it to be used with very small objects. We also show in our human performance evaluation that, in the case of eye contact detection, humans themselves are actually inaccurate 9–40% of the time. Third, their work addresses only the specific application of infant–parent interaction for a single subject, and is not generalizable for human–object interaction with arbitrary humans and objects. We explore the concept of gaze locking, introduce several representative applications, and demonstrate that a very simple classifier can yield robust results with arbitrary humans and objects.

Gaze Perception
A number of studies evaluating people's perception of gaze have been performed, starting with Gibson and Pick's study [16] using six subjects and an in-person gazer. It concludes that, at 2 m, people sense eye contact when others are looking between the left and right edges of their face, but the authors urge a repeat of the experiment using a model (e.g., a set of photographs) as stimulus instead of a live person. Cline's in-person study [9] using a half-mirror incorporates several head poses and eye occlusion, confirming Gibson and

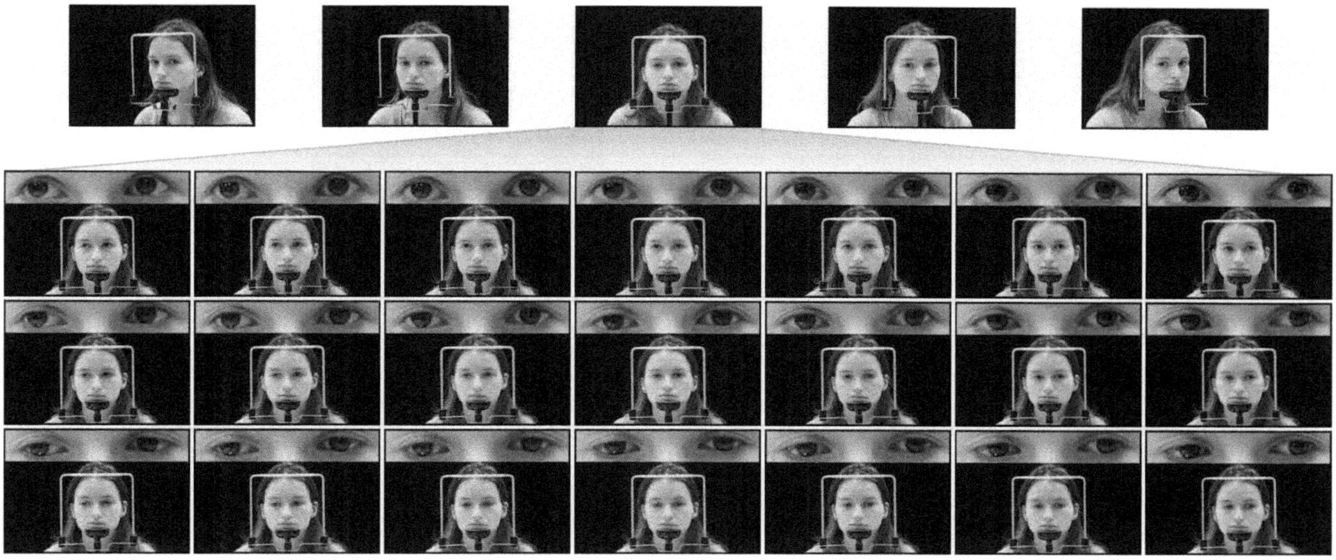

Figure 2. Sample data set images. Our gaze data set includes 56 subjects and five different head poses (shown on top): 0°, ±15°, and ±30° horizontally. For each subject and head pose, there are 21 different gaze directions (shown on bottom for the 0° head pose): the combinations of seven horizontal ones (0°, ±5°, ±10°, ±15°) and three vertical ones (0°, ±10°). For each of these, we also show a cropped area of the eye region.

Pick's eye contact results and measuring errors in the perception of gaze direction in general. Gamer and Hecht [14] explore the effects of distance, eye occlusion, and the presence of a second head as well, while Martin and Jones [21] examine the effects of distance and lighting intensity from a signal detection standpoint. Symons et al. [35] focus on triadic eye gaze acuity (the ability to judge where someone is looking in space) rather than dyadic eye gaze acuity, and verify that digital photographs are a good substitute for in-person gazers. Gemmell et al. [15] and Chen [8] explore how the design of videoconferencing systems can promote gaze awareness without using special-purpose hardware.

Gaze-Based Interactive Systems

The pursuit of more natural, ubiquitous user interfaces has been an important goal for the HCI community. A new class of user interfaces, called *attentive* user interfaces, aims to facilitate more social interactions between users and devices by treating users' attention as a valuable resource [38]. In doing so, they must (a) sense users' attention, (b) make inferences about what users want to do, and (c) negotiate "turns" amongst themselves, as Vertegaal and Shell describe [39].

To date, however, these interfaces have been limited by current gaze tracking techniques, making it difficult to sense users' attention. Although sensing attention through eye contact alone would be ideal, many systems incorporate either gesture-based control [5], manual input [43], or intrusive head-mounted cameras [32] as a workaround. Shell et al., however, did in fact propose standalone eye contact sensors [31], but they use active infrared illumination. They also interfere with each other if placed within 80° of visual angle of each other. They extend Morimoto et al.'s PupilCam design [25] (which locates pupils by reflecting infrared light on them) by comparing the location of a corneal glint (i.e., the first Purkinje image) with that of the pupil reflection. Our gaze locking technique is completely passive, is not prone to interference, and is accurate at long range. We compare the two techniques directly in the Experiments section.

Omron's commercial OKAO Vision system [28] includes a passive gaze tracker, and Ye et al. [42] combine this with an active and intrusive head-mounted camera in order to determine mutual gaze (simultaneous eye contact) between the person wearing the camera and another person. However, Ye at al. find OKAO Vision's gaze tracker to be inaccurate and sensitive to head pose. Their resulting system has an MCC of 0.72, was only tested on one pair of subjects, and was not shown to work over long distances. Our gaze locking approach is accurate, passive, non-intrusive, robust to head pose, and achieves an MCC of over 0.83 at distances of 18 m.

GAZE LOCKING IN PEOPLE

People seem to have an uncanny ability to tell when others are looking at them. In this section, we describe a two-part experiment that we performed to show how accurate people really are. First, we created a gaze data set, then we asked a set of "players" to determine which of those images are gaze locking and which ones are not. Our experiment revealed some very interesting trends in human vision, and we used those to guide the design of our gaze locking approach.

Creating a Gaze Data Set

Data Set Statistics

Our data set contains a total of 5,880 high-resolution images of 56 different people (32 male, 24 female), and each image has a resolution of 5,184×3,456 pixels. 21 of our subjects were Asian, 19 were White, 8 were South Asian, 7 were Black, and 4 were Hispanic or Latino. Our subjects ranged from 18 to 36 years of age, and 21 of them wore prescription glasses.

	McMurrough et al.	Gi4E	Weidenbacher et al.	Our Data Set
# Subjects:	20	103	20	56
# Fixed Gaze Targets per Subject per Head Pose:	16	12	2-9	21
# Fixed Head Poses:	1	N/A	19	5
Head Pose Calibration?	N/A	No	Yes	Yes
Resolution (px):	768×480	800×600	1600×1200	5184×3456
Total # Images:	N/A	1,236	2,220	5,880

Figure 3. Gaze data set comparison. A comparison of our gaze data set with ones recently made for gaze tracking. McMurrough et al.'s data set is video-based and includes precise head pose measurements rather than simply calibrating head pose. The Gi4E data set does not stabilize subjects' head pose. Weidenbacher et al.'s data set offers a wide variety of fixed head poses, but many have only two corresponding gaze directions.

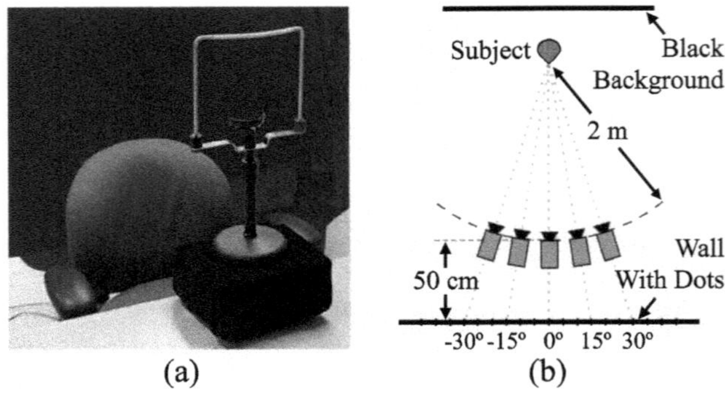

Figure 4. Setup for image capture. (a) Subjects were seated in front of a black background and used a chin rest to stabilize their face. (b) We captured images from five different camera positions asynchronously. Each position represented a (horizontal) head pose. The subjects focused on a grid of dots placed on the wall behind each camera location.

As shown in Figure 2, for each subject, we acquired images for each combination of five horizontal head poses (0°, ±15°, ±30°), seven horizontal gaze directions (0°, ±5°, ±10°, ±15°), and three vertical gaze directions (0°, ±10°). Note that this means we collected five gaze locking images (0° vertical and horizontal gaze direction) for each subject, one for each head pose. Figure 3 compares our gaze data set with data sets recently made by McMurrough et al. [23], Ponz et al. [29], and Weidenbacher et al. [41] for gaze tracking.

Collection Procedure

We recorded each image with a Canon EOS Rebel T3i camera and a Canon EF-S 18–135 mm IS f/3.5–5.6 zoom lens. As shown in Figure 4, subjects were seated in a fixed location in front of a black background, and a grid of dots was attached to a wall in front of them. The dots were placed in 5° increments horizontally and 10° increments vertically. There were five camera positions marked on the floor (one for each head pose), and each position was 2 m from the subject. The dots were organized in such a way that each camera position had a corresponding 7×3 grid.

The subjects used a height-adjustable chin rest to stabilize their face and position their eyes 70 cm above the floor. The camera was placed at eye height, as was the center row of dots. For each subject and head pose (camera position), we took three to six images of the subject gazing (in a raster scan fashion) at each dot of the pose's corresponding grid of dots. To ensure the subject was in focus, not blinking, and looking in the correct direction, we viewed each image at full resolution afterwards and kept the best one from each set of three or six.

Human Accuracy

Experimental Setup

After creating our gaze data set, we asked 52 "players" (27 male, 25 female) to play a computer-based quiz to determine which of those images are gaze locking and which of those are not. The players were all paid volunteers and were mostly university students. We asked the players to state whether or not the subject in each image was looking directly at him or her, a simple yes/no response. Each gaze-locking image was seen by an average of 8.8 players and each non-gaze-locking image was seen by an average of 3.96 players. Each player participated in one 40-minute session, viewing 440 images in the process.

The players viewed our images on a computer monitor, so we needed the subjects to appear at the same resolution as they would if seen in person for the results to be accurate. In addition, each image was captured at a distance of 2 m from the subject, so we created four more copies of each image to serve as a proxy for distances of 6 m, 10 m, 14 m, and 18 m. The appendix describes how we scaled the images—taking the acuity of the human eye into account—to solve both of these problems. We did not find a statistical difference in people's accuracy when we used a small sample of "true" 6-18 m images instead of our scaled images.

Human Accuracy Results

Figure 5 highlights some of our observations. We use the Matthews correlation coefficient (MCC) [22] to represent accuracy in Figure 5(a) and Figure 5(b) since it is widely used in machine learning for assessing binary classification performance with uneven class sizes. An MCC of 1.0 represents perfect classification, an MCC of -1.0 represents completely incorrect classification, and an MCC of 0.0 represents classification that is no better than random guessing. The MCC is not well-defined when only one class of data is used, so we use percentage accuracies in Figure 5(c).

In Figure 5(a), we find that humans are indeed rather adept at determining when others are looking at them. At distances of 18 m, their MCC can still surpass 0.2. Moreover, even though the size of someone else's face decreases quadratically over distance, humans' gaze locking accuracy decreases only linearly with distance.

In Figure 5(b), we see that humans' accuracy is largely maintained across different head poses, even extreme ones such as ±30° to the side. Shechtman et al. [30] find that a 50° ocular duction (i.e., eye movement) is nearly impossible for many age groups, and we found during our experiments that people are uncomfortable moving their eyes 30° to the side. Hence,

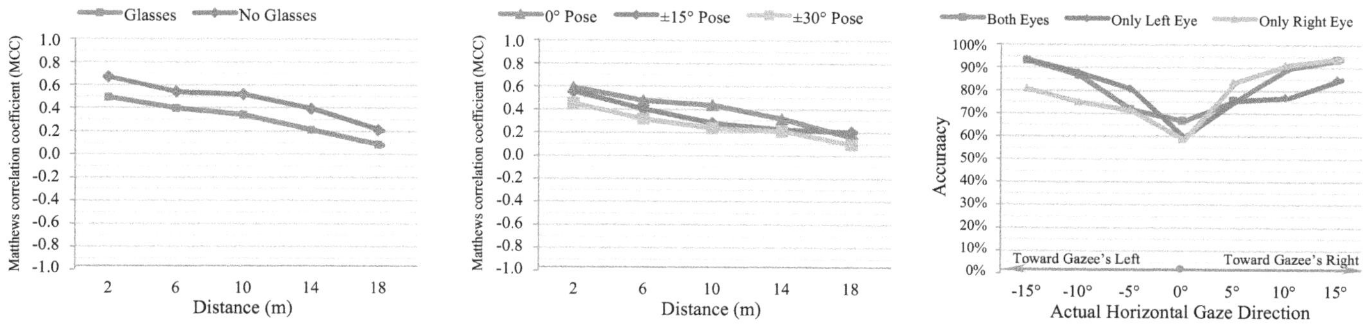

(a) (b) (c)

Figure 5. Gaze locking in people. (a) People are relatively accurate at sensing eye contact, even when the person gazing (i.e., the gazer) is wearing prescription glasses. At distances of 18 m, gazees still achieve MCCs of over 0.2 if the gazer is not wearing glasses. Here, the gazer is at a frontal (0°) head pose. (b) The gazee's accuracy decreases roughly linearly over distance regardless of the gazer's (horizontal) head pose. Head poses that are more off-center (such as ±30°) have slightly lower MCCs. (c) The gazees are least accurate when the gazer is actually looking at them (the 0° case)—that is, the false negative rate is higher than the false positive rate. Interestingly, if the gazer is looking away, the gazee is more accurate when he or she can only see one of the gazer's eyes (the blue line is not strictly above the red and green lines). Each accuracy measurement was calculated over all five distances and head poses. Here, we use percentage accuracies instead of MCCs because each horizontal gaze direction besides 0° is always non-gaze locking by definition and the MCC is not well-defined when only one class of data is used.

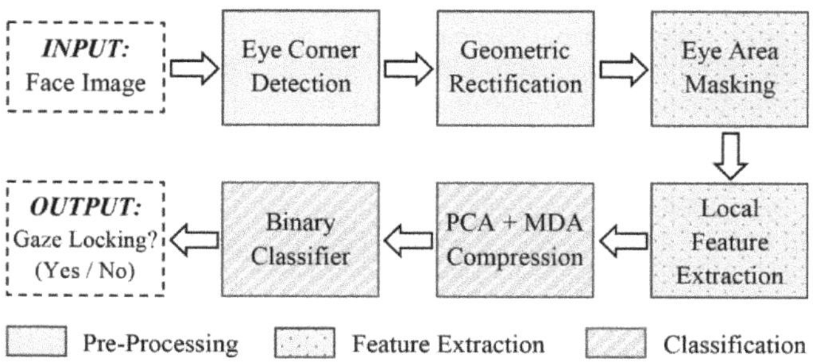

Figure 6. Gaze locking detector pipeline. Our gaze locking detector is comprised of three broad phases, shown here in different colors. In the first phase, we locate the eyes in an image and transform them into a standard coordinate frame. In the second phase, we mask out the eyes' surroundings and assemble pixel-wise features from the eyes' appearance. Finally, we project these features into a low-dimensional space, then feed them into a binary classifier to determine whether the face is gaze locking or not.

eye contact from even a ±30° head pose is unlikely to happen in everyday life.

Lastly, Figure 5(c) shows the results from an extended test that we performed with 10 players. In this test, the players viewed images whose left or right half was cropped off, showing only one of the subject's eyes, in addition to non-cropped images. Interestingly, we found that the players are often more accurate when they can only see one of the other person's eyes. This is the case when the subject is looking away and the visible eye is the one that is looking more off-center.

SAMPLE DETECTOR

Here, we show a simple, lightweight detector design that is nonetheless accurate and robust. It runs at over 20 FPS on a computer with an Intel Core i5-3470 processor, 8 GB of RAM, and an NVIDIA GeForce GTX 660M graphics card.

Given an image, the detector outputs binary decisions that indicate whether each face in the image is gaze locking or not. It is composed of three broad phases, shown in Figure 6. We describe each phase in the subsections below.

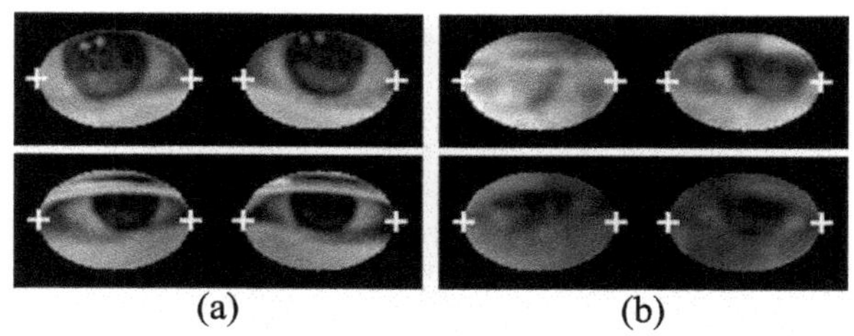

Figure 7. Rectified features and failure cases. (a) Examples of rectified and masked features. Each eye has been transformed to a 48×36 px coordinate frame. The crosshairs signify eye corners detected in the first phase. We mask each eye with a fixed-size ellipse whose shape was optimized offline for accuracy. (b) Two failure cases: strong highlights on glasses (top) and low contrast (bottom).

Pre-Processing Phase

In the first phase, we locate the eyes in an image and transform them into a standard coordinate frame. We find the eyes by taking the eye corner locations output from a commercial face and fiducial point detector [28]. At this point, eye shape varies greatly due to differences in head pose. To remove the influence of head pose, we rectify each eye via an affine transformation to a 48×36 px coordinate frame, then concatenate the two eye regions together to form a 96×36 px image. The low resolution of this image reflects the low resolution encompassed by objects at long distances, making our detector accurate over long distances. Figure 7 shows several examples of rectified features.

Feature Extraction Phase

The most difficult part of using the eyes' appearance for classification purposes is the inherent variance in the eyes' appearance. Both the eyes' shape and degree of openness significantly affect their appearance, even after performing the affine transformation in the first phase. Training our detector with a large number samples helps account for this, but we

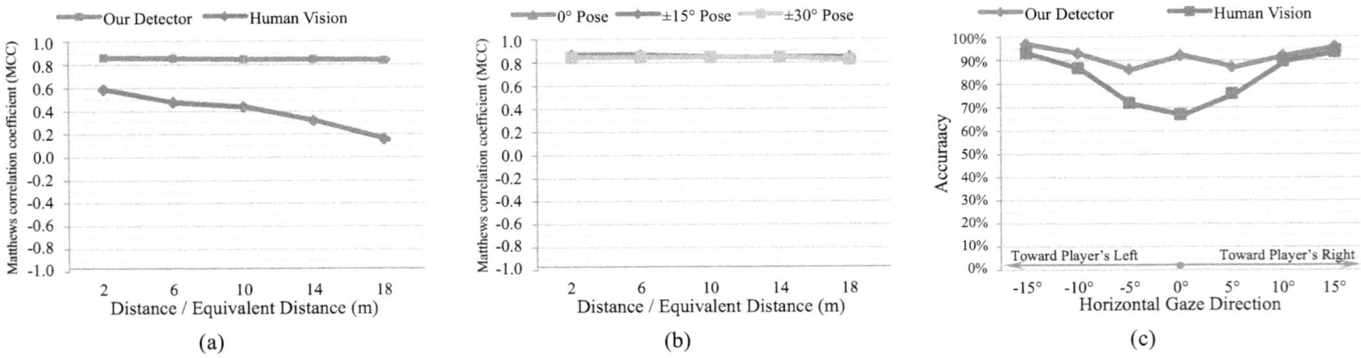

Figure 8. Gaze locking detector performance. As the appendix describes, we downsampled our detector's test images to match the resolution seen by the human fovea at the respective distances. (a) Our detector achieves MCCs of over 0.83 at a distance of 18 m, significantly outperforming humans' accuracy. The detector's accuracy is fairly constant over distance because our method uses features that are of very low resolution. The line representing human performance is an aggregation of the lines from Figure 5(a). (b) Our detector's accuracy is also fairly constant over a variety of (horizontal) head poses. (c) As with human vision, our detector's accuracy is worst when people are looking at or very close to the camera. Our detector significantly outperforms human vision nonetheless. Each accuracy measurement was calculated over all five distances and head poses. As with Figure 5(c), we use percentage accuracies here because the MCC is not well-defined when only one class of data is used.

take the additional step of masking out the areas around the eyes to remove the influence of their variances in appearance.

Our mask (Figure 7) is a fixed-size ellipse whose major axis lies on the line segment connecting the two eye corners. Choosing the size is nontrivial: a larger ellipse reveals more of the eye's surroundings and more information about gaze, but a smaller ellipse is more robust to noise from the surroundings. We used a brute-force search of all possible major and minor axis lengths offline to choose the best size. We chose the values that achieved the best accuracy in our set of training data, which is separate from our testing data.

After applying the mask, we concatenate the remaining pixels' intensity values into a high-dimensional feature vector, then normalize the feature vector to unit magnitude. This unit-magnitude feature vector is our final representation of the eyes' appearance.

Classification Phase

In the final phase, we project the high-dimensional feature vector onto a low-dimensional space via principal component analysis (PCA) [37] and multiple discriminant analysis (MDA) [11], then feed the projected vector into a support vector machine (SVM) [7] that we trained offline. The SVM decides whether the face is gaze locking or not. Since gaze locking is a binary classification problem rather than a continuous one, it is more robust to noise and requires fewer training samples. The Binary Classifier subsection describes the training process.

PCA + MDA Compression

Dimensionality reduction is a common task in appearance matching. It boosts classification speed, removes redundancies in the representations of features, avoids over-fitting, and reduces the effects of noise on classification. Hence, we use PCA to compress our feature vector to roughly 200 dimensions. Afterwards, we employ MDA to form a highly discriminative subspace, compressing our feature vectors even more. We find that a six-dimensional subspace, used to separate seven distinct classes of data, yields the highest accuracy. One class corresponds to gaze locking images and the rest correspond to non-gaze-locking images. This is likely because our training data set comprises seven horizontal gaze directions, one of them gaze locking (0°) and the rest non-gaze-locking.

Binary Classifier

In our sample detector, we use a linear SVM classifier [7] with default parameters (which includes a radial basis function kernel) to output our final binary decision. Even though we use an SVM, any binary classifier (e.g., LDA or neural networks) would work. The kernel allows input features similar to our positive training samples to be "lifted airborne," so to speak, separating them from ones near our negative samples that are still "on the ground." As was the case with the data set statistics described earlier, the number of positive and negative training samples we had was highly unbalanced (280 gaze locking images and 5,600 non-gaze-locking images), so we randomly perturbed our training data to generate 5,000 additional gaze locking samples and 15,000 additional non-gaze-locking samples. We accomplished this by making small, random adjustments to the resolution and detected eye corner positions of our training images.

EXPERIMENTS

We tested our gaze locking detector via leave-one-out cross-validation on a modified version of our gaze data set. The original data set, described earlier in the Creating a Gaze Data Set subsection, comprises five head poses and 21 gaze directions but was captured with a high-resolution camera from a distance of 2 m. The modified data set comprises five downsampled copies of each of the original data set's 5,880 images, where the resolution of each copy matches that seen by the human retina at distances of 2 m, 6 m, 10 m, 14 m, and 18 m. Equation 1 in the appendix describes how we downsampled the images. Note that even the 2 m image is downsampled by a factor of 58.0%. Our supplementary video shows how

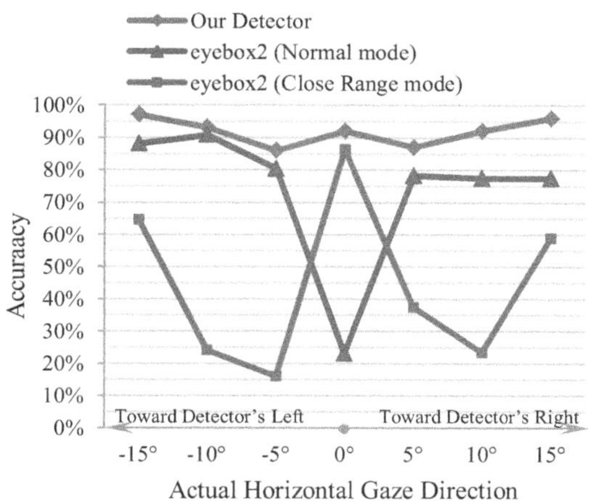

Figure 9. Comparison with an active system. A comparison of our sample detector with an eyebox2, which implements Shell et al.'s active approach to eye contact detection, in both Normal (6 m) and Close Range (2 m) modes. Though passive, our detector is more accurate than the eyebox2. The eyebox2's Normal mode seems to be tuned toward reducing false positives, and its Close Range mode seems to be tuned toward reducing false negatives.

our detector performs on raw footage from webcams and iPad video feeds.

Comparison with Human Vision

Figure 8 shows our sample detector's performance and compares it with human vision's performance (from Figure 5). We again use the Matthews correlation coefficient (MCC) [22] to represent accuracy since it is widely used in machine learning for assessing binary classification performance with uneven class sizes. Although our detector uses a very standard set of tools, it achieves an MCC of over 0.83 at a distance of 18 m, significantly outperforming the 0.15 MCC of human vision (Figure 8(a)). This high accuracy over long distances is a result of using very low-resolution feature vectors. As we see in Figure 8(b), this accuracy is maintained across different horizontal head poses, even fairly extreme ones such as $\pm 30°$.

Figure 8(c) shows our detector's accuracy with respect to a person's actual gaze direction. As with human vision, our detector is least accurate when a person is looking at or very near the camera (i.e., at the borderline between gaze locking and "almost gaze locking"). However, even in this case, our detector is much more accurate than human vision (86% versus 67%). We use percentage accuracies instead of MCCs here because each horizontal gaze direction besides 0° is always non-gaze locking by definition and the MCC is not well-defined when only one class of data is used.

Comparison with an Active System

Here, we compare our sample detector's accuracy with that of the eyebox2 [12], a leading commercial implementation of Shell et al.'s active approach to eye contact detection. Recall that our approach is completely passive and hence does not use active illumination or special hardware like the eyebox2 does. The eyebox2 is specified to work best at a range of 5–10 m in Normal mode and 1.3–3.3 m in Close Range mode, so we asked six people to sit (indoors using a chin rest) 6 m in front of it in Normal mode and 2 m in front of it in Close Range mode. They stared at the eyebox2 and six dots placed horizontally around it (at $\pm 5°$, $\pm 10°$, and $\pm 15°$) for ten seconds apiece. To analyze the eyebox2's accuracy, we measured the proportion of time the eyebox2 claimed they were making eye contact.

Figure 9 shows the results. Our sample detector is more accurate than the eyebox2 regardless of the actual gaze direction. In Normal mode, the eyebox2 seems tuned toward reducing false positives—although we adjusted its illuminator position, threshold setting, and focus setting as the manual instructed, its output was very jittery in the gaze locking case. We also found its range for reliable tracking to be around 5–7 m, and that it does not work well for people with glasses (the participants represented in Figure 9 did not wear glasses). In Close Range mode, the eyebox2 seems to be tuned toward reducing false negatives—it usually claims that people are looking at it unless they are looking at least 15° away. Our gaze locking approach works for a greater range of distances (at least 2–18 m) without separate modes of operation, is more robust to eyeglasses, and can be applied to any image, including existing images.

Failure Cases

As with all appearance-based recognition systems, our approach can be prone to errors when a feature's visual appearance (in our case, that of the eyes) differs significantly from that of average features. For example, even though 22 of 56 subjects in our training data set wore glasses, our detector may not work well for all types of glasses over all head poses, given the large variety. This, however, is also true for active techniques that rely on reflections. Our approach is also prone to errors when the eyes are severely occluded (e.g., if a person's hair blocks an eye), when the illumination is extreme (e.g., strong highlights or profile illumination), or when there is very low contrast in the image. Figure 7(b) highlights two of our sample detector's failure cases.

APPLICATIONS OF GAZE LOCKING

We now demonstrate a few of the applications that gaze locking facilitates. For each of these applications, we recorded video feeds from the respective devices (iPads, webcams, and a DSLR camera) and ran our detector on them offline. Our accompanying video shows the output of our detector on the feeds and images from Figures 10–13.

Human–Object Interaction

Cameras are becoming increasingly small and inexpensive to produce. By embedding cameras in everyday devices and objects, the devices and objects can be selected or activated simply by looking at them.

As an example, Figure 10 shows a proof of concept system that we created with 3rd generation iPads. We process the videos from the iPads' built-in cameras (which have a 640×480 px resolution) to sense when they are looked at,

Figure 10. Human–object interaction. Our gaze locking approach allows people to interact with objects just by looking at them. In this proof of concept, we process the videos from the embedded cameras of three iPads to sense when the iPads are being looked at. Here, the woman is looking at the iPad in the middle. Since the iPads' cameras are on their extreme left, she was instructed to look at the iPads' left halves. Our accompanying video shows our detector's output on the actual video feeds.

Figure 11. User analytics. Two ordinary webcams are placed above two ads for the same product. By counting the number of times each advertisement is viewed, we can gauge which one is more effective. The counts incremented when the viewers looked at the ads' top halves. Our accompanying video shows our detector's output on the actual video feeds.

then display relevant content such as news headlines or reading lists. As another example, a museum exhibit or department store item could be rigged with a small camera to inform passersby about them when they look at them.

Some smartphones (e.g., the Samsung Galaxy S III and the Samsung Galaxy S4) already include "smart pause" and "smart scroll" features to pause videos by looking away from the phone and scroll documents by looking up and down. However, we found that both features on the Galaxy S4 seem to work reliably only when a user moves his or her entire head, although the system also responded sometimes to large eye motions alone. Our technique can distinguish eye contact from a subtle $\pm 5°$ gaze away, and it works over long distances.

User Analytics

Several commercial systems [12, 13] embed cameras in product displays or advertisements as a means of measuring consumer attention, but these systems employ active infrared illumination. As Figure 11 shows, our method offers a completely passive alternative that is robust to distance and does not require special hardware.

Figure 12. Image search filter. Our approach is completely appearance-based and can be applied to any image, including existing images such as ones from the Web. Hence, we can sort these images (A–D) by degree of eye contact to quickly find one where everyone is looking at the camera. These are actual decisions made by our detector.

Figure 13. Gaze-triggered photography. By incorporating a gaze locking detector in a consumer-level camera, the camera could automatically take a picture when the entire group is looking straight back, allowing the photographer to join the group and still capture a perfect photo. Our accompanying video shows our detector's output on the camera's feed.

As with the commercial systems, our method has a reasonably sized tolerance for what it considers gaze locking, allowing it to work for cameras placed adjacent to regions of interest as well. Our detector was trained to distinguish between $0°$ and $\pm 5°$ horizontally and between $0°$ and $\pm 10°$ vertically, so we estimate its tolerance to be roughly $2.5°$ in either direction horizontally and $5°$ in either direction vertically. This corresponds to a 8.7×17.5 cm target at a distance of 1 m and a 43.7×87.5 cm target at a distance of 5 m.

Image Filtering

Unlike active methods, our method can be used to detect eye contact in existing images such as ones from the Internet. There are billions of images on the Internet, and over 300 million photos are uploaded to Facebook alone each day [20]. Hence, as Figure 12 shows, we can sort and filter photos by degree of eye contact with our method to improve image search.

Gaze-Triggered Photography

With today's cameras, taking a group photo can be difficult since everyone must be looking at the camera at the right moment. With our technology, however, cameras can incorporate a gaze trigger that works as follows: the photographer would initiate the function, then join the group as the camera waits to see another face (the photographer's) enter the frame. As soon as this is detected, the camera would take a picture when the entire group is looking straight back. Figure 13 and our supplementary video demonstrate this concept.

Already, many consumer-level cameras (e.g., the Sony Cyber-shot W650) feature an anti-blink function that helps users capture photos when subjects are not blinking. Other cameras (e.g., the Canon PowerShot XS160 IS) also include face self-timers that release the shutter only when an additional face (the photographer's) enters the frame. By sensing eye contact instead of simply sensing blinking or the presence of faces, our technology can make cameras aware of when people are actually looking straight back.

DISCUSSION

Contributions

In this work, we have created a passive approach for sensing eye contact from a live camera or an existing still image or video recording and demonstrated several of the applications that it facilitates, such as human–object interaction and gaze-triggered photography. We also performed a study on how accurately humans can perform the same task, finding several interesting results. Lastly, we created a large gaze data set. Unlike existing gaze tracking approaches, our approach exploits the special appearance of direct eye gaze, making it largely robust to distance and pose, even though it is passive, non-intrusive, and calibration-free. Furthermore, it does not require any special hardware.

Toward embeddable gaze lockers

There is great potential for future work in gaze locking using embedded cameras. Our sample detector consists of fairly simple mathematical operations, so future efforts could create a "gaze locker"—a camera module with a system-on-chip for gaze locking. This gaze locker would be small, cheap, and computationally efficient. Systems-on-chip already exist in cameras for applications such as exposure compensation and image compression.

Moreover, our gaze locking approach is passive and, as a result, energy-efficient. Hence, gaze lockers may even be able to employ energy-harvesting techniques like RFID tags do. We could also use gaze lockers to aid the blind and deaf by sensing when others are looking at them. Furthermore, if we place gaze lockers in many objects, they would collectively form a cloud that serves as a ubiquitous gaze tracker that is accurate over distance. For all of these reasons, we believe gaze lockers could be the perfect platform for bringing gaze-based interactive systems into everyday use in the future.

ACKNOWLEDGMENTS

This research was supported in part by ONR Award No. N00014-11-1-0285. Brian A. Smith was supported by the Department of Defense (DoD) through the National Defense Science and Engineering Graduate Fellowship (NDSEG) Program.

REFERENCES

1. Argyle, M., and Dean, J. Eye-contact, distance and affiliation. *J. Sociometry 28*, 3 (1965), 289–304.
2. Baluja, S., and Pomerleau, D. Non-intrusive gaze tracking using artificial neural networks. Tech. rep., Department of Computer Science, Carnegie Mellon University, 1994.
3. Beymer, D., and Flickner, M. Eye gaze tracking using an active stereo head. In *Proc. CVPR 2003*, IEEE Press (2003).
4. Blackwell, H. R. Contrast thresholds of the human eye. *J. Opt. Soc. Am. 36*, 11 (1946).
5. Bolt, R. A. Put-that-there: Voice and gesture at the graphics interface. In *Proc. SIGGRAPH 1980*, ACM Press (1980), 262–270.
6. Cadavid, S., Mahoor, M., Messinger, D., and Cohn, J. Automated classification of gaze direction using spectral regression and support vector machine. In *Proc. ACII 2009*, IEEE Press (2009), 1–6.
7. Chang, C., and Lin, C. LIBSVM: a library for support vector machines. *ACM Trans. Intell. Syst. Technol. 2*, 3 (2011), 27:1–27:27.
8. Chen, M. Leveraging the asymmetric sensitivity of eye contact for videoconferencing. In *Proc. CHI 2002*, ACM Press (2002), 49–56.
9. Cline, M. G. The perception of where a person is looking. *Am. J. Psychol. 80*, 1 (1967), 41–50.
10. Curcio, C. A., Sloan, K. R., Kalina, R. E., and Hendrickson, A. E. Human photoreceptor topography. *J. Comp. Neurol. 292*, 4 (1990), 497–523.
11. Duda, R., Hart, P., and Stork, D. *Pattern classification*, vol. 2. Wiley-Interscience, 2001, 114–124.
12. eyebox2™ impressions™ for signage. `https://www.xuuk.com/Images/eyebox2productspecs.pdf`.
13. EyeTech™ VT2 XL. `http://www.eyetechds.com/vt2-xl.shtml`.
14. Gamer, M., and Hecht, H. Are you looking at me? measuring the cone of gaze. *J. Exp. Psychol. [Hum Percept.] 33*, 3 (2007), 705–715.
15. Gemmell, J., Toyama, K., Zitnick, C., Kang, T., and Seitz, S. Gaze awareness for video-conferencing: a software approach. *IEEE Multimedia 7*, 4 (2000), 26–35.
16. Gibson, J. J., and Pick, A. D. Perception of another person's looking behavior. *Am. J. Psychol. 76*, 3 (1963), 386–394.
17. Hansen, D., and Ji, Q. In the eye of the beholder: A survey of models for eyes and gaze. *IEEE Trans. Pattern Anal. Mach. Intell. 32*, 3 (2010), 478–500.
18. Hansen, D. W., and Pece, A. E. C. Eye tracking in the wild. *Comput. Vis. Image Und. 98*, 1 (2005), 155–181.
19. Kendon, A. Some functions of gaze direction in social interaction. *Acta Psychol. 26* (1967), 22–63.
20. Kiss, J. Facebook hits 1 billion users a month. `http://www.guardian.co.uk/technology/2012/oct/04/facebook-hits-billion-users-a-month`, Oct 2012.
21. Martin, W. W., and Jones, R. F. The accuracy of eye-gaze judgement: A signal detection approach. *Brit. J. Soc. Psychol. 21*, 4 (1982), 293–299.
22. Matthews, B. Comparison of the predicted and observed secondary structure of T4 phage lysozyme. *BBA-Protein Struct." 405*, 2 (1975), 442–451.
23. McMurrough, C. D., Metsis, V., Rich, J., and Makedon, F. An eye tracking dataset for point of gaze detection. In *Proc. ETRA 2012*, ACM Press (2012), 305–308.
24. Morimoto, C., Amir, A., and Flickner, M. Detecting eye position and gaze from a single camera and 2 light sources. In *Proc. ICPR 2002*, IEEE Press (2002), 314–317.
25. Morimoto, C., Koons, D., Amir, A., and Flickner, M. Pupil detection and tracking using multiple light sources. *J. Image Vision Comput. 18*, 4 (2000).

26. Morimoto, C., and Mimica, M. Eye gaze tracking techniques for interactive applications. *Comput. Vis. Image Und. 98*, 1 (2005), 4–24.

27. Nishino, K., and Nayar, S. The world in an eye. In *Proc. CVPR 2004*, IEEE Press (2004), 444–451.

28. Omron. OKAO vision. `http://www.omron.com/r_d/coretech/vision/okao.html`.

29. Ponz, V., Villanueva, A., and Cabeza, R. Dataset for the evaluation of eye detector for gaze estimation. In *Proc. UbiComp 2012*, ACM Press (2012), 681–684.

30. Shechtman, D., Riordan-Eva, P., and Hardigan, P. Maximum angle of ocular duction during visual fixation as a function of age. *Strabismus 13*, 1 (2005), 21–26.

31. Shell, J. S., Vertegaal, R., Cheng, D., Skaburskis, A. W., Sohn, C., Stewart, A. J., Aoudeh, O., and Dickie, C. ECSGlasses and EyePliances: using attention to open sociable windows of interaction. In *Proc. ETRA 2004*, ACM Press (2004), 93–100.

32. Smith, J. D., Vertegaal, R., and Sohn, C. ViewPointer: lightweight calibration-free eye tracking for ubiquitous handsfree deixis. In *Proc. UIST 2005*, ACM Press (2005), 53–61.

33. Stiefelhagen, R., Yang, J., and Waibel, A. A model-based gaze tracking system. In *Proc. IEEE Intelligence and Systems 1996*, IEEE Press (1996), 304–310.

34. Stiefelhagen, R., Yang, J., and Waibel, A. Tracking eyes and monitoring eye gaze. In *Proc. PUI 1997* (1997).

35. Symons, L. A., Lee, K., Cedrone, C. C., and Nishimura, M. What are you looking at? acuity for triadic eye gaze. *J. Gen. Psychol. 131*, 4 (2004), 451–469.

36. Tan, K.-H., Kriegman, D. J., and Ahuja, N. Appearance-based eye gaze estimation. In *Proc. WACV 2002*, IEEE Press (2002), 191–195.

37. Turk, M., and Pentland, A. Face recognition using eigenfaces. In *Proc. CVPR 1991*, IEEE Press (1991), 586–591.

38. Vertegaal, R. Attentive user interfaces. *Comm. ACM 46*, 3 (2003), 31–33.

39. Vertegaal, R., and Shell, J. Attentive user interfaces: the surveillance and sousveillance of gaze-aware objects. *Soc. Sci. Inf. 47*, 3 (2008), 275–298.

40. Vertegaal, R., Slagter, R., van der Veer, G., and Nijholt, A. Eye gaze patterns in conversations: there is more to conversational agents than meets the eyes. In *Proc. CHI 2001*, ACM Press (2001), 301–308.

41. Weidenbacher, U., Layher, G., Strauss, P.-M., and Neumann, H. A comprehensive head pose and gaze database. In *Proc. IE 2007*, IET Press (2007).

42. Ye, Z., Li, Y., Fathi, A., Han, Y., Rozga, A., Abowd, G. D., and Rehg, J. M. Detecting eye contact using wearable eye-tracking glasses. In *Proc. UbiComp 2012*, ACM Press (2012), 699–704.

43. Zhai, S., Morimoto, C., and Ihde, S. Manual and gaze input cascaded (MAGIC) pointing. In *Proc. CHI 1999*, ACM Press (1999), 246–253.

APPENDIX

Scaling Data Set Images

In our human test, the players viewed our images in front of a computer screen, but we needed the subjects in the images to appear as they would in person for the results to be accurate. We also needed to represent a variety of distances (2 m to 18 m) properly for both the human and sample detector experiments. Hence, we took the parameters of our camera, computer monitor, and even the acuity of the human eye into account to scale the images accordingly and display them at the proper resolution. The calculations are described here.

Human Test

An "eye pixel" is the smallest area of the human fovea that can distinguish a point or a line pair [4, 10]. In our human experiments, if the player were to view the subject directly from a distance of d_o, the subject's face would subtend E of the player's eye's pixels in width, where:

$$E = \frac{w}{2d_o \tan(\theta_e/2)}. \quad (1)$$

w is the width of the subject's face (usually ≈14 cm). θ_e is the angular resolution of the human eye fovea, and is roughly 0.3 arc-minutes (or 0.005° per eye pixel) [4, 10].

When the subject is captured by a camera instead, his or her face subtends C camera pixels in width, where:

$$C = \frac{P_c w}{w_c(u/f - 1)}. \quad (2)$$

P_c is the camera's horizontal pixel count, w_c is the width of the image sensor, f is the camera's focal length, and u is the distance from the subject to the camera.

Then, if the player views the captured image on a screen, the subject's face would subtend S eye pixels in width:

$$S = \frac{\alpha C w_s}{2d_s P_s \tan(\theta_e/2)}, \quad \text{where} \quad \alpha \leq 1. \quad (3)$$

α is the factor by which the image dimensions are scaled on the screen (1 represents 100%), P_s is the screen's horizontal pixel count, w_s is the screen's width, and d_s is the distance from the player to the screen.

For the player to view the subject on the screen without a loss in resolution compared to seeing the subject in person, both C and S must be greater than or equal to E. This was true in our configuration, in which u = 2 m, f = 85 mm, P_c = 5184 px, d_c = 22.3 mm, P_s = 2560 px, d_s = 664 mm, D = 508 mm, and the corresponding (d_o, α) pairs (i.e., the scale factors we used to represent each distance) were (2 m, 19.5%), (6 m, 6.5%), (10 m, 3.9%), (14 m, 2.8%), and (18 m, 2.2%).

Sample Detector Experiments

When testing the accuracy of our sample detector, we wanted the detector to "see" each image as if they were being viewed by a person at the appropriate distance d_o. That is, the subject's face in each image should be of the same resolution that the human retina would see it at a distance of d_o. Hence, we can simply downsample our data set's images to a resolution of E via Equation 1 to get versions of them that correspond to different distances d_o.

Open Project: A Lightweight Framework for Remote Sharing of Mobile Applications

Matei Negulescu*
University of British Columbia
mnegules@cs.ubc.ca

Yang Li
Google Research
yangli@acm.org

ABSTRACT
The form factor of mobile devices remains small while their computing power grows at an accelerated rate. Prior work has explored expanding the output space by leveraging free displays in the environment. However, existing solutions often do not scale. In this paper we discuss Open Project, an end-to-end framework that allows a user to "project" a native mobile application onto a display using a phone camera, leveraging interaction spaces ranging from a PC monitor to a public wall-sized display. Any display becomes projectable instantaneously by simply accessing the lightweight Open Project server via a web browser. By distributing computation load onto each projecting mobile device, our framework easily scales for hosting many projection sessions and devices simultaneously. Our performance experiments and user studies indicated that Open Project supported a variety of useful collaborative, sharing scenarios and performed reliably in diverse settings.

Author Keywords
Remote sharing; protocol and architecture design; mobile interaction; computer vision; projection-based interaction.

ACM Classification Keywords
H.5.2 [Information interfaces and presentation]: User Interfaces: Input Devices and Strategies, Interaction Styles.

INTRODUCTION
Mobile devices grow rapidly in computational power and ubiquity. However, their small form factor, though highly portable, offers a limited interaction bandwidth. In particular, touchscreens, as the major modern input and output medium, suffer from finger occlusion and restricted view areas in spite of their high resolutions (e.g., an Apple iPhone 4s affords a 3.5" touchscreen with a 960x640 resolution). They are awkward to use especially when more than one user wants to interact with the device, e.g., viewing pictures together or playing a multiplayer game.

To address these problems, handheld projectors have shown promise in enlarging the output area of a mobile application [4,5,8,9,15]. However, handheld projectors are often additional hardware to carry and also require special sensors (e.g., a depth camera) for detecting user input in the physical space [8,24]. In addition, projector-based solutions suffer from physical limitations such as hand tremor which makes stabilizing a projection during interaction difficult.

To leverage the intuitiveness of projector-based interaction and overcome the above issues, recent work has explored mobile content sharing using software-based projection (e.g. [3,7,10,16]). For example, Deep Shot allows a user to "post" mobile content onto a remote registered display using a built-in phone camera [10]. More recently, Baur et al.'s Virtual Projection allowed users to share a mobile application by providing continuous feedback on the target display to simulate a projection effect [3]. However, these previous solutions face several challenges.

First, previous systems generally consider predefined target displays for sharing. To set up a target display, the user would need to install the required software component on the display and also register the display before using it. In contrast, we focus on ephemeral sharing scenarios on a variety of displays, especially in a collaborative or public setting, which desire little deployment overhead.

Second, previous solutions conduct computationally intensive tasks such as computer vision on the server or on the target display. This architectural design avoids complex communication protocols and vision processing on low-end mobile hardware. However, it does not scale for hosting many target displays and simultaneous sharing sessions.

Last, previous systems that employ camera-based sharing techniques detect vision features of the screenshot image on the remote display. Although this solution is more seamlessly integrated with the interaction environment, it does not scale for realistic scenarios that often involve sharing from varying distances and angles to remote displays in different lighting conditions.

To address these issues, we developed Open Project, a lightweight, highly scalable framework that allows users to leverage the input and output capabilities of other available devices, such as a large display, for interacting with mobile applications. Similar to prior work, it allows a user to share a running mobile application onto a target display by "projecting" it via a mobile phone camera (see Figure 1). However, it goes beyond prior work in several ways.

UIST'13, October 8–11, 2013, St. Andrews, United Kingdom.
ACM 978-1-4503-2268-3/13/10.
http://dx.doi.org/10.1145/2501988.2502030

* This work was done while the author was an intern at Google Research.

a) A user starts by aiming the phone camera at the barcode that uniquely identifies the display.

b) The barcode, once identified, changes to a checkerboard marker that continuously shifts as the user orients the phone toward a target position, as if it were projected from the phone.

c) The user taps the phone screen to project the application at the checkerboard position, and interacts with the application via either the phone or its projection on the display. The barcode reappears for other users to project their applications.

Figure 1. A user projects a foreground application running on the phone (e.g., Photo Gallery) onto a wall-size display for a larger view of it. To do so, the user activates Open Project on the phone that (a) identifies a specific display, (b) selects a target position and size, and (c) sharing the application.

First, we developed a web-based framework for supporting multiple users simultaneously sharing content on one or many displays. With the easily-accessible nature of web services, any display can become *immediately projectable* once it accesses the Open Project server in its web browser and can support any number of sharing sessions—deployment is as simple as opening a webpage. A mobile device is paired automatically with a target display once the user identifies the display's 2D barcode, requiring no authentication or pre-registration.

Second, we designed a *decentralized architecture* and communication protocol for scalable mobile sharing. All intensive computation—mainly realizing camera-based projection and executing applications—is performed locally on each individual mobile phone; when sharing, a video feed of the application is transferred to the remote display. This enables our framework to easily accommodate an arbitrary number of projection devices and target displays.

Third, we created *a robust "camera projection" algorithm* for creating a projection effect for users to select sharing positions and dimensions on a target display. The algorithm uses a dedicated checkerboard pattern, instead of relying on screenshots, such that it performs reliably at great ranges, varying lighting conditions and angles. Our algorithm functions when the target screen is blank or has a background image. It performs robustly against on or off-screen distracters. A thorough evaluation of the projection algorithm and the system as a whole provided solid findings for how this kind of system performs in a realistic scenario.

RELATED WORK

In addition to projecting mobile screens onto a physical surface (e.g. [4,5,8,9,15]), prior work investigated mobile sharing to remote displays. One solution of sharing is to send user data or application states to the target machine, e.g., [7,10,12,14,16,19]. The other category of sharing is to stream live copies of UIs—images—to the target machine, and redirect user input to the originating device, e.g., [1,3,7,21,23]. Although transferring files or application states allows better performance on the target machine, it requires the target machine to handle the data or execute the application which introduces security concerns when using a shared or public display—our focus scenario. As a result, we chose to share live screen images but keep data and computation on the mobile device.

XICE [1] allows developers to share live views of mobile apps onto other displays using a custom UI rendering framework. While this approach allows less latency, it is incompatible with existing mobile UI frameworks (e.g., on Android or iPhone). Modifying mobile apps to leverage the framework requires significant developer effort. Open Project allows developers to enable remote sharing of any mobile application with fewer than thirty lines of Java code.

An important step in sharing is to specify a target on a remote display. Previously, using a built-in phone camera for direct pointing has shown promise for WYSIWYG selection of distant targets [2,3,6,10,18]. For example, past work has used a grid of static markers as anchors on the remote screen to estimate where the phone is pointing [2,18]. Open Project uses a single marker, which provides continuous feedback and visual synchronization for targeting.

Open Project is closely related to Virtual Projection [3], which used the projection metaphor to share a smartphone's display via its camera. However, the two techniques are different both in focus and in design. Open Project is aimed at enabling impromptu sharing on arbitrary displays with minimal deployment effort. It is particularly designed for remote sharing on public, shared displays where authentication or pre-registration should be avoided. In particular, Open Project employs a web-based architecture

Figure 2. Multiple users simultaneously projecting their mobile applications (left: Maps and right: Photo Gallery).

to allow lightweight instantaneous deployment and easy access to the projection service.

While Virtual Projection centralizes computation to the server and the target display, Open Project employs a distributed architecture that keeps most of the computation on each individual mobile device; this approach can easily scale for many simultaneous projection devices. In addition, instead of relying on visual features of the screenshot of a target display (e.g., [3,10]), Open Project employs a QR code and a camera-propelled marker to indicate a specific position on a remote display. The marker allows reliable and efficient tracking on mobile hardware, and performs at great ranges with varying lighting conditions and angles or when the target display has no visual features.

Using camera frames to estimate motion is widely used in computer vision. Rather than relying on a static scene (e.g., [22]), Open Project uses detected motion to propel a tracking target to simulate the projection effect. We designed a visual synchronization protocol to coordinate two asynchronous but dependent movement processes.

REMOTE SHARING WITH OPEN PROJECT

A handheld projector allows a user to project content at a specific location and size on a large, physical surface. Open Project leverages the projection metaphor so that users can easily share an arbitrary, native mobile application at a desired position on a target display such as the wall-sized display in Figure 1. Instead of relying on the screenshot of the target display (e.g. [3,10]), we use the phone's camera to drive a marker on the remote display to locate where to project—simulating physical projection. This approach functions even when the screen has no visual features in its background—a blank screen. Once the user identifies a projection region, we send screen pixels to be rendered on the remote display instead of the application itself, which allows the sharing of an arbitrary, native application. As the focus of our system is scalability and multi-user collaborative scenarios, Open Project also implements a visual handshake protocol to register users with any display showing a browser pointed at the Open Project server.

To better describe our interaction flow, consider Angela and Ben, two users at a mall. Angela wants to show Ben her vacation pictures on her smartphone. Instead of giving Ben her phone, Angela decides to use the nearby public display to browse these pictures. To do so, Angela enables Open Project in her Photo Gallery application, which starts a camera view for her to capture the marker. Angela identifies the public display by capturing its QR code (see Figure 1a). Once the QR code is identified, it changes into a checkerboard marker. The blue rectangle centered on the marker represents the target region into which the mobile application will be projected into (see Figures 1b) and moves according to where Angela points her phone's camera. To change the target projection size, Angela slides her finger in a circular motion on the touchscreen (as in [20]): moving counterclockwise to enlarge and clockwise to shrink the projection region.

Once satisfied with the location and size of the projection on the display, Angela taps on the phone's touchscreen to affix the projection, which exits the camera view and returns to the Photo Gallery. Meanwhile, the Photo Gallery is shared at the size and location indicated by the projection region on the remote display. Further movement of the phone will not affect the projection. At this point, the QR code reappears at the center of the display ready for other users' projection (see Figure 1c).

The users can now interact with Photo Gallery through both the application running on the phone and its remote projection. As Angela flicks through the pictures by swiping on her phone, the changes take effect in realtime in the mirrored remote representation. When Ben wants to select an image, he swipes the projection directly on the large touch-enabled display. Ben's remote touch input is relayed to Angela's phone to select the image. Should Angela want to maintain control over her application, she can disable remote input through a menu option.

Meanwhile, a third user captures the QR code using Open Project and shares his Maps application. All users occupy different parts of the display to interact with their applications; all computation occurs on their respective mobile devices (Figure 2). Open Project is able to host multiple concurrent projections on a display and the display space is allocated in a First-Come-First-Serve manner. A projection owns its region on the display—no other projections can be placed on top of it—until the user stops the projection from the phone.

THE OPEN PROJECT FRAMEWORK

We designed the framework to satisfy several important goals. First, the framework should support common collaborative and sharing scenarios for mobile users. Second, the system should be usable for off-the-shelf mobile devices, without requiring additional hardware or sensors, should require minimal computation and infrastructure, and should be robust in various settings. Third, the system should be easy to deploy and incorporate. To minimize deployment costs, Open Project requires neither the installation of a custom kernel on mobile devices nor additional software on the remote display.

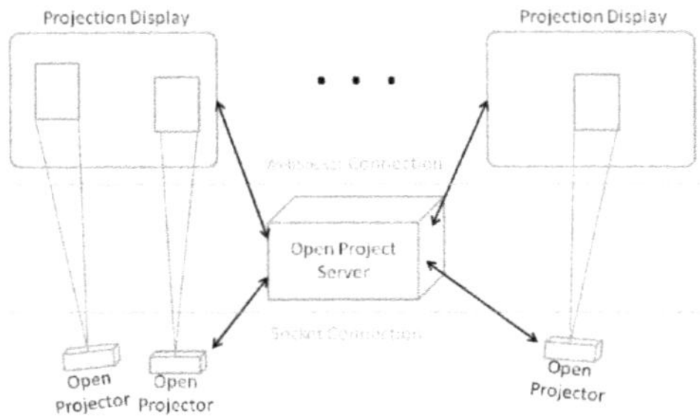

Figure 3. The Open Project runtime architecture.

Instead, Open Project allows developers to project their mobile content by simply adding an Android library while any remote display is share-capable by pointing a browser at our URL.

The Runtime Architecture

The runtime architecture of the Open Project framework consists of three components (see Figure 3): 1) Open Project Server—a web service running on a centralized server for managing projection sessions, 2) Open Projector—a library running on the smartphone for projecting the mobile application, and 3) Projection Display—a web application running in a browser on the display's computer for serving one or multiple projections.

Open Project allows an arbitrary display to become projectable. The owner of the display simply starts a browser on the display's computer and accesses the Open Project Server on the web, i.e., via an HTTP request. This runs Projection Display in the browser. Projection Display starts with a QR code shown at the center of the screen that encodes an ID for identifying the display. Multiple displays can make requests to Open Project Server at the same time and each will be assigned a unique ID.

Note that this lightweight deployment can be as simple as clicking on a bookmark that points to the Open Project Server. The owner of the display can also choose to have a background image or a blank screen. For example, on a public display in a train station, a static background image or dynamic graphics (such as ads) can be displayed as usual, and a projection will be rendered on top of it.

In front of a display, a user activates Open Projector on the phone, e.g., via a menu, while the application of interest is running in the foreground. There are three steps to project a mobile application: *identifying a target display* via the QR code, *adjusting the projection region* on the display, and *sharing the phone screen* on the selected projection region.

Identifying a Target Display

Open Projector starts by invoking the camera functionality on the phone to search for a valid QR code in the scene. It brings up a camera view on the phone for the user to aim the camera at the QR code on the target display. Once Open Projector detects a QR code, it decodes the display ID from the QR code and requests the Open Project Server to create a projection session. The server then notifies both the Projection Display, identified by the decoded ID, and the Open Projector with a session ID. Thereafter, the Projection Display and Open Projector communicate with each other through the Open Project Server using the assigned session ID, which allows messages to be correctly routed when multiple sessions are active (see Figures 2 & 3). Once Projection Display receives a new session ID, it responds by turning the QR code into a checkerboard marker for the user to adjust the projection region.

Adjusting the Projection Region

Once the Open Projector sees the checkerboard marker, it calculates how much the detected marker deviates from the center of the camera view. It then sends the Projection Display the deviation as the amount of adjustment that the marker has to make on the display so that the marker can return to the center of the camera view. As the user moves or orients the phone towards a target position on the display, the marker adjustment is continuously sent to the Projection Display, and the position change of the marker on the display is fed back to the phone visually through the camera. We will elaborate on the details in the next section.

As mentioned earlier, a user can slide her finger on the phone's touchscreen in a circular motion to enlarge or shrink a projection denoted by the blue bounding box. Note that the size and orientation of the marker remain constant. A user may rotate the phone to switch between landscape and the portrait orientations, which will change the orientation of the projection region accordingly.

Sharing the phone screen

Once a user taps the camera view on the phone, the camera view exits and the projection region is affixed. The system now enters the sharing stage. In this stage, the phone's position and orientation become irrelevant to the projection on the display. As the Open Projector has returned control to the application (from the camera view), a user can now interact with the application. Meanwhile, the Open Projector periodically polls the screen image of the application, compresses and sends the image to the display if the screen has been updated. The Projection Display receives the screenshot of the application, scales and renders it according to the determined projection region.

A user can interact with the mobile application on the phone as usual and the UI changes will be reflected on both the local phone screen and the remote projection. In addition, Open Project allows users to directly operate the application via the projection if the display supports user input. When a pointing event occurs, such as a mouse or touch event, the Projection Display verifies if it is within the boundary of an affixed projection, and if so, relays the event to the paired Open Projector using its session ID. This allows the Projection Display to dispatch pointing events to appropriate projections when multiple projections exist on the same display. Additionally, the Projection Display also acts as a window manager and ensures that projections do not overlap, nor are moved off screen.

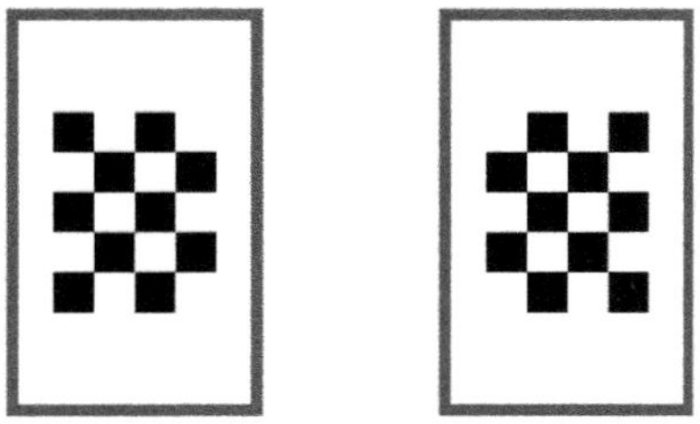

Figure 4. The two checkerboard patterns used for positioning. One is the negation of the other in colors.

The Open Projector receives input events from its projection on the display, and re-dispatches the events to the UI of the application that is being projected. The application responds to the events as if these events were originated locally from the phone, and the UI changes will be displayed on both sides as discussed earlier.

Algorithms for "Camera Projection"

An important step in Open Project is to position a target projection region on a remote display. Open Project emulates a handheld projector through "camera projection", a technique that allows a user to physically target their desired location on the remote display using a built-in phone camera instead of a real projector. To scale for many simultaneous projecting mobile devices and displays, our architecture distributes the computation required for camera projection onto each mobile device.

The fundamental intuition behind the camera projection algorithm is that a designated pattern on the display (e.g., a checkerboard in our current design), as the projection from the camera, should stay at the center of the camera view. When a user moves or orients the phone camera towards a new location on the display, the pattern will deviate from the center of the camera view. Based on the amount of observed deviation, we can calculate how much the target pattern should be moved on the display so that it is centered in the camera view again.

Designing a Target Pattern

An important issue for the algorithm to work is to design an appropriate target pattern that is easy and reliable to detect by a phone camera. A common solution has been detecting features in a screenshot image (e.g. [3,13]). However, such a solution is dependent upon having an appropriately feature-rich screenshot, is constrained under different viewing conditions and at larger distances, and can become complicated when the screen is highly dynamic (e.g., when other simultaneous projections are constantly updating).

Alternatively, checkerboard patterns have been extensively used in computer vision for camera calibration (e.g. [17]). Checkerboards are distinctive markers that are detectable in many lighting conditions, amongst complex distractors, and at various angles. Additionally, such a marker can be dynamically scaled depending on the size and resolution of the display to enable interaction at large distances. Finally, reliable detection of checkerboard markers can be achieved efficiently on low-powered devices such as smartphones, making it ideal for Open Project.

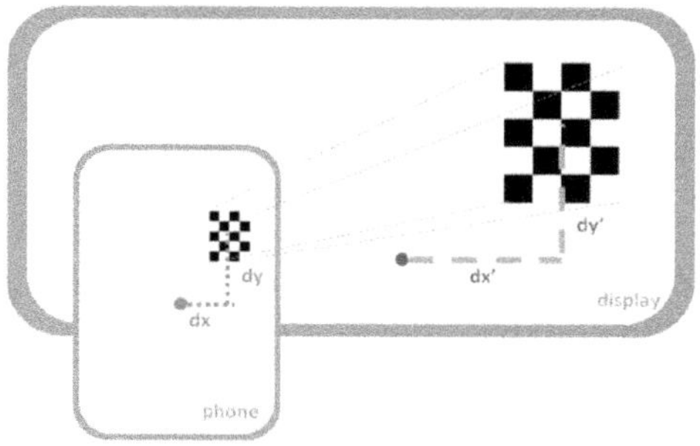

Figure 5. Transforming the offset in camera coordinates, *dx* and *dy*, to an offset in display coordinates, *dx'* and *dy'*.

In our specific design, we use a 5-by-4 checkerboard pattern (see Figure 4) that is resilient of false positives and gives more than enough inner intersection points for calculating a homography matrix. Furthermore, the asymmetric design of the checkerboard helps determine the orientation of the camera with relation to the display.

Detecting a Checkerboard Pattern

Our checkerboard detection algorithm is based on OpenCV, a popular computer vision open source library [25]. In particular, OpenCV provides a set of functions for camera calibration by estimating camera parameters from a series of frames containing a checkerboard pattern. While this algorithm is effective for one-time camera calibration, it is focused on accuracy over speed by continuously iterating its search for quads whose intersections form the inner points of a checkerboard. The algorithm is less suitable when realtime tracking is needed on a smartphone processor. Thus, we tailored the OpenCV algorithm in two ways. First, we eliminate quads quickly by aggressively thresholding based on size and proximity. Second, we eliminate the original algorithm's iterative approach for finding intersection points by expanding quads. A pilot study showed that iterating the search has diminishing returns that do not justify the time cost.

Transforming Deviation from Camera to Display Coordinates

The output of the checkerboard detection algorithm is a set of twelve internal intersection points in camera coordinates. Let dx and dy be the offsets of the centroid of these points from the center of the camera view on the horizontal and vertical axis (see Figure 5). We need to transform these offsets to display coordinates to find how much the checkerboard must be moved on the display (Equation 1).

$$w\begin{bmatrix} dx' & dy' & 1 \end{bmatrix}^T = H\begin{bmatrix} dx & dy & 1 \end{bmatrix}^T \quad (1)$$

where H is a 3-by-3 projective transformation, i.e., a homography matrix, from camera to display coordinates.

Typically, a homography H can be calculated using a RANSAC approach [11], which iteratively finds the best mapping and the transformation matrix between two sets of points, in our case the 12 checkerboard points detected in camera coordinates and on the display. However, this process can be simplified for our use. We can determine the correspondences between the two sets of points, by sorting the detected checkerboard points based on the phone's orientation (detected via built-in accelerometers) and their order in the horizontal and vertical axis. Once the correspondences are known, we can find the homography H by calculating the least square solution of a linear system (see Equation 2), which is much faster than RANSAC.

$$T = H\,O \tag{2}$$

where O is a 3-by-12 matrix whose columns are each the homogeneous coordinates of a checkerboard point observed in camera coordinates. T captures the coordinates of the 12 checkerboard points on the display. In fact, we do not need to know the absolute position of the checkerboard points on the display due to the following deduction. Each point can be represented as a relative coordinate, $T_{relative}$, to the checkerboard center, T_{center}. We do the same for the observed checkerboard points O. Thus,

$$T_{center} + T_{relative} = H\,(\,O_{center} + O_{relative}\,) \tag{3}$$

Because $T_{center} = H\,O_{center}$ is redundant for the calculation, we acquire Equation 4.

$$T_{relative} = H\,O_{relative} \tag{4}$$

However, $T_{relative}$ still requires us to know the physical size of the checkerboard on the display which is constant during projection. One solution is to use a predetermined fixed checkerboard size for all displays. However, this is inappropriate for diverse projection constraints, e.g., a large checkerboard might be used for a wall-size display to allow long-range projection while a small one can suffice on a PC monitor. A second solution is to let Projection Display pass the checkerboard size being used to the Projector on the phone at runtime—an extra step. Instead, we can eliminate this requirement by further deduction. We can take the size factor, S, out of $T_{relative}$:

$$S\,T_{unit} = H\,O_{relative} \tag{5}$$

where S is a 3x3 scaling transformation matrix and T_{unit} is the set of checkerboard points at a unit scale, independent of the actual physical size and position of the checkerboard. We then acquire:

$$T_{unit} = S^{-1}\,H\,O_{relative} \tag{6}$$

We can calculate $S^{-1}\,H$ as a whole, but not individually. However, we can use the expression as a whole, based on Equation 1, to transform dx and dy. This gives us the amount of adjustment needed at the unit scale. Once the Projection Display—which knows the actual size of the checkerboard S—receives this adjustment it can recover dx' and dy' by applying S to scale up the unit scale adjustment.

Synchronizing by Alternating Checkerboard Patterns

Generating updates on the phone and updating the checkerboard on the display are two asynchronous but dependent processes. An update is relative and applied to the marker's current position; the updated position is then used by the phone to generate the next update. As a result, when an update is sent to the Projection Display over the network, the phone has to wait for it to be processed by the Projection Display before analyzing a new frame and generating another update. This requires the two processes to be synchronized so that only one of them runs at a time.

To determine if an update has been processed, i.e., the checkerboard has been moved, we cannot rely on the checkerboard's deviation change observed through the camera as the phone is in constant motion even when not intended by the user. Thus, the Display must indicate that an update has been processed explicitly. Though it is possible to send this message to the phone over the network, it complicates the protocol and increases latency.

Instead, we use a visual synchronization mechanism by alternating between two distinct checkerboard patterns that share the same dimension (see Figure 4). When the display moves the checkerboard in response to an update request, it flips the checkerboard pattern to visually acknowledge. Once the phone detects the checkerboard switch, it starts to process a new frame and sends a new update.

Generating an update only when a checkerboard pattern flips synchronizes the processes well. However, it is possible that, before an update is processed or received by the display, the phone is already in a new position or orientation due to system latency and fast motion of the user's hand. To maximally follow the user motion, we choose to constantly generate updates, without waiting for the pattern to switch, but with an important enhancement. Each update is sent with the type of the pattern that it applies to, i.e., either type 1 or 2 (Figure 4). When an update reaches the display, the display checks its pattern type, applies the one that is consistent with the checkerboard pattern being shown and at the same time flips the pattern that will discard subsequent inconsistent updates. This ensures that a correct update is used for the current checkerboard position and is based on the assumption that in general an update would not take too long, i.e., longer than two pattern switches, to arrive at the display. This approach allows a later update to override an earlier unprocessed one, and leverages nondeterministic ordering of messages over the network (e.g. a late update can arrive early).

IMPLEMENTATION

We implemented Open Projector as a library based on the Android 4.0 platform. We employed the Zxing library [26] to detect the QR marker, and customized the OpenCV library to detect the checkerboard marker. Most of the computation for processing a frame and generating updates is written in C++ and performed natively to improve performance. It is then integrated via Android NDK with the rest of the library written in Java. Developers can enable Open Project for their Android application by using the Java API of the library (see Figure 7).

Figure 6. Example applications shared with Open Project: a) Maps, b) Photo Gallery, c) TicTacToe, and d) a drawing pad.

For sharing an application, the library grabs the drawing cache of the application at an empirically determined rate of 10fps to avoid overloading the phone processor. A new screen bitmap is compressed as a JPEG and sent over the network as an encoded Base64 byte stream. User input such as touch or mouse events from the remote display is converted as an Android TouchEvent and dispatched to the application's UI (view) hierarchy. The library communicates with the Open Project Server through a regular socket connection, which can be implemented with Web Sockets in the future.

The Projection Display is implemented as a web application and is automatically deployed on a target display when the browser points to the Open Project Server. We use a full screen HTML5 canvas in the browser for rendering projections and listening for user events. The web application is connected with the server via Web Sockets. Our server is implemented based on Tomcat, an open source web server [27]. The server merely routes messages and image data from mobile devices to screens. With the exception of decoding messages, it does not perform any additional computation, improving scalability. Web applications require no deployment and can easily respond to simultaneous requests from many different users–in this case, mobile devices. Finally, as all the computation is performed efficiently on the individual mobile device, the Open Project Server and the Projection Display need only limited hardware infrastructure for wide deployment.

```
// Instantiate a VirtualProjection instance
VirtualProjection projector = new OpenProject(activity);
// Start a projection
projector.startProjection (new OpenProjectCallback() {
  public void onSharingStarted () {
    // The user has selected a projection region and the sharing
    // stage is started
  }
  public void onCanceled () {
    // The projection is canceled by the user
    // before the sharing is started
  }
  public void onFinished () {
    // The sharing is ended by the user
  }
  public void onFailed () {
    // VirtualProjection failed to find a target display region
  }
 }
});
```

Figure 7. An example code snippet for enabling Open Project in an application.

ENABLING A MOBILE APPLICATION FOR PROJECTION

A developer can easily hook their mobile application into the Open Project framework. Although our current implementation is based on the Android platform, the API framework can be generalized for other platforms.

To add Open Project to an application, a developer instantiates the *OpenProject* class by passing it a reference to the current activity—a screen on the Android platform (see Figure 7). Open Projector will extract the root of the UI hierarchy for capturing the UI rendering cache and dispatching events from the remote display. A developer can select how to start projecting e.g., through a menu item. Remote input can be disabled on demand through a function call to maintain user control over the application.

To start a projection, a developer calls *startProjection* with *OpenProjectCallback* which allows the developer to handle a status change in the projection process. These callbacks give the developer the option to update the UI or signal the user, e.g., beeping when the sharing stage is started.

To demonstrate our API's ease of use, we added Open Project support to several sample applications provided by the Android SDK (see Figure 6): a Maps application, a Photo Gallery, a TicTacToe game, and a Drawing application. Based on these examples, we estimate that developers can add Open Project to their Android applications with less than 30 lines of Java code.

EVALUATIONS

In addition to demonstrating the usefulness of Open Project in a set of sample mobile applications, we evaluated Open Project in two ways. We first investigated the performance of our checkerboard updating algorithms. We then performed a user study to gauge user reactions to the tool.

Performance Experiments

We intended to find out, under different conditions, the effective range of the checkerboard marker detection and how fast we can update its position.

Apparatus

We used a Thinkpad T420s as our server (running Ubuntu Linux 10.04), a Galaxy Nexus smartphone for running Open Projector (with 11.8cm diagonal size at a resolution of 1280x720), and a PC connected to five Samsung displays (each is 68x120 cm) tiled by Windows 7 (see Figure 1). The PC showed a fullscreen Chrome browser running Projection

Display. Each display had a resolution of 900x1600, totaling 4500x1600 over five screens. The width of the two bezels between adjacent displays is 5cm. All devices were connected to a Belkin N750DB router's Wi-Fi network.

Experimental Design & Procedures

To find the effective range of our checkerboard detection and the time duration for updating the checkerboard position, we evaluated the system at various distances, angles, background distractors, and lighting (see Figure 8).

The major factors for the checkerboard detection include the checkerboard marker's size, the viewing distance and angle from the phone camera. The angle is critical due not only to perspective distortion but also foreshortening. Therefore, we tested our system for three angles: 90°, 60° and 30°. Note that at an acute angle of 30° we consider a range that is closer to the display (140-240cm) to take into account the significant perspective foreshortening. For each angle, we used six distances that cover the available space in the laboratory room. We used a fixed checkerboard marker—a 5x4 array of 3cm black and white squares. The small marker size was selected so as to detect the threshold distance within our small testing environment.

We also took into account two common factors for a computer-vision system: background distracters and lighting. For distracters, we tested three representative conditions: the marker is shown on a white screen, the marker is displayed on top of a full-sized background image, and the marker is surrounded by three distracter projections (a Maps app, a Contacts app, and a YouTube app). Two lighting conditions were tested: on and off.

Measures

In each condition, we mounted the phone such that the center of its camera view sat at a height of 115cm, perpendicular to the ground in portrait mode, with its center aligned with that of the checkerboard. The checkerboard marker was fixed on the display to maintain the designated spatial configuration. We then calculate two measures by processing 200 consecutive camera frames. We define the *detection rate* as the percentage of frames in which the algorithm finds the marker. This reflects how reliably our algorithm can detect the marker. We also measure the *update time* by looking at the duration between two adjacent checkerboard pattern switches detected by the algorithm—an update cycle. The update time includes the frame processing time, and other time costs such as the time to update the camera view, transmit an update over the network and render the new pattern on the display. Note that the update and detection rate are two correlated measures, i.e., when the detection rate is low, it takes a longer time to generate an update, and vice versa.

Results

We summarize Open Project's detection rate and update time performance under different conditions in Figure 8. When the update time is above 500ms, our algorithm is too slow to catch up to a regular user's motion, and we mark such a condition red in Figure 8. Otherwise, we mark it green. The checkerboard detection algorithm is most reliable when the lights are on, when there is less distraction at more straightforward angles. For example, with our very small marker size at 90° or 60°, a user can comfortably stay at a distance of 280cm and experience update times well below 500ms. We expect distance to scale linearly with the physical size of the rendered checkerboard marker which can be dynamically modified.

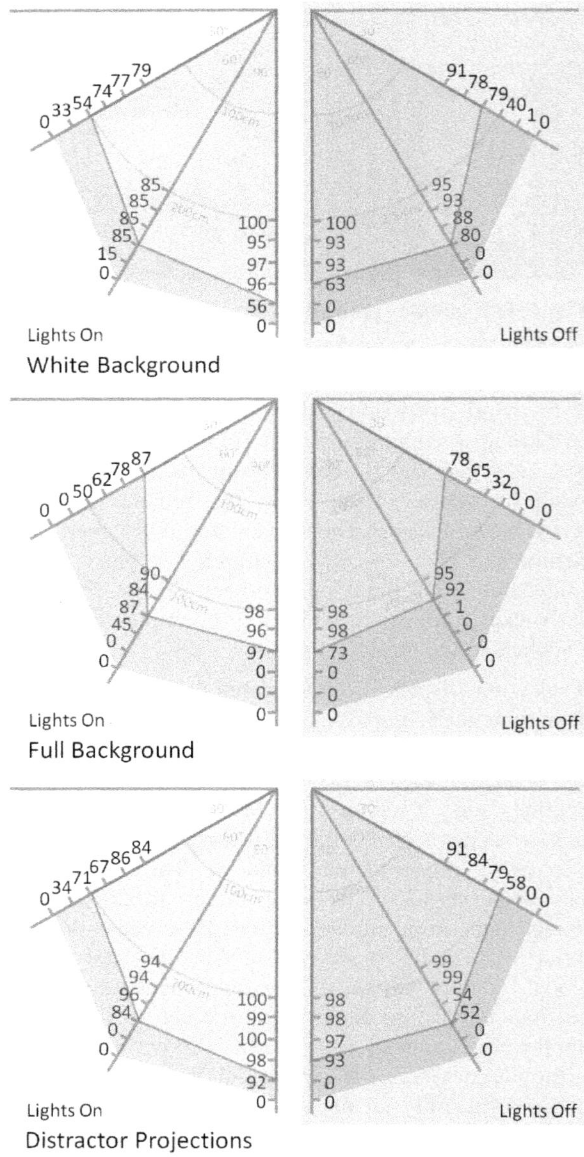

Figure 8. The detection rate (%) and update times in different conditions (green represents less than 500ms update time). Distances at 90° and 60° range from 200cm to 300cm. Distances at 30° range from 140cm to 240cm. They all have even increments of 20cm.

User Studies

We intended to find out 1) if a user can use our camera projection technique to adjust a target projection region on the display, and 2) how mobile users react to our system as a whole. We recruited 10 participants (2 females, 8 males, with a mean age of 22.4) from an IT company, all highly experienced smartphone users. Only one participant had experience with handheld physical projection systems.

Experimental Design

To answer these questions, our study consisted of two sessions. First, a participant moved and resized the projection region on the five-display setup used in our performance experiment. After a warm-up session, a participant starts the task by enabling Open Project on a test application. Starting from the center of the display, the participant must move the projection region to a given location, randomly selected from two categories: those nearby, or at most 68cm away; and those far away, or greater than 170cm. The initial projection dimensions are 22x37cm. A participant needs to scale the projection region up to one of two scales: 31x52cm, and 44x74cm (i.e. 1.4 times or twice the original dimensions). We marked each target location and size on the display. Participants confirm the final projection region and complete a trial by clicking on a button on the smartphone. Participants performed the task 12 times for each setting.

In the second session, participants were asked to project three Open Project-enabled applications onto a 68x120cm touch-sensitive display running at 900x1600 resolution. For this session, we used a citywide free wi-fi network instead of a dedicated network as previous, to experience a realistic network configuration. A participant first played a game of Tic-Tac-Toe with the computer. Then, the participant used the Gallery to find an image of a dog randomly positioned from a list of 15 distractor images. Last, the participant used Maps to find downtown Seattle and Vancouver from San Francisco using only panning and zooming. For a good understanding of the interaction, participants performed the tasks twice: once interacting on their smartphone, and once using the touch-sensitive large display. Participants were asked to think aloud and give qualitative feedback.

Results

Using a within-subjects analysis of variance with distance and scale as factors, we found both factors have a significant effect on the task completion time ($p < 0.05$). Participants took longer to position the projection farther away (M=12s, SD=4s) than closer to the starting position (M=11s, SD=3s). Tasks including scaling to twice the dimensions took 12s on average (SD=4s) while those requiring minor scaling took 11s (SD=4s). Task completion times include acquiring the Stop button for each trial.

To find out how accurately participants positioned the projection region, we calculated the distance from the final projection to the target. Participants were able to accurately position the projection both nearby (offset M=2.1cm, SD=1.5cm) and far away (offset M=2.6cm, SD=2.6cm), i.e., a mean error of 3% of the total distance traveled.

We evaluated how accurately participants were able to scale the projection to match the target size, by considering the percentage amount the participant's projection differed from the target dimensions. Similar to positioning, participants were highly accurate in scaling. When scaling to 1.4 times the original dimensions, participants resized their projection to within 5.3% of the target size (SD=4.6%). When scaling to twice participants had a mean error of 4%. (SD=3.4%).

Qualitative Feedback

Overall, participants were highly positive regarding Open Project for sharing media, collaborate with others or expanding the output space. On a five-point Likert scale, participants rated Open Project highly useful for applications such as presentations (M=4.4), collaborating tasks (M=3.9), and for sharing media with others (M=4.4). Participants rated Open Project as very easy to understand (M=4.3) and easy to use (M=3.7). Participants saw Open Project as somewhat useful for mobile gaming (M=3.6).

In terms of qualitative feedback, participants saw Open Project as a useful addition to their mobile experience. Participants praised the ability to share information quickly and efficiently on a nearby display.

> *"It's difficult to share stuff regularly. Only one person can view the screen at a time. It's a turn-based experience."* [P2].

In terms of the specifics of Open Project, participants found the physical positioning with the camera projection technique to be *"a natural instinct"*. Participants also saw Open Project as a way to control the privacy of their mobile device while still sharing some information.

> *"I am nervous to hand over my phone. With [Open Project], I don't have to hand over my phone that has a lot of private data. [...] It's nice to have control over what is shared."* [P10]

However, our participants did notice the performance was lacking for our current implementation.

> *"In terms of mobile gaming the performance needs to improve. However the concept is useful. With a better frame rate I would change my score accordingly."* [P1]

Finally, participants suggested using Open Project to enable the smartphones as a central repository of data and computation, streaming information to various outputs. Participants thought of our web framework as effectively replicating common hardware used to stream music or video to remote devices with minimal deployment effort.

DISCUSSION

Open Project performs as much computation as possible on the mobile device, maintaining a lightweight server that simply acts as a router. Our current implementation achieves a similar image transmission frame rate to previous techniques (e.g. [3]). However, performance suffers in dynamic applications such as video sharing or realtime gaming. To improve the frame rate, future work can take better advantage of mobile hardware (e.g. using the GPU for marker detection) and use dedicated libraries for content streaming such as VNC. As VNC is a point-to-point protocol, the Open Project Server will have to set up direct connections between a display and its remote clients.

The projection metaphor allows users to easily access any part of the display with radial movement of the arm and wrist. However, physical projection suffers from poor stability and angle-dependent distortion dependent on viewing angle. Open Project's marker-based positioning embodies a partial projection metaphor that takes advantage of the intuitive physical targeting but stabilizes the projection when the user interacts with the projected app. We can strengthen the projection metaphor, e.g., by adding a live view of the projected content to the marker while positioning. We can also enable multiple phones to simultaneously position their content by embedding a unique identifier (e.g., a QR code) into the marker.

Finally, the Open Project framework enables vision-based digital sharing at a large scale with minimal effort. The web-based architecture means that any display capable of showing a browser can be turned into an output device without installation. It is also possible to implement Open Projector (the mobile component in our framework) as a built-in function of a mobile platform for improved performance and simple invoking, e.g., via a hard button.

CONCLUSION

We presented Open Project, an open, web-based framework for enabling mobile sharing and collaboration at a large scale. It employs an intuitive, projection-based metaphor for a user to easily share a mobile application by projecting it onto a target large display. Open Project can turn any computer display projectable instantaneously and without deployment, and its "camera projection" algorithm, for simulating a projection effect, performs reliably in various viewing conditions. Developers can add support for Open Project in native mobile apps by simply linking our library, requiring no additional hardware or sensors. Our study participants responded highly positively to Open Project-enabled applications for mobile sharing and collaboration.

REFERENCES

1. Arthur, R. and Olsen,Jr., D.R. XICE windowing toolkit: Seamless display annexation. *ACM Trans. Computer-Human Interaction. 18*, 3 (2011), 14:1–14:46.
2. Ballagas, R., Rohs, M., and Sheridan, J.G. Sweep and point and shoot: phonecam-based interactions for large public displays. *CHI '05 Extended Abstracts*, 2005, 1200–1203.
3. Baur, D., Boring, S., and Feiner, S. Virtual projection: exploring optical projection as a metaphor for multi-device interaction. *Proc. of CHI'12*, ACM (2012), 1693–1702.
4. Beardsley, P., van Baar, J., Raskar, R., and Forlines, C. Interaction using a handheld projector. *Computer Graphics and Applications. IEEE 25*, 1 (2005), 39 –43.
5. Blasko, G., Feiner, S., and Coriand, F. Exploring Interaction with a Simulated Wrist-Worn Projection Display. *Proc. of Wearable Computers*, IEEE Computer Society (2005), 2–9.
6. Boring, S., Jurmu, M., and Butz, A. Scroll, tilt or move it: using mobile phones to continuously control pointers on large public displays. *Proc. of OzCHI'09*, 2009, 161–168.
7. Bragdon, A., DeLine, R., Hinckley, K., and Morris, M.R. Code space: touch + air gesture hybrid interactions for supporting developer meetings. *Proc. of ITS'11*, 2011, 212–221.
8. Cao, X. and Balakrishnan, R. Interacting with dynamically defined information spaces using a handheld projector and a pen. ACM Press (2006), 225.
9. Cao, X., Forlines, C., and Balakrishnan, R. Multi-user interaction using handheld projectors. *Proc. of UIST'07*, ACM (2007), 43–52.
10. Chang, T.-H. and Li, Y. Deep shot: a framework for migrating tasks across devices using mobile phone cameras. *Proc. of CHI'11*, ACM (2011), 2163–2172.
11. Fischler, M.A. and Bolles, R.C. Random sample consensus: a paradigm for model fitting with applications to image analysis and automated cartography. *Commun. ACM 24*, 6 (1981), 381–395.
12. Greenberg, S. and Rounding, M. The notification collage: posting information to public and personal displays. *Proc. of CHI'01*, ACM (2001), 514–521.
13. Herbert, L., Pears, N., Jackson, D., and Olivier, P. Mobile Device and Intelligent Display Interaction via Scale-invariant Image Feature Matching. *PECCS*, 2011, 207–214.
14. Izadi, S., Brignull, H., Rodden, T., Rogers, Y., and Underwood, M. Dynamo: a public interactive surface supporting the cooperative sharing and exchange of media. *Proc. of UIST'03*, ACM (2003), 159–168.
15. Molyneaux, D., Izadi, S., Kim, D., et al. Interactive Environment-Aware Handheld Projectors for Pervasive Computing Spaces. *Pervasive*, (2012), 197–215.
16. Rekimoto, J. and Saitoh, M. Augmented surfaces: a spatially continuous work space for hybrid computing environments. *Proc. of CHI'99*, ACM (1999), 378–385.
17. Remondino, F. and Fraser, C. Digital camera calibration methods: considerations and comparisons. *Photogrammetry, Remote Sensing and Spatial Information Sciences*, (2006).
18. Rohs, M. Real-world interaction with camera phones. *Proc. of UCS'05*, Springer-Verlag (2005), 74–89.
19. Shen, C., Everitt, K., and Ryall, K. UbiTable: Impromptu Face-to-Face Collaboration on Horizontal Interactive Surfaces. *Proc. of UbiComp 2003*, (2003), 281–288.
20. Smith, G.M. and schraefel, m. c. The radial scroll tool: scrolling support for stylus- or touch-based document navigation. *Proc. of UIST'04*, ACM (2004), 53–56.
21. Tan, D.S., Meyers, B., and Czerwinski, M. WinCuts: manipulating arbitrary window regions for more effective use of screen space. *CHI '04 extended abstracts*, 2004, 1525–1528.
22. Wang, J., Zhai, S., and Canny, J. Camera phone based motion sensing: interaction techniques, applications and performance study. *Proc. of UIST'06*, ACM (2006), 101–110.
23. Wigdor, D., Jiang, H., Forlines, C., Borkin, M., and Shen, C. WeSpace: the design development and deployment of a walk-up and share multi-surface visual collaboration system. *Proc. of CHI'09*, ACM (2009), 1237–1246.
24. Wilson, A.D. and Benko, H. Combining multiple depth cameras and projectors for interactions on, above and between surfaces. *Proc. of UIST'10*, ACM (2010), 273–282.
25. OpenCV. http://opencv.org/.
26. zxing - 1D/2D barcode image processing library. http://code.google.com/p/zxing/.
27. Apache Tomcat http://tomcat.apache.org/.

Surround-See: Enabling Peripheral Vision on Smartphones during Active Use

Xing-Dong Yang[2], Khalad Hasan[1], Neil Bruce[1], Pourang Irani[1]

[1]University of Manitoba
Winnipeg, MB, Canada, R3T 2N2
{khalad, bruce, irani}@cs.umanitoba.ca

[2]University of Alberta
Edmonton, AB, Canada, T6G 2E8
xingdong@cs.ualberta.ca

ABSTRACT

Mobile devices are endowed with significant sensing capabilities. However, their ability to 'see' their surroundings, during active use, is limited. We present Surround-See, a self-contained smartphone equipped with an omni-directional camera that enables peripheral vision around the device to augment daily mobile tasks. Surround-See provides mobile devices with a field-of-view collinear to the device screen. This capability facilitates novel mobile tasks such as, pointing at objects in the environment to interact with content, operating the mobile device at a physical distance and allowing the device to detect user activity, even when the user is not holding it. We describe Surround-See's architecture, and demonstrate applications that exploit peripheral 'seeing' capabilities during active use of a mobile device. Users confirm the value of embedding peripheral vision capabilities on mobile devices and offer insights for novel usage methods.

Author Keywords

Peripheral mobile vision, mobile 'seeing', mobile surround vision.

ACM Classification Keywords

H5.2 [Information interfaces and presentation]: User Interfaces. - Graphical user interfaces.

INTRODUCTION

Smartphones are equipped with powerful sensors, such as accelerometers, GPS and cameras that facilitate a variety of daily tasks. On commercial and research platforms, such sensors have been utilized in numerous contexts such as for distinguishing user activity [26], for sensing on, behind and around a mobile device [5, 41], for context awareness [46] and for interactive document exploration [13]. The integration of an ever expanding suite of embedded sensors is a key driver in making mobile devices smarter [26]. However, current capabilities are mostly focused on *sensing*. We distinguish 'sensing' from 'seeing' in that the latter facilitates some higher level of recognition or interpretation of objects, people and places in the mobile device's surroundings. What new applications might be possible if mobile devices had advanced *seeing* abilities?

UIST'13, October 08 - 11 2013, St Andrews, United Kingdom
Copyright 2013 ACM 978-1-4503-2268-3/13/10…$15.00.
http://dx.doi.org/10.1145/2501988.2502049

We explore the above theme of empowering mobile devices with enhanced peripheral vision capabilities. Our prototype, Surround-See, consists of a smartphone fitted with an omnidirectional lens that gives the device peripheral vision, of its surroundings (Figure 1). During active use, Surround-See effectively extends the smartphone's limited field-of-sight provided by its front- and back-facing cameras. With an ability to 'see' the rich context of the region around the device, smartphones can trigger environment specific reminders and can respond to peripheral interactions, such as pointing at a smart-appliance for efficient access to its control panel on the mobile device.

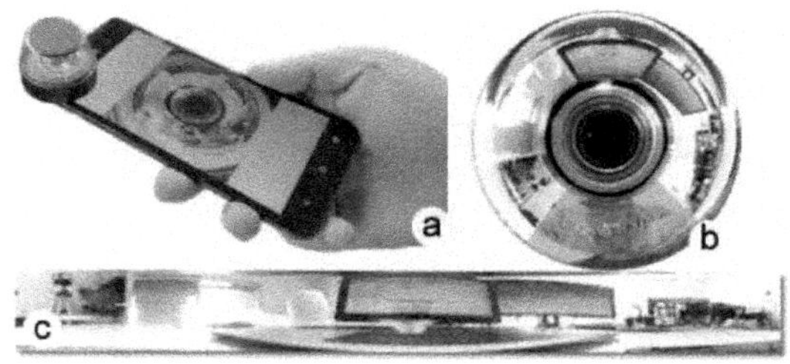

Figure 1 - (a) Surround-See enables peripheral 'sight' on smartphones by means of an omni-directional mirror attached to the mobile device's front facing camera. (b) Surround-See image shows the corresponding scene. (c) The unwrapped image can be used for recognizing the device's peripheral environment (after removing the user's body – shaded in red)

The scenario below captures some of the rich applications Surround-See enables. John, a professional is often using his mobile device. In the morning, he reads the news on Surround-See while his car engine warms-up. Recognizing this, Surround-See triggers a reminder on the danger of eyes-busy mobile use and driving. Later, as he settles into his office while checking email on Surround-See, he points at the speakers in the office, which Surround-See recognizes and provides a control panel to increase the speakers' volume. Laura, a colleague enters his office and asks about his weekend. John picks up his smartphone to show Laura pictures on the phone which Surround-See reorients as the device is positioned closer to Laura. Finally, Laura asks John for directions to the restaurant, which John draws using a stylus and his finger to erase, both of which are recognized as distinct by Surround-See. Shortly after doing some work he decides to step out for only a few minutes. Surround-See recognizes this activity and asks whether he wishes to take his device. As he is uninterested, he declines by gesturing to the device remotely and Surround See sets the mobile into voicemail mode.

The above scenario captures the various possibilities made available when augmenting a mobile device with peripheral vision. During active use Surround-See can (a) trigger reminders based on an environment it recognizes, (b) it can perceive specific objects in the mobile device's periphery (i.e. speakers), which the user can control by (c) pointing at them. In idle mode, such as when resting on a table, Surround-See can also identify certain activities in the vicinity of the device, such as (d) when the user walks away from it or (e) if the user is remotely waving at it to alter its state, i.e. setting it to voicemail mode.

Our contributions include: (a) the concept of enabling mobile devices to 'see' their surroundings; (b) a demonstration of its value through an implementation of a self-contained proof-of-concept prototype, Surround-See; and (c) a set of applications that demonstrate Surround-See's unique capabilities over current smartphone usages.

RELATED WORK

Mobile 'sensing'

Researchers have investigated the possibility of embedding sensors on mobile devices to facilitate tasks in the background. An extensive review on mobile sensing is available in [36]. We briefly discuss state and context awareness enabled by mobile sensors. Hinckley et al.'s [25] seminal work on sensing techniques for mobile interaction opened a new wave of interfaces that exploit a mobile device's state, such as its orientation. Such capabilities, among others, have enabled a significant suite of interactions including the ability to control virtual objects on a mobile screen [47], for automatically reorienting images [25], to support navigation in applications [15], or to facilitate different gesture based interactions [28]. Many of the sensors proposed in these earlier systems are now common on commercial mobile devices, and have been used to create a wide ecosystem of applications that depend on sensing a device's state.

Researchers have also demonstrated methods to sense a mobile device's environment to alter the state of the device. Schmidt et al. [46] augmented mobile devices with tilt, light and heat sensors to identify if the device is resting on a table, is in a pocket, or is being used outside. Such sensor-based information can be used for automatically changing the device state such as lowering its volume. Context information is also possible with geo-locating sensors that incorporate information about the user's location to provide more relevant and targeted services [15, 34].

Beyond sensing a device state or context, researchers have introduced novel sensor-based interaction techniques to facilitate input outside the device's physical space, in its periphery. Single finger interactions around a device are possible with SideSight [5] and HoverFlow [35] which use IR distance sensors to capture gesture-based interactions above and to the sides of the device. Similarly, Abracadabra [21] facilitates input by activating states of a magnetic sensor and maps these to menu and cursor control. This results in occlusion-free input on small devices such as watches. For the most part, sensor-based interaction metaphors are confined to a specific suite of tasks.

Camera-based mobile interaction

On mobile devices, vision-based systems have advanced to the point of complementing basic sensing mechanisms in real-time. Self-contained mobile-based augmented reality (AR) applications have flourished [50]. Examples include Wagner et al.'s [50] marker-based AR system, Paelke et al.'s [41] hand-held AR soccer game and Hansen et al.'s [20] camera-equipped mobile device to establish a spatial relationship between a virtual environment and the physical space to form a mixed reality space.

Camera based input also been shown to work for 2D [51] and 3D navigation [19], for tracking the user's face for zooming/scrolling documents [48], for detecting where users are standing and reorienting the screen accordingly as the device is placed closer to them [8, 9] or for generating input events (e.g., click, double-click) in real-time [31].

In general, most camera-based interactions require that interactive features be used in exclusion of other tasks, as the user has to explicitly point the front- or back-facing camera at the object of interest. Ideally, vision-based methods on mobiles can include the devices' periphery which contains rich context information. This can open new possibilities for integrating users' interactions naturally into the ecosystem of daily mobile applications facilitating a broader range of implicit interactions that build on Buxton's vision for foreground/background interaction [6].

Peripheral vision

Researchers have explored methods for extending a camera's limited field-of-view without significantly changing its form factor. For example, omni-directional cameras have been applied to robotics problems to give robots 'sight' of their periphery. Applications include estimating a robot's motion [16], revealing a robot's location [10], recognizing its surroundings [45], and navigating around obstacles [33]. Very little work has considered the applications of embedding peripheral vision on smartphones for advanced interactions.

Walking User Interfaces

There is a growing trend toward building interfaces to support walking user interfaces (WUIs) [17], including methods to improve text-entry accuracy to user safety. Surround-See, is particularly of value for WUIs, as it allows users to perform additional actions while using the device.

HARDWARE DESIGN OPTIONS

To enable a smartphone with peripheral vision capabilities during active use led us to explore different hardware options. We frame our exploration in terms of the level of 'sight' enabled by various sensing technologies, from coarse to fine. Coarse 'seeing' can detect the presence of an object, with limited ability to detect its motion. Finer 'seeing' involves recognizing different objects and the ability to detect changes in the smartphone's surroundings.

Sensor Options

We first considered sensors that can fit on current smartphones. A second requirement was to implement and explore use-cases with a self-contained prototype.

Proximity sensor

Proximity sensors (capacitive, infra-red, or ultrasound) detect the presence and distance of objects away from it (giving them coarse 'sight'). Multiple proximity sensors in a sensor array can detect the motion of an object in a 2D or 3D space [5]. However, such sensors cannot distinguish between different objects or detect the changes in their surrounding environment. The placement of proximity sensors is also challenged by how users hold the device without occluding them.

Magnetic Sensor

Magnetic sensors detect the presence and angular location of a magnet, such as on a ring, in an emitted field (giving them coarse 'sight'). A magnetic sensor array can detect the 2D or near surface 3D motion of an object [38], but like proximity sensors, they do not distinguish specific objects or content changes in the environment.

Image Sensor

Image sensors (CCD or CMOS) are standard on smartphones. They sense an optical image, which can be processed using computer vision techniques to detect the presence of an object in the image, the motion of an object in either 2D or 3D (with a 3D depth sensing camera), or recognize different objects in the surrounding environment.

Sensing Range

Sensors' limited range can be alleviated by forming an array of multiple sensors (e.g. proximity sensor array or camera array). The increased field-of-operation however, comes with a size tradeoff which makes such solutions impractical for mobile devices. Other more practical methods for enlarging the field-of-view consists of using a wide-angle or omni-directional lens, which can capture a good portion of the 360° around a device's periphery.

Sensor Installation and Form Factor Implications

Proximity or magnetic sensor arrays can be placed above or under an open surface on a smartphone [5, 38]. This allows them to sense the entire space around the smartphone without significantly impacting the device's form factor. However, during active use, these become unusable as the user's hand occludes these sensors.

While the built-in smartphone cameras can be used for the purpose of 'seeing', during active use, the front and back cameras face the sky and ground, respectively. The narrow field-of-view of such built-in cameras (43°-56° on the high-definition smartphone camera we used), does not allow these to capture the smartphone's surrounding space (Figure 2). This limitation can be addressed by mounting a wide-angle or omni-directional lens on the built-in cameras.

Figure 2 – (a) the environment where Figure 1b was taken from; (b)-(c) images taken from the phone's back and front facing cameras respectively.

SURROUND SEE HARDWARE

To explore the interaction space for peripheral vision on a smartphone we create a self-contained proof-of-concept system, Surround-See. The prototype is a HTC Butterfly smartphone with an omni-directional lens from Kogeto [1] mounted on its front-facing camera (Figure 1a). The front was chosen as placing the lens on the back may make the phone unstable at rest, thus precluding a significant number of interactions.

The smartphone runs the Android operating system on a Quad-core 1.5 GHz Krait CPU with 2GB of RAM. The front camera has a maximum resolution of 2MP. For real-time image processing, we down-sampled the resolution to 960×720. The omni-directional lens has a 360° and 56° field-of-view in the horizontal and vertical planes, respectively. The final prototype captures a real time RGB image of the 360° surrounding view of the device. Figure1b-c shows an omni-directional image captured by the prototype, and its unwrapped counterpart.

SURROUND-SEE CAPABILITIES

We implemented three primary capabilities with Surround-See: 1) to recognize the device's peripheral environment; 2) to recognize objects around the device; and 3) to recognize user activities in vicinity to the device. We implemented these features using OpenCV4Android, a JAVA wrapper that allows the OpenCV library to be used on Android platforms. It is worth mentioning that there are many choices for computer vision algorithms for implementing Surround-See features. We used and present those that have shown effective results in the literature and that can be implemented on a self-contained mobile device prototype.

Recognizing the Device's Peripheral Environment

Recognizing the users' peripheral environment was implemented using Local Binary Patterns (LBP) [40] and a machine learning classifier [7]. Before the recognition process starts, we pre-processed the raw omni-directional image by un-wrapping it to a panoramic image using the method described in [11]. While not technically necessary, unwrapping the image makes the rest of the processing easier. Once unwrapped, the bottom of the panoramic image was cropped so that it did not contain the body of the user (about 1/4 of the panoramic image). The resulting image from this pre-process contains only a wide view of Surround-See's surrounding environment (Figure 1).

We then used LBP to describe the image using a unique feature vector. LBP detects microstructures inside an image (e.g. lines, edges). The histogram of the microstructures forms a feature vector of the image. LBP is orientation and luminance invariant, making it robust in describing images taken from different angles and different lighting conditions. The algorithm was originally proposed to classify textures (e.g. cloth). It has, however, been shown to be effective in detecting landmarks too [23]. The feature vector was used to train a machine learning classifier or to recognize a peripheral environment. We collected 20 samples for each of the 5 peripheral environments we recognized (lab, office, desk, hallway, and car). We took ten images for each, the morning and afternoon, with the phone in active use position. To train the classifier, we used Chang and Lin's LIBSVM library using the Support Vector Machine (SVM) [7]. We used a RBF Kernel with parameters that gave the highest 5-fold cross-validation scores (e.g. 96%). The trained model was loaded when the system starts. For every 60 seconds, the system sampled an image of the peripheral environment for recognition. The recognition process runs in a background thread, causing no interference to the phone's normal activities.

In contrast to a phone's built-in GPS, Surround-See can detect subtle changes in its location, e.g. movement inside or outside of a room or at a specific location in a room. When combined with GPS data, Surround-See can detect contextual changes happening within the GPS-sensed location, e.g. a crowed street vs. an empty street.

Recognizing Peripheral Items

Our implementation focuses on two general types of peripheral items: surrounding items and the user's hand.

Recognizing an Object in the Smartphone's Environment

An object in the device's environment is recognized using feature point matching using the ORB algorithm [44]. ORB searches each input frame for a desired object using a reference image. The reference image contains only the object to be searched for (see Figure 3a-b). When the system starts, ORB extracts a set of feature points for the reference image. A feature vector (or descriptor) was then generated for every feature point to uniquely describe the characteristics of that feature point. ORB was then used to search for similar feature points in the input frames. If an object in the input frame contained at least a certain number of matching points (e.g. 1/8 of the total matching set), it was recognized as the desired object. We used OpenCV's *FeatureDetector* class for feature point detection, and *DescriptorMatcher* class feature point matching.

ORB is color invariant. It also performs well with objects at different scales. However, we found it to be error prone to changes of the device's orientation. It could fail to identify the object if it appears at a different orientation in the input frame than that in the reference image. This would require the user to hold the device at the same orientation as when the reference image was sampled, which is impractical. We resolved this using the device's built-in compass. When the system starts, Surround-See loads a list of reference images and their corresponding phone orientations when the images were taken. These initial orientations were used to rotate the input frames during the recognition process. In our implementation, we used one sample image for each desired object while multiple samples per object at different orientations is also possible. Our process however does not incur any performance overhead.

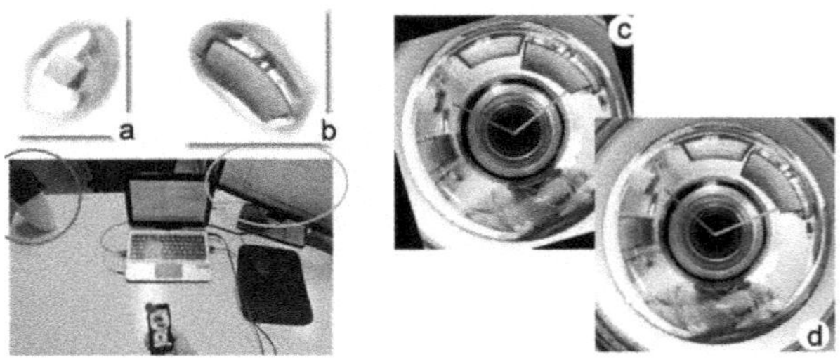

Figure 3 - Reference images: (a) speaker and (b) monitor; (c) rotated input frame for more precise object detection; (d) recognized objects (the blue and green lines indicate the locations of the recognized objects – speaker and monitor).

Recognizing the User's Hand

Explicit mid-air user input is possible, in Surround-See's periphery. Surround-See detects the user's hand using a skin color model in YCbCr color space [30, 42]. A skin color pixel was detected if its Cr and Cb values fall into the ranges [140, 166] and [135, 180] respectively. The resulting input frame formed a black&white binary image with its white region indicating the skin color pixels Figure 4 top).

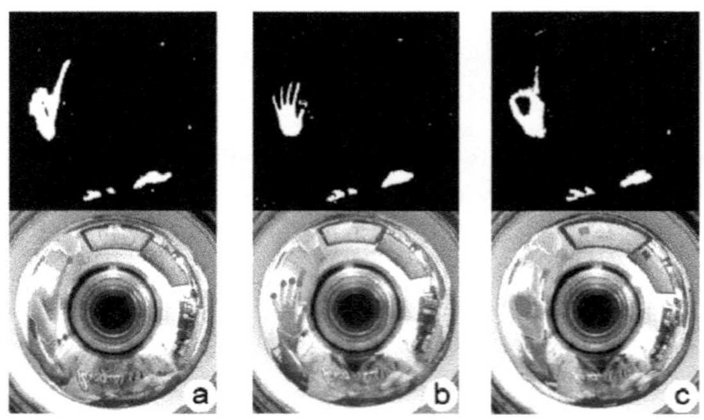

Figure 4– Top: binary image of skin-color pixels; Bottom: (a-b) track fingertip (red dot); (c) detect pinch (red ellipse).

The user's hand was detected by looking for blobs that are larger than a threshold size. We found this method to be effective but also error prone when the background contains colors close to that of the user's skin. We thus dynamically filtered out the background noise by removing the blobs that appeared in the same location for a certain fixed number of frames (e.g. 30 in our application). Finally, the hand contour was obtained by approximating a polygon of the detected hand blob using OpenCV's *approxPolyDP* function (Figure 4 bottom).

Tracking fingertips: Upon extracting the user's hand contour, the user's fingertips were detected by searching through the contour points, and identifying those with a curvature less than a threshold value (e.g. 50°) [3] (Figure4 a-b) In an omni-directional image, the position of the detected fingertip indicates the position of the real finger around the camera (Figure 5). Surround-See can also detect the finger's up-and-down (vertical) motion. This is achieved by calculating the distance from the detected fingertip to the center of the omni-directional image, where an increase in the distance indicates that the finger is moving upward, and a decrease means the opposite.

Figure 5- tracking finger position in the device's periphery.

Recognizing hand postures: A hand posture is recognized by counting the number of detected fingertips. This method is simple and fast. It allows 6 different hand postures in total – fist and 1 to 5 fingers. Other methods are also possible in cases where more hand postures are needed [12, 32, 49, 52]. In our implementation, the '1' posture, with the index finger is reserved for pointing.

Detecting 'pinch'-ing: Pinch is detected using Wilson's method [53], where a pinch is recognized when there is a connected blob inside a hand contour (Figure 4c) Pinch can be used as a 'mouse click' to confirm an action or to trigger a command. Once a pinch is detected, the hand posture recognition method is disabled until the pinch is released.

Detecting User Activities in the Periphery

We implemented three different peripheral activity detection capabilities: whether the user is moving the device away from them, whether the user is stepping away from the device and remotely gesturing at the device.

Proximity to User

During active use, Surround-See uses the user's upper body as a reference point to determine its proximity to the user. We demarcated a rectangular region of interest containing only the user's body to detect the smartphone's perpendicular motion relative to the user (Figure 6 left). Motion detection was implemented using optical flow [14], where the spreading of the motion vectors indicated that Surround-See was being placed closer (Figure 6b) to the user and the gathering of the motion vectors indicated that Surround-See was being moved away from the user (Figure 6a). We found this method reliable especially in differentiating between the perpendicular motion and the other motions such as moving left or right. Unlike previously proposed methods (e.g. [4]), Surround-See is self-contained. It does not need overhead cameras or require users to wear sensors on their body. This is extremely important for mobility.

Figure 6 – Left: ROI contains user's body; Right: (a)-(b) optical flow vectors showing the phone is moving away and closer respectively.

It is worth noting that sensing user proximity cannot occur by simply using the smartphone's built-in sensors (e.g. accelerometer or built-in cameras). For example, the accelerometer can tell the direction in which the smartphone accelerates but cannot tell whether or not the user is moving with the smartphone. Similarly, the smartphone's built-in front or back camera may detect its motion but cannot tell whether or not the user is moving at the same time, e.g. walking when holding the phone, as the user is mostly outside the view of these cameras.

Detecting User Activity within a Region of Interest

In idle mode, i.e. when resting on a horizontal surface, Surround-See can detect the user's activity within a user-defined region of interest (ROI). Surround-See can dynamically track the user-defined ROI using the same method described in Figure 3. Once defined, the user's activities within the ROI were detected using optical flow. In our current implementation, Surround-See detects four user activities, including the user's movement in the horizontal and in the perpendicular directions (Figure 7). Additional activities, such as rapid or groups movements can be detected using sophisticated methods (e.g. [39]).

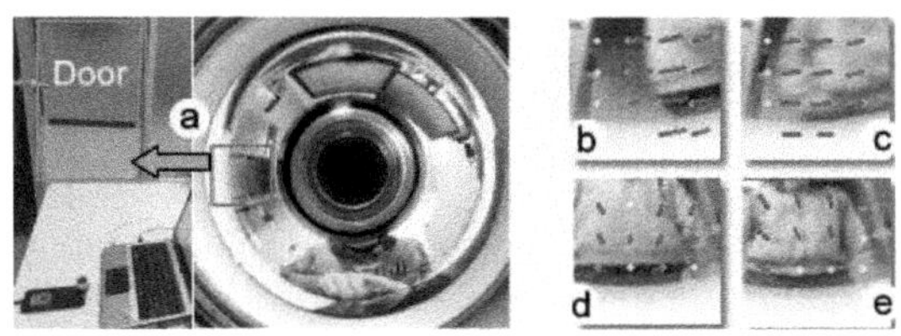

Figure 7 - ROI at the door (a); user moving from left to right (b) and right to left (c); user moving away (d) and closer (e).

Remote Gesturing

In idle mode, Surround-See also allows hand gestures to be carried out when the user is at a short distance away from the phone. This is convenient for situations when the phone is left behind on a desk and the user does not wish to walk up to grab it to invoke a simple command (e.g. turn on the voice mail). Remote gesturing assumes the phone is sitting on a stable platform such as a table and that the view is uncluttered. This allows us to use background subtraction to remove any skin-color noise in the background. This is particularly helpful as a hand blob will appear much smaller in the camera view when the user is not holding the phone, making the blob-size based noise removal error prone. Surround-See uses a real-time adaptive background subtraction based on a Gaussian Mixture Model [29] (implemented in the *BackgroundSubtractorMOG* class in OpenCV). The algorithm updates the background dynamically such that if a moving object in the foreground stalls for several frames, it will be classified as a part of the background. This creates an effective mechanism for determining the start and end of a hand gesture. For example, when standing still, the user is classified as a part of the background. When the user starts to wave his/her hand, the moving part of the user's body becomes the foreground. This indicates the start of a gesture After the user stops moving the hand, Surround-See observes no moving object and gradually classifies the user's body as background. If the user does not move the hand again, s/he will eventually be classified as the background in several frames. This indicates the end of the gesture.

To track the user's hand trajectory, Surround-See finds the user's hand in the foreground using the same skin-color model described earlier A hand trajectory is composed of the temporal and spatial displacement of the center of the detected hand blob. In our current implementation, Surround-See uses a simple gesture recognition algorithm, which identifies hand gestures based on the hand's moving direction, e.g. moving left, moving right, or waving (move left then right or vice versa). More sophisticated algorithms would increase the remote gesture vocabulary set but could also demand higher processing power [37, 54].

SURROUND-SEE INTERACTIONS

We have implemented a number of interaction techniques to demonstrate several key Surround-See features. Each technique serves as an example of one or more of Surround-See's capabilities. Many of the applications are novel while a few others show how previously proposed techniques can be implemented in a mobile and self-contained prototype.

Pen vs. Touch Input

Capacitive stylus is a valuable addition to the user's finger for handwriting or drawing on smartphones and tablets. However, smartphones' touchscreens cannot distinguish a user's touch from that of a capacitive stylus. This problem can easily be solved with Surround-See as it can recognize objects in the environment. Surround-See can easily distinguish the stylus from the finger when interacting with the touchscreen. We implemented a simple drawing application to demonstrate this unique capability. Users can use a stylus to draw on the touchscreen and use the finger to erase the drawing (Figure 8a). Tracking the pen was implemented using the color model similar to the one used for detecting the user's hand.

Off-screen Pointing

Accessing off-screen objects is often considered a tedious and time consuming task due to the repeated invocation of panning or scrolling operations [27]. Recent research has shown that such a task can be made more efficient by directly pointing in mid-air at the location of the object in the around-device space [22]. Limited work exists on identifying the most appropriate sensing methods to facilitate around-device pointing. We implemented a restaurant search application to demonstrate Surround-See off-screen pointing potential (*Tracking User Finger*). When a restaurant of interest is located outside the map view, users can acquire information about it by directly pointing at its off-screen location indicated by an arrow shown on the screen (Figure 8b). We developed two selection mechanisms, dwell and back-tap (tapping on the back of the phone, sensed by the built-in accelerometers). The user can then select the restaurant to trigger an action, e.g. to retrieve a discount coupon. The user can toggle between off-screen objects in the general direction pointed at by the user by moving the finger up or down vertically (another dimension). In comparison to techniques using infrared proximity sensors [5], Surround-See is capable of tracking continuous finger movement at the corners of the smartphone, which is difficult for an array of range sensors. Furthermore, unlike sensors placed on the side to achieve this task [5], Surround-See's range is not occluded by the user's grip.

Remote Operation

Current smartphones can only be used when the user is directly interacting and in contact with the phone (e.g. by touching the phone's touchscreen). It is, however, quite often that the user may want to operate the phone, even briefly, from a short distance. For example, in a meeting with clients, the user may leave the phone on the meeting table when giving a presentation at the podium. If the phone rings during the presentation, the user may want to be able to mute the phone without having to leave the podium. Surround-See allows the phone to be operated remotely (*Remote Gesturing*). The user can simply wave at the phone to mute it. This operation cannot be carried out with smartphones' existing front or back camera when the phone is in a natural idle position. In our implementation, we map the user's hand gestures to common functions, e.g. wave right to mute the phone, wave right-then-left to unmute it, and wave left to turn on the voice mail (Figure 8c).

Controlling Remote Objects (Physical Shortcut)

Objects recognized in Surround-See's periphery can be used to carry out contextual actions. We created a remote control application, which uses physical objects (e.g. speaker or monitor) as a handler to trigger their corresponding controller on the user's smartphone. Users can point at a speaker to open a volume controller window on Surround-See to remotely adjust the speaker's volume (Figure 8d) (*Tracking Finger* and *Recognizing Environmental Objects*). Users can also point at a monitor to remotely turn it on or off. Here the surrounding objects serve as 'physical shortcuts' for launching applications on Surround-See. Users can also create paper stickers as disposable shortcuts [55]. The mapping between the commands and the physical objects relies on the semantics of the physical objects (intrinsic mapping [55]). This makes learning shortcuts easy, which is often time-consuming especially when there is a large number of them [18].

Posture for Speed-dialing

Hand postures can be used as an easy and intuitive method to rapidly trigger a command on the smartphone. In our implementation, we used hand postures to trigger speed-dialing on Surround-See (*Recognizing hand postures*) (Figure 8e). We mapped 5 phone numbers to the 5 hand postures (from 1 to 5). To avoid unintentionally making calls, we allow the users to enable or disable *Posture Speed-dial* based on their needs. Unlike the other applications we describe here, hand posture is not exclusive to Surround-See, and can be carried out using the phone's front or back facing cameras. Surround-See provides an alternative, allowing postures to be used when the hand is already in the peripheral space.

Location-based Messaging

When in active use, Surround-See can perform contextual actions based on its location. We implemented a location-based messaging application, which displays a reminder or warning message on the screen (*Recognizing Peripheral Environment*). For example, when the application first recognizes that Surround-See is by the user's office desk, it asks whether the user wishes to "*Sync your phone?*" as a reminder. When it first recognizes the phone is being used in a shared space, such as a lab, the application asks whether to "*Mute your phone?*". Finally, it warns the user to stop using the phone by showing "*Don't use your phone when driving*" on the screen when it recognizes the user is behind the wheel (Figure 8f). Such reminders can be included for safe utilization of the phone while walking and texting, for example [24]. Note that location detection based on 'sight' extends previous approaches using a proximity sensor [5], i.e. the system can distinguish car-A from car-B.

Proximity-based Screen Rotation

Showing others the content of the screen of a smartphone can sometimes be cumbersome because the user needs to reorient the phone to fit the viewer's field-of-view. The existing approach reorients the content when the phone is tilted. This method is error prone as it does not distinguish between tilt towards and away from the viewer. It is, however, natural for the user to stretch their arm to place the phone closer to the viewer so that the content on the screen can be clearly visible. Based on this observation, we created an image browsing application, which can automatically rotate the orientation of the image by 180° when it detects the phone is being moved away from the user (*Proximity to User*) (Figure 8g). It can also rotate the image back to its initial orientation when it detects the phone is being moved back to the user.

Notify to Take the Phone

Occasionally, users may forget to take their cell phone when leaving their home or office. We created a notification application to notify the user when this happens. When Surround-See is idle, e.g. sits on a desk (*Recognize Peripheral Environment*), the application is on. It monitors users' activities around the door of the user's office (*Detecting User Activity within a User-defined Region of Interest*), by detecting the motion of the moving object within the door region. Upon detecting that the user is moving out of the door (implemented using the same optical flow algorithm as described in *Detecting Proximity to User*), it plays a voice message "*Did you forget your phone?*" to notify the user (Figure 8h). The user may choose to go back to the desk to take the phone or make a hand gesture to turn on the voice mail (*Remote Gesture*).

ELICITING USER APPROVAL

We conducted a user survey as an initial step towards assessing users' approval of Surround-See as a concept that can co-exist with common smartphone usage. Our goal was

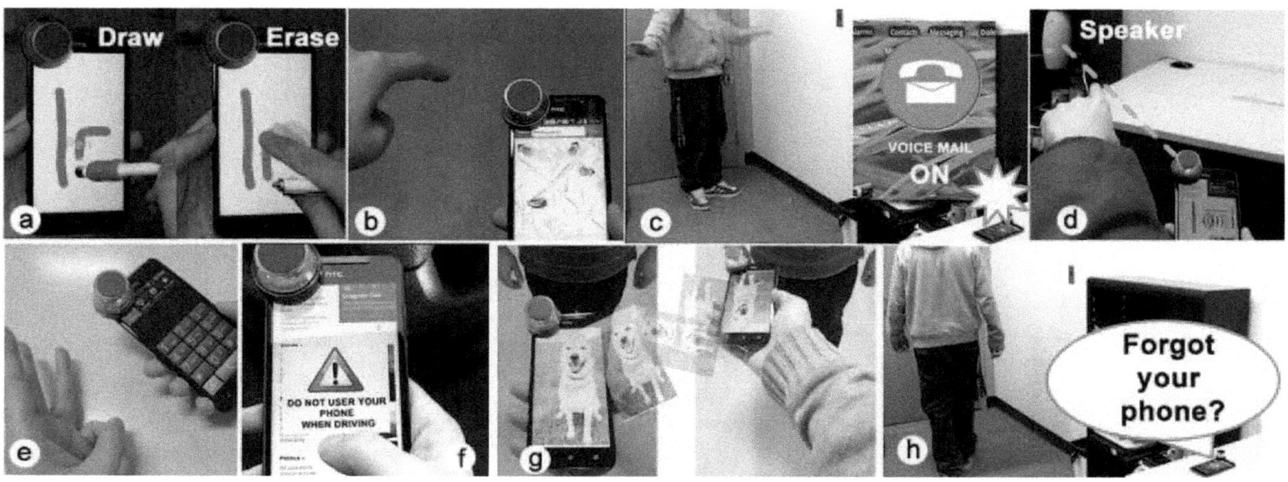

Figure 8 – (a) Left: use pen to draw; Right: use finger to erase; (b) Picking restaurant stored in the off-screen space; (c) Remote gesture to turn on voice mail; (d) Point at a speaker to open a volume controller window; (e) Hand posture for speed-dial; (f) Show a warning message when the user uses the phone behind the wheel; (g) Auto screen rotation based on the proximity to user; (h) Remind the user to take the phone when detects that the user is moving out of the door.

to examine the value proposition of Surround-See's capabilities, our interaction techniques and users' privacy concerns. We adapted the feedback method introduced in [43] and participants made judgments by watching a video showing the Surround-See prototype (same video as the one included in this submission).

Participants

Seventeen computer science students (15 male, ages between 21 and 35) participated in our survey. All of them were smartphone users. Seven participants have used a smartphone for more than 3 years.

Procedure

The participants were shown a video presenting the prototype and all of Surround-See's capabilities. They were also shown the interaction techniques one at a time. For each interaction technique, they filled out a 7-point Likert scale questionnaire (1: strongly dislike and 7: strongly like), and gave reasons to justify their answers. After ranking the interaction techniques, the participants were asked to rank overall how useful they think the techniques are. Finally, they ranked their level of comfort about smartphones that had 'seeing' abilities and held by others, such as family, friends or strangers.

Overall, participants welcomed the idea of making the smartphone more 'sight' enabled during active use. They mostly like the intelligent features (*Notify to Take the Phone* and *Location-based Messaging*) that could help them with common daily slips such as forgetting to take the phone, to mute it in a classroom and features to support remote operations (*Controlling Remote Objects and Remote Operation*). These 4 features were ranked amongst the highest with an average score higher than 6. Three participants commented that they always forgot to mute their phone and another commented that *Location-based Messaging* is a useful feature because "*it could take control, when you forget to do something*". People like the convenient features that allow them to control objects at a distance and indicated that these should become standard on smartphones. A participant commented that *Remote Operation* is "*good because most of the time I leave the phone away and need to return briefly only to set it*". User reports suggest that even when users are not holding their smartphones they still wish to maintain a link with their devices, even at a distance.

Three features (*Proximity-based Screen Rotation*, *Posture for Speed-dialing*, and *Pen vs. Touch Input*) received weaker approval scores between 5 and 6. Most participants agreed that these are handy features to have on top of the phone's existing functions but they also felt these features are limited to a small set of applications. For example, one participant said *Pen vs. Touch Input* is "*useful for drawing apps on my phone. I'd like to see how else it could be used though*". Finally, participants gave a neutral score (4.7, s.e. 0.37) to *Off-screen Pointing*. Most participants did not see high value for this feature in their daily smartphone usage.

Overall, participants did not complain about privacy issues when other people use Surround-See. They felt most comfortable when Surround-See is used by people they know. The user's level of comfort decreases when Surround-See is used by people they know less. They feel neutral (4.3, s.e. 0.24; with 7 being strongly comfortable) when Surround-See is used by a stranger but also expressed a demand for feedback to show that Surround-See is turned on (5.3, s.e. 0.52) (Figure 9). Interestingly, participants wished to also receive feedback if family members had devices with peripheral vision (4.18, s.e. 0.5). This needs to be considered in the design of such devices.

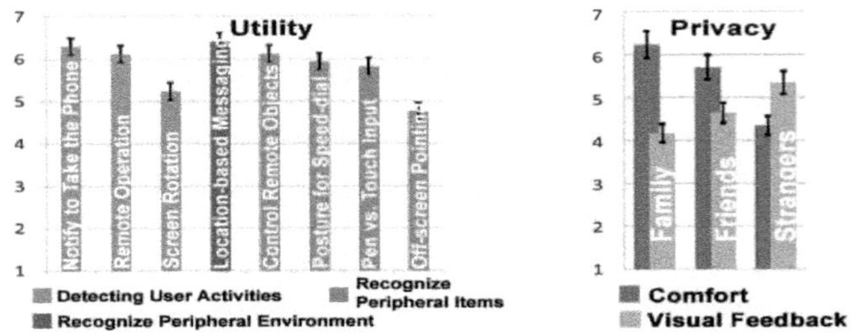

Figure 9 – Left: average user rating for Surround-See's interaction techniques; Right: average user ratings for potential privacy concerns.

DISCUSSION AND LIMITATIONS

In this section, we discuss the lessons we learned and insights we gained from our experience. We also present limitations of our approach.

Omni-directional lens: the omni-directional lens we used provides a 360° view of the peripheral space but presents pixel loss. First, the image from an omni-directional lens is distorted, especially towards the center of the concentric circles. During our implementation, we did not observe major issues caused by this distortion. However, the degree of distortion may vary from lens to lens. Calibration may be considered (e.g. checkerboard calibration) when implementing with different lenses. Second, the object seen from the omni-directional lens is smaller than what can be seen with a normal lens. Smaller objects have fewer pixels to describe their characteristics. This has made object recognition harder. These issues might be resolved by using wider angle omni-directional lenses.

Field-of-view: we believe Surround-See's capabilities can be further extended if its field-of-view went beyond the phone's peripheral space, ideally covering the entire 360° spherical space around the phone. With our current prototype, peripheral objects may not completely fall into the camera's view, an issue that can be addressed with different omni-directional mirror styles and capabilities.

A wider field-of-view allows the system to gain a better 'picture' of its surrounding environment. For example, when the phone is in active use, the user's face is mostly invisible. A complementary top view may allow Surround-See to run face detection on the missing pixels and check if it is the authorized user who is using the phone. This can also allow the users to use the original function of the front facing camera, which we had to sacrifice in our current prototype. Equally important is the wide-angle view from the back camera. It complements what is seen from the front camera, and completes the knowledge of the phone's surrounding space. With more advanced image sensing technologies, we may see true 360° cameras such as [2] that could be mounted on mobile devices.

Depth sensing: Surround-See can also benefit from depth sensing. With knowledge about peripheral objects' distance, Surround-See can alert the user about incoming people or traffic not only in the front [24] but also from the side during eyes-busy interaction. A stereo omni-directional image may be obtained by using 2 sets of cameras and an omni-directional lens. This setup is mainly used on larger platforms, e.g. robotics. Further work is needed to explore this possibility.

User recognition: user recognition could be a useful addition to Surround-See capabilities. Recognizing who is using the phone can be helpful for increasing its security. Knowing who is in the periphery also allows richer interactions to be carried out, e.g. multi-user input. Future work will explore different ways to recognize users. It is worth noting that beyond a certain distance from the phone, complex pattern recognition tasks are challenging due to inadequate pixel resolution. The set of interactions possible will only increase with improved technology.

Computer vision: the performance of Surround-See relies on several factors, including the mobile devices' computing power, the quality of the camera (including lens), and the choice of computer vision algorithms. Given that smartphone cameras don't typically offer nearly the sensor sizes that appear in more traditional vision applications, and also have a small fixed aperture, one would expect that the robustness of most algorithms will suffer somewhat. On the other hand, the limitations of processing capabilities of mobile devices also places limits on the set of vision algorithms that can be used in the proposed applications. However, these issues will become less significant with advances in mobile imaging and processing capabilities.

Battery life: mobile devices' battery life is a concern in our implementation as batteries drain quickly when the camera is active. This issue can also be less problematic with newer ultra-low-power image sensing chips and improvements in battery technology.

Form factor: The form factor of the current prototype can be improved. The 'useful' lens in our off-the-shelf sensor is far smaller than its casing, which can be removed to better integrate the lens in a future device. The lens can be further engineered to hide inside the smartphone when the front or back facing cameras are needed for other tasks.

System evaluation: Surround-See warrants careful investigation of its interaction and recognition techniques. This will be helpful for understanding its practical usability across different environments and scenarios.

CONCLUSION

We introduced the concept of enabling mobile devices to 'see' their surroundings during active use. We created a proof-of-concept system, Surround-See, by mounting an omni-directional lens on the device's front facing camera. We explored Surround-See's capabilities, and implemented a number of interaction techniques to demonstrate its unique features. In an informal setting, users welcomed the idea of having smartphones with advanced 'seeing' abilities. Future work will focus on increasing Surround-See's field-of-view to its entire surroundings and enabling 3D depth sensing. These will include exploring hardware options and software applications that integrate seamlessly with daily mobile tasks.

REFERENCES

1. Kogeto http://www.kogeto.com/say-hello-to-dot
2. Ricoh's 360-degree camera http://www.ricoh.com/
3. Argyros, A. A. & Lourakis, M. I. A. Vision-Based Interpretation of Hand Gestures for Remote Control of a Computer Mouse. *ECCV'06*, 40-51.
4. Ballendat, T., Marquardt, N. &Greenberg, S. Proxemic Interaction: Designing for a Proximity and Orientation-Aware Environment. *ITS'10*. 10 pages.
5. Butler, A., Izadi, S. & Hodges, S. SideSight: multi-touch interaction around small devices. *UIST'08* 201-204.
6. Buxton, W. Chunking & Phrasing and the Design of Human-Computer Dialogues. *IFIP'86*. 475-480.
7. LIBSVM--A Library for Support Vector Machines. http://www.csie.ntu.edu.tw/~cjlin/libsvm.
8. Cheng, L.-P., Hsiao, F.-I., Liu, Y.-T. & Chen, M. Y. iRotate: automatic screen rotation based on face orientation. *CHI'12*. 2203-2210.
9. Dearman, D., Guy, R. & Truong, K. Determining the orientation of proximate mobile devices using their back facing camera. *CHI'12*. 2231-2234.
10. Drocourt , C., Delahoche, L., Pegard, C. & Clerentin, A. Mobile robot localization based on an omnidirectional stereoscopic vision perception system. *ICRA'99*. 1329-1334.
11. El Kadmiri, O. An omnidirectional image unwrapping approach. *ICMCS'11*, 1 - 4.
12. Erol, A., Bebis, G., Nicolescu, M., Boyle, R. D. & Twombly, X. Vision-based hand pose estimation: A review. *CVIU'07*, 108 (1-2), 52-73.
13. Eslambolchilar, P. & Murray-Smith, R. Tilt-Based automatic zooming and scaling in mobile Devices-A State-Space implementation. *LNCS'04*. 120-131.
14. Farneback, G. Two-frame motion estimation based on polynomial expansion. *SCIA'03*. 363-370.
15. Gasimov, A., Magagna, F. & Sutanto, J. CAMB: context-aware mobile browser. *MUM'10*, 1-5.

16. Gluckman, J. & Nayer, S. K. Ego-motion and omnidirectional camera. *ICCV'98*. 999-1005.

17. Goel, M., Findlater, L. & Wobbrock, J. WalkType: using accelerometer data to accomodate situational impairments in mobile touch screen text entry. *CHI'12*. 2687-2696.

18. Grossman, T., Dragicevic, P. & Balakrishnan, R. Strategies for accelerating on-line learning of hotkeys. *CHI'07*, 1591-1600.

19. Hachet, M., Pouderoux, J. & Guitton, P. A camera-based interface for interaction with mobile handheld computers. *I3D'05*. 65-72.

20. Hansen, T. R., Eriksson, E. & Lykke-Olesen, A. Mixed interaction space: designing for camera based interaction with mobile devices. *CHIEA"05*. 1933-1936.

21. Harrison, C. & Hudson, S. E. Abracadabra: wireless, high-precision, and unpowered finger input for very small mobile devices. *UIST'09*. 121-124.

22. Hasan, K., Ahlström, D. & Irani, P. AD-Binning: Leveraging Around Device Space for Storing, Browsing and Retrieving Mobile Device Content. *CHI'13*. 899-908.

23. Heikkilä, M., Pietikäinen, M. & Schmid, C. Description of interest regions with local binary patterns. *Pattern Recognition*, 42 (3), 425-436.

24. Hincapié-Ramos, J. D. & Irani, P. CrashAlert: Enhancing Peripheral Alertness for Eyes-Busy Mobile Interaction while Walking. *CHI'13*. 3385-3388.

25. Hinckley, K., Pierce, J., Sinclair, M. & Horvitz, E. Sensing techniques for mobile interaction. *UIST '00*. 91-100.

26. Hinckley, K. & Sinclair, M. Touch-sensing input devices. *CHI'99*. 223-230.

27. Irani, P., Gutwin, C. & Yang., X.-D. Improving selection of off-screen targets with hopping *CHI'06* 299-308.

28. Jones, E., Alexander, J., Andreou, A., Irani, P. & Subramanian, S. GesText: accelerometer-based gestural text-entry systems. *CHI'10*. 2173-2182.

29. KaewTraKulPong, P. & Bowden, R. An Improved Adaptive Background Mixture Model for Real-time Tracking with Shadow Detection. *AVBS'01*.

30. Kakumanu, P., Makrogiannis, S. & Bourbakis, N A survey of skin-color modeling and detection methods. *Pattern Recognition*, 40 (3), 1106-1122, 2007.

31. Kang, Y. & Han, S. Improvement of smartphone interface using an AR marker. *VRCAI'12*. 13-16.

32. Khan, R. Z. & Ibraheem, N. A. Survey on Gesture Recognition for Hand Image Postures. *CIS*, 5(3), 110-121.

33. Kim, J. & Suga, Y. An Omnidirectional Vision-Based Moving Obstacle Detection in Mobile Robot. *IJCAS'07*, 5 (6), 663-673.

34. Kjeldskov, J. & Paay, J. Just-for-us: a context-aware mobile information system facilitating sociality. *MobileHCI'05*. 23-30.

35. Kratz, S. & Rohs, M. Hoverflow: exploring around-device interaction with IR distance sensors. *MobileHCI'09*, 1-4.

36. Lane, N. D., Miluzzo, E., Lu, H., Peebles, D., Choudhury, T. & Campbell, A. T. A survey of mobile phone sensing. *CM*, 48 (9), 140-150.

37. Li, Y. (2010). Protractor: A Fast and Accurate Gesture Recognizer. *CHI'10*. 2169-2172, 2010.

38. Liang, R.-H., Cheng, K.-Y., Su, C.-H., Weng, C.-T., Chen, B.-Y. & Yang, D.-N.. GaussSense: Attachable Stylus Sensing Using Magnetic Sensor Grid. *UIST'12*. 319--326.

39. Masoud, O. & Papanikolopoulos, N. A method for human action recognition. *IVC'03*, 21 (8), 729-743.

40. Ojala, T., Pietikäinen, M. & Mäenpää, T. Multiresolution Gray-Scale and Rotation Invariant Texture Classification with Local Binary Patterns. *PAMI'02*, 24 (7), 971-987.

41. Paelke, V., Reimann, C. & Stichling, D. Foot-based mobile interaction with games. *ACE'04*. 321-324.

42. Ramakers, R., Vanacken, D., Luyten, K., Coninx, K. & Schöning, J. Carpus: a non-intrusive user identification technique for interactive surfaces. *UIST'12*, 35-44.

43. Rico, J. & Brewster, S. Usable Gestures for Mobile Interfaces: Evaluating Social Acceptability. *CHI'10*. 887-896.

44. Rublee, E., Rabaud, V., Konolige, K. & Bradski, G. ORB: an efficient alternative to SIFT or SURF. *ICCV'11*. 2564-2571.

45. Runschotem, R. & Krose, B. Robust scene reconstruction from an omnidirectional vision system. *ToRA'03*, 19 (2), 351-357.

46. Schilit, B., Adams, N. & Want, R.. Context-Aware Computing Applications. *MCSA'94*.

47. Seo, B.-K., Choi, J., Han, J.-H., Park, H. & Park, J.-I. (2008). One-handed interaction with augmented virtual objects on mobile devices. *VRCAI'08*. 1-6.

48. Sohn, M. & Lee, G. ISeeU: camera-based user interface for a handheld computer. *MobileHCI'05*, 299-302.

49. Stergiopoulou, E. & Papamarkos, N. Hand gesture recognition using a neural network shape fitting technique. *EAAI'09*, 22 (8), 1141-1158

50. Wagner, D. & Schmalstieg, D. First steps towards handheld augmented realit. *ISWC'03*. 127 - 13.

51. Wang, J. & Canny, J. (2006). TinyMotion: camera phone based interaction methods. *CHIEA* '06, 339-344.

52. Wang, R. Y., Paris, S. & Popovic:, J. (2011). 6D hands: markerless hand-tracking for computer aided design. *UIST'11*. 549-558.

53. Wilson, A. Robust Vision-Based Detection of Pinching for One and Two-Handed Input. *UIST'06*. 255-258.

54. Wobbrock, J., Wilson, A. & Li, Y. Gestures without libraries, toolkits or Training: a $1.00 Recognizer for User Interface Prototypes. *UIST'07*. 159-168.

55. Yang, X.-D., Grossman, T., Wigdor, D. & Fitzmaurice, G. Magic Finger: Always-Available Input through Finger Instrumentation. *UIST'12*. 147–156.

GIST: a Gestural Interface for Remote Nonvisual Spatial Perception

Vinitha Khambadkar
vkhambadkar@cse.unr.edu

Eelke Folmer
efolmer@cse.unr.edu

Department of Computer Science and Engineering
University of Nevada, Reno
Reno, NV 89557

ABSTRACT
Spatial perception is a challenging task for people who are blind due to the limited functionality and sensing range of hands. We present GIST, a wearable gestural interface that offers spatial perception functionality through the novel appropriation of the user's hands into versatile sensing rods. Using a wearable depth-sensing camera, GIST analyzes the visible physical space and allows blind users to access spatial information about this space using different hand gestures. By allowing blind users to directly explore the physical space using gestures, GIST allows for the closest mapping between augmented and physical reality, which facilitates spatial interaction. A user study with eight blind users evaluates GIST in its ability to help perform everyday tasks that rely on spatial perception, such as grabbing an object or interacting with a person. Results of our study may help develop new gesture based assistive applications.

Author Keywords
Spatial Perception,Visual Impairment, Gestures.

ACM Classification Keywords
H.5.2 Information Interfaces and Presentation: Voice I/O; I.4.m Image Processing and Computer Vision: Miscellaneous

INTRODUCTION
Vision plays a major role in spatial perception [11], e.g., the human ability to evaluate how objects are arranged in space. For spatial perception, the haptic modality is largely redundant with the visual modality [33] and is therefore extremely valuable for users who are blind, who must rely on the use of their hands or a cane for spatial perception. Spatial perception using the tactile sense is significantly slower and more limited than using the visual sense. Where vision allows identifying multiple objects at a distance, hands have a limited sensing range, which can only be slightly extended through the use of a cane. Hands must process objects sequentially as to identify relations between them. Though the haptic sense can read Braille or embossed text, it is unable to sense color, which sighted people use to identify remote objects.

UIST'13, October 6–9, 2013, St. Andrews, United Kingdom.

ACM 978-1-4503-2271-3/13/10 $15.00.
http://dx.doi.org/10.1145/2501988.2502047

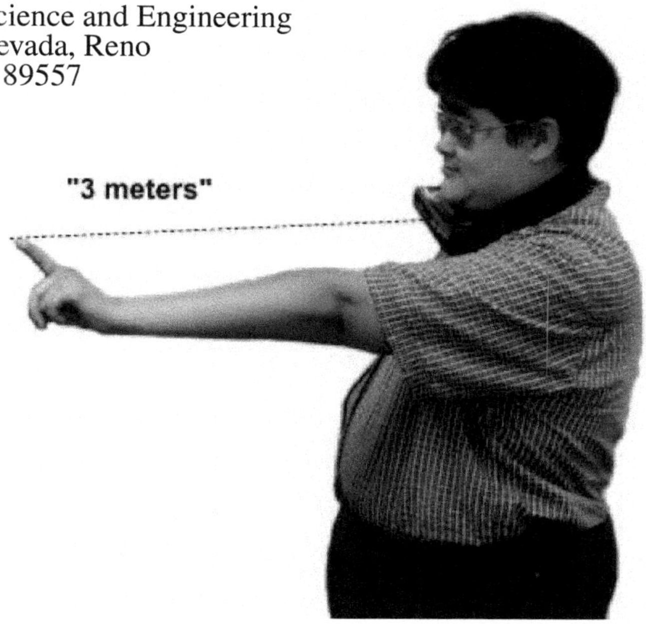

Figure 1. Using a wearable depth-sensing camera, spatial information is provided depending on where the user's arm is pointed at. Different finger gestures access different types of spatial information, such as color, depth or the presence of a human.

Computer vision has been successfully explored to enhance the perception capabilities of users who are blind [30]. Techniques have been developed that extend the sensing range of a cane [39, 16]. Mobile sensing applications have been developed for detecting color, reading signs [36] or identifying currency [28]. Though these techniques help with spatial perception, few support basic spatial interaction tasks, such as grabbing an object from a specific location [19], as this typically requires using a combination of perceptual functions, e.g., remotely sensing an object by a specific property, such as color, and then sensing the distance to the object.

We present GIST; a novel Gestural Interface for remote Spatial percepTion. GIST was inspired by MIT's "Sixth Sense" project [32]; a technique that augments the physical space around the user using wearable micro-projectors and which allows for different hand gestures to interact with that information. GIST offers the *inverse* functionality, i.e., using a wearable depth-sensing camera blind users acquire spatial information using speech about their visible physical space using different hand gestures, thus providing "fifth sense" like functionality (see Figure:1). GIST integrates a number of different perception functionalities, which include, color, human presence, depth and depth range sensing, into a single solution that facilitates spatial interaction.

RELATED WORK

Numerous camera phone applications have been developed for blind users that offer perception functionality, e.g., currency [28], face [25], text [35] or human-powered general purpose recognition [4]. Our survey of related work is limited to *spatial perception* technologies, i.e., *where* something is, using computer vision.

Various approaches extend the sensing range of a cane. Several cane like devices have been developed that use a laser and a camera [3] or sonar [1] to measure the distance to what it is pointing at. Some techniques [39, 18] can also identify the presence of objects, transitions, and edges and convey their presence using audio or haptic feedback. The required hardware and computing equipment that is integrated in such canes makes these solutions rather bulky to wield comfortably for extended periods. This problem can be avoided by using an external depth sensing camera that tracks the tip of a regular white cane [20]. This technique has been specifically developed for blind wheel chair users and allows them to use their cane to probe their environment for obstacles, which are then indicated using sound. Fingersight [9] mounts a laser, a camera, a coil and solenoid on a finger, where distance, reflectance, orientation and color sensed determine the strength of the reflection; allowing for basic edge detection. These techniques are all limited to single-point probing of distance.

Multipoint probing systems facilitate obstacle avoidance. The ultrasonic eyeglasses [23] uses ultrasound to turn distance information into audio using sensory substitution [2], where frequency is used to indicate the presence and distance of objects. The Tacit Haptic glove [16] is a wrist mounted device that uses sonar to measure the distance to objects, which is conveyed to the user as pressure on the user's wrist. Two systems use a haptic belt to convey the presence and distance of obstacles where obstacles are detected either using sonar [5] or using a depth-sensing camera mounted on the user's head [40]. These techniques convey whether an object is within range but they don't identify what the object is.

Recently, several computer vision applications for spatial perception using mobile devices were developed. The Crosswatch system [21] can identify crosswalks from a camera phone image and provides their location and orientation to a blind user. A similar mobile application performs real-time sign recognition [36] to allow blind users to locate signs and conveys what is on the sign using synthetic speech. A similar system for detecting specific markers as part of a navigation system was evaluated with eight blind users [29]. Exploring environments with a phone camera was found to be challenging to perform due to the their limited field of view and the need for the user to rotate their phone [29] . All these systems provide audio cues to indicate the direction to the object of interest, once it is recognized, but as mobile cameras cannot sense depth, providing a distance to the object of interest is limited to objects with a known size, which limits its general applicability.

A number of wearable camera techniques use sensory substitution [2] to convey visual images using haptic or audio feedback. The vOICe [31] has users wear eyeglasses with an integrated camera and a portable computer converts images into sound using headphones. The vOICe conveys images with a resolution of 64x64 pixels and 16 colors per pixel and produces soundscapes at a rate of 1 per second. Visual information from objects to the wearer's left and right are fed into the left and right ear respectively. Bright objects are louder, and frequency denotes whether an object is high up or low down in the visual field. The software also works on smartphones using the integrated camera. Brainport [37] uses a similar setup as the vOICe but instead of audio converts video into electrical pulses that are provided to the user's tongue. Brianport offers a resolution of 400 by 600 pixels with 3 different colors presented at approximately 30 frames per second.

The visual modality has a significantly larger spatial and temporal resolution than the haptic modality; and a larger spatial resolution than the audio modality, therefore these techniques are restricted in the amount of information that can be conveyed. Sensory substitution techniques take a significant amount of practice for users to learn to use [27], as it takes time for the user's brain to adapt to the remapping of sensory modalities. Two sensory substitution devices are most closely related to our approach as they exploit gesture-based spatial exploration.

Israr [19] presents a touchscreen device with a camera mounted on its back. Objects of interest are identified by color and rendered using tactile sensations on the touchscreen using the TeslaTouch [38] technology. Though this technique doesn't convey the distance to an object, users wield this device like a hand mirror, allowing them to infer the approximate location of an object. Preliminary experiments demonstrate the feasibility of this technique to locate and grab objects. This technique is limited to exploring spaces using a single finger. Tactile feedback is limited in how many different types of objects can be conveyed. Touchscreen devices are significantly heavier than mobile phones, so it may be strenuous for a user to use this device for extended periods.

Gomez [12] presents a similar device that uses a depth-sensing camera (Kinect) mounted on the users head. Using up to two fingers, users can explore the color and depth of each pixel captured by the camera using sonification provided using headphones. Different instruments are used to convey color where rhythm encodes depth information. Both techniques offer a more direct mapping between augmented and physical reality using an intermediary touch screen device. However, spatial exploration is confined to the size and touch resolution of the touch screen, which is considerably smaller than the physical space seen by the camera. Due to the surjective mapping, it may be difficult to find objects that are small or far away. The location of the camera makes it challenging to convert a 2D position on the touchscreen to a 3D position in the physical space.

A number of non-visual techniques have been developed for conveying spatial relations. For example, virtual environments providing haptic or audio feedback have been used for conveying the presence and shape of virtual objects [22] thus allowing blind people to map spaces [26]. None of these techniques allow for real time spatial exploration.

SPATIAL PERCEPTION SURVEY

In order to acquire a better understanding of the limitations that users with visual impairments currently face in spatial perception in indoor environments, as well as to gauge the potential usefulness of GIST, we conducted an email survey among 14 blind individuals (7 female) through a local chapter of the National Federation of the Blind (NFB). Twelve respondents were totally blind and two legally blind. All but one used a cane for navigation, with one person also using a guide dog. Only five respondents used a smartphone of which four occasionally used a mobile sensing application for recognizing currency or sensing colors.

Some self-reported limitations of a cane for spatial interaction included: (1) limited usefulness in small or crowded spaces; (2) it can detect the presence of an object but not what it is; (3) inability to detect obstacles above waist level; and (4) risk of damaging objects or accidentally hitting people; To familiarize themselves with the contents and layout of a room, eleven respondents would first use a cane to identify large tactile features, such as walls, doors and windows, and then revert to using their hands to recognize objects such as chairs, tables, trashcans, sinks or objects on a table. Two respondents didn't use a cane at all for this task but rather used both hands for exploration where one legally blind subject relied on using his limited eyesight. In addition to identifying tactile features, sounds and smells also played a minor role in the cognitive mapping of spaces for some respondents.

To find a specific object, such as a phone or a cup, eleven respondents said they mostly relied on their memory for storing and recalling the global location of an object. One respondent gave the example that if a cup's last known location were on the table, she would start exploring the surface of the table with her hands as to locate it. Ten respondents said they knew the color of objects they frequently used, e.g., the color of their favorite coffee cup or the color of their phone. In case an object cannot be found, all respondents indicated they would ask a sighted person for help, when available. Eight respondents noted that –when available– they would also rely on a sighted person to help them understand the contents and layout of an indoor space, for example, when entering a new room. Some of the questions they would ask a sighted person included: (1) the shape and layout of the room; (2) how many people are present; (3) what the seating arrangement is; and (4) the safest way to navigate the room.

When presenting the idea of GIST, all respondents thought this technique could be useful for them. Some possible features that were suggested for GIST included: (1) pointing at an object and have it be identified or have properties such as color or size be conveyed; and (2) pointing at a person and s/he be identified by name or gender.

DESIGN OF GIST

The main requirement for GIST–beyond spatial perception– was to facilitate spatial interaction. To this end the following design decisions were made.

Spatial interaction: GIST allows blind users to directly explore the visible physical space using gestures, thus removing the need for an intermediary sensory substitution device, such as a tablet [12, 19]. This design allows for a closer mapping between augmented and physical reality and enables leveraging the *proprioceptive sense*, i.e., the human ability to sense the position and orientation of their limbs without using eyes or ears. When a blind user explores the physical space using their arms and finds an object of interest, for example, by color, their arm functions like a display as it will point to the object. The user then only has to extend their arm in the direction it is pointing to interact with the object (Figure 2). This interaction is similar to "tactile-proprioceptive displays" [8] though that technique uses haptic feedback to point out virtual objects using the user's own arm, where we use audio. Another benefit of this type of interaction is that it takes advantage of the fact that blind people have a superior proprioceptive acuity [34] due to cross modal plasticity, which extends to the proprioceptive sense [10].

Figure 2. GIST allows a blind user to remotely sense the presence of an object, for example, using color. GIST specifically leverages the proprioceptive sense as the user only has to reach forward in the direction their arm is pointing to interact with the object.

Camera position: GIST uses a wearable depth sensing camera that hangs from the user's neck and rests on the sternum to analyze the visible physical environment as well as for tracking both hands. This setup has several benefits over using handheld approaches or wearing a camera on the user's head:

(1) *Hands free.* Our survey identifies that hands play a major role in spatial interaction. Where handheld approaches are useful when no spatial interaction with an object is required, for example, reading a sign [36], for grabbing or touching an object it is desirable to leave the user's hands free as the tactile sense is most commonly used to identify what the object is. This setup also allows for bimanual spatial exploration, which may be more efficient than when using a single hand.

(2) *Field of view:* a camera placed on the chest sees a large part of the user's FOV, especially considering that depth sensing cameras have a wider FOV than handheld cameras. It is challenging for Blind people to aim a camera at an object independently [4] and the camera's limited FOV makes it easy to miss objects that are close by. Their limited FOV also requires users to rotate the camera when looking for objects, which has been found to be inefficient and cumbersome [29]. A study revealed that blind users prefer wearing a camera over holding a camera for spatial exploration [29]. With depth sensing cameras decreasing in size, they could eventually be worn as a pendant like device [32], which is much less obtrusive than wearing a camera on the head [12]. Placing the camera between both shoulder joints allows the camera to see what each arm is pointing towards; thus optimally leveraging the proprioceptive sense for spatial interaction.

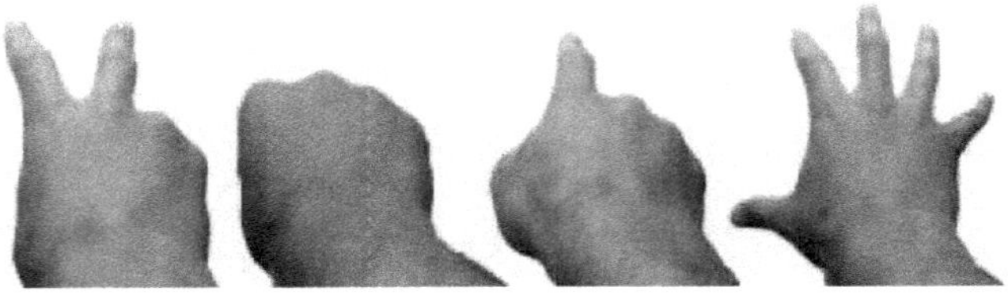

Figure 3. Four different hand gestures access different perception functions (from left to right): (A) color sensing (B) human presence sensing (C) point depth-sensing (D) area depth-sensing.

Interaction: GIST provides spatial information using synthetic speech. Though spatial information could be conveyed using sonification [12, 31] or haptic feedback [19, 2], sensory substitution techniques typically take a considerable amount of time to learn [27]. People who are blind are also very proficient at processing time-compressed speech at significantly higher rates than sighted people [13], which allows for conveying large amounts of information efficiently without users having to learn the meaning of complex patterns. Feedback can be provided discreetly through a wireless earpiece, while still allowing a blind person to hear ambient sounds or speech.

GIST consists of a: (1) mapping mode and a (2) gesture mode. In mapping mode, GIST creates a map of the area with color and depth information for each pixel. Though 3D object recognition algorithms could be implemented for recognizing objects, such as a light-switch or a door handle, GIST currently only implements an algorithm for detecting human presence. Because humans are typically grounded, we only mark the horizontal range a person occupies on the map during mapping. Up to six humans can be identified. Prior to mapping, users are instructed to put their hands down. After the map has been created, GIST switches to gesture mode and informs the user it is ready to accept gestures. Users need to stretch their arm and provide different hand gestures to access different spatial perception functions.

For GIST to work correctly, users are required to stand still and to keep the same facing direction; to avoid acquiring spatial information from an invalid map. Using a pixel-by-pixel comparison, GIST periodically checks whether the map has significantly changed and engages into mapping mode when necessary. When mapping, users will be asked to lower their arms to avoid occlusion problems. As the human activity recognition is computationally intensive, mapping and gesture recognition are separated into two separate modes to boost performance.

Based on the available map information, GIST currently supports four different spatial perception functions: (1) color sensing, (2) human presence sensing, (3) point depth-sensing, and (4) range depth-sensing, which are described below.

Color sensing: the "V" gesture using index and middle finger acts as an color sensing tool. The index and middle finger define a square and the dominant color of that area is extracted from the color information in our map. Colors are read out to the user, e.g., "green" or "white". A basic palette of 11 colors is supported but larger palettes can be used. Users can change the distance between both fingers to allow for more precise or larger area color sensing.

Human presence sensing: the fist gesture (e.g. no fingers) allows for sensing for the presence of a human. Upon detecting this gesture, GIST checks the map and reports to the user how many people are detected to avoid unnecessary probing. GIST will look up the position of the user's middle finger knuckle in the map to see if a human is present at this position. As humans are typically grounded, the user only needs to scan the horizontal range to detect their presence. When the fist doesn't point at a human GIST will state: "no person", otherwise it will state: "person found".

Point depth-sensing: pointing with the index finger conveys the distance to the object or human the arm is pointing at. An area of 20 by 20 pixels at the center of the index finger is sampled from the map to report the average depth information. Distance is reported in meters or feet depending on the user's preference. "Nothing within range" is reported when the depth information is not available as it exceeds the depth-sensing range of the camera. If the human presence or color sensing gesture is held in the same position for three seconds, GIST will automatically switch to point depth sensing.

Area depth-sensing: the open hand gesture (five fingers) is an extension of point depth-sensing but instead of a 20x20 pixel area a rectangular area defined by the user's thumb, middle and ring finger is sampled. Rather than averaging the depth information GIST reports the smallest depth in this area. This gesture may be useful to find objects that cannot be found by color (e.g., a white cup on a white table), but which only stand out by looking at depth. This is also a dynamic gesture that allows for sampling a larger or smaller area by contracting or expanding the fingers.

Users can combine gestures to create filter-like spatial perception functionality. For example, to find a person in a red dress in a room full of people (assuming no occlusion) a blind users can iteratively scan for a person, switch to the "V" gesture to detect the color of their clothes, and upon finding a red color switch to pointing as acquire how far away that person is. This sequence of gestures provides sufficient information to allow a blind person to approach and interact with that person. The color of an object of interest needs to be known a priori, but our survey indicates blind people know the color of their everyday objects. A benefit of this design is that a user can rapidly switch between perceptual functions, something that is difficult to achieve using mobile sensing applications, which also cannot provide depth information.

To best leverage the proprioceptive sense, it is important that the finger gestures are pointing in the direction the arm is pointing and that users scan the physical space using their arm and not using their hand or fingers. Users can issue gestures with both hands at the same time, where an offset is implemented for each arm. This offset helps align where the user's arm is pointing at and what the sensor sees from the center of the user's chest, to more optimally leverage the proprioceptive sense in spatial interaction. For conveying spatial information, we did not find lag to be a significant issue Figure 3 shows an overview of the finger gesture used to access the spatial perception functions.

USER STUDY

A user study with blind users focused on analyzing the performance of GIST with regards to being able to perform two different tasks that rely on spatial perception functionality. We also conducted a brief qualitative study to understand the usability and usefulness of GIST and to collect suggestions for improvement.

Participants

We recruited eight participants (3 female, average age 42.00, SD= 15.10) through a local NFB chapter to participate in our user study. All participants were visually impaired with four subjects being totally blind (TB), three subjects being legally blind (LB) and one subject with low vision (LV). All but the low vision subject used a cane for navigation. None had any self-reported impairments in mobility or hearing. Seven participants were right-handed.

Instrumentation

GIST is implemented using the Windows Kinect sensor, which is a controller-less input device used for playing video games. This sensor consists of an RGB camera and infrared (IR) depth sensor. This sensor measures 28.0x6.3x3.8 cm and weighs 1.4 kg. This sensor can sense depth of up to 6 meters, with an angular FOV of 62° horizontally and 48.6° vertically, allowing the camera to see objects in a $\pm 60m^3$ area. RGB video is captured in a 640x480 resolution at 30fps with 8-bit colors. This sensor can track up to six humans by projecting a speckle pattern onto the users skin using an IR laser projector. A 3D map of the users body is then created by measuring deformations in the reference speckle pattern. This technique is restricted to detecting humans that are standing or sitting. GIST was developed for Windows and was tested on an Intel Core i5 (3.1GHz). The OpenCV library was used to recognizing hand gestures and we take advantage of the camera's near mode, which allows for tracking objects as close as 40 cm in front of the camera. For the mapping mode, the Kinect SDK is used to get color, depth and skeletal information. Retrieving skeletal information typically takes a few seconds, upon which GIST switches to gesture mode.

During GIST's development, a number of preliminary trials were conducted with one subject who was legally blind and several blindfolded subjects. The different spatial perception functions were tested, which allowed for identifying issues with the camera offset, two-handed operation and recognizing gestures. When a single hand is visible, the system assumes the user operates GIST with their dominant hand and sets the offset for the camera accordingly. When two hands are detected it may be difficult to detect which hand is which, especially when only the pointing gesture is used. Upon detecting two hands, we split the sensor's visible area into a left and right region and set each offset according to which region the hand is detected in. We issue a warning to the user when two hands are detected in the same region. Detecting finger gestures is sometimes hard, for example, when the user is pointing their fingers down and they are occluded by the back of the user's hand or when the hand moves outside of the visible range of the camera. The Kinect SDK doesn't support finger recognition and the OpenCV library we used is unable to take advantage of available depth information, which could possibly significantly improve finger recognition.

Figure 4. Setup used for the touch a colored object task. The whiteboard is divided into a 3x3 grid with four different colored papers placed in different cells.

When in gesture mode and GIST doesn't see any gestures for more than 5 seconds, we issue a warning to the user so they can adjust the visibility of their fingers, for example, by pointing them slightly upwards. For the user study, we removed the foot of the Kinect sensor to reduce weight. We attached a Velcro strap to the sensor, which allows the user to wear it like a necklace (see Figure 1). This setup forces the sensor to keep pointing forward; allowing it to capture the users field of view. For the user studies GIST is tethered using an USB extension cable and connected to a desktop computer to avoid the user having to wear heavy computing equipment. Audio feedback is provided using computer speakers.

Procedure

Subjects were asked to perform two different spatial interaction tasks: (1) sensing the location of an object of a certain color and touching it; and (2) sensing the presence of a human in a room and approaching this person. For this study, both tasks were restricted to two-dimensional target acquisition.

Task 1: Touching a Colored Object

For the first study the spatial perception task involves finding the position of a colored object in a vertical plane, perpendicular to the floor, that is defined by the camera's horizontal and vertical FOV. This task represents the practical task of finding and grabbing an object [19]. For this study, we used a large whiteboard that was divided into a 3x3 grid that spanned the entire visible range of the camera when it was placed at 1.0-meter distance from the whiteboard. Due to the camera's angular FOVs, this grid was approximately 1.2 x 0.9 meters. We placed each subject at 1.0-meter distance from the whiteboard facing the center of the grid. At this distance subjects can do one step forward and touch any object in the grid with their hand. Except for an object in the center, objects are at approximately the same distance from the subject; thus minimizing the effect that distance has on the spatial interaction task. This was done on purpose as to constrain spatial perception to the X,Y dimensions. At this distance subjects were unable to accidentally touch the whiteboard when issuing gestures.

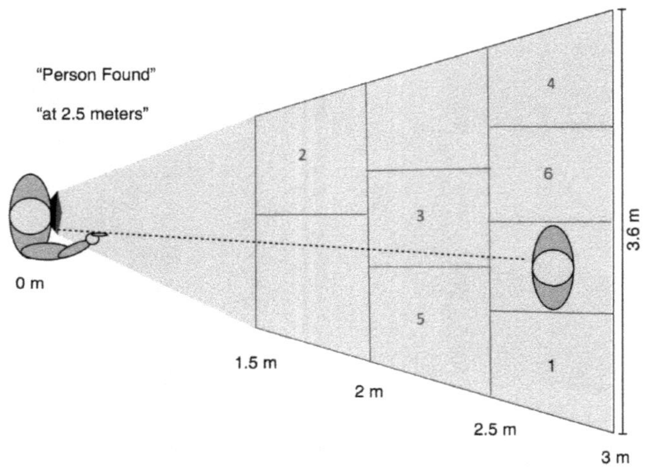

Figure 5. Setup used for the approaching a human task. An area is divided into 9 cells with a target person placed in one of the 6 cells.

For objects, we used six colored papers (red, green, blue, yellow, brown, black) whose size was approximately the size of a cell of our grid (40 x 30 cm). These colors were chosen as they were most easily recognized under varying lighting conditions. Nine different search tasks were created such that: (1) the target location was each one of the nine grid cells picked at random; (2) the target color was picked at random from the six available colors; and (3) three of the remaining eight cells were randomly chosen and filled by one of the remaining five colors at random. The same sequence of search tasks was used for each subject. Papers were attached to the whiteboard using transparent tape. Figure 4 shows the physical setup used for task 1.

Subjects were asked find the target colored object using the color sensing gesture with their dominant hand. Upon sensing the target color, subjects were asked to touch the target object by doing a step forward and extending their arm in the direction it was pointing. We wanted to avoid ambiguity and not have the results of our study to rely on GIST's ability to recognize gestures; therefore the pointing gesture was appropriated for color sensing, as in preliminary trials this was found to be most easily recognized. A 10x10 pixel area is sampled to determine the dominant color that is centered at the subject's index finger. Occasionally a thumb would be visible but GIST will ignore this. To leverage the proprioceptive sense in being able to touch the target object, subjects were specifically instructed to keep their finger pointing in the direction their arm was pointing and only scan for colors using their arm and not with their hand. If the index finger wasn't recognized, subjects were asked to slightly point their index finger upwards (but still pointing in the extension of their arm). Because the whiteboard is white, this color is filtered out to optimize the color detection. We ensured lighting conditions were optimal for the sensor to recognize colors. Prior to the test, subjects were instructed what the search task would involve. Subjects were familiarized with the sensor and the dimensions and layout of the whiteboard. The sensor was attached to the subject's neck using the Velcro strap where we ensured subjects felt comfortable wearing

Figure 6. A blind subject sensing the direction and distance to a person.

it. Subjects that had some residual vision were asked to wear a blindfold for the trials to balance the conditions between subjects. We positioned subjects at 1.0-meter from the whiteboard (measured from the camera) and marked their location by putting a piece of paper under their feet. We calibrated the position of the grid based on their height and marked each corner on the whiteboard using a marker. Four papers were attached to each corner cell. Subjects were asked to find each paper using the pointing gesture using their dominant arm and -upon finding it- to touch each paper. This process allowed us to fine tune the camera offset for their arm, which would typically vary based on their height. This task also allowed subjects to familiarize themselves with the search space in which the target had to be found. Before each search task, we made sure that the map contained the entire grid on the whiteboard and we calibrated the subject's position and the direction the camera was pointing, if necessary. We asked subjects to keep facing the whiteboard and stand still while issuing gestures. For the user study, GIST's ability to check whether the map was invalid was disabled. An observer was present, which would announce the target color to be found and who would record the time it took for the subject to touch the target object from when the target color was announced. As soon as the subject found the target color and started moving towards the whiteboard, GIST's feedback was muted to avoid confusing the subject, as the provided feedback would be incorrect. In addition to saving each map, GIST would log the location of the subject's index finger and time stamp during each search task. If the subject failed to touch the target object, we marked the search task as a failure. Subjects were then required to perform the failed task again after performing the next search task as to minimize the risk of subjects memorizing the layout of objects on the whiteboard.

Task 2: Approaching a Human

For the second study, we simulate the practical task of finding and approaching a person in a room. Interacting with another person typically relies on the willingness of a sighted person to let their presence and location be known using sound. A blind person could ask if another person is present, but we believe sensing human presence using GIST is more discrete and can lead to a greater independence and new opportunities for socialization. The spatial perception task involves finding the position of a human in a horizontal plane that is defined by the camera's horizontal field of view and its depth-sensing range. Because humans are typically grounded, spatial per-

Table 1. *Results (stdev) for the task 1.*

Subject ID	#Attempts	Search Time	Time to Touch
1	1.44 (.53)	8.1 (6.0)	3.7 (1.5)
2	1.11 (.33)	7.4 (5.6)	4.5 (1.0)
3	1.22 (.44)	12.1 (7.6)	4.3 (1.1)
4	1.77 (.83)	16.0 (15.2)	3.9 (1.7)
5	1.55 (.73)	24.5 (28.7)	5.2 (2.0)
6	1.00 (.00)	6.5 (4.1)	5.2 (1.2)
7	1.33 (.50)	9.4 (6.6)	4.8 (1.3)
8	1.44 (.73)	13.1 (13.4)	4.3 (2.3)
Average	1.35 (.25)	12.2(5.9)	4.52 (0.5)

Table 2. *Average search attempts (stdev) for each cell for task 1.*

1.13 (.25)	1.38 (.74)	1.25 (.46)
1.38 (.74)	1.25 (.46)	1.75 (.71)
1.38 (.74)	1.38 (.52)	1.25 (.46)

Table 3. *Average scanning time (stdev) for each cell for task 1.*

15.2 (11.6)	12.0 (7.7)	10.1 (5.6)
32.6 (29.3)	7.8 (7.7)	7.3 (8.9)
11.6 (7.8)	6.5 (4.9)	7.9 (5.8)

Table 4. *Results (stdev) for task 2.*

Subject ID	#Attempts	Total task time
1	1.17 (.41)	16.7 (3.8)
2	1.00 (.00)	13.0 (3.0)
3	1.33 (.52)	24.8 (8.3)
4	1.33 (.82)	20.3 (15.9)
5	1.17 (.41)	20.0 (8.2)
6	1.17 (.41)	16.0 (1.6)
7	1.17 (.41)	13.4 (5.7)
8	1.00 (.00)	13.5 (2.4)
Average	1.17 (0.13)	17.2 (4.2)

Table 5. *Avg search attempts (stdev) for each cell for task 2.*

<table>
<tr><td rowspan="2">1.00 (.00)</td><td></td><td>1.13 (0.35)</td></tr>
<tr><td rowspan="2">1.13 (0.35)</td><td>1.50 (0.75)</td></tr>
<tr><td rowspan="2"></td><td></td></tr>
<tr><td>1.13 (0.35)</td><td>1.13 (0.35)</td></tr>
</table>

Table 6. *Avg scanning time (stdev) for each cell for task 2.*

<table>
<tr><td rowspan="2">16.9 (5.9)</td><td></td><td>14.7 (5.6)</td></tr>
<tr><td rowspan="2">17.0 (5.1)</td><td>25.3 (11.1)</td></tr>
<tr><td rowspan="2"></td><td></td></tr>
<tr><td>15.3 (10.2)</td><td>15.5 (10.2)</td></tr>
</table>

ception for this task is constrained to the X,Z dimensions. Though the Kinect sensor can track depth up to 6.0 meter, a higher accuracy is achieved for ranges up to 3.5 meters [24]. Due to the camera's 62° horizontal angular FOV, an isosceles triangular area with a base of 3.6 meters and a height of 3.0 meters was defined on the floor of a room used for user studies. This area was divided into a grid consisting of nine cells of approximate equal size, which we marked with tape on the floor. For the search tasks six randomly selected target positions were determined (see Figure 5). The same sequence of search tasks is used for each subject. For this task, subjects need to use two different spatial perception functions: (1) human presence sensing; and (2) point depth sensing. Again to avoid ambiguity, the pointing gesture was made to activate human presence sensing and when pointed at a person and held in approximately the same location for three seconds, the distance to that person is conveyed in whole feet, which was already a feature of GIST. Subjects were instructed to scan horizontally with their arm using the pointing gesture to find the location of the person. When the person was found, subjects were asked to wait for GIST to convey the distance and then walk to the person by following the direction their arm was pointing using the distance provided (see Figure 6).

Prior to each search task, a person would assume their target cell in the search grid silently as to not give away their position using audio. We made sure the map contained the entire grid and that a person was detected in the target cell, where we calibrated the subject's position and camera when necessary. Once GIST announced it was ready for gestures, the subject could start their search. The person in the target cell would tap the finger of the subject when s/he would cross their cell to indicate to the subject that the search task was successful. If the subject failed to cross the target cell, we marked the search task as a failure and subjects could try again after the next search task. In addition to the map, GIST would log the location of the subject's finger and a timestamp. An observer recorded the time from when the subject started their search to successfully touching the person. After the user study, subjects were interviewed about their experiences and suggestions for improvements were collected.

Results

Task 1. Table 1 shows the average results for task 1 for each subject. Task time has been split in search time, i.e., the time it took to scan to the target color, and time to touch, i.e., the time it took from finding the target color to physically touching the target object. Because an observer recorded time, all times reported are rounded to 1/10 of a second accuracy. It took an average of 1.36 attempts (SD=.25) to find each target object. In all failed searches, subjects were able to find the target color but failed to touch the target object. In most cases subjects were close to the target, e.g., within 10cm. The average search time for a scanning a target search was 12.2 seconds (SD=5.9) and it took 4.52 seconds (SD=0.5) to touch the target object upon finding the target color.

To analyze task performance with regards to the layout of the grid, tables 2 and 3 show the number of search attempts and scanning time for each cell. We transposed the left and right column for the left-handed subject to be able to compare the results with the right-handed subjects.

Due to the small number of subjects used in our test, A Friedman test found no statistically significant difference between cells for average search attempts ($\chi^2(5) = 5.807$, $p = .325$) but did find a significant difference for average scanning time

($\chi^2(8) = 21.404$, $p < .05$). Pairwise comparisons using a Bonferroni correction found significant differences for the cell tuples: (4,5) and (4,8). As task 1 can be considered to be a pointing task, it can be modeled using Fitts' law [7]. We analyzed search time as a function of the index of difficulty, where only distance to the target is modeled due to our target's fixed size. We found a Pearson correlation of .32 between target distance and time to touch.

Task 2. Table 4 shows the average results for task 2 for each subject. For the left-handed subject, we used a horizontally mirrored version of the grid to allow for combining the results with the other subjects. It took an average of 1.17 attempts (SD=.13) to complete task 2, with average task completion time of 17.2 seconds (SD=4.2). To analyze task performance with regards to the layout of the grid, tables 5 and 6 show the number of attempts and total task time for each cell. A Friedman test found no statistically significant difference between cells for average search attempts ($\chi^2(5) = 6.212$, $p = .286$) but did detect a significant difference for scanning time between cells ($\chi^2(5) = 16.929$, $p = .0.05$) Pairwise comparisons using a Bonferroni correction found significant differences for the cell tuples: $\{(5,6),(1,6),(4,6)\}$.

Qualitative results. After the trial, non-directed interviews with open-ended questions were used to collect qualitative experiences as to understand the usability of GIST and to identify areas for improvement. Overall, all subjects enjoyed using GIST, and thought it could be useful in their everyday lives. All subjects liked the speech feedback provided and none found this to be overwhelming. Two participants said they wouldn't mind GIST to provide speech feedback at a higher rate, especially for human presence sensing, as they used screen readers at a significantly higher speech rates than the speech rate that was implemented for GIST. Half of the subjects found the color perception functionality to be the most useful feature and the other half the human presence sensing. Two subjects stated they experienced some minor discomfort during the trials because the camera became quite warm, causing them to sweat. One subject expressed a minor concern as how issuing gestures using GIST would make them appear to sighted people. Two subjects asked whether GIST could be used when walking with a cane or guide dog. Some suggestions to improve GIST included: (1) being able to recognize specific objects; (2) recognizing a specific individual in a room full of people; (3) being able to recognize certain human properties, such as gender, race or height; (4) being able to use both hands for spatial perception; and (5) support for Braille or haptic feedback so GIST may be used in noisy environments.

DISCUSSION

Where previously it had been argued that spatial interaction tasks such as grabbing an object are difficult to perform using existing assistive technologies [19], our user study demonstrates that the innovative use of the hands for spatial perception can help blind users perform basic tasks, such as grabbing an object or interacting with a person.

Comparison: Contrasting our results with preliminary data from a comparable touchscreen based spatial perception technique [19] shows that we achieved better results for touching a colored object, though an accurate comparison is difficult due to a difference in experimental conditions and number of subjects tested. Other hand held approaches [29, 36] don't report any comparable data. It is reasonable to assume that the task performance in our study will be affected by an object's size (task 1) or the distance and the size of the person (task 2). Our study did not collect evidence for this assumption, as we used fixed target sizes for task 1. For task 2 we found some evidence that it is harder to locate a person that is farther away, e.g., their representation in the map is smaller than when a person is close. For a person that is located farther away, we observed subjects sometimes to skip over their location, which may explain the significant higher scanning times for target cells that were located farthest away.

Social Acceptance: it is important to recognize how using GIST could affect the perception of individuals who are blind. It took decades for the white cane to become a symbol of blindness beyond a tool for navigation. The gestural interaction required by GIST could be considered socially awkward, yet with the increasing popularity of mobile and wearable computing, interacting with eyes free interfaces, using speech and gestures may become more socially acceptable over time. Eyes-free mobile interfaces have been proposed [14] that involve similar speech and gesture based interaction.

Limitations: Our user study did identify a limitation of using gestures. When a subject crossed the sagittal plane with their arm, i.e., the vertical plane dividing the body into a left and right halve, it will cause their upper arm to press against their chest, which then leads to users slightly turning their torso. For GIST this is undesirable as it moves the camera away from the user's FOV, which then invalidates the map. Though we tried to correct subjects when we observed this to occur, it does explain why we found significantly higher scanning times for targets in the left column of our grid for task 1. To some extent the relative bulkiness of the Kinect sensor plays a role in this as well, as we observed the subject's arm to press the sensor away when subjects were scanning on their non-dominant side. With a smaller sensor this effect could possibly be mitigated. By placing the sensor at a different location, e.g., on the user's head [12, 40], this problem could also be avoided but then GIST is unable to leverage the proprioceptive sense to facilitate spatial interaction, as the sensor doesn't see along the user's arms. A more practical solution, which is already supported by GIST, would be to use both arms for spatial perception, constraining each arm to explore its half of the camera's FOV in which it can move unconstrained.

FUTURE WORK

Future work will investigate the following issues:

Robustness. GIST was evaluated under highly controlled conditions as to evaluate how well hands could be used for spatial perception. Lighting conditions were optimal and colors for the targets were chosen such to optimize their recognition. To avoid ambiguity, only the pointing gesture was used in our study as this was most easily recognized. We anticipate being able to make GIST more robust and improve the gesture and color recognition significantly using the recently announced Kinect 2.0 sensor. This sensor offers precise finger recognition that can take advantage of depth information. It also has an improved near mode as well as active infrared, which allows for the sensor to work under varying lighting conditions.

Two-handed spatial exploration. To overcome the limitation of moving the sensor out of the FOV of the user, future user studies will explore spatial perception using both hands. For conveying spatial information sensed by each hand, speech feedback could be provided to the left and right ear depending on the hand that is used. A benefit of using both hands is that spatial perception may be twice as fast for locating objects or that two objects can be found simultaneously. It may also be possible to define new perceptual functions that use both hands, for example, a zoom function could be activated for an area that is defined using a frame gesture defined by the index finger and thumb of both hands.

Target sizes. To evaluate GIST, we used fixed size targets with a relative large size (40 x 30 cm) for task 1. This size may reflect the size of certain objects, such as a coat, that a blind user may want to find, but it is not representative for smaller objects, such as a coffee cup. Future studies will evaluate sensing smaller sized targets. Of specific interest is evaluating the user's ability to adjust the area that is sampled for color. Sampling a larger area may allow for finding a smaller object of a specific color, but when the sample area is too large, we run the risk of the object getting lost in its background as that may become the dominant color for the area sampled. A solution here could be for GIST to analyze a scene and determine what the dominant background color is, for example, the color of the walls of a room and then automatically filter out the background color of a scene. This facilitates color sampling of a larger area and sensing the location of an object faster (assuming the object has a different color from its background).

Real-time mapping. To optimize gesture recognition, mapping and gesture recognition are split into two separate processes, which requires the user to stand still while engaging in spatial perception. It may be possible to facilitate real-time mapping by continuously switching the sensor between near and regular mode. However, this requires solving occlusion problems, as the hands will block part of the camera's visible area. For some spatial perception functions this may not be a problem, as the sensor can sense RGB and depth information around the user's hands, but for human presence detection, GIST requires an unobstructed view of the scene. A benefit of real-time mapping would be that when a user approaches a or object person, updated distance information could be provided.

Implementation. GIST is currently implemented on a desktop computer, but we envision future implementations to be mobile using a tablet device that can be worn in a backpack. Recently, depth-sensing camera's have become available that are significantly smaller and lighter than the Kinect sensor used in our study. The Kinect camera used in our study uses infrared, therefore GIST is limited to being used indoors, as in outdoor environments there is too much infrared light from the sun. However, new camera's have become available that use laser light, which may allow outdoor use. It is also anticipated that depth-sensing technology will become available in mobile devices [15] in the near future, which may allow a blind user to wear GIST like a pendant [32], with no additional computing equipment required.

Applications. Our study lays the groundwork for developing novel assistive augmented reality applications. A significant benefit of a depth-sensing camera is that it can take IR and RGB photos of objects, which can easily segmented from a background or a flat surface due to the available depth information. This may allow for training a classifier that can recognize objects with higher accuracy than using RGB alone. Taking advantage of the excellent speech recognition abilities of the Kinect due to its integrated microphone array, we envision extending GIST with "intelligent personal assistant" like functionality that can answer basic spatial queries pertaining to objects recognized using a natural language interface. Blind users can train this classifier in real-time by holding an object in front of the camera from various viewpoints, while naming the object, e.g., "this is a coffee cup". The user can then place the object on a table in front of them, and ask: "where is my cup", upon which GIST could answer: "the cup is right in front of you" if it can recognize the cup. Blind users can train their own personal library of objects, which combined with some form of indoor localization and mapping [17, 6], could allow for answering basic spatial questions. This approach would also allow GIST to provide the names of objects the user is pointing at and further justifies using synthetic speech as the feedback modality for GIST.

CONCLUSION

We present GIST, a gestural interface that allows users who are blind to probe their field of view using their hands, as to sense the presence and properties of remote objects and people. GIST combines a number of spatial perceptions functions that currently exist as separate solutions into a single technique. GIST is a useful, low-cost technology that can potentially give greater independence to users with visual impairments, as it may help them perform everyday tasks, such as grabbing an object or approaching a person that are difficult to perform using existing assistive technologies.

ACKNOWLEDGEMENTS

This work is supported by NSF Grant IIS-1118074.

REFERENCES

1. Allman, T. *From Bat Sonar To Canes For The Blind.* Imitating Nature. KidHaven Press, 2005.
2. Bach-y Rita, P., and Kercel, S. Sensory substitution and the human-machine interface. *Trends in Cognitive Sciences 7:12*, (2003), 541–546.
3. Benjamin, J. M., A. N. A., and Schepis, A. F. A laser cane for the blind. In *Proc. of the San Diego Biomedical Symposium*, vol. 12 (1973), 53–57.
4. Bigham, J. P., Jayant, C., Ji, H., Little, G., Miller, A., Miller, R. C., Miller, R., Tatarowicz, A., White, B., White, S., and Yeh, T. Vizwiz: nearly real-time answers to visual questions. In *Proc. of UIST*, (2010), 333–342.

5. Cardin, S., Thalmann, D., and Vexo, F. A wearable system for mobility improvement of visually impaired people. *Vis. Comput. 23:2*, (2007), 109–118.

6. Fallah, N., Apostolopoulos, I., Bekris, K., and Folmer, E. The user as a sensor: navigating users with visual impairments in indoor spaces using tactile landmarks. In *Proc. of CHI*, (2012), 425–432.

7. Fitts, P. The information capacity of the human motor system in controlling the amplitude of movement. *J. Exp Psychol 47*, 6 (Jun 1954), 381–91.

8. Folmer, E., and Morelli, T. Spatial gestures using a tactile-proprioceptive display. In *Proc. of TEI*, (2012), 139–142.

9. Galeotti, J., Horvath, S., Klatzky, R., Nichol, B., Siegel, M., and Stetten, G. Fingersight™: fingertip control and haptic sensing of the visual environment. In *Proc. of SIGGRAPH new tech demos*, (2008), 16:1.

10. Gaunet, F., and Rossetti, Y. Effects of visual deprivation on space representation: immediate and delayed pointing toward memorised proprioceptive targets. *Perception 35:1*, (2006), 107–24.

11. Ghirardelli, T., and Scharine, A. *Helmet-mounted displays: Sensation, perception and cognition issues*. US Army Aeromedical Research Lab, 2009, ch. Auditory-Visual Interactions, 599–618.

12. Gomez, J. D., Bologna, G., and Pun, T. Spatial awareness and intelligibility for the blind: audio-touch interfaces. In *Proc. of CHI EA* (2012), 1529–1534.

13. Gordon-Salant, S., and Friedman, S. A. Recognition of rapid speech by blind and sighted older adults. *J. Speech Lang Hear Res 54:2*, (2011), 622–31.

14. Gustafson, S., Bierwirth, D., and Baudisch, P. Imaginary interfaces: spatial interaction with empty hands and without visual feedback. In *Proc. of UIST*, (2010), 3–12.

15. Hardesty, L. Mit news: 3-d cameras for cellphones, `http://web.mit.edu/newsoffice/2011/lidar-3d-camera-cellphones-0105.html`.

16. Hoefer, S. Tacit haptic glove: Hand-mounted haptic feedback sonar obstacle avoidance assistance device, `http://grathio.com/2011/08/meet-the-tacit-project-its-sonar-for-the-blind/`, 2011.

17. Hub, A., Diepstraten, J., and Ertl, T. Design and development of an indoor navigation and object identification system for the blind. In *Proc. of ASSETS*, (2004), 147–152.

18. Iannacci, F., Turnquist, E., Avrahami, D., and Patel, S. N. The haptic laser: multi-sensation tactile feedback for at-a-distance physical space perception and interaction. In *Proc. of CHI*, (2011), 2047–2050.

19. Israr, A., Bau, O., Kim, S.-C., and Poupyrev, I. Tactile feedback on flat surfaces for the visually impaired. In *Proc. of CHI-EA*, (2012), 1571–1576.

20. Ivanchenko, V., Coughlan, J., Gerrey, W., and Shen, H. Computer vision-based clear path guidance for blind wheelchair users. In *Proc. of ASSETS*, (2008), 291–292.

21. Ivanchenko, V., Coughlan, J., and Shen, H. Crosswatch: a camera phone system for orienting visually impaired pedestrians at traffic intersections. *Proc. of ICCHP*, (2008), 1122–1128.

22. Jansson, G., Fanger, J., Konig, H., and Billberger, K. Visually impaired person's use of the phantom for information about texture and 3d form of virtual objects. In *Proc. of the 3rd PHANToM Users Group Workshop* (1998).

23. Kay, L. Ultrasonic eyeglasses for the blind. *Journal of the Accoustic Society of America 108:5*, (2000), 2514–2514.

24. Kinect. Kinect for windows, `http://www.microsoft.com/en-us/kinectforwindows/`, url access date: 5-4-2012.

25. Krishna, S., Little, G., Black, J., and Panchanathan, S. A wearable face recognition system for individuals with visual impairments. In *Proc. of ASSETS*, (2005), 106–113.

26. Lahav, O., and Mioduser, D. Multisensory virtual environment for supporting blind persons' acquisition of spatial cognitive mapping – a case study. In *Proc. of ED-MEDIA* (2001), 1046–1051.

27. Lenay, C., Gapenne, O., Hanneton, S., Marque, C., and Geouelle, C. *Touching for Knowing, Cognitive psychology of haptic manual perception*. 2003, ch. Sensory Substitution: limits and perspectives, 275–292.

28. Liu, X. A camera phone based currency reader for the visually impaired. In *Proc. of ASSETS*, (2008), 305–306.

29. Manduchi, R. Mobile vision as assistive technology for the blind: An experimental study. In *Proc. of ICCHP*, (2012), 9–16

30. Manduchi, R., and Coughlan, J. (computer) vision without sight. *Commun. of the ACM 55:1*, (2012), 96–104.

31. Meijer, P. An Experimental System for Auditory Image Representations. *IEEE Trans. on Biomedical Engineering, 39:2*, (1992), 112–121.

32. Mistry, P., and Maes, P. Sixthsense: a wearable gestural interface. In *SIGGRAPH Sketches*, (2009), 11:1.

33. Newell, F. N., Woods, A. T., Mernagh, M., and Bülthoff, H. H. Visual, haptic and cross-modal recognition of scenes. *Experimental Brain Research 161* (2005), 233–242.

34. Ozdemir, R. A., Pourmoghaddam, A., and Paloski, W. H. Sensorimotor posture control in the blind: Superior ankle proprioceptive acuity does not compensate for vision loss. *Gait & Posture* (2013).

35. Peters, J.-P., Thillou, C., and Ferreira, S. Embedded reading device for blind people: A user-centred design. In *Proc. of AIPR*, (2004), 217–222.

36. Shen, H., and Coughlan., J. Towards a real-time system for finding and reading signs for visually impaired users. In *Proc. of ICCHP)* (2012).

37. Upson, S. Tongue vision. *IEEE Spectr. 44:1*, (2007), 44–45.

38. Xu, C., Israr, A., Poupyrev, I., Bau, O., and Harrison, C. Tactile display for the visually impaired using teslatouch. In *Proc. of CHI EA*, (2011), 317–322.

39. Yuan, D., and Manduchi, R. Dynamic environment exploration using a virtual white cane. In *Proc. of CVPR 1:1*, (2005), 243–249.

40. Zöllner, M., Huber, S., Jetter, H.-C., and Reiterer, H. Navi: a proof-of-concept of a mobile navigational aid for visually impaired based on the Microsoft Kinect. In *Proc. of INTERACT*, (2011), 584–587.

YouMove: Enhancing Movement Training with an Augmented Reality Mirror

Fraser Anderson[1,2], Tovi Grossman[1], Justin Matejka[1], George Fitzmaurice[1]
[1]Autodesk Research, Toronto, ON, Canada
{firstname.lastname}@autodesk.com
[2] University of Alberta, Edmonton, AB, Canada
frasera@ualberta.ca

ABSTRACT
YouMove is a novel system that allows users to record and learn physical movement sequences. The recording system is designed to be simple, allowing anyone to create and share training content. The training system uses recorded data to train the user using a large-scale augmented reality mirror. The system trains the user through a series of stages that gradually reduce the user's reliance on guidance and feedback. This paper discusses the design and implementation of YouMove and its interactive mirror. We also present a user study in which YouMove was shown to improve learning and short-term retention by a factor of 2 compared to a traditional video demonstration.

Author Keywords
Movement; full body; 3D; learning; training; augmented reality; motor learning; guidance.

ACM Classification Keywords
H.5.2 [Information interfaces and presentation]: User Interfaces. - Graphical user interfaces.

INTRODUCTION
Mastering new postures and motions is a crucial component of many physical activities such as dancing, martial arts, and sports. Learning these motor skills can be challenging, requiring hours of training and repetitive practice [38]. Often, learning involves enrolling in classes where an instructor leads a group through a set of exercises. Ballet dancers often use mirrors to receive visual feedback in addition to coaching [7]. While there may be no replacement for expert coaching, less formal self-paced learning may be more desirable for in-home practice, to supplement professional coaching, or for hobbyists.

Technology has enabled movement training to occur at home. Prior to the Internet, trainees could practice along with instructional VHS tapes, such as exercise videos. Now, online video sites, such as YouTube, offer thousands of movement training videos, for skills ranging from surgery to jiu-jitsu. While videos for a variety of skills are available, the use of video as a training medium is limited. Videos offer no feedback, do not capture 3D movement information, and offer no personalized motivation.

UIST'13, October 08 – 11, 2013, St Andrews, United Kingdom.

http://dx.doi.org/10.1145/2501988.250204

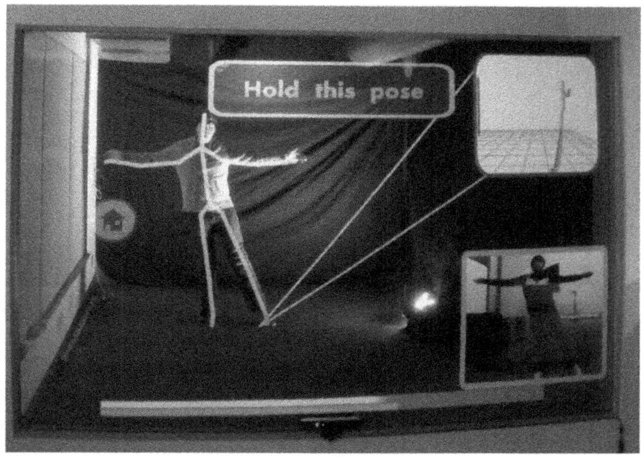

Figure 1: YouMove allows users to record and learn physical movement sequences. An augmented reality mirror provides graphic overlays for guidance and feedback. Note that for this photo the virtual viewpoint was vertically repositioned to account for the offset of a head-mounted camera, and floor lighting was used to reduce glare.

There has also recently been an emergence of fitness and dance video games that use game consoles with tracking technology such as the Microsoft Kinect [6]. While these games may improve some movement skill, their target is entertainment and exercise. In these games, movements are constrained to pre-programmed sequences, and the feedback is limited, often consisting of a simple 2D outline.

In this paper, we present YouMove (Figure 1), a system for learning full body movements. YouMove is comprised of a Kinect-based recording system, and a corresponding training system. The recording system is designed to be easy to use, so anyone can capture movement sequences and annotate them for learning, without the need for complicated motion capture hardware or software. The training system uses the recorded video and 3D movement data to guide the trainee through a series of interactive stages. The training system augments a traditional 'ballet mirror' experience by using a half-silvered mirror with graphic overlays for guidance and feedback. The use of a mirror allows for zero latency, high fidelity feedback. In a user study we find YouMove improves movement learning and short-term retention by a factor of 2 compared to traditional video demonstrations. As implemented, YouMove is immediately beneficial for several domains of movement, such as yoga, dance, and physical therapy, with more domains possible with further advances in sensing.

This paper provides several contributions. First, we provide the first generalized full-body movement training system, YouMove. Next, we provide design guidelines, implementation details, and interaction techniques for a whole-body, interactive, augmented reality mirror. Third, we provide an evaluation demonstrating YouMove's effectiveness over a traditional video approach. Last, we analyze learning and preferences with YouMove and provide directions for future work.

RELATED WORK

This work is influenced by prior work in motor learning, technology-mediated skill learning, and display technology.

Motor Learning

Within the domain of motor learning, there is substantial research on the effects of various factors on motor skill acquisition. The amount of deliberate practice has been shown to have the greatest effect on learning [38]. However, several factors influence the effectiveness of the practice. In particular, the availability and modality of feedback can greatly impact skill acquisition [30].

Nearly all training systems and research involve various manipulations of feedback, see Sigrist et al. for a thorough review [30]. Audio has been shown to be beneficial in learning timing [28]. Summary feedback (feedback at the end of a series of trials) can improve learning compared to feedback shown after each trial [26]. Allowing learners to control when they see feedback is also beneficial [13].

Technology-Based Motor Skill Training

Virtual reality has been leveraged for training movement in a number of specific domains. Various surgical simulators have shown promise in improving surgical skill [14]. A virtual ping-pong trainer showed positive effects of training [32]. The use of a virtual 'ghost' for training 3D hand movements showed that a VR environment was no worse than real-world training [43]. Several other VR-based trainers have had similar results showing a custom system performing at least as well as a traditional method [16]. In each of these cases, the system is designed to support very specific movements, leading to a lack of generalizability.

Physical therapy has driven the use of technology for movement learning [12]. These typically focus on re-training simple movements and improving range of motion. A number of systems have been developed around gaming and VR platforms in an effort to make the otherwise monotonous or painful movements motivating [40]. There is evidence suggesting that the major benefits of technology-based therapy tools are in their ability to motivate and encourage adherence to training schedules [1].

Within the HCI literature, several systems for learning gestures for computer input have been developed and studied. Octopocus provides a dynamic, real-time guide for learning 2D stroke gestures [3]. ShadowGuides provides a similar guide for learning multi-touch gestures and hand postures [9]. Users of both systems showed improvement in learning the mapping of gestures. Anderson and Bischof studied various gesture guides and found high guidance can hinder learning of the motor component [2].

Additional work within the HCI community has focused on movement guidance. Henderson and Feiner developed an HMD-based augmented reality system providing real-time guidance for assembly tasks [11]. LightGuide used on-body projections to guide a user's hand through 3D space [31]. With this approach, feedback is only available for a single hand, and only when the hand is visible. ModelMA allows a performer to record a repeated movement using the Kinect, which an observer can then practice with, however, learning is not addressed and is left as future work [35]. These systems were limited to guiding a small set of movements. In contrast, YouMove supports full-body movement learning using interactive, gamified training.

Novel Display Technologies

Half-silvered mirrors (HSMs) have been used in a number of interactive scenarios. The i-mirror used a projector to allow users to apply virtual makeup, and provided artificial 'night vision' on a small display [33]. The aware-mirror and MR-mirror use an LCD display behind a HSM, displaying news and information, or playing games [10, 25]. In the Haunted Mansion at Walt Disney World, a large display is placed equidistant from the viewer, opposite a HSM, allowing the viewer's reflection and the virtual content to be displayed on the same focal plane [8]. The Holoflector used the same technique coupled with a Kinect to enable 'holographic' interaction with virtual content [19]. This configuration allows reflection-aligned content from multiple viewpoints, but requires a substantially larger configuration space and requires users to maintain a fixed distance from the screen.

Our work is also guided by research on free-hand interaction with large displays. VideoPlace allowed users to visualize their body movement on a large projection screen [15]. Shadow reaching extended this concept by allowing users to use their shadow to select targets that were previously out of reach [29]. Several works have also explored methods for selection on large displays [22, 36].

INSIGHTS ON TRADITIONAL INSTRUCTION

To gain insights that could inform the design of YouMove, we observed professional yoga and ballet classes.

Our observations were consistent with the strategies discussed in the recent work of Velloso et al. [35]. We observed a feedback loop between trainer and trainee consisting of demonstration, performance, and feedback. For example, both the ballet and yoga instructors would demonstrate the movement sequence, then have the trainees repeat the sequence as they made comments and physical corrections to the trainees' movements.

We also observed the ballet instructor using an adaptive guidance approach, reducing the amount of guidance as the class progressed. The trainees started at the barre, then moved to the mirror, and finished the class with more complex sequences without the use of the mirror. In both classes instructors provided timing cues, motivation, and alternative metaphors for thinking about the movement.

DESIGN GUIDELINES

Based on our observations of instruction strategies and a review of previous literature, we have developed a set of design goals to guide the development of the YouMove system. We believe these guidelines are applicable to movement training systems in general.

Leverage Domain Knowledge

Experienced trainers have more knowledge than what can be expressed in a recorded movement. Our observations indicated that feedback from instructors is based on domain knowledge. The experts know how to segment movement, and which parameters of the movement are important. The authoring system should support the capture of this domain knowledge with minimal effort.

Motivate the User

Engagement and motivation is an important part of learning [4]. The training system should provide feedback on the user's progress, encourage the user to continue with their practice, and make it an enjoyable experience.

Simple Presentation, Low Cognitive Load

While practicing, the users should maintain a low cognitive load [34]. The user's attention should be on the movement, not on interpreting complex UI elements. A direct representation of the movement and simple scoring measures should focus the user on learning the movement.

Adaptive guidance

Excessive guidance and video demonstrations can hurt learning, as users come to rely on the guides [21, 27]. Guidance should be reduced as the user learns

Summary Feedback

Feedback on individual movements can cause trainees to focus on small errors, rather than the larger systemic errors. Aggregating feedback from several performances allows trainees to see systemic errors in their movement [39].

User driven learning

Trainees have varying skill levels and preferences that will dictate their training needs. The system should allow users to progress at their own pace to maximize learning [41].

AUGMENTED REALITY MIRROR IMPLEMENTATION

While there have been previous implementations of virtually enhanced physical mirrors [8, 19], we are unaware of a technical setup similar to our own in the research literature. This section contributes a technical description of our Augmented Reality Mirror setup, which could have implications that go beyond the YouMove system.

Our use of the mirror for YouMove is inspired by the floor-to-ceiling mirrors often found in ballet studios. These mirrors allow dancers to see their movements, providing them with immediate visual feedback [7]. By augmenting a traditional mirror with interactive content, we provide additional information that helps trainees learn a movement.

Configuration

The configuration of the Augmented Reality Mirror is illustrated in Figure 2. The display consists of a 3.2m x 1.8m pane of glass with a half-silvered mirror film applied to one side, and a diffuse film applied to the other. The mirror film is applied to the surface facing the user. The film[1] transmits 16% of the visible light, and reflects 58%, resulting in a highly reflective surface while still allowing projected light to pass through. Several other mirror films were tested, but the others absorbed more of the projector light, or did not reflect the user's image as clearly. The diffuse film serves to diffuse the light from a rear-mounted projector (Mitsubishi FD630U, 1920x1080 pixels).

A Microsoft Kinect is mounted below the mirror to track the user. The location of the mirror is specified in the coordinate space of the Kinect. The position of the user's head and the corners of the mirror define an asymmetric projection matrix used to render on-screen content.

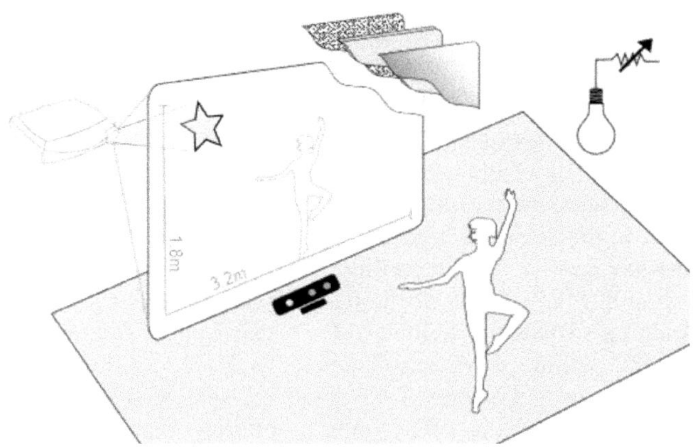

Figure 2: Overview of system design showing projector, layered screen, dynamic lighting, Kinect and user location.

Lighting

While the system is usable in varying ambient lighting conditions, the experience is improved by being in an environment with controlled lighting. With bright ambient light and a dark projection image, the user focuses solely on their reflection in the mirror. With low ambient light and a bright projection, the user's reflection disappears. With a moderate amount of ambient light, the user's reflection and the projected image are both visible (Figure 1). The ability to control lighting allows the system to shift the user's attention between the relevant images (virtual or reflected).

To manipulate the ambient light, a servo motor was mounted to a light's dimmer switch and connected to the PC through an Arduino over USB. The servo motor was mounted using modular building blocks (LEGO), allowing

[1] Supreme Silver 20 – www.apexfilms.ca

the motor to be easily removed and accurately replaced later. The physical actuation of existing dimmer switches would not require the end user to modify any existing wiring or manually adjust the lighting.

Interaction

Mirror-based augmented reality offers unique opportunities for interaction. The user's reflection can be used to directly activate on-screen components, allowing for direct manipulation of a 2D interface from 3D free-space. This *reflection selection* provides zero latency feedback on hand position, allowing quick positioning [20]. Buttons are activated by dwelling the hand over the button. During the dwell period, the button expands providing feedback and increasing the activation area in case the user's hand drifts.

We implemented two types of buttons. Global menu buttons are located on the left side of the mirror, so they will not be triggered accidently during training. The vertical location of the global buttons adapts to the user's height, so that menu items are not out of reach. Quick-access contextual buttons are presented near the user's head, and only appear when required. These buttons are convenient, and their body-centric positioning allows them to be activated by a 'gesture posture', as their location relative to the body is constant, similar to Virtual Shelves [18].

YOUMOVE IMPLEMENTATION

YouMove is composed of a simple program to record data, and a separate training system for playback of that data. The authoring and training system are designed to run independently. The recording software is written in C#, using the WPF framework and the Kinect SDK (v1.6). The training software is written in C++, using openFrameworks, OpenGL, and the Microsoft Kinect SDK v1.6. All software was run on a Window 7 PC, with 12 GB of RAM and a dual core processor. The only calibration required for the training system is to specify the location of the mirror when it is first set up.

YOUMOVE AUTHORING SYSTEM

We developed custom software to capture a trainer's movement and domain knowledge. By simplifying capture, YouMove allows experts to contribute learning material without the need for complicated motion capture hardware or software. The recording system allows authors to record themselves performing the movement. The system captures video, audio and 3D skeleton movement data of the author.

Recording

After launching the software, the author is presented with a screen that has a single 'Record' button as well as the current video stream from the Kinect with a skeleton overlay. To capture movement, the author presses record, performs the movement, and then presses the stop button. Pressing stop takes the author to the editing interface.

Editing

The editing interface (Figure 3) allows authors to trim the recording to eliminate unwanted data – such as walking to or from the capture volume. The author can also specify global parameters for the movement, i.e., timing, smoothness, precision, or stability. These parameters are used by the training system when providing feedback.

Authors then specify keyframes for the recorded movement. Keyframes are postures within the movement that are particularly important for a trainee to match during the movement. For example, a keyframe for a baseball throw may be when the hand reaches peak extension.

Keyframes are specified by navigating to the desired frame and then directly clicking on joints to specify the *important joints* for that keyframe. When a joint is selected, the current frame becomes a keyframe. These keyframes and important joints will be used in the training system to provide tailored guidance and feedback.

Authors can also associate an additional audiovisual recording with individual keyframes, allowing the trainer to provide additional information regarding the movement. This annotation is done by clicking the 'record' and 'stop' buttons below each keyframe marker. Annotations can be used to provide information that may not be immediately obvious to a trainee from seeing the author's movement, or to discuss common pitfalls to avoid. For example, to throw a baseball, an author may annotate the keyframe with a short clip explaining that the elbow should be at approximately 90 degrees.

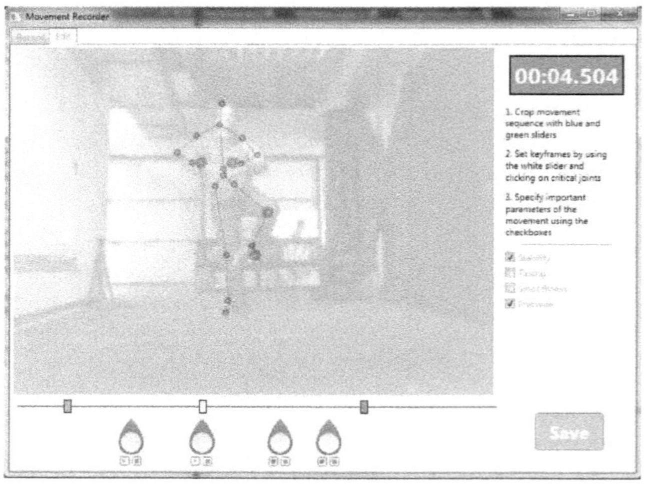

Figure 3: The editing interface allows authors to specify keyframes and global movement parameters. Each keyframe specifies the important joints for that moment, and can be associated with a recording that provides detail.

Saving and Sharing Captures

The user saves the capture by clicking the Save button. The data is saved as media files (mp4 video and wav audio) and plain-text files containing timestamped skeleton locations and keyframe metadata used to synchronize the data.

YOUMOVE TRAINING SYSTEM

The training system is used to teach the movements previously recorded with the authoring system.

Movement Gallery

The initial screen of the system presents a gallery of movements that the user may wish to learn (Figure 4). All buttons and icons throughout the entire system are selected using the reflection selection technique.

Figure 4: The movement gallery allows users to change profiles, query by example, and select a movement.

Query by Example

Selecting the magnifying glass allows users to search for a movement by example. The search screen instructs users to hold a representative posture of the desired movement. Once the user stays still, the system searches the movements in the library for the best match, presenting the most similar movements in a grid for the user to select.

The posture similarity heuristic used for the search is the same as what is used for the scoring measure used in training. That is, it takes a 'snapshot' of the posture the user performing, and compares it to each of the keyframes in each movement of the library. The ability to query by movement may also be useful to search for movements where the movement is emphasized, rather than the pose.

Skeleton Alignment

A fundamental feature of the YouMove training system is guidance and feedback based on a comparison of the author's and trainee's skeleton. The Kinect provides skeleton tracking, reported as 20 joints, with 3D positions updated at 30Hz. The tracked joints include large body parts, such as the hands, arms, torso, legs and the head, but fine movements (e.g., the fingers) are not tracked.

To properly calibrate the author's training skeleton to each user, it must be scaled and translated to match the user's size and position. This is necessary for the skeleton-driven feedback and for accurate scoring. The spatial alignment is done by aligning the hips of the author skeleton with the hips of the trainee. Orientation is not aligned, as it is assumed that the trainee and trainer will be performing the movements in the same orientation relative to the Kinect.

Scaling the skeleton is achieved by dynamically resizing each bone in the trainee skeleton to match the size of the corresponding bone in the trainer. This scaling is done hierarchically from the hips to propagate changes throughout the skeleton. This method is necessary as a simple uniform scaling would not accommodate users with proportionally different limb lengths. We have found that this skeleton algorithms works robustly, and allows the system to work well even when the trainee has a significantly different age, height or weight from the author.

Scoring and Stage Progression

The YouMove system incorporates several elements of gamification designed to motivate the user [17]. Training is composed of a series of stages, and each stage scores the user's performance based on the similarity between their movement and the target movement. If their performance is high enough, they get a gold star and are allowed to progress to the next stage. To avoid frustration, a stage is also unlocked if they repeat the stage twice.

Each keyframe is scored based on the joint with the maximum error, measured by Euclidean distance. Only *important joints* specified in the authoring tool are used to compute the score. To allow for small errors in timing, a window of 0.5s on each side of the target frame is searched to find the best matching posture. If the author has specified that timing is important in the authoring tool, this window is decreased to 0.25s. The maximal Euclidean distance is mapped to a score using a linear mapping, with 0 error being a perfect 10, and 0.15m of error resulting in the score of 7.5 needed to get a gold star and unlock subsequent stages. If precision is specified as a global parameter, this mapping is modified so 0.10m results in a score of 7.5. These values were determined by experimentation.

Training Stages

Once a movement is selected from the gallery, the system progresses through five stages: *Demonstration*, *Posture Guide*, *Movement Guide*, *Mirror*, and *On Your Own*. The user can navigate through the stages using a selection screen (Figure 5, left), although the locking mechanism forces the user to initially perform the stages in order.

The stages progressively introduce the movement to the trainee, and gradually reduce their reliance on guidance and feedback. Each stage presents the user with unique challenges and a different context to perform the movement in, reducing the negative impact of specificity of learning [24]. The Posture Guide repeats twice, and the Movement Guide, Mirror and On Your Own repeat five times, allowing users to practice without being interrupted.

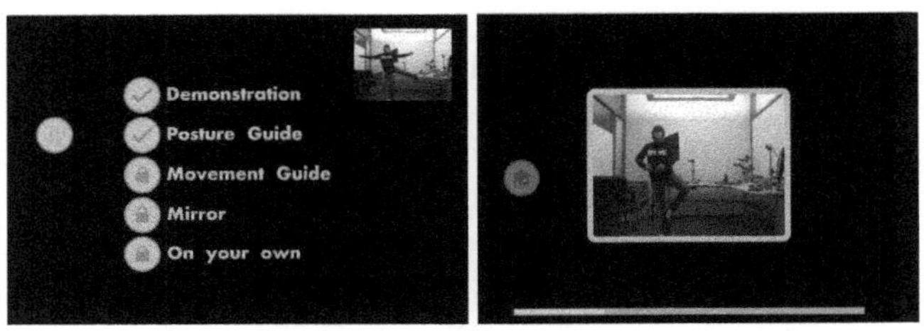

Figure 5: Left) Stage selection interface allowing users to begin one of the unlocked stages. Right) Demonstration stage.

Demonstration

The demonstration stage plays the recorded video for the trainee (Figure 5, right). This stage is designed to be simple and familiar, so the focus is on the movement to be learned.

Audio is played alongside the video to help with timing. At the start of the movement, a pre-recorded voice speaks the word 'And', and each keyframe is counted out in sequence, i.e., 'One', 'Two', etc. The use of numbers (rather than a metronome click) helps trainees remember each movement in the sequence. This counting is present in all other guides except for the 'On Your Own' guide. A progress bar on the bottom of the screen is synched to the video playback.

Posture Guide

The posture guide (Figure 6) helps trainees refine their body position by pausing the movement at each keyframe and providing real-time feedback on their errors. This stage is inspired by the tutorial system found in Pause and Play [23], as it halts the tutorial and allows trainees to work at their own pace. The stage pauses until the user holds a stable position for one second, or until five seconds have elapsed. An additional progress bar on the bottom of the screen represents the amount of time they have currently been stable. If stability is specified as a global parameter in the authoring tool, the threshold for detecting stable movement is lowered from 5 to 3 cm per frame.

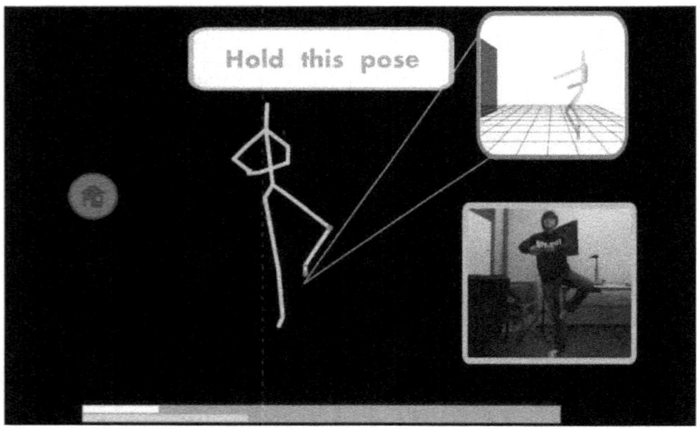

Figure 6: The posture guide requires trainees to maintain a stable posture, matching the position of the trainer. Errors in joint position are indicated by red circles. The callout (top right of figure) can be used to resolve depth ambiguities.

In this stage, ambient lighting is increased and the trainer's skeleton is virtually aligned to the trainee on each rendered frame. Trainees are instructed to match their reflection with the trainer's green skeleton, as in Figure 1. Errors in positioning are shown as red circles overlaid on the user's joints, with the circle radius proportional to the joint error. If the largest error is found to be in the z-axis (depth), then a call-out window appears that shows the trainee a side-view of their body position superimposed on the trainer movement. The author's original video is also displayed on the screen for additional visual reference. The video is automatically cropped based on the location of the trainer's skeleton within the video to preserve on-screen space.

Movement guide

The movement guide (Figure 7) provides a skeleton similar to that of the posture guide, but it moves in real-time and does not pause on the keyframes. In addition, the trainer's skeleton is aligned relative to the starting location of the trainee on each repetition – forcing the trainee to move with the skeleton to maintain alignment.

The movement guide also provides 'cue ribbons' – 3D trajectories that help the user with timing by visualizing the upcoming movements. The ribbons display the trajectory of the hands and feet 300ms ahead of the current frame, with the ribbon becoming more opaque the farther it is in the future. To reduce visual complexity, the ribbons are only displayed if the joint is going to surpass a velocity threshold of 75 cm/s within the subsequent 300 ms. If smoothness is specified as an important parameter, the ribbons are extended to movement 500m/s in the future, to allow trainees to better prepare their upcoming trajectories.

Figure 7: The movement guide encourages the trainee to match the trainer's movements at full speed, using green ribbons (inset) to cue upcoming movements.

Mirror guide

The mirror guide encourages the trainee to focus on their reflection, and does not provide any visual cues to guide the movements. A black screen is projected onto the mirror, and the ambient lighting is increased to enable the trainee to see a clear reflection of themself in the mirror. Audio cues are present to help with timing. This type of guide is similar to a ballet class, where the student practices in front of the mirror with the instructor counting the beats.

On your own

The 'On Your Own' guide mimics a real-world performance scenario where the trainee relies only on what they have learned. The ambient lighting is off, and a white image is projected onto the mirror, preventing the trainee from seeing any reflection. The only audio cue provided is the word 'and', used to indicate the start of the movement.

Post-Stage Feedback

Trainees can view their performance using the Post-Stage Feedback screen (Figure 8). This screen is displayed after each of the training stages, except the Demonstration. This screen summarizes the each of the previous repetitions and presents the aggregate data for each keyframe. Trainees can navigate between keyframes to see an average score for that keyframe, as well as their body pose and a summary video for that frame. During Post-Stage Feedback, ambient lighting is kept at a moderate level, and the projected background is grey. This enables the trainee to see the on-screen content, while allowing them to see their reflection and use reflection-based buttons.

Error in posture is represented by two skeletons: the average skeleton of the trainee for all repetitions (blue), and the trainer skeleton (green). The same circles used in the posture guide are used for feedback to indicate relative joint error. While viewing the feedback, trainees can rotate the 3D view of the skeletons by walking left or right, allowing them to see errors in all dimensions.

A summary video is also provided for each keyframe, allowing the trainee to quickly assess their movements and compare them to the trainer. The trainer video is a static image taken from the recorded video, while the trainee video is an animated sequence of images, each taken from one repetition of the movement, displayed for 0.5s each. By animating the images, trainees can easily see the variations in their movement from frame to frame.

A group of 5 contextual buttons are displayed around the user, allowing them to re-perform the previous stage, advance to the next stage, navigate between keyframes, or view a video annotation if one has been associated with the current keyframe.

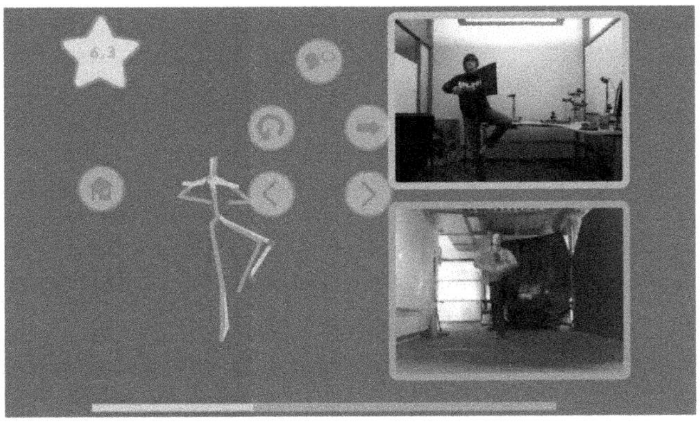

Figure 8: The Post-Stage Feedback screen, showing trainees their overall score, average position (skeleton), and video for each keyframe.

EVALUATION

A controlled study was conducted to compare YouMove to traditional video-based instruction methods. Effectiveness of movement instruction was compared using the results of retention scores after training with each system. Subjects also provided qualitative feedback on the YouMove system, and the use of a mirror as an interactive display.

Participants

Eight participants (2 female) between 21 and 51 years old, ($\bar{x}$ = 30.1 years) were recruited from within the organization, but external to the group. No participants had prior knowledge of, or experience with the system or study, or a dance background.

Study Movements

An author of this paper recorded four movements for the study – two ballet movements and two abstract movements. The ballet movements (variations on the Tendu and Developpe) were easier to conceptualize and only required a moderate amount of movement. The abstract movements were more difficult to perform, as they were a series of postures with no clear structure and required substantial movement. All movements used 4 keyframes.

Conditions

The two conditions for the study were *YouMove* and *Video*. The YouMove condition consisted of the YouMove system as previously described. None of the movements contained multimedia annotations or had global movement parameters specified. The *Video* condition consisted of a video being projected on the mirror screen at the same size as the Demonstration guide (102 x 76 cm), with the area on the screen around the video projected white to prevent the participants from seeing their reflection.

Design

The study was conducted as a two factor repeated-measures design, with each participant learning two movements using YouMove (one abstract followed by one ballet), and two by using just the demonstration video. The condition order and movement pair to condition mapping was fully counterbalanced across the 8 participants.

Procedure

Each participant was introduced to the YouMove system using a simple tutorial movement. The experiment began once participants were comfortable with the system.

Each movement began with a pre-test phase, in which the participant watched a video of the movement twice, and then performed the movement five times during the 'On Your Own' guide. Next, the participant trained using either the full YouMove system, or just the Video. During training, the participant practiced 45 times, either by practicing along with the video, or by practicing with the various guides of the YouMove system. In the YouMove condition, users were free to navigate to any of the unlocked training stages.

Participants completed a short-term retention test five minutes after completing the training. The test consisted of watching the demonstration video once to review the movement, then performing the movement five times during the 'On Your Own' guide. The Kinect recorded the participant's movements in all stages of the study.

A short questionnaire was given to participants after completing the tasks to elicit qualitative feedback. The study took approximately two hours to complete.

Results

A repeated measures ANOVA with two independent variables: *condition* (YouMove, Video), and *movement type* (Ballet, Abstract) was performed. Performance (Figure 9) was measured by computing the RMSE between the space-and-time aligned user skeletons and the target skeleton, using the neck, hands, elbows, knees and feet. These joints were chosen because they are reliably tracked and capture the majority of the information in the movements. Similar analyses were conducted using only the joints specified by the content author, as well as using the joint that has maximal error (the measure used in computing the in-game score). All of these analyses produced equivalent statistical findings, and so we only present the RMSE analysis.

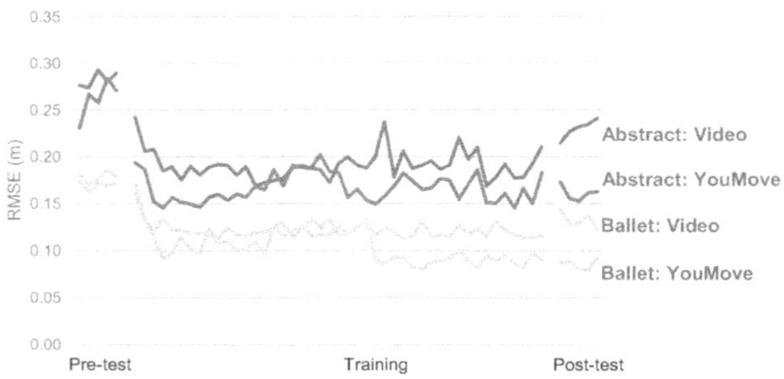

Figure 9: Performance on each trial, for each of the conditions, averaged over all 8 subjects.

The change from pre-test to post-test was significant ($F_{(1,7)} = 9.98$, $p = 0.02$), with YouMove scores improving by an average of 0.10m (44%), and the Video condition improving scores by 0.05m (20%), representing a medium-large effect size ($\eta^2 = 0.13$). The effect of movement type on the change was not significant ($F_{(1,7)} = 0.24$, $p > 0.6$), nor was the interaction between movement type and condition ($F_{(1,7)} = 0.23$, $p > 0.7$), indicating that YouMove's effectiveness is not dependent on movement difficulty.

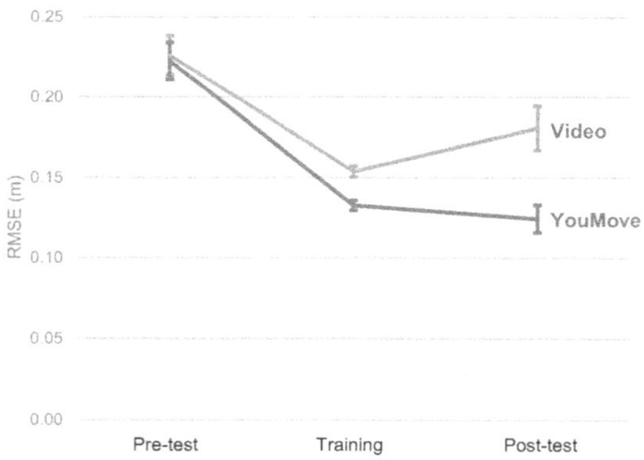

Figure 10: Pre-test, training, and post-test scores for the YouMove and Video conditions.

An ANOVA was also conducted on the post-test scores. The condition was significant ($F_{(1,7)} = 9.96$, $p = 0.02$) with scores of 0.12m for YouMove and 0.18m for Video, an improvement of 33% (Figure 10). The movement type was also significant ($F_{(1,7)} = 114.2$, $p < 0.01$), with scores of 0.10m for ballet movements and 0.19m for abstract movements, indicating that ballet movements were easier.

Stage Usage Analysis

For the *YouMove* condition, most participants performed the training guides in sequence, although some participants did choose to replay guides before continuing. After unlocking all stages, there was no clear preference, but users seemed less likely to return to the posture guide. This is likely due to the increased time the posture guide requires. The guide use by trial is visualized in Figure 11.

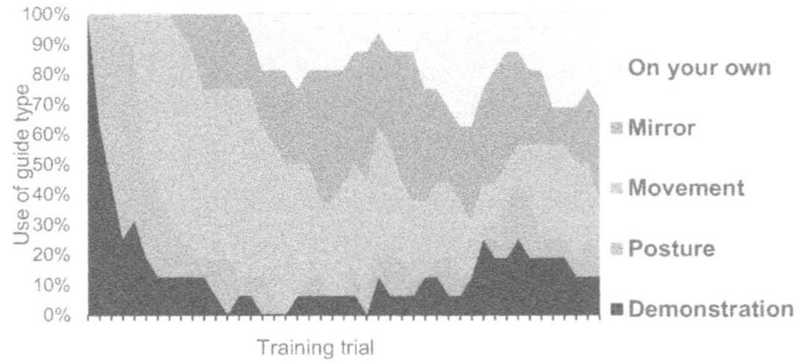

Figure 11: Frequency of use for each guide type for all participants during training with the YouMove system.

DISCUSSION

Overall, we were pleased to see that when comparing pre-test and post-test results, learning increased by more than a factor of 2 (44% vs. 20%) with the YouMove system.

Analysis of learning

Across all conditions, participants appeared to learn the movement within the first few training trials (Figure 9) and then reached a plateau, with relatively constant performance. In the case of the video condition, this was likely because the trainee had truly plateaued, and learned all of the usable information from the video. With the YouMove condition, however, the gradual reduction of guidance meant that the trainee was continually learning the movement and making up for the lack of guidance with increased skill, resulting in consistently high performance.

The retention scores show improved learning with YouMove, as performance is maintained on the retention tests. In contrast, retention scores for video are worse than in training, evidenced by the upward slope in Figure 10.

While training with the YouMove system took longer (i.e., average of 20 minutes compared to 11 minutes with video), this cannot fully explain the results of learning, as the number of exposures to the movement remained constant. Additionally, performance on the video condition plateaued after approximately 8 repetitions, and unlike the YouMove condition, the stimuli did not change and so it is unlikely that any additional learning would occur if the video condition had been repeated for 20 minutes.

Mirror interaction

Dynamic lighting allowed the system to shift the attention of the user, and did not seem to distract participants. The dynamic lighting provided the intended effect and enabled the screen to be multiplexed, allowing the trainee to use both their reflection and the projected guide.

Some participants had difficulty lining up the reflection of their hand with the buttons for the reflection selection technique. To mitigate these problems, we have since added virtual cursors that appear if the system has been waiting more than five seconds for a selection to be made. These cursors provide novice users with the necessary feedback to correct their movement, yet do not interfere with the efficient reflection-based interaction.

Query by example

While the ability to search for similar movements was not tested in the user study, during informal use it proved to be fairly robust and useful. For novices, this feature will allow querying of large databases without having to know the name of the movement. This is especially useful in domains that have complex or cryptic names for their movements.

During training, the trainee's performance is recorded in the same format as the trainer's. This allows users to upload their movements for others to learn from, and enables them to review their prior performances at a later date.

Authoring

The authoring system proved to be easy to use. No formal study was conducted, but it was sent to an untrained user and they were able to record and annotate several movements with minimal effort. The movements were successfully transferred and used in our training system.

The authoring system benefits experts as it allows for content expansion. One minute of content creation generates approximately ten minutes of unique training content through the use of stages which vary the method of presentation and provide feedback. This allows experts with limited time to produce a useful quantity of content with minimal time investment.

Training stages

The Demonstration stage was well liked by users. This is likely due to familiarity with video as a teaching tool, and the ability for participants to easily understand the content. Some participants did, however, comment on the difficulty in judging limb placement and depth from video.

The Posture Guide allowed users to correct the movement, and many errors in positioning were corrected using the posture guide and depth callout. Though similar in nature to the posture guide, the movement guide was one of the most preferred guides. It provides practice guidance at full-speed while still providing useful feedback.

The Mirror Guide and 'On Your Own' guide were clearly valuable. Many participants felt that they had learned the movement, but when the guides were taken away they struggled to remember the sequence.

The Post-Stage Feedback was also well received. Five participants explicitly mentioned that the ability to move back and forth to change the viewpoint of the skeleton was a useful feature. The utility of the feedback is evident in the fact that many participants spent a substantial amount of time on this stage. They were aware that the amount of exposures to the movement was kept constant, and that any time spent on the feedback screen would lengthen the experiment, yet many participants still examined each keyframe.

LIMITATIONS AND FUTURE WORK

The evaluation captures the combined effects of many novel elements. More work is needed to analyze each component and its contribution to learning. Long-term learning and retention are also important areas to explore.

One limitation of the system is related to the skeletal tracking of the Kinect. In particular, the Kinect has difficulty tracking movements that cause large amounts of occlusions. One possible improvement would be to leverage multiple Kinects [5]. Improvements in sensing technology will open new domains of training. Playing musical instruments, surgery, many sports, and other motor-skill based domains could benefit from such a system.

The use of RMSE as a measure of learning is limiting, as real world movements may differ in positioning, but convey the same movements. More work is needed to accurately model and assess full body movement similarity.

Another limitation is the large mirror required for the training system. While the presented implementation uses a half-silvered mirror as a display, the software could also run as a traditional video-based augmented reality system, as in [35]. This would be more accessible to users, but does not provide the real-time feedback that the mirror does. It would be interesting to better understand any learning difference between a mirror and video based system on various devices (large screen, small screen, etc.).

The addition of social features and richer gamification could also greatly help YouMove. One can imagine online yoga, dance or martial arts classes, with competition from online peer groups, but more work is needed to achieve this.

CONCLUSION

We have presented *YouMove*, a novel full-body movement training system. Our work contributes an augmented reality mirror implementation, a content creation system that allows anyone to easily record full-body movements, and a training system that uses the recorded movements to instruct a trainee using a series of stages of increasing difficulty. We have also presented a user study that shows that YouMove results in better short-term retention scores than a video-based learning approach. As implemented, the system is immediately useful for a number domains, such as therapy, yoga, and many types of dance. Adapting the techniques presented here to a wider range of movements opens new avenues for future research.

REFERENCES

1. Anderson, F., Annett, M. & Bischof, WF. (2012). Tabletops in motion: the kinetics and kinematics of interactive surface physical therapy. *CHI EA*, 2351-2356.
2. Anderson, F., & Bischof, WF. (2013). Learning and Performance with Gesture Guides. *CHI* 1109-1118.
3. Bau, O. & MacKay, W., (2008). OctoPocus: a dynamic guide for learning gesture-based command sets. *UIST*, 37-46.
4. Bederson, BB. (2004). Interfaces for staying in the flow.*Ubiquity* 5(27).
5. Butler, D. A., Izadi, S., Hilliges, O., Molyneaux, D., Hodges, S., & Kim, D. (2012). Shake'n'sense: reducing interference for overlapping structured light depth cameras. *CHI* 1933-1936.
6. Dance Central. (2010). *Harmonix*, Massachusetts, USA.
7. Dearborn, K., & Ross, R. (2006). Dance learning and the mirror: comparison study of dance phrase learning with and without mirrors. *Dance Education*, 109-115.
8. Doctorow, C. (2011). Haunted Mansion Hitchhiking Ghosts go digital, play high-tech pranks on riders. *http://boingboing.net/2011/04/06/haunted-mansion-hitc.html.*
9. Freeman, D., Benko, H., Ringel Morris, M. & Wigdor, D. (2009). ShadowGuides: visualizations for in-situ learning of multi-touch and whole-hand gestures. *ITS*, 167-172.
10. Fujinami, K., Kawsar, F. and Nakajima, T. (2006). AwareMirror: A Personalized Display Using a Mirror. In *Proc. Pervasive Computing,* 316-332.
11. Henderson, SJ. & Feiner, SK. (2011). Augmented reality in the psychomotor phase of a procedural task. *ISMAR*, 191-200.
12. Holden, MK. (2005). Virtual environments for motor rehabilitation: review. *Cyberpsychology*, 8(3), 187-211.
13. Janelle, CM., Barba, DA., Frehlich, SG., Tennant, LK., & Cauraugh, JH. (1997). Maximizing performance feedback effectiveness through videotape replay and a self-controlled learning environment. *Research Quarterly for Exercise and Sport*, *68*(4), 269-279.
14. Judkins, TN., Oleynikov, D. & Stergiou, N. (2005). Real-time augmented feedback benefits robotic laparoscopic training. *Stud. Health Tech.* 119, 243-248.
15. Krueger, MW. (1977). Responsive Environments. *AFIPS*, 423-433.
16. Lehmann, KS., Ritz, JP., Maass, H., Çakmak, HK., Kuehnapfel, UG., Germer, CT., & Buhr, HJ. (2005). A prospective randomized study to test the transfer of basic psychomotor skills from virtual reality to physical reality in a comparable training setting. *Annals of surgery*, 241(3), 442.
17. Li, W. Grossman, T. & Fitzmaurice, G. (2012). GamiCAD: A gamified tutorial system for first time autocad users. *UIST*, 103-112.
18. Li, FCY, Dearman, D, & Truong, KN. (2009). Virtual shelves: interactions with orientation aware devices. *CHI,* 125-128.
19. Microsoft Research, (2012). Holoflector. *research.microsoft.com/apps/video/dl.aspx?id=159487.*
20. Ng, A., Lepinski, J., Wigdor, D., Sanders, S., & Dietz, P. (2012). Designing for low-latency direct-touch input. *UIST,* 453-464.
21. Palmiter, S., & Elkerton, J. (1991). An evaluation of animated demonstrations of learning computer-based tasks. *CHI,* 257-263.
22. Pierce, JS. Forsberg, A., Conway, M, Hong, S. & Zeleznik, R. (1997). Image Plane Interaction Techniques in 3D Immersive Environments. *I3D*, 39-43.
23. Pongnumkul, S., Dontcheva, M., Li, W., Wang, J., Bourdev, L., Avidan, S., & Cohen, MF. (2011). Pause-and-play: automatically linking screencast video tutorials with applications. *UIST.* 135-144.
24. Proteau, L., Marteniuk, RG., & Lévesque, L. (1992). A sensorimotor basis for motor learning: Evidence indicating specificity of practice. *Exp. Psych.*, 44(3), 557-575.
25. Sato, H., Kitahara, I., & Ohta, Y. (2009). MR-mirror: a complex of real and virtual mirrors. *VMR*, 482-491.
26. Schmidt, RA. (1991). Frequent augmented feedback can degrade learning: Evidence and interpretations. *Tutorials in motor neuroscience*. 59-75.
27. Schmidt, R. A., & Wulf, G. (1997). Continuous concurrent feedback degrades skill learning: Implications for training and simulation. *Human Factors*, 39(4), 509-525.
28. Shea, C. H., Wulf, G., Park, JH., & Gaunt, B. (2001). Effects of an auditory model on the learning of relative and absolute timing. *Motor behavior*, *33*(2), 127-138.
29. Shoemaker, G., Tang, A., & Booth, K. S. (2007). Shadow Reaching: A New Perspective on Interaction for Large Wall Displays. *UIST,* 53-56.
30. Sigrist, R., Rauter, G., Riener, R. & Wolf, P. (2012). Augmented visual, auditory, haptic and multimodal feedback in motor learning: A review. *Psych. Bull.Rev.*, 1-13.
31. Sodhi, R., Benko, H. & Wilson, A. (2012). LightGuide: Projected visualizations for hand movement guidance. *CHI*, 179-188.
32. Todorov, E., Shadmehr, R. & Bizzi, E. (1997). Augmented feedback presented in a virtual environment accelerates learning a difficult motor task. *Motor Behavior* 29(2) 147-158.
33. Ushida, K., Tanaka, Y., Naemura, T., & Harashima, H. (2002). i-mirror: An Interaction / Information Environment Based on a Mirror Metaphor Aiming to Install into Our Life Space. *Artificial Reality and Telexistence*, 113-118.
34. Van Merriënboer, J. J., & Sweller, J. (2005). Cognitive load theory and complex learning: Recent developments and future directions. *Educational psychology review*, *17*(2), 147-177.
35. Velloso, E., Bulling, A. & Gellerson, H. (2013). MotionMA: Modelling and Analysis by Demonstration. *CHI* 1309-1318.
36. Vogel, D. & Balakrishnan, R. (2005). Distant freehand pointing and clicking on very large, high resolution displays. *UIST*, 33-42.
37. Vogel, D. & Balakrishnan, R. (2004). Interactive public ambient displays; transitioning from implicit to explicit, public to personal, interaction with multiple users. *UIST*, 137-146.
38. Ward, P., Hodges, NJ., Williams, AM., & Starkes, JL. (2004). Deliberate practice and expert performance. *Skill acquisition in sport: Research, theory and practice*, 231.
39. Winstein, CJ., & Schmidt, RA. (1990). Reduced frequency of knowledge of results enhances motor skill learning. *Exp. Psych.: Learning, Memory, and Cognition*, 16(4). 677-691.
40. Wollersheim, D., Merkes, M., Shields, N., Liamputtong, P., Wallis, L., Reynolds, F., & Koh, L. (2010). Physical and psychosocial effects of Wii video game use among older women.*International Journal of Emerging Technologies and Society*, 8(2), 85-98.
41. Wulf, G. Raupach, M. & Pfeiffer, F. (2005). Self-controlled observational practice enhances learning. *Research Quarterly for Exercise & Sport,* 76, 107-11.
42. Wulf, G., Shea, C. & Lewthwaite, R. (2010). Motor skill learning and performance: a review of influential factors. *Medical Education*, 44, 75-84.
43. Yang, U. & Kim, GJ. (2002). Implementation and evaluation of just follow me: An immersive, VR-based, motion-training system. *Presence 11(*3) 304-323.

Skillometers: Reflective Widgets that Motivate and Help Users to Improve Performance

Sylvain Malacria[1] **Joey Scarr**[1] **Andy Cockburn**[1] **Carl Gutwin**[2] **Tovi Grossman**[3]
[1]University of Canterbury, Christchurch, New Zealand
[2]Department of Computer Science, University of Saskatchewan, Saskatoon, Saskatchewan, Canada
[3]Autodesk Research, Toronto, Ontario, Canada
sylvain@malacria.fr, {joey, andy}@cosc.canterbury.ac.nz, gutwin@cs.usask.ca, tovi.grossman@autodesk.com

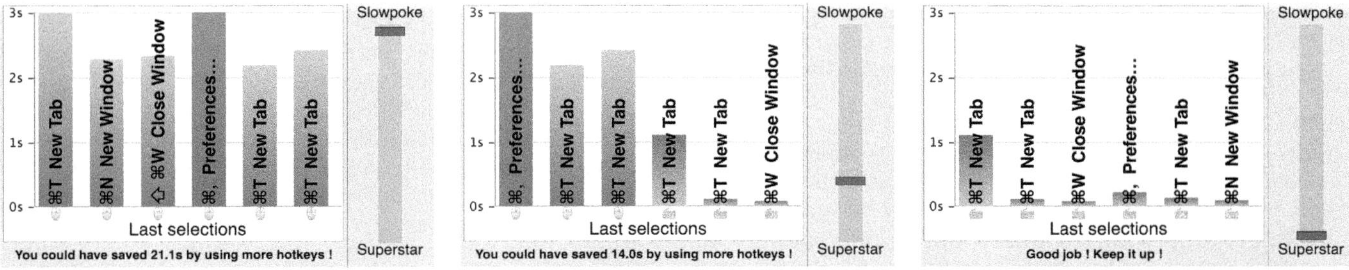

Figure 1. Three snapshots of a skillometer designed to encourage hotkey use. At first (left), the user mostly relies on mouse selections for activating commands. The skillometer indicates that he could save time by using hotkeys, and displays the appropriate hotkey bindings. As he begins to increase his hotkey use (center), the skillometer shows the benefits of the switch, encouraging him to use more hotkeys (right).

ABSTRACT
Applications typically provide ways for expert users to increase their performance, such as keyboard shortcuts or customization, but these facilities are frequently ignored. To help address this problem, we introduce *skillometers* – lightweight displays that visualize the benefits available through practicing, adopting a better technique, or switching to a faster mode of interaction. We present a general framework for skillometer design, then discuss the design and implementation of a real-world skillometer intended to increase hotkey use. A controlled experiment shows that our skillometer successfully encourages earlier and faster learning of hotkeys. Finally, we discuss general lessons for future development and deployment of skillometers.

Author Keywords
Expertise; hotkeys; learning; reflection.

ACM Classification Keywords
H.5.2. Information Interfaces and Presentation: User Interfaces. - Graphical user interfaces.

General Terms
Human Factors; Design; Measurement.

ACM 978-1-4503-2271-3/13/10...$15.00.
http://dx.doi.org/10.1145/2501988.2501996

INTRODUCTION
In modern applications, users have many opportunities to enhance their productivity. They can alter their environment (e.g., customizing the interface to suit their workflows and bring frequently-used commands close to hand), or they can alter themselves by learning new skills and techniques for the application. These new techniques can dramatically improve performance, but a major problem in many systems is that users ignore these opportunities [23, 27]. For example, many users opt to "satisfice" [38] and stick with the interaction procedures they learnt as novices, even when they are aware of the expert features [12].

This behavior is not unreasonable. Adopting a new mechanism or strategy could require a significant investment of time and effort, possibly outweighing any efficiency gains; if the user has no way of estimating these costs and benefits, then they should not be expected to switch. Critically, it is the user's *perception* of the new mechanism that matters [35], rather than its actual properties – therefore, if we could inform the user about the benefits of adopting a new mechanism or strategy, they might be more inclined to do so.

In this paper, we present and analyse the design potential of using *skillometers* as a solution to these problems. Skillometers are widgets designed to accelerate the development of UI expertise by allowing the user to visualize their past and potential future performance. While the term 'skillometer' has been used in the domain of intelligent tutoring systems to reflect the system's model of the user's understanding (e.g., [4, 5]), we are unaware of their use for interface performance, except for Linton and Schaefer's proposal to use a "Skill-O-Meter" to visualize command vocabulary [26]. Other related systems are reviewed later in the paper. The specific skillometer implemented and evaluated in this paper, shown in Figure 1, displays a visualization of a user's interaction efficiency (in this case, with menus and keyboard shortcuts), and suggests ways in which efficiency could be improved.

This paper makes three specific contributions. First, we present a general skillometer framework which can be used to inform the design of future skillometers. Second, we discuss the design of HotkeySkillometer, a skillometer for encouraging hotkey use, and describe its implementation. Finally, we present the results of a controlled experiment, where participants performed tightly constrained tasks in Apple Keynote. Results demonstrate that the HotkeySkillometer motivates users to increase their use of hotkeys. We conclude by discussing the lessons learned and issues of generalisation.

SKILLOMETER DEFINITION

Reflective interfaces, which inform the users about their own behavior, have been well-studied in the area of tutoring systems (e.g. [5, 24]), which are specifically designed to help the user develop skills and knowledge. In the context of interaction, Linton and Schaefer [26] proposed a reflective visualization called a 'Skill-O-Meter', which displays the user's command vocabulary compared to others in their peer group. However, the effect of this feedback on user behavior was not evaluated. More recently, Bateman et al. [8] developed a 'Search Dashboard' that gave users information about their search habits, including comparison of their behaviors to those of typical and expert users. By displaying information about expert behavior, the Search Dashboard was able to broaden users' knowledge of search engine features.

In this paper, we define a *skillometer* as a reflective widget that motivates and helps the user increase their level of performance with an interface. Importantly, as reflective widgets, skillometers support the user in understanding meta-level aspects of their own interaction. Typically, the meta-level aspect of interaction revealed by a skillometer will concern the user's level of performance, although others may be revealed, such as the user's task strategy or interaction modalities used to select commands (examples follow later in the paper).

Under this definition, a tooltip that displays a hotkey binding would not be considered to be a skillometer because although it assists the user in increasing their level of performance (by helping the user learn the hotkey), it does not facilitate understanding of performance at a higher level. In contrast, the widget shown in Figure 1 is a skillometer because it displays the user's level of performance (a meta-level aspect of interaction) as well as showing hotkey bindings that might be used to complete pointer-based selections (shown in red).

TARGET DOMAINS OF USER PERFORMANCE

Skillometers can be deployed to improve four different target domains of user performance with interfaces: *intramodal*, *intermodal*, *vocabulary extension*, and *strategic*. Each of these domains is described with respect to potential skillometer design and prior work in upcoming subsections. In brief, *intramodal* improvement addresses the rapidity of skill acquisition within one particular interactive method for one particular function (e.g., assisting the user to improve their performance with a novel pointing device); *intermodal* improvement addresses ways to assist users to switch to faster methods for accessing a particular function (e.g., switching from cursor-based pointing to hotkeys); *vocabulary extension* methods focus on broadening the user's knowledge of the range of functions available through the interface; and *strategic* methods address higher level issues of how users combine interface functions to accomplish tasks.

Domain 1: Intramodal Improvement

Human skill acquisition has been shown to reliably follow a 'power law of practice' [31] across a wide range of activities, including interaction with computer systems. The law of practice shows that performance improves quickly at first, gradually leveling off with experience. In many interaction contexts, such as cursor-based selection of menu items, this effect is easily explained: users who are unfamiliar with the interface must initially rely on visual search to identify likely targets, but can gradually use faster methods for interaction based on spatial, muscular and procedural memory. After extensive experience with any particular interaction modality, users will approach a performance ceiling representing the limit of the user's capability for that modality.

While performance improvement within any particular interaction modality will follow a power law of practice, research in the psychomotor literature clearly shows that different forms of practice and training can yield different rates of skill acquisition – see [36] for an extensive review. For example, there are reliable experimental effects for various practice manipulations, including the timing and distribution of practice, the mental effort associated with processing trained material, the specificity of the training material, and various feedback effects.

Accelerating the rate of skill acquisition is one opportunity for skillometers to improve performance. For example, some psychology literature suggests that *knowledge of performance* can improve skill acquisition (although results can vary [36]), and this effect might be employed by a skillometer. A touch-typing skillometer, for instance, might show a real-time line chart of the user's word-per-minute rate (Figure 2a). Additionally, many psychology and sports studies shows that appropriate goal-setting can improve skill acquisition (again, see [36]). This result might be incorporated into the skillometer by continually showing the user's peak typing rate as another line on the chart above their current rate.

Domain 2: Intermodal Improvement

Most interfaces support more than one interaction modality for accessing the same function: for example, the 'Bold' function might be activated by selecting it from a menu, clicking a toolbar button, choosing it in a dialog box, or pressing Ctrl+B. The rate of skill acquisition for each independent modality is the concern of *intramodal* improvement. *Intermodal* improvement, in contrast, concerns the transition from slower modalities to faster ones that ultimately offer a higher performance ceiling.

Many studies have observed that expert interface modalities are often unused or only lightly used. Carroll [12] attributed

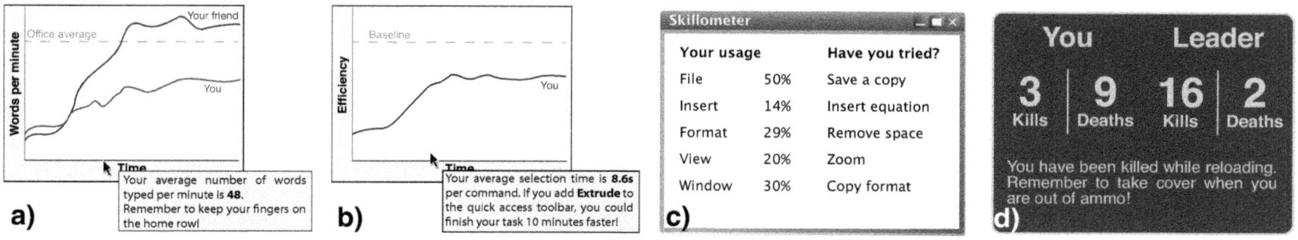

Figure 2. Concept sketches of skillometers for a) typing speed (intramodal), b) interface customization (intermodal), c) command awareness (vocabulary extension) and d) video game training (strategic).

the effect to the *paradox of the active user*, noting that users tend to be too engaged in their primary task to put cognitive effort into learning more efficient ways to accomplish that task. This behavior is an example of a wider human phenomenon called *satisficing* [38], where people make do with sufficient, but suboptimal, strategies due to limited cognitive resources: typical users do not have the necessary information to determine whether learning hotkeys will be a worthwhile investment, nor can they spare the substantial effort required to acquire that information. In related work, Scarr et al. [35] further examined users' failure to make a transition to higher-performance expert modalities, noting that a temporary 'performance dip' while gaining familiarity with a new modality can deter users from switching to a new method.

Several factors act as deterrents or barriers to users switching to modalities that can offer a higher performance ceiling, including the user's lack of awareness of other modalities, their perception of performance with other modalities, and their lack of motivation to use them. Each of these is described below, with particular reference to the opportunities for skillometers.

Awareness of Other Modalities

There are many ways to increase awareness of advanced interaction modalities. For example, keyboard shortcuts are sometimes displayed to the right of menu labels, or in tooltips that appear after a dwell. However, Grossman et al.'s results suggest that even when shortcuts are displayed in dropdown menus, they are commonly ignored by users [20]. This may be attributable to the fact that the shortcut is not displayed until the user has already done most of the work for selecting the command with the mouse, so they have no incentive to learn the hotkey. Malacria et al. [28] and Tak et al. [39] both developed successful systems that provide "feedforward" information about hotkeys when a modifier key (e.g. Ctrl) is held down, displaying hotkey mappings when they are needed rather than after the fact, with both systems increasing hotkey use. Krisler and Alterman showed improved hotkey learning with their HotKeyCoach [22], which displayed a pop-up window that needed to be explicitly dismissed every time the user selected a command with the mouse. However, explicit awareness techniques often come at the cost of undue distraction, and one of the goals of our skillometer is to minimise interference and disruption of normal interaction (explicit dialog boxes clearly violate this goal). Scarr et al.'s "calm notification" [35] technique provides awareness in a less intrusive fashion by using an ambient dialog in the corner of the screen that does not require user response and that automatically fades away if ignored.

The visual presentation of a skillometer widget can incorporate awareness information about appropriate expert modalities. Using a skillometer as the location for this information has two important advantages over other methods: first, it provides a consistent location for feedback on higher-performance methods for completing recent actions; second, the skillometer can show performance over time, allowing users to compare past and potential future performance (e.g., the skillometer in Figure 1 shows information about the last six commands).

Perception of Performance with Other Modalities

In their framework of interface expertise, Scarr et al. [35] note that the user's *perception* of their potential performance in a modality (both over the short and the long term) is a critical factor influencing their decision of whether to switch. However, a user's perception of future performance is often unreliable [13]. In the context of command selection, studies have consistently shown that keyboard shortcuts offer a higher performance ceiling than mouse selection [23, 32], yet Tak et al. found that some participants failed to use known hotkeys because they believed the toolbar buttons to be faster [39].

Appropriate skillometer design may assist with communicating accurate perceptions of the relative potential and actual performance gains of using different modalities. For example, a skillometer might show the actual time taken to select the 'bold' command in a ribbon or menu (calculating time from completing a text selection and selecting the item) and also show the estimated keystroke time for the associated hotkey. Alternatively, time estimates might be aggregated and/or projected to future total time savings, based on the frequency with which particular commands have been used in the past (e.g., the tooltip in Figure 2b). Such information might assist the user in making rational judgements concerning the costs and benefits of changing modality.

Lack of Motivation

The user's motivation for improving performance is another important factor. There are many elements of motivation at play in a user's decision to learn new skills and techniques, and skillometer design can make use of both intrinsic and extrinsic elements. First, intrinsic motivation concerns the user's own interest in improving, and here it is important for the skillometer to clearly visualize the potential for future improvement. However, designers must recognize that the user's performance goal may depend upon the context – for example, a user browsing the Internet at home may be less concerned with fast command selection than an office worker who carries out the same tasks throughout the day. Interestingly, however, Tak et al. [39] found that increased time pressure did not lead to increased hotkey use, suggesting that workload alone is not sufficient to encourage adoption of more efficient methods (reflecting Carroll's paradox).

Extrinsic motivation can also be used in skillometer design – in particular, there are interesting opportunities for skillometers to use social factors, social learning, and gamification (discussed later) as motivation. For example, recent results from Banovic et al. [7] showed that social influence was important for encouraging tool palette customization. Similarly, Peres et al. [33] found that users were more likely to use keyboard shortcuts if they worked with others who did so, and Bateman et al. [8] found that having knowledge of expert search engine use led people to change their own behaviour.

Domain 3: Vocabulary Extension

Many interfaces allow access to extensive functionality, but users are often unaware of functions that may assist their performance (see [30] for a review of the problem). For example, in a photo editing suite a user may be familiar with a tool for painting filled circles and may use it to remove red-eye from photographs, unaware that a more effective dedicated red-eye removal function is available. Existing interface mechanisms such as 'tip of the day' can assist in extending the user's vocabulary of commands, but the information they provide is typically unconnected with the user's current task, and may therefore be viewed as an unwanted distraction.

The conceptual deterrents and barriers to vocabulary extension are similar to those described for *intermodal improvement* described above. The opportunities for skillometers to assist with overcoming these deterrents and barriers are also similar to those described for intermodal improvement, although there are additional challenges in determining the functional relationships between groups of commands. While it is straightforward for a skillometer to determine and display intermodal relationships (such as the availability of a hotkey when a menu item is selected by pointing), determining functional relationships is likely to benefit from some semantic knowledge of the user's task objective. For example, a skillometer could only represent the efficiency of the 'red-eye' example above if it correctly identified that the user's manipulation of the circle painting tool was directed at that specific task rather than some other activity.

However, skillometers are not restricted to displaying information about task completion times. Rather, they might be used to promote reflection about other meta-level aspects of interaction, such as the range of commands used. In such a deployment, a skillometer might depict the set of commands that the user employs, grounded by a depiction of the set of commands used by other users – Linton's 'Skill-O-Meter' proposal [26] and Bateman's 'Search Dashboard' [8] are examples. Furthermore, the skillometer might incorporate information about the frequency of use of commands among a community of users, thereby alerting a user to unknown commands that others find useful (e.g., Figure 2c). CommunityCommands [30] and Patina [29] were directed at these objectives, with Patina's interface representation using a heatmap stencil overlay on top of the user interface to show the frequency of command use among a community of users.

Domain 4: Strategic Improvement

Strategic improvement involves helping the user to optimize their sequence of actions – i.e., choosing a better *strategy* to complete the task. While vocabulary extension often facilitates strategic improvement (e.g., invoking 'Align Left' is a better strategy than using drag-and-drop to manually left-align items), users may need more guidance than simply providing broader awareness of application functionality. We refer the reader to Bhavnani et al. [10] for a detailed analysis of strategic aspects of computer use, but we use one of their examples to illustrate interaction strategies. Consider a user interacting with a drawing package to create a series of identical arched windows. A novice user might use a 'sequence-by-operation' strategy, first drawing all of the arcs for the window arches (arc operation), then drawing all of the vertical lines for the window sides (line operation), and finally drawing the horizontal lines for the window bases. An experienced user, in contrast, might use a 'detail-aggregate-manipulate' strategy, first drawing the arc and lines for one window (detail), then grouping the lines (aggregate), and finally copying and pasting multiple replicates (manipulate).

In theory, a skillometer targeted at strategic improvement would detect inefficient interaction strategies and suggest better ones. In general, detecting suboptimal user interaction strategies is a difficult problem. However, in some applications (particularly games), there are points where it is easy to tell that the user has performed poorly. For example, a strategic skillometer for a first-person shooter game might analyse players' deaths and give targeted advice such as 'remember to take cover while reloading' or 'keep your movements unpredictable' (Figure 2d).

SKILLOMETER INTERFACE: GOALS AND MECHANISMS

As discussed above, skillometers may be targeted at any of four different domains of user interface performance. However, regardless of the target domain, there are four goals that apply to the user interface of any skillometer, as follows.

Goal 1: Visualize the Possibility for Improvement

A skillometer interface should clearly communicate to the user that their performance can be improved. This can mean different things, depending on the purpose of the skillometer. An *intramodal* skillometer might display a graph of the user's performance compared to a theoretical optimum. For an *intermodal* skillometer, this means making the user aware of different modalities and their benefits – for example, displaying the user's performance compared to their performance if they used hotkeys. Skillometers aimed at *vocabulary extension* and *strategic improvement* might suggest new functionality and interaction strategies to the user, and demonstrate how these might improve efficiency or quality of work.

Goal 2: Provide Specific Details on How to Improve

As well as making the user aware of the possibility of improving their performance, a skillometer should also provide specific guidance to the user about how that improvement could take place. For example, an intermodal skillometer would provide details of how to perform commands with a better modality, such as showing the hotkey bindings for each command performed.

Goal 3: Motivate the User to Improve

Motivation can be provided by a skillometer in several different ways. A skillometer's visualization should stimulate the user's intrinsic motivation: as discussed in Goal 1, it should enable the user to quantify the benefits of improvement. However, there are additional methods available to motivate and persuade users, discussed below.

Social Influence and Competition

As mentioned earlier, social influence can be an important extrinsic motivation for changing user behavior (e.g., [7, 8, 33]). A skillometer could make use of this by comparing the user's performance, modality use, command knowledge, or interaction strategies to others in their peer group. For example, a touch-typing skillometer could display extra lines on the graph representing the typing speeds of co-workers. However, care must be taken, as some users may react negatively to unfavorable comparison with others.

Exaggeration of Benefits

Since the point of a skillometer is to persuade users to change their behavior, one option would be to exaggerate the advantages of doing so. This is a case of *benevolent deception* [3], where an interface lies in order to provide some benefit to the user. As with competition, care needs to be taken with this approach to avoid negative effects – if the deception is too obvious, the user will lose trust in the system and stop attending to the feedback.

Gamification

Gamification is a broad research topic, and we refer readers to [14] and [21] for a review of gamification techniques. In brief, game elements have been demonstrated to enhance the effectiveness of training with software systems (e.g., [15, 25]), and gamification has been deployed to assist learning of commercial software interfaces (e.g., Microsoft's Ribbon Hero [2]). Gamified interactive components could be used as part of a skillometer, such as scoreboards, achievements, and progression-based elements equivalent to game levels.

Goal 4: Minimize Disruption to Normal Interaction

While providing feedback on user performance can be beneficial, it has also been shown to degrade learning if given too frequently [34]. A skillometer should therefore aim to provide information when it is most useful to the user, and minimize disruption of the user's normal workflow. Research by Bødker [11] suggests that there are two types of task interruption: *breakdowns* and *focus-shifts*. Breakdowns result in severe disruption and force the user's attention to a new activity, while focus-shifts cause only a brief attention switch and have a minimal effect. Systems resulting in a breakdown, such as Microsoft's *Clippy*, have been shown to be quickly abandoned after a few untimely interruptions [37].

Ideally, skillometer feedback would be transient, unintrusive, and require no user response, eliciting a focus-shift rather than a breakdown from the user. However, this presents a difficult trade-off: in order for a skillometer to counteract Carroll's *active user paradox*, a certain amount of disruption is necessary to draw attention to the skillometer.

Manipulating the *locus of control* is one way that a skillometer could avoid this tradeoff. Push notifications, such as a window popping up on screen, can be distracting and interrupt the user's workflow. However, if the locus of control rests with the user, they can choose to request the feedback at a time that suits them, and ignore it when they are busy. The risk of this approach is that the user may never request the feedback – so a possible compromise is a small ambient display in the corner of the screen, which constantly displays a performance overview and provides more detailed information and guidance only on demand.

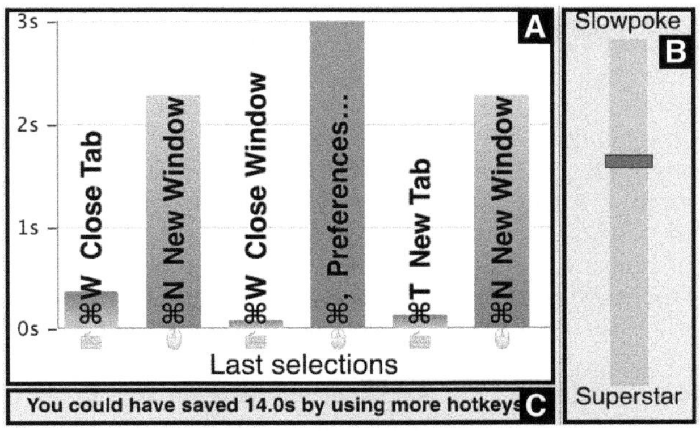

Figure 3. The visual design of HotkeySkillometer.

A SKILLOMETER FOR PROMOTING HOTKEY USE

To gain practical experience with the challenges of designing and implementing skillometers, and to gain initial insights into the validity using skillometers to assist expertise development, we constructed and evaluated a system called HotkeySkillometer. The system, shown in Figure 3, is directed at target domain #2, *intermodal improvement* – it aims to motivate and assist users in transitioning from mouse-driven interaction methods (menu and toolbar selections) to hotkeys [20, 28, 6]. We chose to examine hotkey intermodal improvement because hotkeys are widely available in commercial software, yet they are known to be lightly used [23].

Overview of HotkeySkillometer

HotkeySkillometer monitors the user's interaction with graphical desktop applications, analysing and depicting their level of performance, and displaying alternative and faster hotkey methods for executing commands whenever they are available. Its display consists of three parts, labelled A, B, and C in Figure 3. Part A (Fig. 3, left) uses a bar chart to show the time taken to select each of the six most recently used commands (the Implementation section below details how selection times are calculated to determine each bar's height).

When a new command is selected, an animation slides a new bar item into view, scrolling all other items leftwards. Each bar is coloured dependent on the selection modality (red for mouse, green for hotkey), and an icon below each bar also depicts the modality. Additionally, each bar is overlaid with text showing the name of the command and its hotkey.

Part B (Fig. 3, right) is a meter that grades the user's performance based on the modality used for the last 6 command selections – if all selections were made with hotkeys, the slider will be at the 'Superstar' end; if all used the mouse, it will be at the 'Slowpoke' end. The value of the slider is determined by a weighted interpolation, where more recently selected commands have more weighting – this gives the bar a more noticeable 'swing' toward the positive end each time a hotkey is used, or the negative end with each mouse selection.

Part C (Fig. 3, bottom) shows motivational text advising the user that hotkey selections are faster. It also quantifies, across the past 6 selections, how much time could have been saved if the selections were performed with hotkeys instead (based on a KLM-derived value of 200ms for each hotkey selection).

By default, HotkeySkillometer is a transient window located at the bottom left (or right, based on user preference) of the display. As soon as the user selects a command or presses the Command key, the window fades in and remains until the user stops selecting commands. When the user mouses over the window, it fades out revealing the content beneath it. While the mouse-over fading enables users to interact with underlying content, it also prohibits intentional interaction with components within the skillometer – this design choice is appropriate for HotkeySkillometer, but will be inappropriate for other designs where the user needs to be able to explicitly request information associated with skillometer components (e.g., the roll-over tips shown in Figure 2a).

With respect to the interface goals, HotkeySkillometer supports *Goal 1: Visualize the possibility for improvement* and *Goal 3: Motivate the user to improve* in both the height of mouse-based bar chart items (suggesting poor performance) and through the performance meter, which quickly moves towards the 'Slowpoke' end following mouse selections. It supports *Goal 2: Provide specific details on how to improve* in Part C's text and by the hotkey overlay on the bar chart. *Goal 4: Minimize disruption to normal interaction* is supported by using a transient window that only appears after each command selection and which quickly fades out with inactivity.

IMPLEMENTATION OF HOTKEYSKILLOMETER

The implementation of HotkeySkillometer requires three fundamental building blocks. First, it has to be able to monitor and detect command selections. Second, it has to determine which modality (e.g., mouse or hotkey) was used to select the command. Third, it has to calculate and display the user's performance. Our implementation, HotkeySkillometer, is a Mac OS X application, developed using Objective-C and the Cocoa framework. It uses Apple's Accessibility API [1] to browse and access GUI control elements; all Mac OS X applications implementing this interface can therefore be observed by our skillometer. Details of how HotkeySkillometer achieves each of the three building blocks follow.

Monitoring and Detecting Command Selections

HotkeySkillometer uses two separate components for menus and toolbar selections.

Menu Items

When an application first receives focus, HotkeySkillometer dynamically adds global action listeners to all the menu items located within an application's menu bar and context menus. These action listeners are triggered as soon as the user selects a command (either by clicking on the menu item, or using its associated hotkey), and the listener is provided with all the accessibility attributes of the menu item, which includes the command name and keyboard shortcut.

Toolbar Buttons

Handling toolbar selections is more complicated, since Apple does not provide a global listener for toolbar buttons. Unlike the menu bar, toolbar buttons are often custom widgets that do not implement the Accessibility API, which complicates identifying widgets and accessing any associated hotkey.

To circumvent this limitation, HotkeySkillometer uses a hard-coded description of the mapping between toolbar buttons and their equivalent menu items for each of the client interfaces it monitors. It then uses a combination of a global mouse event listener (that intercepts mouse-up actions) and the Accessibility API to identify the widget located beneath the mouse cursor and thus determine which command was executed. An alternative approach, not used in HotkeySkillometer, would use code injections for extending existing method of the applications at runtime [16]. However, this method would be limited to Cocoa applications and would require a plugin for each monitored application.

Determining the Modality Used

Since toolbar selections use a different detection mechanism to menus, they are easily distinguished. However, for menu items that also possess hotkeys, the same action listener is called for both pointer and hotkey selections. To discriminate between selection modalities, HotkeySkillometer listens to global mouse and keyboard events and checks whether the key corresponding to the keyboard shortcut character was pressed immediately before command selection. If so, the command is recorded as a hotkey selection.

Calculating User Performance

HotkeySkillometer measures pointing time using an Objective-C implementation of Evans and Wobbrock's Input Observer [18], which assumes that a user's current pointing action began with the most recent ballistic movement. The time to select a toolbar item therefore begins at the user's most recent ballistic motion, and ends when the toolbar button is clicked. Menu item selection time is calculated as the sum of the time taken to point to the top-level menu bar item, and the time spent in the menu (and submenus) prior to command selection. For context menus, selection time is simply the time spent in the menu prior to selection.

For keyboard shortcut selections, HotkeySkillometer simply measures the time between the first modifier keypress (or the last command selection in the case of consecutive keyboard shortcut activations) and the command selection time.

Note that both of these measures exclude the time for mental preparation and for precursor movements such as homing the hand to the mouse or key. Consequently, both measures represent the lower-bound of the selection time.

EXPERIMENTAL STUDY

We performed a lab experiment using HotkeySkillometer to gain initial insights into the validity of the skillometer approach to performance improvement. The experimental tasks were conducted using Apple's Keynote software in a between-subjects design, with half of the participants having access to HotkeySkillometer and the other half not.

Participants and Apparatus

24 participants were recruited from a local university (20 male, 4 female). The experiment was performed on an Apple Macbook Pro running Mac OS 10.8. Participants were provided with a standard mouse and QWERTY keyboard, and a 24" screen running at 1920×1080 pixels.

Since Keynote ordinarily lacks keyboard shortcuts for many commands, we used the Mac OS System Preferences to add custom hotkeys for all of the commands used in the experiment. Each shortcut was composed of a single modifier key (Command) followed by one of the 18 alphabetic keys from the left part of the keyboard. No hotkey letter was the same as the first or last letter of the command name.

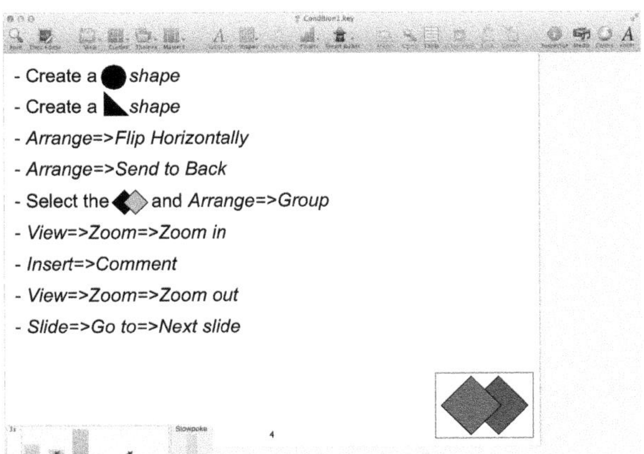

Figure 4. The initial state of a slide used in the experiment. Participants performed tasks on the slide surface, and the instructions were included as a background image. The skillometer appeared at bottom left.

Procedure

Participants were pseudo-randomly assigned to either the *skillometer* or *control* condition (*control* having no access to HotkeySkillometer). Participants were introduced to the Keynote software and to the experimental procedure – they were instructed that they would be completing 'a repetitive series of tasks'. In the *skillometer* condition, participants were additionally given a brief description of the skillometer, explaining the visual presentation of parts A, B, and C shown in Figure 3. To reduce the risk of introducing bias, the skillometer instructions did not mention its overall goal. Participants in both conditions were informed that hotkeys existed for all commands (with labels shown next to menu items). Finally, they were instructed to complete tasks as accurately and quickly as possible.

Each participant performed eight formatting commands on a Keynote slide, then selected a 'next slide' command. They repeated the same eight commands (and next slide) ten times, giving a total of $10 \times 8 = 80$ logged command selections. Instructions for the eight formatting commands were presented in a Keynote slide (Figure 4), and each command involved manipulating components within the slide or view to achieve a particular effect – for example, zooming in or flipping items on the slide. The 'next slide' command initiated the next set of 8 commands on a new slide identical to the preceding one. Timing for each command selection consisted of the elapsed time since the previous correct command selection. All user actions were logged, and the whole experiment took participants 15 minutes on average. To gain insight into the behavior of our participants, we collected post-experiment comments using a short questionnaire. We had considered using a think-aloud protocol to achieve this, but since think-aloud protocols achieve the same goal as skillometers (i.e., promoting reflection during interaction) [17], it would have likely confounded our experimental objectives.

Design and Hypotheses

The experiment was designed as a 2×10 mixed-design ANOVA, with between-subjects factor *Interface* {*skillometer, control*} and within-subjects factor *Repetition* {*1..10*}. *Interface* was a between-subjects factor to minimize unintended learning effects. The two key dependent variables were proportion of hotkey use and task time (the time between command selections). Our primary hypotheses concerning skillometers were as follows:

H1: Proportion of hotkey use will be higher for *skillometer* than for *control.*
H2: Task time will be lower for *skillometer* than for *control.*
H3: There will be an *Interface* × *Repetition* interaction, showing more rapid hotkey adoption with *skillometer.*

Additionally, we wanted to ensure that the skillometer was addressing an appropriate target domain of user performance, leading to **H4:** hotkey selections will be faster than menu and toolbar selections.

Results

Hotkey Use

Figure 5-left shows the proportion of command selections completed using hotkeys for the control (left) and HotkeySkillometer (right) conditions across the ten repetitions. With HotkeySkillometer the mean rate of hotkey use across all repetitions was 50% compared to 28% for the control condition, giving a significant main effect of *Interface* ($F_{1,22} = 4.52$, $p < 0.05$) and supporting **H1**. There was

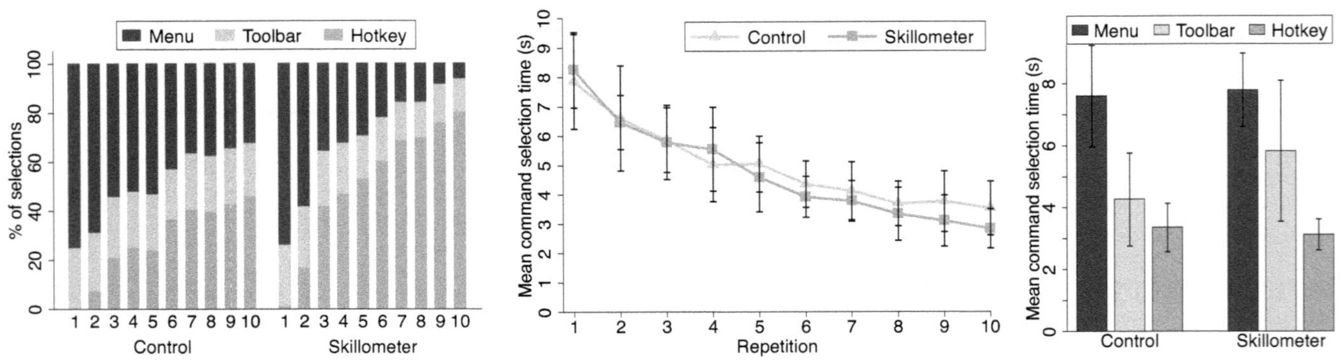

Figure 5. Percentage of selections per modality per repetition in both Control and Skillometer conditions (left). Mean command selection time across all repetitions (center). Mean command selection times across modalities and conditions (right).

also a significant interaction effect of *Interface*×*Repetition* ($F_{9,198} = 3.13$, $p < 0.01$), with participants making an earlier and more substantial switch to hotkeys when using the skillometer, with 80% of commands completed using hotkeys by the 10th repetition, compared to 42% with the control.

Command Selection Time

Figure 5-center summarizes the results for command selection time, showing that selections were initially marginally faster with the control but marginally faster in the skillometer condition across the later repetitions. Given a suggested cross-over effect, it is relatively unsurprising that there is no significant main effect for *Interface* ($F_{1,22} = 0.27$, $p = 0.6$). However, there is no significant *Interface*×*Repetition* interaction ($F_{9,198} = 0.55$, $p = 0.8$). We therefore reject **H2** (with caveats described in the Discussion).

Although there is no significant evidence that the skillometer reduced command selection time, analysis of variance for *Modality* (hotkey, menu, and ribbon) confirms that hotkey selections were much faster than toolbar or menu selections, with mean selection times of 3.3, 5.2 and 7.7 s respectively ($p < 0.001$). We therefore accept **H4**.

Figure 5-right, which shows the mean selection time for each modality in the control and skillometer condition, offers an explanation for the apparent inconsistency between the skillometer resulting in higher use of fast hotkeys, yet *not* resulting in a significant overall performance improvement. Specifically, it shows that toolbar selections were slower with the skillometer present (5.8 s compared to 4.2 s with the control).

One explanation for slow toolbar selections when using the skillometer is that users engaged in additional activities (mental and/or perceptual) in order to memorize and learn the hotkeys associated with commands, and that these activities consumed additional task time. Additionally, Figure 5-center suggests that skillometer users were still improving their performance and Figure 5-left further suggests that they were still increasing in the proportion of hotkeys used. Consequently, we suspect that participants' performance in the skillometer condition would have continued to improve as more hotkeys were learned and routinely executed. However, further empirical work is necessary.

DISCUSSION

To briefly summarise, skillometers are intended to be a widely applicable interface technique that motivates and assists users to increase their level of performance with an interface. They do so by encouraging users to reflect about their level of performance and by assisting them in understanding the performance benefits attainable by altering aspects of their interaction. We described four different domains of performance that skillometers can aim to improve (intramodal performance, intermodal performance, vocabulary extension and user strategies), and we identified four interface goals that any skillometer should seek to achieve (visualize the possibility to improve, provide details on how to improve, motivate the user to improve, and minimize disruption). We then described the design, implementation and evaluation of one specific skillometer addressing intermodal performance improvement – from point and click modality with menus and toolbars to hotkeys. Results of a lab study showed that users quickly learned and used more hotkeys with a commercial software product when presented with an accompanying skillometer.

While the experimental results are encouraging, they are preliminary and cover only a small subset of the potential domains into which skillometers could be deployed. In the following sections we discuss design refinements, explanations for our experimental results, and issues of generalisation.

Understanding and Refining HotkeySkillometer

In designing and implementing HotkeySkillometer, we followed the four interface design goals described earlier in the paper. Although the experimental results showed that the overall design successfully achieved increased hotkey use, it is difficult to know the relative contribution of each of the design goals in that success. This is an important question because the different interface design goals tend to pull the designer in different directions – for example, 'goal 4: minimize disruption' leads to subtle and transient visual effects that may go unnoticed, while goals 1-3 all encourage visual effects that are readily noticeable. Similarly, we are currently unable to determine whether each of goals 1-3 are crucial to the overall success of the system, or whether any one on its own would have had the same effect. For example, it is possible that the display of the hotkey bindings on the bar chart (motivated by 'goal 2: provide specific details') accounts for all of the increase in hotkey adoption because it made hotkeys more salient in the display.

We attempted to mitigate some of these concerns in our experimental method by displaying only the last six commands within the skillometer (and therefore the previous use of any particular hotkey was not inside the view when next needed). We consider it unlikely that our results are attributable solely to the increased saliency of hotkey bindings, since previous research has failed to find benefits for such techniques [20]. We also attempted to understand the relative importance of different skillometer components by asking for subjective feedback on each, but this feedback yielded few strong insights. In general, participants viewed the history chart and overlaid hotkeys as being most useful, and the performance meter and motivational text least useful, with two stating that they did not look at the motivational text at all. We also noticed some participants tilting their head to read the text, suggesting that a horizontal chart would have been easier to read.

To elicit further feedback on the design we gave a real-world implementation of HotkeySkillometer to eight people to use on their personal computers for a week. While the lack of global toolbar support (see the Implementation section) reduced the usefulness of the tool, we received several comments on the design. One participant said he wanted to "measure improvement or long term performance", suggesting that the performance meter might have a configurable time component. Several participants suggested that the skillometer should not show hotkey selections, because it increases distraction when the user already knows the hotkey (counter to interface goal 4) and because it consumes space in the skillometer that might otherwise be dedicated to unknown hotkeys. However, two of the participants in the lab study would have disagreed with this recommendation, as they stated that hotkey feedback in the skillometer was useful for confirming which command was executed if they suspected an error was made. A related issue was raised regarding the inclusion of repeated command selections in the skillometer – a richer vocabulary of available hotkeys would be displayed if only the most recent repetition was displayed.

A final variation to the design of HotkeySkillometer that we are keen to pursue would blend the *feedback* methods that it currently employs with *feedforward* display techniques. HotkeySkillometer currently 'pushes' data to the user in response to their command selections. However there are rich interaction opportunities in supporting users who wish to explicitly 'pull' assistance prior to completing command execution. For example, ExposeHotkey [28] and OctoPocus [9] demonstrate improved learning of expert interface techniques by providing feedforward assistive information in response to partially complete interactions. A skillometer might use equivalent feedforward methods, such as displaying a list of frequent commands that have not been previously selected by hotkeys in response to the user pressing the command key.

Improving User Performance with Skillometers

An important issue for skillometers in general is whether they do in fact help users to improve overall performance – and in particular, why did this not occur in our initial evaluation? There are two main points for discussion in this issue.

First, the difference in completion time for toolbar selections between the skillometer and control groups may have arisen because groups were attempting to learn both the hotkeys and the toolbar locations at the same time – and in the skillometer condition, participants may have allocated more of their cognitive resources to learning the hotkeys, leading to less effective learning of the toolbar. There are often costs associated with learning new interaction modalities [35] – and it is worth noting that the skillometer group did not suffer any 'performance dip' as they switched to the new mode. More research is needed, however, to determine why the skillometer group continued to use the toolbar (or menu) in some instances – there may have been other types of 'interaction inertia' that future skillometer design could attempt to counteract.

Second, it is clear that hotkeys are substantially faster than the other two interaction modalities, so the observed slowdown in toolbar use for the skillometer group would likely be overcome by the hotkey advantage over a longer term than our 15-minute study (a trend that is also suggested by the divergence of the lines in Figure 5-center).

Challenges in Designing Skillometers for Other Domains

Although we provided design suggestions for each target domain earlier in the paper, it is clear that substantial challenges arise in designing and implementing skillometers for domains other than intermodal improvement, particularly for strategic deployments.

However, even in the complex domain of strategic improvement, there are realistic opportunities for successful deployment. In particular, computing systems are increasingly capable of capturing and usefully processing large pools of meta-information about users' interaction, both at individual and societal levels. These data repositories can be put to use to predict the user's intention and needs, and the predictions facilitate new forms of interaction to assist users in completing their tasks. For example, Fitchett and Cockburn [19] introduced the 'AccessRank' algorithm and demonstrated that it outperformed a variety of previous algorithms for predicting upcoming user actions across a wide range of user tasks. A skillometer could use such predictions to gain an understanding of the user's task, and suggest alternative methods for achieving it when alternatives are known. But again, interesting design questions emerge on whether the skillometer's role extends beyond identifying and suggesting better interactive alternatives (as we have described them), or whether they could additionally provide a shortcut method for achieving the predicted intention (which we see as beyond their scope).

Platform Requirements for Engineering Skillometers

Accessibility APIs remain the best solution for implementing systems like skillometers on a generic level. However, the main goal of these APIs is to be able to provide better access to interfaces for individuals with disabilities. These APIs are therefore usually limited to a shallow description of the UI components, and it is complicated (often impossible) to access deeper information such as the actions associated with toolbar buttons. Ideally, the next generation of UI toolkits would provide an improved connection between UI components and their semantics.

CONCLUSIONS AND FUTURE WORK

Users have many opportunities to enhance their productivity in modern applications, one of them being to transition to expert modalities such as hotkeys. Yet users tend to stick to their familiar methods and strategies for interaction, rather than trying to improve. As a solution to this problem, this paper introduced the use of *skillometers*, a type of reflective interface that motivates and helps users to increase their level of performance. We provided a framework examining the domains of interaction that can be targeted for improvement, and discussed interface design goals for skillometers. We then described the design and evaluation of HotkeySkillometer, an exemplar skillometer that motivates and helps people to use more hotkeys. A preliminary lab study provided positive results, with experimental participants exposed to the skillometer learning more hotkeys than those in the control condition.

There are two main directions for future work. First, we will refine the design of HotkeySkillometer based on feedback from our study participants, and perform a longer-term, application-specific study with a complex application. Second, we will study skillometers in other settings and for other target domains, such as strategic improvement.

ACKNOWLEDGMENTS

This research was partially funded by Royal Society of New Zealand Marsden Grant 10-UOC-020.

REFERENCES

1. Apple accessibility api. https://developer.apple.com/library/mac/#documentation/Accessibility/Conceptual/AccessibilityMacOSX/OSXAXIntro/OSXAXintro.html.
2. Ribbon hero 2. http://www.ribbonhero.com/.
3. Adar, E., Tan, D., and Teevan, J. Benevolent deception in human computer interaction. In *CHI '13*, ACM (2013).
4. Aleven, V., Koedinger, K., Sinclair, H., and Snyder, J. Combatting shallow learning in a tutor for geometry problem solving. In *Intelligent Tutoring Systems*, Springer (1998).
5. Anderson, J., Corbett, A, Fincham, J., Hoffman, D., and Pelletier, R. General principles for an intelligent tutoring architecture. *Cognitive approaches to automated instruction* (Jan 1992).
6. Bailly, G., Pietrzak, T., Deber, J., and Wigdor, D. J. Métamorphe: augmenting hotkey usage with actuated keys. In *CHI '13*, ACM (2013).
7. Banovic, N., Chevalier, F., Grossman, T., and Fitzmaurice, G. Triggering triggers and burying barriers to customizing software. In *CHI '12*, ACM (2012).
8. Bateman, S., Teevan, J., and White, R. The search dashboard: how reflection and comparison impact search behavior. In *CHI '12*, ACM (2012).
9. Bau, O., and Mackay, W. Octopocus: a dynamic guide for learning gesture-based command sets. In *UIST '08*, ACM (2008).
10. Bhavnani, S., Peck, F., and Reif, F. Strategy-based instruction: Lessons learned in teaching the effective and efficient use of computer applications. *ACM Trans. Comput.-Hum. Interact. 15*, 1 (May 2008).
11. Bødker, S. Applying activity theory to video analysis: how to make sense of video data in human-computer interaction. In *Context and consciousness*, Massachusetts Institute of Technology (1995).
12. Carroll, J., and Rosson, M. Paradox of the active user. *Interfacing thought: Cognitive aspects of human-computer interaction* (1987).
13. Czerwinski, M., Horvitz, E., and Cutrell, E. Subjective duration assessment: An implicit probe for software usability. In *IHM-HCI '01*, vol. 2 (Jan 2001).
14. Deterding, S., Dixon, D., Khaled, R., and Nacke, L. From game design elements to gamefulness: defining "gamification". In *MindTrek '11*, ACM (2011).
15. Dong, T., Dontcheva, M., Joseph, D., Karahalios, K., Newman, M., and Ackerman, M. Discovery-based games for learning software. In *CHI '12*, ACM (2012).
16. Eagan, J., Beaudouin-Lafon, M., and Mackay, W. Cracking the cocoa nut: user interface programming at runtime. In *UIST '11*, ACM (2011).
17. Ericsson, K., and Simon, H. How to study thinking in everyday life: Contrasting think-aloud protocols with descriptions and explanations of thinking. *Mind, Culture, and Activity 5*, 3 (1998).
18. Evans, A., and Wobbrock, J. Taming wild behavior: the input observer for text entry and mouse pointing measures from everyday computer use. In *CHI '12*, ACM (2012).
19. Fitchett, S., and Cockburn, A. Accessrank: predicting what users will do next. In *CHI '12*, ACM (2012).
20. Grossman, T., Dragicevic, P., and Balakrishnan, R. Strategies for accelerating on-line learning of hotkeys. *CHI '07*, ACM (2007).
21. Kapp, K. *The Gamification of Learning and Instruction: Game-based Methods and Strategies for Training and Education*. Pfeiffer, 2012.
22. Krisler, B., and Alterman, R. Training towards mastery: overcoming the active user paradox. *NordiCHI '08*, ACM (2008).
23. Lane, D., Napier, H., Peres, S., and Sandor, A. Hidden costs of graphical user interfaces: Failure to make the transition from menus and icon toolbars to keyboard shortcuts. *International Journal of Human-Computer Interaction 18*, 2 (2005).
24. Lesgold, A., Eggan, G., Katz, S., and Rao, G. Possibilities for assessment using computer-based apprenticeship environments. *Cognitive approaches to automated instruction* (Jan 1992).
25. Li, W., Grossman, T., and Fitzmaurice, G. Gamicad: a gamified tutorial system for first time autocad users. In *UIST '12*, ACM (2012).
26. Linton, F., and Schaefer, H.-P. Recommender systems for learning: building user and expert models through long-term observation of application use. *User Modeling and User-Adapted Interaction 10*, 2.
27. Mackay, W. Triggers and barriers to customizing software. In *CHI '91*, ACM (1991).
28. Malacria, S., Bailly, G., Harrison, J., Cockburn, A., and Gutwin, C. Promoting hotkey use through rehearsal with exposehk. In *CHI '13*, ACM (2013).
29. Matejka, J., Grossman, T., and Fitzmaurice, G. Patina: Dynamic heatmaps for visualizing application usage. In *CHI '13*, ACM (2013).
30. Matejka, J., Li, W., Grossman, T., and Fitzmaurice, G. Communitycommands: command recommendations for software applications. In *UIST '09*, ACM (2009).
31. Newell, A., and Rosenbloom, P. Mechanisms of skill acquisition and the law of practice. *Cognitive skills and their acquisition* (1981).
32. Odell, D., Davis, R., Smith, A., and Wright, P. Toolglasses, marking menus, and hotkeys: a comparison of one and two-handed command selection techniques. In *GI '04*, Canadian Human-Computer Communications Society (2004).
33. Peres, S., Tamborello, F., Fleetwood, M., Chung, P., and Paige-Smith, D. Keyboard shortcut usage: The roles of social factors and computer experience. *the Human Factors and Ergonomics Society Annual Meeting 48*, 5 (2004).
34. Salmoni, A., Schmidt, R., and Walter, C. Knowledge of results and motor learning: A review and critical reappraisal. *Psychological Bulletin 95*, 3.
35. Scarr, J., Cockburn, A., Gutwin, C., and Quinn, P. Dips and ceilings: understanding and supporting transitions to expertise in user interfaces. In *CHI '11*, ACM (2011).
36. Schmidt, R., and Lee, T. *Motor Control and Learning: A Behavioral Emphasis*. Human Kinetics, 2011.
37. Shroyer, R. Actual readers versus implied readers: role conflicts in office 97. *Technical Communication 47*, 2 (2000).
38. Simon, H. Satisficing. *The new Palgrave: a dictionary of economics 4* (1987).
39. Tak, S., Westendorp, P., and van Rooij, I. Satisficing and the use of keyboard shortcuts: Being good enough is enough? *Interacting with Computers* (2013).

MenuOptimizer: Interactive Optimization of Menu Systems

Gilles Bailly[1] Antti Oulasvirta[1] Timo Kötzing[2] Sabrina Hoppe[1]
[1]Max Planck Institute for Informatics and Saarland University [2]University of Jena

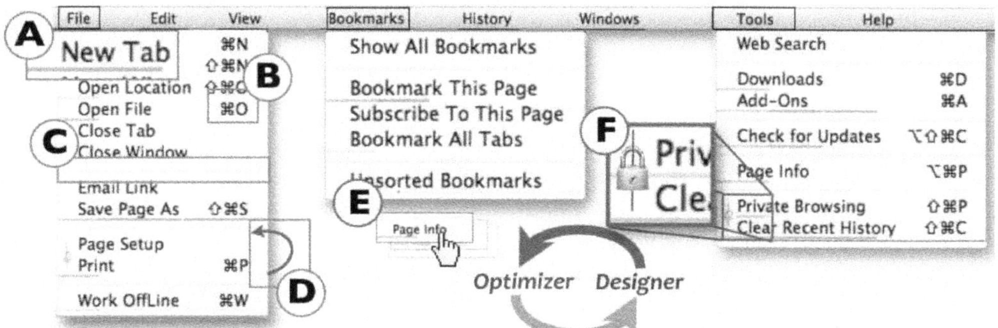

Figure 1: MenuOptimizer assists in the design of menus: While the designer edits the menu (action in red), a model-based optimizer updates itself to provide feedback and suggestions (in blue): A) Item feedback indicates the frequency (line width) and user performance over time (color gradient). B–C) Hotkeys and separators are automatically assigned. D) Item placements to improve user performance are suggested. E) Designers can normally edit items (move, delete, etc.) and also F) lock items to constrain them together to accelerate optimization.

ABSTRACT

Menu systems are challenging to design because design spaces are immense, and several human factors affect user behavior. This paper contributes to the design of menus with the goal of interactively assisting designers with an optimizer in the loop. To reach this goal, 1) we extend a predictive model of user performance to account for expectations as to item groupings; 2) we adapt an ant colony optimizer that has been proven efficient for this class of problems; and 3) we present MenuOptimizer, a set of interactions integrated into a real interface design tool (QtDesigner). MenuOptimizer supports designers' abilities to cope with uncertainty and recognize good solutions. It allows designers to delegate combinatorial problems to the optimizer, which should solve them quickly enough without disrupting the design process. We show evidence that satisfactory menu designs can be produced for complex problems in minutes.

Author Keywords

Menus; Predictive models; Interactive optimization.

ACM Classification Keywords

H.5.m. Information interfaces and presentation (e.g., HCI): Miscellaneous.

INTRODUCTION

Menu systems, consisting of menus, hotkeys or toolbars, are widespread interfaces for selecting commands. Interface design strongly affects their usability. However, despite apparent simplicity, designing usable menu systems is challenging because the number of alternative designs grows superexponentially as a function of the number of commands. For instance, a linear menu with n items can, in theory, be organized in $n!$ ways. However, professional applications comprise hundreds of items organized in hierarchical menus. A menu hierarchy can be organized in about $(2n)!$ ways. For 50 items, the size of the search space is a whopping $100! \approx 10^{158}$. Design heuristics, such as placing frequently used items at the top [5], may be effective for small n but fail with larger n or if additional human factors such as semantic relationships among items are considered. Although experts can quickly generate a handful of solutions to hard design problems [6], they cannot examine all promising solutions. Novices, known to search the space depth-first [3], are likely to get stuck in a local search space.

Combinatorial optimization methods (e.g., [29]) have been successfully used to generate user interfaces such as virtual keyboards [8,21,24,34]. These methods explore a large number of designs in order to find ones that minimize or maximize a pre-specified objective function. Computation time is on a scale of hours, days, or weeks. While empirical evidence confirms improvements in usability in other contexts (e.g., [24,34]), there is reason to suggest that they may be impractical for the design of menu systems. First, designers cannot be expected to wait days or weeks for a solution. Moreover, designers may not be able to define the optimization problem completely in advance. Interaction design, in general, is rather more an iterative process of redefinition and refinement. Finally, predictive models for menu systems performance are only just emerging [5,20,25], are limited to linear menus, and have yet to cover all important human factors that affect design choices.

UIST'13, October 8–11, 2013, St. Andrews, United Kingdom.
Copyright © 2013 ACM 978-1-4503-2268-3/13/10...$15.00.
http://dx.doi.org/10.1145/2501988.2502024

This paper contributes the *design of a user interface and an optimization method for interactively assisting in menu design with an optimizer in the loop*. MenuOptimizer illustrates our approach by integrating an optimizer into QtDesigner, a widely used design tool. The goal is to improve the quality of process and outcomes in the design of menus. The key challenges are, on the one hand, how to support designers' abilities to cope with uncertainty, define constraints, and recognize good solutions and, on the other hand, to allow designers to delegate combinatorial subproblems to an optimizer that should solve them rapidly enough not to disrupt the process of design.

Figure 1 reviews the concept of designer–optimizer interactions in MenuOptimizer. At present, it supports the design of static hierarchical menus. Two design scenarios are supported: 1) In the *updating* of existing menus, user behavior is partially known from logs or interviews. 2) *Sketching* novel menus involves assumptions about usage and objective, which can change during the design phase. Both scenarios are supported with the same functionality: Designers can edit menus by adding, renaming, or moving commands in it, and every edit updates the optimizer to work with the present menu design. The optimizer provides suggestions at item level (optimal placement for an item), menu level (improvements made by moving items), and the menu system level (menu templates). Designers can specify and change their assumptions about use and users by editing distribution graphs directly. To direct the optimizer, designers can also change the objective function by setting the relative weight of user performance, consistency (expectations as to item locations), and edit distance to the present design. With multiple optimization objectives, the optimizer's suggestions are plotted in real time on a Pareto front plot. Designers can also lock items, which restricts the optimizer's search space.

To realize the interactions in MenuOptimizer, we extended a state-of-the-art predictive model of user performance (*Search–Decision–Pointing; SDP* [5]) with a model of expected item groupings; the system proposes logical groups and hierarchies that are statistically consistent with other applications. Furthermore, we show that the menu design problem can be formulated as a known optimization problem. We then describe an ant colony optimizer, a method proven to be efficient for this class of problem.

After presenting MenuOptimizer, we show evidence from several evaluations. We consider two realistic design cases. The first is the optimization of Mozilla Firefox from logs collected on regular users; the second involves the image editing software Seashore. We report on the short- and long-term performance of the optimizer, showing that it can rapidly produce satisfactory suggestions for menus. Moreover, data from a preliminary study suggests that interactions with MenuOptimizer can help novice designers to design menus with less editing effort. Finally, we detail further directions for interactive optimization of menu systems.

MOTIVATION AND FORMATIVE STUDY

Designing user interfaces is, in general, a complex, expensive, and time-consuming process [6,26,28,32]. Some reasons cited in existing literature are related to the issue of combinatorial explosion as described above: 1) Designers cannot explore the space of possible interface designs manually [14,26]. 2) Designers underestimate the diversity of the user population [15]. 3) They have difficulties in demonstrating the advantages of a design to others [26]. 4) Finally, designers find it difficult to analyze a design's efficiency [32]. For instance, in the evaluation of a design, there is a tendency to favor aesthetics over efficiency [32].

Because we were unable to find literature on such problems specific to *menu systems*, we conducted a pre-study. Six experienced designers were interviewed. They all work in the industry as designers or usability professionals. They stated that they design between zero and three *complex* (~1,000-item) menu systems per year in the context of software or Web applications and 1–5 intermediately complex menu systems (~100 items) a year. Their reported range of command sets is 50 to 1,000 commands. They stated their main design goals as being "understandability" and "allowing users to find what they want." However, item selection time for experienced users (users who already know item locations) appears not to be among their main concerns because they need to satisfy the immediate expectations of their clients.

The interviewees confirmed that designing large menu systems is "very difficult" and involves "trial and error in the beginning." Several design challenges were mentioned, among them "labeling top-level menus," "coherence between commands and their labels," and "choosing the best placements for items." They described their design process as "iterative" and involving feedback from final users. They also confessed that they do not always seek the best solutions. For instance, "it happens that we put commands in two places because they are not in a perfect location in either. However, we know that this also introduces confusion." To solve the problems mentioned above, the designers considered important "the logic of the software," "experience," and "feedback from customers." None of the designers mentioned collecting logs for individual users, but they do use analytical tools (e.g., Google Analytics) to learn about frequency distributions for commands. We learned that updating the hierarchy of commands (links on Web sites) in line with visitors' expectations was a frequent task.

Finally, when asked what kind of support they would desire, the designers stated tools that "provide alternative versions of the current menu system" so that they "can compare designs." They also wanted to "check whether all commands are in the menu system."

While this pre-study interviews included only professionals, we believe that designing small-to-intermediate menus must involve a large number of applications and designers.

RELATED WORK

MenuOptimizer contributes to the areas of automatically generated interface*s* [11,17,28], mixed-initiative design [16] and, in particular, to optimizer-assisted design. We concentrate on optimizer-assisted design here, identifying three sub-areas: 1) designs generated by one-shot (offline) optimizers, 2) design guided by the output of an offline optimizer, and 3) design optimization with a human in the loop.

1. *Offline (non-interactive) optimization* has been used in HCI in the context of widget layouts [31], text entry [21,24,34], menus [14,23], accessibility [1213], and dialog layout [9]. Regarding menus, Goubko et al. [14] proposed a framework for optimizing menus on cellular phones. However, they impose a constraint on the menu structure, use a contrived predictive model [20], and describe neither the optimization method nor evaluate its outcomes. Matsui et al. [23] proposed an optimizer for hierarchical menus on mobile devices that is based on genetic algorithms and simulated annealing. As the objective function, they used the SDP model [5] and introduced two costs: that of favoring proximity between semantically related items and a granularity cost to favor balanced hierarchies. Our optimization method also builds on the SDP model, but we introduce several necessary improvements, including a model of consistency that can suggest item groupings. Importantly, we reject the constraint of balanced hierarchies, making the task harder but more realistic.

2. *Optimization results can be seeds for the design process.* AIDE [32] initially computes a layout that the designer can then edit. At all times, the designer can compare the present layout with the precomputed optimum generated with the branch and bound method. In the design of Template Gallery (see Figure 2B), we follow the idea of comparing the present menu with the best known. MenuOptimizer also continuously provides suggestions during editing.

3. *To involve the designer in the optimization process* [3,27,30]: Quiroz et al. proposed an interactive genetic algorithm for generating widget layouts when no predictive models are available [27]. In each iteration, the designer chooses the best three designs out of ten to guide the optimizer. While not addressing UI design, Scott et al. [30] proposed a technique in which the user can guide an optimizer by constraining its search space during optimization.

To our knowledge, *interactive* optimization of menus has not previously been studied. MenuOptimizer builds on ideas from the three areas mentioned above. 1) The optimizer can be used in offline mode; after defining items and user behavior, the optimizer searches for the best solutions. 2) MenuOptimizer also provides a visualization of suggestions that the designer can choose to follow, and guidance is offered via comparison of the current menu with the best known. 3) MenuOptimizer does not assume perfect knowledge in the predictive model. Several interactions allow the designer to guide and focus the optimizer.

WALKTHROUGH

We introduce MenuOptimizer in a design scenario. The interface elements in parentheses refer to Figures 1–5. The scenario is divided into two stages: global and local editing.

1. Global editing: *Kim is designing a menu system for image editing software with a set of 50 commands. Kim first states her command set by typing commands in an empty menu. Then, she explicates her assumptions about users and their frequencies of command selections* (User Profile Panel). *She uses a slider to indicate that she prefers to optimize for consistency instead of performance* (Objective Panel). *Now the optimization problem has been set, the optimizer starts to propose menu designs, which are visible* (Template Gallery). *Kim examines the gallery as the suggestions appear and selects one with four submenus and large logical groups. Two menus have titles that are given automatically.*

2. Local editing: *Kim is not happy with the* Crop item *being far away from* Select, *so she moves the two together by drag-and-drop. The optimizer shows that this placement decreases a user's average selection performance by 1.5%. Nevertheless, Kim moves the items because she wants to keep them together. Then, Kim follows the optimizer's suggestion to move* Select *to the* Edit *menu* (Suggestions). *Kim then marks* Undo, Redo, *and a few other items with* Locks *because she wants to keep these items together. From now on, the optimizer only suggests designs maintaining this group. Finally, Kim finalizes the design by asking* MenuOptimizer *to assign hotkeys. As the menu is created in* QtDesigner, *it can be easily instantiated in the application.*

This scenario should take about 15 minutes, with the time for the global and local phases split roughly half and half. To realize this scenario, we need 1) a predictive model of menu performance, 2) an optimization method, and 3) interactions between the designer and the optimizer. We now present these three components.

ADAPTING A PREDICTIVE MODEL FOR MENUS

Model-based optimization critically relies on a valid and comprehensive *predictive model*. Several models of menu performance have been proposed [1,2,5,20,25]. We implement and extend the most recent model: the SDP model [5]. It covers four human factors: target acquisition, visual search, decision-making, and learning (see below).

To assist the designer better, two adaptations have been made to the existing model. First, we extend the model to user performance with hierarchical menus attached to the menu bar. Second, the grouping of commands into submenus or logical groups (marked by separator lines) is central to menus. Such decisions should be informed by a notion of "semantics", indicating which commands belong together. Our informal tests suggested that user *expectations* of item groups from previous applications are central. Both designers and users expect certain commands to be together (e.g., Undo and Redo). Having these adaptations in the optimizer frees the designer from the work of grouping items.

SDP: A Predictive Model for Linear Menus

SDP (Search–Decision–Pointing) is a three-component linear regression model that predicts the selection time of an item in a menu [5]: **Search**, the time to localize an item, increases linearly with the number of items in the menu. **Decision** is the time to decide from among items given the "entropy" determined by the frequencies of previous selections and given by the Hick-Hyman law. **Pointing** is based on Fitts' law and predicts that items closer to the top are faster to select. Search and decision are modulated by the number of repetitions of an item. With practice, performance shifts from being dominated by search (linear) to decision (logarithmic). Our model parameters are the same as [5], but the designer can change them to test hypotheses.

Adaptation 1: Menus Attached to the Menu Bar

To deal with a menu system, a model must account for two aspects: 1) steering from one submenu to another and 2) menu bars. For the former, we use a *steering cost,* proposed in [1], that penalizes designs with deep submenu structures. For the latter, we assume that at the beginning of a selection, the cursor is on the left side of the screen and in the middle and that items have a width four times their height.

Adaptation 2: Consistency Score for Grouping Items

Here we propose a model that allows the optimizer to produce logical groups and hierarchies that are statistically consistent with other applications. To allow this, we built a database of item co-occurrences. The database currently has 3,290 commands and 111,859 command pairs collected by a menu-logger tool [22] from 68 applications in Mac OS X. Using this database, we compute a score for the expected relative position of command pairs in a selected set of prior applications. Each command pair i, j has an expectation score $E(i, j)$ between 0 and 1, representing the two commands' tendency to be close in prior menus. A higher score is given to pairs that tend to be in the same submenu and the highest to pairs that are always in the same logical group (e.g., Undo and Redo). The expectation score $E(i, j)$ for a given menu is computed as follows:

$$E(i,j) = \frac{0.33}{1+D_{ij}}(Hierarchy(i,j) + Menu(i,j) + Group(i,j)) \quad (1)$$

where $Hierarchy(i,j)$, $Menu(i,j)$, and $Group(i,j)$ each returns 1 if i and j are in the same hierarchy (have a common ancestor), menu, or logical group, respectively; and 0 otherwise. D_{ij} is the shortest path in the hierarchy to reach j from i. Therefore, for command pairs that tend to be in a child–parent relationship in the menu tree, the score is between 0 and 1/3. The score is above 1/3 if they are in the same submenu and greater than 2/3 if they are in the same group. For commands that are *not* in the database, we use a simple lexical similarity score: the number of shared words.

$$E_{lexical}(i,j) = \frac{commonWords(i,j)}{\max(\,length(i), length(j))} \quad (2)$$

For instance, E(Show All Bookmarks, Hide Bookmarks) is 1/3. For item pairs not sharing words, we assign a score of 0.0. To calculate the average expectation score $E_{average}$, we average the expectation scores over selected applications.

Evaluating the consistency of a given menu: Now, the computed $E_{average}(i, j)$ score can be used for determining a score for the consistency of a given menu system C_{menu} over pairwise comparisons with its expectation score E_{menu}:

$$C_{menu} = \frac{\sum_{i=1}^{n}\sum_{j=i+1}^{n} |\, E_{menu}(i,j) - E_{average}(i,j)\,|}{n(n-1)/2}, \quad (3)$$

where n is the number of items in menu system M.

This score has several desirable effects on the optimizer (one result is shown later in Figure 4):

1. Item pairs that tend to be in the same logical groups are "pulled" together.
2. Item pairs that cannot be positioned to match $E_{average}$ are penalized, with the penalty depending on how far from the expected position they end up.
3. Unrelated items are bumped from submenus whose other items are cohesive.

In summary, we augment the SDP model with a consistency model to allow the optimizer to suggest item groups and form hierarchies. Optimizing consistency was our primary goal according to the results of the formative study. However, speed is also important for many users because even experienced ones do not always switch to hotkeys [19]. Moreover, improving speed does not always take place at the expense of groupings. For instance, an entire group can be moved. The optimizer must propose designs according to this dual objective.

OPTIMIZER DESIGN

In this section, we show that the problem of designing menu systems can be formulated as the *Quadratic Assignment Problem* (QAP). Developed in operations research, the QAP is the task of assigning n facilities to n locations on a factory floor. The QAP is NP-hard, and optima for problems with $n > 20$ cannot be expected to be found [33]. Analogously, menu design is about assigning items to slots in submenus in a menu tree. This observation is important because it allows us to adapt an existing optimization method known to work well for this problem.

Feedback latency (s)	Search space	Response	Algorithm
10^{-1}	n	Predicted command and menu performance	Exhaustive search
10^{0}	n^2	Optimal command placement	Exhaustive search
10^{1}	n^3	Menu swap/move suggestions	Exhaustive search
10^{0}	n^3	Improvement in menu designs	Heuristic generation
10^{1}	$(2n)!$		Hill-climbing
10^{2}	$(2n)!$		Ant colony optimizer
10^{3}	$(2n)!$	▼	

Table 1: Optimizer responses on different time scales. n = number of items in the menu system.

Problem Formulation: Menu System Design as the QAP

The *letter assignment problem* (i.e., virtual keyboard design) has been shown to be the QAP [4]. There, n letters must be positioned in m locations (keyslots) so as to minimize typing times for a language. The goal is to minimize the cost c_{ij} of typing letter j when starting from letter i, typically given by Fitts' law, and weighted by the probability p_{ij} in the digraph distribution. More formally, the goal is

$$\min_{\psi \in P(n,m)} \sum_{i=1}^{n} \sum_{j=1}^{n} p_{ij} c_{\psi(i)\psi(j)}, \quad (4)$$

where $C = [c_{sr}]$ is an m x m matrix and $P = [p_{ij}]$ is an n x n matrix; $P(n,m)$ is the set of all 1–1 (injective) mappings from $\{1, \ldots, n\}$ to $\{1, \ldots, m\}$, corresponding to the placement of the letters in these locations; and, $\psi(i)$ is the location of letter i in the current solution $\psi \in P(n,m)$. Now, $p_{ij} c_{\psi(i)\psi(j)}$ is the *cost contribution* of assigning letter i to location $\psi(i)$ and letter j to $\psi(j)$. This problem can be formulated with a quadratic objective function [33]: Let x_{ij} be a binary variable that is 1 if letter i is assigned to location j, and 0 otherwise. Now, Eq. 4 is equivalent to

$$\min \sum_{i=1}^{n} \sum_{j=1}^{n} \sum_{k=1}^{n} \sum_{l=1}^{n} p_{ij} a_{kl} x_{ik} x_{jl}, \quad (5)$$

where a_{kl} is the cost of using keyslot l after keyslot k.

The design of menu systems is a QAP, too: n commands are assigned to slots in k submenus that form a tree. Three differences must be addressed for treating menu system design as the QAP. First, instead of transitioning from a previous command j in Eq. 4, SDP assumes each selection to start from the *same* position; no changes are needed to Eq. 4. Second, every additional factor in the cost function adds a sum term to Eq. 4. However, the formula collapses back to the quadratic form when one allows a larger cost matrix C. In the case of SDP, we have four coefficients: 1) the number of items in the menu, 2) the position of the target item, 3) the number of trials for that item, and 4) decision entropy in that menu. Hence, a four-dimensional cost matrix is necessary. We also need to consider that menus form *hierarchies* (trees). If there are k submenus and n items, they can be organized in $(n + k)^{n+k-2}$ ways into a tree. It can be shown that, although this vastly expands $P(n, m)$ (the set of mappings of items to locations in the tree), Eq. 4 still applies.

Multi-scale Interactive Optimization

We follow the *multi-scale approach* presented in Table 1: The goal is to generate immediate responses to the designer's edits but improve them when more time is given:

- **Item-level responses in 10^{-1}–10^{1} seconds**: The effects of edits on user performance are computed by an exhaustive search in $O(n^2)$. User Performance Graph and item-level feedback for a case of n = 25 takes about 600 ms on a normal laptop. Move/Swap Suggestions are computed in $O(n^3)$. To provide first suggestions rapidly, we start computation with the most frequent items. For a description of these UI features, please see the next section.
- **Rapid menu-system-level responses in 10^{0}–10^{1} s**: First, a *heuristic menu generator* provides the initial suggestions by arranging commands in a frequency-based order and creating menu hierarchies of depth 3 with a minimum of three commands per submenu. With optimization for consistency, related commands are also moved to be together. A *greedy hill-climbing algorithm* is initialized by the best designs found. It improves them by generating h x 10 designs by random local edits and taking the h best solutions for the next iteration (we use h=3). It runs for about 30s before handing over to the ant colony.

The Ant Colony Optimizer: 10^{2}–10^{3} seconds

Although the greedy search produces reasonable solutions rapidly (see below), they are limited to a local optimum. To search globally, we apply a method that is known to work particularly well for the QAP. *Ant colony optimization* (ACO) [7] is based on the biological metaphor of an ant colony foraging for food. Multiple searchers cooperate to produce solutions according to a memory of past solutions.

Implementation for Menu Systems

To our knowledge, ACO has not yet been applied to menus. We use the *Max-Min Ant System* (MMAS) variant [33]. It ensures the exploration of the search space by imposing upper and lower bounds τ_{max} and τ_{min} (respectively) to the pheromone level. To increase efficiency, only the best ants add pheromone. The pseudo-code for MMAS is:

```
Initialize pheromone trails to τ_max
WHILE (not converged) DO
    FOR each ant
        FOR each element i
            PlaceElement i
    UpdateTrails
```

In initialization, pheromone trails are set to τ_{max}. In each iteration, the odds of placing command i in slot j are

$$p_{ij} = \frac{\tau_{ij}(t)}{\sum_{(i,j)\in N(s^p)} \tau_{il}(t)}, \quad (6)$$

where $N(s^p)$ is the set of feasible placements and $\tau_{ij}(t)$ is the pheromone value for location j. In the subsequent iteration, pheromone is updated for the best ants according to

$$\tau_{ij}(t+1) \leftarrow \rho\, \tau_{ij}(t) + \Delta\tau_{ij}^{best}, \quad (7)$$

where $\rho < 1$ is the *evaporation factor*, $\Delta\tau_{ij}^{best} = 1/f(S^{best})$, and S^{best} is the best global solution.

Hierarchies complicate optimization. Previous work has made simplifications to make the problem more tractable (see [14,23]) but did not explore unconstrained hierarchies or use a realistic cost function. To represent hierarchies, we use *pointers* to mark the locations of submenus in the parent menu. We also found the following techniques useful:

1. **Compression**: Because the ants randomly place commands, sparse placements arise. We "compress" menus by removing empty slots before pheromone deposit.
2. **Penalties for illegal structures**: Ants generating menus wherein some commands are not accessible are penalized by a decrease in pheromone values for their solutions.

3. **Two-phased search**: We first develop pheromone structures for valid hierarchies (all items included) and only then move on to focus on command assignment.
4. **Pheromone diffusion**: Pheromone deposition is *diffused* 1) for items close in consistency score and 2) to positions in neighboring submenus.

Multi-Objective Optimization

We implemented three scalarizations that collapse the normalized objectives into a single variable: weighted sum, weighted Tchebycheff scalarization, and weighted square root sum. In our experience the weighted square root sum offers the most stable performance in the Pareto frontier.

Parameter Setting

Parameters were set by testing 1,152 combinations for the number of ants, ρ, the number of winners, and diffusion heuristics. Each was tested for 5,000 iterations for the Firefox problem (see below). The winning configuration was further fine-tuned manually for a larger set of problems.

USER INTERFACE DESIGN

MenuOptimizer augments QtDesigner, a C++/Qt graphical user interface builder used by novice and expert software designers alike. MenuOptimizer can be used exactly like the regular QtDesigner. A designer can manipulate a menu system by adding, removing, and moving items, groups, and submenus by direct manipulation. The optimizer-produced features are reviewed here in three main categories. An overview of the UI is provided in Figure 2.

Model-based Feedback for Design Choices

Metrics and visualizations that summarize the current status of an interface arguably help designers to take into account elements that can be difficult to perceive; they inform and justify design choices; and they can be referred to when one is communicating a design to others [32]. MenuOptimizer provides SDP-based feedback at two levels:

Items: The user performance and selection frequency for each item are visually represented in a place underneath it (see Figure 1A). The width of the line indicates frequency: more frequent commands have longer lines. The color gradient indicates user performance over time for the item.

Menu system: User Performance Graph (see Figure 2E) shows the average selection times for each user over time. The Template Gallery plot in Figure 2C shows the currently chosen menu against suggestions by the optimizer.

Suggestions for Improvement

A major feature of MenuOptimizer is its improvement suggestions. A key difference from previous systems [32] is that *several* suggestions are offered both locally and globally (a multi-scale approach). Menu-level suggestions are updated whenever the optimizer finds a better solution.

Menu system: Template Gallery (Figure 2C) is a key feature of MenuOptimizer: It updates the optimizer's suggestions (templates) for menu systems that have a higher objective score than the present design does. Three features assist the designer in decision-making and exploration:

1. *Pareto front plot*: Templates are organized in a scatter plot to emphasize the tradeoff between *selection time* (y-axis, predicted by SDP) and *consistency* (x-axis, from Eq. 2). The plot shows the evolution of the *Pareto optimality frontier*: the frontier where it is not possible to improve for one objective without being worse for the other.
2. *Distance* of a template to the menu system currently edit-

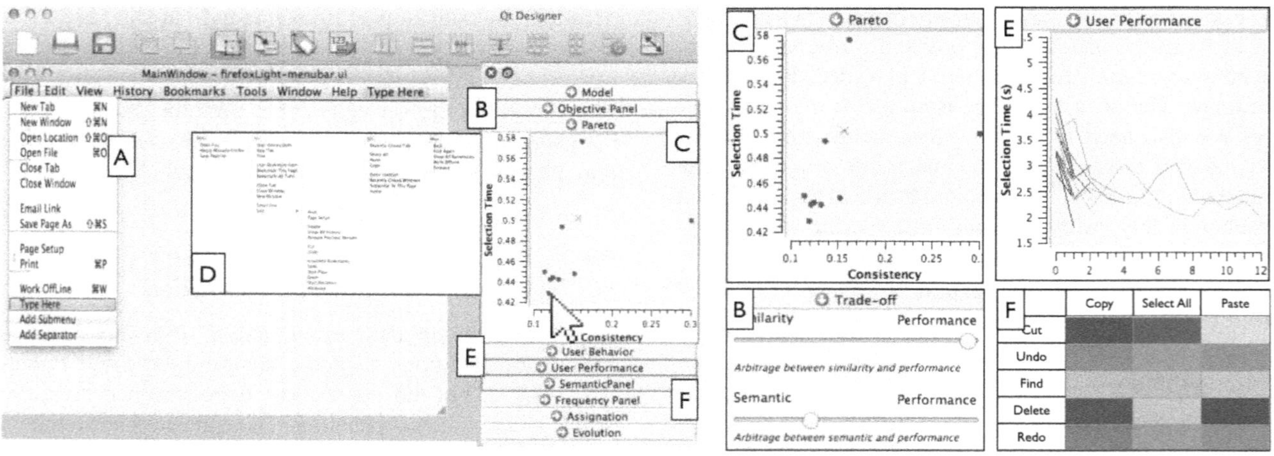

Figure 2: MenuOptimizer integrates optimizer-based assistance into the QtDesigner interface: A) The menu is edited. B) Objective Panel allows the designer to set the weights for three optimization objectives: performance, consistency, and similarity to the present menu. C) Template Gallery shows new menu system suggestions (•) on a Pareto front plot with user performance (y-axis) and consistency (y-axis) and (D) a preview of the menu. The current menu system (×) is shown to aid in comparison. E) User Profile Graph shows predicted performance for each user. F) Association Panel allows editing of assumptions about how closely related command pairs are.

ed is indicated by the size of the marker. A small circle indicates that only a few changes (moves of items) distinguish the two designs. This dimension is useful for designers who may at a later stage of design, want to constrain improvement suggestions to local changes.

3. *Preview*: The template content is previewed when the mouse is hovered over the marker. By clicking, the designer replaces the current menu with the proposed template. Figure 2D shows the preview.

Submenus: MenuOptimizer provides Move/Swap Suggestions for a submenu (Figure 1D) and between submenus. The arrows indicate where to move an item to improve the user's average selection time. Swap suggestions are marked with a double-headed arrow. A box adjacent to the arrow indicates the percentage gain. So as not to overload the display, we display only the three best suggestions at a time.

Items: Designers can also select a command in the menu (click with timeout), and the system renders a colored line next to each item to indicate whether that position would improve or worsen the current menu design.

Separator assignment: On the basis of a predefined threshold for consistency score $C(i, j)$, MenuOptimizer automatically assigns *separators* that mark groups of adjacent items. Computation is done in linear time by comparing consistency scores for adjacent items. Examples of outcomes are shown later in the paper, in Figure 4.

Hotkey Assignment: Upon request, MenuOptimizer assigns hotkeys. Because this important feature is not taken into account by the predictive model, we use a rule-based approach: First, we assign the most common command–hotkey associations (e.g., Ctrl+S for Save), to maintain consistency with expectations. We then assign hotkeys in frequency-based order, using the first letter of the command. Modifiers (e.g., Shift) are added if collisions occur.

Title suggestions: We use the command database to derive candidate *titles* for submenus. For each submenu, we choose the label that is shared by the most commands (voting) as a title. The strategy is conservative: In the case of multiple candidates, no title is suggested to avoid forcing the designer to make corrections. An example is shown in Figure 4.

Editable Objectives and Assumptions

Key aspects of the objective function are directly editable. This forces designers to explicate their assumptions and let them see the implications of these assumptions in real time as the optimizer updates its search problem and visualizations accordingly. It allows them to test different design ideas and explore the robustness of their design with different assumptions about users.

User profiles: The optimality of a menu depends on the target users and their assumed selection behavior. MenuOptimizer allows an arbitrary number of users, each with unique distribution of selections. Internally, a user is represented as a sequence of item selections. User Profile Panel lets designers add users and choose different frequency distributions for commands by clicking and dragging their distribution graphs (Figure 3). An additional feature is the loading of distributions from log files: CSV-formatted log files rendered as distributions that are also directly editable.

Figure 3. User Profile Panel shows directly editable distributions of item selections by users. Designers can change the frequency (A) and the distribution (B).

Locking of item groups: At some point, the designer may want to keep certain items together. Locks (Figure 1F) can be used to constrain items to groups [30] such that subsequent suggestions by the optimizer keep them intact. This mechanism also accelerates optimization because the locked groups reduce the size of the search space.

Submenu optimization: The user can ask the optimizer to optimize only a submenu. The submenu is made inactive for about 10 seconds, during which the optimizer searches for local improvements to this submenu. The suggested improvement can be previewed in place before acceptance.

Association Panel: Designers can edit the automatically suggested co-occurrence scores for command pairs to affect the groupings of items (Figure 2F). They can mark two commands as "Strongly related," "Related," "Slightly related," or "Unknown" simply by clicking the cells.

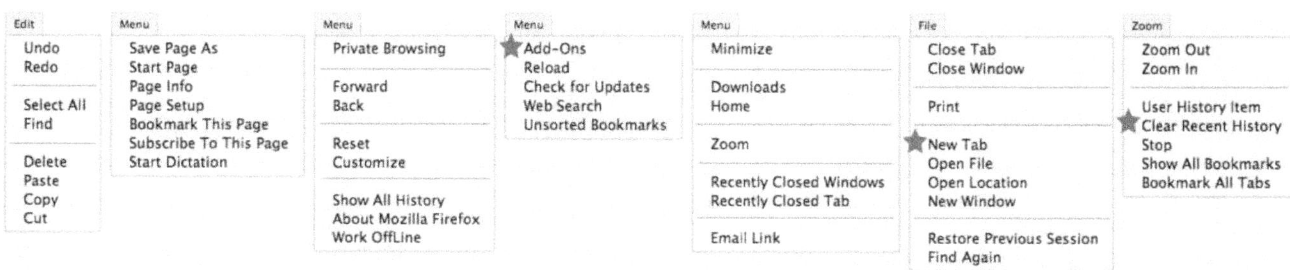

Figure 4: A menu system for the Firefox case proposed after 20,000 iterations (~15 minutes). The objective function had a weight of 75% for consistency and 25% for user performance (asterisks indicate the 3 most frequent items from 50 users' logs).

IMPLEMENTATION

To maintain a high level of interactivity in the editing interface, we use a client–server architecture wherein the optimizer runs on a second computer and communicates its suggestions over XMPP. The optimizer is implemented in Python. Ants are parallelized to accelerate the search. The optimizer is fast enough to run on a regular laptop. We use a MacBook Pro 2.8 Ghz with 8 GB of RAM for all examples reported in this paper.

TECHNICAL ASSESSMENT

This section reports on qualitative and quantitative evaluations of the optimizer system. Because the desirable tradeoff between quality and speed is designer- and application-dependent, we report tests for short-to-mid-term performance and also a benchmark for long-term performance.

Case Studies: SeaShore and Firefox

To assess the quality of the suggestions of the optimizer, we show outputs for two cases: a browser (Firefox) and an image editor (Seashore). Both have ~50 items. The goal for Firefox was to improve its menu design, given logs of real users [10], from which we chose a random sample of 50. Seashore emulates the case wherein a designer is creating a menu system from scratch. The input is a list of commands and our estimates of user behavior. To avoid bias, we use a database for consistency scores (Eq. 2) that does not include the two applications. Output for Firefox after 20,000 iterations (or 15 minutes on a laptop), is presented in Figure 4 (not handpicked). We can observe the following:

- A system with seven submenus was created with no sub-submenus.
- There are many logical groups that are consistent with other applications (e.g., Undo, Redo). The group Delete-Paste-Copy-Cut is interesting. The four are grouped together (consistency) so that users can find them. Moreover, Paste has been moved up because it is the most frequently of the four.
- Because 15 minutes is not sufficient to explore the entire search space, some groups are not optimal (e.g book-marking commands)
- Three menus were given a title by the optimizer. The others would require edits by the designer.
- Because consistency was preferred (75%) for this case, some frequently used items are not prominently placed.

We give examples for Seashore in *Appendix*. The observations are similar and show that the optimizer is not over-calibrated to the Firefox problem. Runtimes for Seashore are about one third due to fewer users.

Temporal Performance

Parameters of the optimizer system were originally calibrated to a scenario allowing a few minutes. To evaluate its ability to improve designs over time, we performed 25 runs of 10,000 iterations (~10 min) for the two optimizers in the system: the greedy searcher and ACO. Seashore and Firefox were used as cases. Figure 5 shows the average temporal performance of the ant colony optimizer against greedy search. A crossover is seen at around 300 iterations (~20 s). After that, ACO is preferable.

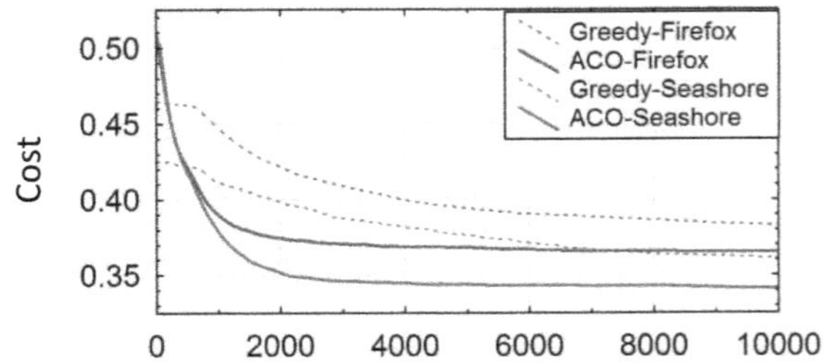

Figure 5: Temporal performance of the optimizer system for the Firefox and Seashore case. In our test setup, 10,000 iterations takes about 10 minutes.

However, the optimizer should, in theory, be useful for different classes of interface problems as long as they can be subsumed to the QAP. We therefore tested it in the context of virtual keyboards. This test is indicative of the performance of ACO when calibrated for a long-term task. Our benchmark is the *Metropolis keyboard* optimized in [34]. We created a version of ACO that uses exactly the same objective function: Fitts' law parameters for stylus movement and digraph frequencies. Parameters were set in a separate trial; we then conducted runs of 50,000 iterations.

Figure 6 shows the distribution of best-found solutions, in comparison to the Metropolis keyboard. The best-found keyboards from ACO were systematically better than Metropolis. The best, *JUSTHCI*, named for the sequence of the first letters on the second row, improves on Metropolis's words per minute (WPM) by 1.8 percent.

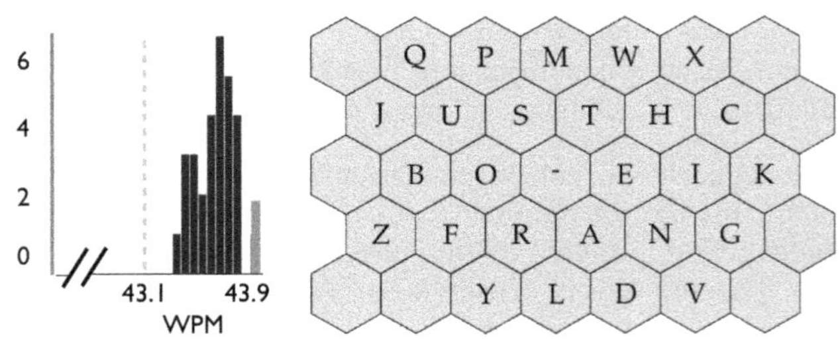

Figure 6: Results of long-term optimization benchmarked against the Metropolis keyboard [34]. The JUSTHCI keyboard (43.9 WPM) outperforms Metropolis (43.1 wpm).

PRELIMINARY USER STUDY

The focus of our user study was on the *joint performance* of the designer and MenuOptimizer. We compared novice designer performances with and without MenuOptimizer in the task of designing medium-complexity (37 and 52 items for Arduino and Seashore, respectively) menus, with a focus on the effect of the functionality that we hypothesized would help the most: using the menu design suggestions appearing in Template Gallery as a basis for editing a menu. We were also keen to understand *how* users use Template Gallery and learn about their rationale for edits.

Participants. Twelve participants without background in menu design (5 females) aged 22 to 44 were recruited from the local university. They received a compensation of 15€.

Experimental design: The study follows a 2 x 2 within-subjects design with *Condition* (MenuOptimizer vs. QtDesigner) and *Task* as the factors (see below). The order of the two factors was counterbalanced.

Tasks. The stated task was to organize commands *in a usable menu system such that its users will easily "understand it" and be able to "quickly select commands."* To avoid order effects, two versions were created: Seashore and Arduino. The first had 52 commands related to image manipulation, the second 37 concerning electronics programming. Tasks were presented on a sheet of paper showing a list of commands with definitions and frequencies.

Procedure. Participants were first instructed in the task and training was carried out with a predefined menu (different from those used during the experiment) for 15 minutes. In both conditions, a single menu was initially filled in with all the commands to let participants focus on organizing commands rather than on entering their names in the interface. Participants could freely move, insert, and remove items and submenus. With MenuOptimizer, they could also use in-place item-level feedback, User Performance Graph, Evolution Graph, and Template Gallery. Participants had 25+15 minutes to perform the task with each system. A semi-structured interview was performed after the study.

Results

For statistical analysis, we used 2 (Condition) x 2 (Task) ANOVA. The effect of *Condition* on time on task was not significant (M=23 mins). Users in both conditions spent about the same amount of time editing their menus. Users were also equally satisfied with their designs in both conditions: the difference in quality ratings between QtDesigner menus (mean Likert rating: 4.4, σ=1.4) and MenuOptimizer menus (M=4.1, σ =1.5) was not statistically significant. However, users made significantly fewer *edits* (37.5%) when using MenuOptimizer than with QtDesigner ($F_{1,20}$=8.15, p =.01), as shown in Figure 7.

User-produced menus were evaluated against model-based predictions of 1) selection time and 2) consistency score (see Figure 8). The same statistical test was used as above, but one menu design was excluded due to a technical problem. First, designs produced with the help of MenuOptimizer (M=2.36s, SE=0.018) are faster than QtDesigner (M=2.41s, SE=0.017) but the statistical test was borderline-significant ($F_{1,19}$ =4.30, p=0.052). Second, the consistency score of MenuOptimizer designs is the same than the one of QtDesigner (both M=0.088, SE=0.005). However, an interaction effect was observed, $F_{1,19}$=5.37, p=0.032. Menus designed with MenuOptimizer had slightly better consistency scores for the more complex task (Seashore; M=0.078 versus 0.094, respectively), whereas scores were worse for the simpler task (Arduino) (M=0.099 versus 0.083). (lower score is better.)

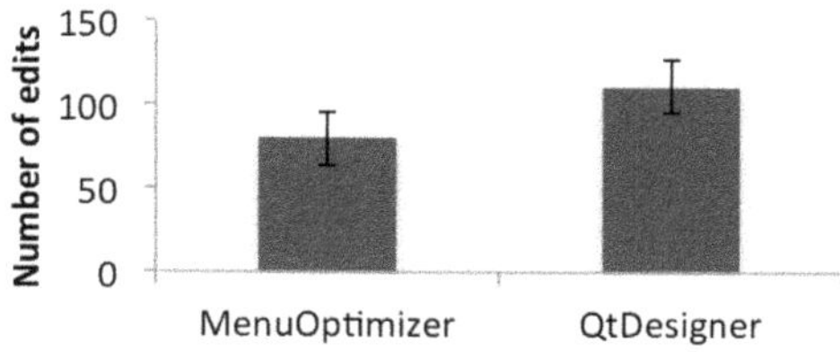

Figure 7: Number of edits required for completing the task.

Observations

Workflow. All users adopted a top-down cascade strategy. They started by using the template gallery. Then, they performed sub-menu level optimization and edits.

Template Gallery. Template Gallery was used differently by different users. Some did not have the patience to wait for good designs and instead selected the first available template and started editing it. Some selected several templates before starting to edit, sometimes only guided by scores in the Pareto plot. Finally, some users used the templates only for inspiration. For instance, one user intensively compared the current menu with suggested templates.

Item Feedback. Users reported that the item-level performance feedback (Figure 1A) is useful because it reminded them to focus also on the performance objective, and it motivated them to move frequent items to the top of groups or menus. However, most users did not understand the color coding. According to the SDP model, the selection time of an item decreases as a function of repetitions rather than as a function of position in the menu. It is, therefore, possible to have a green line for frequent items even if they are deep in the hierarchy. This was found to be confusing.

Rationale for edits. Most users mentioned focusing on groupings rather than selection time because this is the most important objective. One participant mentioned focusing on groupings here because the hierarchy was "quite small" but would focus more on selection time for large ones. All users except one started by grouping items and only afterwards, if at all, focused on selection time.

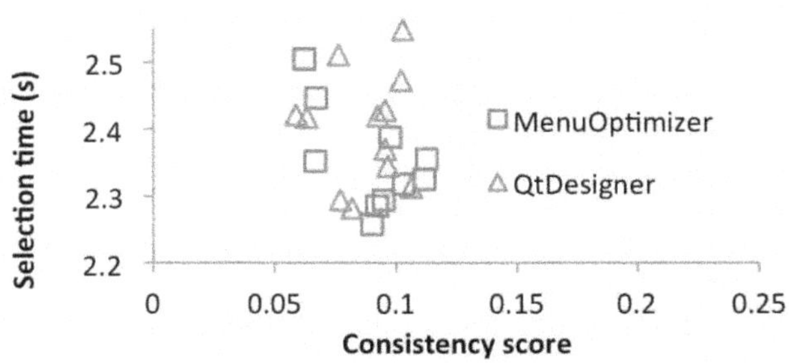

Figure 8: Selection time and consistency score for user-produced designs. Bottom left designs are better.

Discussion

This study is a first step to understand interactive optimization. Our experimental design had to adhere to the constraint of lab studies, and only 15 minutes of practice was given to explain MenuOptimizer. However, novice designers already produced designs they were equally happy with significantly less effort.

The study also provides useful recommendations for the design of MenuOptimizer and more generally interactive optimization systems. First, item feedback should stay simple enough that it does not introduce confusion. For instance, encoding only frequency would probably have been sufficient. Second, the optimizer should even quicker provide a first acceptable design to start with because many users do not have the patience to wait for better designs. Third, many designers seemed to favor the quality of groupings over performance in the beginning stages of design. Our heuristic first-response optimizer worked better for the performance objective but there is room to improve on the grouping aspect to make the suggestions more readily usable. Finally, while MenuOptimizer lets designers compare menu designs with produced templates, it seems important to provide more comparative tools. For instance, by comparing existing designs with previous ones at different levels (menu systems, submenus).

This study also has several limitations requiring additional evaluations and, in particular, longitudinal studies. The time for designing a menu was limited to 30 minutes. With more time, designers can probably better handle functionalities and refine their strategies. Moreover, the evaluation was performed by novice users with medium size menus. More work is needed to understand the needs and behaviors of professional designers. Finally, the 24 produced menus should be experimentally evaluated by final users to evaluate the real impact of MenuOptimizer on user performance.

CONCLUSION AND FUTURE WORK

This paper has investigated interface and optimizer design for the *interactive optimization of menus*. We extended the predictive model of menu performance by introducing a metric for consistency that allows the generation of menu hierarchies and item groups. We proposed MenuOptimizer, an interface providing feedback methods and proactive suggestions to operate menus at different levels of granularity: items, menus, and menu systems. This changes the design process. Instead of organizing items one by one, the designer specifies the problem and starts the design process on the basis of a template, and the system assists the designer in further edits. We have shown that the menu design problem can be formulated in terms of a QAP problem and we proposed an adaptation of the ant colony meta-heuristic that better matches the requirements of interactive and iterative design.

There are two kinds of evidence for the usefulness of this approach: 1) A user study shows that novice designers generate designs that equally satisfy them but with 38% less editing. 2) The temporal response curve of the optimizer system better suits interactive editing tasks than the prevailing "fire or forget" approach.

Finally, we see several opportunities to improve our approach.

Menu systems. The present work is limited to linear menus and should be extended to cover hotkeys, ribbons and palettes. We are currently working on a predictive model of learning and adoption of hotkeys.

Semantics. "Semantics" is a strong factor in menu use. Our approach was to use the consistency of item collocation as a secondary optimization objective. Although it allows grouping items and setting a hierarchy, it does not take into account the fact that semantics is actually a cognitive factor (or many). Ideally, semantics would be part of the predictive model. Improvements are possible via integration of knowledge of relationships like synonyms, antonyms, or tools such as Wordnet or LSA. Previous work in modeling users' navigation in hierarchies could also provide a useful starting point for this work [18].

Predictive model. More generally, developing predictive models is the key to understanding user behavior and developing optimization methods. Existing models should be empirically validated in the field: The question is still open whether behavior predicted by such models actually hold for end-users in longer-term use.

Scalability. Our optimizer presently deals well with medium size menu systems (~50 items). We are yet to see how it scales up as the number increases to hundreds. We believe that for such cases, both the optimizer and the interface will need to better guide the designer to partition a problem. For instance, the Layer menu in PhotoShop has 30 items, and is a design problem of its own.

ACKNOWLEDGMENTS

We thank R. Kirsten, H. Du, A. Roudaut, C. Coutrix, P-O. Kristensson, A. Jameson, M. Löchtefeld, K. Hornbaek, A. Krueger, H-J. Mueller for help and comments. This work has partially been funded by the Cluster of Excellence Multimodal Computing and Interaction within the German Federal Excellence Initiative.

REFERENCES

1. Ahlstrom, D. Modelling and improving selection in cascading pull-down menus using Fitt's law, the steering law and force fields. ACM CHI'05. (2005), 61-70.
2. Ahlstrom, D., Cockburn, A., Gutwin, C., Irani, P. Why it's quick to be square: modeling new and existing hierarchical menu designs. ACM CHI'10. (2010), 1371-1380.
3. Anderson, D., Anderson, E., Lesh, N., Marks, J., Mirtich, B., Ratajczak, D. and Ryall, K. 2000. Human-guided simple search. AAAI'00, 209-216.
4. Burkard,R.E.,and Offermann,D.M.J .Entwurf von schreibmaschinentastaturen mittels quadratischer zuordnungsprobleme. Zeitschrift für Operations Research 21, 4 (1977), B121–B132.
5. Cockburn, A., Gutwin, C. and Greenberg, S. A predictive model of menu performance. ACM CHI '07, (2007), 627-636.

6. Cross, N. Expertise in design: an overview. Design studies 25, 5 (2004), 427–441.
7. Dorigo,M.,Birattari,M.,and Stutzle,T.Ant colony optimization. Computational Intelligence Magazine 1, 4 (2006), 28–39.
8. Eggers,J.,Feillet,D.,Kehl,S.,Wagner,M.,and Yannou,B. Optimization of the keyboard arrangement problem using an ant colony algorithm. European Journal of Operational Research 148, 3 (2003), 672–686.
9. Fogarty, J., Hudson, S. E. GADGET: a toolkit for optimization-based approaches to interface and display generation. ACM UIST'03. (2003), 125-134.
10. https://testpilot.mozzilalabs.com/testcases/menu-item-usage/
11. Gajos, K. and Weld, D. S. SUPPLE: automatically generating user interfaces. ACM IUI'04, (2004), 93-100.
12. Gajos K., Wobbrock, J. O. and Weld, D. S. Automatically generating user interfaces adapted to users' motor and vision capabilities. ACM UIST'07, (2007), 231-240.
13. Gajos, K, Wobbrock, J. O and Weld, D. S. Improving the performance of motor-impaired users with automatically-generated, ability-based interfaces. ACM CHI '08, (2008), 1257-1266.
14. Goubko M. V. and Danilenko A. I. An automated routine for menu structure optimization. ACM EICS'10, (2010), 67-76.
15. Gould J. D. and Lewis, C. Designing for usability: key principles and what designers think. Commun. ACM 28, 3, (1985), 300-311.
16. Horvitz, E.. Principles of mixed-initiative user interfaces. ACM CHI '99, (1999), 159-166.
17. Kim, W. C. and Foley, J. D. Don: user interface presentation design assistant. ACM UIST '90, (1990), 10–20.
18. Kitajima, M., Blackmon, M., Polson, P. A comprehension-based model of web navigation and its application to web usability analysis. *People and Comp. XIV*, Springer (2000), pp. 357-373.
19. Lane, D., Napier, A., Peres, C., and Sandor, A. The Hidden Costs of Graphical User Interfaces: The Failure to Make the Transition from Menus and Icon Tool Bars to Keyboard Shortcuts. IJHCS. 18 (2005), 133--144.
20. Lee, E. MacGregor, J. Minimizing user search time in menu retrieval systems. Hum. Fact. 27, 2, (1985), 157-162
21. Light,L.W.,and Anderson,P.G. Typewriter keyboards via simulated annealing. AI Expert (1993).
22. Malacria, S., Bailly, G, Harrison, J., Cockburn, A. and Gutwin, C. 2013. Promoting Hotkey use through rehearsal with ExposeHK. ACM CHI '13, (2013),, 573-582.
23. Matsui S. and Yamada, S. Genetic algorithm can optimize hierarchical menus. ACM CHI'08, (2008) 1385-1388.
24. Oulasvirta,A. et al. Improving two-thumb text entry on touchscreen devices. ACM CHI'13, (2013).
25. Paap,K.,and Cooke,N.Designing menus,(1997).
26. Poltrock, S. E. and Grudin, J. Organizational obstacles to interface design and development: two participant-observer studies. ACM TOCHI'94. 1, 1, (1994) 52-80.
27. Quiroz, J. C., Louis, S. J. and Dascalu S. M. Interactive evolution of XUL user interfaces. ACM GECCO '07, (2007), 2151-2158.
28. Raneburger, D., Popp, R., and Vanderdonckt, J. 2012. An automated layout approach for model-driven WIMP-UI generation. ACM EICS'12, 91-100.
29. Rao, S. S. Engineering Optimization: Theory and Practice, (2009).
30. Scott, S. D., Lesh, N., Klau, G. W. Investigating Human-Computer Optimization. ACM CHI'02. (2002), 155-162.
31. Sears. A. 1993. Layout Appropriateness: A Metric for Evaluating User Interface Widget Layout. IEEE Trans. Softw. Eng. 19, 7 (July 1993), 707-719.
32. Sears, A. AIDE: a step toward metric-based interface development tools. ACM UIST '95, (1995), 101-110.
33. Stutzle,T.,and Dorigo,M. ACO algorithms for the quadratic assignment problem. New Ideas in Optimization (1999), 33–50.
34. Zhai, S., Hunter, M., and Smith, B. A. The metropolis keyboard - an exploration of quantitative techniques for virtual keyboard design. ACM UIST '00, (2000), 119-128.
35. Zhai,S., Sue,A.,and Accot,J. Movement model, hits distribution and learning in virtual keyboarding. ACM CHI'02, (2002), 17–24.

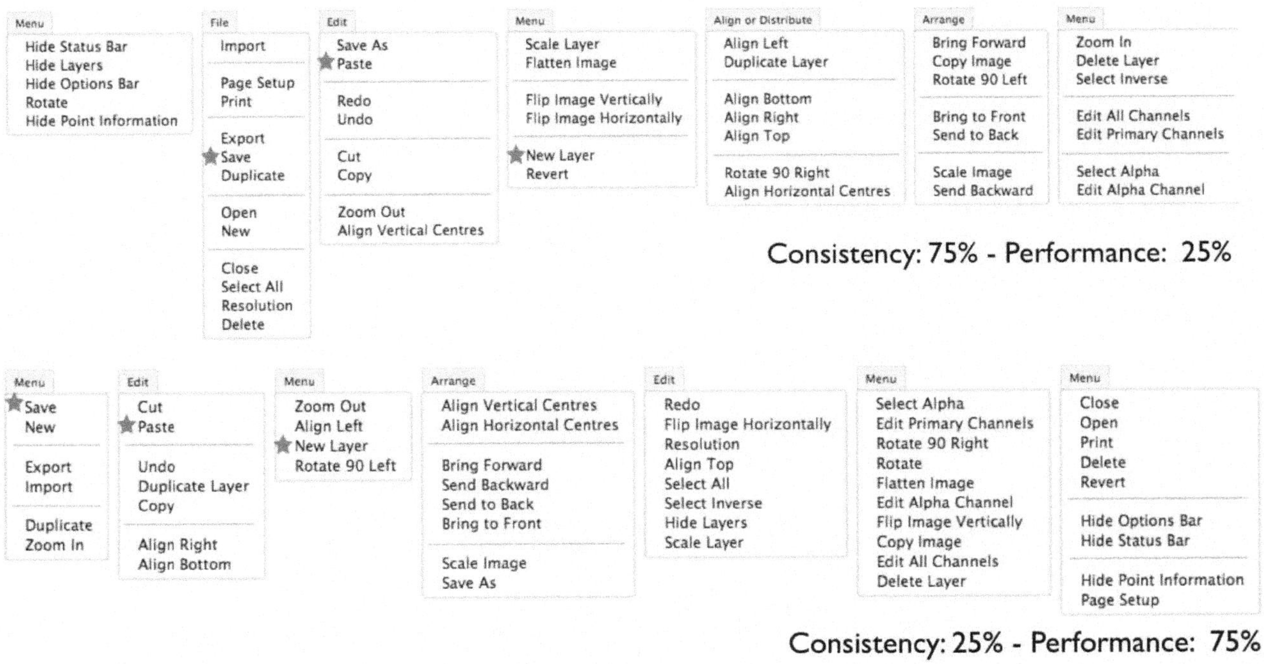

The Auckland Layout Editor: An Improved GUI Layout Specification Process

Clemens Zeidler, Christof Lutteroth
University of Auckland
Auckland 1010, New Zealand
{clemens,christof}@cs.auckland.ac.nz

Wolfgang Stuerzlinger
York University
Toronto, Canada M3J 1P3
wolfgang@cse.yorku.ca

Gerald Weber
University of Auckland
Auckland 1010, New Zealand
gerald@cs.auckland.ac.nz

ABSTRACT

Layout managers are used to control the placement of widgets in graphical user interfaces (GUIs). Constraint-based layout managers are among the most powerful. However, they are also more complex and their layouts are prone to problems such as over-constrained specifications and widget overlap. This poses challenges for GUI builder tools, which ideally should address these issues automatically.

We present a new GUI builder – the Auckland Layout Editor (ALE) – that addresses these challenges by enabling GUI designers to specify constraint-based layouts using simple, mouse-based operations. We give a detailed description of ALE's edit operations, which do not require direct constraint editing. ALE guarantees that all edit operations lead to sound specifications, ensuring solvable and non-overlapping layouts. To achieve that, we present a new algorithm that automatically generates the constraints necessary to keep a layout non-overlapping. Furthermore, we discuss how our innovations can be combined with manual constraint editing in a sound way. Finally, to aid designers in creating layouts with good resize behavior, we propose a novel automatic layout preview. This displays the layout at its minimum and in an enlarged size, which allows visualizing potential resize issues directly. All these features permit GUI developers to focus more on the overall UI design.

ACM Classification Keywords

H.5.2 User Interfaces: Graphical user interfaces (GUI)

Author Keywords

GUI builder; layout editing; constraint-based layout; layout manager

INTRODUCTION

The use of graphical user interfaces (GUIs) is widespread, including on web and mobile platforms. WYSIWYG GUI builders facilitate the creation of GUIs by designers. In such tools, widgets are dragged and dropped from a palette onto a GUI canvas. Subsequently, they are selected, moved, resized, and adjusted in order to compose the final GUI layout.

UIST'13, October 8–11, 2013, St. Andrews, United Kingdom.

http://dx.doi.org/10.1145/2501988.2502007

Nowadays the same application may be used across a wide range of screen sizes, such as desktop machines, tablets and mobile phones. Resizable GUIs are also recommended by modern GUI guidelines[1]. Consequently, it is important that a GUI stays sound at different sizes. To create resizable GUIs with dynamic layouts, a *layout manager* can be used. A layout manager implements a *layout model* that defines how objects in a layout, the *widgets*, can be arranged and how their resize behavior can be specified.

Constraint-based layout models are naturally powerful: with the notable exception of flow layouts, many other layout models, including gridbag layout [26], can be reduced to constraint-based layouts (see also Figure 1). For example, the "LCD" display in iTunes[2] is always centered at the top of the window between other widgets, but this is usually not possible with other layout models. Many other layout managers rely on a hierarchy of nested layouts to define more complex layouts. Within nested layouts, widgets typically cannot be aligned across different levels of the hierarchy. In contrast, constraint-based layout models greatly reduce the need for nested layouts, even for visually hierarchical layouts. Constraints can align widgets that are situated in different parts of a visually hierarchical layout [17]. Constraint-based layout managers use a dedicated or off-the-shelf constraint solver to compute widget positions and sizes.

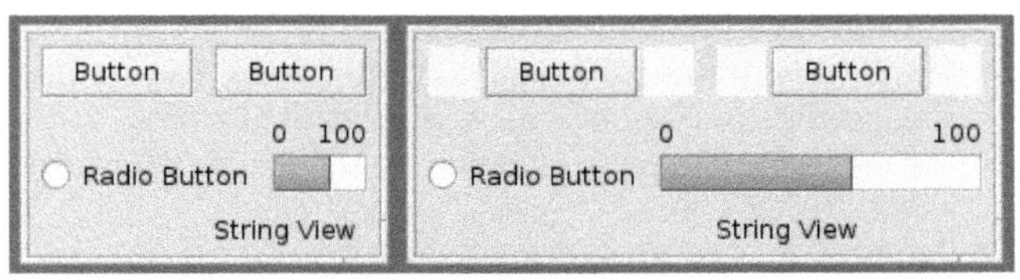

Figure 1. Example constraint-based layout. The behavior of the middle row is independent from the top and bottom rows when resizing. This is impossible to achieve with a single gridbag layout.

While constraint-based layouts are more powerful, their creation may be more complex and poses challenges. General constraints are difficult to visualize and even harder to manipulate directly. Specifying individual constraints can be tedious and error-prone, as they are situated at a low level of abstraction. Thus widgets may overlap each other (Figure 2)

[1] `developer.android.com/training/multiscreen/screensizes.html`
`msdn.microsoft.com/en-us/library/windows/desktop/aa511331.aspx`
[2] `apple.com/itunes`

or become over-constrained, i.e., the layout may have no solution. This makes it harder for GUI designers to leverage the advantages of constraints.

The novel Auckland Layout Editor (ALE) addresses these issues and simplifies the creation and modification of constraint-based layouts. Here, we present a complete description of ALE's layout edit operations, which maintain constraints automatically and hence require fewer operations to configure widgets correctly. In particular, we present a new method for automatically identifying all constraints necessary to maintain a given layout, based on a tiling of orthogonal polygons into rectangles, and we explain how this method is used during layout editing. The output of this method ensures that layouts stay non-overlapping for all sizes and that they always have a unique solution. While ALE's edit operations enable quick creation of the most common layouts, arbitrary constraints can also be added via auxiliary dialogs. We demonstrate how ALE's edit operations can work together with general constraint editing while keeping the layout specifications sound, i.e., non-overlapping and solvable. A recent user study found that ALE's edit operations can make layout creation and editing significantly faster than other modern GUI builders [29]. Furthermore, we present a novel approach to visualizing the resize behavior of a window. Layout design usually happens at a fixed size, yet the resulting layout should also look good at different sizes. Currently this requires explicit manual testing by the designer. To help the designer to better evaluate the resize behavior, we present a new preview that automatically shows appropriately shrunk and enlarged versions during editing.

Contributions

We present several innovations and improvements to the GUI layout creation process. In particular, we introduce:

- Detailed specifications of edit operations for constraint-based layouts that automatically keep a layout sound and solvable and speed up layout editing.
- A new algorithm that automatically adds constraints at design-time to prevent widget overlap at all sizes.
- An extension to permit manual constraint addition and editing in the system.
- A novel way to visualize the resize behavior of a layout during the design phase.

REQUIREMENTS FOR LAYOUT EDITING

In this section we specify our design goals for ALE. These are derived from related work, existing usability guidelines, and our own experience with layout creation. We also define requirements for all layout specifications that can be created with a GUI builder. We differentiate between concrete layouts, as they are rendered on a screen, and *layout specifications*, which can be rendered at many different sizes and hence lead to many concrete layouts. Our design goals can be subdivided into usability, completeness, and soundness requirements. Common usability guidelines [14, 18] naturally apply to GUI builders. In particular, a builder should be intuitive, easy to use, and edit operations should lead to predictable results. Common GUI design guidelines, such as [6], emphasize that it is not desirable to place widgets completely "freely", i.e., at an arbitrary position in a layout. Aligned layouts are more compact and easier to understand [9]. Consequently, widgets should be easy to align and the system should automatically maintain such alignments.

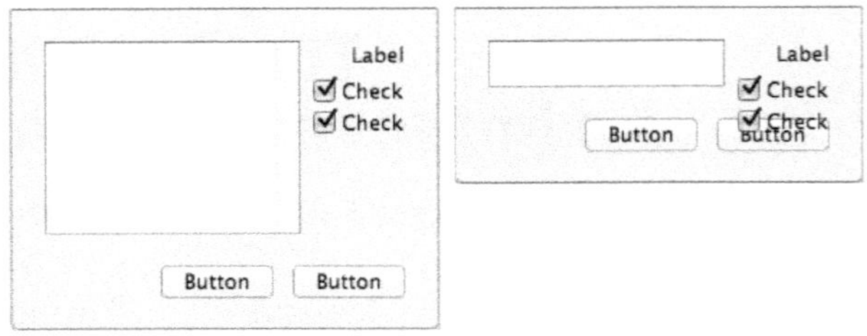

Figure 2. The constraint-based layout on the left appears sound. Yet, at the smaller size shown on the right, widgets overlap due to a missing constraint. The constraint-based GUI builder used, Apple Xcode, gave no indication of this issue.

Completeness guarantees that every correct layout specification that is both possible in the underlying layout model and appropriate in practice can actually be created.

Soundness ensures that every layout specification that can be created is correct and adequate, i.e., no erroneous layouts can be created. Here we use three soundness requirements.

Unique Solution A layout specification must have exactly one solution. When computing a layout, the underlying specification needs to be *solved*, i.e., a concrete visual layout needs to be generated. If the specification contains conflicts, then there is no solution. If there is more than one solution, then the layout may behave non-deterministically. For example, if the position of a widget is underspecified it may "randomly" change its position during resizing, which is undesirable.

Non-Overlap A layout specification must be non-overlapping, i.e., in all layouts derived from the specification, widgets may not intersect each other or the boundaries. This property ensures that all widgets are completely visible and accessible at all GUI sizes. A widget that is overlapped by another may be inaccessible and thus useless (Figure 2).

Well-Defined Layout Sizes Each layout specification must have a single minimum, preferred, and maximum layout size. It is theoretically possible for a layout specification to have multiple valid extreme sizes (Figure 3). Yet, such situations are not desirable. First, window managers support only a single minimum and maximum window size. Secondly, in order to keep the layout non-overlapping, "or" constraints must be used, which are difficult to solve. Last, a layout with multiple extreme sizes potentially has a very different appearance at different sizes, which may confuse users. Note that we still permit discrete layout specification changes at runtime. For example, when the screen is rotated one can switch between different layout specifications with different extreme sizes.

RELATED WORK

Myers [19] summarized various non-constraint-based techniques for creating GUIs, including graphical tools for placing interface objects on screens. IBuild [25] enabled the cre-

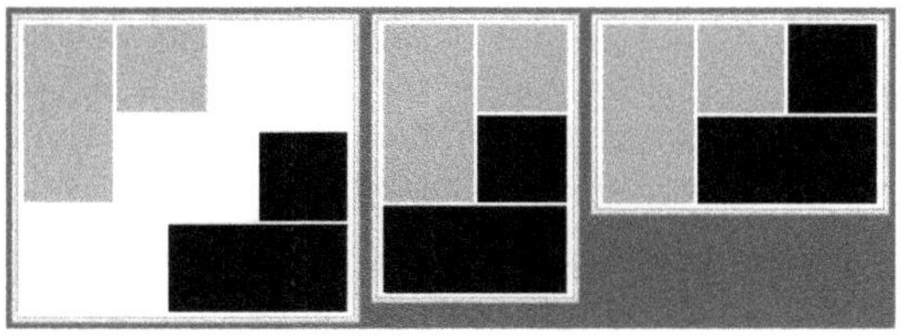

Figure 3. Layout with two possible minimum sizes.

ation of complex GUIs in a WYSIWYG manner. It already supported nested layouts, spring-like layout elements, and interactive testing of resizing. Druid [23] predicted intended alignment and spacing of a widget during editing, facilitating placement. FormsVBT [1] supported simultaneous editing of a textual and a graphical representation of a layout.

Some GUI builders permit manual constraint editing. OPUS used tabstops for specifying constraints [10]. Lapidary [27] provided rich constraint editing functions. In the Gilt system [8], widgets could be aligned relative to user-specified tabstops or other widgets. In the Intui GUI builder [22], constraints can be toggled between struts and springs, between and inside widgets. Yet, only one constraint per widget side is supported, which can make it impossible to create non-overlapping layout specifications. Peridot [20] analyzes objects drawn by the user and guesses constraints to be added. The user then has to confirm the proposed constraints. Rockit [16] automatically proposes constraints based on the "gravity field" of other objects. The user can select the desired constraints from a set. This is similar to previous work where constraints are inferred by snapping graphical objects relative to other objects [11]. In ALE widgets can be snapped to others in order to set up the corresponding constraints. However, ALE adds more powerful edit operations, such as inserting a widget between others and swapping widgets. Bramble [7] connects objects using a set of interactors, which establish non-linear constraints. While this can be used to prevent overlap, the user has to add interactors manually. ALE adds such constraints automatically.

Today, there are many open-source GUI builders, such as WindowBuilder Pro[3], Matisse/Swing[4], and Qt Designer[5]. There are also commercial GUI builders, such as MS Expression Blend[6] and Visual Studio[7]. Most of them support aligning widgets via snapping, but do not maintain alignment when objects are moved or resized. Also, layouts must be resized manually in order to evaluate their resize behavior. In contrast, ALE's edit operations keep widgets aligned by default. ALE also provides an automatic preview of resize behavior.

Apple added support for constraints to the Xcode Interface Builder[8] in 2012. It aligns objects via snapping, but also permits free placement of widgets. Constraints between widgets can be added manually but are removed upon conflict. All the abovementioned constraint-based approaches require that the user knows how to specify constraints manually. In contrast, ALE enables the creation of many interesting layouts without exposing a single constraint to the user. Moreover, the edit operations automatically maintain all constraints for snapped items and for non-overlap. ALE disables conflicting manual constraints to support error diagnosis. Finally, a recent comparison between Xcode and ALE confirms that our new approach results in better usability [29].

Adaptive document layout [12] in the print and web domains is somewhat similar to GUI layout. However, the flow of a document constrains placement differently than a GUI. Documents typically arrange text and images in a sequential manner, and support more flexibility in the layout using algorithms for figure placement, line-break, and pagination. Grid-based [15] as well as constraint-based [3, 13] methods have been used for document layout.

Firefox's responsive design view[9] can simulate a GUI at different screen sizes. Also Android Studio[10] shows layouts at different device sizes. However, this does not take an optimally enlarged layout size into account. FormsVBT [1] supports a graphical and a textual edit view as well as a result view. However, the result and graphical edit views are displayed at a fixed size and give no indication of how a layout would look at a different size. In contrast, ALE shows a live preview of the layout at the minimum and an optimally enlarged layout size. This reduces the potential for user errors, as the resize behavior is visualized immediately and directly. ALE's layout previews are targeted particularly at situations where enough constraints exist, but do not lead to the desired resize behavior. In these situations, displaying all constraints clutters the design view, which does little to help the designer quickly identify the problem.

THE AUCKLAND LAYOUT EDITOR (ALE)

Similarly to other GUI builders, ALE uses a component palette and an editing canvas (Figure 4). Widgets are dragged from the palette into the editing canvas, where the designer can change the layout using a rich set of edit operations. We first describe the constraint system used in ALE, which is conceptually similar to other such systems.

A layout consists of various types of *layout items*, such as widgets and nested layouts. In the following and for brevity, we refer to all layout items simply as widgets. Each widget has an intrinsic *minimum*, *preferred*, and *maximum size*. A widget assumes its preferred size if there are no other constraints for it, similarly to the behavior of a sponge. ALE includes a special type of widget that can act as a strut or spring.

Layout items are connected via constraints. ALE supports two types of linear constraints: *hard* constraints, which have

[3] `eclipse.org/windowbuilder`
[4] `netbeans.org/features/java/swing.html`
[5] `qt.nokia.com`
[6] `microsoft.com/expression/products/Blend_Overview.aspx`
[7] `microsoft.com/visualstudio/en-us`
[8] `developer.apple.com/technologies/tools`
[9] `developer.mozilla.org/en-US/docs/Tools/Responsive_Design_View`
[10] `developer.android.com/sdk/installing/studio.html`

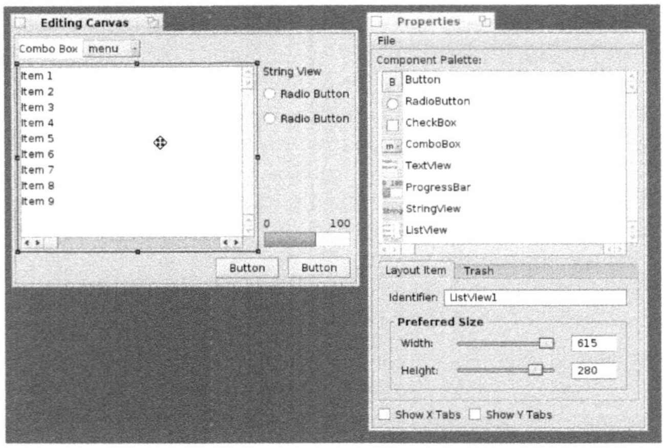

Figure 4. Screenshot of the ALE GUI builder. New widgets can be inserted into the editing canvas on the left via drag and drop from the component palette on the right.

to be satisfied, and *soft* ones, which may be violated if necessary. We support both equality and inequality constraints.

Variables in a constraint are called *tabstops* and represent horizontal or vertical grid lines. Other frequently used names for the same concept are aligners, guides, and snap or anchor lines. Each window defines tabstops for its four borders, so that they can be used for alignment. Tabstops are reference counted, which allows unused ones to be removed automatically.

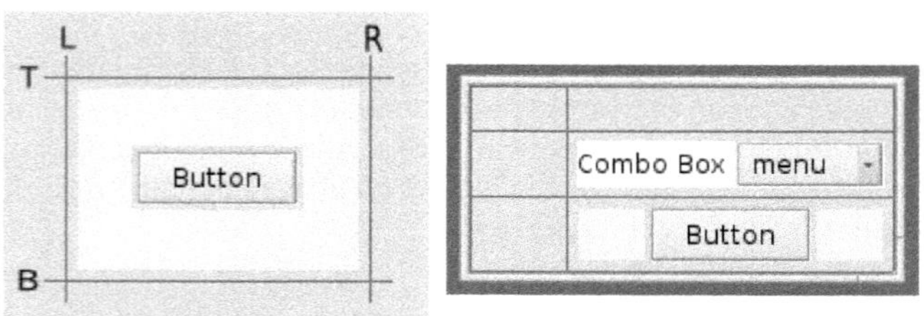

Figure 5. Left: Widgets are by default automatically centered in their layout area (light gray). The area is surrounded by a margin and four tabstops. ALE shows tabstops as blue lines. Right: A combo box and a button are connected to the same vertical tabstops. As the combo box cannot shrink further, the button is centered.

Within the overall layout, each widget is associated with a rectangular *layout area* that is surrounded by four tabstops. As most layouts use margins, there is by default a small margin between the layout areas and their tabstops (Figure 5). When inserting a widget into a layout, some constraints are automatically derived from the intrinsic sizes of a widget: a hard inequality for the minimum, a soft equality for the preferred, and a soft inequality for the maximum size. These constraints are defined both horizontally and vertically and are managed by the associated layout area. Consequently, users do not need to manage constraints for intrinsic sizes manually. The preferred size of a widget can be fine-tuned in the properties window. This is comparable to changing the "weight" of a row or column in a gridbag layout. If the size of the layout area is between a widget's minimum and maximum size, the widget uses the whole space of the area. If the widget cannot grow, it is centered in the area by default (Figure 5). The user has the option to align the widget to any border or corner of the layout area. Also, the user can fine-tune widget positions by changing the margins.

In contrast to most other systems, ALE uses a quadratic optimization function with an active set solver [5]. This method is fast enough for GUI problems [4]. We found that solving layouts with 30 widgets can be done in the order of 10 ms (Intel Core 2 Duo 3GHz). Soft preferred size constraints together with a quadratic optimization function ensure that there is a unique layout solution, as a convex objective function has a unique minimum. A linear optimization function cannot ensure this, as there is in general an infinite number of solutions for the soft constraints, which leads to underdetermined widget sizes [28].

Many useful layouts can be specified simply by aligning layout areas with each other. Such layouts naturally reuse tabstops for multiple layout areas and thus need no additional constraints. See, e.g., Figure 5, where the top tabstop of the button is reused as the bottom tabstop of the combo box. A layout consisting of fully connected layout areas is always solvable as long as the containing window is large enough, because the maximum constraints are soft and thus no conflicts can occur (e.g., in Figure 5 the button's maximum size constraint is violated, as it has a fixed size).

ALE LAYOUT EDIT OPERATIONS

Ideally, a GUI builder should make the creation of a constraint-based layout easy and intuitive. If a GUI builder exposes each constraint, margin, tabstop, strut or spring directly to the user, this significantly increases the complexity of layout editing. In other words, the user has to create, correctly configure, and maintain a substantially larger number of entities to achieve a given result. To avoid this, ALE's layout edit operations were designed to automate the construction and maintenance of the layout specification as much as possible, while still ensuring that the operations are sufficient to create and edit complex GUIs.

As in most GUI builders, a GUI can be created and edited by drag and drop operations. The edit operations provided are moving, swapping, resizing, inserting, and removing of a layout area and the widget contained therein. All operations try to connect layout areas to existing tabstops through snapping, and create as few new tabstops as possible. Reusing tabstops leads to good alignment and simpler layout specifications that are easier to understand. Only the intrinsic size constraints are updated when a layout area is connected to new tabstops, and new constraints are added only in a few cases. Furthermore, all operations are designed to leave an initially sound layout in a sound state. Thus no overlap between widgets can be generated. In the following sections and for brevity, we describe only the horizontal case for each operation. Vertical cases are handled analogously.

Edit operations are started by dragging a widget or a border of a selected widget. Then, ALE checks at each mouse position whether an operation can be applied and gives corresponding visual feedback (Figure 6). This is done by applying the operation tentatively in the background and checking the result. If an operation is applicable, the user can commit it by "dropping" the widget, and the result becomes visible. In general, edit operations can affect multiple widgets and a layout may differ in several places after an operation. To help the user understand the changes, a short animation visualizes how affected widgets are altered. All edit operations can be reverted using undo. Inserting, removing, moving and swapping of widgets are done via dragging the widget; dragging a border is used for resizing.

Inserting a Widget

New widgets can be inserted into the layout by drag and drop from the widget palette into the edit canvas. When dragging a widget, it is visualized as a dotted rectangle, the *dragged widget outline*, which has the preferred size of the dragged widget. We limit the size of the dragged widget outline to a reasonable one to avoid problems with very large widgets. Two cases need to be considered when inserting a new widget into the layout. A widget can be inserted into an empty area (Figure 7) or it can be placed between an existing tabstop and a widget adjacent to that tabstop (Figure 8).

Inserting into an Empty Area

A widget can be inserted into an empty area if the mouse position is in that empty area. Dropping the dragged widget into an empty area must constrain that widget to at least two tabstops, one in each direction, because of the requirement for a unique solution. If an edge of the widget is close to a tabstop, the widget is snapped to that tabstop. If the widget can only be snapped to a single tabstop in one direction, a new tabstop is created at the opposite widget edge.

If the widget cannot be snapped to any existing tabstop in a given direction, we solve the problem in a novel way. In this case, the largest rectangular empty area that completely contains the dragged widget outline is identified (Figure 6). If the outline overlaps another non-empty layout area, i.e., no rectangular empty area completely contains the outline, the largest empty rectangular area that contains the mouse position is used. For the direction in question, the widget is then connected to the outer tabstops of this largest rectangular empty area. This is also an easy way to fill a whole rectangular empty area with a resizable widget.

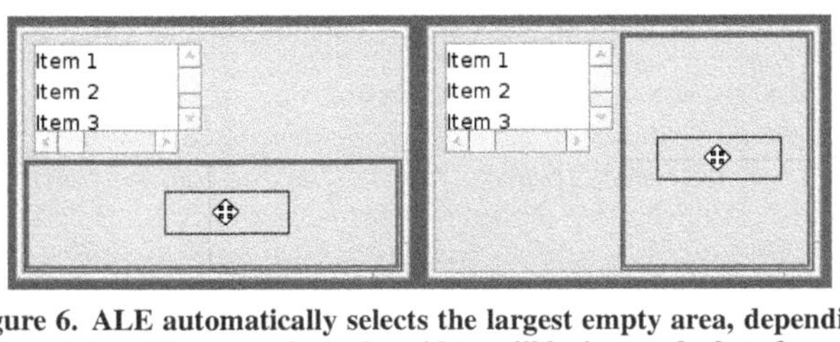

Figure 6. ALE automatically selects the largest empty area, depending on user input. The area where the widget will be inserted when dropped is highlighted in green. Here, the widget is entirely within the lower empty area (left) or within the right one (right). In the lower-right quadrant, the larger (right) area would be used.

These rules enable the user to select the desired area in an intuitive way. The combination of being able to use the full extent of an empty area or simply to snap a widget to one corner or border makes this operation quite versatile (Figure 7), see also the Tk pack model[11].

Figure 7. A widget can be inserted at various positions within an empty rectangular area. Left: Far from the tabstops, the dragged widget fills the whole empty area. Middle: When close to only the left tabstop, the widget snaps to that tabstop and resizes vertically. The right edge creates a new tabstop. Right: When close to the left and bottom tabstops, the widget is constrained to the corner.

Inserting between Tabstop and Area

A widget can be inserted at any existing tabstop. To trigger this operation, the mouse position must be over an existing widget and close to a tabstop, i.e., an edge, of that widget. One edge of the new widget then aligns with that existing tabstop, while a new tabstop is created for the opposite edge. The existing widget is connected to the new tabstop (Figure 8). Initially, the size of the new widget is *temporarily* set to zero, as the final size is determined later by the solver.

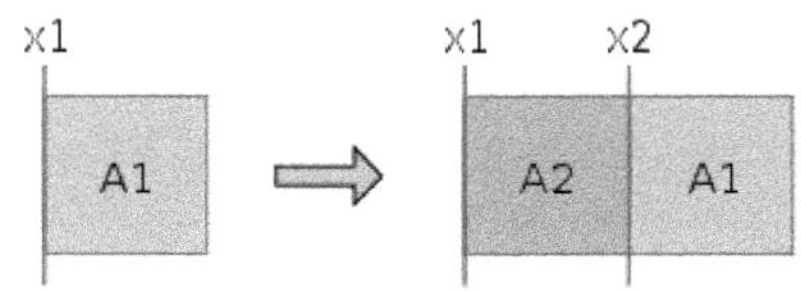

Figure 8. When inserting a new widget $A2$ between area $A1$ and tabstop $x1$, a new tabstop $x2$ is added.

Once the new widget has been inserted at an existing tabstop in one direction (say horizontal), it must also be connected in the other (vertical) direction. If its preferred height is smaller than the height of the existing widget, the new widget is either connected to the top or the bottom tabstop of the existing widget, whichever is closer. In this case, a new tabstop is added at the opposite vertical side of the new widget. Figure 9 shows such an example where a small button is inserted beside a larger text view. If the preferred height of the new widget is larger or close to the height of the existing widget, the new widget is connected to both the top and the bottom tabstop of the existing widget. Because the maximum size constraints of the existing widget are soft, this never generates a conflict.

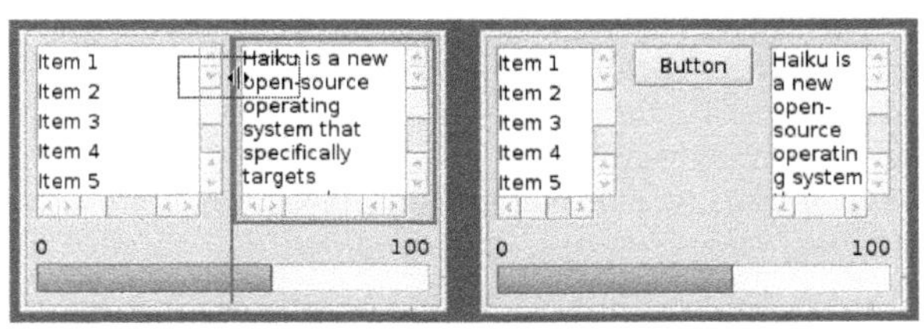

Figure 9. Inserting a small button at an existing tabstop between a list and a text view. The existing tabstop and widget are highlighted in green. As the button is dropped close to the top of the text view, it is connected to its top tabstop.

[11] `tcl.tk/man/tcl8.6/TkCmd/pack.htm`

Removing Widgets

A widget is removed from the layout by dragging it outside the edit canvas. Any created gaps are filled, see below.

Moving Widgets

When moving a widget, a valid position for the insertion is determined and then the widget is moved from its original place. Here the same logic is used as for insertion. However, when looking for an insertion position the area occupied by the moving widget is ignored. This makes it impossible to snap a widget to itself, for example.

Swapping Two Widgets

Dropping one widget onto another swaps the positions of the two widgets. Here it is sufficient to connect the moved widget to the tabstops of the other one and vice versa.

Resizing a Widget

When a widget is connected to wrong/undesired tabstops, the user can adjust this with a resize operation. Resizing is done by dragging one of the borders or corners of a widget. During resizing, all relevant tabstops are visualized as light blue lines to aid alignment. There are two cases to consider. First, a widget may be resized to an existing tabstop, via snapping (Figure 10). Here, the system ensures that the resized widget does not overlap with any other one; otherwise, the resize operation is not permitted. Secondly, a widget can be resized to match its preferred size. This occurs when the dragged border is released in an empty area, i.e., without snapping. In this case, a new tabstop is created for the dragged border (two for a corner). This can also be interpreted as detaching a widget from a tabstop. Preferred sizes can be adjusted via the properties window (Figure 4 bottom right).

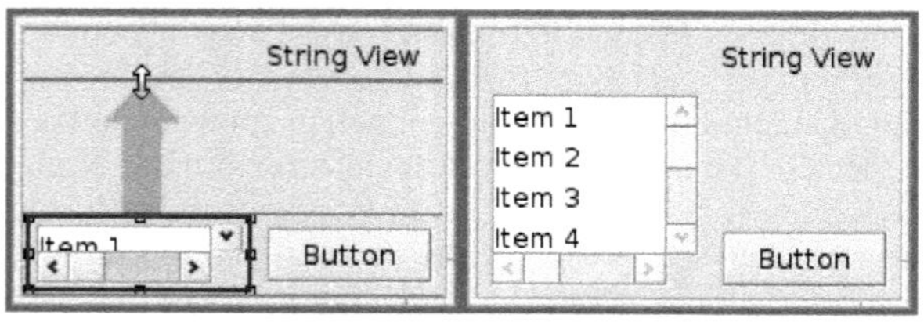

Figure 10. Resizing the top of the list widget to the bottom of the string.

Filling Gaps

A move, resize, or remove operation can detach adjacent widgets as one or more widgets may lose their connection to a tapstop. This is usually visible as a "gap". Such "gaps" and the associated "floating" widgets violate the unique solution requirement (Figure 11). ALE avoids this by checking for unconnected widgets after remove, move and resize operations. If the layout contains parts that are unconnected, all "floating" widget groups are moved one after another into the direction where the removed widget has been located. For example, if a group was connected to the right side of the removed or resized widget, the group is moved to the left. When the foremost widget of the floating group hits the border of another widget, it is connected with the corresponding tabstop of the other widget (Figure 11). During this process the moved group may become connected to another floating group. Groups are moved until they are connected directly or indirectly to at least one horizontal and one vertical layout border.

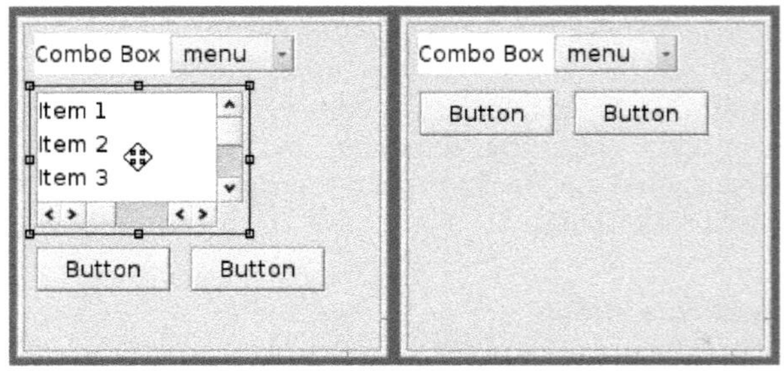

Figure 11. Filling gaps: Upon removal of the list widget, the two buttons both "float" vertically. Moving the button group up fills the gap. The tops of the buttons are connected to the bottom of the combo box.

NON-OVERLAPPING LAYOUTS

We start with a formal definition of *non-overlap* to explain how ALE guarantees non-overlapping layouts. A widget is *completely left* of another if the right side of the first widget is left of the left side of the other widget. Two widgets are called *horizontally non-overlapping* if either one is completely left of the other. *Vertically non-overlapping* is defined analogously. Two widgets are *non-overlapping* if they are horizontally or vertically non-overlapping. A layout is non-overlapping if all possible pairs of widgets are non-overlapping.

While a given layout may be non-overlapping, this does not imply that the underlying specification produces only non-overlapping layouts. This is a central problem in GUI layout. For example, the layout on the left of Figure 2 is non-overlapping. Yet, as the size is reduced, the check box starts to overlap the button due to a missing constraint. Any specification that produces only non-overlapping layouts is a *non-overlapping specification*.

The main idea of the non-overlap algorithm presented here is that for a given non-overlapping layout, the underlying specification can be made non-overlapping by adding additional *non-overlap constraints*. These are simple hard linear constraints that ensure a non-negative distance between two widgets. In the following, we show that all layouts created using ALE's operations are non-overlapping. Moreover, we explain where non-overlap constraints are added.

Non-Overlap of Created Layouts

All edit operations transform a non-overlapping layout so that it stays non-overlapping. Starting from the naturally non-overlapping empty layout we prove via structural induction that all layouts evolving from there are non-overlapping. Inserting or moving a widget into an empty area keeps the layout non-overlapping by definition. When inserting or moving a widget horizontally between a tabstop and another widget, it does not overlap the involved widget as a new "column" is created between the tabstop and the existing widget, and the new widget is temporarily assigned zero size. Furthermore, the new widget does not overlap any existing widgets above or below in a vertical direction because per definition

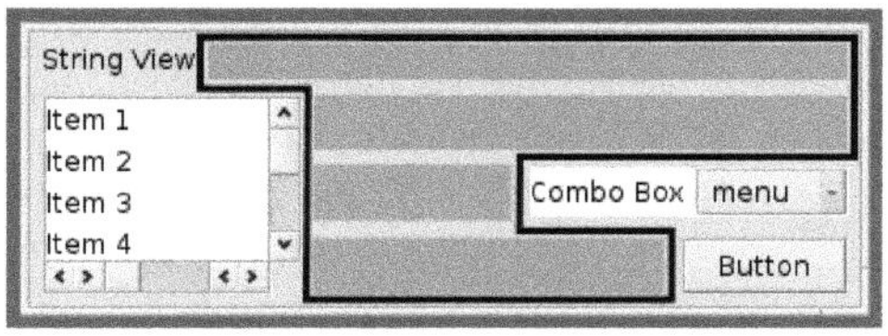

Figure 12. The empty area is an orthogonal polygon (black outline) that is filled with tiles (red). Each tile has a minimum size of zero, which guarantees a non-overlapping layout specification.

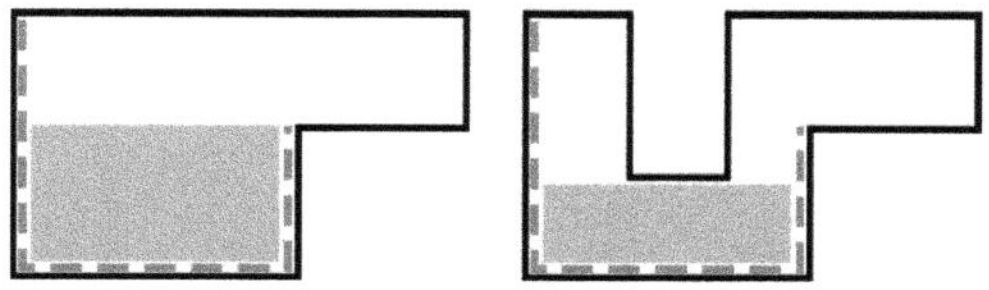

Figure 13. Empty polygon (black outline). An identified U-shape is visualized as a red dotted line. Left: The U-shape is tiled up to the shorter leg (red tile). Right: A widget extends into the U-shape and the U-shape is tiled only partially.

of the operation it has at most the height of the existing widget, and this widget did not overlap any other widgets before. Swapping two widgets does not change the topology of the tabstops and thus works as well. When increasing the size of a widget, the system always verifies that the resized widget does not intersect with another; otherwise the operation fails. Decreasing a widget's size also keeps the layout non-overlapping because the resulting widget is always smaller than the old one.

The last case that has to be considered is gap filling. When filling a gap, floating groups are moved one after another into the direction of the removed widget. Because a floating group is only moved until it hits another widget, this operation also keeps the layout non-overlapping. Given that each edit operation leaves the layout non-overlapping, the system can never get into a state where the layout has overlaps. Thus ALE is suitable for creating and editing a concrete layout under the non-overlap requirement. In the next section we discuss how we expand this to keep all layout specifications non-overlapping.

Non-Overlapping Layout Specifications

To maintain the non-overlap requirement of a layout specification during all resize operations, one needs to ensure that all pairs of widgets are non-overlapping. Yet, checking all pairs would be inefficient, so we propose a more sophisticated approach. We first recall that in *full layouts*, i.e., layouts without empty space, all widgets share tabstops with all neighbors. Thus the layout is non-overlapping.

Tiling of Empty Areas

It remains to argue what to do if a layout has one or more empty area(s). If two visually adjacent widgets do not share a tabstop, the gap between the two widgets is treated as an empty area with no extent. Otherwise, the empty area(s) are orthogonal polygons. Our solution is to tile these orthogonal polygons by introducing new, virtual, empty rectangular widgets (Figure 12). Each such virtual rectangular widget is connected to existing tabstops. These virtual widgets only need a minimum size of zero to guarantee non-overlapping layout specifications.

We now discuss the algorithm for tiling all empty areas. All empty areas are orthogonal polygons. In general, such polygons can be tiled in $O(n^{3/2} \log n)$ time [24] (n being the number of polygon edges), producing $O(n)$ tiles. As discussed later, the algorithm presented here permits a choice of the shape of the inserted tiles, which affects the resizing behavior of the layout. In a first step, all U-shaped segments in the orthogonal polygons are identified. A U-shape has a horizontal edge and two upwards-pointing vertical legs, the two neighboring edges. In general, the length of the legs can differ (Figure 13). In a second step, the identified U-shapes are tiled. Each U-shape is tiled up to its shorter leg (Figure 13 left). As depicted on the right of Figure 13, it is possible that a widget may extend into a U-shape. In this case the U-shape is only filled up to this widget. When inserting a new tile, new U-shapes may be created and these U-shapes must be added to the list of U-shapes.

After tiling all U-shapes, all orthogonal polygons are completely tiled and the layout becomes non-overlapping. Moreover, the requirement that a layout has well-defined layout sizes is satisfied, as the inserted tiles conserve the topology of the widgets relative to each other. When tiling U-shapes, the inserted tiles become "row-like" (Figures 12 and 13). By choosing C-shapes instead, tiles become "column-like". This may affect the resize behavior, i.e., if widgets move horizontally or vertically relative to each other. By default, ALE produces "row" tiles, but the user can toggle this.

If there are n widgets in the layout, then the empty areas cannot have more than $4n + 4$ corners. This gives us a small linear bound on the number of necessary constraints, as we need only two minimum size constraints per tile. In general, the tiling will have to be recomputed if a layout is modified.

After adding all non-overlap constraints identified by this algorithm the layout becomes non-overlapping. Moreover, the requirement that a layout can only have a single minimum and preferred size is satisfied, as the inserted tiles keep the orientation of the widgets towards each other constant.

When to Add Non-Overlap Constraints

For all edit operations discussed above and to test an operation for applicability, the operation is temporarily applied, the resulting specification solved, and then it is verified for soundness. As a first step, all existing non-overlap constraints are removed from the current layout so as not to interfere with the change. After the layout operation is temporarily applied, non-overlap constraints are inserted for the new specification. If the resulting specification is solvable, the operation can be applied. Otherwise the previous layout and non-overlap constraints are restored. As a last step of a successful operation, the solver recalculates the minimum, maximum and preferred layout sizes. If necessary, the parent window size is updated to fit the modified layout.

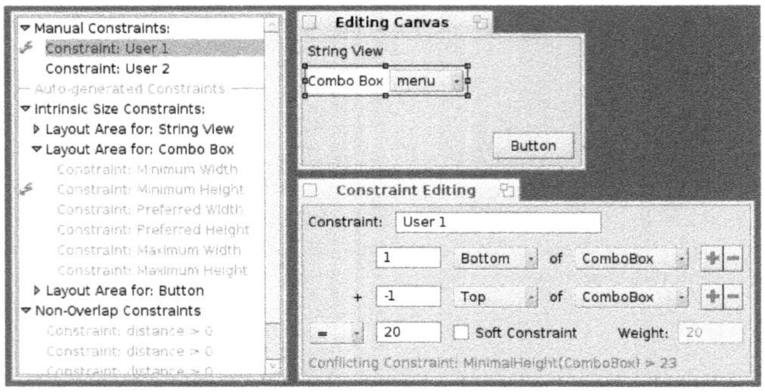

Figure 14. Left: Constraint list. Top-right: Editing canvas. Bottom-right: Constraint edit dialog. The selected constraint "User 1" ($ComboBox_{height} = 20$) conflicts with the minimum height constraint of the combo box ($ComboBox_{height} \geq 23$). Conflicting constraints are marked in the list and the corresponding widget is highlighted.

GENERAL CONSTRAINT EDITING

Using the new edit operations described above it is already possible to specify a large set of layouts. However, it may be necessary to add additional constraints manually in order to achieve certain layout specifications. For example, the width of a widget may be specified to be a multiple of the width of another. Another case is placing a widget globally centered in a layout, between other widgets. To fulfill the completeness requirement, such general constraint editing has to be supported. This section describes how manual editing techniques for linear hard and soft constraints can work together with the new edit operations. Moreover, we discuss how a layout can still be kept sound (non-overlapping and solvable).

The first step towards general constraint support is to permit the creation of arbitrary horizontal or vertical tabstops, not associated with widgets. Adding new tabstops relative or absolute to other tabstops in a constraint-based layout has been proposed [8]. In existing constraint-based GUI builders, constraints can be specified between two tabstops of different widgets. For general constraint editing, one only has to extend this to support arbitrary tabstops and also a (theoretically) unlimited number of tabstops. It is still possible to use the new edit operations introduced above, as they do not rely on every tabstop being connected to a widget. However, we still have to discuss how a layout specification can be kept non-overlapping. Furthermore, the creation or modification of manual constraints may create conflicts with other constraints. Figure 14 shows ALE's constraint editing interface with an example. Conflicting manual constraints are marked in the constraint list.

Ensuring Non-Overlapping Layouts

With our new edit operations it is only possible to connect widgets to others in the layout. Thus all widgets are directly or indirectly connected to a horizontal and a vertical layout border tabstop. With arbitrary tabstops it is possible to position a widget so that it is not directly or indirectly connected to a layout border tabstop. For example, a widget can be aligned to a tabstop at a two-thirds position in an otherwise empty layout. However, unconnected widgets are not a problem when calculating the constraints for non-overlapping layout specifications. The constraint-generation algorithm described above works for all layouts that are initially non-overlapping. Although a manually added constraint may affect the position of widgets, the generated non-overlap constraints still prevent all widgets from overlapping at all times.

Ensuring Solvable Layouts

There are two types of conflicts that may occur with general constraints. First, a manually added constraint may conflict with other manually added constraints or with those of layout areas, e.g., violate the minimum size constraint of a widget. Secondly, when performing an edit operation, the resulting layout may conflict with manually added constraints. Only hard constraints can cause conflicts and ALE uses these only for minimum sizes and non-overlap. There are several possible strategies to detect and handle conflicting constraints. Here we outline our solution.

By solving the layout after each edit operation on a manual constraint, it is possible to determine whether the constraint causes a conflict. If a manual constraint edit operation triggers a conflict, the simplest solution is to disable the manual constraint. If one of the new edit operations triggers a conflict with a manual constraint, we search for conflicting manual constraints and disable them. We choose to disable conflicting manually added constraints, so that the user can recover from conflicts more easily (Figure 14). This is less drastic than Xcode, where manual constraints are *removed* automatically when a widget is moved to a problematic position. ALE also shows conflicts in the constraint list to make it easier for the user to understand the problem.

In general, isolating conflicting constraints is a hard problem, known as maximum feasible subset (MaxFS). One simple solution is to remove one or more constraints from the system and test whether the conflict exists in the remaining system. This has to be repeated until the smallest set of constraints that makes the layout solvable again has been removed. Since the system has to be solved for each step, this is expensive. However, conflicts are relatively rare, and the common case where no conflict is introduced can be detected by solving only once. A single conflicting constraint can be found in $O(\log n)$ solving steps, using a binary-search-like algorithm. Furthermore, for our new edit operations and manually added constraint edits, all involved constraints and affected tabstops are known. We know which tabstops have possibly caused the conflict and search for conflicting manual constraints that (directly or indirectly) use these tabstops. This simplifies the problem and makes the search more efficient. In practice, the search usually completes in less than 100ms.

PREVIEW OF RESIZE BEHAVIOR

When constructing a user interface, designers usually construct a reasonably sized instance of the layout. Current GUI builders then permit designers to test the window resize behavior manually. However, this is error-prone, as the designer may forget to test all aspects of the resize behavior. A common problem scenario is that the user has connected a widget to a wrong tabstop. An automatic preview of the resized user interface, for both increased and decreased sizes, can reveal

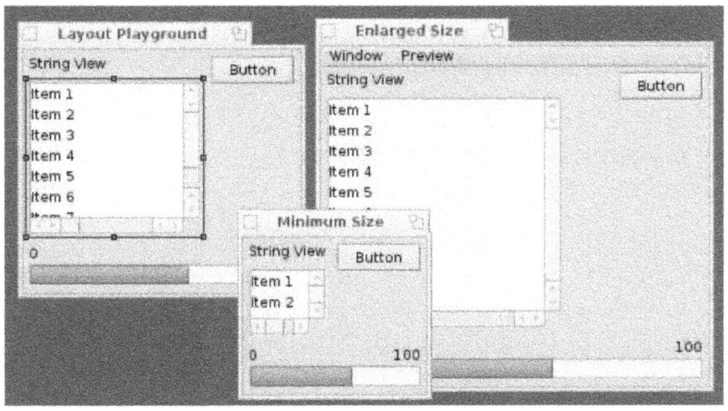

Figure 15. Enlarged and minimum size preview for a layout. The left window shows the preferred size, the bottom the minimum size and the right the enlarged size. Here it becomes visible that the list and the button are not connected to each other.

this. Yet, such preview windows consume precious screen real estate. Also, a small increase or decrease may only yield differences that are not big enough to (easily) see. To address this, we introduce the idea of *optimal resize previews*. The goal of these previews is that the user is able to see the resize behavior of the layout quickly, using minimal screen real estate. Such an optimal resize preview shows the window both at the minimum size and at another size, with a clearly visible size difference relative to the construction window for every widget or constraint, so that the user can see whether the layout specification is correct.

The minimum layout size shows the layout in the most compact form. To determine this size, the hard constraint for the overall layout size is replaced by a strong soft constraint that sets the layout size to zero. This makes the layout as small as permitted by its hard constraints, i.e., minimum size ones. One option for a larger size would be the preferred layout size. However, this is non-optimal, as this size may not significantly differ from the minimum size in all aspects. Thus, we show a second preview that is enlarged enough to enable the user to easily see all size changes relative to the construction window. The just noticeable difference between two simultaneously visible line segments is less than 5 percent of the length [21]. To ensure that our resize visualization is above this threshold, we double the increase by default to 10% and also introduce a minimum increase, at least 10 pixels larger. The user can adjust these two parameters according to preferences and screen pixel densities. To calculate the enlarged size for each widget, we temporarily change the preferred size of every widget to be 10% larger and at least 10 pixels larger than the size in the construction window. Then we compute the size of this modified layout and show it (Figure 15).

DISCUSSION

Here we discuss some of the consequences of the design decisions behind ALE in more detail. ALE uses layout areas to place widgets, and these areas automatically manage all necessary size constraints. This makes editing simpler as all corresponding constraints are hidden from the user. Our use of a quadratic objective function ensures that the preferred size soft constraints are uniquely determined. This makes it impossible to create under-constrained GUIs and makes layouts created with ALE predictable. Also, this approach leads to aesthetically more pleasant layouts [28].

The new edit operations make it easy to create and edit layouts quickly. For example, automatically moving existing widgets aside saves significant time. Also, inserting a widget into the whole available empty space simplifies some tasks. In general, users need to perform fewer steps. Our previous user study confirms this [29]. Since all non-overlap constraints are handled by the system, there is no need to visualize them. There is also no need to display intrinsic size constraints. Thus only manually added constraints are shown, as appropriate. Furthermore, ALE displays tabstops only on demand, and only those that are relevant for the current operation. This leads to a less cluttered design view and permits designers to concentrate on the layout itself.

Moreover, ALE automatically generates non-overlapping layout specifications. This not only reduces the number of constraints that have to be created and maintained, but also reduces the potential for design errors. Tiling the empty space prevents widgets from overlapping, and has the side effect that the extreme layout sizes are well-defined. The designer has some control over this by toggling the tiling algorithm to work horizontally or vertically.

With an increasing number of widgets, the number of tabstops also increases and it may become difficult to select the correct tapstop in a "dense" area. In our experience, this is only rarely the case. One solution is to use snap-and-go [2], as long as each tabstop is at a distinct location. Another is to automatically merge all tabstops at the same location. We will explore whether this leads to unexpected results in future work.

Our current implementation of the active set method is not optimal, as it uses a dense matrix representation. The constraint system has to be solved each time the layout is resized, which happens fast enough. Yet during the edit process the layout has to be solved even more frequently in order to tentatively test a new layout specification. In ALE this usually takes less than 100ms (Intel Core 2 Duo 3GHz), which is sufficient for interactive use and keeps the system responsive and usable at all times. Also, our implementation of the algorithm for generating non-overlapping layout specifications does not guarantee a minimal set of constraints, as some unnecessary constraints may be inserted. Since the runtime performance of an application is more important than the editing process, a pre-solve process could remove redundant constraints.

ALE's source code is available on github [12]. At a recent open-source meeting (BeGeistert, November 2012) we received much positive feedback on ALE.

CONCLUSION

This paper has presented ALE, a GUI builder that makes it possible to create and edit constraint-based layouts with simple operations. ALE's new edit operations automatically keep the layout sound and solvable. They also keep widgets aligned relative to each other, which leads to well-structured

[12] `https://github.com/czeidler/haiku`

layouts. Through a new algorithm that automatically generates non-overlap constraints, ALE can create layouts that are guaranteed to be non-overlapping for all possible layout sizes. We have also discussed how ALE's edit operations can be combined with general constraint editing, and how conflicts are resolved. This keeps common layout editing tasks easy, while making arbitrary constraint-based layouts possible. Moreover, we have introduced optimal resize previews to help GUI designers validate the resize behavior of a layout specification. These real-time previews show the layout at a minimum and a sufficiently enlarged size, which optimizes the screen space used for the previews.

In the future, we plan to integrate a sparse matrix representation into the active set solver to accelerate interactions in the GUI builder further. This is a fairly common optimization. Moreover, we plan to add a pre-solver to prune the constraint system further and improve performance. In exceptional cases designers may want widgets to overlap, and we might explore this in the future. Furthermore, the interface for manual constraint editing could be improved, e.g., to make it easier to center widgets globally in the layout, similar to Xcode.

REFERENCES

1. Avrahami, G., Brooks, K. P., and Brown, M. H. A two-view approach to constructing user interfaces. *SIGGRAPH* (1989), 137–146.
2. Baudisch, P., Cutrell, E., Hinckley, K., and Eversole, A. Snap-and-go: helping users align objects without the modality of traditional snapping. CHI (2005), 301–310.
3. Borning, A., Lin, R. K.-H., and Marriott, K. Constraint-based document layout for the web. *Multimedia Syst. 8*, 3 (Oct. 2000), 177–189.
4. Borning, A., Marriott, K., Stuckey, P., and Xiao, Y. Solving linear arithmetic constraints for user interface applications. UIST (1997), 87–96.
5. Fletcher, R. *Practical methods of optimization; (2nd ed.)*. Wiley-Interscience, 1987, ch. 10.3.
6. Galitz, W. *The essential guide to user interface design: an introduction to GUI design principles and techniques*. Wiley, 2007.
7. Gleicher, M. A graphics toolkit based on differential constraints. UIST (1993), 109–120.
8. Hashimoto, O., and Myers, B. A. Graphical styles for building interfaces by demonstration. UIST (1992), 117–124.
9. Heim, S. *The resonant interface: HCI foundations for interaction design*. Pearson, 2007, ch. 6.6.
10. Hudson, S. E., and Mohamed, S. P. Interactive specification of flexible user interface displays. *ACM Trans. Inf. Syst. 8*, 3 (July 1990), 269–288.
11. Hudson, S. E., and Yeatts, A. K. Smoothly integrating rule-based techniques into a direct manipulation interface builder. UIST (1991), 145–153.
12. Hurst, N., Li, W., and Marriott, K. Review of automatic document formatting. DocEng (2009), 99–108.
13. Hurst, N., Marriott, K., and Moulder, P. Cobweb: a constraint-based web browser. Australasian Computer Science Conference (2003), 247–254.
14. International Organization for Standardization. ISO 9241-10: Ergonomic Requirements for Office Work with Visual Display Terminals (VDT) – Part 10: Dialogue Principles, 1996.
15. Jacobs, C., Li, W., Schrier, E., Bargeron, D., and Salesin, D. Adaptive document layout. *Commun. ACM 47*, 8 (Aug. 2004), 60–66.
16. Karsenty, S., Landay, J. A., and Weikart, C. Inferring graphical constraints with Rockit. HCI'92 (1993), 137–153.
17. Lutteroth, C., Strandh, R., and Weber, G. Domain Specific High-Level Constraints for User Interface Layout. *Constraints 13*, 3 (2008).
18. Molich, R., and Nielsen, J. Improving a human-computer dialogue. *Commun. ACM 33*, 3 (Mar. 1990), 338–348.
19. Myers, B. A. User-Interface Tools: Introduction and Survey. *IEEE Software 6* (1989), 15–23.
20. Myers, B. A., and Buxton, W. Creating highly-interactive and graphical user interfaces by demonstration. SIGGRAPH (1986), 249–258.
21. Ono, H. Difference threshold for stimulus length under simultaneous and nonsimultaneous viewing conditions. *Perception & Psychophysics 2* (1967), 201–207.
22. Scoditti, A., and Stuerzlinger, W. A new layout method for graphical user interfaces. IEEE (2009), 642–647.
23. Singh, G., Kok, C. H., and Ngan, T. Y. Druid: a system for demonstrational rapid user interface development. UIST (1990), 167–177.
24. Soltan, V., and Gorpinevich, A. Minimum dissection of a rectilinear polygon with arbitrary holes into rectangles. *Discrete & Computational Geometry 9*, 1 (1993), 57–79.
25. Vlissides, J. M., and Tang, S. A unidraw-based user interface builder. UIST (1991), 201–210.
26. Weber, G. A reduction of grid-bag layout to Auckland layout. Australasian Software Engineering Conference (ASWEC) (April 2010), 67 –74.
27. Zanden, B. V., and Myers, B. A. The Lapidary graphical interface design tool. CHI (1991), 465–466.
28. Zeidler, C., Lutteroth, C., and Weber, G. Constraint solving for beautiful user interfaces: how solving strategies support layout aesthetics. CHINZ (2012), 72–79.
29. Zeidler, C., Stuerzlinger, W., Lutteroth, C., and Weber, G. Evaluating direct manipulation operations for constraint-based layout. INTERACT'13 (to appear).

SeeSS: Seeing What I Broke – Visualizing Change Impact of Cascading Style Sheets (CSS)

Hsiang-Sheng Liang*, **Kuan-Hung Kuo***, **Po-Wei Lee**†
Yu-Chien Chan†, **Yu-Chin Lin**†, **Mike Y. Chen***
Mobile and HCI Research Lab, National Taiwan University
*{r01922036, b97115, mikechen}@csie.ntu.edu.tw †{b98705027,b98901204,b99705011}@ntu.edu.tw

ABSTRACT
Cascading Style Sheet (CSS) is a fundamental web language for describing the presentation of web pages. CSS rules are often reused across multiple parts of a page and across multiple pages throughout a site to reduce repetition and to provide a consistent look and feel. When a CSS rule is modified, developers currently have to manually track and visually inspect all possible parts of the site that may be impacted by that change. We present SeeSS, a system that automatically tracks CSS change impact across a site and enables developers to easily visualize all of them. The impacted page fragments are sorted by severity and the differences before and after the change are highlighted using animations.

Author Keywords
Development Tools; Toolkits; World Wide Web and Hypermedia; Web Development; Cascading Style Sheet

ACM Classification Keywords
H.5.m. Information Interfaces and Presentation (e.g. HCI): Miscellaneous

INTRODUCTION
Cascading Style Sheet (CSS) is a fundamental web language for describing the presentation of web pages, such as colors, fonts, and layout. It is primarily designed to enable the separation of content from presentation, and has been a W3C standard since 1996 [11, 18].

One of its key benefits is reusing the same CSS files and rules on the same page and across multiple web pages, which reduces repetition, increases download speed, provides a consistent look and feel, and improves maintainability. CSS reuse is a common practice. For example, on Apple and McDonald's US websites, each CSS file is referenced by an average of 22.8 and 6.1 HTML files respectively.

When modifying a CSS rule, developers need to first visually check that the intended change has been correctly implemented. Then they need to verify that the change does not introduce unintended bugs on all parts of the site that reference the modified CSS files and reuse the modified CSS rules [9]. Figure 1 shows an example where a simple change to fix an alignment bug of the Login button on one page breaks the layout of other buttons elsewhere on the site.

UIST'13, October 8–11, 2013, St. Andrews, United Kingdom.

ACM 978-1-4503-2268-3/13/10 $15.00.
http://dx.doi.org/10.1145/2501988.2502006

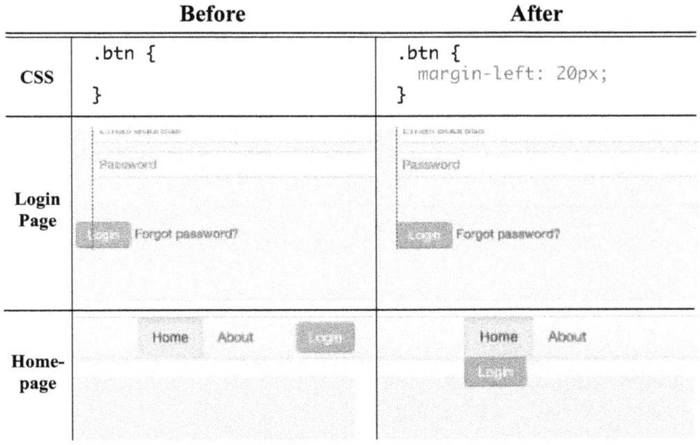

Figure 1. Modifying a CSS rule may fix a bug on the current page, but introduce bugs elsewhere: a developer fixes the "Login" button alignment by adding a `margin-left` property to the login page; however, such change breaks the "Login" button layout in the navigation bar on the home page. This bug is not immediately visible to developers using currently available tools.

Many tools have been developed for web programming: inspector tools such as Firebug [7] and Chrome and Safari's built-in tools [4] help developers inspect rendered web pages individually, but do not help track changes across a site. Web UI testing tools such as Selenium [17], Sahi [16], and Sikuli [19] support UI automation when performing functional testing of web pages, but may not detect non-functional problems introduced through CSS changes. Mogotest [13] is a web-based regression testing tool that visualizes changes on pages individually, but do not support interactive development nor multi-page visualization.

We present SeeSS, a system that automatically tracks CSS change impact across a website and visually presents all parts of the site that have changed due to the CSS code modification. As shown in Figure 2, SeeSS computes and shows all visible changes before and after the modification, and sorts them based on how much has changed in each of the cropped regions. Our SeeSS prototype currently tracks HTML and CSS references of a static site when documents are opened

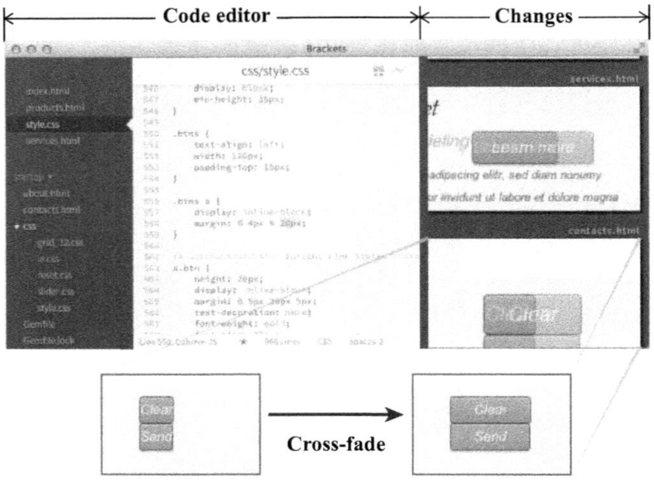

Figure 2. SeeSS graphical user interface: the left panel corresponds to the code editor, and the right panel shows a list of visual changes associated with the most recent CSS modifications.

and saved. It also renders and stores snapshots of all pages across the entire site, and compares them across revisions.

We conducted a small lab-based user study with 4 developers and the initial results were promising. Participants all reported that they were faster at fixing CSS problems with SeeSS and all would like to continue using SeeSS as their regular web development tools.

RELATED WORK

Web Browser Developer Tools

Modern desktop browsers like Google Chrome, Safari, Firefox, and Internet Explorer have built-in inspectors [4, 7] that help developers view, debug, inspect, and profile individual web pages [8]. The Document Object Model (DOM) inspector enables developers to select specific elements on the current page, view all the CSS attributes applied to these elements and locate the CSS files containing each associated CSS rules. While the DOM inspector can help developers locate and modify a particular CSS rule, developers still need to manually track all HTML files that reference the corresponding CSS file, and check all parts of the site which are impacted by a modification of this rule.

Web UI Testing Automation Tools

Selenium [17] and Sahi [16] are designed for automating functional tests of web pages. Pre-recorded input sequences, such as mouse and keyboard events, are fed to the website, then assertions are used to check if responses matches expected patterns (e.g. if certain text exists). Sikuli [3] takes a visual approach: screenshots are used to depict input sequences and help visually check the resulting patterns.

While these tools help test the functionality of websites, they are not well supported for CSS programming. First, in the case of dynamic web applications, some of the visual programming may happen independent of the functional programming. For example, the HTML/CSS/Javascript may be developed by front end developers, while the functional programming is done by the back end developers. Second, the desired states for CSS are often described by wireframes before the final visual mockups are ready. SeeSS facilitates iterative CSS development without a functional website and before the final mockup of the site is ready.

Web Regression Testing Tools

Regression testing shows change impact and ensures that the intended behavior is preserved after modification [6]. Mogotest [13] is a web-based consistency testing service that provides regression testing across multiple browsers. It compares the current DOM snapshots of the site with previous versions. For each page, it shows a side-by-side view of two versions if it detects a change.

Instead of visualizing individual and entire pages, SeeSS is designed to identify the exact set of regions that changed and to enable users to visualize all of them at once. This enables developers to verify the intended changes and to spot any unintended changes at a glance. In addition, SeeSS is integrated with a code editor and analyzes changes upon every file save in order to provide immediate feedback revealing errors before they accumulate.

SYSTEM DESIGN

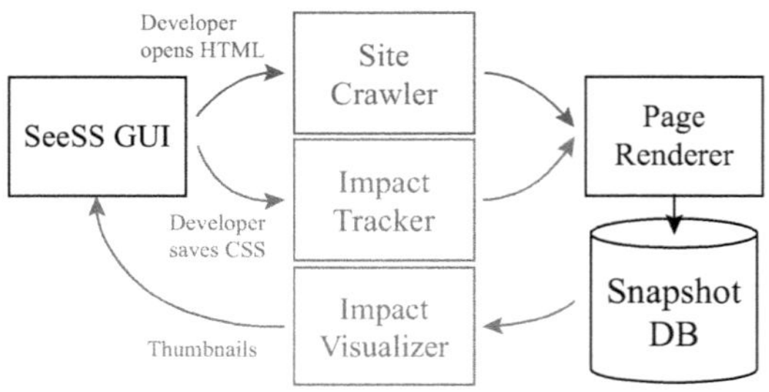

Figure 3. SeeSS system architecture and data flow.

In order to support the tracking of CSS change impact, SeeSS needs to: (a) track what pages are part of the current site, (b) detect all visual changes across the site due to a CSS modification, and (c) visualize the differences. Figure 3 shows the system architecture and data flow.

SeeSS GUI

The SeeSS GUI supports editing of HTML and CSS files, listens to HTML and CSS file open and save events, and displays the rendered visual changes as a series of *thumbnails*. A thumbnail represents a rendered page region that has visible differences between the current and the last snapshots. It consists of two cropped snapshots representing how the region looks *before* and *after* the CSS change.

The thumbnails support the following two user interactions: a) when the mouse hovers over the left half of a thumbnail, the animation stops and the previous version of page fragment is shown. When the mouse hovers over the other half, the current version is shown; b) clicking on the thumbnail opens the corresponding HTML document in the editor window.

Site Crawler

When an HTML page is opened in the GUI, the file is passed to the Site Crawler, which performs a recursive traversal of the hyper-links in the file. In addition to calling the Page Renderer to take initial snapshots for each crawled page, the crawler also records all CSS files that are referenced by each page. The dependency graph between the HTML files and the CSS files is used to track change impact.

Impact Tracker

When a CSS modification has been saved, the Impact Tracker looks up the set of HTML files referencing the changed CSS file using the dependency graph. It calls the Page Renderer to render the HTML files and save the snapshots to the database, and then calls the Impact Visualizer to detect differences.

Impact Visualizer

For each HTML file that references the changed CSS, the Impact Visualizer fetches the current and the last snapshots and calculates their visual differences. Because a CSS modification may impact multiple regions of a page, bounding boxes are calculated to capture the areas where the two versions differ. The bounding boxes are used to crop the snapshots and the results are displayed in the GUI. An animation is used to help highlight the visual differences to developers. Details about the animation are given in the implementation section.

IMPLEMENTATION

We implemented the SeeSS GUI using the Brackets open-source text editor [2] with a custom SeeSS extension. The extension is implemented using HTML, CSS, and Javascript. It is a resizable sidebar on the right side of the editor window. It displays the visual differences using CSS cross-fade animation, a common approch used to smoothly transition between two states [1, 5].

The other components are implemented using Node.js v0.8.8 [14], a Javascript-based server framework, running on Mac OS X 10.7. They communicate with the SeeSS Brackets extension via socket.io, a Javascript library for real-time communication. PhantomJS v1.9 [15], a headless WebKit rendering engine, is used to render the HTML pages. A pool of PhantomJS processes is used to crawl the site and to render multiple pages in parallel. The snapshots are full-page screenshots captured using PhantomJS.

The current implementation of the impact ranking algorithm is the mean square error of the RGB values of the pixels between the two versions, which is the sum of squared difference of each pixel's red, green, and blue values, divided by the area of each bounding box.

DEVELOPER FEEDBACK

We conducted a small lab study to understand how SeeSS supports web developers' workflow [10]. Given the small number of participants and the large number of potential factors that could affect task completion time and error, our goal was to collect feedback rather than quantitative comparisons.

Study Design

We created two websites with CSS problems, and asked each participant to debug one site then the other. The study used a within-subjects design; the order of the websites and the order of whether SeeSS was used were counter-balanced. We asked the participants to think-aloud while fixing the CSS problems. Afterwards, participants filled out questionnaires, and discussed their experience in semi-structured interviews.

Each site had 5 CSS tasks that the participants needed to complete. The tasks were designed to cover the following CSS programming challenges: (T1) modifying rules such as font-family and layout widths that are typically used throughout the site; (T2) modifying rules that apply to elements with multiple occurances on the same page, such as the appearance of buttons and widgets; (T3) tinkering with `position` and `z-index`, which are affected by attribute settings of ancestor elements; (T4) overriding existing rules, which requires the knowledge of selector specificity, style cascading, and style inheritance; (T5) avoiding ineffective modifications, such as applying `height` attribute to an inline element.

The experiment setup mimicked typical web development environment, with a code editor to make edits and a browser window to visually check and inspect the results. The experiment was carried out on a Mac Mini equipped with Intel CoreDuo 2.53GHz and 8GB DDR3 RAM.

Participants

After a pilot study with 3 users, we recruited 4 participants (1 male) on average of age 22 who had CSS programming experience from our university. The participants self-rated their HTML and CSS proficiency between 3 and 4 on a 5-point Likert scale (average 3.3) with 5 being an 'expert'. The participants used Sublime Text and Vim as their primary code editor, and none had experience with the Brackets editor.

Results

The post-experiment questionnaire and interviews showed positive perception and promising results. On a 5-point Likert scale indicating levels of agreement, all four participants rated SeeSS a 4 on helping them fix CSS problems more quickly. They also all rated a 4 when asked if they would use SeeSS as their regular web development tools.

However, when asked if SeeSS' speed was acceptable, three participants rated it 3 and one rated it 2. We analyzed the system logs and saw that SeeSS took an average of 5.7 seconds to display the thumbnails (standard deviation was 4 seconds), which was significantly slower than the sub-second rendering time of a browser page reload.

DISCUSSION

Waiting for Thumbnails

We observed that participants sometimes came to a short halt after saving a file. When asked about what they were waiting for, participants reported that they were waiting for the SeeSS thumbnails to display. P1 thought that he made a mistake several times, when it was the system that was too slow to display the thumbnails. This was a behavioral change owing to the latency of SeeSS, but also suggests that SeeSS provided sufficient utility for participants to be willing to wait. In any case, SeeSS' speed should be significantly improved and the user interface should provide a progress indicator.

Using File Search

P2 and P3 used the "Find in Project" command to look up all HTML files that referenced the modified CSS file. Interestingly, they only used it when SeeSS was not available, and never used it when SeeSS was available. They reported being cautious about making edits because the code was written by someone else and the impact of each CSS rule was unknown. The situation is similar for collaborative projects, especially for new team members who are not yet familiar with the dependencies among various HTML and CSS files. SeeSS can play an important role in helping developers become familiar with new projects and avoid breaking other developers' code.

Designing Thumbnails

Two of the participants reported difficulty in matching elements in the thumbnails to pages they are viewing in the browser. They suggested limiting the thumbnail scaling to a maximum of 1:1, and show more surrounding elements to provide more context when possible.

All the participants commented that the most important thumbnail was at times not the first on the list. P2 and P3 suggested grouping thumbnails from the same page together and sort them by their y-position on the page. This may also make it easier to locate elements in the document. Clustering similar changes may also help summarize the thumbnails.

LIMITATIONS AND FUTURE WORK

Dynamic Sites

Our current implementation of SeeSS only supports static websites, and do not support server-generated content such as web application framework like Ruby on Rails, Django, and Google App Engine. We are extending the Site Crawler to understand the local file layout of popular frameworks as well as supporting crawling over http.

Another limitation is dynamically loaded content such as those loaded via AJAX and generated by Javascript. UI automation techniques such as Crawljax [12] could be used to enumerate possible UI states, perform javascript-based navigation, and generate dependency graphs between the dynamic HTML elements and CSS. However, for dynamic HTML elements that depend on user input, such as login forms and chat messages, test cases need to be provided by developers using test case authoring tools such as Sikuli [3] and Selenium [17].

Performance and Scalability

Participants reported that they sometimes had to wait for the thumbnails to appear to confirm their CSS changes. We are experimenting with DOM tree-based impact tracker and impact visualizer, which are significantly faster than the image-based trackers implemented in our original prototype. Our recent benchmarks have shown a 5 times speed increase, which helps to scale up to larger sites.

Thumbnail Animations and Representations

Our prototype currently supports cross-fade animation. DOM tree-based analysis, in addition to the original pixel-based approach, can be used to identify the change of dimensions, position and other properties of the individual DOM elements. Such an approach affords the support of a richer animation vocabulary that conveys complex changes such as text reflow, style change and glyph transforms in a similar fashion as so done in the markup code editor Gliimpse [5].

Ranking change impact is still an open research problem that requires large-scale user studies and real cases of CSS bugs. We plan to release SeeSS and collect some real statistics that can help provide insights to this problem. On the other hand, we are also seeking alternative representations to a ranking list. We plan to add a full-screen, hotkey-activated view that tiles up all the thumbnails in order to provide developers with a holistic view of the CSS change.

CONCLUSION

We have presented SeeSS, a system that automatically tracks CSS change impact across an entire website and helps developers visualize them. A preliminary, 4-person study showed promising results with participants all indicating fixing CSS problems more quickly with SeeSS, and all would like to use SeeSS as their regular web development tools. We are exploring alternative thumbnail visualizations, and techniques to improve performance and to support dynamic websites.

REFERENCES

1. Bezerianos, A., Dragicevic, P., and Balakrishnan, R. Mnemonic rendering: an image-based approach for exposing hidden changes in dynamic displays. UIST '06 (2006), 159–168.
2. Brackets - open-source code editor. `http://brackets.io/`.
3. Chang, T.-H., Yeh, T., and Miller, R. C. Gui testing using computer vision. CHI '10 (2010), 1535–1544.
4. Chrome Developer Tools. `https://developers.google.com/chrome-developer-tools/`.
5. Dragicevic, P., Huot, S., and Chevalier, F. Gliimpse: Animating from markup code to rendered documents and vice versa. UIST '11 (2011), 257–262.
6. Evans, R. B., and Savoia, A. Differential testing: a new approach to change detection. ESEC-FSE companion '07 (2007), 549–552.
7. Firebug. `http://getfirebug.com/`.
8. Geneves, P., Layaida, N., and Quint, V. On the analysis of cascading style sheets. WWW '12 (2012), 809–818.
9. Keller, M., and Nussbaumer, M. Cascading style sheets: a novel approach towards productive styling with today's standards. WWW '09 (2009), 1161–1162.
10. LaToza, T. D., and Myers, B. A. Designing useful tools for developers. PLATEAU '11 (2011), 45–50.
11. Lie, H. W. *Cascading style sheets*.
12. Mesbah, A., van Deursen, A., and Lenselink, S. Crawling Ajax-based web applications through dynamic analysis of user interface state changes. TWEB '12 (2012), 3:1–3:30.
13. Mogotest. `http://mogotest.com/`.
14. Node.js. `http://nodejs.org/`.
15. PhantomJS. `http://phantomjs.org/`.
16. Sahi. `http://sahi.co.in/`.
17. Selenium. `http://docs.seleniumhq.org/`.
18. W3C Recommendation of Cascading Style Sheets, Level 1, 1996. `http://www.w3.org/TR/CSS1/`.
19. Yeh, T., Chang, T.-H., and Miller, R. C. Sikuli: using gui screenshots for search and automation. UIST '09 (2009), 183–192.

Capturing On Site Laser Annotations with Smartphones to Document Construction Work

Jörg Schweitzer
RheinMain University of Applied Sciences
Unter den Eichen 5
65195 Wiesbaden, Germany
mail@jschweitzer.de

Ralf Dörner
RheinMain University of Applied Sciences
Unter den Eichen 5
65195 Wiesbaden, Germany
ralf.doerner@hs-rm.de

ABSTRACT
In the process of construction work, taking notes of real world objects like walls, pipes, cables and others is an important task. The ad hoc capturing of small information pieces on such objects on site can be challenging when there is no specialized technology available. Handwritten or hand drawn notes on paper are good for textual information like measurements whereas images are better to capture the physical state of objects. Without a proper combination however the benefit is limited. In this paper we present an interaction system for taking ad hoc notes on real world objects by using a combination of a smartphone and a laserpointer as input device. Our interface enables the user to directly annotate objects by drawing on them and to store these annotations for later reviewing. The deictic gestures of the user are then replayed on a stitched image of the scene. The users voice input is captured and analyzed to integrate additional Information. The user can mark positions and place hand taken measurements by pointing on the objects and speaking the corresponding voice commands.

Author Keywords
Handheld Devices; Image Alignment; Stitching; Visualization;

ACM Classification Keywords
H.5.2 [Information Interfaces and Presentation]: Input devices and strategies; H.5.1 [Multimedia Information Systems]: Animations - Audio input/output

General Terms
Human Factors; Design.

ACM 978-1-4503-2271-3/13/10...$15.00.
http://dx.doi.org/10.1145/2501988.2502010

INTRODUCTION AND RELATED WORK
Construction work on professional level as well as small scale private projects usually require notes to be taken about the involved real world objects and the tasks related to them. Our partners in construction work and facility management provided us with scenes where pre-work or mid-work data acquisition is needed for making decisions. A tool to draw an 'enhanced snapshot' of the on site state and integrate further information from the visit is desired. Standard software like CAD programs provide features to model complex objects and processes but are often not efficiently usable on site and with mobile devices. Even when such software is available on mobile platforms like Autocad WS [4] its modelling process requires too much additional work to be used for fast note taking. A variety of Smartphone apps provide more appropiate user interfaces, like Bosch Toolbox [5], D-Photo Measures [7], Measure & Sketch [8] that allow the user to take photos and annotate them by drawing measures and simple graphical elements. Usually those tools are unable to create a more complex reconstruction of the scene and rely on single images instead. Sankar et al. [17] have shown capturing of indoor scenes with image based methods utilizing smartphones and replaying those scenes to review the situation. Other applications involve the use of Augmented Reality by letting the user place a printed marker in the scene [11] or use referential objects as as a base for calculations [20]. Such markers help for tasks like image registration or measuring, still most tools rely on an additional data entry step like drawing on a taken photograph. Gauglitz et al. [9] included real world objects through a mobile portal for annotation and collaboration. Palmer et al. have shown the benefits of annotations viewable on physical objects [15]. Patel et al. [16] presented 'iCam' to geometrically analyze and annotate indoor scenes including laser-based distance calculations. Kurz et al. used projectors as a backwards channel for tracked laserpointers [10].

In this work we present a system that captures annotations on real world objects and converts them to reusable data objects in the form of stitched images and animated videos. The user directs a smartphone that has been equipped with a laserpointer to the objects he wants to take notes of. The system captures deictic gestures via camera and creates a stitched overview to draw the laserpointers path upon. Image matching algorithms are used to convert the frames from the captured video into a stitched panoramic image. The position of the laserdot is used to draw position annotations and path annotations on top of the stitched image. The voice of the user is captured and replayed with the resulting video. Addition-

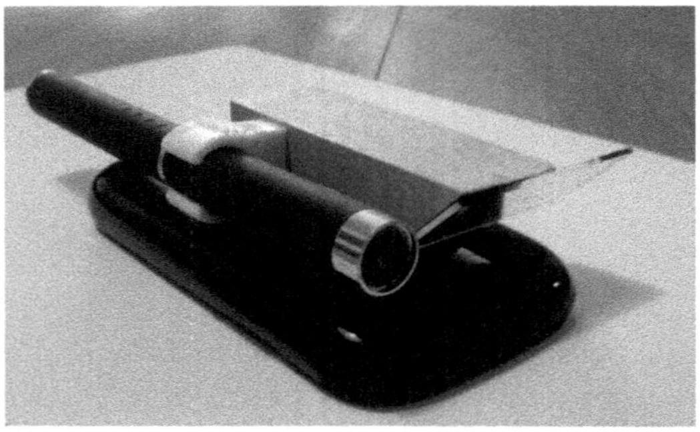

Figure 1: The laserpointer and mirror mounted on a removable back cover.

ally speech analysis is used to convert certain keywords into graphical elements to further annotate the captured objects.

APPLICATION OVERVIEW

So far our work has been tested on android smartphones but could easily be implemented on IOS based phones or other comparable platforms too as long as the phone provides a back camera. A common smartphone is extended with a laserpointer that aims in the direction of the smartphone cameras center. A physically comfortable setup can be achieved by attaching a laserpointer and a small mirror to an additional back cover which is then attached to the phone. 1 The laserpointer is therefore directed similar to the beam of an infrared remote control pointing 'out' from the top of the smartphone. The mirror is used to adjust the camera angle by 90° so that the direction of camera and laserpointer are aligned. The user directs the laserpointer at the real world objects to highlight positions and paths. At the same time the internal camera of the smartphone captures a video of the scene. The laserpointer stays active all the time to make it easier for the user to navigate on objects because the laserdot is always visible to him. However, this also eliminates the possibility to use the appearance of the laserdot in a videoframe as a marker to start extracting a path. To add such basic information and other delimiters a simple application on the smartphone is used. The user presses a button on the phone and thereby creates a time based annotation corresponding to the video. This annotation is used to mark the start or end of a path drawn with the laserpointer. This way the captured video can be separated into multiple parts which contain multiple different strokes or gestures. After capturing all the users input the system reconstructs the scene. A stitched image is created from the frames of the captured video. On this image the path of the laserdot is drawn. Annotations from extracted voice input are calculated and also drawn on the stitched image. The end result can then be watched as a single image representing the whole scene or as a video replay of the annotation process. The image is aimed at creating a condensed overview of the scene with the vital information included. The video replay is used to convey the full information containing of the audio data and the deictic gestures drawn with the laserpointer.

RECONSTRUCTION OF THE SCENE

Stitching

The basic task to create panoramic views is the image registration, which means finding a transformation that maps separate images into a common coordinate system. Szeliski et al. [19] distinguish between direct methods that work on similarity of pixel values and feature based methods that extract a set of descriptive points and match those. We decided for a feature based approach as we found that to be more robust for handling rotations and more flexible for recognizing panoramas. Our scenes are closely related to spherical panoramas but also include translation to some degree. Other than with unordered picture collections like used by [18] we can assume that the similarity between frames of a video capture is higher the closer those frames are positioned to each other in the video. Hence we decided for a sequential approach examining transformations between neighbouring frames instead of a full comparison of all possible image pairs. This also greatly reduces the 'brute force' complexity from matching every pair of frames $O(n^2)$ that structure-from-motion systems like 'Bundler' [1] have as a base to $O(n)$. This decision was also made with aiming for a potential implementation on a smartphone in the future, since global alignment for each image based on bundle block adjustment even with optimizations takes from minutes to hours on a standard PC as the number of images goes from tens to hundreds. So far our algorithms were implemented on a standard PC using methods from the OpenCV library [6].

Scale-invariant feature transform (SIFT) features [12] were widely used over the last years to work on image correspondence problems with some of the most prominents usages being the Phototourism project [3] and the Photosynth application [13]. We used SIFT features to analyze and match the videoframes in our scenes, primarily relying on the 'Fast Library for Approximate Nearest Neighbours'. After the detection, matches are filtered by the average distance between them and still remaining non-injective matches are removed. In the next step the filtered matches are used to calculate the perspective transformations between neigbouring images. For a video with n frames this results in $2 * (n - 1)$ transformations combining the transformations for all 'next' and 'previous' neighbours. This set of transformations allows us to use any frame in the video as the base frame and map all other frames into its coordinate system by following the chain of 'previous' or 'next' transformations. Figure 2 shows a reconstructed scene, with an overview image (a) for comparison and two stitched panoramas (b) and (c) created from a video of that scene taken with a mobile phone undergoing a sideways panning motion. The panoramas were created using a subset of 50 frames from a video with 200 frames. Panorama (b) shows our own results in image stitching. Panorama (c) shows the same images stitched by Microsoft Research Image Composite Editor [2].

Locating the laserpointer

Finding the visible dot from the laserpointer is a basic task in the area of image processing. It usually consists of a first step where qualified pixels are extracted based on their values, to

(a) Single Image (b) Our stitching result (c) Stitching from Microsoft ICE

Figure 2: Comparison of an overview image and reconstructed panoramas of the same scene

create a number of candidates. In a second step the candidates are ranked by some metrics to find the most promising one. A set of different filters is usually applied to enhance certain features of the images to support one or both steps. In case of a red laserpointer the color and brightness are the most promising properties to extract qualified pixels. For more convenience when defining filters, all frames were transformed into HSV color space. Then the most basic approach is to look for the maximum intensity value (V) in the image. Since the laserpointer usually creates a very bright dot, this simple tracking works very well in some of scenes.

Problems occur with high reflective surfaces like glass or polished metal where the brightest values get 'stolen' from different pixels in the image. Another obstacle is that the laserpointer does not always create a strong red color value (H) but an almost white one instead. Therefore we tried a filter based on a wide angle around red color in HSV color space in combination with filtering an upper percentage (20%) of intensity. To rank the resulting candidates their position, size and form was also analyzed. The dot should be centered, round and relatively small. Image 3 shows a reconstructed path based on the described tracking pipeline. The outer right image frame reflected bright sunlight so that only logical analysis of position, size, form and translation over multiple frames could extract the correct location.

Locating the laserpointer with variations of the described pipeline sometimes gave good and sometimes completely unusable results. Depending on the scene we encountered tracking problems like Stuerzlinger et al. described [14] for example with shiny objects. Such a tracking created a single point of failure while feature based stitching proved to be a lot more robust in the same scenes. Additionally the extracted position of the dot was never noticeably better than the implicit known position close to the center of the image. We therefore decided to switch to an approach, where calibration is done once before using the system. We direct the pointer to the images center at a maximum distance and get its position from a sequence of images. In case of the shown examples calibration distance was 5m to 8m, hence somewhat longer than the interaction distance. This approach results in drifting of the dot when pointing at objects farther away or very

Figure 3: Reconstructed path from a sideways panning motion.

much closer than calibrated. However, in our tests the pointing precision was never a problematic issue. The users own pointing precision decreases with longer distance to objects (small objects in relation to hand movements) and was not restricted by drift. We therefore do see this approach as superior over image based tracking. Image 4 shows a scene where the pointer is dragged over pipes covered in tinfoil. The reflections completely change the appearance of the dot and make any attempt on extracting it very difficult. Image 5 shows another reconstructed path in a scene with a curved water pipe installation. The user has encircled two areas with the laserpointer to mark them. Both images (6, 7) show good results in recreating the the drawn path on the real world objects.

Integrating audio data

When the path of the laserpointer is successfully reconstructed its movement can be replayed on the panoramic image as a video in combination with the original audio data. This already allows for a very good understanding of the scene. To further improve the results the audio data can be analyzed with speech recognition systems. We convert simple and clearly spoken words to text with Googles Speech API [21]. As the most basic method we place the text close to the laserdot. Since the replay is created offline by redrawing all frames of the scene the text elements can be made to

Figure 4: Reconstructed path on a reflective surface.

Figure 5: Path with encircled areas of interest.

appear instantly from the time when the corresponding word starts in the audio data. Image 6 shows a simple scene where the words 'one', 'two', 'three', 'four' were extracted from the audio data and drawn on the stitched image. As the next step in using audio data we use a voice command to create markers along the path of the laserdot. The keyword 'mark' is used to reference a frame and therefore position on the path were a marker should be placed. The next word in the extracted text is used as a description for the marker. Image 7 shows again the scene with the curved water pipe installation where two markers are created by voice input. Different than shown in image (7) the user now does not have to encircle the areas of interest anymore. Additionally the marker is known to the system as an object and can be used as a reference point to attach metadata or to navigate the video. Image 8 shows another usage of voice based markers. In this scene, three circuit breakers are marked inside a control cabinet. The words 'five', 'two' and 'seven' correspond to the circuit breakers that are of interest. As another feature our system supports the voice based creation of measurement annotations. Measuring distances is one of the most integral tasks in construction work. Our system enables the user to integrate hand measured distances into the scene by using a voice command. The keyword 'measure' is used to set the starting point of the measurement. The next word marks the end point and is converted to numerical representation if possible. In the resulting image and video two markers and a connection line is drawn with the supplied measurement value next to the line. In image 9 the scene with the water pipe installation is shown again. This time being annotated with two measurements that were taken before and integrated by voice commands.

Figure 6: Textual labels created from speech recognition.

Figure 7: Graphical markers created from voice command.

EVALUATION

Interaction

Even though our proposed system relies on a smartphone as data recording tool, the user does not have to look at the device. He can continuously look at the real world scene and the objects he is interested in without having to switch between information spaces like real world, paper or drawing software

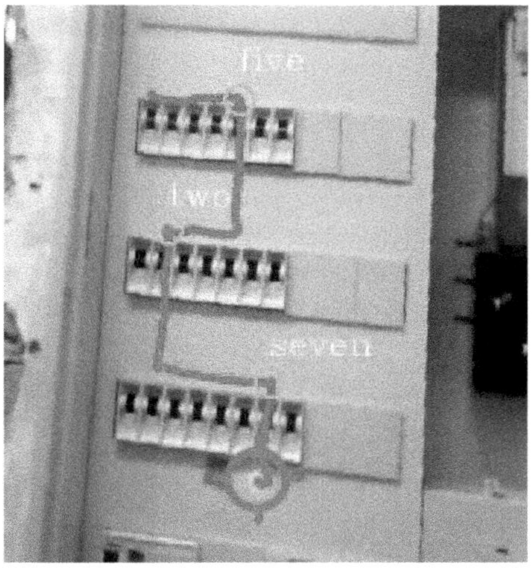

Figure 8: Graphical markers to reference circuit breakers.

Figure 9: Graphical measurements created from voice command.

The only direct interaction with the smartphone while pointing is by touching its surface without looking. Furthermore the user needs only one hand to create deictic gestures and annotations. The other hand is free to interact with the environment. This is very helpful, because it allows to manipulate objects according to the taking of notes, like holding open the door of a cabinet. It can be even more important in hazardous situations where the user needs a free hand to ensure his safety like holding on to a rail.

After taking the notes the replay videos are created automatically. The user does not have to rework his collected data and manually create a combined result. The stitched images are used as the background and the extracted annotations are drawn above them. This provides the user with a complete overview of the scene eliminating the workload of ordering lists of single images or navigating them in a viewer software. We found that visual quality of less sucessful stitched images is not necessarily a problem as long as the overall scene was understandable. Actually the cleaner and better aligned panoramas sometimes turned out to be irritating, because they can give the impression of a single image, but at the same time break the expected physical metrics. If a stitched image is not clearly recognized as such then the user can be irritated by the perspective distortion and start to doubt angles and directions.

The continuous recording time of individual paths is considerably slow. Most of our testvideos did not break the 15 second mark. Accordingly we see the biggest advantages in taking 'snapshots' of certain states of the real world objects incorporating explanations about measures or other visible parts. We think this interface can provide very useful data for decision making at crucial points in the construction process. Capturing short scenes with explanations of certain states of the construction work, is a fast and efficient way to create a history of events without having to switch to a computer or extensively transferring handwritten notes into another data format.

Scene Reconstruction

We tested our application by creating stitched images and replays in several different scenes provided from our partners. Technical installations typically provide a lot of non-uniform surfaces and therefore a good base to extract the features. Still the sequential approach bears the weakness of clutching and chained errors. As an intermediate step we see a global analysis of matches over the whole sequence after pairwise matching as promising. Such an analysis would also help to address the task of combining multiple strokes. So far our stitched images are created from one consistent movement. By matching these stroke images to each other we can find a rough estimate of the relative locations of the contained single images. Based on this initial guess, promising pairs of images from the two paths could be found for further processing and a full registration.

Audio

The integration of audio data proved to be very useful. As a first benefit it creates a very immersive replay in combination with the deictic gestures. In the audio channel the user can also store a lot of information that cannot be visually represented in a comfortable way, like longer verbal instructions. This way our application prevents the need of writing down information that cannot be drawn with the common set of graphical markers (points, lines, text) that many other applications use. Furthermore text entry can be a tiresome process on mobile devices. With our application the user can input his voice annotations with normal dictating speed. The additional use of voice commands further enhances the level of detail of integrated information. The user does not have to explicitly select a certain type of graphical marker and place it somewhere in the scene by interacting with the small surface of a mobile device. Instead he just 'tells' our application to create a certain element at the position he is pointing at.

CONCLUSION AND FUTURE WORK

We presented a novel interaction system to take short notes on real world objects by drawing on them and additionally using voice commands to place positional markers and measurements. Our system enables the user to directly draw on the objects of interest allowing intuitive annotations with using deictic gesturing. With this form of interface, the user can continuously look at the real world scene and therefore the shared communication space is left intact. Other attending people can watch him taking notes and give feedback to support him. Unlike typical smartphone Applications the user does not have to go through a secondary data entry step, like drawing on a photograph. Instead the real world annotations are directly captured and turned into panoramic images and videos allowing the user to review the notes afterwards.

For future development we see the automatic combining of multiple stitched paths as a priority. With this the user would gain the freedom to annotate a scene, take a break and and then continue in the same scene. As another step, features for automatic measuring would make a useful addition. Taking measures is a basic task in construction work. Our pointing device enables the user to reference positions he cannot reach physically, thus it would be very helpful to create measurements from the referenced points. However we agree with our partners that automatic measuring will only be useful if the accuracy can be trusted. We plan to evaluate different ways of automatic measurements like the usage of the point clouds created from Bundler/Photosynth as well as other technologies like laser projections or laser distance meters. Lastly, with the ongoing growth of calculation performance on mobile devices the full integration of the software on a smartphone should be considered.

ACKNOWLEDGEMENTS

This research was funded by the promotional program "Forschung für die Praxis" (Research for the Practice) of the Hessian Ministry for Science and Art in the context of the project "kARbon".

REFERENCES

1. Bundler. `http://phototour.cs.washington.edu/bundler/`. [Online; accessed 05-April-2013].
2. Microsoft research image composite editor. `http://research.microsoft.com/en-us/um/redmond/groups/ivm/ice/`. [Online; accessed 05-April-2013].
3. Photo tourism. `http://phototour.cs.washington.edu/`. [Online; accessed 05-April-2013].
4. Autodesk. Autocad ws. `https://www.autocadws.com/`. [Online; accessed 05-April-2013].
5. BOSCH. Bosch toolbox. `http://www.bosch-professional.com/de/de/news-extras/toolbox-app/toolbox-app.html`. [Online; accessed 05-April-2013].
6. Bradski, G. The OpenCV Library. *Dr. Dobb's Journal of Software Tools* (2000).
7. D-Solutions. D-photo measures. `https://play.google.com/store/apps/details?id=com.dsol.dmeasures`. [Online; accessed 05-April-2013].
8. druidlab. Measure & sketch. `https://play.google.com/store/apps/details?id=com.druidlab.mymeasure`. [Online; accessed 05-April-2013].
9. Gauglitz, S., Lee, C., Turk, M., and Höllerer, T. Integrating the physical environment into mobile remote collaboration. In *Proceedings of the 14th international conference on Human-computer interaction with mobile devices and services*, MobileHCI '12, ACM (New York, NY, USA, 2012), 241–250.
10. Kurz, D., Hantsch, F., Grobe, M., Schiewe, A., and Bimber, O. Laser pointer tracking in projector-augmented architectural environments. In *Proceedings of the 2007 6th IEEE and ACM International Symposium on Mixed and Augmented Reality*, ISMAR '07, IEEE Computer Society (Washington, DC, USA, 2007), 1–8.
11. Laboratories, T. I. Happy measure 3d zollstock. `https://play.google.com/store/apps/details?id=de.tlabs.maren.furnishing.client2.android`. [Online; accessed 05-April-2013].
12. Lowe, D. G. Distinctive image features from scale-invariant keypoints. *Int. J. Comput. Vision 60*, 2 (Nov. 2004), 91–110.
13. Microsoft. Microsoft photosynth. `http://photosynth.net/`. [Online; accessed 05-April-2013].
14. Oh, J.-Y., and Stuerzlinger, W. Laser pointers as collaborative pointing devices. In *Graphics Interface* (2002), 141–150.
15. Palmer, D., Adcock, M., Smith, J., Hutchins, M., Gunn, C., Stevenson, D., and Taylor, K. Annotating with light for remote guidance. In *Proceedings of the 19th Australasian conference on Computer-Human Interaction: Entertaining User Interfaces*, OZCHI '07, ACM (New York, NY, USA, 2007), 103–110.
16. Patel, S. N., Rekimoto, J., and Abowd, G. D. iCam : Precise at-a-Distance Interaction in the Physical. 272–287.
17. Sankar, A., and Seitz, S. Capturing indoor scenes with smartphones. *Proceedings of the 25th annual ACM symposium on User interface software and technology - UIST '12* (2012), 403.
18. Snavely, N., Seitz, S. M., and Szeliski, R. Photo tourism: Exploring photo collections in 3d. In *SIGGRAPH Conference Proceedings*, ACM Press (New York, NY, USA, 2006), 835–846.
19. Szeliski, R. Image alignment and stitching: A tutorial. Tech. rep., MSR-TR-2004-92, Microsoft Research, 2004, 2005.
20. vistech.projects. Partometer3d. `https://play.google.com/store/apps/details?id=com.vistechprojects.partometer3d`. [Online; accessed 05-April-2013].
21. www.google.com, G. Web speech api demonstration. `http://www.google.com/intl/en/chrome/demos/speech.html`. [Online; accessed 05-April-2013].

Crowd-scale Interactive Formal Reasoning and Analytics

Ethan Fast[1], Colleen Lee[1], Alex Aiken[1], Michael S. Bernstein[1], Daphne Koller[1], Eric Smith[2]
Stanford University[1], Kestrel Institute[2]
{ethan.fast, clee0, aiken, msb, koller}@cs.stanford.edu, eric.smith@kestrel.edu

ABSTRACT
Large online courses often assign problems that are gradable by simple checks such as multiple choice, but these checks are inappropriate for domains in which students may produce an infinity of correct solutions. One such domain is *derivations*: sequences of logical steps commonly used in assignments for technical, mathematical and scientific subjects. We present DeduceIt, a system for creating, grading, and analyzing derivation assignments across arbitrary formal domains. DeduceIt supports assignments in any logical formalism, provides students with incremental feedback, and aggregates student paths through each proof to produce instructor analytics. DeduceIt benefits from checking thousands of derivations on the web: it introduces a *proof cache*, a novel data structure which leverages a crowd of students to decrease the cost of checking derivations and providing real-time, constructive feedback. We evaluate DeduceIt with 990 students in an online compilers course, finding students take advantage of its incremental feedback and instructors benefit from its structured insights into confusing course topics. Our work suggests that automated reasoning can extend online assignments and large-scale education to many new domains.

Author Keywords
MOOC, theorem prover, formal logic, online education

ACM Classification Keywords
H.5.2 Information Interfaces and Presentation: Graphical user interfaces

General Terms
Human Factors; Design

INTRODUCTION
As online courses enroll thousands of students [22], course staff are unable to provide feedback on assignments and instead turn to automatic grading systems. Automatic grading works well for multiple choice quizzes, but it remains difficult in domains where students may construct many correct solutions [2, 10]. *Derivations*, or sequences of logical steps where each step follows from its predecessors, are one popular assignment type that technical, mathematical, or scientific subjects often assign in their offline problem sets. However, because derivations encode open-ended reasoning, they are uncommon in large online courses today.

With derivation assignments, it is important to provide *personalized, realtime feedback* to students and instructors. While a grading system can report whether an answer is correct (e.g., through multiple choice or string matching), it doesn't know enough about a student's reasoning to provide guidance for a wrong answer. Most grading systems offer limited feedback that is unassociated with the intermediate steps of a solution [1]. But derivations are prone to a great deal of internal variation, and often have many right answers [3], so we face the challenge of providing *constructive* suggestions [9]. Similarly, students tend to learn better when subject to *real-time* feedback loops [8], for example help from human TAs in a traditional course setting [9, 3, 30]. However, theorem prover calls are expensive computations [14] and often do not complete at interactive speeds. Instructors, only seeing the final product, also remain largely uninformed about the paths that students take to construct derivations.

In this paper, we pursue large-scale online derivation assignments for any formal domain and at any level of abstraction. Critically, we suggest that *hosting these derivations online, at large scale, allows realtime personalized feedback for students and detailed analytics for instructors*. Unlike previous work focused on single domains like calculus (e.g., [31, 23]), we allow instructors to support derivations in *any* formal domain: for example, compilers, regular expressions, or mathematics. Instructors may also specify levels of proof detail for an assignment; for instance, they may require that students report some derivation rules but elide others.

Our approach illustrates the interface benefits that follow from the scale of online courses. Rather than provide slow feedback based entirely on proof search, we create a *proof cache* that saves other students' previous attempts at the derivation and can thus provide realtime feedback and guidance to students. By aggregating these paths, we enable instructors to analyze student progress and challenges.

In this paper we present:

- *DeduceIt*: A web-based system which allows instructors to to specify a general class of derivation exercises, scales to a large workload of students, and enables students to complete assignments at varied levels of abstraction. DeduceIt provides students with constructive and real-time feedback.

UIST'13, October 8–11, 2013, St. Andrews, United Kingdom.

http://dx.doi.org/10.1145/2501988.2502028

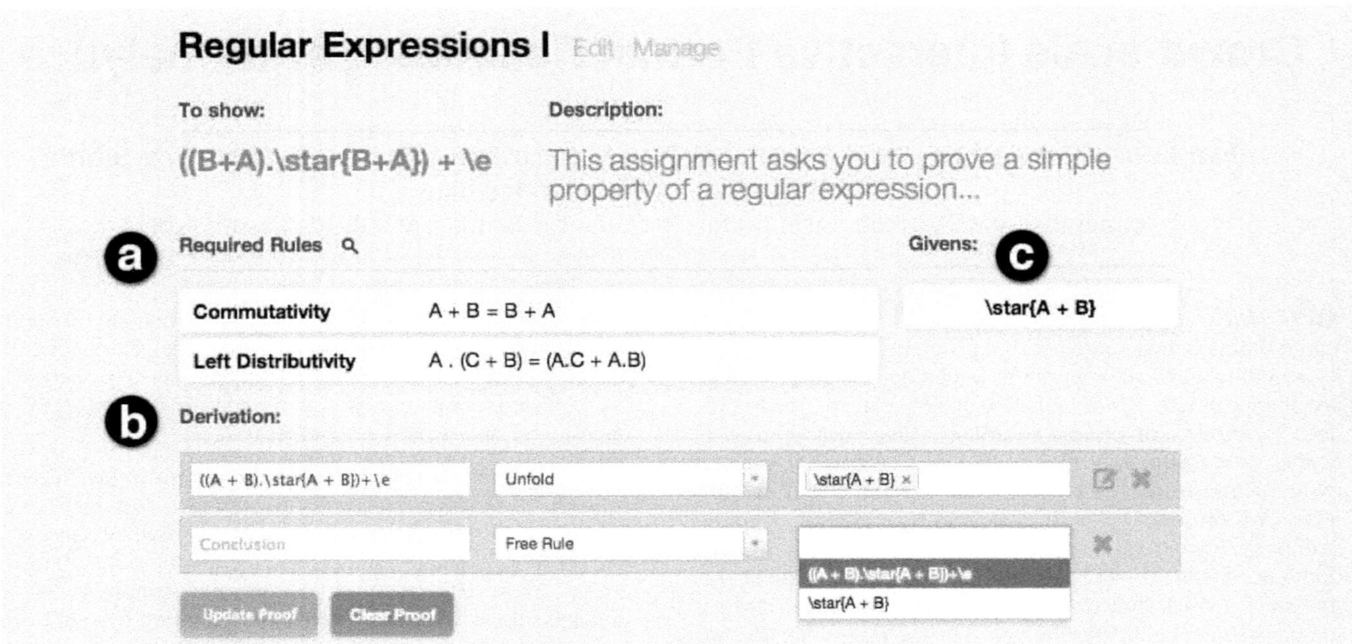

Figure 1: The DeduceIt interface: (a) set of available rules (b) interactive derivation component (c) set of given assumptions

- The *proof cache*: A novel data structure which records the history of every attempted derivation, reusing computations from previously derived steps. We show that this cache increases derivation-checking efficiency by 87% and provides feedback in less than one second, much faster than what is possible in a single user system.
- An *empirical evaluation* of DeduceIt: a deployment of DeduceIt to 990 students online for assignments in type checking, regular expressions, finite automata, and several other topics. We detail how: 1) students take advantage of DeduceIt's incremental feedback for exploration, and 2) instructors use DeduceIt to obtain structured insights into confusing course topics.

The rest of this paper is organized as follows: we begin with related work and a motivating example, then we present DeduceIt's interface and capabilities. Next, we describe the implementation of the system and provide an empirical evaluation, using data collected from students in an online class. We close with reflections, conclusions, and future work.

RELATED WORK

At its core, DeduceIt is an interactive proof solving system. Many existing tools provide users with rich and automated feedback as a form of proof assistance [23, 6, 24, 21, 15, 4, 25, 31], but they are tied to specific formalisms or require background knowledge generally not assumed in a MOOC audience. For instance, some tools allow users to explore complex problem domains, but they require knowledge of an underlying programming language that students or instructors may find difficult to understand (e.g., [23, 24]); other tools present a more pedagogically oriented interface, but they are limited in the kinds of formalisms they can support (e.g, [31]).

Automated theorem provers have been applied to educational settings [27, 28, 25, 4], and the idea of using theorem provers to enable education has engendered much discussion among researchers [10, 2]. However, systems designed to address educational use have also tended toward interfaces designed for a single domain (e.g., geometry [25]) or present unstructured interactions that are designed for users already familiar with programming (e.g., ProveEasy [4]). DeduceIt aims to support constrained interactions across many (incomplete) formalisms at just enough depth for students to explore.

Other work addresses automatic feedback and grading systems with a more domain specific focus. Simple forms of automatic grading have been studied in both physical and online classrooms [12]. These systems tend to restrict an assignment's answer domain with assumptions like multiple choice answers, concrete-valued answers (e.g., answers that match against a string or numerical value), or a set of test cases to evaluate a programming assignment. Tools can assist with formal reasoning tasks like model checking or logical inference [18], but these tools aren't designed toward pedological ends. Further, automated grading and plagiarism detection systems have long evaluated student program code—where solutions may be unstructured and creative—in computer science departments [5, 26], but we are concerned with a system that works across all kinds of derivations.

Finally, crowdsourcing research has enabled new forms of problem-solving and evaluation. For instance, peer consistency evaluation can be used to effectively judge the accuracy—and grade—of a student's answer, even in the absence of a ground truth [13] and crowd-based peer assessment has been successfully applied to grade student assignments

[29, 17]. DeduceIt does not require human evaluation; it instead uses crowds to guide its exploration of the proof space.

SCENARIO

DeduceIt provides students with feedback and support for any formal domain, and allows instructors to specify the level of abstraction at which a student may work though a derivation. In this section, we demonstrate these ideas.

Regular Expressions I is an assignment we use to introduce students to DeduceIt. Here, students must show that two regular expressions are equal: $(A+B)* \equiv ((B+A).(B+A)*)+\epsilon$. We assign the syntax $+$, $*$, ϵ, and . as union, Kleene closure, empty string, and concatenation. Students must derive the expression $((B+A).(B+A)*)+\epsilon$ starting from a set of givens, in this case the single expression $(A+B)*$, using given properties of regular expressions.

Constraints on the Derivation Interface

DeduceIt limits the actions available to students at each step of the derivation. Students may freely enter expressions into the conclusion box of a derivation, but the rules and givens input fields are constrained to lists of possibilities. This offers students a form of guidance.

Since our student has been given only $(A + B)*$ from which to start her derivation, she reasons that she must select this expression from the givens input field on the first step. From the rule field she must select a rule from the list of assignment rules, and in the conclusion field she must enter a newly derived expression. She selects the "Unfold" rule, which expands a Kleene star expression. She then tries Unfold on the full starting expression, mentally applying the rule to the given and typing out $((A + B).(A + B)*) + \epsilon$ in the conclusion. She submits the step.

The derivation returns with her step highlighted in green: it was successful. A new set of input fields lies below her previous entry, querying her for the next step.

Working at Specifiable Levels of Abstraction

Since our student's previous conclusion is nearly identical to the goal, she wants to use it for her next step. If she can transform its two sub-expressions $A + B$ to $B + A$, then she will have proven the goal and completed the assignment. She decides to apply Commutativity to each of the two $A + B$ sub-expressions, entering her result in the conclusion input box on the next line of the derivation. This new conclusion is identical to the goal expression: $((B + A).(B + A)*) + \epsilon$

She selects "Commutativity" from the rule input field, selects $((B + A).(B + A)*) + \epsilon$ from the givens field, and submits the step. DeduceIt checks her derivation, infers through proof search that she means to apply Commutativity twice—on the two appropriate sub-expressions—and responds that her derivation is correct. She has completed this assignment.

Here our student *interacts with DeduceIt at a relatively high level of abstraction*: she applies Commutativity twice, simultaneously, in a single derivation step. Under a different assignment setup she might be required to enter each application of Commutativity separately; or alternatively, she might be allowed to apply Commutativity freely without needing to specify it as a separate proof step.

Providing Constructive and Real-time Feedback

Immediate feedback is critical to the design of interactive educational systems [8]. If DeduceIt were running locally on her computer, the student would have needed to wait up to four seconds for each incremental piece of feedback. Instead, feedback is available in under one second, which allows her to move from one step to another with confidence that her prior reasoning is correct. This acceleration is possible because DeduceIt can utilize proof steps that other students computed previously.

Displaying Analytics and Hints

The instructor opens the analytics interface. He sees that many students are struggling to complete an easy exercise, and in particular that they are often veering into a dead-end proof path, so he annotates that subtree of the derivation with a hint suggesting why the direction will not be fruitful. When a student next tries this direction, she receives the feedback and reroutes, saving herself some frustration.

DEDUCEIT

DeduceIt is an online derivation system that supports arbitrary formal domains and specifiable levels of abstraction. It takes advantage of large courses by creating a cache of proofs that it uses to optimize verification and power derivation analytics for the instructor.

Interacting with a DeduceIt Derivation

Each DeduceIt assignment contains an interactive derivation (Figure 1). To move forward in the derivation, a student must derive a conclusion by applying the selected rule on the selected givens(s).

On each derivation step, DeduceIt responds with one of several kinds of *feedback*: if the derivation is so far valid, all its steps will turn green; if the system cannot parse the conclusion of some step in the derivation, that step will turn yellow; or if the system can parse but not prove the conclusion of some step in the derivation, that step will turn red. Each valid step preceding an invalid step will remain green.

DeduceIt derivations have *constraints* that aim to make it easier for students to complete derivations while avoiding syntactical mistakes that are unrelated to learning. Students may only select expressions they have already derived (or members of the set of starting givens) from the givens input field. Likewise, students may only select rules which are associated with the current assignment from the rules input field.

Finally, if an invalid step has any *hint annotations* on the proof tree, a hint appears adjacent to that step. Hints take the form of a question mark, expanding into text on mouseover.

Assignment Analytics on the Proof Tree

Because many students complete each derivation, DeduceIt can give instructors real-time access to assignment analytics. DeduceIt creates a *proof tree* for each assignment (Figure 2), which tracks the history of all associated derivations. These

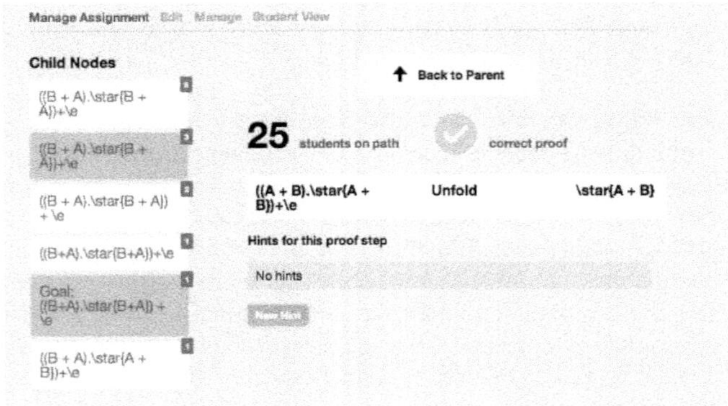

Figure 2: Annotating a node on the proof tree.

derivations share a common root node, and each step in a derivation maps from a parent node to a child node via a step in the proof. Every node keeps track of derivation state information and a count of how many students have traversed it. An instructor may annotate any node in the tree with hints, and these will be visible to a student if she enters upon that path in her own derivation. An instructor may also use this tree to override the behavior of the underlying derivation checker, e.g., forcibly label a given derivation step valid. This can be useful for steps which make use of particularly long chains of free rules that aren't discovered and verified because of limitations in proof search.

Extensions to the Derivation Interface

Based on our experiences with DeduceIt, we have developed several other forms of derivation feedback which we have not yet deployed for an online class.

Displaying the Proof Path

DeduceIt maintains aggregate data about every derivation, so the system knows when students are proceeding down well-traveled paths in a derivation, down correct but—so far—more lengthy paths, or down paths which have not yet led to the goal. DeduceIt can optionally display this information with a status indicator, a colored circle of green, yellow, or orange at the top of the derivation, indicating whether students are on a common path, an uncommon but successful path, or an as yet unsuccessful path.

DeduceIt could provide students even more fine-grained information: the exact number of other successful or unsuccessful students who have worked to the current state of their derivation; or detection of the exact step in their derivation where they left the well-traveled path. It is also possible to further process the proof tree. By collapsing some nodes which are syntactically different but semantically equivalent (e.g., the expressions $(1 + 2) + 3$ and $1 + (2 + 3)$) we could construct a more meaningful notion of a derivation path.

Providing Automatic Hints

DeduceIt allows instructors to set up hints for any derivation step by annotating an assignment's proof tree. Optionally, DeduceIt can construct these hints automatically using proof search by holding the rule and assumption fields constant and searching for alternative valid conclusions.

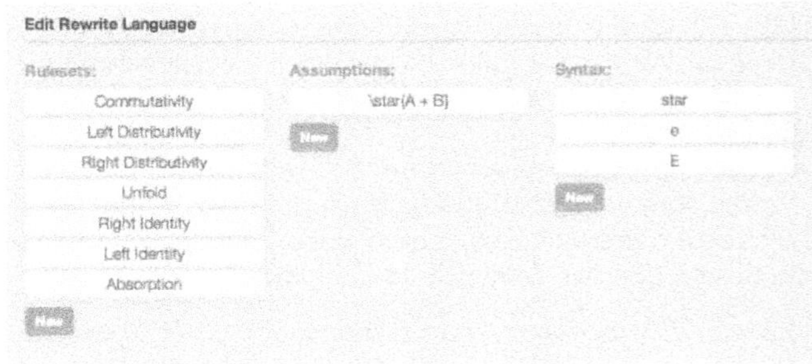

Figure 3: Instructors must specify a rewrite language for each assignment.

For instance, suppose that students enter $x = 3 + 1$, *Balance Equation*, and $x + 1 = 3$ in the fields for conclusion, rule, and assumptions. This is an incorrect step, so DeduceIt will highlight it in red. But the hint-generating DeduceIt is able to give students more specific feedback, e.g., "Balance Equation can be applied, but your conclusion is incorrect." Here proof search finds a viable alternative conclusion, $x = 3 - 1$, so DeduceIt knows it is possible to apply the selected rule upon the selected given.

Other hint-generating systems might hold constant different parts of the derivation (e.g., searching for rules and assumptions to match a given conclusion), or draw inspiration from Model-Tracing Tutors [11].

Background: Term Rewriting Systems

To understand the instructor's authoring interface, we begin by reviewing the major concepts behind *term rewriting systems*. DeduceIt uses a term rewriting system to verify student derivations. Term rewriting systems consist of a set of expressions with nested sub-expressions, and relations which define transformations on those expressions; each transformation is called a *rewrite rule* [19, 24]. Term rewrite rules have a left side, which must match a term for the rule to be applied, and a right side, which defines the new expression produced by the rule. Variables may appear in the rule (declared in the system with \$ notation) which binds to the term or its subexpressions. For example, in a language which supports integers, symbols, and the binary operators $+$, $-$, and $=$ (this happens to be a subset of the default DeduceIt language), one such rule might be: $(\$x + \$y = \$z) \rightarrow (\$x = \$z - \$y)$. The system can apply this rule to the expression $2 + 1 = 3$ to produce $2 = 3 - 1$.

Assignment Creation Across Arbitrary Formalisms

Taking advantage of term rewriting systems, instructors can use DeduceIt to define nearly any kind of formal assignment. To create an assignment, an instructor must specify four things:

1. Rewrite language: Every assignment has a default rewrite language composed of variables, symbols, integers, and several common unary and binary operators. In many assignment domains this will be sufficient, but an instructor

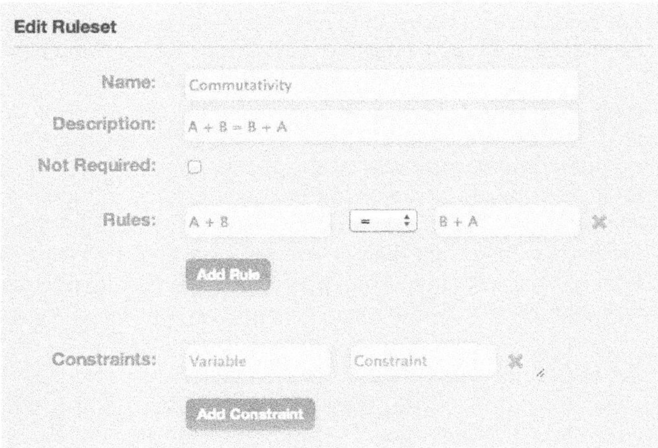

Figure 4: Editing a ruleset on the instructor interface.

may optionally augment the language with extra syntax for functions and constants (Figure 3).

2. Rulesets: Named sets of rewrite rules which a student may apply while working through an assignment's derivation. One ruleset corresponds to many underlying rewrite rules. This is necessary because an instructor may want to refer to several distinct rules by the same name (e.g., $1 * X \rightarrow X$ and $X * 1 \rightarrow X$ are two distinct rewrite rules describing the multiplicative identity.)

3. The given expression(s): A set of expressions which serve as the starting point of a derivation.

4. The goal expression: The desired result of a derivation.

Most assignments have a small number of rulesets and given expressions, because DeduceIt is designed for pedagogical purposes and not large, general proofs. This makes debugging fairly straightforward, and in practice assignments take between 5 and 30 minutes to prepare and up to another 30 to test, as reported by the TA for the class in our evaluation.

Customizing an Assignment Language

Instructors can customize an assignment's language, allowing students to use familiar notation. By default DeduceIt provides the unary operators ~ and $-$, and the binary operators ., &, |, ,, $*$, \, $+$, $-$, $=$, $\neq$, $\leq$, $\geq$, $<$, $>$, $=>$, $:=$, and $\rightarrow$, listed in order of precedence. DeduceIt also supports variables (only used when defining rewrite rules), symbols, and integers. For example, three expressions in the rewrite language are: "$\$p, (\$p => \$q) \rightarrow \$q$", "$a.b.b.a$", and "$x + 2 = y$".

Note that with several exceptions (the notation specific to rewrites: $:=$, $\rightarrow$, and \$) the operators used in expressions have no meaning without an accompanying set of rules; they simply determine the parsing of an expression.

Instructors may add two kinds of syntax to DeduceIt's standard rewrite language: constants and functions. This is convenient in many domains, where familiarly named functions and constants enhance the readability of an assignment. For these custom functions and constants, constants appear as a symbol value preceded by a backslash, e.g., $\backslash e$. Functions look much the same, except they have arguments which they accept in brackets, e.g., $\backslash sin\{x\}$.

Defining an Assignment Domain with Rulesets

To control the level of abstraction at which students complete an assignment, instructors define a ruleset for each student-facing rule. A ruleset defines a *set* of transformations that a student may use in a derivation, because each rule often requires multiple rewrite rules for its implementation, e.g., $1 * X \rightarrow X$ and $X * 1 \rightarrow X$ for the multiplicative identity. Each ruleset has a name, a student-facing description, a set of rewrite rules, and an optional set of constraints (Figure 4). The name and description of a ruleset are all a student sees when using DeduceIt; students do not need to understand rewrite rules.

To allow students to elide less important proof steps, the instructor may choose whether a ruleset is *required* or *free*. Required rulesets must be named explicitly when a student uses them in a derivation. Free rulesets, however, may be elided. Behind the scenes, DeduceIt will attempt to fill in free steps automatically through proof search. This is useful when a student must use trivial transformations which are necessary to the derivation but unimportant to the assignment.

Instructors can define both *strict* and *context independent* rewrite rules. To apply a strict rule, its left side must match exactly on an expression, whereas a context independent rule may be applied to an expression or any of its subexpressions. For many assignments a single context independent rule can take the place of many strict rules. This eases the burden on an instructor and usually speeds up proof search. However, strict rewrite rules cannot be entirely replaced with context independent rules. Some transformations may be context dependent (e.g., lexing character values of a string). Moreover, *strict rewrite rules allow instructors to simulate complex assignment domains which would otherwise lie outside the scope of a typical rewrite rule based system.*

For example, we use strict rewrite rules to define a type checking assignment over a specific domain of input $\backslash type\{t\}\{expr\}$. Because we tailor such rules specifically to the context of this assignment, we do not need the power of full type analysis: rewrite rules are sufficient. Further, as students see only the description of each rule, which tends to be general, and not the underlying implementation as rulesets, which is often more specific, DeduceIt appears to have expressive capability far beyond rewrite systems. Instructors would use a similar approach to deploy assignments in domains like parsing or multivariate calculus.

Sharing Rewrite Languages

Some rewrite languages are common enough that it makes sense to share them among different assignments: for instance, many assignments might use the languages defined for basic algebraic manipulation, predicate logic, or the expansion of regular expressions. DeduceIt allows instructors to reuse a rewrite language across assignments.

IMPLEMENTATION AND PROOF CACHE

The core implementation challenge of DeduceIt is to run a large-scale theorem prover in real time. DeduceIt is a system formed of three distinct components: a frontend interface, a backend theorem prover, and a database. The frontend manages all user interactions (for both students and instructors) as described in the previous section, the backend theorem prover exposes an online API which the frontend calls—when necessary—to check student derivations, and the database stores all the data associated with users and assignments, including the various proof trees which together constitute the proof cache.

The frontend is a Ruby on Rails web application deployed on Heroku, the backend is a Haskell application also deployed on Heroku, and the database is a MongoDB installation running on MongoHQ. Each of these components can be scaled to serve arbitrary numbers of students.

Theorem Prover

To verify student derivations, DeduceIt applies proof search over a term rewriting system. DeduceIt's theorem prover also includes a parser which is constructed dynamically on each theorem prover call, allowing instructors to define custom assignment syntax.

The Theorem Prover API

The DeduceIt prover is wrapped in a web server which can be queried via an API over the following arguments: *rulesets*, *assumptions*, *syntax*, and *conclusion*. To every query the prover will respond with either "proven", "unproven", or "syntax error." The frontend uses this API to assess the validity of each step in a derivation.

The *syntax* argument defines any new syntax on the default rewrite language. The rest of the parameters are used for proof search: DeduceIt tries to prove the provided *conclusion* expression using the set of rewrite rules defined in *rulesets* on the starting expressions in *assumptions*.

Proof Search

Proof search applies rewrite rules iteratively upon a group of expressions to generate new expressions. In general, a search may be considered either *forward*, starting from the known expressions and working toward the desired expressions, or *backward*, starting from the desired expressions and working toward the known expressions with an inverted set of rules. DeduceIt supports both kinds of search.

In practice, DeduceIt conducts one round of forward search and one round of backward search; the two rounds of search then meet in the middle, i.e., they check for terms generated in common. We introduce backward search to ensure DeduceIt will correctly check rewrite languages which allow the introduction of new symbols, e.g., predicate logic and the rule $\$a \rightarrow \$a \vee \$b$ (note here that $\$b$ is a variable in the rewrite rule which binds to *any expression*, so forward search cannot enumerate every possible value of $\$b$). Moreover, the meet-in-the-middle approach tends to be more effective than two rounds of only forward or backward search [14].

We find the system is limited to two rounds of search under reasonable time constraints, with an upper bound of 4 seconds for students interacting with a web application. At each iteration of search DeduceIt applies the set of available rewrite rules—defined by the collection of rulesets—non-deterministically and exhaustively. Notably, this delay falls into the third classification of Nielsen's work on response times, below the ten-second limit for keeping a user focused on his or her dialog with the system [20]. While the theorem prover could be made more efficient, the next section will demonstrate that in many cases this is unnecessary.

Proof Cache

DeduceIt introduces the idea of a *proof cache*, which takes advantage of other students' explorations to make the entire system run at more interactive speeds.

The proof cache tracks all responses that the frontend application receives from the prover. This cache is composed of many proof trees, one for each assignment, and together these proof trees track the aggregate history of every attempted derivation. Proof trees are a useful tool for managing assignments, but they can also, by acting as a cache, dramatically improve the overall performance of the system.

DeduceIt's bottleneck is in its prover; proof search is by far the most computationally expensive aspect of the system. A proof cache can limit the outbound queries to the prover and so, intuitively, increase the performance of the system.

To check a new derivation step using the proof cache, DeduceIt queries the proof tree for that derivation's assignment: if the new step already exists in the tree, then the system doesn't need to query the prover; it simply returns the stored result.

Besides the benefits of providing an infrastructure for hints and a summary of how well students are doing in an assignment, the proof cache has a very significant performance benefit for two reasons:

1. Most students complete derivations with steps that other students have used previously or future students will use.

2. It is more efficient to reuse the intermediate results of one student's derivation to check the validity of a derivation step than to check every derivation step with the prover.

An average prover call takes $810ms$, whereas a typical cache lookup takes only $23ms$. This improvement moves DeduceIt up a level on Nielsen's scale of responsiveness, under one second, to the level at which a user's flow of thought is uninterrupted [20]. We evaluate the performance impact of the proof cache more fully in the next section.

EVALUATION

DeduceIt hypothesizes that online derivation systems can scale to many students, across formal domains, and provide useful instructor analytics. To evaluate DeduceIt, we deployed it in the winter 2013 offering of Coursera's *Compilers* class, assigning several DeduceIt problems every week of the course. Out of the 7625 students who enrolled, 990 of them completed at least one DeduceIt assignment.

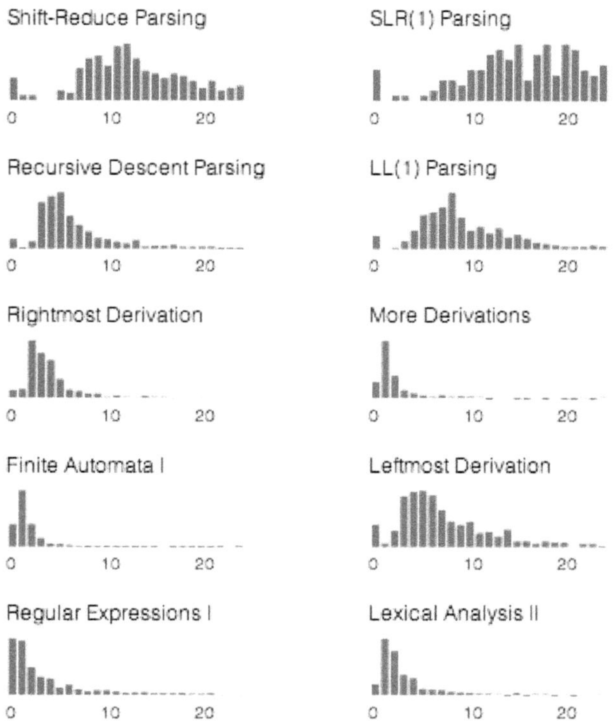

Figure 5: Normalized histograms show student time distributions for each assignment. The x-axis measures time in minutes. These time distributions are approximately normal with right skew and centered upon a fixed time value which tracks loosely with an assignment's difficulty.

In this section we provide evidence for two claims:

1. *Students successfully use DeduceIt for derivations.* We show through data analysis and user feedback that students engage with DeduceIt to solve problems.
2. *DeduceIt provides instructors with insights that translate into future course improvements.* Here we provide examples from our experience with the Compilers course.

We run several analyses over ten DeduceIt assignments, measuring the distribution of students' time spent on assignments and derivation steps, the success rate of students, the average number of student errors, and the performance impact of the DeduceIt's proof cache.

Assignment Time Distributions

First, we analyze the amount of time students spent on each assignment. These time distributions are approximately normal with right skew and centered upon a fixed time value which tracks loosely with an assignment's difficulty (Figure 5). For example, in the *Rightmost Derivation* assignment students are clustered around 4 minutes, and in the *Shift-Reduce Parsing* assignment they are clustered around 10 minutes; the *Rightmost Derivation* assignment is generally considered easier by students than *Shift-Reduce Parsing*. This relation holds true among the remainder of the assignments. To determine assignment difficulty in offline courses, instructors would typically need to guess or to ask students, who may have faulty recall. DeduceIt could easily be expanded to support knowledge-tracing [7] and provide instructors with more detailed analytics.

Rule Time Distributions

We also observe the time distribution which governs rule application across assignments. Supposing some rules are easier or more natural to apply than others, we can use DeduceIt to find rules associated with longer elapsed time between steps, revealing what parts of the course material are more likely to confuse students. On average, it takes students 163 seconds (roughly 3 minutes) between derivation steps.

Rule time distributions may also help instructors diagnose problematic derivation paths. For example, "Nonterm Y input end" is the rule associated with the longest elapsed time (1482s). This rule comes from *LL(1) Parsing* and represents an operation on a lookup table. Most students using "Nonterm Y input end" have entered a valid but misleading conclusion on the previous derivation step, which is an ideal candidate for hint annotation on the assignment proof tree (e.g., a hint which suggests, "While this step is correct, it doesn't lead to the solution.").

For a second use-case of this data, we examine the assignment *Regular Expressions I*. Here, the rules "Left Identity" and "Right Identity" are used by students most quickly, at about 100 seconds between applications. Students apply the "Unfold" rule most slowly, at approximately 400 seconds in its application. This suggests Unfold may be the most challenging property of regular expressions for students.

More generally, these analytics grant the instructors fine-grained insight into students' understanding, even on complex assignments. Instructors might use such information to better focus the emphasis of their lectures.

Student Success Rates

Next, we examine the success rates of students across assignments. These results are displayed in Table 1. Success rates are uniformly high, ranging from 93% to 99%, and these rates track reported assignment difficulty in a manner consistent with time distributions.

High success rates do not necessarily suggest that students are *learning* from these assignments, but we have received feedback that supports this idea. Several students told us that they found DeduceIt's derivation constraints (e.g., a list of available rules and givens, and step-by-step validation) useful for understanding the domain of a problem. One student mentioned, "Being able to step through the parsing actions and 'be' the parser and know immediately when I made a mistake was incredibly helpful in coming to truly understand how the different parsing styles work." However, these constraints beget certain tradeoffs: DeduceIt trades flexibility in assignment notation for ease of verification, and other students told us that assignment syntax got in the way, that DeduceIt "is difficult to use since you have to learn the syntax of each problem before actually applying what you know." An

Assignment Name	Description	Min	Total	Rules	Cache	Success	Valid	Syn.	Sem.
Regular Expressions I	Prove two regexes are equivalent	2	185	7	3412	96%	55%	11%	34%
Lexical Analysis II	Show the sequence of moves of a lexer	6	119	4	5963	97%	63%	6%	30%
Finite Automata I	Show that an automaton accepts a string	5	53	10	4589	98%	73%	3%	23%
Leftmost Derivation	Perform a leftmost derivation	10	97	3	10857	95%	56%	6%	38%
Rightmost Derivation	Perform a rightmost derivation	10	78	3	10857	98%	81%	1%	17%
More Derivations	Parse a sequence of roman numerals	6	61	9	9042	99%	81%	1%	18%
Recursive Descent Parsing	Show each state of a recursive descent parse	13	155	4	9465	96%	69%	1%	29%
LL(1) Parsing	Derive string using parse table	13	69	11	4750	99%	83%	1%	15%
Shift-Reduce Parsing	Show a shift-reduce parse of a string	20	151	8	6894	94%	85%	2%	12%
SLR(1) Parsing	Parse string using SLR(1) action table	15	99	33	4815	93%	60%	2%	36%

Table 1: *Min* is the shortest observed derivation path. *Total* is the observed number of unique derivations paths. *Rules* is the number of rules in the assignment. *Cache* is the size of the proof cache, e.g., the observed number of unique steps. *Success* is the success rate among students who attempted the assignment. *Valid* is the percentage of derivation steps which are valid. *Syn.* and *Sym.* are the percentages of observed syntax and semantic errors, respectively. (Note: Leftmost and Rightmost Derivation share the same subset of the proof cache.) Assignments are listed in the order they were assigned.

analysis of learning is outside the scope of this paper, but on balance we consider the feedback promising.

Student Error Rates

We next compute the rate of student mistakes, where an error is a conclusion which doesn't follow from the givens. Error rates among derivation steps for all the DeduceIt assignments are substantial—on average 29.4%, or approximately one error for every three correct steps—despite the high overall success rates reported in Table 1. We expect this result: students will always get some things wrong. Learning rarely takes place without error, whether indeliberate or exploratory as students use the system as a means of externalizing cognition [16]. Ideally, we might distinguish between two classes of error: errors which stem from a misunderstanding of course material, and errors which stem from misunderstandings (or exploratory actions) with DeduceIt.

To approximate the impact of these two classes of error, we divide student mistakes into two categories: syntax errors, and semantic errors (*Syn.* and *Sem.*, Table 1). Syntax errors arise from entering an expression which DeduceIt cannot parse, whereas semantic errors arise from parseable derivation steps which cannot be proven. While semantic errors are certain to contain faulty logic, this is not obviously true for syntax errors: a student might have intended to write a correct step and simply failed to use the system properly. We use the rates of student syntax errors as a proxy for measuring rates of student confusion with the DeduceIt system.

Across all assignments syntax errors are low, never exceeding 11%. Notably, the highest rate of syntax errors occurred in the first class assignment, *Regular Expressions I*, despite the fact that students generally considered this assignment the easiest. The syntax error rates of subsequent assignments never exceeded 6%, although these later assignments were much more difficult. In fact, in the last 6 assignments, the average syntax error rate was only 1.3%. This is likely a result of students learning to use the system. Low overall rates among syntax errors suggest that DeduceIt did not confuse students to the detriment of assignment completion and correctness.

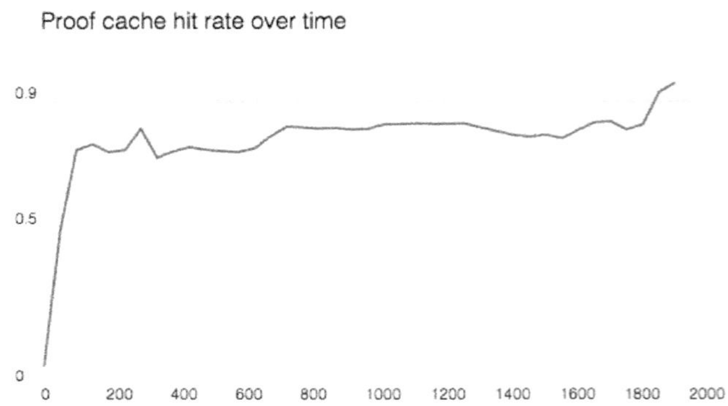

Figure 6: The x-axis measures the total number of derivation steps entered into the system. The y-axis measures the cache hit rate as a percentage.

Performance Impact of the Proof Cache

We test a hypothesis which provides the general intuition behind the proof cache: *most derivations contain steps that other students have previously used or will use in the future.* Of 50,099 total derivation steps in the class, only 5,407 (10%) of them are unique. So, 90% of derivation steps are reused, which indicates that a proof cache may be useful.

Next, we examine our second hypothesis: *it is more efficient to use the proof cache than to check every derivation step with the prover.* To test this hypothesis, we measured the overall proof cache hit rate. In Figure 6, we show the cache hit rate plotted against time. By the 1900th student interaction, the cache has reached a hit rate of 90%. Since the average theorem prover call takes $810ms$ and the average cache lookup takes $23ms$, we can compute an average time of $810ms * 0.10 + 23ms * 0.90 = 101.7ms$. This represents a cost savings of 87% and qualitatively improves usability: running the cache allows DeduceIt to move up one level on Nielsen's hierarchy of responsiveness [20]. As DeduceIt adds more attempted derivation steps to the cache, the hit rate should continue to climb, albeit at a slower rate.

Further, the proof cache has benefits over memoization in a single user system. The proof cache hit rate is high because many students tend to enter the same derivation steps. A single student is less likely to enter the same derivation step more than once. Collectively, students reuse 90% of derivation steps, whereas on average, individual students reuse fewer than 17% of steps.

LIMITATIONS AND FUTURE WORK

In our Compilers course we encountered several notable limitations and tradeoffs in the DeduceIt system.

First, supporting arbitrary formalisms is a challenging design goal for a pedagogical system. DeduceIt achieves this goal by encouraging instructors to create *incomplete* instead of full formalisms. When necessary, complex rewrite rules that are difficult to implement generally are instead handled by assignment-specific rules, providing students with an illusion of working in a more general theory. In this way, DeduceIt trades completeness for expressiveness and simplicity, making it easier for instructors to create and debug assignments at the expense of totally covering a domain. However, other valuable systems might approach this tradeoff differently.

Second, a DeduceIt assignment must adopt the syntax of the default rewrite language. This works well for many kinds of assignments (e.g., algebra, basic calculus, predicate logic, regular expressions, and type checking), since instructors can still define custom functions and constants. However, in some assignments, natural notation differs more considerably from DeduceIt's rewrite language (and its possible extensions); this creates unnecessary friction on the derivation interface. For example, *LL(1) Parsing* uses a series of rules to define a lookup table: one student commented that some such rules were defined in "less than ideal notation." This is an issue we hope to fix in future versions of DeduceIt. Expressions and rules in the rewrite language do not need to be rendered as text on the student view; customizable HTML trees would allow instructors far more latitude in defining the appearance of assignment notation.

Third, while DeduceIt responds to students with information about semantic errors, syntax errors, correct steps, and annotated hints, some students felt the system wasn't offering them sufficient guidance. One student mentioned, "I spent more than half an hour trying to understand why DeduceIt was not accepting my derivations." Our ongoing work in hint generation addresses this concern. In the current system, not every incorrect step on the proof tree can be annotated by an instructor; an improved system might generate such hints automatically or notify instructors when several students reach in a dead end of the proof tree, encouraging them to add a hint in real-time.

Fourth, student interactions are constrained by proof search. Although instructors can mark rules as free, and this allows students to elide those rules in their derivations, the system is currently limited to two rounds of search. In future work we might improve the efficiency of our theorem prover or distribute proof search client-side, passing a larger share of computation onto the students' machines.

Fifth, although DeduceIt's proof cache provides a dramatic performance benefit, there are several ways the design of the cache can be improved. For instance, changing the cache representation from a tree into a directed acyclic graph (DAG) would be faster and more space efficient. Likewise, collapsing semantically equivalent derivation steps would also make lookups faster and improve the cache hit rate.

Finally, this paper does not directly address DeduceIt's effect on teaching outcomes: that is, how the system compares with traditional educational tools, and how it impacts student learning. We hope to study this question in future work.

CONCLUSION

For online education to succeed, it must move beyond simple multiple-choice problems to the kinds of open-ended assignments used by real courses. Peer grading holds promise but is difficult to apply in many domains [13, 17]. For many online courses that use formal, structured reasoning, automated systems can provide guidance through interactive assignments. We have presented DeduceIt, a system exploring this potential for student derivations in arbitrary formal domains.

DeduceIt enables instructors to set up reusable assignments for any kind of formal derivation, which can be completed by students at specifiable levels of abstraction. The system provides students with constraints — rules that may be applied only to the set of proven or given expressions — which provide support as the students work, and DeduceIt responds in real-time with information about the correctness of each derivation step: whether a mistake is due to a syntactic or semantic error, and hint annotations.

Students and instructors are successfully engaging with DeduceIt. Out of the 990 students who used DeduceIt in our online Compilers class, we observe an overall assignment completion rate of 96.5% and an average time to completion of 12.7 minutes over 10 assignments. Similarities in student proofs allow us to provide feedback to students at speeds that would be impossible using standalone systems. Further, instructors are using DeduceIt to perform course analytics that were quite difficult to track before. By analyzing assignment data using structures like DeduceIt's proof tree, instructors can determine which parts of an assignment are most difficult for students to complete, or which course concepts are least well understood.

DeduceIt suggests that online education might allow for assignments with complex reasoning requirements and multiple correct answers. Generalizing the system beyond formal derivations, or asking students to check and approve each others' claims, might create opportunities for more general instances of structured reasoning in domains such as chemistry, physics, or even law. DeduceIt and the compilers course are available at `http://www.coursera.org/course/compilers`.

ACKNOWLEDGMENTS
Special thanks to Joel Brandt and our colleagues at Stanford. We'd also like to thank Coursera, for helping us deploy our Compilers course; the Compilers course students, for their hard work and feedback; and finally our reviewers for their very useful suggestions.

REFERENCES
1. Coursera support documentation. `http://support.coursera.org`.
2. Bennett, R. E., and Bejar, I. I. Validity and automated scoring: It's not only the scoring. *Educational Measurement: Issues and Practice 17*, 4 (1998), 9–17.
3. Bennett, R. E., Steffen, M., Singley, M. K., Morley, M., and Jacquemin, D. Evaluating an automatically scorable, open-ended response type for measuring mathematical reasoning in computer-adaptive tests. *Journal of Educational Measurement 34*, 2 (1997), pp. 162–176.
4. Burstall, R. Proveeasy: Helping people learn to do proofs. *In Proc. ENTCS 2000* (2000), 16 – 32.
5. Cheang, B., Kurnia, A., Lim, A., and Oon, W.-C. On automated grading of programming assignments in an academic institution. *Comput. Educ. 41*, 2 (2003), 121–131.
6. Clavel, M., Durán, F., Eker, S., Lincoln, P., Martí-Oliet, N., Meseguer, J., and Quesada, J. Maude as a metalanguage. *In Proc. WRLA 1998 15* (1998).
7. Corbett, A., and Anderson, J. Knowledge tracing: Modeling the acquisition of procedural knowledge. *In Proc. UMUAI 1994* (1994), 253–278.
8. Corbett, A. T., and Anderson, J. R. Locus of feedback control in computer-based tutoring: impact on learning rate, achievement and attitudes. In *Proc. CHI '01* (2001).
9. Gallien, T., and Oomen-Early, J. Personalized versus collective instructor feedback in the online courseroom: Does type of feedback affect student satisfaction, academic performance and perceived connectedness with the instructor? *International Journal on E-Learning 7*, 3 (2008), 463–476.
10. Hearst, M. The debate on automated essay grading. *Intelligent Systems and their Applications, IEEE 15*, 5 (2000), 22–37.
11. Heffernan, N. T., Koedinger, K. R., and Razzaq, L. Expanding the model-tracing architecture: A 3rd generation intelligent tutor for algebra symbolization. *Int. J. Artif. Intell. Ed.* (2008), 153–178.
12. Hernan-Losada, I., Pareja-Flores, C., and Velazquez-Iturbide, A. Testing-based automatic grading: A proposal from bloom's taxonomy. *In Proc. ICALT 2008* (2008), 847–849.
13. Huang, S.-W., and Fu, W.-T. Enhancing reliability using peer consistency evaluation in human computation. *In Proc. CSCW 2013* (2013), 639–648.
14. Kaindl, H., and Kainz, G. Bidirectional heuristic search reconsidered. *Journal of Artificial Intelligence Research 7* (1997), 283–317.
15. Kaufmann, M., and Moore, J. S. An industrial strength theorem prover for a logic based on common lisp. *IEEE Trans. Softw. Eng. 23*, 4 (1997), 203–213.
16. Kirsh, D., and Maglio, P. P. On Distinguishing Epistemic from Pragmatic Action. *Cognitive Science 18*, 4 (1994), 513–549.
17. Kulkarni, C., Pang, K., Le, H., Chia, D., Papadopoulos, K., Cheng, J., Koller, D., and Klemmer, S. Peer and self assessment in massive online design classes. *ACM TOCHI* (2013).
18. Lapets, A., Skowyra, R., Bassem, C., Kfoury, A., and Bestavros, A. Towards an infrastructure for integrated accessible formal reasoning environments. *In Proc. UITP 2012*.
19. Mart-Oliet, N., and Meseguer, J. Rewriting logic: Roadmap and bibliography. *J. Log. Algebr. Program. 81* (2001).
20. Nielsen, J. *Usability Engineering*. Morgan Kaufmann, 1993.
21. Nipkow, T., Wenzel, M., and Paulson, L. C. *Isabelle/HOL: a proof assistant for higher-order logic*. Springer-Verlag, Berlin, Heidelberg, 2002.
22. Pappano, L. Massive open online courses are multiplying at a rapid pace. `http://www.nytimes.com/2012/11/04/education/edlife/massive-open-online-courses-are-multiplying-at-a-rapid-pace.html`.
23. Paulin-Mohring, C. Inductive definitions in the system coq rules and properties. *TLCA 1993* (1993).
24. Paulson, L. C. The foundation of a generic theorem prover. *Journal of Automated Reasoning 5* (1989).
25. Ritter, S., Towle, B., Murray, R., Hausmann, R., and Connelly, J. A cognitive tutor for geometric proof. *In Prof. ITS 2010* (2010), 453–453.
26. Schleimer, S., Wilkerson, D. S., and Aiken, A. Winnowing: local algorithms for document fingerprinting. *In Proc. ACM SIGMOD 2003* (2003), 76–85.
27. Suppes, P. The next generation of interactive theorem provers. *7th International Conference on Automated Deduction 170* (1984), 303–315.
28. Suppes, P. Student use of an interactive theorem prover. *Contemporary Mathematics 29* (1984).
29. Tosic, M., and Nejkovic, V. Trust-based peer assessment for virtual learning systems. *In Proc. SocInfo 2010* (2010), 176–191.
30. VanLehn, K. The relative effectiveness of human tutoring, intelligent tutoring systems, and other tutoring systems. *Educational Psychologist 46*, 4 (2011), 197–221.
31. Windsteiger, W. Theorema 2.0: A graphical user interface for a mathematical assistant system. *CEUR Workshop Proceedings* (2012), 73–81.

A Tongue Training System for Children with Down Syndrome

Masato Miyauchi Takashi Kimura Takuya Nojima
Graduate School of Information Systems, University of Electro-Communications
1-5-1 Chofugaoka, Chofu
Tokyo, 182-8585 Japan
{m_miyauchi, tkimura}@vogue.is.uec.ac.jp, tnojima@computer.org

ABSTRACT

Children with Down syndrome have a variety of symptoms including speech and swallowing disorders. To improve these symptoms, tongue training is thought to be beneficial. However, inducing children with Down syndrome to do such training is not easy because tongue training can be an unpleasant experience for children. In addition, with no supporting technology for such training, teachers and families around such children must make efforts to induce them to undergo the training. In this research, we develop an interactive tongue training system especially for children with Down syndrome using SITA (Simple Interface for Tongue motion Acquisition) system. In this paper, we describe in detail our preliminary evaluations of SITA, and present the results of user tests.

Author Keywords

Tongue training; myofunctional therapy; Down syndrome; depth camera; tongue-computer interface

ACM Classification Keywords

H5.2 [Information interfaces and presentation]: User Interfaces. - Input devices and strategies.

General Terms

Human Factors

INTRODUCTION

Many children with Down syndrome have several symptoms such as speech and swallowing disorders. To improve these symptoms, myofunctional therapy (MFT) [1,6], which is a collection of mouth and tongue training, is considered to be beneficial. However, such training is too simple and monotonous to maintain the attention of children.

One of the MFT methods for training the tongue muscle, called the "lip tracer" method, involves protruding the tongue and then moving it along the contour of the upper lip, as if the tongue were tracing the lip. Another training method is to open the mouth with the tongue at the roof of the mouth. In addition to these methods, MFT includes a variety of training sets, such as "swallowing training" (i.e., swallowing water while opening the mouth and biting a straw), "orbicularis oris muscle and buccinator muscle training" (i.e., opening the mouth horizontally, closing it, and then inflating the cheeks). It would seem that these MFT training sets are so simple that children with Down syndrome would be able to easily train their tongues using such methods. However, this simplicity means that the training does not have any mentally stimulating or interesting aspects from the perspective of children, such as visual or acoustic effects. During the training, children simply move their tongues. This results in little motivation for children to engage in the training. In addition, to motivate children with Down syndrome to do such training, the support of their teachers or families is necessary; they must constantly check to ensure that the children are able to do the training properly.

To increase children's motivation to perform the training, and to simultaneously reduce the amount of work required to monitor and supporting the training, an interactive system to detect tongue motion is needed. For such an interactive system, tongue motion should be detected in a non-contact way. In particular, because the target users of the system are children with Down syndrome, no devices should be worn or put around the mouth (1) to avoid accidental ingestion, (2) to maintain hygiene, (3) and to reduce any unnecessary effort. We developed the SITA (Simple Interface for Tongue motion Acquisition) system to satisfy these conditions [5]. In addition, we also developed a tongue training game to better attract the attention and interest of such children.

RELATED WORK

To measure tongue motion, a number of methods have been suggested. Huo et al. proposed a tongue-computer interface using a magnet on the tongue and magnet sensors outside of the mouth [3]. The magnet is placed on the tip of the tongue, and its magnetic field changes according to the motion of the tongue, which is measured by magnet sensors around the mouth. Saponas et al. have proposed a tongue-sensing dental retainer used as a computer interface for patients with paralyzing injuries [8]. The system is able to recognize simple tongue gestures by using proximity sensors embedded on a dental retainer. Salem et al. have proposed a tongue pointing system using a pressure sensitive isometric joystick [7]. Furthermore, Slyper et al. have proposed three types of tongue input devices: a sip/puff switch, a bite sensor, and a tongue joystick [10]. However, while these research

UIST'13, October 08 - 11 2013, St Andrews, United Kingdom

http://dx.doi.org/10.1145/2501988.2502055

systems are capable of detecting various types of tongue motion, they require users to put certain devices inside and around the mouth, which runs the risk of accidental ingestion. In addition, maintaining these devices hygienically can be a burden for people around children with Down syndrome. Therefore these systems are not very suitable for use by such children. Hueber et al. have proposed a lip and tongue motion recognition system based on ultrasound and optical images [2]; originally designed as a segmental vocoder, the system is able to recognize tongue motion without installing any special devices on a user's body. However, the system requires an ultrasound sensor that is not commonly accessible to the public. Li et al. also proposed a non-contact method using an RGB camera [4]. Their method can detect six states of the tongue and mouth, but it is not able to measure continuous tongue motion, which is important in tongue training.

PRELIMINARY SYSTEM

Tongue motion recognition method

Figure 1 shows the hardware setup for our proposed SITA system. A Kinect (Microsoft) is placed 70cm in front of the user and captures the user's facial RGB image and depth data.

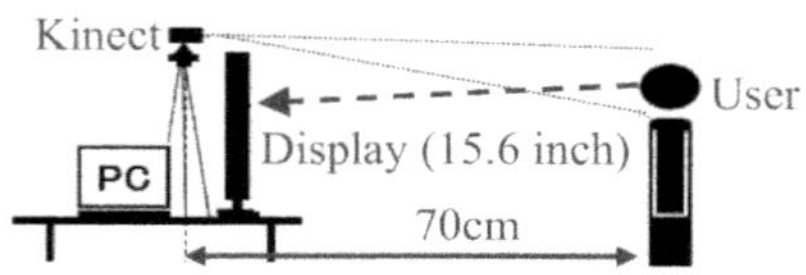

Figure 1: Hardware setup for preliminary system.

Eye recognition followed by facial recognition is applied to the captured image to search the eye area using the OpenCV Haar-like feature detection library. Then, the nose and mouth areas are determined from the structural characteristics of the face. As shown in Figure 2(a), a rectangular mouth area is placed approximately 20 pixels below the highest point of the nose area, which is placed at the center of the eye area.

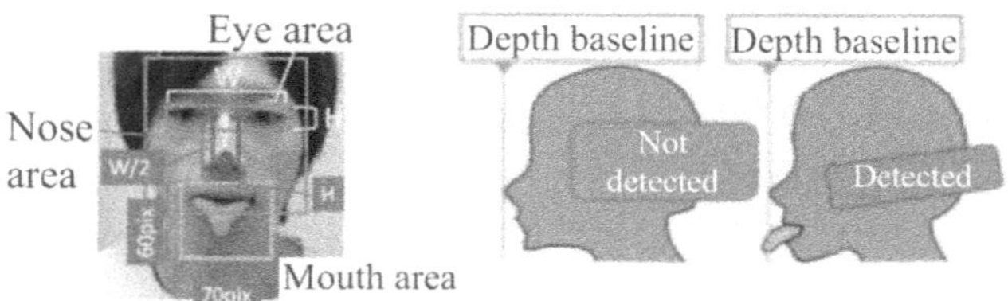

(a) Face segmentation (b) Tongue detection

Figure 2: Basic face segmentation and tongue detection.

Inside the mouth area, the SITA system continuously seeks the highest point. If this highest point inside the mouth area is higher than that of the nose area, then SITA assumes that the tongue has been thrust out of the mouth (Figure 2(b)).

Pointing accuracy evaluation

Experimental setup

An overview of the experimental setup is shown in the left side of Figure **3**. The setup consists of the Kinect, a chin support, and an acrylic plate, though the chin support and the acrylic plate are not necessary during actual use. The chin support is used to fix the participant's head. Then the acrylic plate is placed in front of the participant in a position that can barely be reached by the participant's protruded tongue. Then the Kinect is fixed at 70 cm away from the acrylic plate. On the plate, a matrix of 4 by 7 dots is engraved at 1cm intervals(Figure **3** right, lower, "Normal view"). The participants are asked to indicate one of the dots on the plate with their tongue by using the haptic cues of their tongue. Then, we measure the position of the tip of the tongue based on our proposed method. The acrylic plate is transparent under visible light as well as infrared light, allowing the core part of the tongue motion acquisition algorithm to work properly. Before conducting the experiment, we captured the dot positions with the Kinect's RGB camera to be used as a reference. Because these dots are small, we lighted up the acrylic plate from the side to illuminate them. Then the camera is able to capture a clear image of the dots (Figure **3** right, upper, "Illuminated dots").

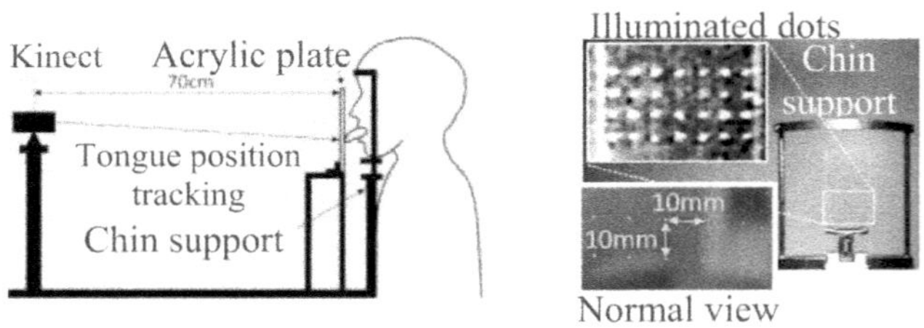

Figure 3: Left: Special setup for evaluation experiments; Right: Chin support and acrylic plate.

Accuracy evaluation procedure and results

Five males in their 20s participated in this experiment. After each participant's head was fixed onto the chin support and the Kinect was placed in an appropriate position, the participants pointed out certain dots on the plate with their tongue and maintained the motion for 5 seconds. Each point was selected randomly. No dots were selected that a particular participant would not be able to indicate with his tongue. All points were measured 3 times for each participant. The results are shown in Figure 4.

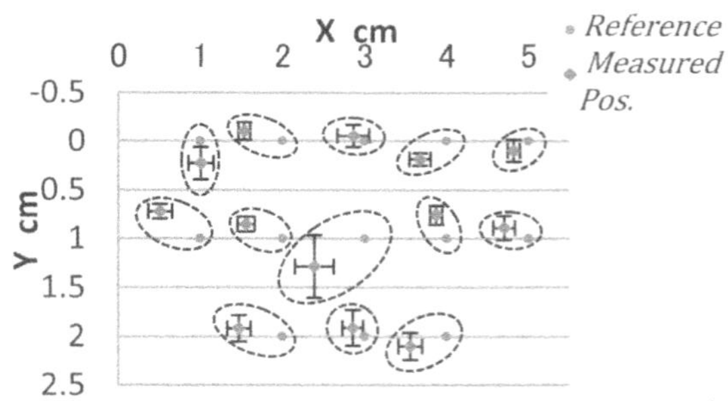

Figure 4: Accuracy of measured positions.

In the figure, it may appear that several points of data are missing. This is because some of the matrix points were too far away from the participants' tongues to comfortably indicate them, and thus these points were eliminated from the results. Nonetheless, from the obtained results, the proposed algorithm has the ability to measure the position of the tip of the tongue with an accuracy of within 0.5cm. Among the various above mentioned training exercises in the MFT, the "lip tracer" is one that requires accurate motion. It is an exercise that traces the upper lip by the tongue. A tongue motion measuring system should therefore be able to measure such motion. Considering the typical thickness of the lip (about 1cm), the accuracy of our proposed system (about 0.5cm) should be sufficient for this purpose.

Preliminary user test

Following the accuracy evaluation, a simple shooter game controlled by tongue motion was developed (Figure 5). The center green circle indicates a player (participant). The circle automatically shoots bullets at regular intervals in a specific direction controlled by the player's tongue. The game's objective is to shoot the surrounding target circles. Once all of the targets on the screen are shot and destroyed, then smaller targets appear.

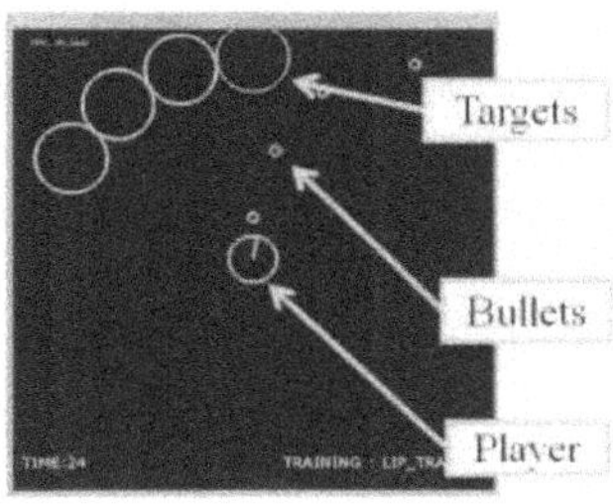

Figure 5: Screenshot of preliminary game application.

For the user test, 7 students of different types of disorders (four males and three females, including two Down syndrome) attending the Tokyo Metropolitan Chofu Special Support School were allowed to play this application freely while we and their teachers observed them. From the observations, we identified several points to be improved, as follows. (1) A larger display was preferred; small displays and small images tended to cause the children to physically approach the display, which resulted in sensor detection problems due to the sensor range. (2) Robustness with respect to the orientation of a user's face needed to be improved. In addition, the gap between the positions of the Kinect camera and the display easily caused errors in face recognition to occur. (3) The shooting game application did not seem sufficient to attract the participants' attention. Based on these observations, therefore, we developed a second version of our game system.

SECONDARY DEVELOPED SYSTEM

In response to the observations made during the first user test, we developed a second version and conducted the test again.

System components

In this second, revised version of our system, we used a more compact RGB and depth camera (Xtion PRO LIVE, ASUS). In Figure 6 left, the camera was placed in the center of the 21.5 inch wide LCD display, using a transparent mounting device, to recognize the user's face and tongue effectively.

Figure 6: Left: Hardware layout of secondary system; Right: Screenshot of the revised second application.

Improvements in tongue motion recognition method

We applied the following improvements to our tongue motion recognition method. We changed the face recognition module from the OpenCV library to Facetracker [9], to recognize the nose and mouth areas directly. At the same time, face orientation data provided by the library enabled the proposed method to adjust the face rotation (Figure 7, left). A face orientation notifier was also implemented (Figure 7, right). This notifier informs the player (participant) whether his/her face orientation is within acceptable limits. If the face position exceeds any acceptable limit, then the game is paused and a notification image is shown to notify the player to correct their face orientation.

Figure 7: Left: robust recognition for rotation. Right: face orientation notifier (red circle: OK, blue cross: FAIL).

Application and user test

The objective of this revised, second application is for the user to catch fish through tongue movement (Figure 6, right). The pink circle in the center of the figure is a tongue-controlled cursor used to catch the fish. A fish can be caught if the distance between the cursor and the fish becomes less than 50 pixels. When all of the fish have been caught, a sound effect is generated and the user proceeds to the next stage. A second user test was conducted at the same special support school as the first test. The subjects were 4 children (two 5th grade (10-11 years old) girls and a boy and a girl of the 1st grade (6-7 years old)) with Down syndrome. The experiment was carried out in 3 separate days. All of the children could freely move their tongue forward, right and left, as well as up and down. The experiment duration was 3 to 5 minutes. During the experiment, the children's behavior was observed and notes were taken. The results are as follows.

Student 1 (Girl with moderate Down syndrome, 5th grade): She seemed to be very interested in playing the game. Every time she caught a fish, she smiled and gave out a scream of delight. However, sometimes the facial recognition failed because she physically approached the display. Both of her teachers agreed that she displayed substantial tongue movement and enjoyed this application. ***Student 2*** (Girl with mild Down syndrome, 1st grade): At the beginning of the trial, she was hesitating to play the game. Then we did a demonstration to show her how to play that. After the demonstration, she played the game happily and caught all the fish. Her teacher commented that she was enjoying the game and has a good understanding of the application. ***Student 3*** (Boy with moderate Down syndrome, 1st grade): He did not play the game at all. He kept his head hanged down during the experiment. His teacher commented that he is too shy to play the game in unfamiliar situations. However, he sometimes watched the display and got excited. His teacher also noted that he is sure interested in the game. ***Student 4*** (Girl with severe Down syndrome, 5th grade): Although she appeared interested in the game, she pushed her tongue forward only a few times during her 3 minute session. Her teacher noted that keeping her tongue protruded is difficult for her. In addition, she appeared distracted by the people around her.

This secondary experiment shows that the proposed system is completely safe and secure from both physic and hygienic aspects. In addition, Children with Down syndrome are able to play the game if they could understand the rules of the game. However, all the children had some sort of difficulty in understanding the rule and how to play that. Then more appropriate instructions are necessary for easier understanding. Actually, Student 1 and 2, children with moderate or mild Down syndrome, are able to understand and play the game but they need an additional short instruction from their teachers. Student 3 and 4 had more difficulty in understanding the game. In the case of Student 3, it was not because of his symptoms but because of his shyness. In his case, several trials should help him to understand the game. Adding to that, carefully designed instruction should be necessary especially for the child with severe Down syndrome, Student 4. The system encounters difficulty in measuring tongue motion when a player move his/her head and body aggressively. Thus the design of the game should be improved that could reduce unwanted player's motion, along with an improved detection algorithm.

Teacher's comments

After the conclusion of the tests, the teacher observers provided the following feedback. Several stages of the game with different levels of difficulty should be created. Each child has a different degree of ability to control their tongue. Thus, the availability of different difficulty levels which match each student's ability would help motivate them to play the game. Background images should be simplified because children can be easily distracted. To allow them to better concentrate on playing the game, simpler background images should therefore be used. Distinct screen images as well as a cursor icon that suits game context is preferable for easier comprehension of the game situation. Finally, more impressive visual and auditory effects should be added to better attract the children's attention.

Teachers also commented that this revised, second version of the game was more attractive than the first version. It was also mentioned that some of the students could use this application for their daily training exercises.

CONCLUSION AND FUTURE WORK

In this paper, the basic mechanisms of our newly developed non-contact tongue motion acquisition (SITA) system were described. Our accuracy evaluations showed that our SITA system has sufficient accuracy to be used as a game interface. Then, we developed a tongue training system for children with Down syndrome using the proposed SITA system. Through user tests, we could confirm the applicability of the SITA system as useful for tongue training. In our future work, we plan to develop more attractive and easier applications for children with Down syndrome to use in their independent play. To this end, we plan to conduct long-term user tests to evaluate the usability and training effects of our system.

ACKNOWLEDGEMENTS

We thank all of the teachers, staff, and students at Tokyo Metropolitan Chofu Special Support School, and the students' parents who supported our user tests.

REFERENCES

1. Gallerano, G., Ruoppolo, G. and Silvestri, A. Myofunctional and speech rehabilitation after orthodontic-surgical treatment of dento-maxillofacial dysgnathia. *Progress in Orthodontics 13*, 1(2012), 57-68.
2. Hueber, T., Benaroya, E., Chollet, G., Denby, B., Dreyfus, G. and Stone, M. Development of a silent speech interface driven by ultrasound and optical images of the tongue and lips. *Speech Communication 52*, 4 (2010), 288-300.
3. Huo, X., Wang, J. and Ghovanloo, M. A Magneto-Inductive Sensor Based Wireless Tongue-Computer Interface. *IEEE Transactions on Neural Systems and Rehabilitation Engineering 16*, 5 (2008), 497-504.
4. Liu, L., Niu, S., Ren, J. and Zhang, J. Tongible: a non-contact tongue-based interaction technique. In *Proc. ASSETS 2012*, ACM Press, (2012), 233-234.
5. Miyauchi, M., Kimura, T. and Nojima, T. Development of a non-contact tongue-motion acquisition system. *Proc. UIST Adjunct 2012*, ACM Press (2012), 75-76.
6. Profitt, W.R. and Mason, R.M. Myofunctional therapy for tongue-thrusting: background and recommendations. *The Journal of the American Dental Association 90*, 2 (1975), 403-411.
7. Salem, C. and Zhai, S. An isometric tongue pointing device. In *Proc. CHI 1997*, ACM Press (1997), 538-539.
8. Saponas, T.S., Kelly, D., Parviz, B.A. and Tan D.S. Optically Sensing Tongue Gestures for Computer Input. In *Proc. UIST 2009*, ACM Press (2009), 177-180.
9. Saragih, J., Lucey, S. and Cohn, J. Deformable Model Fitting by Regularized Landmark Mean-Shift, *International Journal of Computer Vision 91*, 2 (2011), 200-215.
10. Slyper, R., Lehman, J., Forlizzi, J. and Hodgins, J. A Tongue Input Device for Creating Conversations, In *Proc. UIST 2011*, ACM Press (2011), 117-126.

A Mixed-Initiative Tool for Designing Level Progressions in Games

Eric Butler, Adam M. Smith, Yun-En Liu, and Zoran Popović
Center for Game Science
Department of Computer Science & Engineering, University of Washington
{edbutler,amsmith,yunliu,zoran}@cs.washington.edu

ABSTRACT
Creating game content requires balancing design considerations at multiple scales: each level requires effort and iteration to produce, and broad-scale constraints such as the order in which game concepts are introduced must be respected. Game designers currently create informal plans for how the game's levels will fit together, but they rarely keep these plans up-to-date when levels change during iteration and testing. This leads to violations of constraints and makes changing the high-level plans expensive. To address these problems, we explore the creation of mixed-initiative game progression authoring tools which explicitly model broad-scale design considerations. These tools let the designer specify constraints on progressions, and keep the plan synchronized when levels are edited. This enables the designer to move between broad and narrow-scale editing and allows for automatic detection of problems caused by edits to levels. We further leverage advances in procedural content generation to help the designer rapidly explore and test game progressions. We present a prototype implementation of such a tool for our actively-developed educational game, *Refraction*. We also describe how this system could be extended for use in other games and domains, specifically for the domains of math problem sets and interactive programming tutorials.

Author Keywords
Game design; design tools; AI-assisted design; educational games.

ACM Classification Keywords
H.5.0 Information Interfaces and Presentation: General

INTRODUCTION
The design of interactive experiences that consist of a sequence of episodes building in complexity is an intricate, multi-dimensional design problem that often takes experts a long time to complete. This is particularly apparent in game design. Designing just a single gameplay element (e.g., puzzles, challenges, encounters, levels) requires many iterations and interactive playtests to uncover a satisfying result. Crafting a coherent and effective sequence of these elements into an entire game, called a *progression*, is even more involved because the experience of playing the game is highly dependent on the way individual components are connected. As game designers adjust their game at these different scales—altering details of a single gameplay element and scheduling appropriate introduction of those details across the game's entire progression—they wrestle with a mixture of formal and informal requirements. Keeping all of these concerns in mind while designing each level is difficult.

Game designers have adopted semi-structured practices for addressing this complexity. They often create informal notes and plans that capture a sketch of the progression's overall properties and then consult this document while designing individual levels. Although developers often create complex in-house tools for authoring game content (e.g., the Dragon Age Toolset[1]), these tools focus on individual levels and rarely explicitly model progressions. As designers improve their level designs in response to testing, the progression plan is rarely updated and the high-level structure of the final level progression is not articulated in general terms again.[2] As a result, the coherence and intent of the original plan can be lost.

We propose the creation of progression design tools that aid game designers through all stages of design: sketching, rapid exploration, iteration, and final authoring of a complete game progression while keeping the progression plan in-context and up-to-date. Such tools should allow editing of both individual elements and progressions over those elements. Building on the ideas of mixed-initiative planning and constraint-based game content generation and verification, we demonstrate a prototype tool using the educational game *Refraction* that combines existing single-level editors into a mixed-initiative progression design tool.

Our focus on tools for designers contrasts with current trends in game design automation research. Many projects aiming to reduce designer burden offer fully automatic generators for individual levels, often focusing on optimizing a fixed metric for the quality of the level [24]. These systems are not designed to optimize the relative placement of levels within a

UIST'13, October 6–9, 2013, St. Andrews, United Kingdom.

ACM 978-1-4503-2271-3/13/10...$15.00.
http://dx.doi.org/10.1145/2501988.2502011

[1]`http://social.bioware.com/page/da-toolset`

[2]In a very interesting exception to this trend, fans sometimes recreate visual progression plans for popular games, such as Piotr Bugno's detailed outline of the story and level progressions for *Portal 2*: `http://www.piotrbugno.com/2012/06/portal-2-timelines/`

progression. Other fully automated generators explicitly take user-configurable constraints as input [17, 20]. These generators are directable down to a fine scale but still require an external progression plan. Zook et al. [25] describes a system for fitting a progression of generated challenges in a training game to an ideal player performance curve; however, the system requires all design input to take the form of formally modeled properties such as evaluation functions and causal coherence constraints. We are interested in allowing the designer input at all scales, so fully automated methods will not suffice. Mixed-initiative design tools, such as Tanagra [21] and SketchaWorld [18], pair generative techniques with an interactive editing interface that allows the human and machine to take turns editing a shared level design. Such tools help the designer prototype new ideas and check constraints for quality assurance while still allowing designers to craft levels with subtle properties that are difficult to formalize. These tools focus on creating single levels, whereas we want to create a tool that allows designers to work at multiple scales. However, we follow similar design process pattern for the problem of designing coherent progressions of detailed levels.

Effective progression design tools could provide valuable assistance to the same expert designers who would normally have designed levels without such support. We expect that they would be almost required for very large, complex progressions where manual exploration becomes intractable. More importantly, however, they would open up possibilities for end-user progression design. Consider an experienced teacher who wants to directly manipulate which concepts will be used in a progression tailored to their class. They might prefer that the tool automatically generate the relevant challenges at the scale of individual puzzles everywhere except where one or two key levels should visually resemble examples previously shown in class. This property is unlikely to be supported by any fully automated system.

In this paper, we discuss the requirements of a progression design tool, and present our prototype implementation for our actively-developed educational game, *Refraction*, illustrating its utility through several case studies. We expect that these ideas might be explored in domains outside of games such as interactive programming tutorials and high-school algebra exercises. This paper makes the following contributions:

- We identify the need for progression design tools and describe their impact with respect to current practices.
- We sketch a general architecture for progression design tools, including the use of generative techniques on a per-level basis where available.
- We present a prototype implementation of our design tool, attached to our own active design project, *Refraction*.

REFRACTION

Refraction is a puzzle game, intended for use with elementary education of fractions, that involves splitting and combining laser beams to form beams of fractional power. The game consists of a sequence of puzzles in which the player must direct lasers into targets, a task that requires both spatial and mathematical problem-solving skills. A sample puzzle is shown in Figure 1.

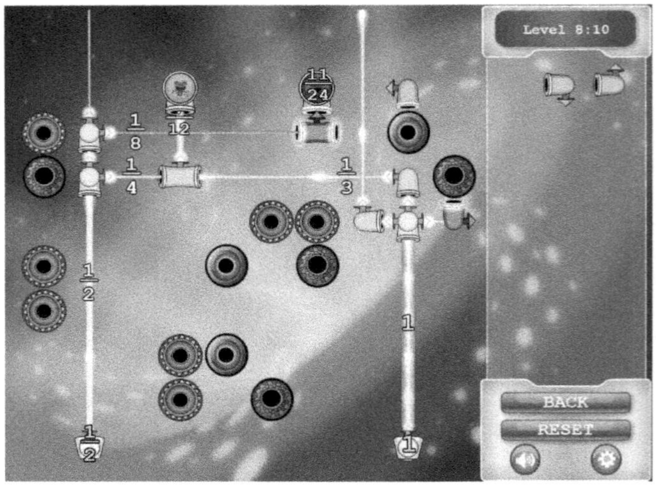

Figure 1. A level of *Refraction*, our actively developed game. We continue to create and release new level progressions for the game, driving our need for progression design tools.

Though *Refraction* has already been released to a wide audience, it is still under active development. We frequently need to create new level progressions for ongoing classroom studies and experiments, often involving adapting the game for different age groups or testing new mechanics. Thus, we personally have a strong need for tools that allow us to effectively and rapidly explore and iterate level progression designs.

CURRENT PRACTICES

Game developers have created a wealth of guidelines and best-practice suggestions for creating effective level progressions in games. In this section, we review current practices and discuss which aspects our system aims to improve. These practices are not well-documented, and there is not a clear accepted plan for tackling these challenges. Industry magazines such as Gamasutra[3] archive articles and discussions on game development written by industry members, from which we draw our information.

Level Progressions

Many games consist of a sequence of distinct elements (e.g., levels, stages, challenges, scenarios or puzzles) that the player encounters. We call this sequence a *progression*. In *Refraction*, the elements are the individual puzzles (involving 2-5 minutes of play), and the progression is the entire sequence of puzzles (2-5 hours of play). There are many ways to discretize a game progression; puzzles in *Refraction* are very short so make a reasonable choice, but larger games might model progressions over smaller elements. In this paper, we will generally refer to the individual elements as *levels*. Levels cannot be designed entirely in isolation; how they relate to each other is critical for effective game design. Much of the effort spent during the iteration process focuses on altering individual levels to improve the overall progression.

As a result, game design often happens at multiple scales. At a broad scale, designers create a *progression plan*, which

[3]`http://gamasutra.com`

documents the features they want each of their levels to have. These features might include, for example, which mechanics appear in a level or which key dramatic events occur in the game's narrative for a story-oriented game. In *Refraction*, there are several different types of pieces the player may use, such as bending pieces, splitting pieces, and adding pieces. The pieces required to solve any particular level are a feature we consider during the design process. At a narrow scale, designers are editing the levels themselves, trying to craft levels that have the complex properties they desire.

There are many design considerations when creating progression plans. For example, many games introduce different mechanics slowly and deliberately to allow the player to learn each of them without becoming overwhelmed. Game designer Dan Cook associates these mechanics with *skill atoms* [6] and suggests diagramming the dependence between atoms to better understand how a game works. In many cases, the introduction of a new skill atom may depend on the player having previously mastered another. For example, in Nintendo's *Super Mario Bros.*, the player should learn to jump before they can learn to jump on an enemy. Similarly, overusing a certain atom can lead to burnout, and avoiding this requires additional constraints between levels to be checked. In *Refraction*, we wish to introduce pieces in a particular order and pace. Skill atoms may also have intra-level considerations: in *Refraction*, for example, some types of pieces cannot be used unless another type of piece is present in the level.

Another important design consideration of progressions is pacing. *Pacing* describes how elements such as complexity, difficulty, and intensity vary over the course of the game. Game designer Jenova Chen writes [5] about how Csikszentmihalyi's concept of *Flow* [7] applies to game progressions. If the difficulty increases too quickly, players can become frustrated; too slowly, they become bored and disengaged. Many articles have been written on Gamasutra analyzing and discussing techniques for effective game pacing [4].

Design Practices

Designers understand the value in explicitly planning their games' progressions. Progression design considerations and progression plans are often sketched out in a design document or whiteboard before production of levels. Designers have written articles endorsing planning game progressions before production, writing that teams that do not explicitly create progression plans often end up redoing work after user testing reveals problems with their progressions, resulting in a worse final product[5]. However, the progression may change greatly during production, user testing, and iteration of levels; levels and mechanics may be reordered, or mechanics may be dropped entirely or new ones added. So while planning progressions beforehand is very useful, if left unaltered, the progression plans become increasingly inaccurate. Although game developers frequently spend great effort creating in-house editors and other authoring tools for their games[6], to the best of our knowledge, they do not create editors for their progression plans that automatically sync with their levels. For designers to continue to work at this broad scale during development, they must first evaluate the current progression manually, a significant task[7]. After production, sometimes developers (or even players) recreate visualizations of the progression realized in the final game. While these may be used in post-mortem analysis, they are still created mainly by hand, and are of little utility for design of that game, since it has already been published and is unlikely to undergo large changes. Integrating an up-to-date progression plan as part of the standard editing environment could help the designer more effectively work at multiple scales.

Because the information about the progression plan is cumbersome to keep in sync with the actual level progression, ensuring that the current levels meet all progression design considerations is an expensive, error-prone task. Edits to levels frequently change their properties in ways which may, for example, disrupt desired pacing, or introduce game mechanics too quickly or in the incorrect order. If not noticed by the designer, these problems will eventually be discovered in user testing, a relatively expensive resource. Automated detection of these problems may save time and effort by finding issues quickly, without designer effort.

We expect having the ability to rapidly explore different progression plans would enhance the design process. However, if the designer wishes to make a minor adjustment to the progression, say moving the introduction of a mechanic to a later point in the game, this might require significant modifications to existing levels. While a large portion of game developers create level editors to help author levels, these adjustments are still expensive to make. Because of this, designers can be limited in how easily they can explore the design space.

Current design practices result in several problems we wish to overcome in the design of our system. Designers are not able to easily explore progressions because level authoring is time-consuming. Designs for progressions plans are often abandoned after level creation begins because they are too cumbersome to keep up-to-date. As a result, level edits often introduce problems that are not discovered without significant inspection and user testing.

PROGRESSION DESIGN TOOLS

In this section, we formalize our design problem and discuss our goals for an effective game progression design system.

Definitions

We will use *levels*, *progressions*, and *progression plans* as defined previously. Each level has several *properties*, features that the designer cares about. Examples include which game concepts are used in a particular level, or whether a particular narrative event occurs in a level. There are often a huge

[4]e.g., `http://www.gamasutra.com/view/feature/134815/` or `http://www.gamasutra.com/view/feature/132415/`

[5]e.g., `http://www.gamasutra.com/view/feature/3848/`

[6]For example, players can create complex mods and scenarios using *Starcraft 2*'s in-house level editor: `http://us.battle.net/sc2/en/game/maps-and-mods/`

[7]Recommendations to do just that come from `http://www.gamasutra.com/view/feature/132256/`

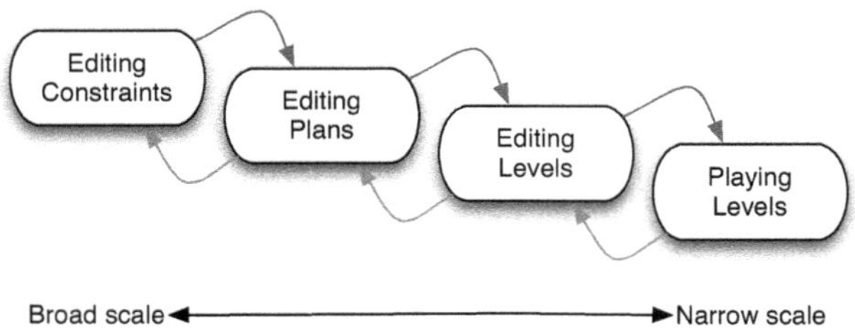

Figure 2. The ideal workflow for our system (a waterfall-like pattern). Designers must iterate at multiple scales, so our tool aims to allow the designer to move freely between broad and narrow-scale editing.

number of possible levels that share a particular set of properties. Likewise, there are many progressions that conform to a particular progression plan. The designer may have particular considerations for their game's progression, such as pacing or the ordering in which mechanics are introduced. We refer to all of these considerations definable at the level of the progression plan as *progression constraints* (or just *constraints*). We use the term (loosely) in the sense of optimization problems: the designer has a set of constraints in mind, and the design problem is to generate a progression best satisfying those constraints. Constraints may be hard (never to be violated), soft (flexible in exchange for satisfying other constraints at some cost), or unmodeled (not tracked by the tool). Again, there will generally be many progression plans that equally satisfy a particular set of constraints.

Goals of the Design Tool

The tool is intended to be a full-fidelity game editor and for authoring the final levels seen by players. The system should support rapid iteration and exploration at multiple scales of the design: progression constraints, progression plans, and individual level designs. Designers should be able to playtest the current progression. Figure 2 demonstrates the desired workflow for the system. Many constraints and properties can be formally modeled, so we would like to draw on advances in procedural content generation to automate generation and analysis of content where possible. Level generation is not an option for all types of games, so it is an optional component of our tool. It is important to note that many critical design considerations, such as the moment-to-moment difficulty or affective impact on players, are subjective or cannot be easily modeled. Thus human editing *must* be available at all scales, so the system should integrate existing level editors that game designers already create. As the designer changes from broad-scale progression planning to narrow-scale level editing and back, the system should automatically keep other parts updated: Edits to levels should be reflected in the progression plan, and edits to the plan should notify the designer if plan-level constraints are violated.

APPLICATION TO REFRACTION

To ground this discussion about progressions, levels, and constraints, we discuss how these ideas apply in the design of our game, *Refraction*. In this section, we discuss progression constraints and level properties specific to *Refraction* that we currently use as well as which game-specific components we

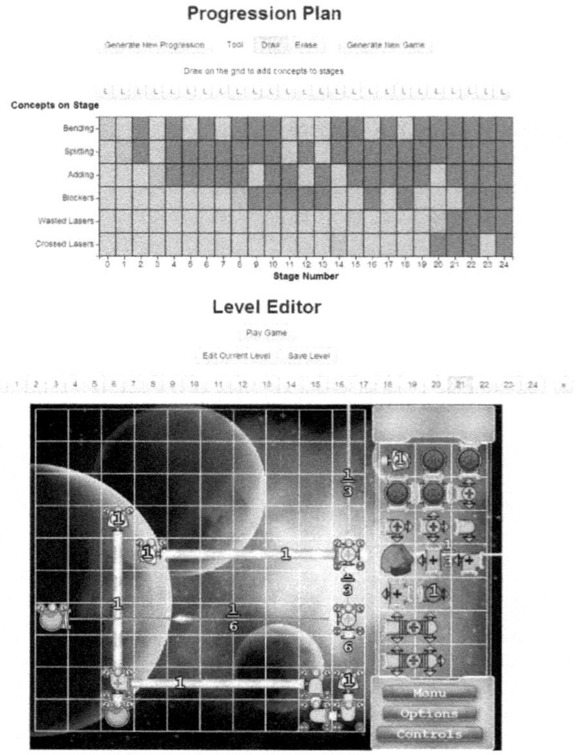

Figure 3. Screenshots of two of the three browser-based editing environments of our tool, each for editing the game at a different scale. On top is the *progression plan editor*, used for directly manipulating the plan. On the bottom is the *level editor*, which embeds *Refraction*'s custom editor. There are additional views for editing constraints and playtesting.

needed to provide for the implementation. Figure 3 shows screenshots from our prototype intended to demonstrate how a designer might control and view plans and levels. We delay discussing the system components until the next section.

Constraints and Properties

All level properties we model in this prototype describe whether a particular gameplay *concept* (or *skill atom*, to use Cook's [6] terminology) is required to solve a level. Table 1 lists a sample of these concepts. Because we currently only model concepts, all of our level properties are binary, describing whether a concept is required. Many additional properties have not yet been modeled, such as how closely the pieces must be placed together in all possible solutions. Some can-

Concept	Description
Bending	Must use bending pieces
Splitting	Must use splitting pieces
Adding	Must use adding pieces
Blockers	Must contain obstructive pieces
Wasted Laser	Leaves some laser beams unused
Crossed Laser	Laser beams are unavoidably crossed

Table 1. A sample of the properties we model for levels in *Refraction*. These properties are binary, describing whether or not a particular gameplay concept is required to solve a level.

not be directly modeled, such as whether a level is fun or aesthetically pleasing. Though not tracked by our tool, these can still be addressed through manual edits to level designs.

We have implemented four types of progression constraints.

Prerequisites
Prerequisites are *inter*-level constraints that define a partial ordering over the introduction points of the concepts. For concepts A and B, if A is a *prerequisite* of B, then the level of A's first appearance must precede the level in which B first appears. For example, we want to introduce pieces that bend the laser before introducing pieces that split the laser.

Corequisites
Corequisites are *intra*-level constraints on which concepts can appear together. A is a corequisite of B if A must show up in any level that has B. For example, one concept is to require that the laser be looped around to cross itself. This is only generally possible if bending pieces are available. Thus, "Bending" is a corequisite for "Crossed Laser."

Concept Count
For each level in the progression plan, we compute a illustrative proxy measure for "level intensity" (a term often occurring in other designers' progression plans) as a sum of the concepts that are in the level. Although this metric does not correspond directly with real-world difficulty, it is nevertheless useful for controlling pacing of the progression at a broad scale with a few quick adjustments. The constraint assigns target number of concepts for each level. Our interface allows control via a spline editor, as seen in Figure 5.

Concept Introduction Rate
This constraint controls the rate at which new concepts are introduced, describing, for each point in the progression, the number of concepts that should have been introduced by that point. This constraint, expressed via spline editor, can be used to ensure concepts are introduced at a pace allowing the player to master one before proceeding, as well as roughly showing how the complexity of the game changes at a glance.

Clearly, these concepts are specific to *Refraction*. However, the progression constraints are quite general. Given another game's set of gameplay concepts, we imagine that prerequisites and corequisites will still be meaningful for shaping progression plans. The designer could specify constraints that apply to properties related to categories other than gameplay, such as aesthetics. For example, a designer might want to specify that aesthetic properties like background music and graphical tileset should change in groups, corresponding to movements to different places in the game's fictional world.

Game-Specific System Components
Using these particular properties for level generation and analysis in *Refraction* requires a subtle technical approach. Ensuring that a concept is *required* to solve the level entails checking that *all* possible solutions of the puzzle (there are generally many) use the concept, a computationally difficult problem. For example, in a level in which the player is expected to split a laser in two then later add it back together, careless design might enable the player to use only bending

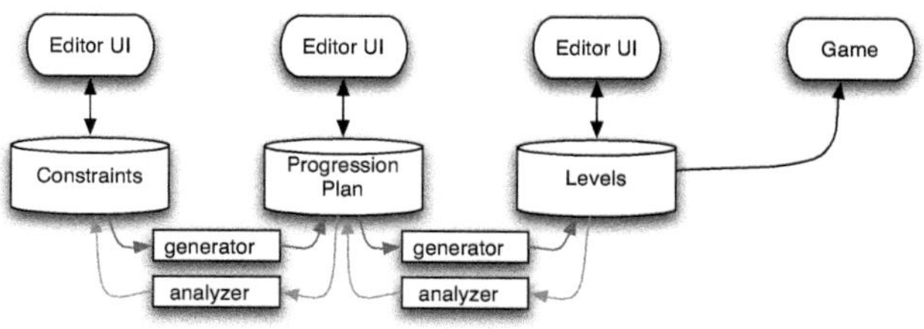

Figure 4. The pieces of our system. Cylinders are models. Ovals represent editing/viewing interfaces that correspond to the four elements of the workflow outlined in Figure 2. The square components are the automated parts that ensure consistency across scales.

pieces to bypass the splitting and adding altogether. Smith et al. [19] developed a level generator (with *Refraction* as the example application) that can enforce this type of constraint on its outputs. The generator uses *answer set programming* (ASP), a declarative constraint-programming technology, to ensure that specified concepts must be used in all possible solutions. In addition to reusing this generator in our system, we extended it to use the same formal game model to determine if a designer-altered level requires each gameplay concept. This level analyzer is used to update the progression plan after levels are manually edited.

We created a progression plan generator using ASP's ability to solve constrained optimization problems. Progression constraints (e.g., prerequisites) are expressed as soft constraints and manual edits locked by the designer as hard constraints. Soft constraints are implemented with an integer-valued penalty function. The generator searches for plans satisfying all hard constraints with the minimal penalty for soft constraints. We include additional soft constraints that add variation to the plan by penalizing repetition. We implemented (in Javascript) a corresponding analyzer that, given a progression plan, checks for violated constraints.

SYSTEM DESCRIPTION
In this section we describe in detail each of the system components we built for our *Refraction*-based prototype. For each component, we discuss its role and how our implementation works. Some of our implementations of these components are game-specific, while others could be directly reused for other games. Of course, all parts of the system can be extended or replaced in the interest of better supporting the designer. Figure 4 illustrates how the system components fit together.

Model
The model that the tool manipulates consists of three parts, which directly correspond to the scales of the workflow: the progression constraints, the progression plan, the progression itself (the sequence of concrete level designs). The designer can also output the playable game from the tool.

Working with Progression Plans
The broad-scale iteration loop takes place between manipulating progression constraints and the progression plan. The system has a set of user interface components used to display and manipulate the progression constraints. Figure 5

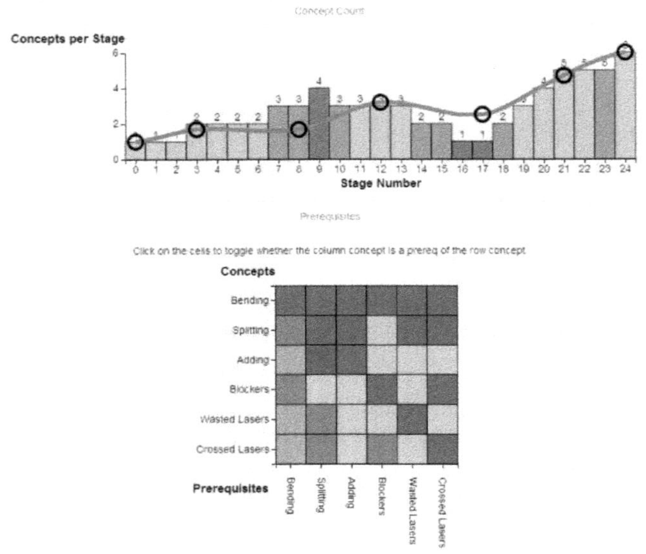

Figure 5. View of the two types of constraint editors in our implementation, which allow manipulation of the various constraint parameters. Each interface type is used for multiple constraint types, e.g., the grid is used for both prerequisites and corequisites. If the current progression plan violates these constraints, the violations are displayed in red. On top, the *concept count* graph shows us that several levels have too many or too few concepts. The blue curve is the target, and the bars are the values of the current plan. On bottom, the red cell of the *prerequisite* chart shows us that the "adding" concept is erroneously introduced before the "splitting" concept. Blue indicates an active constraint (dark is manual, light is inferred via transitivity), while dark gray indicates an unselectable constraint (e.g., two concepts may not be mutual prerequisites).

shows the set used in our implementation. These components are responsible both for letting the designer adjust the constraint parameters and showing whether the current progression plan violates these constraints. As the designer changes the constraint values, the component interfaces update to display whether the current progression plan satisfies the new constraints.

The primary component for manipulating the progression plan is the *progression plan editor*, shown at the top of Figure 3. For our implementation, this consists of a grid showing level properties of each level, where the cells are the current value of the property for that level. The user can directly manipulate this grid to change level properties. As the designer edits the plan, the *progression analysis* component checks whether the constraints are still satisfied. This is then reflected in the constraint editors in real time.

The designer manually manipulates the constraints and progression plan in order to produce a plan that matches their intent. However, the *progression generation* component can be used for rapidly populating the plan and sampling alternatives. When manually activated by the designer, the progression generator creates a new progression plan (overwriting any existing) that best satisfies the current constraints.[8] In order to prevent any manual edits from being overwritten by generation, our system allows the designer to "lock" a particular level. The generators will not modify these levels or their corresponding entries in the property matrix.

Thus, the full iteration loop for this scale is: set values of the constraints, optionally generate a new progression, manually edit the progression, check whether these edits violate any new constraints or unmodeled design criteria, repeat.

Working with Levels

The narrow-scale iteration loop involves manipulating the progression plan and the levels themselves. The structure of components at this scale corresponds with the structure above. First is the previously described progression plan editor. Like the constraint editors, manipulation of the progression plan does not immediately change the levels below.

The *level editor* is used for editing individual levels. Because levels are always game-specific, a single-level editor must be supplied by the game's developers. Developers must also provide a *level analyzer* that computes the relevant design properties for each level. The difficulty of producing such an analyzer scales with the subtlety of the properties checked: determining if a level uses a particular piece or is set to use a particular graphical tileset is easy, but determining the level of strategy needed to complete the level is harder. When the designer edits a level, the level analyzer is used to immediately reflect the changes in the progression plan. These changes are propagated further up to the progression constraints.

For the purposes of automation, the developers may optionally provide a *level generator*. Though the designer could manually edit levels, certain games, including *Refraction*, have generators that divert significant burden from the designer. The level generator, if it exists, can be triggered by the designer to create levels that match the properties described in the current plan. Any levels that are "locked" are not overwritten, so manually-tuned levels can be preserved.

This iteration loop corresponds to the one above: edit the progression plan, optionally generate levels, manually edit levels, check how the progression (and the progression constraints) changed based on these edits, repeat.

Testing the Game

The final component of the system allows for playtesting the levels directly. Thus the game must have an interface that accepts new level progressions to be played immediately.

EVALUATION

Our implementation of the prototype system was intended for internal use by the authors. We evaluate the general architecture and our game-specific implementation through a set of case studies, exploring new design techniques that our system enables. The first case study requires the game-specific level generator, but the others do not require such technology.

Rapid Exploration at a Broad Scale

[8]As there are often many progression plans that achieve an equivalent score with respect to the stated constraints, we have configured the progression generator to make liberal use of randomness in the interest of exploring diverse solutions.

Assuming the system has a level generator, this tool enables game designers to rapidly explore different progression plans and test the plans in playable games. For example, consider a scenario for *Refraction* early in the design phase of a new progression for a new, younger audience. We do not know how this set of players will respond, so we wish to rapidly explore and playtest several possible progressions. We might want to remove "addition pieces" from the game entirely and avoid introducing the "crossed laser" concept (see Table 1) until late in the progression. Our tool allows the designer to quickly sketch these modifications into the progression plan, generate a new set of levels satisfying the plan, and test these levels immediately. While these generated levels may lack some of the unmodeled properties the designer desires, this is acceptable at an early stage of rapid exploration. The designer also has the ability to edit the generated levels to suit their needs, which can be easier than creating new levels from scratch. Previously, creating even an initial progression with the key gameplay concepts removed would have entailed massive effort before the first round of tests.

This rapid exploration applies at the broader constraint scale as well. Suppose in *Refraction* we wish to add an additional prerequisite constraint that "laser crossing" must come after introducing "splitting pieces." The tool can automatically create a progression plan in conformance with this constraint. It then populates a sequence of levels compatible with that plan, allowing a game satisfying the new constraint to be played with minimal designer effort. Without our system, the designer would have to first manually evaluate where the existing plan failed, devise a new plan for an adjusted progression (in notes outside of the editor), then create several new levels, either by hand or by manually configuring the level generator. We expect this reduction in friction to enhance rapid prototyping of progressions.

Automatic Detection of Problems during Iteration

As discussed, levels and progressions undergo a great deal of iteration during the development process. One of the dangers of changes during iteration is breaking previously expressed planning intents, both global progression constraints and level property constraints.

Consider an example in *Refraction* where, late in the development process, the designer wishes to make a minor adjustment to the mathematical portions of the fifth level of the progression. They exchange a "splitter piece" with two outputs for one with three outputs. However, this extra output introduces what we call a "wasted laser," or a laser that is not used in the solution. 'Wasted lasers" is one of the concepts controlled in the system and is constrained via the prerequisite constraint to first appear after another concept, "crossed lasers," which has not been introduced by this level. This could be corrected by adding additional pieces (a new target to absorb the extra laser), but may go unnoticed by the designer. However, upon saving the change in our tool, the system will automatically update the progression plan to reflect that wasted lasers appear in this early level. Since a prerequisite constraint is now violated, the constraint editor highlights this problem to notify the designer. The designer may then take steps to fix it: one option is moderately editing the offending level. If the designer prefers to keep the level as-is, they can generate a new plan for surrounding levels or remove this prerequisite constraint. We believe that this feature can make managing large design projects easier by notifying the designer of automatically detected problems.

Global Optimization of Progression Properties

A designer often needs the progression to satisfy many complex time-varying properties simultaneously. For large progressions this task is difficult to do manually. For example, suppose a designer for *Refraction* is trying to control the pacing of the progression. They are interested in controlling aggregate properties: the number of concepts per level, and the rate at which new concepts are introduced during the progression. The designer wants new concepts to be introduced at an even rate, but they want the number of concepts per level to vary significantly between levels. These constraints are modeled in our system, so the designer may directly edit curves (see Figure 5) to control the constraints. Our system's built-in progression generator can find the closest feasible solution through global optimization. As the designer refines these curves, they can quickly see possible solutions and adjust parameters appropriately. The designer may also rely on the fact that all design changes that were manually introduced can be preserved through the optimization process. We expect this to ease the process of creating progression plans that satisfy several complex constraints.

DISCUSSION

We believe that ideas from this system can be applied to a wide range of games. Some components are game-specific, such as the level editor and generator. The others, particularly those at the broader scale of progression constraints and plans, can be reused between games; the pairing of the our constraint editing interfaces with a generic constrained optimization tool on the back end are generic. The modularity of our framework allows it to be extended for new games and for additional functionality. In this section we discuss some of the limitations and some of the possible ways in which the system could be extended. We then discuss how these ideas might be explored in other, non-game domains.

Limitations and Extensions

We have defined progression plans as a sequence of level properties. In our implementation, these properties are binary values indicating whether a level contains a particular concept, but more nuance is certainly possible. For example, we may be concerned with *how many* bending pieces appear or the overall size of the player's solution. Having numeric knobs instead of binary values would enable the designer to specify even more precise progression plans. The system is also extendable to address some aesthetic concerns; for example, we might give the designer control of the average distance between pieces to allow them to create dense or open-feeling levels. We have already explored constraints on symmetry, balancing, and packing for *Refraction* levels, but elided those properties from the prototype presented here. These new constraints are significantly more detailed than the current set and will require new display mechanisms to make them easy to see and manipulate.

Our prototype supports only a linear progression, limiting its application to some games. For example, in Nintendo's *Super Metroid*, the player explores a large, nonlinear open world. The player finds "power ups" in this world that unlock new abilities, allowing the player to explore previously inaccessible locations. Therefore, the "progression" is defined over which abilities the player has unlocked and which mechanics they understand how to use, rather than a single number describing how many levels they have completed. While extensions to the system to support other progression structures are plausible, most require finding a natural visual depiction for such structures. Currently, our ability to generate progressions and levels under hard and soft constraints exceeds our ability to present useful interfaces that would allow a designer to guide these generators in directions that would satisfy some external intent, so more research must be done to explore how to depict and interactively manipulate these more abstract progression mechanisms.

Refraction is a game of relatively small scope, but we believe this system could be used for much larger games. To remain tractable, one strategy would be to only model the most salient properties of levels and solutions. If complex levels can be created by connecting detailed tiles (e.g., pre-authored chunks of terrain in an 3D adventure game), then the representation used in progression planning can remain discrete and visually manageable. Another strategy would be modeling at additional scales. For *Refraction* it was feasible to work at two scales because puzzles are short enough to be treated as atomic objects. However, many games have very large "levels," such as the single-player campaign missions of real time strategy games like Blizzard Entertainment's *Starcraft*. While designers may wish to model progressions over the entire game's missions, the levels themselves are quite long, and the designer may wish to model an "intra-level" progression of a single level, or perhaps even modeling the progression over individual encounters within a level. Such progressions could be modeled by hierarchically nested progression diagrams: scales for each encounter, mission, and overall game.

We have supplied a small example of possible progression constraints, but they can be extended or new ones introduced. Luckily, many progression constraints apply generally to a broad class of games and so can be reused. This is in contrast with level constraints, which are almost always game-specific. For example, many games are concerned with the order mechanics are introduced, so our *prerequisite* constraint can be used in those games. Likewise, many games require care with pacing, so a constraint dealing with how long concepts should be practiced after introduction before moving on to new concepts would be generally useful.

The existing user interfaces for constraint editing can be repurposed for different kinds of constraints. For example, in addition to prerequisites and corequisites, we might use the same interface for constraints such as: *mutual exclusion*, where concepts A and B shall not show up in the same level; *sequential exclusion*, where if A was used in a previous level, B cannot be used in the current level; or *sequential introduction*, where A must be introduced immediately preceding B.

Similarly, the spline editing interface can be reused for many designer-specified functions. For example, we can model a sense of "scale" for *Refraction* levels by measuring the minimal number of pieces required to complete the level. Our *concept count* constraint gives a very primitive idea of level intensity, and as long as a designer can usefully employ edits of this curve in place of lower-level tweaks, it is valuable. However, it would be desirable to use a function more representative of real-world difficulty and player experience. Backing the spline editor with more sophisticated functions, such as a learning rate derived from an externally-validated learner model, is an obvious and enticing avenue of future work.

Our system has basic support for preserving manual edits by "locking" entire levels as fixed with respect to the generators, but better methods could be applied to make the tool more useful. An obvious first step is allowing more fine-grained locking by locking only particular concepts: for example, the designer may want to ensure that splitting shows up in levels 2–5 but wants to allow the generator to make other decisions for those levels. Allowing the generators to reorder existing levels or minimally modify levels while preserving designer-specified features may also make the locking tool significantly more useful.

Finally, the generators and analyzers can be replaced as technology improves. Depending on the game, many existing level generation technologies would fit in the system. While answer set programming fit our game well for both level and progression plan generation, we could explore many other optimization or planning techniques. For example, for level generation, a game with continuous physics like Rovio Entertainment's *Angry Birds* might use a generate-and-test system that uses the game's internal physics engine. Many relatively simple techniques, such as making an approximate query against a database of previously authored and annotated plans and levels, are likely to be fruitful as well.

Application to Other Domains

We believe these ideas can be explored in other domains beyond games. Here we propose some potential applications of this system, looking at two other domains in closer detail.

Example Domain: Teaching Programming

As one example, we consider an interactive application that teaches programming, similar to *Codecademy*[9]. "Levels" in this domain are individual programming exercises. We speculate a designer may be concerned with properties such as which programming concepts (e.g., recursion, conditionals) are explained or introduced in the exercise, or which concepts the user is assumed to already know. Another may be the complexity of the exercise, either by number of lines of code required or whether certain library function calls are required. Other properties are subjective in nature, such as the directness of suggestions given to find the solution, the narrative used to give context to the user, or the visual layout of the exercise in the application and access to related examples.

[9]http://www.codecademy.com

A designer may wish to ensure several global progression constraints over the exercises. Concepts should not be used until an exercise where they are intentionally introduced. Complexity should vary between exercises to prevent frustration or boredom. Concepts are revisited to give users sufficient practice, and should be recombined with other concepts; for example, designers may wish for each concept to be used with at least three other concepts.

This problem domain shares many of the characteristics of our game design problem (indeed, many of these concerns map exactly into Cook's discussion of skill atoms) so it should likely benefit from using a progression design tool. As most of our tool components can be directly reused, the designers need only supply an editor for exercises and tools to compute properties of crafted puzzles. For the computationally complex task of determining if there are alternate solutions to a programming task that avoid the use of certain concepts, program synthesis techniques could be used to search the constrained space of small programs in a language that fit a specification [3].

Example Domain: High-School Algebra Problems

We consider creating a homework assignment containing a progression of algebra problems. There are several level properties a curriculum designer may wish to control, some modelable, others subjective: which algebraic concepts are used (e.g., factoring, cancellation, distribution), how many steps a particular problem takes to solve, or whether the problem resembles in-class examples.

We consider several progression constraints a designer might wish to enforce, such as the partial ordering of concepts (e.g., properties of roots before properties of logarithms). Designers may want to introduce new concepts in isolation to allow students to master them before combining them with others. They may also wish to ensure the supporting text for each problem is thematically coherent with nearby problems.

There is existing work moving towards being able to analyze and generate such math problems automatically. For instance, Andersen et al. [1] created a framework capable of automatically generating example problems and progressions for elementary and middle school mathematics. Given a hand-authored problem, their system can report which pathway through a mental algorithm the student is likely to take, thus allowing a metric for analysis and synthesis of problems, which is also suitable for our progression designer.

More generally, we suspect that the progression designer could be useful for analysis of the entire math or science curricula through 13 years of K–12 education, or design of a problem-based learning course.

RELATED WORK

There is a long history of creating design tools in HCI research. Many tools have been created to support rapid exploration and prototyping at an early stage. Sketch-based tools such as Silk [13] and Denim [14] allow the designer to sketch interfaces with a stylus. Suede [12] explored the rapid creation of prototypes of speech-based user interfaces using wizard-of-oz techniques. Similar techniques could be used to prototype progression design tools in domains where automation similar to that which we built on is not yet available. In this case, the ability to sketch in broad-scale properties of a progression (e.g. a target pacing curve) and sample alternative plans is still useful even if per-level design is done by hand.

Systems like d.tools [10] support an iteration loop of creating, testing and analyzing interface prototypes. Because user testing and iteration is critical when creating game levels and progressions, our system also aims to support these kinds of iteration loops, but a manner specific to our domain.

Juxtapose [11] and Side Views [23] are examples that allow the user to quickly explore alternatives to the current design. Our tools tries to support this though sampling randomly generated alternatives under constraints, though adopting a literal side-by-side view could be more effective.

Much work has been done using constraint solvers in user interfaces, such as Cassowary [2] and the engine in Amulet [15]. In contrast to familiar applications of geometric layout constraints on interface elements, many of our constraints are much more abstract in nature, such as the nonexistence of shortcut solutions for a level that is supposed to introduce a new gameplay concept. Even so, we strongly separate the definition of the constraint (as driven by the interface of the design tool) from the back-end search technology used to find satisfying solutions. Creating generators and analyzers for *Refraction* involved setting up constraints and passing these to a domain-independent solver from the Potassco project [8].

There is also a rich history of work in mixed-initiative planning and collaboration tools. COLLAGEN increased the ease with which users could create mixed-initiative planning tools [16]. The framework specifies an interface with goals, recipes, and steps, to be implemented by domain-specific planners. COLLAGEN would then provide a dialogue system capable of conversing with the end-user, using the underlying planner. More generally, the SHARED-PLAN architecture underlying COLLAGEN allows computer and human agents to collaborate together in groups to satisfy goals, such as planning or interface design [9]. Our tool is more visually oriented, rather than relying on dialogue as a method of interaction; in addition, we optimize directly while planning subject to constraints instead of requiring recipes to search for solutions.

Mixed-initiative planners have also been used in other domains. NASA's MAPGEN is actively used to create daily activity plans for Mars rovers [4]. OZONE was designed to be a mixed-initiative constraint-based planning framework with pluggable components and was used to plan military resource allocation and transport tasks [22]. Our domain is different in that designers must both create plans and levels.

CONCLUSION

In this paper, we have identified the potential utility of mixed-initiative progression design tools for games, described how such systems could work, and created an implementation to be used with our own deployed game. Progressions and levels are both very difficult to design, and it is arduous to juggle *all* design considerations while working at multiple scales. For several types of games, many of these considerations can be formally modeled, so we can use computation to automate portions of the process. At the same time, many design concerns are completely subjective, so there is a strong need to retain human involvement in the creation of final progression plans and levels for deployment. We expect that game progression design tools can significantly enhance the game creation process. There are many other domains where interactive experiences are composed of scaffolded episodes. Practically all educational and general training environments fit this paradigm to some extent. We describe how given a breakdown of key concepts and the ability to automatically generate levels from parametric specification other domains directly map to our progression design process.

There are several areas of future work, in addition to potential extensions mentioned earlier. Experience with this prototype has already prompted a number of game-specific and general directions to explore next. For example, in addition to adding more details to the progression plan (properties and curves), we want to investigate how concrete patterns discovered in the level editors (such as a commonly used cluster of pieces) can be upgraded into plan-scale properties without additional programming. Meanwhile, broader user studies are required to determine the effectiveness of this model before we can make progress on deploying progression design tools for an audience beyond experienced level designers. More study is needed to discover how well this system applies to a wider class of games. Finally, we propose exploring these ideas in other, non-game domains.

ACKNOWLEDGMENTS

This work was supported by the University of Washington Center for Game Science, DARPA grant FA8750-11-2-0102, the Bill and Melinda Gates Foundation, the William and Flora Hewlett Foundation, and an NSF Graduate Research Fellowship under Grant No. DGE-0718124.

REFERENCES

1. Andersen, E., Gulwani, S., and Popovic, Z. A trace-based framework for analyzing and synthesizing educational progressions. CHI (2013).
2. Badros, G. J., Borning, A., and Stuckey, P. J. The cassowary linear arithmetic constraint solving algorithm. *ACM Trans. Comput.-Hum. Interact. 8*, 4 (Dec. 2001), 267–306.
3. Basin, D., Deville, Y., Flener, P., Hamfelt, A., and Nilsson, J. F. Synthesis of programs in computational logic. In *PROGRAM DEVELOPMENT IN COMPUTATIONAL LOGIC*, Springer (2004), 30–65.
4. Bresina, J. L., Jónsson, A. K., Morris, P. H., and Rajan, K. Mixed-initiative planning in mapgen: Capabilities and shortcomings. In *Proceedings of the ICAPS-05 Workshop on Mixed-initiative Planning and Scheduling, Monterey, CA*, Citeseer (2005), 54–61.
5. Chen, J. Flow in games (and everything else). *Communications of the ACM 50*, 4 (2007), 31–34.
6. Cook, D. The chemistry of game design. *Gamasutra* (2007).
7. Csikszentmihalyi, M. *Flow: The Psychology of Optimal Experience*. Harper & Row Publishers, Inc., 1990.
8. Gebser, M., Kaufmann, B., Kaminski, R., Ostrowski, M., Schaub, T., and Schneider, M. Potassco: The potsdam answer set solving collection. *AI Communications 24*, 2 (2011), 107–124.
9. Grosz, B. J., Hunsberger, L., and Kraus, S. Planning and acting together. *AI Magazine 20* (1999), 23–34.
10. Hartmann, B., Klemmer, S. R., Bernstein, M., Abdulla, L., Burr, B., Robinson-Mosher, A., and Gee, J. Reflective physical prototyping through integrated design, test, and analysis. In *Proceedings of the 19th annual ACM symposium on User interface software and technology*, UIST '06, ACM (2006), 299–308.
11. Hartmann, B., Yu, L., Allison, A., Yang, Y., and Klemmer, S. R. Design as exploration: creating interface alternatives through parallel authoring and runtime tuning. In *Proceedings of the 21st annual ACM symposium on User interface software and technology*, UIST '08, ACM (2008), 91–100.
12. Klemmer, S. R., Sinha, A. K., Chen, J., Landay, J. A., Aboobaker, N., and Wang, A. Suede: a wizard of oz prototyping tool for speech user interfaces. In *Proceedings of the 13th annual ACM symposium on User interface software and technology*, UIST '00, ACM (2000), 1–10.
13. Landay, J. A. Silk: sketching interfaces like krazy. In *Conference Companion on Human Factors in Computing Systems*, CHI '96, ACM (1996), 398–399.
14. Lin, J., Newman, M. W., Hong, J. I., and Landay, J. A. Denim: finding a tighter fit between tools and practice for web site design. In *Proceedings of the SIGCHI conference on Human Factors in Computing Systems*, CHI '00, ACM (2000), 510–517.
15. Myers, B., McDaniel, R., Miller, R., Ferrency, A., Faulring, A., Kyle, B., Mickish, A., Klimovitski, A., and Doane, P. The amulet environment: new models for effective user interface software development. *Software Engineering, IEEE Transactions on 23*, 6 (1997), 347–365.
16. Rich, C., and Sidner, C. Collagen: A collaboration manager for software interface agents. *User Modeling and User-Adapted Interaction 8*, 3-4 (1998), 315–350.
17. Schanda, F., and Brain, M. Diorama. `http://warzone2100.org.uk/`, Apr. 2013.
18. Smelik, R., Tutenel, T., de Kraker, K. J., and Bidarra, R. Integrating procedural generation and manual editing of virtual worlds. In *Proceedings of the 2010 Workshop on Procedural Content Generation in Games*, PCGames '10, ACM (2010), 2:1–2:8.
19. Smith, A., Butler, E., and Popović, Z. Quantifying over play: Constraining undesirable solutions in puzzle design. In *FDG '13: Proceedings of the Eighth International Conference on the Foundations of Digital Games* (2013).
20. Smith, A. M., Andersen, E., Mateas, M., and Popović, Z. A case study of expressively constrainable level design automation tools for a puzzle game. In *Proceedings of the International Conference on the Foundations of Digital Games*, FDG '12, ACM (2012), 156–163.
21. Smith, G., Whitehead, J., and Mateas, M. Tanagra: Reactive planning and constraint solving for mixed-initiative level design. *Computational Intelligence and AI in Games, IEEE Transactions on 3*, 3 (2011), 201–215.
22. Smith, S., Lassila, O., and Becker, M. Configurable, mixed-initiative systems for planning and scheduling. In *Advanced Planning*, AAAI Press (1996), 235–241.
23. Terry, M., and Mynatt, E. D. Side views: persistent, on-demand previews for open-ended tasks. In *Proceedings of the 15th annual ACM symposium on User interface software and technology*, UIST '02, ACM (2002), 71–80.
24. Togelius, J., Yannakakis, G., Stanley, K., and Browne, C. Search-based procedural content generation: A taxonomy and survey. *Computational Intelligence and AI in Games, IEEE Transactions on 3*, 3 (2011), 172–186.
25. Zook, A., Lee-Urban, S., Riedl, M. O., Holden, H. K., Sottilare, R. A., and Brawner, K. W. Automated scenario generation: toward tailored and optimized military training in virtual environments. In *Proceedings of the International Conference on the Foundations of Digital Games*, FDG '12, ACM (2012), 164–171.

BodyAvatar: Creating Freeform 3D Avatars using First-Person Body Gestures

Yupeng Zhang[1,2], Teng Han[1,3], Zhimin Ren[1,4], Nobuyuki Umetani[1,5], Xin Tong[1], Yang Liu[1], Takaaki Shiratori[1], Xiang Cao[1,6]
[1]Microsoft Research Asia, [2]University of Science and Technology of China, [3]University of Bristol, [4]University of North Carolina, [5]The University of Tokyo, [6]Lenovo Research & Technology
yupengzhang@outlook.com; hanteng1021@gmail.com; zren@cs.unc.edu; n.umetani@gmail.com; {xtong, yangliu, takaakis}@microsoft.com; xiangcao@acm.org

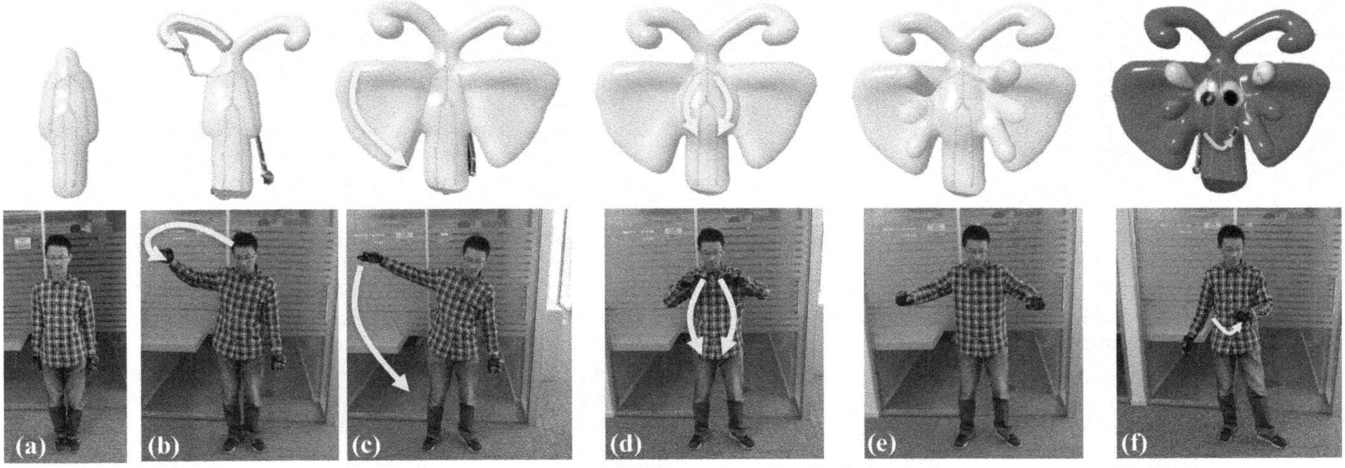

Figure 1. Creating a 3D butterfly using BodyAvatar.
(a) Scan the initial shape. (b) Drag antennas. (c) Sweep wings. (d) Sculpt a big belly. (e) Grow legs. (f) Paint color.

ABSTRACT
BodyAvatar is a Kinect-based interactive system that allows users without professional skills to create freeform 3D avatars using body gestures. Unlike existing gesture-based 3D modeling tools, BodyAvatar centers around a first-person "you're the avatar" metaphor, where the user treats their own body as a physical proxy of the virtual avatar. Based on an intuitive body-centric mapping, the user performs gestures to their own body as if wanting to modify it, which in turn results in corresponding modifications to the avatar. BodyAvatar provides an intuitive, immersive, and playful creation experience for the user. We present a formative study that leads to the design of BodyAvatar, the system's interactions and underlying algorithms, and results from initial user trials.

Author Keywords
3D avatar; body gesture; first-person; creativity.

ACM Classification Keywords
H.5.m. Information interfaces and presentation (e.g., HCI): Miscellaneous.

INTRODUCTION
3D avatars, i.e. onscreen virtual characters representing players/users, are common in video games and online virtual worlds. Especially, with the popularity of Kinect™, these avatars can now directly mimic players' body movement, making the experience ever more immersive. These 3D avatars are usually designed by professional game artists, with only limited player customization available such as by selecting from a collection of predesigned body parts, colors, and accessories. However, if one likes to be more creative and build an imaginary 3D character of non-predefined forms as their avatar, they usually have to master complex 3D modeling software, much beyond the skills of typical game players.

Motivated to fill this gap and exemplified in a typical Kinect gaming setting, we present BodyAvatar, a system to allow any user to easily create their freeform 3D avatar out of imagination, using full-body gestures as the input language like they do when playing Kinect games. These avatars may also be animated by the user's body similar to in Kinect games. Given that avatars typically take forms of living creatures, BodyAvatar focuses on creation of organic-looking 3D shapes but without structural constraints.

BodyAvatar is unique from other gesture-based 3D modeling systems [e.g. 13, 15, 17], in that it centers around a first-person "you're the avatar" interaction metaphor. This metaphor is directly based on the fact that the user is creating a virtual representation of themselves. Instead of treating the 3D model as a separate passive object, the user considers their own body as a physical representation, or proxy, of the avatar being created. Based on an intuitive body-centric mapping, the user performs gestures to their own body as if wanting to modify it, which in turn results in corresponding modifications to the avatar.

UIST'13, October 8–11, 2013, St. Andrews, United Kingdom.
Copyright © 2013 ACM 978-1-4503-2268-3/13/10...$15.00.
http://dx.doi.org/10.1145/2501988.2502015

The typical workflow of BodyAvatar starts with the user posing their body to set the initial shape of the avatar (e.g. a simple stick or a four-legged animal) (Figure 1a). The avatar can then be "attached" to the user's body and continuously animated by body movement. Under the attached status, the user performs various gestures to their own body to edit the avatar progressively, e.g., dragging from their head to give the avatar an antenna, or gesturing around their stomach to grow a fat belly for the avatar (Figure 1b, d). In addition, two users may create an avatar collaboratively in a similar fashion.

BodyAvatar enables free 3D avatar creation without requiring professional skills. It aims at an intuitive, immersive, and playful experience for the user - its first-person metaphor provides both an *intuitive* frame of reference for gesture operations and an *immersive* "you're the avatar" feeling, and its game-like interaction style offers a *playful* atmosphere.

RELATED WORK

Creating models of digital 3D objects is a common task in engineering, design, and film. It is however typically done using complex software based on conventional GUI, thus remains the privilege of trained professionals. As such, much research has been conducted to make this process accessible to novices, mostly falling into two categories:

Sketch-based: a common approach is to interactively interpret the user's 2D sketches into 3D shapes. For example, SKETCH [20] supports constructing 3D scenes by sketching geometric primitives. In a more "organic" style, Teddy [7] lets the user create rotund 3D objects by drawing their 2D silhouettes, as well as supporting operations like extrusion, cutting, and bending. In a style similar to Teddy, ShapeShop [16] supports creation of more complex and detailed 3D solid models through sketch. ILoveSketch [1] instead maintains the original sketch strokes and lets the user draw models consisted of 3D curves. Sketch-based tools leverages people's natural drawing abilities, hence is more intuitive for novice users than using mouse and keyboard to create shapes indirectly. However, expressing 3D shapes via 2D drawing still requires the mental skills of spatial projection and rotation, especially when the process involves frequent perspective changes. In addition, sketching normally requires pen input thus is mainly suitable for desktop settings.

Gesture-based: other systems aim to allow the user to construct and manipulate 3D shapes using hand gestures performed in 3D space, often based on a virtual sculpting metaphor. For example, Nishino et al. [13] use two-handed spatial and pictographic gestures, and Surface Drawing [15] uses repeated marking of the hand to construct 3D shapes. Such systems are more direct than sketch-based systems in that they do not require conversion between 2D and 3D. However, gesturing in the air without physical references or constraints pose challenges for the user to align their gestures to the virtual 3D object. To address this, McDonnell et al. [11] use a PHANTOM device to simulate haptic feedback from the virtual object, and Rossignac et al. [14] propose using a shape-changing physical surface to output the 3D shape being edited. Instead of generating actuated active feedback, Sheng et al. [17] use an elastic sponge as a passive physical proxy of the 3D model, which provides a frame of reference as well as allows gestures to be directly performed on it with passive kinesthetic and tactile feedback. Going a step further, KidCAD [5] projects a 2.5D model on malleable gel, which also serves as the input device for using tangible tools and gestures to edit the model. However, this setup cannot support full 3D. BodyAvatar is inspired by these works in that the user's body also serves as a physical proxy for the 3D avatar to receive gesture operations. In our case the proxy is neither actively actuated by the system [14] nor passively manipulated by the user [17] – it *is* the user.

Also related to gesture-based modeling is Data Miming [6], which allows using freehand gestures to describe an existing 3D shape in order to *retrieve* it from a database. Especially, Data Miming was designed based on an observation study of how people describe man-made objects and primitive shapes. BodyAvatar was designed following a similar user-centered process, with a complementary focus on *creating* organic avatars from imagination.

Another relevant research area is animating an arbitrarily shaped 3D model using human body movements. Traditionally this has aimed at mapping professional motion capture data to 3D meshes [2] or articulated characters [18]. Most recently, KinÊtre [4] allows novice users to use Kinect and their own body to animate a diversity of 3D mesh models, including those scanned from real-world objects. Note that animation has almost always been treated as a separate process from modeling, and often supported by different tools. In contrast, BodyAvatar unifies modeling and animating under the same first-person metaphor, and fuses them into one seamless activity.

FORMATIVE STUDY

BodyAvatar was designed through a user-centered process. Our exploration started from an abstract concept: to let a user create the shape of a 3D avatar using their full body in ways most intuitive to them. To concretize what those ways may be, we learned from our prospective users through a formative study.

Procedure

The goal of the study is to identify common patterns in how people intuitively express 3D shapes using their body. To do so, we adopted a Wizard-of-Oz [8] style method. The "system" was simulated by a researcher drawing 2D sketches of 3D shapes on a whiteboard in front of the participant, representing the avatar being created (Figure 2a). The participant used any body actions they felt appropriate to generate and modify the avatar until satisfied, while thinking aloud to explain the anticipated effect of each action. The researcher drew and modified the sketch according to the participant's actions and explanations.

Nine volunteers (2 female) participated. We included both young adults and children (aged 7 to 25) who are likely (but not the only) prospective user groups of BodyAvatar. Only one had experience with 3D modeling software. The participant was asked to "create" 5 avatars from a blank canvas using their body. For the first 4, the participant was asked to reproduce 4 example cartoon characters shown to them as 2D images (Figure 2b), and for the last one they created an avatar out of their own imagination. We refrained from giving any concrete instruction on how they should achieve the tasks, and only gave high-level hints when they were out of ideas, e.g. "you may pretend yourself to be the avatar", "try using your arm or leg to do something to change it". Each study session lasted 50-60 minutes. We observed and recorded both the workflow and the individual actions they took to create the avatars.

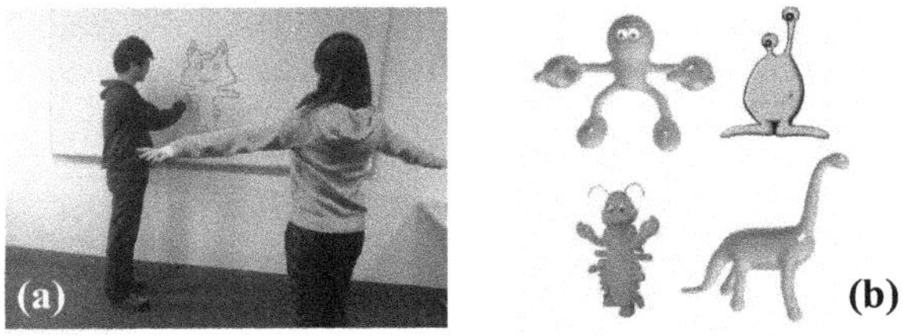

Figure 2. Formative study. (a) Setup. (b) Example characters.

Observations

The majority (seven) of the participants were dominated by a first-person mentality, i.e. they fantasized themselves as the avatar they were creating, and performed actions on or around their own body. One participant instead adopted a third-person style, i.e. imagining the avatar being in front of him, and performed actions in the air where he imagined the avatar to be. Another participant combined both styles.

Almost all participants treated the avatar as a single entity to be continuously built upon, hence they naturally followed a general "generating basic shape → adding features/details" workflow. The only exception was the one participant with 3D modeling experience, who combined this workflow together with cases where he first created subparts and then assembled them to the main entity.

For generating the basic shape, two strategies were observed: posing their full body to mimic the intended shape (8 participants, Figure 3a); and sketching the 2D silhouette in the air using their finger (2 participants). One participant used both strategies.

Several common actions were observed for adding features and details to the basic shape:

Growing a new limb was fairly common. Many participants expressed this by extending their arms or legs outwards, mimicking the shape of the expected limb (Figure 3b).

Figure 3. Participant actions. (a) Posing the body to mimic a dinosaur. (b) Extending arms to grow new limbs.

For adding thinner features, such as an antenna on the head, many participants used a *pinching* gesture, starting from the respective part of their own body and moving away, as if pulling the feature out. Unlike growing limbs, here participants expected the shape of the new feature to follow the path of their hand movement. This also allowed the participant to create more complex geometric features than they can directly mimic using arms or legs.

Tracing an imaginary shape to express it was frequently observed. Participants tended to use a finger to trace a curve, and use palms to trace a surface (either a free hanging surface, or the surface surrounding a volume traced using both hands, such as a big belly).

Another interesting action we observed was semantically *pointing* to one's own body features, e.g. pointing to their eyes with a finger to indicate a pair of eyes should be added to the avatar. Such actions were frequently used by participants to add human facial features such as eyes, mouth, nose, and ears.

Other than adding features, some participants also used their hand like a knife to cut unwanted parts. One participant used his hand like a brush on his body in order to paint color on the avatar.

Bimanual actions were commonplace, where participants simultaneously used both hands/arms to perform the same type of actions, mostly in a geometrically symmetric fashion. There were also occasional observations of asymmetric bimanual actions, e.g., two participants used one hand to describe the shape of a feature, and the other hand to point to their body where they would like the feature to be added.

Despite not seeing a real system, most participants already expressed much fondness in the concept of creating avatars using their body during brief interviews after the study. They thought the actions they came up with were quite intuitive. Not surprisingly, the young children among the participants turned out to be more creative (if less predictable) in their body expressions; while the adults demonstrated more stepwise planning in their workflow.

DESIGN

We now present the interaction design of BodyAvatar, which is directly based on principles and elements provided by the formative study. In the next section we will explain the underlying algorithms to enable these interactions.

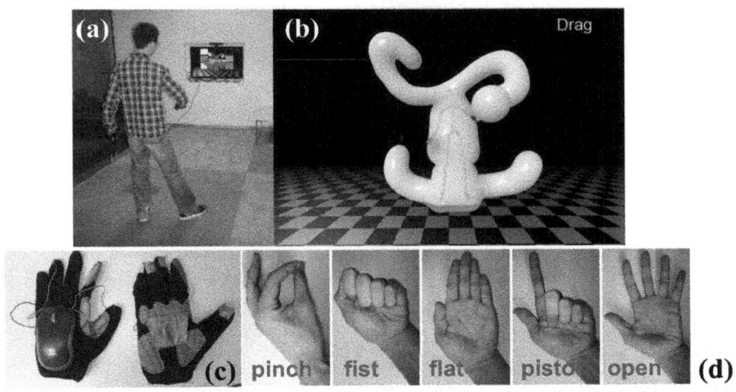

Figure 4. (a) BodyAvatar setup. (b) Software interface. (c) Gesture gloves. (d) Hand poses (shown without glove for clarity).

General Setup

BodyAvatar employs a typical Kinect gaming setup, where the user stands in front of the Kinect sensor and the screen displaying the software interface (Figure 4a). The user can walk freely inside the Kinect sensing range and make all kinds of body movements which are tracked by Kinect. Given that current Kinect SDK does not yet support view-independent recognition of multiple hand poses except open and close hands, we made a pair of very low-cost "gesture gloves" (Figure 4c) that can detect 5 different hand poses (Figure 4d) used for triggering different gesture operations. We took an off-the-shelf pair of gloves, and attached several flexible electrodes (made of conductive cloth) at strategic locations on each glove. These electrodes are connected to the circuit of a wireless mouse which is also attached to the glove. When the user makes certain hand poses, certain combinations of electrodes contact each other, and in turn change the mouse button states that are wirelessly transferred to the computer. We envision the use of gloves will be replaced by Kinect sensing itself in the near future with technology advances [9]. In addition, we use automatic speech recognition to support a few abstract commands.

The software interface (Figure 4b) shows a virtual stage, on which a 3D body skeleton is displayed to represent the user tracked by Kinect, as if the user is looking into a mirror. Hence in some contexts we will use the phrases "user" and "body skeleton" interchangeably. On the same virtual stage also shows the 3D avatar being created, which may be either moving together with the body skeleton or static, depending on its status (to be detailed later). To help the user judge the spatial relationship between themselves and the avatar, parts of the body skeleton behind the avatar are occluded, and the parts inside the avatar are shown semi-transparently. Textual information tips are shown above the scene at times to indicate current statuses and operations.

Workflow

Consistent with what we observed in the formative study, the BodyAvatar workflow consists of two stages: generating the initial shape; and further editing it to the final result. For the first stage, we adopt the action used by most participants, i.e. posing their body to mimic the shape they want. We call this stage *Scan*.

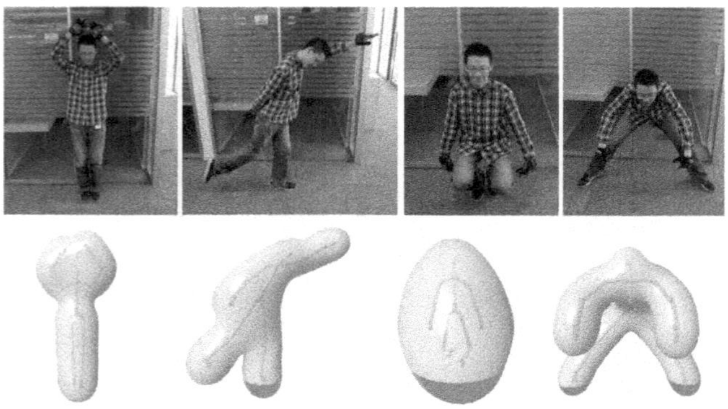

Figure 5. Creating various initial shapes through scan.

Scan

BodyAvatar always starts in *Scan* stage, where the user sees a 3D blobby shape that surrounds their body skeleton and deforms like a viscous fluid as they move (Figure 5). The "fatness" of the shape, i.e. the radius from the skeleton to its surrounding surface, is adjustable by the user by saying "bigger" or "smaller". The user can keep deforming the shape using their body. When satisfied they say "scan" to freeze the shape as the initial avatar and enter *Edit* stage.

Edit

In *Edit* stage, the user performs a variety of gestures (to be detailed later) to edit the avatar. They may also return to *Scan* stage at any point by saying "scan", so that they can regenerate the initial shape.

Metaphors

BodyAvatar includes interactions under two metaphors: *first-person* and *third-person*. The first-person metaphor characterizes BodyAvatar from other systems, and is used predominantly; the third-person metaphor is included as a supplement to support necessary operations that are less convenient to perform as first-person. Besides *Scan* stage which is always first-person, in *Edit* stage the avatar may have two statuses to switch between: *attached* or *detached* to the user's body (or equivalently the user may think of their body attached or detached to the avatar), corresponding to the first-person and third-person metaphors respectively.

First-Person

Under the first-person metaphor, the onscreen avatar and the user's body are considered embodiments of each other. In addition to *Scan* stage where the onscreen shape directly mirrors the user's body pose, this metaphor is further reflected in the attached status in *Edit* stage. In this status, the avatar is continuously animated by the user's body motion in a style similar to KinÊtre [4], i.e. the body skeleton is embedded inside the avatar, and different body parts are attached to different surrounding sections of the avatar in a user-defined manner (we use the word "section" to refer to any subset of the avatar shape that can be animated individually, to differentiate from "body parts" that are parts of the user's body). For example, the avatar walks, jumps, bends, and turns around as the user does so, enforcing the perception that "you're the avatar". Note this does not assume geometric or structural similarity between the body and the avatar.

The user's two arms are treated specially, in that each arm (or both arms) can be individually detached from the avatar by a quick arm swing as if to "fling off" the attached avatar section, so that the arm is "freed up" to perform editing gestures to the rest of the body that remains attached. To attach the arm again, the user keeps it inside an avatar section for 3 seconds to "stick to it", then the arm becomes attached to the avatar section and animates it as usual.

In the attached status, the user's body serves as a physical proxy for the avatar to receive editing gestures. The user performs a hand gesture at a position on or around their body, and the editing effect is applied to the corresponding position on the avatar, e.g. dragging from their head to create a horn from the top section of the avatar (Figure 6a), based on a *body-centric mapping* in relation to the body part. This is true even if the body part is in motion itself, e.g. the user may use a detached hand to drag out a tentacle from the other (attached) hand when both hands are moving. Since the user's gestural movement is visualized by the body skeleton inside the avatar, it also creates an impression that the avatar is editing itself.

By doing so, the user's body provides an intuitive frame of reference that is both physical and semantic, making alignment of the editing gestures much easier than doing it in open 3D space. By looking at how the avatar moves following their body, the user can easily derive the mapping between the two, and use it to guide their actions. For avatar sections not directly attached to a body part, e.g. additional limbs, the user may use nearby attached body parts as a reference and extrapolate the mapping into the neighboring 3D space. For example, if the avatar has a horn that sticks forward from a limb attached to the user's arm, the user can put the other hand in front of that arm to reach the tip of the horn. Note that the user does not need to look at their body or hand to operate. Instead they can quickly put their hand near a body part through proprioception, and the visualization of their body skeleton and the avatar provides continuous feedback to further guide them to reach the exact target location. To further assist alignment, a green highlight (see

Figure 4b) is shown on the avatar's surface when the user's hand is near the surface, indicating the target location.

One potential challenge for first-person editing is when the avatar becomes too large in one or more dimensions, so that the user cannot reach its boundary. When this happens, the system automatically scales up the body skeleton's arm length so that the hand can always reach outside the avatar by a small distance when fully extended. The scaling factor is adjusted based on the elbow angle, so that when the user straightens the arm they can achieve maximal extended reach, but when bending the arm back to touch their body the action remains truthful to the physical arm pose.

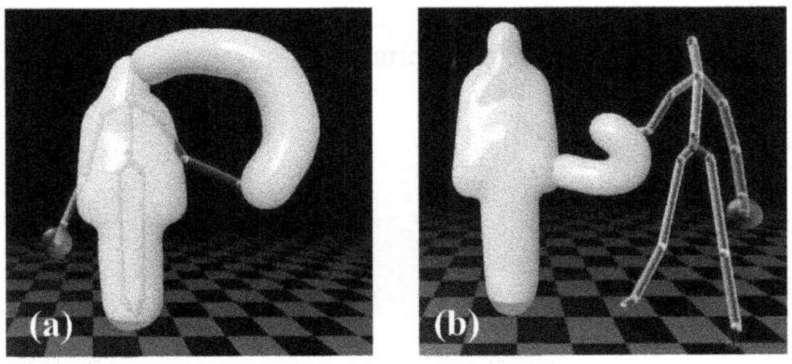

Figure 6. (a) First-person editing. (b) Third-person editing.

Third-Person

The detached status of the avatar symbolizes the third-person metaphor, where the avatar remains still as a separate passive object to be operated on, and the user acts as the operator that can freely move around or through the avatar. Provided as a supplement to first-person interactions, this status allows the user to do certain operations that are less convenient to perform in the first-person status, such as scaling and 3D rotation of the avatar model, and editing regions of the avatar that are harder to reach under the body-centric mapping due to human anatomy constraints, e.g. its backside.

For editing gestures in this detached status, an absolute *spatial mapping* is used, in that the location of the editing effect is the same as that of the user's hand, regardless of its spatial relationship to the body or the avatar (Figure 6b). Editing under this mapping is similar to most existing freehand gesture-based 3D modeling systems (e.g. [13, 15]) and may suffer similar challenges in aligning the gesture to the 3D avatar, thus is meant to be used sparingly.

When the avatar is detached, the user can also *manipulate* it as a whole. This is done in a style similar to the handle bar metaphor [19], where two hands moving in 3D space are used to rotate, scale, and translate a virtual 3D object as if it is skewered on a bimanual handle bar. To trigger manipulation, the user makes a *fist* pose in both hands and moves the hands in 3D, and ends the manipulation by opening the hands. To reduce mental complexity, manipulation is constrained to one dimension at a time (scaling; translation along x, y, or z axis; rotation around x, y, or z axis) which is determined by the type of movement the user makes in the beginning.

Switching between Metaphors

For switching between attached (first-person) and detached (third-person) statuses, we adopt an intuitive physical analogy. While attached, the user can "jump out" of the avatar by making a large hop to the side to *detach* from it; and while detached, the user can "walk into" the avatar and stay inside for 3 seconds to *attach* to it again. During the attaching step, the user can freely define the mapping between their body and the avatar similarly to KinÊtre [4], by posing their body and aligning certain body parts to certain avatar sections. In the beginning of *Edit* stage, the initial avatar generated by *Scan* also starts in a detached status, so that the user can freely define the initial mapping by attaching to it. As mentioned before, the user can also individually attach and detach their arms to various avatar sections using a similar physical analogy.

Detaching and attaching again (and optionally manipulating the avatar between the two steps) also provides the user an easy process to modify the body-to-avatar mapping on the fly for both animating and editing purposes. To make it easier to attach to the avatar in a semantically sensible manner, during manipulation the avatar is constrained to be always grounded on or above the virtual stage, and the user can snap its scale to be of the same height of their body.

Editing Gestures

Directly inspired by actions observed in the formative study, BodyAvatar offers the following gestural operations to edit the avatar (Figure 7). Each gesture is triggered by a specific hand pose, and ended by opening the hand(s). The editing effect is continuously previewed during the operation.

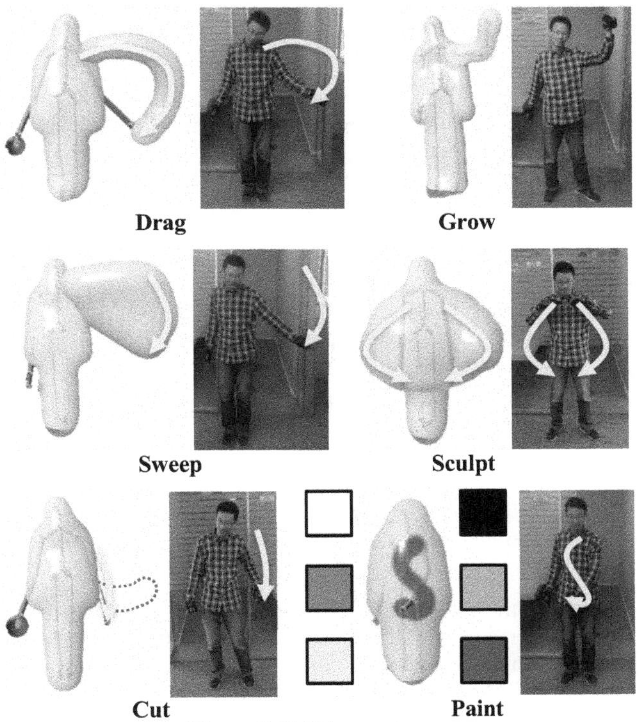

Figure 7. Editing gestures.

Drag

Using a *pinch* hand pose, the user places the hand near the surface of the avatar and then moves the hand in an arbitrary 3D trajectory, as if dragging out a thread. This operation adds a curved tube shape that follows the hand trajectory, e.g. an antenna. *Drag* can be performed in both first-person and third-person fashions. It unifies pinching and finger tracing actions observed in our formative study. Incidentally, *Drag* may also be appropriated as a more general "3D drawing tool" to create other 3D shapes by filling the volume with 3D "strokes" (i.e. tubes).

Grow

Using a *fist* hand pose, the user places their arm (or part of the arm) outside the avatar in any pose, as if pushing out from a shell. This operation adds a multi-segment cylindrical shape based on the pose of the arm segments outside, e.g. to make an additional limb. Unlike *Drag* which follows the hand trajectory, *Grow* only reflects the current arm pose, thus can be seen as a partial *Scan* only of the arm. *Grow* is derived from participant actions shown in Figure 3b, and is restricted as a first-person operation since it assumes the user to reside inside the avatar.

Sweep

Using a *flat* hand pose, the user sweeps their arm in space to traverse a 3D surface, which adds the surface (with a given thickness) to the avatar, e.g. to create a wing.

Sculpt

Using also the *flat* hand pose but with both hands simultaneously, the user traces around the outer side of an imaginary rotund volume rooted on their body, as if shaping a piece of clay. The system infers the volume and adds it to the avatar. For example, one can sculpt around their stomach to give the avatar a big belly. *Sculpt* acts as an incremental operation in that the volume is always added upon the existing avatar surface regardless of the starting points of the gesture, so that the user can sculpt repeatedly to create a volume beyond normal hand reach.

Both *Sweep* and *Sculpt* operations are inspired by how participants used their palms to trace surfaces (free hanging or surrounding a volume). Although conceptually such actions could be also performed in free space in a third-person manner, in practice this would cause considerable ambiguity in interpreting the boundary of the surface or volume. Instead, under first-person metaphor, the user's body naturally serves as a boundary to close the under-defined surface or volume. Therefore, we keep *Sweep* and *Sculpt* as first-person only operations.

Cut

Using a *pistol* hand pose, the user moves the hand across any region of the avatar, as if cutting through it. Any volume in the cutting path is removed, as well as sections that become disconnected from the avatar's main body afterwards. *Cut* can be performed in both first-person and third-person fashions.

Paint

Saying "Paint" opens a color palette shown on both sides of the screen, using which the user can add colors to the avatar. Placing their hand inside a color block picks the color, then the user either makes a *fist* hand pose to fill the entire avatar with the color at once, or uses the hand like a paintbrush to paint on the avatar with a *pistol* hand pose. Saying "Edit" closes the color palette and then the user can make other editing gestures as usual.

Except for *Sweep* and *Sculpt* that are differentiated by the number of hands used, the user may freely perform bimanual operations combining the same or different types of editing gestures. Similarly to *Scan*, the user can say "bigger/smaller" to adjust the size parameter used for certain operations, including diameter of the tube/cylinder in *Drag*/*Grow*, thickness of the surface in *Sweep*, and diameter of the paintbrush in *Paint*. When not performing gestures, a sphere is shown on each hand of the user, the size of which indicates this size parameter. Saying "Cancel" triggers undo of the most recent operation.

These editing gestures provide a complete set of operations that allow the user to create curves, surfaces, and volumes on the avatar, as well as trim and color it, resulting in a diverse range of avatars that can be created (Figure 8). Compared to existing gesture-based 3D modeling systems, some of our gestures are unique to the first-person metaphor, e.g. *Grow*; others take on a new meaning (e.g. *Sculpt*) under the first-person metaphor. There are also other interesting actions from the formative study that are less straightforward to support but we would like to explore in the future, such as semantic pointing and using one's legs to edit.

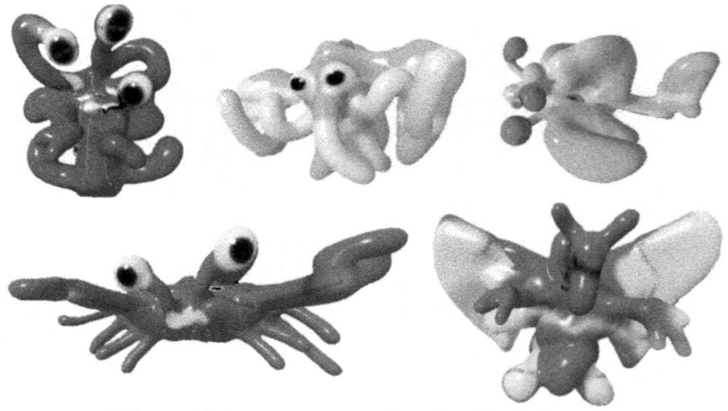

Figure 8. Avatars created using BodyAvatar.

Two-Person Creation

Based on the same functionalities described above, BodyAvatar also allows two people to collaboratively create an avatar (Figure 9). In *Scan* stage, two users can join their bodies to scan into a more complex initial shape than a single user can possibly pose. In *Edit* stage, the avatar is attached to one user who can animate it and perform first-person editing, while at the same time the second user may perform third-person editing to the avatar but using the first user's body as a proxy. This interaction style combines merits from both first-person and third-person metaphors – the first user can animate the avatar to position and orient it for the convenience of the second user, and the second user can make edits that are inconvenient for the first user to perform, yet still have the benefit of a physical frame of reference.

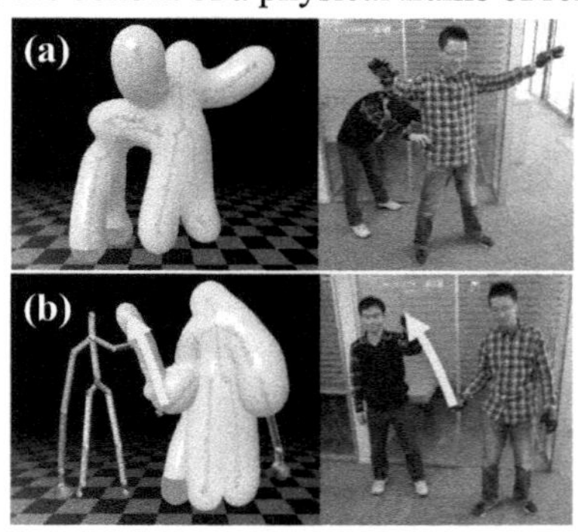

Figure 9. Two-person creation. (a) Scan. (b) Edit.

ALGORITHM

Avatar Model Representation

The avatar's static 3D shape is modeled by an implicit surface constructed from a number of meta-balls in 3D space

[12]; and its kinematic structure is represented by a tree-structured skeleton (referred to as "avatar skeleton" to differentiate from the "body skeleton" of the user). A triangle mesh is used to render the avatar. The mesh is generated from the meta-ball model using the marching-cube algorithm [3] and animated by the avatar skeleton. A texture map is used for coloring. Figure 10 illustrates.

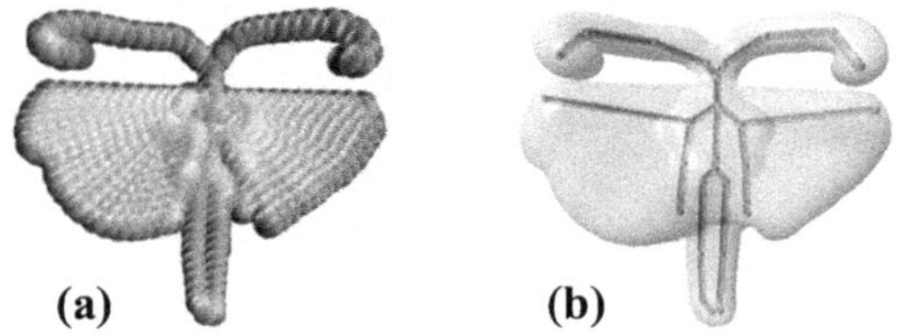

Figure 10. Avatar model representation. (a) Meta-ball model. (b) Rendered avatar mesh (without texture) and skeleton.

A meta-ball is an approximate spherical 3D Gaussian function, and the implicit surface is an iso-surface in the accumulated function of all meta-balls. We choose the meta-ball representation because of its flexibility in supporting ad hoc modification; it also naturally results in a smooth "organic" 3D shape that fits our context of creating avatars.

The avatar skeleton is made of a number of line segments ("bones") connected by joints. Each bone has a fixed length, and dynamically maintains its rotation angles relative to its parent joint.

At the time of its creation, each meta-ball is associated to one of the avatar bones. This allows us to also use meta-ball functions to calculate animation weights for the bones, to be detailed later.

The *Scan* stage generates an initial avatar model based on the user's body pose. The avatar skeleton is generated by replicating the user's body skeleton (both structure and pose), and meta-balls are placed along each bone with equal radius and distance (0.875 times the radius) (Figure 12a). This initial model is updated at every frame, until the user says "scan" to freeze the result. The avatar mesh is also regenerated from the meta-balls at every frame, which gives the avatar a fluid feeling during preview, and its topology may be changed on the fly by joining and separating certain body parts. "Bigger/smaller" speech commands adjust the meta-ball radius and in turn the fatness of the model.

Once the avatar model is frozen and passed to *Edit* stage, we define its pose at this time as the "default" (i.e. before animation) pose, which is used as the standard representation of the model. All further edits to the avatar are to be applied to this default model, after appropriate transform if applicable.

Animation

When the avatar is attached to the user in *Edit* stage, it is continuously animated by the user's body movement. Unlike in *Scan* stage where the meta-balls continuously change positions and regenerate the avatar mesh, here we directly animate the existing mesh because we need to maintain the general shape and structure of the avatar. To do so, we adopt the well-known skinning animation [10] technique, where each mesh vertex is moved by blending motion from one or several avatar bones. To calculate the blending weight of each bone for the vertex, we make use of function values (indicating "influence") of the meta-balls associated with the bones again. Calculated under the default pose, for each bone we sum the function values at the vertex position from all meta-balls associated with the bone, and use this accumulated influence as its weight (after normalization across all bones). By doing so, we obtain smooth animation results directly consistent with the mesh geometry, since it is also determined by the meta-balls.

Then to map the user's body motion to motion of the avatar bones, we need to establish an association between bones of the user's body skeleton ("body bones") to avatar bones. This association is determined by the user's *attach* action when the user poses their body inside the avatar. Each body bone searches for the closest avatar bone (considering both position and orientation) and attaches to it. If no avatar bone is sufficiently close (i.e. < 0.15 meter in distance and $< 60°$ in separation angle), the body bone remains unattached. The root joints of both skeletons (body and avatar) are attached to each other by default. When the user moves, global translation and rotation of their body is applied to the avatar through the root joints, and rotation angles of each body bone is applied to their attached avatar bone if applicable. Unattached avatar bones preserve their original rotation angles.

Body-Centric Mapping

Key to BodyAvatar's first-person editing is a body-centric mapping to transform a position p_w in the world space (where the user and the animated avatar reside) to a position p_m in the model space defined by the default avatar pose (where the edit takes effect), based on current poses of the user and the avatar. This allows the user to always think of their editing gesture to be relative to their body regardless of its pose.

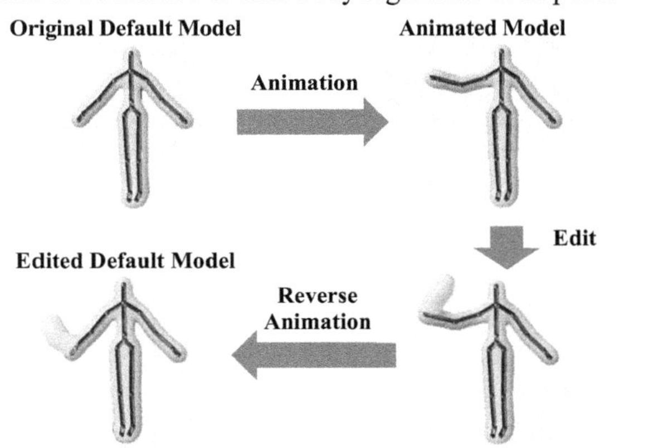

Figure 11. Body-centric mapping. (added shape is highlighted)

In general, this mapping is achieved by a "reverse animation" mechanism. We can imagine the new 3D shape (e.g. horn) being added by an editing gesture as rigidly bound to the nearby avatar section (and in turn the body part that animates the section). Then for each point p_w in the gesture trajectory, we calculate where it should move to (i.e. p_m) if that avatar section is to be animated back to its default pose (Figure 11). To enable this reverse animation, we follow a process similar to animating avatar mesh vertices. However, instead of blending from multiple bones, here we require all points in the gesture trajectory to be driven by one and the same avatar bone, so that the transform remains rigid and unambiguous to the user. To choose which bone to use, we take the "root point" of the added shape (for *Drag* and *Sculpt* this is the starting point of the gesture, and for *Grow* and *Sweep* this is the shoulder joint of the user's arm), and again calculate the accumulated influence of each avatar bone based on the function values of their associated meta-balls at this root point. Note that to facilitate this calculation, in this step meta-balls are temporarily moved from their default positions to match the current avatar pose. We then select the bone with the largest influence to drive the reverse animation for all points in the gesture trajectory. Again, using meta-ball functions to choose the bone takes the geometry of the avatar into account implicitly. Note although the same bone is used for all points in the gesture trajectory, the actual reverse animation transform for each point may differ depending on the pose of the bone at the time each point is created, hence any motion of the avatar section (and in turn the body part that animates it) during the gesture is also taken into account as mentioned before.

Additional considerations are taken for *Drag* and *Sculpt*. *Drag* requires the created tube to always start on the surface of the avatar, hence needs to first project the starting point p_s of the gesture to the nearby surface. If p_s is outside the avatar (by a small distance, otherwise *Drag* is not allowed), this is simply done by finding the closet point on the surface; if p_s is inside the avatar, we first find the nearby avatar bone using the same method in the previous paragraph, then cast a ray from the bone through p_s to hit the surface and take the intersection point. For *Sculpt*, given its incremental nature, we not only project starting points of both hands onto avatar surface in a similar fashion, but also translate the rest of the gesture trajectory by the same displacement caused by the projection, so that it feels the gesture is always performed on top of the existing surface. For both *Drag* and *Sculpt*, after projection and/or displacement, points in the gesture trajectory are transformed using reverse animation as usual.

Editing Operations

All shape-adding operations (Figure 12b-e) are supported by adding meta-balls to the default model. New avatar bones may be added as needed to associate with the newly added meta-balls, and are connected to the closest joint in the avatar skeleton. Reverse-animated gesture trajectory is used in first-person editing, and original gesture trajectory is used in third-person editing. The avatar mesh is regenerated from the meta-ball model after each operation is completed.

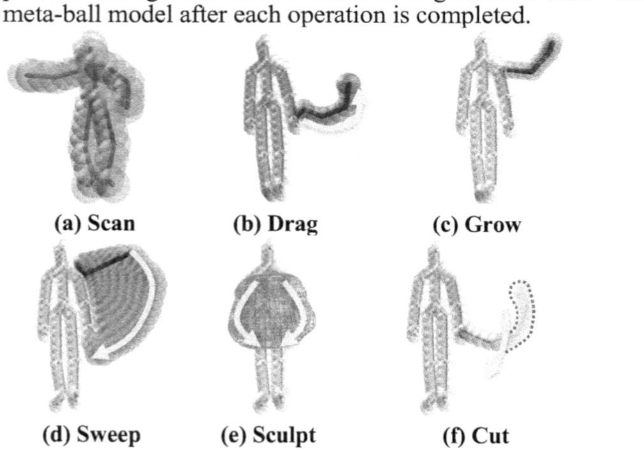

Figure 12. Operation effects on the avatar model. (affected meta-balls and bones are highlighted)

Drag adds a chain of meta-balls along its trajectory, along with a chain of 4 bones sampled from the trajectory.

Grow generates meta-balls along the arm in a fashion similar to *scan*. A replication of the body bones of the arm is added to the avatar skeleton.

Sweep tessellates the surface swept by the arm with a grid of meta-balls. This surface is defined by joining the line segments connecting the user's hand and shoulder at each frame during the gesture. The surface is treated as rigid, thus only one bone is added to animate it as a whole.

The "bigger/smaller" speech commands affect the radius of the meta-balls created by *Drag*, *Grow*, and *Sweep*.

Sculpt requires generating a rotund volume from two 3D hand trajectories only. To infer this volume, we take each pair of points along the two trajectories, and use them as the endpoints to define a 120° arc, whose radius points towards the user's body. Joining all these arcs results in a 3D curved surface that defines the outer side of the target volume (shown as a wireframe in Figure 12e). The inner side is defined by the existing surface of the avatar. Then a number of meta-balls are added to approximate this volume, using a greedy algorithm to fill the space with as few and as large meta-balls as possible.

Cut deletes all meta-balls the gesture trajectory intersects with. If all meta-balls associated with an avatar bone are deleted, the bone will also be deleted. If the model breaks into several disconnected components after the cut, the component containing the earliest created meta-ball or a bone closest to the root joint is kept as the main body, and the other components are deleted.

Unlike other operations, *Paint* affects the avatar's texture map but not the geometry or structure. Instead of using reverse animation, here we adopt a screen-based 2D painting metaphor since the color is always applied to the avatar surface. Taking the user's hand position, we find a point on the avatar surface that occupies the same 2D location on the screen, by casting a ray from the virtual rendering camera through the hand to hit the avatar surface. The texture color at this position is modified accordingly.

IMPLEMENTATION

The BodyAvatar software is implemented in C++ and runs on Windows OS in real-time. It uses Kinect for Windows SDK for body tracking, DirectX 11 for graphics rendering and GPU acceleration, and Microsoft Speech Platform for speech command recognition.

USER TRIAL

To understand the effectiveness of BodyAvatar, we conducted an initial user trial. Six volunteers (3 female), aged 22-23, participated in the trial (noted as P1-P6). Three had experience with 3D modeling software (P1 for 4 years, P2, P5 each for 1 year), two had drawing experience (P1 for 14 years, P5 for 3 years), and 5 had played Kinect games. Although the current participants were from a relatively uniform age group due to availability, they represented a major prospective user population for BodyAvatar, i.e. young adults. In the future we plan to conduct further trials with children and other age groups.

Procedure

Each participant participated in the trial individually. The BodyAvatar interface is displayed on a 32-inch LCD screen. The participant stood and walked between 2.8-4.5 meters in front of the screen determined by the sensing range of Kinect. Considering variable accents of the participants, to prevent them from being distracted by recognition errors of speech commands, a researcher entered correct commands through hotkeys according to their speech when necessary.

The researcher first gave a demonstration of BodyAvatar, then walked the participant through each operation by letting them try themselves. Some examples the researchers created using BodyAvatar were also shown as inspirations. The participant then spent 5 minutes to freely explore the system until comfortable.

The participant was asked to create 3 avatars: (1) to mimic any one of three example avatars shown to them: a butterfly, a lobster, and a horned monster; (2) to create an avatar based on any one of four abstract textual descriptions: dragon, fish, big-headed baby, and alien; (3) to freely create any avatar they specified themselves. Note that although we provided candidate tasks in (1) and (2), these were merely used to inspire the participant to gradually open up their creativity, and we were not concerned about how faithfully the avatar created matches the chosen subject.

For a conceptual comparison, after the BodyAvatar trial, the participant also tried ShapeShop [16], a fully functional sketch-based 3D modeling tool. The participant watched a demo video and was walked through the main functions of ShapeShop. They were then asked to explore the tool and do a free creation of any 3D model they like.

The participant was asked to think aloud throughout the entire trial. We observed their behaviors such as workflow, frequent actions, engagement, etc. After the session, we interviewed the participant about their experience. Each participant session lasted 75 to 100 minutes in total.

Findings

All the participants completed 3 avatars using BodyAvatar without difficulty. They spent on average 11 minutes 33 seconds creating each avatar, of which 6 minutes 48 seconds was for modeling the shape and 4 minutes 45 seconds for painting colors (we should note that an earlier, less robust version of the coloring algorithm was used in the user trial, which contributed to the overrepresented time spent on painting). Participants were satisfied with their creations for 17 of the total 18 avatars. Figure 13 shows examples.

Figure 13. Avatars created during user trial.

Intuitiveness, Immersion, Playfulness

BodyAvatar successfully achieved its goal to be intuitive, immersive, and playful:

Intuitive: participants all found the concepts and operations natural, simple, and straightforward to understand and perform. None had difficulties understanding the 3D structure of the avatar and the effects of the gestures. Five of the 6 participants said the system was very easy to learn. The only exception P1 said she needed some time to memorize the mapping between gestures and operations, especially when the same hand pose is reused for different operations under different contexts (e.g. *Grow* and *Fill Color*). This challenge was partially due to the limited set of hand poses we can detect using the gesture glove, and may be overcome with future technologies. Indeed, we did not observe the participants' learning speed of BodyAvatar to be dependent on their existing experience with 3D modeling, drawing, or Kinect gaming. In comparison, the 3 participants with 3D modeling experience (P1, P2, P5) succeeded in creating a simple rigid model using ShapeShop (e.g. a toy car), while the other 3 found it difficult to judge the 3D structure of the object and perform operations to their desired effects, and gave up as a result despite the fact that they all appreciated the higher precision offered by ShapeShop's interface.

Immersive: the first-person metaphor resulted in a high degree of immersion for the participants, as they felt themselves to be the avatar. As P1 put: "*I even forgot where I was. I imagined I was right in there (the screen), messing around in that closed space about myself.*"

Playful: the entire creation process was filled with laughter of all participants throughout – when they finished their avatar, when they achieved a good result from their gesture, and even when they got an unexpected result. The feeling that they were looking into a mirror and fiddling with themselves seemed to have made everything laughable. During the interview, every participant expressed that using BodyAvatar was a very enjoyable experience.

In fact, immersion and playfulness together resulted in a high level of engagement from the participants, side-evidenced by their perception of time. During the interview we asked the participant how long they thought they spent with BodyAvatar, and all quoted a much lower number than the actual time passed - "*I didn't feel that long had passed, so was amazed when I saw it was half past eight.*" (P3)

First-Person Metaphor

We were particularly interested in participants' experience of the first-person metaphor in BodyAvatar. Although we did not have access to other gesture-based 3D modeling tools for comparison, the third-person operations in BodyAvatar captured some of their aspects, thus can be considered as a delegation for informal conceptual comparison.

All the participants agreed that first-person operations were easy and helpful for the creation process ("*you can feel your avatar is really alive in the first person mode, and it's much easier to control it than in the third person mode*", P3). The foremost advantage of first-person operations was the intuitive physical frame of reference. When making edits in third-person style, all the participants encountered challenges in positioning their hand relative to the avatar especially along the depth dimension, and had to try the gesture several times before confirming – a typical issue in gesture-based 3D modeling tools. Such difficulties did not happen in the first-person status: participants simply looked at the screen and used their proprioception to reach the appropriate position. As a result, participants were more active and confident in first-person status, and showed no hesitation when performing gestures.

Although the avatar could be moved and rotated in both first-person (by walking and turning one's own body) and third-person (manipulating using gestures) style, participants used these two ways for very different purposes. First-person rotation was used very frequently, almost subconsciously, by all participants to examine the 3D structure of the avatar, as if turning around in front of a mirror to check new clothes – an intuitive action directly from everyday life. In contrast, third-person rotation was almost only used to prepare for an editing operation, and participants always had to pause to think about the desired rotation before performing it – similar observations were made with ShapeShop, where participants seldom rotated the model for examining its 3D structure.

On the other hand, aside from inherent limitations of the first-person metaphor such as the difficulty to edit the backside of the avatar, technical limitations of Kinect body tracking capability also made some first-person operations vulnerable to tracking noise/error when certain body parts occluded or contacted each other (e.g., bending down to touch one's foot). Third-person manipulation and editing operations helped participants to circumvent these issues.

Two-Person Creation

In addition to the main user trial that focused on the single user experience, we conducted an informal trial session afterwards with a pair of users (who also participated in the main trial) on the two-person creation experience, which again yielded positive feedback. In particular, the two-person editing style (Figure 9b) made some editing steps considerably easier. Even when the avatar section being edited (e.g. rear legs of a centaur) was somewhat offset from the first user's body, the second user could still use the first user's body as a starting point to quickly extrapolate and locate the section in space, without trying repeatedly like in a pure third-person metaphor.

DISCUSSION & CONCLUSION

Current BodyAvatar interactions are most suited for creating organic-shaped avatars, not necessarily for models with polyhedral features. This is consistent with our objective to create living creatures representing the user. If a user wishes to create mechanical-looking objects instead, a different interaction style or system may be preferable, e.g. one that is based on assembling primitives. On the other hand, there is no algorithmic limitation in the range of shapes that can be modeled using our meta-ball representation together with potential technical extensions such as blob-trees as demonstrated by ShapeShop [16].

The level of detail that BodyAvatar can create could be limited by the physical granularity of the gestures (both in terms of the user's motor control capability and in terms of Kinect's sensing capability) under the first-person metaphor, where the user and the avatar are typically close to a one-to-one scale. However, under the third-person metaphor the user may freely scale up the avatar to do detailed edits on a portion of it, although this may again highlight the gesture alignment challenge as seen in other gestural 3D modeling systems. Considering all factors, we believe our choice to focus on the first-person metaphor is rational given our goal to support novice users' creation, where intuitiveness and simplicity takes priority over precision and sophistication.

There exist many possible extensions to BodyAvatar. For example, in the future we are interested in incorporating other elements into the avatar, such as real-world objects (e.g. a hat) scanned by Kinect, or predesigned components (e.g. facial features or polyhedral primitives) retrieved using gestures (similarly to [6]). These will further expand the range of avatars BodyAvatar can create, making it more generalizable to other application domains, such as designing 3D-printed articulated toys, interactive storytelling, or prototyping characters and animations for movie production.

In conclusion, BodyAvatar provides an intuitive, immersive, and playful experience for novice users to create freeform 3D avatars using their own body. Its first-person interaction metaphor is unique from existing gesture-based 3D modeling tools, and well accepted by our users.

ACKNOWLEDGEMENTS

We sincerely thank Jaron Lanier, Shahram Izadi, and Jiawen Chen for invaluable research discussion and help, and anonymous participants of the user trial.

REFERENCES

1. Bae, S-H, Balakrishnan, R., Singh, K. (2008). ILoveSketch: as-natural-as-possible sketching system for creating 3D curve models. *UIST*. p. 151-160.
2. Baran, I., Popovic, J. (2007). Automatic rigging and animation of 3D characters. *SIGGRAPH.*
3. Bloomenthal, J. (1988). Polygonization of implicit surfaces. *Computer Aided Geometric Design*, 5(4), p.341-355.
4. Chen, J., Izadi, S., Fitzgibbon, A. (2012). KinÊtre: animating the world with the human body. *UIST*, p. 435-444.
5. Follmer, S., Ishii, H. (2012). KidCAD: digitally remixing toys through tangible tools. *CHI*. p. 2401-2410.
6. Holz, C., Wilson, A.D. (2011). Data miming: inferring spatial object descriptions from human gesture. *CHI*, p. 811–820.
7. Igarashi, T., Matsuoka, S., Tanaka, H. (1999). Teddy: a sketching interface for 3D freeform design. *SIGGRAPH*, p.409-416.
8. Kelley, J. F. (1984). An iterative design methodology for user-friendly natural language office information applications. *Transactions on Office Information Systems*, 2(1), p. 26–41.
9. Keskin, C., Kirac, F., Kara, Y.E., Akarun, L. (2012). Hand pose estimation and hand shape classification using multi-layered randomized decision forests. *ECCV*. p. 852-863.
10. Lewis, J. P., Cordner, M., Fong, N. (2000). Pose space deformations: a unified approach to shape interpolation and skeleton-driven deformation. *SIGGRAPH*. p. 165–172.
11. McDonnell, K., Qin, H., & Wlodarczyk, R. (2001). Virtual clay: A real-time sculpting system with haptic toolkits. *I3D*. p. 179-190.
12. Nishimura, H., Hirai, M., Kawai, T., Kawata, T., Shirakawa, I., Omura, K. (1985). Object modeling by distribution function and a method of image generation. *Electronics Communications Conference*, p. 718–725.
13. Nishino, H., Utsumiya, K., & Korida, K. (1998). 3D object modeling using spatial and pictographic gestures. *VRST*. p. 51-58.
14. Rossignac, J., et al. (2003). Finger sculpting with digital clay: 3D shape input and output through a computer-controlled real surface. *Shape Modeling International*. p. 229-234.
15. Schkolne, S., Pruett, M., & Schroeder, P. (2001). Surface drawing: creating organic 3D shapes with the hand and tangible tools. *CHI*. p. 261-268.
16. Schmidt, R., Wyvill, B., Sousa, M. C., Jorge, J.A. (2005). ShapeShop: sketch-based solid modeling with blobTrees. *Eurographics Workshop on Sketch-Based Interfaces and Modeling*. p. 53-62.
17. Sheng, J., Balakrishnan, R., Singh, K. (2006). An interface for 3D sculpting via physical proxy. *GRAPHITE*. p. 213-220.
18. Shin, H.J., Lee, J., Shin, S.Y., Gleicher, M. (2001). Computer puppetry: an importance-based approach. *Trans. on Graphics*. 20(2), p. 67-94.
19. Song, P., Goh, W.B., Hutama, W., Fu, C., Liu, X. (2012). A handle bar metaphor for virtual object manipulation with mid-air interaction. *CHI*. p. 1297-1306.
20. Zeleznik, R.C., Herndon, K., & Hughes, J. (1996). SKETCH: an interface for sketching 3D scenes. *SIGGRAPH*. p. 163-170.

VizlCal: Accurate Energy Expenditure Prediction for Playing Exergames

Miran Kim[1] mirank@unr.edu
Jeff Angermann[2] jeffa@unr.edu
George Bebis[1] bebis@unr.edu
Eelke Folmer[1] efolmer@unr.edu

[1]Department of Computer Science and Engineering
[2]School of Community Health Sciences
University of Nevada, Reno

ABSTRACT
In recent years, exercise games have been criticized for not being able to engage their players into levels of physical activity that are high enough to yield health benefits. A major challenge in the design of exergames, however, is that it is difficult to assess the amount of physical activity an exergame yields due to limitations of existing techniques to assess energy expenditure of exergaming activities. With recent advances in commercial depth sensing technology to accurately track players' motions in 3D, we present a technique called Vizical that uses a non-linear regression approach to accurately predict energy expenditure in real-time. Vizical may allow for creating exergames that can report energy expenditure while playing, and whose intensity can be adjusted in real-time to stimulate larger health benefits.

Author Keywords
Machine Learning, Computer Vision, Exergames, Gestures, Exercise, Health, Energy Expenditure, Physical Activity.

ACM Classification Keywords
I.2.10 Vision and Scene Understanding: Motion

INTRODUCTION
Recent studies show that short bouts of high-intensity training, such as the popular CrossFit workouts, have great potential to significantly improve fitness levels [32]. Though the durations are shorter than typical aerobic activities, the benefits are usually longer lasting and the improvements to cardiovascular health and weight loss are more significant [5]. These findings are particularly interesting in the context and design of *exergames*, e.g., video games that use exertion-based interfaces to promote physical activity, fitness, and gross motor skill development [26]. As exergames typically involve short bouts of upper and whole body gestures, they may be considered as a form of high-intensity training and could yield similar associated health benefits. As video games are considered powerful motivators, many researchers have argued that exergames could be an important tool in fighting the current childhood obesity epidemic [29].

UIST'13, October 8–11, 2013, St. Andrews, United Kingdom.

ACM 978-1-4503-2268-3/13/10...$15.00.
http://dx.doi.org/10.1145/2501988.2502009

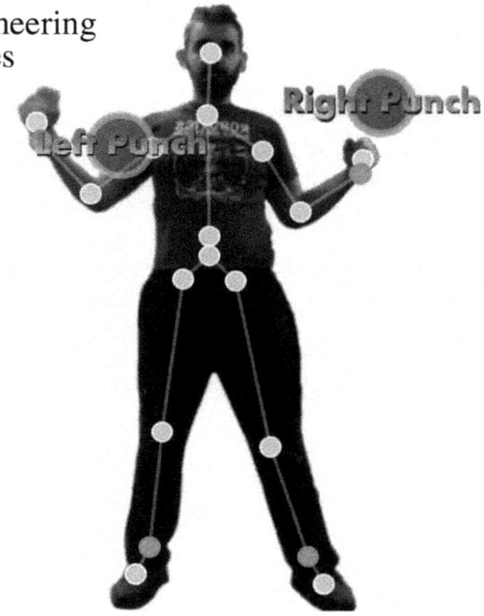

Figure 1: Recent commercially available depth sensing cameras, such as Microsoft Kinect, allow for accurately tracking skeletal joint positions of a user playing an exergame.

Recent studies reveal that popular exergames, such as Nintendo Wii, stimulate greater energy expenditure (EE) than when playing sedentary video games [14, 22], but they don't achieve levels of physical activity that are comparable with conventional types of exercise [15, 10] or the sports they simulate [13]. Though exergames have been introduced in some physical education programs [28], interest in using them beyond entertainment purposes seems to be waning [2].

A challenge in the design of exercise games is that it is difficult to measure the amount of EE an exergame yields. This is due to a number of limitations of existing methods for measuring EE, for example, the use of heart rate is limited as it can be influenced by psychological factors, such as excitement. Wearable activity monitors predominantly measure locomotion and are limited in being able to capture upper body motions, which are often used in exercise games. EE can be more accurately measured using calorimetric techniques such as metabolic gas analysis systems, but these techniques are expensive and require a significant amount of training.

We present Vizical, a low-cost and easy to use technique for accurately assessing the EE of exergames. Vizical takes advantage of recent advances in motion sensing input controller technology (Microsoft Kinect) to accurately track a player's movements in 3D (See Figure 1). Vizical may be used to design exergames that: (1) stimulate higher levels of physical activity, (2) report current or total EE; and (3) can adjust their intensity in real-time.

BACKGROUND AND RELATED WORK

Total energy expenditure (TEE) of humans has three components: (1) basal metabolic rate (BMR), thermic effect of food (TEF); and the energy expenditure of activity (AEE). A complete review of all different types of energy expenditure assessment techniques is beyond the scope of this paper, though a comprehensive overview is provided by Levine [24]). In general, EE can be measured using three different approaches. We will discuss the most popular methods for each approach and discuss their limitations in being able to assess EE of exergames.

Direct calorimetry methods measures the rate of heat loss from a subject using a calorimeter. A calorimeter is typically implemented in the form of an isothermal or adiabatic chamber. Because these systems are extremely expensive to build and require enormous expertise to operate, these techniques are typically only used in highly specialized labs [24].

Indirect calorimetry methods measures oxygen consumption and/or CO2 production and convert this into EE using various formulas. Various techniques exist, for example, total collection systems, such as the Douglas bag [33] can be used to collect expired air from a subject wearing a mask. Confinement systems, such as a respiratory chamber, have the subject contained in gas-tight room. For both approaches, oxygen consumption can be measured by changes in volume and/or composition of the expired air. These systems are very accurate but not portable. Also, they do require extensive training to use the systems. Because the response time to observe changes in oxygen consumption is typically high ($>$10 minutes), these systems are typically used to measure EE over longer periods of time. Different from the above mentioned systems, metabolic gas analysis systems are considered to be more practical and preferable; the systems require subjects to inhale air through a mask and expire via a non-return valve in order to measure oxygen consumption (VO2) and/or CO2 production (VCO2). In recent years, portable VO2 metabolic systems have been developed [23]. Such portable systems operate untethered and transmit data wirelessly for various physical activities outside a laboratory setting. These systems are very accurate and have fast response times ($<$ 30s), but they are expensive and do require extensive training. Additionally, subjects may experience respiratory discomfort using metabolic systems while exercising.

Non-calorimetric methods predict EE by extrapolating physiological or kinematic measurements. These methods are often calibrated against calorimetric techniques [24]. Because heart rate typically increases when users engage in physical activity, it can be used as a proxy for physical activity [12]. Heart rate monitors are portable, low-cost, and unobtrusive, and they can be used over longer periods of time. Heart rate is subject to large individual variation and is a poor proxy for exertion for children due to developmental considerations [8]. The most significant limitation of this method in context of exergames is that heart rate is affected by psychological factors, such as excitement. This is problematic as playing (non-active) video games have been found to elevate heart rate [16], without users actually getting physically active. The energy cost of physical activities can also be assessed using kinematic measurements, typically in the form of wearable accelerometers. Approaches for EE estimation using wearable accelerometers can be classified in two categories: (1) physical-based [17], and (2) regression-based [9] approaches. Physical-based approaches rely on a model of the human body, where velocity or position information is estimated from accelerometer data and kinetic motion and/or segmental body mass is used for estimating EE. Regression-based approaches, on the other hand, estimate EE by directly mapping accelerometer data to EE. The simplest regression-based approach is to estimate EE from a single accelerometer placed at the hip using linear regression. This approach has been extended to using non-linear regression models (i.e., to fully capture the complex relationship between acceleration and EE) [36] and multiple accelerometers (i.e., to account for upper or lower body motion which is hard to capture from a single accelerometer placed at the hip) [37]. Combining accelerometers with heart rate monitors [30] has been shown to improve EE estimation significantly.

In the context of exergames, a limitation of using accelerometers is in their ability to capture total activity, as accelerometers only selectively record movement of the part of the body to which they are attached. Accelerometers worn on the hip are primarily suitable for gait or step approximation, but they cannot capture upper body movement; if worn on the wrist, locomotion is not accurately recorded. Exergames typically involve whole body motions, such as punches and kicks. Increasing the number of accelerometers will increase the accuracy of capturing total body movement, but it is often inconvenient and not practical, due to cost. Another limitation is that accelerometers can't report EE in real time and they have a limited sensitivity (e.g., due to band pass filters they only detect accelerations between 0.05 and 2G, which prevents them from detecting light activities or discriminating between levels of vigorous activities [7]).

Exergaming studies. A recent analysis [3] of exergaming studies reveals that most exergames are only able to engage children into light-to-moderate levels of physical activity with games involving whole body gestures stimulating larger amounts of EE than games that only involve upper body gestures. The Center for Disease Control recommends children should engage into 60 minutes of moderate-to-vigorous levels of activity daily, including 20 minutes of vigorous activity [1]. Given these criteria, current exergames do not stimulate types and amounts of physical activity required to maintain cardiorespiratory fitness. The majority of these studies used heart rate and accelerometers to predict EE. The only two studies [38, 25] that found moderate levels of physical activity for whole body exergames, used VO2 metabolic systems to measure EE. These findings seem to support our claim that the recent exergaming criticisms are to an extent unfounded, as techniques with significant limitations are being used to assess EE of exergames.

Related work. Four unique approaches closely related to ViziCal were identified. Krohn and Boisclair assessed the metabolic cost of fish swimming in an aquarium by tracking their motions using a stereo camera while measuring their total oxygen consumption [21]. Image analysis was used to measure the swimming speed of each fish, which was subsequently used as a feature in predicting EE. This technique is not well suited for assessment of human activity, as the continuous motion of forced swimming is not applicable to the rapid and sporadic movements typically associated with exergaming. In another approach utilizing video analysis, Kaneko et al. assessed EE in spacelab astronauts performing gymnastic exercises during spaceflight [18]; this approach is not applicable to our problem since the astronaut's motions are significantly different from how our exergames are played. Ogsnach et al. employed video analysis to model and calculate EE in professional soccer players [27], but their experimental design only accounted for running performance. Botton et al. estimated EE in tennis using computer vision [4]. Their approach classified tennis EE as one of five different types of activities, i.e., walking, running, returning, serving, and sitting down. Each of these activities has a different amount of EE associated with it, which was measured using a portable VO2 metabolic system. Overall EE was then calculated by sequencing the activity using video analysis. As this approach was limited to activity segregation and classification, it does not approximate the continuous range of motion movement accounted for in our model.

VIZICAL

We have developed a non-calorimetric technique called Vizical that can predict EE of exergaming activities using the rich amount of kinematic information acquired using a commercially available 3D camera (Kinect). Kinect is a controller-less input device used for playing video games and exercise games for the Xbox 360 platform. This sensor can track up to six humans in an area of $6m^2$ by projecting a speckle pattern onto the users body using an IR laser projector. A 3D map of the users body is then created in real-time by measuring deformations in the reference speckle pattern. A single depth image allows for extracting the 3D position of 20 skeletal joints at 200 frames per second. This method is invariant to pose, body shape and clothing [34]. The joints include hip center, spine, shoulder center, head, shoulder, elbow, wrist, hand, hip, knee, ankle, and foot (See Figure 1). The estimated joint locations include the direction that the person is facing, which allows for distinguishing between the left and right joints for shoulder, elbow, wrist, hand, hip, knee, ankle and foot. Studies have investigated the accuracy of Kinect [19, 11], which found that the depth measurement error ranges from a few millimeters at the minimum range (70cm) up to about 4 cm at the maximum range of the sensor (6.0m).

We adopt a regression based approach by directly mapping kinematic data collected using the Kinect to EE, since this has shown good results without requiring a model of the human body [30, 37]. The EE of playing an exergame is acquired using a portable VO2 metabolic system, which provides the ground truth for training a regression model (see Figure 2). Given a reasonable amount of training data, the regression model can then predict EE of exergaming activities based on kinematic data captured using a Kinect sensor (see Figure 3). Accelerometer based approaches typically estimate EE using a linear regression model over a sliding window of one-minute

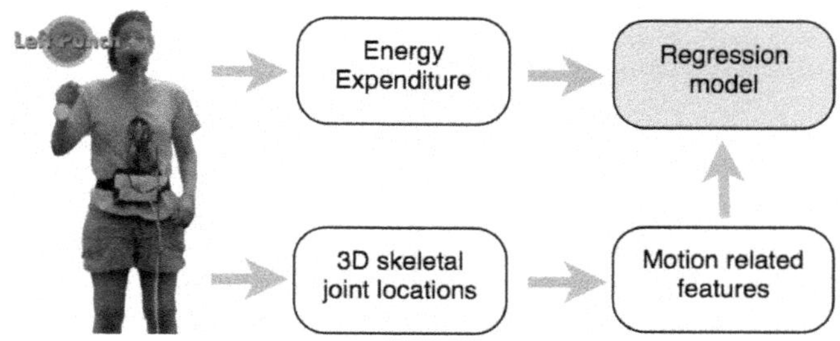

Figure 2: Kinematic information and EE of a subject playing an exergame is obtained using a portable VO2 metabolic system. From the skeletal joint location data, various motion related features are extracted to train a regression model using the collected ground truth data.

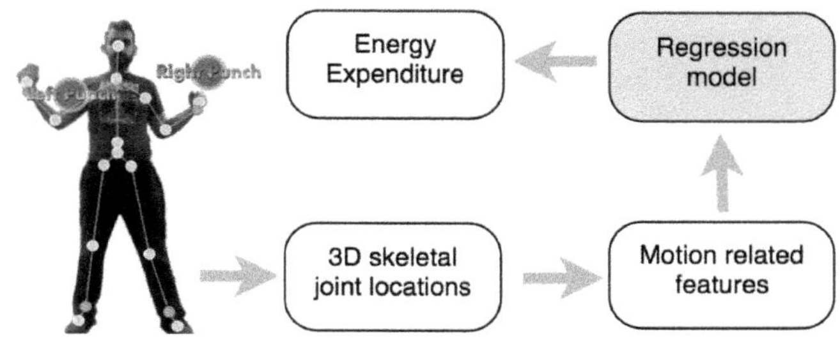

Figure 3: Based on kinematic information the regression model can then predict the EE of an activity.

length using the number of acceleration counts per minute [9] (e.g., the sum of the absolute values of the acceleration). A recent study found several limitations for linear regression models to accurately predict EE using accelerometers [20]. This study further suggests nonlinear regression models may be able to better predict EE associated with upper body motions and high-intensity activities.

For ViziCal, we employ Support Vector Regression (SVR)[35], a popular regression technique that has good generalizability and robustness against outliers and supports non-linear regression models. SVR can approximate complex non-linear relationships using kernel transformations. Kinect allows for recording human motion at a much higher spatial and temporal resolution. Where accelerometer based approaches are limited to using up to five accelerometers simultaneously, ViziCal can take advantage of having location information of 20 joints. This allows for detecting motions of body parts that do not have attached accelerometers such as the elbow or the head. Though accelerometers sample at 32Hz, they report accumulated acceleration data in 1 second epochs. Their sensitivity is also limited (0.05 to 2 G). Because ViziCal acquires 3D joint locations at 200Hz, accelerations can be calculated more accurately and with a higher frequency. Besides using acceleration, features from more powerful, view-invariant, spatial representation schemes of human motion can be used, such as histograms of 3D joints [40]. Besides more accurate EE assessment, ViziCal has a number of other benefits: (1) Accelerometers can only be read out using an external reader, where ViziCal can predict EE in real time, which may allow for real-time adjustment of the intensity of an exergame; (2) Subjects are not required to wear any sensors, though they must stay within range of the Kinect sensor; and (3) Accelerometers typically cost several hundreds of dollars per unit whereas a Kinect sensor retails for $150.

EXPERIMENT

An experiment was conducted to demonstrate the feasibility of Vizical to accurately predict the EE of playing an exergame. This experiment provides insight into the following two research questions: (1) What type of features are most useful in predicting EE? (2) What is the accuracy of ViziCal compared with accelerometer based approaches?

Instrumentation

For our experiment, the Kinect for Windows sensor is used, which offers improved skeletal tracking over the Kinect for Xbox 360 sensor. Though studies have investigated the accuracy of Kinect, these were limited to non-moving objects [19, 11]. We measured the accuracy of the Kinect to track moving joints using an optical 3D motion tracking system with a tracking accuracy of 1mm. We anticipated the arms to be most difficult to track, due to their size; therefore, we attached a marker at the wrist of subjects, close to wrist joints in the Kinect skeletal model. A number of preliminary experiments with two subjects performing various motions with their arms found an average tracking error of less than 10 mm, which we deem acceptable for our experiments. EE is collected using a Cosmed K4b2 portable gas analysis system, which measures pulmonary gas exchange with an accuracy of $\pm 0.02\%$ (O_2), $\pm 0.01\%$ (CO_2) and has a response time of 120ms. This system reports EE in Metabolic Equivalent of Task (MET); a physiological measure expressing the energy cost of physical activities. METs can be converted to calories by measuring an individual's resting metabolic rate.

An exergame was developed using the Kinect SDK 1.5 and which involves destroying virtual targets rendered in front of an image of the player using whole body gestures (See Figure 1 for a screenshot). This game is modeled after popular exergames, such as EyeToy:Kinetic and Kinect Adventures. A recent criticism of exergames is that they only engage their players in light and not vigorous levels of physical activity, where moderate-to-vigorous levels of physical activity are required daily to maintain adequate health and fitness [1]. To allow for ViziCal to distinguish between light and vigorous exergames, a light and a vigorous mode was implemented in our game. The intensity level of any physical activity is considered vigorous if it is greater than 6 METs and light if it is below 3 METs. Using the light mode, players destroy targets using upper body gestures, such as punches, but also using head-butts. We included gestures with the head, as this type of motion is difficult to measure using accelerometers, as they are typically only attached to each limb. We play tested this version with the portable metabolic system using a number of subjects to verify that the average amount of EE was below 3 METs. For the vigorous mode, destroying targets using kicks were added, as previous studies show that exergames involving whole body gesture stimulate larger amounts of EE than exergames that only involve upper body gestures [3]. After extensive play testing, jumps were added to assure the average amount of EE of this mode was over 6 METs. A target is first rendered using a green circle with a radius of 50 pixels. The target stays green for 1 second before turning yellow and then disappears after 1 second. The player scores 5 points if the target is destroyed when green and 1 when yellow as to motivate players to destroy targets as fast as possible. A jump target is rendered as a green line. A sound is played when each target is successfully destroyed. For collision detection, each target can only be destroyed by one specific joint (e.g., wrists, ankles, head). A text is displayed indicating how each target needs to be destroyed, e.g.,"Left Punch"(see Figure 1).

An initial calibration phase determines the length and position of the player's arms. Targets for the kicks and punches are generated at an arm's length distance from the player to stimulate the largest amount of physical activity without having the player move from their position in front of the sensor. Targets for the punches are generated at arm's length at the height of the shoulder joints with a random offset in the XY plane. Targets for the head-butts are generated at the distance of the player's elbows from their shoulders at the height of the head. Jumps are indicated using a yellow line where the players have to jump 25% of the distance between the ankle and the knee. Up to two targets are generated every 2 seconds. The sequence of targets in each mode is generated pseudo-randomly with some fixed probabilities for light (left punch:36%, right punch:36%, two punches:18%, head-butt:10%) and for the vigorous mode (kick:27%, jump:41%, punch:18%, kick+punch:8%, head-butt:5%). Targets are generated such that the same target is not selected sequentially. All variables were determined through extensive play testing as to assure the desired METs were achieved for each mode. While playing the game the Kinect records the subject's 20 joint positions in a log file every 50 milliseconds.

Participants

Previous work on EE estimation [31] has shown that subject independent EE estimation is more difficult than subject dependent estimation. This is because commonly employed regression models fail to account for physiological differences between subject data used to train and test the regression model. For this experiment, we are primarily interested in identifying those features that are most useful in predicting EE. EE will vary due to physiological features, such as gender and gross phenotype. To minimize potential inter-individual variation in EE, which will allow us to concentrate on identifying those features most useful in predicting EE; we collected data from a homogeneous healthy group of subjects, which would allow us to concentrate on The following criteria were used: (1) male; (2) body mass index less than 25; (3) body fat percentage less than 17.5%; (4) age between 18 and 25; (5) exercise at least three times a week for 1 hour. Subjects were recruited through flyers at the local campus sports facilities. Prior to participation, subjects were asked to fill in a health questionnaire to screen out any subjects who met the inclusion criteria but for whom we anticipated a greater risk to participate in the trial due to cardiac conditions or high blood pressure. During the intake, subjects' height, weight and body fat were measured using standard anthropomorphic techniques to assure subjects met the inclusion criteria. Fat percentage was acquired using a body fat scale. A total of 9 males were recruited (average age 20.7 (SD=2.24), weight 74.2 kg (SD=9.81), BMI 23.70 (SD=1.14), fat % 14.41 (SD=1.93)). Our number of subjects is comparable with related regression based studies [39, 36]. Subjects were paid $20 to participate.

Data Collection

User studies took place in an exercise lab. Subjects were asked to bring and wear exercise clothing during the trial. Before each trial the portable VO2 metabolic system was calibrated for volumetric flow using a 3.0L calibrated gas syringe, and the CO2 and O2 sensors were calibrated using a standard gas mixture of O2:16% and CO2:5% according to the manufacturer's instructions. Subjects were equipped with the portable metabolic system, which they wore using a belt around their waist. Also they were equipped with a mask using a head strap where we ensured the mask fit tightly and no air leaked out. Subjects were also equipped with five Actical accelerometers: one on each wrist, ankle and hip to allow for a comparison between techniques. Prior to each trial, accelerometers were calibrated using the subject's height, weight and age. We assured there was no occlusion and that subjects were placed at the recommended distance (2m) from the Kinect sensor. Subjects were instructed what the goal of the game was, i.e., score as many points as possible within the time frame by hitting targets as fast as possible using the right gesture for each target. For each trial, subjects would first play the light mode of the game for 10 minutes. Subjects then rested for 10 minutes upon which they would play the vigorous mode for 10 minutes. This order minimizes any interference effects, e.g., the light bout didn't exert subjects to such an extent that it is detrimental to their performance for the vigorous bout. We limit our data collection to ten minutes, as we consider exergaming activities to be anaerobic and for this experiment are not interested in predicting aerobic activities.

Training the Regression Model

Separate regression models are trained for light and vigorous activities as to predict METs, though all data is used to train a single classifier for classifying physical activities. Eventually when more data is collected, a single regression model can be trained, but for now, the collected data represents disjunct data sets. An SVM classifier was used to classify an exergaming activity into being light or vigorous; only kinematic data and EE for such types of activities was collected. We implemented our classifier and regression models using the LibSVM library. Using the collected ground truth, different regression models are trained as to identify which features or combinations of features yield the best performance. Using the skeletal joint data obtained, two different types of motion-related features are extracted: (1) Acceleration of skeletal joints; and (2) Spatial information of skeletal joints.

Acceleration: acceleration information of skeletal joints is used to predict the physical intensity of playing exergames. From the obtained displacement data of skeletal joints, the individual joint's acceleration is calculated in 50ms blocks, which is then averaged over one-minute intervals. We choose to partition our data in one-minute blocks as to allow for comparison with the METs predicted by the accelerometers. Though the Kinect sensor and the Cosmed portable metabolic system can sample with a much higher frequency, using smaller time windows won't allow for suppressing the noise, which exists in the sampled data. There is a significant amount of correlation between accelerations of joints (e.g., when the hand joint moves, the wrist and elbow often move as well as they are linked). To avoid over-fitting our regression model, the redundancy in the kinematic data is reduced using Principal Component Analysis (PCA) where we end up selecting five acceleration features that preserve 90% of the information for the light and 92% for the vigorous model. PCA was applied only because our vectors were very large and we wanted to optimize the performance of training our SVR. We verified experimentally that applying PCA did not affect prediction performance significantly.

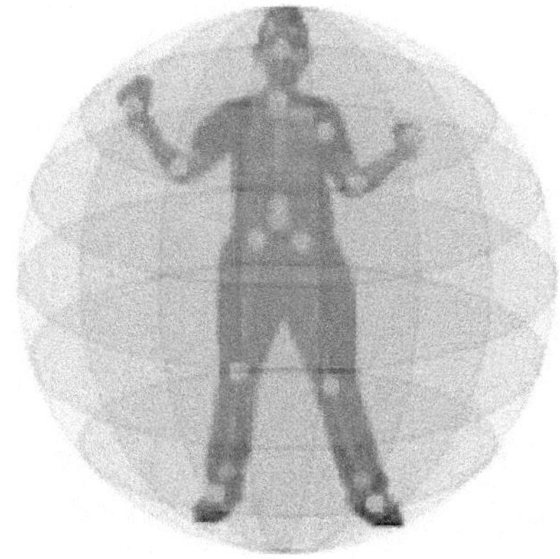

Figure 6: A visual representation of the sphere and its partitioning into bins for the joint binning process.

Spatial: to use joint locations as a feature, we employ a view-invariant representation scheme called joint location binning [40]. Unlike acceleration, joint binning can capture specific gestures, but it cannot discriminate between vigorous and less vigorous gestures. As acceleration already captures this, we explored joint binning as a complementary feature to improve performance. Joint binning works as follows: 3D space is partitioned in n bins using a spherical coordinate system with an azimuth (θ) and a polar angle (ϕ) that is centered at the subject's hip and surrounds the subject's skeletal model (see figure 6). The parameters for partitioning the sphere and the number of bins that yielded the best performance for each regression model were determined experimentally. For light, the best performance was achieved using 36 bins where θ and ϕ were partitioned into 6 bins each. For vigorous, 36 bins were used where θ was partitioned into 12 bins and ϕ into 3 bins. Binning information for each joint is managed by a histogram with 36 bins; with a total of 20 histograms for all joints were used as a feature vector. Histograms of bin frequencies are created by mapping the 20 joints to appropriate bin locations over one-minute time interval with a 50 ms sampling rate. When bin frequencies are added, the selected bin and its neighbors get votes weighted linearly based on the distance of the joint to the center of the bin it is in. To reduce data redundancy and to extract dominant features from the 20 histograms, PCA is used to extract five features retaining 86% of information for light and 92% for the vigorous activities. As the subject starts play-

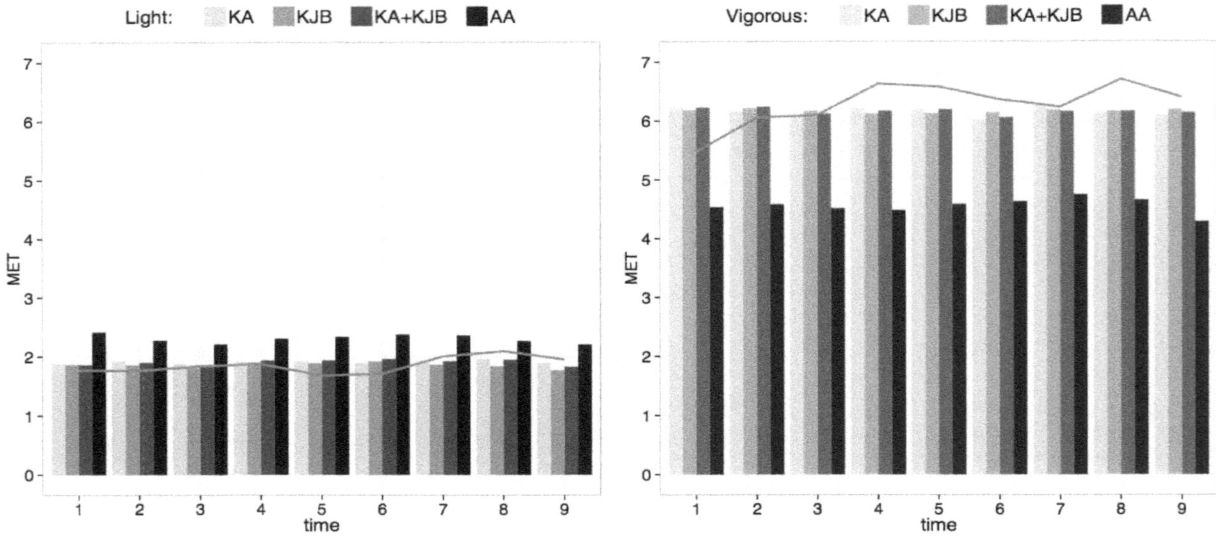

Figure 4: Predicted METs versus ground truth. Figures show predicted METs in one-minute intervals for light (left) and vigorous (right) using three different regression models with each model using the following features: KA uses acceleration; KJB uses joint position; and KA+KJB uses both acceleration and joint position. AA shows predicted MET using the wearable accelerometers. MET's are averaged over 9 subjects. The blue lines show the ground truth MET collected using the portable metabolic system.

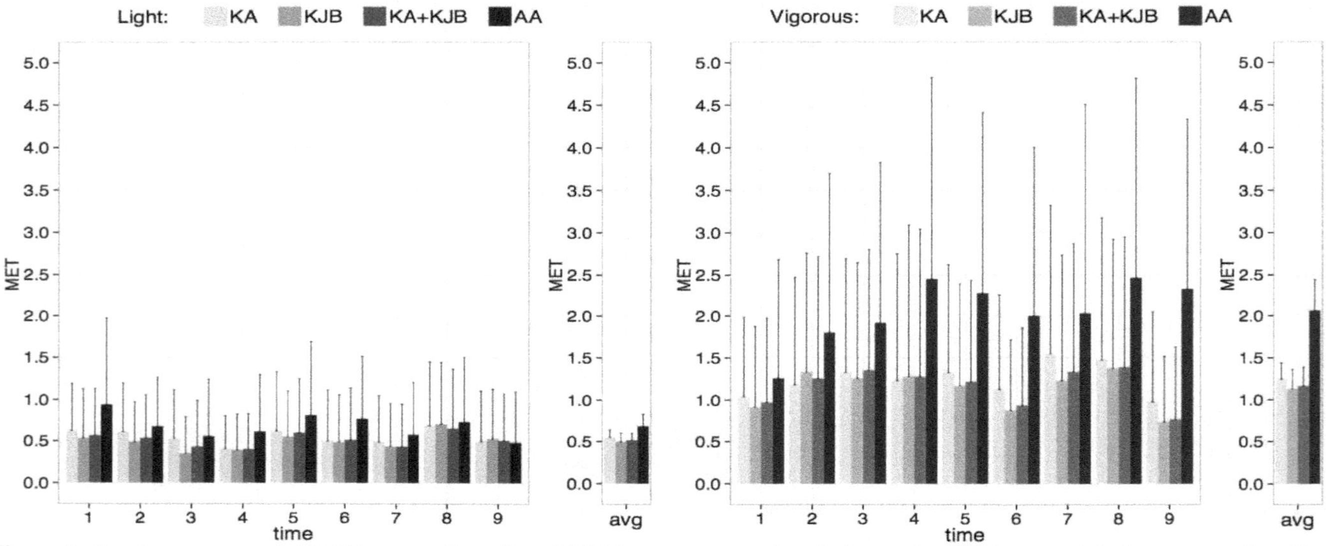

Figure 5: Root mean square (RMS) error of predicted MET versus ground truth for each technique and their averages (see Fig 5 for the legend). Error bars display standard deviation of the RMS error between subjects.

ing the exergame, it takes some time for their metabolism and heart rate to increase; therefore the first minute of collected data is excluded from our regression model. A leave-one-out approach was used to test the regression models, where data from eight subjects was used for training and the remaining one for testing. We repeat this process so that each subject was used once to test the regression model.

Results

Figure 4 shows the predicted METs of the light and vigorous regression models using three sets of features: (1) acceleration (KA); (2) joint position (KJB) and (3) both (KA+KJB). For the accelerometers (AA), METs are calculated by averaging the METs of each one of the five accelerometers used according to manufacturer's specifications. METs are predicted for each subject and then averaged over the nine subjects; METs are reported in one-minute increments. On average the METs predicted by our regression models are within 17% of the ground truth for light and within 7% for vigorous, where accelerometers overestimate METs with 24% for the light and underestimate METs with 28% for vigorous. These results confirm our assumption that accelerometers predict EE of exergames poorly. We calculate the root mean square (RMS) error as a measure of accuracy for each technique (see Figure 5). A significant variance in RMS error between subjects can be observed due to physiological differences between subjects. Because the intensity for each exergame is the same throughout the trial, we average METs over the nine-minute trial and compare the performance of all techniques using RMS [39]. For the light exergame, a repeated-measures ANOVA with a Greenhouse-Geisser correction found no statistically significant difference in RMS between any of the techniques ($F_{1.314,10.511} = 3.173$, $p = .097$). For the vigorous exergame, using the same ANOVA, a statistically significant difference was found ($F_{1.256,10.044} = 23.964$, $p < .05$, partial $\eta^2 = .750$). Post-hoc analysis with a Bonferroni adjustment revealed a statistically significant difference between MET predicted by all regression techniques and the accelerometers ($p < .05$). Between the regression models, no significant difference in RMS between the different feature sets was found ($p = .011$).

Classifying Exergame Intensity

To be able to answer the question whether an exergame engages a player into light or vigorous physical activity, we also trained an SVM using all the data collected in our experiment. A total of 162 data points were used for training and testing with each data point containing one-minute of averaged accelerations for each of the 20 joints. Using 9-fold cross-validation we achieved an accuracy of 100%. Once an activity is classified, the corresponding regression model can be used to accurately predict the associated METs.

DISCUSSION AND FUTURE WORK

For vigorous exergaming activities ViziCal predicts MET more accurately than accelerometer-based approaches. This increase in accuracy may be explained by an increase in spatial resolution that allows for capturing gestures, such as head-butts more accurately, and the ability to calculate features more precisely due to a higher sampling frequency. The increase in performance has to be put in context, however, as our regression model was trained and tested using a restricted set of gestures, where accelerometers are trained to predict MET for a wide range of motions, which inherently decreases their accuracy.

We anticipated joint binning to be able to outperform joint acceleration, as it allows for better capturing of specific gestures; but our experiment showed no significant difference in RMS error between both features and their combination. Joint binning however, may yield a better performance for exergames that include more sophisticated sequences of gestures, such as sports based exergames. A drawback of using joint binning as a feature is that it restricts predicting MET to a limited set of motions that were used to train the regression model. The histogram for joint binning for an exergame containing only upward punches looks significantly different from the same game that only contains forward punches. The acceleration features for both gestures, however, are very similar. If it can be assumed that their associated EE do not differ significantly, acceleration may be a more robust feature to use, as it will allow for predicting MET for a wide range of similar gestures that only vary in the direction they are performed, with far fewer training examples required than when using joint binning. Because SVM uses acceleration as a feature, it may already be able to classify the intensity of exergames, who use different gestures from the one we used in our experiment; something we will investigate.

The exergame used for training our regression model uses a range of different motions, but it doesn't cover the gamut of gestures typically used in all types of exergames, which vary from emulating sports to dance games with complex step patterns. We also limited the intensity of our exergame for training the regression models to two extremes, light and vigorous, as these are considered criteria for evaluating the health benefits of an exergame. Rather than having to classify an exergame's intensity a priori, a single regression model that can predict MET for all levels of intensity would be more desirable, especially since moderate levels of physical activity are also considered to yield health benefits [1].

Though no difference was found in performance between acceleration and joint position, there are techniques to refine these features. For example, acceleration can be refined by using coefficient of variation, inter-quartile intervals, power spectral density over particular frequencies, kurtosis, and skew [31]. Joint binning can be refined by weighing bins based on the height of the bin or weighing individual joints based on the size of the limb they are attached to. Since the emphasis of this work was on identifying a set of features that would allow us to predict energy expenditure, we did not perform comparisons using different regression models. In future work, we plan to evaluate random forests regressors, which are used by the Kinect [34] and which typically outperform SVR's for relatively low dimensionality problems spaces like ours [6].

A high variance in RMS error between subjects was observed despite our efforts to minimize variation in EE by drawing our subjects from a homogeneous population. Demographic data should be considered to train different regression models to compensate for inter-individual variations. Alternatively we could possibly calibrate the regression result by incorporating demographic information as input to the regression model or correcting the regression estimates to compensate for demographic differences. Since exergames have been advocated as a promising health intervention technique to fight childhood obesity, it is important to collect data from children. There is an opportunity to use the Kinect to automatically identify demographic data, such as gender, age, height and weight, and automatically associate a regression model with it, without subjects having to provide this information in advance. Future work will also investigate whether we can interpolate between regression models in the case that no demographic match can be found for the subject.

CONCLUSION

In recent years, exercise games have been criticized for not yielding levels of physical activity that are high enough to be considered healthy. We present ViziCal, a tool for accurately predicting energy expenditure (EE) of exergaming activities that doesn't require the user to wear any sensors. Experiments show a significant increase in being able to predict EE for exergames with vigorous motions in comparison with a conventional accelerometer based approach. ViziCal can be used to design exercise games that yield greater health benefits; thus addressing some of the current criticisms of exergames.

ACKNOWLEDGMENTS

This work is supported by NSF Grant IIS-1118074.

REFERENCES

1. Center for Disease Control, how much activity do you need? `http://www.cdc.gov/physicalactivity/everyone/guidelines/children.html`.
2. New York Times, 'exergames' don't make children fitter, `http://parenting.blogs.nytimes.com/2012/06/25/exergames-dont-make-children-more-fit/`.
3. Biddiss, E., and Irwin, J. Active video games to promote physical activity in children and youth: a systematic review. *Arch Pediatr Adolesc Med 164:7*, (2010), 664–672.
4. Botton, F., Hautier, C., and Eclache, J.-P. Energy expenditure during tennis play: a preliminary video analysis and metabolic model approach. *J Strength Cond Res 25:11*, (2011), 3022–3030.
5. Buchan, D. S., Ollis, S., Young, J. D., Thomas, N. E., Cooper, S.-M., Tong, T. K., Nie, J., Malina, R. M., and Baker, J. S. The effects of time and intensity of exercise on novel and established markers of cvd in adolescent youth. *Am J Hum Biol 23:4*, (2011), 517–526.
6. Caruana, R., Karampatziakis, N., and Yessenalina, A. An empirical evaluation of supervised learning in high dimensions. In *Proc. of ICML*, (2008), 96–103.
7. Chen, K. Y., Janz, K. F., Zhu, W., and Brychta, R. J. Redefining the roles of sensors in objective physical activity monitoring. *Med Sci Sports Exerc 44*, (2012), 213–223.
8. Corder, K., Ekelund, U., Steele, R. M., Wareham, N. J., and Brage, S. Assessment of physical activity in youth. *J Appl Physiol 105:3*, (2008), 977–987.
9. Crouter, S. E., and Bassett, Jr, D. R. A new 2-regression model for the actical accelerometer. *Br J Sports Med 42:3*, (2008), 217–224.
10. Daley, A. J. Can exergaming contribute to improving physical activity levels and health outcomes in children? *Ped. 124:2*, (2009), 763–771.
11. Dutta, T. Evaluation of the kinect^{TM} sensor for 3-d kinematic measurement in the workplace. *Appl Ergon 43:4*, (2012), 645–654.
12. Gondoni, L. A., Titon, A. M., Nibbio, F., Augello, G., Caetani, G., and Liuzzi, A. Heart rate behavior during an exercise stress test in obese patients. *Nutr Metab Cardiovasc Dis 19:3*, (2009), 170–176.
13. Graves, L., Stratton, G., Ridgers, N. D., and Cable, N. T. Comparison of energy expenditure in adolescents when playing new generation and sedentary computer games. *BMJ 335:7633*, (2007), 1282–1284.
14. Graves, L. E. F., Ridgers, N. D., and Stratton, G. The contribution of upper limb and total body movement to adolescents' energy expenditure whilst playing nintendo wii. *Eur J Appl Physiol 104:4*, (2008), 617–623.
15. Graves, L. E. F., Ridgers, N. D., Williams, K., Stratton, G., Atkinson, G., and Cable, N. T. The physiological cost and enjoyment of wii fit in adolescents, young adults, and older adults. *J Phys Act Health 7:3*, (2010), 393–401.
16. Irwin, A. R., and Gross, A. Cognitive tempo, violent video games, and aggressive behavior in young boys. *J Fam Viol 10:3*, 337–350.
17. Jang, Y., Jung, M., Kang, J., and Chan Kim, H. A wearable energy expenditure analysis system based on the 15-channel whole-body segment acceleration measurement. *Proc of IEEE Eng Med Biol Soc 4* (2005), 3834–3840.
18. Kaneko, M., Miyatsuji, K., and Tanabe, S. Energy expenditure while performing gymnastic-like motion in spacelab during spaceflight: case study. *Appl Physiol Nutr Metab 31:5*, (2006), 631–635.
19. Khoshelham, K., and Elberink, S. O. Accuracy and resolution of kinect depth data for indoor mapping applications. *Sensors 12:2*, (2012), 1437–1454.
20. Kozey, S. L., Lyden, K., Howe, C. A., Staudenmayer, J. W., and Freedson, P. S. Accelerometer output and met values of common physical activities. *Med Sci Sports Exerc 42:9*, (2010), 1776–1784.
21. Krohn, M. M., and Boisdair, D. Use of a stereo-video system to estimate the energy expenditure of free-swimming fish. *Canadian Journal of Fisheries and Aquatic Sciences 51:5*, (1994), 1119–1127.
22. Leatherdale, S. T., Woodruff, S. J., and Manske, S. R. Energy expenditure while playing active and inactive video games. *Am J Health Behav 34:1*, (2010), 31–36.
23. Leprêtre, P. M., Weissland, T., Paton, C., Jeanne, M., Delannaud, S., and Ahmaidi, S. Comparison of 2 portable respiratory gas analysers. *Int J Sports Med 33:9*, (2012), 728–33.
24. Levine, J. A. Measurement of energy expenditure. *Public Health Nutr 8:7A*, (2005), 1123–1132.
25. Maddison, R., Mhurchu, C. N., Jull, A., Jiang, Y., Prapavessis, H., and Rodgers, A. Energy expended playing video console games: an opportunity to increase children's physical activity? *Pediatr Exerc Sci 19:3*, (2007), 334–343.
26. Mueller, F. F., Gibbs, M. R., and Vetere, F. Taxonomy of exertion games. In *Proc. of OZCHI*, (2008), 263–266.
27. Osgnach, C., Poser, S., Bernardini, R., Rinaldo, R., and di Prampero, P. E. Energy cost and metabolic power in elite soccer: a new match analysis approach. *Med Sci Sports Exerc 42:1*, (2010), 170–178.
28. Papastergiou, M. Exploring the potential of computer and video games for health and physical education: A literature review. *Computers & Education 53:3*, (2009), 603 – 622.
29. Penko, A. L., and Barkley, J. E. Motivation and physiologic responses of playing a physically interactive video game relative to a sedentary alternative in children. *Ann Behav Med 39:2*, (2010), 162–171.
30. Rosenberger, M. E., Skrinar, G., Haskell, W. L., Intille, S. S., and Tapia, E. M. Multiple wireless accelerometers and heart rate accurately predict energy expenditure during level walking. *Medicine and Science in Sports and Exercise, 40:5*, (2008), S62–S63.
31. Rothney, M. P., Neumann, M., Béziat, A., and Chen, K. Y. An artificial neural network model of energy expenditure using nonintegrated acceleration signals. *J Appl Physiol 103:4*, (2007), 1419–1427.
32. Schmidt, W. D., Biwer, C. J., and Kalscheuer, L. K. Effects of long versus short bout exercise on fitness and weight loss in overweight females. *J Am Coll Nutr 20:5*, (2001), 494–501.
33. Shephard, R. J. A critical examination of the Douglas bag technique. *J Physiol 127:3*, (1955), 515–24.
34. Shotton, J., Fitzgibbon, A., Cook, M., Sharp, T., Finocchio, M., Moore, R., Kipman, A., and Blake, A. Real-Time Human Pose Recognition in Parts from Single Depth Images *Proc. of CVPR*,(2011), 1297-1304.
35. Smola, A. J., and Schölkopf, B. A tutorial on support vector regression. *Statistics and Computing 14:3*, (2004), 199–222.
36. Su, S., Wang, L., Celler, B., Ambikairajah, E., and Savkin, A. Estimation of walking energy expenditure by using support vector regression. *Conf Proc IEEE Eng Med Biol Soc 4* (2005), 3526–3535.
37. Swartz, A. M., Strath, S. J., Bassett, Jr, D. R., O'Brien, W. L., King, G. A., and Ainsworth, B. E. Estimation of energy expenditure using CSA accelerometers at hip and wrist sites. *Med Sci Sports Exerc 32:9*, (2000), 450–456.
38. Tan, B., Aziz, A. R., Chua, K., and Teh, K. C. Aerobic demands of the dance simulation game. *Int J Sports Med 23:2*, (2002), 125–134.
39. Vathsangam, H., Emken, A., Schroeder, E. T., Spruijt-Metz, D., and Sukhatme, G. S. Determining energy expenditure from treadmill walking using hip-worn inertial sensors: an experimental study. *IEEE Trans Biomed Eng 58:10, (2011), 2804–2819.*
40. Xia, L., Chen, C.-C., and Aggrawal, J. K. View invariant human action recognition using histograms of 3d joints. *Proc. of HAU3D*, (2012), 20–27.

Imaginary Reality Gaming: Ball Games Without a Ball

Patrick Baudisch, Henning Pohl*, Stefanie Reinicke, Emilia Wittmers,
Patrick Lühne, Marius Knaust, Sven Köhler, Patrick Schmidt, and Christian Holz
Hasso Plattner Institute, Potsdam, Germany
{firstname.lastname}@hpi.uni-potsdam.de
*University of Hannover, Germany
Henning.Pohl@hci.uni-hannover.de

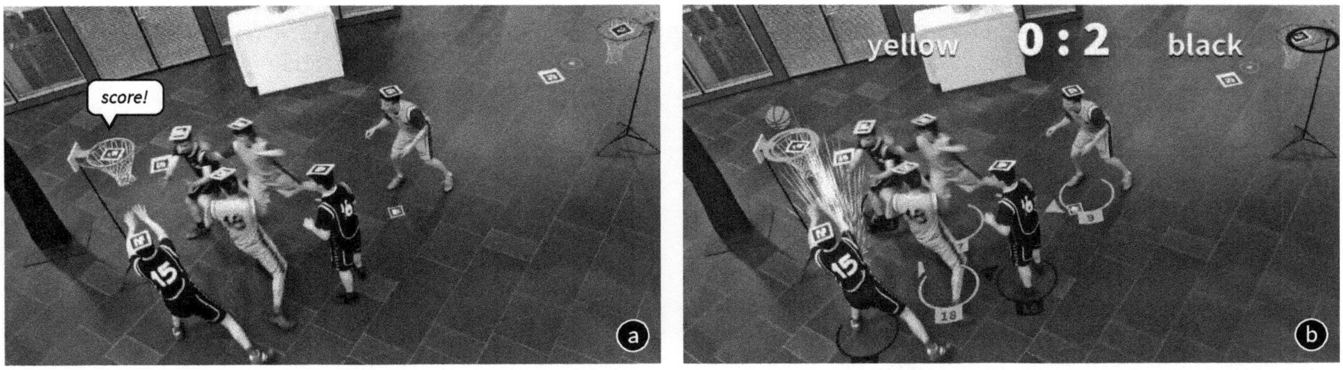

Figure 1: (a) Six players in a game of *Imaginary Reality Basketball*. Player 15 on the Black team has thrown the *imaginary ball* at the basket and scored. There is no visible ball; players get all information from watching each other act and a small amount of auditory feedback. (b) Under the hood & invisible to the players, the system represents the imaginary ball as a large number of *ball particles*, each of which represents one plausible ball trajectory. Players are tracked using accelerometers and an overhead camera.

ABSTRACT
We present *imaginary reality games,* i.e., games that mimic the respective real world sport, such as basketball or soccer, except that there is *no visible ball*. The ball is virtual and players learn about its position only from watching each other act and a small amount of occasional auditory feedback, e.g., when a person is receiving the ball.

Imaginary reality games maintain many of the properties of physical sports, such as unencumbered play, physical exertion, and immediate social interaction between players. At the same time, they allow introducing game elements from video games, such as power-ups, non-realistic physics, and player balancing. Most importantly, they create a new game dynamic around the notion of the invisible ball.

To allow players to successfully interact with the invisible ball, we have created a physics engine that evaluates hundreds of plausible ball trajectories in parallel, allowing the game engine to select the trajectory that leads to the most enjoyable game play while still favoring skillful play.

ACM Classification: H5.2 [Information interfaces and presentation]: User Interfaces.

Keywords: Physical gaming; augmented reality gaming; probabilistic; imaginary interfaces; motion capture.

INTRODUCTION
Sports, such as soccer or basketball, offer many wonderful qualities. They are highly immersive, lead to physical exertion, and create immediate social interaction between players. Unfortunately, physical games are limited by the constraints of the real world, restricting their game mechanics to what is physically possible.

Researchers have tried to merge physical and virtual play in display-based augmented reality games such as Human Pacman [5] or AR Quake [16]. These games overlay a virtual world onto the physical world using hand-held or head-mounted see-through displays. This allows these games to introduce virtual game elements, such as power-ups (e.g. [22]) or creating virtual game elements that are not limited by the rules of physics (e.g. [20]).

Unfortunately, the use of displays takes away many of the qualities of physical sports, as players now perceive the world only indirectly through displays, which are of limited resolution, limited field of view, and exhibit inevitable lag. This causes many subtleties to be lost, such as details of body language, facial expressions, and co-player actions taking place in the user's visual periphery.

In this paper, we propose a different approach: We drop the displays, thus creating a sort of "screenless AR". Instead, players obtain most of the information they need to play from watching co-players' positions, movements, and gestures. In addition, but only where necessary, we provide a small amount of auditory feedback to disambiguate. So rather than trying to give players a high-fidelity representation of the virtual game world, we embrace the uncertainty and develop it into a new game mechanic. The result is a new class of interactive games. While these games maintain the ability to have virtual game elements, such as power-ups and non-physical objects, they bring back some of the qualities of physical sports games, as players again interact *directly* with each other.

UIST'13, October 8–11, 2013, St. Andrews, United Kingdom.
Copyright © 2013 ACM 978-1-4503-2268-3/13/10...$15.00.
http://dx.doi.org/10.1145/2501988.2502012

IMAGINARY REALITY GAMING

Figure 1a shows a scene from imaginary reality basketball, one of the games we have implemented. Like every imaginary reality game, it mimics the respective real world sport—except *there is no visible ball.* Players learn about the position of the virtual ball by watching each other act. Occasionally, players *hear* the ball make contact with a physical object or being played by a person, which disambiguates the ball's location. In between, the ball position is *uncertain.* At the shown moment, Player *15* on the Black team is throwing the imaginary ball at the basket, scoring.

Figure 2: A game sequence leading up to a slam-dunk.

Figure 2 shows a slightly longer example. (a) Player *9* on the Orange team (top left) chest passes the ball towards his teammate *18*. (b) *18* receives it (Audio: "eighteen") and (c) tries to pass it back to *9*. (d) Unexpectedly, *16* from the Black team intercepts the pass (Audio: "sixteen"). He starts running towards the basket and (e) dunks the ball. (Audio: "Score! Two-zero for Black").

Figure 3: Imaginary reality games can offer non-physical elements in the form of power-ups: here the "get-ball" power-up.

As mentioned earlier, imaginary reality games cannot only emulate real-world sports, but they also allow us to introduce power-ups and non-physical behavior, thereby introducing some of the richness of video games into physical sports. Figure 3 and Figure 4 illustrate this at the example of the "get-ball" and the "safe" power-ups, which appear periodically with an audio announcement over the marked center location of the playfield. Both figures use the "debug" view of our system, which reveals the ball etc; the players do not see any of this additional information.

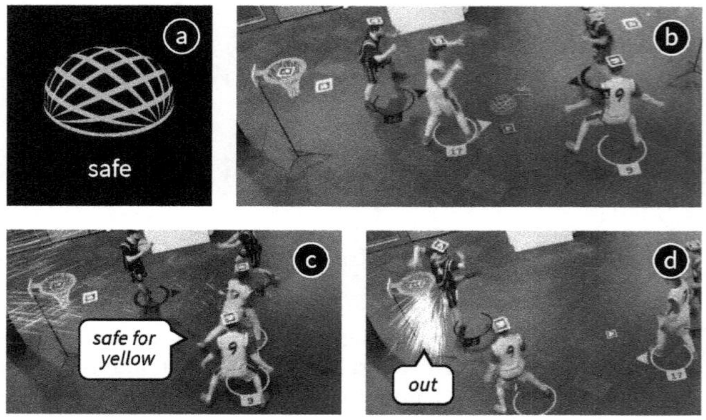

Figure 4: The "safe" power-up protects a team's basket. This prevents the opposing team from scoring.

SYSTEM ARCHITECTURE

As illustrated by Figure 5, the imaginary reality games system consists of three main components. The *tracking system* tracks players and their gestures (as well as playfield boundaries, baskets, and power-up locations). It reports player moves to our custom physics engine, which we call *quantum engine*. The quantum engine simulates the imaginary ball, computes the probabilities of outcomes, and reports these to the *game engine*. The game engine refines probabilities by applying handicaps and power-ups, etc. It then determines the outcome of the game move randomly based on these probabilities. Finally, the game engine conveys its decision to the players using auditory feedback.

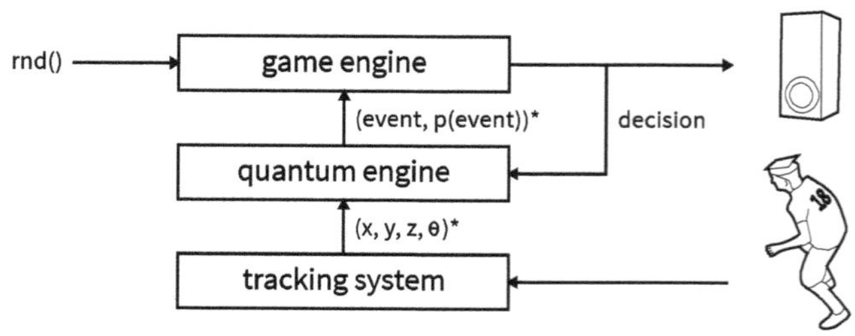

Figure 5: Imaginary reality games system

Figure 6 shows the tracking solution we have created for imaginary basketball. An overhead camera (Microsoft LifeCam 1080p) monitors the 6×4m playfield. It tracks players' head position and orientation based on head-worn ALVAR markers [1]. To allow the system to sense gestures, players wear tiny accelerometers with radio senders on their hands and belts (*Axivity* [2]). A simple peak detection algorithm extracts players' game gestures, such as jumping, throwing, or catching a ball.

Note that the tracking is incomplete. For example, it does not allow sensing in what direction a player passes a ball—it merely approximates this direction based on the player's head orientation. This conscious design decision allows us to run the game on moderate tracking hardware accessible to a broader audience (unlike, say, a commercial motion capture system). The system copes with the lack of tracking information, as we explain in the following section.

Figure 6: Our Tracking is based on (a) *ALVAR* markers [1], (b) a webcam, and (c) hand-worn accelerometer (*Axivity* [2]).

IMAGINARY PHYSICS

The quantum engine is the key component of the imaginary reality system. It allows players to successfully play the ball, despite the uncertain ball location and despite the only approximate tracking.

Traditional approaches of handling imprecise input, such as enlarging targets, area cursors, sticky targets and target gravity techniques [3] do not work for imaginary reality games, as they interfere with gameplay when scaled to this level: as illustrated by Figure 7, enlarged or magnetic players tend to fully "occlude" players behind them, preventing those players from *ever* getting the ball.

The quantum engine therefore takes a different approach: it first samples *all* plausible outcomes of the current move and their probabilities *and then* makes a well-informed decision, i.e., it chooses in *hindsight* which of the possible outcomes to "make real".

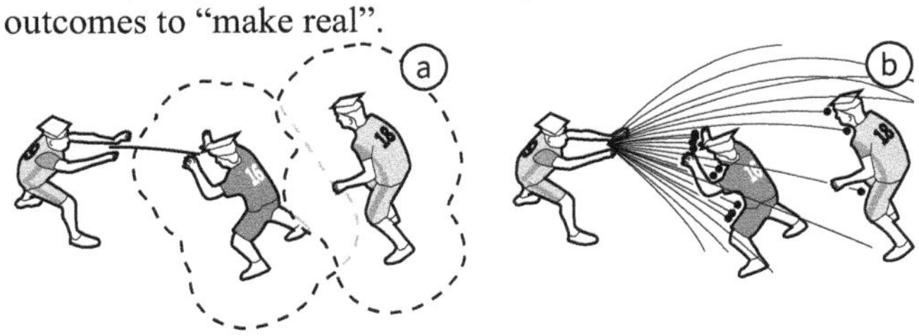

Figure 7: (a) Traditional enlarging of players helps pass the ball but also prevents the player on the left from *ever* passing past the opposing player in the middle. (b) The quantum engine instead samples all plausible ball trajectories, allowing it to pick outcomes that lead to enjoyable game play.

Rather than computing the trajectory of *the* ball, it computes the trajectories of *many versions of* the same ball (500 of them). It does so by representing the ball as a collection of *ball particles*, each of which represents one plausible trajectory of the ball. The system's debug view (e.g., Figure 1b) reveals the trajectories of ball particles as white lines. The quantum engine evaluates each particle using regular Newtonian physics. It then aggregates the probabilities of each outcome and passes them on to the game engine, which applies modifiers, and decides on the outcome.

As illustrated by Figure 7b, our particle approach allows handling situations with multiple competing targets. As the shown player passes the ball, some ball particles hit the teammate, some the opposing player, and some go out. The quantum engine determines the raw probabilities of the three outcomes by simply counting particles. In order to increase the probability of enjoyable gameplay, the game engine now increases the probability of the pass to the teammate and decreases the probability of the ball going out. Finally, it makes the decision randomly according to these probabilities and announces it to the players.

Benefits of the Quantum Engine Approach

While the original objective behind the development of the quantum engine was to help players acquire the invisible ball, it ended up providing a lot of additional value to our games:

1. *Optimize gameflow:* The quantum engine provides the game engine with choice. This choice allows the game engine to favor outcomes that lead to enjoyable gameplay, such as those that keep the ball in the game, enable multiplayer combos, etc.

2. *Hindsight:* Unlike traditional gaming systems that use a visible ball, imaginary reality games do not have to commit to a trajectory until players receive feedback [17]—which is not until the ball has been *received* or until it hits an object. This extra time allows the engine to consider the *entire* move when optimizing for gameflow. This also allows players to increase the chance of being passed to—by performing a great *receiving* gesture. This is another unusual game mechanic enabled by imaginary reality gaming.

3. *Forgiveness:* The quantum engine spreads particles broadly. As a result, even inexperienced players will always catch a few particles, even though they misread the body language of co-player or poorly extrapolate ball trajectories. Combined with a handicap system, this allows the system to help inexperienced players get into the game.

4. *Favor skillful play:* Despite all the modifications, the main contributor to any outcome is always a player's skill: by aiming better, moving into the most likely trajectory of a pass, and by receiving the ball at the perfect moment, skillful play leads to success. This creates an incentive to focus and to practice, adding a long-term incentive to imaginary reality gaming.

IMAGINARY REALITY GAMES ALLOW FOR COMPLEXITY

Despite the low bandwidth of their auditory feedback channel, imaginary reality games allow implementing reasonably complex games, such as basketball or soccer. The reason is that imaginary reality games (1) leverage players' experience with real-world sports and (2) allow them to extract information from mutual observation.

Learning Non-Trivial Rules—by Transfer

Despite the weakness of the auditory feedback channel, imaginary reality games can be learned quickly, because they allow players to transfer skills from the corresponding real-world sports (*transfer learning*, e.g., [7]).

To invite this type of knowledge transfer, we designed imaginary reality games to appear as similar as possible to their real-world counterpart. In particular, we hide the probabilistic inner workings and portray the games as if they were based on a single physical (yet invisible) ball. To do this: (1) we design auditory feedback so as to always refer to a single ball and never mention particles or probabilities. (2) The game engine never breaks the illusion of a single physical ball, by producing only game moves that are plausible under a single-ball interpretation.

Based on a foundation of rules transferred from real-world sports, designers of imaginary reality games are then free to (carefully) challenge players with power-ups and modes.

Following the Invisible Ball—by Observation

Imaginary reality games allow for *fast* gaming action primarily because what players see of the physical world, such as co-players' moves, *implies* the invisible ball position.

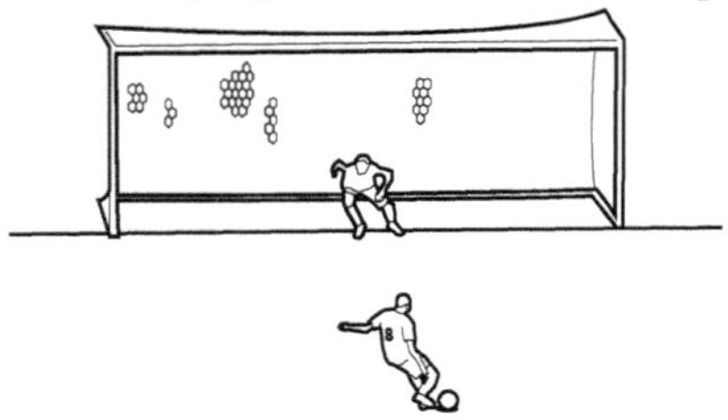

Figure 8: The goalie has to read the strikers body language to decide where to go. (Interestingly, as spectators we do the same. Even before this ball is being kicked, we can already tell that this one will probably go in, as the striker's body posture suggests that he is aiming right, while the goalie has his weight shifted in the opposite direction).

Interestingly, players are typically already trained in the main imaginary reality gaming skills, because these skills are similar to those involved in real-world sports. Consider Figure 8. To maximize his chances of saving the ball, the goalie *anticipates* the shot by (1) reading the opposing player's body posture, (2) imagining possible ball trajectories, and then (3) quickly moving to the expected ball location. A goalie in imaginary reality soccer performs essentially the same process (except that he cannot monitor the flying ball and instead has to solely rely on extrapolation).

CONTRIBUTION

The main contribution of this paper is the concept of imaginary reality gaming—games around an invisible ball.

Imaginary reality games maintain many properties of physical sports, such as physical exertion and *immediate* social interaction between players. At the same time, they allow introducing game elements from video games, such as power-ups, non-realistic physics, and player balancing.

Imaginary reality games produce a new game dynamic. Different not only from most traditional video games, but also from most display-based AR games, players do not look at screens or mobile devices anymore. Instead, our main game element is observation and imagination, as players engage in the shared illusion of an invisible ball.

Our main engineering contribution is the quantum engine, a parallel physics engine that (1) allows optimizing gameplay, (2) can make decisions in hindsight, and (3) helps beginners get into the game, yet that (4) favors skillful play.

IMAGINARY REALITY GAMES—A FAMILY OF GAMES

Imaginary reality gaming is a general gaming concept that applies to a range of games and can be implemented on a range of form factors and tracking systems. In our process towards imaginary reality basketball, we implemented imaginary reality versions of the tabletop games air hockey (tracked using Microsoft Kinect) and foosball (tracked on diffuse illumination) both shown in Figure 9. Both were instrumental in our overall design evolution as they offered easier debugging and allowed for faster design iteration, testing, and tweaking of game mechanics and algorithms, all of which are reflected in imaginary reality basketball.

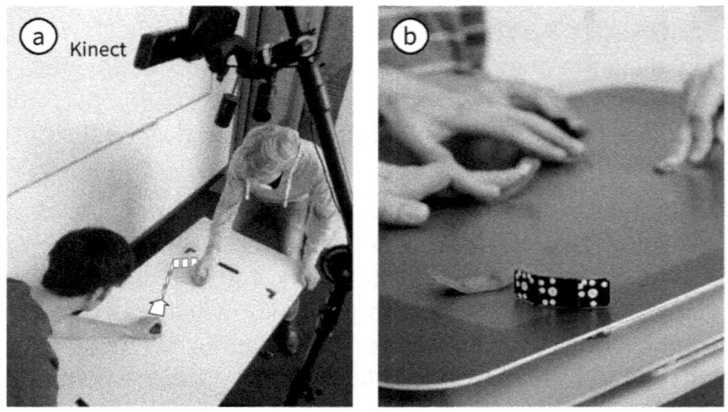

Figure 9: (a) A game of imaginary reality air hockey tracked using a Kinect. Here the blue player scores via the left wall. (b) Imaginary reality foosball tracked on a diffused illumination table. Players kick the ball by performing tilt gesture sequences using our custom *Band-aid* paddles.

RELATED WORK

Imaginary reality games build on physical games, probabilistic simulation, and spatial/non-visual interaction.

Physical World vs. Virtual World in HCI

In human-computer interaction, the disconnection between virtual and physical has been investigated in a wide range of contexts. In particular, the field of augmented reality is bridging this gap by merging a visual representation of the virtual world into the physical world users see.

Imaginary reality games draw inspiration from *imaginary interfaces* [6], i.e., interfaces that allow for spatial, non-visual interaction on mobile devices. Gustafson et al. showed that users can learn an imaginary interface based on previous experience with a physical device of identical layout (*transfer learning* [7]). Imaginary reality games might be considered a form of *shared* imaginary interfaces. While imaginary interfaces leave out display to achieve a preferable form factor (*ultra-mobile* devices), imaginary reality games leave out displays to create a new game mechanic—one that cannot be obtained with screens.

Probabilistic Simulation

The quantum engine presented in this paper takes a probabilistic approach to ball trajectories. Probabilistic approaches have been used in a variety of contexts, including processing uncertain input to user interfaces [18]. In graphics, Chenney et al. used Markov chains to generate plausible-looking animations that satisfy a given set of constraints [4]. Twigg and James allow users to create animation sequences by first generating many sequences and then eliminating those that do not meet a given constraint [21].

Games that Combine the Virtual and the Physical

Several researchers explored how to add virtual properties to physical ball games. Ichikawa and Nojima presented a ball than can change its trajectory by ejecting gas [8]. Izuta et al. added challenge to a ball game by occasionally making the ball invisible by turning its illumination off [9].

Virtual game objects in physical games have been explored by mixed reality and pervasive games [12]. *Airhockey Over a Distance* locally re-enacts the shots of an opponent located at a remote site [14]. Players of *AR²Hockey* use physical mallets to shoot a puck that is only visible on head-mounted displays [15]. Jeong et al. use a haptic cave to enable users to pass virtual balls to virtual co-players [11]. Jebara et al. display hints for how to tackle the current shot in pool billiard on a head–mounted display [10].

VI games are games for visually impaired users. Like imaginary reality games, many are inspired by real-world sports. VI games substitute the visual channel, e.g., with vibro-tactile or audio (e.g., [13, 19]). VI Pong is a spatial game that uses vibro-tactile feedback to guide players to the point where the pong ball will hit [19]. When playing VI Tennis, in contrast, players try to perform a swing gesture at the right moment [13]. Paralympics games for the visually disabled are closer renditions of real-world sports—they use audio-enhanced balls. Imaginary Reality games resemble VI games in that the ball is invisible. However, they *rely* on players' ability to see, which allows players to strategize around the locations and current actions of co-players and to anticipate ball trajectories. This comes at the expense of not being playable eyes-free.

ALGORITHM OF THE QUANTUM ENGINE

To allow readers to implement *their* quantum games, we now provide a detailed description of the algorithm. The goal of the algorithm is to place ball particles where players and spectators expect the ball to be located—more particles at more likely positions. For consistency, we use language from imaginary reality basketball, but the mechanism applies to all types of 2D and 3D imaginary reality games we have built. The quantum engine uses the following rules:

Initialization At the beginning of the game a single particle is dropped into the game at a physically marked respawn location, such as the playfield center.

Splitting If the probability *p* of a particle is above a global threshold, say 1/250, the particle splits into two new particles, each of which represents half the original probability. Repeated application of the rule causes the initial particle to spawn the desired number of particles, e.g. 512.

Brownian Motion If a ball drops on the ground, players' knowledge of the ball location tends to "blur" over time. By letting particles move slowly but randomly, the ball "spreads" over time, helping players to find the ball; eventually this allows players to pick up the ball anywhere.

Collisions based on probe lines Figure 10a illustrates the algorithm—here the engine has to decide whether Player 16 intercepts the ball, whether the pass goes to teammate 18, or whether the ball goes out.

To allow for the most informed decision, the game engine delays its decisions as long as possible, i.e., until events that may result in auditory output. This is the case at time t_1, when particles reach Player 16. The game engine now has to make its first decision. It may either implement the intercept or run with "whatever the future might bring".

The quantum engine therefore computes the raw probability of the intercept: if Player 16 has intercepted, say, 200 of 500 particles, (the engine computes this as a collision of the particles with a cylinder surrounding the player) this player has intercepted the actual ball with a raw probability of 40%. However, to optimize gameplay the game engine adjusts raw probabilities based on how desirable the individual outcomes are. The immediate outcome of Player 16 intercepting the ball is well defined—it receives the probability adjustment for "intercepts".

In order to estimate how desirable "whatever the future might bring" is, the quantum engine extrapolates particles' trajectories into the future using what we call *probe lines*. Probe lines predict the future under the assumption that players do not move, but this assumption tends to be reasonable on the involved time scales. Here, the probe lines find a possible collision with Player 18 (say 20%) and a possibility for the ball to go out (40%). The game engine adjusts these probabilities. It then normalizes probabilities, and decides randomly based on the resulting probabilities.

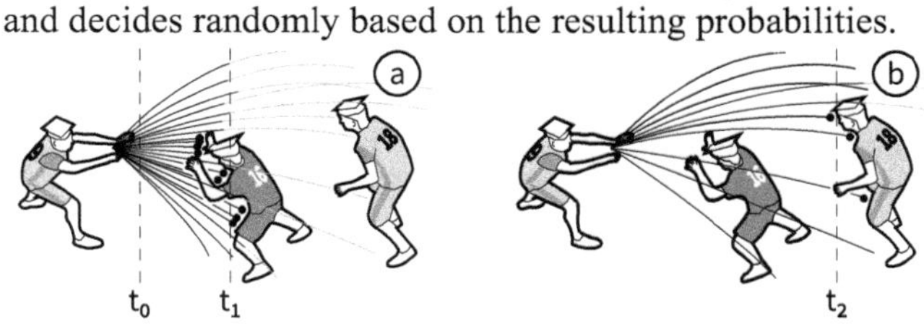

Figure 10: (a) t_0: Player 9 on the left is passing the ball. At t_1, the ball has reached Player 16 and the quantum engine makes its first decision; here it lets be ball through. (b) t_2: The ball has reached Player 18 and the engine decides again.

Let's imagine that the outcome is that Player 16 does not intercept the ball. The particles intercepted by Player 16 now die off and the engine awaits the next collision. At time t_2 the game engine has to decide again: complete the pass to teammate Player 18 or choose the remaining future. All remaining probe lines predict that the ball will go out, which is an undesirable event. The game engine adjusts probabilities accordingly, making the completed pass more likely than the ball going out, i.e., the game engine will most likely complete the pass to teammate 18.

Elastic collisions If the ball collides with an elastic object, the engine picks one particle as the *primary outcome*. This particle determines the auditory feedback. The quantum engine now preserves all particles that would have produced *similar* auditory feedback in *roughly* the same timing. It deletes all other particles, as the auditory feedback has made them *implausible*.

Power-ups In addition to power-ups that modify space, imaginary reality games allow for a range of power-ups that can be implemented by simply increasing or decreasing probabilities. *Penalty:* the probabilities of particles hitting a player are reduced. If set to a very low value, the player is essentially "out", as this player cannot receive the ball anymore. *Attract:* the probabilities of particles hitting a player are increased, helping this player to receive passes and intercept the ball. *Goal seeker:* increases the probabilities of particles that hit the opposing basket, etc. Handicaps work the same way, but persist throughout the game, while most power-ups expire after a few seconds.

EVALUATION

We conducted a brief qualitative study with 30 participants (aged 18–25, 7 female) in the form of five 3 vs. 3 imaginary basketball matches on the 6×4m court. Before each match, the players were introduced to the game rules, but not the underlying mechanisms. They then practiced passing for about 2min. Each participant then played for about 20min.

Results

On a Likert scale (1 = unpleasant, 7 = enjoyable), participants rated game play as 5.9, so clearly enjoyable. They judged that "skillful play" contributed slightly more than "random" (4.2), one player called it "a realistic balance between random and skill." This supports our claim of "enjoyable gameplay while still favoring skillful play."

Five players felt that imaginary basketball was "surprisingly realistic" or "close to actual Basketball." Many players wanted to play longer and one wrote: "We had team spirit and wanted to beat the other team." Four participants described imaginary basketball as "more tiring than I imagined" and one "faster than real basketball." Asked which game element they liked best, nine participants chose power-ups and eight passing.

Two participants said that "keeping the overview [felt] similar to actual basketball." However, one player mentioned that, compared to actual basketball, "feedback isn't enough." With respect to learning the game, two players mentioned that imaginary basketball was "confusing at first, but actually easy to learn" and "intuitive after a few passes." Two players stated that in imaginary basketball, "height [is] not important", allowing "people of different skill levels to play together."

CONCLUSIONS

In this paper, we presented imaginary reality games, physical ball games without a visible ball. Our main contribution is the game concept itself, which creates a class of games around an invisible ball. We also demonstrate how to implement the concept using a custom probabilistic physics engine. As future work, we plan to explore the concept more broadly, to create more instances of imaginary reality games on a variety of platforms and at different scales.

ACKNOWLEDGEMENTS

We thank Tobias Mohr, Vasily Kirilichev, Dietmar Funck, Konstantin Kaefer, Marvin Killing, Max Plauth, Christoph Sterz, Stefanie Platz, Philipp Tessenow, Katherine Isbister.

REFERENCES

1. Alvar. http://virtual.vtt.fi/virtual/proj2/multimedia/alvar.html
2. Axivity. Wax3 motion sensor. http://www.axivity.com.
3. Bateman, S., Mandryk, R.L., Stach, T., and Gutwin, C. Target assistance for subtly balancing competitive play. *Proc. CHI'11,* 2355–2364.
4. Chenney, S. & Forsyth, D., Sampling plausible solutions to multi-body constraint problems. *Proc. Siggragh'00*, 219–228.
5. Cheok, A., Goh, K., Liu, W., Farbiz, F., Fong, S., Teo, S., Li, Y., & Yang, X. Human Pacman: A mobile wide-area entertainment system based on physical, social, & ubiquitous computing. *Personal & Ubiquitous Computing* 8(2), 2004:71–81.
6. Gustafson, S., Bierwirth, D., and Baudisch, P. Imaginary interfaces: Spatial interaction with empty hands and without visual feedback. *Proc. UIST'10*, 3–12.
7. Gustafson, S., Holz, C., and Baudisch, P. Imaginary phone: Learning imaginary interfaces by transferring spatial memory from a familiar device. *Proc. UIST'11*. 283–292.
8. Ichikawa, T., and Nojima, T. Development of the Motion-Controllable Ball. *Proc UIST'10,* 425-426.
9. Izuta, O., Sato, T., Kodama, S., and Koike, H. Bouncing Star Project: Design and Development of Augmented Sports Applications Using a Ball Including Electronic and Wireless Modules. *Proc. AH'10,* 22:1-22:7.
10. Jebada, T., Eyster, C., Weaver, J., Starner, T., & Pentland, A. Stochasticks: Augmenting the billiards experience with probabilistic vision and wearable computers. *ISWC'97*, 138–145.
11. Jeong, S., Hashimoto, N., and Makoto, S. A Novel Interaction System with Force Feedback Between Real – and Virtual Human. *Proc. ACE'04,* 61-66.
12. Magerkurth, C., Cheok, A.D., Mandryk, R.L., and Nilsen, T. Pervasive games: Bringing computer entertainment back to the real world. *Computers in Entertainment*, 3(3), 2005:1–19.
13. Morelli, T., Foley, J., Columna, L., Lieberman, L., and Folmer, E. VI-Tennis: a vibrotactile/audio exergame for players who are visually impaired. *Proc. FDG '10*, 147-154.
14. Mueller, F., Cole, L., Brien, S., and Walmink, W. Airhockey over a distance. *Proc. ACE'06*, Article number 70.
15. Ohshima, T., Satoh, K., Yamamoto, H., and Tamura, H. AR^{2}Hockey: A case study of collaborative augmented reality. *Proc. VRAIS'98*. 268–275.
16. Piekarski, W., and Thomas, B. ARQuake: The outdoor augmented reality gaming system. *CACM* 45(1), 2002:36–38.
17. Schrödinger, E. Die gegenwärtige Situation in der Quantenmechanik. *Die Naturwissenschaften*, 23(49), 1935:823-828.
18. Schwarz, J., Mankoff, J., and Hudson, S.E. Monte Carlo methods for managing interactive state, action and feedback under uncertainty. *Proc. UIST'11*, 235–244.
19. Strachan, S., Zophoniasson, H., and Anastassova, M. ViPong: Probabilistic Haptic Gaming for the Visually Impaired. *Proc. HAID'12,* 10-12.
20. Sugano, Y., Mochizuki, Y., Usui, T., & Okude, N. Shootball: Ball Sport Using Dynamic Goals. *Proc. ACE'07,* 262-263.
21. Twigg, C.D., and James, D.L. Many-worlds browsing for control of multibody dynamics. *TOG* 26(3), 2007:14:1–14:8.
22. Yamabe, T., Iwate, T., Shichinohe, T., and Nakajima, T. Prototyping Augmented Traditional Games: Concept, Design and Case Studies. *Proc. GPC'11,* 105-116.

MagGetz: Customizable Passive Tangible Controllers On and Around Conventional Mobile Devices

Sungjae Hwang, Myungwook Ahn, Kwang-yun Wohn
Graduate School of Culture Technology
Korea Advanced Institute of Science and Technology
{best, chapi, wohn}@kaist.ac.kr

ABSTRACT
This paper proposes user-customizable passive control widgets, called *MagGetz*, which enable tangible interaction on and around mobile devices without requiring power or wireless connections. This is achieved by tracking and analyzing the magnetic field generated by controllers attached on and around the device through a single magnetometer, which is commonly integrated in smartphones today. The proposed method provides users with a broader interaction area, customizable input layouts, richer physical clues, and higher input expressiveness without the need for hardware modifications. We have presented a software toolkit and several applications using *MagGetz*.

Author Keywords
Tangible User Interface (TUI), Around Device Interaction (ADI), pressure input, magnetometer, mobile device.

ACM Classification Keywords
H.5.2 [Information interfaces and presentation]: User Interfaces. – Input devices and strategies.

INTRODUCTION
Physical objects in real life provide users with intuitive tactile clues through its physical artifacts so that users can conduct low-attention and vision-free interactions. However, flat touchscreens, commonly used on conventional mobile devices, have several interaction issues. First, users' fat fingers [19] frequently occlude the content of interest. Second, the virtual controls lack tactile clues and require visual attention. Third, the touchscreen device merely detects touch coordination and the binary touch state (i.e., touch and release). Based on these issues, researchers have since long attempted to increase this input space by adding other types of tangible objects. These pioneering methods include the usage of a capacitive foot print [4, 10, 15, 21, 22], camera markers [2, 11], palettes that embedded conductive layers [5, 20], and magnetic augmentations [1, 6, 12, 13, 14, 17, 18]. However, some approaches do not alleviate the occlusion problem (e.g., 4, 10, 15, 21), some need additional special hardware (e.g., 1, 2, 5, 17, 20, 21), or some do not have any tactile clues (e.g., 6, 12, 13, 14, 18).

Figure 1: *MagGetz* enables tangible interaction on and around mobile devices without requiring power or wireless connections

In this paper, we have introduced a set of tangible control widgets to provide users with richer tactile clues, higher input expressiveness, and a wider interaction area without the need for hardware modifications (Figure 1). The goal of this research is to show how the magnetically driven tangible controllers can be successfully integrated for conventional mobile devices. The rest of the paper introduces the *MagGetz*, with the technical novelty and benefits of this approach. The second part of this paper describes the possible applications using the *MagGetz* and indicates future avenues of our research.

RELATED WORK
Here, we present separately in the next three sections the previous work on each of the three related fields.

Tangible Interactions for Mobile Devices
Tangible user interfaces (TUIs) provide physical forms of digital information and computation, facilitating the direct manipulation of bits [8]. However, touchscreen devices do not support this beneficial tactile clue. With this background, the

UIST'13, October 08 - 11 2013, St Andrews, United Kingdom
Copyright 2013 ACM 978-1-4503-2268-3/13/10...$15.00.
http://dx.doi.org/10.1145/2501988.2501991

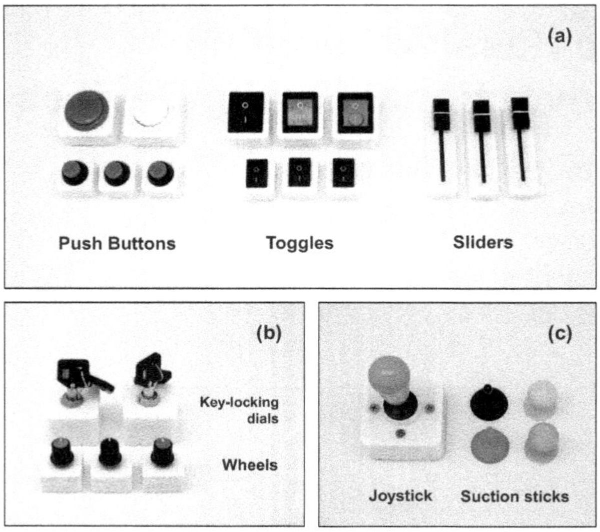

Figure 2: Three types of *MagGetz* controllers: (a) linear movement type, (b) curved movement type, and (c) 2D plane movement type.

	Type	Magnet orientation (to the ground)	Magnet size (mm)	Magnetic strength (uT)	Max. working distance (mm)	Input expressiveness
Button (Small)	Linear	Horizontal	2ø, 5T	300	100	Analog
Button (Large)			5ø, 3T	500	100	Analog
Toggle (Small)			5ø, 3T	500	150	Binary
Toggle (Large)			8ø, 5T	800	200	Binary
Slider		Vertical	8ø, 3T	600	200	Analog
Key lock	Curved	Vertical	2ø, 5T	300	120	Binary
Wheel					120	Analog
Joystick	2D plane	Horizontal	10ø, 5T	1500	400	Analog
Suction Stick			5ø, 3T	500	100	Analog

Table 1: Comparison of *MagGetz* control widgets.

research community has proposed a variety of methods to enable tangible interaction for touchscreen devices. The first approach relies on capacitive markers [4, 10, 15, 21, 22]. Yu et al. [21] suggested a technique that senses and tracks objects on a capacitive touchscreen by simulating finger touches using passive materials and active modulation circuits embedded inside tangible objects. Later, they introduced a passive controller, called a Clip-on gadget [22], which clips on the bezel to reduce screen occlusion. Similarly, Kratz et al. [15] presented a passive rotary knob controller that works with a capacitive touchscreen. Chan et al. [4] introduced tangible blocks that allow an underlying capacitive touchscreen to identity different blocks or stacking heights. Jansen et al. [10] explored the tangible remote controllers for a wall-size display. They explored the benefits of using tangible sliders on a table as a remote controller by comparing a virtual and tangible slider. These studies enabled tangible interactions on capacitive multi-touch devices without requiring any hardware modifications. However, the interaction area is confined within the touchscreen, which results in occlusion problems. In addition, the passive widgets are invisible to the touchscreen when it is untouched, and the active widgets need circuit hardware and a power.

The second approach of enabling tangible interaction for mobile devices is using cameras [2, 11]. Portico [2] is a portable system for enabling tangible interaction on and around table computers. In that study, the authors used two cameras on small foldable arms to recognize a variety of physical objects placed on and around the tablet. In addition, Kato et al. [11] introduced a tangible joystick that realizes continuous analog input by tracking a marker at the top end of a controller with the device's inertial camera. This approach successfully extends its interaction area with richer tactile clues. However, the cameras do not work properly in the dark environment. Moreover, the cameras and foldable arms are very bulky [2], or the controller's location is fixed and limited with regard to the location of camera [11].

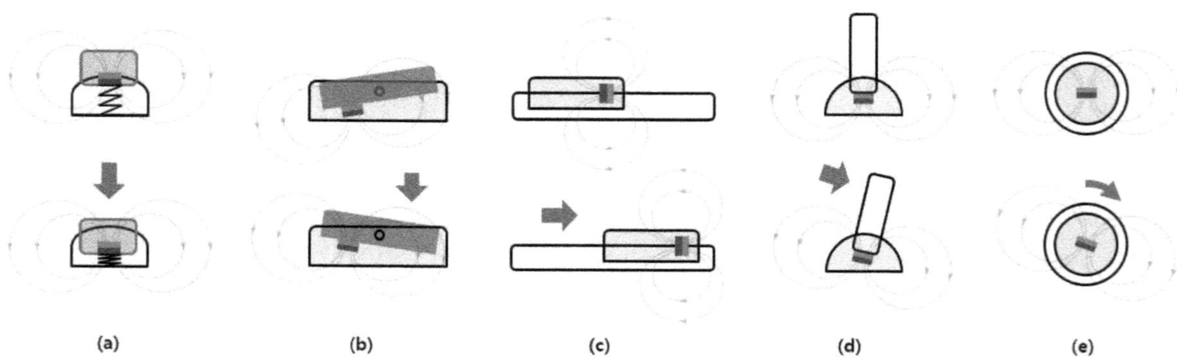

Figure 3: The location of a magnet and the visualization of magnetism for each control element. The side view of push button (a), toggle switch (b), slider (c), and joystick (d). The top view of the rotational wheel (e).

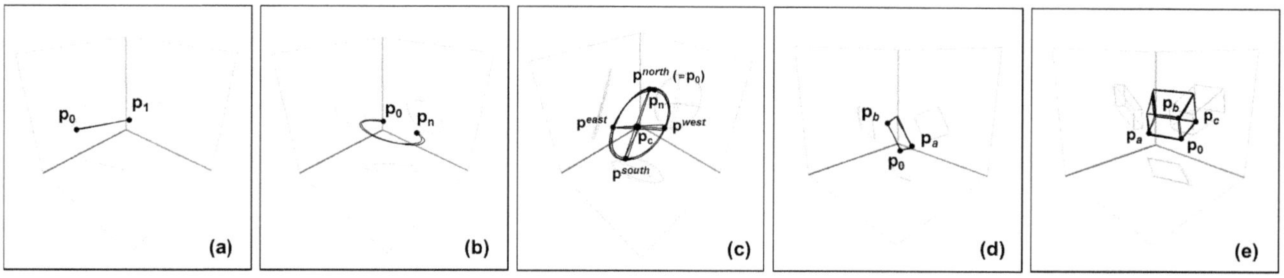

Figure 4: Magnetic traces for different control widgets: (a) a button, (b) a wheel, and (c) a joystick. The combination of multiple widgets: (d) two buttons, and (e) three toggle switches.

Magnetically Driven Input for Mobile Devices

Magnets are very cheap, small, and robust, do not require power, and their positions and orientations can be easily detected wirelessly using magnetometers embedded in modern phones [3]. Moreover, they do not easily degrade over time. For these reasons, a number of input techniques using magnetism have been introduced, attempting to expand the interacting surface beyond the physical bounds of devices [6, 12, 13, 14, 18]. Harrison and Hudson [6] described an input interaction around the small device through a finger-attached magnet. Similarly, Ketabdar et al. [12] proposed a gestural interaction for playing music through a small magnet worn on the finger. They used a magnetometer embedded in typical smartphones for interaction with music-related applications. Besides these, magnetic-based interfaces have been successfully applied to many tasks such as hand-writing [13], turning pages and zooming [14] or gestural authenticating [18]. These approaches definitely improve usability by expanding the interaction beyond the bounds of the device screen. However, the main limitation is that they do not provide users with tactile clues.

More recently, Ashbrook et al. [1] presented a subtle input with a magnetically tracked finger ring. They introduced a unique input method that makes a selection by twisting the ring and clicks by sliding it along the finger. Liang et al. [17] introduced GaussSense, which is a back-of-device sensing technique for enabling input on an arbitrary surface using a stylus. While these approaches provide users with tactile clues through their tangible tokens (e.g., ring [1] and stylus [17]), they need additional sensing hardware (e.g., a wrist-worn tracking bracelet [1] and a magnetic sensor grid [17]). Besides these approaches, magnets are successfully used in more constrained ways. For instance, Mobile ActDresses [9] uses the specific spatial properties of a magnet attached onto slip-on device covers to customize the visual theme. Moreover, many devices in the market already have an automatic wake and sleep feature triggered by a magnet (e.g., Nexus7 and iPad2).

Customizable physical Interfaces

Unlike virtual controls on screens, physical controllers provide richer tactile clues through their rigid shapes and predetermined layouts. However, the physicality of these interfaces makes them static, limiting the customization of the interfaces they can support. To address this issue, researchers have attempted to support the customization of physical interfaces [5, 7, 16, 20]. Phidgets (physical widgets) [5] constitute a general toolkit of physical user interface components. The toolkit provides a developer with a collection of controls, sensors, and actuators to design and customize physical interfaces. Similarly, Calder [16] and d.tools [7] are toolkits for supporting product designers in the process of developing rapid prototypes of their ideas. Later, Villar et al. [20] introduced a malleable control structure made up of a set of controls that users can freely arrange. In their study, the individual controls can be actively added, removed, and rearranged on a flexible substrate that embeds conductive layers and custom-designed coaxial connectors.

While these studies support a rapid prototyping and deployment of custom interfaces, they need wires or wireless connections with electric powers. Moreover, they do not support the real-time adaptation of the physical layout.

THE DESIGN OF MAGGETZ

Building on previous works, we take advantage of magnets and suggest unpowered, low-cost, and user-configurable magnetic tangible controllers on and around mobile devices using them. Here, we describe our system, which comprises both hardware and software.

Hardware Design

MagGetz constitutes a set of tangible control widgets made from traditional physical input elements (~15 US$) covered with an acrylic case. In order to track the physical movement of control widgets, we attached a permanent magnet on the appropriate position of each widget (see Figure 3). We then covered it with an acrylic case that we designed using computer-aided design (CAD) and attached a 3M restickable adhesive tape (R100) underneath the case in order for the magnet to be individually attached, detached, and rearranged on various surfaces (e.g., desks, back of mobile phones, or phone holders). Basically, we have implemented three different types of *MagGetz* based on the magnetic movement: linear type (e.g., push buttons, toggle switches, and sliders), curve type (e.g., rotational wheels, and key-locking dials), and two-dimensional (2D) plane type (e.g., a joystick, and suction-cup sticks). The control widgets of each type are shown in Figure 2. These controls act as input blocks that can be combined to create a custom control environment. For instance, the user can attach three different control widgets surrounding the device as shown in Figure 1. To make a noticeable difference in the magnetic field when the user changes the states of controllers (e.g., pushing the button, rotating the wheel, or turning the toggle switch on and off), we chose an appropriate permanent magnet and embedded it on a place where it moves as much as possible (see Figure 3). We used Neodymium coin magnets with 3~5mm in thickness and 2~10mm in diameter for different widgets (300 ~1500uT).

The comparison of *MagGetz* control widgets is shown in Table 1. Referring to this, the working distance varies depending on how we arrange the magnet: The distance that the magnetic pulse reaches increased when the base side of the magnet is heading for the sensor (e.g., the wheel's working distance is much longer than the small button's). The working distance is the maximum distance between the sensor of the device and the controller at which they work properly. With this setup, the system could measure a change in the magnetic field according to the state of each controller.

Software Design

We developed a general toolkit on Android 4.0.4. (SHV-E160S, Samsung Galaxy Note) using Java. We also implemented a three-dimensional (3D) Visualizer using OpenGL library for developers to examine a change in the magnetic field. Our software used an inertial three-axis magnetometer that senses the magnetic field strength along with x, y, and z directions at a sampling frequency of 100 Hz. To mitigate sampling noise, we used a fixed size buffer; the movement vector from the last reading to its predecessor is computed and normalized. This process generates a 3D vector that reflects the variations of the magnetic field around the mobile device.

Figure 4 shows the magnetic traces for different control widgets that a three-axis magnetometer sensed. These traces are: (a) a straight line when a small button was pressed, (b) a curved line when a wheel was rotated, and (c) a circular plane when a joystick was controlled (all directional points and four right-angled directions from center). As shown in this visualization, the magnetism around the control widget differs according to its physical movement. Basically, our system relies on this phenomenon and determines the current states of widgets by comparing a current magnetic value with the reference magnetic values stored in the calibration procedure. In order to determine the status of widgets, tangible widgets have to be static with respect to the device. For the calibration, our system stores a trace of magnetic values according to the change of the widgets' states (e.g., pressing a button, or rotating a wheel).

In the case of linear type, the system stores two end-points (e.g., when a button is fully pressed and released) rather than all points at a regular interval distance (see Figure 4a). It then infers the state of the widget by using a ratio for the distances between the current point and the two end-points. To do so, the software projects a new point vector onto the vector between two end points and calculates relative position within the vector between two end points, which denotes the state of a widget. For instance, pressure level l applied on a button widget when we have a new input $\mathbf{x}$ is computed using the following formula:

$$l = \frac{|\mathbf{x}' - \mathbf{p}_0|}{|\mathbf{p}_1 - \mathbf{p}_0|} \quad (1)$$

where $\mathbf{p}_1$ is a last reference point (e.g., a point when the button is fully pressed), $\mathbf{p}_0$ is a first reference point (e.g., a point when the button is not pressed), and $\mathbf{x}'$ is a vector that new point $\mathbf{x}$ projected onto $\mathbf{p}_0\,\mathbf{p}_1$.

In the case of the curved type, the system captures and stores reference points at a regular interval distance, which is different from the linear type (see Figure 4b). Our system records every magnetic point that changes more than 10uT. For instance, the system could capture 30 points for a wheel while it rotates. Later, the system infers the state of the wheel by finding the nearest one among 30 points to a current point and then considering it as the state of the wheel. The level of rotation l for a wheel is calculated using the following formula:

$$l = \frac{\sum_0^k |\mathbf{p}_{i+1} - \mathbf{p}_i|}{\sum |\mathbf{p}_{i+1} - \mathbf{p}_i|} \quad (2)$$

where $\mathbf{p}_i$ is i[th] reference point from starting point $\mathbf{p}_0$ (e.g., minimum rotation of a wheel), k is a sequence of the reference point closest to a new magnetic input point.

For the 2D plane type, our system stores a center point (e.g., the default state of a joystick), four right-angled directional points (e.g., east, west, south, and north), and other directional points (e.g., the arc between east and north) at a regular interval as reference points (see Figure 4c). In order to minimize errors when the circle is distorted, the system infers the state of the joystick by finding a vector closest to a new point among vectors between a center point and directional reference points. The pressure level l on a joystick when we have a new input $\mathbf{x}$ is calculated using the following formula:

$$l = \frac{|\mathbf{x}'_k - \mathbf{p}_c|}{|\mathbf{p}_n^k - \mathbf{p}_c|} \quad (3)$$

where $\mathbf{p}_c$ is a center point, $\mathbf{p}^k$ is a vector that is closest to a new input point $\mathbf{x}$ among vectors between a center point $\mathbf{p}_c$ and directional reference points ($\mathbf{p}^0$~$\mathbf{p}^n$), $\mathbf{p}^k_n$ is the last point of vector $\mathbf{p}^k$ starting from $\mathbf{p}^k_0$ (= $\mathbf{p}_c$), and $\mathbf{x'}_k$ is a vector that new point $\mathbf{x}$ projected onto $\mathbf{p}_c\mathbf{p}^k_n$. The direction of a joystick can be obtained by applying k of $\mathbf{p}^k$ to equation (2).

Besides the inference of a single widget, our system can track the multiple widgets simultaneously. To do so, our system needs to store magnetic traces for all widgets. In particular, the system stores a point when all widgets are deactivated and points when each widget is activated. Figure 4(d) shows an example of a magnetic trace that two widgets generate (button a, and button b). In order to calibrate them, for instance, a user needs to attach them around the device and tell the type of widgets to the system. The user then stores three conditions of the widgets by clicking a virtual button on the screen after changing the states of widgets one by one: a condition when the button a and b are released, a condition when the button a is fully pressed while the button b is released, and the button b is fully pressed while the button a is released (needs N+1 conditions for using N widgets). In this case, the trace of two buttons generates a 2D-filled square plane and the pressure level applied on button a (l_a) and the pressure level for button b (l_b) are calculated by the following equation:

$$\mathbf{x} = l_a|\mathbf{p}_a - \mathbf{p}_0| + l_b|\mathbf{p}_b - \mathbf{p}_0| \quad (4)$$

where $\mathbf{x}$ is a new magnetic point according to the user's input, $\mathbf{p}_a$ is a reference point of button a with maximum pressure, $\mathbf{p}_b$ is a maximum point of button b, and $\mathbf{p}_0$ is a reference point of button a and b with minimum pressure. By using the Gauss elimination method, our system can infer the states of each widget's pressure level (l_a, and l_b) simultaneously. This equation can also be applied to a hexahedron graph that three linear-type widgets generate, as shown in Figure 4(e). Our system can individually track the states of control widgets that generate up to three dimensional shapes (e.g., a set of three pressure-sensitive buttons, a set of a joystick and a pressure-sensitive button). For instance, our system does not work properly for a set of four sliders because magnetic traces of them are overlapped each other.

MAGGETZ APPLICATIONS

In this section, we introduce a series of applications using the *MagGetz* toolkit and their potential interactions.

Control Cover for Mobile Devices

If the controllers are fixed on the mobile device, physical movement of the device does not affect the relative position to the sensor. We have built a series of mobile phone holders that contain some unpowered control widgets. Figure 5(a) shows a game control pad that has a joystick and two buttons. Figure 5(b) shows a cover for taking a photo that consists of a pressure-sensitive button and a wheel.

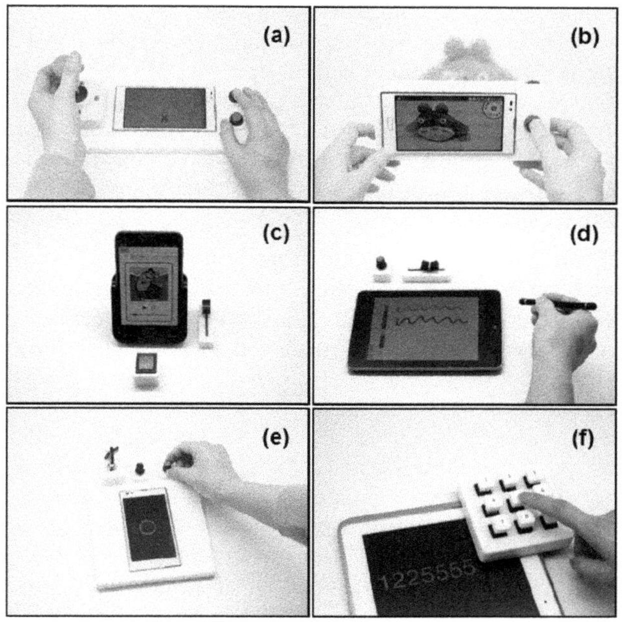

Figure 5: Various forms of *MagGetz* Applications: (a) joystick pad cover, (b) photo-taking cover, (c) music player, (d) drawer, (e) *MagGetz* for authentication, and (f) *MagGetz* number pad

This setup enables users to use a halfway push with their thumbs and to adjust an aperture with their index fingers. In this way, a user can take a photo through pressure-sensitive interaction, and no occlusions result from this process.

User Customizable Controllers

One of the features of *MagGetz* is a customization of controls. We have implemented some applications under the user-customized controllers: a music player and a drawer. Figure 5(c) shows a music player with a toggle switch for controlling the power and a slider for adjusting the volume. Besides this custom setup, the user can rearrange and replace the toggle switch and slider. For instance, the user can change a slider to a wheel for controlling the volume and rearrange the toggle switch on the back of the device. Another possible application is a drawer, as shown in Figure 5(d). In this case, we designed software that allows the user to control the thickness of a pen through the wheel and to change the color of the pen through the slider.

MagGetz Authentication

Similar to the previous work that uses magnetic gestures for authentication [18], we proposed an application that uses magnetic control widgets for the authentication purpose. Figure 5(e) shows an example setup that consists of two wheels and a key lock. With this setup, the user places his/her mobile device on the slot and unlocks the system by adjusting the wheels and key locks at a right angle.

Multiple Widgets with Binary States

We can use more than three controllers simultaneously through the binary input control widgets. We have implemented a simple calculator application with a physical number pad that contains nine binary buttons, as shown in Figure 5(f). In this case, the system stores nine reference points for nine keys that are pressed and compares them with an incoming value.

DISCUSSION AND CONCLUSION

We have presented a *MagGetz* toolkit and various applications using it, which provide users with a wider interaction area, higher input expressiveness, and a customizable layout of richer physical clues. *MagGetz* do not need power, a wireless connection, or the hardware modifications of mobile devices in order to operate. We believe that *MagGetz* toolkit can be successfully integrated for conventional mobile devices. On the contrary, *MagGetz* do have limitations: First, the magnetism involved might damage the objects (e.g., magnetic stripes on credit cards and magnetic hard disks.) when the objects are very close to the magnets. However, magnets do not affect flash memories on modern mobile devices or IC chips on credit cards. Second, the magnetometer we used occasionally reports a large offset in the data or a stuck pointing in one direction. In this case, user should wave the device in figure eight to get back on track. This technical glitch, however, will be undoubtedly solved as sensor technology improves. For future work, we plan to design different shapes and forms of input control widgets (e.g., deformable, stretchable, or elastic properties) and consider using magnetic shields to enhance performance.

REFERENCES

1. Ashbrook, D., Baudisch, P., White., S., Nenya: subtle and eyes-free mobile input with a magnetically-tracked finger ring. *In Proc. of CHI*, (2011), 2043-2046.
2. Avrahami, D., Wobbrock, J. O., Izadi, S., Portico: tangible interaction on and around a tablet. *In Proc. of UIST*, (2011), 347-356.
3. Bianchi, A., Oakley, I., Designing Tangible Magnetic Appcessories, *In Proc. of TEI*, (2013), 255-258.
4. Chan, L., Müller, S., Roudaut, A., Baudisch, P., CapStones and ZebraWidgets: sensing stacks of building blocks, dials and sliders on capacitive touch screens. *In Proc. of CHI*, (2012), 2189-2192.
5. Greenberg, S., Chester F., Phidgets: easy development of physical interfaces through physical widgets. *In Proc. of UIST*, (2001), 209-218.
6. Harrison, C., Hudson, S. E., Abracadabra: wireless, high-precision, and unpowered finger input for very small mobile devices. *In Proc. of UIST*, (2009), 121-124.
7. Hartmann. B., Klemmer. S. R., Bernstein. M., Mehta. N., d.tools: Visually Prototyping Physical UIs through Statecharts. *In Proc. of UIST*, (2005).
8. Ishii, H., Tangible bits: Beyond pixels. *In Proc. of TEI*, (2008).
9. Jacobsson, M., Fernaeus, Y., Nylander, S., Mobile ActDresses: programming mobile devices by accessorizing. *In Proc. of CHI EA*, (2012), 1071-1074.
10. Jansen, Y., Dragicevic, P., Fekete, J. D., Tangible remote controllers for wall-size displays. *In Proc. of CHI*, (2012), 2865-2874.
11. Kato, H., Kato, T., A camera-based tangible controller for cellular phones. *In Proc. of MobileHCI*, (2009).
12. Ketabdar, H., Haji-Abolhassani, A., Yüksel, K.A., Kehribar, I., Ercil, A., Digital Music Performance for Mobile Devices Based on Magnetic Interaction, *IEEE Transactions on Instrumentation and Measurement*, (2011), vol.60, no.11, 3524-3533.
13. Ketabdar, H., Roshandel, M., Yüksel, K.A., MagiWrite: towards touchless digit entry using 3D space around mobile devices. *In Proc. of MobileHCI*, (2010), 443-446.
14. Ketabdar, H., Yüksel, K., A., Roshandel, M., MagiTact: interaction with mobile devices based on compass (magnetic) sensor. *In Proc. of IUI*, (2010), 413-414.
15. Kratz, S., Westermann, T., Rohs, M., Essl, G., CapWidgets: tangile widgets versus multi-touch controls on mobile devices. *In Proc. of CHI EA*, (2011), 1351-1356.
16. Lee, J. C., Avrahami, D., Hudson, S. E., Forlizzi, J., Dietz, P. H., Leigh, D., The calder toolkit: wired and wireless components for rapidly prototyping interactive devices. *In Proc. of DIS*, (2004), 167-175.
17. Liang, R.H., Cheng, K.Y., Su, C.H., Weng, C.T., Chen, B.Y., Yang, D.N., GaussSense: Attachable stylus sensing using magnetic sensor grid. *In Proc. of UIST*, (2012), 319-326.
18. Shirazi, A.S., Moghadam, P., Ketabdar, H., Schmidt, A., Assessing the vulnerability of magnetic gestural authentication to video-based shoulder surfing attacks. *In Proc. of CHI*, (2012), 2045-2048.
19. Siek, K. A., Rogers, Y., Connelly, K.H. Fat Finger Worries: How Older and Younger Users Physically Interact with PDAs. *In Proc. of INTERACT*, (2005), 267-280.
20. Villar, N., Gellersen, H., A Malleable Control Structure for Softwired User Interfaces. *In Proc. of TEI*, (2007), 49-56.
21. Yu, N., Chan, L., Tsai, S., Hsiao, I., Tsai, D., Hsiao, F., Cheng, L., Chen, M., Huang, P., Hung, Y. TUIC: enabling tangible interaction on capacitive multi-touch displays. *In Proc. of CHI*, (2011), 2995-3004.
22. Yu, N., Tsai, S., Hsiao, I., Tsai, D., Lee, M., Chen, M., Hung, Y. Clip-on Gadgets: expanding multi-touch interaction area with unpowered tactile controls. *In Proc. of UIST*, (2011), 367-372.

inFORM: Dynamic Physical Affordances and Constraints through Shape and Object Actuation

Sean Follmer* **Daniel Leithinger*** **Alex Olwal** **Akimitsu Hogge** **Hiroshi Ishii**
MIT Media Lab
75 Amherst Street, Cambridge, MA 02139, USA
{sean, daniell, olwal, ishii}@media.mit.edu

Figure 1: inFORM enables new interaction techniques for shape-changing UIs. *Left to right:* On-demand UI elements through *Dynamic Affordances*; Guiding interaction with *Dynamic Constraints*; Object actuation; Physical rendering of content and UI.

ABSTRACT

Past research on shape displays has primarily focused on rendering content and user interface elements through shape output, with less emphasis on dynamically changing UIs. We propose utilizing shape displays in three different ways to mediate interaction: to *facilitate* by providing dynamic physical affordances through shape change, to *restrict* by guiding users with dynamic physical constraints, and to *manipulate* by actuating physical objects. We outline potential interaction techniques and introduce *Dynamic Physical Affordances and Constraints* with our inFORM system, built on top of a state-of-the-art shape display, which provides for variable stiffness rendering and real-time user input through direct touch and tangible interaction. A set of motivating examples demonstrates how dynamic affordances, constraints and object actuation can create novel interaction possibilities.

Author Keywords

Shape-changing User Interfaces, Shape Displays, Actuated Tangible Interfaces, Token and Constraint Interfaces.

ACM Classification Keywords

H.5.2 User Interfaces: Graphical user interfaces, Input devices and strategies, Interaction styles.

*The first two authors contributed equally to this work.

UIST'13, October 8–11, 2013, St. Andrews, United Kingdom.

ACM 978-1-4503-2268-3/13/10...$15.00.
http://dx.doi.org/10.1145/2501988.2502032

INTRODUCTION

The rich variety of physical forms found in everyday life often serve both functional and aesthetic roles. These physical objects have features that not only provide functionality, but also suggest possible uses, or confine the ways we may interact with them; Norman labels these as perceived affordances [30]. This notion of perceived affordances has been long appropriated by the HCI field, particularly in the context of Graphical User Interfaces (GUI) and Tangible User Interfaces (TUI) [17]. While GUIs have the ability to change perceived affordances rapidly to adapt them to different content and context, TUIs primarily exploit the affordances inherent in physical form, as well as their physiological and cognitive advantages [21]. For example, the Token and Constraint framework introduced by Ullmer uses mechanical constraints to provide physical affordances for interacting with tangible controllers, such as tokens [38]. However, TUIs, such as those outlined by Ullmer, are often limited by the static nature of most man-made physical artifacts, and thus cannot easily change their form. Therefore, many projects in this area are commonly single-purpose and do not physically reflect changing program states well [15].

To overcome these limitations, we seek to bring the dynamism of visually perceived affordances of GUIs to physical interaction by utilizing shape-changing UIs (see Figure 1). This paper explores Dynamic Affordances which can transform shape, size, location and orientation, in addition to being able to appear and disappear. They provide appropriate affordances on demand by changing their physical properties based on program states and the context of the user or other objects in the interaction area to *facilitate* interaction. Buttons can, for example, grow in size to ease target acquisition, or move out of the way of an object. We also introduce Dynamic Constraints, which help mediate interaction between the interface and tangible tokens or tools. Dynamic Constraints not only provide affordances to the user, but also serve to mechanically *restrict* object motion. Constraints limit the degrees of freedom through which users interact with the system, allowing for more precise input in each dimension. These build on and expand Ullmer's Token and Constraint work [38].

In addition to creating affordances and constraints for physical objects and tools, we also show how shape change can be utilized to *manipulate* passive objects. Mechanical forces can push objects, causing them to roll, slide, or tumble in one direction or another. Other constraints can be programmed to rotate or raise passive objects. Passive tangible tokens can be moved to maintain state, and devices, such as phones, can be raised to draw attention to them. Our techniques allow for a wide variety of physical objects to be actuated. This opens up interaction possibilities that point towards tabletop systems that can more easily interact with the world around us.

To explore these techniques and interactions, we introduce the inFORM system, a state-of-the-art 2.5D shape display that enables dynamic affordances, constraints and actuation of passive objects. Shape displays allow for more general-purpose shape change than many other actuated or shape-changing interfaces, and thus are ideal research platforms. The inFORM system supports fast 2.5D actuation, malleable input, and variable stiffness haptic feedback. While shape displays still remain limited in scale and cost, this work is an exploration of the interaction capabilities and is meant to inspire further research in this area. Our belief is that shape-changing interfaces will become increasingly available in the future, and this work tries to push towards creating a vocabulary and design space for more general-purpose interaction for shape displays, including rendering of both content and UI elements.

In this paper, we first review related work in physical affordances and constraints, as well as shape-changing interfaces and dynamic affordances. Next, we discuss the design space of Dynamic Affordances and Dynamic Constraints, and provide methods for using these concepts to also actuate objects. We describe three implemented demonstration applications that highlight different aspects of our concepts, followed by a technical overview of our system. Finally we discuss the implications, limitations, and future potential of the inFORM system.

CONTRIBUTIONS

- An exploration of the design space of dynamic affordances and constraints.
- Actuation of physical objects through shape displays.
- State-of-the-art system for fast, real-time 2.5D shape actuation, co-located projected graphics, object tracking, and direct manipulation.
- Three applications that demonstrate the potential of these interaction techniques for HCI.

RELATED WORK

Our work draws heavily from the rich history of affordances. Gibson introduced the theory of affordances as "what [an object or environment] offers the animal, what it provides or furnishes, either for good or ill." This can be viewed as the set of action potentials for an object [11]. Norman first applied affordance to design and HCI, focusing on "perceived affordances" that the designer creates to provide interaction clues, or suggestions, to the user [30]. Gaver [9] defines his technology affordances as "properties of the world that are compatible with and relevant for people's interactions." He emphasizes the importance of perceptible affordances, since mismatched or hidden affordances interfere with the interface's legibility, which may confuse the user and result in improper operation. Gaver highlights that these affordances can be perceived visually, tactilely, or aurally. He also expands on sets of affordances: *nested affordances*, which are grouped spatially, and *sequential affordances*, which are grouped temporally. Sequential affordances are often used in GUI based interaction, where graphical perceived affordances can be rendered quickly and then disappear.

Hartson elaborates on Norman and Gaver's work describing four types of affordances as *cognitive affordance*, "Design features that helps users in knowing something", *physical affordance*, "Design features that helps users in doing a physical action in the interface", *sensory affordance*, "Design features that helps users sense something " and *functional affordance*, "Design features that helps users accomplish work (i.e., the usefulness of a system function)" [13]. Kaptelinin further splits both cognitive and physical affordances in two parts, describing the *handling affordance*, the affordances a user interacts with, and the *effecter affordance*, the affordances a tool manipulates an object with. They suggest that these must be tightly coupled [20]. Feedback and feedforward also play a large role in affordance, and Vermeulen positions feedforward in the context of affordance, and reviews feedback and affordances [40].

In this paper, we focus on rendering both *cognitive affordances* and *physical affordances* through a shape display. These affordances can be perceived both tacitly and visually. Physical form can be used as a cognitive affordance, i.e., rendering a physical play button shaped like a triangle, which could be primarily perceived visually but also tactilely. But, we also render *physical affordances* on demand, which help guide the user's motion physically or mechanically. These physical affordances can be both handling affordances or effecter affordances, which is often the case with dynamic physical constraints. Our dynamic affordances also draw heavily on Gaver's sequential affordances.

Static Affordances: Tangibles and Graspables

Fitzmaurice et al. [7] demonstrate the benefits of graspable UIs with Bricks, where physical affordances are mapped to the control and representation of virtual objects and abstract actions. SLAP widgets [44] demonstrate how passive controls can provide control and input affordances through optical tracking and sensing.

DataTiles [35] are tangible toolglasses [3], which can be arranged on a screen and act as transparent lenses or props that guide the user's pen interaction with the underlying virtual content. The different tile types embed grooved widgets that physically steer the user's interaction through motion constraints. The Token+constraint framework [38] explores this design space further, highlighting the importance of mechanical constraints, and allows users to build database queries by arranging tangibles where rules and meaning are inferred from spatial relationships.

Haptics

In Haptics [37], a proxy device is typically used to render tactile illusions of physical touch, collisions and constraints in the interface. Electromagnetism can, for example, be used to control a finger or device with an attached magnet [43, 41]. Such haptic interfaces can effectively provide guidance and feedback, but lack perceivable affordances in their static state; the system can only suggest operation during interaction or movement. Tagged handles [27] approach this limitation by having the user experience tangibles with functional form attached to the actuated devices to enhance perceptibility.

Actuated and Dynamically Controlled Objects

A natural extension to user manipulation of TUIs is the ability to computationally control them through actuation. The Actuated Workbench [31] uses electromagnetism for 2D movement of tracked tangibles on an interactive surface, while Madgets [42] extends the concept to enable height actuation, control of mechanical mechanisms, and to power circuits through induction, in passive tangible assemblies. PICO [32] introduces mechanical constraints as a direct way for the user to specify behavior and rules for actuated tangibles. While the system can communicate system constraints through graphics and object actuation, it is limited in its ability to manifest mechanical constraints; only the user can create those. Other techniques for moving objects on a 2D surface include vibration [36] and robotics [22].

Dynamic, Computationally Controlled Affordances

There is even more interesting potential in the computational control of physical form to adapt and change affordances as a response to both context and user. Coelho and Zigelbaum [5] and Rasmussen et al. [34] review the design spaces for shape-changing interfaces, where actuation actively modifies the shape of an interface or object. Ishii describes his vision of Radical Atoms, and suggests Dynamic Affordances as an interesting area of further research [16]. Most current shape-changing interfaces that address on-demand affordances provide a specific transformation, which limits their use for general purpose UIs and 3D interaction. The haptic chameleon by Michelitsch et al. [29] introduces the concept of shape-changing control devices and reports on experiments with early prototypes. Hemmert et al. [14] manipulate tapering and weight shift in conceptual mobile devices. Bubblewrap [2] embeds electromagnetic actuators in textiles to control form, while MudPad [19] uses magnetorheological fluid to manipulate viscosity. Jamming User Interfaces can change the stiffness of an input device to change its affordances through particle jamming [8]. Harrison and Hudson [12] employ pneumatics, whereas Tactus Technologies [4] use microfluidics, to inflate predefined physical buttons, for on-demand tactile affordances on touch screens. Madgets also provide affordances dynamically, by moving them around a surface or mechanically raising or locking elements [42].

Shape displays, which enable more general topologies and greater degrees-of-freedom, tend to primarily focus on content representation through graphics and shape; the generated shapes can respond to the user's touch [18], gestures [25], or other objects' presence [23]. Poupyrev et al. do, however, mention the potential for on-demand UI elements in the description of Lumen, a 13×13 array of actuated illuminated rods [33].

This work builds on the rich literature of affordances and also strongly on the Token+constraint framework [38], but expands on it by considering dynamic changes. The use of a general-purpose 2.5D shape display allows us to support dynamic adaptation of the form, based on user interaction, application context and scenario. The combination of dynamic surface topologies, actuated control of passive tangible objects, user sensing, and object tracking, provides a rich set of capabilities for dynamically controlled perceptible affordances that can optimize user guidance and interaction.

DYNAMIC AFFORDANCES AND CONSTRAINTS

Past research on shape displays has primarily focused on rendering content through shape output, with less emphasis on investigating dynamically changing UI elements. We propose an analysis of dynamically generated physical features with specific affordances that guide the user on how the system can be used and provide passive haptic feedback, enabling interaction at a lower cognitive cost [21]. We believe that shape displays need to provide three types of functionality for creating dynamic UIs: to *facilitate* through Dynamic Affordances, to *restrict* through Dynamic Constraints, and to *manipulate* passive objects through shape change.

Facilitate: Dynamic Physical Affordances

Dynamic Affordances function both as perceived affordances and "real" affordances, as they are rendered physically and provide mechanical support for interaction. We can combine graphical perceived affordances with Dynamic Affordances, or switch between these states.

In the inFORM system, these affordances are physical elements that the user can touch. Depending on how they are rendered by the system, they either directly react to touch, or react to displacement from the user pushing or pulling them. Figure 2 depicts a set of different dynamic affordances rendered on our system. Examples of UI controls with dynamic affordances that our system supports are:

Binary Switches: Buttons

Buttons are formed by raising pins from the surrounding surface. Users activate a button by touching it or by pushing it into the surface, which is registered as a binary input.

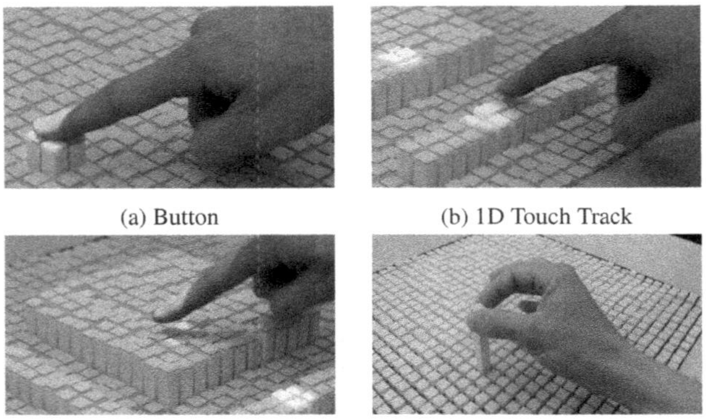

(a) Button (b) 1D Touch Track (c) 2D Touch Surface (d) Handle

Figure 2: *Dynamic Physical Affordances* transform the UI to facilitate interactions.

(a) Well (b) Slot (c) Ramp (d) Surface

Figure 3: *Dynamic Physical Constraints* guides the user by limiting possible interactions.

1D input: Touch tracks

Touch tracks consist of a line or curve of adjacent raised pins, which the user can touch at different locations, or slide over. These touch points are registered in one input dimension.

2D input: Touch surfaces

Touch surfaces are created using multiple pins, which are aligned to form surfaces. These surfaces, which can be non-planar, map each touch point to two dimensions.

Handles

Handles provide interaction in the Z dimension. These raised pins can be grabbed, and then pulled up or pushed down along one dimension.

Interactions with Dynamic Affordances

Affordances can change shape to reflect a changing program state. For example, when a user presses a play button (triangle shape) it can transform into a stop button (square shape).

Shape-changing affordances can also enable smooth transitions between input dimensions. For example, pressing a button could cause it to transform into a 2D touch panel.

It can be advantageous to let the user's proximity inform shape change. Affordances can, for example, increase in size as a user's hand approaches them, making them easier to acquire according to Fitt's law [28].

Affordances can also move out of the way of physical objects, or rearrange to provide more space for interaction. Besides avoiding physical objects, affordances can compliment them to increase their functionality. As a physical object is moved, the affordances can appear or follow it. For example, as a device is placed on the table, relevant physical UI controls can appear; a phone could be complemented with a large answer button next to it, or a tablet could have buttons to control games appear around it.

The inFORM system is particularly well-suited to guide complex interactions and adapt the affordances, when the user may perform multiple actions using the same controls. Gaver refers to *sequential affordances* [9] in situations where the affordances change based on the interaction, to enable new possibilities or restrict actions. A UI control can, for example, be rendered with different stiffness to provide further affordances. Two flat surfaces might appear the same, and both afford touching, but once the user touches their surface, a stiff surface affords touch interaction, where a more compliant surface affords pressing. More interestingly, with systems like inFORM, such qualities can be dynamically changed and updated based on interaction and context.

Restrict: Guiding Interaction with Dynamic Constraints

While Dynamic Affordances facilitate user interactions, Dynamic Constraints limit the possibilities, making some interactions difficult or impossible to perform. These Dynamic Constraints make the system more legible, but also guide the user in performing certain interactions through physical interaction with the constraints. They can also help mediate interaction through tangible tokens or tools.

When an object is placed on a shape display, it physically interacts with the shapes generated by the display. In the context of our work, we refer to the physical objects as tokens and the shapes interacting with them as constraints. Figure 3 depicts different types of constraints. Constraints like wells, slots and ramps limit the movement of the token through their shape, thus guiding user interaction, similar to [38].

As our system can sense how tokens interact with constraints, it can dynamically modify their parameters (shape, size, location, orientation) to adapt to user input or to reflect changing program states. Examples of techniques to guide interactions using shape change:

Holding Tokens and Sensing Presence: Wells

Wells act as containers to hold objects. Placing an token inside a well or removing it, is sensed as a binary action. The shape of the well and the shape of the token determine if the token can be rotated in the well, which adds another degree of freedom.

Restricting Movement to 1D: Slots

Slots are grooves which constrain the direction in which a user can move a token. In addition to the same actions that are supported by the wells, tracked tokens can also be moved in the slots to, for example, control a 1D parameter.

Affecting Movement: Ramps and Curved Surfaces
The surface geometry can be changed to make it easier or harder for the user to move tokens in a certain direction. Ramps can, for example, be used to faciliate or restrict movement of a token due to gravity.

Interaction with Dynamic Physical Constraints
Wells can transform in size and shape to adapt to the size, shape and number of tokens. They can also deepen to move tokens outside the users reach (see Figure 4).

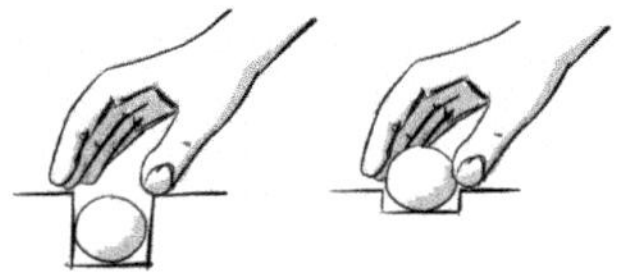

Figure 4: The depth of a well affords if the user can grasp a token contained in it.

Slots change in size, shape and location to reflect a changing program state. A user can, for example, place a token inside a well, which is equivalent to selecting a top level menu item. The well then transforms into a slot, similar to an expanding menu. As the user moves the item inside the well, its shape can transform and branch out to present selectable options.

Slots can also transform their shape to promote the movement of tokens in a certain direction or to hinder it. An example is shown in Figure 5 (right), where a ramp-shaped slot allows users to roll a token with ease in the direction sloping downwards, while requiring deliberate effort to move it in the upwards direction. In addition to ramps, slots can contain further constraints to provide haptic feedback as the user moves the token through the slot. Such feedback can be provided through slots with detents at the bottom (Figure 5, left), ramps with drops, or vibration of the entire slot.

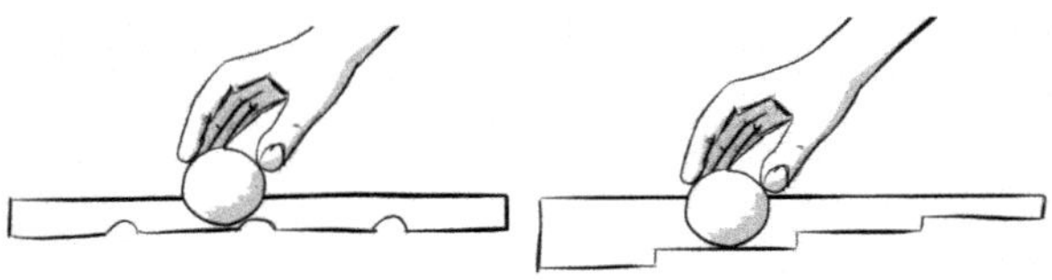

Figure 5: Slots with indentations and ramps can be used to guide the user's interaction or to provide haptic feedback.

Manipulate: Actuating Objects with Shape Displays
Shape displays can appropriate passive objects by independently actuating and manipulating them to create dynamic affordances and constraints. This way, passive objects can be augmented with dynamic capabilities, expanding their possible use as tangible tokens or tools that represent program state or other functionality.

The shape display can apply mechanical force to an object and cause it to move in a variety of ways. This greatly expands opportunities for interaction, and inter-material interaction, as well as solving a problem inherent in passive tangible systems: keeping tokens' physical state synchronized with the digital state. Additionally, it allows the shape display to output greater degrees of freedom (e.g., lateral movement), and enables greater degrees of freedom afforded to the user for input. Our techniques for actuating passive objects do not require an active or special material (such as magnets), but instead manipulate geometrical shapes, with the limitation that certain geometries (such as a ball) are easier to move than others. Other factors to consider include the mass of the object, the force of the motors, and the friction between the shape display surface and the passive object.

Manipulating Objects on the Surface through Actuation
Any object can be lifted vertically by the system as long as the actuation force is sufficient (1.08 N/actuator for inFORM). Objects placed on the table can also be tilted to lean in one direction, with computational control of tilt angle and orientation. This can be used, for example, to orient an object's surface towards a user.

In addition to lifting and tilting, objects can be translated on the X-Y surface through three techniques. Firstly, objects can be lifted and caused to slide or roll down an inclined plane rendered by the surface, essentially using gravity to cause it to move (see Figures 1 and 9). Secondly, given the right shape, the vertical actuator movement can push an object sideways or induce rolling (see Figure 6). This works by applying a force on the object offset from its center of mass, inducing a moment on the object, either causing it to roll or slide out of the way. This actuation method works best for objects with angled or rounded features, like spheres, cones and cylinders. To ensure overlap with at least four pins at a time, our current system actuates spherical objects of at least 25.4 mm diameter. Thirdly, tilt can be used for controlled tumbling of objects about the X- or Y-axis, by alternating tilting and catching, to move the object on the surface. Tumbling works well for cubes or other angular geometry. These different techniques have varying levels of legibility to the user—the inclined plane, for example, makes it clear where the ball will move.

Objects can also be rotated about the surface's Z-axis through similar techniques as used for X-Y translation. Currently only certain objects, with conical or rectangular shapes can be rotated. However, a simple surface feature to allow locking an object at an anchor point could allow for rotation through the aforementioned methods of pushing-induced sliding.

In-air movement through Ballistics
Objects can be projected ballistically from the table into air. The use of multiple pins allows the launch angle to be computationally controlled. With sufficient tracking, the object could also be smoothly caught to dampen impact and avoid subsequent bounces. Currently, we are able to launch a 7 g ball with 20 mm diameter, approximately 80 mm above the maximum pin height of the surface.

Figure 6: inFORM can lift, translate, tilt, or rotate objects on the surface by changing the surface geometry. Here, a ball is moved on the surface.

Vibrations for Haptic Feedback or Attention
Vibrations by the actuators underneath an object can cause the object to shake. This can provide haptic feedback or draw attention to that object.

User Interaction with Actuated Objects
Similar to PICO [32], users can physically stop the interface from actuating objects by lifting them or holding them in one position. This can be used to control interface behavior of moving parts. In addition, users can place static physical barriers on the table to prevent tokens from moving. These objects can be of arbitrary shape or make use of the space inbetween the actuators. An example is a wall barrier made from a cardboard sheet, or a cup that is placed over an object to prevent it from being moved. The constraints defined by the shape display surface could also be user defined, for instance, by deforming the shapes directly with bare hands.

Parameter space
The physical properties of a UI element strongly influence its perceived and real affordances. In his definition of affordances, Gibson [10] lists a number of such properties: "When the constant properties of constant objects are perceived (the shape, size, color, texture, composition, motion, animation, and position relative to other objects), the observer can go on to detect their affordances." This definition includes dynamic parameters like motion and animation, which static TUIs do not possess as real affordances. Shape-changing interfaces, on the other hand, have the ability to add such parameters, and can be categorized as changes in orientation, form, volume, texture, viscosity, spatiality, adding/subtracting, and permeability [34].

We find it attractive to utilize 2.5D shapes display to render physical affordances, as their hardware capabilities enable simultaneous control over multiple parameters. In the following list, we identify parameters that both contribute to affordances and can be dynamically controlled by inFORM.

Shape: The shape of UI elements can provide multiple affordances, real affordances (how the shape can be touched), and cultural affordances (what the shape represents). Their quality and expressiveness is tightly coupled to the possible resolution and degrees of freedom [25]. This creates interesting interface design challenges that must be considered, in particular, for 2.5D shape display hardware.

Size: The size of a UI element is constrained by the user's physiology and available space. It has to be sufficiently large for the user to manipulate, while also small enough to fit in the interface. While static physical UIs have to compromise between these two factors, dynamically resizing UI elements can enable better ergonomics and use of space, given that they can provide sufficiently smooth and continuous transitions at their spatial and temporal resolution.

Position and Orientation: The spatial relationship between objects is an important parameter for TUIs. While these can be dynamically modified, users cannot easily grasp, lift and rearrange objects on 2.5D shape displays. Therefore, we propose to complement them with passive physical tokens that enable these interactions, while they can also be constrained and actuated by the display surface shape.

Color: Color and visual texture can be applied to provide additional graphical perceived affordances, using embedded display [33], projection [25], or augmented reality [24].

Haptic feedback: The material and haptic feedback of an element communicates to the user if it affords actions like deformation. Systems with mechanical actuation can provide haptic feedback by dynamically changing the resistance of a pin when pressed by the user.

Visibility: By rapidly changing the size of a dynamically rendered element, it can appear and disappear. An advantage compared to static systems is that physical objects can be rendered in succession, rather than having to permanently share valuable space. The rate of change is hardware dependent.

Motion: Motion describes the change of the above parameters over time. While motion to switch between predefined static affordances has been explored previously [12], carefully choreographed motion adds a compelling dimension to the interaction. If the UI element transforms continuously as the user interacts with it, the motion itself turns into an expressive affordance. The quality of motion in the context of HCI has previously been described by the path, volume, direction, and velocity of an object [39].

DEMONSTRATION APPLICATIONS

3D Model Manipulation (handles, constraints, context)
The 3D Model Manipulation application demonstrates how the inFORM system's dynamic capabilities can be used to render physical representations of 3D models that the user can flip through, and then use tokens and tools to transform, edit or paint (see Figure 7).

Users move a token through a slot to browse the different 3D models (Figure 1) and can select it by placing the token in an adjacent well (Figure 7a). When the token is placed in the well, it transforms into a slot. Moving the token to any end of the slot will select the function of the token; rotation, translation or scale. The slot transforms again to represent the degrees of freedom of the current mode. In rotation mode, the slot is a circle circumscribing the model (Figure 7c), scale mode uses a linear slot (Figure 7b), while translation mode has no constraints. As the token is moved in these constraints, the object dynamically transforms. To exit the current mode, the user places the token in the *select well*.

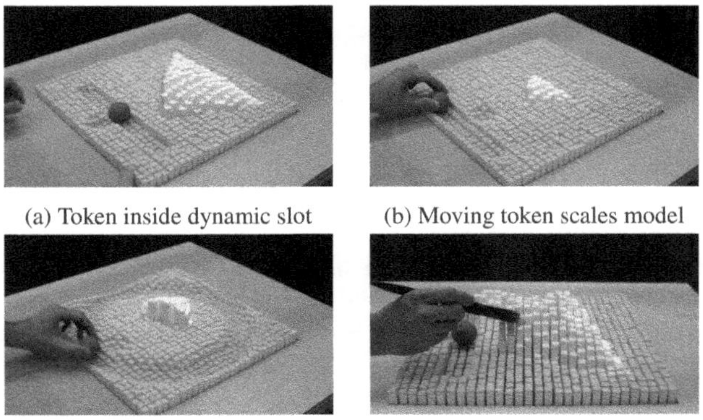

(a) Token inside dynamic slot (b) Moving token scales model (c) Rotation in circular slot (d) Painting geometry with tool

Figure 7: The 3D Model Manipulation application uses tokens and tools to browse, transform and edit physical representations of 3D models.

The user can also use a 3D brush tool to add geometry, erase geometry, or paint on the 3D model, as shown in Figure 7d. To change modes for the brush, the user presses a foot pedal to activate a context menu which is rendered physically as a 2D Dynamic Affordance. The menu appears offset from the current location of the brush in 3D space, allowing for quick selection. The bristles of the brush move smoothly over the shape display surface, while being optically tracked by the system.

Marble Answering Machine

The Marble Answering Machine [6], is a tangible interface to receive, store and play back voice messages that are represented as physical marbles. Its iconic form, sketched by Durrell Bishop, is a continuous surface with a raised hill and a hole in it. Our homage to the original design, implemented with the inFORM system, uses a dynamically changeable form, and demonstrates how Dynamic Physical Constraints transform to reflect changing program states (Figure 8).

New messages are represented by marbles, which are ejected from the hole (Figure 8b) to roll into a newly formed well that stores messages (Figure 8c). To listen to a message, users pick up a marble from the *new message well* and place it inside the *play well* (Figure 8d). The play well transforms into a slot, and as the message is played back, the marble is moved inside the slot, representing its relative playback position. At any given time, users can pick up the marble to stop the message, or scrub it in the playback slot to replay parts of the message. Once the message is played, the machine moves the marble to the *old message well*. Dropping the marble back into the hole on top of the machine erases it.

This system demonstrates the ability to render both aesthetic form and UI elements. In addition, it highlights the ability for the user to directly intervene while an object is being actuated. In the spirit of PICO [32], the user can also introduce mechanical constraints to control computational behavior. By placing a rigid sheet in the path of the playback track, the user can limit message playback to the beginning of the audio file.

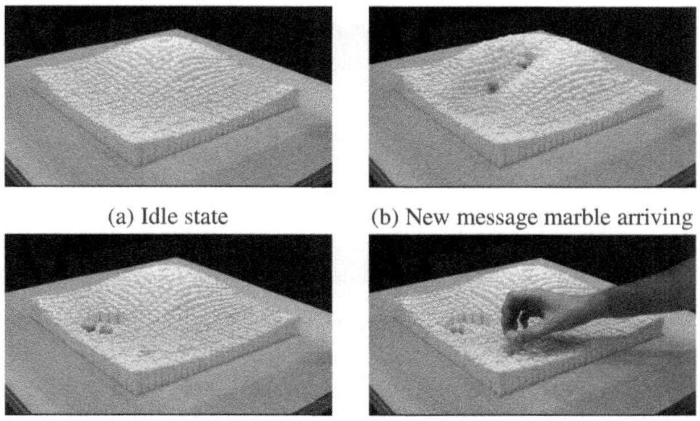

(a) Idle state (b) New message marble arriving (c) New messages in well (d) Moving marble to *play well*

Figure 8: inFORM's version of the Marble Answering Machine uses dynamic shape and constraints to reflect program state.

Actuating Interactive Devices on the Surface

Beyond passive tokens, we can also actuate interactive devices, such as phones or tablets. Such devices can be similarly moved, tilted, rotated, and vibrated. A smartphone could, for example, be tilted towards the user upon a phone call or alert (see Figure 9), or to preserve privacy in a collaborative session when private information should not be seen by others.

Figure 9: inFORM can actuate devices, for example, by sliding and tilting a tablet towards the user.

The dynamic capabilities of inFORM could be used to render physical UI elements on-demand, for example, by having physical buttons and touch elements emerge when a tablet is placed on the surface. These UI elements provide physical affordances for applications on the tablet. Vibration and haptic feedback could be used to augment gameplay, for instance.

IMPLEMENTATION

Shape Display

The system uses 30×30 motorized white polystyrene pins, in a 381×381 mm area. The pins have a 9.525 mm^2 footprint, with 3.175 mm inter-pin spacing, and can extend up to 100 mm from the surface. Push-Pull rods are used to link each pin with an actuator, to enable a dense pin arrangement independent of actuator size, giving the system a height of 1100 mm. The linkage, a nylon rod inside a plastic housing (Sullivan Gold-N-Rods), transmits bi-directional force from a motorized slide potentiometer (ALPS RSA0N11M9A07), through a bend. Six slide potentiometers are mounted onto a custom-designed PCB, powered by an Atmel ATMega 2560, and TB6612FNGCT-ND motor drivers. The linear positions are read by the 10-bit A/D converters on the microcontroller, and allow for user input, in addition to servoing their position using PID control.

150 boards are arranged in 15 rows of vertical panels, each with 5×2 boards. The boards communicate with a PC over five RS485 buses bridged to USB. The system has a 60 Hz refresh rate, determined by the 115200 bps RS485 bus speed, the 8 byte control message, and 30 boards on each RS485 bus.

For each pin, we can update both position and PID terms to provide haptic feedback and variable stiffness, for example, to create haptic detents or buttons that are harder to press. This control also allows us to limit power consumption per pin to avoid burning out the motors.

Pin height and stiffness is represented in software as an 8-bit height map, which can be produced by OpenGL shaders, through different shape primitive classes, or by directly writing data. The height map is then sent to the microcontrollers. Similarly, all 900 pin heights can be received over the RS485 bus, and used to track user's surface deformations as input.

Each pin can exert a force of 1.08 Newtons (equivalent to 100 g weight), which was measured using a precision digital scale. The effective average upwards and downwards speeds (0.644 m/s and 0.968 m/s, respectively) were measured using a high speed camera.

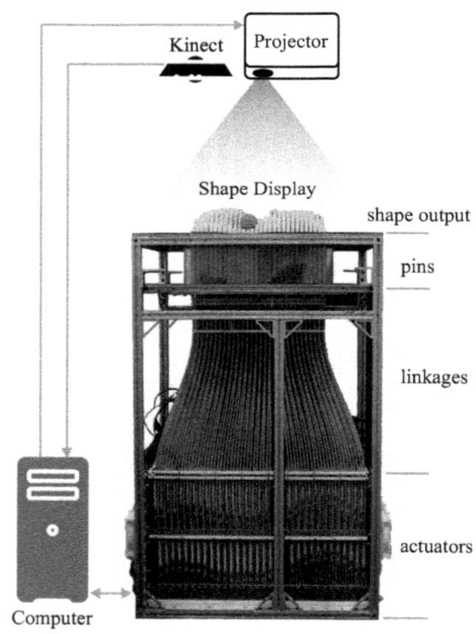

Figure 10: The inFORM system actuates and detects shape change with 900 mechanical actuators, while user interaction and objects are tracked with an overhead depth camera. A projector provides visual feedback.

In theory, the system's 900 pins could consume up to 2700 W due to a peak 3 W power consumption per actuator. In practice, however, we measure the effect to approximately 700 W when in motion. Due to friction, the pins maintain their static position unpowered. Therefore, the power consumption to maintain a shape is less than 300 W (mainly due to the 83 % efficiency of our 12 V power supplies). Heat dissipation remains a critical design criteria for the actuation assembly and we use two rows of five 120 mm fans to cool the actuators.

User and Object Tracking

Our current system uses an overhead depth camera to track users' hands and surface objects, as shown in Figure 10. A Microsoft Kinect with a 640×480 pixel depth sensor is mounted 1200 mm above the surface and calibrated for extrinsic and intrinsic camera parameters. We combine a static background image of the table surface with the surface's real-time height map to form a dynamic background image that is used for subtraction and segmentation. The height map is scaled and a homography is applied to warp the image into camera space. We find all pixels above the computed dynamic background model, and threshold the image. For hand and fingertip tracking, we use OpenCV to compute contours of the threshold image, followed by convex hull and convexity defects. The 3D finger tip coordinates are transformed to surface space, and an arbitrary number of finger tip contacts can be tracked and detected to trigger touch events. For object tracking, we currently rely on color tracking in the HSV space. However, other approaches to object tracking would be straightforward to implement. Objects and finger positions are tracked at 2 mm resolution in the 2D surface plane, and at 10 mm in height. The touch tracking can be combined with input from the slide potentiometers to, for example, distinguish button presses from light touch.

Graphics and Projection

Graphics are rendered using OpenGL and openFrameworks. The projector's world coordinates were determined after calibration with the Kinect color camera, while distortion coefficients and intrinsic parameters were recovered using ProCamCalib [1]. The projector's 1400×1050 pixel output is then warped to correct for the parameters and projected over an 87×66 cm area.

Limitations

As an alternative to the limited depth camera touch tracking, it may be interesting to embed touch sensors, e.g., capacitive or optical, directly in the pins. More sophisticated object tracking, for example, using multiple cameras, markers, or sensing in the electromagnetic or RF domain, could be used to address user occlusion, object identification, and color interference with projector.

The limited scalability due to the current architecture with one actuator per pin, has significant implications on cost and footprint to move beyond the current relatively low resolution. Also, the current implementation is limited to 1D input and output for each pin, which would be difficult to increase without significantly increasing complexity. While stiffness can be controlled, pin shape, spacing and material choices limit the affordances and constraints that the system can generate and how they interact with external objects. We, however, believe that the system's spacing, resolution and the interactive speeds rendered, are sufficient to allow the prototyping of many interactions that would be challenging on other existing shape displays. The current cost and scale of our shape display hardware limits its primarily use to research.

DISCUSSION AND FUTURE WORK

Shape displays allow for new ways to create physical interfaces, beyond functionality alone. Aesthetic form is an important part of many of the devices and objects that we interact with on a daily basis. Shape displays begin to let interface designers create radically different physical forms for different applications. The Marble Answering Machine example points towards this type of use, where form is more than functional; it is also evocative and emotional. This introduces an opportunity for physical motion design. It also points towards uses of shape displays for prototyping new physical interfaces.

While we have yet to perform a formal quantitative user evaluation, the system has been used by roughly 50 people and we have collected qualitative feedback from these encounters. Users tried the 3D Model Manipulation application and an example program to move passive objects on the surface autonomously. Initial feedback was generally very positive, with users commenting on the advantages of having physical UI elements appear and transform on demand, as well as expressing general delight with the autonomous movement of passive objects on the table. However, we observed that in the 3D Model Manipulation application, users sometimes struggled with physically overlapping content and UI elements. While we believe the main reasons to be the limited resolution of the shape display hardware and the software not adapting well to content changes, solving the physical overlap of content and interface elements rendered both as shapes is a very interesting new challenge of such interfaces.

We also noticed on multiple occasions how rapid shape transitions were jarring to users, an observation we have made in earlier studies as well [24]. The question remains how to best communicate shape transitions to the user before they occur, to avoid surprise. We see this question as an important next step for research on shape displays. One potential solution is for smooth, slow transitions, that can be explored calmly, as in Lumen [33].

Smooth transitions may not suffice to adequately inform the user; possibilities for shape change may need to be more legible. As Gaver explains: "Affordances are not passively perceived, but explored" [9] and we must find a way for these new affordances to gracefully be explored, potentially by more tightly coupling their motion to the motion of the user. We think this is a rich area for future exploration. For example, it can be viewed as a feedforward problem [40]. Or, one potential direction to explore legibility for potential shape change could be to combine shape change with augmented reality, similar to [24]. More theoretically, considering the shape display as an autonomous agent, may suggest looking towards research in human—robot interaction, where robots may want to convey to the user how they will move through more subtle means.

Along these lines, the legibility of how a passive object will move on the table is of interest. We described two ways to move a ball on the shape display surface: pushing the ball or rolling it down a slope. Rolling down a slope is much more legible to the user; toy marble runs are very legible, because the marble only has one path and the user can easily follow its trajectory, which is powered only by gravity. A designer, using the inFORM system, can make a ball's trajectory more legible by creating a slot that it will move in. But, such features for legibility alone may take up space and not scale well. New interaction techniques can be explored to address this legibility.

We believe that the *facilitate*, *restrict* and *manipulate* techniques described here are merely one part of a larger space of Dynamic Physical Affordances, which will emerge as shape-changing UIs mature. The Dynamic Physical Affordances in this paper focus on affordances rendered on a 2.5D surface. However, it is interesting to look at the larger space of possibilities for actuation and shape change: the user, the tool handle, tool, object, and physical surface must be considered. In this work, we have focused on dynamically changing the physical surface, but these other areas and their combinations provide many interesting possibilities for new interactions. For example, a tool can change shape as the interaction surfaces change shape as well. It is at these intersections between different materials and different interaction elements where shape change and actuation begin to open new opportunities for human—computer interaction. This suggests the importance of considering the whole ecology of interaction and interactive devices. We believe that proxemic interaction for shape-changing UIs is another important area to explore, as well as multi-user collaboration, co-located and remote.

CONCLUSIONS

In this work we have explored the design space of Dynamic Physical Affordances and Constraints, and described methods for actuating physical objects on actuated shape displays. Many prior approaches to shape-changing user interfaces have relied on special-purpose or bistable shape change. Instead, we explored dynamic shape change's more general-purpose role, similar to the flexibility of a bitmap screen for GUIs. This opens possibilities for using shape change both for content and as a UI elements. Dynamic Physical Affordances and Constraints encompass a large space of features that we hope will inspire designers when creating shape-changing interfaces.

ACKNOWLEDGMENTS

We thank Ryan Wistort, Guangtao Zhang, Cheetiri Smith, Alyx Daly, Pat Capaloung and Jason Moran for work on inFORM hardware, and Mark Feldmeier for advice. This research was supported in part by the National Science Foundation Graduate Research Fellowship under Grant No. 1122374. Alex Olwal was supported by a Swedish Research Council Fellowship and a Blanceflor Foundation Scholarship.

REFERENCES

1. Audet, S., and Okutomi, M. A user-friendly method to geometrically calibrate projector-camera systems. In *IEEE CVPR 2009* (2009), 47–54.

2. Bau, O., Petrevski, U., and Mackay, W. Bubblewrap: a textile-based electromagnetic haptic display. In *CHI EA '09*, ACM (2009), 3607–3612.
3. Bier, E. A., Stone, M. C., Pier, K., Buxton, W., and DeRose, T. D. Toolglass and magic lenses: the see-through interface. In *SIGGRAPH '93*, ACM (1993), 73–80.
4. Ciesla, C. M., and Yairi, M. B. User interface system and method, 07 2009.
5. Coelho, M., and Zigelbaum, J. Shape-changing interfaces. *Personal Ubiquitous Comput. 15*, 2 (Feb. 2011), 161–173.
6. Crampton Smith, G. The hand that rocks the cradle. *ID magazine* (1995), 60–65.
7. Fitzmaurice, G. W., Ishii, H., and Buxton, W. A. S. Bricks: laying the foundations for graspable user interfaces. In *CHI '95*, ACM Press/Addison-Wesley Publishing Co. (1995), 442–449.
8. Follmer, S., Leithinger, D., Olwal, A., Cheng, N., and Ishii, H. Jamming user interfaces: programmable particle stiffness and sensing for malleable and shape-changing devices. In *UIST '12*, ACM (2012), 519–528.
9. Gaver, W. W. Technology affordances. In *CHI '91*, ACM (1991), 79–84.
10. Gibson, J. J. *The Senses Considered as Perceptual Systems*. Houghton Mifflin Co., 1966.
11. Gibson, J. J. *The ecological approach to visual perception*. Psychology Press, 1986.
12. Harrison, C., and Hudson, S. E. Providing dynamically changeable physical buttons on a visual display. In *CHI '09*, ACM (2009), 299–308.
13. Hartson, R. Cognitive, physical, sensory, and functional affordances in interaction design. *Behaviour & Information Technology 22*, 5 (2003), 315–338.
14. Hemmert, F., Hamann, S., Lwe, M., Wohlauf, A., Zeipelt, J., and Joost, G. Take me by the hand: Haptic compasses in mobile devices through shape change and weight shift. In *NordiCHI '10* (2010).
15. Ishii, H. Tangible bits: beyond pixels. In *TEI '08*, ACM (2008), xv–xxv.
16. Ishii, H., Lakatos, D., Bonanni, L., and Labrune, J.-B. Radical atoms: beyond tangible bits, toward transformable materials. *interactions 19*, 1 (Jan. 2012), 38–51.
17. Ishii, H., and Ullmer, B. Tangible bits: towards seamless interfaces between people, bits and atoms. In *CHI '97*, ACM (1997), 234–241.
18. Iwata, H., Yano, H., Nakaizumi, F., and Kawamura, R. Project feelex: adding haptic surface to graphics. In *SIGGRAPH '01*, ACM (2001), 469–476.
19. Jansen, Y., Karrer, T., and Borchers, J. Mudpad: tactile feedback and haptic texture overlay for touch surfaces. In *ITS '10*, ACM (2010), 11–14.
20. Kaptelinin, V., and Nardi, B. Affordances in hci: toward a mediated action perspective. In *CHI '12*, ACM (2012), 967–976.
21. Klemmer, S. R., Hartmann, B., and Takayama, L. How bodies matter: five themes for interaction design. In *DIS '06*, ACM (2006), 140–149.
22. KOJIMA, M., SUGIMOTO, M., NAKAMURA, A., TOMITA, M., INAMI, M., and NII, H. Augmented coliseum: An augmented game environment with small vehicles. In *TABLETOP '06*, IEEE Computer Society (2006), 3–8.
23. Lee, N., Kim, J., Lee, J., Shin, M., and Lee, W. Molebot: mole in a table. In *SIGGRAPH '11*, ACM (2011), 9:1–9:1.
24. Leithinger, D., Follmer, S., Olwal, A., Luescher, S., Hogge, A., Lee, J., and Ishii, H. Sublimate: State-changing virtual and physical rendering to augment interaction with shape displays. In *CHI '13* (2013).
25. Leithinger, D., Lakatos, D., DeVincenzi, A., Blackshaw, M., and Ishii, H. Direct and gestural interaction with relief: a 2.5d shape display. In *UIST '11*, ACM (2011), 541–548.
26. Macknik, S. L., King, M., Randi, J., Robbins, A., et al. Attention and awareness in stage magic: turning tricks into research. *Nature Reviews Neuroscience 9*, 11 (2008), 871–879.
27. MacLean, K. E., Snibbe, S. S., and Levin, G. Tagged handles: merging discrete and continuous manual control. In *CHI '00*, ACM (2000), 225–232.
28. McGuffin, M., and Balakrishnan, R. Acquisition of expanding targets. In *CHI '02*, ACM (2002), 57–64.
29. Michelitsch, G., Williams, J., Osen, M., Jimenez, B., and Rapp, S. Haptic chameleon: a new concept of shape-changing user interface controls with force feedback. In *CHI '04 Extended Abstracts on Human Factors in Computing Systems*, CHI EA '04, ACM (New York, NY, USA, 2004), 1305–1308.
30. Norman, D. A. *The Psychology of Everyday Things*. Basic Books, Inc., 1988.
31. Pangaro, G., Maynes-Aminzade, D., and Ishii, H. The actuated workbench: computer-controlled actuation in tabletop tangible interfaces. In *UIST '02*, ACM (2002), 181–190.
32. Patten, J., and Ishii, H. Mechanical constraints as computational constraints in tabletop tangible interfaces. In *CHI '07*, ACM (2007), 809–818.
33. Poupyrev, I., Nashida, T., and Okabe, M. Actuation and tangible user interfaces: the vaucanson duck, robots, and shape displays. In *TEI '07*, ACM (2007), 205–212.
34. Rasmussen, M. K., Pedersen, E. W., Petersen, M. G., and Hornbaek, K. Shape-changing interfaces: a review of the design space and open research questions. In *CHI '12*, ACM (2012), 735–744.
35. Rekimoto, J., Ullmer, B., and Oba, H. Datatiles: a modular platform for mixed physical and graphical interactions. In *CHI '01*, ACM (2001), 269–276.
36. Reznik, D., and Canny, J. A flat rigid plate is a universal planar manipulator. In *IEEE ICRA 1998*, vol. 2, IEEE (1998), 1471–1477.
37. Salisbury, K., Conti, F., and Barbagli, F. Haptic rendering: introductory concepts. *Computer Graphics and Applications, IEEE 24*, 2 (2004), 24–32.
38. Ullmer, B., Ishii, H., and Jacob, R. J. K. Token+constraint systems for tangible interaction with digital information. *ACM Trans. Comput.-Hum. Interact. 12*, 1 (Mar. 2005), 81–118.
39. Vaughan, L. C. Understanding movement. In *CHI '97*, ACM (1997), 548–549.
40. Vermeulen, J., Luyten, K., van den Hoven, E., and Coninx, K. Crossing the bridge over norman's gulf of execution: revealing feedforward's true identity. In *CHI '13*, ACM (2013), 1931–1940.
41. Weiss, M., Remy, C., and Borchers, J. Rendering physical effects in tabletop controls. In *CHI '11*, ACM (2011), 3009–3012.
42. Weiss, M., Schwarz, F., Jakubowski, S., and Borchers, J. Madgets: actuating widgets on interactive tabletops. In *UIST '10*, ACM (2010), 293–302.
43. Weiss, M., Wacharamanotham, C., Voelker, S., and Borchers, J. Fingerflux: near-surface haptic feedback on tabletops. In *UIST '11*, ACM (2011), 615–620.
44. Weiss, M., Wagner, J., Jansen, Y., Jennings, R., Khoshabeh, R., Hollan, J. D., and Borchers, J. Slap widgets: bridging the gap between virtual and physical controls on tabletops. In *CHI '09*, ACM (2009), 481–490.

Traxion: A Tactile Interaction Device with Virtual Force Sensation

Jun Rekimoto
Interfaculty Initiative in Information Studies, The University of Tokyo
7-3-1 Hongo, Bunkyo-ku, Tokyo 113-033, Japan
Sony Computer Science Laboratories, Inc.
3-14-13 Higashigotanda, Shinagawa-ku, Tokyo 141-0022, Japan
rekimoto@acm.org

ABSTRACT
This paper introduces a new mechanism to induce a virtual force based on human illusory sensations. An asymmetric signal is applied to a tactile actuator consisting of an electromagnetic coil, a metal weight, and a spring, such that the user feels that the device is being pulled (or pushed) in a particular direction, although it is not supported by any mechanical connection to other objects or the ground. The proposed tactile device is smaller (35.0 mm × 5.0 mm × 7.5 mm) and lighter (5.2 g) than any previous force-feedback devices, which have to be connected to the ground with mechanical links. This small form factor allows the device to be implemented in several novel interactive applications, such as a pedestrian guide system that includes a finger-mounted tactile device or an (untethered) input device that features virtual force. Our experimental results indicate that this illusory sensation actually exists and the proposed device can switch the virtual force direction within a short period. We combined this new technology with visible light transmission via a digital micromirror device (DMD) projector and developed a position guiding input device with force perception.

Author Keywords
Input devices; tactile interactions; force feedback; perception; illusion

ACM Classification Keywords
H.5.2. Information Interfaces and Presentation (e.g. HCI): User Interfaces

General Terms
Input devices; Tactile interactions; Illusion

INTRODUCTION
Haptic sensations play a very important role in our daily life. The sense of touch enables us to physically manipulate an object smoothly, rapidly, and accurately. We naturally and extensively use this sense every day during moments of physical interaction. Several systems have been proposed for incorporating haptic feedback into human-computer interactions. While normal graphical user interfaces (GUIs) rely mainly on visual information, these systems use synthetic haptic sensations as one facet of human-computer interaction.

There are two types of haptic feedback. In one type, which we call "force-feedback," a real-world physical force is created. Devices belonging to this category often use mechanical rods [8, 10], motor-controlled strings [6], or other physical mechanisms. In the second type, called "tactile-display," physical sensations are created as an additional feedback method. Examples of devices in this category include mice or gamepads with vibrators and touch panels with an actuator that adds a tactile "click" feeling to an interaction [5, 12]. Both types have their own advantages and disadvantages. Force-feedback type devices normally require a mechanical component linked to heavier objects, or to the ground. Its working space is therefore limited, and because of its bulkiness, mobile use is not practical. In contrast, tactile-display devices can be smaller and lighter, but they can create only a vibration, not a force.

There have been a few previous attempts to create force without using mechanical support. We can feel a force when trying to rotate a friction wheel because of a "gyro" effect. Nakamura et al. combined two or three eccentrically weighted rotors to generate an illusory sensation of force [14, 11, 4]. Amemiya et al. also proposed a device that creates a perceptual attraction force, based on the asymmetric actuation of a mechanical weight [2, 3]. These devices are based on the asymmetry of the relationship between stimulation and perception in the human. When people use such a device, they can perceive a traction force, although there are no mechanical links between the device and other objects. However, since these devices are based on the mechanical movement of a crank, the form factor of the device is much bigger and heavier than those of tactile displays. For example, the size of the prototype device that Amemiya developed is 70 mm × 200 mm × 48 mm, its weight is 250 g, and it consumes about 30 W [2] of power for one-dimensional (1D) traction synthesis. If two or more of these devices were combined to create a two- or three-dimensional (2D or 3D) traction force, it would become even bigger and heavier.

UIST'13, October 6–9, 2013, St. Andrews, United Kingdom.
Copyright © 2013 ACM 978-1-4503-2271-3/13/10...$15.00.
http://dx.doi.org/10.1145/2501988.2502044

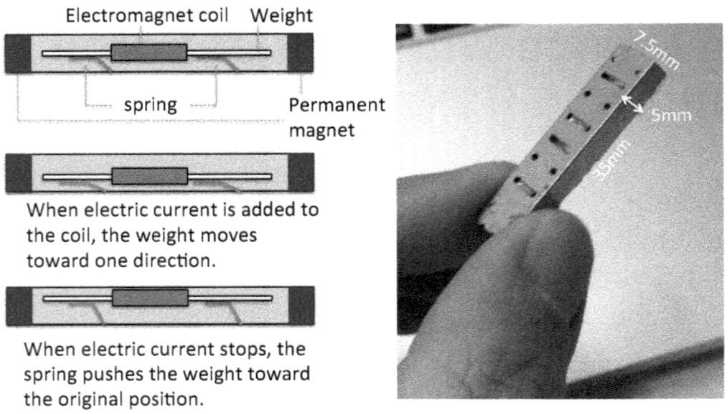

Figure 1. Configuration of the "force-reactor" tactile device

In this paper, we propose a novel device that creates a virtual force without any mechanical links to the ground being required. Furthermore, it is significantly smaller and lighter than any previous virtual force devices. Our proposed mechanism uses human illusory sensation to create the perception of a virtual force. The weight of our virtual force creation device is about 5.2 g and the size is 7.5 mm × 35.0 mm × 5.0 mm. This small form factor allows the development of several new applications using virtual force. For example, a user can be guided to a particular location by being virtually "pulled" by a device in which it is implemented. We named this tactile architecture "traxion."

TRAXION OPERATION PRINCIPLE

Traxion is a combination of an existing tactile actuator and a novel way to actuate it. We currently use an ALPS "force-reactor" [1] as the tactile actuator. This component has a structure in which electromagnet coils are attached to a metal sheet supported by a spring (Figure 1). The metal sheet is placed between two permanent magnets. When a wave signal is transmitted to the coils, the metal sheet responds to it by vibrating. After the signal stops, this vibration is suspended by the spring and the magnets within 50 ms. This short suspension time contributes to the accuracy and crispness of the tactile sensation.

While this device is effective as a tactile display, normally it does not create a force. However, we found that when an asymmetric signal is transmitted to the coils, it causes a virtual force such that the user feels as if an invisible force is pulling the device in a particular direction, or pushing it in the opposite direction. In this case, the current is applied to the electromagnet for a short period (e.g., 2 ms) to move the weight in one direction, and then is suspended. When the weight returns to the original position (which takes around 6 ms), the current is applied to the electromagnet again and the process is repeated. As a result, the movement of the weight becomes asymmetric, i.e., the movement caused by the electromagnet is fast, and the movement caused by the spring is slow. We experimented with various asymmetric signal patterns that can create a virtual force in two opposite directions. We consider that a human feels this virtual force because of the non-linearity of human force perception: the difference in the accelerations in the movement of the weight caused by the electromagnetic coils and by the spring is not offset. Thus, the user feels a (virtual) force in one direction. By changing the duty ratio of the signal, the user can also feel a force in the opposite direction. We currently use 2 ms (ON) and 8 ms (OFF) cycle for producing a virtual force.

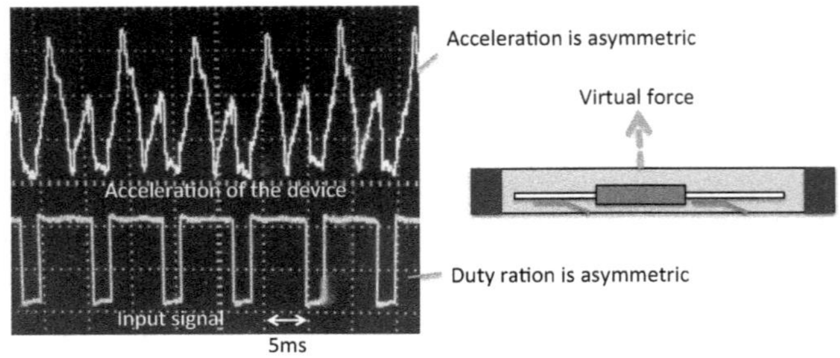

Figure 2. Operation principle of Traxion: Asymmetric electric current is added to the coil in the actuator.

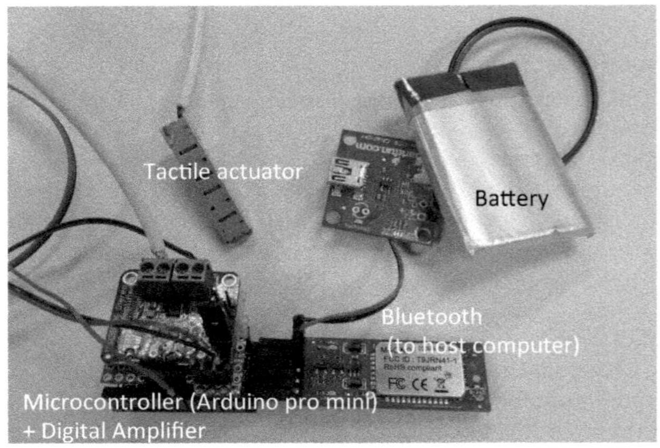

Figure 3. Traxion system configuration: the digital amplifier unit connected to Arduino microcontroller board creates a signal to drive a tactile device.

Since there is no mechanical component that connects the device to the ground, there is obviously no actual force; instead, there is a sensory illusion of force that the user perceives. A possible explanation for this illusion is based on the nonlinearity of human tactile sensation. As described above, the weight is moved asymmetrically by carefully controlling the ratio of the actuation signal. We assume that this asymmetric vibration causes the human sensory illusion that the object is being pulled in a particular direction.

We also found that the direction of the virtual forces, i.e., the pull force and the push force, can be changed by controlling the ratio of the electric current. This makes it possible to construct a tactile interaction device that pulls people in two directions (i.e., a bidirectional 1D virtual force device).

System configuration

The configuration of an actual virtual force-inducing system is shown in Figure 3. A microcontroller board (Arduino [9]) is connected to a digital amplifier unit that drives tactile actuators. The communication between the microcontroller and the host computer is transmitted by either a wired (i.e., USB serial) or wireless (Bluetooth serial) connection.

Comparison with previous virtual force devices

Since Amemiya et al. and Nakamura et al.'s devices also create virtual force based on human illusory sensation, it is necessary here to discuss the difference between their device and ours. The major difference is in the structure of the device. Earlier devices used a mechanical crank or rotating wheels, the size and weight of which were much larger than those of our device. In contrast, the smallness of our device allows several potential configurations, such as a finger-mounted navigation device or a tablet stylus with virtual force. In addition, the movement of the mechanical crank created an undesired vibration that masked the intended vibration to create force, and the wheel rotation created a moment effect that also caused an unintended force. Therefore, Amemiya et al. had to construct a "tandem" version in which two symmetric components were embedded to offset this undesired motion; however, the device then became even bigger and heavier.

When a mechanical wheel and cranks are used, it is also difficult to change the rotation direction (i.e., to change the direction of a virtual force) in a short period. Thus, in practice, the device is a one-way force device. This limits the possibility of using this method for interactive applications. In contrast, our device can change the virtual traction direction in a very short period (less than 10 ms) and acts as a bidirectional force feedback device. Furthermore, the smallness of our device potentially allows two or more components to be combined to conform to a 2D or 3D force feedback device within a reasonable form factor.

EVALUATION

1D virtual force: To confirm that this virtual force effect actually exists, we conducted an evaluation. Ten subjects, all students in the computer science department, participated in this experiment. A subject held the device with two fingers and electric signals were transmitted to the device to create a virtual force. The (intended) direction of the virtual force was selected randomly. The durations of stimulations were 640 ms, 320 ms, 160 ms, 80 ms, and 40 ms, and the order of the duration was also randomized. The used duty cycle was 2 ms:6 ms thus a 40 ms stimulus consists of 5 cycles. The subjects participated in five trials for each duration, and the task was to indicate when they felt a force and its direction, using a game controller stick. To avoid any possible effect from aural or visual stimuli, participants were blindfolded with a sleep mask and wore noise-cancelling headphones (Figure 4 (left)).

The results are shown in Figure 4 (right). As shown in the graph, the illusory sensation actually exists, and participants could very accurately distinguish both virtual force directions, even when the duration of the stimuli was short.

In interviews held after the experiment, most participants insisted that when they moved the device in the direction of the induced virtual traction force, the perceived force was much stronger. To illustrate a possible explanation for this phenomenon, we present an example. Assume that a real force is added to an object that a participant is holding. When the participant moves the device toward that force, the perceived force should become weaker. For example, if an object is pulled by a spring, moving the object toward the spring reduces the perceived force. In contrast, when a participant feels a virtual force, the perceived force does not alter, even when the participant moves the object toward that force. Since they did not feel the expected reduction in force, the participants therefore inferred that the added force was *stronger* than before (meaning that the decrease in the perception of the force strength is offset by the increase in the added force).

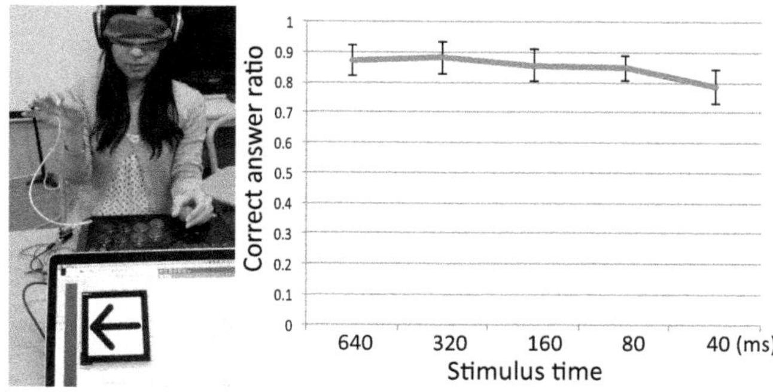

Figure 4. 1D virtual force experimental results.

Figure 5. Configuration of 2D force device.

2D virtual force: The experimental results demonstrated that our proposed tactile device can create a virtual force in two directions (i.e., 1D force feedback). We also examined the possibility of combining two devices to create a 2D virtual force device. Figure 5 shows the physical configuration of such a device. We transmitted two asymmetric signals to both the devices and evaluated how the synthetic force vector was perceived.

The same ten subjects participated in this experiment as in the previous experiment and were asked to hold the device with two fingers. This time, the task was to select which of eight possible force directions they sensed. The duration of each stimulation was fixed to 640 ms, and the same duty cycle (2 ms:6 ms) was used.

Figure 6 shows the results. As shown in the graph, the correct answer ratio of the perceived direction was not as good as that in the 1D experiment, although the ratio exceeds that of random guess. This means that just combining two actuators to create a merged force vector does not suffice to realize a virtual force in arbitrary directions. This issue needs to be studied further.

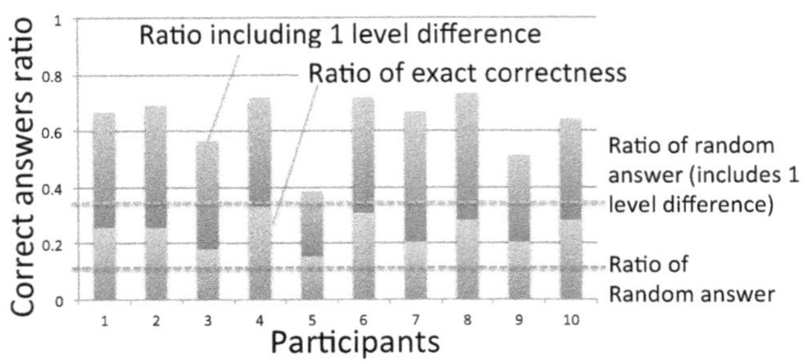

Figure 6. 2D virtual force experimental results.

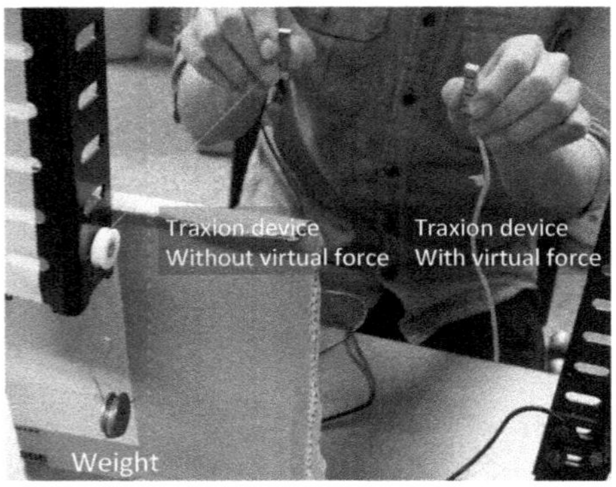

Figure 7. Estimation of virtual force strength

Estimation of virtual force strength

It should also be worthwhile to investigate the strength of the virtual force. First, as a pilot study, we designed an evaluation environment. In this experiment, a participant was asked to hold two Traxion devices, one in each hand. One device was arranged such that it induced a virtual force (using 2 ms:6 ms duty cycle), and the second device generated only a normal vibration (i.e., 5 ms:5 ms duty cycle); however, the latter device was connected to weights by a thin Nylon thread. Then, the participant was asked to compare the virtual and real force exerted by the weights (Figure 7).

The same 10 subjects participated in this experiment as in the previous ones. The average weight perceived as matching the virtual force was 29.8 g (0.292 N) and its standard deviation was 8.5 g (0.083 N).

APPLICATIONS

Virtual way finder: We feel that this device is adequate for guiding pedestrians, especially visually impaired people. By mounting the device on a user's finger, it is possible to guide the user when he or she has to turn to the left or right. We examined this possibility using the "Wizard-of-Oz" method, in which a blindfolded user with the device is guided by another user through tactile sensation (Figure 8(left)). When the pedestrian reaches the corner of a corridor, another user remotely turns on the actuator to guide the pedestrian in the intended direction.

Force-inducing input devices: Another possible application is to include virtual force in the construction of input devices. For example, a stylus for use on an interactive surface can feature force feedback without any mechanical link being used. Figure 8(right) shows such an input device. In this case, we also mounted a photo sensor and amplifier on the device to receive light from the projector.

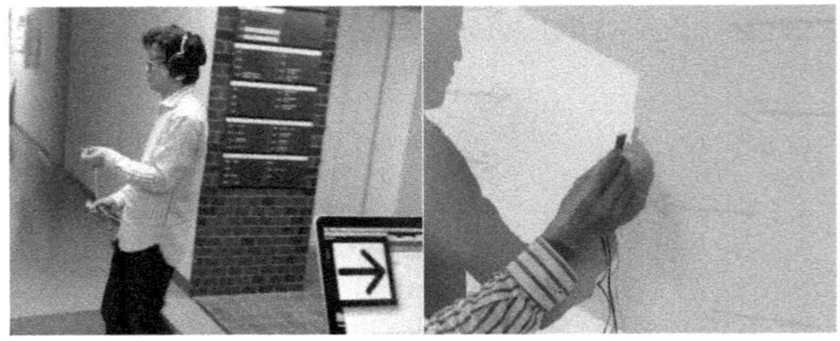

Figure 8. Traxion applications: (left) Pedestrian guide application.(right) "Virtual Force Field": An input device with virtual force feedback. A DMD projector emits a light pixel with a different temporal pattern according to its color. When the tactile device decodes this pattern and generates a virtual force accordingly, the user can feel this force.

A light projected from a DMD (digital micromirror device) projector has its own turn-on/turn-off pattern according to the color of the light. When a device can decode this pattern, and thus a virtual force is generated, it is possible to guide a user to a particular position on the screen [13] through the device. A user feels as if a virtual force is pushing or pulling the device, until it reaches to the correct position.

Although this prototype is preliminary, we consider that it is possible to develop various surface computing systems equipped with untethered force feedback input devices.

RELATED WORK

Tactile Direction Guide Systems: As discussed above, Amemiya et al. developed a virtual force feedback system based on a mechanical wheel and weight. Although this system essentially constitutes a one-way force feedback device, multiple devices can be combined to create a traction force that can be used for guiding a pedestrian [2, 3]. ActiveBelt is a tactile navigation system consisting of multiple vibrators attached to a belt [15]. When worn around the user's waist, the belt indicates a direction to the user by actuating the vibrator corresponding to the relevant direction. Our Traxion device can also indicate direction by inducing left and right virtual force to the user's finger.

Tactile Actuators: Many researchers and manufactures have developed touch panels with haptic feedback [5, 12]. We are currently using an ALPS force-reactor [1] as an actuator device, but it would be worthwhile to investigate how the asymmetric actuation of other types of tactile devices can create a virtual force, as we described in this paper. Another very different method of creating haptic sensations in free space has recently been developed [7]. This method is an extension of "spotlight audio," a technique for localizing or directionalizing audio signals using an array of transducers. In this method, a decrease in the signal frequency enables people to feel haptic sensations instead of hearing sound. Its main advantage is that no finger-mounted unit is required. Although this method is very interesting and has potential, the parameters, e.g., accuracy, sensing delay, and transducer-hand distance, that have currently been achieved are still not of a sufficiently high quality to allow realistic applications to be created.

CONCLUSIONS AND FUTURE WORK

In this paper, we proposed a tactile device that can create virtual force feedback based on human illusory sensations. Although no real force exists, users perceive that the device is pulled (or pushed) in the direction intended by the system. Since the form factor of this tactile device is smaller and lighter than that of any other previously proposed devices, it creates the possibility of developing mobile applications and untethered input devices that provide virtual force feedback. Our experimental results demonstrated that people could correctly perceive two opposite directions of virtual force.

Currently we are using only an existing tactile device and controlling a transmitted signal to create virtual force. The configuration of this device itself is asymmetric (i.e., the electromagnet is attached to one side of the metal weight and the spring is attached to the other), and therefore, the metal weight cannot be completely controlled. We feel it would be worthwhile to examine whether the electromagnet can be attached to both sides of the metal weight and whether two separate signals can be transmitted to allow the metal weight to be controlled more precisely. In addition, since the extension of our 1D system to a 2D system in which two tactile devices were combined was not very successful, we may have to create a device that has a structure in which a single controlled weight is moved in various directions, so that we can eliminate the necessity of synthesizing two vibrations.

We are also considering a system in which visible light communication and this device are combined. As briefly demonstrated in the Applications section, if the device can decode a light signal transmitted from a projector, a "virtual force field" can be created whereby a device under the projected light is guided toward a particular location. For example, an input device can be guided toward a particular object on a screen by virtual force. Surgery is another possible domain where a virtual force field can be applied to provide important support. For example, a virtual force unit can be attached to a surgical knife. This would enable the surgeon to feel the "cut-path" as a haptic sensation by means of a light line projected onto the patient's body. This cut-path information system can also be applied to other medical sensing technologies, such as ultrasonic sensing or magnetic resonance imaging.

ACKNOWLEDGMENTS

I am indebted to all the reviewers for valuable suggestions and comments to improve this paper. I also thank Ayaka Sato for video production support.

REFERENCES

1. ALPS. Alps Electric Press Release Force Reactor™. http://www.alps.com/e/news release/2005/0608 01.html, 2008.
2. Amemiya, T., Ando, H., and Maeda, T. Phantom-drawn: direction guidance using rapid and asymmetric acceleration weighted by nonlinearity of perception. In *Proceedings of the 2005 international conference on Augmented tele-existence*, ICAT '05 (2005), 201–208.
3. Amemiya, T., Ando, H., and Maeda, T. Directed force perception when holding a nongrounding force display in the air. In *Proc. of EuroHaptics 2006* (2008), 317–324.
4. Badshah, A., Gupta, S., Morris, D., Patel, S., and Tan, D. Gyrotab: a handheld device that provides reactive torque feedback. In *Proceedings of the SIGCHI Conference on Human Factors in Computing Systems*, CHI '12 (2012), 3153–3156.
5. Fukumoto, M., and Sugimura, T. ActiveClick: Tactile feedback for touch panels. In *CHI 2001 summary* (2001), 121–122.
6. Hirata, Y., and Sato, M. 3-dimensional interface device for virtual work space. In *IEEE/RSJ International Conference on Intelligent Robots and Systems* (1992), 889–896.
7. Iwamoto, T., Tatezono, M., and Shinoda, H. Non-contact method for producing tactile sensation using airborne ultrasound. In *Proc. EuroHaptics 2008*, vol. 5024 of *LNCS*, Springer (2008), 504–513.
8. Iwata, H. Artificial reality with force-feedback: development of desktop virtual space with compact master manipulator. *SIGGRAPH Comput. Graph. 24*, 4 (1990), 165–170.
9. Mellis, D. A., Banzi, M., Cautielles, D., and Igoe, T. Arduino: An open electronics prototyping platform. In *CHI '07 Extended Abstracts*, ACM (2007).
10. Minsky, M., young Ming, O., Steele, O., Frederick P. Brooks, J., and Behensky, M. Feeling and seeing: issues in force display. *SIGGRAPH Comput. Graph. 24*, 2 (1990), 235–241.
11. Nakamura, N., and Fukui, Y. An innovative non-grounding haptic interface 'gyrocubesensuous' displaying illusion sensation of push, pull and lift. In *ACM SIGGRAPH 2005 Posters*, SIGGRAPH '05 (2005).
12. Poupyrev, I., Maruyama, S., and Rekimoto, J. Ambient touch: designing tactile interfaces for handheld devices. In *ACM UIST 2002* (2002), 51–60.
13. Rekimoto, J. SenseableRays: Opto-haptic substitution for touch-enhanced interactive space. In *CHI '09 extended abstracts*, ACM (2009).
14. Tanaka, Y., Sakai, M., Y.Khono, Fukui, Y., Yamashita, J., and Nakamura, N. Mobile torque display and haptic characteristics of human palm. In *ICAT 2001* (2001), 115–120.
15. Tsukada, K., and Yasumura, M. Activebelt: Belt-type wearable tactile display for directional navigation. In *in Lecture Notes in Computer Science. Springer-Verlag GmbH, Oct 2004*, Springer (2004), 384–399.

Human-computer Interaction for Hybrid Carving

Amit Zoran
Responsive Environments
MIT Media Lab
amitz@media.mit.edu

Roy Shilkrot
Fluid Interfaces
MIT Media Lab
roys@media.mit.edu

Joseph Paradiso
Responsive Environments
MIT Media Lab
joep@media.mit.edu

ABSTRACT
In this paper we explore human-computer interaction for carving, building upon our previous work with the FreeD digital sculpting device. We contribute a new tool design (FreeD V2), with a novel set of interaction techniques for the fabrication of static models: personalized toolpaths, manual overriding, and physical merging of virtual models. We also present techniques for fabricating dynamic models, which may be altered directly or parametrically during fabrication. We demonstrate a semi-autonomous operation and evaluate the performance of the tool. We end by discussing synergistic cooperation between human and machine to ensure accuracy while preserving the expressiveness of manual practice.

Author Keywords
Computer-Aided Design (CAD); Craft; Digital Fabrication; Carving; Milling.

ACM Classification Keywords
H.5.2 Information interfaces and presentation: User Interfaces; I.3.8 Computer Graphics: Applications

INTRODUCTION
This paper contributes an application of a digital sculpting device for hybrid carving, using a revised version of the FreeD tool (FreeD V2), previously discussed in [21]. FreeD enabled users to make physical artifacts with virtual control, and FreeD V2 adds manual and computational design modification *during* fabrication, rendering a unique 3D model directly in a physical material. Our intention is to explore a territory where artifacts are produced in a collaborative effort between human and machine, incorporating subjective decision-making in the fabrication process and blurring the line between design and fabrication.

In the course of our work, we discuss different hybrid interaction methodologies. Not only does the tool assist inexperienced makers carving complex 3D objects (static-model mode, see Figure 1), it also enables personalizing and changing of the underlying model (dynamic model mode). In the latter case, FreeD doubles as an input device, where the user moves and the computer reacts. We present several novel

UIST'13, October 08 - 11, 2013, St. Andrews, United Kingdom.
Copyright © 2013 ACM 978-1-4503-2268-3/13/10...$15.00.
http://dx.doi.org/10.1145/2501988.2502023

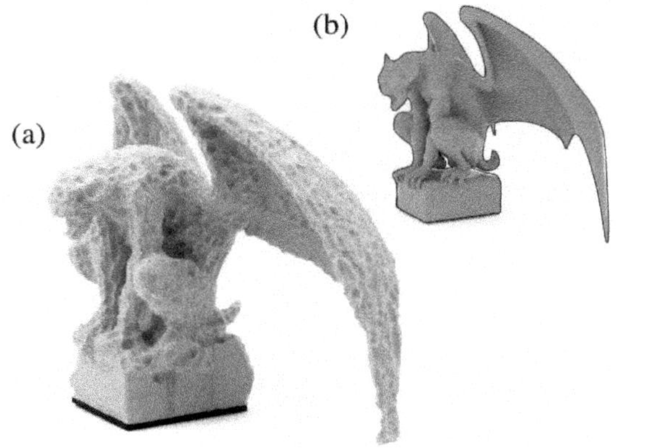

Figure 1. A gargoyle sculpture (with a wingspan of 280mm) made with the FreeD V2 (a) based on a complex CAD model (b).

modes of interaction such as switching between virtual models through the work; overriding the computer; deforming a virtual model while making it; or searching interactively for an optimal parametric model. In addition, the new tool can operate independently for tasks such as semi-automatic texture rendering.

In the next section, we discuss our previous efforts and related work, and in the subsequent section titled *The FreeD V2 Design*, we present the new version of the FreeD, focusing on revisions from the early version. In *Modes of collaboration and interaction*, we present three operational modes: static (rigid) model, dynamic model (a computational virtual model that responds to the users actions), and a semi-autonomous mode of tool operation. Finally, in *Performance and exploration*, we discuss the experience of working with the tool.

RELATED WORK
Today, we tend to see design and fabrication as two distinct digital practices, where design is the creative stage and fabrication is the automatic production stage. Unlike in contemporary digital practice, in traditional craft, the intuitive engagement in fabrication directly influences the result [11]. Following traditional craft practices and carving techniques, we presented the FreeD, a handheld digital milling device, monitored by a computer that controls the speed and alignment of the shaft while preserving the maker's gestural freedom. In [21] we discussed our concept, compared traditional craft and modern processes, and reviewed related work in artistic expression and handheld digital fabrication tools.

Relevant concepts in hybrid design and fabrication were previously implemented by digitally monitored 3D clay sculpting with bare hands or manual tools [16, 14]. We found CopyCAD by Follmer et al. [7] especially interesting, as it allows users to copy 2D elements of physical objects, then re-assemble and re-fabricate these elements in a new 2D shape.

FreeD V2 can be used to modify the virtual model during fabrication. Gustafson et al. studied the use of hand-gestures in free-air as a control input for a virtual shape without visual feedback [8], Song et al. [18] used annotation squiggles with a pen, Arisandi et al. [3] employed specialized hand-held tools, and Cho et al. [5] used a depth camera to track hand-gestures in shaping a virtual object using a virtual pottery wheel. Recently, similar ideas were integrated with fabrication technologies, such as laser cutters [10, 12], a RepRap 3D printer [13] and specialized fabricators [20].

THE FREED V2 DESIGN

In this section, we introduce the new design to readers unfamiliar with our previous work and detail its additional capabilities: an overriding button, LEDs, sonic control, and an addition of two degrees of freedom (DOF) of shaft deflection, which allows additional semi-automatic movements. The device is one element of a system (see Figure 2) that contains the handheld tool, a magnetic motion tracking system (MMTS), the fabricated object, a computer, and software distributed over the laptop and the tool. The tool is usually held with a single hand, while the user is free to move it in 3D, limited only by the length of power cables and the MMTS.

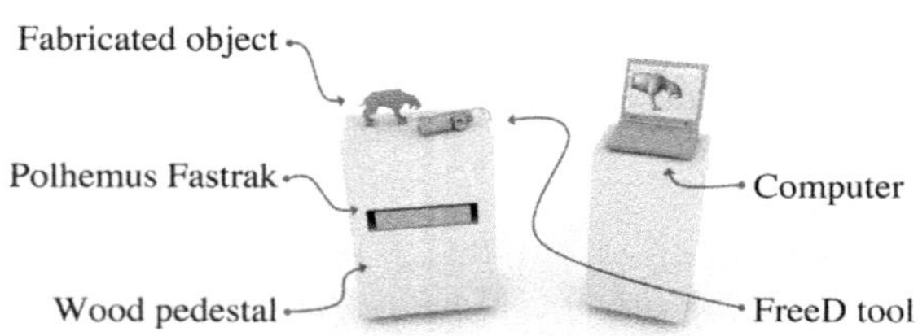

Figure 2. The FreeD, work environment, computer, and MMTS.

Tool design and motor control

The FreeD V2 contains a custom milling mechanism (spindle) built on top of a long shaft (Figure 4) with a 12V DC motor (Micro-Drives M2232U12VCS with up to 10,000 RPM with no load, and up to 5.2mNm torque). A custom 3D bearing mechanism is located underneath the handle, sitting above the titanium shaft and enabling three DOF movements at an approximate spherical volume of 20 mm (see Figure 3). Three servomotors (MKS 6125 mini servos, with up to 5.8 kg-cm for 6V), aligned perpendicular to the shaft near the spindle motor, determine the shaft's position. An electronic circuit on the PCB (with an ATmega328 microprocessor and a MC33926 motor driver, powered with 5V and 12V signals) communicates with the computer via Bluetooth to control the shaft movement and the spindle speed.

A force-sensing resistor (FSR) sensor is located on the handle, allowing the user to override the computer. The DC motor speed (Sp, where 1 is the maximum value) is a function of the pressure read from the FSR (Pr, where 1 is maximum value) and the risk to the model (Rs, 1 is maximal risk - see

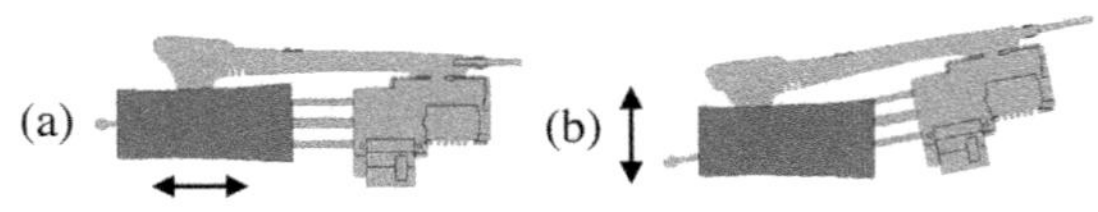

Figure 3. The multiple-axis bearing allows the milling bit to move in 3 degrees of freedom: 2 in the carving-plane, and a forward-backward motion.

Figure 5 (a)-(c)):

$$Sp = 1 - Rs(1 - Pr) \qquad (1)$$

Two LEDs are located on the tool to provide the user with visual feedback. The first LED's blinking frequency correlates to the pressure detected by the FSR. The second LED corresponds to the distance between the bit and the surface of the model (when the bit touches the model's surface, the light is constant). In addition, the operating frequency of the DC motor (PWM), controlled by the motor-driver, changes from ultrasonic to an audible range (arround 2KHz) to give the user an alarm when the bit is within 4mm of the model surface.

The major part of the computation is done on a computer (Alienware M14x Laptop with i7-3740QM Intel core, 12GB DDR3, and 2GB NVIDIA GeForce GT 650M graphic card). The computer also provides the user with a visual feedback on the screen (see Figure 5 (d-f)). For tracking (MMTS) we use the Polhemus FASTRAK system, an AC 6D system that has low latency (4ms), high static accuracy (position 0.76mm / orientation 0.15° RMS), and high refresh rate (120Hz).

On the computer, where the virtual model resides, the software runs in Grasshopper and Rhino. The input is the 6D location and orientation of the tool, and the outputs are commands to the control PCB on the FreeD. A prediction of the next position of the bit is extrapolated by a spline of the 4th order (using the current location and the 3 previous ones). The software calculates the distances (D) to the CAD model (using rhinoscript MeshCP()) from both the current location and the predicted one, estimating which point puts the model at higher risk (i.e., which is closer to the model). While the DC motor's speed is calculated on the tool as a factor of Pr and Rs, the latter is calculated by the main control software (values in mm):

$$Rs = \begin{cases} 0 & \text{if } D <= 100 \text{ } and \text{ } D > 4; \\ D/8 & \text{if } D <= 4 \text{ } and \text{ } D > 0; \\ 1 & \text{elsewhere.} \end{cases} \qquad (2)$$

The default shaft position is fully extended, with a 20mm potential to absorb the offset and retract. Unlike our early work, in the FreeD V2 we now use the servos for independent tool operation rather than as a penetration protection mechanism.

Method of Operation

Operation of the FreeD V2 is similar to that discussed earlier: the user sits in front of the material (Balsa foam), which is attached to a wooden stand (see Figure 2). The physical working area is calibrated to the virtual workspace. She is free to investigate any milling approach, such as milling lines, drilling holes, trimming surfaces, or using an arbitrary

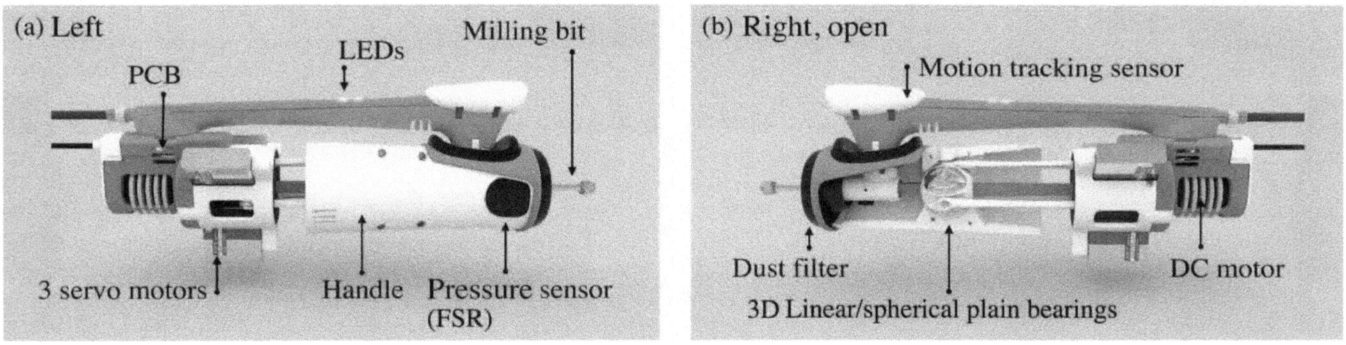

Figure 4. FreeD V2 is a handheld digital milling tool: (a) a left view of the tool, with its main components, and (b) a right view of the opened device.

pattern. The computer slows down the spindle as the bit approaches the model, stopping it completely before it penetrates the virtual model (see Figure 5 (d-f)). This enables the user to cut along the boundary of the virtual model where desired. She can leave parts of the model unfinished or override the computer using the pressure sensor. Further, in some modes of operation, the system can dynamically alter the model based on user actions or operate autonomously.

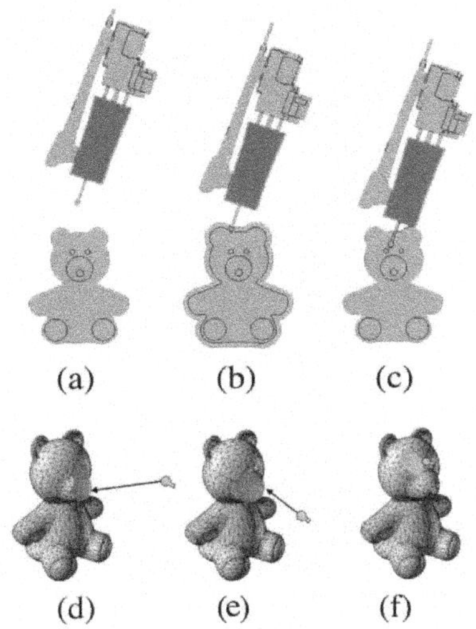

Figure 5. Risk management with the FreeD. (a-c) Low, High and penetration level of risk. (d-f) Heatmap visualization of the risk zone.

MODES OF COLLABORATION AND INTERACTION

In this section, we survey several original interaction modes with FreeD V2: the static CAD model mode where the computer assists only by preventing the user from damaging the model (the first part of this section, *Toolpath personalization*, was partially discussed in our early work); a dynamic mode where the computer numerically controls the model, responding to the user's actions; and the autonomous mode where the computer can operate independently of the user for tasks such as semi-automatic texture rendering. Together, these modes span a new space, where both human and computer work in synergy and contribute to the final product.

Fabrication of static models

In the fabrication of a static model, the user cannot alter the CAD model, and the boundary of the virtual object remains static. This approach resembles traditional digital fabrication technologies, where the virtual model is fixed and prepared beforehand. Here however, the user (rather than an automatic process) determines the toolpath. This enables personalization of the work, and may also circumvent complicated CAD challenges such as merging 3D elements into a single object.

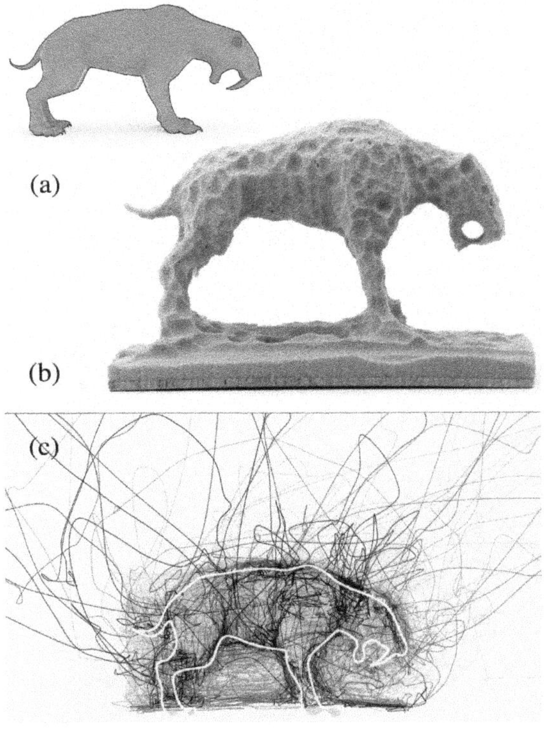

Figure 6. Sculpting a static model of a sabertooth tiger (80 min fabrication time, length 125mm). (a) The 3D model, (b) the end result of the sculping process, (c) and the toolpath projection. The tool is capable of achieving a smoother surface (see Figure 16), with deliberate intent.

Toolpath personalization

As discussed earlier, FreeD gives the user direct control over the milling toolpath. The final surface smoothness and resolution are determined by the size and shape of the endmill and the toolpath. Usually in fabrication, a manual process renders a chaotic surface pattern whereas an automatic process renders an organized network of marks. This is mainly because in a manual toolpath, a product of the maker's dexterity and patience, the operation never repeats itself and evolves into a unique texture, for example in the fabrication of a saber-tooth tiger model (Figure 6 (a)). The final texture (b) reflects the user toolpath (c), properties of the material, milling bit size, and latency of the system. The parts left unfinished (the legs) demonstrate decisions made during the work.

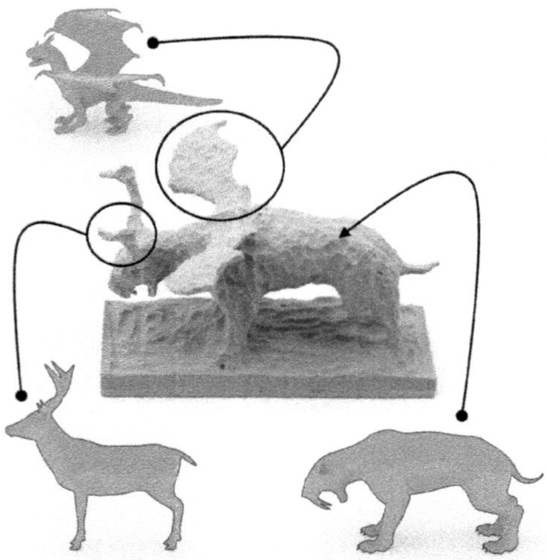

Figure 7. Hybridization of meshes while sculpting (100 min fabrication time, model length 120mm). The final 3D shape does not exist virtually; it only exists in the fabricated model.

Physical merging

As FreeD encourages the user to work creatively and intuitively, the user can manually switch between different reference virtual models *during* the work. The fusion of these models need not be determined numerically but physically, relinquishing the need to solve mesh intersection problems in making a single CAD model, as in the merging of a saber-tooth tiger with dragon wings and deer horns (Figure 7).

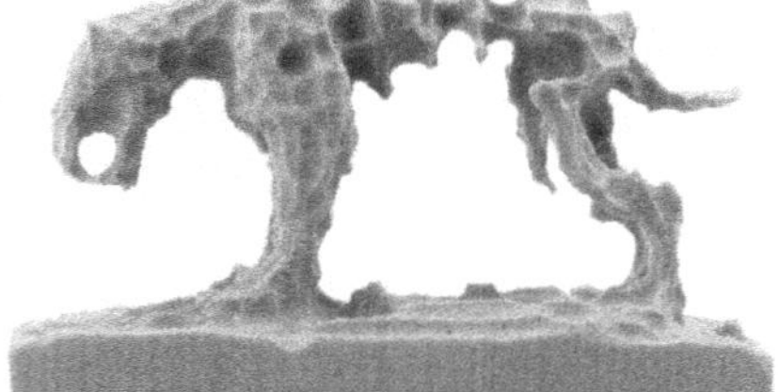

Figure 8. The result of overriding computer guidance is a completely different design (90 min fabrication time, model length 120mm). The artist takes risks and produces a unique artifact.

Manual override

Here, we present an approach foreign to most digital fabrication methods: allowing *intentional destruction* of the fabricated model. By overwriting the computer, the user minimizes digital control on the shaft while keeping the advantage of digital guidance with an aural alarm and LED. In addition to leaving parts unfinished, the maker can intentionally "damage" the model, working around or *inside* the virtual shape, allowing for physical improvisation. Beyond Figure 6b, in Figure 8, the user continued to manually remove parts of the model to achieve a unique artifact.

Fabrication of dynamic models

Today, digital fabrication technologies require models to be designed beforehand and no changes can be made during fabrication, as in the static approach presented in the last section. In contrast, craftpersons are free to deform the subject during the creation process, as long as the remaining material allows. Aiming to recreate this freedom, we present a novel capability to allow the modification of dynamic virtual models during fabrication, exploring three types of interaction with dynamic models: Direct shape deformation, Volume occupancy optimization, and Data-driven shape exploration.

Direct shape deformation

The first order dynamics in our interaction model is to allow for direct deformation of a CAD model. Unlike manual overriding of a static model, in direct shape deformation the computer keeps track of subtracted material: when the user presses the override button and penetrates the virtual model, the computer deforms the mesh to ameliorate the penetration.

Recent related methods of mesh deformation [19] seek to preserve local features under deformation. Here, we used a simplified weighting scheme for local deformation with respect to the user's action. As the weights for the offset vector of vertices ($\vec{O_v}$, where v is the vertex index) we use a Gaussian decay over the distance from the nearest vertex to the bit, to create an effect of a smooth deformation:

$$\vec{O_v} = \vec{T_v} * e^{\frac{-(d_v/S)^2}{0.005(10-Pr)^2}} \quad (3)$$

Where Pr is the value read from the override FSR button (0 is no pressure and 1 is maximal pressure), $\vec{T}$ is the penetration vector (the vector between the point of first contact to the deepest bit position), d_v is the distance from v to the penetration point, and S is the number of affected vertices, a constant number that can be defined by the user (and thus define the affected area). See Figure 9 for an example of deforming a mesh while fabricating.

Volume occupancy optimization

Further examining the art of carving, we face a common challenge: fitting a shape to a given volume of material, for example in the case of an irregular piece of wood, where the artist may try to maximize the volume of the shape while bounded by the material. FreeD allows the user to work in this fashion, using optimization of volume occupancy.

We illustrate the idea of volume occupancy optimization through a simple parametric bowl with three parameters: inner and outer radii (r_i, r_o) and height (c). Let us denote $\Theta = \{r_o, r_{in}, c\}$. Spheres and cubes were used to create the model of the bowl with constructive solid geometry (CSG) boolean operations (using the Carve CSG library [17]). See Figure 10 (e) for examples of parametic bowls.

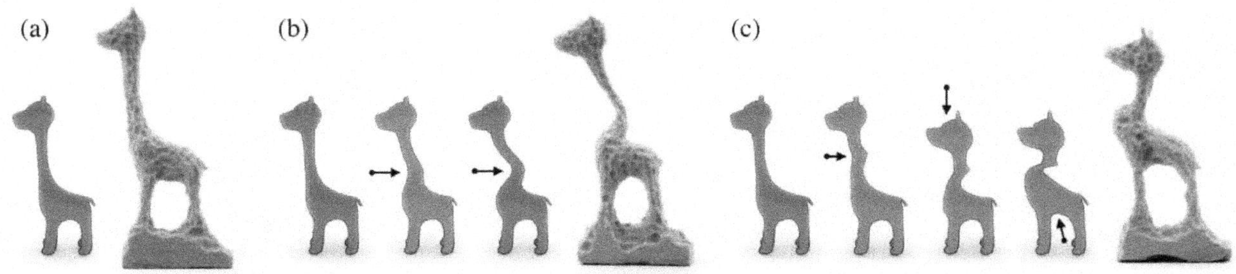

Figure 9. Model deformation while carving using the override mechanism. The model is smoothly deformed in proportion to the bit's penetration of the material. (a) The original model, (b) deformation from the left, (c) and deformations of the model from multiple directions.

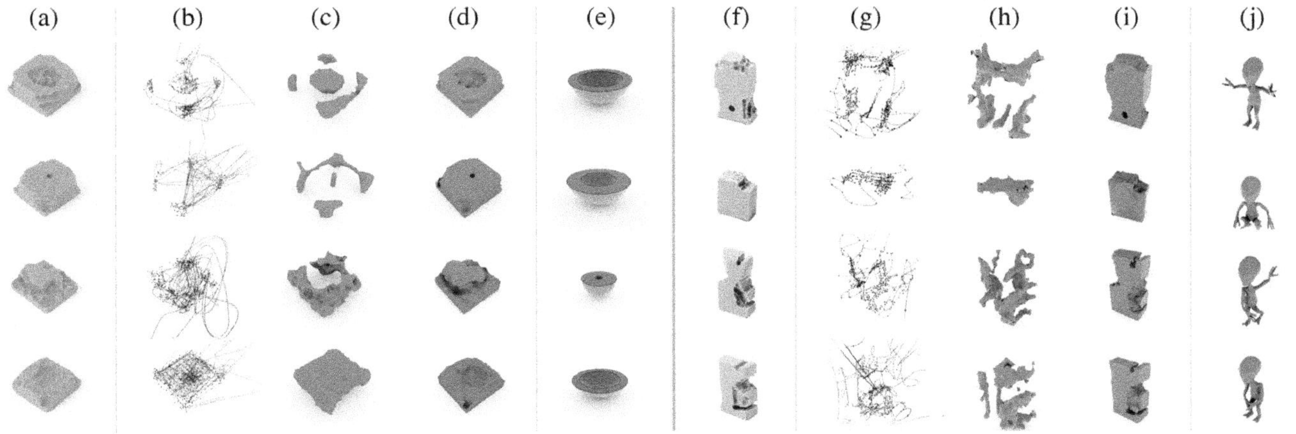

Figure 10. An initial iteration in a parametric fitting process of bowl and humanoid forms: (a), (f) the physical carved material, (b), (g) renderings of the toolpath, (c), (h) simulations of the material *removed* by the tool, (d), (i) simulations of the remaining material, (e), (j) result of the fitting algorithm.

In order to fit a shape in the material, we first determine the remaining volume. After the FreeD carves out a part of the material, the toolpath is bounded so only the points inside the volume in question are left (see Figure 10 (b)). Each point describes only the center of the bit, therefore 10 points were randomly sampled on a sphere with radius 3.2mm (the real bit size) to simulate the whole bit as it passed through space. A solid shape is created out of the point cloud using the Alpha Shapes method [6] (see Figure 10-(c)). Once the removed portion is established, the remaining volume is easily obtained with a boolean CSG operation (see Figure 10-(d)).

A parametric bowl is then fitted inside the remaining volume by a score function vector, whose norm should be minimized:

$$f_1(\Theta) = w_1 * V_{remain}(\Theta)$$
$$f_2(\Theta) = w_2 * V_{out}(\Theta)$$
$$f_3(\Theta) = w_3 * (1 - c)$$
$$f_4(\Theta) = w_4 * (1 - r_{in})$$
$$F(\Theta) = [f_1(\Theta); f_2(\Theta); f_3(\Theta); f_4(\Theta)]$$

The $V_{remain}(\Theta)$ marks the remaining volume of material after the bowl was subtracted and $V_{out}(\Theta)$ marks the volume that the bowl takes *outside* the remaining volume, i.e. out in the air. These measures should be minimized so to maximize occupancy and minimize escape. The bowl is made as high and thick as possible using the final two residuals. We used a non-linear least-squares solver [2] to find the solution for the canonical optimization problem: $\arg\min_\Theta \|F(\Theta)\|^2$. Due to the CSG operations, the function is evaluated numerically.

Data-driven shape exploration

In this dynamic-model mode we strive to simulate the unbounded amount of possible outcomes that manual carving allows. Using a vast database, the tool guides users while exploring the shape-space in an interactive process.

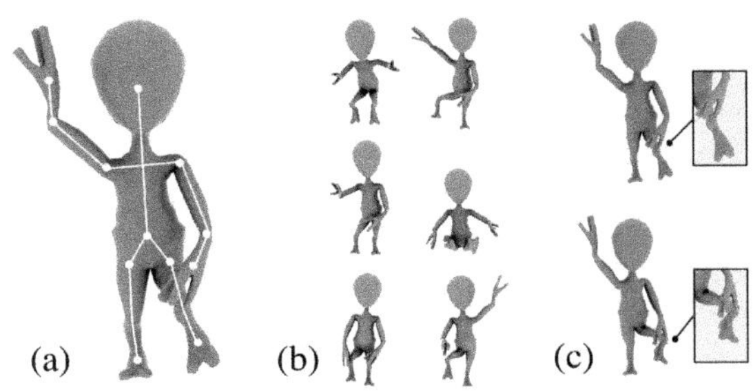

Figure 11. The parametric skeleton model of a humanoid creature: (a) skeleton of 14 joints, (b) sample of the database of possible poses, (c) fine-tuning process recovers the best pose to fit the remaining material.

We work with a hierarchical database of over 4000 examples of human poses that were recorded with the Kinect sensor via the OpenNI software stack [1]. The poses were clustered using a K-Means variant, to 50 clusters (meta-poses) of varying sizes, using WEKA [9]. Then, we use the method from [4] to auto-rig the humanoid alien model to a skeleton model that corresponds with the Kinect. For deformation of the mesh, we used the canonical Linear Blend Skinning method. Figure 11-(a) and (b) illustrates the database of skeleton poses.

The process of finding the remaining volume (see the previous section) is repeated. Then, an exhaustive search over the database is performed to find the meta-pose that has the least amount of escape from the remaining volume (V_{out}), followed by a search within the best-found cluster. Several options for advancement are presented to the user to choose from in each iteration. After the database search, fine tuning ensues, for the position of the limbs and for small translations of the entire shape in respect to the volume. Figure 11-(c) shows an example of finely tuning the alien pose.

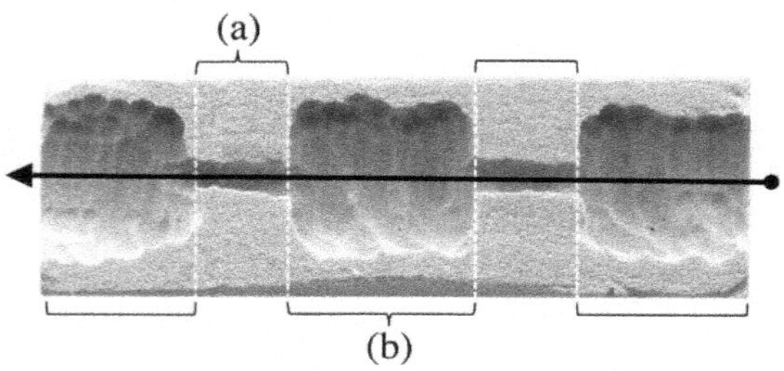

Figure 12. Automatic tool operation in a straight line. In (a) regions there is no autonomous movement, while in (b) regions the shaft programmatically removes more material resulting in a bigger *virtual bit*.

Autonomous operation mode

Digital fabrication technologies incorporate several degrees of automatic motion, while common hand-held devices do not automatically move but are manually controlled. The use of automatic motion in hand-held devices is rarely considered. Lately this is changing, as was demonstrated by Rivers et al. [15], by integrating 2D actuation mechanism to correct the user's path, and in [21] , where shaft retraction prevents the user from accidental penetration of the model.

An independent actuation of the shaft operates semi-autonomously: while the user holds FreeD and makes large-scale movements, the tool makes autonomous smaller-scale movements. For example, the tool is operated as a semi-autonomous milling device (CNC, see Figure 12). In Figure 13 we demonstrate a semi-autonomous texture rendering: when the bit is closer than 4mm to the fur segment, the servos operate with a linear pecking movement (4Hz, 5mm movement range) to achieve a fur texture. The user continues to operate the tool freely, unconstrained by the shaft actuation.

PERFORMANCE AND EXPLORATION

In this section, we first present statistical performance measurements collected while working with the FreeD V2, before discussing our experience using the tool.

System performance

The FreeD V2 system was used (mostly by us) in the fabrication of 11 complete artifacts, in addition to several 3D sketches and a few preliminary sculptures in our early studies. We tested the tool with carving in both high and low

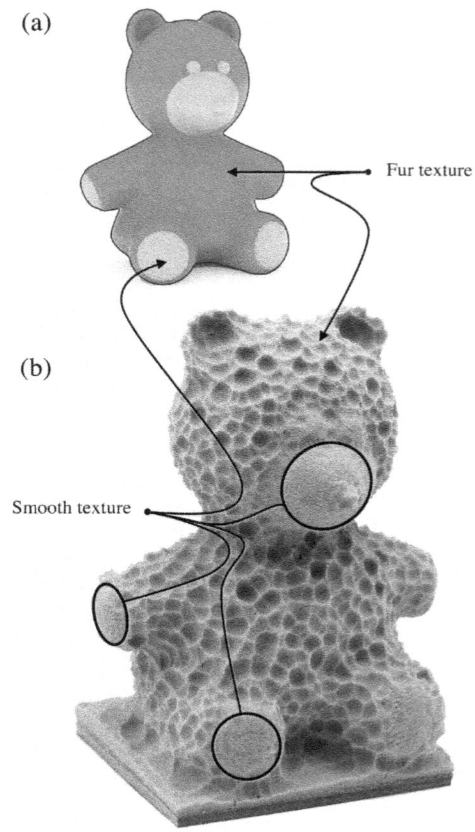

Figure 13. Teddy bear model (height 147mm) (a) embellished with fur textures. The mesh is encoded with a rough or smooth texture. The rough texture causes the shaft to move back and forth, creating dimples in the material that simulate fur (b).

density balsa foams, basswood, and carving wax. All of the studies presented in this paper were done in foam, since it took up to 10 times longer to machine wax and wood. The control software updated at a frame rate varying between 10 to 20 frames per second (FPS). We worked with mesh models of 150 vertices (humanoid) to 5370 vertices (gargoyle), lengths between 120mm (giraffe) to 280mm (gargoyle), and with production times of 40 minutes (giraffe) to 5 hours (gargoyle). The static-bit accuracy (measured by holding the bit in one place while rotating the tool around it) varies between 0.05 mm RMS (20cm from the magnetic field generator) to 0.4mm RMS (70cm away).

While in our work we seek personalization of artifact rather than production accuracy, here we test how accurately the FreeD can reconstruct a predesigned virtual model. The surface accuracy depends on the frame rate, tool movement speed, and material density. For example, with 15 FPS and 350mm/sec attack speed, the bit penetrated 3.5mm in a dense balsa foam before the system shut down the spindle rotation.

To empirically evaluate the accuracy of FreeD V2 we designed a model with non-straight angles and a sphere (Figure 14 (a)), fabricated it with FreeD, and then scanned it with Konica Minolta VIVID 910 scanner so to computationally es-

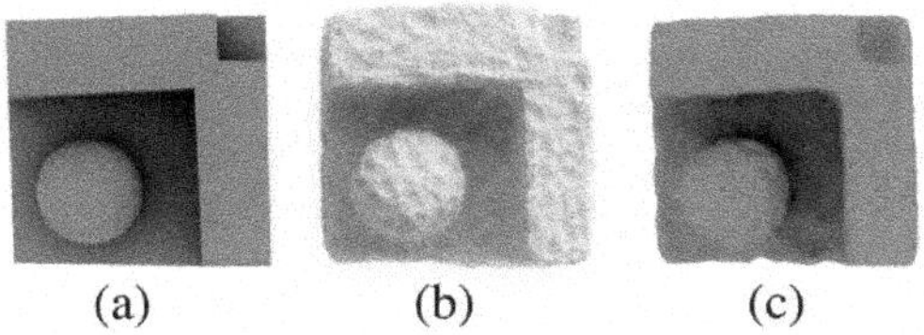

Figure 14. An examination of the FreeD V2's accuracy measure. (a) the virtual model (53mm length) , (b) the model fabricated with FreeD, (c) a 3D scanning of the fabrication. The RMS error is less than 0.5mm.

timate the error. We present the following results only to give a general sense of accuracy, as the adherence of the resulting surface to the virtual model is greatly a factor of the maker's dexterity and patience, a complex concept to quantify. The resulting error was smaller than 0.5mm RMS (samples for this measurement were taken within a grid of less than 1mm resolution). As expected because of the bit size, FreeD fails to clear out material from sharp corners; however all subtractive fabrication methods suffer from this drawback.

Experimentation

Here we discuss the making of a larger-scale model that incorporates most of the functionalities of the tool. We made a humanoid model, an alien figure, which features a large head and elongated arms. The work began by interactively exploring the skeleton database in the same manner we discussed earlier (see section). Figure 15 (b-d) shows the different poses fetched from the database while carving out material. When a satisfying pose was found, we began removing larger chunks of material. Using the shape deformation method described earlier, we created a dent in the model to emphasize the sideways motion of the hips (see Figure 15-(e)). We then kept removing material until the general form was fleshed out (see Figure 15-(f) for an illustration) and moved on to texturing and decorating. On the computer we set the alien's head to have a rough texture that will resemble hair. Finally, we used the override mechanism to create completely unguided carvings of the mouth and navel, and decided to leave part of the model unfinished.

Discussion

Extended user studies will be conducted to validate the tool's capabilities in supporting creative processes. Yet, using the tool ourselves and allowing five other participants to collaborate on single carving (see Figure 16), we have a few initial reflections. In projects presented in this paper, the tool was guided along lines away from the object, removing material from one side to another. When the model becomes recognizable, the operation changed to tracking the surface manifolds. Changes in spindle speed, when the bit approaches the model surface, inform the users on the relative location of the tool with respect to the model and help build intuition. Several participants noted it took them a while to trust the tool in protecting the object from a wrong movement.

On the screen, a virtual mark represents the current position of the FreeDs milling bit (see Figure 5 (d)-(f)). Occasionally, we relied on this mark in the initial stage where the virtual shape is not yet revealed in the raw material. However, the

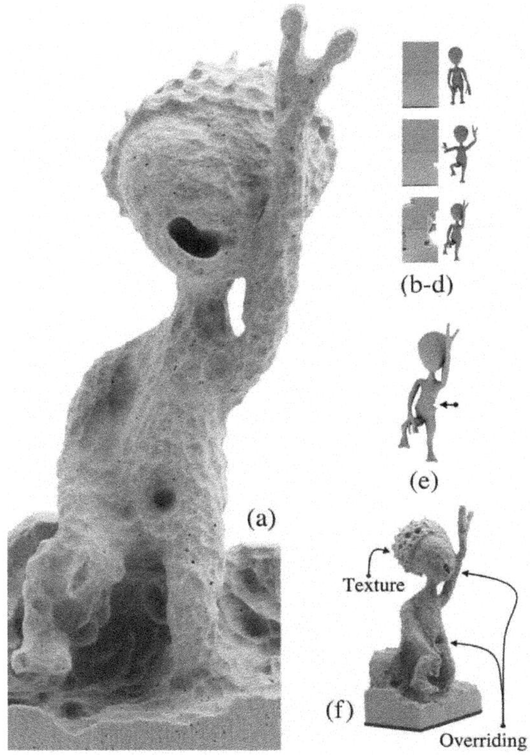

Figure 15. Fabrication of a humanoid model (height 222mm) illustrating all methods. (a) The final artifact. (b-d) Evolution of the model as material is removed. (e) Smooth deformation. (f) Texturing hair and deliberate penetration of the model to carve a mouth and navel.

main limitation of the FreeD, as indicated by several users, is a lack in visual feedback of the virtual model projected on the material. On the other hand, this drawback helped develop a physical intuition for the digital guidance. Nevertheless we find there is a place to consider such a visualization method in a future work.

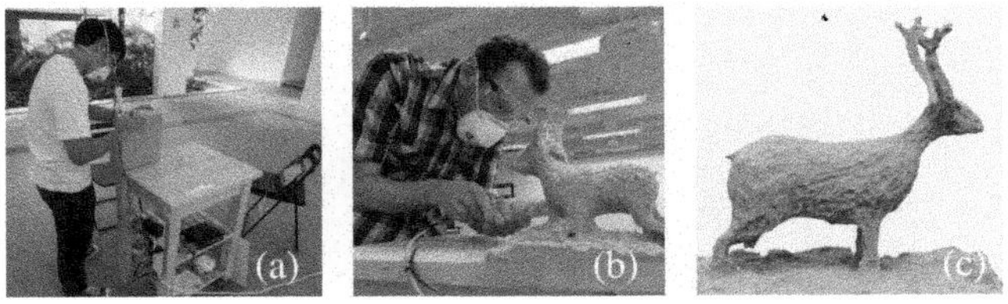

Figure 16. Collaborative effort (a), (b) in creating (c) a deer artifact.

CONCLUSION

We propose a new technique where digital capabilities integrate with handheld carving tools to assist inexperienced makers in carving complex 3D objects, as well as to enable interpretation and modification of a virtual model while fabricating it. The FreeD keeps the user's subjective toolpath as a signature embedded in the texture. In addition, it is capable of completing tasks in a semi-automatic mode, generating a physical texture independently of the user. Since design manipulation is integrated within a tangible carving experience, the nature of this work resembles the process of traditional craft, while allowing risk management and quality assurance.

We wish FreeD to enable creative work in a domain yet unexplored, a new hybrid territory of artifacts produced by both machine and man, fusing automated production with human subjectivity. Blending design with fabrication and automatic process with manual control, we believe the collaborative technology presented here has the potential to alter some of the dominant paradigms in contemporary digital fabrication processes. By introducing traditional approaches to the digital making of artifacts, we hope this intimate collaboration between man and machine will pave the path for a new paradigm in human-computer interaction.

Acknowledgements

Many thanks to our collegues and friends who supported us during the work: T. Rucham, J. Steimle, A. von Kapri, D. Mellis, NW Gong, P. Schmitt, C. Xia, K. Ran, M. Feldmeier, A. Petron, B. Mayton, M. Levin, S. Follmer, Y. Sterman, G. Dublon, N. Gershenfeld, F. Durand, Y. Gingold, L. Liu, M. Gharbi, K. Bala, R. Jaroensri, H.V. Shin, S. Nanayakkara, K.P. Yeo, D. Cohen-Or, and all the craftspersons who shared their knowledge. The CAD models were purchased from turbosquid.com, and the renderings were made with VRay.

REFERENCES

1. Openni user guide. `http://www.openni.org/documentation`, November 2010. Last Checked December 14, 2012.
2. Agarwal, S., and Mierle, K. Ceres solver: Tutorial & reference. `http://code.google.com/p/ceres-solver`, 2012. Last Checked December 14, 2012.
3. Arisandi, R., Takami, Y., Otsuki, M., Kimura, A., Shibata, F., and Tamura, H. Enjoying virtual handcrafting with tooldevice. In *Adjunct proceedings of the 25th annual ACM symposium on User interface software and technology*, ACM (2012), 17–18.
4. Baran, I., and Popović, J. Automatic rigging and animation of 3d characters. In *ACM Transactions on Graphics (TOG)*, vol. 26, ACM (2007), 72.
5. Cho, S., Heo, Y., and Bang, H. Turn: a virtual pottery by real spinning wheel. In *ACM SIGGRAPH 2012 Emerging Technologies*, SIGGRAPH '12, ACM (New York, NY, USA, 2012), 25:1–25:1.
6. Edelsbrunner, H., and Mücke, E. P. Three-dimensional alpha shapes. *ACM Trans. Graph. 13*, 1 (Jan. 1994), 43–72.
7. Follmer, S., Carr, D., Lovell, E., and Ishii, H. Copycad: remixing physical objects with copy and paste from the real world. In *Adjunct proceedings of the 23nd annual ACM symposium on User interface software and technology*, UIST '10, ACM (New York, NY, USA, 2010), 381–382.
8. Gustafson, S., Bierwirth, D., and Baudisch, P. Imaginary interfaces: spatial interaction with empty hands and without visual feedback. In *Proceedings of the 23nd annual ACM symposium on User interface software and technology*, UIST '10, ACM (New York, NY, USA, 2010), 3–12.
9. Hall, M., Frank, E., Holmes, G., Pfahringer, B., Reutemann, P., and Witten, I. H. The weka data mining software: an update. *SIGKDD Explor. Newsl. 11*, 1 (Nov. 2009), 10–18.
10. Johnson, G., Gross, M., Do, E. Y.-L., and Hong, J. Sketch it, make it: sketching precise drawings for laser cutting. In *Proceedings of the 2012 ACM annual conference extended abstracts on Human Factors in Computing Systems Extended Abstracts*, CHI EA '12, ACM (New York, NY, USA, 2012), 1079–1082.
11. McCullough, M. *Abstracting Craft: The Practiced Digital Hand*. MIT Press, Cambridge, MA, USA, 1998.
12. Mueller, S., Lopes, P., and Baudisch, P. Interactive construction: interactive fabrication of functional mechanical devices. In *Proceedings of the 25th annual ACM symposium on User interface software and technology*, UIST '12, ACM (New York, NY, USA, 2012), 599–606.
13. Patel, N. Gestural printing: Jumping the shark on kinect hacks. `http://bit.ly/dLiheh`, 2011. Last checked 11 December, 2012.
14. Rivers, A., Adams, A., and Durand, F. Sculpting by numbers. *ACM Trans. Graph. 31*, 6 (Nov. 2012), 157:1–157:7.
15. Rivers, A., Moyer, I. E., and Durand, F. Position-correcting tools for 2d digital fabrication. *ACM Trans. Graph. 31*, 4 (July 2012), 88:1–88:7.
16. S., C., and Rehg, J. M. Shapeshift: A projector-guided sculpture system. In *Adjunct proceedings of the 20nd annual ACM symposium on User interface software and technology*, UIST '07, ACM (Newport, Rhode Island, USA, October 2007).
17. Sargeant, T. carve. `http://code.google.com/p/carve/`, 2012. Last Checked December 14, 2012.
18. Song, H., Guimbretière, F., Hu, C., and Lipson, H. Modelcraft: capturing freehand annotations and edits on physical 3d models. In *Proceedings of the 19th annual ACM symposium on User interface software and technology*, UIST '06, ACM (New York, NY, USA, 2006), 13–22.
19. Sorkine, O., Cohen-Or, D., Lipman, Y., Alexa, M., Rössl, C., and Seidel, H. Laplacian surface editing. In *Proceedings of the 2004 Eurographics/ACM SIGGRAPH symposium on Geometry processing*, ACM (2004), 175–184.
20. Willis, K. D., Xu, C., Wu, K.-J., Levin, G., and Gross, M. D. Interactive fabrication: new interfaces for digital fabrication. In *Proceedings of the fifth international conference on Tangible, embedded, and embodied interaction*, TEI '11, ACM (New York, NY, USA, 2011), 69–72.
21. Zoran, A., and Paradiso, J. A. Freed – a freehand digital sculpting tool. In *Proceedings of the 2013 ACM annual conference on Human Factors in Computing Systems*, CHI EA '13 (Paris, 2013).

PacCAM: Material Capture and Interactive 2D Packing for Efficient Material Usage on CNC Cutting Machines

Daniel Saakes [1] daniel@saak.es
Thomas Cambazard [1] thomas.cambazard@epfl.ch
Jun Mitani [1,2] mitani@cs.tsukuba.ac.jp
Takeo Igarashi [1,3] takeo@acm.org

[1]JST ERATO Igarashi Design Interface Project [2]University of Tsukuba [3]The University of Tokyo

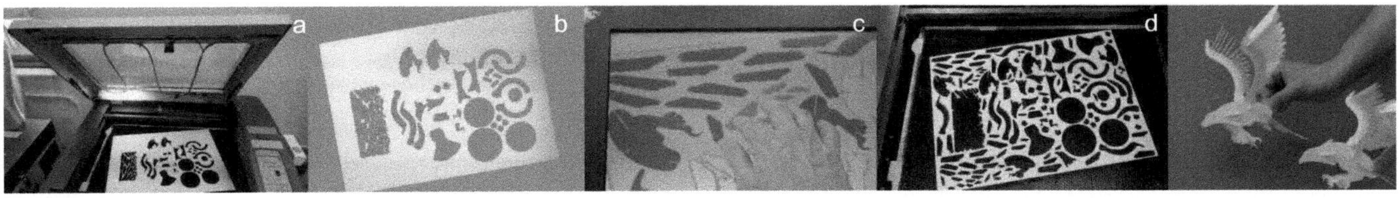

Figure 1. PacCAM supports users in packing 2D parts by capturing materials in a CNC machine (a) and using the captured materials (b) in a dedicated user interface based on 2D rigid body simulation and snapping (c), resulting in optimized utilization of material for efficient fabrication (d).

ABSTRACT

The availability of low-cost digital fabrication devices enables new groups of users to participate in the design and fabrication of things. However, software to assist in the transition from design to actual fabrication is currently overlooked. In this paper, we introduce PacCAM, a system for packing 2D parts within a given source material for fabrication using 2D cutting machines. Our solution combines computer vision to capture the source material shape with a user interface that incorporates 2D rigid body simulation and snapping. A user study demonstrated that participants could make layouts faster with our system compared with using traditional drafting tools. PacCAM caters to a variety of 2D fabrication applications and can contribute to the reduction of material waste.

Author Keywords

Design Tool, Fabrication, 2D Shape Packing

ACM Classification Keywords

H.5.2 Information Interfaces and Presentation: User Interfaces. - Graphical user interfaces.

INTRODUCTION

Many objects are composed out of raw materials that enter the fabrication process flat; as sheets or in rolls. Computer numerical control (CNC) fabrication devices such as plotters, routers, and cutters transform these materials into multiple parts that make up 3D objects. Specialists optimize the process of fabricating physical parts with many goals, such as efficient material use, avoid complex tooling, and minimization of machine time. Although there are fast and advanced algorithms [4, 7] (NP-hard) for packing 2D shapes, there are certain cases that automatic methods can not handle. For instance, source materials that contain graphics or have spatially varying quality require complicated trade-offs between function, aesthetics and efficient material use. In cases with such soft constraints, layout is performed by hand.

With the proliferation of decentralized [22] and personal [11] digital fabrication, new groups of occasional designers/makers are emerging. However, material usage is far from optimized in this emerging user community. We visited numerous fablabs, hackerspaces, and university labs and found piles of partly used materials as shown in Figure 1b. In this paper, we present a new system that is specifically aimed at manual packing of shapes to reduce material waste.

When designing physical objects that are composed of flat materials, designers encounter and switch between multiple representations: a) the intended 3D object, b) the decomposition of the object in 2D parts, and c) the layout and fitting of the 2D parts for actual fabrication on the sheets/rolls. A multitude of research and commercial software exists to support the user or automate the transition from step a to b [2, 14, 17, 18, 19, 23, 24]. However, the transition from step b to c is is currently overlooked. This final step from design to actual manufacturing is a one way process, only output. We ultimately aim to make this final step bi-directional: both output and input by using material features as a creative constraint in the design of an object.

Our contribution is a dedicated user interface for making overlap-free 2D layouts. Our solution consists of capturing materials inside the CNC machine that serve as a guide and constraint in a packing and layout task. On the basis of observed natural behavior, we adapt existing ideas of 2D rigid body simulation in tabletop computing and extend research on snapping with collision-snapping. We evaluate the performance of collision-snapping in a small user study and compare performance improvement in simple tasks with a traditional interface.

UIST'13, October 6–9, 2013, St. Andrews, United Kingdom.
Copyright © 2013 ACM 978-1-4503-2271-3/13/10...$15.00.
http://dx.doi.org/10.1145/2501988.2501990

RELATED WORK

In general, the notion of a material is lost when using computer aided design software [25]. Only a few applications [10, 29, 30] consider the imperfections of materials as an artistic expression. In industries that work with natural materials such as leather, defects influence the price [4], and therefore, craftsmen make trade-offs to minimize the visibility of a defect in the final product while ensuring efficient material use.

A discrepancy exists between a virtual representation during design and spatial impact in the real world [3]. Interactive fabrication [26] aims to automate all the steps of design and fabrication to make a direct connection between human input and machine output. CopyCad [9] is a camera projector system on a CNC device that aims to integrate physical objects into CAD. The Visicut project [21] employs a camera in a laser cutter for a WYSIWYG preview and positioning of graphics on objects. However, these methods do not address layout or packing problems directly.

In computer graphics, various tools are offered to the user for mapping a 2D texture on a 3D model. For instance, in UV texture mapping, the artist switches between a texturemap view and the 3D object. Other tools that assist occasional users in the transition from 3D concept to 2D parts. For instance, in the sketchchair [23] application, the user sketches a chair and the software constructs the 3D shape of the chair and calculates the 2D parts for fabrication. Autodesk 123D software [2] assists the user in fabricating 3D objects and provides a number of ways to decompose a 3D shape into 2D parts. However, these applications do not provide intelligent support for interactive manual packing or provide bidirectional feedback to inform design choices.

Bridging paper and electronic documents has been addressed by various prior art. Early systems aimed to simplify the process of digitizing paper documents [15]. Later, systems such as PADD [13] focused on interexchange, i.e., combining the affordances of both paper and digital documents. Our effort to capture and layout parts on materials is similar to the interexchange of physical and digital documents.

Within the domain of fabrication, a large body of work exists for machine optimization of layouts, bin-packing of rectangular shapes, or irregular shape nesting in the domain of fabrication [4, 7]. Machine packing is an NP-hard problem and algorithms are typically intended for mass production of shapes in clothing or metal industries. These algorithms cannot handle nontrivial or conflicting constraints present in many real-world design scenarios. Manual layout allows the user to leave material in a certain shape intentionally when using only part of the material. Users may layout parts considering their structure, e.g., grouping related parts together, which is helpful in the subsequent manual assembly process. Finally, when a design does not fit the material, interactive packing helps the user to decide which parts to remove, how to modify its shape, or how much additional material is necessary. Therefore, we focus on manual and interactive packing.

CAD drafting tools or 2D vector illustration tools (e.g. Adobe Illustrator, Rhino and Autocad) are regularly used for making layouts. Although direct manipulation of translation is supported, rotation generally requires activation via a button. Therefore, a packing task with combined manipulation of orientation and positioning [16] is less supported. Research into multitouch and tabletop computing has introduced natural interaction using physics simulation. For instance, the Bumptop system [1] allows informal organization of desktop icons using simulation of dragging and pushing motions for creating piles. Other systems have introduced 2.5D interfaces, such as the simulation of cards sliding over each other [27], or use whole-hand gestures to sweep objects [28]. Although all these systems contain collision detection and physical simulation, none are optimized specifically for packing tasks.

Other related work has focused on snapping and smart guides to assist users in layout tasks. The common implementation in 2D vector illustration software is magnetic snapping [6]; when an object is near a snapping opportunity, the object snaps into place. The snap-and-go system [5] argues that this behavior leads to inaccessible areas and proposes to change the mapping from motor space to screen space temporarily. However, these mapping systems only work via indirect manipulation (mouse + pointer). In addition, current snapping methods only support either rotation, position or scaling, and only function for specific angles (orthogonal/diagonal). Fitting irregular shapes requires manipulation of both position and orientation and snapping to arbitrary objects.

MATERIAL CAPTURE

Capturing material shape and fitting a design is an essential part of the packing task. For accurate capturing, we implemented two methods: an overlooking camera, similar to Visicut [21], and using the toolhead of a laser cutter to scan materials on the table. Both methods are shown in Figure 2.

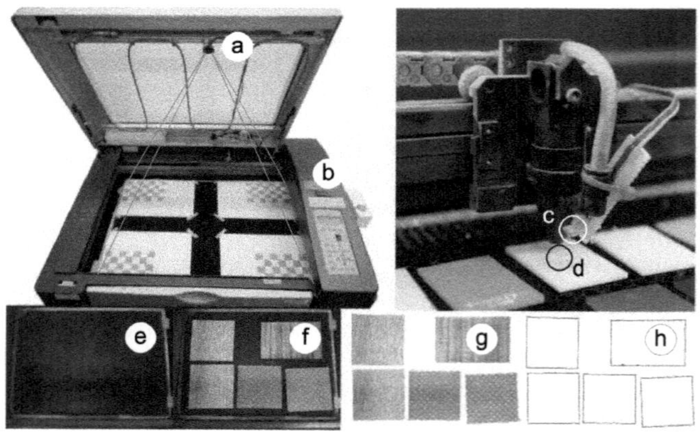

Figure 2. Top Left: an overlooking camera (a), mounted in the lid of a laser cutter for capturing materials, activated by a remote control attached to the side (b). Top right: a method for capturing that uses a photodiode (c) mounted on the toolhead of the laser cutter. The presence of material is detected by the reflection (d) of the sensing laser. Bottom row: a captured empty (e) and full table (f), the transformed and masked material (g), and the extracted edges (h).

Overlooking Camera

An overlooking camera is a commonly implemented method (e.g. [9, 10, 20, 21, 29]) when merging physical objects and virtual representations. Using projective transformation a pixel x,y in the camera image space is mapped to a point x,y on the CNC table. Our prototype is implemented on a laser cutter (7050-60w Commax Co. Ltd.) with a table size of 695mm × 495mm. We mounted a calibrated Logitech C905 webcam (960 × 720 pixels) to the lid of the laser cutter, as shown in Figure 2a. The camera captures the entire table when the lid is open, resulting in a resolution of 1 pixel to 1.17 mm.

Extrinsic calibration is performed once, when the camera is installed. White cardboard is placed in the corners of the table. The laser cutter prints calibration patterns using rastering and the homography matrix is calculated using OpenCV as shown in Figure 2. This eliminates the need for manual or visual alignment. The accuracy of this method is established in a reverse process by first cutting a grid of test patterns on cardboard that covers the entire table. A picture is taken and the perspective transformation is calculated for a number of points (N = 48). The x,y positions are then compared to the coordinates on the table. This results in a mean error of 0.83 mm and a standard deviation of 0.50 mm.

In everyday use, users capture two pictures, one of the empty table and one of the material on the table. To enable this, we attached a remote control (Figure 2b) to the side of the laser cutter. Simple background subtraction results in a mask that indicates the presence of the material (Figure 2efg). The OpenCV findContours function is used to detect the edges of the material, as shown in Figure 2h. The resulting polylines are simplified, cleaned and saved in an SVG file that contains both bitmap and vector representations. The SVG file can be used with 2D layout software to include the material position and orientation as a constraint in the design process.

Scanning Laser

An exact but slow method to acquire material on the CNC table is to use the toolhead both to cut parts and scan material. Thus, the presence of a material is directly correlated to the coordinate system of the device without prior calibration. In addition to the burning laser, a laser cutter has a low-power laser for previewing a programmed toolpath. We assume that the low-power laser is in perfect alignment with the high-power laser. As shown in Figure 2cd, an inexpensive photodiode is mounted on the toolhead and is directed toward the point where the laser hits the source material.

For each x,y position on the table, the material is sensed (non-contact) by detecting the reflection of the laser, which is measured by a 10bit analog-to-digital converter. The intensity of the reflection is dependent on the wavelength of the laser and the color of the material. This technique is accurate, but because the toolhead must be moved to probe a point, it is slow, depending on the resolution. We currently employ a serpentine scanning algorithm prototyped on a pen-plotter. Intelligent and adaptive scanning, possibly guided by the overlooking camera will speed up this process.

INTERACTIVE 2D PACKING

The interactive packing user interface makes use of a physics simulation. Parts have friction and can collide and are translated and orientated by means of a virtual spring/damper joint. In addition, basic layout functionality has been implemented such as copy, cut, paste, duplicate, grouping, parts margins, flipping parts, locking position and fixing orientation. The captured material is loaded as a background image. Around the material and inside its cavities, invisible and static boundary parts are created that collide with the parts through 2D rigid body simulation. Parts are initially placed and orientated as in the original drawing. In case of overlap with other parts or boundary parts, parts begin in a *ghost* state, i.e. no collision detection is performed, and they are drawn translucent. Ghost parts are constantly and automatically checked for overlap, and if possible, are fit in the physics simulation.

Observation Study

To obtain inspiration when designing the packing interface, we asked several people (N=8, all male, computer graphics and architecture students) to solve two packing tasks and observed the process. First, the packing of a sketchchair [23] and second, a standard problem [7] from the clothing industry often used to benchmark packing algorithms. For the observation study, we laser cut the parts from acrylic. From our observations, we extracted a number of patterns that people use when manipulating parts. 1) grouping similar parts together in subsolutions 2) compacting a group of parts by pushing parts, 3) fitting groups or parts together by subtle testing of angles and positions, and 4) using both hands. On the basis of these observations, we designed a new interface that has a foundation in both earlier physical simulation work and snapping.

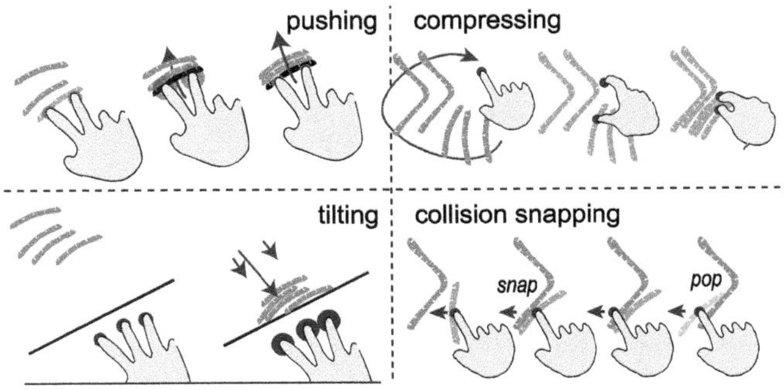

Figure 3. User Interface for making layouts. Shown are single handed multitouch ideas: (top left) a press with two fingers to push parts with the selection; (top right) a pinch gesture that compresses the selection; (bottom left) pressing on the side with three fingers initiates a tilt and all parts move towards the fingers; (bottom right) collision snapping is a combination of parts colliding and sliding over each-other.

Interaction Techniques

It was observed that users mostly gently drag parts without pushing, and that their actions consist of subtle sliding and rotating motions, and testing. Therefore, in the interface, the default behavior is that parts moved by the user collide and slide with other parts but do not alter the position or orientation of other parts. In the simulation, we temporarily lower the weight of selected parts.

Pushing. Pushing (Figure 3) to move parts was also observed. This is a default behavior in many user interfaces with physical simulation. For example, in the Roomplanner application, Wu and Balakrishnan [28] used a vertical hand motion to sweep and push objects. Likewise, Wilson et al. [27] used multiple fingers to push objects. We implemented pushing or sweeping objects as a *push* state of the selection. Activated with a modifier key or by applying pressure, the selected objects change color and push and move other objects.

Compress. Another often observed behavior was the grouping of parts into subsolutions and packing these parts tightly together in a sequence of small pushes of the outer parts. This roughly compares to building piles [1], A lasso selection selects a number of parts and is followed by a command that piles the objects. We implemented a similar compress function to pack parts together. The current prototype implementation determines the centroid of mass of the selection and applies a force toward that center for each part.

Tilt. The tilt operation lets gravity slide all the parts towards the same direction. When activated, tilt applies a force (gravity) to all parts in the layout parallel towards the position of the mouse. This is useful for moving and compressing all parts in a corner or side of the material.

Collision snapping. Dragging and pushing shapes alone is insufficient for making a 2D layout. Shapes often have to cross obstacles or move inside cavities. Therefore, the ability to *pick up*, move around, and *put back* a shape is required. As shown in Figure 4, this is achieved through the *ghost* state, which excludes a part from collision detection. In this manner, shapes can be temporarily stored in the vicinity of a target location before actually being used in the solution.

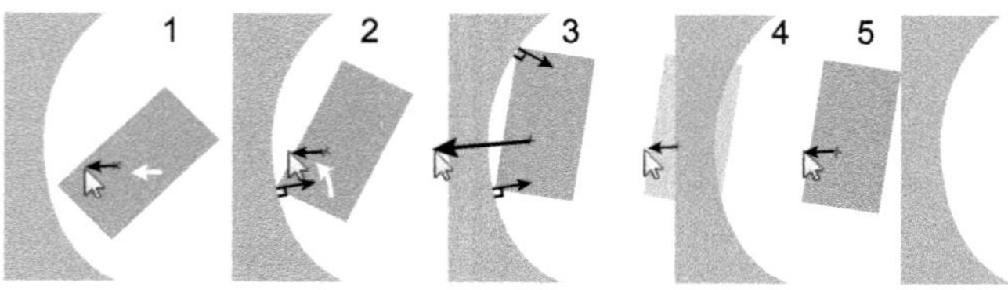

Figure 4. Collision snapping in action. From left to right: 2) The part snaps to the boundary. 3) the force in the spring between the cursor and registration point increases; 4) the part pops into ghost state; and 5) when the part has no overlap, it pops back into collision detection.

The popping back and forth from and into collision detection is implemented for mouse input interfaces. When the user drags a selection, a spring/damper joint is attached between the cursor and the selected parts. When the selection collides with other parts, the force in the spring is measured. If it exceeds a threshold value, e.g., the distance between the cursor position and part is too large, the selection pops into the ghost state and snaps to the mouse pointer. While in the ghost state, parts still have friction with the ground but do not collide. In addition, when ghost parts become overlap free, they are automatically popped back into collision detection.

Implementation

The prototype system is implemented using the Qt toolkit and supports basic functionality such as the import and export of SVG and DXF drawings and printing layouts directly to the lasercutter using the Qt printer driver. Box2D [8] is used as the physics engine. For performance, parts are simplified using polyline optimization and approximate convex decomposition [12]. We support a variety of input methods, traditional mouse, pen, and single-hand multitouch. The system is currently running in our lab and is used regularly.

EVALUATION OF THE USER INTERFACE

A full-fledged evaluation of the proposed system is beyond the scope of this paper. However, we evaluated the performance of collision snapping in a small user study. We asked participants to complete three small packing tasks for three conditions in a 3×3 experiment design. The first condition is a **traditional** drafting interface with rotation handles, as shown in Figure 5 left. The second condition involved a **fluid dragging** interface with fluid integration of rotation and translation [16]. The third condition added **collision** snapping to fluid dragging. We expected that subjects would be faster using the proposed interface when manipulating parts in the fluid condition compared with that in the traditional interface. We also expected that collision would render the fastest completion times because it reduces that need for precision manipulations.

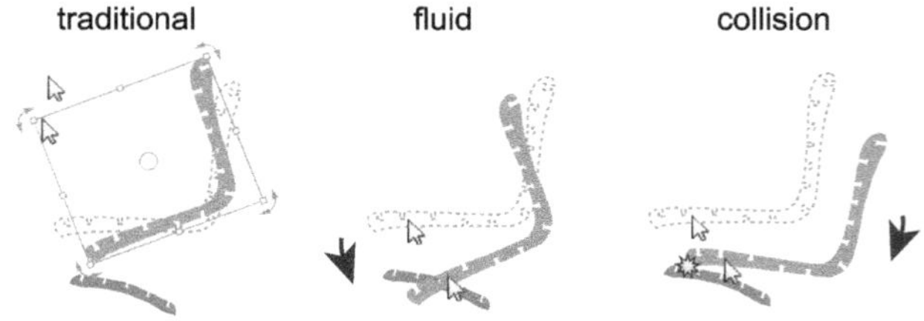

Figure 5. The user study consisted of a 3×3 design. Three conditions are shown: traditional modal drafting interface (traditional), fluid integration of rotation and translation (fluid), and collision snapping (collision).

Within each condition, we asked the participants to complete three tasks, as shown in Figure 6. In each task, a participant drags the given parts from a start position into a target area. The participants were instructed to avoid overlap in their solution. The task order was fixed: 1) dragging with simple target area, 2) dragging with irregular target area, and 3) compacting parts.

We chose a within-subjects design to reduce the error variance that we expected to find in a packing task. The three conditions were ordered semirandomly, and all permutations of the conditions were distributed among the participants. The observations during a pilot study using packing tasks revealed that we had to address carry-over effects. Therefore, we specifically chose simple tasks with minimal packing challenge and measured completion time and not utilization. The exactly same tasks were chosen for all three conditions. To counteract task knowledge and suppress exploration time, we showed the task and solution beforehand and provided time to practice the tasks at the start of each condition.

Setup

Twelve participants (2 female, 10 male), ranging in age from 19 to 33, were recruited from local universities. All participants had prior experience with vector drawing software, and some participants had experience with digital fabrication.

One participant (participant 13) did not understand the assignment and was excluded from the results.

Each evaluation took approximately 30 minutes. The software consisted of a subset of the functionality because it only allowed single-part manipulation. The software ran on a 13-inch MacBook Air. The packing task was presented to the users in full-screen mode on a 20-inch display (SyncMaster 204B). The participants used a standard wireless mouse (Logitech M310) for input. Time was measured from the mouse-down of the first drag operation to the mouse-up of the last drag operation when the participants indicated they had completed the task. The study was performed in a meeting room.

Result

In the first task we tested the performance of simple packing. As depicted in Figure 6, eight almost convex shapes of various sizes had to be fit into a rectangular target area without overlapping. The required utilization of the solution was 42%. Three parts had to be rotated to fit into the target area. The repeated measures analysis of variance showed significant effects on completion time, as observed in Figure 7, ($F(2, 22) = 14.43, P<.0005$) as shown in Figure 7. Post-hoc tests using the Bonferroni corrections showed a significant effect between the collision and traditional conditions (collision<traditional, P<.0005) and between the collision and fluid conditions (collision<fluid, P<.05). However, no significant difference was found between the fluid and traditional conditions.

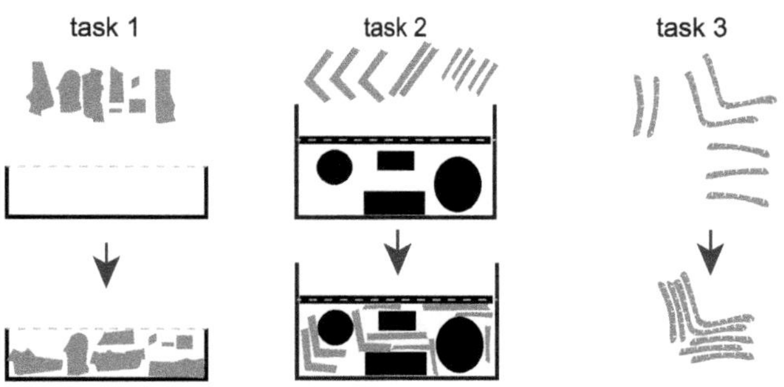

Figure 6. Within each condition of the user study, participants executed three packing tasks that involved moving parts to a target area. Top: task start and bottom: suggested solution.

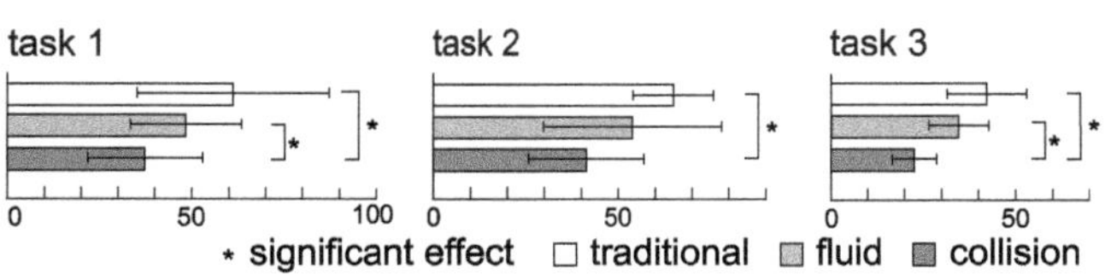

Figure 7. Results of the user study. Completion time was measured in seconds (faster is better).

The second task consisted of fitting concave shapes into an irregular shaped target area as depicted in Figure 6. Although utilization was only 30%, the target area required the user to reorient the majority of ten parts to make them fit. This task was specifically designed to test collision snapping because all parts had to be popped into the target area, with static boundary parts (drawn in black) blocking the entrance.

The repeated measures analysis of variance showed significant effects on completion time ($F(2, 22) = 4.08, P<.05$) . Post-hoc tests using the Bonferroni correction showed a significant effect between only the collision and traditional conditions (collision<traditional, P<0.05).

The final task consisted of compacting seven shapes. This task was straightforward and did not leave much room for creative packing behavior. The task was specifically designed to test snapping and orientation. All users completed this task in less than 1 minute. A repeated measures analysis of variance determined that completion time differed significantly between the conditions ($F(2, 22) = 17.96, P<.0005$) . Post-hoc tests using the Bonferroni correction revealed a significant difference between the collision and the traditional conditions (collision<traditional, P<.005), and collision and fluid dragging (collision<fluid, P<.05). However, no significant difference was found between the fluid and traditional conditions.

Discussion

Collision snapping resulted in significantly faster completion time over the traditional interface because it does not require the precise manipulations to position and orient parts. The first two tasks, in which the participants started puzzling and optimizing their solution between the conditions, allowed for multiple solutions, and therefore, they yielded less clear results compared with the third task. Nevertheless, the results indicate that although having little prior experience with the proposed improvements, our subjects performed the tasks faster than the status quo. The results also indicate that collision snapping plays a significant role in completing time for such tasks.

A number of participants noted that the fluid dragging implementation had too little friction; i.e. the parts rotated too quickly and center of mass had to be estimated to translate parts without reorientation. In future, it will be better to allow the user to adjust the magnitude of friction and the pop-force threshold in collision snapping. A few of participants reported that they preferred the traditional interface for precision manipulation.

Task 2 (irregular target area) was reported to be confusing. Because of the noncolliding ghost parts and their tight fit with the boundary parts in the target area, ghosts often remained floating and did not snap or collide with other parts. We think an improved version of the collision-snap should involve a local search to test overlap on parts in ghost state, i.e. testing for small rotation and translation variants. Then, when a fit is found, ghost parts should automatically reorient and be placed back into the simulation. We see this as a first step towards a hybrid interface.

CONCLUSION AND FUTURE WORK

We presented a system that integrates current technologies found in sensing, computer vision, physics simulations, and desktop user interfaces to assist users in packing tasks for manufacturing. A small user study indicated an increase in performance using the proposed user interface over the traditional interface.

In this paper we focused on manual layouts. The results of the second task suggest combining the collision-snapping technique with automatic packing into a hybrid interface. In the future we plan to implement hybrid solutions that offer suggestions throughout the process of making manual layouts, as well as start, finish or suggest solutions. A new avenue of research is integrating the proposed system into design software and using the features of a material and packing constraints as input for the creative process, which will allow visualization of the relationship between materials and design decisions.

Packing is a generic problem that has many applications outside the field of fabrication with 2D materials, such as in transportation and storage. We hope that our efforts will contribute to human-in-the-loop solving of open-ended spatial layout problems across various domains.

ACKNOWLEDGEMENTS

We thank the anonymous reviewers for their suggestions and ideas. We also thank Masahiro Furukawa for arranging participants for the user study. The eagle model was designed by user jtronics and is available at thingiverse.com/thing:30990.

REFERENCES

1. Agarawala, A., and Balakrishnan, R. Keepin' it real: pushing the desktop metaphor with physics, piles and the pen. In *Proc. CHI'06* (2006), 1283–1292.
2. Autodesk. Autodesk 123d. `http://www.123dapp.com`.
3. Azuma, R. A survey of augmented reality. *Presence 6*, 4 (1997), 355–385.
4. Baldacci, R., Boschetti, M. A., Ganovelli, M., and Maniezzo, V. Algorithms for nesting with defects. *Discrete Applied Mathematics* (2012). In Press.
5. Baudisch, P., Cutrell, E., Hinckley, K., and Eversole, A. Snap-and-go: helping users align objects without the modality of traditional snapping. In *Proc. CHI '05* (2005), 301–310.
6. Bier, E. A., and Stone, M. C. Snap-dragging. In *Proc. SIGGRAPH '86* (1986), 233–240.
7. Bounsaythip, C., and Maouche, S. Irregular shape nesting and placing with evolutionary approach. In *Proc. SMC '97*, vol. 4 (1997), 3425–3430.
8. Catto, E. Box2d: A 2d physics engine for games. `http://box2d.org`. Accessed: 25/01/2013.
9. Follmer, S., Carr, D., Lovell, E., and Ishii, H. Copycad: remixing physical objects with copy and paste from the real world. In *Adj. proc. UIST'10* (2010), 381–382.
10. Fukuchi, K., Jo, K., Tomiyama, A., and Takao, S. Laser cooking: a novel culinary technique for dry heating using a laser cutter and vision technology. In *Proc. CEA '12* (2012), 55–58.
11. Gershenfeld, N. *Fab: The Coming Revolution on Your Desktop–from Personal Computers to Personal Fabrication*. Basic Books, Inc., 2007.
12. Ghosh, M., Amato, N. M., Lu, Y., and Lien, J.-M. Fast approximate convex decomposition using relative concavity. *CAD 45*, 2 (Feb. 2013), 494–504.
13. Guimbretière, F. Paper augmented digital documents. In *Proc. UIST'03* (2003), 51–60.
14. Hildebrand, K., Bickel, B., and Alexa, M. crdbrd: Shape fabrication by sliding planar slices. *Comp. Graph. Forum 31*, 2 (May 2012), 583–592.
15. Johnson, W., Jellinek, H., Klotz, Jr., L., Rao, R., and Card, S. K. Bridging the paper and electronic worlds: the paper user interface. In *Proc. INTERACT '93 and CHI '93* (1993), 507–512.
16. Kruger, R., Carpendale, S., Scott, S. D., and Tang, A. Fluid integration of rotation and translation. In *Proc. CHI '05* (2005), 601–610.
17. McCrae, J., Singh, K., and Mitra, N. J. Slices: a shape-proxy based on planar sections. *ACM Trans. Graph. 30*, 6 (Dec. 2011), 168:1–168:12.
18. Mitani, J., and Suzuki, H. Making papercraft toys from meshes using strip-based approximate unfolding. *ACM Trans. Graph. 23*, 3 (Aug. 2004), 259–263.
19. Mori, Y., and Igarashi, T. Plushie: an interactive design system for plush toys. In *Proc. SIGGRAPH '07* (2007).
20. Mueller, S., Lopes, P., and Baudisch, P. Interactive construction: interactive fabrication of functional mechanical devices. In *Proc. UIST'12* (2012), 599–606.
21. Oster, T. Visicut: An application genre for lasercutting in personal fabrication. RWTH Aachen Univ., 2011.
22. Rifkin, J. *The third industrial revolution: how lateral power is transforming energy, the economy, and the world*. Palgrave Macmillan, New York, NY, USA, 2011.
23. Saul, G., Lau, M., Mitani, J., and Igarashi, T. Sketchchair: an all-in-one chair design system for end users. In *Proc. TEI '11* (2011), 73–80.
24. Schwartzburg, Y., and Pauly, M. Fabrication-aware design with intersecting planar pieces. *Comp. Graph. Forum 32*, 2pt3 (2013), 317–326.
25. Vallgårda, A., and Sokoler, T. A material strategy: Exploring material properties of computers. *IJDesign. 4*, 3 (2010).
26. Willis, K. D., Xu, C., Wu, K.-J., Levin, G., and Gross, M. D. Interactive fabrication: new interfaces for digital fabrication. In *Proc. TEI'11* (2011), 69–72.
27. Wilson, A. D., Izadi, S., Hilliges, O., Garcia-Mendoza, A., and Kirk, D. Bringing physics to the surface. In *Proc. UIST '08* (2008), 67–76.
28. Wu, M., and Balakrishnan, R. Multi-finger and whole hand gestural interaction techniques for multi-user tabletop displays. In *Proc. UIST '03* (2003), 193–202.
29. Yoshida, H. Bridging synthetic and organic materiality: graded transitions in material connections. In *ACM SIGGRAPH 2011 Studio Talks* (2011), 10:1–10:1.
30. Zoran, A., and Paradiso, J. The freed: a handheld digital milling device for craft and fabrication. In *Adj. proc. UIST'12* (2012), 3–4.

Sauron: Embedded Single-Camera Sensing of Printed Physical User Interfaces

Valkyrie Savage, Colin Chang, Björn Hartmann
University of California, Berkeley
Berkeley Institute of Design, Computer Science Division
valkyrie@eecs.berkeley.edu, colinichang@berkeley.edu, bjoern@eecs.berkeley.edu

ABSTRACT
3D printers enable designers and makers to rapidly produce physical models of future products. Today these physical prototypes are mostly *passive*. Our research goal is to enable users to turn models produced on commodity 3D printers into interactive objects with a minimum of required assembly or instrumentation. We present Sauron, an embedded machine vision-based system for sensing human input on physical controls like buttons, sliders, and joysticks. With Sauron, designers attach a single camera with integrated ring light to a printed prototype. This camera observes the interior portions of input components to determine their state. In many prototypes, input components may be occluded or outside the viewing frustum of a single camera. We introduce algorithms that generate internal geometry and calculate mirror placements to redirect input motion into the visible camera area. To investigate the space of designs that can be built with Sauron along with its limitations, we built prototype devices, evaluated the suitability of existing models for vision sensing, and performed an informal study with three CAD users. While our approach imposes some constraints on device design, results suggest that it is expressive and accessible enough to enable constructing a useful variety of devices.

Author Keywords
Prototyping; Fabrication; 3D Printing; Vision-Based Sensing

ACM Classification Keywords
H.5.2 User Interfaces (D.2.2, H.1.2, I.3.6): Prototyping

General Terms
Design, Human Factors

INTRODUCTION
Our environment is replete with products that have dedicated physical user interfaces like game controllers, musical instruments or personal medical devices. While the ubiquity of

UIST'13, October 8–11, 2013, St. Andrews, United Kingdom.
ACM 978-1-4503-2268-3/13/10.
http://dx.doi.org/10.1145/2501988.2501992

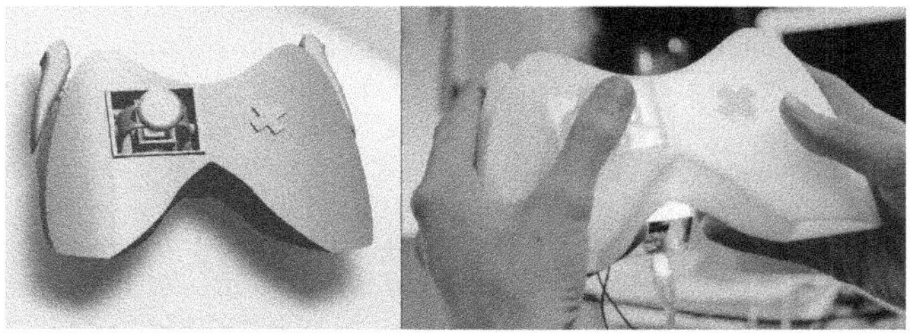

Figure 1. With Sauron, designers create a 3D CAD model of an input device and place a virtual camera in the model. Once printed, they attach a matching physical camera to sense user input on the device.

smart phones has led to a rise in touchscreen applications, retaining physicality has important benefits such as tactile feedback and high performance manipulation [11]. For example, gamers prefer physical input for speed and performance, musicians for virtuosity and control.

Rapid additive manufacturing technologies enable designers and makers (we will refer to both groups jointly as "designers" for the remainder of this paper) to quickly turn CAD models of such future devices into tangible prototypes. While such printed form prototypes can convey the *look and feel* of a physical device, they are fundamentally passive in that they do not sense or respond to manipulation by a user. Building integrated prototypes that also exhibit interactive *behavior* requires adding electronic sensing components and circuitry to the mechanical design.

Existing research has developed electronic toolkits that lower the threshold of making physical prototypes interactive [2, 7]. However, such toolkits still require designers to manually assemble printed parts and sensors. Such assembly may also require significant changes to a 3D model (e.g., to add fasteners or split an enclosure into two half shells). Detailed electro-mechanical co-design is time-consuming and cumbersome and mismatched with the spirit of rapid prototyping. Alternatively, designers may instrument the environment with motion capture [1] or depth cameras [25] to add interactivity, but these approaches limit designers to testing prototypes inside the lab in small, restricted areas.

Our research goal is to facilitate the creation of *functional* physical interface prototypes on commodity 3D printers with minimal additional instrumentation or assembly (Figure 1). In this paper, we present an embedded machine vision-based approach for sensing human input on 3D-printed physical prototypes. Our system, Sauron, enables designers to 3D print a complete interactive device in a single step. After printing, designers add a miniature camera with integrated ring light to their prototype. After an interactive registration step, Sauron can track the motion and position of buttons, sliders, joysticks, and other input devices through machine vision performed on the user's computer.

Sensing all input components on a device with complex shape can be challenging, as components may be outside the viewing frustum of a single camera or blocked by the device's geometry. To address such challenges, we introduce automatic visibility analysis and model modification to translate human input into visible movement that can be accurately tracked with standard computer vision algorithms. We first determine which components will be visible to the camera by placing a virtual camera into a CAD model during the design phase. For components that are not visible, Sauron can modify the component model's internal geometry to extend motion into the camera's viewing frustum using parameterized extrusions. Next, Sauron uses raytracing to determine how optical mirrors may be placed to make motion visible in cases where geometry modification fails because of mechanical interference. We implement these techniques by extending commercial parametric CAD software.

While computer vision research traditionally strives to uncover information about an unknown environment, our approach seeks to modify a known environment to facilitate computer vision. Prior work has demonstrated how 3D printed mechanisms can be used to detect physical motion with optical sensors [24]; we believe we are the first to automatically modify them based on analysis of a 3D design.

Our approach has some important assumptions and limitations: first, we require a 3D printer that can deposit sacrificial support material to print designs with moving parts in a single pass. Most professional machines support this, but few hobbyist machines do today. Second, for printers that cannot deposit multiple colors simultaneously, a user has to perform some manual marking of a printed model with either reflective or dark pigment. Third, our implementation of the CAD plugin can currently only process certain types of hollow models and is not guaranteed to succeed. Fourth, our current model modification techniques only work for a subset of input components. Despite these limitations, Sauron enables construction of a useful variety of devices.

To evaluate the expressivity of our approach, we describe functional prototypes created with Sauron. Three knowledgable CAD users were asked to design DJ mixing boards with our sensing approach in mind. In all cases the users were able to focus on the usability of their prototype interfaces without being impeded by the sensing techniques. We also evaluated ten pre-made models downloaded from the internet and determined that even designers who did not have vision sensing in mind while designing would have been able to use Sauron for their prototypes in seven of ten cases.

Our main contribution is a design tool enabling users to rapidly turn 3D models of input devices into interactive 3D-printed prototypes where a single camera senses input. This comprises three parts:

1. A method for tracking human input on physical components using a single camera placed inside a hollow object.
2. Two algorithms for analyzing and modifying a 3D model's internal geometry to increase the range of manipulations that can be detected by a single camera.
3. An informal evaluation of Sauron, a system that implements these techniques for models constructed in a professional CAD tool.

The remainder of this paper is organized as follows: we present related work, then a description of our approach. We offer details of our initial implementation. We present a collection of prototypes, created by us, to test Sauron's CAD modification capabilities, and the results of an informal user study using Sauron. Finally, we discuss the limitations of Sauron and conclude with directions for future work.

RELATED WORK

Sauron is informed by prior work in three distinct areas: electronic toolkits for rapid prototyping of functional physical user interfaces; computer vision approaches for sensing interaction; and techniques and systems that leverage digital fabrication.

Electronic Prototyping Tools

Electronic prototyping platforms like Arduino [2], Calder [3], Phidgets [7], and d.tools [8] enable designers to quickly create new tangible computing devices by offering accessible software abstractions for working with sensing, actuation, and display hardware. These platforms focus on working with electronic components, but offer little support for integrating such components into printed devices. Modifying a device CAD model to accommodate such hardware can be a time-intensive process: users have to address constraints like mount points and clearances for each component. Enclosures and components must then be manually assembled, which may again require CAD redesign to make assembly possible, e.g., by breaking the shell into multiple pieces and adding fasteners.

Some recent projects seek to lower this barrier: .NET Gadgeteer's CAD plug-in automatically generates mounting bosses and cut-outs for connectors [21], and Enclosed allows users to interactively design enclosures around pre-designed electronics [22]. Sauron takes inspiration from such systems; in addition, its vision sensing can also eliminate electromechanical integration and assembly steps and enable designers to print an entire device as a single object.

Computer Vision

Vision-based design tools like Papier-Mâché offer high-level event models to facilitate design of tangible interfaces [12]. Eyepatch [13] and Crayons [6] offer direct-manipulation interfaces to train vision classifiers without programming.

Some systems place cameras in the environment to track objects and users' interaction with those objects for rapid prototyping, e.g., depth cameras in SketchSpace [9] or motion

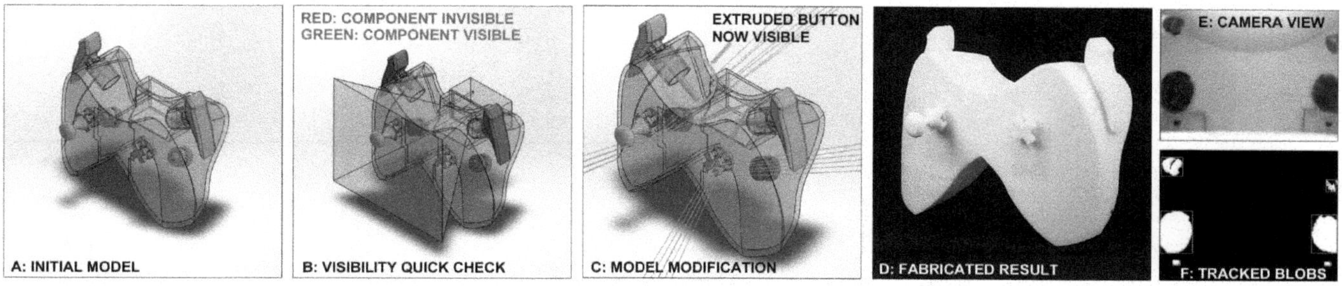

Figure 2. When designing with Sauron, a designer begins with his model (A), then inserts a virtual camera and runs quick check for visibility (B). A full model modification pass (C) performs extrusions and suggests mirror placement to bring invisible controls into the camera's view. He fabricates his design (D), then colors the inside and inserts the camera and mirrors (E). The computer vision software tracks the motion of components (F) and forwards events on to control software, such as a game.

capture systems in Display Objects [1]. In contrast to these projects, we embed the camera inside the designer's device so testing is not confined to a controlled laboratory setting. This embedding approach has also been taken by some hardware devices, e.g., the Rockin' Mouse [4], Mouse 2.0 [20], Digits [10] and Rock-Paper-Fibers [17], though these systems do not contribute general prototyping tools.

Sauron's approach shares the greatest similarity with Döring's work-in-progress on embedding a camera and projector system into product mockups [5]. We extend their work by providing visibility analysis and automatic CAD model modification techniques. We also share an approach with SLAP widgets [23] – fabricated controls that can be placed on an interactive tabletop, where controls are tracked by the tabletop's vision system. Sauron generalizes the intuition behind SLAP widgets beyond tabletop computing and offers a tool to design custom widget configurations in CAD software.

CAD & Digital Fabrication

Finally, Sauron relates to prior work in augmenting CAD tools and leveraging digital fabrication for prototyping.

ModelCraft [19] introduced techniques to edit digital 3D models based on digital pen annotations performed on folded paper versions of the model. Our goal of prototyping interactivity is orthogonal to providing new interaction techniques for model editing.

Willis's work on printed optics describes how to combine optical sensors with light guides printed using transparent materials to fabricate interactive components like buttons and sliders [24]. Their prototype requires inserting electronics at print time. With Sauron, a single camera is added after printing is complete. In addition, while Willis's work is inspirational in delineating a design space for optically sensed physical manipulation, the authors do not provide a tool for the design of such objects.

Midas fabricates capacitive touch sensors using a CNC cutter based on high-level specifications [18]. Our contribution is complementary, as Sauron focuses on vision sensing of mechanisms rather than touch input.

DESIGNING WITH SAURON

We will describe the process of designing and fabricating models for single-camera sensing with a running example: a designer wishes to prototype a new video game controller with buttons, a joystick, and a direction pad. He wants to explore ergonomics – how the controller feels to hold and how it will feel during gameplay. He follows the steps in Figure 2.

Modeling: The designer creates a 3D model of his controller in a CAD tool like SolidWorks, placing buttons and joysticks from a library of available controls Sauron provides (Figure 2A). Each library element is parameterized and customizable.

Adding a virtual camera: Using the Sauron CAD plug-in, he adds a 3D model of Sauron's camera to his assembly. This camera can be positioned anywhere on the model's surface, pointing inwards, into the interior of the hollow model. The designer then adds mount points for the camera so it can be attached with screws once he fabricates his controller.

Visibility analysis: Sauron provides a "quick check" feature which allows the designer to quickly determine if components are directly within view of the camera or if they will require model modifications (Figure 2B). In our example, the joystick and direction pad in front of the camera are visible, so they are colored green. The bumper and rear buttons are not: they lie outside the camera's field of view and are marked red.

Model modification: To make the remaining components visible to the camera, the Sauron plugin automatically extrudes the interior portion of the bumper buttons to extend into the camera's field of view (Figure 2C). The rear buttons cannot be extended, as the extrusions would intersect the controller's shell. Detecting this interference, Sauron casts rays from the camera into the 3D scene, reflecting them off the interior of the body, and determines locations where placement of two small mirrors will make the rear buttons visible in the camera image. The plugin visualizes these locations to guide the designer during manual assembly.

Fabrication and assembly: The designer sends his file (without the camera model) to his 3D printer (Figure 2D). Once the print is completed, an automatically generated instruction sheet guides him through the process of marking the interior of input components, e.g., with black marker (Figure 2E). Last, he screws the camera into its mounts.

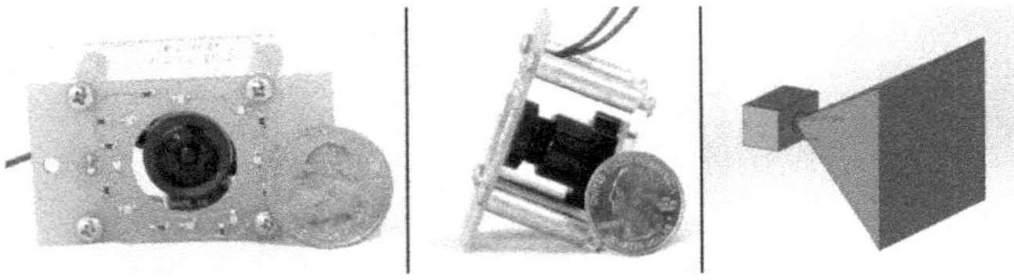

Figure 3. Left: Sauron's USB camera and ring light. Right: Our virtual model of the camera and its field of view.

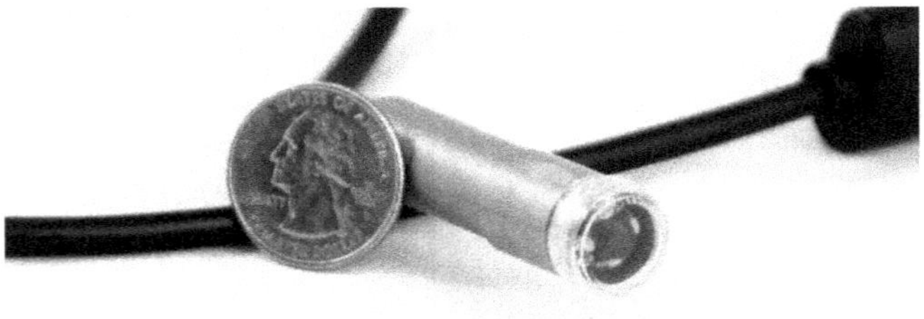

Figure 4. The hardware can be miniaturized, as in this pipe inspection camera with integrated LEDs.

Registration and Testing: Finally, the designer registers the components with the vision system one at at time: his CAD tool prompts him which component to move, and he moves each through its full range of motion to configure its component-specific recognizers. The system then tracks each component separately (in Figure 2E & F, components are: extruded bumper buttons on top; joystick and d-pad in the middle, reflected rear buttons in mirrors below). Once all the components are registered, he is ready to test his controller. Sauron sends input event data as OpenSoundControl messages, a format that software tools can understand and map to game controller events. Sauron can also deliver events over WebSockets to applications written in HTML and JavaScript.

IMPLEMENTATION

In this section, we describe Sauron's camera, CAD component architecture, algorithms for modifying internal geometry, and vision pipeline.

Physical and Virtual Cameras

Sauron uses a single camera to sense input on a physical device. In order to determine visibility of input components inside the CAD environment, Sauron uses a virtual camera that matches the physical camera's measurements and optical characteristics. We empirically measured the field of view of the camera with a geometric test pattern, and we then generated model geometry corresponding to this field of view as a reference for designers (Figure 3).

Our current implementation uses a 640x480 USB camera with a retrofitted 110 degree M12 lens (Sentech STC-MC36USB-L2.3). The interior of the model is illuminated by a ring light with eight surface-mount white LEDs. This hardware may be too bulky for handheld devices; however, there are no technological barriers to miniaturization. We have also built prototypes using a commercial pipe inspection camera (Figure 4) which is much smaller, but suffered from a low video frame rate and shallow depth of field .

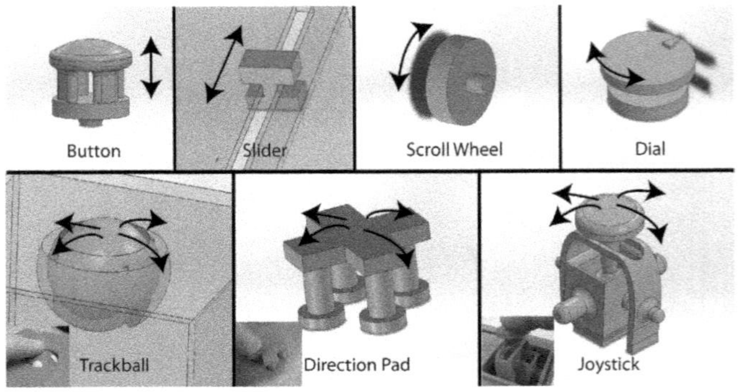

Figure 5. Sauron currently supports seven types of input components. The various components have different types of motion trackable by Sauron, from binary up/down of a button, to one-dimensional slider input, to two-dimensional input from a trackball or joystick. Extrusion features of components are highlighted in red.

Component Library and Architecture

Sauron provides a library of components with buttons, sliders, scroll wheels, dials, trackballs, direction pads, and joysticks (Figure 5). These components, when printed, will be tracked through contrasting material applied in a specific pattern or location. For many of the components, this location is in the base, which is tagged in our models. We require that designers use components with tagged geometry in their devices so our plugin understands which portions need to be visible to the camera as well as how to perform modifications. Our base components are parametric models for the SolidWorks CAD software.

Because Sauron models are parametric, designers already have significant freedom in modifying them to suit their needs. As long as the tagged geometry (on the interior, facing the camera) is kept, the exterior of the models can be changed. As an example, a designer creating a video game controller may make some buttons oblong rather than circular: the long buttons on the side of the controller in Figure 2 were built from the same parametric model as the rear circular buttons.

To create a new Sauron-compatible component, the component must exhibit visible motion on the inside of a prototype that can be tracked by the camera. Second, the component must be paired with a suitable vision algorithm to extract its state from visible changes. These two requirements can be decoupled. For example, both toggle switches and momentary switches can use the same algorithm extracting a single state bit from a change in position.

Modifying Components

Users' CAD models are modified based on an analysis of which input components fall within the field of view of the virtual camera. The two basic modifications our software considers are extrusion and mirror placement. The software which performs model modifications is implemented in C# as a SolidWorks 2012 plugin.

Extrusion

In order to perform modifications, our initial step is to extend the virtual camera's field of view feature to infinity while maintaining its angles. We revert this after all modification steps are complete. We determine visibility through collision detection between tagged model geometry and the virtual camera's field of view feature. When components are outside the field of view, e.g., on a side wall (Figure 6C), Sauron attempts to extend the component's base through extrusion (Figure 6A-B). This technique is not applicable to scroll wheels or trackballs. The model parts Sauron can extrude are shown in red in Figure 5.

To calculate extrusion depth, we first cast a ray from the component's base and determine if it intersects the field of view. If not, then we cannot reach the field of view with extrusion. We then measure the distance from the base along its normal to the field of view and update our extrusion to that depth. We next iterate through possible positions of the component (e.g., simulate a slider's motion along its track) and check that we are not intersecting any other components or the body of the device, and that we continue to meet the field of view. We iteratively extend our extrusion if we fall outside the cone and perform mechanical interference checks at all positions at each length. If we avoid collisions, the component has been successfully modified. Failure cases of this algorithm are shown in Figure 7.

Extrusion need not be limited to a single direction straight down from a component's base. We have built proof-of-concept components like the button in Figure 8, which have multiple possible extrusion directions. This increases the applicability of extrusion to more complicated geometries. Our prototype does not automatically extrude such components yet, but a designer using the camera's virtual field of view reference can make these modifications manually.

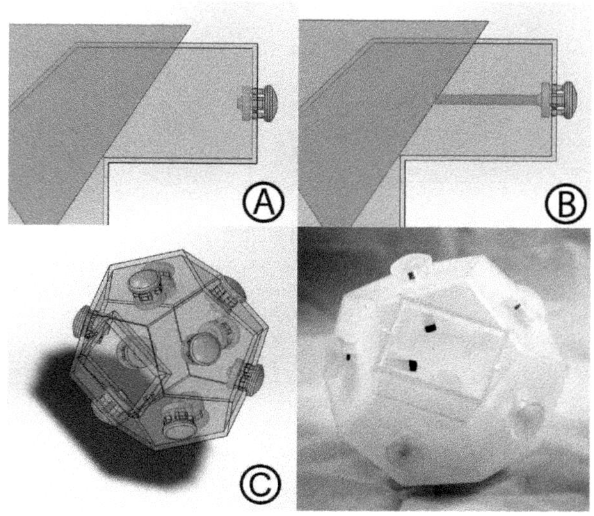

Figure 6. We measure the distance from the button to the virtual camera's field of view–highlighted in blue (A), then extrude the bottom of the button that distance (B). This technique is useful when creating objects where input components on many faces point different directions, like this dodecahedral ball of buttons (C).

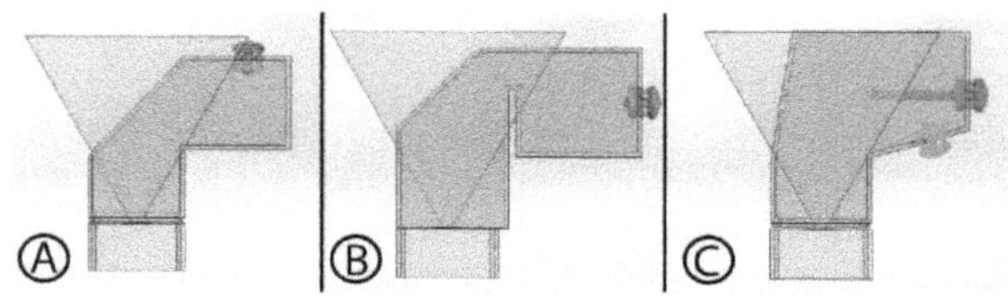

Figure 7. Extrusion does not work in some cases. The component's base may not point at the camera's field of view (A). The component's base may point at the field of view, but be blocked by the main body (B). One component's base (green), if extruded, would intersect the another component (red) (C).

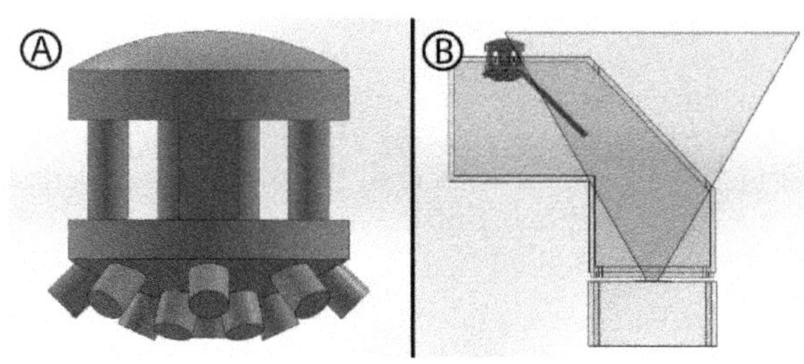

Figure 8. This prototype component (A) can be extruded in multiple directions to meet the camera's FOV cone (B).

Visibility Check, Raytracing, and Mirror Placement

Designers can check visibility of their components by seeing whether they fall within the field of view geometry of the virtual camera. However, the virtual camera's field of view shown to the user has limited depth so it does not interfere with other modeling tasks. Using raycasting, Sauron provides immediate visibility feedback by highlighting all components that are directly visible to the camera. We cast a ray from the center of the camera to the bottom of each component and determine whether that ray falls inside the field of view. If so, we perform the same check in the maximum and minimum positions of the component (e.g., we slide sliders to each end of their tracks).

We use raytracing to determine how to place mirrors for components where extrusion failed (Figure 9). The designer has to manually insert these during post-print assembly.

Each ray is cast from the camera to the body of the device, and from there reflected based on the surface normal of the body at the intersection point: i.e., we assume that during assembly the mirror will be placed tangent to the body's inner face. The reflected rays are traced to determine if they intersect any components which were not successfully modified in the extrusion step. If such a component is encountered by the reflected ray, the location on the body that it was reflected from is marked. This leaves a cloud of points per component, which informs the designer where to place mirrors during assembly (see Figure 2). Our prototype traces a coarse grid of 20x20 rays because of limitations of the SolidWorks API, in which a single trace takes up to 250ms. A more efficient reimplementation can increase rays to one per camera pixel.

The raytracing algorithm also finds occlusions. If a component is not the first object hit by any direct rays cast or any rays reflected off the main body, the user is alerted that the component needs to be moved or manually modified because it is out of the camera's view. For example, in a case with two buttons in a row and the camera's view parallel to the row, if mirror placement is not possible then the rear button would

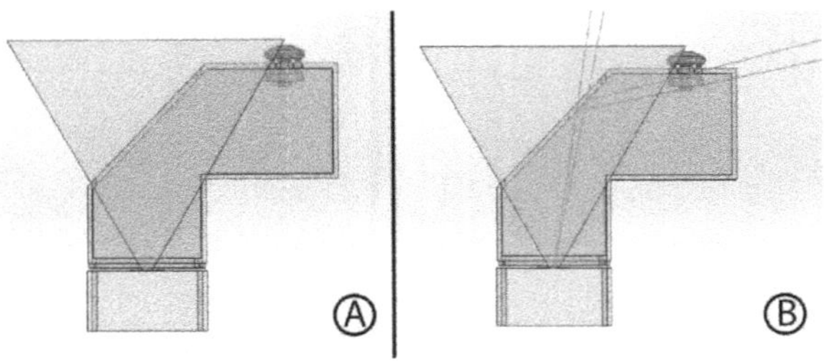

Figure 9. An illustration of the raytracing algorithm used for mirror placement. Note that the button in the figure cannot be extruded to meet the field of view cone. A mirror will be glued at the spots where the rays successfully reflect (seen in B) during assembly.

trigger this alert because all rays cast from the camera hit the front button first.

Mirrors can also be used to redirect motion to increase its visibility. For example, buttons moving along the Z-axis (toward the camera) are harder to track than buttons that move in the XY plane. A 45 degree mirror placed next to the button can redirect visible motion. Our prototype does not automatically calculate the locations of these mirrors yet.

Post-Print Assembly

Due to the nature of our sensing approach, we require that designers' models be hollow and contain a hole of suitable size for the lighting and camera rig to be inserted. Many prototypes are designed to be hollow because such designs conserve printing material. However, this requirement places some restrictions on how other elements, e.g., an LCD screen, can be placed inside the model.

We also require a few steps of assembly to make the prototype suitable for use with our vision pipeline. To increase visibility of the input components versus the background, we require the addition of some distinctive material to the input components. This material can be printed in multi-color 3D printers. Alternatively, coloring the bottoms of the input components with a pen is sufficient. We use a silver permanent pen on dark model material or a black permanent pen on light model material (see Figure 10).

Because most current materials used for 3D printing are too brittle to create small compliant parts, users must add springs manually after printing (e.g., to restore buttons after being pressed). This limitation is not unique to Sauron. We designed our buttons to allow for insertion of springs using tweezers. Any mirrors will need to be inserted as well. We

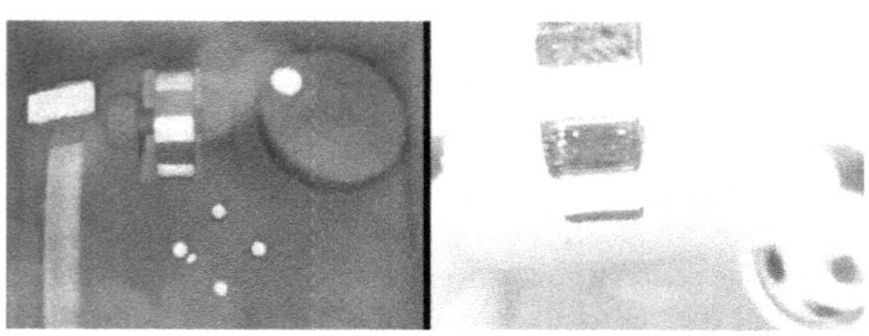

Figure 10. Components with reflective ink on black material (left) and black ink on white material (right).

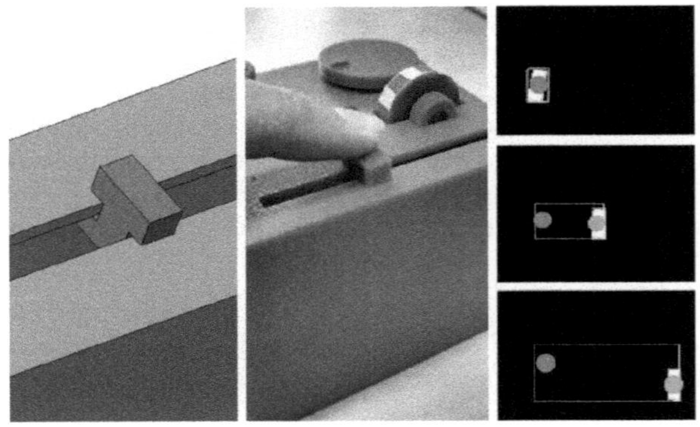

Figure 11. Sauron's SolidWorks plugin highlights each model component in turn and asks the designer to move it. The vision software creates a bounding box as the component moves through its range and also saves any information required by the component type. For example, to determine slider position later the vision software saves the two most extreme tracked center points (the red and green dots).

use small craft mirrors which we affix to the printed device's interior surface with epoxy.

Sauron generates a basic set of step-by-step instructions, automatically displayed in the designer's browser, to assist in correct model assembly. These instructions include automatically-created screenshots of the model highlighting parts that require their attention and example images showing them how to apply mirrors and how to mark components.

Machine Vision

A computer vision pipeline tracks user manipulations of components once they have been printed. We run each camera frame through a series of steps: binarization, connected components detection, and previous frame differencing. This highlights movement of components between frames.

Registration

Users have to register components before they can be tracked. During the registration process, regions of interest for each component are determined. A designer is prompted by SolidWorks to actuate each of his components in turn, and a bounding region is created that encompasses all the points through which the component moved (Figure 11). These regions determine the relative position of the component within its bounds during the testing phase.

In future work, we would like to explore more detailed simulation in the CAD environment. This could eliminate the physical registration phase by either generating and printing visual markers (and using sensing similar to [5]) in a contrasting material, or by predicting the position of the components in the camera's image and sending that information to the vision software.

Tracking

After registration, different detection algorithms apply to each input component. The techniques we use for each component are visualized in Figure 12. For *buttons*, we extract one bit of status from movement of its tracked blob. The direction pad generalizes this approach to track four cardinal directions, while the *joystick* tracks movement of X and Y

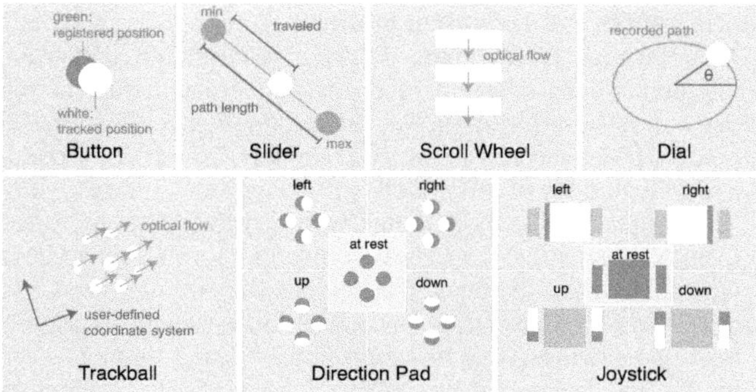

Figure 12. The different types of components in the Sauron library require tailored computer vision tracking approaches to extract state information.

axes separately. We find the absolute position of a *slider* in a unit interval by finding its blob on a line connecting the minimum and maximum positions observed during calibration (see also Figure 11). The *dial* tracks position as orientation of a blob around an elliptical path, while *scroll wheel* and *trackball* use optical flow to determine amount and direction of relative movement.

We currently do not correct for perspective in our images, which leads to non-linear behaviors in components like the slider and dial. It would be possible to account for perspective analytically since we know position and orientation of a component with respect to the camera in the model. For example, a slider follows a known line through $(x_{min}, y_{min}, z_{min})$ and $(x_{max}, y_{max}, z_{max})$ in the CAD model. Given a slider located at (u, v) in the image, we can find the point that is mutually closest (in a least-squares sense) to the line from the focal point through the image plane at (u, v) and the line of the slider's movement.

The vision component of our prototype is implemented in C++ and runs at interactive speeds (>32fps) on a 2011 Macbook Pro. We rely on the open-source computer vision library OpenCV [15] and OpenFrameworks [16]. Messages are passed between SolidWorks and OpenFrameworks via the OpenSoundControl (OSC) protocol. OSC messages are sent over UDP and contain an address (e.g., *"/button/1"*) and payload (e.g., "on" or "off"). Our prototype uses these messages to communicate processed events, to start and stop test mode, and to start and stop registration of a particular component (see Figure 13).

Testing

Sauron can deliver input events to application using either OpenSoundControl or WebSocket messages.

Existing third-party tools can transform OSC messages into keyboard, mouse, or game controller events, without the need to write code. For example, using the third-party program OSCulator, a designer could simply assign messages coming from */joystick/x* to move the mouse cursor in the X direction and from */joystick/y* to move it in the Y direction. This strategy can also be employed to generate USB HID game controller events and key presses automatically without code.

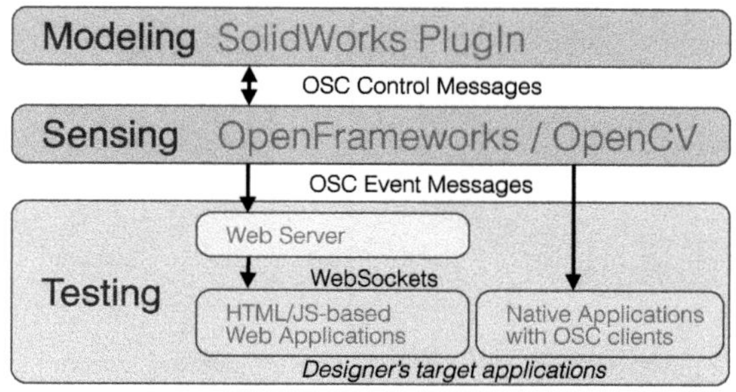

Figure 13. SolidWorks and OpenFrameworks exchange messages via OpenSoundControl. OpenFrameworks also sends OSC messages containing processed data to a WebSockets server to deliver events to a user's application.

For designers who wish for more control and who are familiar with programming, we enable event consumption in web applications written in HTML and Javascript. Leveraging web applications as a platform allows interface prototyping on any device with an internet-connected web browser. We use a node.js server which exposes processed events over WebSockets. We adopt this strategy from Midas [18].

EVALUATION

To evaluate the feasibility and expressivity of the Sauron sensing approach, we asked experienced CAD users to design Sauron devices; we also checked the suitability of various models found online for vision sensing; and we printed and tested several prototypes.

Modeling with Sauron

We performed an informal evaluation with three mechanical engineers. All were proficient SolidWorks users. We first explained how Sauron works and demonstrated a printed prototype containing examples of all our input components. We then asked them to prototype a disk jockey (DJ) controller that could be tested with Sauron. Common functions on such controllers are volume and EQ control knobs, large "scratch" wheels for two audio channels, and a crossfader. We emphasized thinking aloud, as we wished to determine how the constraints of our vision-based system affected their design process. Participants did not run the plug-in itself during the modeling sessions due to time constraints, but we ran it on the resulting models and fabricated one of their designs (see Figure 17).

All of our participants modeled DJ mixing boards that could be successfully used with our vision-based sensing approach (Figure 14). They followed different approaches to place the camera – though all showed concern for the aesthetics of their design and accordingly tried to mount the camera inside the main enclosure or otherwise out of the way. One user mounted the camera sideways (Figure 14A), but at a location such that the mixer's components would not occlude each other; another created a very deep box at the start, stating that he preferred "to focus on the user side, rather than the camera because I don't care about the box size" (Figure 14B). The most ingenious design mounted the camera on the top, pointing down, so that all components would be visible in

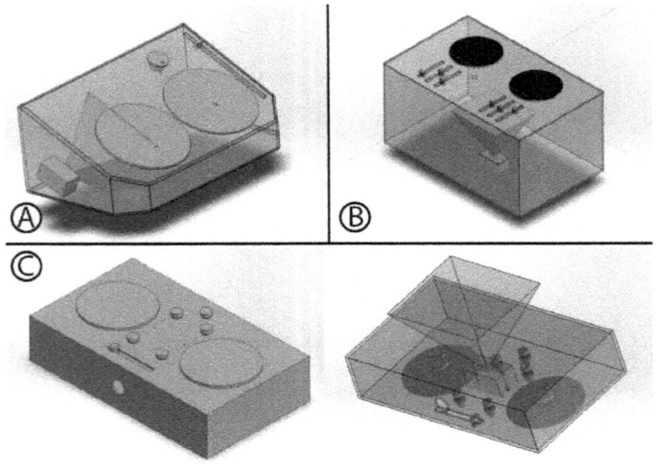

Figure 14. Our three user study participants prototyped DJ mixing boards using our component library. Each had a very different strategy for ensuring the camera could see all components. The assembly on the bottom (with interior cutaway view at right) was designed to have the camera inside reflecting off mirrors placed on the back wall.

a single large mirror placed at the bottom of the controller (Figure 14C). In aggregate, while users had to plan for the visibility constraints of camera sensing in their design, these constraints were not seen as overly burdensome.

One user wished that an interactive design checker was available to test his design iteratively for visibility. A complete model modification pass currently requires ~5 minutes to process a non-rectilinear model with 10 components, because of slow calls to the SolidWorks API. Based on this feedback we implemented the "quick check" feature which highlights components that are immediately within the viewing area without performing ray-tracing or extrusion.

Participants also successfully modified the library of parameterized components. One participant stated that it was important to her that the sensing portion of each component was decoupled from the user-facing portion. For example, the scratch wheels are large on the user's side to enable users to place their entire hand on them, while the internal dial diameter is small so it can be seen by the camera in its entirety (see Figure 14C). The same user also wished that there was better documentation for the component library, describing how large holes for mounting needed to be.

Analysis of Pre-Designed Models

To determine if designers working without our constraints in mind would create prototypes that are compatible with our vision-based system, we downloaded several online 3D models and analyzed them. The models, which comprised a deduplicated set of all models with keywords "interactive" or "controller" on the model-sharing site grabCAD.com, ranged from XBOX and Guitar Hero controllers to interactive desks with keyboards. None of the devices that we analyzed were designed for 3D printing, but rather for rendering or as engineering drawings. Our first step in processing them was estimation of the internal geometry of the bodies, for which we assumed simple shelling (i.e., no internal supports, wall thickness approximately .1", interior curves following the curves of the outside of the body). After this was done, we selected several candidate camera locations which would not interfere with what we understood to be the user-facing functions of the device, and we measured which components would be visible to the camera directly, which via extrusion, and which via reflection.

Out of 10 devices we analyzed, we believe that 7 of them could be successfully processed by Sauron. Three devices were too thin – this caused serious occlusion problems between components. Their bodies also did not allow space for the inclusion of mirrors to solve the occlusion problem (Figure 15). One of the failing devices, a steering-wheel-style device, had two handle areas with buttons at their far ends and thin, continuously-curving surfaces bending away from the main body. Using just one mirror bounce, it would be impossible to see around these bends to the buttons at the ends.

Example Devices

We also fabricated three prototypes that display the range of interactive components our prototype system offers.

Ergonomic Mouse

Our ergonomic mouse (see Figure 16) has a trackball the user can manipulate with his thumb as well as two buttons and a scroll wheel. We configured the mouse to control the mouse cursor on a laptop using OSCulator. Due to large tolerances in our model, the scroll wheel tended to oscillate between "up" and "down" states after being released. This problem could either be addressed through modifications to the model or by double thresholding in our computer vision component.

DJ Mixer

We constructed a DJ mixing board – based on a study participant's design – in two pieces to fit on our 3D printer's bed

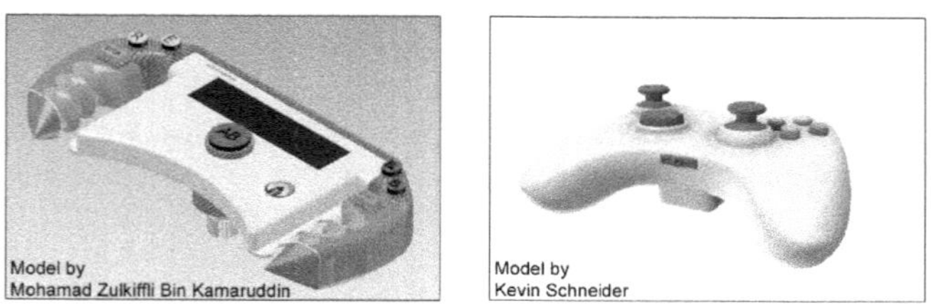

Figure 15. These models found online were too shallow to sense with Sauron—occlusion and curvature would prevent correct sensing with computer vision.

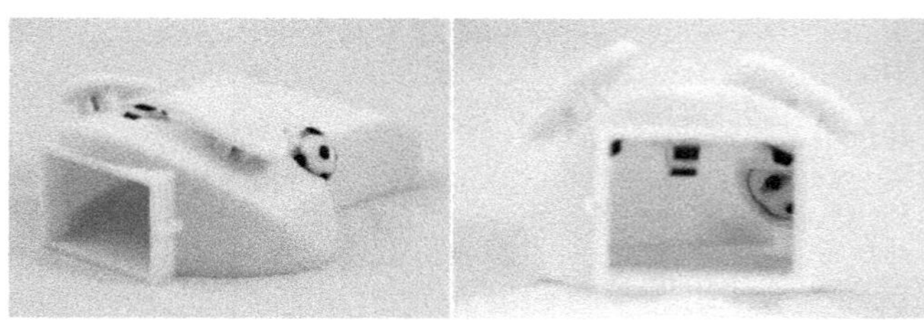

Figure 16. Our ergonomic mouse prototype has a trackball the user can manipulate with his thumb as well as two buttons and a scroll wheel. On the right is the camera's view of the inside of the mouse.

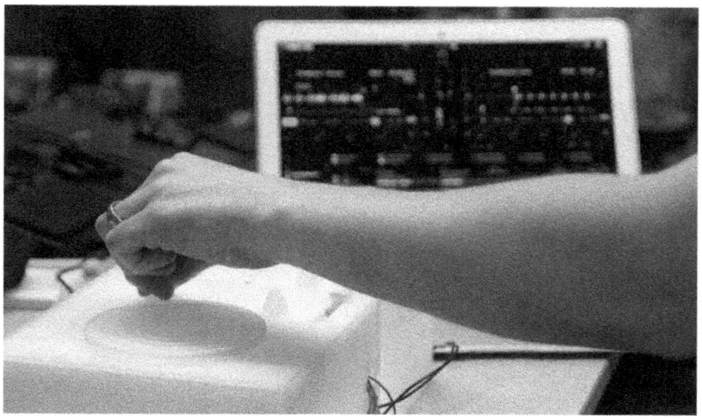

Figure 17. Our DJ mixing board, based on one of our users's designs, has sliders and two dial configurations: raised knobs for easy manipulation of volume, and a larger flat wheel for seeking and scratching songs. The different types of dials share a sensing algorithm, however, as their interior parts are similar.

size. We converted the OSC messages sent out by Sauron's vision software to MIDI messages to control Traktor, a professional DJ application (see Figure 17). One issue this prototype raised was that disparities between the virtual and physical camera parameters affected visibility. While the components were designed to fit within the virtual camera's field of view, an offset between the lens axis and the center of the sensor on our (manually-modified) camera led to some components falling outside the physical field of view. We are confident that better calibration and measurement can overcome such problems.

Game Controller

We developed two versions of a video game controller, shown in Figures 1 and 2. To test responsiveness, we built a simple browser-based game to accept data from Sauron's WebSockets server. The controller moves the player character around (joystick) and shoots fireballs (buttons). We found the game was playable, although detection of the joystick position was noisy. This seems to be due to the fact that the blobs tracked for the main base and the two flanks were lumped together when the joystick was in certain configurations, e.g., at extreme right. We believe this is not a fundamental issue and could be mitigated by iterating on the joystick's interior design or by using a higher-resolution camera.

LIMITATIONS

Currently, our prototypes still require some post-printing assembly for marking components and inserting mirrors. However, we believe this step is significantly less time-consuming than the process of wiring up a prototype with discrete electronic components.

A second limitation is the required registration process after printing. In future work we plan to create more sophisticated algorithms which can pre-determine bounding boxes of printed components using the digital model, or which can generate visual markers to denote end points and motion type. This would allow designers to skip the registration step.

Because we currently use visible light sensing, environmental lighting can interfere with our algorithms. For example, our prototypes behave erratically when tested with bright fluorescent lights directly overhead. Some components, like the slider and joystick, require a certain amount of clearance around them to move properly. When bright light shines through these gaps, vision tracking can become problematic. One remedy is to move sensing into the infrared spectrum.

Our algorithms do not deal with cases where chaining of model modifications is required: i.e., if a component could be seen by first extruding, then reflecting, it will not be correctly processed by our algorithm. We provide the field of view of our camera as a reference to designers so that they can correct cases like this on their own, however more complex automatic interior geometry modifications are possible.

Finally, we support only a limited library of components, and not all components can be modified through extrusions. However, this library is extensible by expert users who can define and label faces for extrusion and who can choose or program appropriate tracking algorithms. Our informal evaluation suggests though that configuring and changing existing components to suit the needs of a particular prototype may be sufficient to cover a useful design space.

FUTURE WORK

Current Sauron prototypes are all tethered to a PC. There are opportunities to explore interactive devices not connected to computers. For example, tangible peripherals for mobile device could also be prototyped using our system. Modern smartphones have on board cameras and LED flashes, and enough on-board processing to perform computer vision. Modeling the phone and its camera parameters could enable mobile prototypes designed to encase the phone.

We believe that an exciting use for Sauron is in the development of entirely novel input devices which are not supported by traditional electronics. One example is a curved slider: electronics typically measure either linear or rotary motion, but a slider on a curved or irregular track would be easily prototyped using Sauron.

The creation of interactive prototypes also need not be limited to 3D printed plastic. Digital fabrication opens the doors to many new areas of exploration: any process which fabricates material according to a model created in software could be processed similarly. One such promising technology is laser cutting, where we already see the ability to create 3D models through sliceforms or layering of 2D cross-sections of an object. Laser Origami [14] has pushed the bounds further, and it is not difficult to imagine fully laser-cuttable mechanisms that could be tracked by Sauron.

For future work we hope to test our tool more extensively with designers in the context of a workshop or class. We are also planning to explore tools to simplify the physical design process for users unfamiliar with CAD tools.

CONCLUSION

In this paper, we presented Sauron, a system to assist designers creating interactive physical prototypes without the need for wiring or an augmented environment. Sauron uses a camera to track input on moving physical components. Sauron can check visibility of model components at design time and modify component geometry. Several 3D printed objects created by the authors demonstrate the range of capabilities of the prototype system. Feedback from early users also suggests improvements to be made as the work continues. Beyond Sauron, we will expand our future research agenda to assist people in the creation of interactive objects by leveraging the ubiquity and power of digital fabrication tools.

ACKNOWLEDGEMENTS

This material is based upon work supported by the National Science Foundation under Grant No. DGE 1106400, a Microsoft Graduate Women's Fellowship and an Alfred P. Sloan Fellowship. The authors would also like to thank Mark Oehlberg for help with electronics.

REFERENCES

1. Eric Akaoka, Tim Ginn, and Roel Vertegaal. DisplayObjects: prototyping functional physical interfaces on 3D styrofoam, paper or cardboard models. In *Proceedings of the International Conference on Tangible, Embedded, and Embodied interaction*, TEI '10, pages 49–56. ACM, 2010.
2. Arduino : an open-source electronics prototyping platform. http://arduino.cc/. Accessed: July 2013.
3. Daniel Avrahami and Scott E. Hudson. Forming interactivity: a tool for rapid prototyping of physical interactive products. In *Proceedings of the ACM Conference on Designing Interactive Systems*, DIS '02, pages 141–146. ACM, 2002.
4. Ravin Balakrishnan, Thomas Baudel, Gordon Kurtenbach, and George Fitzmaurice. The Rockin'Mouse: integral 3D manipulation on a plane. In *Proceedings of the ACM SIGCHI Conference on Human factors in computing systems*, CHI '97, pages 311–318. ACM, 1997.
5. Tanja Doering, Bastian Pfleging, Christian Kray, and Albrecht Schmidt. Design by physical composition for complex tangible user interfaces. In *CHI '10 Extended Abstracts on Human Factors in Computing Systems*, CHI EA '10, pages 3541–3546. ACM, 2010.
6. Jerry Fails and Dan Olsen. A design tool for camera-based interaction. In *Proceedings of the SIGCHI Conference on Human Factors in Computing Systems*, CHI '03, pages 449–456. ACM, 2003.
7. Saul Greenberg and Chester Fitchett. Phidgets: easy development of physical interfaces through physical widgets. In *Proceedings of the ACM Symposium on User Interface Software and Technology*, UIST '01, pages 209–218. ACM, 2001.
8. Björn Hartmann, Scott R. Klemmer, Michael Bernstein, Leith Abdulla, Brandon Burr, Avi Robinson-Mosher, and Jennifer Gee. Reflective physical prototyping through integrated design, test, and analysis. In *Proceedings of the ACM Symposium on User Interface Software and Technology*, UIST '06, pages 299–308. ACM, 2006.
9. David Holman and Hrvoje Benko. SketchSpace: designing interactive behaviors with passive materials. In *CHI '11 Extended Abstracts on Human Factors in Computing Systems*, CHI EA '11, pages 1987–1992. ACM, 2011.
10. David Kim, Otmar Hilliges, Shahram Izadi, Alex D. Butler, Jiawen Chen, Iason Oikonomidis, and Patrick Olivier. Digits: freehand 3D interactions anywhere using a wrist-worn gloveless sensor. In *Proceedings of the ACM Symposium on User Interface Software and Technology*, UIST '12, pages 167–176. ACM, 2012.
11. Scott R. Klemmer, Björn Hartmann, and Leila Takayama. How bodies matter: five themes for interaction design. In *Proceedings of the ACM Conference on Designing Interactive Systems*, DIS '06, pages 140–149. ACM, 2006.
12. Scott R. Klemmer, Jack Li, James Lin, and James A. Landay. Papier-Mâché: toolkit support for tangible input. In *Proceedings of the SIGCHI Conference on Human Factors in Computing Systems*, CHI '04, pages 399–406. ACM, 2004.
13. Dan Maynes-Aminzade, Terry Winograd, and Takeo Igarashi. Eyepatch: prototyping camera-based interaction through examples. In *Proceedings of the ACM Symposium on User Interface Software and Technology*, UIST '07, pages 33–42. ACM, 2007.
14. Stefanie Mueller, Bastian Kruck, and Patrick Baudisch. LaserOrigami: Laser-Cutting 3D Objects. In *Proceedings of the SIGCHI Conference on Human Factors in Computing Systems*, CHI '13, pages 2585 – 2592. ACM, 2013.
15. OpenCV : open source computer vision. http://opencv.org/. Accessed: July 2013.
16. OpenFrameworks : an open-source C++ toolkit for creative coding. http://www.openframeworks.cc/. Accessed: July 2013.
17. Frederik Rudeck and Patrick Baudisch. Rock-paper-fibers: bringing physical affordance to mobile touch devices. In *Proceedings of the SIGCHI Conference on Human Factors in Computing Systems*, CHI '12, pages 1929–1932. ACM, 2012.
18. Valkyrie Savage, Xiaohan Zhang, and Björn Hartmann. Midas: fabricating custom capacitive touch sensors to prototype interactive objects. In *Proceedings of the ACM Symposium on User Interface Software and Technology*, UIST '12, pages 579–588. ACM, 2012.
19. Hyunyoung Song, François Guimbretière, Chang Hu, and Hod Lipson. ModelCraft: capturing freehand annotations and edits on physical 3D models. In *Proceedings of the ACM Symposium on User Interface Software and Technology*, UIST '06, pages 13–22. ACM, 2006.
20. Nicolas Villar, Shahram Izadi, Dan Rosenfeld, Hrvoje Benko, John Helmes, Jonathan Westhues, Steve Hodges, Eyal Ofek, Alex Butler, Xiang Cao, and Billy Chen. Mouse 2.0: multi-touch meets the mouse. In *Proceedings of the ACM Symposium on User Interface Software and Technology*, UIST '09, pages 33–42. ACM, 2009.
21. Nicolas Villar, James Scott, Steve Hodges, Kerry Hammil, and Colin Miller. .NET gadgeteer: a platform for custom devices. In *Proceedings of the International Conference on Pervasive Computing*, Pervasive '12, pages 216–233, Berlin, Heidelberg, 2012. Springer-Verlag.
22. Christian Weichel, Manfred Lau, and Hans Gellersen. Enclosed: a component-centric interface for designing prototype enclosures. In *Proceedings of the International Conference on Tangible, Embedded and Embodied Interaction*, TEI '13, pages 215–218. ACM, 2013.
23. Malte Weiss, Julie Wagner, Yvonne Jansen, Roger Jennings, Ramsin Khoshabeh, James D. Hollan, and Jan Borchers. SLAP widgets: bridging the gap between virtual and physical controls on tabletops. In *Proceedings of the SIGCHI Conference on Human Factors in Computing Systems*, CHI '09, pages 481–490. ACM, 2009.
24. Karl Willis, Eric Brockmeyer, Scott Hudson, and Ivan Poupyrev. Printed optics: 3D printing of embedded optical elements for interactive devices. In *Proceedings of the ACM Symposium on User Interface Software and Technology*, UIST '12, pages 589–598. ACM, 2012.
25. Andrew D. Wilson. Using a depth camera as a touch sensor. In *ACM International Conference on Interactive Tabletops and Surfaces*, ITS '10, pages 69–72. ACM, 2010.

PAPILLON: Designing Curved Display Surfaces With Printed Optics

Eric Brockmeyer [1], Ivan Poupyrev [1], Scott Hudson [2]

[1] Disney Research Pittsburgh,
4720 Forbes Avenue,
Pittsburgh, PA 15213 USA
{eric.brockmeyer, ivan.poupyrev}
@disneyresearch.com

[2] HCI Institute,
Carnegie Mellon University
5000 Forbes Avenue,
Pittsburgh, PA 15213 USA
scott.hudson@cs.cmu.edu

ABSTRACT

We present a technology for designing curved display surfaces that can both display information and sense two dimensions of human touch. It is based on 3D printed optics, where the surface of the display is constructed as a bundle of printed light pipes, that direct images from an arbitrary planar image source to the surface of the display. This effectively decouples the display surface and image source, allowing to iterate the design of displays without requiring changes to the complex electronics and optics of the device. In addition, the same optical elements also direct light from the surface of the display back to the image sensor allowing for touch input and proximity detection of a hand relative to the display surface. The resulting technology is effective in designing compact, efficient displays of a small size; this has been applied in the design of interactive animated eyes.

ACM Classification: H.5.2 [Information interfaces and presentation]: User Interfaces - Graphical user interfaces; Input devices and strategies.

Keywords: 3D printing, fabrication, touch sensing, finger input, gestures, interactive characters, alternative displays.

INTRODUCTION

There has been rapidly growing interest in departing from traditional flat rectangular paradigm of todays display technology, and in exploring alternative display forms and shapes for interactive applications. These include but are not limited to, the design of spherical, polyhedra and volumetric displays [2, 3, 9, 13, 21, 24], the exploration of bendable, deformable and elastic displays [23, 17, 18, 7] as well as actuated displays that change their shape dynamically [14, 19, 20].

PAPILLON is a technology for designing *3D curved display surfaces* that both act as information display and sense two dimensions of human touch. There are formidable challenges in designing curved visual displays. Traditional displays commonly used in consumer electronic devices such

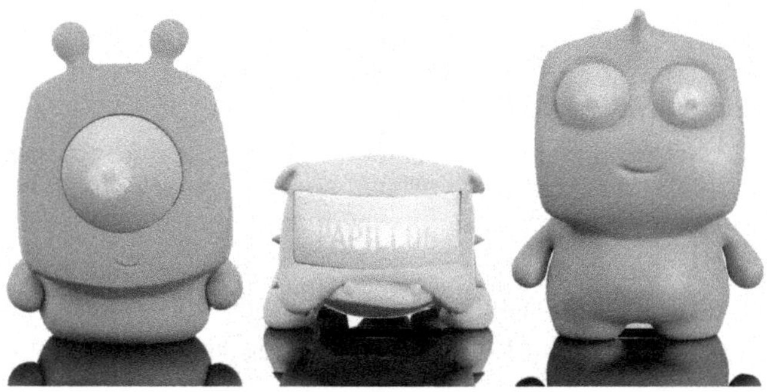

Figure 1. Curved displays are embedded into the characters to design interactive eyes. The characters are passive and do not have any electronics embedded.

as liquid crystal displays (LCD), can not be easily manufactured as arbitrary 3D shapes. Flexible displays, such as organic light emitting displays (OLED) and electrophoretic displays [17] can be bended and twisted, but can not be formed into an arbitrary shape, e.g. a spherical cap. Projecting images onto curved screens allows for the display of various forms [3, 5]. However, due to the size of a projectors, focal length and the need for an unobstructed optical path, it is often difficult to use them in small devices, e.g. interactive characters and toys. Additionally, enhancing all these approaches with touch sensitivity introduces yet another level of complexity and design challenges.

PAPILLON addresses many of these challenges by exploring a recently proposed *printed optics* approach [26], where the surface of display is constructed as an array of printed optical elements, i.e. 3D light pipes, that direct images from an image source to the surface of the display (Figure 1). The choice of the image source is arbitrary and it could be a traditional projector or an LCD screen. Crucially, the display surface and display driving electronics are effectively *decoupled,* which allows arbitrary curved display surfaces to be designed and iterated without modifying the conventional planar image source. In addition, the same optical elements can also direct light from the display surface to an image sensor allowing position and proximity of user hand to be tracked. Touch, proximity and position sensitivity of *PAPILLON* is an important contribution of this work.

PAPILLON represents a significant new application and development of *Printed Optics* that further explores its vi-

UIST'13, October 08 - 11 2013, St Andrews, United Kingdom

ACM 978-1-4503-2268-3/13/10$15.00.
http://dx.doi.org/10.1145/2501988.2502027

sion of creating tools for designing highly customizable interactive devices. The original printed light pipes displays described in [26] were limited to flat surfaces. As we discuss later, designing curved display surfaces with printed optics technique is a not a trivial problem. This is due to the fact that classic square pixel grids can not be remapped onto a curved surface without introducing significant image distortions. Investigating, designing and implementing the algorithms that allow to compute pixels arrangements for curved display surfaces is a contribution of this paper.

The design of *PAPILLON* was motivated by a specific application: designing highly expressive animated eyes for interactive characters, robots and toys. Expressive eyes are essential in any form of face-to-face communication [3] and designing them has been a challenge [1]. *PAPILLON* provides effective and efficient solution to this challenge.

The rest of the paper describes the design of the *PAPILLON* approach and it's contributions are as follow:

1. A set of fundamental techniques for producing spherical display surfaces using printed optics approach and alternative, non-rectangular pixel arrangements.
2. A technique for bi-directional touch, position and proximity sensing on curved surfaces using printed optics.
3. An application of display and sensing for designing animated eyes in interactive characters and toys.

RELATED WORK

There is a rich history of exploring display shapes in designing user interfaces. Some of the relevant explorations include volumetric displays [9], non-planar displays such as spherical, cubic or polyhedral [3, 21, 24], displays distributed in environments [22], collocated or embedded in everyday objects [11], actuated displays that change their shapes dynamically [7, 19, 20] and even biological displays where the change of appearance of biological species is used as a display modality [6, 16]. The overall goal is to find new forms for effective information presentation, exploring novel aesthetic qualities or designing displays appropriate for specific application limitations.

One of the key challenges in designing and exploring alternative display form-factors is creating technologies to display information on non-planar, *curved surfaces*. In this paper we will discuss the two classes of curved displays:

Ruled display surfaces are those that can be produced by sweeping a single line in Euclidean 3D space. Intuitively they can be understood as surfaces that could be produced by bending and twisting a flat plane, such as a sheet of paper, without tearing or stretching it (Figure 2).

Doubly curved display surfaces are those that can produce arbitrary surfaces with curves across both surface subdivision directions, such as spherical or parabolic shells.

There are three technological approaches that can be used to create curved displays surfaces. First, is *projection* on the curved or flexible surfaces [3, 5] which allows for the creation of an arbitrary display surface but requires embedding the projector in the device limiting the applications of these displays. Second, *assembling curved surfaces* out of smaller planar displays or even single pixels [24, 22, 21] which

Figure 2. Classes of curved display surfaces.

limits the resolution and form factor of the displays and has high design complexity. Third, using flexible displays to create desired shapes [11] which allows for high quality displays, but is limited to ruled display surfaces. In this paper we introduce a fourth approach, which is designing curved display surfaces using *3D printed optical elements*, which allows for the creation of both ruled and spherical display surfaces and unlike projection based curved displays it can be used with a variety of display devices, e.g. projectors, tablet computers and interactive tables. We chose to use spherical cap as a step towards arbitrary doubly curved surfaces, which we have not yet resolved.

Implementing touch and gesture sensitivity is another challenge in designing curved display devices. Traditional touch sensing techniques, i.e. projective, capacitive, optical or acoustic surface waves were designed for flat surfaces and fail on the irregular shaped displays. Computer vision techniques based on infrared illumination, FTIR and depth tracking are effective [1, 27], but require a clear optical path from the user touching the surface to the vision sensor, i.e. it has to "see" the curved surface. This could be a limiting factor, e.g. it makes it difficult designing interaction with very small curved displays. Recognizing touch and gesture events from sound is another possibility, but it does not allow precise position tracking [10]. Creating overlay sensors for curved surfaces has also been proposed [12], but in many cases it obstructs the surface or introduces significant additional complexity. The most relevant touch sensing approach is using embedded optical pathways between object surface and the sensor, so that the user touch could be seen "through" the object [7, 15, 28]. In *Papillon* we use the same 3D printed optical structures both for display and touch sensing, making sensing completely seamless and requiring very little instrumentation of the device.

Multiple applications of curved displays were proposed, including data visualization and group interaction, innovative interfaces for consumer electronic devices, advertisement, labeling and packaging [3, 11, 17, 21, 24]. The current work was motivated by challenges in designing animated eyes for interactive characters, toys and robots. The classic approach to designing eyes, in the movie and location-based entertainment industry, is to build mechanically actuated, animatronic eyes [1] that tend to be realistic but complex, expensive and difficult to scale down to fit into small characters, where space for motors and driving electronics may not be available. Furthermore, the animatronic approach is not applicable to fictional characters from animated movies, comics and cartoons whose eye expressions are non-realistic and highly exaggerated.

Rear-projection images of eyes and faces allows for the design of animated and highly expressive eyes for large-

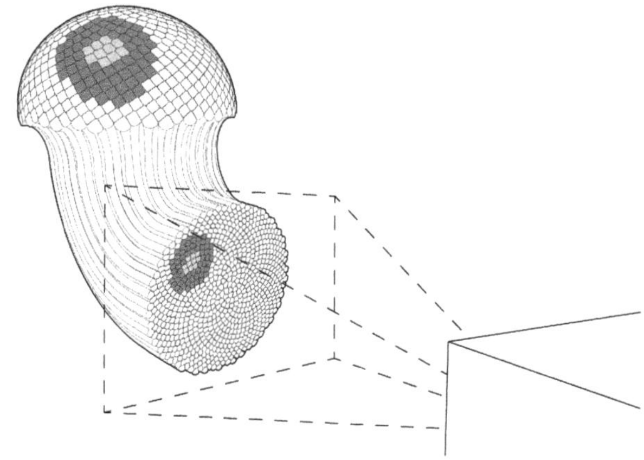

Figure 3. *Papillon* curved display design.

scale characters and robots [3]. It is, however, not scalable to small characters due to limited space. Furthermore, popular characters often take on a broad variety of appearances, from a talking sea sponge to a chameleon, with complex faces and bodies, where eyes could be sunk deep inside or stick out. Designing free air optical paths for these characters is difficult and often impossible unless we can design a technology that can effectively guide light between any two locations on the body of the character. The *Papillon* technology allows us to achieve that.

PAPILLON CURVED INTERACTIVE DISPLAYS

Papillon provides curved display surfaces using printed optics technology [26]. The surfaces are 3D printed as bundles of light pipes using transparent UV cured photopolymers separated by a translucent support material. The light pipes guide images from the receiving end of the bundle to the top of the surface (Figure 3).

The key advantage to this approach is that the design of the curved display surface is largely *decoupled from the image source* allowing for the use of projectors, LCD and OLED displays, LED arrays, laser projectors, etc. Another important advantage of this approach is that it allows for *spatial separation* of the image source and displayed image, which is important when designing embedded displays for small objects such as interactive characters (Figure 1).

Early explorations of the printed optics demonstrated feasibility of this approach but were limited to *planar surfaces*. Extending it to curved displays, however, is not trivial. It requires consideration of pixel topologies that allow to 1) transmission of images with minimum distortion and 2) allow effective packing of 3D light pipes.

Designing Light Pipes Topologies

The fundamental challenge in *PAPILLON* is designing an arrangement of pixels on a spherical display surface that satisfies the following requirements:

Isotropic pixel arrangements on a surface, i.e. the distances between all neighboring points on both input and output surfaces have to be uniform. On the receiving side it would sample the provided image uniformly. On the display side it would produce a consistent, uniform image with minimal gaps or distortions.

Isomorphic mapping between pixels on a sampling plane and pixels on the curved surface, in particular the relative arrangement and order of pixels on the bottom should correspond to the same arrangement and order on the top. This way we can assume that the image is undistorted, e.g. not reversed when displayed on the curved surface.

Pipes diameter and spacing must be within the tolerances that are possible with current 3D printing technology.

Design of the isotropic pixel arrangements depends on the properties of the geometric surface and will be different for ruled and spherical surface design.

Pixel topologies for ruled display surfaces.

Ruled display surfaces can be remapped to the plane surfaces without tears and stretching and, therefore, any classic 2D lattice, can be effectively used for pixel arrangements. A 2D Bravais lattice is a set of points created by generative discrete translations operations defined as:

$$\Lambda = n_1 \cdot \overrightarrow{a_1} + n_2 \cdot \overrightarrow{a_2} \quad (1)$$

where n_1 and n_2 are any integer number. It was demonstrated that there are only five types of lattices defined by Equation 1: oblique, rectangular, rhombic, hexagonal, and square [4]. These five latices represent basic pixel topologies for ruled display surfaces, e.g. Figure 4 and the middle character on Figure 1 demonstrate the surfaces based on rectangular and hexagonal lattices.

Pixel topologies for doubly curved surfaces.

There are no standard lattices that are effective for any arbitrary doubly curved surfaces, each pixel arrangements has to be designed individually for each surface. In this paper we develop pixel arrangements for *spherical display surface* that is one of the most common surfaces used in broad variety of applications [e.g. 3, 23].

Traditional rectangular lattices (Equation 1) produce significant distortions when mapped on spherical or general doubly curved surfaces, the resulting points will not be

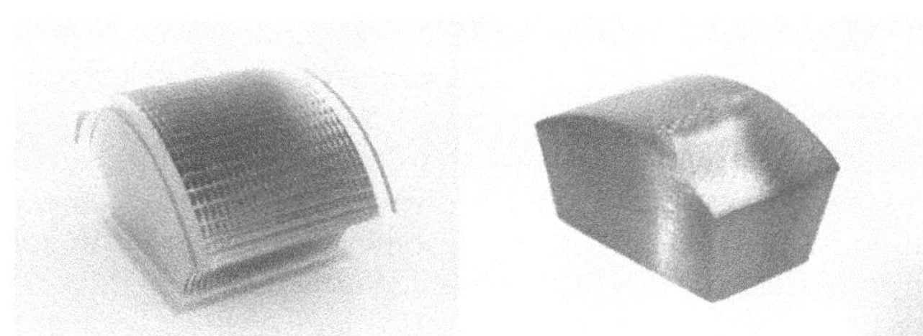

Figure 4. Ruled display surfaces with square (left) and hexagonal (right) pixel arrangements.

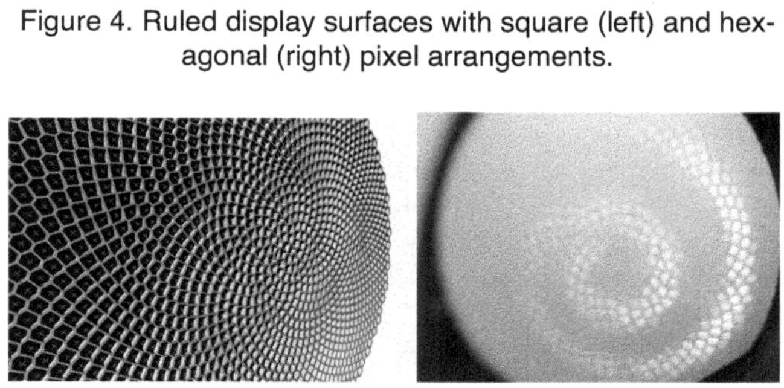

Figure 5. spheric display surfaces with Fibonacci pixel arrangements.

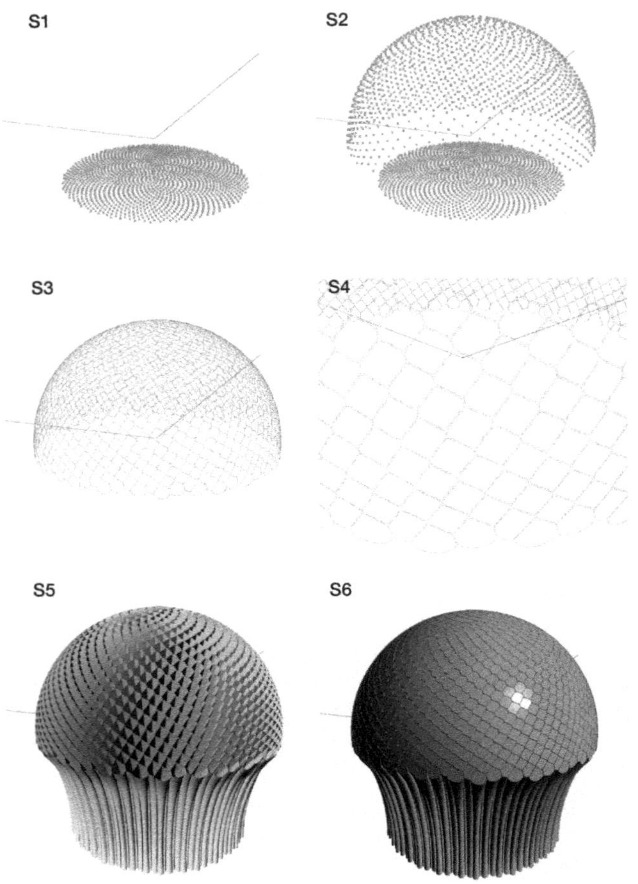

Figure 6. *PAPILLON* production pipeline.

spaced uniformly [7]. In computer graphics such spherical projection distortions can be controlled by warping 2D images before projection so that they appear normal when seen on spherical screen [3]. In case of printed optics implementing spherical warping in physical form is challenging and an alternative pixel topology has to be designed.

To address this challenge for spherical surfaces we use *generative Fibonacci lattices*. The points of the Fibonacci lattice are arranged along a tightly wound spiral on a sphere and can be calculated as follows [8]. Let N be any natural number and i an integer ranging from $-N$ to N. The number of points is $P = 2N + 1$ and i-th point of the Fibonacci spiral in spherical coordinates is computed as follows:

$$lat_i = arcsin\left(\frac{2i}{2N+i}\right), \qquad (2)$$
$$lon_i = 2\pi i \phi^{-1}.$$

The resulting pixel topology is evenly spaced occupying roughly the same area. We can easily control the density of pixels by changing N. Figure 5 demonstrates the spherical pixel topology with 756 points. This technique does not directly translate to arbitrary 3D surfaces and part of our future work includes integrating methods such as simulated annealing with our approach. However, for spherical solutions the Fibonacci pattern allows for a direct mapping of points from the 2D to 3D surface without any twisting of the pipes, i.e. the center line of the pipes are all in plane with the origin.

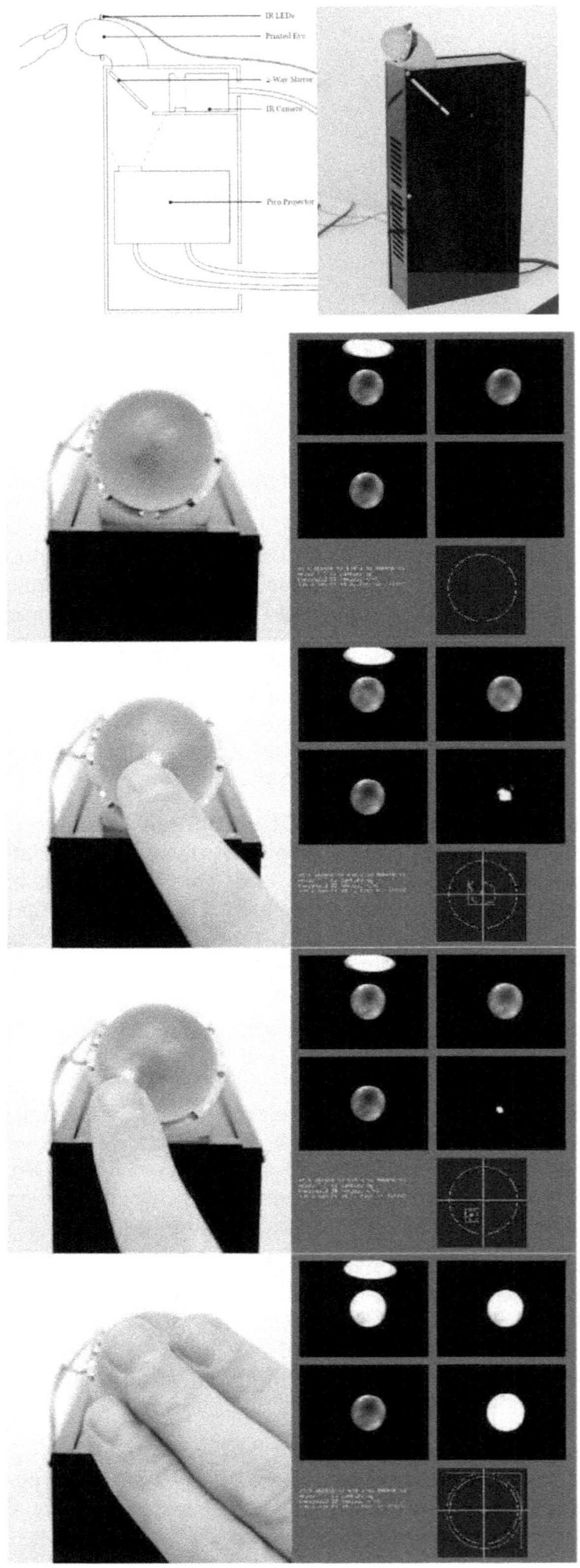

Figure 7. Position sensing on curved display

Curved Display Production Pipeline

Figure 6 outlines a basic production pipeline for spherical, curved display surfaces. All geometric computations were performed using Rhino 5.0 3D modeling environment extended with Grasshopper 9 parametric modeling toolset. Each step in the pipeline were computed using custom written Python scripting component.

In *Step 1* the pixel distribution is computed on the planar surface using Equation 2. This pixel distribution forms the base of the pipelines that is used to sample images to be displayed on the curved display surface. In *Step 2* the pixel distribution is computed on the spherical surface using the same Equation 2. Note that pixel clouds computed on Step 1 and Step 2 are isomorphic.

The Voronoi tessellation of the spherical surface is computed in *Step 3* forming a spherical mesh. The support material area around the mesh is computed in *Step 4* and polygons forming the top of the light pipes are computed. The light pipes walls are extruded from the curved surface into the bottom plane in *Step 5* creating areas where support material will be printed. The light pipes are filled with the optical clear material in *Step 6* producing final model that is 3D printed.

Touch Sensing with PAPILLON

The printed light pipes allow bi-directional curved surfaces where the same structures are used both to display an image and measure touch location. We chose to use diffuse IR illumination and camera based sensing, because this allows to preserve the physical decoupling between the interactive touch display and sensing apparatus.

We implemented touch and position sensing by augmenting 3D printed sphere with 8 infrared LEDs with a wavelength of 850 nm (Figure 7). As the user finger is approaching the spherical surface, infrared light bounces from the finger into the light pipes and onto a two-way mirror. A mirror, which is an acrylic sheet coated with aluminum oxide, is 50% transparent passing the light from the projector creating an image on the surface of the sphere. At the same time the mirror reflects IR image from the light pipes onto a PointGrey Flea3 monochrome camera outfitted with 2.1 mm wide angle lens. A Kodak No87 Wratten IR filter removes visible light from the projector and the environment. To track the position of finger the infrared image captured by the camera is filtered, the background is subtracted and resulting image is thresholded to improve the image clarity. The image is then dilated to account for the spacing between printed light pipes, producing contiguous shapes detected with blob detection algorithms (Figure 7).

The resulting design allows us to both display images on the surface of the 3D printed sphere and sense position of human finger touching its surface. This technique is generic and can be extended to any other 3D printed curved display surface of the similar size. As with most diffuse illumination touch displays, ours is designed to detect actual surface contact, it can see the finger about 10mm above the surface.

APPLICATION: INTERACTIVE CHARACTERS

There are multiple applications of 3D printed curved interactive surfaces. We explored applications of PAPILLON for designing highly expressive animated eyes for interactive characters, robots and toys (Figures 8, 9). Our technology has a number of advantage when compared with alternative approaches.

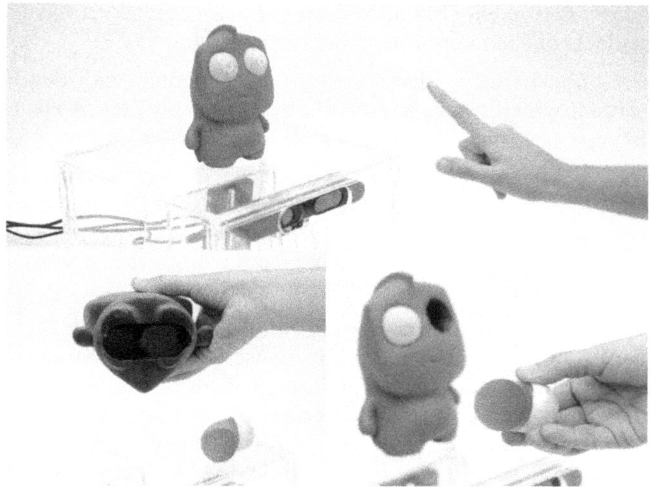

Figure 8. Interactive characters with *PAPILLON*.

Figure 9. Dynamic animated eyes with PAPILLON.

Arbitrary eye shapes and placements. Our eye elements are digitally designed and 3D printed, therefore, they can take any shape and location that is required by the character. They also extend to characters with a multitude of eyes.

Passive, non-instrumented characters. The characters and toys implemented with *Papillon* technology do not have any interior active electronic elements, moving parts, wires and power requirements. They are completely passive and all the images are projected from the outside into the character (Figure 8) This allows creating engaging, yet easily replaceable and very robust interactive characters.

Rich interactivity. Characters are instrumented with depth camera which tracks presence of the user as well as basic interactions, such as pointing or extending the hand.

Rich communication and expressiveness. Because images are projected into the character's eyes, they can communicate a rich set of emotions and intentions (Figure 8). The expressions that our characters create can not be produces by traditional animatronic technologies.

We evaluated our characters in informal studies with children 6 to 8 years old and the response was extremely positive. Children had no difficulties in recognizing the emotions and "facial expressions" communicated by our characters via animated eyes. They found our characters to be fun and engaging.

CONCLUSIONS

PAPILLON opens new and exciting opportunities in creating novel interactive devices. In particular it allows for the design and exploration of novel form factors for display devices and their applications. This paper establishes basic approaches to designing and developing novel display form factors using a printed optics approach. We hope that it will provide foundation and encourage researchers and practitioners in future experimentation and development and may be applied to a broader range of surface topologies and applications.

ACKNOWLEDGMENTS

We thank Karl Willis for his advice and insight. We are also thankful to Mo Mahler, Jonna Dauner and James Krahe for their help in designing the characters and eye animations.

REFERENCES

1. Basset, K., Hammon, M., Smoot, L. A Fluid-Suspension, Electromagnetically Driven Eye with Video Capability for Animatronic Applications, In IEEE Humanoid Robots, 2009. pp. 40-46
2. Baudisch, P., Becker, T., and Rudeck, F. Lumino: Tangible blocks for tabletop computers based on glass fiber bundles. In CHI '10, ACM (2010), 1165–1174.
3. Benko, H., Wilson, A., Balakrishnan, R. Sphere: multi-touch interactions on a spherical display. In ACM UIST'08, 2008, 77-86.
4. Davey, B. Introduction to Lattices and Order. Cambridge University Press. 2 ed. 2002. 310 p.
5. Delaunay, F., de Greeff, J., Belpaeme., T. A Study of a Retro-Projected Robotic Face and its Effectiveness for Gaze Reading by Humans. In IEEE Human-Robot Interaction, 2010. pp. 39-44
6. Cheok, A., Kok, R., Tan, C., Fernando, O., et al. Empathetic living media. In ACM DIS'08. 2008. pp. 465-473.
7. Follmer, S., Leithinger, D., Olwal, A., Cheng, N., Ishii, H. Jamming user interfaces: programmable particle stiffness and sensing for malleable and shape-changing devices. In ACM UIST'12. 2012. pp. 519-528.
8. González, A. Measurement of Areas on a Sphere Using Fibonacci and Latitude–Longitude Lattices. Mathematical Geosciences, 1 (42). 2010. pp. 49-64.
9. Grossman, T., Balakrishnan, R. The design and evaluation of selection techniques for 3D volumetric displays. In ACM UIST '06. 2006. pp. 3-12.
10. Harrison, C., Schwarz, J., Hudson, S. TapSense: enhancing finger interaction on touch surfaces. In Proceedings of ACM UIST '11. 2011, pp. 627-636
11. Holman, D., Vertegaal, R., Altosaar, M., Troje, N., Johns, D. Paper windows: interaction techniques for digital paper. In ACM CHI'05, 2005. pp. 591-599.
12. Holman, D., Vertegaal, R. TactileTape: low-cost touch sensing on curved surfaces. In UIST '11 Adj. pp. 17-18.
13. Hoover, P., Cabrera, L. E., and Aumiller, C. Augmented reality, surface style: Extending displays through fiber optics. In Ext. Abstracts CHI '10, ACM (2010), 2681–2684.
14. Iwata, H., Yano, H., Nakaizumi, F., and Kawamura, R. Project FEELEX: adding haptic surface to graphics. In ACM SIGGRAPH'01. 2001. pp. 469–476.
15. Jackson, F., Bartindale, T., Olivier, P. FiberBoard: compact multi-touch display using channeled light. In ACM ITS '09, pp. 25-28.
16. Kuribayashi, S., Wakita, A. PlantDisplay: turning houseplants into ambient display. In ACM ACE '06. Article 40.
17. Lahey, B., Girouard, A., Burleson, W., Vertegaal, R. PaperPhone: Understanding the Use of Bend Gestures in Mobile Devices with Flexible Electronic Paper Displays. In ACM CHI'11. 2011. pp. 1303-1312.
18. Leithinger, D., Ishii, H. Relief: a Scalable Actuated Shape Display. In ACM TEI '10. pp. 221-222.
19. Leithinger, D., Lakatos, D., DeVincenzi, A., Blackshaw, M., Ishii, H. Direct and Gestural Interaction with Relief: a 2.5D Shape Display. In ACM UIST '11. pp. 541-548.
20. Poupyrev, I., Nashida, T., Maruyama, S., Rekimoto, J., Yamaji, Y. Lumen: Interactive visual and shape display for calm computing. ACM SIGGRAPH Emerging Technologies, 2004. p. 17.
21. Poupyrev, I., Newton-Dunn, H., Bau, O. 40: Interaction with Multifaceted Display Devices. In ACM EA CHI'06, 2006, 1241-1246.
22. Sato, M., Suzuki, Y., Nishizaka, S., Torigoe, Y., et al. Large-scale displays for public spaces---constellation of departure: presenting the impression of airplanes taking off above an airport departure lounge. Computers in Entertainment. ACM. 2011. 9, 1, Article 4.
23. Schwesig, C., I. Poupyrev, E. Mori. Gummi: a bendable computer. In ACM CHI'2004, 2004, pp. 263-270.
24. Stavness, I., Lam, B., Fels, S. pCubee: a perspective-corrected handheld cubic display. In ACM CHI'10, 2010, pp. 1381-1390.
25. Stevenson, A., Perez, C., Vertegaal, R. An inflatable spherical multi-touch display. In ACM TEI'11. 2011. pp. 289-292.
26. Willis, K., Brockmeyer, E., Hudson, S., Poupyrev, I. Printed Optics: 3D Printing of Embedded Optical Elements for Interactive Devices. In ACM UIST 2012, pp. 589-598
27. Wilson, A. Using a Depth Sensor as a TouchSensor. In ACM ITS'10. pp. 69-72
28. Wimmer, R. FlyEye: grasp-sensitive surfaces using optical fiber. In ACM TEI'10, 2010. pp. 245-248.

The Dog Programming Language

Salman Ahmad
Massachusetts Institute of Technology
saahmad@mit.edu

Sepandar D. Kamvar
Massachusetts Institute of Technology
sdkamvar@mit.edu

ABSTRACT
Today, most popular software applications are deployed in the cloud, interact with many users, and run on multiple platforms from Web browsers to mobile operating systems. While these applications confer a number of benefits to their users, building them brings many challenges: manually managing state between asynchronous user actions, creating and maintaining separate code bases for each desired client platform and gracefully scaling to handle a large number of concurrent users. Dog is a new programming language that provides a solution to these challenges and others through a unique runtime model that allows developers to model scalable cross-client applications as an imperative control-flow — simplifying many development tasks. In this paper we describe the key features of Dog and show its utility through several applications that are difficult and time-consuming to write in existing languages, but are simple and easily written in Dog in a few lines of code.

Author Keywords
Programming Languages; Application Development

ACM Classification Keywords
D.3.3. Programming Languages: Language Constructs and Features; H.5.0.Information Interfaces and Presentation

INTRODUCTION
In the last few years, we have seen an unprecedented growth of the Internet and of mobile devices. Over two billion people now use broadband Internet, up from 50 million a decade ago [3]. And just six years after the original iPhone was introduced, half of Americans own a smartphone [26], and over a quarter of Americans use their phone as their primary Internet device [25]. Consequently, many modern software applications are deployed in the cloud, interact with many users, and run on multiple client platforms such as Web browsers, iOS, and Android.

Unfortunately, these applications can be difficult to design, build, and maintain. The interactive applications enabled by modern Javascript and mobile operating systems are inherently stateful, and running them over a stateless protocol like HTTP requires developers to resort to various tricks to manage state between asynchronous web requests. Some of these tricks include: sessions, cookies, and most prominently, mapping application logic onto a persistent data model. This manual bookkeeping drastically increases the complexity of otherwise straightforward applications.

```
define chat_with: user as: username do
  forever do
    listen to user for messages
    on message do
      message = username + ": " + message
      notify: "chatroom" of: message
    end
  end
end

define pick_username_for: user do
  listen to user for usernames
  on username do
    return username
  end
end

listen to anyone for entrances
on each entrance do
  user = person from entrance
  username = pick_username_for: user
  chat_with: user as: username
end
```

Figure 1. Dog makes it easy to build social applications. This example shows how to create a real-time chatroom application.

For mobile applications in particular, much of the interaction code ends up being shifted to the client. This further obscures an application's underlying logic, which is now split between the server and the client, and requires new code to be written for each client platform.

The consequence of all of this is that programs that are conceptually simple and easily described even by the nonprogrammer often require sophisticated architectures, the use of advanced programming techniques, and careful planning to implement in practice. This is particularly true for those programs (and parts of programs) that encode interaction flows and social processes.

Continuation passing Web frameworks are a notable previous attempt to shield developers from HTTP's statelessness. Instead of registering callback functions to process HTTP requests, these frameworks pause and resume a program's execution, implicitly capturing application state [20]. This approach is considered to be simpler and numerous frameworks have been proposed [19, 27, 23]. However this style of devel-

UIST'13, October 8–11, 2013, St. Andrews, United Kingdom.

http://dx.doi.org/10.1145/2501988.2502026

opment has fallen out of practice because of continuations' consumption of server-side resources and the trends towards rich client-side interfaces.

We developed Dog to address these shortcomings and provide a more modern approach to simplifying Web-based application development. Dog is a new dynamically-typed procedural programming language that simplifies creating interactive, multi-user, and cross-client software applications through two key contributions:

1. Dog allows server-side code to be written as an imperative control flow that spans multiple requests and shields developers from HTTP's statelessness while not sacrificing scalability.

2. Dog facilitates cross-client development by allowing server-side logic to control client-side interactions through a scripting protocol that minimizes code duplication while enabling developers to take advantage of platform-specific UI affordances.

Together, these two features allow programs that take hundreds of lines of code in current languages to be written in just a few lines of Dog code, without sacrificing performance or scalability. To achieve this, we built a unique runtime environment for Dog that incorporates three core features:

1. An asynchronous execution model that allows complex event-driven code to be written in a structured and imperative manner.

2. A concurrency model that features lightweight threading constructs called tasks, which are managed by the runtime, enforce immutable memory semantics, and are backed by *persistent* continuations so they can pause indefinitely.

3. A distributed runtime model that allows a program's execution to be run across multiple machines.

We begin this paper by describing the two core principles behind Dog: Workflow-Centric Programming and Server-Client Scripting. We then provide an overview of Dog's syntax, and demonstrate Dog's utility through several diverse applications. Then, we describe the details of the Dog runtime and provide a technical overview of its reference implementation, which compiles to JVM bytecode.

WORKFLOW-CENTRIC PROGRAMMING

Conventional Approach: Manual State Management

Conventional Web-based applications break up logic across multiple asynchronous URL handlers. Developers specify server-side logic that is executed in response to an incoming URL request. For example, PHP associates logic with a URL by placing a PHP script at a matching file system path while Java Servlets and Ruby Rack-based applications (including the popular Rails framework) use a more sophisticated routing mechanism that pairs a URL pattern with a handler object. We refer to this style of programming as *resource-centric programming* (Figure 2b).

(a) Pseudocode

```
Allow a user to try to login. If the password does not
match, then give them 3 more chances before suggesting
that they submit a 'Forgotten Password' request.
```

(b) Resource-Centric Code (Ruby + Sinatra)

```
get "/login" do
 session.delete("login_tries")
 render "login_form.html"
end

post "/login" do
  user = params["user"]; password = params["pass"]
  if authenticate(user, password) then
    session["user"] = user
    session.delete("login_tries")
    redirect_to("/dashboard")
  else
    if session["login_tries"] == nil then
      session["login_tries"] = 0
    end
    session["login_tries"] += 1

    if session["login_tries"] >= 3 then
      redirect_to("/forgot_password")
    else
      flash["message"] = "Wrong password. Please try again."
      render "login_form.html"
    end
  end
end

```

(c) Workflow-Centric Code (Dog)

```
listen to everyone for logins

on each login do
  user = person from login
  repeat 3 times
    if user: login.user has_password: login.pass then
      signin: login.user
      show_dashboard_for: user
    else
      message = "Wrong password. Try again."
      show message to user
      listen to user for logins
      on login do
        user = person from login
      end
    end
  end
  reset_password_for:user
end
```

Figure 2. Server-side code to implement login logic. Workflow-centric programming allows for code to be written as a straightforward imperative control flow. State is manage implicitly by the program's execution using familiar techniques like control structures and local variables. In resource-centric programming, state between individual server requests is manually preserved by storing data in the session.

This style of server-side programming plays a specific and limited role: it inspects incoming HTTP requests and produces an HTTP response. Multistep logic that spans multiple requests needs to manually store state so that the relevant information is available during a future request-response cycle (Figure 2b shows an example using sessions). This manual bookkeeping complicates many development tasks, for example, ensuring confirmation before changing a user's email address, choosing a different billing method before making an online purchase, or viewing the next page from paginated results.

Dog: Automatic State Management

Instead of writing code as a series of URL endpoints, Dog applications are written as imperative control flows that directly represent the user interaction flow across multiple request-response cycles. Developers rely on familiar state management features like local variables, condition statements, loops, and functions. State is implicitly captured by the program's execution and developers are afforded compilation warnings, stack-based debugging, well-defined function APIs, as well as easier ways to write test cases. We refer to this style of programming as *workflow-centric programming* (Figure 2c).

Workflow-centric programming is a natural and familiar way to write applications and allows developers to focus on the interactions they want to create rather than low-level technical details. In fact, many designers and programmers already use workflows as a prototyping tool to describe an application's intended behavior [14]. To confirm our intuition that workflow-centric programming is a good fit for Web programming, we ran a simple study asking participants which of two pseudocode implementations of a popular online service they preferred. One implementation was written using a workflow-centric programming model and the other was resource-centric. The service described in the study included YouTube, ZipCar, and Tumblr. Participants overwhelmingly preferred the workflow-centric model by a margin of 21 to 2.

Operationally, workflow programming is similar to console-based programming. Instead of calling `print` and `readLine` to send and receive data from a terminal, Dog developers use Dog's built-in `show` and `listen` commands to send and receive data to a Web-accessible API. The `show` command (Figure 2c line 11) makes a particular variable visible to the client, and the `listen` command (Figure 2c lines 1 and 12) opens a "channel" that clients can use to send data back into the program.

A program can open multiple channels and selectively wait until information is sent using the `on` block (Figure 2c line 13). Execution will stop when it reaches an `on` block and wait for a message to be sent over the specified channel (just like a console-based program blocks on `readLine` until the user provides input). In certain cases, it is convenient to delegate work to a handler to avoid complicating the application's primary control flow. To address this, Dog includes the `on each` block (Figure 2c line 3), which registers a code block to be executed when data arrives over a channel.

Authentication and security are built into `listen` and `show`. Both commands accept a predicate[1] that designates which users can view the shown data or send input on the listen's channel (Figure 2c line 1 shows an example where anyone is allowed to login). By default, a client is assumed to be an anonymous user. Users are logged into the system when the application calls the `signin:` function (Figure 2c line 7).

Dog's workflow-centric programming model provides a structured approach for managing state that helps to elucidate application logic and reduce informal state management conventions that require additional code. The resulting code is not only more writable, but also more understandable.

[1]Predicates are discussed later in the syntax section.

```
<script id="login" type="text/x-dog-template">
  <h3>Please Login</h3>
  {{#listenForm listens.login}}
    <input type="text" name="login">
    <input type="password" name="pass">
    <input type="submit" name="submit" value="Log In">
  {{/listenForm}}
</script>
```

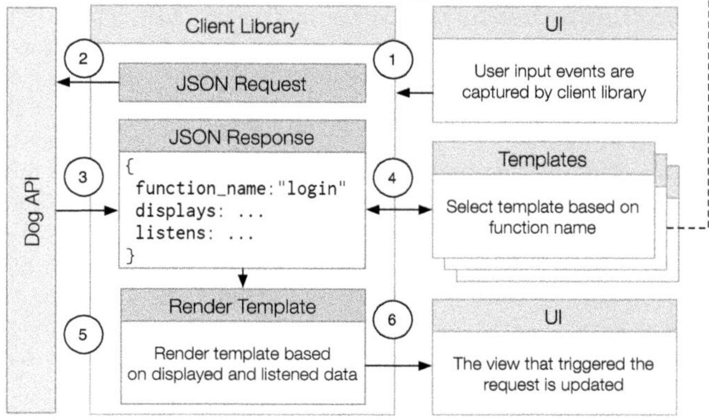

Figure 3. Dog's client-side libraries are built around templates. Here, we show the Javascript client library. Developers create templates using Handlebars.js but other templating languages are supported as well.

SERVER-CLIENT SCRIPTING

With the rise of mobile OSes, developers are increasingly deploying native client applications on multiple platforms. While most of the client applications are often similar, they currently need to be reimplemented for each platform.

With Dog, an application's high-level logic is written server-side rather than client-side. Clients connect to the server and the server "tells" the client what they should do and when they should do it. Communication between the client and the server is done through a server-client scripting protocol that exposes what a program has `shown` and `listened` for.

Dog's model provides a clean separation between back-end business logic and front-end design. The client has complete control over the application's aesthetics and is free to leverage platform-specific UI features and design conventions. However, the client is not burdened with reimplementing the application's high level interaction and navigational flows. We felt that this was a sensible separation of concerns that reduces duplicated code while providing engaging experiences on a variety of platforms.

In terms of its implementation, the server-client-scripting protocol is built on top of a JSON-based RESTful API. The API allows clients to inspect the runtime state of any *task*[2] in a Dog program that is waiting for user input. Tasks are identified by a special 128-bit *id*, but if the client is connecting for the first time, it asks the API for a special root task, which corresponds to the top-level scope in the Dog program. The server responds with the name of the current function that the task is waiting in, the data that the function wants the client to show (specified by `show`) and the inputs that the function wants back from the user (specified by `listen`).

[2]Tasks are a special concurrency construct in Dog and are discussed in the Runtime section.

When the client sends input to the API, the API passes that data into the task and continues its execution until the task waits again. The API then returns the new state of the task to the client, which likely contains a new set of `shows` and `listens` (Figure 3).

To further simplify development, Dog provides a series of client libraries to automatically talk to the API. The official client libraries included in the Dog distribution are available for Web browsers (Javascript), iPhone, and Android. These libraries are primarily template based. Whenever the client library gets a response, it inspects the "function_name" field (Figure 3) and automatically renders an associated template. If no template is available, the client library will auto-generate one based on the information that has been `shown` and `listened`. Thus, client-side development only requires developers to create a template for the functions they define in their program. Of course, developers are not restricted to only using templates and can opt to use the API directly. However, this is considered an advanced use case.

SYNTAX

Overview

Our goal in designing Dog's syntax was to make it possible to write code that is understandable even to a non-programmer who has never seen Dog. In practice, this meant designing a syntax that allows and encourages English-like readability [17], minimizes intimidating punctuation [16] and includes built-in libraries and language constructs that are already easy-to-read.

A hallmark feature of Dog's syntax is its use of named parameters with functions, a feature popularized by Smalltalk [5]. The definition of the "substring" function in Dog looks like:

```
define substring: str from: start to: finish do
  ...
end
```

The argument names are actually part of the function name itself. Thus, the function above is actually called `substring:from:to:`. This allows the definition of another substring function with different semantics in an unambiguous way. For example, it is possible to have another substring function called `substring:from:length:`.

Calling a function requires specifying all of the arguments:

```
hello = substring: "Hello, World" from: 0 to: 5
```

While this syntax may seem verbose, it is designed to be understandable. Other languages may use:

```
substring("Hello, World", 0, 5)
```

In this case, it is unclear if the "5" is the length of the substring or the ending syntax. Dog's function invocation is unambiguous.

Dog's data model has four built in primitive types: nulls, booleans, numbers, and strings. Values can be assigned to variables using the equals operator. Primitives can be grouped into a composite data type called structures. Structures are dynamic containers for key-value pairs. They can be nested and have either strings or numbers as keys. A structure's contents can be accessed using both the "dot" and "bracket" operators (similar to Javascript objects). Dog does not have an explicit array data type, however, since the keys of a structure can be numbers, structures can be used to store array information.

```
my_struct = {
  string = "String Value"
  number = 3.14159
}

my_struct.string == my_struct["string"] # true
```

All values in Dog are immutable and there are no shared variable references in the language. Consequently, the only data a Dog function can access are its arguments and all arguments follow "pass-by-value" semantics. This is an important feature of Dog that supports concurrent programming and is discussed at length later in the paper.

Almost every Web application incorporates the use of a database of some sort [21, 7]. While Dog eliminates shared variable references, modeling applications around a centralized data store is common in practice. Therefore, as an added convenience, Dog features "collections". Collections are globally scoped containers that hold structures. They can be thought of as a database but do not require pre-defined columns and can hold structures of any structure type. Since there are no shared *variable* references, a value in a collection does not change until the program explicitly re-saves it.

The example below shows the basic usage for collections in Dog:

```
define collection games

sonic = {
  title = "Sonic The Hedgehog"
  platform = "Genesis"
}

insert: sonic into: games
```

To query collections, Dog has built-in syntactic support for SQL-like predicates similar to LINQ [13]. Predicates in Dog are created using the `where` keyword. When a predicate is paired with a collection identifier, it is compiled as a `query` that can be passed to the built-in `find:` function to retrieve matching structures:

```
sega_games = find: games where platform == "Genesis"
```

Built-in support for predicates allows some of the most common operations in Web applications to be written in a manner that is easily readable. In particular, predicates are used heavily with the `listen` command. The following snippet opens a channel that is only visible to users that have a their "teacher" property set to true:

```
listen to people where teacher == true for grades
```

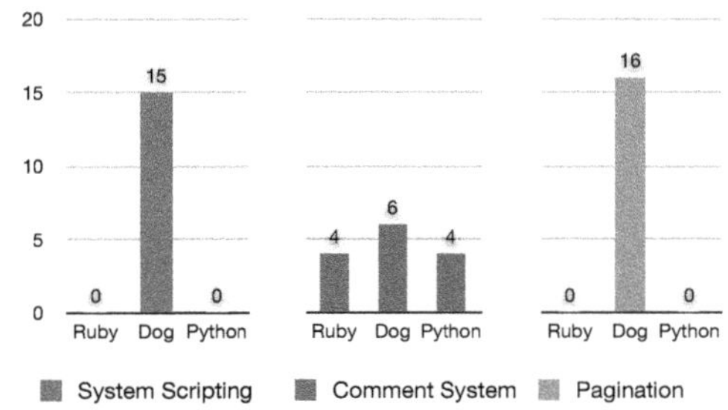

Figure 4. Results from asking users to identify the code they prefer for solving different tasks.

The `listen` command accepts a query into the `people` collection, a special system managed collection that stores all user profiles. When a client submits a request, the API ensures the client is authenticated on behalf of a user that is matched by that query. To accept all users, developers can use `everyone` instead of a query.

Dog's core language constructs and named-parameter function invocation syntax allow developers to write English-like programs that reduce code ambiguity to simplify development. While much of a language's ease-of-use is out of the hands of the designers and depends on the authors of libraries, by emphasizing understandability in the standard libraries we hope to cultivate a community that values readability and intuitive API design.

Syntax Evaluation

To evaluate our syntax decisions, in particular our choice to use named parameters we ran a small study that compared programs written in Dog to the same program written in either Ruby or Python. The programs were explained in plain English and participants were asked which implementation they preferred and if they had any prior experience with programming. Three programs were used during this experiment. The first was a portion of a Web application that handled pagination, an example that lends itself to workflow-centric programming. The second was a commenting system that allowed users to post comments on an online board, an example that lends itself to resource-centric programming. The third was a system-scripting program that sequentially renamed all JPG files in a directory, an example of something that Dog was explicitly not designed for. The Ruby and Python implementations were written using best practices, widely accepted idioms, and relevant frameworks. Participants preferred the Dog implementations by a wide margin (Figure 4). Participants with little to no programming experience frequently commented that the English-like language constructs (like `on` and `listen`) as well as the "long but descriptive" function names were the reason for their preference of Dog. On the flip side, participants with programming experience, frequently commented favorably about how Dog programs exhibit little "hidden state" and that they didn't need to guess the purpose of particular function calls.

USING DOG

In this section, we present a series of applications to demonstrate the usefulness of Dog and its programming model.

Real-Time Messaging: GroupChat

GroupChat is a real-time chatroom application. The program begins by `listening` for users to enter a chatroom:

```
define chat_with: user do
  ...
end

listen to anyone for entrances
on each entrance do
  user = person from entrance
  chat_with: user
end
```

Once the user enters, we use the `person from` command to get the current user and then call the `chat_with:` function that loops forever listening for messages from that user:

```
define chat_with: user do
  forever do
    listen to user for messages
    on message do
      notify: messages of: message
    end
  end
end
```

Notice the use of `on` instead of `on each` when waiting for messages. When waiting for entrances, we used `on each` because we wanted to track each user independently of one another. Whereas, in this case, we used `on` because we wanted to continue execution with the current user.

Once we receive a message, we will want to broadcast it to all other users in the chatroom. Real-time applications like this call for "push" networking rather than HTTP's typical "pull" request-response cycle. As a solution to this common and difficult problem, Dog provides a built-in notification library that allows the server to push messages to all subscribed clients. All the official client libraries fully support push notifications either through a background network connection or by polling the server. The call to `notify:of:` will push the message to all tasks waiting on the "messages" channel except for the calling task.

To build a browser-based client for GroupChat, we use dog.js, the Javascript client library. Dog.js, like the other client libraries, is template-driven — all we need to do is create templates that the library will render automatically. The UI is specified in an `index.html` file that is placed in a directory called `public` that is located along side the Dog program. The Dog runtime will automatically serve any files inside the `public` directory, including resources like images and stylesheets. `index.html` is shown below:

```
<html>
  <script src="/dog/dog.js" />
  <script id="root" type="text/x-dog-template">
    <h2>Welcome to GroupChat</h2>
    {{#listenLink listens.entrances}}Enter{{/listenForm}}
  </script>
  <script id="chat_with:" type="text/x-dog-template"
    data-notifications="chatroom">
    <ul>
      {{#each notifications.messages}}
        <li>{{this}}</li>
      {{/each}}
```

Figure 5. GradeBook is a peer assessment application written in Dog. Dog's cross-client development model allows server-side code to drive multiple client side applications.

```
    </ul>
    {{#listenForm listens.messages}}
      <input type="text" name="message">
      <button type="button">Send</button>
    {{/listenForm}}
  </script>

  <div data-dog-viewport="true" />
</html>
```

Dog.js uses Handlebars.js for rendering templates [11]. Templates are contained inside `script` tags with a content type of `text/x-dog-template`. The template has access to the variables that have been `shown` and `listened`. Templates are defined on a per-function basis. Thus, in this case, we have two: one for the root function and another for the `chat_with:` function. Templates are associated with a function using their `id` attribute. The `chat_with:` template is decorated with the `data-notifications` attribute, which tells the client library to re-render the template whenever a "chatroom" notification is received. Templates are rendered and placed inside "viewports". When a template sends a request to a server-side listen, the server's response is rendered by a new template and replaces the viewport that sent the original request. In most application, only a single viewport is needed, as is the case with GroupChat. The full source code is shown in Figure 1.

Native and Browser Development: GradeBook

GradeBook is a peer assessment application. When a student submits an assignment, the application will require another student to grade the submission. Once the grader is done, the assignment is forwarded to the professor who can take the grader's feedback into consideration before providing the final grade. The main application logic is shown below. Some of the application's code is abstracted into functions that are not shown.

```
listen to people where role == "student" for assignments

on each assignment do
  submitter = person from assignment
  if user:submitter already_submitted:assignment then
    error = "You may only submit your assignment once..."
    show error to submitter
  else
    grades = ask_peers_of:submitter to_grade:assignment
    teacher = people where role == "teacher"
    final_grade = ask:teacher to_grade:assignment using:grades
    assignment.grade = final_grade
    save: assignment
  end
end
```

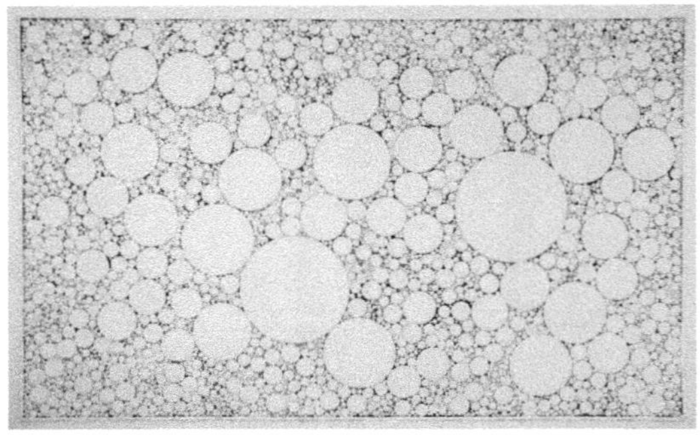

Figure 6. Tangent is a socially created art installation where a Dog program coordinated the activities of many individual contributors. Zoom for detail. Graphite on canvas. 8ft. × 5ft.

The application can be easily changed to handle new requirements. For example, the code for having 3 students grade each assignment is:

```
grades = []
repeat 3 times
  grade = ask_peers_of:submitter to_grade:assignment
  grades = append:grade to:grades
end
```

In addition to a browser-based client, we also created an iPhone application using the the Cocoa Dog client library (Figure 5).

Crowdsourcing: Tangent

Dog originated as a domain-specific language for parallel human computation [2]. It has evolved into a more general-purpose programming language, but is still useful for programming crowdsourcing systems. As an example, we used Dog to create a number of crowdsourced art pieces for a recent exhibition.

One such installation was a geometric art piece called Tangent. Participants used "child-friendly" tools like stencils and color pencils to draw circles that were tangent to each other and then color the negative space between them. The installation can be seen in Figure 6. The entire code for the application is shown below, although certain instructional message strings have been shortened for brevity.

```
# Functions

define confirm: message index: index do
  show index to everyone
  show message to everyone
  message = "Is there any space available?"
  listen to everyone for confirmation
  wait on confirmation
  confirmation == "no"
end

define confirm: message do
```

```
  show message to everyone
  listen to everyone for confirmation
  wait on confirmation
end

define draw_circle do
  confirm: "...draw a circle using a stencil..."
end

define ask: user to_draw_circle_tangent: index do
  confirm: "...draw a circle tangent
    to another circle..." index: index
end

define ask: user to_color_negative_space: index do
  confirm: "...color in any enclosed
    space that is not a circle..." index: index
end

# Main

draw_circle

count = 1
while !done do
  done = ask: someone to_draw_tangent_circle: count
  count = count + 1
end

count = 1
while !done do
  done = ask: someone to_color_negative_space: count
  count = count + 1
end
```

During the time of the exhibit, Tangent has had hundreds of collaborators. The application ran on a kiosk next to a canvas and gave visitors instructions on how they could contribute. The kiosk connected to a centrally hosted server which enabled remote tweaks to the application while it was deployed in another country.

Social Networking: Aardvark

Dog is also capable of building applications using protocols other than HTTP. For example, we built an Aardvark-clone in Dog that allowed users to interact with the application over IM and email. Aardvark [9] is a social question-answer site that routes user submitted questions to somebody in the user's extended social network. Instead of submitting questions using a Web page, Aardvark allows users to naturally submit questions via instant message or email. Dog's standard library has built-in support for handling SMTP and XMPP connections by overloading the `listen` command with `via instant_message` making Aardvark's implementation straightforward. The follow code also makes use of the `wait on` command, which is the same as the `on` block except inline.

```
listen to everyone via instant_message for questions
on each question do
  message = "Hey! I'll try to find someone to answer that..."
  send_message: message to: asker

  category = classify: question
  ranked_users = people where expertise == category
  answered = false
  for each user in ranked_users do
      response = ask:user if_able_to_answer_question_on:category
      if response == "yes" then
        send_message: "Great, here it is: " to: user

        listen to user via instant_message for response
        wait on response

        send_message: "Thanks. I'll send that along." to: user
        send_message: "I got an answer from #{user}." to: asker
        send_message: response to: asker

        answered = true
        break
      else
        send_message: "Thanks for your help." to: user
      end
    end

    if !answered then
      message = "I couldn't find anyone. Please try again."
      send_message: message to: asker
    end
  end
```

RUNTIME

Most existing languages have runtimes that provide coarse-grained concurrency primitives, execute instructions in a blocking manner, and require application-level coordination for distributed execution. These properties make it difficult to efficiently implement Dog's workflow programming model. To address this, we built a custom runtime environment for Dog that provides solutions to these limitations.

Existing Limitation: Thread-Only Concurrency

Many applications need to coordinate the activities of multiple concurrent and independent users. Threads are the conventional solution to concurrency. In theory, a developer could create a separate thread to manage each user. Unfortunately, threads require significant amounts of system resources. If an application creates a new thread whenever it is waiting for a user to submit input, the system will quickly run out of memory.

Some languages, like Ruby and Python, provide green-threads or coroutines that execute at the language level rather than at the OS level and generally use less memory. However, even green-threads are not suitable for coordinating individual users. First, despite their reduced memory consumption, green-threads cannot handle Web-scale traffic if each user is backed by a thread. Second, since thread state is stored in memory, all user progress will be lost when the application server lives behind a load balancer or is restarted (during a crash or routine maintenance). Third, green-threads do not change the fact that creating multi-threaded applications and coordinating access to shared memory is challenging for even the most experienced developers [15]. Fourth, at a practical level, most languages that provide green-threads also impose a Global Interpreter Lock (GIL) which only allows a single thread to run at a time to avoid problems with libraries that are not thread safe (e.g. Python, Ruby, Javascript). As a result, these languages are unable to take advantage of multi-core CPUs.

Dog's Solution: Task-Based Concurrency

Dog provides a concurrency primitive called *tasks*. A task is a green-thread that is backed by a persistent continuation. This means that a task waiting for input can be saved to disk to reduce memory contention and survive past server restarts. Saved continuations are automatically deleted from disk after a configurable timeout, which, by default, is 1440 seconds. An exception to this is the root task, which is never deleted.

Additionally, all values in Dog are immutable and the runtime prevents shared memory references. This memory model not only simplifies the understandability and predictability of Dog programs but also facilitates multithreaded programming by eliminating the need for locks and avoiding unintended side effects. Cross-task communication is coordinated by special, uni-directional, FIFO channels. Lastly, since there is no shared state, Dog does not impose a GIL and Dog programs take advantage of multicore CPUs. While immutability makes parallel execution easier, certain sequential programming tasks are harder. As an example, iterators are less efficient and can be awkward since changes to enumerated elements are lost unless explicitly re-saved.

Existing Limitation: Blocking Execution Semantics

Almost all existing languages' runtimes are synchronous and execute instructions in a blocking manner that waits for the current instruction to finish before proceeding. In conjunction with thread-only concurrency, when an application attempts to access input from a user, the entire thread will block. This has two negative consequences. First, as previously mentioned, it increases the memory demand on the machine. Second, this will lead to a large number of system threads, result in significant context switching overhead, and slow the machine.

Additionally, many applications may need to respond to multiple sources of user input. For example, a survey application may want to send out a single task to hundreds of people and wait for the responses. With blocking execution semantics, only a single task can be sent at a time even though the tasks are independent of one another and can be done in parallel. Using a separate thread (or even a Dog task) to solve this problem requires application control to be broken up into multiple worker threads and joined back, which is challenging for even experienced developers [15].

Dog's Solution: Asynchronous Execution

Synchronous runtimes provide a straightforward, "strictly consistent" guarantee: the program always finishes executing a statement before moving to the next. Dog's runtime, on the other hand, is asynchronous and provides a slightly different, "causally consistent" guarantee: a statement's output will be written by the time that the output is needed. In general, this nuanced distinction can be ignored as it often does not impact the *correctness* of a program[3]. However, it does allow the runtime to execute code in non-deterministic ways to improve performance. Certain function calls in Dog do not immediately return an output value but rather return a special future that promises to eventually hold the output. When a program attempts to access a future the current task will automatically block and the runtime will swap it out so another task can execute. The moment the promised value is provided, all tasks waiting on that future will resume execution. This allows Dog programs to wait for multiple users in the same task without fear of blocking the task from doing other operations.

[3] This is only true because of Dog's immutable memory model.

Existing Limitation: Process-Bound Execution

A key problem facing current applications is distributing traffic across multiple machines to handle large numbers of users. This poses a problem for workflow-programming with existing languages because virtually all existing runtimes are process-bound and only execute in a single process on a single machine. Distributing execution over many nodes requires architecting applications around a centralized database and manually managing state between machines.

Dog's Solution: Dynamic Distributed Load Balancing

The Dog runtime is designed to naturally scale across multiple machines and readily tolerate machine failures. When a Dog program begins, the runtime starts, connects to a distributed task queue and waits for a task to be scheduled. Adding new machines to a Dog cluster is as simple running the Dog program on a new machine and specifying the task queue as a command line flag. When a task is scheduled for execution, the task queue will evenly distribute them across the available machines. Tasks can be distributed across machines without worry of deadlock, race conditions, or consistency errors, because of the runtime's non-shared and immutable memory semantics. Thanks to persistent continuations, machines in a Dog "cluster" can fail without worry. If a machine crashes in the middle of executing a function, some other machine will eventually pick up where the machine left off and continue execution. In fact, the runtime has a "crash-only" design — gracefully stopping a runtime instance and yanking the power cable from the box have the same effect. Additionally, because continuations are persistent and requests can be handled by any machine, deploying and scaling Dog applications is mostly trivial — simply run the application on a new machine and place that machine behind a standard load balancer like nginx or HAProxy. No special configuring or routing (e.g. sticky load balancing) is needed.

IMPLEMENTATION

The standard reference implementation for Dog compiles to Java Virtual Machine (JVM) bytecode. Targeting the JVM was a natural choice given its performance, stability, and widespread adoption [12]. As a result, developers can natively interoperate with any existing Java library.

Compiler

The Dog compiler is written in Java and uses an LL(*) parser [22] generated from a grammar written using ANTLR [18]. The parser produces a Dog abstract syntax tree that the compiler transforms into a flat array of Dog Virtual Machine Instructions. The Dog Virtual Machine is a register-based machine [24] and has an instruction set modeled after Lua [10].

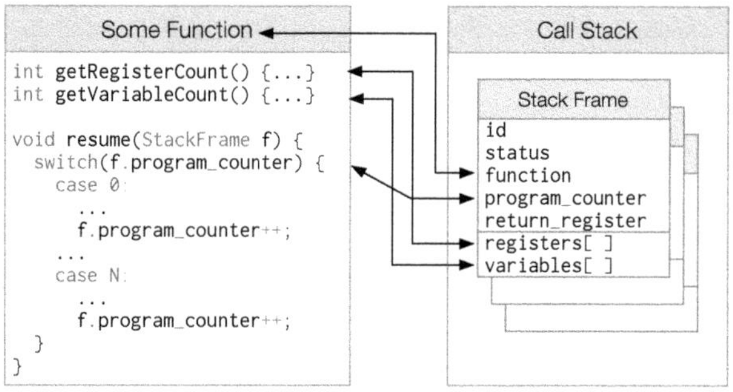

Figure 7. Dog implements persistent continuations by subverting the JVM stack and using custom, heap-allocated, stack frames. Every function is backed by a class that reports the number of necessary registers and variable slots. A stack frame object is instantiated accordingly and passed into the function's resume method.

The assembler emits the appropriate JVM bytecode for each Dog VM instruction. Internally, each Dog VM instruction is modeled as a class that overrides the `toJVMBytecode` method. This code architecture allows reuse of the compiler front-end by multiple runtime back-ends, making it possible to target other runtime environments in the future[4]. Lastly, the generated JVM bytecode is written to disk as a *bark* file, which is a ZIP file that holds metadata used by the Dog runtime to begin execution.

Persistent Continuations

The JVM (like most languages) does not provide support for continuations that are both serializable and portable. Thus, Dog subverts the JVM stack and forces the runtime to use a continuation passing style with custom stack frames. All Dog functions are compiled to Java classes that override the `resume` method. When the resume method is called, it receives a heap-allocated stack frame object that is dynamically created with the correct amount of registers and variable slots that the function needs to run (Figure 7). During compilation, all the JVM instructions are instrumented so they interact with the Dog stack instead of the JVM stack.

To resume a function the compiler inserts special *checkpoints* into the JVM bytecode stream. These checkpoint atomically increment a special *program-counter* in the stack frame (Figure 7). At the start of the function, the compiler inserts a jump table (implemented as a JVM `tableswitch` instruction) that inspects the program-counter and jumps to the correct instruction in the function's bytecode. The checkpoints are inserted such that the code between checkpoints is guaranteed to be idempotent. Thus, if the machine crashes while the runtime is between checkpoints, the function can still be safely resumed.

Scheduler

The scheduler connects to the distributed task queue, waits for tasks to be scheduled, and then coordinates their execution. Each runtime has at least one scheduler but, by default, the reference implementation creates single scheduler for every core that is available on the system to maximize performance on multicore CPUs. The task queue is implemented on top of MongoDB [1].

[4]Currently, Dog has an existing implementation in Ruby. Additionally, a Javascript runtime is being explored.

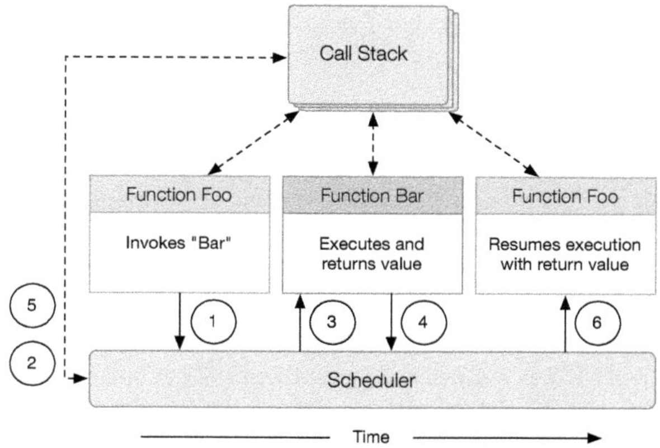

Figure 8. Dog uses a "trampoline" to call and return from functions. Function Foo calls Bar by returning a signal object to the scheduler (1). The scheduler inspects the signal, allocates a new stack frame for Bar and pushes it onto the call stack (2). The scheduler then calls Bar and passes the current call stack as an argument (3). Function Bar executes and returns another signal object with its return value (4). The scheduler pops the stack frame from the call stack, and inserts the return value into Foo's stack frame (5). The scheduler then resumes execution of Foo from where it left off (6).

An important part of the scheduler is managing function invocations using a technique called a "trampoline" [4]. Instead of a caller function directly invoking a callee function, the caller simply returns a "signal" to the scheduler with a reference to the callee (Figure 8). The scheduler inspects the signal, resolves the function reference, dynamically creates a custom stack frame for the callee, sets the callee's stack frame's parent to the caller's stack frame, and then invokes the callee. When the callee returns, the scheduler takes the return value, inserts it into the caller's stack frame's `return_register` (Figure 7), and resumes execution of the caller. The use of a trampoline greatly simplifies the implementation of Dog's persistent continuations.

When a task attempts to access a future or begins waiting on a channel it throws a `WaitException` which is caught by the scheduler. The task is then persisted to the task queue until the data become available.

PERFORMANCE EVALUATION

While Dog was not designed specifically for execution speed, it is important to achieve a certain threshold of performance to be useful in practice. Consequently, we ran a standard set of benchmarks on Dog and compared its results with other languages:

Benchmark	Dog v0.4	Ruby v1.9	Python v2.7
fib	1.722s	2.357s	6.385s
prime	14.974s	3.985s	15.993s
mandelbrot	11.410s	8.780s	1.080s
substring	15.222s	28.016s	22.724s

As shown in the table above, Dog is competitive with Ruby and Python, faster on the benchmarks that involve frequent memory access (substring) and slow on the benchmarks that require complex mathematics (mandelbrot).

In terms of network performance, which is more important for Web applications, Dog has a clear advantage thanks to the JVM's robust network stack. The GradeBook application written in Ruby on Rails with various performance optimizations is able to process an average of 229.08 requests per second while the Dog version is able to process 937.62 requests per second.

All tests were run on a 2.4 GHz Intel Core i5 CPU with 8GB of RAM. It is important to note that performance-critical portions of a Dog program can always be written natively with Java.

RELATED WORK

Dog is most closely related to continuation passing Web frameworks like Seaside, Apache Cocoon, and Tir [19, 27, 23]. While these frameworks provide a similar model to workflow-centric programming they lack the flexibility of Dog's server-client scripting API. All output content is sent as raw HTML intended only for Web browsers and all input must be sent back through special form tags that force the entire screen to be re-rendered. Dog's approach facilitates targeting multiple clients beyond the browser and enables developers more control over the user experience. Furthermore, all application state in these frameworks must remain in local memory unlike Dog which supports persistent continuations. As a consequence, these frameworks are difficult to scale as they require special load balancing to route HTTP requests to the same process on the same machine (i.e. sticky load balancing), often leading to unequal load distribution. Additionally, if an application server crashes or is removed for maintenance, all application state on that server is lost.

Many of Dog's features were inspired by other languages and systems. Its syntax with named parameters heavily influenced by Smalltalk, its data model with only a single composite "structure" type by Lua, its register-based virtual machine instruction set by Lua, its immutable memory model by Clojure, and its runtime concurrency features like tasks and channels by Go and Stackless Python [5, 10, 8, 6, 28].

CONCLUSION

Dog introduces a new way of building applications that simplifies many development tasks. Its unique runtime model provides solutions to asynchronous state management, cross-client development, and scalable deployment. As such, Dog represents a useful tool for developing interactive Web-based applications that coordinate the activities of many users across multiple different client platforms.

ACKNOWLEDGMENTS

We thank and the anonymous reviewers for their helpful comments and suggestions.

REFERENCES

1. 10Gen Inc. MongoDB. `http://www.mongodb.com`.
2. Ahmad, S., Battle, A., Malkani, Z., and Kamvar, S. The Jabberwocky Programming Environment for Structured Social Computing. In *Proceedings of the 24th annual ACM Symposium on User Interface Software and Technology*, ACM (2011), 53–64.
3. Andreesen, M. Why Software Is Eating The World. *The Wall Street Journal* (2011).
4. Bothner, P. Kawa: Compiling Dynamic Languages to the Java VM. In *Proceedings of the annual conference on USENIX Annual Technical Conference* (1998), 41–41.
5. Goldberg, A., and Robson, D. *Smalltalk-80: The Language and its Implementation*. Addison-Wesley Longman Publishing Co., Inc., 1983.
6. Google Inc. Go. `http://golang.org`.
7. Google Inc. Google web toolkit. `https://developers.google.com/web-toolkit/`.
8. Hickey, R. Clojure. `http://www.clojure.org`.
9. Horowitz, D., and Kamvar, S. D. The Anatomy of a Large-Scale Social Search Engine. In *Proceedings of the 19th International Conference on World Wide Web* (2010), 431–440.
10. Ierusalimschy, R., De Figueiredo, L. H., and Celes, W. The implementation of Lua 5.0. *Journal of Universal Computer Science 11*, 7 (2005), 1159–1176.
11. Katz, Y. Handlebars.js: Minimal Templating on Steroids. `http://handlebarsjs.com`.
12. Lindholm, T., and Yellin, F. *Java Virtual Machine Specification*, 2nd ed. Addison-Wesley Longman Publishing Co., Inc., 1999.
13. Meijer, E., Beckman, B., and Bierman, G. LINQ: Reconciling Object, Relations and XML in the .NET Framework. In *Proceedings of ACM SIGMOD* (2006), 706–706.
14. Myers, B., Park, S. Y., Nakano, Y., Mueller, G., and Ko, A. How Designers Design and Program Interactive Behaviors. In *Visual Languages and Human-Centric Computing* (2008), 177–184.
15. Ousterhout, J. Why Threads Are A Bad Idea (for most purposes). In *Presentation given at the 1996 Usenix Annual Technical Conference*, vol. 5 (1996).
16. Pane, J. F., Myers, B. A., and Miller, L. B. Using HCI Techniques to Design a More Usable Programming System. In *Proceedings of the IEEE Symposium on Human Centric Computing Languages and Environments* (2002), 198–206.
17. Pane, J. F., Ratanamahatana, C., Myers, B. A., et al. Studying the Language and Structure in Non-Programmers' Solutions to Programming Problems. *International Journal of Human-Computer Studies 54*, 2 (2001), 237–264.
18. Parr, T. J., and Quong, R. W. ANTLR: A Predicated-LL(k) Parser Generator. *Software Practice and Experience 25* (1994), 789–810.
19. Perscheid, M., Tibbe, D., Beck, M., Berger, S., Osburg, P., Eastman, J., Haupt, M., and Hirschfeld, R. *An Introduction to Seaside*. Software Architecture Group (Hasso-Plattner-Institut), 2008.
20. Queinnec, C. Inverting Back the Inversion of Control or, Continuations Versus Page-centric Programming. *ACM SIGPLAN* (2003), 57–64.
21. Rails Core Team. Ruby on Rails. `http://www.rubyonrails.org`.
22. Rosenkrantz, D. J., and Stearns, R. E. Properties of deterministic top down grammars. In *Proceedings of the First Annual ACM Symposium on Theory of Computing*, STOC '69, ACM (1969), 165–180.
23. Shaw, Z. Tir Web Framework. `http://tir.mongrel2.org`.
24. Shi, Y., Casey, K., Ertl, M. A., and Gregg, D. Virtual Machine Showdown: Stack versus Registers. *ACM Transactions on Architecture and Code Optimization 4*, 4 (2008), 2:1–2:36.
25. Smith, A. Smartphone Adoption and Usage. *Pew Research Center* (2011).
26. Smith, A. Nearly half of American adults are smartphone owners. *Pew Research Center* (2012).
27. The Apache Cocoon Project. Cocoon. `http://cocoon.apache.org/`.
28. Tismer, C. Continuations and Stackless Python. In *Proceedings of the 8th International Python Conference* (2000), 2000–01.

Interactive Record/Replay for Web Application Debugging

Brian Burg[1], Richard Bailey[1], Andrew J. Ko[2], Michael D. Ernst[1]

Computer Science and Engineering[1]
University of Washington
{burg, rjacob, mernst}@cs.washington.edu

The Information School[2]
University of Washington
ajko@uw.edu

ABSTRACT
During debugging, a developer must repeatedly and manually reproduce faulty behaviors in order to inspect different facets of the program's execution. Existing tools for reproducing such behaviors prevent the use of debugging aids such as breakpoints and logging, and are not designed for interactive, random-access exploration of recorded behavior. This paper presents Timelapse, a tool for quickly recording, reproducing, and debugging interactive behaviors in web applications. Developers can use Timelapse to browse, visualize, and seek within recorded program executions while simultaneously using familiar debugging tools such as breakpoints and logging. Testers and end-users can use Timelapse to demonstrate failures *in situ* and share recorded behaviors with developers, improving bug report quality by obviating the need for detailed reproduction steps. Timelapse is built on Dolos, a novel record/replay infrastructure that ensures deterministic execution by capturing and reusing program inputs both from the user and from external sources such as the network. Dolos introduces negligible overhead and does not interfere with breakpoints and logging. In a small user evaluation, participants used Timelapse to accelerate existing reproduction activities, but were not significantly faster or more successful in completing the larger tasks at hand. Together, the Dolos infrastructure and Timelapse developer tool support systematic bug reporting and debugging practices.

Author Keywords
Debugging, deterministic replay, web applications

ACM Classification Keywords
D.2.5 Software Engineering: Testing and debugging

General Terms
Human Factors; Design

INTRODUCTION
Debugging is often an iterative process in which developers repeatedly adjust their view on a program's execution by adding and removing breakpoints and inspecting program state at different times and locations. This iteration requires a developer to repeatedly reproduce the behavior they are inspecting, which can be time-consuming and error-prone [36]. In the case of interactive programs, even reproducing a failure can be difficult or impossible: failures can occur on mouse drag events, be time-dependent, or simply occur too infrequently for a developer to easily reach a program state suitable for debugging.

Deterministic record/replay [5] is a technique that can be used to record a behavior once and then deterministically replay it repeatedly and automatically, without user interaction. Though it seems that the capability to record and replay executions should be useful for debugging, no prior work has described actual use cases for these capabilities, or how to best expose these capabilities via user interface affordances. At most, prior systems demonstrate feasibility by providing a simple VCR-like interface [18, 33] that can record and replay linearly. Many record/replay systems have no UI, and are controlled via commands to the debugger or special APIs [9, 11, 27]. Finally, prior work does not consider how record/replay capabilities can interoperate with and enhance existing debugging tools like breakpoints and logging. Prior tool instantiations [18, 25, 1] are inappropriate for debugging because they can interfere with program performance, determinism, and breakpoint use, and they are difficult to deploy.

This paper presents Timelapse, a developer tool for capturing and replaying web application behaviors during debugging, and Dolos, a novel record/replay infrastructure for web applications. A developer can use Timelapse's interactive visualizations of program inputs to find and seek non-linearly through the recording, and then use the debugger or other tools to understand program behavior. To ensure deterministic execution, Dolos captures and reuses user input, network responses, and other nondeterministic inputs as the program executes. It does this in a purely additive way—without impeding the use of other tools such as debuggers—via a novel adaptation of virtual machine record/replay techniques to the execution environment of web browsers. Debugging tools are particularly important for interactive web applications because the web's highly dynamic, event-driven programming model stymies traditional static program analysis techniques.

This paper makes the following contributions:

- Dolos: a fast, scalable, precise, and practical infrastructure for deterministic record/replay of web applications.
- Timelapse: a developer tool for creating, visualizing, and navigating program recordings during debugging tasks.
- The first user study to explore how and when developers use record/replay tools during realistic debugging tasks.

Dolos and Timelapse are free software: our source code, study materials, and data are available on the project website[1].

We first discuss the design of Timelapse, and use a scenario to illustrate how Timelapse supports recording, reproducing, and debugging interactive behaviors. Next, we present the design and implementation of the underlying Dolos record/replay infrastructure. We discuss the results of a small study to see how developers use Timelapse in open-ended debugging tasks. Finally, we conclude with related work and present several implications for future interactive debugging tools.

REPRODUCING AND NAVIGATING PROGRAM STATES

The Timelapse developer tool is designed around two activities: capturing user-demonstrated program behaviors, and quickly and repeatedly reaching program states within a recording when localizing and understanding a fault. The novel features we describe in this section support these activities by making it simple to record program behavior and by providing visualizations and affordances that quicken the process of finding and seeking to relevant program states without manually reproducing behavior.

To better understand the utility of replay capabilities during debugging, we first conducted a small pilot study with a prototype record/replay interface. Using contextual inquiry, we found that developers primarily used the prototype to isolate buggy output, and to quickly reach specific states when working backwards from buggy output towards its root cause. Towards these ends, we saw several common use cases: "play and watch"; isolating output using random-access seeking; stepping through execution in single-input increments, and reading low-level input details or logged output.

This section introduces the novel features of the Timelapse developer tool by showing how a fictional developer named Claire might use Timelapse's features while debugging.

Debugging Scenario: (Buggy) Space Invaders

Claire, a new hire at a game company, has been asked to fix a bug in a web application version of the Space Invaders video game[2]. In this game, the player moves a defending ship and shoots advancing aliens. The game's implementation is representative of modern object-oriented interactive web programs: it uses timer callbacks, event-driven programming, and helper libraries. The game contains a defect that allows multiple player bullets to be in flight at a time; there is only supposed to be one player bullet at a time (Figure 1).

Reproducing Program Behavior

Claire is unfamiliar with the Space Invaders implementation, so her first step towards understanding and fixing the multiple-bullet defect is to figure out how to reliably reproduce it. This is difficult because the failure only occurs in specific game states and is influenced by execution conditions outside of her control, such as random numbers, the current time, or asynchronous network requests.

[1] `http://github.com/burg/timelapse/`

[2] `http://matthaynes.net/playground/javascript/glow/spaceinvaders/`

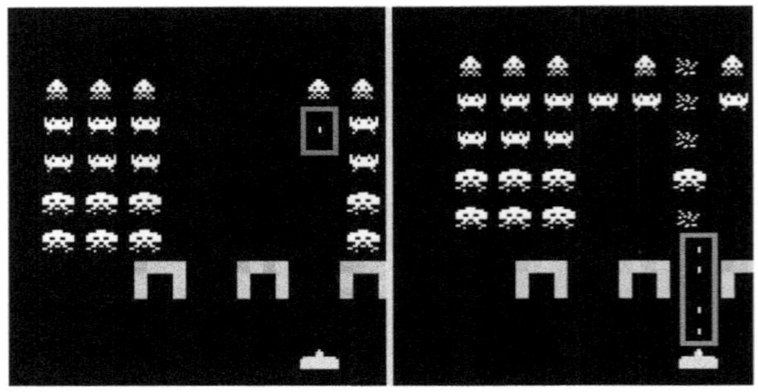

Figure 1. Screenshots of normal and buggy Space Invader game mechanics. Only one bullet should be in play at a time (shown on left). Due to misuse of library code, each bullet fires two asynchronous `bulletDied` events instead of one event when it is destroyed. The double dispatch sometimes enables multiple player bullets being in play at once (shown on right). This happens when two bullets are created: one between two `bulletDied` events, and the other after both events.

With Timelapse, Claire begins capturing program behaviors with a single click (Figure 2-6), plays the game until she reproduces the failure, and then finishes the recording. Recordings created by Timelapse are compact, self-contained, and serializable, so Claire can attach her recording to a bug report or share it via email.

To reproduce the defect with traditional tools, Claire would have to multitask between synthesizing reproduction steps, playing the video game, and reflecting on whether the reproduction steps are correct. Once Claire finds reliable reproduction steps, she could then use breakpoints to further understand

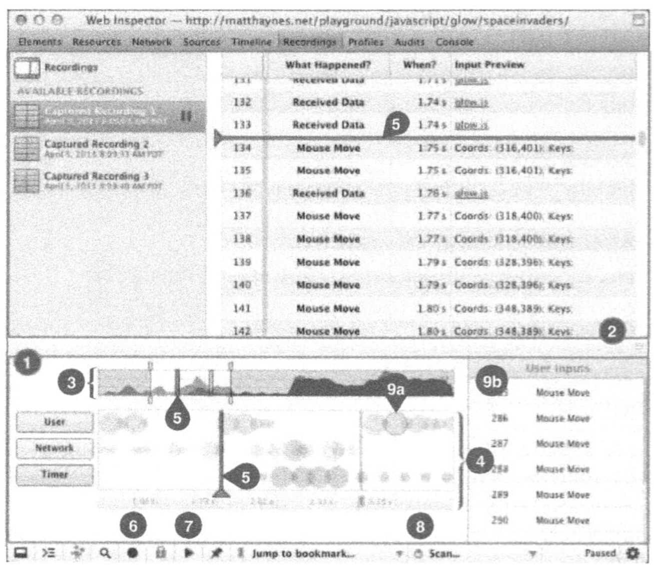

Figure 2. The Timelapse tool interface presents multiple linked views of recorded program inputs. Above, the timelines drawer (1) is juxtaposed with a detailed view of program inputs (2). The recording overview (3) shows inputs over time with a stacked line graph, colored by category. The overview's selected region is displayed in greater detail in the heatmap view (4). Circle sizes indicate input density per category. In each view, the red cursor (5) indicates the current replay position and can be dragged. Buttons allow for recording (6), 1× speed replay (7), and breakpoint scanning (8). Details for the selected circle (9a) are shown in a side panel (9b).

the defect. But, breakpoints might themselves affect timing, making the defect harder to trigger or requiring modified reproduction steps.

Navigating to Specific Program States

To focus her attention on code relevant to the failure, Claire needs to know which specific user input—and thus which event handler invocations—caused the second bullet to appear.

Claire uses Timelapse's visualization and navigation tools (Figure 2) to locate and seek the recording to an instance of the multiple bullets failure. First, Claire limits the zoom interval to when she actually fired bullets, and then filters out non-keystroke inputs. She replays single keystrokes with a keyboard shortcut until a second bullet is added to the game board. Then, she seeks execution backward by one keystroke. At this point, she is confident that the code which created the second bullet ran in response to the current keystroke.

Without Timelapse, it would not be possible for Claire to isolate the failure to a specific keystroke and then work backwards from the keystroke. Instead, she would have to insert logging statements, repeatedly reproduce the failure to generate logging output, and scrutinize logged values for clues leading towards the root cause.

Navigation Aid: Debugger Bookmarks

Having tracked down the second bullet to a specific user input, Claire now needs to investigate what code ran, and why.

With Timelapse, Claire sets several *debugger bookmarks* (Figure 3-6) at positions in the recording that she wants to quickly revert back to, such as the keystroke that caused the second bullet to appear or an important program point reached via the debugger. Debugger bookmarks support the concept of temporal focus points [28],which are useful when a developer wants to relate information [13]—such as the program's state at a breakpoint hit—that is only available at certain points of execution. Timelapse restores a debugger bookmark by seeking to the preceding input, setting and continuing to the preceding breakpoint, and finally simulating the user's sequence of debugger commands (step forward/into/out).

With traditional tools, Claire must explore an execution with debugger commands such as "step into", "step over", and "step out". This is frustrating because these commands are irreversible, and Claire would have to manually reproduce the failure multiple times to compare multiple instants or the effects of different commands.

Navigation Aid: Breakpoint Radar

Once Claire finds the code that creates bullets, she needs to understand why some keystrokes fire bullets and others do not.

With Timelapse, Claire first adjusts the zoom interval to include keystrokes that did and did not trigger the failure. Then, she sets a breakpoint inside the `Bullet.create()` method and records and visualizes when it is actually hit during the execution using the *breakpoint radar* feature (Figure 3-3a). Breakpoint radar automates the process of replaying the execution, pausing and resuming at each hit, and visualizing when

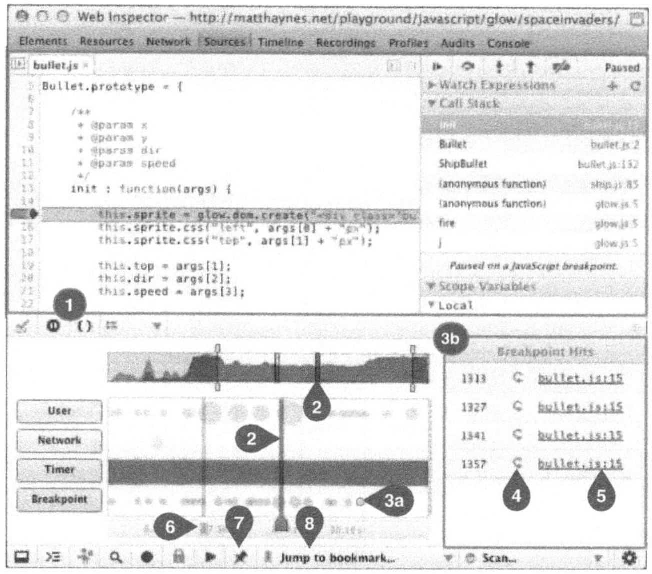

Figure 3. Timelapse's visualization of debugger status and breakpoint history, juxtaposed with the existing Sources panel and debugger (1). A blue cursor (2) indicates that replay execution is paused at a breakpoint, instead of between user inputs (as shown in Figure 2). Blue circles mark the location of known breakpoint hits, and are added or removed automatically as breakpoints change. A side panel (3b) shows the selected (3a) circle's breakpoints. Shortcuts allow for jumping to a specific breakpoint hit (4) or source location (5). Debugger bookmarks (6) are set with a button (7) and replayed to by clicking (6) or by using a drop-down menu (8).

the debugger paused. Claire can easily see which keystrokes created bullets and which did not.

With traditional tools, Claire would need to repeatedly set and unset breakpoints in order to determine which keystrokes did or *did not* create bullets. To populate the breakpoint radar timeline, Claire would have to manually hit and continue from dozens or hundreds of breakpoints, and collect and visualize breakpoint hits herself. For this particular defect, breakpoints interfere with the timing of the bullet's frame-based animations, so it would be nearly impossible for Claire to pause execution when two bullets are in flight.

Interacting with Other Debugging Tools

Once Claire localizes the part of the program responsible for the multiple bullets, she still needs to isolate and fix the root cause. To do so, Claire uses debugging strategies that do not require Timelapse, but nonetheless benefit from it. Timelapse is designed to be used alongside other debugging tools such as breakpoints[3], logging, and element inspectors; its interface can be juxtaposed (Figure 3) with other tools.

Through code inspection, Claire observes that the creation of a bullet is guarded by a flag indicating whether any bullets are already on the game board. The flag is set inside the `Bullet.create()` method and cleared inside the `Bullet.die()` method. To test her intuition about the

[3]To prevent breakpoints from interfering with tool use cases, Timelapse tweaks breakpoints in several ways: breakpoints are disabled when recording or seeking, and enabled during real-time playback.

code's behavior, she inserts logging code and captures a new execution to see if the method calls are balanced. The logging output in Figure 4 is synchronized with the replay position: as Claire seeks execution forward or backward, logging output up to the current instant is displayed. Logging output is cleared when a fresh execution begins (i.e., Timelapse seeks backwards) and then populated as the program executes normally.

Claire has discovered that the multiple-bullet defect is caused by the `bulletDied` event being fired twice, allowing a second replacement bullet to be created if the bullet "fire" key is pressed between the two event dispatches. In other words, the failure is triggered by firing a bullet while another bullet is being destroyed (by collision or leaving the game board).

With basic record/replay functionality, affordances for navigating the stream of recorded inputs, and the ability to easily reach program states by jumping directly to breakpoint hits, Timelapse both eliminates the need for Claire to repeatedly reproduce the Space Invaders failure and frees her to focus on understanding the program's logic. Our user evaluation explores these benefits further.

RECORD/REPLAY INFRASTRUCTURE

Dolos is the underlying record/replay infrastructure that enables the Timelapse tools and user interfaces. For Timelapse to be useful during debugging tasks, Dolos must not disrupt existing developer tools and workflows. Concretely, this entails the following four design goals:

1. **Low overhead.** Recording must introduce minimal performance overhead, because many interactive web applications are performance-sensitive. Replaying must be fast so that users can quickly navigate through recordings.

2. **Deterministic replay.** Recordings must exactly reproduce observable program behavior when replaying. Replaying should not have external effects.

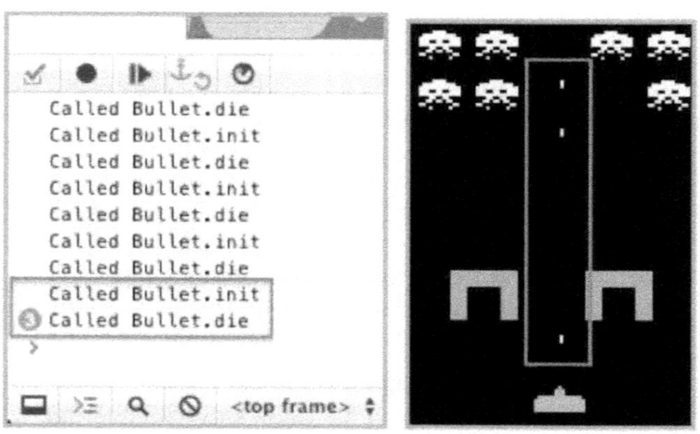

Figure 4. Screenshots of the logging output window and the defect's manifestation in the game. Claire added logging statements to the `die` and `init` methods. At left, the logging output shows the order of method entries, with the blue circle summarizing 3 identical logging outputs. According to the last 4 logging statements (outlined in red), calls to `die` and `init` are unbalanced. At right, three in-flight bullets correspond to the three calls to `Bullet.init`.

3. **Non-interference.** Recording and replaying must not interfere with the use of tools such as breakpoints, watchpoints, profilers, element inspectors, and logging.

4. **Deployability.** Recording and replaying must require no special installation, configuration, or elevated user privileges.

To the best of our knowledge, no prior record/replay tool satisfies all of these constraints. Source-level instrumentation of JavaScript [16] can perturb performance [25] and relies on hard-to-deploy[4] proxies to perform source rewriting. Rewriting techniques can interfere with a developer's expectations by obfuscating source code or by causing the debugger to unexpectedly interact with code the developer did not write. User-space record/replay library tools [18, 27] execute in the same address space as the target program and use wrappers to interpose on nondeterministic APIs (such as the `Date` constructor). These tools are inherently incompatible with breakpoint debuggers: because they piggyback on the target program, pausing at a breakpoint will also prevent the record/replay library's mechanisms from executing. Virtual machine replay debugging [33] ensures deterministic execution of the entire browser instead of one page context—preventing the use of built-in debugging tools which cannot run independently from other browser components. Macro-like replay tools such as Selenium WebDriver [31], CoScripter [15], or Sikuli [34] are commonly used for workflow automation; towards that end, they only record and replay user input, and not other program inputs such as network traffic, dates and times, and other sources of non-determinism. Replaying only user input is not deterministic enough to consistently reproduce web application behaviors. These external tools are unaware of internal system state or external server state: for example, they may try to provide input while the program is paused at a breakpoint, or cause the program to ask a server for resources that are no longer valid.

Web Browser Architecture

We use the term *web interpreter* to refer to the interpreter-like core of web browsers. The web interpreter processes inputs from the network, user, and timers; executes JavaScript; computes page layout; and renders output. We do not consider features that do not affect the results of computation, such as bookmarks and a browser's address bar. The web interpreter schedules asynchronous computation using a cooperative single-threaded event loop. It communicates with embedders (Safari, Google Chrome) and platforms (Linux, Mac OS X) via embedder and platform APIs (Figure 5). Both APIs are bidirectional: the web interpreter can call "out" to collect environmental information from the platfrom or delegate security policies to the embedder; the platform and embedder can call "in" to schedule computation (asynchronous timers, user input, network traffic) in the web interpreter's event loop.

[4]Proxies used for instrumentation and debugging like Fiddler [29] require elevated privileges, manual configuration, and intentional man-in-the-middle attacks to subvert SSL encryption.

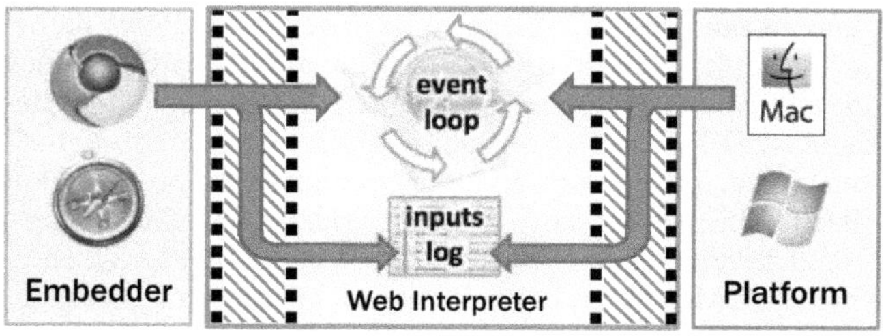

Figure 5. The flow of inputs while recording execution. Boxes delineate module boundaries. Arrows indicate the flow of program inputs. The web interpreter receives input and sends output via embedder and platform APIs (thick lines). During recording, input shims (striped regions) record program inputs delivered via the public APIs, and pass on the inputs to the unmodified event loop.

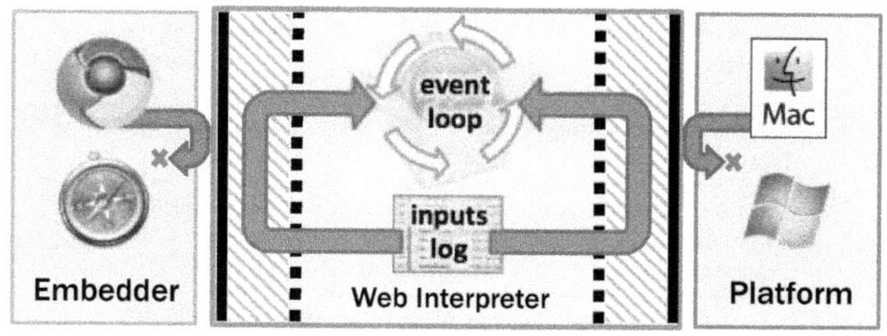

Figure 6. The flow of inputs while replaying execution. During replay, the interpreter's replay controller uses the input log to simulate the sequence of recorded public API calls into the interpreter (blue arrows). External calls to public APIs are ignored (solid black line) to prevent user interactions from causing a different execution. Calls from the web interpreter to platform APIs (i.e., to get the current time) use memoized return values and do not have external effects.

Design

Our requirements of low overhead, deterministic replay, non-interference, and deployability are closest to the design goals of virtual machine-based record/replay systems. Well-known systems in this space, such as ReVirt [7] and VMWare Replay Debugging [33], achieve deterministic record/replay via the "instruction-counting trick". A hypervisor interposes on nondeterministic machine instructions, but executes ordinary instructions natively on the bare-metal processor. Interrupts are captured and injected accurately by counting their position in the instruction stream. This technique satisfies our four design goals: it is fast, ensures precise replay, is compatible with debuggers, and requires minimal modifications to the runtime environment.

The execution model of web programs does not have machine instructions or interrupts, but there are parallels between virtual machines and web browsers. The Dolos infrastructure makes the following novel substitutions to make the "instruction-counting trick" work for the web's execution model:

- Instead of simulating deterministic hardware, Dolos simulates deterministic responses from embedder and platform when the web interpreter calls out to them.
- Instead of hardware interrupts, Dolos captures and simulates the subset of inbound embedder and platform API calls that trigger computation within the web application.
- Instead of counting instructions as a unit of execution progress, Dolos counts DOM event dispatches—precursors to the execution of JavaScript code—that may have deterministic or nondeterministic effects.

Implementation

The Dolos infrastructure is a modified version of the WebKit browser toolkit. We chose WebKit because it contains the most widely-deployed web interpreter (WebCore) and developer toolchain (Web Inspector). Our deployment model is straightforward: a version of WebKit built with Timelapse and Dolos support is distributed as a dynamic library, and can be used with existing WebKit embedders such as Safari or Google Chrome by adjusting the dynamic library load path.

Recording and replaying

Hypervisors (and record/replay systems based on them) are fast in part because most execution occurs at full speed on bare hardware. Similarly, Dolos achieves high record/replay performance in part by using the same code paths as normal execution when recording and replaying program inputs. Dolos captures and replays calls to the embedder and platform APIs using *shims*—thin layers used to observe external API calls or simulate external API calls from within. During recording (Figure 5), the shims record all API calls that affect program determinism. During replay, these API calls are simulated (Figure 6) to deterministically reproduce the recorded program behavior. To prevent user interactions from causing a different execution during replay, the shims block external API calls while allowing simulated calls to proceed.

During recording, Dolos saves the timing, ordering, and details of inbound calls to the web interpreter that are pertinent to the recorded web program's execution. During replay, these inbound calls are simulated by Dolos, rather than actually being issued by the embedder or platform. Dolos's approach to capturing and replaying computation-triggering calls is applicable to programs implemented using an event-loop-based UI framework. Dolos can seek to and/or pause execution prior to any simulated inbound call. Because the event loop is transparent to web programs, Dolos "pauses" execution without using breakpoints by simply not simulating the next computation-triggering inbound call. One can use breakpoints to pause JavaScript execution at any statement, but cannot use them to pause execution before the web interpreter interprets an inbound call.

Program inputs

Like hypervisor record/replay systems, Dolos classifies inputs to the web interpreter—that is, relevant inbound and outbound embedder and platform API calls—as either interrupts or environmental nondeterminism. Table 1 enumerates the major sources of interrupt-like inputs and environmental inputs. Conceptually, interrupts cause computation to happen, while environmental inputs embody nondeterministic aspects of the environment. Interrupts are API calls *from* the embedder or platform to the interpreter; environmental inputs are API calls *to* the embedder or platform from the interpreter.

Input	Classification	DOM Derivatives
Keyboard strokes	Interrupt	keyboard events
Mouse input	Interrupt	mouse events
Timer callbacks	Interrupt	(none)
Asynchronous events	Interrupt	animation events
Network response	Interrupt	AJAX, images, data
Random values	Environment	Math.random
Current time	Environment	Date.now
Persistent state	Environment	cookies, local storage

Table 1. Major classes of input as defined by Dolos.

Dolos records and replays embedder/platform API calls rather than individual DOM events [18, 21, 25] which result from the web interpreter's interpretation of inbound API calls. For example, instead of recording individual DOM `click` events, Dolos captures the embedder's calls to the web interpreter's `handleMousePress` API. This in turn may trigger one, many, or no DOM event dispatches, depending on the interpreter's state. Dolos's strategy reduces log size, runtime overhead, and implementation complexity because it does not require event targets to be serialized when recording or re-targeted when replaying.[5]

Dolos captures and replays network traffic in the same way that other event loop callbacks are handled. When capturing, Dolos caches the HTTP headers and raw data of network responses as they are passed from the embedder to the web interpreter. When replaying, Dolos blocks outbound network requests from actually reaching the network. Dolos simulates deterministic network responses by reusing cached HTTP headers and data. For example, when loading images asynchronously on Flickr, Dolos caches all image data when capturing. When replaying, Dolos simulates network responses by reusing cached image data, and never communicates with Flickr servers.

For environmental inputs, Dolos uses shims to memoize the web interpreter's C++ calls to the platform or embedder APIs rather than memoizing calls to nondeterministic JavaScript functions. For example, Dolos does not record the return value of JavaScript's `Date.now()` function; instead, Dolos memoizes the JavaScript engine's calls to the `currentTimeMS()` platform API inside the implementation of `Date.now()`.

Replay fidelity

The Dolos infrastructure guarantees identical execution when recording and replaying, up to the order and contents of DOM events dispatched. JavaScript execution is completely deterministic. There is no guarantee regarding number of layout reflows or paints due to time compression or internal browser nondeterminism. This is unimportant because visual output cannot affect the determinism of JavaScript computation: JavaScript client code can ask for computed layout data, but will block until the layout algorithm runs on the current version of the DOM tree. Rendering and painting activity is not exposed to client code at all.

To the best of our knowledge, Dolos is the first web record/replay infrastructure that *detects* execution divergence. Timelapse warns users when divergences are detected or when known-nondeterministic APIs are used, and allows them to abort replay, ignore divergences, or report feature requests to the Dolos developers. Dolos uses differences in measures such as DOM node counts and event dispatch counts to detect unexpected execution divergences caused by bugs in Dolos itself. This has helped us find and address obscure sources of nondeterminism, such as resource caching effects, asynchrony in the HTML parser, implicit window size and focus state, and improper multiplexing of inputs to nested `iframe` elements.

[5] Guo et al. [9] report on the space and time benefits of memoizing application-level API calls instead of low-level system calls [27].

The Dolos prototype does not address all known sources of nondeterminism, such as the Touch, Battery, Sensor, Screen, or Clipboard APIs, among others. There are no conceptual barriers to supporting these features: they are implemented in terms of standardized DOM events and interfaces, making them relatively easy to interpose upon using techniques described in this paper. Each new program input requires local changes to route control flow through a shim, plus a helper class to serialize and simulate the program input.

Engineering cost

Dolos's design scales to new platforms, embedders, and sources of nondeterminism because inputs are recorded and replayed at existing module boundaries. Implementing Dolos required minimal changes to WebKit's architecture: namely, the insertion of shims just beneath the web interpreter's public embedder and platform APIs (shown in Figure 5 and in Figure 6). The Dolos infrastructure consists of 7.6K SLOC (74 new files, 75 modified files). For comparison, WebKit contains about 1.38M SLOC.

Overhead

Dolos's record/replay performance slowdown is unnoticeable ($< 1.1\times$) for interactive workloads and modest ($\leq 1.65\times$) for non-interactive benchmarks without any significant optimization efforts (Table 2). Recording overhead and the amount of data collected scales with user, network, and nondeterministic inputs, not CPU time.

We report the geometric mean of 10 runs (except for interactive runs, which were recorded once but replayed 10 times). We cleared network resource caches between executions to avoid memory and disk cache nondeterminism. We used local copies of benchmarks to avoid network nondeterminism.

Recording has almost no time overhead: execution times are dominated by the subject program. Replaying at $1\times$ speed is marginally slower than a normal execution due to extra work performed by Dolos, and seeking (fast replaying) is much faster because it elides user and network waits from the recorded execution.

While being created or replayed, recordings are stored in-memory and consume modest amounts of memory (first column in the data size section of Table 2). When serialized, the recordings are highly compressible. A recording's length is limited only by main memory; in our experience, users attempt to minimize recording length to reduce the number of irrelevant inputs. Timelapse's linear presentation of time does not scale well to long executions. This could be ameliorated by using nonlinear time scaling techniques [32, 14].

Program			Run Time						Data Size (KB)	
Name	Description	Workload	Bottleneck	Baseline	Disabled	Recording	Replaying	Seeking	Log	Site
JSLinux	x86 emulator	Run until login	network	10.5s	1.00×	1.65×	1.65×	0.37×	24.7 / 71.4 / 8.5	4500
JS Raytracer	ray-tracer	Complete run	CPU	6.3s	1.00×	1.01×	1.17×	1.02×	24.0 / 69.4 / 10.2	5.9
Space Invaders	video game	Scripted gameplay	timers	25.8s	1.00×	1.03×	1.22×	0.25×	247 / 683 / 56.8	712
Mozilla.org	home page	Read latest news	user	22.3s	1.00×	1.00×	1.09×	0.23×	187 / 502 / 29.5	2800
CodeMirror	text editor	Edit a document	user	16.6s	1.00×	1.00×	1.03×	0.07×	57.6 / 163 / 17.1	168
Colorpicker	jQuery widget	Reproduce defect	user	15.3s	1.00×	1.00×	1.07×	0.13×	112 / 302 / 26.7	577
DuckDuckGo	search engine	Browse results	user	14.1s	1.00×	1.00×	1.08×	0.19×	119 / 309 / 29.6	1900

Table 2. Overhead for three non-interactive and four interactive programs. "Baseline" is unmodified WebKit, and "Disabled" is Dolos when neither record nor replay is enabled. Log size is given for the in-memory representation, the uncompressed log file, and the compressed log file. Site content is images, scripts, and HTML.

Limitations

Dolos only ensures deterministic execution for *client-side* portions of web applications; it records and simulates client interactions with a remote server, but does not directly capture server-side state. Tools that link client- and server-side execution traces [35] may benefit from the additional runtime context provided by a Dolos recording. Dolos cannot control the determinism of local, external software components such as Flash, Silverlight, or other plugins. However, plugins interact via the embedder API; Dolos could handle plugin nondeterminism in the same way that other embedder nondeterminism is handled.

Web interpreters provide many API calls that do not affect program determinism. For example, WebKit's web interpreter includes APIs for usability features like native spell-checking, in-page search, and accessibility. Dolos does not record or replay these API calls because a developer may wish to use such features differently during replay, and these features do not affect the determinism of the web program.

Dolos's hypervisor-like record/replay strategy relies on the layered architecture of WebKit. It is not directly applicable to systems without clear API boundaries between the embedder, platform, and web interpreter. For example, the Gecko web interpreter used by Firefox is implemented by dozens of decoupled components rather than a monolithic module. This design makes it easy to extend the browser, but difficult to record and replay only the subset of components that affect the specific web program's execution, as opposed to those are used by browser features, browser extensions, or several web programs at once. Shims for Gecko would have the same behavior as Dolos's shims, but they would be placed throughout the web interpreter rather than at coarse abstraction boundaries.

HOW DO DEVELOPERS USE TIMELAPSE?

Prior work [7, 18, 27] asserts the usefulness of deterministic record and replay for debugging. In this section, we present a formative user study that investigates when, how, and for whom record/replay tools and specifically Timelapse are beneficial. Our specific research questions were:

RQ 1 How does Timelapse affect the way that developers reproduce behavior?

RQ 2 How do successful and unsuccessful developers use Timelapse differently?

Study Design

We recruited 14 web developers, 2 of which we used in pilot studies to refine the study design. Each participant performed two tasks. We used a within-subjects design to see how Timelapse changed the behavior of individual developers. For one task, participants could use the standard debugging tools included with the Safari web browser. For the other task, they could also use Timelapse. To mitigate learning effects, we randomized the ordering of the two tasks, and randomized task in which they were allowed to use Timelapse.

The goal of this study was to explore the variation in how developers used Timelapse, so the tasks needed to be challenging enough to expose a range of task success. To balance realism with replicability, we chose two tasks of medium difficulty, each with several intermediate milestones. Based on our results, our small exploratory study was still sufficiently large to capture the variability in debugging and programming skill among web developers.

Participants

We recruited 14 web developers in the Seattle area. Each participant had recently worked on a substantial interactive website or web application. One half of the participants were developers, designers, or testers. The other half were researchers who wrote web applications in the course of their research. We did not control for experience with the jQuery or Glow libraries used by the programs being debugged.

Programs and Tasks

Space Invaders. One program was the Space Invaders game from our earlier example scenario. The program consists of 625 SLOC in 6 files (excluding library code) and uses the Glow JavaScript library[6]. We chose this program for two reasons: its extensive use of timers makes it a heavy record/replay workload, and its event-oriented implementation is representative of object-oriented model-view programs, the dominant paradigm for large, interactive web applications.

We asked participants to fix two Space Invaders defects. The first was an API mismatch that occurred when we upgraded the Glow library to a recent version while preparing the program for use in our study. In prior versions, a sprite's coordinates were represented with `x` and `y` properties; in recent versions, coordinates are instead represented with `left` and `top` properties, respectively. After upgrading, the game's hit detection

[6] `http://www.bbc.co.uk/glow/`

code ceases to work because it references the obsolete property names. The second defect was described in the motivating example and was masked by the first defect.

Colorpicker. The other program was Colorpicker[7], an interactive widget for selecting colors in the RGB and HSV colorspaces (see in Figure 7). The program consists of about 500 LOC (excluding library and example code). The widget supports color selection via RGB (red, green, blue) or HSV (hue, saturation, brightness) component values or through several widgets that visualize dimensions of the HSV colorspace.

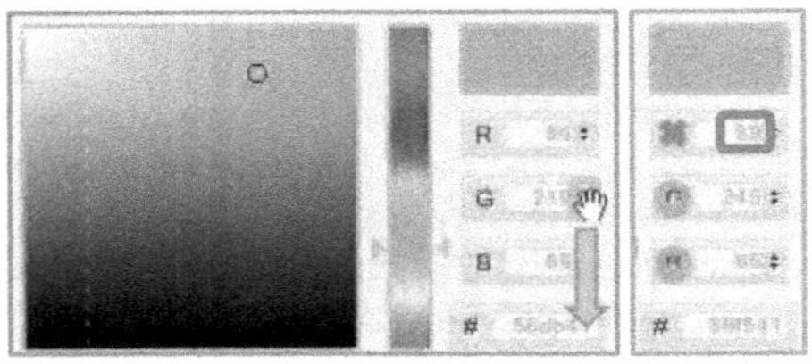

Figure 7. The Colorpicker widget.

We chose this program because it makes extensive use of the popular jQuery library, which—by virtue of being highly layered, abstracted, and optimized—makes reasoning about and following the code significantly more laborious.

The Colorpicker task was to create a regression test for a real, unreported defect in the Colorpicker widget. The defect manifests when selecting a color by adjusting an RGB component value, as shown in Figure 7. If the user drags the G component (left panel, orange), the R component spontaneously changes (right panel, red). The R component should not change when adjusting the G component. The bug is caused by unnecessary rounding in the algorithm that converts values between RGB and HSV color spaces. Since the color picker uses the HSV representation internally, repeated conversions between RGB and HSV can expose numerical instability during certain patterns of interaction.

We claim that both of these faults are representative of many bugs in interactive programs. Often there is nothing wrong with the user interface or event handling code *per se*, but faults that are buried deep within the application logic are only uncovered by user input or manifest as visual output. The Space Invaders faults lie in incorrect uses of library APIs, but manifest as broken gameplay mechanics. Similarly, the Colorpicker fault exists in a core numerical routine, but is only manifested ephemerally in response to mouse move events.

Procedure

Participants performed the study alone in a computer lab. Participants were first informed of the general purpose and structure of the study, but not of our research questions to avoid observer and subject expectancy effects. Immediately prior to the task where Timelapse was available, participants spent 30 minutes reading a Timelapse tutorial and performing exercises on a demo program. In order to proceed, participants were required to demonstrate mastery of recording, replaying, zooming, seeking, and using breakpoint radar and debugger bookmarks. Participants could refer back to the tutorial during subsequent tasks.

[7] `http://www.eyecon.ro/colorpicker/`

Each task was described in the form of a bug report that included a brief description of the bug and steps to reproduce the fault. At the start of each task, the participant was instructed to read the entire bug report and then reproduce the fault. Each task was considered complete when the participant demonstrated their correct solution. Participants had up to 45 minutes to complete each task. We stopped participants when they had demonstrated successful completion to us or exceeded the time limit.

After both task periods were over, we interviewed participants for 10 minutes about how they used the tool during the tutorial and tool-equipped task and how they might have used the tool on the other task. We also asked about their prior experience in bug reproduction, debugging, and testing activities.

Data Collection and Analysis

We captured a screen and audio recording of each participant's session, and gathered timing and occurrence data by reviewing the video recordings after the study concluded.

Our tasks were both realistic and difficult so as to draw out variations in debugging skill and avoid imposing a performance ceiling. We measured task success via completion of several intermediate task steps or critical events. For the Space Invaders task, the steps were: successful fault reproduction, identifying the API mismatch, fixing the API bug, reproducing the rate-of-fire defect, written root cause, and fixing the rate-of-fire defect. For the Colorpicker task, the steps were: successful fault reproduction, written root cause, correct test form, identifying a buggy input, and verifying the test.

We measured the time on task as the duration from the start of the initial reproduction attempt until the task was completed or until the participant ran out of time. We recorded the count and duration of all reproduction activities and whether the activity was mediated by Timelapse (automatic reproduction) or not (manual reproduction). Reproduction times only included time in which participants' attention was engaged on reproduction, which we determined by observing changes in window focus, mouse positioning, and interface modality.

Results

Below, we summarize our findings of how Timelapse affects developers' reproduction behavior (RQ1) and how this interacts with debugging expertise (RQ2).

Timelapse did not reduce time spent reproducing behaviors. There was no significant difference in the percentage of time spent reproducing behaviors across conditions and tasks. Though Timelapse makes reproduction of behaviors simpler, it does not follow that this fact will reduce overall time spent on reproduction. We observed the opposite: because reproduction with Timelapse was so easy, participants seemed more willing to reproduce behaviors repeatedly. A possible confound is that behaviors in our tasks were fairly easy to reproduce, so Timelapse only made reproduction less tedious, not less challenging. We had hoped to test whether Timelapse is more useful for fixing more challenging bugs, but were forced to reduce task difficulty so that we could retain a within-subjects study design while minimizing participants' time commitment.

8–25% of time was spent reproducing behavior. Even when provided detailed and correct reproduction steps, developers in both conditions spent up to 25% (and typically 10–15%) of their time reproducing behaviors. Participants in all tasks and conditions reproduced behavior many times (median of 22 instances) over small periods. This suggests that developers frequently digress from investigative activities to reproduce program behavior. These measures are unlikely to be ecologically valid because most participants did not complete all tasks, and time spent on reproduction activities outside of the scope of our study tasks (i.e., during bug reporting, triage, and testing) is not included.

Expert developers incorporated replay capabilities. High-performing participants—those who successfully completed the most task steps—seemed to better integrate Timelapse's capabilities into their debugging workflows. Corroborating the results of previous studies [26, 22], we observed that successful developers debugged methodically, formed and tested debugging hypotheses using a bisection strategy, and revised their assessment of the root cause as their understanding of the defect grew. They quickly learned how to use Timelapse to facilitate these activities. They used Timelapse to accelerate familiar tasks, rather than redesigning their workflow around record/replay capabilities. In the Colorpicker task, participant 11 used Timelapse to compare program state before and after each call in the `mousemove` event handler, and then used Timelapse to move back and forth in time when bisecting the specific calls that caused the widget's RGB values to update incorrectly. Participants in the control condition appeared to achieve the same strategy more slowly by interleaving changes to breakpoints and manual reproduction.

Timelapse distracted less-skilled developers. Those who only achieved partial or limited success had trouble integrating Timelapse into their workflow. We partially attribute this to differences in participants' prior debugging experiences and strategies. The less successful participants used ad-hoc, opportunistic debugging strategies; overlooked important source code or runtime state; and were led astray by unverified assumptions. Consequently, even when these developers used Timelapse, they did not use it to a productive end.

Summary In our study, developers used Timelapse to automatically reproduce program behavior during debugging tasks, but this capability alone did not significantly affect task times, task success, or time spent reproducing behaviors. For developers who employed systematic debugging strategies, Timelapse was useful for quickly reproducing behaviors and navigating to important program states. Timelapse distracted developers who used ad-hoc or opportunistic strategies, or who were unfamiliar with standard debugging tools. Timelapse was used to accelerate the reproduction steps of existing strategies, but did not seem to affect strategy selection during our short study. As with any new tool, it appears that some degree of training and experience is necessary to fully exploit the tool's benefits. In our small study, the availability of Timelapse had no statistically significant effects on participants' speed or success in completing tasks. Figure 8 shows task success and task time per task and condition. In future work, we plan to study how long-term use of Timelapse during daily development affects debugging strategies. We also plan to investigate how recordings can improve bug reporting practices and communication between bug reporters and bug fixers.

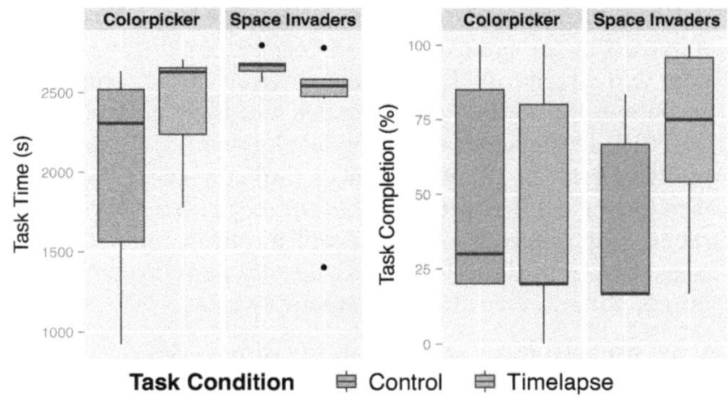

Figure 8. A summary of task time and success per condition and task. Box plots show outliers (points), median (thick bar), and 1st and 3rd quartiles (bottom and top of box, respectively). There was no statistically significant difference in performance between participants who used standard tools and those who had access to Timelapse.

RELATED WORK

Visualizing and Exploring Recordings and Traces

In contrast to the dearth of interactive record/replay tools, there have been many tools [12, 24] to visualize, navigate, and explore execution traces[8] generated by logging instrumentation. This is because execution traces are several orders of magnitude larger and contain very low-level details: the only way to understand them is to use elaborate search, analysis, and visualization tools. While Timelapse visualizes an execution as the temporal ordering of its inputs, trace-based debugging tools [12, 32] infer and display higher-level structural or causal relationships observed during execution. Timelapse's affordances primarily support navigation through the recording with respect to program inputs, while trace-based tools focus directly on aids to program comprehension (such as supporting causal inference or answering questions about what happened [12]).

Unfortunately, the practicality of many trace-based debugging tools is limited by the performance of modern hardware and the size of generated execution traces. Modern profilers, logging, and lightweight instrumentation systems [2] (and visualization tools [32] built on top of them) have acceptable performance because they capture infrequent high-level data or perform sampling. In contrast, heavyweight fine-grained execution trace collection introduces up to an order of magnitude slowdown [12, 20]. Generated traces and their indices [23, 24] are very large and often limited by the size of main memory.

Supporting Behavior Reproduction and Dissemination

To the best of our knowledge, deterministic record/replay systems that support dissemination of behaviors have only been

[8] *Execution traces* consist of intermediate program states logged over time, while Dolos's recordings consist only of the program's inputs.

widely deployed as part of video game engines [6]. Recordings of gameplay are artifacts shared between users for entertainment and education. These recordings are also a critical tool for debugging video game engines and their network protocols [30]. In the wider software development community, bug reporting systems [8] and practices [36] emphasize the sharing of evidence such as program output (e.g., screenshots, stack traces, logs, memory dumps) and program input (e.g, test cases, configurations, and files). Developers investigate bug reports with user-written reproduction steps.

While we have focused on the utility of record/replay systems for debugging, such systems are also useful for creating and evaluating software. Prior work has used record/replay of real captured data to provide a consistent, interactive means for prototyping sensor processing [3, 19] and computer vision [10] algorithms. More generally, macro-replay systems for reproducing user [31] and network [29] input are used for prototyping and testing web applications and other user interfaces. Dolos recordings contain a superset of these inputs; it is possible to synthesize a macro (i.e, automated test case) for use with other tools. The JSBench tool [25] uses this strategy to synthesize standalone web benchmarks. Derived inputs may improve the results of state-exploration tools such as Crawljax [17] by providing real, captured input traces.

CONCLUSION AND FUTURE WORK

Together, Timelapse and Dolos constitute the first toolchain designed for interactively capturing and replaying web application behaviors during debugging. Timelapse focuses on browsing, visualizing, and navigating program states to support behavior reproduction during debugging tasks. Our user study confirmed that behavior reproduction was a significant activity in realistic debugging tasks, and Timelapse assisted some developers in locating and automatically reproducing behaviors of interest. The Dolos infrastructure uses a novel adaptation of instruction-counting record/replay techniques to reproduce web application behaviors. Our prototype demonstrates that deterministic record/replay can be implemented within browsers in an additive way—without impacting performance or determinism, impeding tool use, or requiring configuration—and is a platform for new debugging aids.

Prior work assumes that executions are in short supply during debugging, and that developers know a priori what sorts of analysis and data they want before reproducing behavior. In future work, we want to disrupt this status quo. On-demand replay (in the foreground, background, or offline) could change the feasibility of useful program understanding tools [12] or dynamic analyses [4] that, heretofore, have been considered too expensive for practical (always-on) use. Using the Dolos infrastructure, we intend to transform prior works in dynamic analysis and trace visualization into on-demand, interactive tools that a developer can quickly employ when necessary. We believe that when combined with on-demand replay, post mortem trace visualization and program understanding tools will become *in vivo* tools for understanding program behavior at runtime.

ACKNOWLEDGEMENTS

This material is based in part upon work supported by the National Science Foundation under Grant Numbers CCF-0952733 and CCF-1153625. Any opinions, findings, and conclusions or recommendations expressed in this material are those of the author(s) and do not necessarily reflect the views of the National Science Foundation.

REFERENCES

1. Andrica, S., and Candea, G. WaRR: A tool for high-fidelity web application record and replay. In *DSN* (2011).
2. Cantrill, B. M., Shapiro, M. W., and Leventhal, A. H. Dynamic instrumentation of production systems. In *USENIX ATC* (2004).
3. Cardenas, T., Bastea-Forte, M., Ricciardi, A., Hartmann, B., and Klemmer, S. R. Testing physical computing prototypes through time-shifted and simulated input traces. In *UIST* (2008).
4. Chow, J., Garfinkel, T., and Chen, P. M. Decoupling dynamic program analysis from execution in virtual environments. In *USENIX ATC* (2008).
5. Cornelis, F., Georges, A., Christiaens, M., Ronsse, M., Ghesquiere, T., and Bosschere, K. D. A taxonomy of execution replay systems. In *SSGRR* (2003).
6. Dickinson, P. Instant replay: Building a game engine with reproducible behavior. In *Gamasutra* (July 2001).
7. Dunlap, G. W., King, S. T., Cinar, S., Basrai, M. A., and Chen, P. M. ReVirt: enabling intrusion analysis through virtual-machine logging and replay. *SIGOPS Oper. Syst. Rev. 36*, SI (Dec. 2002), 211–224.
8. Glerum, K., Kinshuman, K., Greenberg, S., Aul, G., Orgovan, V., Nichols, G., Grant, D., Loihle, G., and Hunt, G. Debugging in the (very) large: Ten years of implementation and practice. In *SOSP* (2009).
9. Guo, Z., Wang, X., Tang, J., Liu, X., Xu, Z., Wu, M., Kaashoek, M. F., and Zhang, Z. R2: An application-level kernel for record and replay. In *OSDI* (2008).
10. Kato, J., McDirmid, S., and Cao, X. DejaVu: Integrated support for developing interactive camera-based programs. In *UIST* (2012).
11. King, S. T., Dunlap, G. W., and Chen, P. M. Debugging operating systems with time-traveling virtual machines. In *USENIX ATC* (2005).
12. Ko, A. J., and Myers, B. A. Extracting and answering why and why not questions about Java program output. *ACM Trans. Softw. Eng. Methodol. 20*, 2 (Sept. 2010), 4:1–4:36.
13. Ko, A. J., Myers, B. A., Coblenz, M. J., and Aung, H. H. An exploratory study of how developers seek, relate, and collect relevant information during software maintenance tasks. *IEEE Trans. Softw. Eng. 32*, 12 (Dec. 2006), 971–987.
14. Kuhn, A., and Greevy, O. Exploiting the analogy between traces and signal processing. In *ICSM* (2006).

15. Leshed, G., Haber, E. M., Matthews, T., and Lau, T. CoScripter: Automating and sharing how-to knowledge in the enterprise. In *CHI* (2008).

16. Mesbah, A., and van Deursen, A. Invariant-based automatic testing of AJAX user interfaces. In *ICSE* (2009).

17. Mesbah, A., van Deursen, A., and Lenselink, S. Crawling Ajax-based web applications through dynamic analysis of user interface state changes. *ACM Transactions on the Web (TWEB) 6*, 1 (2012), 3:1–3:30.

18. Mickens, J., Elson, J., and Howell, J. Mugshot: deterministic capture and replay for JavaScript applications. In *NSDI* (2010).

19. Newman, M. W., Ackerman, M. S., Kim, J., Prakash, A., Hong, Z., Mandel, J., and Dong, T. Bringing the field into the lab: Supporting capturing and RePlay of contextual data for design. In *UIST* (2010).

20. O'Callahan, R. Efficient collection and storage of indexed program traces, 2006. `http://www.ocallahan.org/Amber.pdf`.

21. Oney, S., and Myers, B. FireCrystal: Understanding interactive behaviors in dynamic web pages. In *VL/HCC* (2009).

22. Parnin, C., and Orso, A. Are automated debugging techniques actually helping programmers? In *ISSTA* (2011).

23. Pothier, G., and Tanter, E. Summarized trace indexing and querying for scalable back-in-time debugging. In *ECOOP* (2011).

24. Pothier, G., Tanter, E., and Piquer, J. Scalable omniscient debugging. In *OOPSLA* (2007).

25. Richards, G., Gal, A., Eich, B., and Vitek, J. Automated construction of JavaScript benchmarks. In *OOPSLA* (2011).

26. Robillard, M. P., Coelho, W., and Murphy, G. C. How effective developers investigate source code: an exploratory study. *IEEE Trans. Softw. Eng. 30*, 12 (Dec. 2004), 889–903.

27. Saito, Y. Jockey: a user-space library for record-replay debugging. In *AADEBUG* (2005).

28. Sillito, J., Murphy, G. C., and Volder, K. D. Asking and answering questions during a programming change task. *IEEE Trans. Soft. Eng. 34* (2008), 434–451.

29. Telerik. Fiddler web debugging proxy, 2013. `http://www.fiddler2.com/fiddler2/`.

30. Terrano, M., and Bettner, P. 1500 Archers on a 28.8: Network programming in Age of Empires and beyond. In *Gamasutra* (March 2001).

31. The Selenium Project. Selenium WebDriver documentation, 2012. `http://seleniumhq.org/docs/03_webdriver.html`.

32. Trümper, J., Bohnet, J., and Döllner, J. Understanding complex multithreaded software systems by using trace visualization. In *SOFTVIS* (2010).

33. VMWare, I. Replay debugging on Linux, October 2009. `http://www.vmware.com/pdf/ws7_replay_linux_technote.pdf`.

34. Yeh, T., Chang, T.-H., and Miller, R. C. Sikuli: Using GUI screenshots for search and automation. In *UIST* (2009).

35. Zaidman, A., Matthijssen, N., Storey, M.-A., and van Deursen, A. Connecting client and server-side execution traces. *Empirical Software Engineering (EMSE) 18*, 2 (2013), 181–218.

36. Zimmermann, T., Premraj, R., Bettenburg, N., Just, S., Schrter, A., and Weiss, C. What makes a good bug report? *IEEE Trans. Soft. Eng. 36*, 5 (September 2010), 618–643.

Authoring Multi-Stage Code Examples with Editable Code Histories

Shiry Ginosar, Luis Fernando De Pombo, Maneesh Agrawala, Björn Hartmann
Computer Science Division, University of California, Berkeley
shiry@cs.berkeley.edu, lfdepombo@berkeley.edu, maneesh@cs.berkeley.edu, bjoern@cs.berkeley.edu

ABSTRACT
Multi-stage code examples present multiple versions of a program where each stage increases the overall complexity of the code. In order to acquire strategies of program construction using a new language or API, programmers consult multi-stage code examples in books, tutorials and online videos. Authoring multi-stage code examples is currently a tedious process, as it involves keeping several stages of code synchronized in the face of edits and error corrections. We document these difficulties with a formative study examining how programmers author multi-stage code examples. We then present an IDE extension that helps authors create multi-stage code examples by propagating changes (insertions, deletions and modifications) to multiple saved versions of their code. Our system adapts revision control algorithms to the specific task of evolving example code. An informal evaluation finds that taking snapshots of a program as it is being developed and editing these snapshots in hindsight help users in creating multi-stage code examples.

Author Keywords
Examples; tutorials; programming; editable histories

ACM Classification Keywords
H.5.m. Information Interfaces and Presentation (e.g. HCI): Miscellaneous

INTRODUCTION
Programmers can find technical material needed for specific programming tasks by searching for community-generated content online. While novice programmers may mostly look for syntactic help, more advanced developers often need to acquire strategies for combining smaller library functions and APIs to create full programs. One way to learn such strategies is through *multi-stage code examples* which present multiple versions of a program where each stage increases the complexity of the overall example [33].

Indeed, teaching materials often use multi-stage code examples such as the one presented in Figure 2 (on the next page). This simplified example introduces elements of an interactive drawing program one-by-one. The first stage shows how to draw a single line. The second shows how to set drawing parameters such as canvas size and color. The third stage adds interactivity by drawing lines to the cursor position. Finally, the last stage clears the screen so only a single line is drawn while the mouse is dragged.

UIST'13, October 8–11, 2013, St. Andrews, United Kingdom.
ACM 978-1-4503-2268-3/13/10.
http://dx.doi.org/10.1145/2501988.2502053

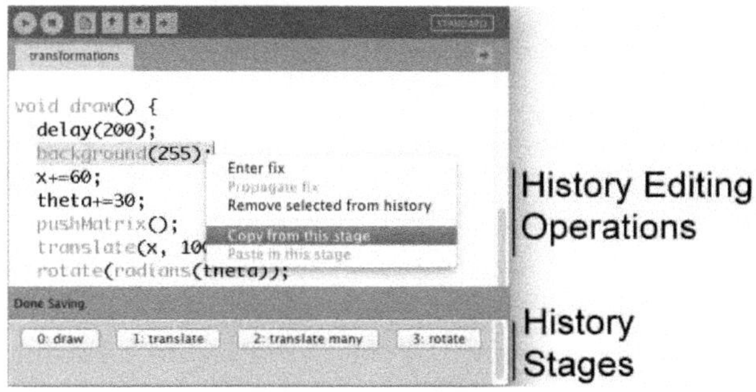

Figure 1. We introduce an editor that facilitates the construction of multi-stage code examples through a set of history editing operations and the management of history stages.

Creating multi-stage code examples requires keeping track of multiple versions of code and the edits between them. In a formative study where we observed coders as they created such examples, we found that authors have difficulty planning example stages from beginning to end. They often go back and forth in stage history, making changes over multiple versions. For example, if the lines in an example designed for print are difficult to see because they are too thin (Figure 2), the author would have to modify stages 2-4 to consistently update the thickness parameter.

Revision control systems like git [13] or Subversion [36] provide tools for controlling multiple versions of code. However, their user interface is insufficient to support the specific task of authoring code examples. For instance, after committing several revisions of a program, there is no easy way to add a block of code to the existing sequence of revisions without requiring the user to intervene and resolve conflicts. A tool that assists users with such editing operations would ideally be integrated into an Integrated Development Environment (IDE) to make for a seamless development and editing experience (Figure 1). Our formative study suggests that this type of editor should support an addition operation so that authors can make changes to multiple versions of code. It should also enable authors to remove or fix existing blocks of code throughout the history of example stages. Ultimately, for seamless authoring of multi-stage code examples, pro-

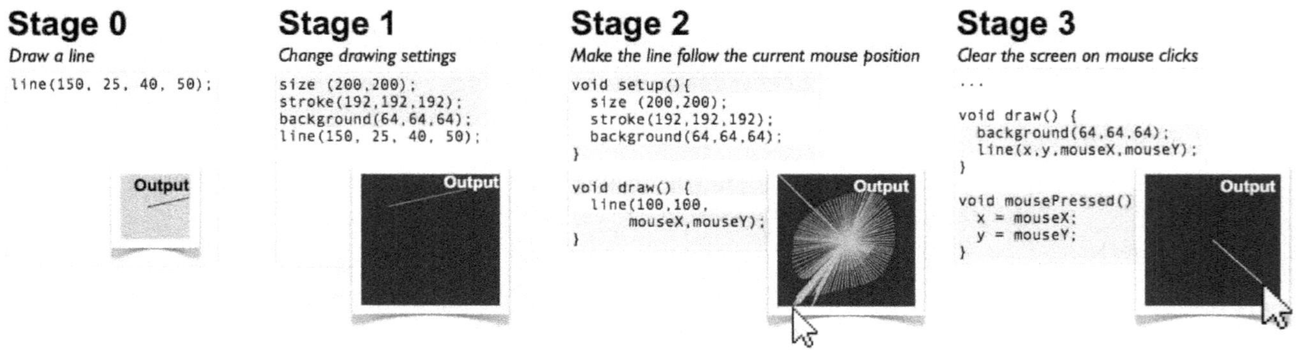

Figure 2. In multi-stage examples, each stage builds upon the existing code and adds new functionality (highlighted). Stage 0 shows how to draw a single line. Stage 1 shows how to set drawing parameters such as canvas size and color. Stage 2 adds interactivity by drawing lines to the cursor position. Finally, Stage 3 clears the screen so only a single line is drawn while the mouse is dragged. (Adapted from the Processing.org).

grammers need to be able to edit the history of their code, propagating changes across stages.

We present an authoring tool that facilitates the creation of multi-stage code examples (Figure 1). Our tool extends a standard IDE, and captures a rich representation of code into an underlying version control system. It introduces IDE interaction techniques that enable example authors to edit the example history by propagating edits across stages. The techniques we use are based on differencing algorithms that identify the point in history where a change was introduced, and the most likely location of code blocks in other stages of the example program. Some of these algorithms are included in revision control tools and others, like the ability to add code to previous revisions, extend the functionality of these tools.

Authors can use our system to convert a set of code stages to multi-stage code examples that can be directly consumed by learners. We take inspiration from code examples in books, tutorials and websites, and demonstrate the generation of one output format as a proof of concept. In this HTML format we highlight the differences in the lines of code between stages and we include the running output of each stage as it is viewed directly in the web page. Additionally, learners can easily navigate between example stages.

We conducted an informal study of our tool with seven participants and found that they frequently saved snapshots of their code as stages while writing examples (up to 11 stages per example). Additionally, they successfully edited across stages to modify or fix their examples.

BACKGROUND

Several different types of learning materials use multi-stage code examples to teach strategies of program construction. For example, programming books and online tutorials often start with a simple construct and develop a more complicated example over several chapters. Many video tutorials begin with an empty project and develop a working program. However, these often do not demonstrate discrete, working code in separable stages [37]. In this section, we review people's programming learning strategies to motivate the importance of supporting the authoring of multi-stage examples.

How Programmers Use Code Examples

Programmers face different barriers when trying to write code in a new environment [20]. *Use barriers* represent difficulties in determining how to work with a programming interface. *Coordination barriers* concern the rules for combining individual building blocks to achieve complex behaviors. Both barriers are well addressed by concrete code examples. Coordination strategies in particular can be taught by introducing many examples of programs as they are being developed [33]. By following these examples, a learner can observe how others combine smaller structures to create a working program.

Users are not inclined to read lengthy training materials; their particular goals and concerns often differ from the careful ordering of chapters in a training procedure [6]. This trend also holds for programmers: when programmers find tutorials online they often experiment with the included code samples rather than take the time to read the accompanying explanation. Moreover, programmers often begin adapting code before they completely understand it [4]. When a developer feels that the information he already collected is sufficient to complete a given task, the developer may drop out of the comprehension process and switch to implementing a solution with found information [21]. In line with these observations, Minimalist Instruction Theory [6] calls for designing materials as small, self-contained units representing real tasks that can be read in any order. Multi-stage examples share similarities with early Minimalist systems as they break the experts' program creation process into discrete chunks. Each of these chunks has a well defined effect on the output of the program enabling out-of-order access and exploration by the learners. By exporting multi-stage examples to interactive formats like HTML they allow for the presentation of output formats similar to Carroll's ViewMatcher that presented example programs in an interactive tool together with their output [7] and to Victor's designs that make the state of the program visible [40].

RELATED WORK

Our work builds on two primary areas of prior work; tools for authoring and using code examples, and tools for visualizing and editing operation histories.

Authoring and Using Code Examples

Like our work, JTutor [22] focuses on code changes over time; it permits record-and-replay of code edits, but does not offer the history editing we provide. The commercial Codeplayer [37] records and replays coding sessions at the character level. Like single-take screencasts, such performances require careful planning on the author's part. Our history editing techniques enable example authors to make modifications to different stages at any point.

Augmented examples provide additional information beyond a static view of a piece of source code. JTourBus [28] lets developers record annotated "tours" through a project to highlight important code locations to others. WebEx allows teachers to produce example code with line-wise explanations [5]. HyperSource [17] and Codetrail [14] save relevant URLs along with source code as a form of design rationale. Our work instead focuses on capturing additional temporal information on how code evolves.

Several researchers have investigated how to help learners find, extract or synthesize code examples [3, 8, 24, 25, 34]. Other systems aim to make example code reuse easier [29, 30, 42]. In contrast, we focus on example authoring.

Researchers have investigated how to author examples and tutorials for other domains besides programming. Many studies concentrate on image manipulation and 3D modeling applications because of the complexity of their interfaces. Several systems generate tutorials for such interfaces from demonstrations [1, 10, 15]. Given a structured representation of a step-by-step procedure, such systems can also observe a user's actions and synchronize the display of instructions with those actions [1, 2, 31]. Demonstrations in 3D Modeling or photo manipulation can comprise hundreds of operations and therefore call for intelligent techniques for aggregating or navigating steps [11, 15, 16]. The dependence or independence of different actions in an editing sequence can be captured by revision control functions adapted to image manipulation [9]. Our system is unique with respect to these prior works as none of these systems are designed to build multi stage code examples.

Editable Histories

Editable code histories in our work are closely related to editable graphical histories, which provide authors with tools to modify prior document states. Researchers built such systems for vector graphics [23, 35], photo manipulation [9], information visualization [18], and other domains. Common actions supported by these tools, like ours, are navigation to prior states and editing a prior state to propagate changes forward in time. We also allow editing later states and propagating changes back. More importantly, our work differs in that the final product of our tool is not a single document but rather a sequence of documents over time. In this sense, the collected history is the final artifact.

The ability to edit multiple code stages is related to Linked Editing, a technique to link duplicate code blocks in a program and edit them simultaneously [38]. However, unlike multi-stage code examples, the Linked Editing model does not capture a sequential history of modifications.

The Git rebase command also enables programmers to apply changes and additions of code to a chain of commits [13]. However, our system can better resolve conflicts when we propagate the addition of code to past stages since (1) we assume there is one author who is guided to only merge in additive changes and (2) we let the user impose location constraints on both ends (start and end) of the propagation.

FORMATIVE STUDY

To better understand the challenges programmers face when producing multi-stage code examples, we conducted a formative study with seven participants. We asked each participant to produce a multi-stage code example that describes how to program the classic Pong game in Processing, a Java variant [32]. We chose Processing as the language of our study for several reasons. First, Processing is designed for creating images, animations and interactive graphical sketches. Graphical programs have visual output and allow for at least one straightforward way to define different stages of program construction as points at which the visual output changes. Second, simple programs can be expressed very concisely in Processing, while complex projects remain possible.

Participants in the formative study were students at our institution already familiar with Processing. We gave them a program editor that we linked to a revision control system, so that we could simulate a tool that makes it easy to snapshot any stage of the development of a program by committing a revision to the system. We provided participants with paper printouts of the snapshots of their code so that they could view their snapshots side by side and thereby simulate the ability to switch between stages in the editor.

Our participants all made high-level plans to subdivide the study task into meaningful example stages. In practice, they created an average of 4.4 stages ($\sigma = 1.9$) as they developed their program. However, they did not always follow their initial plans. At times the plans contained mistakes and they had to re-plan the stages. In other cases they had to fix minor code errors in earlier stages. All participants faced multiple instances where they realized that earlier implementation decisions had to be modified in order to proceed. On average, participants indicated that they would have edited previous revisions an average of 1.6 times ($\sigma = 0.89$) while programming Pong.

Types of Modifications to Previous Revisions

We noted two types of modifications that users indicated that they wanted to perform on earlier stages of the code.

Modifications for Pedagogical Reasons

The goal of some modifications was to construct a flow of stages that learners could easily follow. For instance, one participant defined the ball velocity in the first stage as a per-second velocity. However, when developing later stages she decided that it would be more instructive to refer to velocities as per-frame velocities, as these require fewer unit conversions when writing frame-based rendering routines. She then wished to change the definition of the velocity variable and add an extra frame rate variable to her first stage.

Modifications as a Result of an Error

Other modifications were the result of errors in the code that programmers did not notice at first, but later wanted to fix. For example, one participant noticed that she had accidentally swapped the window width and height variables throughout her program. She wished to modify all the earlier versions of the code in which the variables were switched.

The Need for Editable Histories

Making such modifications using a regular IDE would require propagating the change to all relevant stages manually. In some cases, this process of change propagation was complex enough that some participants remarked that they would have preferred to jettison much of their work and restart from an earlier point. In contrast to editing code for the purpose of the final program, participants had to not only think about refactoring the current state of the code, but also check that the flow across stages remained consistent.

In essence, while participants were able to formulate high-level plans, detailed decisions were made just-in-time based on existing code. Producing multi-stage examples is thus fundamentally a non-linear process that requires making modifications to multiple stages of the code project.

Design Guidelines

Based on our formative study we devised the following design guidelines to support multi-stage editing inside an IDE.

Enable Easy Addition of Stages

Programmers should be able to capture snapshots of the current state of their code without interfering with their coding workflow. When we provided participants with this ability, they took full advantage of it and saved multiple snapshots.

Enable Easy Navigation and Execution of Stages

Programmers have to be able to access all stages in the editor with minimal effort. Participants frequently went back to saved snapshots of their code in order to remind themselves of how they got to the current state. A natural extension to this guideline is to allow programmers to execute the code as it exists in each stage in order to see the resulting output.

Enable Edits of Any Stage

Programmers must be able to modify any stage of their code. We distinguish between three different types of edits that we observed in the formative study:

- **Propagate code fixes across stages:** allowing errors such as the switched height and width to be fixed.
- **Add code across stages:** allowing omissions such as variable definitions to be included where they belong.
- **Remove code across stages:** allowing participants to change their minds in hindsight about existing code such as the introduction of the ball in the very first stage.

Enable the Removal of Stages

Based on the experience of at least one participant it seems worthwhile to be able to remove a saved stage such that the previous stage flows directly to the next without the intervening one. This would have allowed participants to delete stages they later determined had no educational value.

AUTHORING A MULTI-STAGE CODE EXAMPLE

To illustrate how these design guidelines may be expressed in a tool for editing code histories consider the following example. The task is to show the drawing primitives necessary to build a program that rolls an object off the screen using translation and rotation (Figure 3).

Adding a Stage to the History

A programmer begins by making a high level plan and breaking down the task she is working on into small testable units. The programmer chooses to start by drawing a circle (Figure 3A). Once this code is tested the programmer saves a snapshot of the current state of the code. A dialog box lets the programmer specify the title for the stage (Figure 4A).

The programer adds a second stage where she translates the circle to a new location and a third stage where she animates the repeated translation of the circle (Figure 3B). We borrow Kurlander's approach [23] and add a button in the history panel for every new stage (Figure 4B). The programmer can click this button to view a previous stage.

Modifying Code Across Stages

A programmer can modify code in any stage in two ways. They can make changes to the latest stage and selectively propagate them to past stages, or they can make changes to a past stage and selectively propagate them to later ones.

Fixing Blocks of Code Across Stages

The programmer next wants to rotate the object as it rolls off the screen. However, because of the circle's rotational symmetry she decides to change her object to a square (Figure 3C). She can either fix her choice of a shape in the stage where the circle was introduced and propagate the fix to future stages, or fix it in her current code and propagate the fix to all previous stages. In this case, she chooses the latter. She selects and highlights the line creating the circle and right clicks on the **Enter fix** option (Figure 4C). She then edits the code in place to change the shape to a square and propagates the change back to all other stages using **Propagate fix** (Figure 4D). Finally, she adds code to rotate the square as it is translated, to simulate rolling off the screen (Figure 3D).

Adding Blocks of Code Across Stages

Viewing the current output of her program, the programmer realizes that the demonstration of rotation is not clear enough, since the square also has a rotational symmetry. She decides to transform the square into a more complex shape – in this case a robot face. Thus she adds shapes representing the eyes and mouth of the robot to all stages of the example.

Adding code to a different stage is a form of a copy-paste operation where a block of text is copied from the present and is pasted in a past stage, or vice versa. Once it is pasted, it is also included in all intermediate stages. The programmer decides to add the drawing of facial features in the current code. She then selects and highlights the code she just added, right

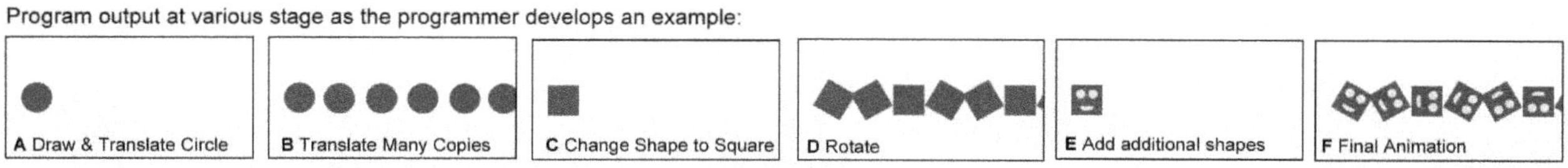

Figure 3. A programmer takes different steps during the development of the example, reverting and adding to earlier decisions.

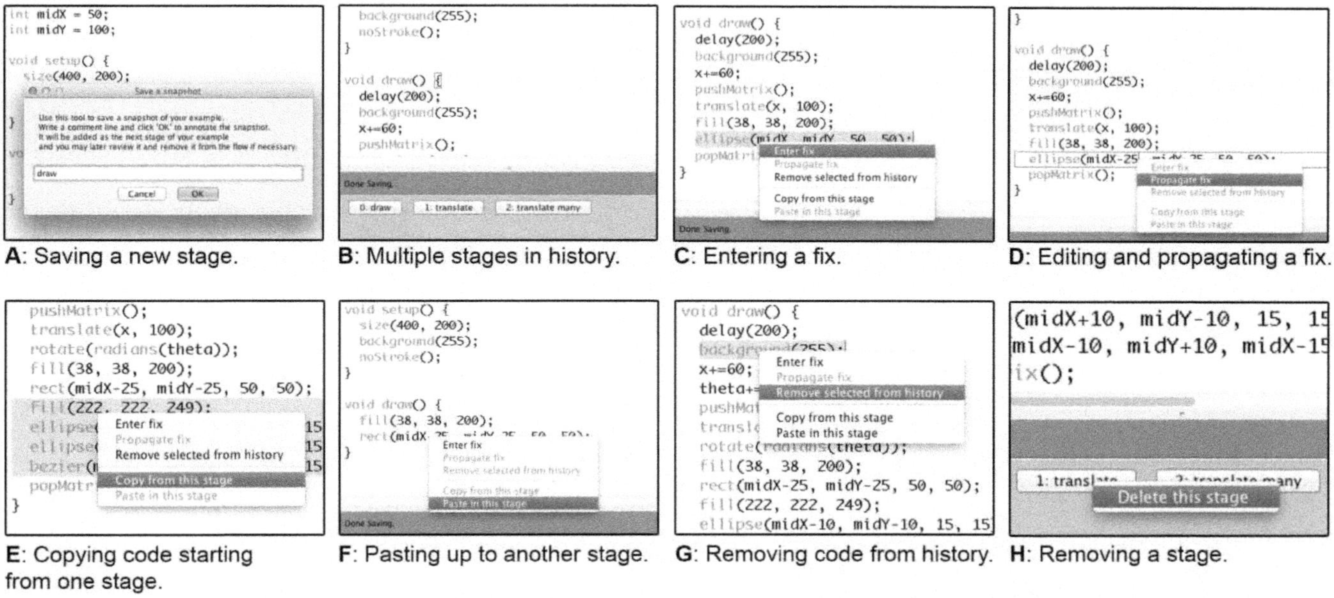

Figure 4. The Multi-stage example editor offers functions to manage code stages and functions to perform edits across multiple stages.

clicks and chooses the **Copy from this stage** option (Figure 4E). Navigating to the very first stage, the programmer points to the end of the line after which she would like to paste and chooses the **Paste in this stage** option (Figure 4F). The copied code is pasted in the past stage and propagated to all the stages in between. As a result the robot is drawn in all stages. If the programmer attempts to paste in a location that conflicts with the location of the code in the current stage the operation fails and an error message is displayed. This could occur, for instance, if the programmer were to copy code from the bottom of the file at the current stage and paste it at the very top of the file in a past stage.

Removing Blocks of Code from History
The programmer next decides that she would like to better emphasize the result of each rotation operation for educational purposes. She therefore removes the line that clears the window each time the drawing function is called. She selects and highlights the line that clears the background, and selects the **Remove selected from history** option (Figure 4G). The deleted code is removed from the stage in which it was introduced and onwards. Alternatively, the programmer could have navigated to the stage where the code was introduced, removed it from there and propagated the fix to later stages.

Presenting Negative Effects of Edits
As the number of stages in the example increases, the programmer is more likely to make mistakes when editing across stages. For example, removing a declaration of a variable from all stages may break a past stage that includes code to increment that variable. Before performing any change that affects multiple stages, our tool simulates the changes and re-compiles each affected stage. If any compilation fails the programmer is notified that her change would break the corresponding stage in history. The programmer can then decide whether to approve or cancel the edit. While this check can detect compile-time problems it cannot detect runtime errors.

Removing a Stage from the Code History
On a final read-through of her complete example, the programmer decides that the stage where she translated the shape by a fixed amount is superfluous. She right-clicks on the stage's button and chooses the **Delete this stage** option (Figure 4H). This option deletes the snapshot of the state of her code at that point of history. However the edits from the deleted stage are still reflected in subsequent stages.

Publishing Examples
The purpose of writing multi-stage code examples is to produce materials that learners can easily consume. Important design considerations for such materials are how to enable *navigation* between the various stages, and how to present *changes* between stages. In our implementation, when the programmer is finished authoring a code example, she may publish it as an interactive web page. Learners can then navigate between stages using a draggable control. In order to convey the differences between stages, we highlight the changed lines between subsequent stages and include the running output of the program at each stage (Figure 5).

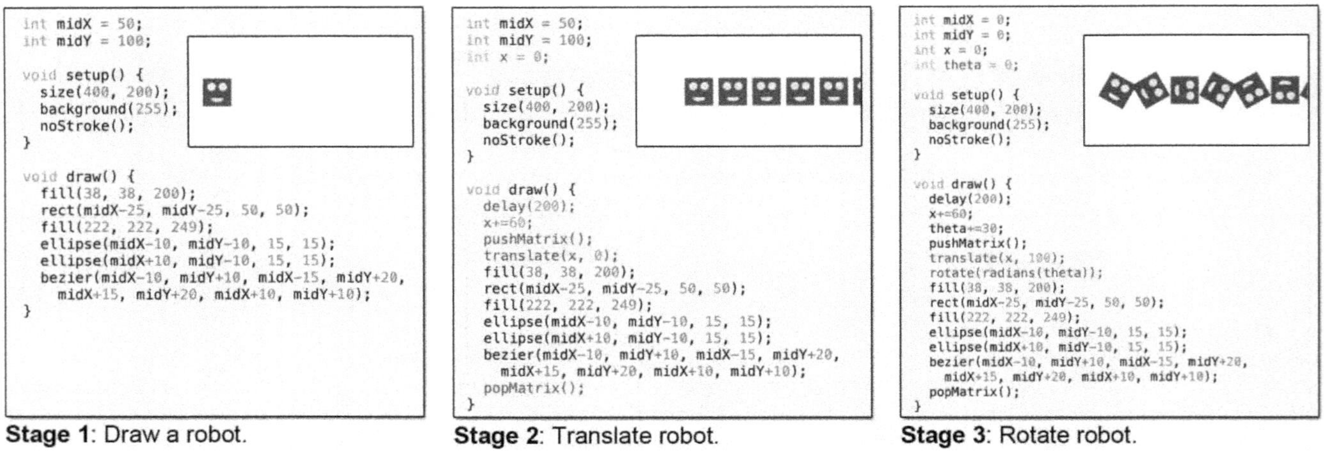

Figure 5. The exported learning materials enable viewers to navigate stages and see changes in source as well as program output. The export format was reformatted here for the sake of presentation.

The example format presented here is merely a proof of concept. Given the rich representation of the program history collected by our system we believe that many other output formats may be possible. We leave the problem of finding the optimal format for displaying multi-stage code examples as future work.

IMPLEMENTATION

We wrote our authoring tool in Java as an extension of the open source Processing IDE [32]. However, the principles behind our algorithms are not tied to any particular language or editor. In addition to the IDE's representation of the program, we maintain a separate representation of the code in a git repository [13]. This allows us to use revision control operations as the basis for our history editing algorithms.

Adding a Stage to the History

Example stages are snapshots of code in time. Saving such snapshots are the bread and butter of revision control systems and we therefore delegate snapshotting to git [13]. When the programmer opens a new file to author a Processing program (called a "sketch"), a repository is initialized in the sketch folder to track a copy of the code in a text file. Each time the programmer takes a new snapshot of her code for a stage, its current state is committed to git as a new revision.

Modifying Code Across Stages

We support several types of edits across sequences of stages.

Fixing Blocks of Code Across Stages

In order to allow a programmer who is working on the current stage to fix an existing block of code (Figure 6A, code highlighted in orange) in all stages where it appears (Figure 6A, code highlighted in yellow), we must first locate the stage where the author introduced it. This is the earliest place where we should propagate the fix. Similarly, when a programmer directly edits a past stage and propagates code fixes to later stages, we must locate the last stage where the code appears. We look for exact copies of the code (ignoring whitespace) because modified lines of code may have different semantics. Propagating changes to stages where the author has modified the relevant block of code would require

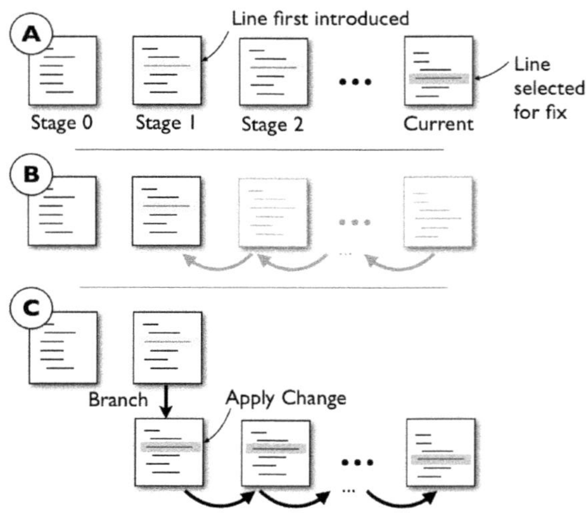

Figure 6. Fixing existing code. A. When the fix is propagated to the past, the revision where the code first appeared is located using git pickaxe. B. The code is rolled back. C. A new brach is created where the fix is applied, and the code is rolled forward to the current state.

additional user input to disambiguate how changes should be propagated to different lines, as our tool cannot decide this automatically for the users.

In our system we use the git pickaxe utility to identify the stages where each line in a block of code that is to be fixed across stages appears. Given each line to fix in the code, the pickaxe utility returns all revisions that changed that line (Figure 6A). If the fix is propagated to a past stage, the system rolls back to the first revision where the line appeared (Figure 6B). The system then creates a new branch where the line is fixed and recommitted (Figure 6C). The fix is rolled forward to the current revision by applying all subsequent changes from the original branch. The operation is similar when the fix is propagated to a later stage.

Removing code is just a special case of fixing as it can be expressed as a fix where the new version is an empty line.

Adding Blocks of Code Across Stages

Adding a block of code across a sequence of stages requires additional constraints from the user: the first and last stage where the addition should occur, and the exact lines in these stages where the code should be added. These constraints are needed in operations such as taking a new line X that is between lines A and B in the present and adding it at a past stage before A or B were introduced. In this case, there may be several possible locations of line X in the past stage and we use the provided location to resolve the ambiguity.

We allow addition of new lines of code to a sequence of revisions ranging from some past revision up to the present state. This supports both the case where the user is copying from the present and pasting to a past stage and the case where the user is editing a past stage and propagating to the present. The difference lies only in the user interface. In order to implement this forward propagation, we introduce a new algorithm for adding blocks of code to code histories through a modified three-way merge process.

Generally, three-way merge algorithms [12] reconcile independent changes in two files under the assumption that they share the third file as a common origin. If the changes are compatible and would not conflict by altering the same lines, then a new file will be produced. If not, then the algorithm attempts to identify the cause of the failure. Users of revision control systems, where two or more programmers may independently change the current revision, commonly experience such failures. In our tool, copying and pasting a chunk of code from one stage to another can be thought of as a similar situation. While the paste location is given by the user, we must determine how this new change can be merged into the existing flow of changes from stage to stage. For example, in Figure 7 if we are pasting changes into Stage 1 (Figure 7A) then the first two files to be merged would be Stage 1 after pasting ("Stage 1P") and "Stage 2", and the common origin would be "Stage 1" (Figure 7B).

Our implementation uses the three-way merge capability of the UNIX diff3 tool [12]. When merging two sets of changes into an original there is only a small set of cases where there is no ambiguity concerning the ordering of lines and therefore a guaranteed correct merge. General purpose tools like diff3 are conservative in what they will accept as a non-conflicting merge and report a conflict whenever there is an ambiguity. To shield developers from having to manually resolve such conflicts, we can take advantage of user-provided position constraints and the knowledge that all edits are additions.

We automatically resolve the conflicts that the three-way merge identifies. Unlike the general three-way merge problem, we have an advantage when propagating pasted code forward. Here the original stage with the paste applied may only contain additional lines of code (Figure 8) as fixes and deletions are covered by the previous techniques. Our merge therefore resolves the conflict by accepting all changes to the original code (stage 1 in Figure 8) introduced by the next stage (e.g., the removal of line A in Figure 8, stage 2), and only using pasted additions (line B in Figure 8, stage 1P) in the resulting merge.

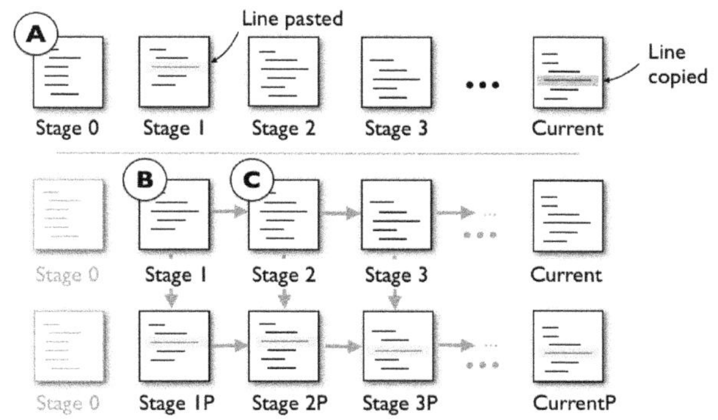

Figure 7. Adding a block of code to past stages using a copy-paste operation. A. The programmer wants to introduce a new block of code at an earlier stage. She copies it from the current local changes and pastes it in the past stage. B. The first step of propagating the paste to all stages in between. At every step we perform a three-way merge between an example stage (Stage 1), the stage with the pasted code (Stage 1P) and the next stage in history (Stage 2). The result of the merge is a modification of Stage 2 containing the pasted code (Stage 2P). C. In the next step stages 2, 3 and the previous result 2P are merged.

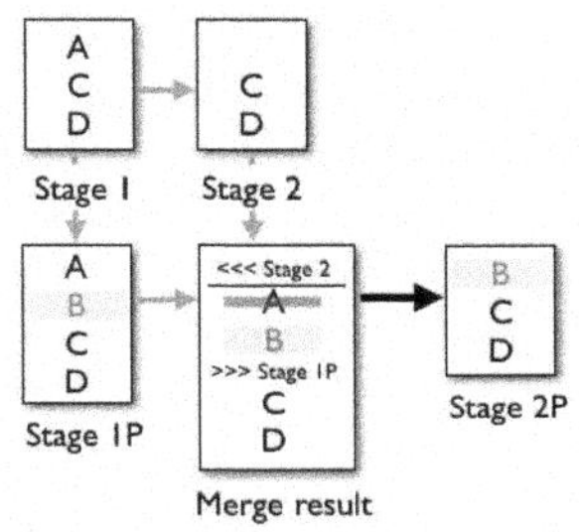

Figure 8. We resolve conflicts by only looking at the original file with the code pasted in it (stage 1P) for the location in which to paste the code. All other changes from stage 1P (like adding line A) are discarded.

We can recursively apply this process until we reach the current stage. In each step of the recursion, the result of the previous merge (e.g. "Stage 2P" in Figure 7C) serves as one of the three files to merge. To check if the propagation succeeded we compare the result of the final merge against the correct state of the current stage. We consider all possible places to paste the additional code in each stage and ultimately select the sequence of placements that results in the correct state of the code, if such a selection exists. It may not always be feasible to find the right sequence of paste positions, for instance if the user copied the last line of a stage and pasted it as the first line of the previous stage.

Presenting Negative Effects of Edits

In order to warn the user of potential negative effects of her actions, we optimistically apply the edit and ensure that all stages still compile. This background compilation test is performed on a copy of the code file and using a clone of the git repository. If all stages of the edited example compile successfully, the edit is applied to the code. If the edit breaks a stage, we inform the user of the failure and undo the edit. Furthermore, the system directs the user to the first stage that did not compile when attempting to apply the edit.

Removing a Stage from the Code History

At times, programmers take snapshots of key points in the construction of the code that later no longer seem essential for the sake of the example. When a previously saved stage is removed we roll back all stages up to and including it. Next we apply the changes from the stage to be removed and the next one then commit these changes together. Lastly, we roll forward to the current revision. The final artifact in this case does not change, only the sequence of stages.

Publishing Examples

We chose to publish finished code examples in HTML as a demonstration of one possible output format. The log extracted from git is parsed by a Python script and converted to HTML using the Jinja2 templating library [19].

Since the published examples are designed to be consumed by learners, we allow easy navigation between stages using an extension of the Tangle kit [41], a Javascript library for creating reactive documents that offers draggable controls to show or hide objects from view on a web page [39].

We employ two strategies in order to help learners understand what changed from stage to stage. First, we highlight the changed lines between stages when moving from one to the other using JQuery utilities. Second, we use Processing.js to embed in the page the running interactive output of the program at every stage, so that even without reading the code itself the effect of each stage is immediately visible.

EVALUATION

To evaluate the effectiveness of our system for authoring multi-stage code examples we conducted an informal use study. We asked participants to use our tool to modify an existing multi-stage example and to generate a code example of their own.

Participants

We recruited seven participants, all graduate students at our institution, with prior expertise in Processing. The six Computer Scientists and one Mechanical Engineer, ages 22 to 28, all rated themselves as expert programmers. Six were male; one female. Two of the participants took part in our formative study. Only one participant self reported to be an expert in tutorial writing; the rest had at most passing knowledge.

Methodology

Each two hour session in our lab consisted of a warm-up task, two experimental tasks, and a post-study survey. In the warm-up task, we first introduced participants to the features of our system using step-by-step instructions for constructing a simple code example. The goal of this task was to acquaint participants with the propagation features of our system. A preliminary version of our system that only included one propagation direction for each kind of operation was tested. This initial version also did not include background compilation to show potential problems of edits.

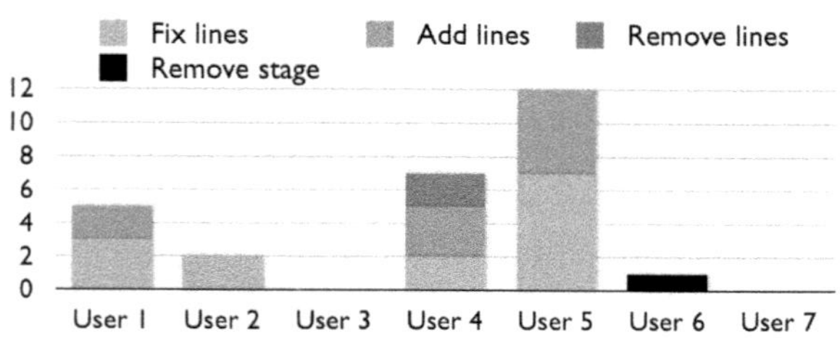

Figure 9. The number of history editing operations used by the evaluation study participants during the multi-stage example generation task.

In the second task, we asked participants to make various changes to a given multi-stage code example for the game of Pong. The example exhibited several poor design and didactic choices that we asked participants to improve, such as the proportion of the sizes of the ball and paddle, the contrast of colors, and the inclusion of superfluous example stages. Participants edited the example such that the changes were reflected throughout the history of its construction using the operations of our system.

In the third task, we asked each participant to create their own multi-stage code example using our system. This task was designed to mimic real-world use of the system. To check that our propagation tools are applicable in a variety of contexts, we assigned a different programming assignment to each participant. We asked some of the participants to write games, such as Snake and a raindrop catching game. Others built tools, such as a color picker. Others created motion simulations of objects and particles.

Results

All participants successfully completed the warm-up task. They all used all available features during the second modification task as participants successfully translated our edit suggestions into appropriate history editing operations. Following our modification suggestions, participants used each feature once, except for fixing code which they used 4 times.

When authoring their own code examples during the third task, all participants structured their code in a modular, multi-stage fashion, and saved between 3 and 11 stages ($\mu = 6.4, \sigma = 2.5$). While programming, all participants frequently navigated back to previous stages to remind themselves of the state of the code at that time, either by reading or executing the code, and often by doing both. Given the variety in the examples they authored and the individual differences in the writing process between people, it was not surprising that different participants used a different subset of the modification features. Participants used an average of 3.86 history editing features during the generation task (Figure 9). In the third task users 3 and 7 did not use any features of our tool because one implemented his example correctly on the first trial, and the other was not able to construct a full example in the allotted time.

In order to assess whether the user view of the available operations matched the system view [26], participants rated whether the effects of each operation matched their expectations and the average match rating was relatively high. Detailed results are presented in Figure 10.

Strengths

When asked which operation was the most useful to them in authoring a multi-stage code example, participants' answers covered the whole range of available operations. This result suggests that all the operations are necessary. All participants attested that they would be very likely to use this tool for authoring multi-stage examples.

The ability to save snapshots and navigate between them: In our post-study survey, participants noted that the main advantage of using our tool for authoring multi-stage code examples was the ability to easily save snapshots of their code. Participants also mentioned the value in being able to switch rapidly between the stages and re-run the code at each stage. One participant noted that being able to save snapshots helped him remember to partition his task into concrete subtasks.

The ability to edit past stages: Participants liked the fact that they didn't have to make all design decisions from the very start since they could make changes and reflect them in previous versions on-the-fly. Thus, they could focus on the main goal for each stage, rather than worry about each little detail. One person noted that he felt he could almost write the code as he would for his own purposes, while producing a tutorial at the same time.

The ability to publish examples: An additional advantage reported by participants is the ability to publish their examples directly into a format that is consumable by readers without any post-processing other than possibly adding explanatory text. During the modification task participants used publication in a way that we did not anticipate. When trying to understand the example given to them, participants exported the example to HTML format in order to view the differences between each stage and observe the running output. We interpret this usage as a sign that our output format is valuable for sharing examples between authors as well as with learners.

Shortcomings

Participants identified possible improvements of features.

Support directly editing past stages: In the version of our tool used in the evaluation, all our modification operations required the user to modify code in the present and then propagate the changes back to the past. This metaphor worked for some users, but not for others who would rather have the ability to edit the code in past stages directly and propagate the edits forward (Cognitive Science has established that different people prefer different metaphors for reasoning about time [27]). During the study, these users found it more natural to reason about modifications in a chronological order. They tended to switch back through earlier stages each time they propagated a modification, effectively checking that the system behaved as expected. In fact, our underlying architecture allows for edit propagation in any direction. Following the study, we realized that we should enable edits to past stages - adding it only required a simple change to the UI.

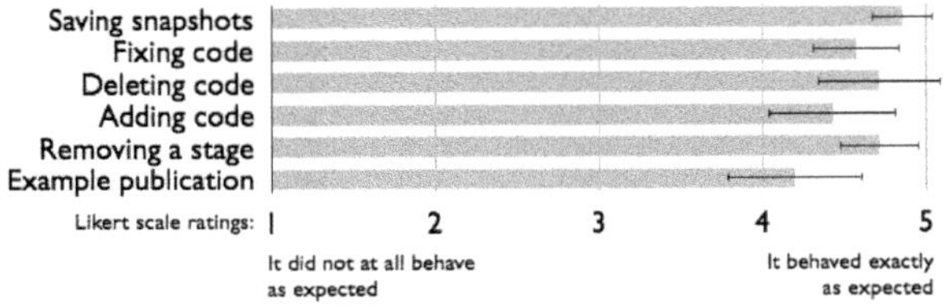

Figure 10. Post-experiment questionnaire results. Error bars indicate $\frac{1}{2}$ standard deviation in each direction.

Need for improved interaction techniques for editing: Two users would have preferred not to indicate when they are about to enter code fixes. Instead, they wanted the system to infer the fix from the local changes in the code. Other users identified shortcomings in the usability of the current features, specifically a lack of visual feedback. For instance, one user suggested that all local unsaved changes in an example stage be highlighted to make it easier to remember what may be propagated back. Another user suggested highlighting all allowable places in the past where a copied piece of code could be pasted. Users also expressed interest in the ability to rename a stage, the ability to add a new stage between two existing past stages, and the ability to split their current local changes into two separate stages.

LIMITATIONS

Our approach has some inherent limitations that limit its generality; our prototype's implementation places additional restrictions on users.

Our matching algorithm does not have any semantic understanding of the code – all operations are performed at the character or line-level although the UI allows for aggregate operations on blocks of code. As a result, our modification algorithm will not attempt to propagate fixes to any lines that do not match the original line being modified by the user. Future work could investigate if comparisons at the abstract syntax tree (AST) level could relax this restriction.

We assume that stages represent a linear progression of code development. Alternatively, programmers may wish to develop modular examples where viewers can enable or disable different aspects of an example interactively. This investigation is left to future work.

CONCLUSION

We presented a set of interaction techniques and underlying algorithms that permit programmers to propagate code changes to multiple history stages. These techniques were motivated by a formative study that found that programmers needed to make such modifications to fix mistakes and adjust didactic strategies when writing multi-stage examples. An informal evaluation of our initial implementation for the Processing IDE showed that programmers can successfully use our techniques to author and modify code across stages. An open empirical question for future work is how to best present the resulting examples to different communities of learners online. More generally, we are interested in pursuing additional work on creating tools that benefit both authors as well as consumers of learning materials for programming.

ACKNOWLEDGMENTS

This material is based upon work supported by the National Science Foundation Graduate Research Fellowship under Grant No. DGE 1106400 and NSF Award IIS-1149799.

REFERENCES

1. Bergman, L., Castelli, V., Lau, T., and Oblinger, D. Docwizards: a system for authoring follow-me documentation wizards. In *Proceedings of UIST*, ACM (2005), 191–200.
2. Berthouzoz, F., Li, W., Dontcheva, M., and Agrawala, M. A framework for content-adaptive photo manipulation macros: Application to face, landscape, and global manipulations. *ACM Transactions on Graphics. 30*, 5 (Oct. 2011), 120:1–120:14.
3. Brandt, J., Dontcheva, M., Weskamp, M., and Klemmer, S. R. Example-centric programming: integrating web search into the development environment. In *Proceedings of CHI*, ACM (2010), 513–522.
4. Brandt, J., Guo, P. J., Lewenstein, J., Dontcheva, M., and Klemmer, S. R. Two studies of opportunistic programming: interleaving web foraging, learning, and writing code. In *Proceedings of CHI*, ACM (2009), 1589–1598.
5. Brusilovsky, P. Webex: Learning from examples in a programming course. In *WebNet'01* (2001), 124–129.
6. Carroll, J. M. *The Nurnberg funnel: designing minimalist instruction for practical computer skill.* MIT Press, 1990.
7. Carroll, J. M., Singer, J. A., Bellamy, R. K. E., and Alpert, S. R. A view matcher for learning smalltalk. In *Proceedings of CHI*, ACM (1990), 431–437.
8. Chang, K. S.-P., and Myers, B. A. Webcrystal: understanding and reusing examples in web authoring. In *Proceedings of CHI*, ACM (2012), 3205–3214.
9. Chen, H.-T., Wei, L.-Y., and Chang, C.-F. Nonlinear revision control for images. In *ACM SIGGRAPH 2011 papers*, ACM (2011), 105:1–105:10.
10. Chi, P.-Y., Ahn, S., Ren, A., Dontcheva, M., Li, W., and Hartmann, B. Mixt: automatic generation of step-by-step mixed media tutorials. In *Proceedings of UIST*, ACM (2012), 93–102.
11. Denning, J. D., Kerr, W. B., and Pellacini, F. Meshflow: interactive visualization of mesh construction sequences. In *ACM SIGGRAPH 2011 papers*, ACM (2011), 66:1–66:8.
12. UNIX diff3. http://www.unix.com/man-page/FreeBSD/1/diff3/.
13. Git Distributed Version Control System. http://git-scm.com/.
14. Goldman, M., and Miller, R. C. Codetrail: Connecting source code and web resources. *Journal of Visual Languages and Computing 20*, 4 (2009), 223–235.
15. Grabler, F., Agrawala, M., Li, W., Dontcheva, M., and Igarashi, T. Generating photo manipulation tutorials by demonstration. *ACM Transactions on Graphics 28*, 3 (July 2009), 66:1–66:9.
16. Grossman, T., Matejka, J., and Fitzmaurice, G. Chronicle: capture, exploration, and playback of document workflow histories. In *Proceedings of UIST*, ACM (2010), 143–152.
17. Hartmann, B., Dhillon, M., and Chan, M. K. Hypersource: bridging the gap between source and code-related web sites. In *Proceedings of CHI*, ACM (2011), 2207–2210.
18. Heer, J., Mackinlay, J. D., Stolte, C., and Agrawala, M. Graphical histories for visualization: Supporting analysis, communication, and evaluation. *IEEE Transactions on Visualization and Computer Graphics 14*, 6 (2008), 1189–1196.
19. Jinja2. http://jinja.pocoo.org/docs/.
20. Ko, A. J., Myers, B. A., and Aung, H. H. Six learning barriers in end-user programming systems. In *Proceedings of VLHCC*, IEEE (2004), 199–206.
21. Ko, A. J., Myers, B. A., Coblenz, M. J., and Aung, H. H. An exploratory study of how developers seek, relate, and collect relevant information during software maintenance tasks. *IEEE Transactions on Software Engineering 32*, 12 (Dec. 2006), 971–987.
22. Kojouharov, C., Solodovnik, A., and Naumovich, G. Jtutor: an eclipse plug-in suite for creation and replay of code-based tutorials. In *Proceedings of eclipse technology eXchange*, ACM (2004), 27–31.
23. Kurlander, D., and Feiner, S. Editable graphical histories. In *IEEE Workshop on Visual Languages* (oct 1988), 127 –134.
24. Mandelin, D., Xu, L., Bodík, R., and Kimelman, D. Jungloid mining: helping to navigate the API jungle. In *Proceedings of PLDI*, ACM (2005), 48–61.
25. Mooty, M., Faulring, A., Stylos, J., and Myers, B. A. Calcite: Completing code completion for constructors using crowds. In *Proceedings of VLHCC*, IEEE (2010), 15–22.
26. Norman, D. A., and Draper, S. W. *User Centered System Design; New Perspectives on Human-Computer Interaction.* L. Erlbaum Associates Inc., 1986.
27. Nunez, R. E., Motz, B. A., and Teuscher, U. Time after time: The psychological reality of the ego- and time-reference-point distinction in metaphorical construals of time. *Metaphor and Symbol 21*, 3 (2006), 133–146.
28. Oezbek, C., and Prechelt, L. Jtourbus: Simplifying program understanding by documentation that provides tours through the source code. In *ICSM*, IEEE (2007), 64–73.
29. Omar, C., Yoon, Y., LaToza, T. D., and Myers, B. A. Active code completion. In *Proceedings of ICSE*, IEEE Press (2012), 859–869.
30. Oney, S., and Brandt, J. Codelets: linking interactive documentation and example code in the editor. In *Proceedings of CHI*, ACM (2012), 2697–2706.
31. Pongnumkul, S., Dontcheva, M., Li, W., Wang, J., Bourdev, L., Avidan, S., and Cohen, M. F. Pause-and-play: automatically linking screencast video tutorials with applications. In *Proceedings of UIST* (2011), 135–144.
32. Reas, C., and Fry, B. Processing: programming for the media arts. *AI Society 20*, 4 (Aug. 2006), 526–538.
33. Robins, A., Rountree, J., and Rountree, N. Learning and teaching programming: A review and discussion. *Computer Science Education 13* (2003), 137–172.
34. Stylos, J., Faulring, A., Yang, Z., and Myers, B. A. Improving api documentation using api usage information. In *Proceedings of VLHCC*, IEEE (2009), 119–126.
35. Su, S. L., Paris, S., Aliaga, F., Scull, C., Johnson, S., and Durand, F. Interactive visual histories for vector graphics. Tech. Rep. MIT-CSAIL-TR-2009-031, Massachusetts Institute of Technology, Computer Science and Artificial Intelligence Laboratory, June 2009.
36. Apache Software Foundation. Subversion. http://subversion.apache.org//.
37. The code player. http://thecodeplayer.com/.
38. Toomim, M., Begel, A., and Graham, S. L. Managing duplicated code with linked editing. In *Proceedings of VLHCC*, IEEE (2004), 173–180.
39. Victor, B. Explorable explanations. http://worrydream.com/ExplorableExplanations/.
40. Victor, B. Learnable programming. http://worrydream.com/LearnableProgramming/.
41. Victor, B. Tangle. http://worrydream.com/Tangle/.
42. Wightman, D., Ye, Z., Brandt, J., and Vertegaal, R. Snipmatch: using source code context to enhance snippet retrieval and parameterization. In *Proceedings of UIST*, ACM (2012), 219–228.

A Colorful Approach to Text Processing by Example

Kuat Yessenov
MIT
Cambridge, MA

Shubham Tulsiani
IIT Kanpur
Kanpur, India

Aditya Menon
UCSD
San Diego, CA

Robert C. Miller
MIT
Cambridge, MA

Sumit Gulwani
Microsoft Research
Redmond, WA

Butler Lampson
Microsoft Research
Cambridge, MA

Adam Kalai
Microsoft Research
Cambridge, MA

ABSTRACT

Text processing, tedious and error-prone even for programmers, remains one of the most alluring targets of Programming by Example. An examination of real-world text processing tasks found on help forums reveals that many such tasks, beyond simple string manipulation, involve latent hierarchical structures.

We present STEPS, a programming system for processing structured and semi-structured text by example. STEPS users *create and manipulate hierarchical structure by example*. In a between-subject user study on fourteen computer scientists, STEPS compares favorably to traditional programming.

Author Keywords

Programming by Example; Text Processing.

ACM Classification Keywords

D.1.2 Programming Techniques: Automatic Programming; H.5.2 Information Interfaces and Presentation: UI

INTRODUCTION

Text processing (TP) is a problem of importance to programmers, data analysts, and other knowledge workers who have to handle data in many formats. Modern programming languages and text processing tools generally use regular expressions, string manipulation primitives, and parser generators. In contrast, the programming by example (PBE) approach (also called programming by demonstration) allows the user to edit example text by hand, and the system produces a program automatically [2, 13, 3, 7]. PBE systems are easier to learn and lack the arcane syntax of programming languages. Even for programmers, a sufficiently-powerful PBE system should have superior usability.

A number of PBE systems address repetitive TP tasks, such as reformatting a bibliography, from short demonstrations.

UIST'13, October 8–11, 2013, St. Andrews, United Kingdom.
Copyright © 2013 ACM 978-1-4503-2268-3/13/10...$15.00.
http://dx.doi.org/10.1145/2501988.2502040

These systems face challenges and advance the state of the art in HCI, Program Synthesis, and Machine Learning aspects of PBE.

A key difficulty, revealed by our examination of tasks from TP user forums, is that many tasks *crucially rely on latent hierarchical structure*. Previous PBE systems, based on patterns for cursor movement, string manipulation, or multiple selections, fail to capture these structures.

Almost every text file has structure. Reformatting a bibliography involves manipulating deeply nested structures including different entry types like books or articles, each with lists of author names that can be further decomposed into surnames, etc. For a simpler motivating example, consider a text file of multi-line records, e.g.:

```
TRB1006:
   Company: Yamaha
   Kind: Bass
   Year: 2006
COX15SA:
   Kind: Guitar
   Company: Yamaha
   Year: 2005
...
```

There is a structure obvious (to humans) here that may or may not be necessary to uncover, depending on the task at hand. For example, consider the following three tasks:

1. Sort the records by year.
2. Capitalize the company names.
3. Delete the year field from records where the company is "Yamaha" (because they have been discovered to be erroneous).

Only the second task may be accomplished without referring to structure. A system like SmartEdit [1] may quickly learn to repeat: *move the cursor to the end of the string "Company:", select to the end of the line, and then capitalize the selection.*

However, for the first and third tasks, repetitive cursor movements with string manipulation are insufficient, and these tasks cannot be implemented by example using prior systems. How can one enable users to expose and manipulate such structure in a simple fashion, by example?

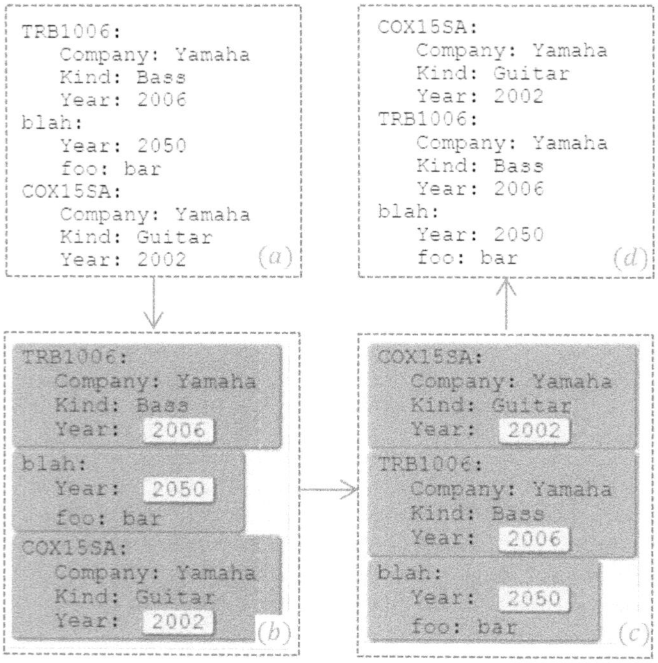

Figure 1. Sorting by year in STEPS. Mock input/output pairs[1] specify each step; nested colored blocks represent structure.

Our work is partly inspired by LAPIS [16], a system for text editing that incorporates "lightweight structure" and PBE. The multiple selection and simultaneous editing features of LAPIS, on the second task above, would enable one to select all company names and then simultaneously capitalize them, all by example. In LAPIS, patterns match arbitrary regions that may even partially overlap, such as the patterns *sentence* and *line of text*. This makes different patterns difficult to simultaneously display, and LAPIS users cannot easily create or manipulate hierarchical structure by example. The TP help forum posts we examined discussed hierarchical structure far more often than overlapping patterns.

STEPS and HSS

We introduce a Sequential Transformations by Example Programming System (STEPS) that, through a sequence of steps, modifies a hierarchically structured string (HSS). This HSS is displayed using nested colored blocks, as in Figure 1.

A STEPS user begins with a possibly-large text file and specifies explicit steps by input/output pairs. On the ith step, the user illustrates a function f_i through an example of input HSS x_i and output HSS y_i such that $f_i\ x_i\ = y_i$. The system attempts to infer likely candidate functions mapping x_i to y_i. The output of a successful session is the modified text file and a standalone script that may be run on future data.

Figure 1 illustrates the first task in STEPS: first add structure, coloring the records red and the years yellow $(x_1 = a, y_1 = b)$, then sort red blocks by their yellow

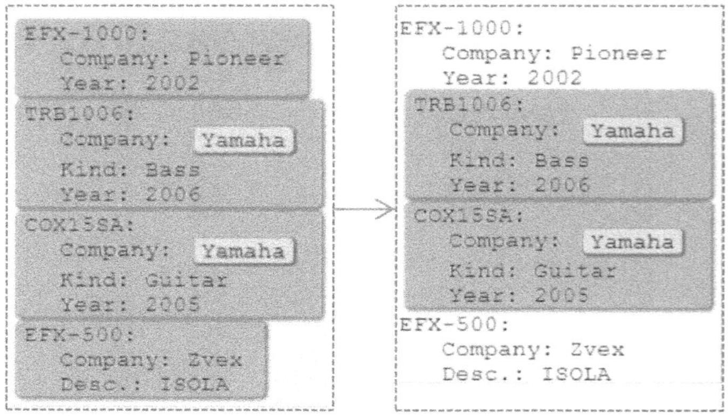

Figure 2. Un-coloring red blocks that do not contain blue blocks. This is a step in deleting year fields from Yamaha records (after coloring records in red and "Yamaha" string in blue).

blocks $(x_2 = b, y_2 = c)$, and finally remove the colors $(x_3 = c, y_3 = d)$.[1] Text and colored blocks are created and manipulated in a fashion similar to standard text editing operations. To color a block, one selects the text to be colored and then clicks on the desired color from a palate. This is similar to highlighting text in a rich text editor, but only nested (nonoverlapping) blocks are permitted.

For the third task, a user might try to delete the yellow blocks from red blocks containing "Yamaha." If the system fails to infer the correct transformation, additional colors and steps provide a recourse, e.g., color records in red, color the word Yamaha in blue, un-color red blocks that do not contain blue blocks (illustrated in Figure 2), and finally color and delete the year lines from the red blocks.

Demonstration vs. (mock) input/output examples

Each step is defined by an input-output pair of HSS's; the keystrokes and mouse movements used to generate this pair are not recorded. In contrast, the original PBE dream is that the system will simply observe the user perform actions and generalize their intention.

Demonstrations can be faster and more natural than the copying and pasting required to provide explicit before and after HSS's, but the ability to *correct* a PBE system is essential as described by Lau's study of why PBE systems fail [11]. Input/output examples ease debugging, since subtle mistakes can be identified and fixed by inspecting and editing a static artifact rather than replaying a trace.

Additionally, interaction through mock examples is a single technique that encompasses a variety of types of operations, unlike demonstration. How do you demonstrate sorting (or removing duplicates or counting) for a large file – do you manually search for the alphabetically first entry? Or suppose a user edits the 1st, 2nd, and 17th records – this may

---

[1] This STEPS program can be displayed succinctly because the output to each step is the input to the next, i.e., $y_i = x_{i+1}$ for all i. In general, this need not be true.

or may not be a signal that the 3rd-16th records should not change. Lau also advises "presenting a model users can understand" [11], and input/output pairs make transparent the information on which the system bases its inference.

Simplified *mock* examples that hide inessential information or convey corner cases are common on TP help forms. Editable input/output pairs similarly enable users to easily construct ad-hoc artificial examples without changing the underlying file. For example, in Figure 1, the second record was created artificially as a response to the fact that the pattern first learned by the system for year was "200?", i.e., a number starting with 200. In a large file, the user may not find the entries where this is not the case. Hence, she creates a mock entry with a year of 2050, and the system infers the pattern of a number following "Year:". Also, since her data format permits arbitrary field order within a record, she places the year first even though the year happened to be last in all records in her file, so that the resulting script will correctly generalize to future data.

Finally, for proficient users, mock examples may provide surprisingly simple input-output pairs, e.g., the operation of Figure 2 may be defined by:

and counting may be illustrated by:

Scope

STEPS is a programming system targeted at an audience of people who program or have once programmed. These users can benefit from such a tool, especially those who use languages such as Java or C++ where TP is notoriously awkward. The scope of STEPS is what one could accomplish with "a short Perl/AWK script," which most programmers interpret to mean a precise syntactic or structural transformation rather than a fuzzy knowledge-based operation. Most text transformations found on TP forums are in the scope of STEPS. One type of exception is tasks that require multiple input files, and extending STEPS to handle multiple files would increase its utility.

More fundamentally, STEPS is poorly suited for probabilistic transformations like spelling correction, which may be more suited for systems such as Google Refine [8]. The types of errors that are rampant in unstructured data entered by humans may require too many steps. For example, in correcting addresses, STEPS would likely require a separate step for correcting each type of error, such as adding "NY" state fields to entries labeled with a city "New York" (or even "New Yrok") but where the state was omitted.

That said, STEPS is easily extensible. If the underlying library of functions included, say, a mapping zip codes to city names, then STEPS programs could easily employ this mapping. STEPS does not acquire and extract rich data from the web. However, the programmers posting on Perl/AWK TP forums rarely expected such fuzzy, probabilistic operations, suggesting that one can convey to programmers the types of tasks appropriate for STEPS.

If the data at hand is tabular in nature, spreadsheet processing software such as Excel, Google Refine [8] or Data Wrangler [9] may be more appropriate. However, the coloring feature of STEPS can be trivially applied to importing spreadsheets, coloring respective cells.

The hope is that systems like ours may also serve as stepping stones towards the dream of popular end-user systems with rich semantic capabilities. However, for the systems built en route to be useful, it is important to establish user expectations that are reliably met.

Contributions

This paper makes the following contributions:

- hierarchical structure coloring and manipulation as a user interface technique for PBE;
- mock input/output examples as a user interface technique for PBE;
- STEPS, a web-based PBE system that incorporates these techniques;
- a Domain Specific Language for manipulating hierarchically structured strings
- a user study of programmers showing that STEPS is faster than conventional programming, on tasks that have been out of reach for other PBE systems.

The remainder of this paper proceeds with a discussion of related work, the tasks used in our user study, a description of the interface, and a short description of the synthesis architecture. Finally, we discuss the user study.

RELATED WORK

A number of PBE systems for simple string manipulation *that do not expose or manipulate structure by example* exist, such as EBE [18], Tourmaline [17], Cima [14], TELS [19], Visual Awk [10], DEED [5], SmartEdit [12], and Flash Fill [6].[2] The lack of exposed structure limits the scope of these systems, as discussed earlier.

Additional tools consider the structure of text documents for purposes other than text processing. The PADS project [4] learns structure for ad-hoc data sources in domain specific languages designed for programmers. It produces very precise format specifications capable of identifying any errors in a data file, at a cost of increased complexity. It does not permit structural manipulations by example.

Data Wrangler extracts data from a text file and imports it into a spreadsheet program that supports some PBE [9]. For

[2] Flash Fill has been released in Microsoft Excel 2013.

Mock Input	Mock Output

TRB1006:
  Company: Yamaha
  Kind: Bass
  Year: 2006
EFX-1000:
  Company: Pioneer
  Year: 2005
COX15SA:
  Company: Yamaha
  Kind: Guitar
  Year: 2002
	COX15SA:
	  Company: Yamaha
	  Kind: Guitar
	  Year: 2002
	EFX-1000:
	  Company: Pioneer
	  Year: 2005
	TRB1006:
	  Company: Yamaha
	  Kind: Bass
	  Year: 2006

System response
FAILED TO FIND PATTERN. Perhaps see an example of sorting.

Figure 3. Though STEPS fails to infer a pattern, it is able to guess that the desired function may be sorting, and it provides context-specific help.

data that is inherently tabular, the powerful spreadsheet manipulations offered provide an alternative to PBE for many tasks. However, the loss of formatting information in the import process and the inability to manipulate hierarchical structure may limit applicability to general TP.

For synthesis and ranking, we use the framework of Menon *et al.* [15]. We also borrow ideas from Gulwani's pattern matching algorithm [6], which in turn borrows ideas from the Version Space Algebra approach to PBE [12].

For a recent overview of Programming by Example interaction paradigms, see [7].

TASKS

Following Gulwani's analysis of Excel help forums [6], we began by examining a large number of (single-file) text-processing tasks from a Unix shell script help forum [1] from which we created over one hundred benchmark tasks. Common practice on forums was to include input/output examples. Real and artificial examples were both prevalent.

Below are some typical scenarios of how STEPS can be used for text processing. These also happen to be the tasks we used to evaluate STEPS, which we describe later.

User Study Task 1: Remove digits (warm up)

Delete digits, as illustrated below.

Al~~123~~
John~~45~~
...

This task can be done by most prior PBE systems and regular-expression search-and-replace in some editors. STEPS requires users to color text before deleting it; the first step is selecting what is to be deleted and the second step is simply deleting it (for which STEPS provides a shortcut).

x_1	y_1
Al123 John45	Al123 John45

x_2	y_2
Al123 John45	Al John

The argument for not allowing direct deletion in one step is that it is surprisingly hard to debug: visually inspecting the result of a deletion is difficult because one does not see what has been deleted, while inspecting the results of coloring is easy. Alternatively, one could modify the system to allow deletion in one step and show deleted text in strikeout, as in earlier systems such as SmartEdit.

User Study Task 2: Replace / with \ in Location field

The data consists of records separated by blank lines, and the goal is to replace / with \ in `Location` fields only, not in other fields such as `Last Modified`. The first two records are:

```
Acrobat 6.0.2 Professional:

Version: 6.0.6
Last Modified: 18/10/2003 00:11
Kind: PowerPC
Location: /Apps/Acrobat/Professional.app

LiveUpdate:

Version: 3.0.1
Last Modified: 17/04/2003 12:00
Location: /Apps/Norton/LiveUpdate.app
```

To accomplish this task, one first adds structure and then performs the replacement. So, if the above data is the first mock input x_1, then a possible first mock output y_1 is:

```
Acrobat 6.0.2 Professional:

Version: 6.0.6
Last Modified: 18/10/2003 00:11
Kind: PowerPC
Location: / Apps / Acrobat / Professional.app
```

```
LiveUpdate:

Version: 3.0.1
Last Modified: 17/04/2003 12:00
Location: / Apps / Norton / LiveUpdate.app
```

After replacing / with \, one removes all color (for which the interface provides a shortcut). Note that adding the three colors above in STEPS would actually require three steps because STEPS currently limits users to adding one new color per step. Throughout this paper, we keep the presentation succinct by adding multiple colors simultaneously.

User Study Task 3: List fonts by style

Each font entry has a style. Sort the styles, and then list fonts with that style in the order they occur, each followed by a semicolon. Sample data:

```
AquaKana:
  Family: .Aqua Kana
  Style: Regular
  Version: 1.0
  Designer: JIYU-KOBO Ltd.
  Embeddable: Yes
Courier:
  Family: Courier
  Style: Regular
  Version: 5.1d1e1
  Embeddable: Yes
Courier-Bold:
  Family: Courier
  Style: Bold
  Version: 5.1d1e1
  Embeddable: Yes
```

Sample output:

```
Bold: Courier-Bold;
Regular: AquaKana; Courier;
```

This task, by far the most difficult, merits a more detailed walk through, which we give in the next section.

The fourth and final user study task involves searching an HTTP log file and extracting URL components that meet multiple criteria. In hindsight, it would have provided more variety to replace this task with one operating on semi-structured data that is not purely record based. We recently used STEPS for such tasks in response to a journal editor who requested a script to format-check journal submission files. The tasks include a number of tests on a latex file, such as verifying that the section titles are in "title case".

AVOIDING "DEAD ENDS"

Every PBE system will inevitably fail in some cases; the key question is how to proceed. There was nothing more frustrating to our users than a failure message with no suggestion of how to make progress, as Lau also reports [11]. *Search failures*, such as in Figure 3, occur when the system fails to find any useful transform mapping x to y that is "reasonable" (i.e., other than the trivial transform that always outputs the constant string y). *Ambiguity failures* occur when the computer finds too many transforms.[3] Users can often address ambiguity failures by providing longer mock examples or weeding through suggested transformations. Furthermore, a system good at *ranking* candidate transforms may also avoid ambiguity failures.

[3] The example of Figure 3 is ambiguous in many ways: it could be sorting records by year (or ID) or reversing records. It is also ambiguous because it will not even be clear how to segment further records.

One participant in our user study reported, "I was surprised that I never reached a dead end." In our experiments, dead ends did occur sometimes, and they were usually caused by search failures. STEPS employs several strategies to avoid dead ends.

First, the STEPS philosophy is to decompose complex transforms into smaller steps. Adding further colored blocks often makes progress.

Second, in the case of search failure, STEPS still attempts to identify the *type* of transform being illustrated, to provide useful feedback in the form of documentation or examples. Some examples of operations that are easier to recognize than to precisely infer include: sorting (mock output is a permutation of mock input), deleting, adding or removing color, extending or shrinking color, and counting (numbers in the mock output but not mock input).

In such cases, context-specific help can be given. For example, in sorting records, suppose that a user first tries to accomplish the entire task in a single step, as in Figure 3. The fact that the lines in the mock input and output are permutations of one another is a clue that sorting may be the primary operation. Hence feedback on how to sort suggests to the user that she might first color records. (Note that if the user is trying to do something besides sorting, such as reversing records, such feedback may still be helpful because she still needs to segment records.) As we shall see, it turns out that the clues of Menon *et al.* [15] perfectly model the problem of guessing the transformation type.

Third, when exact matches to $f\ x\ = y$ are not found, STEPS returns functions f that are approximately correct, i.e., $f\ x\ \approx y$. (Our notion of approximation considers differences in white space to be of minimal importance.) This can address small user typos and also may lead to unanticipated but more productive alternative suggestions.

STEP-BY-STEP WALK THROUGH

Bart, a fictitious user, is asked to write a program for User Study Task 3, namely grouping and listing fonts by style. Bart first pastes the data sample into the system in a text area, and the clicks a "START SCRIPT" button. For the first step, Bart tries:

Mock Input x_1	Mock output y_1
AquaKana:↵ ··Family:·.Aqua·Kana↵ ··Style:·Regular↵ ··Version:·1.0↵ ··Designer:·JIYU-KOBO·Ltd.↵ ··Embeddable:·Yes↵ Courier:↵ ··Family:·Courier↵ ··Style:·Regular↵ ··Version:·5.1d1e1↵ ··Embeddable:·Yes↵	AquaKana:↵ ··Family:·.Aqua·Kana↵ ··Style:·Regular↵ ··Version:·1.0↵ ··Designer:·JIYU-KOBO·Ltd.↵ ··Embeddable:·Yes ↵ Courier:↵ ··Family:·Courier↵ ··Style:·Regular↵ ··Version:·5.1d1e1↵ ··Embeddable:·Yes ↵

Note that the system displays white space (spaces, tabs and newlines) with visible characters. Bart also employs a STEPS feature by which he names the grey color as "font."

After he hits the "Auto-code" button, the system offers Bart only one suggestion of a program with an English description of "Mark from capital letter to 'Yes' as font." It also gives him an opportunity to preview the transform before executing it. Bart examines the data, and it looks good. It appears that all the records end in "Embeddable: Yes." However, Bart, like the participants in our study, is not intimately familiar with the data. He is not sure if "Embeddable" will always be followed by "Yes," so he changes the mock pair so the second record ends in "No." The computer is forced to generalize.

Mock Input x_1	Mock output y_1
AquaKana:↵ ··Family:·.Aqua·Kana↵ ··Style:·Regular↵ ··Version:·1.0↵ ··Designer:·JIYU-KOBO·Ltd.↵ ··Embeddable:·Yes↵ Courier:↵ ··Family:·Courier↵ ··Style:·Regular↵ ··Version:·5.1d1e1↵ ··Embeddable:·No↵	AquaKana:↵ ··Family:·.Aqua·Kana↵ ··Style:·Regular↵ ··Version:·1.0↵ ··Designer:·JIYU-KOBO·Ltd.↵ ··Embeddable:·Yes ↵ Courier:↵ ··Family:·Courier↵ ··Style:·Regular↵ ··Version:·5.1d1e1↵ ··Embeddable:·No ↵

The new program generated is, "Mark from capital letter to 'Embeddable: ', word as font." Bart looks at the resulting preview, is satisfied, and continues. Several points worth making are:

1) Bart preferred to create an artificial mock example (actually modify an example) rather than spend the time searching for an example with "Embeddable: No" in the data.
2) In fact, all the data at hand did happen to end in "Embeddable: Yes." However, since Bart wanted a program that generalized well to future examples, his efforts were not in vain.
3) When this task was used in the user study, about half of the study participants examined the data preview and accepted the first program, and about half made the artificial "No" example. Two participants exerted further effort on segmentation because they were concerned about the fact that records may end in a completely different field than "Embeddable."
4) The suggestions and ranking of the system could be better on this example (i.e., perhaps a better pattern would be to recognize that records start on nonindented lines), but nonetheless users succeed with mock examples and additional colors.

In the second step, Bart introduces a new color, green, which he calls "name." For the mock example, he takes the first two records and colors "AquaKana" and "Courier" in green. The system provides three possible programs along with the ability to preview them in a dialog, shown below.

Each of these programs is presented by its English description alone; the code is collapsed.[4] By clicking on any of these options, Bart sees a preview of its effect. The first

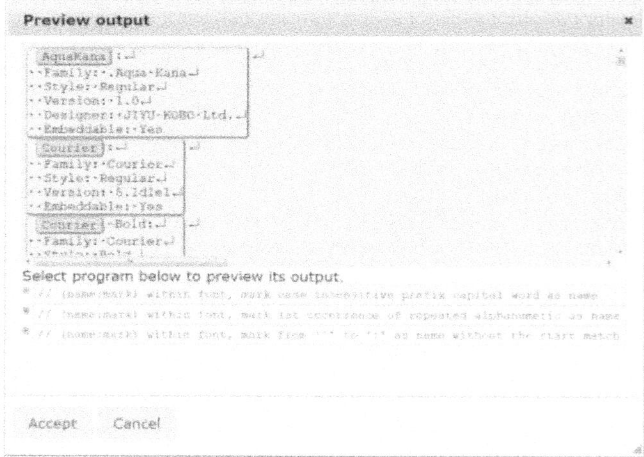

one is clearly wrong, as Bart intended the entire "Courier-Bold" to be green. But the third program is exactly what Bart wanted. He clicks "Accept" and moves on to the next step.

He then introduces a new color called style and marks the styles in a similar fashion. He then simplifies matters by replacing each record with just the name and style. The program generated is, "Within font, keep only name, style" and the resulting data is as follows,

```
AquaKana Regular ↵
Courier Regular ↵
Courier-Bold Bold ↵
GeezaPro-Bold Bold ↵
GeezaPro Regular ↵
```

...

Bart then sorts the records by style. For mock input he finds four records that are out of order (two would have sufficed):

```
Helvetica-Oblique Oblique ↵
AbadiMT-CondensedExtraBold Regular ↵
AmericanTypewriter-Condensed Condensed ↵
AmericanTypewriter-Light Light ↵
```

The mock output are these four records sorted by their blue style. The generated program is "Sort font by style in alphabetical order."

[4] Moreover, there are typically multiple programs yielding exactly the same output on the data, and these are all collapsed into a single group. In earlier versions, we had them expanded by default, but no user was editing the code or selecting amongst multiple programs that yield the same output.

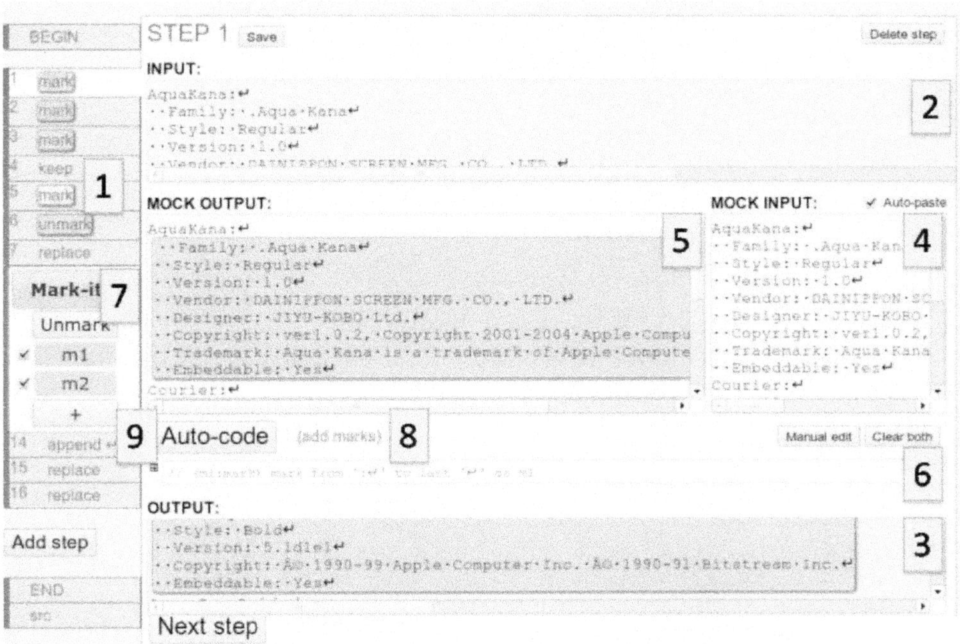

Figure 4. The STEPS interface. Steps are shown in separate tabs. Visible are:

1. List of steps
2. Step input data
3. Step output data
4. Mock input
5. Mock output
6. Editable code
7. Draggable palette
8. Feedback
9. Auto-code button

Grouping

For the crucial step, Bart creates a new color called "styleGroup". He finds six consecutive fonts and groups them into four groups based on equivalent styles.

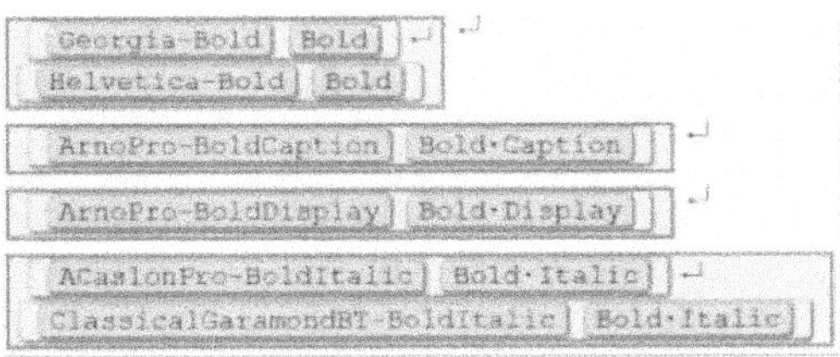

Above is the mock output (the mock input is the same without the yellow color). The generated program is "Group font by style as styleGroup."

Wrap-up

The rest of the task is straightforward. Bart keeps only the first occurrence of the style within each yellow group, deleting the rest, and then appends semicolons and removes newlines, as was required in the task.

Note that grouping was the most difficult step for most users in the study, as we will discuss. This is probably because the tutorial we had given them had examples of sorting but no examples of grouping. Nonetheless, all but one of the participants tried grouping on their own, and the other participant found an alternative solution. (Also note that no participant renamed any colors or edited the style declarations.)

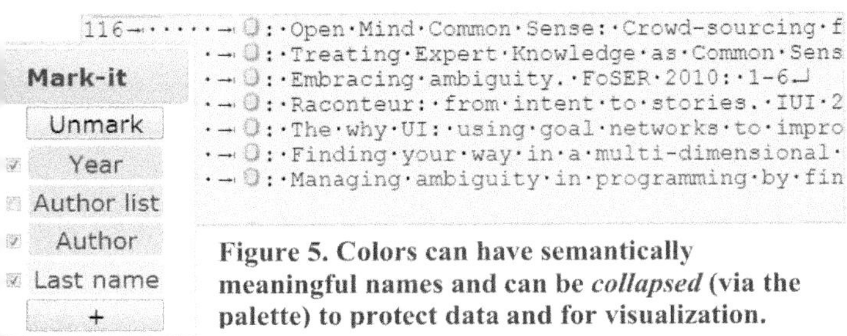

Figure 5. Colors can have semantically meaningful names and can be *collapsed* (via the palette) to protect data and for visualization.

INTERFACE

STEPS is a web application that works inside a browser window. Figure 4 shows a typical session consisting of a list of step tabs shown on the left side (1). The session starts by pasting raw text into the BEGIN tab and ends by copying the output text in the END tab. Step tabs enable the user to revisit and debug steps. Changes to a step automatically propagate throughout all following tabs, and changes to the data in the BEGIN tab propagate all the way to the END tab.

Each step has resizable panes for its *input (2)*, *output (3)*, *mock input (4)*, and *mock output (5)*. Spaces, tabs, and newline characters are displayed with visible glyphs.[5] Our earlier designs, which placed the mock input to the left of the mock output (or above the mock output), led users to mistakenly edit the mock input when they meant to edit the mock output. The code for the step is shown above the output and collapsed to a human-readable comment by default (6).

[5] Using the browser's built-in search functionality, searching for strings that include spaces fails when space characters are replaced with visible characters. Instead, one may create a new font where the standard space character is visible.

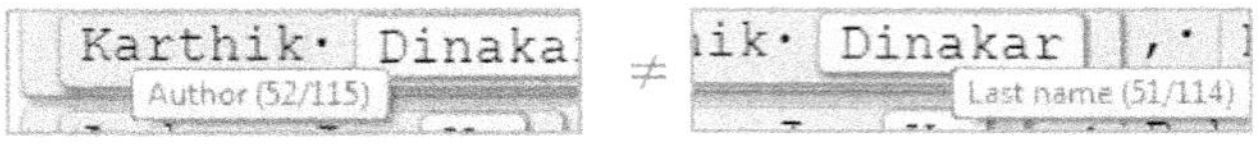

Figure 6. Tooltips appear when you hover over a colored block, indicating region name and block index/total count. Mismatches in numbers can be useful for debugging.

IMPLEMENTATION

We apply the synthesis and ranking approach of Menon *et al* [15]. To instantiate it, we need to define a domain specific language, and a number of *clues*, functions which generate candidate program fragments based the mock input and mock output. A clue might suggest, for example, that if a month name is present, the system should increase the likelihood of date transformations.

Domain Specific Language

We have designed a domain specific language, implemented as a small JavaScript library, which defines a colored string data type together with a small set of operations. A colored string is a string in which some regions are marked with a *tag*, an arbitrary string associated with a color. They must be nested as in XML: each tagged string consists of a sequence of tagged and plain substrings. The library will be made available online and is the only requirement to use the synthesized scripts outside of STEPS.

The core set of operations is shown in Table 1 and makes up the language of STEPS. These operations were chosen because they have natural English descriptions and also are general enough to cover a large number of input-to-output examples. For simplicity, each proposal that our system generates corresponds to exactly one command in the language, which we present in a direct English translation.

Generality is achieved by supplying a variety of options that slightly alter the behavior of the operations. For example, `mark-between` can optionally find the start or the end non-greedily or in nested fashion and drop either the start or the end match; the `sort` command takes an option to specify which comparison to use, etc.

The library also defines a pattern language for tagged strings. This language extends regular expressions with matching by tags and/or containment of another pattern, excluding certain tags by hiding them, and selecting matches by occurrence. The substitution mask for the `replace` operation can refer back to parts of the match to build a new tagged string.

Clue generation

The clue generation is primarily guided by the nature of the operation, e.g., adding colors, removing colors, or editing text. The nature can be determined by a quick inspection of the mock pair.

Then, for each command, STEPS generates a number of candidates for the parameters and the options. For pattern inference, it uses a library of common regular expression

Operation	Params	Description
`mark`	p, t	mark matches to pattern p as tag t
`split`	p, t	mark between consecutive matches to pattern p as tag t
`mark-between`	p_1, p_2, t	mark between matches to p_1, p_2 as t
`within`	p, f	apply function f to each match of tag pattern p
`retag`	p, t	re-tag matches to p as t
`untag`	p	un-tag matches to the tag pattern p
`shrink`	t, p	shrink tags t to a match of p
`extend`	t, p	extend tags t to a match of p
`sort`	t, p	sort substrings of tag t by matches to p (which can be a tag itself)
`group`	t_1, t_2, p	consecutive matches to t_1 with the same match to p as t_2
`replace`	p, m	replace matches to p by a substitution mask m
`remove`	p	remove matches to p
`keep`	p	keep only matches to p

Table 1: STEPS operations and their required parameters.

patterns, existing text and tags in the mock pair, and their combination. The space of all candidate programs is exhaustively explored, and all solutions that approximately match the mock pair are presented.

USER STUDY

We performed a between-subject user study on fourteen computer scientists, doctoral students or postdocs, at a major software research laboratory. It would be difficult to get a true sample of "typical" programmers, but as Figure 7 shows, the participants had a variety of levels of programming experience.

The tasks, from the Task section above, were presented through a web-based form. Each task had an input file, and correctness was judged solely on the output produced for that input file (to avoid judging correctness of programs in general). The data varied in length from 200-830 lines.

Submitted answers were automatically judged and participants were informed whether their answer was correct or not and thus had an opportunity to "debug" submissions. (Otherwise it would not be clear when to move to the next problem or double check one's work.)

Seven participants were randomly assigned to each of the two conditions. In the STEPS group, participants were given a 20-minute overview of STEPS including a hands-on tutorial of some of the major types of features. Note that *grouping* was not covered in the tutorial since we wanted to

	Age	Gender	Programming Experience	Task 1	Task 2	Task 3	Task 4
Control	24	M	High	1	2	16	6
	25	M	Medium	12	12	29	12
	29	M	Medium	6	4	20	*
	29	M	Low	11	7	*	*
	28	M	Low	19	10	*	*
	26	M	Low	14	19	*	*
	26	F	High	36	8	*	*
STEPS	25	M	Medium	1	3	14	3
	28	M	High	3	7	17	16
	30	F	Medium	2	5	30	11
	27	M	Medium	3	12	*	13
	27	F	Low	2	5	54	*
	23	M	Low	2	8	56	*
	29	M	Medium	3	8	*	*

Figure 7. User study results. Task times are in minutes.

see if participants could discover how to do it on their own. They were then given a maximum of 70 minutes to work on the tasks.

In the control group, participants were allowed to accomplish the tasks using whatever means they wished, be it programming, manual editing, or using other tools such as word processors or spreadsheets. Prior to the experiment, they were told that they were to be given text-processing tasks and were allowed to prepare a machine of their choice (typically either a personal laptop or a company-provided desktop). They were also given 70 minutes for the tasks.

Participants identified their programming experience as low: "learned to program," medium: "spent a good bit of time programming," or high: "worked on large projects or been have been employed as a programmer."

Results

STEPS users completed **82%** of the tasks compared to **68%** for the control group. Everyone completed the first two tasks. Therefore, we performed an ANOVA of completion times for the first two tasks with task and condition as independent factors. The times were log-transformed to make the distribution closer to normal. We found a significant main effect of condition ($F=5.22$, $p< 0.032$), in which STEPS users were faster than the control on tasks 1 and 2, but no significant effect of task or interaction between task and condition.

Discussion

In the STEPS group, a minority of the steps (the ones that were accepted) were simply prefixes of the data. For task 3, grouping was a key step that six out of the seven participants discovered on their own even though our tutorial did not mention this operation. For this task, the remaining participant used STEPS for partial automation, finding a way to perform what most do in grouping using only five marking steps (though this would not have scaled well to larger data).

Participants were asked to compare STEPS to programming or something else they were familiar with. Several compared STEPS to "playing a game" or "solving a puzzle," one user compared it to using a spreadsheet, and one participant responded that using STEPS was like programming in an unfamiliar language. The latter participant found STEPS frustrating and wished she could just program instead, but the other participants used positive words such as "cool." Several participants requested access to STEPS for their personal use.

On the negative side, participants uniformly expressed frustration at not knowing what the possible primitive operations were, i.e., what it could do and what it couldn't do. In hindsight, this might have been improved at the cost of a longer tutorial, or by better exposition such as is found in LAPIS and SmartEdit.

In the control group, people used a variety of programming languages, partial automation (e.g., for the first task several participants opened the data in a text editor and ran 10 search-and-replace commands, replacing each digit with an empty string), and in some cases even manual editing. Presumably this was done when they thought it would be faster than programming, and hence forcing them to program (or program in a specific language) would present the comparison to STEPS in an even better light.

It is well known that most of the time in programming is spent debugging and understanding one's data. Anecdotally, this was true for our control participants as well. It seems quite likely that the speed-ups we observed were partly due to how STEPS makes it easier to visualize, understand, and debug the data, compared to programming.

CONCLUSION AND FUTURE WORK

For more than a decade, progress has stalled on what used to be considered one of the most interesting challenges in end user programming: performing sophisticated text edits, such as reformatting a bibliography, by example. Examination of tasks found on TP help forums sheds light on the difficulty: many TP tasks require exposing and manipulating *hierarchical structure* present in text files. This paper introduced STEPS, a system for manipulating hierarchical structures by example.

Our user study demonstrates that STEPS is faster than other alternatives, at least for computer science graduate students and postdocs. It also became clear that STEPS can be improved in terms of the way in which it displays the inferred operations and set of possible operations, both of which have been addressed by previous work.

Looking forward, a central question is to what extent *end users* would adopt a HSS manipulation system like STEPS. In order for this to happen, STEPS inference must be improved to handle single steps that are more complex. Also, ways must be found to teach the end users about key concepts in STEPS. One possible approach is to allow demonstrations alongside input-output pairs, meaning that a user can demonstrate a step on their data while the system generates and displays the corresponding input-output pair. This might be a useful way to introduce the concept of input-output pairs.

A caution raised by Lau [11] and Gulwani [7] is to compare the perceived value of automation with its bottom-line cost, as users may be unwilling to incur the burden of switching out of one application into a separate PBE system. To this end, it may be wise to incorporate such a system into a programming IDE, which may also set certain expectations by explicitly presenting STEPS as an alternative to traditional programming.

REFERENCES

[1] The UNIX and Linux forums: Shell programming and scripting. http://www.unix.com/shell-programming-scripting.

[2] Allen Cypher, editor. *Watch What I Do: Programming by Demonstration*. MIT Press, 1993.

[3] Allen Cypher, Mira Dontcheva, Tessa Lau, and Jeffrey Nichols. *No Code Required: Giving Users Tools to Transform the Web*. Morgan Kaufmann Publishers Inc., San Francisco, CA, USA, 2010.

[4] Kathleen Fisher and David Walker. The PADS project: an overview. In *ICDT*, 2011.

[5] Yuzo Fujishima. Demonstrational automation of text editing tasks involving multiple focus points and conversions. In *Proceedings of the International Conference on Intelligent User Interfaces (IUI '98)*, pages 101–108, 1998.

[6] Sumit Gulwani. Automating string processing in spreadsheets using input-output examples. In *Proceedings of the 38th ACM SIGPLAN-SIGACT Symposium on Principles of Programming Languages (POPL 2011)*, 317-330, 2011.

[7] Sumit Gulwani. Synthesis from Examples: Interaction Models and Algorithms. In *Proceedings of the 14th International Symposium on Symbolic and Numeric Algorithms for Scientific Computing (SYNASC)*, 8-14, 2012.

[8] David Huynh and Stefano Mazzocchi. Google Refine. http://code.google.com/p/google-refine/.

[9] Sean Kandel, Andreas Paepcke, Joseph Hellerstein, and Jeffrey Heer. Wrangler: interactive visual specification of data transformation scripts. In Desney S. Tan, Saleema Amershi, Bo Begole, Wendy A. Kellogg, and Manas Tungare, editors, *CHI*, pages 3363–3372, 2011.

[10] Jurgen Landauer and Masahito Hirakawa. Visual AWK: a model for text processing by demonstration. In *Proceedings of the 11th International IEEE Symposium on Visual Languages '95*, pages 267–274, 1995.

[11] Tessa Lau. Why programming-by-demonstration systems fail: Lessons learned for usable AI. *AI Magazine*, 30(4):65–67, 2009.

[12] Tessa Lau, Steven Wolfman, Pedro Domingos, and Daniel Weld. Programming by demonstration using version space algebra. *Machine Learning*, 53(1-2), 2003.

[13] H. Lieberman. *Your Wish Is My Command: Programming by Example*. Morgan Kaufmann, 2001.

[14] David Lawrence Maulsby. *Instructible agents*. PhD thesis, Calgary, Alta., Canada, Canada, 1995. UMI Order No. GAXNN-03114.

[15] Aditya Krishna Menon, Omer Tamuz, Sumit Gulwani, Butler Lampson, and Adam Tauman Kalai. A Machine Learning Framework for Programming by Example. *Proceedings of the 29th International Conference on Machine Learning, 2013*.

[16] Robert C. Miller. *Lightweight structure in text*. CMU PhD thesis, Pittsburgh, PA, USA, 2002..

[17] Brad A. Myers. Watch what I do. chapter Tourmaline: text formatting by demonstration, pages 309–321. MIT Press, Cambridge, MA, USA, 1993.

[18] Robert P. Nix. Editing by example. *TOPLAS*, 7(4):600–621, 1985.

[19] Sun Wu and Udi Manber. Agrep – a fast approximate pattern searching tool. In *Proceedings of the Winter USENIX Technical Conference*, pages 153–162, 1992.

UltraHaptics: Multi-Point Mid-Air Haptic Feedback for Touch Surfaces

Tom Carter[1], Sue Ann Seah[1], Benjamin Long[1], Bruce Drinkwater[2], Sriram Subramanian[1]
Department of Computer Science[1] and Department of Mechanical Engineering[2]
University of Bristol, UK
{t.carter, s.a.seah, b.long, sriram.subramanian, b.drinkwater}@bristol.ac.uk

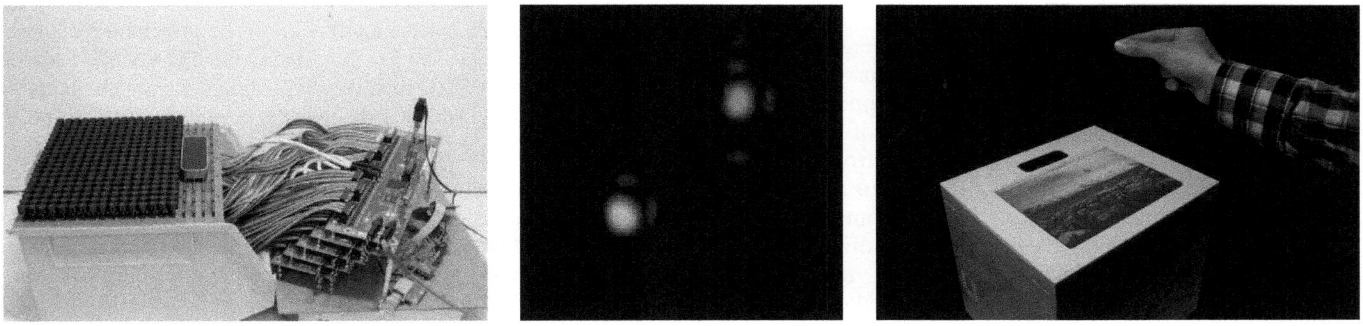

Figure 1: The UltraHaptics system. Left: the hardware. Centre: a simulation of two focal points, with colour representing phase and brightness representing amplitude. Right: receiving two independent points of feedback while performing a pinch gesture.

ABSTRACT
We introduce *UltraHaptics*, a system designed to provide multi-point haptic feedback above an interactive surface. *UltraHaptics* employs focused ultrasound to project discrete points of haptic feedback through the display and directly on to users' unadorned hands. We investigate the desirable properties of an acoustically transparent display and demonstrate that the system is capable of creating multiple localised points of feedback in mid-air. Through psychophysical experiments we show that feedback points with different tactile properties can be identified at smaller separations. We also show that users are able to distinguish between different vibration frequencies of non-contact points with training. Finally, we explore a number of exciting new interaction possibilities that *UltraHaptics* provides.

Author Keywords
Haptic feedback; touch screens; interactive tabletops.

ACM Classification Keywords
H.5.2. Information Interfaces and Presentation: User Interfaces

UIST'13, October 8–11, 2013, St. Andrews, United Kingdom.
Copyright © 2013 ACM 978-1-4503-2268-3/13/10...$15.00.
http://dx.doi.org/10.1145/2501988.2502018

INTRODUCTION
Multi-touch surfaces have become common in public settings, with large displays appearing in hotel lobbies, shopping malls and other high foot traffic areas. These systems are able to dynamically change their interface allowing multiple users to interact at the same time and with very little instruction. This ability to 'walk-up and use' removes barriers to interaction and encourages spontaneous use. However, in return for this flexibility we have sacrificed the tactile feedback afforded by physical controls.

Most previous research has focused on recreating this feedback on interactive surfaces. This can be achieved through vibration [2, 4] or by physically changing the shape of the surface [19, 20, 15].

There are situations when receiving haptic feedback before touching the surface would be beneficial. These include when vision of the display is restricted, such as while driving, and when the user doesn't want to touch the device, such as when their hands are dirty. Providing feedback above the surface would also allow for an additional information channel alongside the visual. Previous methods capable of providing this feedback have involved a device worn upon the user's body [33, 30, 32].

In this paper, we introduce *UltraHaptics*, a system that provides haptic feedback above interactive surfaces and requires no contact with either tools, attachments or the surface itself. Instead, haptic sensations are projected through a screen and directly onto the user's hands. It employs the principle of *acoustic radiation force* whereby a phased array of ultrasonic transducers is used to exert forces on a target in mid-air.

There are three aspects to the creation of the *UltraHaptics* system. First, when augmenting an interactive surface with ultrasonic feedback, it is useful for the array generating the acoustic field to also double as a projected display device. Finding a fitting projection material is not trivial, as it must efficiently permit ultrasound through while also appropriately reflecting incoming light. Through a series of technical evaluations we show that display surfaces with 0.5mm holes sizes and 25% open space reduce the impact on any focusing algorithm while still creating a high performance projection surface.

Second, most existing approaches to generating acoustic fields suffer from secondary maxima that surround the central focus. We need an algorithm that can suppress these secondary maxima while allowing the creation of multiple focal points. We do this by using a concept of control points to define a target for the algorithm by telling it to maximise and minimize the intensity selectively at these control points. Finally, there are no studies on users' ability to discriminate different focal points generated using *acoustic radiation force*. Because focal points do not have well defined edges we cannot rely on the results of discrimination studies done with pins and vibrators. We conduct a series of psychophysical studies to demonstrate feedback points with different tactile properties can be distinguished at smaller separations and that users can identify different tactile properties with training.

We present four main contributions:

1. We outline the principles, design and implementation of an ultrasonic, mid-air haptic feedback system for touch surfaces.

2. We investigate the desirable properties of an acoustically transparent display surface that allows the haptic feedback to be projected through the display from below.

3. We present a series of psychophysical studies that demonstrate feedback points with different tactile properties can be distinguished at smaller separations and that users can identify different tactile properties with training.

RELATED WORK

Previous research related to *UltraHaptics* can be divided into two categories: alternative haptic feedback methods and previous ultrasonic haptic feedback systems.

Haptic Feedback Methods

Researchers have explored a wide variety of haptic systems for interactive surfaces. One direction has been to vary the friction coefficient of the surface, either through vibrating the surface with ultrasound [4] or through the use of electrovibration, as demonstrated by TeslaTouch [2]. These approaches are only capable of providing one haptic sensation at a time and apply it across the entire surface. In the case of TeslaTouch, haptic feedback cannot be felt with a stationary point of contact.

Another method is to physically change the shape of the touch surface. FEELEX uses a pin array to deform the surface into a relief image [19]. Alternatively, a fluid layer embedded within the display can be manipulated through the use of electromagnets [20] or pneumatics [15] to alter its shape. These systems require the user's hand to be in direct contact with the surface. In many scenarios, it would be preferable to receive the haptic feedback as the hand approaches the surface.

Separating the visual and haptic displays has been proposed as a solution to this problem. The use of a tool enables users to interact with the system without needing to touch the surface. The haptic pen combines a pressure sensitive stylus with a physical actuator to provide vibrotactile feedback [23]. Similarly, haptic feedback can be provided by a separate static device, such as the SensAble PHANTOM [26] or maglev haptics [3]. However, exploring a virtual environment through a tool creates a disconnect between the user and the content.

Wearable attachments, such as data gloves [33], enable haptic feedback to be provided above the surface while still letting users move their hands freely. SensableRays transfers haptic feedback to an actuator on the user's hand wirelessly through modulated light [30]. Similarly, FingerFlux alters a magnetic field to stimulate the user's finger through an attached magnet [32]. These attachments maintain constant contact with the user's skin and so are always providing some tactile sensation. They also require the user to adorn their hands with the device prior to use, thus limiting the potential for spontaneous interaction.

Ultrasonic Haptic Feedback

The use of focused ultrasound to stimulate receptors in the human body was investigated as an alternative that requires no physical contact. Research originated in the field of biological sciences in the early 1970s where it was used to diagnose neurological and audiological disorders by analysing changes in perceptual thresholds [9]. By stimulating neuroreceptors within the skin, it has been demonstrated that focused ultrasound is capable of inducing tactile, thermal, tickling, itching and pain sensations [13].

It is important to note that there are two different methods to stimulating receptor structures through ultrasound. The first takes advantage of the *acoustic radiation force*: the force generated when ultrasound is reflected. The ultrasound is focused onto the surface of the skin, where it induces a shear wave in the skin tissue. The displacement caused by the shear wave triggers mechanoreceptors within the skin generating a haptic sensation [11]. The second method bypasses the receptors entirely and directly stimulates the nerve fibres [12]. However, this method requires powerful acoustic fields that penetrate the skin, making it unsuitable for applications designed for prolonged use. We therefore focus on ultrasound incident upon the skin surface.

The use of acoustic radiation force to generate tactile sensations was first demonstrated by Dalecki et al. [5]. A nonfocusing ultrasonic transducer submerged in a water bath was used to emit ultrasound onto the finger of a user. To provide haptic feedback, the radiated ultrasound is modulated down to a frequency detectable by the receptors in the human hand. By moving from using water-based ultrasound to airborne ultrasound the potential range of applications of this technology were broadly increased [18].

The introduction of two-dimensional phased arrays of ultrasound transducers allowed for a dynamic system, with ultrasound focused to a point that can be moved along two axes [17]. While this technique creates a strong focal point, it suffers from the creation of four secondary maxima surrounding the central focus. When the focal point is above the centre of the array, the secondary maxima have about 5% of the intensity of the central focus according to [17], but as the focal point moves further from the centre of the array this value increases considerably. Randomly distributing the transducers across the array rather than arranging them in a grid has been shown to significantly reduce the intensity of secondary maxima [10]. However, this creates an inefficient array in terms of maximising the intensity of the focal points while minimising the footprint of the array.

Previous attempts to create two or more focal points used spatial or temporal multiplexing [1]. The former has the drawback that the secondary maxima of multiple focal points will often constructively interfere with each other creating extra regions of perceivable haptic feedback. Temporal multiplexing on the other hand involves rapidly switching between focal points. This necessarily shortens the duration of ultrasound radiation for each focal point, reducing its intensity accordingly. Both multiplexing methods also risk residual ultrasound from a focal point destructively interfering with other focal points.

When combining ultrasonic haptic feedback with a visual display, various arrangements of transducers have been investigated. They have been positioned in four small arrays along the edges of the display [25], in two columns either side of the display [16] and on the back of the display [1]. Ideally, the direction of the resultant force of the feedback would come from the corresponding visual element. However, these configurations incorporated traditional displays, which are acoustically opaque and so restrict the positioning of the transducers.

ULTRAHAPTICS

Current systems with integrated interactive surfaces can allow users to walk-up and use them with unadorned hands. Our goal is to integrate haptic feedback into these systems without sacrificing their simplicity and accessibility. To achieve this, we designed a system consisting of an ultrasound transducer array positioned beneath an acoustically transparent display. This arrangement enables the projection of focused ultrasound through the interactive surface and directly onto the users' bare hands. By creating multiple simultaneous feedback points, and giving them individual tactile properties, users can receive localised feedback that corresponds to their actions. The design of our system was guided by two primary requirements: an acoustically transparent display and independent points of feedback.

Acoustically Transparent Display

With the transducer array positioned behind, the display surface must allow ultrasound to pass through without affecting the focusing and with minimal attenuation. The ideal display would therefore be totally acoustically transparent. Other considerations include being solid to the touch and providing a high quality projected image.

Acoustic metamaterials are materials whose structure is designed to manipulate waves of sound. By artificially creating a lattice structure within a material, it is possible to correct for the refraction that occurs as the wave passes through the material [24]. This enables the creation of a solid material that allows a certain frequency of sound to pass through it. A pane of glass manufactured with this technique would provide the perfect display surface. Furthermore, it has been proven that such a material could enhance the focusing of the ultrasound by acting as an acoustic lens [28].

As such metamaterials are not yet commercially available, we looked to cinema for inspiration. Cinema screens face a similar challenge as speakers are placed behind the screen for optimal synchronisation between the audio and video. They must therefore remain acoustically transparent while providing a high quality picture. Traditionally, perforated screens have been used. Small holes allow the screen to be permeable to sound, but are too small to adversely affect picture quality. Studies show that smaller and closer holes provide better transparency at higher frequencies, although testing was limited to 20kHz [31]. However, the regular patterns of holes can cause moiré and there is a limit to how small the holes can be made. Once this limit had been reached, woven fabric was investigated as a solution [8]. A fine weave creates very small holes and a large percentage of open area, making for an effective cinema screen.

We tested a range of perforated and woven screens with different properties. Details of these tests are presented in the technical evaluation section.

Independent Feedback Points

In order to relate points of haptic feedback to on-screen elements, users must be able to identify the presence of multiple feedback points. If users are able to distinguish between points with different tactile properties, meaning can then be attached to them. There are both technical and perceptual issues associated with this.

Technical Issues

Previous studies positioned focal points 50mm apart [1]. At this distance, interface elements would have to be sparsely distributed if they are to provide haptic feedback. Furthermore, the problems associated with both spatial and temporal multiplexing increase as the distance between focal points is reduced, rendering these approaches unworkable. We therefore decided to adapt and extend an alternative focusing method so that each element of the transducer array can contribute to multiple focal points at the same time. This approach was then evaluated by taking measurements of the created acoustic field.

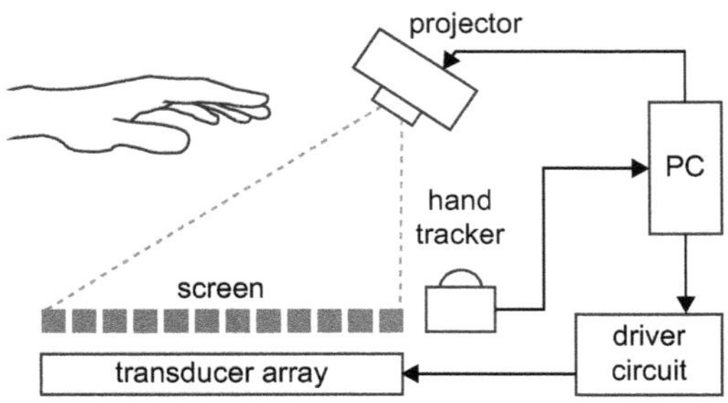

Figure 2: Overview of the UltraHaptics system.

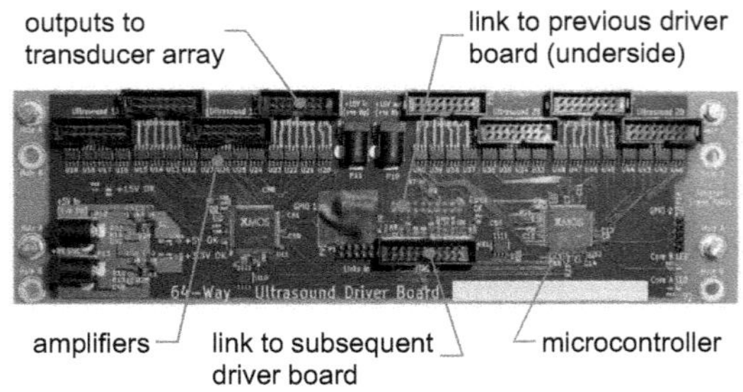

Figure 3: An UltraHaptics driver board.

Perceptual Issues

The human hand is not capable of detecting vibrations at 40kHz. Vibration is detected by mechanoreceptors within the skin. The mechanoreceptors within the skin are responsive to vibrations in the range 0.4Hz to 500Hz [14]. We modulate the emitted ultrasound in order to create vibrations within the optimum frequency range detectable by the human hand. By changing the modulation frequency, we also change the frequency of the vibration on the hand and this can be used to create different tactile properties. Modulating different focal points at different frequencies can give each point of feedback its own independent 'feel' [27]. In this way we are not only able to correlate haptic and visual feedback, but we may also attach meaning to noticeably different textures so that information can be transferred to the user via the haptic feedback.

The minimum distance between points of ultrasonic stimulation at which the human hand can identify them as separate is unknown. It is also unknown whether users are able to distinguish between points at different modulation frequencies. Previous perception studies in haptic stimulation used physical actuators placed on the skin but a non-contact scenario has never been studied. We therefore decided to conduct a series of user studies to establish the limitations of our design.

IMPLEMENTATION OF ULTRAHAPTICS

In order to evaluate our design we built a prototype system, which is outlined in Figure 2. Challenges in building the UltraHaptics system included constructing the hardware, computing amplitudes and phases for each transducer such that multiple focal points are formed, and modulating simultaneous focal points at different frequencies.

Haptic Feedback Loop

Our transducer array has 320 muRata MA40S4S transducers arranged in a 16x20 grid formation. The transducer units are 10mm in diameter and positioned with no gap between them to minimise the array footprint. We chose this type of transducer as they produce a large amount of sound pressure (20 Pascals of pressure at a distance of 30cm), have a wide angle of directivity (60 degrees) and are widely available due to their common use as car parking sensors.

When haptic feedback is required, a phase delay and amplitude is calculated for each transducer to create an acoustic field forming the desired focal points. A lookup table of phase delays and amplitudes is then assembled on the host PC and sent to the driver circuit via an Ethernet connection. The computation determines the frame rate of the feedback. On a PC with an Intel Core 2 Quad 2.4GHz CPU and an NVIDIA GeForce GTX 480 we achieved speeds of up to 60fps.

The driver circuit consists of a chain of custom-made driver boards (Figure 3). Each driver board features two XMOS L1-128 processors running at 400MHz. They are designed to be stackable, so that a system can be scaled up or down simply by adding or removing driver boards. All connected boards have synchronised clocks driving their outputs at 10MHz. The output signal from the processors to the transducers is a square wave and is amplified from 5V to 15V. Other waveforms could be used but the resonant nature of the transducers mean that a sine wave will always be emitted.

The visual content is projected onto the display surface from above. As users interact with this content, the positions of their hands are tracked by a Leap Motion controller and fed into the application running on a PC. The Leap Motion controller provides the 3D coordinates of the fingertips and palm of the users' hands at up to 200 frames per second. It also provides properties including directional vectors, normals and width of the fingers, which are sufficient to build up an accurate model of the hands. Finally, with 150-degree field of view and eight cubic feet of tracked space, it is very well-suited to detecting input above a touch surface.

Computing Phases and Amplitudes

Our algorithm to compute the amplitude and phase for each transducer has been adapted from that proposed by Gavrilov [10]. Rather than a focal point, the approach is able to form 2D focal shapes such as letters of the alphabet. A concept of control points is used to define a target for the algorithm, telling it to maximise the intensity of the ultrasound at these control point positions.

There are three steps to the algorithm [6, 7]. First, the acoustic field generated by a single transducer is calculated to create a large modelled volume. This makes it possible to determine the phase and amplitude at any point within the modelled volume by offsetting the sample transducer for the position, phase and amplitude of each of the transducers in the real array and combining the values.

The control points are then defined upon a 2D plane so that they form the desired shape. Finally, the optimal phases are calculated using a minimum norm solver so that the resulting acoustic field is as close to that specified by the control points as possible. There is more than one solution that will create optimal focusing to the control points but some create a higher intensity than others. Solutions are therefore iteratively generated to find the one that creates the highest intensity at the focal shape.

While Gavrilov arranged the control points into a shape, positioning single control points some distance apart creates multiple high intensity points. There is also no reason the control points must lie on a plane. Instead, we can position them to create multiple focal points at different heights. We also extended the control point concept to include null control points. These perform the opposite role to normal control points, instructing the algorithm to generate zero amplitude at that point. By positioning a null control point at each of the positions where unwanted secondary maxima would be expected, we were able to minimise their intensity while optimising the efficiency of the array by having the greatest density of transducers.

Algorithm 1 Our Waveform Algorithm

```
modelledVolume ← integralRayleighSommerfeld()
transducers ← transducerArrayLayout(modelledVolume)
loop
  controlPoints ← positionControlPoints()
  repeat
    phasesAndAmplitudes ←
        minimumNormSolver(transducers, controlPoints)
  until error < ϵ
  send phasesAndAmplitudes to transducer array
end loop
```

Modulating Multiple Focal Points

The human hand is not capable of detecting vibrations at 40kHz. We modulate the emitted ultrasound in order to create vibrations that are detectable by the human hand. Modulating multiple focal points at different frequencies is achieved by time multiplexing scenes with different numbers of focal points. For example, in a scenario with two focal points, we must generate four scenes: an empty scene, one with only focal point A, one with only focal point B and one with both focal points. We then move between the scenes as depicted in Figure 4. The amplitude of a single focal point is more than one of a pair of focal points. Therefore, after calculating

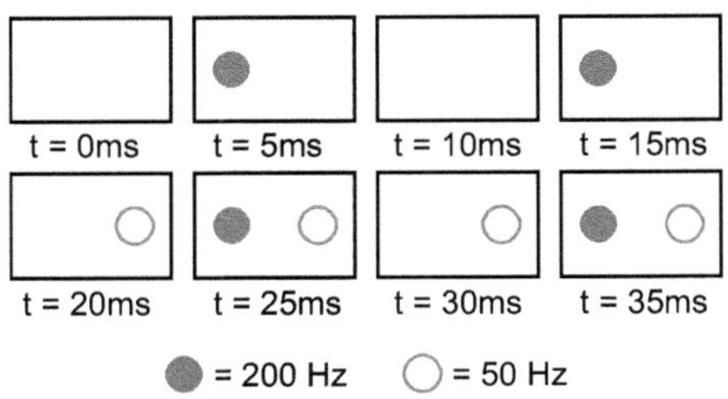

Figure 4: Multiplexing two focal points with different modulation frequencies.

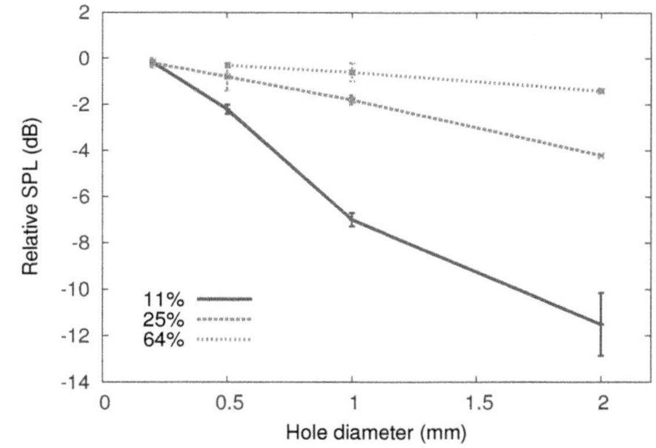

Figure 5: Attenuation of ultrasound through perforated screens with various hole diameters and percentage of open space.

the phases and amplitudes for every scene, we scale the amplitudes of the transducers so that the amplitudes of the focal points remain constant.

TECHNICAL EVALUATION

There are three main factors that affect the performance of our system: the acoustic and visual properties of the display surface, the strength of the feedback and the formation of the focal points. In order to evaluate our system, we carried out a technical analysis of each factor. All measurements were made using a calibrated Brüel & Kjær 1/8" pressure-field microphone Type 4138-A-015.

Display Surface

We measured the attenuation of the ultrasound as it passed through a selection of perforated sheets and woven fabrics. The display being tested was placed directly on top of a single transducer and the microphone was positioned 20mm above. A digital oscilloscope was used to perform an FFT calculation and extract the 40kHz component in order to isolate the ultrasound from ambient and transient noise. The maximum and minimum values were recorded over a period of 30 seconds and then averaged. The results are presented as a decrease in sound pressure level (relative SPL (dB)) where 0dB is the sound pressure level with no display surface present.

Woven Material

We tested the acoustic impedance of two woven fabrics. The first was muslin, a loosely woven cotton fabric. The second was Screen Excellence Enlightor 4K, a finely woven material designed to act as a projector screen for home theatres that feature speakers located behind the screen. The Enlightor 4k is specified as providing uniform attenuation of just -2.5dB between 500Hz and 20kHz. The results are presented in Table 1.

From the poor performance of the Enlightor 4k, we can conclude that the weave does not have enough open space for 40kHz. Conversely, the single layer of muslin performed very well as it has a high percentage of open space. However, this

Fabric	Relative SPL (dB)
Muslin - 1 layer	-0.25
Muslin - 2 layers	-0.45
Enlightor 4k	-3.60

Table 1: Attenuation of ultrasound through woven fabrics.

same property causes poor performance as a projection surface, leading to a large loss of visual detail.

Perforated Sheet
To further investigate their effect on acoustic transparency, we wanted to control the hole diameter and percentage of open space in the material. We therefore created a set of perforated sheets by laser-cutting small holes into 210 gsm white paper. The results are presented in Figure 5. Both properties have large effects, providing a selection of possible display surface choices that offer minimal attenuation.

Focusing Through the Display
Displays that offer minimal attenuation of ultrasound may still affect the focusing of the sound waves due to diffraction and the incident angle of the waves on the underside of the display surface. We therefore took four of the best performing display surfaces and evaluated them on the full size transducer array. The display was placed directly onto the array and the microphone was positioned 200mm above the centre of the array. A single focal point was created at the microphone with no modulation so that a stable measurement could be taken. Again, we extracted the 40kHz component from the FFT calculation to filter out ambient and transient noise. We recorded maximum and minimum values over a duration of 60 seconds. The averaged results are presented in Table 2. All results show a slightly greater attenuation

Display Surface	Relative SPL (dB)
0.2mm at 11% open space	Undetectable
0.5mm at 25% open space	-2.4
1mm at 64% open space	-4.8
Muslin - 1 layer	-1.2

Table 2: Experimental results of the acoustic impedance of display surfaces to focused 40kHz ultrasound.

than the results in Figure 5, which is to be expected due to a higher total SPL from the full array of transducers. It also indicates that the surfaces do have some affect on the focusing of the sound waves. One result of note is that the surface with 0.5mm holes at 25% open space performed better than the one with 1mm holes at 64% open space. This implies that smaller holes reduce the impact on focusing to a greater extent than open space.

Formation of Focal Points
Our simulations show that our system creates discrete focal points with low amplitude secondary maxima (Figure 6 far left). To verify our simulations, we scanned the microphone across the horizontal plane at a height of 200mm above the transducer array. A single focal point was created at the same height above the centre of the array with no modulation. Measurements of the 40kHz component were at 2mm increments. The results of the scan are presented in Figure 6 centre left with amplitude normalised across the measured region.

In order to maximise the amplitude of multiple focal points, a distance that is a multiple of the wavelength should separate them. This allows individual sound waves to contribute constructively to both focal points. Adjacent focal points must also be positioned at least 1cm apart in order for a low amplitude region to be formed between them. Figure 6 shows a simulation of two focal points separated by this minimum distance, while the far right image represents a microphone scan across the same region. The results show that our system is capable of creating distinct focal points at this separation.

Forming two focal points at different heights is also possible. We simulated two focal points being created at heights of 200mm and 400mm from the transducers, with a horizontal distance of 1cm between them. Figure 7 contains simulations of the acoustic field across the horizontal plane at heights of 200mm (left) and 400mm (right). There remains a large gap between the two focal points and the unfocused point at each height has low amplitude compared to the focal point.

Strength of Focal Points
The greater the number of simultaneous focal points, the weaker any individual focal point will be. To measure this, we created scenarios with 1 to 5 focal points and measured the pressure generated at one of them. All focal points were created at a height of 200mm above the array surface, were unmodulated and were spaced 40mm apart. A perforated display surface with 0.5mm diameter holes and 25% open space was used. As before, only the 40kHz component was measured. The results are presented in Table 3 as a measurement of the absolute sound pressure level.

Number of focal points	Absolute SPL (dB)
1	72.6
2	71.7
3	68.2
4	67.4
5	66.6

Table 3: The strength of focal points when different numbers of points are produced simultaneously.

As can be seen from the table, for increasing numbers of focal points the sound pressure level drops slowly with our approach (a doubling in sound pressure level being a difference of approximately 6dB), showing that our method for creating focal points outperforms the theoretical limitations of both spatial and temporal multiplexing.

USER STUDIES

Identifying the number of focal points
We performed a user study to test the design and implementation of our system in forming discernible focal points. We decided to run a focal point discrimination task to determine

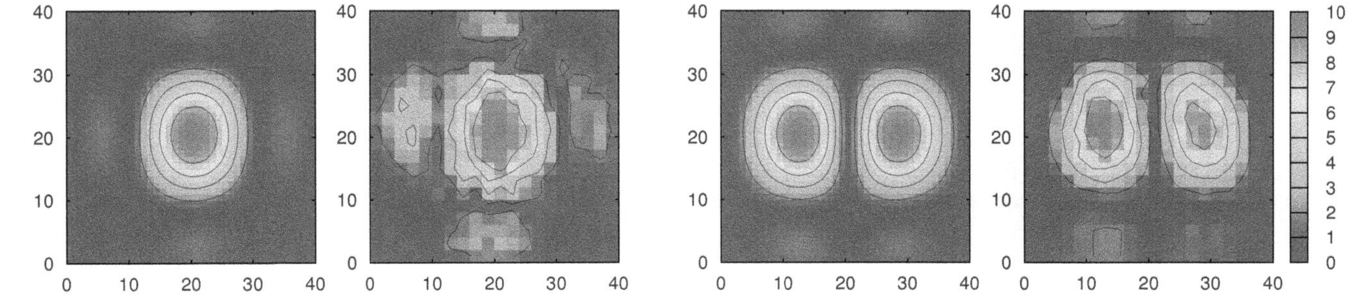

Figure 6: A comparison of the simulated and measured intensities of one and two focal points, each at 200mm from the emitting transducers. Far left: single focal point simulation. Centre left: single focal point measured with a microphone (RMSE 1.30, peak pressure 257 Pascals). Centre right: two focal point simulation. Far right: two focal points measured with a microphone (RMSE 0.77, peak pressure 234 Pascals). All axes are in *mm*.

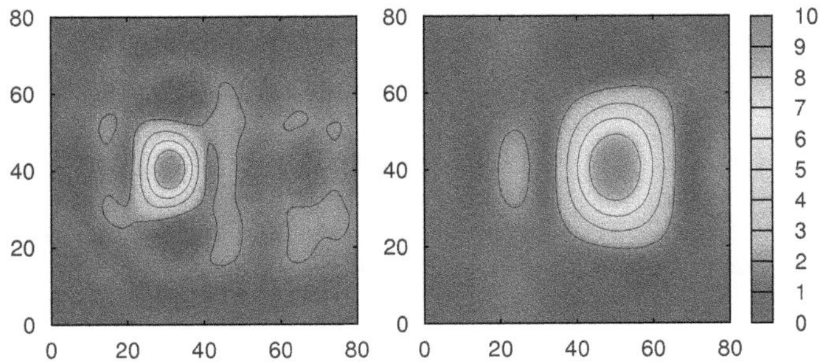

Figure 7: A single simulation containing two focal points placed at different heights. The xy position is kept constant, while the left image is taken at a height of 200mm and the right is taken at 400mm. All axes are in *mm*.

whether participants are able to recognise and discriminate between zero, one and two focal point conditions.

In the technical evaluation, we determined that the system is capable of producing two focal points that are 1cm apart. Although the system is able to produce two discrete focal points that are quite close together, this does not mean that the human hand is capable of resolving these points as separate.

As the system uses 40 kHz ultrasound, the focal points generated are about 1cm in diameter (the wavelength of sound at 40 kHz). Previous studies on two-point discrimination tasks, which measures the minimum separation at which two points are felt instead of one, have used static pins that are about 0.5mm wide, which results in a separation threshold of about 2-3 mm [22]. Perez et al. [29] performed two-point vibration discrimination tasks, but also with comparatively small piezoelectric vibrators with a width of 3mm resulting in discrimination thresholds of 2-5mm depending on the frequency of the vibrators. The static pins and vibrators also has the advantage of sharp edges, which helps in the discrimination of two points as it activates mechanoreceptors in the skin that specializes in spatial acuity [21].

We hypothesised that the separation threshold between two focal points would be significantly higher. This is due to the focal points being larger and not having a well-defined edge, which will degrade a two-point discrimination task. However, one of the ways of improving this task with our system would be to modulate the two focal points at different frequencies. Frequency JND (just-noticeable-difference) thresholds have found that the hand is able to discriminate between 12% to 25% difference in frequencies, and the amount of this difference depends on the reference frequency [2]. The hand is able to perceive the differences since vibration thresholds vary with frequency as different mechanoreceptors are activated [14].

Participants

A total of 9 participants (3 females and 6 males) aged between 23 and 30 years (mean 27.9, SD 4.1) took part in the study. The experiment lasted for about 60 minutes and consisted of 112 trials. Participants were recruited from within the university.

Procedure

We used the system to create either zero, one or two focal points. All the focal points were created at a set height of 200mm above the transducer array. The focal points consisted of modulation frequencies set at 4, 16, 63 or 250 Hz. When there was one focal point, it would be randomly created at locations A, B or C (see Figure 8a) which was set at a distance of either 1 or 2 cm away from the centre of the array. There were 8 conditions of one focal point (two at each frequency).

When there were two focal points, they would be created at locations A and B with a separation of *d* cm between the edges of both focal points (see Figure 8b). The factors of each focal point were: *frequencies - 4, 16, 63, 250 Hz*; *location - A, B*. We carried out a full-factorial design resulting a total of 20 frequency pairs. We repeated all 20 pairs for focal point separations (*d*) of 1, 2, 3, 4 and 5 cm giving a total of 100 two-point trials.

We also added 4 trials of the zero focal point condition. All the conditions were presented in a random order to all the participants.

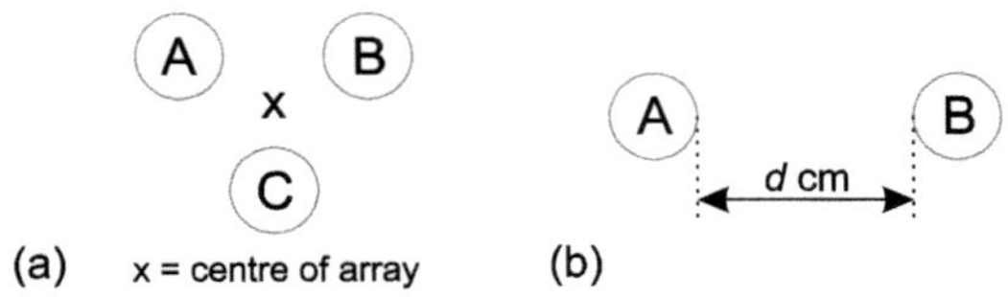

Figure 8: (a) Positions of one focal point condition - A, B or C (b) Separation of *d* cm between edges of two focal points.

The system was set-up using the perforated sheet with 0.5 mm diameter and 25% open space as the display surface. There was no visual feedback provided by the system as it was used without any projection on its surface. Three guides were installed by the side of the system at a height of 200mm to help the participants judge the where to put their hands.

All participants went through a 5-minute practise before the experiment started to make sure that they understood the instructions. They were not prompted if they incorrectly judged the number or the type of focal points in one of the trials as we wanted to test the system in a 'walk-up and use' scenario. Following the practice, participants were asked if they had any questions regarding the study, otherwise they proceeded with the experiment. There were five two-minute breaks during the experiment, at every 20th-trial interval, to allow participants to rest their hands.

Participants were asked to only use their dominant hand during the entire experiment. They were instructed to judge the number of focal points of air pressure created by the system. The participants would start each trial by positioning their hand, at the height of the guides, above the ultrasound transducer array. They were then informed to move their hand anywhere along the horizontal plane to find the focal points. If they felt two focal points, they were asked to report if both the focal points felt the same or different. When the focal points felt different, they were asked to report the point they felt was faster and the point they felt was slower. They were allowed a maximum of one minute to explore, however they never exceeded this time. White noise was played throughout the experiment to mask any audio cues to the participants.

Results

We measured the percentage accuracy that the participants correctly identified the zero, one and two focal point conditions. For the zero focal point conditions, all the participants had an accuracy of 100% (4 out of 4 trials each). For the one focal point conditions, 7 participants had an accuracy of 100% each (8 out of 8) and two participants had an accuracy of 87.5% each (7 out of 8).

Figure 9 shows that participants were able to perceive 2 focal points better if the focal points were of different frequencies. At a separation distance of 3 cm, the mean accuracy of perceiving 2 focal points when the focal points were of different modulation frequencies was 86% (about 10 out of 12) compared to 31% (2.5 out of 8) when the focal points were of the same modulation frequency.

To analyse their ability to discriminate 2 separate focal points, we applied a repeated measures ANOVA with a Greenhouse-

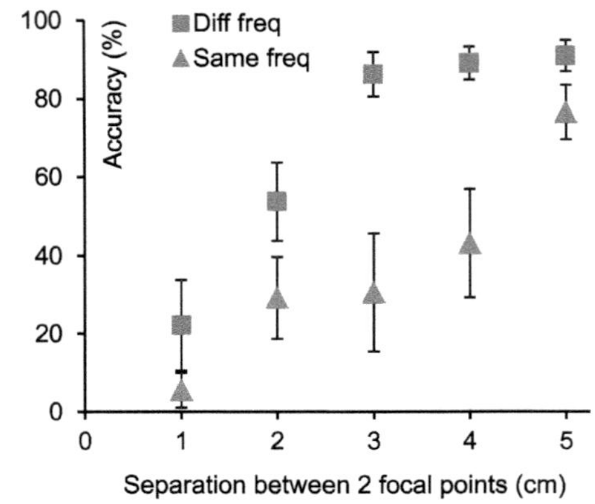

Figure 9: Percentage accuracy of 2-point discrimination when using focal points with the same modulation frequencies and different modulation frequencies (error-bars denote standard error).

Geisser correction on the percentage of correctly identified focal points. We found that there were significant differences in increasing the separation between 2 focal points when both points were of the same modulation frequency ($F_{(4, 32)} = 15.236$, $p < 0.001$) and when both focal points were of different frequencies ($F_{(4, 32)} = 45.416$, $p < 0.001$).

When comparing the results between focal points of the same frequency and focal points of different frequencies, we found that the accuracy of detecting two focal points at separation distances of 2, 3, 4 and 5 cm were significantly higher ($p \leq 0.041$). At 1 cm separation, we found no statistically differences in the results ($p = 0.071$).

It is useful to highlight the differences between this study and that in [1] to avoid the direct comparison of results. The study in [1] consisted of 4 focal points in fixed positions and with constant tactile properties. The participant identified whether each point was on or off and scored out of 4 for each condition. As such, identifying the presence of a single focal point in a condition with two focal points was considered 75% accurate. In our study, the modulation frequency, number and location of the focal points were all varied. Any answer other than the correct number of focal points is considered 0% accurate.

Identifying the frequency of the focal points

From the first study, we found a trend in the ability to identify focal points as being different for certain frequency pairs at distance of 3, 4 and 5 cm. If participants were able to tell the difference between two focal points which are modulated at different frequencies, then different meanings could be assigned to each point.

We decided to perform a second study to test for the participants ability to identify the frequency of the focal points when there are two focal points.

Participants

A total of 4 participants (1 female and 3 males) aged between 23 and 30 years (mean 26.8, SD 3.8) took part in the study.

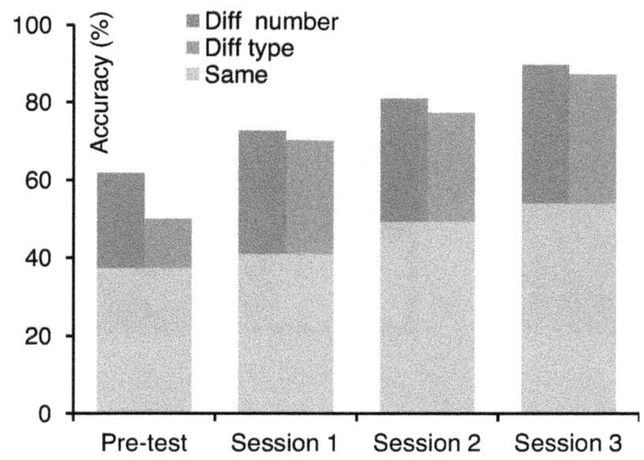

Figure 10: Percentage accuracy of identifying if 2 focal points were of the same frequency (same), were of two different frequencies (diff number) and the type of frequency when there were two different frequencies (diff type).

For each session, the experiment lasted less than 20 minutes and consisted of 42 trials.

Procedure

The second study setup was similar to the first study. All the conditions were two focal points created at a set height of 200mm above the transducer array. We chose to test pairs of 4-63, 4-250, 16-250 Hz and their respective mirrored pairs at separation distances of 3, 4 and 5 cm. We also added two same frequency pairs each of 4, 16, 63 and 250 Hz at all three separation distance making a total of 14 frequency pairs per separation distance.

This time, all the participants went through a 10-minute training before the first session of the experiment. The participants were prompted if they answered incorrectly and were told the correct answer to reinforce learning. There was one 2-minute break in the middle of each session to allow participants to rest their hands.

There were a total of 3 sessions. The first session consisted of the 10-minute training followed by the experiment. This was conducted in the afternoon of Day 1. The second and third sessions were both conducted in the morning and afternoon of Day 2, but with no training before the experiment. During the experiment, the participants were informed after each trial if they were correct or incorrect, but were not told the answer.

Results

Figure 10 shows that participants got better at identifying focal points and determining the frequency of the focal points with training and time. The overall percentage accuracy for correctly identifying the frequency for each focal point increased from a mean of 50% without any training to 88% in Session 3.

DESIGNING APPLICATIONS

Based on the results of our technical evaluations and user studies, we explored the unique interaction possibilities provided by multi-point, above screen haptic feedback. We focused on three areas and created an application for each.

Mid-air Gestures

Currently, mid-air gestures suffer from a decoupling of the user's hands from the interface. Users are solely reliant on audio and visual feedback to determine whether their gesture has been successful. Gesture based interactions are therefore often limited to broad, sweeping movements. With our system, individual feedback can be targeted to each finger or hand involved in the gesture, giving the user a greater sense of control and enabling more reserved motions. In Figure 11 left, a two-finger pinch is used to zoom into an image. A focal point is created on each of the thumb and active finger and the difference in modulation frequency between the two grows as they are moved apart.

Tactile Information Layers

Tactile feedback has previously been employed to provide a layer of non-visual information to a touch screen. However, receiving this feedback requires covering the visual information. By moving the tactile layer into the air above the display, the user can receive both forms of information at the same time. For example, while browsing a map, population density can be projected as a heat map in the air above (Figure 11 centre).

Visually Restricted Displays

There are many scenarios where it is not possible to have visual contact with the display, such as while driving or if the user is visually impaired. In these cases, mid-air haptic feedback can be used to guide the user to the location of an interface element. This is of particular benefit with movable elements, such as sliders, as the user will not be able to learn their position. Figure 11 right, shows the interface for a music player. A strong focal point locates the user's finger above the main controls while a lower intensity point is projected above the volume slider. The user is able to tap on the first focal point to toggle playing or pausing the music and can grab and drag the second point to change the volume.

CONCLUSIONS

This paper introduced a new method for providing multi-point, mid-air haptic feedback above a touch surface. Through technical evaluations, we have demonstrated that the system is capable of creating individual points of feedback that are far beyond the perception threshold of the human hand. We have also established the desirable properties of a display surface that is transparent to 40kHz ultrasound. The results of two user studies demonstrate that feedback points with different tactile properties can be distinguished at smaller separations. It was also shown that users are able to identify different tactile properties with training. Finally, we discussed the new interaction possibilities afforded by the *UltraHaptics* system.

ACKNOWLEDGEMENTS

This work is supported by the European Research Council (Starting Grant Agreement 278576) under the Seventh Framework Programme and by EPSRC (EP/J004448/1) through its responsive mode funding scheme.

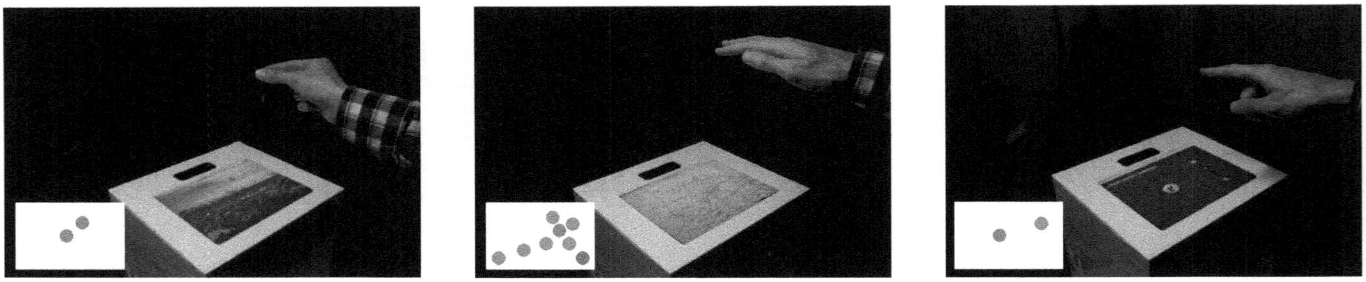

Figure 11: Applications using the UltraHaptics system. Inserts depict focal point locations with different colours representing different tactile properties. Left: a pinch-to-zoom gesture in a photo application. Centre: a tactile information layer conveying population density. Right: a jukebox application with focal points to guide the user to interface elements.

REFERENCES

1. Alexander, J., Marshall, M. T., and Subramanian, S. Adding haptic feedback to mobile tv. In *Ext. Abstracts CHI 2011*, ACM Press (2011), 1975–1980.
2. Bau, O., Poupyrev, I., Israr, A., and Harrison, C. Teslatouch: electrovibration for touch surfaces. In *Proc. UIST 2010*, ACM Press (2010), 283–292.
3. Berkelman, P. J., Butler, Z. J., and Hollis, R. L. Design of a hemispherical magnetic levitation haptic interface device. In *Proc. ASME HAPTICS 1996* (1996), 17–22.
4. Biet, M., Giraud, F., and Lemaire-Semail, B. Implementation of tactile feedback by modifying the perceived friction. *The European Physical Journal Applied Physics 43* (2008), 123–135.
5. Dalecki, D., Child, S., Raeman, C., and Carstensen, E. Tactile perception of ultrasound. *J. Acoust. Soc. Am. 97* (1995), 3165–3170.
6. Ebbini, E. S., and Cain, C. a. Multiple-focus ultrasound phased-array pattern synthesis: optimal driving-signal distributions for hyperthermia. *IEEE T. Ultrason. Ferr. 36*, 5 (1989), 540–548.
7. Filonenko, E. A., Gavrilov, L. R., Khokhlova, V. A., and Hand, J. W. Heating of biological tissues by two-dimensional phased arrays with random and regular element distributions. *Acoust. Phys. 50*, 2 (2004), 222–231.
8. Fukuhara, S., Kageyama, S., Tai, Y., and Yoshida, K. An acoustically transparent screen. *J. Audio Eng. Soc 42*, 12 (1994), 1020–1023.
9. Gavrilov, L. Use of focused ultrasound for stimulation of nerve structures. *Ultrasonics 22*, 3 (1984), 132 – 138.
10. Gavrilov, L. The possibility of generating focal regions of complex configurations in application to the problems of stimulation of human receptor structures by focused ultrasound. *Acoust. Phys. 54* (2008), 269–278.
11. Gavrilov, L., and Tsirulnikov, E. Mechanisms of Stimulation Effects of Focused Ultrasound on Neural Structures: Role of Nonlinear Effects. *Nonlinear Acoust. at the Beginning of the 21st Cent.* (2002), 445–448.
12. Gavrilov, L., and Tsirulnikov, E. Focused ultrasound as a tool to input sensory information to humans (review). *Acoust. Phys. 58* (2012), 1–21.
13. Gavrilov, L. R., Gersuni, G. V., Ilyinski, O. B., Tsirulnikov, E. M., and Shchekanov, E. E. A Study of Reception with the Use of Focused Ultrasound. I. Effects on the Skin and Deep Receptor Structures in Man. *Brain Research 135*, 2 (1977), 265–277.
14. Gescheider, G. A., Bolanowski, S. J., Pope, J. V., and Verrillo, R. T. A four-channel analysis of the tactile sensitivity of the fingertip: frequency selectivity, spatial summation, and temporal summation. *Somatosensory & Motor Research 19*, 2 (2002), 114–124.
15. Harrison, C., and Hudson, S. E. Providing dynamically changeable physical buttons on a visual display. In *Proc. CHI 2009*, ACM Press (2009), 299–308.
16. Hoshi, T. Development of aerial-input and aerial-tactile-feedback system. In *World Haptics Conference, 2011 IEEE* (2011), 569–573.
17. Hoshi, T., Takahashi, M., Iwamoto, T., and Shinoda, H. Noncontact tactile display based on radiation pressure of airborne ultrasound. *IEEE Transactions on Haptics 3*, 3 (2010), 155 –165.
18. Iwamoto, T., Tatezono, M., and Shinoda, H. Non-contact method for producing tactile sensation using airborne ultrasound. In *Proc. EuroHaptics 2008*, Springer-Verlag (2008), 504–513.
19. Iwata, H., Yano, H., Nakaizumi, F., and Kawamura, R. Project feelex: adding haptic surface to graphics. In *Proc. SIGGRAPH 2001*, ACM Press (2001), 469–476.
20. Jansen, Y., Karrer, T., and Borchers, J. Mudpad: localized tactile feedback on touch surfaces. In *Adj. Proc. UIST 2010*, ACM Press (2010), 385–386.
21. Johnson, K. O. The roles and functions of cutaneous mechanoreceptors. *Current Opinion in Neurobiology 11*, 4 (2001), 455–461.
22. Johnson, K. O., and Phillips, J. R. Tactile spatial resolution. i. two-point discrimination, gap detection, grating resolution, and letter recognition. *Journal of Neurophysiology 46*, 6 (1981), 1177–1192.
23. Lee, J. C., Dietz, P. H., Leigh, D., Yerazunis, W. S., and Hudson, S. E. Haptic pen: a tactile feedback stylus for touch screens. In *Proc. UIST 2004*, ACM Press (2004), 291–294.
24. Liu, Z., Zhang, X., Mao, Y., Zhu, Y. Y., Yang, Z., Chan, C. T., and Sheng, P. Locally Resonant Sonic Materials. *Science 289*, 5485 (2000), 1734–1736.
25. Marshall, M., Carter, T., Alexander, J., and Subramanian, S. Ultra-tangibles: creating movable tangible objects on interactive tables. In *Proc. CHI 2012*, ACM Press (2012), 2185–2188.
26. Massie, T. H., and Salisbury, K. J. Phantom haptic interface: a device for probing virtual objects. vol. 55-1 of *Proc. ASME 1994*, ASME (1994), 295–299.
27. Obrist, M., Seah, S. A., and Subramanian, S. Talking about tactile experiences. In *Proc. CHI 2013*, ACM Press (2013), 1659–1668.
28. Pendry, J. Negative refraction makes a perfect lens. *Physical Review Letters 85*, 18 (Oct. 2000), 3966–3969.
29. Perez, C., Holzmann, C., and Jaeschke, H. Two-point vibrotactile discrimination related to parameters of pulse burst stimulus. *Medical and Biological Engineering and Computing 38*, 1 (2000), 74–79.
30. Rekimoto, J. Senseablerays: opto-haptic substitution for touch-enhanced interactive spaces. In *Ext. Absstracts CHI 2009*, ACM Press (2009), 2519–2528.
31. Wakatsuki, T., and Fukunishi, T. Acoustical characteristics of a sound screen for hdtv. In *Audio Engineering Society Convention 95* (10 1993).
32. Weiss, M., Wacharamanotham, C., Voelker, S., and Borchers, J. Fingerflux: near-surface haptic feedback on tabletops. In *Proc. UIST 2011*, ACM Press (2011), 615–620.
33. Wusheng, C., Tianmiao, W., and Lei, H. Design of data glove and arm type haptic interface. In *Proc. HAPTICS 2003* (2003), 422 – 427.

Good Vibrations: An Evaluation of Vibrotactile Impedance Matching for Low Power Wearable Applications

Jack I.C. Lindsay[1,2], Iris Jiang[1], Eric Larson[2], Richard Adams[3], Shwetak N. Patel[2], Blake Hannaford[1]

[1]BioRobotics Lab
[2]Ubicomp Lab
University of Washington
Seattle, WA
{JackICL, IJiang, ECLarson, Shwetak, Blake}@uw.edu

[3]Barron Associates
Charlottesville, VA
{Adams}@barron-associates.com

ABSTRACT
Vibrotactile devices suffer from poor energy efficiency, arising from a mismatch between the device and the impedance of the human skin. This results in over-sized actuators and excessive power consumption, and prevents development of more sophisticated, miniaturized and low-power mobile tactile devices. In this paper, we present the experimental evaluation of a vibrotactile system designed to match the impedance of the skin to the impedance of the actuator. This system is able to quadruple the motion of the skin without increasing power consumption, and produce sensations equivalent to a standard system while consuming 2/3 of the power. By greatly reducing the size and power constraints of vibrotactile actuators, this technology offers a means to realize more sophisticated, smaller haptic devices for the user interface community.

ACM Classification:
H.5.2 [Information interfaces and presentation]: User Interfaces. – Haptic I/O.

Author Keywords
Haptics; Vibrotactile; Vibration Motors

INTRODUCTION
Vibrotacile actuators are used ubiquitously for haptic feedback—they are built into every smartphone and modern game controller and are used for everything from notification to tactile feedback. Most vibrotactile actuators accelerate a mass back and forth at high frequency to produce vibration. These actuators offer a simple means of conveying tactile cues to users, and can be built into large arrays for more sophisticated haptic rendering [1], [2]. However, the perceptibility of haptic sensations is limited by the size of the vibrating mass, and consequently, the

ACM 978-1-4503-2268-3/13/10...$15.00.
http://dx.doi.org/10.1145/2501988.2502051

Figure 1. The prototype impedance adapter in test setup for displacement measurement.

power consumption required to move that mass. This means that miniaturized haptic feedback systems and power-limited mobile devices can only produce a fraction of the possible haptic sensations afforded by vibrotactile actuators.

Overcoming these limitations requires shrinking actuators and cutting power consumption. Unfortunately, vibrotactile devices are fundamentally constrained by the skin's vibrotactile threshold, or the threshold below which vibrations are imperceptible. Surpassing the vibrotactile threshold places constraints on the minimum size of the motor mass and its acceleration. Moreover, as the number of actuators and vibration levels increases, these systems require even more power and size. Because of the relationship between perception, vibration, and power, researchers have recently attempted to maximize transmission of energy from the actuator to the skin.

For instance, Jiang *et al.* use an elastic support structure to manage the load to the motor [2] and increase skin displacement. This system is appropriate for applications like lower leg prosthetics, but is not suitable for tactile stimulation of the hands and fingers in mobile devices because the system requires a large surrounding structure.

In our system, we adopt the theoretical framework of [3], which describes the design of an impedance adapter for optimizing the energy transfer to the skin from a vibrotactile actuator (*i.e.*, using a small motor with minimal

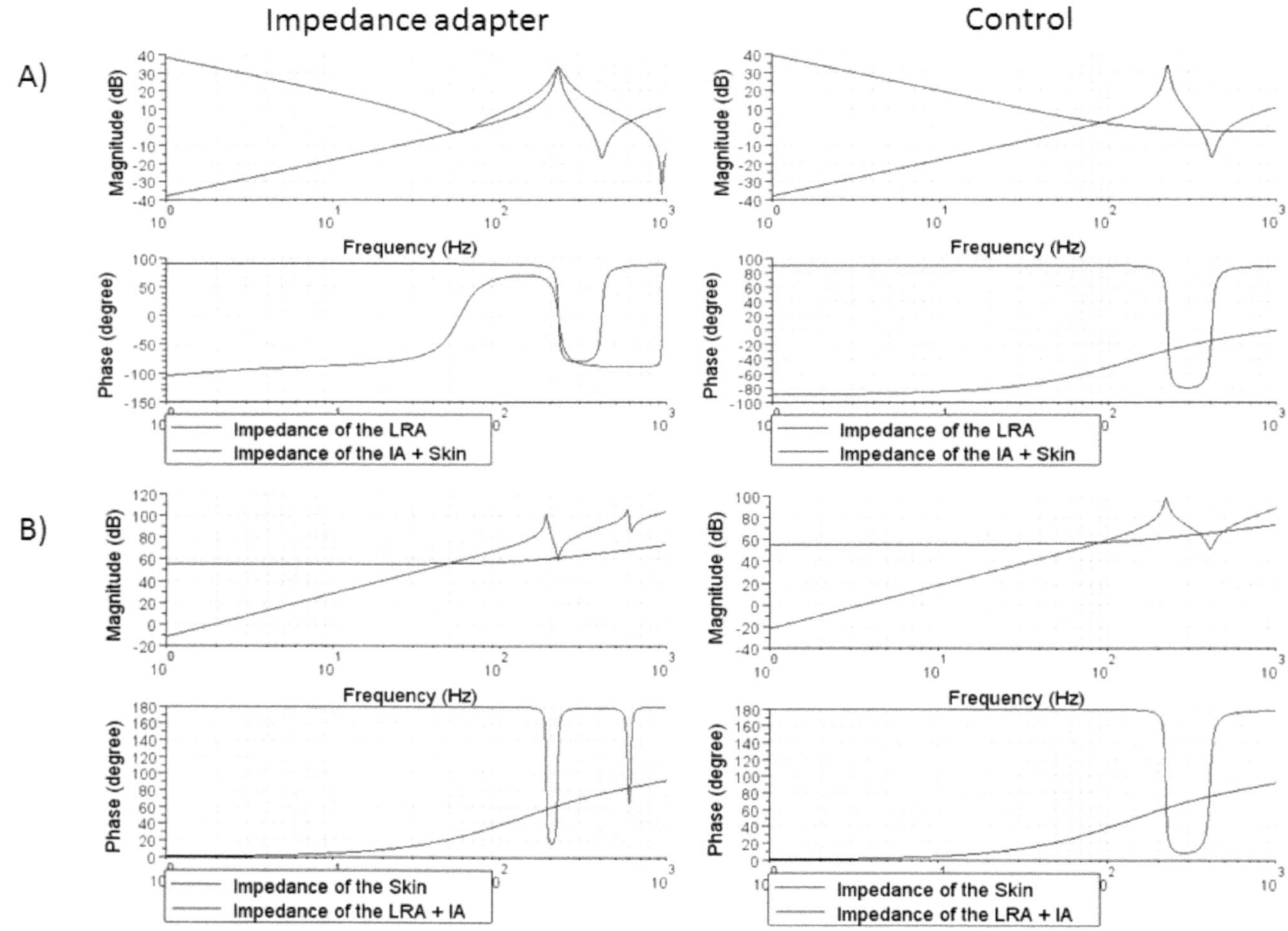

Figure 2. Bode plots of the impedance of different elements of the system. A) Impedance at the interface of the LRA and impedance adapter. B) Impedance at the interface of the impedance adapter and skin. Modeling of the impedance of the control system is performed by setting IA parameters such that it appears as a rigid, massless sheet without damping.

power input). The impedance adapter works in series with the actuator (*i.e.*, it can be worn on the finger or embedded underneath the actuator). This is in contrast to Jiang *et al.* who required the structure around the motor. Applications for this technology include virtual and augmented reality gloves with increased dexterity, rendering fine textures on touch surfaces, and increased haptic capability in numerous mobile devices. The impedance adapter offers a means to greatly miniaturize the size and power of vibrotactile feedback without sacrificing functionality.

In this paper, we describe the implementation of a working prototype and an empirical evaluation of our prototype system with eight users. Our device consists of a mass and spring that match the impedance of the skin to the impedance of the actuator. Our results show a significant decrease in power consumption, and our adapter can generate a four-fold increase in skin displacement. Furthermore, our system can generate vibration on the skin that is perceptually equivalent to a system without an impedance adapter at two-thirds the power—thus increasing the range of haptic sensation in small, wearable devices.

Our contributions are two-fold. We present:

1. A physical prototype of a haptics impedance adapter that is informed by the mathematical model described in [3].

2. An empirical evaluation of the device quantifying skin displacement and the perceived haptic sensation.

Our system places energy transfer as a major priority in haptic design, and stands as a first round prototype in a field that could continue to lead to smaller haptic devices.

THEORY OF OPERATION

In typical operation, vibrotactile actuators supply energy to the skin by producing waves of force directly at the skin's surface. These waves interact with the impedance of the skin, and are either absorbed into the skin through damping or reflected back off. In existing systems, the skin's impedance is significantly different from that of the actuator, and large amounts of energy are reflected backwards and lost, and therefore do not contribute to perception.

The impedance adapter works as a matching network that takes the waves of vibration from the actuator and conditions them to match the impedance of the skin. The matching network has an impedance which matches both the LRA and the skin at their respective interfaces at the operating frequency, as shown in figure 2. This greatly reduces energy reflection, increasing energy absorption and resulting in greater perception. See [3] for a summary of the impedance modeling.

PROTOTYPE AND IMPLEMENTATION DETAILS

Two prototypes were created with different contact areas. This was because simulation results from [3] indicate that maximum displacement is achieved using a contact area of 1 mm^2, while maximum sensation was achieved using a contact area of 64 mm^2. Both impedance adapters include a Precision Microdrives C-10 linear resonant actuator (LRA), a steel compression spring, a plastic base, steel dowel pins, and elastic band 1.25cm wide (see Figure 3). The steel compression spring was cut to length from stock, and its new spring constant was measured. The plastic base was 3D printed and included a mount for the dowel pins, spring, and elastic band. Furthermore, the base had a carefully measured area in contact with the skin. Impedance adapter 1 (IA#1) had a contact area of 64 mm^2 and impedance adapter 2 (IA#2) had a contact area of 1 mm^2. Both plastic bases were fitted with two dowel pins, and weighed 4.6g including the pins.

The complete assembly consisted of the LRA, spring, and base in series with the skin as shown in Figure 3. The elastic band was sewn to the base and wrapped around the finger.

Based on [3] we hypothesized that IA#1 would increase perceived sensation by a factor of 2.5 and IA#2 would produce a four-fold increase in skin displacement.

EXPERIMENTAL EVALUATION

We designed two experiments that evaluated (1) the skin displacement between an impedance adapter and a control and (2) the power requirements for the impedance adapters to provide equivalent perceived sensation as compared to a vibrotactile control.

Skin Displacement

In this evaluation we measured the movement of the skin in response to the actuator with and without the impedance adapter. Skin displacement was measured using a Keyence IL-030 laser distance sensor, which provides a resolution of 0.001mm.

Experiment. In the control condition the laser was focused on the top of the LRA, with the finger directly in contact with the LRA. The finger was assumed to be in constant contact with the LRA. When the impedance adapter was present, the laser was focused on the plastic base sitting directly on the skin. The base was again assumed to be in constant contact with the skin. The base was thick enough that any flex was assumed to be small in comparison to the oscillation of the system, see Figure 1.

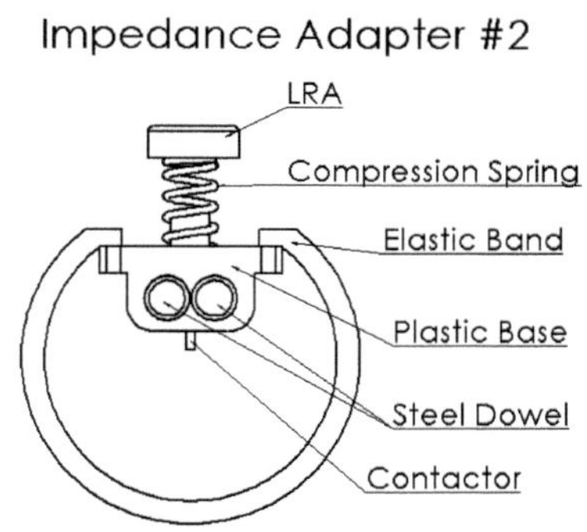

Figure 3. Schematic diagram of an impedance adapter and LRA. The finger is placed through the loop of the elastic band.

In all conditions, the vibrating system was held in contact with the skin using an elastic band. The elastic was sized to loosely hold the system in place, and designed to minimize static pressure against the fingerpad. Paper shims were used to ensure the oversized band fit evenly across participants. The band experienced very little stretch when properly shimmed, and most of the static pressure on the skin was a result of the weight of the impedance adapter and LRA. With a total mass of 7.5g the impedance adapter system produced a gravitational force on the finger of 0.06N, resulting in a displacement of ~0.75mm. However, this displacement should not affect the properties of the finger—other studies have found that this level of static pressure has a minimal effect on the mechanical impedance of the fingertip [4]. Furthermore, work by Lamore and Keemink found no difference in the vibrotactile threshold at high frequencies between static loading conditions [5]. Thus the gravitational force should have no effect on the experiments.

Skin displacement was measured using a stock LRA, an LRA with a 1.1 mm^2 contact area, and both impedance adapters. Eight subjects (four female, four male) were tested in all four conditions, three trials per condition. All tests were conducted using the participant's index finger. The study was approved by the University of Washington Human Subjects Division, approval #44695. The data from the distance sensor were band-pass filtered in the frequency range of interest (20-500Hz) to remove hand tremor and high frequency noise. We then calculated the root-mean-square (RMS) skin displacement for each trial using the filtered data.

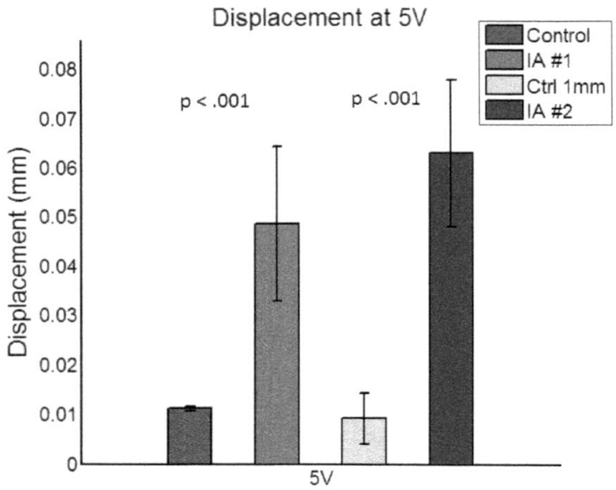

Figure 4: (A) RMS skin displacement for a contactor with a radius >4.5mm. (B) RMS skin displacement for a contactor with a radius of 1mm

Result. IA#1 and IA#2 were able to significantly increase skin displacement as compared to a stock LRA by a factor of 3.26 and 4.25 on average, respectively (based on a paired t-test, $p<0.001$). The mean RMS displacement and standard deviation for all conditions is shown in figure 4.

Implication. Simulations in [3] expected IA#2 to outperform the stock LRA by a factor of 4.40 which is remarkably close to the empirical finding of a 4.25x improvement. IA#1 fared even better than simulation, with an expected improvement of 2.28x and a measured improvement of 3.26x. This demonstrates an error in the model in [3], and suggests that mechanical stiffness and damping do not increase as a 1/3 power law of contact area.

Previous studies in psychophysics have demonstrated that displacement is proportional to sensation, all else being held equal [7]. Thus, doubling displacement will double sensation. With these large gains in skin displacement, we also set out to measure the perceived sensation of these gains in a controlled user study.

Equivalent Perception

All eight subjects also participated in a perceptual equivalence test. Each subject wore the stock LRA on their right index finger. This was used as the reference. On the left index finger, subjects wore one of the four test conditions: a stock LRA, an LRA with $1.1mm^2$ contact area, IA#1, or IA#2. Subjects were instructed to try and match the vibration level felt on the left finger with the vibration felt on the reference finger.

Experiment. The actuators were driven by two separate power supplies. The experimenter would set the voltage of the reference actuator to 1 of 5 settings (1V, 2V, 3V, 4V, or 5V), and provide ~1sec bursts of vibration to both actuators at the same time. Both actuators vibrated at a constant frequency of 175Hz. Subjects would tell the experimenter whether they felt the voltage of the test actuator should be

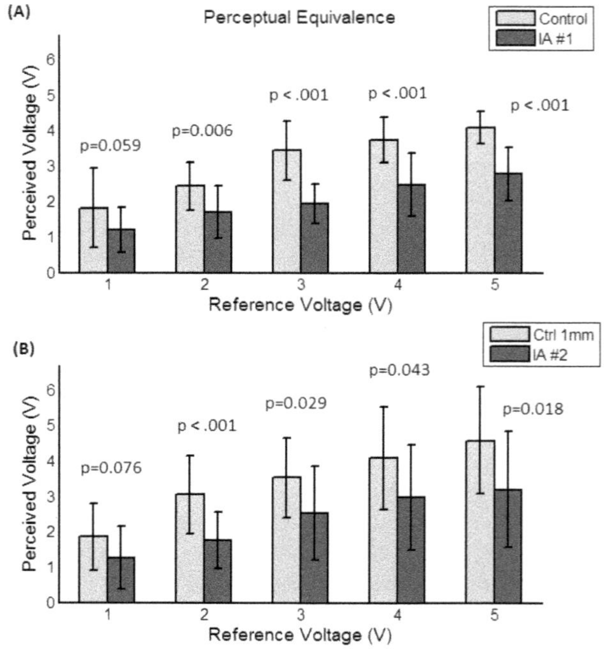

Figure 5. Subjects adjust voltage levels on an LRA on one index finger to match the vibration sensed from an LRA on the other index finger. (A) Shows tests with a large radius, (B) shows tests with a smaller radius.

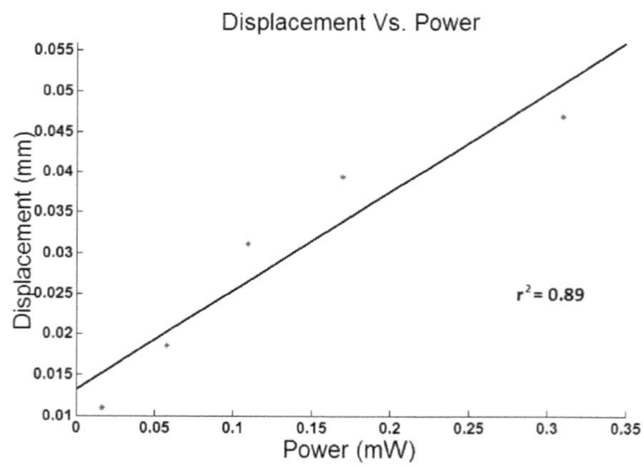

Figure 6: Linearity of the LRA and impedance adapter at power levels.

higher or lower, and the experimenter would adjust the voltage of the test actuator until the subject perceived both actuators to feel the same. Subjects wore earmuffs to block the sound of the vibration and were positioned so they could not see the voltage readings on the power supplies.

Each of the four test conditions was presented in random order. Each voltage level within a test condition was also presented in a random order. It condition consisted of 10 trials (2 trials per voltage level).

Result. The results of the perceptual equivalence study are shown below in figure 5. Figure 5 (A) compares IA#1 to the LRA with the same $64mm^2$ contact area. Figure 5 (B) compares IA#2 to the LRA with the same $1mm^2$ contact area. The results show that subjects set the test voltage 35% lower on average for IA#1 and 32% lower on average for IA#2 than the reference voltage applied to a stock LRA. There was no statistically significant difference between the reference voltages and the test voltages for either control condition.

Subjects' evaluation of equivalent voltage settings varied between low reference voltages and high reference voltages. With a 1V reference, it was not clear whether subjects could distinguish between a system with an impedance adapter and a system without. In both conditions, however, subjects could distinguish between the two systems when the reference voltage was 2V or higher, and subjects applied a significantly lower voltage to the system with an impedance adapter ($p < 0.05$).

Implication. In all cases, the voltage for the system with an impedance adapter was set at approximately 66% of the voltage for the system without an impedance adapter. This suggests that an impedance adapter can be used to lower power consumption by 55% while maintained an equivalent psychophysical sensation. Even so, this is a lower percentage than might be expected based on psychophysical tests by [7], who found a linear relationship between depth of indentation and stimulation. This suggests that the four-fold increase in skin displacement should have resulted in a 75% drop in equivalent power, given a linear relationship between power and displacement.

This difference could be attributed to subjects' inability to discriminate between small changes in voltage level [8]. For instance, when adjusting voltage levels to be equivalent, if the voltage was initially low, the subject would generally say to stop adjusting the voltage at a lower level. If the voltage was initially set high, then the subject would say to stop at a higher voltage. Thus, "equivalence" in our experiments may be artificially high—the true equivalence level for minimizing the power could be ascertained by always adjusting the voltage level up from a lower voltage.

However, the difference could also be attributed to non-linear dynamics in the LRA and impedance adapter at low power levels. To test this latter hypothesis, two subjects participated in a skin displacement test using IA#1 as input voltage was swept from 1V to 5V. The results are shown in Figure 6, illustrating a linear relationship between power and displacement. Thus, the discrepancy in theorized power reduction and actual power reduction is not due to non-linearity in the LRA. It is more likely due to the "resolution" at which subjects could perceive the vibrotactile sensation. Therefore we believe these results show a "worst case" power reduction. The possible power savings are likely much greater than 55% (and might be as high as the theorized 75%).

MINIATURIZATION

The current prototypes are quite large, requiring significantly more volume than a vibrotactile actuator alone. The prototypes, however, are just one realization of the model developed in [3], designed to evaluate whether the simulation results showing improved skin displacement holds up in the real world. The four parameters upon which they are designed could be realized in a much smaller package with a membrane spring and dense masses. Physical constraints allow the design to shrink to less than half the volume of the LRA while still maintaining proper characteristics.

CONCLUSION

Empirical testing of our prototype impedance adapters has demonstrated the significant improvement they offer over a typical system. By matching the impedance of the skin to signal from the actuator, it is possible to greater improve skin displacement—up to a four-fold. We were also able to show the "worst case" power reduction was 55%. In the future, we will make the prototype even smaller as the properties of the impedance adapter depend only on the stiffness of the spring and the mass of the base.

REFERENCES

1. Zelek, J. S., Bromley, S., Asmar, D., & Thompson, D. (2003). A haptic glove as a tactile-vision sensory substitution for wayfinding. *Journal of Visual Impairment and Blindness*, 97(10), 621-632.
2. Jiang, I., Ishikawa, Y., Lindsay, J., Hannaford, B. Design and Optimization of Support Structures for Tactile Feedback, *IEEE World Haptics Conference*, Daejeon, Korea, 2013, In Press.
3. Lindsay, J., Adams, R., and Hannaford, B., Improving Tactile Feedback with an Impedance Adapter, *IEEE World Haptics Conference*, Daejeon, Korea, 2013.
4. Precision MicroDrives, www.precisionmicrodrives.com
5. Moore, T. J., & Mundie, J. R. (1972). Measurement of specific mechanical impedance of the skin: Effects of static force, site of stimulation, area of probe, and presence of a surround. *The Journal of the Acoustical Society of America*, 52, 577.
6. Lamoré, P. J. J., & Keemink, C. J. (1988). Evidence for different types of mechanoreceptors from measurements of the psychophysical threshold for vibrations under different stimulation conditions. *JASA*, 83, 2339.
7. Verrillo, R. T., Fraioli, A. J., & Smith, R. L. (1969). Sensation magnitude of vibrotactile stimuli. *Perception & Psychophysics*, 6(6), 366-372.
8. Gescheider, G. A., Bolanowski, S. J., Hardick, K.R., (2001). The frequency selectivity of information-processing channels in the tactile sensory system. *Somatosensory & Motor Research*, 18(3), 191-201.

The Skweezee System: Enabling the Design and the Programming of Squeeze Interactions

Karen Vanderloock[1,2], Vero Vanden Abeele[1,3], Johan A.K. Suykens[2], Luc Geurts[1,2]

[1]e-Media Lab, Group T
Leuven Engineering College
Vesaliusstraat 13
3000 Leuven, Belgium
{karen.vanderloock,
vero.vanden.abeele,
luc.geurts}@groept.be

[2]KU Leuven
ESAT-SCD
and iMinds Future Health
Departement, Leuven, Belgium
Kasteelpark Arenberg 10
3001 Heverlee, Belgium
johan.suykens@esat.kuleuven.be

[3]CUO | Social Spaces
iMinds/KU Leuven
Parkstraat 45
3000 Leuven, Belgium

ABSTRACT
The Skweezee System is an easy, flexible and open system for designing and developing squeeze-based, gestural interactions. It consists of Skweezees, which are soft objects, filled with conductive padding, that can be deformed or squeezed by applying pressure. These objects contain a number of electrodes that are dispersed over the shape. The electrodes sense the shape shifting of the conductive filling by measuring the changing resistance between every possible pair of electrodes. In addition, the Skweezee System contains user-friendly software that allows end-users to define and to record their own squeeze gestures. These gestures are distinguished using a Support Vector Machine (SVM) classifier. In this paper we introduce the concept and the underlying technology of the Skweezee System and we demonstrate the robustness of the SVM based classifier via two experimental user studies. The results of these studies demonstrate accuracies of 81% (8 gestures, user-defined) to 97% (3 gestures, user-defined), with an accuracy of 90% for 7 pre-defined gestures.

Author Keywords
Soft User Interface; Tangible Interaction; Gesture Recognition; Support Vector Machines; Electronic Textiles

ACM Classification Keywords
H.5.2 Information Interfaces and Presentation

INTRODUCTION
Ever since Marc Weiser unleashed his vision of Ubiquitous Computing [31] as computing "weaved into the fabric of our everyday life", this has encouraged HCI researchers to explore how to enrich every day, mundane objects with computation. In particular, tangible interaction has focused on augmenting computing systems with graspable objects [6,29], that can be manipulated in a similar way as non-computing objects, e.g. lifting, rotating or relocating objects on interactive surfaces. Via embedding a myriad of sensors, via the addition of advanced signal processing and computing, ubiquitous computing becomes 'embodied' or part of our everyday interaction [5,10]. In addition to the classical tangible tabletops enriched with graspable widgets [e.g. 12,28], in the past years, a high number of research projects embedded computation in the objects themselves, not relying on larger surfaces [e.g. 4,21,23].

In the past decade, we also witnessed the introduction of electronic textiles in human-computer interaction [1,2]. The goal is to create computing technologies that are entirely fabric based, and can be worn, washed, dried and folded as normal fabrics. E-textiles have been embraced by the wider "do-it-yourself" (DIY) community, not in the least by publications by Buechley and the workshops/website by Perner-Wilson et al. [2,18,20], who set forth the goal to make a library of materials and techniques available that can form the foundation of DIY electronic textiles.

With the Skweezee System, we combine the idea of making interactive devices of everyday objects with the technology and aspiration of electronic textiles. The System contains both a tangible object and an algorithm. The Skweezees are soft tangible objects, filled with conductive padding. When squeezing (by applying pressure with hands or other body parts) the Skweezee is deformed. In order to detect and discriminate specific deformations, the Skweezee contains (soft) electrodes that are dispersed over the shape (eight electrodes in our prototypes). By measuring the resistance between any pair of electrodes, a number is obtained that is related to the magnitude of deformation between those electrodes. For every deformation, a different pattern of measurements is obtained, which allows the computer to distinguish different deformations. Figure 1 shows several potential candidates for Skweezees, ranging from small objects held and squeezed in one hand, to shapes inviting bimanual interaction or even full-body interaction. In essence, any 'soft' object is a candidate for becoming a Skweezee, by replacing the original stuffing with conductive filling, and inserting the desired number of electrical wires which function as electrodes.

UIST'13, October 8–11, 2013, St. Andrews, United Kingdom.

http://dx.doi.org/10.1145/2501988.2502033

The Skweezee System also includes software which comprises an algorithm that allows to recognize the squeezing gestures and consists of a Support Vector Machine based classifier. With this software, users can record their own deformations or squeezing gestures that have to be recognized. A graphical user interface shows the aforementioned pattern of measurements resulting from the deformation, and the recognized gesture (see Figure 4).

In summary, the Skweezee System enables end-users to design and develop gestural squeeze interactions at any size and configuration (see Figure 1 and Figure 2). It is our aspiration that people without engineering backgrounds (e.g. therapists, instructors, industrial designers or artists) can design and program their own Skweezees to sense those squeeze gestures that are desired for their application domains. Therefore, Skweezees are very much designed with the same aspiration Buechley et al. [19] put forward: to emphasize end-users' creativity, empowerment and self-expression. In this paper, we will specifically focus on the technology underlying the Skweezee System and test its robustness and accuracy.

RELATED WORK

Soft, deformable objects that act as input devices have been suggested before by other researchers. Perhaps, the most simple form of a Skweezee is the felt pressure sensor introduced by Perner-Wilson et al. [18]. The felt pressure sensor contains a blend of regular and resistive yarn. When squeezed, the conductive fibers throughout the sensor improve the electrical connections, lowering the resistance between any two electrodes on the sensor's surface. Skweezees differ from felt pressure sensors: they contain more than two electrodes (eight in the prototypes presented in this paper), and measure the resistance between all possible pairs of electrodes. This way a Skweezee can be considered an N-dimensional pressure sensor (N>1), allowing to detect more complex deformations of the sensor.

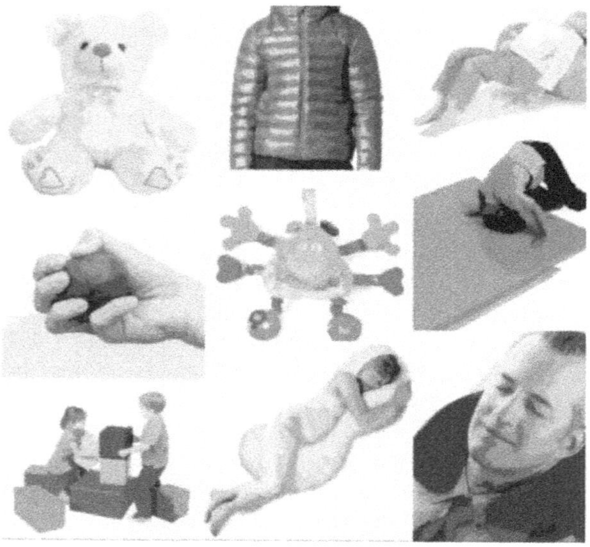

Figure 1. Potential candidates for Skweezees are any objects that are 'soft', and can be filled with conductive padding and electrodes, rendering the application space infinite, e.g. a cuddly toy or baby toy that can be used for training bimanual skills, a feathered jacket that detects physical caresses, a gym roll or mat for rehabilitation purposes, a stress ball, a pregnancy cushion or neck pillow to assess sleeping patterns or big soft blocks to be used for fun and educational purposes.

Figure 2. Four prototypes of Skweezees: the sphere, the cube, the cylinder and the cuboid.

Murakami and Naomasa also investigated soft input devices, and more specifically 3-D deformable shapes [17]. They constructed deformable objects consisting of up to ninety small bars of conductive polyurethane foam. When deformed, the length of several bars will change and thus their resistance as well. By deriving the lengths of all bars from their resistance, the geometric shape deformation of the object can be estimated. Smith et al. used conductive foam as well for their Digital Foam, described as "a new input sensor developed to support clay like sculpting and modeling operations" [26]. Their prototype consists of 162 discrete bars of conductive foam embedded in a sphere, each acting as a unique pressure sensor. Skweezees have a somewhat simpler construction, consisting of a textile covering filled with homogeneous conductive fabric. Skweezees do not aim to determine their exact geometric deformed shape, but rather the gesture causing the deformation, as performed and recorded earlier by the user.

Slyper et al. suggested silicone as base material for their soft sensor [25]. While silicone provides the necessary mechanical properties (deformable and elastic), electrical (non-deformable) switches are placed at several places in the object, and are opened or closed depending on the user's action. The materials used in Skweezees do not limit the deformation, there are no rigid, non-deformable sensors inserted. Moreover, sensing in Skweezees is continuous, as opposed to the discrete nature of the measurements in Slyper's work.

Sensing deformation through measuring changes in conductivity has also been done in the context of bendable interfaces like, for example TWEND [8] or PaperPhone [15]. TWEND consists of two pieces of thin, flexible plastic with a layer of foam in between, in which eight optical bending sensors are embedded. PaperPhone consists of a flexible display, augmented with a layer of bidirectional bend sensors. Both, however, are not fully twistable and can be damaged due to the characteristics of the used material. Skweezees are not limited in the kind of deformations, and cannot 'break'.

Sensor wise, this work could be seen as an extension of the TactileTape sensor [9] to three-dimensional instead of one-dimensional volumes. TactileTape is a one-dimensional touch sensor that looks and behaves like regular tape. However, it is actually a flexible potentiometer, consisting of three surfaces that form an open circuit. When a finger deflects the surface, the circuit closes.

PinStripe [13] resembles our Skweezee technology in that it also relies on the change of resistance. Pinstripe consists of fields of parallel conductive lines sewn onto the fabric. It can be controlled by varying the amount of cloth pinched. However, resistivity measurements between each pair of lines are only binary. In the Skweezee System, the resistivity measurements allow for a continuous range of values. Moreover, the Skweezee System enables 3-D deformations, rather than the two-dimensional sheet of fabric for the PinStripe.

Finally, Sugiura et al. presented the FuwaFuwa sensor module [27], which measures deformation in six orthogonal directions via photo reflectivity. The sensor is "a round, hand-size, wireless device for measuring the shape deformations of soft objects such as cushions and plush toys." To do so, this sensor (a ball with a diameter of 65mm) has to be placed in the soft deformable object. In case more distant deformations have to be measured, the authors suggest to insert another module. In the case of a Skweezee, the object to be deformed *is* the sensor, no extra modules need to be inserted, and the object can take any size or geometric shape.

TECHNOLOGY OF SKWEEZEES

In order to test the feasibility of Skweezees, we made several prototypes intended to be deformed with two hands (see Figure 2). We explored several shapes, materials, electrode fixtures and electrode positions.

Materials

As mentioned before, Skweezees are filled with conductive padding. The Skweezee should be deformable to a large extent (the order of magnitude of deformation runs in centimeters for our prototypes) and return to its rest position when untouched. Therefore, the filling should show considerable elasticity. The filling should be conductive as well; its resistance should drop when pressed together. We found the balance between conductivity and elasticity to be rather delicate. We experimented with nylon filaments suffused with conductive carbon (Resistat F9116, www.resistat.com), conductive wool consisting of steel fibers mixed with normal wool (Bekinox W12/18, www.bekaert.com) and low-density conductive foam. Our experiences gave us a preference for conductive wool, but obviously, one can experiment with other fillings as well, as long as one bears in mind the need for both elasticity and conductivity.

Figure 3. Inside view of the textile casing of a Skweezee, showing the electrode consisting of conductive wire, conductive tape and a sample of the filling, all stitched together with conductive yarn.

Inside the Skweezees, we embedded electrodes, dispersed over the object. In our shapes we embedded eight, but embedding more or less electrodes is possible. The number should be defined by the number of gestures one aims to recognize, by the size and shape of the object, and the targeted accuracy of gesture detection. We will revisit this choice of number of electrodes in the Discussion section.

Different options are possible to fixate the electrodes insight the shape. It is critical that electrodes will not migrate when the shape is deformed and that they have a permanent contact with the conductive padding. Therefore, one should look for a mechanism to keep the electrode in its place and in permanent contact with the filling (see Figure 3). We relied on using conductive tape to fixate the electrode to the outer lining of the shape. To ensure its position, the electrodes were not only taped but also secured by a double stitch with conductive yarn.

Electronics

When deforming a Skweezee the resistance between two or more electrodes will change. We developed a circuit to measure the resistance between every unique pair of electrodes. Our prototypes contain eight electrodes (N=8), so there are 28 (=N*(N-1)/2) unique electrode pairs to be scanned. Two multiplexers – one for each electrode of the pair – are used to select an electrode pair. The multiplexers are driven by the digital outputs of a microcontroller (Arduino UNO). A voltage divider and the microcontroller's A/D converter is used to measure the resistance between the two selected electrodes. All 28 measurements are then sent to the PC.

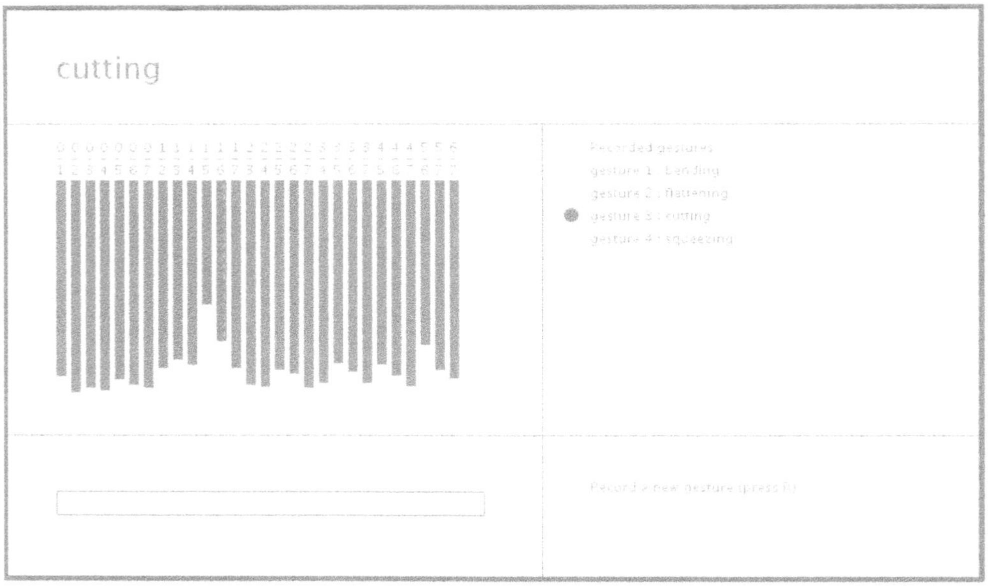

Figure 4. Screenshot of the software showing the 28 measurements (bars at the left) and the names of the recorded gesture (at the right). The recognized gesture is shown at the top.

Software

Software for recording and sensing gestures is written in Processing. The software allows the user to monitor all measurements obtained when deforming the Skweezee, in real time (see the 28 bars on the left side, on the screenshot in Figure 4). The program shows the names of all user-defined gestures (i.e. shape deformations) (see the right side of the screenshot in Figure 4). The name of the recorded gesture that is the most similar to the current one when performing a gesture, is shown at the top of the screen, (see "cutting" on the screenshot in Figure 4).

The user can also record additional gestures. First, s/he gives a name to the gesture, then s/he changes the shape of the Skweezee. During a time interval of 10 seconds, the user can perform the gesture once, or several times, and dynamically change the extent of the deformation. All instances for which the sample values exceed a preset threshold (defined in a pilot test) are stored in memory, and serve as a reference for the gesture.

Gesture recognition algorithm

Every gesture generates different consecutive patterns of 28 measurements that correspond to the measurements across the 28 unique electrode pairs. Some examples of such patterns at a certain moment in time are shown in Figure 5. A classifier algorithm is then needed to discern these patterns. When a new gesture is performed, the classifier has to decide which patterns in the recorded set are most similar to the new gesture. The first implementation was a minimum-distance classifier. However, the performance of this classifier was unsatisfactory, since it could not detect similar gestures with different amplitudes. As a result, the user had to perform the gesture always to the same extent.

To solve this, we opted for a Support Vector Machine (SVM) classifier [24,30]. The features on which the classifier bases its decision are the 28 measurements, recorded continuously from the moment the user starts the deformation until he releases the Skweezee. Each recorded instance corresponds to a single point x_i in a 28-dimensional space. During the recording of a gesture, the data of the 28 measurements are continuously saved, so multiple points x_i are obtained. All these different instances are labeled with the correct gesture y_i. This list of instances are then added to the previous recordings, and so a new training set $\{x_i, y_i\}_{i=1}^{N}$ is obtained. Typically, around 110-170 points are obtained for each gesture. The basic concept of SVMs is the use of a hyper plane to separate data of two classes. To extend the classifier to multiple classes the "one-against-one" method with "max wins" voting is used, based on the comparison in [11].

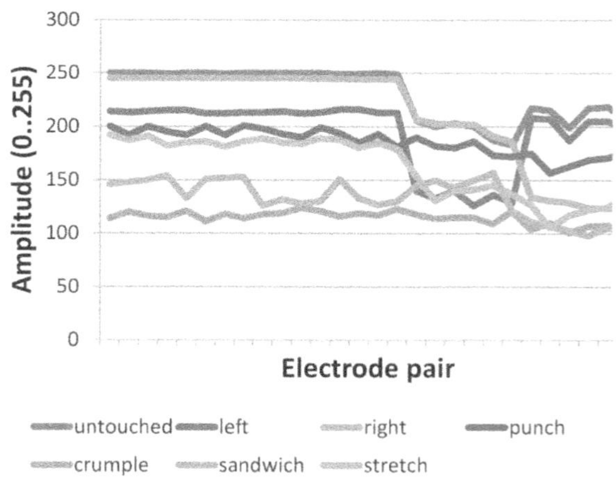

Figure 5. Pattern of measurements corresponding to the gestures shown in Figure 6.

Figure 6. The seven predefined gestures with the cuboid.

The idea behind an SVM classifier is to map the original data points to a high-dimensional, or even infinite-dimensional, feature space so the classification problem becomes easier. The mapping φ is done by an appropriate choice of a kernel function, $K(x_i, x_j) = \varphi(x_i)^T\varphi(x_j)$.

Based on [14] and [16], the radial basis function (RBF) is chosen:

$$K(x_i, x_j) = \exp\left(-\gamma\|x_i - x_j\|^2\right), \gamma > 0.$$

SVMs require the solution of the following optimization problem:

$$\min_{w,b,\xi} \frac{1}{2} w^T w + C \sum_{i=1}^{N} \xi_i$$

Subject to

$$y_i(w^T\varphi(x_i) + b) \geq 1 - \xi_i, i = 1, \ldots, N,$$

$$\xi_i \geq 0, i = 1, \ldots, N.$$

$C > 0$ is the penalty parameter of the error term. The library LIBSVM [3] is used to train the classifier and predict new values. To be able to use the default values for C and γ, each of the 28 measurements of the training set is linearly scaled to the range $[-1, +1]$ using the formula:

$$x_{i,scal}(l) = -1 + 2 * \frac{x_i(l) - \min(feature\ l)}{\max(feature\ l) - \min(feature\ l)},$$

$$l = 1, \ldots, 28\ and\ i = 1, \ldots, N$$

where $x_i(l)$ is the lth element of the 28-dimensional vector x_i and $x_{i,scal}(l)$ is the scaled measurement l. The scaling factors, i.e. the minimum and maximum of each feature of the training data, are saved. The same scaling for each measurement is then applied on each instance of a performed gesture during the test phase.

The best parameters C and γ can be found by doing a "grid-search" using cross-validation. We want to avoid to do this model selection each time a new gesture is recorded, because we want to keep the recording of a new gesture real-time. As a result, we have done a grid-search for C and γ offline, on different data sets. Of course, the optimal parameters change depending on the gestures that are recorded. Following parameters are chosen: $C = 1$ and $\gamma = 0.07$. For this choice, we got offline cross-validations between 89.2% and 100%, depending on the data set.

Finally, we want to stress that the complexity of this SVM classifier is hidden for the user. Users can simply perform and record their gestures in the software, and the classification happens automatically.

EVALUATION OF SKWEEZEES

In order to assess the feasibility of the Skweezee System and more particularly the accuracy of the classifier, we conducted two experiments with two of our prototypes, namely the cylinder and the cuboid (see Figure 2). The cuboid's measurements are 10 cm x 10 cm x 20 cm. The cuboid contains 8 electrodes, each positioned in one of the corners. The cylinder has a diameter of 7 cm and a length of 22 cm. One electrode is positioned at each end, two pairs of three electrodes are equally distributed around the circumference at one third and two third of the length respectively.

Participants

For the first experiment, we invited 20 participants, 14 male and 6 female, with an age between 19 and 59. For the second experiment, we invited 10 other participants, 7 male and 3 female, aged between 19 and 52. None of them had experimented with our Skweezee System before, they were unaware of the characteristics of the Skweezees at hand.

Experiment 1: Pre-defined gesture set

Methods and rationale

The first experiment lasted on average 10 minutes, and consisted of a single test run for one of the two Skweezees. 10 participants tested the cuboid, 10 other participants tested the cylinder. For each Skweezee, a set of gestures was defined by the experimenter before the experiments were carried out. The predefined set consisted of seven gestures. Figure 6 shows the gestures for the cuboid: "untouched", "left", "right", "punch", "crumple",

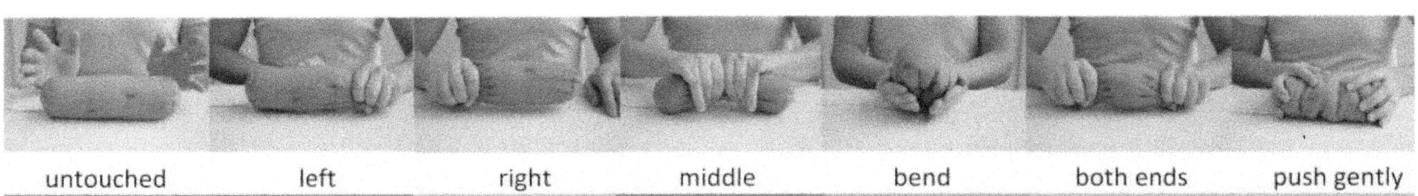

Figure 7. The seven predefined gestures with the cylinder.

"sandwich" and "stretch". The gestures for the cylinder are shown in Figure 7: "untouched", "middle", "bend", "both ends", "push gently", "left" and "right". These gestures were selected and recorded by the experimenter, based on his knowledge of the characteristics of each Skweezee (e.g. the size, the shape and the position of the electrodes). The recorded data were included in the training set of the classifier.

For the experimenter, it was always possible to perform each gestures in such a way that the computer recognized it correctly, an accuracy of 100% was achieved. However, we wanted to find out whether the classifier still performed well when the gestures were performed by other users. Since it was expected that every participant would make the gestures in a slightly different way (size and positioning of the hands, applied force when squeezing,...), it was likely that the accuracy of the classifier would drop (as shown in similar studies, e.g. [22]). The data 'generated' by the participant are considered as the test set of the classifier (and obviously different from the training set).

Procedure

At the start of the experiment, the experimenter demonstrated all gestures, and then asked the participants to make the same gestures with the Skweezee. During this practice phase, the participant was allowed to look at the computer screen to see which gesture was recognized by the classifier. Next, the evaluation phase was carried out, during which no visual or auditory feedback was given to the participant. The researcher called out the name of one of the seven gestures in the set, and then the participant had to perform the according gesture within three seconds, after which the recognized gesture was logged. The gestures were called out randomly, and the researcher ensured that each gesture was called out four times. Hence, after completing, the participant had performed 28 gestures.

Results

On average, a classification accuracy of 90% was obtained for both Skweezees, with a standard deviation of 8%. Two participants succeeded to get a score of 100%. The lowest score measured is 71%.

Experiment 2: User-defined gesture set

Methods and rationale

The motive for the second experiment was to evaluate the Skweezees when users were allowed to create their own gesture set without a specific task in mind. Contrary to other studies [7,22,25], we did not tell the participants which gestures they had to perform. Neither did we inform the participants about the potential and the limitations of the Skweezees, which might inspire (or constrain) the creation of an optimal gesture set. As shown in [32], users can come up with other gestures than the experts and vice versa. However, if the performance of the system would still be acceptable, Skweezees would open up a lot of opportunities for people wishing to use Skweezees for their own applications.

Procedure

The experiment lasted on average 40 minutes, and consisted of three test runs for each of the two Skweezees. For each test run, first there was a recording phase, to generate the training set of the classifier, and next an evaluation phase, to generate test samples for the classifier. During the recording phase, the participant was asked to think of a squeeze gesture, and a corresponding name. When ready, the researcher would type in the name and the participant was asked to perform the actual gesture in order to record it. The recording lasts 10 seconds, so the participant was asked to perform the same gesture a few times, while releasing and regrabbing the Skweezee, to be able to catch different intensities and different ways of grabbing. When four different gestures were programmed, the classifier was automatically trained and we switched to the evaluation phase. During the evaluation phase, the researcher would

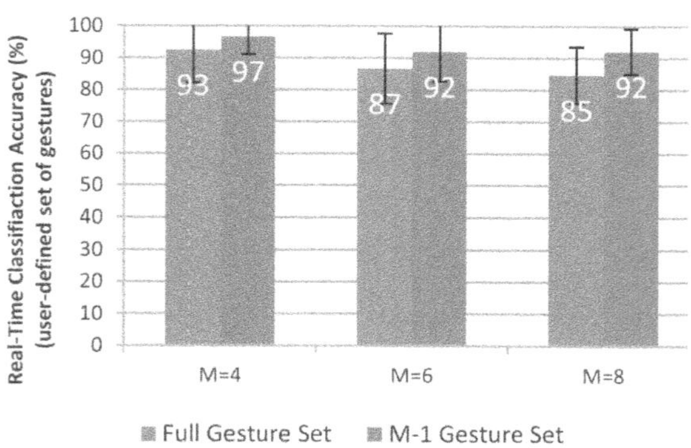

Figure 8. Real-time, per-user classification accuracy for 4, 6 or 8 gestures on the cuboid (in blue). When the 'worst' gesture is removed, scores improved (in red). The error bars represent the standard deviations of these accuracies.

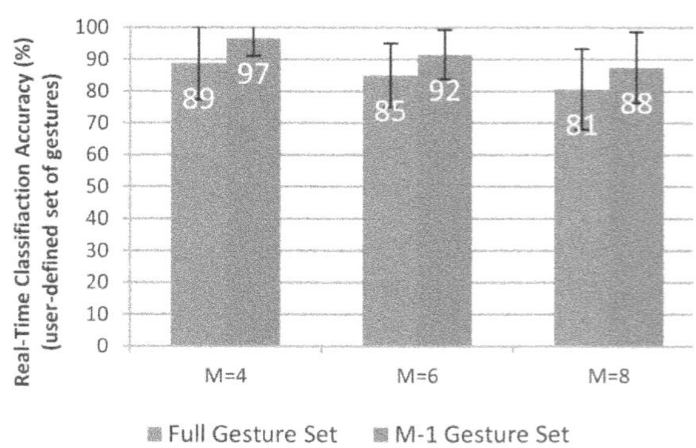

Figure 9. Real-time, per-user classification accuracy for 4, 6 or 8 gestures on the cylinder (in blue). When the 'worst' gesture is removed, scores improved (in red). The error bars represent the standard deviations of these accuracies.

call out the name of one of these four gestures and ask the participant to perform the according gesture. The gestures were called out randomly, and the researcher ensured that each gesture was called out four times. No feedback was given during the evaluation phase, so the participant could not make corrections if an incorrect gesture was recognized. The participant had to complete the gesture within three seconds. Hence, after completing the first trial, the participant performed 16 gestures. In the next test run, two more gestures were added according to the same procedure, hence totaling six gestures. Finally, the third trial consisted of eight gestures. We decided not to continue and add more gestures, since most participants indicated that it was difficult to remember more gestures and to invent new ones. The same procedure was adopted for both Skweezees.

Results

Figure 8 (for the cuboid) and Figure 9 (for the cylinder) show the real-time classification accuracies, averaged across all participants, together with the standard deviations shown as error bars on the figures. As can be inferred from the graphs (in blue), for the cuboid we achieved accuracies between 85% and 93% for the full gesture set (ranging from 4 to 8 gestures). The individual maximum score for 4 and 6 gestures was 100%, and 97% for 8 gestures. For the cylinder, accuracies between 81% and 89% are obtained. For each size of gesture set, an individual accuracy of 100% could be obtained. When the 'worst' gesture is removed, i.e. the results of the gesture with the lowest recognition rate is not included, the scores for the cuboid vary between 92% (7 gestures) and 97% (3 gestures). For the cylinder, these numbers range from 88% to 97%. Removing the worst score is also done in other similar experiments, e.g. [22], and somewhat compensates for the fact that the participants were inexperienced, as discussed below.

DISCUSSION

Accuracy

Our experimental evaluation demonstrates the feasibility of Skweezees, achieving real-time accuracies between 81% and 97%. One needs to keep in mind that these accuracies are obtained by only one recording interval of 10 seconds. From a user perspective, this is a great benefit: the user only has to record each gesture once. However, we expect the recognition rate to increase when taking more samples per gesture type in the user-defined case and data from more participants in the pre-defined scenario.

In addition, we like to stress again that participants had no prior experience with the Skweezees. They did not receive information on how the Skweezees were designed (e.g. where the electrodes were located in the shape and where the greatest resistance changes would be). Henceforth, participants did not have the knowledge on how to create an 'optimal' set of gestures that could easily be discriminated by the Skweezee. The programmed gestures in their set were the result of the participants' own creativity and the perceived and real affordances of the Skweezee only.

Another remarkable observation is the big difference between participants. Especially during the second experiment, some participants really tried to find gestures with a unique pattern and really saw it as a challenge to define different gestures. They enjoyed creating the different gestures. As an example, with 8 user-defined gestures, one participant scored 97% for the cuboid and 100% for the cylinder. We also noted that during the second experiment, some users did find it hard to come up with eight different 'meaningful' gestures. Moreover, users found it hard to remember and faithfully reproduce them later on. Hence, we subsume that user-defined limitations on the amount of gestures that can be memorized and reproduced might have affected our accuracies in a negative way.

Advantages

The Skweezee System has some important advantages over existing technologies for soft interfaces. First, the Skweezee System has a simple construction, consisting of a textile covering filled with homogeneous conductive fabric and some electrodes. The object to be deformed is the sensor. Secondly, they can detect a wide range of variations in deformation. Moreover, the Skweezee System does not determine the exact geometric deformed shape, but rather the gesture causing the deformation, as performed and recorded earlier by the user. As shown in the experimental results, the Skweezee system achieves accuracies between 81% and 97%. Finally, the Skweezee System is easy to use: it can be designed and programmed by those active in the 'field' themselves, coaches, therapists, instructors, etc. We can think of cuddly toys in physical therapy that encourage bimanual actions, input devices that facilitate intuitive 3D drawing or 3D manipulation, or even outdoor furniture that stimulates exergaming. But certainly, end-users can envision even more creative and embodied designs.

Limitations

The most important limitation of the current system is its 'sensitivity'. Sometimes, small changes in the deformation lead to relatively large differences in the obtained pattern of measurements. On the other hand, totally different gestures can result in a quite similar pattern of measurements. This paradoxical observation can partially be explained by the limited resolution of the system. Indeed, a decrease of resistance between two electrodes is due to compressed material in between them, but the system cannot tell where exactly this compression is (close to one of both electrodes, in the middle, equally distributed,...). On the other hand, changes in the intensity of the deformation are easily detected, which explains the high sensitivity to small changes. One way to solve these issues is by increasing the number of electrodes, which in turn will increase the resolution of the Skweezee, and so the accuracy of gesture classification. The underlying technology does not specify that only eight electrodes need to be used. However, there is a trade-off with complexity of the design and with the speed of measurement. With every extra electrode, the number of measurements and computation time increase as well. We have not experimented with more electrodes, therefore we can neither specify the influence on accuracy nor the influence on computational time. Nevertheless, whatever the results of adding electrodes, accuracies will also be defined by the design of the shape (inviting specific gestures through its shape) and the according positioning of the electrodes. Investigating the effect of more electrodes and a higher resolution is part of our future work.

We hope that given the generic nature of the Skweezee System, even novices can easily create a shape that incorporates desired affordances, position electrodes where the measurement would make the most difference, and program the desired squeeze gestures. Further work will include Skweezee workshops with non-experts, to investigate whether designs of Skweezees and the recording of gestures is as straightforward as we hope for.

Another limitation which is not further investigated is the lifetime of the Skweezees. We assume that the conductive wool compresses over time, which will affect the sensor data. Also, the proposed platform only works for soft objects that have no other functions since the inner layer is restricted with the material needed for the sensing.

CONCLUSION

Skweezees are soft, squeezable shapes that are filled with conductive padding and strategically positioned electrodes. Using a Support Vector Machine classifier, the Skweezee System can be programmed, even by non-techies, to sense their shape deformation. Consequently, the Skweezee System enables rich gestural squeeze interaction for the DIY community. Our experimental results show that well designed and crafted Skweezees can easily sense up to 7 different gestures with an accuracy of 90%, without extensive training. Hence, we are convinced that the Skweezee System can become an additional tool to bring ubiquitous computing to the "real world" and help users in their quest for creativity, empowerment and self-expression.

ACKNOWLEDGMENTS

This work is part of the TIII project, a TETRA funded research project by IWT – Flanders (120147). Johan Suykens acknowledges support from KU Leuven, the Flemish government, FWO, the Belgian federal science policy office and the European Research Council (CoE EF/05/006, GOA MANET, IUAP DYSCO, FWO G.0377.12, ERC AdG A-DATADRIVE-B).

REFERENCES

1. Berzowska, J. Programming materiality. *Proceedings of the Sixth International Conference on Tangible, Embedded and Embodied Interaction*, ACM (2012), 23–24.
2. Buechley, L. and Eisenberg, M. Fabric PCBs, electronic sequins, and socket buttons: techniques for e-textile craft. *Personal and Ubiquitous Computing 13*, 2 (2007), 133–150.
3. Chang, C.-C. and Lin, C.-J. LIBSVM: A library for support vector machines. *ACM Trans. Intell. Syst. Technol. 2*, 3 (2011), 27:1–27:27.
4. Collective, B.M. and Shaw, D. Makey Makey: improvising tangible and nature-based user interfaces. *Proceedings of the Sixth International Conference on Tangible, Embedded and Embodied Interaction*, ACM (2012), 367–370.
5. Dourish, P. *Where the action is: the foundations of embodied interaction*. MIT Press, Cambridge, MA, USA, 2001.
6. Fitzmaurice, G.W., Ishii, H., and Buxton, W.A.S. Bricks: laying the foundations for graspable user interfaces. ACM Press/Addison-Wesley Publishing Co. (1995), 442–449.
7. Geurts, L., Van Woensel, A., and Vanden Abeele, V. No sweat, no fun: Large-gesture recognition for computer games. *Proceedings of the fourth international conference Fun and Games 2012*, (2012).
8. Herkenrath, G., Karrer, T., and Borchers, J. Twend: twisting and bending as new interaction gesture in mobile devices. *CHI '08 Extended Abstracts on Human Factors in Computing Systems*, ACM (2008), 3819–3824.
9. Holman, D. and Vertegaal, R. TactileTape: low-cost touch sensing on curved surfaces. *Proceedings of the 24th annual ACM symposium adjunct on User interface software and technology*, ACM (2011), 17–18.
10. Hornecker, E. and Buur, J. Getting a grip on tangible interaction: a framework on physical space and social interaction. *Proceedings of the SIGCHI conference on Human Factors in computing systems*, ACM (2006), 437–446.
11. Hsu, C.-W. and Lin, C.-J. A comparison of methods for multiclass support vector machines. *IEEE Transactions on Neural Networks 13*, 2 (Mar), 415–425.
12. Jordà, S. The reactable: tangible and tabletop music performance. *Proceedings of the 28th of the international conference extended abstracts on Human factors in computing systems*, ACM (2010), 2989–2994.
13. Karrer, T., Wittenhagen, M., Lichtschlag, L., Heller, F., and Borchers, J. Pinstripe: eyes-free continuous input on interactive clothing. *Proceedings of the SIGCHI Conference on Human Factors in Computing Systems*, ACM (2011), 1313–1322.
14. Keerthi, S.S. and Lin, C.-J. Asymptotic behaviors of support vector machines with Gaussian kernel. *Neural computation 15*, 7 (2003), 1667–1689.
15. Lahey, B., Girouard, A., Burleson, W., and Vertegaal, R. PaperPhone: understanding the use of bend gestures in mobile devices with flexible electronic paper displays. *Proceedings of the SIGCHI Conference on Human Factors in Computing Systems*, ACM (2011), 1303–1312.
16. Lin, H. and Lin, C.-J. *A Study on Sigmoid Kernels for SVM and the Training of non-PSD Kernels by SMO-type Methods*. 2003.
17. Murakami, T. and Nakajima, N. Direct and intuitive input device for 3-D shape deformation. *Proceedings of*

the SIGCHI conference on Human factors in computing systems: celebrating interdependence, ACM (1994), 465–470.
18. Perner-Wilson, H., Buechley, L., and Satomi, M. Handcrafting textile interfaces from a kit-of-no-parts. *Proceedings of the fifth international conference on Tangible, embedded, and embodied interaction*, ACM Press (2011), 61.
19. Perner-Wilson, H. and Buechley, L. Making textile sensors from scratch. *Proceedings of the fourth international conference on Tangible, embedded, and embodied interaction*, ACM (2010), 349–352.
20. Perner-Wilson, H. and Satomi, M. How to get what you want. *KOBAKANT DIY Wearable Technology Documentation*. http://www.kobakant.at/DIY/.
21. Ryokai, K., Marti, S., and Ishii, H. I/O brush: drawing with everyday objects as ink. *Proceedings of the SIGCHI conference on Human factors in computing systems*, ACM (2004), 303–310.
22. Sato, M., Poupyrev, I., and Harrison, C. Touche;: enhancing touch interaction on humans, screens, liquids, and everyday objects. *Proceedings of the 2012 ACM annual conference on Human Factors in Computing Systems*, ACM (2012), 483–492.
23. Schiettecatte, B. and Vanderdonckt, J. AudioCubes: a distributed cube tangible interface based on interaction range for sound design. *Proceedings of the 2nd international conference on Tangible and embedded interaction*, ACM (2008), 3–10.
24. Schölkopf, B.S. and Smola, A.J. *Learning With Kernels: Support Vector Machines, Regularization, Optimization and Beyond*. MIT Press, 2002.
25. Slyper, R., Poupyrev, I., and Hodgins, J. Sensing through structure: designing soft silicone sensors. *Proceedings of the fifth international conference on Tangible, embedded, and embodied interaction*, ACM (2011), 213–220.
26. Smith, R.T., Thomas, B.H., and Piekarski, W. Digital foam interaction techniques for 3D modeling. *Proceedings of the 2008 ACM symposium on Virtual reality software and technology*, ACM (2008), 61–68.
27. Sugiura, Y., Kakehi, G., Withana, A., et al. Detecting shape deformation of soft objects using directional photoreflectivity measurement. *Proceedings of the 24th annual ACM symposium on User interface software and technology*, ACM (2011), 509–516.
28. Ullmer, B. and Ishii, H. The metaDESK: models and prototypes for tangible user interfaces. *Proceedings of the 10th annual ACM symposium on User interface software and technology*, ACM (1997), 223–232.
29. Ullmer, B. and Ishii, H. Emerging frameworks for tangible user interfaces. *IBM Syst. J. 39*, 3-4 (2000), 915–931.
30. Vapnik, V.N. *Statistical learning theory*. Wiley, 1998.
31. Weiser, M. The Computer for the Twenty-First Century. *Scientific American 265*, 3 (1991), 94–104.
32. Wobbrock, J.O., Morris, M.R., and Wilson, A.D. User-defined gestures for surface computing. *Proceedings of the SIGCHI Conference on Human Factors in Computing Systems*, ACM (2009), 1083–1092.

Tactile Rendering of 3D Features on Touch Surfaces

Seung-Chan Kim[1,2], Ali Israr[1], Ivan Poupyrev[1]

[1] Disney Research Pittsburgh,
4720 Forbes Avenue,
Pittsburgh, PA, 15213 USA
{kimsc, israr, ivan.poupyrev}
@disneyresearch.com

[2] Department of Mechanical Engineering,
KAIST
291 Daehak-ro, Yuseong-gu, Daejeon
305-701, Korea

ABSTRACT

We present a tactile-rendering algorithm for simulating 3D geometric features, such as bumps, on touch screen surfaces. This is achieved by modulating friction forces between the user's finger and the touch screen, instead of physically moving the touch surface. We proposed that the percept of a 3D bump is created when local gradients of the rendered virtual surface are mapped to lateral friction forces. To validate this approach, we first establish a psychophysical model that relates the perceived friction force to the controlled voltage applied to the tactile feedback device. We then use this model to demonstrate that participants are three times more likely to prefer gradient force profiles than other commonly used rendering profiles. Finally, we present a generalized algorithm and conclude the paper with a set of applications using our tactile rendering technology.

ACM Classification: H5.2 [Information interfaces and presentation]: User Interfaces. - Graphical user interfaces, Input devices and strategies, Haptic I/O.

Keywords: Electrovibration, haptic rendering, friction

INTRODUCTION

Touch and gesture interactions have rapidly proliferated in recent years and have become a de-facto standard in mobile phones, tablet and desktop computers. Consequently, the efforts to develop effective, feasible and inexpensive tactile feedback for touch screen interaction have also increased [15, 19]. The goal of this work is to develop tactile rendering techniques that provide rich, immediate and dynamic tactile feedback to users interacting with touch screens. Such tactile feedback not only increases the effectiveness of touch interactions, but also leads to more realistic and satisfying experience for millions of users.

Early pioneering work on touch screen tactile feedback focused on using mechanical vibrations, where the screen or the entire device would move rapidly to stimulate a user's fingertip [8, 20]. Challenges in designing feasible vibrotactile touch interfaces included cost, reliability, actuator size, power requirements, as well as difficulty in the effective control of the device's mechanical vibrations [2, 16].

Recently, a promising new direction in touch screen haptics has emerged. Instead of creating *vibrotactile* stimulation on a user's finger, it suggests modifying *friction* between a sliding finger and the touch screen surface [2, 11, 29]. It has been demonstrated that such devices allow for the creation of not only a feasible and lightweight tactile feedback apparatus suitable for touch screens, but also provide rich, dynamic and highly satisfying user experiences [2]. These friction displays are particularly suitable to modern touch and gesture interfaces that are based on sliding and flicking fingers on screen.

Despite the rich interaction opportunities that these displays provide, there has been little work done on designing and evaluating fundamental techniques and algorithms for generating rich tactile sensations on friction-based tactile displays. Much of the previous work has focused on the hardware and materials required to build such tactile devices [1, 2, 29]. Levesque et al. [10, 11] used a *squeeze-film* effect to modulate the friction forces between the user's finger and a thin glass plate, where the level of force feedback was proportional to general mathematical functions, such as sinusoid profiles, and their spatial densities. It showed effective-

Figure 1: Tactile bump-rendering algorithm would allow the user to experience rich tactile textures on flat touch screens.

UIST'13, October 8–11, 2013, St. Andrews, United Kingdom.

ACM 978-1-4503-2268-3/13/10...$15.00.
http://dx.doi.org/10.1145/2501988.2502020

ness of friction-based feedback displays in designing user interfaces; however, it did not attempt to convey fine 3D geometric details of the content presented to the user.

In this paper we propose, develop and evaluate an algorithm to render 3D geometrical features on friction-based tactile displays. The algorithm is based on an observation that the haptic perception of 3D features on flat surfaces depends predominantly on *lateral forces* applied on a finger [17, 21]. We formulate a perceptual model that relates the perceived strength of friction as a function of the voltage applied to a friction display. We then utilize this model to modulate the *perceived friction levels* and render differentiating tactile feedback for complex 3D objects; such as textures, facial features, 3D models, surface forms and topographies, etc. Although the proposed algorithm is applicable to all lateral force feedback devices, our development is based on electrovibration-based tactile feedback.

We believe that the development of our tactile rendering algorithms expands the vocabulary of possible tactile representations and allows to render rich tactile information overlaid on visual content. This will lead to new exciting uses of tactile displays technology for touch screen interaction.

BACKGROUND AND RELATED WORK

Given a haptic feedback apparatus, creating a realistic and compelling tactile representation of objects and interactions is an important challenge in haptic research that is not well understood (see e.g., [16]).

One fundamental direction in creating such "tactile content" includes the formation of a set of abstract "tactile primitives" that are perceptually differentiable and can be easily learned and recognized. For example, in 1957 Frank Geldard developed "Vibratese language" that consisted of five vibrators placed at five locations on the back [5]. Variations in location, intensity and timing of the vibrations were coded to represent alphanumerical characters. In more recent work, tactile primitives have been assigned to provide feedback for various interaction events [3, 8]. These tactile primitives were mainly defined for the vibrotactile stimulation and are not scalable to friction-based displays.

Another direction in haptic content generation is the simulation of the dynamic physical properties of objects and environments. Typically, force-feedback devices are used to render inertial, stiffness and viscous elements of simulated objects and environments [17, 23]. "Record and Play" strategies have also been used, where physical features of the object were first measured and then re-played at a later time when the user interacted with virtual objects [22]. These techniques are applicable when the physical deformation models of objects are either available or can be measured. However, in cases where a finger slides over an arbitrary texture, the contact conditions cannot be empirically determined.

Finally, an emerging direction in haptic content generation techniques focuses on *affective* haptic events that neither simulate nor provide information per se, but attempt to communicate a feeling, a mood or a special effect. For example, Yohanan and MacLean [30] used "affective" models to modulate user emotions while users interact with a haptic apparatus. Israr and Poupyrev [9] developed psychophysical models to create, control and modulate a feeling of motion on human skin, resulting in novel feelings and effects that could not be experienced otherwise.

It is important to emphasize that all of these techniques are hardware specific and do not usually scale well either to other modalities of touch perception or to other haptic apparatus. The design of tactile feedback content is invariable tied to the character of haptic actuation. For example, the perceptual characteristics of vibrations cannot be applied to force-feedback applications. Similarly, techniques defined for force-feedback devices cannot be applied to friction-based interactions where the user's finger is actively sliding and exploring the surface of a touch screen.

Most modern friction haptic displays are based on two basic technologies. In tactile displays based on a *squeeze-film effect*, a thin sheet of glass placed on top of the screen is laterally vibrated at an ultrasonic frequency, creating a thin cushion of air under the touching finger [4, 29]. By modulating the frequency and intensity of vibrations, this technology allows for a decrease in physical friction between the glass and sliding finger, making the screen "smoother" on demand.

In tactile displays based on an *electrovibration effect* the friction between the sliding finger and the touch screen is produced by injecting a periodic electrical signal into a conductive electrode coated with a thin dielectric layer [2]. The periodic signal creates an alternating electrostatic force that periodically attracts and releases the finger from the touch surface, producing friction-like rubbery sensations. Varying the frequency and amplitude of the periodic signal varies the quality of sensations along the stick-slip and smooth-rough continuums [2].

The advantage of using electrovibration-based lateral haptics in touch screen interaction is that it can be easily integrated into popular capacitive or optical touch screens and is inexpensive and lightweight. The nature of touch itself is also different – unlike in traditional haptic devices where the stimulus is presented to passive skin, the interactions on the friction tactile displays are "active", where the human hand freely moves on the screen, similar to our natural way of exploring surfaces and textures on real world objects [13]. Furthermore, friction-based displays are expressive and allow for the production of a rich palette of tactile sensations. This is because the frequency bandwidth of these devices is significantly broader than that of traditional electro-mechanical actuators [2].

This paper explores the design of tactile rendering algorithms that allow us to systematically generate rich and effective tactile sensations for lateral friction displays. We believe that the formulation, development and evaluation of such a tactile rendering algorithm are important contributions in the further development of practical and useful tactile displays for touch screen interactions.

TACTILE RENDERING ON A FRICTION DISPLAY

The fundamental observation that is used in designing the tactile rendering algorithm is that *a perception of a physical bump by a finger sliding on a physical surface is defined predominantly by lateral forces applied to the finger.* This hypothesis was initially explored as early as in 1990 [17] and it was experimentally validated in perceptual studies conducted using active forces by Robles-De-La-Torre and Hayward in 2001 [21]. This is both a highly significant fact and an exciting discovery because it means we can create a *perception of 3D tactile features on a flat touch surface by manipulating only lateral forces, such as friction.* In other words, friction-based displays can create tactile percepts of 3D bumps on touch screens.

The algorithmic tactile rendering of a 3D bump on a touch screen opens up a broad range of exciting applications for the tactile display of images, videos and interactive computer graphics on touch screens. This includes, but is not limited to geometric features such as ridges, edges, protrusions, textures, etc.

The rest of the paper is organized as follows. In the next section we discuss *what a tactile bump is* and *how users perceive it*. We discuss experimental studies of bump perception in detail, in particular, the effect of lateral forces. We then continue the discussion of techniques for rendering 3D bumps using electrovibration-based friction-based tactile displays. The design of the algorithm consists of two parts. First, we design and investigate a perceptual model that *links voltages that are used to control friction to the subjective friction strength.* By using this model we can control the perceived strength of friction, which can be useful broadly beyond the scope of this paper. The development and evaluation of this model is one contribution of this paper.

Second, we propose and evaluate a *lateral force profile that creates a perception of the 3D tactile bump.* The proposed force profiles extend the previous work [17, 21] that we have discussed above. We conduct an experiment that demonstrated the effectiveness of lateral friction profiles compared to two other general control schemes. The design and evaluation of control schemes for rendering 3D tactile bumps forms the second contribution of the paper.

Finally, we illustrate the use of developed techniques to algorithmically generate tactile profiles for a variety of visual content. Specifically, we discuss a *one-dimensional case* to generate real world patterns, such as corduroy; the repeating objects, such as book stacks and others. We then generalize our algorithm to a *two-dimensional case* and demonstrate how it can be used to provide tactile feedback for any depth-based imagery, such as 3D computer graphics renderings or real-time images from a depth camera, such as Kinect. Designing such algorithms is the third contribution of this paper. An overview of potential applications concludes the paper.

PERCEPTION OF BUMPS

Before designing algorithms it is important to discuss what haptic bumps are and the mechanisms of their perception.

The human perception of small geometric features such as a bump is often categorized according to object scale, i.e., as features *that fit under the fingertip* or features with contours *that extend beyond the fingertip.*

The features that fit under fingertips are often referred to as *tactile textures.* They are perceived through static skin identation and require little finger motion [12]. When the feature has relatively large contours it cannot be perceived via a static finger and requires active haptic exploration [6] where forces perceived through touch and kinesthetic feedback from the moving finger are temporarily integrated. As the scale of the features increases larger motions are required and eventually also involve wrist and arm movements. In this paper, we are focusing on a medium-scaled geometric feature that can be perceived with only the motion of the wrist. We define such surface features as "*bumps*".

Lateral forces for rendering geometric features

The easiest approach to create the perception of bumps is to simply push or pull the user's finger by means of physical actuation using a vibrator [20], force feedback device [25], or electromagnetic device [27]. This approach, however, is often impractical when it comes to touch screens, as additional movement of the screen and force feedback devices is required.

A number of previous studies have demonstrated that variations in a lateral, horizontal force component experienced while sliding the finger over the surface can provide sufficient information regarding the surface geometry [17, 21]. Moreover, Gordon and Morison showed that the *gradient*, defined by dividing the base-to-peak height by half the surface length, is an effective stimulus for curvature perception, and humans rely on local curvature when perceiving surface [7, 14].

We can conclude that the surface *slope* or *gradient* at the touch point is the most important feature in perceiving curved objects [7]. This has been used early for simulating local geometric features such as bumps with haptic devices. For example, Minsky et al. [17] created an illusion of bumps by calculating the local spring force based on the local gradients of the virtual surface experienced by the user equipped with force-feedback joystick. Based on the observation that the steeper slope of bumps produces stronger resistance, previous researchers utilized slope information when creating a force field for simulating bumps on the surface [21]. A similar approach was also employed by a recent study that calculated the lateral force field based on the gradient of the image intensity function [24]. It is important to note that the earlier research discussed above based on using active force feedback devices and usually does not scale to other tactile feedback technologies, such as electrovibration-based tactile displays used in this paper.

Rendering tactile bumps on touch screens

Creating geometric features, such as bumps, on a flat touch screens without physically moving the touch panel under the user's fingertip has not been explored before. Here, we create a percept of tactile bumps by varying the frictional forces

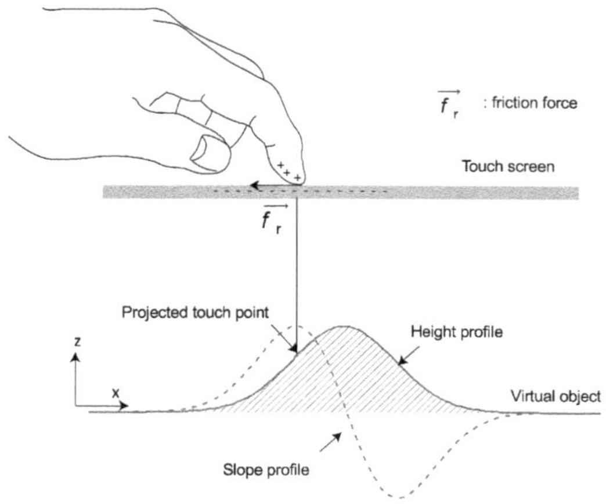

Figure 2: The use of electrovibration to create friction between the finger and the surface.

felt on the surface of the panel by the user's fingertip. More specifically, we propose that resistive forces on the fingertip are proportional to the local *gradient* of the geometric shape displayed on a touch screen, i.e., the steeper the bump – the higher the resistance forces felt on the finger. We create the perception of 3D surface bumps by *modulating the resistance forces as a function of the virtual slope that the user interacts with* (Figure 2).

We utilize an electrovibration tactile feedback devices, where the resistive forces felt by a user are a function of the *voltage* applied to the display [2]. Therefore, the voltage is the main control variable.

Controlling perceived friction forces by electrovibration

In this section, we determine a psychophysical model describing relationship between perceived friction felt by the user and applied voltage.

Apparatus. An electrovibration display similar to the one in Bau et al. [2], was used in this study. The display consisted of a 3M Microtouch surface-capacitive panel used both to track the location of the sliding finger as well as to render haptic feedback on the panel. A simple transistor-based circuit, interfaced via a serial port, was used to control the frequency and amplitude of the voltage applied to the panel. The panel was placed in a wooden frame and connected to a laptop (Figure 3).

Methods. Eleven participants (six males, average age: 23.9 years) took part in the experiment. Experimental procedures for determining subjective force magnitude scales were similar to those presented in [28, 31]. In each trial, participants scanned the touch panel with the index finger and felt the resistance corresponding to the test stimulus applied to the panel electrode. In order to obtain subjective scales for most common interactions on touch-screens, they were instructed to move their index finger freely in approximate linear strokes, thus not constraining their gestures by contact force, direction, velocity and length of stroke. Participants were asked to assign a number between 0 and 100 to describe the subjective friction intensity. Smaller numbers correspond to lower perceived friction.

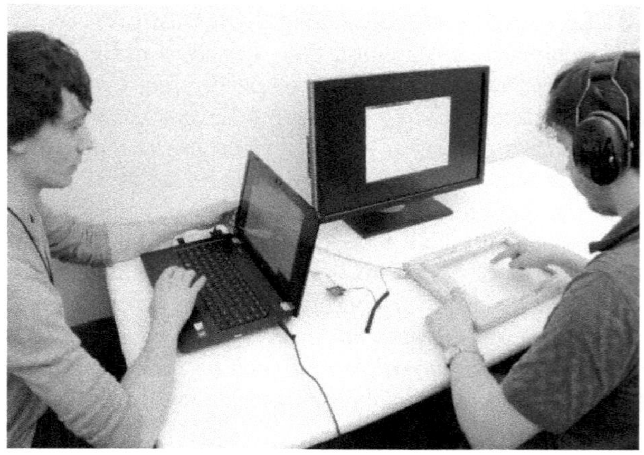

Figure 3: Experimental apparatus and setup.

Subjective friction scales for pure sinusoidal input voltage were determined at three test frequencies, namely 60, 110 and 200 Hz. The stimulus set consisted of ten equally spaced amplitude levels (in the logarithmic scale) at each test frequency. The ratio of two consecutive amplitude levels was set at 1.15, that is a 15 percent increment from the lower level corresponding to 1 JND apart between the two levels [2]. The lowest amplitude was 15 percent above the rough estimation of the absolute detection threshold at each test frequency. The entire stimulus set consisted of 30 test stimuli randomly presented three times in a test session. Each participant completed three test sessions of 90 trials, each with 5-10 minute intersession breaks. The total number of trials in the experiment was 2,970. Before the main experiment, participants familiarized themselves with the device, procedures, and rating scales. They wore earmuffs to block any environmental and/or device noise.

Results and Discussion. In order to reduce inter-participant variability, the raw subjective ratings were normalized by dividing them by the geometric mean of the ratings in the corresponding session and then multiplying the result by the overall geometric mean of the ratings obtained in the entire experiment.

Figure 4 shows normalized force ratings plotted against the voltage applied to the electrovibration display in the log-log scale, a standard way of plotting human subjective scales [28]. Each data point represents the average friction rating assigned to the voltage level by eleven participants, and the error bar represents the standard error of the mean. The entire data is regressed against a straight-line function, represented as a thick dashed line, to determine the best-fit line function between subjective ratings and applied voltage. The straight-line functions yielded high correlation coefficients (R, degree of freedom, $df = 2968$) of 0.69.

The straight-line fit is the first order psychophysical model to relate the applied voltage amplitude and the perceived friction forces, and is estimated in the log-log scale as:

$$Y = 1.24 \cdot X - 1.05 \qquad (1)$$

The estimated model of perceived friction, i.e. the dashed line in Figure 4, is essential in the algorithm to render 3D

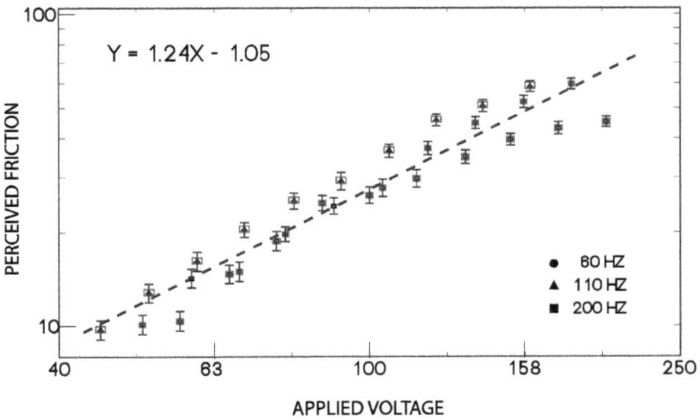

Figure 4: Subjective friction magnitude scales as a function of the voltage applied to the electrovibration-based lateral tactile feedback device.

surface features, such as bumps, holes, ridges and edges. Using the relationship, we can design and implement arbitrary friction force profiles on flat touch screen surfaces. Importantly, this relationship can be scaled to other configurations of electrovibration devices by adjusting the coefficients of Equation 1 according to the hardware specifications, such as thickness of dielectric layer and operating frequency.

Pairwise comparison of lateral force profiles

The main element in our tactile rendering procedure is the choice of a force profile that *maps local geometrical properties of the virtual surface to friction forces.* We conducted a pairwise comparison study to establish subjective preference of force profiles for rendering 3D tactile bumps on a touch screen. Three rendering profiles (S1, S2, S3) were computed for the Gaussian bump and compared (Table 1).

Height profile (S1) maps the depth of the surface geometry from a reference plane, which is usually a touch screen, to friction force. This method is often called *displacement mapping* and is used in force [25, 26] and tactile [29] rendering.

Slope profile (S2) maps the slope of the height profile to friction force adjusted for the direction of finger motion [21].

Rectangular profile (S3) is the most traditional binary on/off profile that has often been used in touch screen tactile feedback interfaces [2, 10].

A standard Gaussian-shaped virtual bump was used in this study, and the goal was to create its tactile representation that would feel like a real, physical bump. The friction force profiles were calculated as a function of displacement along the bump x dimension (Table 1), here A is the height, m is the center, and σ is the width of the virtual bump. The computed friction forces ranged from 1 and 100 in order to match the dynamic range of the electrovibration tactile device. They were then mapped to control voltages using the straight-line perceptual model defined in Figure 4.

Procedures. The same experimental setup was used as in the previous experiment, except that the tactile touch panel was secured directly on top of the monitor screen and placed horizontally on the table to synchronize haptic feedback with visual contents (Figure 5). Ten participants (6

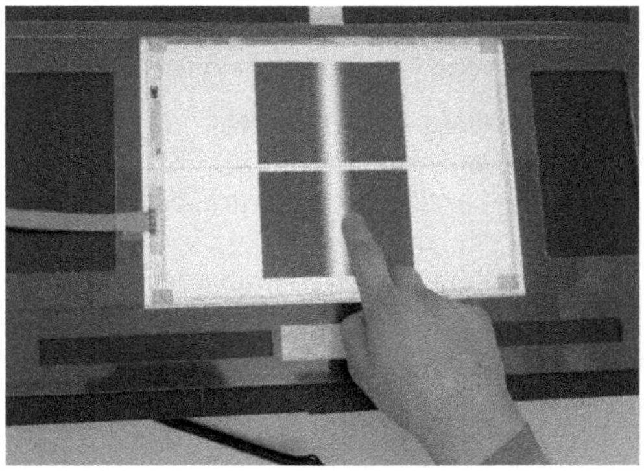

Figure 5. System configuration for the experiment.

males, average age: 26 years) took part in the study. A classic two-interval forced-choice procedure was used to obtain subjective preference. In each trial, participants were presented with two visual representations of bumps. Each bump was overlaid with one of the tactile-rendering profiles S1, S2 or S3. Participants were asked to choose the force profile that most resembled the real physical bump. Two widths ($\sigma = 20$ pixel and $\sigma = 30$ pixel) and two heights ($A = 1$ and $A = 0.8$) were randomly chosen for each profile pair to increase the variety of profiles in comparison trials.

The experimental session was divided into two blocks of 60 trials, separated by a 5-minute break. In each block, 12 comparison pairs (3 profile pairs × 2 widths × 2 heights) were presented 5 times in a random order, thus resulting in a total of 120 trials per participant. The slope profile (*S2*) was compensated to account for the direction of the finger's motion on the bump. The operating frequency for all profiles was set to 60 Hz.

Results and Discussion. The proportion of preferred tactile-rendering profiles is shown in Figure 6. Three pairs of bars represent the three possible pairwise combinations of profiles. Chi-square tests showed that participants' preferences in all comparisons were statistically significant ($p<0.01$) regardless of the width and height variance ($p>0.05$).

Results of the comparison experiments show that 1) participants preferred both the slope (85%) and the height (81%) profiles over commonly utilized rectangular profiles, and 2)

	Geometry to friction force mappings
S1	$G_1(x) = Ae^{-\frac{(x-m)^2}{2\sigma^2}}$
S2	$G_2(x) = \nabla G_1(x) = A'\frac{(x-m)}{\sigma^2}e^{-\frac{(x-m)^2}{2\sigma^2}}$
S3	$G_3(x) = A\big(u(x-(m-\sigma)) - u(x-(m \quad \sigma))\big)$

Table 1: Force rendering profiles

participants preferred slope profiles (73%) to the height rendering profile when compared in same trials.

TACTILE RENDERING ALGORITHM

In this section, we present an algorithm that generates tactile rendering of visual contents on friction-based lateral tactile displays. We first explain the algorithm in a one-dimensional case and then generalized it to a two-dimensional case.

Figure 7 summarizes the rendering algorithm. The input to the algorithm is a geometric representation of a surface to be rendered and the position and direction of motion of the finger sliding on the touch panel. The algorithm first computes the gradient of the surface based on the direction of the user's finger motion, it then determines the amplitude of the voltage that has to be injected into the tactile device using the psychophysical model presented in Equation 1.

One dimensional case

The one-dimensional case is used for defining a tactile profile along a single axis as employed in the pairwise experiment discussed above, and was used in the research presented in [17, 21]. The gradient of the surface $F(x)$ is:

$$\nabla F(x) = dF(x)/dx \quad (2)$$

Let's assume that the finger slides on the touch screen in the positive x-direction. The gradient is normalized by taking the dot product of the gradient and the unit vector along the direction of finger motion. This normalized gradient is scaled to the friction force level and then mapped to the applied voltage using the perceptual model defined by Equation 1 and injected into the tactile feedback device.

Generalized two-dimensional case

A growing body of haptics research utilizes image-based haptic rendering techniques [2, 26]. The purpose of generalization is to accommodate a wide variety of inputs to be rendered using our algorithm.

As an example, we implement the algorithm on a two-dimensional depth map, that can be computed from a 3D model or obtained from a depth camera. The input is a typical 2D grayscale depth image (Figure 8(a)) and a user slides the finger across it. The procedure can be easily extended to other use cases, such as mathematical models for texture synthesis [26].

Step 1: Calculate the 2D gradient field

From the 2D grayscale image, we calculate the gradient of the depth distribution, which is defined as:

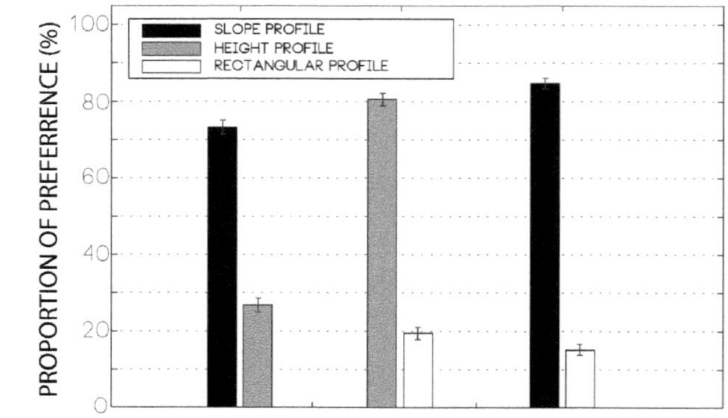

Figure 6: Results of pairwise comparison experiment

$$\nabla F(x,y) = \left(\frac{\partial F}{\partial x}, \frac{\partial F}{\partial y}\right) = \frac{\partial F}{\partial x}\hat{i} + \frac{\partial F}{\partial y}\hat{j} \quad (3)$$

where $F(x,y)$ is the two-dimensional depth distribution. This computation is typically done as a preprocessing step and yields a 2D vector field in xy plane. Each vector points in the direction of increasing depth of F, i.e. represents it steepest ascent Figure 8(b) shows the gradient fields along the x- and y- axis. Figure 8(c) shows the 2D image overlaid with levels of haptic feedback as the user slides the finger on a marked path.

Step 2: Determine the user's finger motion on touch screen

Define a unit *direction vector* of the finger motion in contact with the touch screen as:

$$\bar{\mathbf{v}}_i = \frac{\mathbf{x}_i - \mathbf{x}_{i-1}}{|\mathbf{x}_i - \mathbf{x}_{i-1}|} \quad (4)$$

where $\mathbf{x}_i$ is the finger position vector at the time of t_i. We usually compute a moving average of $\bar{\mathbf{v}}$ in case the touch screen has a low spatial resolution.

Step 3: Calculation of perceptual friction force

Compute the interaction between the static gradient field ∇F computed at Step 1 and user finger motion $\bar{\mathbf{v}}$ as

$$f_i = f_0 |\nabla F| \cos\theta_i = f_0 \nabla F \cdot \bar{\mathbf{v}}_i . \quad (5)$$

Where, f_i is the scalar value representing the *perceptual frictional force* at a given instant t_i, f_0 is a non-zero scale factor, and θ_i is the angle between two vectors.

Step 4: Calculation of controlled voltage for the device

Use the model in Equation 1 to compute the control voltage

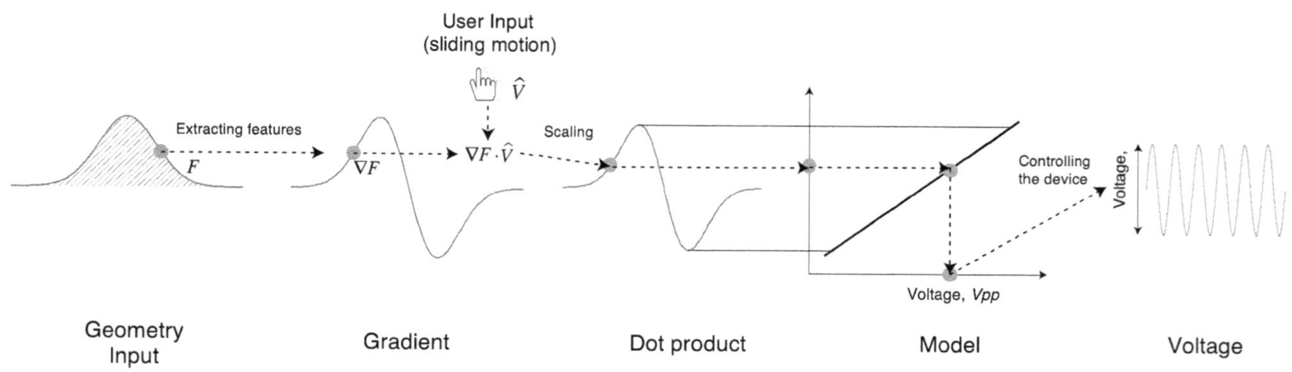

Figure 7: A block diagram summarizing of the tactile rendering algorithm.

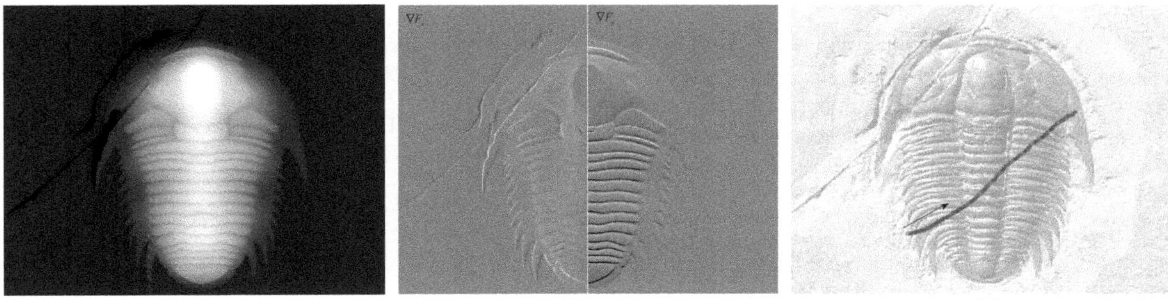

Figure 8: (a) Depth map (input image) extracted from a 3D model, (b) Gradient in the x- and y- direction, ∇F_x, ∇F_y, and (c) The actual 2D image overlaid with the haptic feedback rendered with our algorithm as the user moved in a shown path.

that corresponds to the required friction force *f* computed in Equation 5. In order to utilize the entire range of the device, we can scale friction force values to the range between 0 and 100 corresponding to the minimum and the maximum gradient values of the given input image.

The proposed algorithm is easily extended to render tactile feedback for other forms of input. It can also be easily incorporated into other types of friction-based lateral tactile displays.

Explorations and applications

In this section, we explore the use of our tactile rendering algorithm to create realistic 3D tactile features on a touch screen for a broad variety of images incorporating depictions of everyday objects, textures, patterns, etc. The following scenarios explore the further uses of the algorithm, and are not in any way limiting its use in other applications.

Depth maps

The two-dimensional depth image is one of the most common media used for defining haptic fields [26]. A typical example is its use with the 3D model as shown in Figure 9(a). The 3D information encoded in depth fields is widely used in various types of interactive applications, such as games, navigation, maps, computer graphics, etc. With our algorithm we can enhance depth maps with 3D tactile sensations.

Depth images can be also acquired directly from depth-measuring cameras, which are widely employed in various HCI contexts with the introduction of Microsoft Kinect. Figure 9(b) shows an example of interaction with a depth map stream taken from Kinect. This can be further applied to the systems for the visually impaired, where the direct video stream can be used to render environmental conditions.

Tactile content authoring

Previous studies have addressed the importance of haptic feedback in touch interaction [2]. With this in mind, we applied the proposed algorithm to enhance visual information, by overlaying haptic content on digital pictures. Figure 9(c) shows an example where the user selects books from the virtual library and can feel spine covers rendered as 3D tactile bumps. The tactile experiences can be dynamically adjusted according to information associated with the object in the picture. For example, book thickness or user book preferences can be mapped to different parameters of the Gaussian bump profile that is used for books tactile rendering.

Tactile UI

Oakley et al. [18] augmented the standard GUI components with the haptic effects, such as haptic recess effect, snap-to effect (gravity well), friction, and tactile textures. Similarly, we added 3D tactile bumps to standard GUI components. Unlike in previous work, however, we render 3D tactile bumps *algorithmically* and can *dynamically* change their properties depending on changes in the GUI elements. We expect this approach can be used not only for enriching touch experiences, but also to increase accessibility of the standard GUI components.

3D graphical models

The algorithm can be also applied to 3D models commonly produced in the computer graphics communities. Because the gradient, ∇F, is equivalent to the normal vector of the constructed mesh surface, the Equation 5 can be written as:

$$f = f_0 \bar{\mathbf{n}} \cdot \tilde{\mathbf{v}} \cdot \qquad (6)$$

Where, $\bar{\mathbf{n}}$ is a 1×3 unit normal vector of the mesh that is being touched by the user and $\tilde{\mathbf{v}}$ is the augmented 1×3 movement direction vector, $[\,\bar{\mathbf{v}} \mid 0]^T$. Thus, arbitrary 3D models and the entire dynamic 3D scenes and animations can be 3D haptically rendered in real time, without the need to pre-compute gradient field in advance.

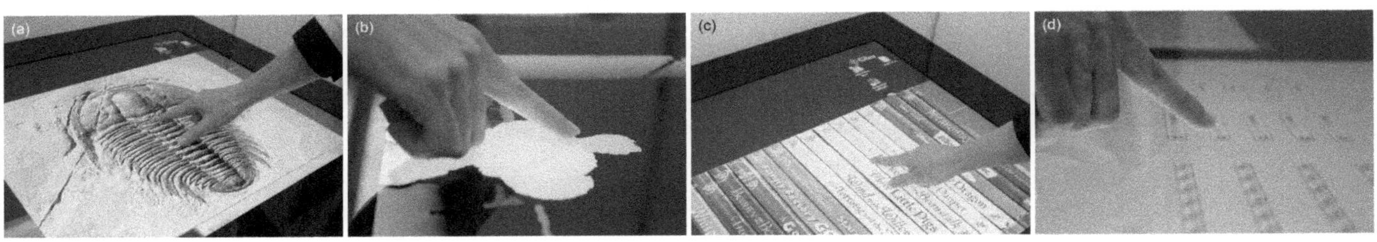

Figure 9. Applications of 3D tactile bumps in various interaction scenarios.

Haptic augmented reality

AR markers and other tracking techniques can be used to obtain the gradients of the geometric field corresponding to the real world around the user. Consequently, the depth and gradient field of the objects and surfaces can be computed and their tactile representations can be rendered using or algorithm.

CONCLUSIONS

In this paper, we present a tactile-rendering algorithm that simulates geometric features such as bumps on flat touch surfaces using only lateral resistance forces produced by the electrovibration effect. We have evaluated algorithm in controlled experimental studies that demonstrated that we can create a realistic and convincing tactile sensations of 3D bumps on a variety of visual content, including photos and 3D models. This functionality can be easily incorporated into touch-based interfaces and allow for the creation of effective and engaging tactile user experiences.

REFERENCES

1. Bau, O. and Poupyrev, I. REVEL: tactile feedback technology for augmented reality. *ACM Transactions on Graphics (TOG)*, *31*, 4 (2012), 89.
2. Bau, O., Poupyrev, I., Israr, A. and Harrison, C. TeslaTouch: electrovibration for touch surfaces. In *Proc. UIST '10*, ACM (2010), 283-292.
3. Brewster, S., Chohan, F. and Brown, L. Tactile feedback for mobile interactions. In *Proc. CHI'07*, ACM (2007), 159-162.
4. Casiez, G., Roussel, N., Vanbelleghem, R. and Giraud, F. Surfpad: riding towards targets on a squeeze film effect. In *Proc. CHI'11*, ACM (2011), 2491-2500.
5. Geldard, F. A. Adventures in tactile literacy. *American Psychologist*, *12*, 3 (1957), 115.
6. Gibson, J. J. Observations on active touch. *Psychological review*, *69*, 6 (1962), 477-491.
7. Gordon, I. E. and Morison, V. The haptic perception of curvature. *Attention, Perception, & Psychophysics*, *31*, 5 (1982), 446-450.
8. Hoggan, E. and Brewster, S. New parameters for tacton design. In *Proc. CHI '07 Extended Abstract*, ACM (2007), 2417-2422.
9. Israr, A. and Poupyrev, I. Tactile brush: drawing on skin with a tactile grid display. In *Proc. CHI'11*, ACM (2011), 2019-2028.
10. Lévesque, V., Oram, L. and MacLean, K. Exploring the Design Space of Programmable Friction for Scrolling Interactions. In *Proc. IEEE Haptics Symposium* (2012), 24-30.
11. Lévesque, V., Oram, L., MacLean, K., Cockburn, A., Marchuk, N.D., Johnson, D., Colgate, J.E. and Peshkin, M.A. Enhancing physicality in touch interaction with programmable friction. In *Proc. CHI'11*, ACM (2011), 2481-2490.
12. Lederman, S. and Klatzky, R. Haptic perception: A tutorial. *Attention, Perception, & Psychophysics*, *71*, 7 (2009), 1439-1459.
13. Lederman, S. J. and Klatzky, R. L. Hand movements: a window into haptic object recognition. *Cognitive psychology*, *19*, 3 (1987), 342-368.
14. Lederman, S. J. and Klatzky, R. L. Haptic perception: A tutorial. *Attention, Perception, & Psychophysics*, *71*, 7 (2009), 1439-1459.
15. Lee, J. C., Dietz, P. H., Leigh, D., Yerazunis, W. S. and Hudson, S. E. Haptic pen: a tactile feedback stylus for touch screens. In *Proc. UIST '04*, ACM (2004), 291-294.
16. MacLean, K. E. Haptic interaction design for everyday interfaces. *Reviews of Human Factors and Ergonomics*, *4*, 1 (2008), 149-194.
17. Minsky, M., Ming, O.-y., Steele, O., Frederick P. Brooks, J. and Behensky, M. Feeling and seeing: issues in force display. *SIGGRAPH Comput. Graph.*, *24*, 2 (1990), 235-241.
18. Oakley, I., McGee, M. R., Brewster, S. and Gray, P. Putting the feel in 'look and feel'. In *Proc. CHI '00*, ACM (2000), 415-422.
19. Poupyrev, I. and Maruyama, S. Tactile interfaces for small touch screens. In *Proc. UIST '03* (2003), 217-220.
20. Poupyrev, I., Rekimoto, J. and Maruyama, S. TouchEngine: a tactile display for handheld devices. In *Proc. CHI '02 Extended Abstract*, ACM (2002), 644-645.
21. Robles-De-La-Torre, G. and Hayward, V. Force can overcome object geometry in the perception of shape through active touch. *Nature*, *412*, 6845 (2001), 445-448.
22. Romano, J. M. and Kuchenbecker, K. J. Creating Realistic Virtual Textures from Contact Acceleration Data. *Haptics, IEEE Transactions on*, *5*, 2 (2012), 109-119.
23. Rosenberg, L. B. Virtual fixtures: Perceptual tools for telerobotic manipulation. In *Proc. Virtual Reality Annual International Symposium, 1993., 1993 IEEE* (1993), 76-82.
24. Saga, S. and Deguchi, K. Lateral-Force-Based 2.5-Dimensional Tactile Display for Touch Screen. In *Proc. IEEE Haptics Symposium* (2012).
25. Salisbury, K., Brock, D., Massie, T., Swarup, N. and Zilles, C. Haptic rendering: programming touch interaction with virtual objects. In *Proc. Proceedings of the 1995 Symposium on Interactive 3D graphics*, ACM (1995), 123-130.
26. Srinivasan, M. and Basdogan, C. Haptics in virtual environments: Taxonomy, research status, and challenges. *Computers & Graphics*, *21*, 4 (1997), 393-404.
27. Weiss, M., Wacharamanotham, C., Voelker, S. and Borchers, J. FingerFlux: near-surface haptic feedback on tabletops. In *Proc. UIST '11*, ACM (2011), 615-620.
28. Wijekoon, D., Cecchinato, M., Hoggan, E. and Linjama, J. Electrostatic Modulated Friction as Tactile Feedback: Intensity Perception. In *Proc. Eurohaptics* Springer Berlin Heidelberg (2012), 613-624.
29. Winfield, L., Glassmire, J., Colgate, E. and Peshkin, M. T-PaD: Tactile Pattern Display through Variable Friction Reduction. In *Proc.World Haptics* (2007), 421-426.
30. Yohanan, S. and MacLean, K. E. Design and assessment of the haptic creature's affect display. In *Proc. HRI '11*, ACM (2011), 473-480.
31. Zwislocki, J. J. and Goodman, D. A. Absolute scaling of sensory magnitudes: A validation. *Attention, Perception, & Psychophysics*, *28*, 1 (1980), 28-38.

SenSkin: Adapting Skin as a Soft Interface

Masa Ogata, Yuta Sugiura, Yasutoshi Makino, Masahiko Inami, Michita Imai

Keio University
{ogata | michita} @ayu.ics.keio.ac.jp, y-sugiura@kmd.keio.ac.jp,
makino@sdm.keio.ac.jp, inami@inami.info

ABSTRACT
We present a sensing technology and input method that uses skin deformation estimated through a thin band-type device attached to the human body, the appearance of which seems socially acceptable in daily life. An input interface usually requires feedback. SenSkin provides tactile feedback that enables users to know which part of the skin they are touching in order to issue commands. The user, having found an acceptable area before beginning the input operation, can continue to input commands without receiving explicit feedback. We developed an experimental device with two armbands to sense three-dimensional pressure applied to the skin. Sensing tangential force on uncovered skin without haptic obstacles has not previously been achieved. SenSkin is also novel in that quantitative tangential force applied to the skin, such as that of the forearm or fingers, is measured. An infrared (IR) reflective sensor is used since its durability and inexpensiveness make it suitable for everyday human sensing purposes. The multiple sensors located on the two armbands allow the tangential and normal force applied to the skin dimension to be sensed. The input command is learned and recognized using a Support Vector Machine (SVM). Finally, we show an application in which this input method is implemented.

Author Keywords
Skin deformation; soft interface; photo-reflectivity; bio-sensing; tactile feedback; tangential force.

ACM Classification Keywords
H.5.2 User Interfaces (D.2.2, H.1.2, I.3.6): Input devices and strategies (e.g., mouse, touchscreen).

INTRODUCTION
Wearable interfaces, such as cheap and useful depth cameras and moduled sensors with easy-to-install microcontrollers for beginner user, and their related interactions are changing along with the new technologies.

UIST'13, October 08 - 11 2013, St Andrews, United Kingdom
Copyright 2013 ACM 978-1-4503-2268-3/13/10...$15.00.
http://dx.doi.org/10.1145/2501988.2502039

As described below, stable and durable sensors can be installed on wearable accessories [9]. After conducting two works on skin sensing technology [9, 6], our focus has progressed to utilizing skin as an interface. Ideas of using a user's body as a part of an input interface were already developed in the field of human-computer interaction [7, 10]. These designs provide tactile feedback to users through their own body. However, previous works have not considered direct input using skin as a surface, but only through camera-based tracking or distance sensors worn on the wrist. In contrast, our method measures the three-dimensional force applied to the skin's surface by a finger, so that the skin can be adapted as a soft interface. When touching their skin, users can feel the area of the skin being touched and can moderate the force they use when they touch it. People can gather information about the clothes they are wearing, whether they are leaning against a wall or a chair, and whether they are wearing a watch by using their tactile sense, without using their eyes. Socially, skin-to-skin contact improves human relationships, and it also offers a sense of reliability (sometimes people pinch themselves to make sure they are not dreaming). The challenge in this study was to establish a method for sensing information that is input using the skin as an interface and measuring the force applied to the skin quantitatively.

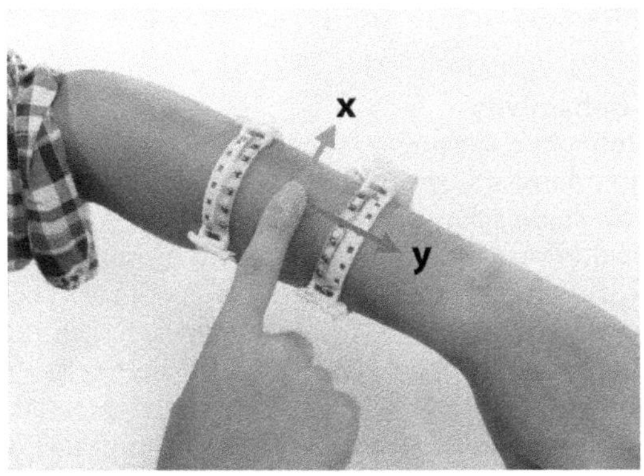

Figure 1. Image of the proposed input interface using skin deformation.

In this paper, we propose a novel method to measure the deformation of the skin surface as bio-information using an IR reflective sensor. This method can be adapted for use on skin on any part of the body. We chose to make our measurements on an arm, because this choice facilitated the sensing and the construction of the device. Only a few operations are required to perform three-dimensional force sensing: the user places the device that carries multiple sensors on his or her arm, and calibrates it. By modeling the tangential force and IR reflection, the force applied to the skin can be quantified. An advantage of the device design is that no devices or sensors cover either the area of the skin that is touched or the finger with which the user touches. Furthermore, the user receives tactile feedback from the skin that he touches when he performs input operations using his own finger and arm skin. This means that the user can control which place he touches and the amount of force that he applies. In short, the device realizes an interface that detects the interactions between the fingers and the skin on any part of the body. We focus on the aspect of the input interface, and show its applications.

RELATED WORKS

On-body Interaction

On-body interaction is becoming popular in HCI [7, 10] along with the progress and market growth of depth cameras and other sensors. Skinput [7] provides a method for turning the human body into an input interface using a bioacoustics microphone to sense the vibration that occurs when the body is tapped. A similar approach that uses a different material was proposed by Sugiura et al. [6], which leverages the photo-reflective sensor, using an elastic fabric as the deformable material. Sugiura et al. developed and investigated a soft interface using a stocking that can be attached to and cover any object. The implant approach [5] is another perspective for using skin as an interface, but requires a surgical process for attaching the device. The idea of SenSkin, which adapts the skin as an input interface, is related to the organic user interface [4], which provides the perspective of equality between function and form. This idea is adapted in this study, because SenSkin directly recognizes the user's finger function such as pull, push, and pinch.

Photo-Reflectivity

Photo-reflective sensing is used in the broad fields of not only environmental measurement but also human sensing. Research studies have been conducted on measuring the biological information of a human body using a nail sensor for measuring pressure applied on a finger [11]. Our previous works are [9, 13, 6]. A similar approach proposed by Sugiura et al. [13] leverages the photo-reflective sensor, using an elastic fabric as the deformable material. They developed a soft interface using a stocking that can be attached to and cover any object. The iRing, which leverages a photo-reflective sensor to detect the gestures of the finger on which the ring is worn, is proposed in [9]. The next step in the approach for adapting IR sensing for the purpose of biological sensing is to apply it for sensing the tangential force of the skin, as done by Makino et al. [6]. They used skin deformation sensing to find the relationship between the sensor's distance from the skin and the tangential force that is applied parallel to the arm bone. In this study, we measured the three-dimensional force applied by a finger to the skin using the same multiple sensors as were used in our previous study, and used SVM learning to train an input interface to recognize finger gestures made on the skin.

Haptic and Force Sensing

Our study focused on a model for measuring the three-dimensional force that is applied when the skin is touched by a finger by sensing the skin deformation. The method requires that sensor bands be attached somewhere on the user's body. However, since no sensor is attached to the finger, and the skin that is touched is not covered by a sensor, users can touch their skin freely and are not aware of the device in everyday use. Nakatani et al.'s method [8] recognizes pressure applied by a finger to the palm without haptic obstacles by measuring finger pad deformation. Yoshimoto et al. [11] developed a skin pressure sensor using electrodes and capacitive sensing. SenSkin realizes the sensing force in an interaction between two skins without haptic obstacle or skin-like material.

SENSKIN

Senskin is a method and technology that uses multiple IR reflective sensors implanted in an armband to allow the skin to be used as a soft input interface. We compared the actual force and the sensor values using an elastic model of the human skin. Our previous work studied the relationship between a one-dimensional force and the values recorded by two photo-reflective sensors. In this study, we found the relationship between a three-dimensional force model and the output of multiple sensors through two lines. In addition, by training an SVM on patterns of skin deformation, the recognition of finger gestures made on skin was achieved.

Principle and Method

Senskin leverages the principle of skin softness and deformation. In fact, the skin deformation when a three-dimensional force is applied is sensed. Skin has folds and wrinkles when the limb that it covers is not extended, and the subcutaneous fat works as a defense when the skin is subjected to an external force. The inner force generated by muscle movement affects the deformation of the skin surface and the extension of the skin. This research also provides a method for measuring the three-dimensional force applied to the skin, which is experimentally verified.

A computational model of skin, including fold and wrinkle deformation, was already studied in [6], according to which the skin can be represented as an elastic membrane, and the principal stresses can be computed using Hooke's law. Skin has three layers: the epidermis, dermis, and subcutaneous tissue. These layers are stretched when a force is applied to the skin surface.

Measurement

A one-dimensional tangential force model was already proposed in a previous work [6]. In this experiment, two IR reflective sensors identified as Sensor 1 and Sensor 2 were used. We measured the difference between the normalized Sensor 1 and Sensor 2 sensor values, and found that the value monotonically increases. By placing sensors along the armband, other tangential forces could be measured. When the finger moves in the right (or left) direction parallel to the armband, the sensors on the right (or left) side of the armband become closer to the finger than those on the other side. In addition, the normal force can also be predicted using this method by comparing the difference between the values recorded by sensors on two armbands. Therefore, using the methods of measuring tangential force that were presented in previous studies, the three-dimensional force applied by a finger to the skin can now be measured.

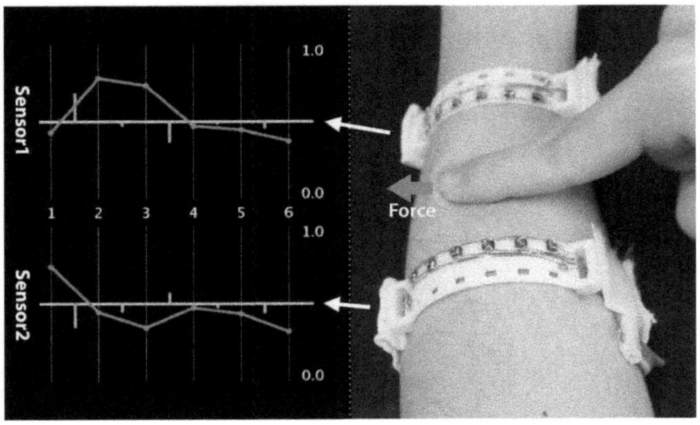

Figure 2. Measurement with multiple sensors.

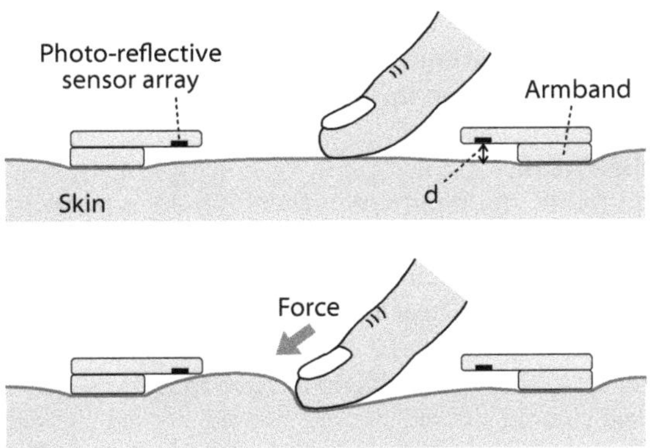

Figure 3. Section image of armband.

Hardware Design

Because of the structure of the skin and its elastic model, a relatively vast area of skin is pulled when force is applied. For example, if the skin is pinched and pulled, the skin on the opposite side of the limb moves. We designed an armband that stops the skin from sliding out from the sensing area, that is, the area between the two armbands. To maintain a distance from the skin, the sensor part of the armband is raised above the level of the surface that is in contact with the skin. By stopping the skin from sliding between the armbands, the skin deformation can be measured quantitatively as the change in its distance from the edge of armband.

The armband device has six IR reflective sensors on each band and an elastic tape with hook-and-eye fasteners to allow easy attachment. The sensors are placed at 10 mm intervals on the band, and each sensor has four pins, all of which are connected to a power supply and an analog–digital converter. The polycarbonate parts on which the six sensors are mounted project over the skin area between the bands at a height of 2 mm.

We selected the SG-105 Photointerrupter [Kodenshi Corp.] as the IR reflective sensor. The sensor consists of an IR LED and IR transistor. We chose a 75 Ohm resistor for the LED and a 30 K Ohm resistor for the transistor to transmit the sensor output to an A/D converter. The 75 Ohm resistor is connected by lines to all six sensor LEDs. The A/D converter is an Arduino Pro Mini (3.3 V) and it is connected to a Bluetooth module to transmit sensing data to a PC.

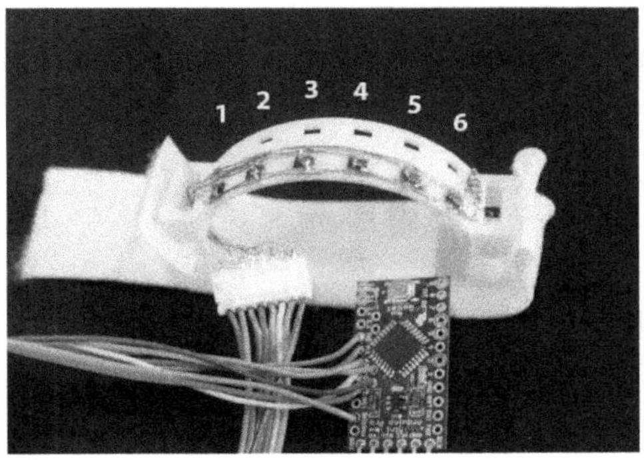

Figure 4. Prototype. (Armband and A/D converter)

Calibration

The main purpose of the calibration is to set a baseline of the sensor value when skin is in normal state, as well as to terminate the range of possible sensor values when it deforms. The procedure is:

- (1) Set the baseline value;
- (2) Put the finger between the two armbands and move it randomly;
- (3) Make sure that all sensors are measured and the upper and lower thresholds were set. At the same time, it is recommended to push the area near the armband and pull the skin toward the armband.
- (4) Set the baseline again in case the skin was moved during the previous processes.

All sensor values are calculated as relative values. The values vary the lowest and highest value determined by calibration with a range from 0.0 to 1.0. The baseline of the relative values is 0.5, because skin deformation is affected by wrinkles, and the levels of pull toward and backward is not equal.

MEASUREMENT

Bearing in mind a related work [6], we tested two types of measurement: the relationship of the horizontal tangential force and the sensor value; and the relationship of normal force applied to the skin surface and the sensor value.

Horizontal Tangential Force

Before presenting the calculation of the sensor values, we describe the index numbers of the sensors on the armbands. The user wears two armbands; the armband near the wrist is called A, and the other is called B. The sensors are given index numbers from 1 to 6 from the left side. Thus, for example, the sensor identified as S_{A1} is the leftmost edge sensor on armband A. The formula for obtaining the horizontal component X is calculated as

$$X_A = \sum_{i=1}^{3} (S_{A(i)} - S_{A(i+3)}), X_B = \sum_{i=1}^{3} (S_{B(i)} - S_{B(i+3)})$$

$$X = \frac{X_A - X_B}{2}$$

Component Y, which is the vertical tangential force, is calculated as

$$Y_A = \sum_{i=1}^{6} S_{A(i)}, Y_B = \sum_{i=1}^{6} S_{B(i)}, Y = \frac{Y_A - Y_B}{2}$$

Component Z, which is the normal force, that is the axis perpendicular to the skin surface, is calculated as

$$Z_A = \sum_{i=1}^{6} S_{A(i)}, Z_B = \sum_{i=1}^{6} S_{B(i)}, Z = \frac{Z_A + Z_B}{2}$$

The measurement of the tangential force of component X was conducted as shown in Figure 5. The measuring direction must remain tangential to the skin surface. The instruments used to take the measurements were a force gauge (A&D Company, Limited; AD-4932A-50N; resolution: 0.01N) and a plastic plate glued to skin. The results are shown in Figure 5. The sensor value is a relative value that varies between the lowest and highest value determined by calibration. The plot shows the linear relationship up to almost 5 N (510 g).

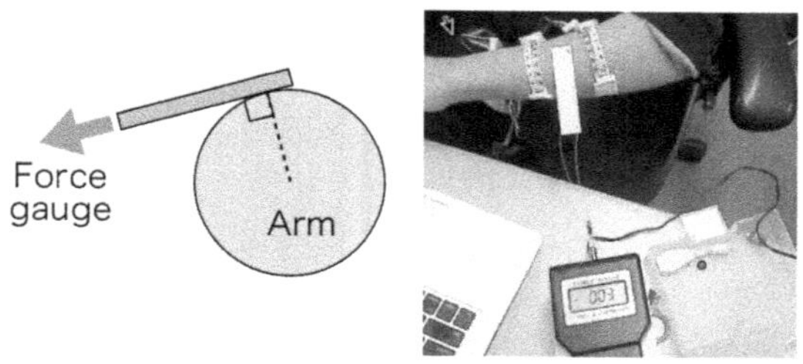

Figure 5. Measuring direction and experimental setup.

Figure 6 shows the data produced with our experimental setting. The first section between zero force and the next force point is relatively smooth, and can be thought of as the slack of rope. The plots rise to near 8N, with an elastic model after 6N. This measurement was done with one participant (author) after two trials: the first was stopped because the device peeled away from the skin because of weak adhesiveness; the second showed the same tendency of elasticity. The plots in Figure 6 terminate at the point when the plate glued to the arm peeled off.

Normal Force

Normal force is the 3rd axis of this system and is the pressure added perpendicularly to the skin surface. This force is estimated from each pair of armband sensors across the sensing area. When the finger touches the skin, the skin deforms along the force level from the finger, and the difference in the value between the pair of armband sensors increases. By sensing these changes, the point on the skin that is touched and the force is calculated.

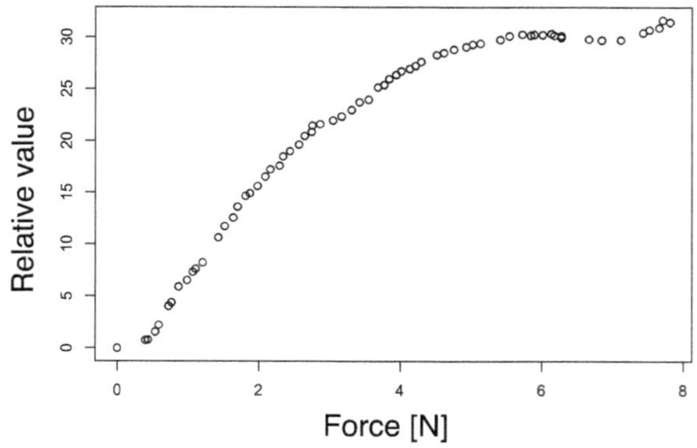

Figure 6. Relationship between sensor value and tangential force (horizontal axis).

RECOGNITION

Recognition of the input command from 12 sensors is first learned using SVM. We tested using three classes: (1) raw data of 12 sensors; (2) ***Diff*$_A$*(i)*, *Diff*$_B$*(i)***: the differences between the values of each sensor, that is, 5 differences for each armband, yielding 10 data; and (3) ***Cross(i)***: 12 raw data and 6 cross difference data of each indexed sensor. The variables were

$$Diff_A(i) = S_{A(i+1)} - S_{A(i)}, i = 1 \sim 5$$

$$Diff_B(i) = S_{B(i+1)} - S_{B(i)}, i = 1 \sim 5$$

$$Cross(i) = S_{A(i)} - S_{B(i)}, i = 1 \sim 6$$

We prepared seven command modes for input: normal, push, pinch, pull-up, pull-down, pull-right, and pull-left. The SVM model was constructed using 145 plots of sensor data including all the command classifications. The recognition rates for these commands for the three classes were: (1) 98.11%, (2) 91.82%, and (3) 98.74% of prediction collection.

DISCUSSION

The recognition rate is sufficient to identify the input command, and it is clear that the SVM model using cross differences (3) is better than that using only 12 sensor data (1). The cross difference component yields better results because skin is considered an elastic model, and the relationship between the sensor data of the two armbands is considered. On the other hand, (2) does not contribute to improving the results. The difference between the values of adjacent sensors is also an important element for recognition, because it represents the differential calculus of the skin deformation shape.

Possible Applications

Because Senskin recognizes finger gestures made on the skin though the skin's deformation, it can be used as a controller for other wearable computers, such as those incorporated in eyeglasses or wearable game devices. However, the device cannot easily be used in a sports situation or on a body part that is at a significant distance from the hand. It can, however, be used in other fields, including the medical and cosmetic, because it senses skin interaction without interfering with the user's activity. In Figure 7, we show an application to cursor and desktop icons using SenSkin as an input controller. Figure 8 depicts a situation where SenSkin is used.

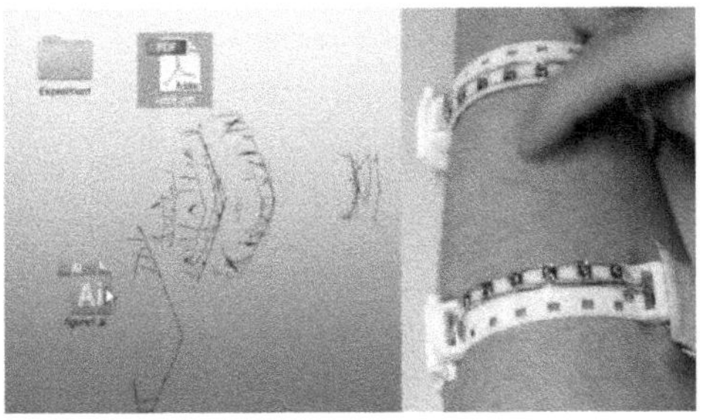

Figure 7. Using Senskin as an input controller.

Limitation

Skin deformation can be caused by joint and muscle movement. To obtain precise data from the sensor data for input recognition, Senskin should be used in conjunction with an accelerometer to detect the joint status to eliminate sensor output chattering. In normal use of the device in normal situations, the IR reflection does not present a problem. However, very strong IR rays emitted by the armband sensors may cause skin disorders in people whose skin is sensitive. Our experiment was done with one participant (author); an experiment with more than two participants may find other limitations or characteristics. Finally, almost all wrinkled skin has lost some subcutaneous tissue, so that it would be difficult for people with very wrinkled skin to use the Senskin device.

CONCLUSION

In this paper, we proposed and described the idea of Senskin, which is a technique for sensing skin deformation, allowing the skin to be used as an input interface. The contributions of this research study are fourfold. (1) An organic interface was proposed that uses soft skin, and provides feedback to the user through his or her own skin. (2) A sensing method and a device design for measuring the tangential force and normal force applied to the skin's surface were presented. (3) The results for command recognition by SVM learning were sufficiently accurate to show that the skin can be used as an input interface. (4) A skin input interface with possible applications was proposed.

ACKNOWLEDGMENTS

This work was supported by Strategic Information and Communications R&D Promotion Programme (SCOPE) of the Ministry of Internal Affairs and Communications, Japan.

REFERENCES

1. Argyros, Antonis A., Lourakis, Manolis I.A. Vision-based interpretation of hand gestures for remote control of a computer mouse. *Computer Vision in Human-Computer Interaction, Lecture Notes in Computer Science* (2006), 40-51.
2. Erol, A., Bebis, G., Nicolescu, M., Boyle, R. D., Twombly, X. Vision-based hand pose estimation: A review, *Computer Vision and Image Understanding 108*, 1-2 (2007), 52-73.
3. Harrison, C., Tan, D., Morris, D. Skinput: appropriating the body as an input surface. In *Proc.CHI 2010*, ACM Press (2010), 453-462.
4. Holman, D., Vertegaal, R. Organic user interfaces: designing computers in any way, shape, or form. *Communications of the ACM 51,* 6 (2008), 26-30.
5. Holz, C., Grossman, T., Fitzmaurice, G., Agur, A. Implanted user interfaces. In *Proc. CHI 2012*, ACM Press, 503-512.
6. Makino, Y., Sugiura, Y., Ogata, M., Inami, M. Tangential force sensing system on forearm. In *Proc. of AH 2013*, ACM Press, 29-34.
7. Mascaro, S., Asada, H. Photoplethysmograph fingernail sensors for measuring finger forces without haptic obstruction. *IEEE Transactions on Robotics and Automation 17*, 5 (2001), 698-708.
8. Nakatani, M., Kawasoe, T. Shiojima, K., Koketsu, K., Kinoshita, S., Wada, J. Wearable contact force sensor system based on fingerpad deformation, *World Haptics Conference,* (2011), 323-328.
9. Ogata, M., Sugiura, Y., Osawa, H., Imai, M. iRing: intelligent ring using infrared reflection. In *Proc. of UIST 2012*, 131-136.
10. Saponas, T.S., Tan, D.S., Morris, D., Balakrishnan, R., Turner, J., Landay, J.A. Enabling always-available input with muscle-computer interfaces. In *Proc. UIST '09*, 167-176.
11. Yoshimoto, S., Kuroda, Y., Imura, M., Oshiro, O. Superimposed skin pressure sensor. In *SIGGRAPH Asia 2012 Emerging Technologies,* SA 2012. 4 pages.
12. Sturman, D.J., Zeltzer, D. A survey of glove-based input. *IEEE Computer Graphics and Applications 14,* 1 (1994), 30-39.
13. Sugiura, Y., Inami, M., Igarashi, T. A thin stretchable interface for tangential force measurement. In *Proc. of UIST '12*, 529-536.

Author Index

www.ingramcontent.com/pod-product-compliance
Ingram Content Group UK Ltd.
Pitfield, Milton Keynes, MK11 3LW, UK
UKHW051416290926
15471UKWH00009B/1632

9 781450 326742